area

Φ

contents

100 graphic designers

010 curators

010 design classics

Phaidon Press Limited
Regent's Wharf
All Saints Street
London N1 9PA

Phaidon Press Inc.
180 Varick Street
New York, NY 10014

www.phaidon.com

First published 2003

ISBN 0 7148 4325 3

A CIP catalogue record of this book is available from the British Library.

Editor: Valérie Vago-Laurer
Project Editor: Patrick Busse
Editorial Assistant: Jesse Donaldson
Designer: Julia Hasting
Production Manager: Karen Farquhar

Printed in China

Acknowledgements

Special thanks are due to the 100 designers and the ten curators: Anthon Beeke, Nick Bell, Ken Cato, Shigeo Fukuda, Fernando Gutiérrez, Werner Jeker, Uwe Loesch, Stefan Sagmeister, Serge Serov, Omar Vulpinari. Special thanks are also extended to Sacha Happee of Studio Anthon Beeke and Elise Bufton of Cato Partners for their invaluable contributions. Thank you to Elisabeth Johnson for copyediting and Heidi Bek, Fay Maruyama, Studio Anthon Beeke, and Alex Padalka for translation. Werner Jeker would like to thank Elisabeth Schwarzenbeck of Les Ateliers du Nord for her assistance in the writing of his texts.

The publisher would also like to thank the following for their assistance in providing the images for various graphic designers and the design classics: *Eye, The International Review of Graphic Design*, London's Transport Museum, Niklaus Troxler, Allain Weill, Elisabeth Schwarzenbeck, and Anne-Claude Lelieur of the Bibliothèque Forney, Paris. Thanks also to Nico Schweizer of Mediadub.com for providing *area*'s typeface Typ 1441.

area is an exhibition in a book dedicated to 100 of the most significant new graphic designers today. It brings together the curatorial input of ten distinguished design leaders from around the world, each asked to select their ten favorite "rising stars"—graphic designers who have emerged and broken new ground over the last five years. The curators are internationally respected teachers, practitioners, and art directors recognized not only for their own work, but also for their active involvement in the current scene. Their choices are organized in an A to Z order with each designer's work represented in four pages, along with an introductory text written by the selecting curator.

area's roster of 100 designers is characterized not by one theme but rather by its diversity. From the rebirth of the elegant, detail-driven Swiss school to an embrace of a more playful, unstructured, and, at times, even vulgar aesthetic; from the glorification of a technology-driven process to the re-emergence of the heroic amateur and the "home-made"; from the development of a truly international, interconnected, and interdisciplinary medium to the rise of regional styles, it documents the trends shaping today's graphic-design culture.

Like all the graphic work featured in this book, *area* is defined by its choices. The curators were limited to a selection of ten and a representative sampling of works from each designer's portfolio. For coherency, Web design and motion graphics were excluded from this study. Yet it is precisely these focused parameters that make it possible to distinguish the key players and ideas in this rich and prolific field.

In addition to their choice of ten designers, all of the curators were asked to pick a "classic"—a piece of graphic design from any era that is of particular significance to them. The curators' choices—and their candid and often humorous texts explaining those choices—are not just indicators of their individual points of view, but also forays into many layers of graphic-design history.

preface

area

Anthon Beeke

is known as the ultimate provocateur, the *enfant terrible* of Dutch graphic design. Largely self-trained, he overturned conventions and created sensational images, relentlessly exposing the human body. He was a partner of the legendary Amsterdam design firm Total Design before creating his own design agency, Studio Anthon Beeke in 1989. He is chief lecturer in the department of People and Information at the Design Academy in Eindhoven, the Netherlands.

Nick Bell

is director of UNA (London) designers, known as Nick Bell Design until 1998 when his practice became associated with UNA in Amsterdam. In 1997 he became the art director of *Eye, The International Review of Graphic Design*, for which he has won numerous design awards. Bell has lectured widely in the United States and Europe. His clients include The British Council, Tate Britain, The Barbican Centre, and The Royal Mail.

Ken Cato

is chairman of Cato Partners, established in Melbourne, Australia in 1970. With eight offices worldwide, it has become the largest design company in the Southern Hemisphere. Cato's work encompasses all facets of design, ranging from graphic and product design, to fashion, to interior and environmental design. An indefatigable advocate of the cause of graphic design worldwide, Cato was president of AGI from 1997 to 2001, and in 1991 created AGIdeas, which has become the world's biggest student graphic design conference.

Shigeo Fukuda

is one of the world's leading contemporary visual artists. With graphic design as his base, he is active in a variety of genres including sculpture and environmental and monument design. Fukuda's playful designs, which are humorous while displaying a sense of irony, have won him international acclaim. Based in Tokyo, Fukuda is a visiting professor at Tokyo National University of Fine Arts and Music, and is currently chairman of the Japan Graphic Designers Association.

Fernando Gutiérrez

is a partner of the international design firm Pentagram, and since 2000 the creative director of *Colors*, the global magazine created for Benetton by Tibor Kalman and Oliviero Toscani. Based in London, Gutiérrez has kept close ties to his homeland, Spain. He is the art director of *Matador*, an annual Spanish literary and photography journal, and frequently works for the national daily newspaper *El Pais*. He is consultant creative director for the Museo Nacional del Prado in Madrid.

Werner Jeker

who founded the Ateliers du Nord in 1984, is one of the most renowned Swiss graphic designers. Based in Lausanne, he works regularly with local cultural institutions and has clients worldwide. He has also worked as an architect and recently designed the "Pavillon Signalschmerz" for the Swiss Expo.02, an acclaimed success. He has taught at the most prestigious design schools and is currently chair of the Visual Communications department at the Hochschule für Gestaltung, Kunst, und Konservierung (HGKK) in Bern.

Uwe Loesch

is acknowledged as one of the world's most important poster designers. In the past twenty years he has won nearly all the existing international poster design awards, and his work is represented in the permanent collections of the world's major museums. Since 1990 a professor of Communication Design at the University of Wuppertal, Germany, Loesch is an eminent teacher, whose work is frequently emulated and who has influenced generations of young designers.

Stefan Sagmeister

was born in Vienna and first moved to New York City in 1987. In 1993 he formed his own company, Sagmeister Inc., focusing on the music industry. He has designed graphics and packaging for the Rolling Stones, David Byrne, Lou Reed, Aerosmith, and Pat Metheny and his work has received four Grammy nominations as well as many international design awards. Sagmeister, who is a frequent lecturer and participant in international graphic design juries, has become an advocate for change in the design world.

Serge Serov

is the foremost spokesperson of graphic design in Russia and Eastern Europe. He is the founding president of the Golden Bee Moscow International Biennale of Graphic Design and since 1998 heads the Graphic Design School of the College of Applied Arts in Moscow. Serov also works as an editor and has curated a number of graphic design exhibitions.

Omar Vulpinari

heads the department of Visual Communication Design at Fabrica in Treviso, Italy, the research and development center for communication created by Luciano Benetton and Oliviero Toscani. He has been a consultant to, among others, the United Nations, Witness, Coca Cola, Nikon, Fuji, Porsche, *The New Yorker* magazine, and MTV. He is a member of the International Society of Typographic Designers.

010 curators

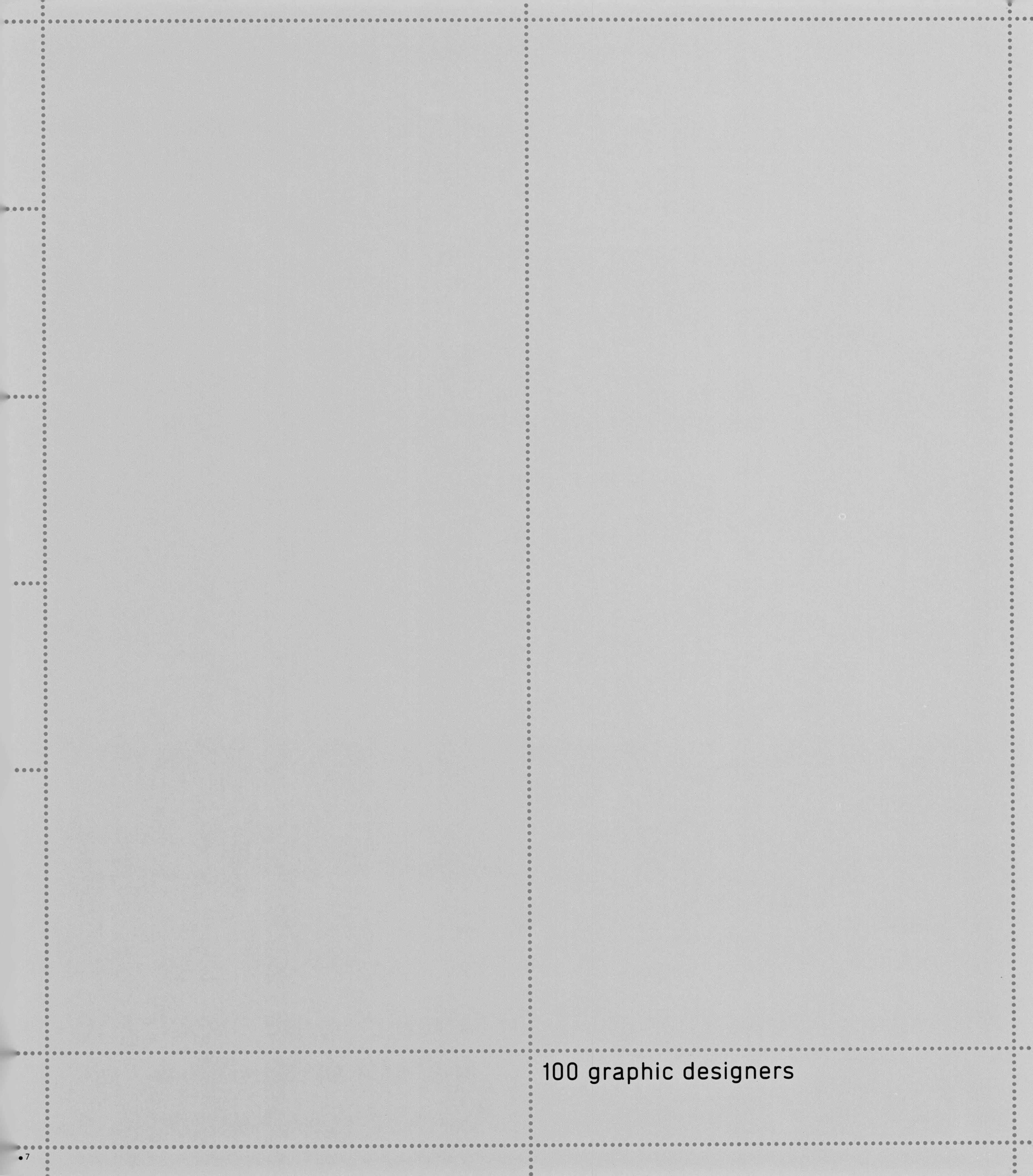

100 graphic designers

In 1972, on a voyage to the distant kingdom of Afghanistan, I passed through Iran and discovered Persia, this fairy-tale land that a long time ago gave the world such grandiose poets as Ferdowsi, Jalal ad-Din ar-Rumi, and Hafez. Iran still has a notable book culture and to this day cultivates the special tradition of calligraphy. •• Thirty years later an invitation by Morteza Momayez allowed me to travel back to Iran. In Tehran he presented me to Majid Abassi, who promptly showed me his work on an old IBM computer in Reza Abedini's studio. I was impressed. •• Abassi works with minimal graphic and typographic means and has perfected the art of forming a relationship between Persian and Latin writing. This allows him to combine his own tradition with new, mostly Western forms of expression and to create something unique. •• Abassi has designed many book covers and posters. Especially with the book covers, he handles image and text with a great deal of craftsmanship. Some of these designs are full of poetry, others full of wit, like the photomontage of a glass eye under a magnifying glass for a detective novel. One of his posters (poster for exhibition of photographs by Sadeq Hedayat) has become so popular that it is becoming an icon of Iranian graphic design. This comes as no surprise, as posters are surely his secret passion, for they provide him with the space to realize his large-scale ideas. •• Abassi was born in Tehran in 1965 and graduated from the fine-arts department of the University of Tehran in 1996. He has received numerous awards at national and international competitions, and over the last few years his work has been represented at all the major poster biennials. •• Uwe Loesch ••

1

2

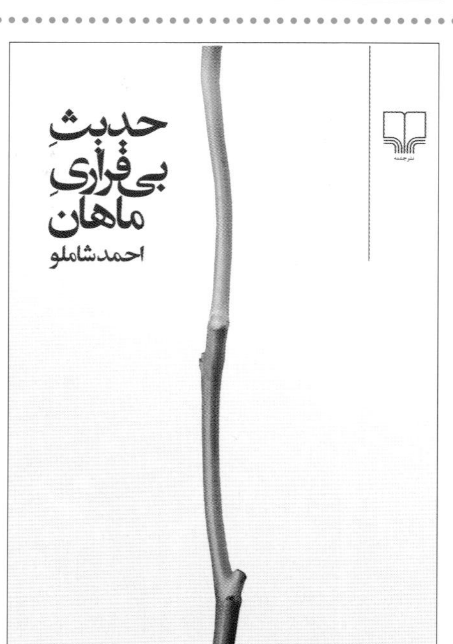

3

4

5

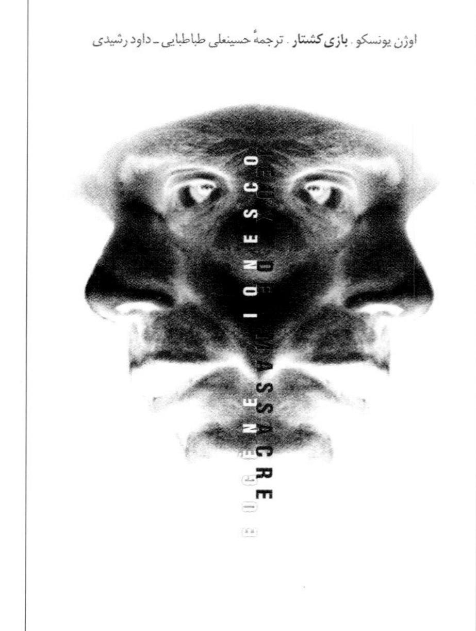

6

1 Book cover, *Iranian Folk Culture* / Cheshmeh Publications / Iran / 1999
2 Book cover, *The Coolness of the Journey's Dawn* / Khojasteh Publications / Iran / 2001
3 Book cover, *Ahmad Shamlou's Poems* / Cheshmeh Publications / Iran / 2001
4 Book cover, *Eye to Eye* / Did Publications / Iran / 2002
5 Book cover, *My Favorite Stories*, Vol. 1 / Cheshmeh Publications / Iran / 2001
6 Book cover, *Jeux de Massacre* / Did Publications / Iran / 2000
7 Poster for the Persian typography exhibition inspired by the novel *Blind Owl* / The 5th Color / Iran / 2002
8 Poster for the book *Graphic Design Iran 1* / Iranian Graphic Designers Society (IGDS) / Iran / 2002
9 Logo / Kajé Construction Company / Iran / 1997
10 Logo / Borzoyeh Medical Publications / Iran / 1994
11 Logo / Doran Publishing / Iran / 1998
12 Logo for Bouda Bana building in Tehran / Tazdgol Company / Iran / 2003
13 Logo / Mehr Publishing / Iran / 2002

Majid Abbasi

Tehran

7

8

9

10

11

12

13

14 Poster dedicated to silkscreen artist Hossein Otroushi / The 5th Color / Iran / 2002
15 Poster for third *Research of the Year* exhibition / Science Ministry / Iran / 2002
16 Poster for *The Keystone* exhibition on eight graphic designers / The 5th Color / Iran / 2002
17 Poster for *Brief Encounters* international poster exhibition / Thierry Sarfis / France / 2002
18 Poster for exhibition of photographs by Sadeq Hedayat / Seyhoun Gallery / Iran / 2001
19 Poster for the play *Hamlet* / Hossein Ali Tabatabai / Iran / 2001
20 Poster celebrating the 100th birthday of Sadeq Hedayat / Cheshmeh and Khojasteh Publications / Iran / 2002

Majid Abbasi

17

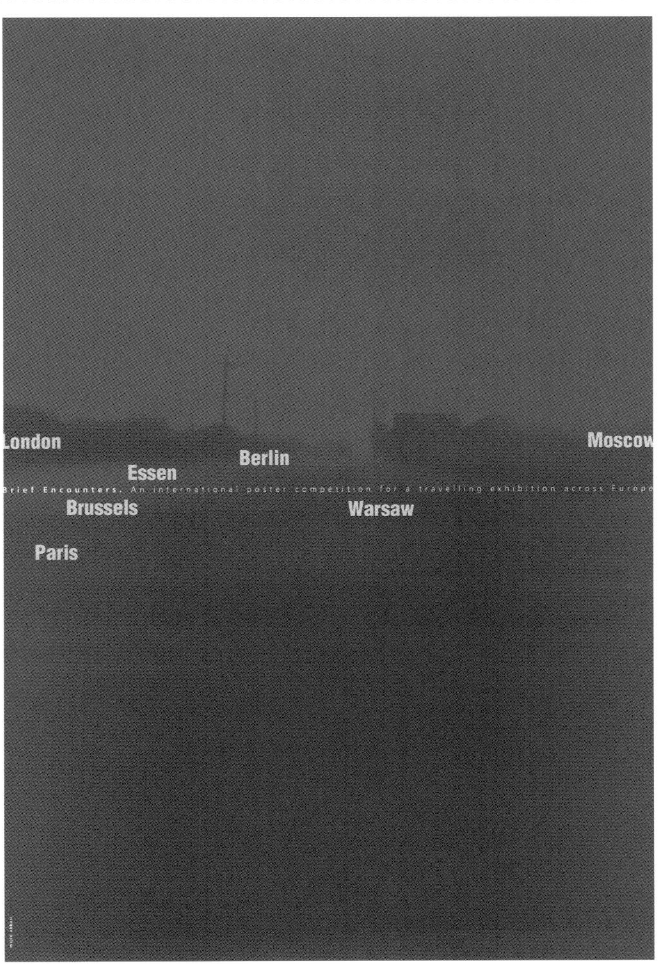
London
Essen
Berlin
Moscow
Brief Encounters. An international poster competition for a travelling exhibition across Europe
Brussels
Warsaw
Paris

18

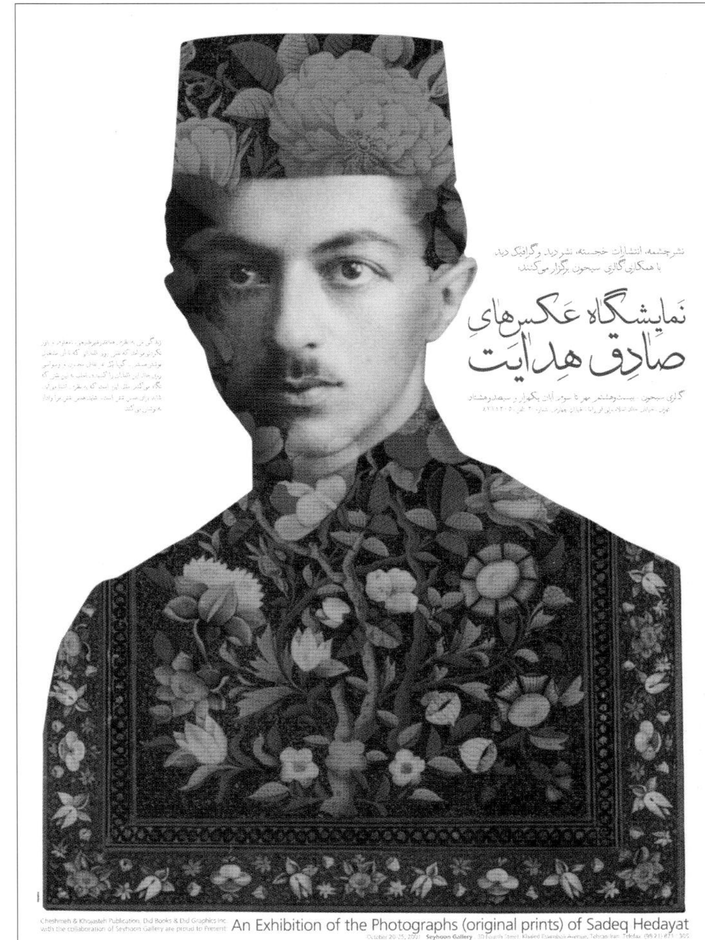
نمایشگاه عکس‌های
صادق هدایت
An Exhibition of the Photographs (original prints) of Sadeq Hedayat

19

اثر ویلیام شکسپیر
هاملت
کارگردان : حسینعلی طباطبایی

20

بمناسبت صدمین سالروز تولد صادق هدایت
(۱۲۸۱ - ۱۳۸۱)

I met the Iranian designer Reza Abedini at the June 2002 biennial in Brno. He was a relatively young man dressed in white with an acute, burning stare. In Tehran, he organizes the biennial of Iranian graphic designers, which he is now planning to make international. He gave me a catalogue of his work, which seemed a bit too small. I flipped through it, and I can't say I liked it much. • • My conception of the three paradigms of graphic design looks something like this: In classical typography, illustration is entirely dictated by text. The range of font in the text sets the standard for the tonal range of the images. They must not contain lines wider than the largest or narrower than the smallest font used: a strong, healthy family, the patriarchy of text. In modern typography, image and text become independent, equal, strong partners. Image is the liberated woman of modernism. She may become the illustration for the text; or she can do without text, creating an independent "visual row," or even become the "visual text" herself. With the postmodern paradigm now beginning to reveal itself, we approach the domination of image, trapping, enveloping, and swallowing the text. • • At the Brno biennial, which showcases the freshest ideas from around the world, even poster slogans now dissolved amid the gentle grids of the image. • • In the works of Reza Abedini I also find the precise embodiment of my conception of stylistic processes in typography worldwide. Abedini's text is almost always not next to the image, but inside it. Dark font on light images, light font on dark images. He leaves tons of free space around for the text. But this is no longer empty whiteness or the blackness of modernist cosmos; this is a living environment of the image that fills all of the surrounding space with itself—an alloy of image and text. • • It was only on revisiting his work that I fully appreciated Abedini's design. On closer look, I see him as a unifying phenomenon, joining national color with international quality, regionalism with globalism, Iran's traditional Farsi writing with the most modern European typography. What's more, this powerful synthesis comes to him with ease and nonchalance. • • Serge Serov • •

1

2

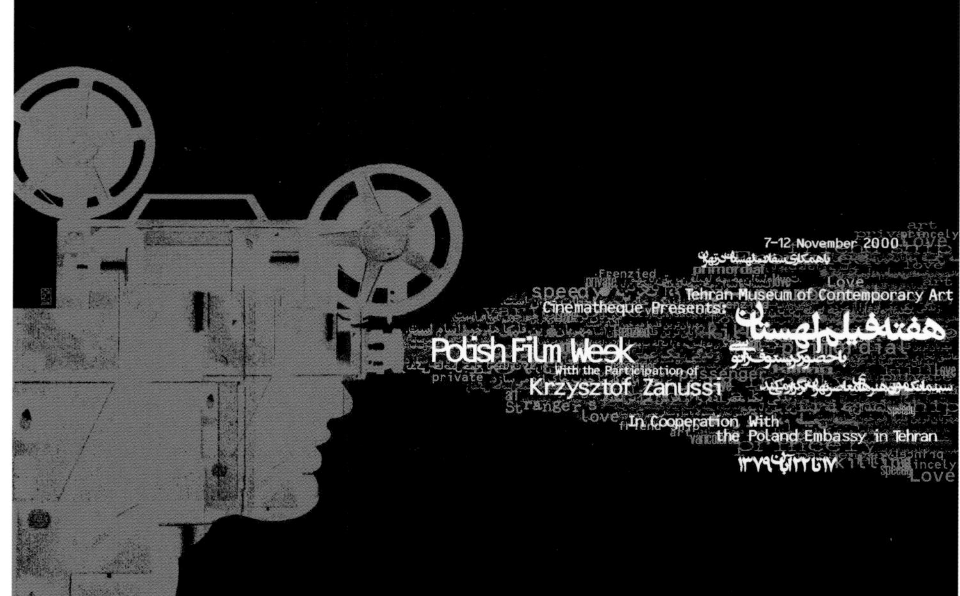

3

1 Book cover, *Raporthaye Yomyeh* / Rozaneh Publishing / Iran / 1999
2 Book cover, *Shere Tanze Emroz Iran* / Rozaneh Publishing / Iran / 1999
3 Poster for Polish Film Week / Tehran Museum of Contemporary Art / Iran / 2000
4 Book cover, *Resale Se Asl* / Rozaneh Publishing / Iran / 1998
5 Poster for personal theatrical project focussing on dance, light, and graphic design / Iran / 2000
6 Book cover, *Resale Delgosha* poetry selection / Rozaneh Publishing / Iran / 2000
7 Poster for lecture on the Iranian poet Mowlana / Marc Bloch University / France / 1999

Reza Abedini

Tehran

4

تصنیف صدرالدین محمد بن ابراهیم شیرازی (ملاصدرا)
به تصحیح دکتر سید حسین نصر
به اهتمام محمدرضا جوزی
رساله سه اصل

5

DANCE AND MESSAGE
COLLECTION OF TEN PLAYS BY THE USE OF: IMAGE MUSIC LIGHT DANCE
DESIGNER AND DIRECTOR
MEHRAN ZAMANI
ART DIRECTOR AND VIDEOGRAPHIC
REZA ABEDINI
10 MAY 2001
CULTURAL CENTER OF TEHRAN

6

گزیدهٔ رساله دلگشا
عبید زاکانی
به اهتمام
سید ابراهیم نبوی

7

Colloque International
Mowlānā Jalāl od-Din Rûmi (Mowlavi)
Université MARC BLOCH - Strasbourg
Faculté des Langues Vivantes.
Departement d'Etudes Persanes.
Academie des Arts -Iran
10-12 Octobre 2001
Palais Universitaire /
Strasbourg/ France
مولانا جلال الدین رومی مولوی

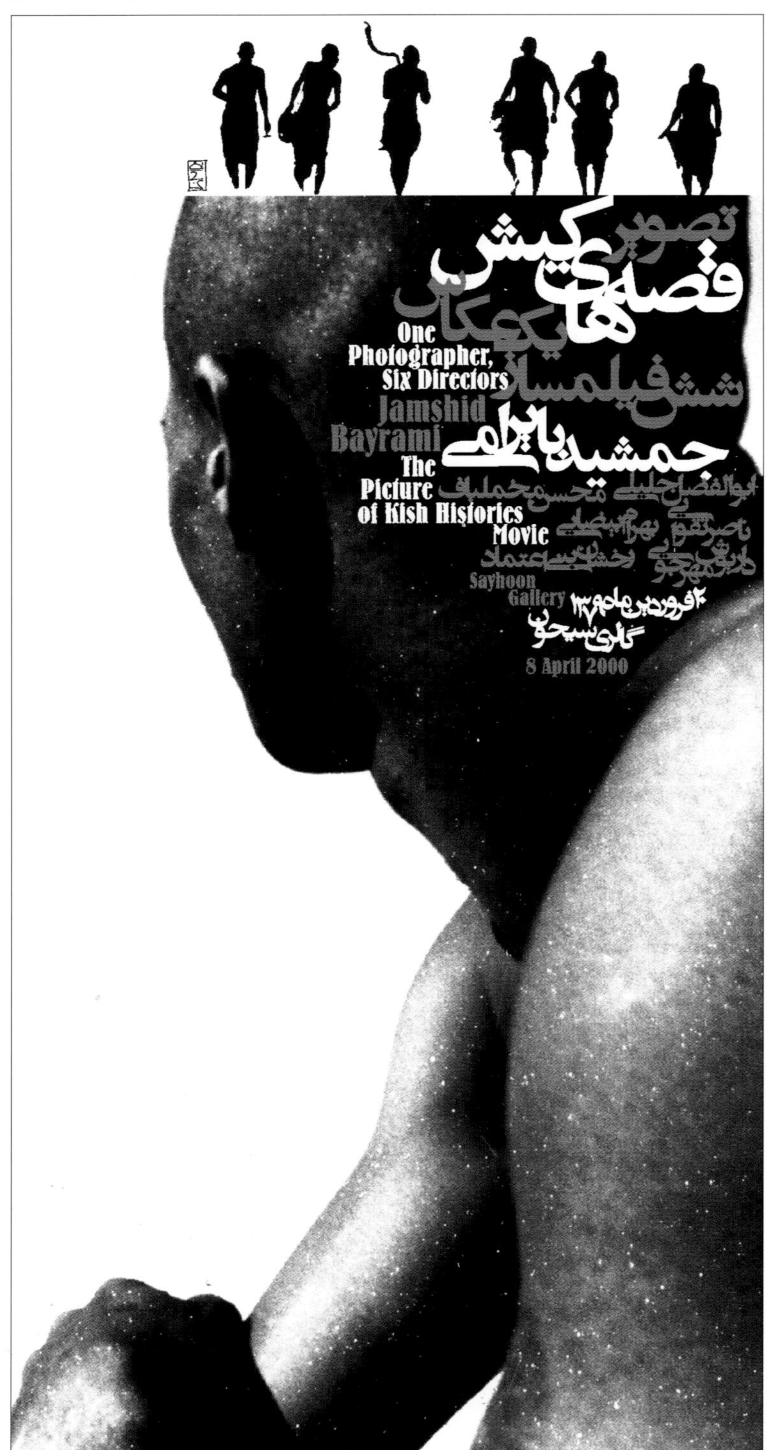

8

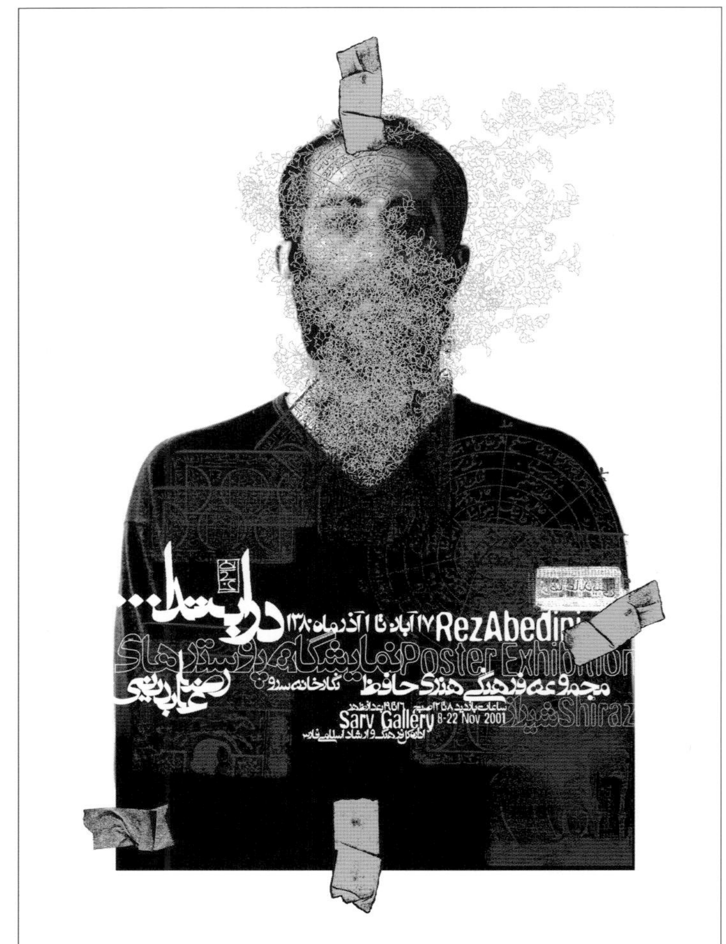

9

10

8 Poster for exhibition of photographs by Jamshid Bayrami / Sayhoon Art Gallery / Iran / 2000
9 Poster for Reza Abedini solo exhibition / Hafiz Cultural Complex / Iran / 2001
10 Poster for *Imagination Through Drawing* exhibition / Iranian Artists House Gallery / Iran / 2002
11 Poster for 7th Biennial of Iranian Graphic Designers / Iranian Graphic Designers Society (IGDS) and Tehran Museum of Contemporary Art / Iran / 2002
12 Poster for International Conference on the Philosophy of Art / Tehran Museum of Contemporary Art / Iran / 2001
13 Poster for International Conference on Post-Modernism and Contemporary Art / Tehran Museum of Contemporary Art / Iran / 2001
14 Poster for The Second International Biennal, Painting of the Islamic World / Tehran Museum of Contemporary Art / Iran / 2002

Reza Abedini

11

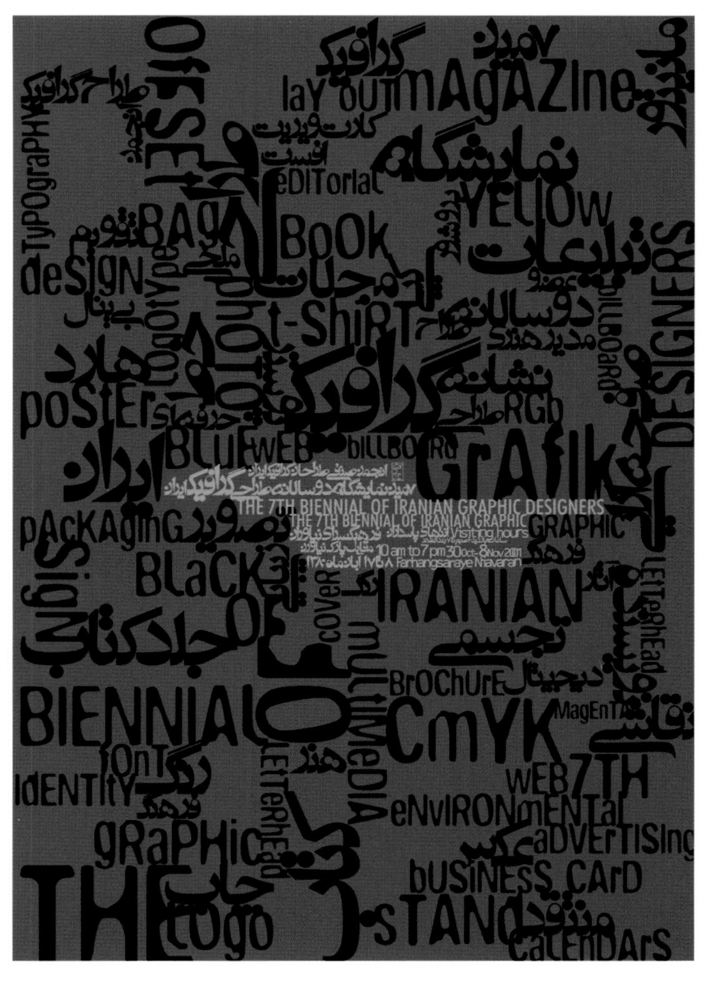
THE 7TH BIENNIAL OF IRANIAN GRAPHIC DESIGNERS
Farhangsaraye Niavaran

12

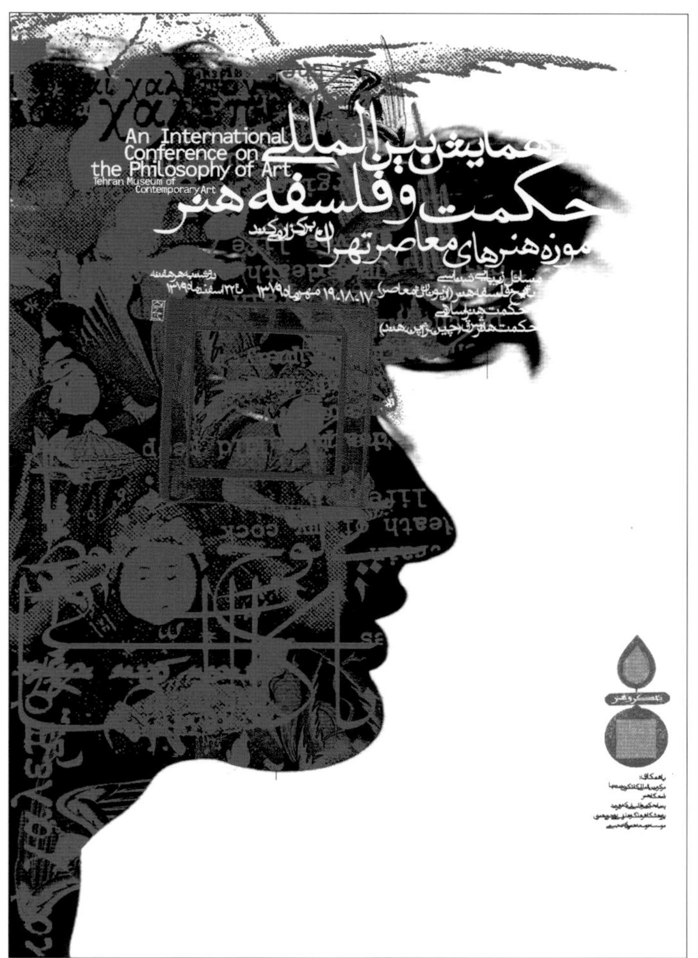
همایش بین المللی
حکمت و فلسفه هنر
An International
Conference on
the Philosophy of Art
Tehran Museum of
Contemporary Art
موزه هنرهای معاصر تهران

13

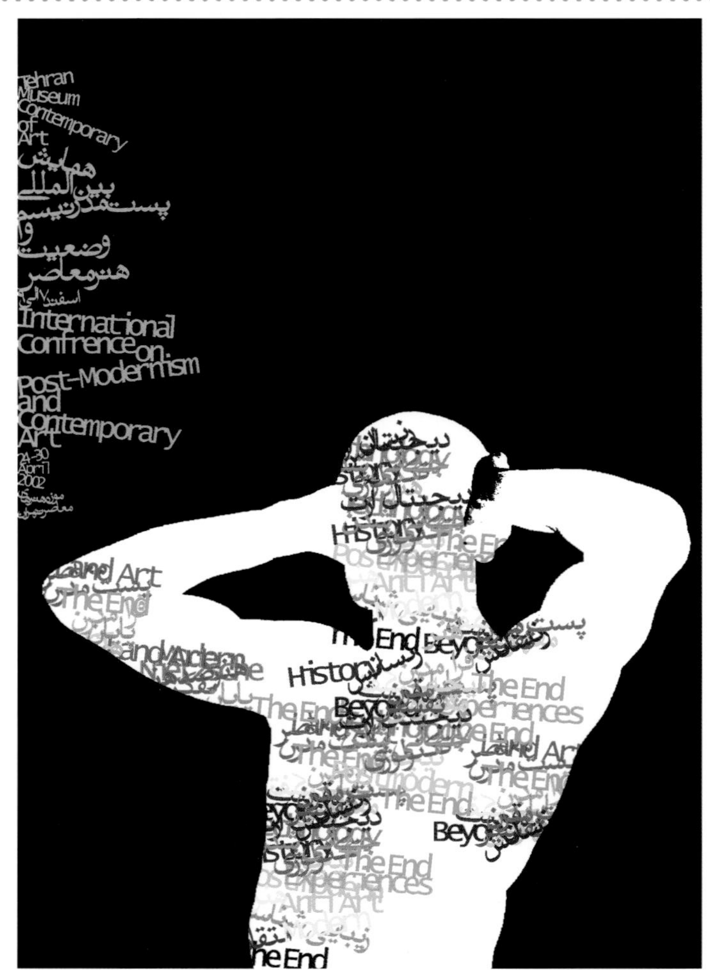
Tehran
Museum
Contemporary
of
Art
International
Confrence on
Post-Modernism
and
Contemporary
Art
24-30
April
2002

14

دومین دوسالانه
بین المللی
نقاشی
جهان اسلام
The Second
International
Biennial
Painting
of the Islamic
World Tehran 2002

I have known Sebastian Campos—a.k.a. Aficionado—for six or seven years, since he was a design student in Barcelona. His approach to work was always considered; he has always had a very specific way of doing things. Since then he has moved to London and established a fine reputation for himself, initially as a partner of the the design trio Praline. He has remained true to his own unique way of working, but living in London seems to have sharpened him up somewhat. • • Recent projects include an identity, packaging, and promotional program for the English punk band Ikara Colt. He describes the project as "an oblique attempt to update and expand 'punk' clichés," which is exactly what he did, with a visual language that expresses the punky, art-rock dynamic of the band. Typography plays an important role, with clear sans-serif type and ordered grids. However, it's the cut-and-paste aesthetic of original punk graphics that is updated to great effect here. Each band member was given a disposable camera to take "on tour" photographs, which were edited by the band and placed in the inner sleeve of the CD as stickers. The front cover and gatefold interior have blank squares with generic captions, leaving the fans to choose their own story. It is a great idea that actively involves both the band and their fanbase. • • The catalogue/poster/invitation Aficionado created with Praline for the exhibition *My Generation: 24 Hours of Video Art* recalls the moving type of video and film credits: The type has been layered and overprinted to create a sense of animation. Everything was designed in modules, so that each plate produced nine flyers/invitations, two posters, and one catalogue (with copy printed on the reverse). This ingenious solution put all the budget into one piece of print, and the results speak for themselves. • • In September 2000, Praline gave a talk that dealt with the theme of "wayfinding" in their work. The poster designed to promote the event employs an arrow-shaped Post-it note, found among their office supplies, and a great bit of copy: "(t)here." Here and there. It is a very direct piece of communication, a problem solved with characteristic logic and clarity. Quiet and unassuming, it does everything it needs to do and nothing more. • • Fernando Gutiérrez • •

1–2 Front and back of unfoldable leaflet/poster for the presentation of the Interactive Surfaces project / Royal College of Art and Harper Mackey Architects / United Kingdom / 2002

3 Invitation to talk by Rebecca Brown and Mike Heath (with Matthew Savidge) / Central Saint Martins College of Art and Design / United Kingdom / 2000

4 Souvenir for talk by Praline at Harper Mackay Architects (with Regine Stefan and David Tanguy) / United Kingdom / 2000

5 Poster for *Graphic Britain* exhibition at Magma Bookshop / United Kingdom / 2002

6 Poster for *Transmission02: Utopia* exhibition and publication (with Regine Stefan and David Tanguy) / :phunk / Singapore / 2001

Aficionado

London

1

2

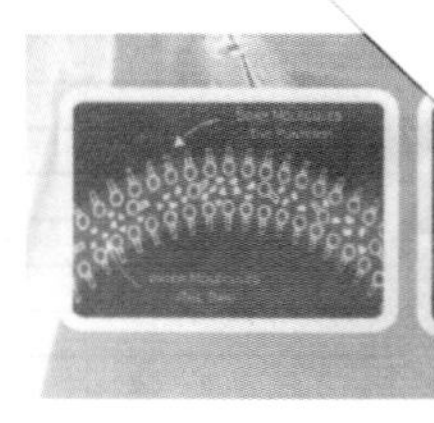

③

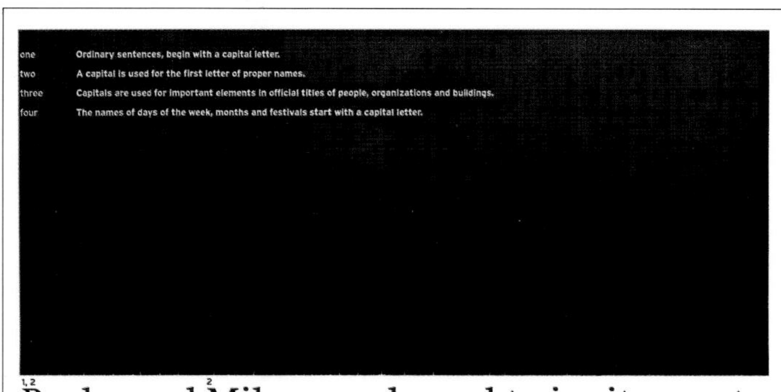

one Ordinary sentences, begin with a capital letter.
two A capital is used for the first letter of proper names.
three Capitals are used for important elements in official titles of people, organizations and buildings.
four The names of days of the week, months and festivals start with a capital letter.

[1, 2] Becky and [2] Mike are pleased to invite you to attend a casual gathering [comma: indicates a short pause or slight interruption] in which they will reveal the conceptual framework that underlies their professional practice [full stop: Used at the end of sentences that express complete statements]

[1, 3] Friday 3rd of [3] March [comma: indicates a short pause or slight interruption] 12 pm [full stop: Used at the end of sentences that express complete statements]

[1, 4] Room 410 [semicolon: A stronger more definite break in a sentence than a comma, less than a full stop] [4] Graphics [comma: indicates a short pause or slight interruption] 3rd year studio [full stop: Used at the end of sentences that express complete statements]

④

Prăliñé

P: 55 Tompion House, Percival St, London, ec1v 0hx
T: +44 20 7689 1372 F: +44 490 2167
E: pralinefamily@hotmail.com

Sebastián Campos M: 07880 638 951
Regine Stefan M: 07818 072 788
David Tanguy M: 07799 842 997

(t)here

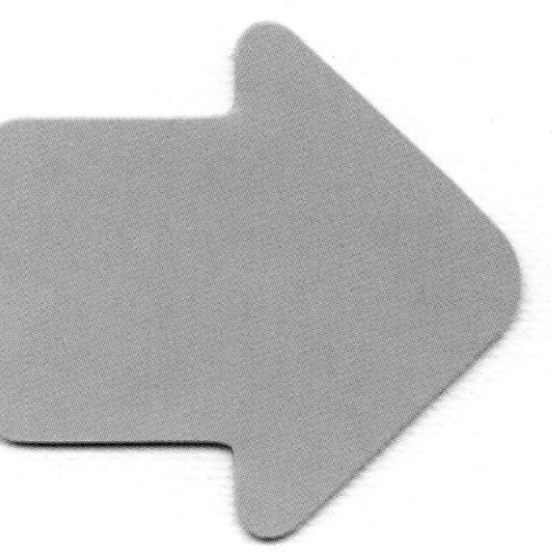

⑤

Elementary Edutainment

⑥

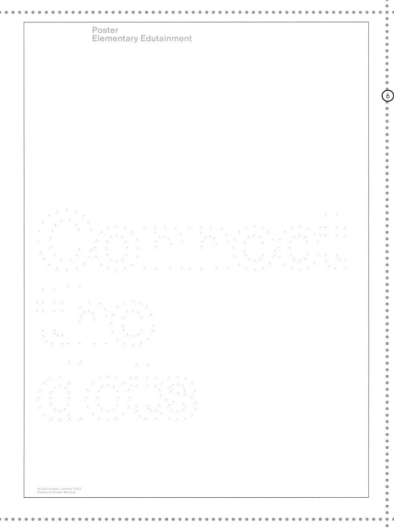

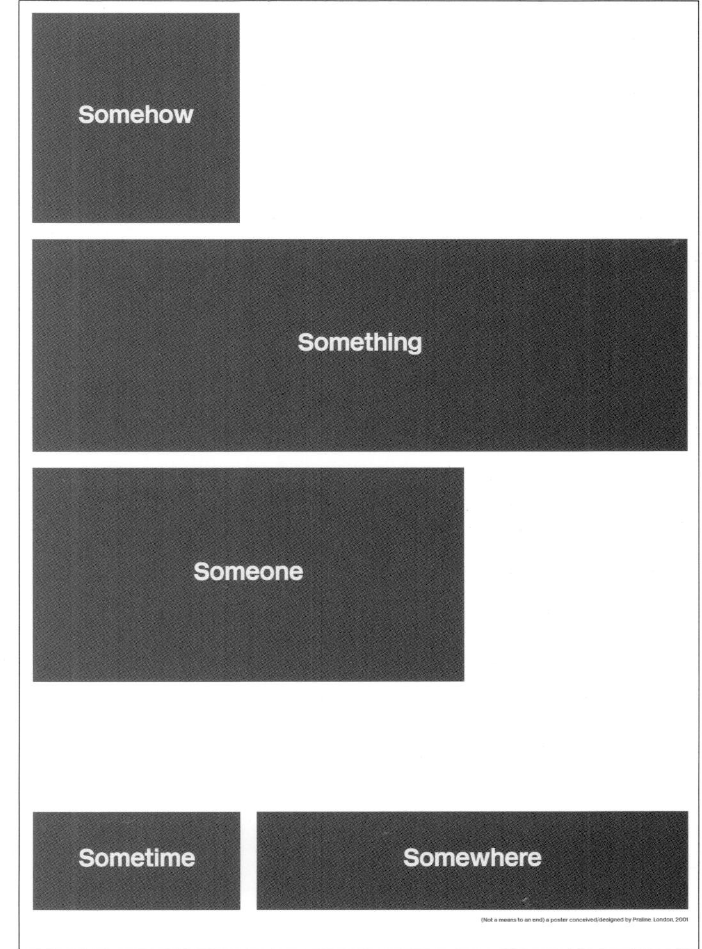

(Not a means to an end) a poster conceived/designed by Praline. London, 2001

7
8

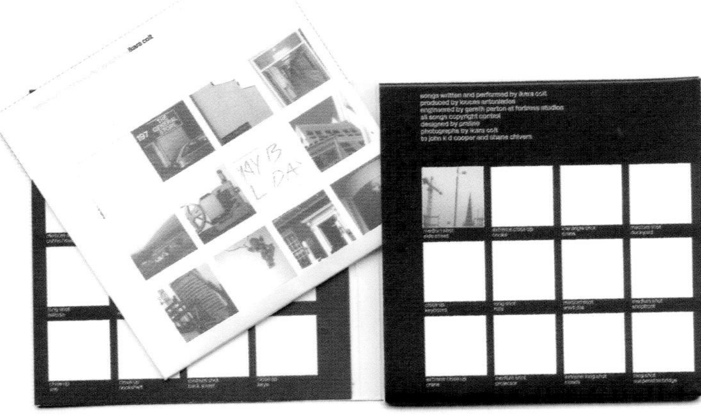

ikara colt

bad photo bad photo bad photo bad photo bad photo bad photo bad photo bad photo bad photo bad photo bad photo bad photo

extendedplay

basic instructions ep

longplay

chat and business

9

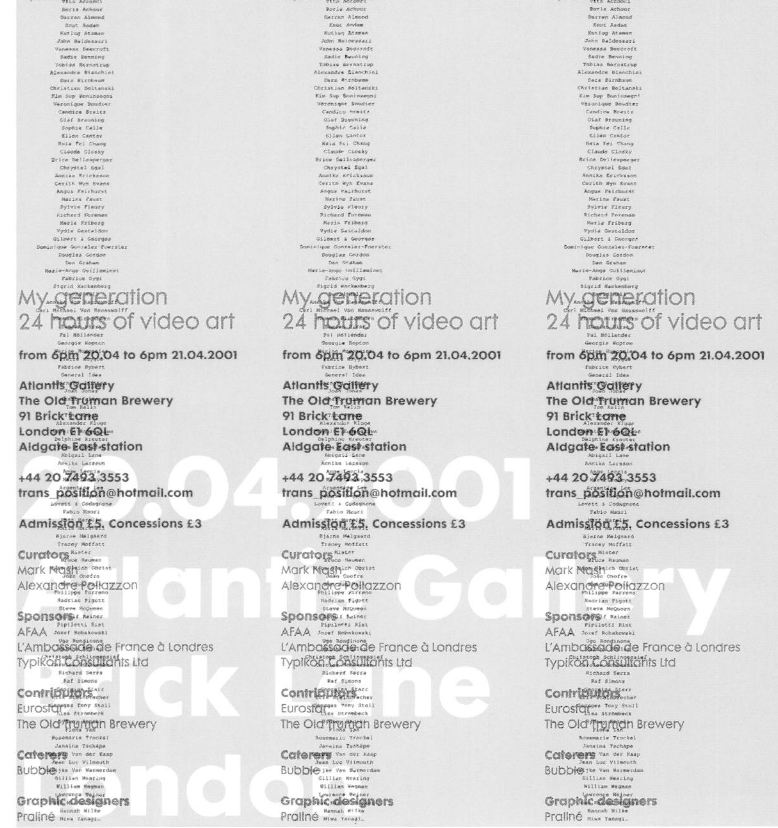

10

7–8 CD packaging, *Chat and Business*, by Ikara Colt / Fantastic Plastic Records / United Kingdom / 2001 / Inner sleeve contains adhesive photographs by the band that can be used to personalize the generic cover.
9 Poster for two recordings by Ikara Colt / Fantastic Plastic Records / United Kingdom / 2002
10 Cover, *My Generation, 24 Hours of Video Art* exhibition catalogue (with Regine Stefan and David Tanguy) / Atlantis Gallery / United Kingdom / 2001 / Catalogue designed as part of a module that allows each print plate to produce nine invitations, two posters, and one catalogue.
11–14 Book design for *The Mobile Effect* by Sadie Plant / Milk Projects and Motorola / United Kingdom / 2001
15–18 Cover and spreads, first issue of *Graphic* magazine, Spring 2003 (with Sam Baker and Inca Starzinsky) / BIS Publishers / United Kingdom and The Netherlands / 2003

on the mobile
credits
page 20

Photography: Dr Sadie Plant (except pp 4, 6, 8, 11-12 Drew Jarrett)

on the mobile
contents
page 21

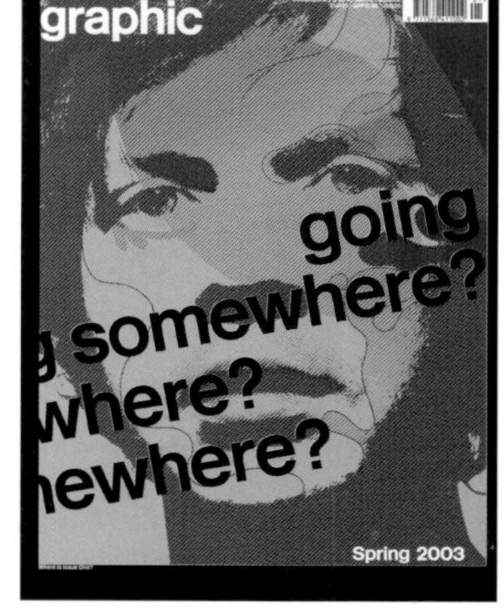

graphic
going
somewhere?
where?
ewhere?
Spring 2003

11
12
13
14

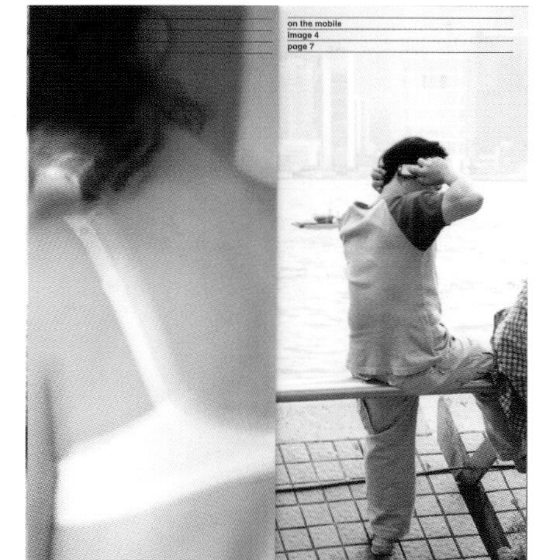

on the mobile
image 4
page 7

15
16
17
18

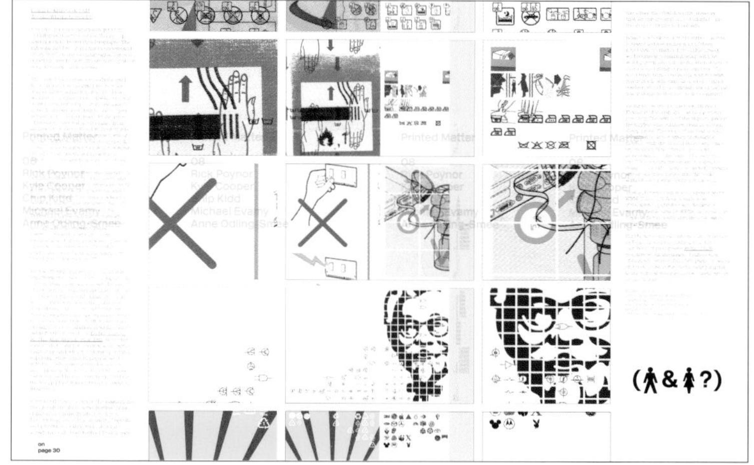

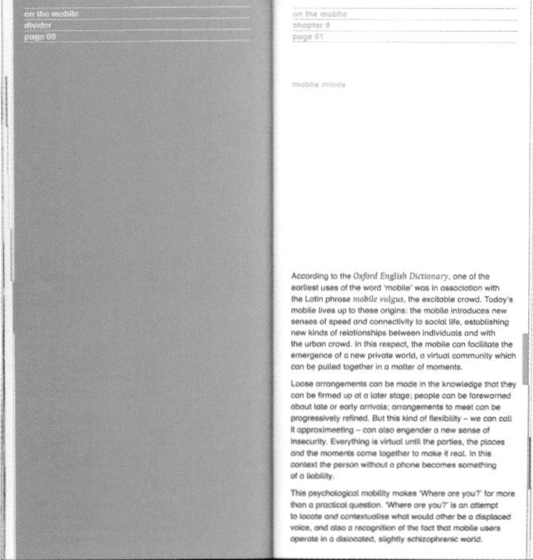

on the mobile
chapter 6
page 61
mobile minds
According to the Oxford English Dictionary, one of the earliest uses of the word 'mobile' was in association with the Latin phrase mobile vulgus, the excitable crowd. Today's mobile lives up to these origins: the mobile introduces new senses of speed and connectivity to social life, establishing new kinds of relationships between individuals and with the urban crowd. In this respect, the mobile can facilitate the emergence of a new private world, a virtual community which can be pulled together in a matter of moments.
Loose arrangements can be made in the knowledge that they can be firmed up at a later stage; people can be forewarned about late or early arrivals; arrangements to meet can be progressively refined. But this kind of flexibility – we can call it approximeeting – can also engender a new sense of insecurity. Everything is virtual until the parties, the places and the moments come together to make it real. In this context the person without a phone becomes something of a liability.
This psychological mobility makes 'Where are you?' for more than a practical question. 'Where are you?' is an attempt to locate and contextualise what would other be a displaced voice, and also a recognition of the fact that mobile users operate in a dislocated, slightly schizophrenic world.

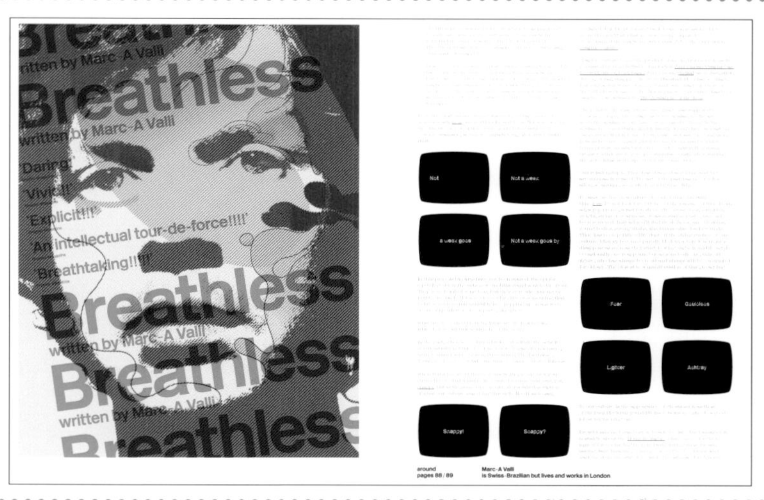

Breathless
written by Marc-A Valli
'Daring'
'Vivid'
'Explicit!!!'
'An intellectual tour-de-force!!!!'
'Breathtaking!!!!!'

on the mobile
chapter 1
page 30

Many people feel irritated and disconcerted by this new electronic soundtrack. All ringing phones are disruptive, even arresting. As Marshall McLuhan observed in *Understanding Media*, an incoming call provokes a sense of expectation, even urgency, which is why usually feel compelled to answer a ringing phone, even when they know the call is not for them. Like a calling bird, a ringing phone demands a response. Public uses of the mobile spread this tension to all those within earshot, while leaving them powerless to intervene: only the person to whom the call is made is in a position to respond.[3]

Mobile calls can come at any time, at any place, and in the company of any number of onlookers and eavesdroppers. The etiquette of handling such interventions has become a matter of some debate, and in many parts of the world, the ability to handle them – on the part of the recipient and all those within earshot – has become an important social skill.[4] A ringing mobile will often take precedence over the social interactions it disrupts: the need or desire to answer a call often outweighs the importance of maintaining the flow of face-to-face conversation. This is why even a silent mobile can make its presence felt as though it were an addition to a social group, and why many people feel that just the knowledge that a call might intervene tends to divert attention from those present at the time. The mobile tends to siphon concentration, demanding attention even when it is not in use; for many couples, its presence can be as powerful and distracting as that of a third person. Some contributors to this research suggested that the mobile functions as a **gooseberry phone** – an unwanted addition to the pair. In the UK, a few people admitted to making **gooseberry calls** to friends out on dates in order to get a progress report.

3
This also accounts for the profound sense of melancholy associated with unanswered calls, especially when, as is often the case in the wake of train crashes, car accidents, or natural disasters, mobile phones keep ringing long after there is anyone to answer them.

4
Peter Laufer, *Wireless Etiquette: A Guide to the Changing World of Instant Communication*, Omnipoint Communications, 1999

on the mobile
chapter 1
page 31

The receipt of a public call tends to be met by one of three responses. These are **flight**, in which users immediately move to absent themselves from their social situation; **suspension**, in which recipients stay put, but stop whatever they are doing for the duration of a call and effectively cut themselves off from their environment; and **persistence**, in which users stay put and engaged with the actual world, as far as possible carrying on with whatever they were doing before they made or took the call.

All these responses run some risk that people who are present at the time will feel abandoned by the person who has answered the mobile, and in so doing has opted to be answerable to the device rather than to them. Several American contributors to this research drew attention to the disempowering effects of situations in which they felt as though they were being dropped and picked up by their companions without any chance to negotiate the terms. As well as regarding the mobile monologues of passing strangers as inappropriate and unwelcome impositions on their personal space, they expected calls to be deferred or at least taken out of earshot when in the company of friends.

Observers tend to be more tolerant of users where mobile use is long-standing and high. Users also tend to be more considerate, more sensitive to their surroundings than their counterparts in countries where the mobile is less integrated into the conduct of everyday life. Users in more mobile countries are also more likely to use their devices for purposes other than telephony, and much of this use is inoffensive and discreet.

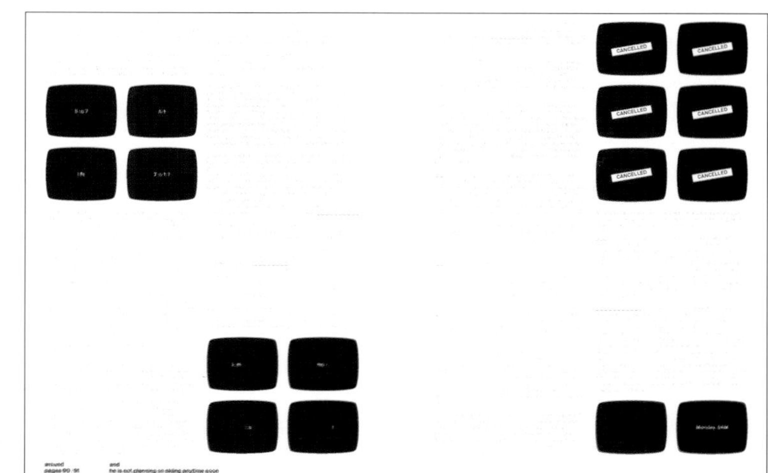

CANCELLED

The posters from Kum Nam Baik's "Recollection" series are filled with countless dots created by brushwork reminiscent of snowflakes in a cold Korean winter gust or petals dancing in the wind of a spring thunderstorm. Using the technique of pointillism, Baik seems to push the underlying meaning of the letters and words deep into the backdrop of the picture. Are they expressions of anger or pain, or of joy? In this group of works we can find the origin of Baik's sensitivities, and within its creative process we can even sense the presence of his hopes and aspirations. • •One can find the same spirit in his posters that contain more concrete visual messages. Among the works of his private exhibition titled *The Style of Korea* one can find deeply felt songs in praise of human creativity through the still, round-shaped motifs—the Korean coins, the wheels, the oval-shaped bamboo basket, the round tiles, and the round pile of hot red peppers. • •In the posters for the exhibition of Korean Buddha statues, Baik's wisdom becomes apparent, for he goes beyond the traditional worshiping of the Buddha from a frontal view, and, by also showing the Buddha in profile, focuses on the beauty of the sculpture itself. • •In one of the posters from the "My favorite Seoul" series, there is a colorful Korean pastry with the face of a fish floating in the sky above the Seoul Tower, a nostalgic symbol of gentle, heartwarming East Asian humor. • •The name "Baik" means "white." The Asian design world of the present day tends to be swallowed into the whirl of the volatile economic realities and the culture of the information age. It is my wish that amid all this turmoil Baik will remain a precious white bastion, reminding us of the importance of true creativity. • •Shigeo Fukuda • •

Kum Nam Baik

Seoul

1–2 Posters for *Exhibition of Korean Buddhism* [sic] *Sculpture* / National Museum of Korea / 2002
3–4 Posters for museum opening / Haein-sa Museum / Korea / 2002
5–6 Posters for museum opening / Gahoe Museum / Korea / 2002

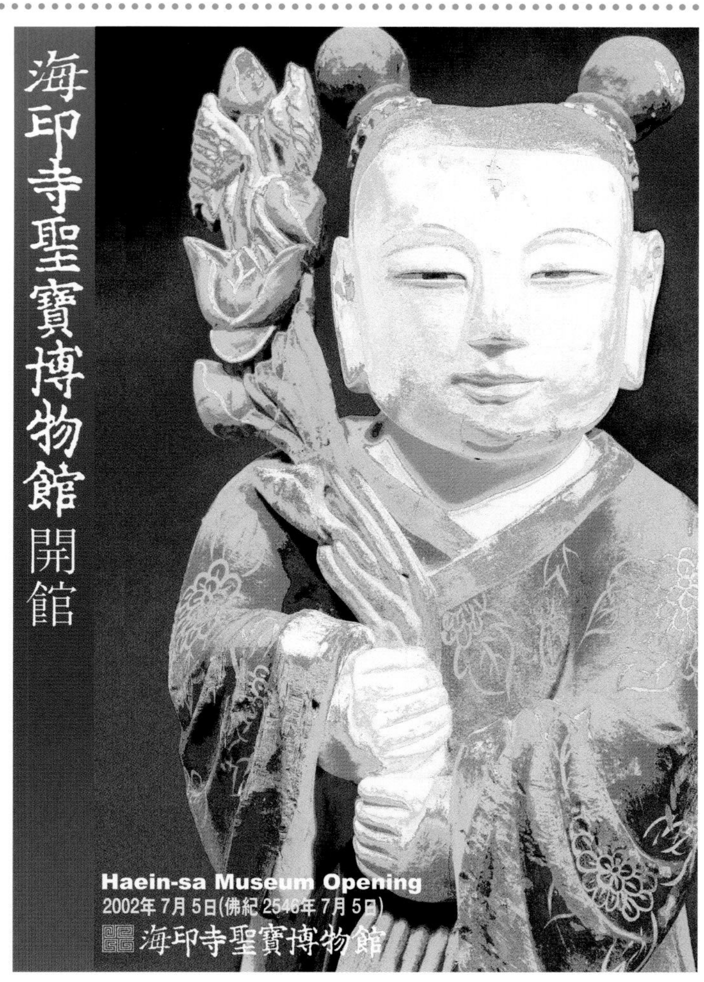
海印寺聖寶博物館開館
Haein-sa Museum Opening
2002年 7月 5日(佛紀 2546年 7月 5日)
海印寺聖寶博物館

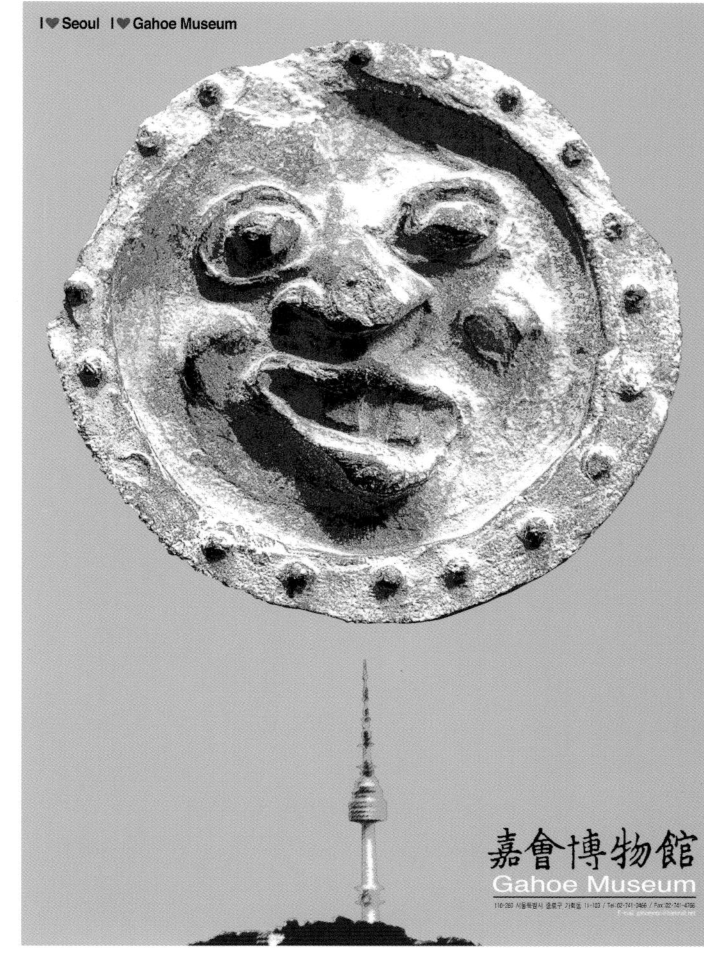
I ♥ Seoul I ♥ Gahoe Museum
嘉會博物館
Gahoe Museum

3
4

5
6

海印寺聖寶博物館開館
Haein-sa Museum Opening
2002年 7月 5日(佛紀 2546年 7月 5日)
海印寺聖寶博物館

嘉會博物館
Gahoe Museum

7 8

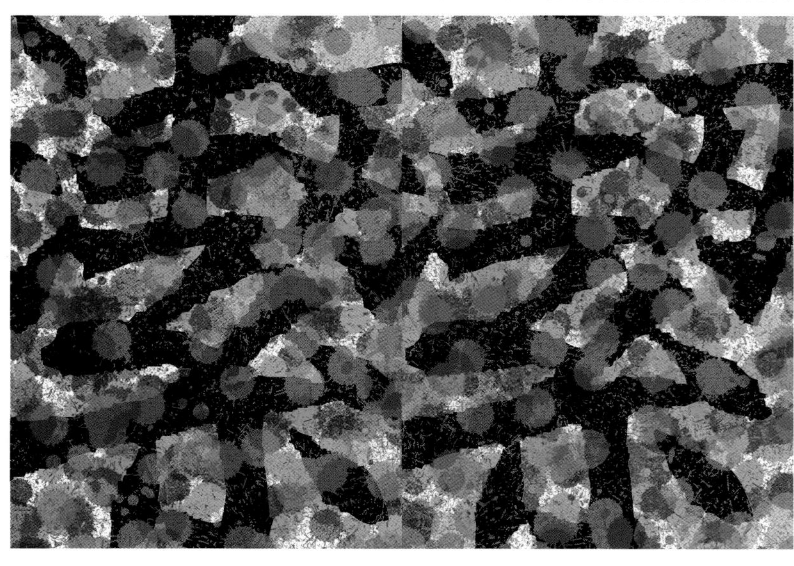

9

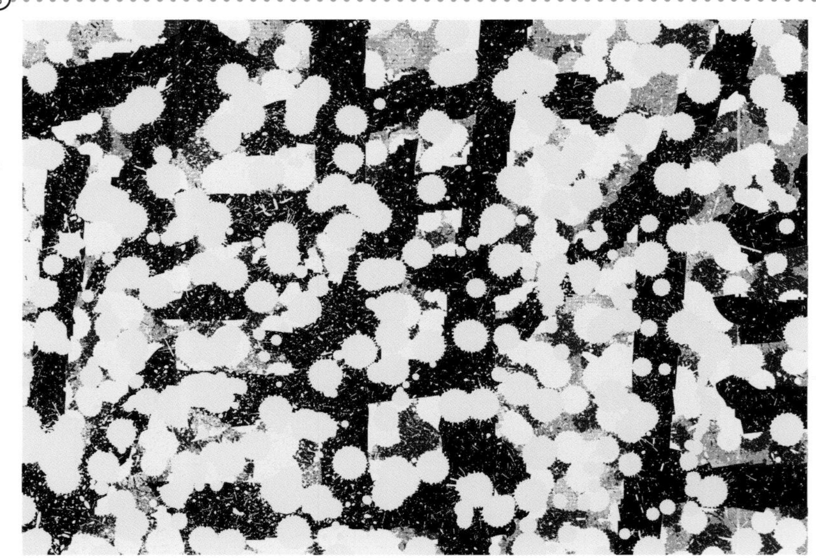

10

Kum Nam Baik

7–8 Self-commissioned poster series "Letter" / Korea / 1984
9–10 Self-commissioned poster series "Recollection" / Korea / 2002
11–19 Self-commissioned poster series "The Style of Korea" / Korea / 2002

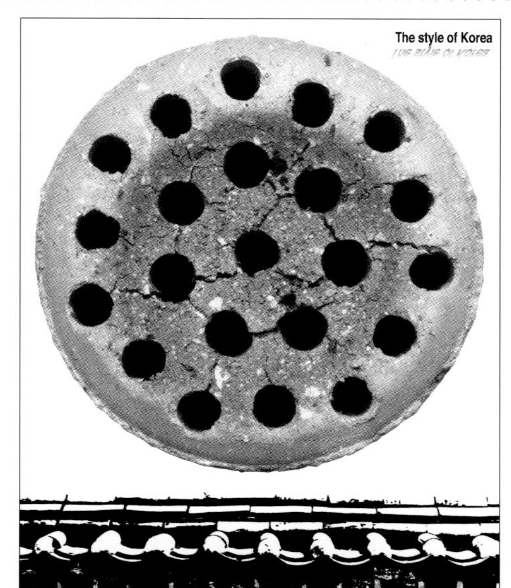

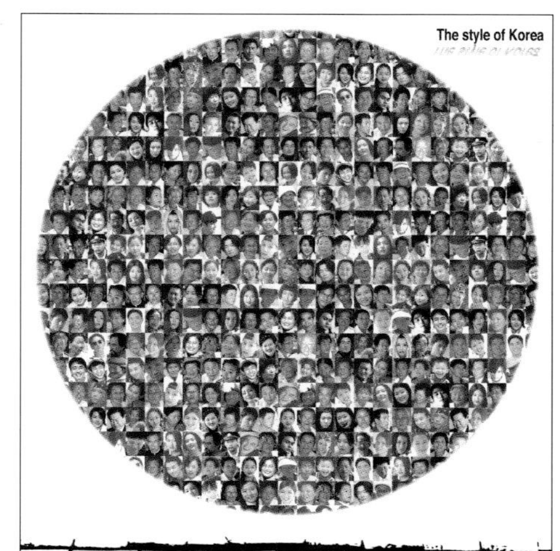

11 12 13

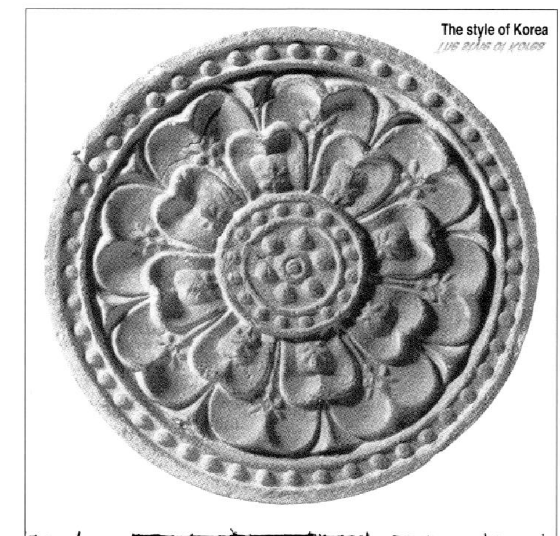

14 15 16

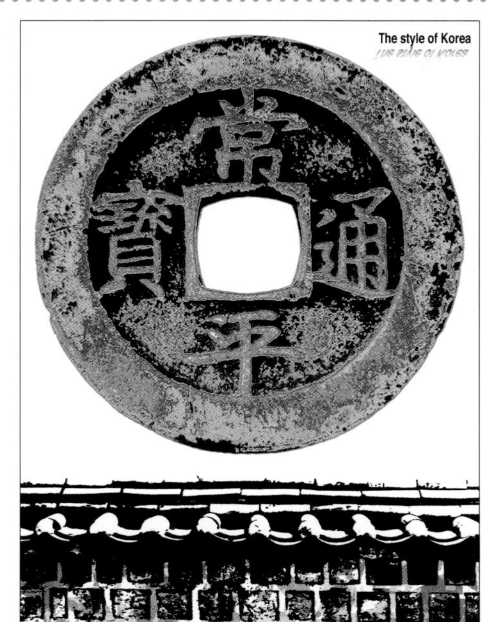

17 18 19

Newut is the name of one of André Baldinger's font designs. It sounds like "*die neue Wut*" (the new rage). Yet this Newut is quite tame, no sign of rage at all. Here somebody has cultivated a rage, abstracted it, safeguarded its essence, and divided it into spatial forms with a clear perception. Baldinger deliberately strips away everything that is inessential and dismisses it. As independent, self-reliant entities, what remains forms his true illustrative starting point. The resulting unobtrusive complexity makes for a linear thinker, who never wants to be didactic with his work. The Newut font cannot deny an affinity to the Nordic. The German characteristic is very much anchored in it, as becomes apparent in the lowercase application of capital letters. Maybe it represents the first steps toward the German adoption of the lowercase for nouns. • • Baldinger likes to expand toward the plane, measure far across spaces, and sit down in these typographical worlds. Three-dimensionality tempts him, and his answers are convincing, because he transports and transposes in an illustrative language that speaks of respect. He is a democrat of forms. • • Turning the world by 90 degrees makes him a "mover of perspectives" in the positive sense, not a magician, but an observer who likes to retell a story. Although, or because, he orients himself with the help of grids, real and metaphoric, the observer feels further planes lurking behind. It is as if a book became transparent and the complete contents could enjoy visual equality. • • Baldinger is distinct, his path seems logical and straightforward. As a typographer he comes from the two-dimensional, further along he turned to three-dimensional exhibition and interior design, and now, in his stage designs, he is adds the element of movement. Precisely because he is a linear thinker and his illustrative deductions are of interest, his work will gain in importance; he is a man of quiet persistence. Yet at times he allows himself to submerge the world in outrageous colors. • • Werner Jeker • •

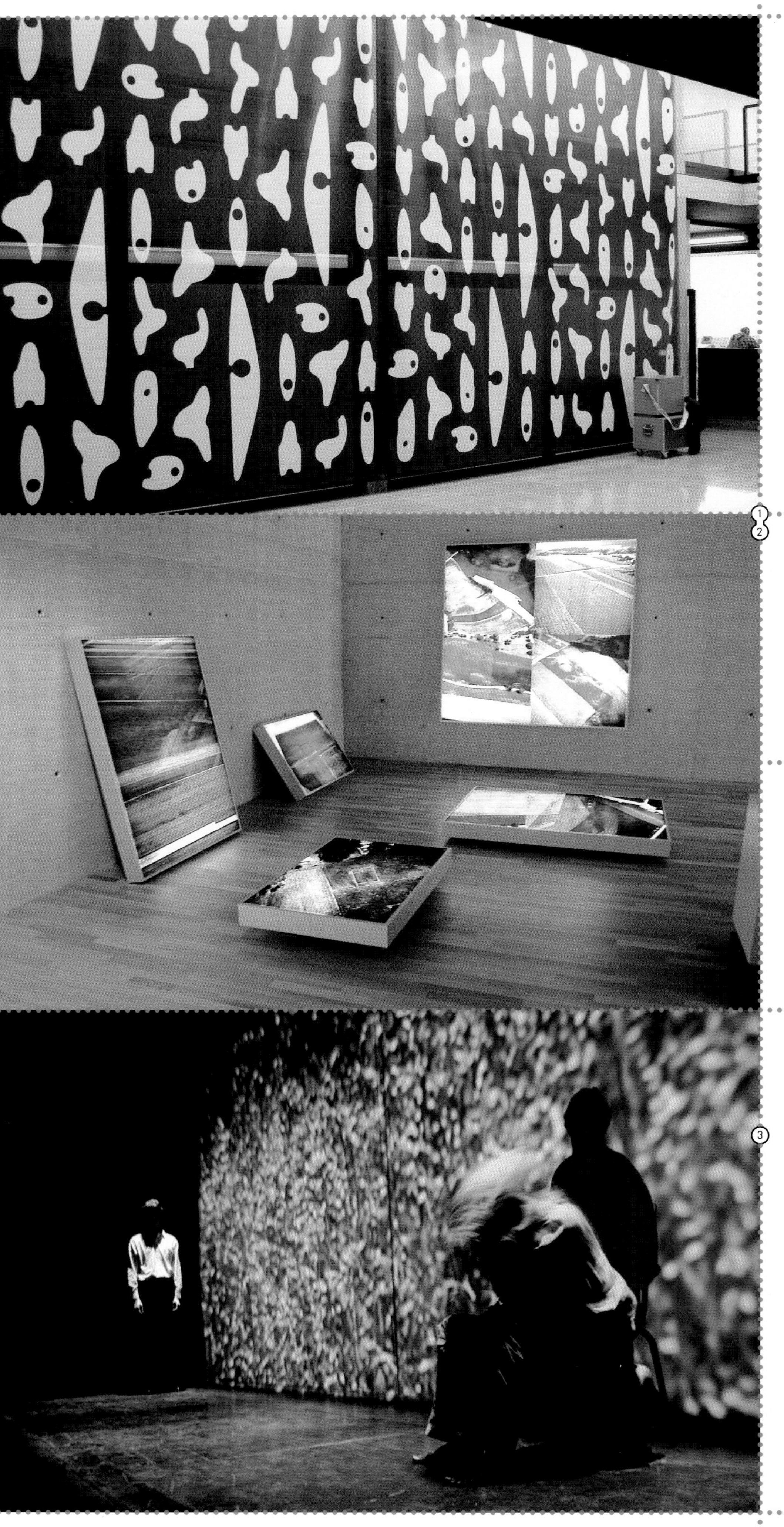

1–2 Entrance wall and light boxes as part of visual conception for the permanent exhibition (with Anne Crausaz and François Rappo) / Musée Latenium, Neuchatel / Switzerland / 2001
3 Stage design for play *Le Triptique de tiberiade*, by Jose Saramago (with Rodolphe Aute) / Le crochet a nuages / Switzerland / 2002
4 Poster for promotion of the Newut typeface / amb+ / Switzerland / 2000
5 Poster for play *La vie est un songe*, by Pedro Calderón de la Barca / Le crochet a nuages / Switzerland / 1996
6 Poster for play *Le Triptique de tiberiade*, by Jose Saramago / Le crochet a nuages / Switzerland / 2002
7 Poster for play *Tandis que j'agonise*, by William Faulkner / Le crochet a nuages / Switzerland / 2000

André Baldinger

Paris/Lausanne

4

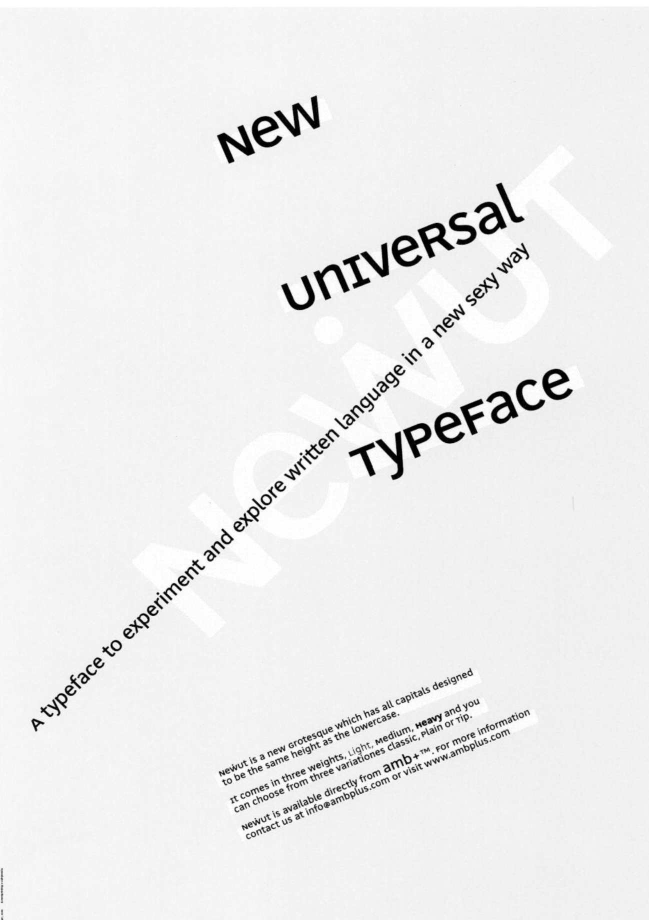
New
uNIVeRsal
TYPeFace
NewUT
A typeface to experiment and explore written language in a new sexy way
NewUt is a new grotesque which has all capitals designed to be the same height as the lowercase.
It comes in three weights, Light, Medium, Heavy and you can choose from three variations classic, Plain or rip.
NewUt is available directly from amb+™. For more information contact us at info@ambplus.com or visit www.ambplus.com

5

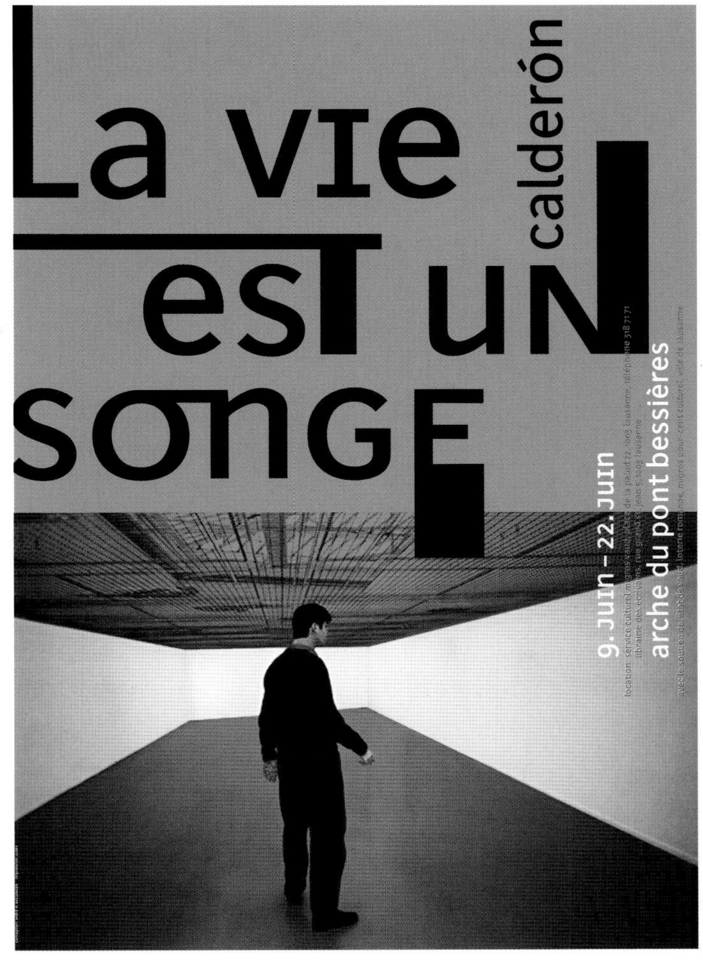
La vIE
esT uN
SONGE
calderón
9. juin – 22. juin
arche du pont bessières

6

LE TRIPTYQUE DE TIBERIADE DE JOSE SARAMAGO
THEATRE PAR LE CROCHET A NUAGES
GRANGE DE DORIGNY DU 3 AU 15 DECEMBRE
LOCATION 021 318 71 71 OU 021 692 21 12
AVEC LE SOUTIEN DE LA VILLE DE LAUSANNE — LA FONDATION NESTLE POUR L'ART — LA LOTERIE ROMANDE

7

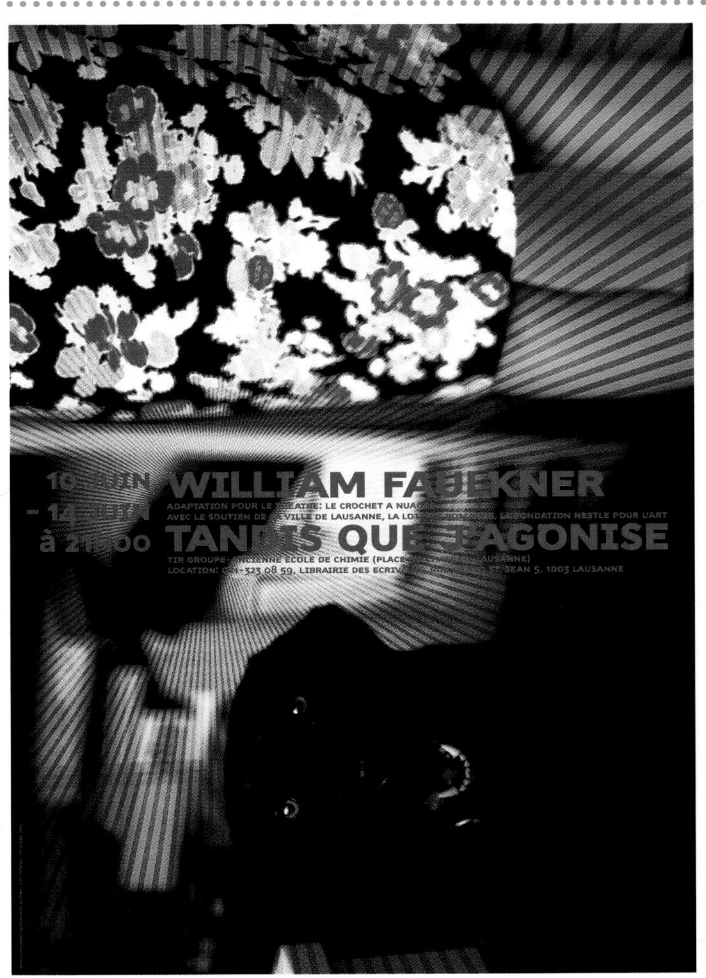
WILLIAM FAULKNER

All signes of amb+ B-Dot shown in Light

Aa Bb Cc Dd Ee Ff Gg Hh Ii Jj Kk Ll Mm Nn Oo Pp Qq Rr Ss Tt Uu Vv
Ww Xx Yy Zz 1234567890¬%‰.,:;-–—·‘’‚“”„‹›«»*/?!¿¡()[]{}
†‡§¶¤¥£ƒ¢$ﬁﬂßæÆœŒøØ&áâàäãåçéêèëíîìïñóôòöõúûùüÿÁÂÀÄ
ÃÅÇÉÊËÈÍÎÏÌÑÓÔÒÖÕÚÛÙÜŸ©®™@▪…‡ªº+-=≠±µ|≤≥ (10)

amb+ B-Dot Light, Regular, Bold, Black

The quick brown fox jumps over the lazy dog 1234567890 ©®™@▪
The quick brown fox jumps over the lazy dog 1234567890 ©®™@▪
The quick brown fox jumps over the lazy dog 1234567890 ©®™@▪
The quick brown fox jumps over the lazy dog 1234567890 ©®™@▪

amb+ B-Dot special

The quick brown fox jumps over the lazy dog 1234567890 ©®™@▪

aa**also**…………B-Dot

André Baldinger

8–9 Lettering on roof of the railway station Interface Flon / Tschumi/Merlini/Ventura Architects / Switzerland / 2000
10 Type sample for the B-Dot typeface / amb+ / Switzerland / 2000
11–12 Cover page and spread, cultural newspaper *Rote Fabrik Zeitung* no. 157 / IG Rote Fabrik / Switzerland / 1999
13 Cover and spreads, *Toit du Monde* / Sigismond de Vajay and Lars Mueller Publishers / Switzerland / 2002

13

Jop van Bennekom is a pure avant-gardist, an artist who uses the medium of a "magazine" as his canvas. His own publication, *Re-Magazine*, is actually visual art. It is the communications instrument of a small group of kindred spirits, but the communication is channeled through bookstores. Another magazine, which he generates with other partners, is the gay zine *Butt*, a demonstrative expression of his own homosexuality. But here too he uses the publication to comment on—or rather to pay homage to—the kind of design amateurism that characterizes such zines: fast, artless typography, improper fonts for headlines. Still, the details show that van Bennekom knows what he's doing; he's just not that interested in the craft. He is an anti-designer. He is a writer, editor, what have you, but he always gets a bit grouchy when you call him a "graphic designer." "Magazine maker" would be more appropriate. Or "artist."•• Van Bennekom's design for the architecture magazine *Forum*, on the other hand, is the complete opposite of the deliberate amateurism of his other publications. He uses carefully balanced texts and images with very readable typography. But here also, he is looking for the edges of what still communicates and what doesn't. All of his work demonstrates he is a good designer who probably thinks that's not enough. In an Andy Warhol–like fashion, working with a loose group of like minds, he experiments with the medium of magazines, with communication, with editorial formats.•• I find it hard to define van Bennekom's work, but I love the research it confronts you with: a *Fluxus*-like approach to "performing" a magazine. *Re-Magazine* is a performance about the medium of magazines. Seeing it in the light of my own background with *Fluxus*, I can't help finding that fascinating.•• Anthon Beeke••

1

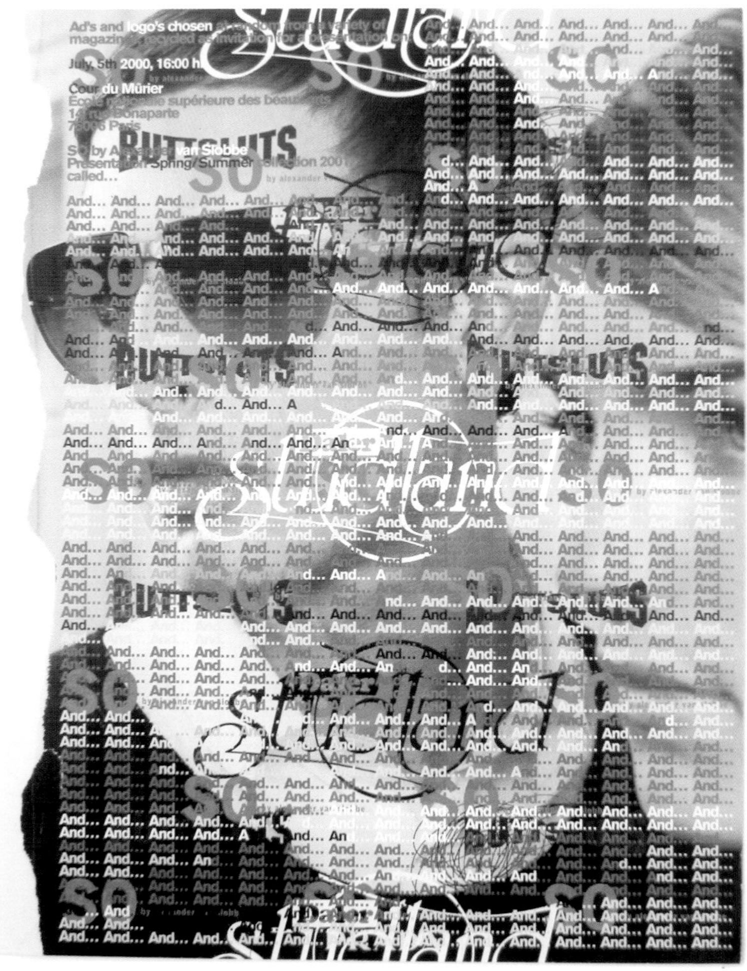

2

1 Invitation for presentation of Droog design at the Salone del Mobile, Milan / Droog Design / Netherlands / 2001 / The invitation also introduced Droog's new house style "droog non id."
2 Invitation for spring/summer collection fashion show / So by Alexander van Slobbe / Netherlands / 2000
3–6 Cover and spreads, *BUTT* magazine no. 3 / Netherlands / 2002 / *BUTT* is a self-published, interview-based gay magazine.
7–8 Cover and spread, *BUTT* magazine no. 5 / Netherlands / 2002
9–10 Spreads, *BUTT* magazine no. 4 / Netherlands / 2002

Jop van Bennekom

Amsterdam

BUTT

BUTT
INTERNATIONAL FAGGOT MAGAZINE FOR INTERESTING HOMOSEXUALS AND THE MEN WHO LOVE THEM

3
4
5
6

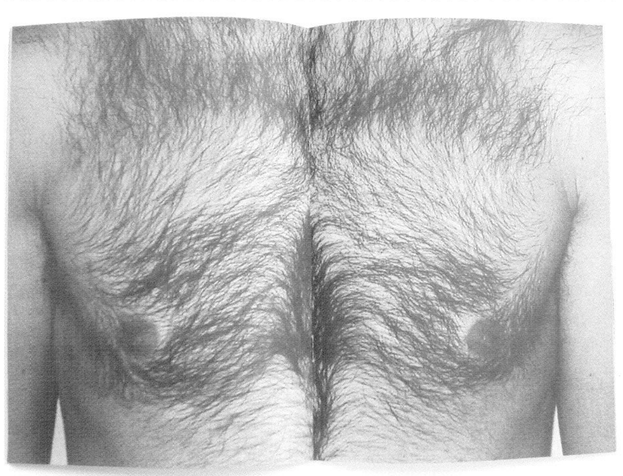

7
8

MATTHIAS VRIENS DUTCH BALLET DANCER TURNS OUT TO BE AMERICAN FASHION PHOTOGRAPHER

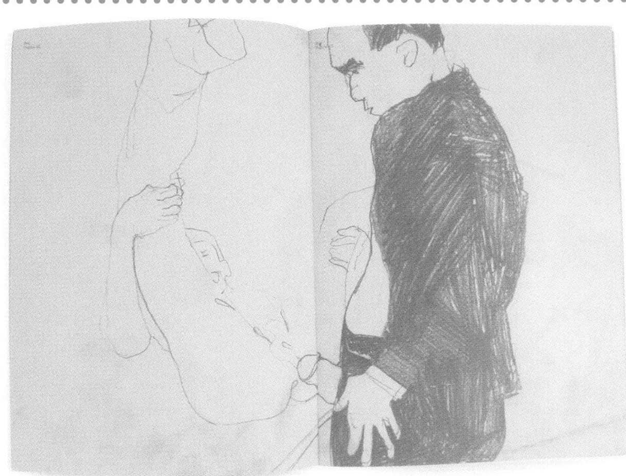

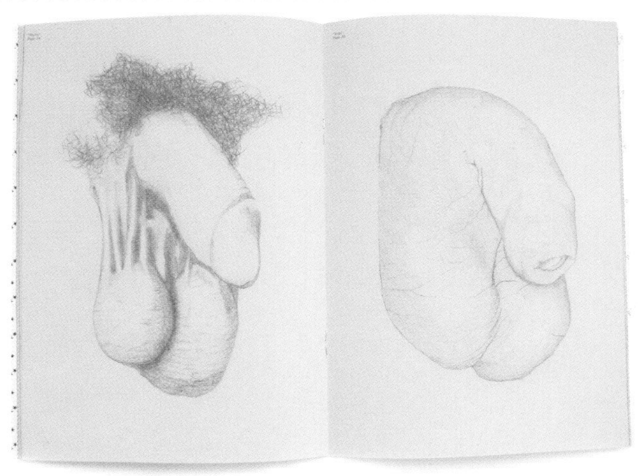

9
10

RECOIL.557
BUREAU AMSTERDAM
trash-à-porter
INEZ IPSC restaurant
Galerie Daniel Buchholz
NOW&WOW
DE PRAKTIJK
SO
THIS ADVERTISEMENT PAGE IS FOR BRUTTO GUSTO

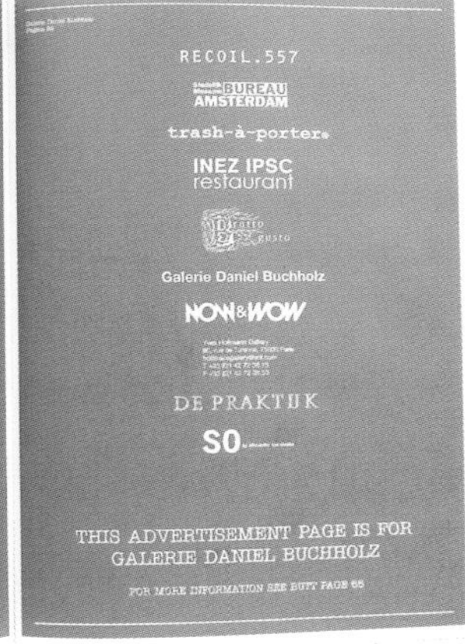
RECOIL.557
BUREAU AMSTERDAM
trash-à-porter
INEZ IPSC restaurant
Galerie Daniel Buchholz
NOW&WOW
DE PRAKTIJK
SO
THIS ADVERTISEMENT PAGE IS FOR GALERIE DANIEL BUCHHOLZ

PATRICK SCHUCKMANN IS SCRIPTWRITER FOR A BLOCKBUSTER SOAP SERIES IN GERMANY AND HAS A LOW VOICE

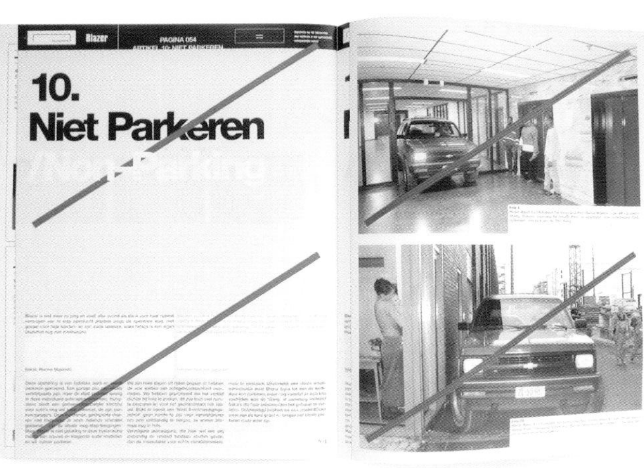

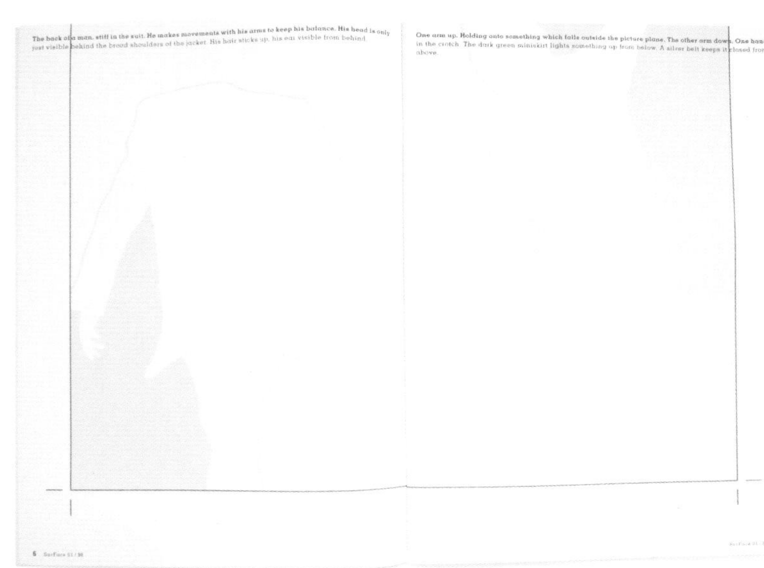

11 12 13

14 15 16

11–13 Spreads, *Forum Magazine* nos. 39 and 40 / Forum magazine and A et A / Netherlands / 1999

14–16 Cover and spreads, *Surface–A Re-make of a Fashion Magazine*, summer 1998 / Surface–Plaatsmaken / Netherlands / 1998 / Surface is an art project published and distributed as a magazine. It shows an abstraction of pages from fashion magazines reprinted in skintone colors.

17–20 Cover and Spreads, *Re-Magazine* no. 8 / Artimo / Netherlands / 2002 / *Re-Magazine* is an intersection of visual culture and editorial experimentation. Issue no. 8, "Re-Magazine # 23: It's Spring 2007," tries to envision a possible near future.

21–24 Cover and Spreads, *Re-Magazine* no. 4 / Jop van Bennekom / Netherlands / 2000 / Issue no. 4, "Boring!," examines the inspiring effects of boredom and nothingness.

Jop van Bennekom

17
18
19
20

21
22
23
24

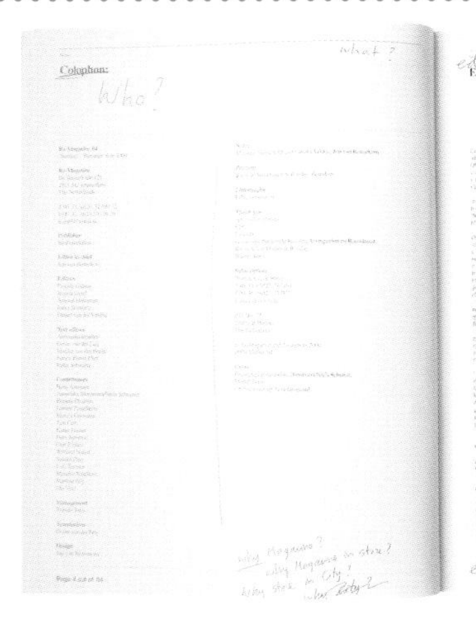

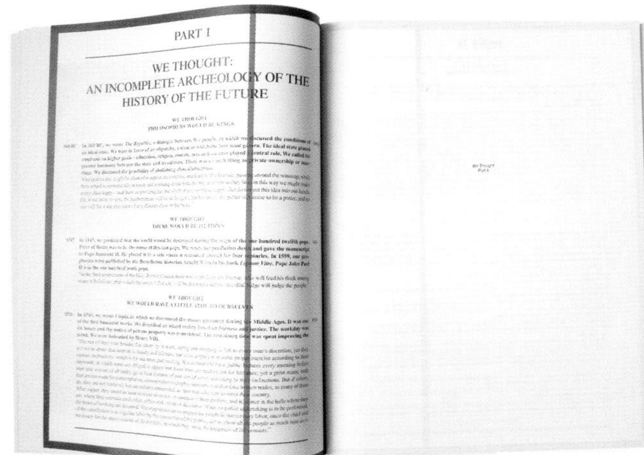

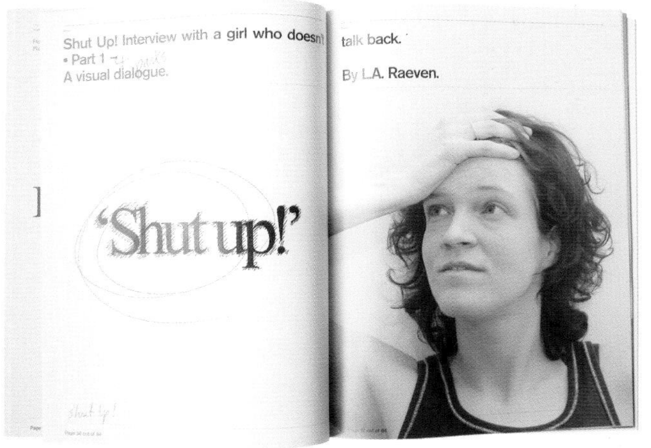

Before Andrew Blauvelt attended Cranbrook Academy of Art, he studied photography and typography. These studies were oriented toward the theoretical, with aspects of semiotics, structuralism, poststructuralism, and postmodernism. At Cranbrook he applied these ideas to design. "This theoretical aspect became the central component of my teaching, writing, and approach to design," he says. "Over the years, the theoretical has broadened to include aspects of sociology and cultural anthropology: more human, less abstract." • • Blauvelt takes design very seriously. He believes that "designers must be open to the entire culture and to history, not to mimic the past or other ideas but to see how design might be changed if it were open to such ways of thinking. I'm more interested in what you might call the history of ideas or a culture of ideas than in designs from the past." At the Walker Art Center in Minneapolis he directs more than one hundred cultural projects a year and thinks deeply and broadly about what is produced. • • In examining projects like *The Indexical Archive*, *365: A Year to View*, and the Design Internship poster, it seems that Blauvelt is focused on transforming overlooked data into fresh, beautiful, informational visual art. "These projects and others come out of a desire to approach design conceptually and systematically. It establishes the parameters, or the rules of the game, and lets the design happen out of these conditions and limitations," he notes. "This was an approach that I had been interested in for many years—which had developed out of a comment I once wrote, 'Why is so much information design so boring?' I was also interested in not being defined by my studies at Cranbrook, which so many people associate with formal excess and visual complexity. It was simply too fashionable to be producing this kind of work." He continues: "I find data and information can be beautiful, especially when it is given visual form: It becomes intelligible in this process. Information is rhetorical, not neutral. It tells a story. For *The Indexical Archive* the story it tells is about a design competition and the many ways in which you can see it; for *365: A Year to View*, it tells of everything the Walker does in one year, it is literal not metaphoric; in the Design Internship poster it shows duration and accumulation, gives an indication of the work produced by the interns. I advocate a simple approach to graphic design but with a complexity of content and information." • • Omar Vulpinari • •

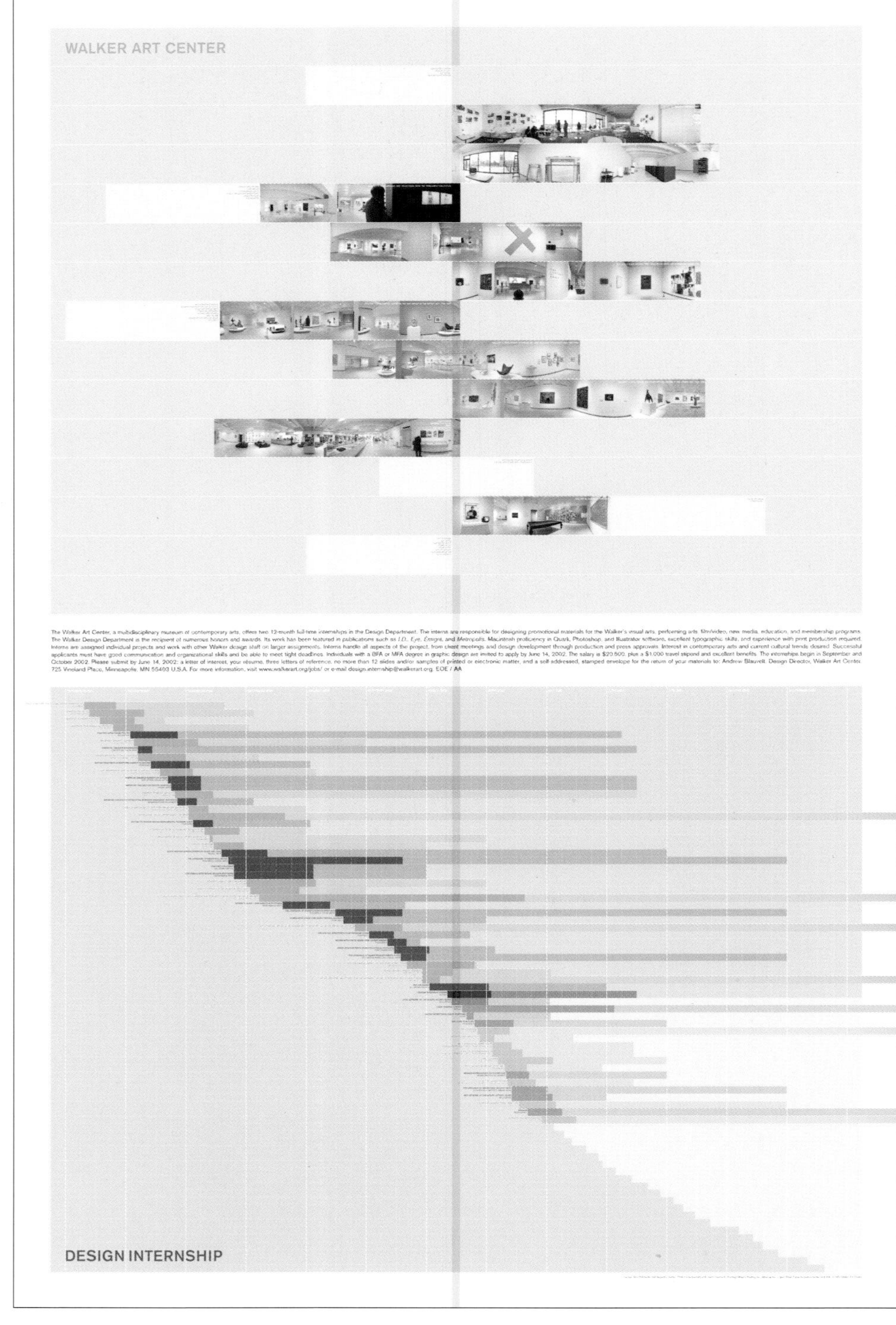

1

Andrew Blauvelt

Minneapolis, Minnesota

1 Poster advertising design internship program (with Alex DeArmond and Alejandro Quinto) / Walker Art Center / USA / 2002
2–4 Cover and spreads, exhibition catalogue *Painting at the Edge of the World* (with Santiago Piedrafita) / Walker Art Center / USA / 2001
5–7 Cover and spreads, exhibition catalogue *Let's Entertain: Life's Guilty Pleasures* (with Santiago Piedrafita) / Walker Art Center / USA / 2000

PAINTING AT THE EDGE OF THE WORLD / DOUGLAS FOGLE / WALKER ART CENTER

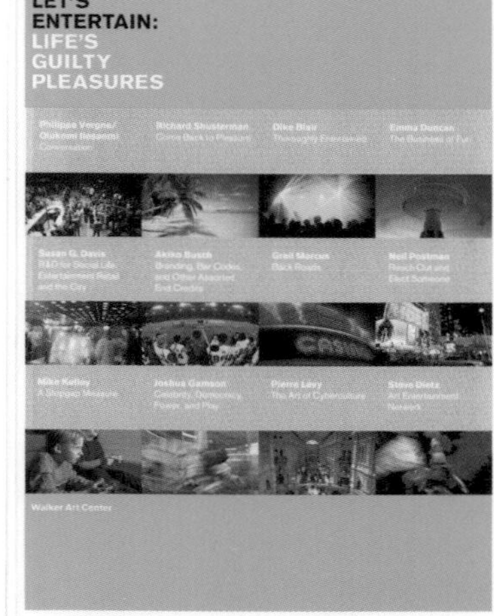
LET'S
ENTERTAIN:
LIFE'S
GUILTY
PLEASURES
Walker Art Center

LET'S
ENTERTAIN:
LIFE'S
GUILTY
PLEASURES
Philippe Vergne/
Olukemi Ilesanmi
Conversation

2
3
4

PAINTING AT THE EDGE OF THE WORLD
28
Painting: The Task of Mourning
Yve-Alain Bois
1986

PAINTING, THE TASK OF MOURNING
29

5
6
7

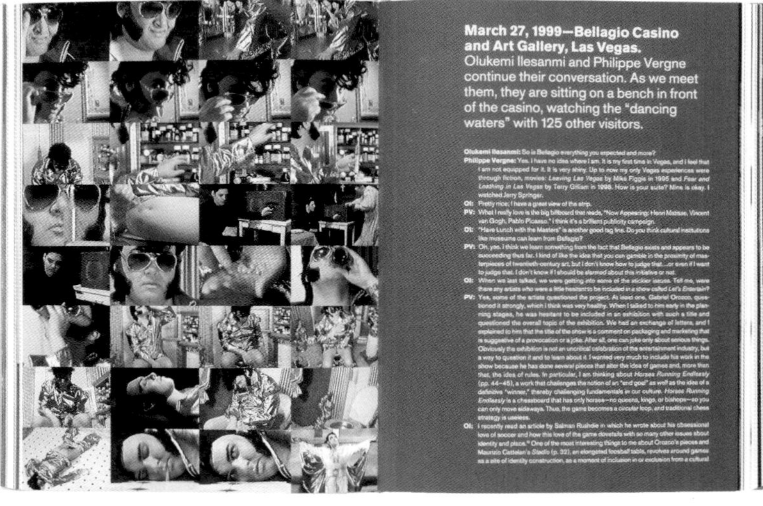
March 27, 1999—Bellagio Casino and Art Gallery, Las Vegas.
Olukemi Ilesanmi and Philippe Vergne continue their conversation. As we meet them, they are sitting on a bench in front of the casino, watching the "dancing waters" with 125 other visitors.

PAINTING AT THE EDGE OF THE WORLD
298
Julie Mehretu
JULIE MEHRETU
301

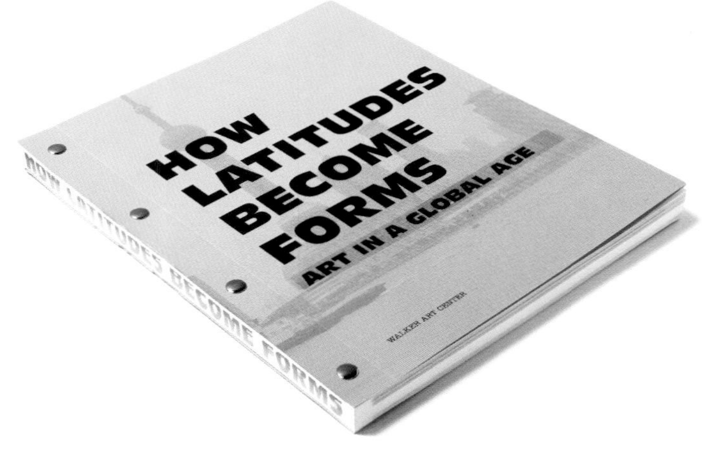

8
9
10

11
12
13
14

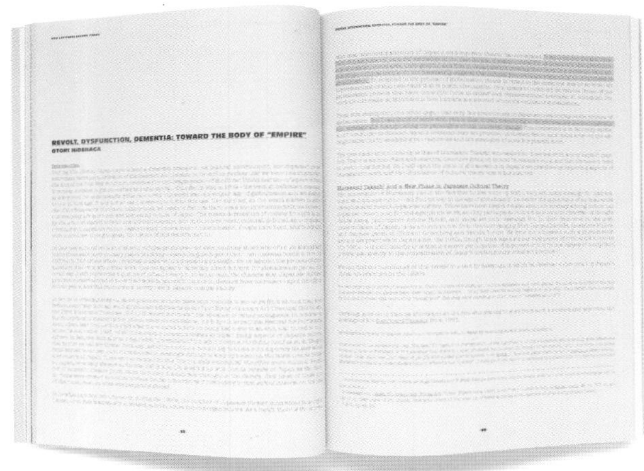

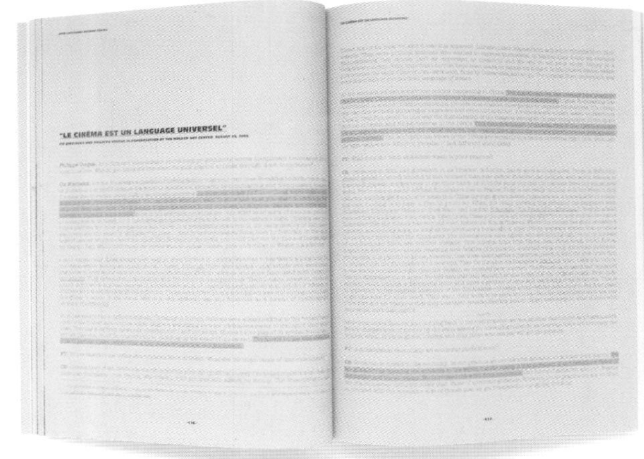

8–10 Cover and spreads, exhibition catalogue *Zero to Infinity: Arte Povera 1962–1972* (with Linda Byrne) / Walker Art Center and Tate Modern / USA and United Kingdom / 2001

11–14 Cover and spreads, exhibition catalogue *How Latitudes Become Forms: Art in a Global Age* (with Chad Kloepfer) / Walker Art Center / USA / 2001

15 "Walk Around Time: Mapping the Artists of the Permanent Collection" gallery guide and poster (with Alejandro Quinto) / Walker Art Center / USA / 2002

16 Spread from *The Indexical Archive*, a publication accompanying the American Center for Design's 21st Annual 100 Show of Excellence (with Santiago Piedrafita) / American Center for Design / USA / 2000

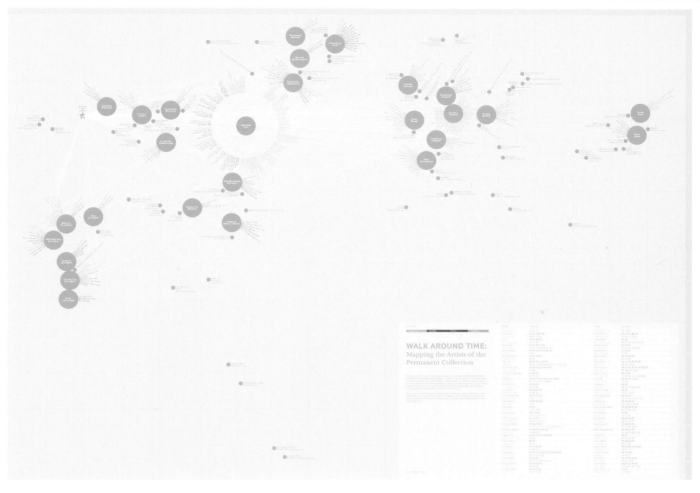

WALK AROUND TIME:
Mapping the Artists of the Permanent Collection

15

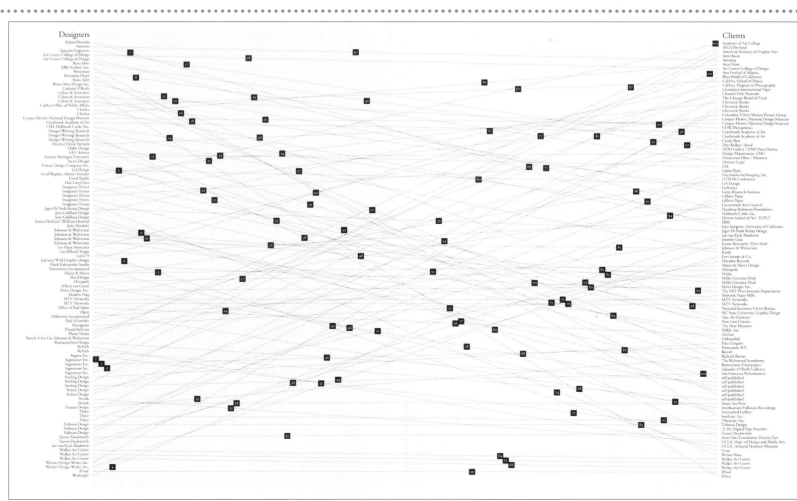

Designers
AdamsMorioka
Antenna
Appetite Engineers
Art Center College of Design
Art Center College of Design
Bates Hori
BBK Studios, Inc.
Behaviour
Benjamin Pham
Brian Tafel
Bruce Mau Design Inc.
Cadmus O'Keefe
Cahan & Associates
Cahan & Associates
Cahan & Associates
CalArts Office of Public Affairs
Charles
Charles
Cooper-Hewitt, National Design Museum
Cranbrook Academy of Art
CSD, Hallmark Cards, Inc.
Design/Writing/Research
Design/Writing/Research
Design/Writing/Research
Drenttel Doyle Partners
Duffy Design
EAI / Atlanta
Eastern Michigan University
Factor Design
Froeter Design Company, Inc.
GA Design
Geoff Kaplan, Martin Venezky
Good Studio
Hui-Ling Chen
Imaginary Forces
Imaginary Forces
Imaginary Forces
Imaginary Forces
Imaginary Forces
Jager Di Paola Kemp Design
Jens Gehlhaar Design
Jens Gehlhaar Design
Jessica Helfand | William Drenttel
John Nordyke
Johnson & Wolverton
Johnson & Wolverton
Johnson & Wolverton
Johnson & Wolverton
Lee Hunt Associates
Lisa Billard Design
Loft219
Lorraine Wild Graphic Design
Mark Rakatansky Studio
Matsumoto Incorporated
Mayer & Myers
MetaDesign
Metropolis
Mikon van Gastel
Mires Design, Inc.
Modern Dog
MTV Networks
MTV Networks
Office of Paul Sahre
Open
Otherwise Incorporated
Paul Schneider
Pentagram
Pittard Sullivan
Plazm Media
Ranch A Go-Go, Johnson & Wolverton
Raymond Jow Design
ReVerb
ReVerb
Segura, Inc.
Sagmeister Inc.
Sagmeister Inc.
Sagmeister Inc.
Sagmeister Inc.
Sterling Design
Sterling Design
Sterling Design
Stoltze Design
Stoltze Design
Swank
Swank
Tenazas Design
Thirst
Thirst
Thirst
Tolleson Design
Tolleson Design
Tolleson Design
Turner Duckworth
Turner Duckworth
Jan van Eyck Akademie
Walker Art Center
Walker Art Center
Walker Art Center
Werner Design Werks, Inc.
Werner Design Werks, Inc.
Wired
Worksight

Clients
Academy of Art College
AIGA Portland
American Institute of Graphic Arts
Anni Kuan
Antenna
Arco Films
Art Center College of Design
Arts Festival of Atlanta
Blue Shield of California
CalArts, School of Dance
CalArts, Program in Photography
Champion International Paper
Channel One Network
The Chicago Board of Trade
Chronicle Books
Chronicle Books
Chronicle Books
Columbia TriStar Motion Picture Group
Cooper-Hewitt, National Design Museum
Cooper-Hewitt, National Design Museum
COR Therapeutics
Cranbrook Academy of Art
Cranbrook Academy of Art
Cuaka Bon
Dan Rolleri / *Speak*
DDD Gallery / DNP Duo Dojima
Design Department, EMU
Dimension Films / Miramax
Discreet Logic
EAI
Edana Reps
Electronics for Imaging, Inc.
FUSE98 Conference
GA Design
GaSonics
Getty Research Institute
Gilbert Paper
Gilbert Paper
Greenwood Arts Council
Pasadena Robinson Foundation
Hallmark Cards, Inc.
Herron School of Art / IUPUI
IBM
Inju Stergeon, University of California
Jager Di Paola Kemp Design
Jan van Eyck Akademie
Jennifer Gray
Joanie Bernstein / Elvis Swift
Johnson & Wolverton
Kiosk
Levi Strauss & Co.
Matador Records
Mayer & Myers Design
Metropolis
Midas
Miller Genuine Draft
Miller Genuine Draft
Mires Design, Inc.
The MIT Press Journals Department
Mohawk Paper Mills
MTV Networks
MTV Networks
National Insurance Crime Bureau
NC State University, Graphic Design
New Art Examiner
New Line Cinema
The New Museum
NIKE, Inc.
NoZone
Oldsmobile
Pina Zangaro
Promotone B.V.
Revolv
Richard Barnes
The Richmond Symphony
Romerturm Feinstpapier
Salander-O'Reilly Galleries
San Francisco Performances
self-published
self-published
self-published
self-published
self-published
self-published
Smart Art Press
Smithsonian Folkways Recordings
Sonnabed Gallery
Steelcase, Inc.
Thirstype, Inc.
Tolleson Design
[T-26] Digital Type Foundry
Turner Duckworth
2wice Arts Foundation, Patricia Tarr
UCLA, Dept. of Design and Media Arts
UCLA, Armand Hammer Museum
Verso
Warner Bros.
Walker Art Center
Walker Art Center
Walker Art Center
Wired
Xilinx

16

Blue Source is a classic, high-quality studio specializing in design for the music industry. While they work for a number of companies and brands outside the music industry, music and its audience are at the core of the studio's identity. • •They are art directors of the highest league (just look at those photographs for Kosheen), original illustrators (check out the images for the self-commissioned film *Hair*), film directors (ditto), competent typographers (see the Union Brand identity and the typography of the Levi's Silver Tab campaign), but most of all just designers who after a decade in the business still seem to have a lot of fun: Their depiction of a wide-eyed couple, Macintosh Power Book in hand, gazing into the future and petting a goat is one of the more original portraits produced in design. • •Blue Source calls their work "media neutral," meaning that they develop ideas in response to each project's unique needs. The idea comes first and is then developed trough the appropriate communications channel. • •The visual series they develop for bands—such as the deconstructed 3-D portraits for Coldplay, the fashion-porn paintings for Dirty Vegas, the strangely inanimate objects for Faultline, the modern psychedelia for the Chemical Brothers, the hyperrealistic photography for Birth, or the architectural landscapes for Travis—have the feel of all-encompassing campaigns. They define the look and feel of a band in a way rarely seen since the heyday of the 12-inch album cover. • •Stefan Sagmeister • •

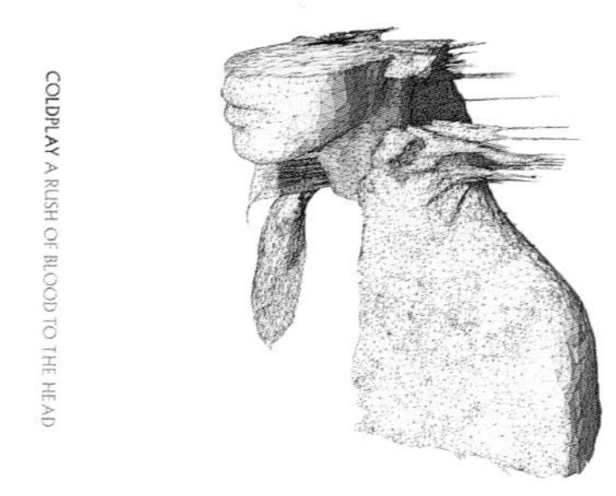

1

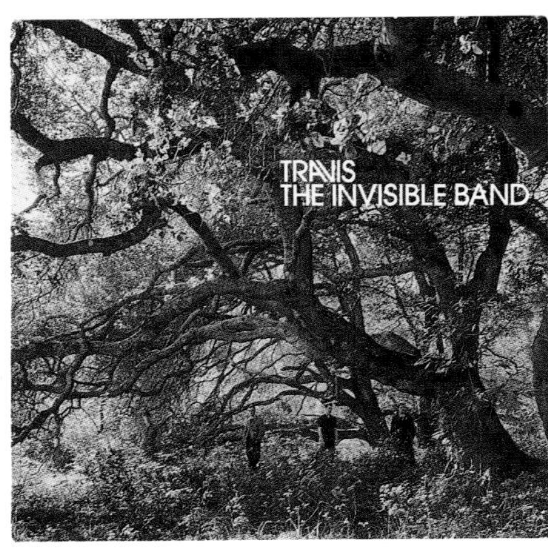

2

3

4

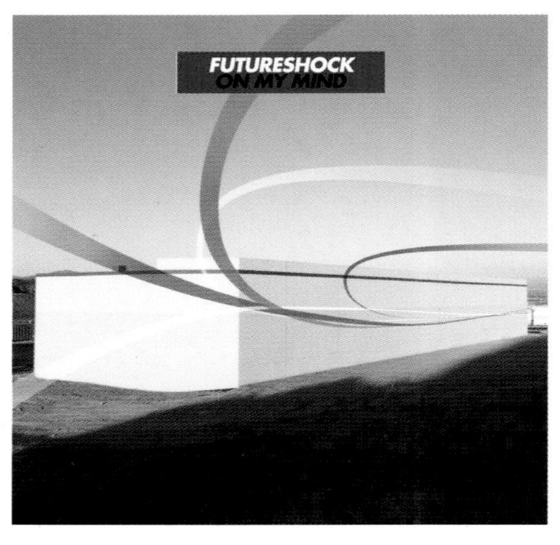

5

6

7

1 Vinyl/CD cover, *A Rush of Blood to the Head*, by Coldplay (photography Sølve Sundsbø) / Parlophone Records / United Kingdom / 2002
2 Vinyl/CD cover, *The Invisible Band*, by Travis (photography Stefan Ruiz) / Independiente / United Kingdom / 2002
3 Vinyl/CD cover, *Star Guitar*, by The Chemical Brothers (artwork Kate Gibb) / Virgin Records / United Kingdom / 2002
4 Vinyl/CD cover, *Resist*, by Kosheen (photography Patrice Hanicotte) / Arista BMG Records / United Kingdom / 2001
5 Vinyl/CD cover, *On My Mind*, by Futureshock (photography Dan Holdsworth) / Parlophone Records / United Kingdom / 2003
6 De-bossed promotional record sleeve with information sticker, *Phantom Theory*, by Futureshock / Parlophone Records / United Kingdom / 2003
7 Vinyl/CD cover, *Phantom Theory*, by Futureshock (photography Dan Holdsworth) / Parlophone Records / United Kingdom / 2003
8 Print advertising campaign for the shoe Star Racer (illustration Kam Tang) / Adidas / Netherlands / 2001
9 Print advertising campaign for the shoe Water Moccasin (artwork James Dimmock) / Adidas / Netherlands / 2001

Blue Source

London

8

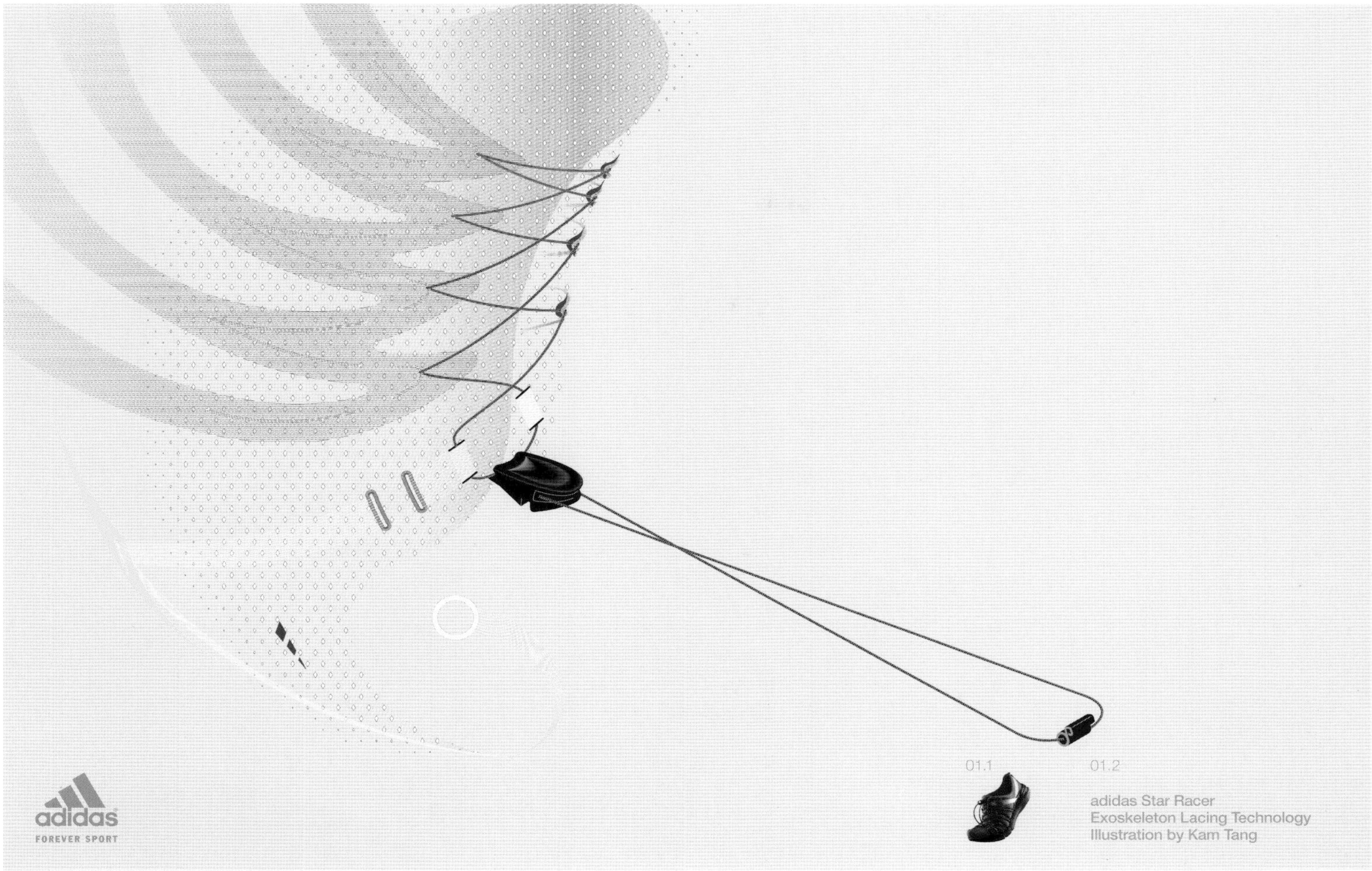

adidas
FOREVER SPORT

01.1 01.2

adidas Star Racer
Exoskeleton Lacing Technology
Illustration by Kam Tang

9

adidas
FOREVER SPORT

03.1 03.2

adidas Water Moccasin
Outsole Grip Technology
Image created by James Dimmock

10

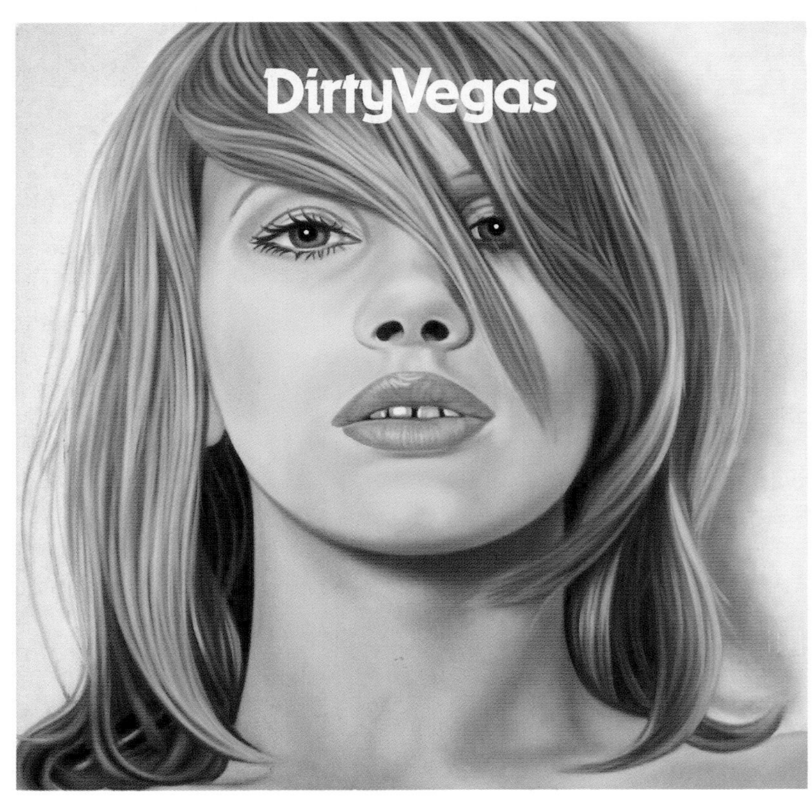

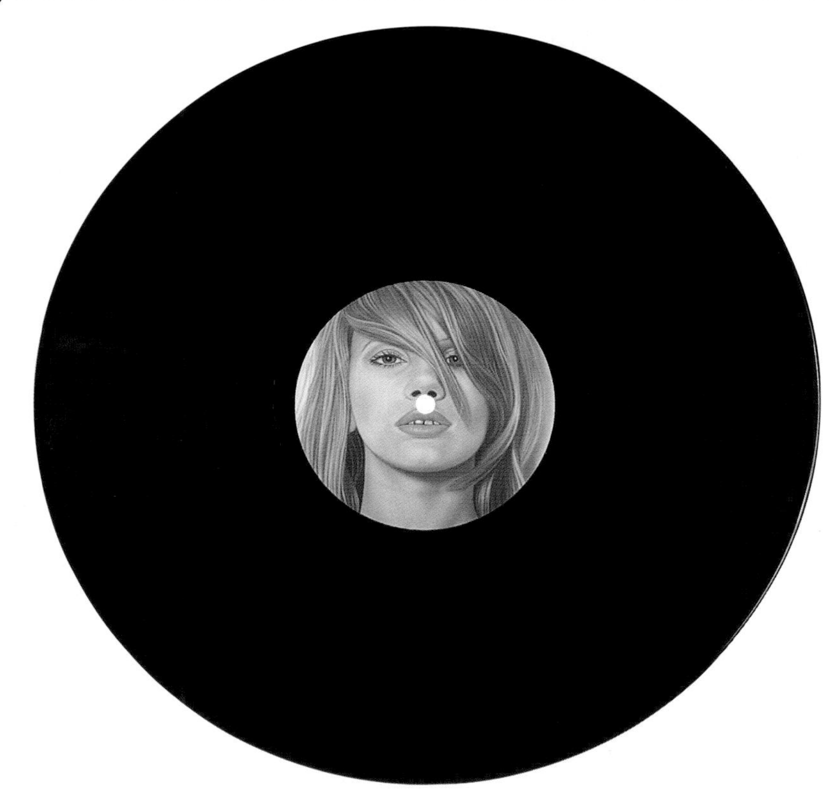

Blue Source

10 Clockwise from top left: Vinyl/CD covers, "Days Go By" single, "Ghosts" single, and self-titled LP by Dirty Vegas (artwork Richard Phillips) / Parlophone Records / USA and United Kingdom / 2003
11–12 Visual identities for music channel The Amp / BSkyB Broadcasting / United Kingdom / 2003
13 Cover illustration, *Gas Book 08–Blue Source* / DesignEXchange / Japan / 2002

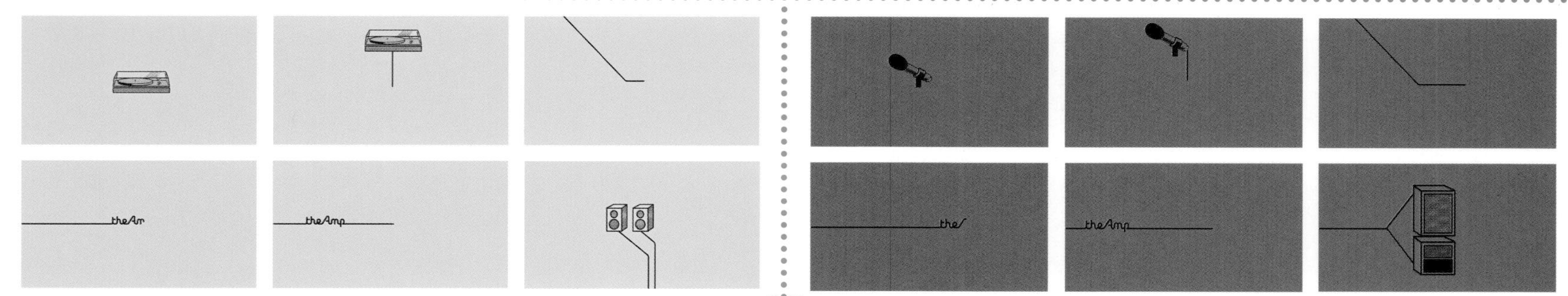

11 12

13

Life is mundane, frequently banal, but it also never fails to surprise or shock. So if your business is communication, your worth can be measured according to how well you can respond to special circumstances with the same tools you've deemed necessary under normal conditions. *The New York Times* has passed this test. The way in which the paper responded to the extraordinary events of 11 September 2001 was exemplary. Particularly impressive was the calm manner in which the paper communicated the numbing enormity of the event and the magnitude of the loss by simply putting into action the basic, sober principles of their trade: "clarity, balance, and modulation." There are aspects of the paper's typography that many would take issue with—the centered headlines in quirky fonts, the old-fashioned use of rules—but somehow since all visual aspects of the paper are in synthesis with the content, those details don't seem to matter. The experience of the whole is such a nourishing one it is possible to forgive the idiosyncrasies—some would say it's those that give the paper its personality. • • One would think a product that is issued every day would depend on a heavy manual of rigid guidelines to standardize the design, but according to assistant managing editor and design director Tom Bodkin, nothing could be further from the truth. Speaking over a year before September 11, he said, "Surprising to some, we don't have a design stylebook. We have guidelines for typography and color palette, but little on paper in any organized form. That is deliberate. What we want is the exercise of individual interpretation and creativity in addressing the ever-changing demands of a newspaper page." • • One doesn't normally expect to see great graphic design emerging from large companies. The quality of *The New York Times'* design is all the more remarkable for the fact that more than one hundred people are under Bodkin's charge. How Bodkin gets all of his team and other departments working together so efficiently cannot be put down merely to practiced tradition. The way he describes his job provides a clue: "I help artists think like editors and editors think like artists, making sure artists never lose sight of content and instructing editors on the importance of form." • • Nick Bell • •

The New York Times

U.S. ATTACKED

HIJACKED JETS DESTROY TWIN TOWERS AND HIT PENTAGON IN DAY OF TERROR

A CREEPING HORROR

President Vows to Exact Punishment for 'Evil'

A Somber Bush Says Terrorism Cannot Prevail

Awaiting the Aftershocks

The New York Times

The Year in Pictures

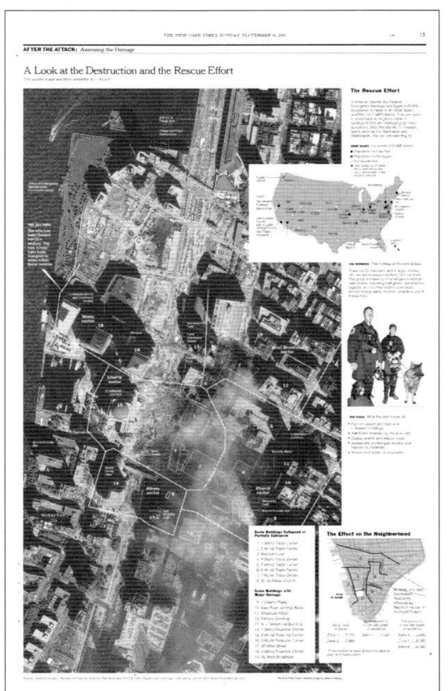
A Look at the Destruction and the Rescue Effort

Towers Lent City a Lift, Adding Postcard Panache And an Air of Resilience

New Yorkers Awake to a World That Now Seems Fragile and Unfamiliar

A Nation Challenged

The New York Times

Stress From Attacks Will Chase Some Into the Depths of Their Minds, and Stay

Bin Laden Operative Is Linked To Suspects

After a War Starts at Home, the Guard Prepares to Take It Abroad

Technology's Role to Grow In a New World of Security

A Nation Challenged

The New York Times

Determined Volunteers Camped Out To Pitch In

From 5,000 Feet Up, Mapping Terrain for Ground Zero Workers

Unpolished Secret Agents Were Able to Hide in Plain Sight

1 Front page, *The New York Times*, 12 September 2001 / The New York Times / USA / 2001
2 Page from "The Year in Pictures" section, *The New York Times*, 31 December 2001
3 Page from *The New York Times*, 16 September 2001
4 Page from *The New York Times*, 13 September 2001
5 Front page, "A Nation Challenged" special section, *The New York Times*, 18 September 2001
6 Front page, "A Nation Challenged" special section, *The New York Times*, 23 September 2001
7, 9 Spreads from "The Year in Pictures" section, *The New York Times*, 31 December 2001
8 Spread from *The New York Times*, 13 September 2001

Tom Bodkin

New York

7

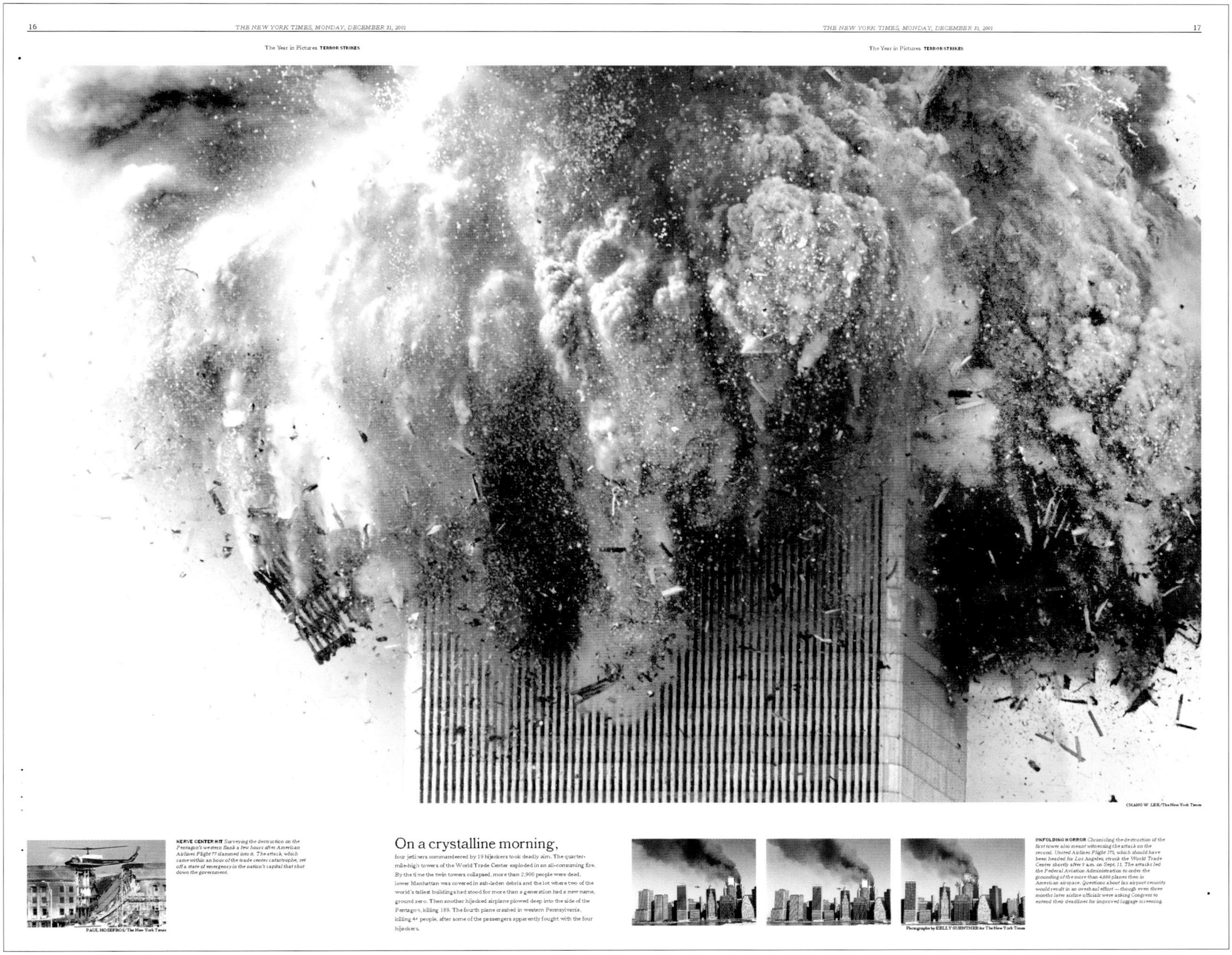

16 THE NEW YORK TIMES, MONDAY, DECEMBER 31, 2001 — THE NEW YORK TIMES, MONDAY, DECEMBER 31, 2001 17

The Year in Pictures **TERROR STRIKES**

CHANG W. LEE/The New York Times

PAUL HOSEFROS/The New York Times

NERVE CENTER HIT *Surveying the destruction on the Pentagon's western flank a few hours after American Airlines Flight 77 slammed into it. The attack, which came within an hour of the trade center catastrophe, set off a state of emergency in the nation's capital that shut down the government.*

On a crystalline morning,

four jetliners commandeered by 19 hijackers took deadly aim. The quarter-mile-high towers of the World Trade Center exploded in an all-consuming fire. By the time the twin towers collapsed, more than 2,900 people were dead, lower Manhattan was covered in ash-laden debris and the lot where two of the world's tallest buildings had stood for more than a generation had a new name, ground zero. Then another hijacked airplane plowed deep into the side of the Pentagon, killing 189. The fourth plane crashed in western Pennsylvania, killing 44 people, after some of the passengers apparently fought with the four hijackers.

Photographs by KELLY GUENTHER for The New York Times

UNFOLDING HORROR *Chronicling the destruction of the first tower also meant witnessing the attack on the second. United Airlines Flight 175, which should have been headed for Los Angeles, struck the World Trade Center shortly after 9 a.m. on Sept. 11. The attacks led the Federal Aviation Administration to order the grounding of the more than 4,000 planes then in American airspace. Questions about lax airport security would result in an overhaul effort — though even three months later airline officials were asking Congress to extend their deadlines for improved luggage screening.*

8

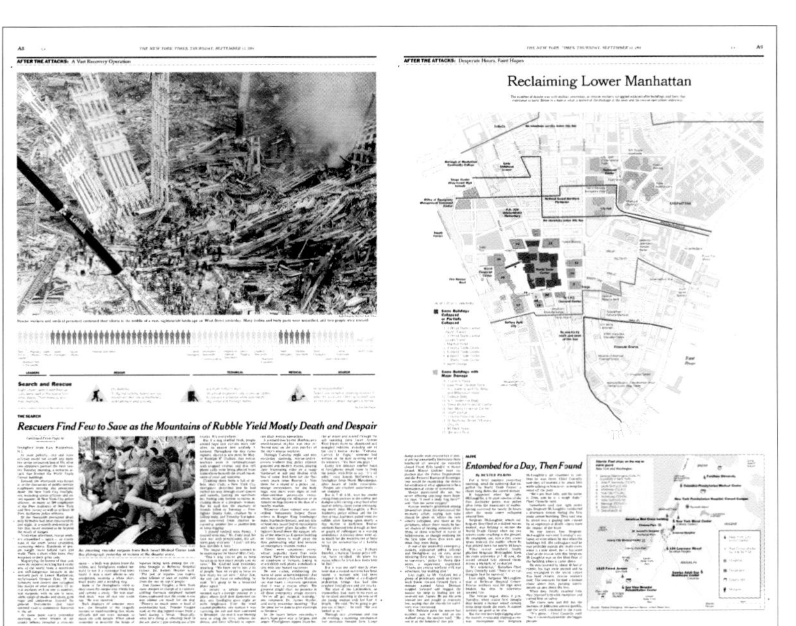

AFTER THE ATTACKS: A Vast Recovery Operation

Search and Rescue

Rescuers Find Few to Save as the Mountains of Rubble Yield Mostly Death and Despair

AFTER THE ATTACKS: Desperate Hours, Faint Hopes

Reclaiming Lower Manhattan

Entombed for a Day, Then Found

9

The New York Times
Week in Review
Section 4

Put 'Em Up

Flag Fever: the Paradox of Patriotism

Walking the line between national pride and jingoism.

An Act Of Terror Reshapes The Globe

Alliances crack. Russia warms to the West. History is on the move.

What do I do in the war, Daddy?
By R. W. Apple Jr. 3

A new landscape for homeland defense.
By Tom Zeller 4

Big is Back
In the wake of terror, a sea change in the role of government . . .
By Robin Toner

. . . and a challenge to the Supreme Court's 10-year drive toward federalism.
By Linda Greenhouse 14

(10)

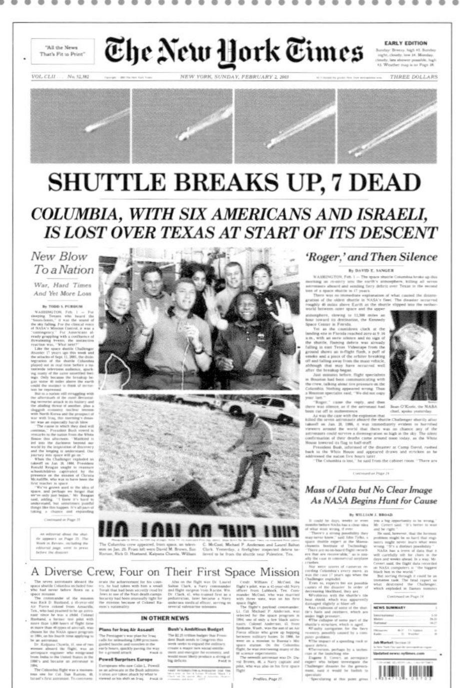
"All the News That's Fit to Print"
The New York Times
EARLY EDITION

SHUTTLE BREAKS UP, 7 DEAD

COLUMBIA, WITH SIX AMERICANS AND ISRAELI, IS LOST OVER TEXAS AT START OF ITS DESCENT

New Blow To a Nation
War, Hard Times And Yet More Loss

'Roger,' and Then Silence

Mass of Data but No Clear Image As NASA Begins Hunt for Cause

A Diverse Crew, Four on Their First Space Mission

INSIDE OTHER NEWS

(12)

The New York Times
The Millennium
YNE C1 E1
SATURDAY, JANUARY 1, 2000

Copyright © 2000 The New York Times

VISIONS OF THEIR WORLD

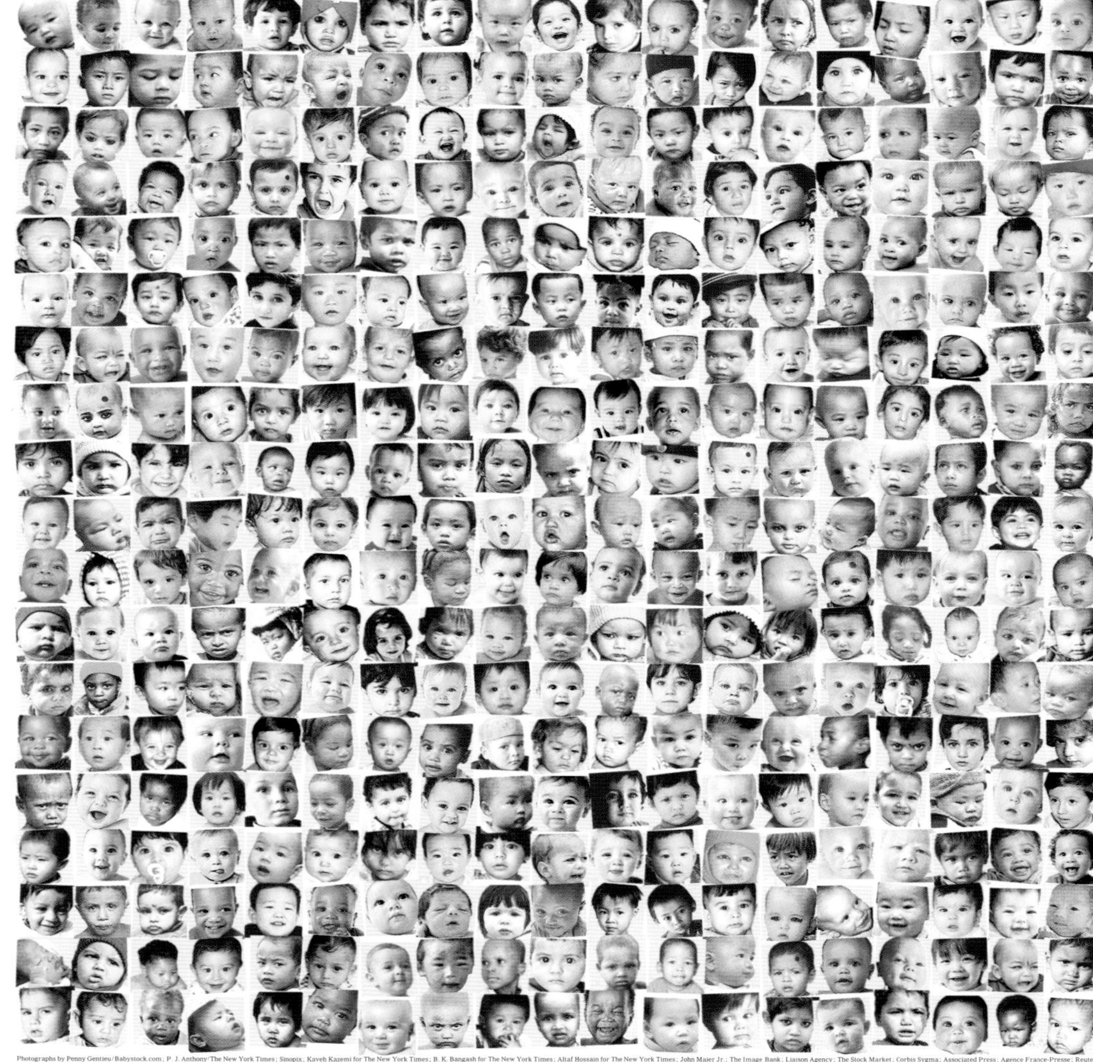

Photographs by Penny Gentieu/Babystock.com; P. J. Anthony/The New York Times; Sinopix; Kaveh Kazemi for The New York Times; B. K. Bangash for The New York Times; Altaf Hussain for The New York Times; John Maier Jr.; The Image Bank; Liaison Agency; The Stock Market; Corbis Sygma; Associated Press; Agence France-Presse; Reuters

THE WORLD'S POPULATION IN 2050 These faces represent a projection of the world's demographic makeup at midcentury. United Nations demographers expect that there will be almost nine billion people on the planet — a 50 percent increase over the next 50 years. Proportionally, there will be many more Africans, and far fewer Chinese and Europeans, than there are today; America will grow at about half the global rate. For the current mix, see the photographs on Page 37. An article by David E. Sanger exploring population trends is on Page 8.

POWER
As a new century begins, America stands astride the globe, with no apparent challengers on the horizon. Get ready to be blindsided.
By R. W. Apple Jr.
2

BIOLOGY
Science will extend our lives to biblical lengths. It may be harder for people to find the wisdom to match their years.
By Pam Belluck and Sheryl Gay Stolberg
7

TECHNOLOGY
If history is any guide, innovation will gallop ahead in the 21st century, dragging a hesitant humanity along behind it.
By Tim Race
12

IDENTITY
Many envision a future that pits a nightmare state against the heroic individual. Sometimes it's hard to know which to fear more.
By Edward Rothstein
21

CITIES
The city of tomorrow will be a maelstrom — a violent, unstoppable, electric center of culture, business and despair. A lot like São Paulo today.
By Roger Cohen
28

A (Very) Early Look at the Front Page of Jan. 1, 2100 **34**

And Reflections on the World We've Known **39**

(11)

Tom Bodkin

10 Front page, "Week in Review" section, *The New York Times*, 30 September 2001
11 Front page, "The Millennium" special section, *The New York Times*, 1 January 2000
12 Front page, *The New York Times*, 2 February 2003
13 Spread from "A Nation Challenged" special section, *The New York Times*, 31 December 2001
14 Spread from *The New York Times*, 16 September 2001
15 Spread from "A Nation Challenged" special section, *The New York Times*, 23 September 2001

13

A NATION CHALLENGED: Portraits of Grief

Victims of the World Trade Center disaster whose sketches have appeared in Portraits of Grief.

THE PORTRAITS

Closing a Scrapbook Full of Life and Sorrow

By JANNY SCOTT

It began as an imperfect answer to a journalistic problem, the absence of a definitive list of the dead in the days after the World Trade Center was attacked. But it evolved improbably in the weeks and months after Sept. 11 into a sort of national shrine.

Three days after the attacks, reporters at The New York Times, armed with stacks of the homemade missing-persons fliers that were papering the city, began dialing the numbers on the fliers, interviewing friends and relatives of the missing and writing brief portraits, or sketches, of their lives.

In the weeks that followed, amid nonstop news coverage of the disaster and the war, reading "Portraits of Grief" became a ritual for people nationwide. In hundreds of e-mail messages and letters to The Times, readers said they read them religiously, rarely missing a day. For some, it was a way of paying homage. Others said it was a means of connecting, a source of consolation.

"One felt, looking at those pages every day, that real lives were jumping out at you," Paul Auster, the novelist, said in an interview about the profiles, which conclude today as a daily feature in The Times. "We weren't mourning an anonymous mass of people, we were mourning thousands of individuals. And the more we knew about them, the more we could wrestle with our own grief."

There was Myrna Yaskulka, the Staten Island grandmother remembered for her pink rhinestone-studded sunglasses, metallic gold raincoat and leopard-skin pants; Kevin Dowdell, the oft-decorated firefighter who sanded floors on his days off to support his family; Diane Urban, who spoke her mind so often that one relative suggested at her memorial service that everyone get T-shirts saying "Diane Urban Told Me Off."

There was Nancy Morgenstern, the bicycle racer and Orthodox Jew, who, faced with the seemingly conflicting requirements of her two passions, embraced both of them completely rather than take the easy way out and give one up. She so impressed a client with her ability as a travel agent that he hired her as his administrative assistant at Cantor Fitzgerald.

There were the traders, firefighters, window washers, chefs and managing directors; the new parents, pairs of siblings, fathers of 10; the avid shoppers, rugby team captains, lovers, fanatical golfers, part-time bouncers and the rare few whose mothers lovingly conceded that they were definitely not saints.

Over time, the profiles helped shed light on the striking number of men and of young people among those who died, the wide geographical range of the neighborhoods affected, and the degree to which the victims made up a telling cross section of the New York region.

It became hard not to notice, too, how many were Irish- and Italian-Americans, the children and grandchildren of immigrants, whom Roman Catholic schools and Wall Street had propelled out of working-class neighborhoods into firms like Cantor Fitzgerald and suburban towns like Basking Ridge, N.J.

Through today's issue, The Times has published more than 1,800 sketches. The official count of those dead and missing in the trade center attacks stands at 2,937. Reporters have contacted, or tried to contact, relatives or friends of nearly every victim the paper was able to locate. Some have declined to give interviews; others said they were not ready to talk. (As more names become known and more families agree to interviews, the editors intend to publish additional profile pages from time to time.)

The portraits were never meant to be obituaries in any traditional sense. They were brief, informal and impressionistic, often centered on a single story or idiosyncratic detail. They were not intended to recount a person's résumé, but rather to give a snapshot of each victim's personality, of a life lived. And they were democratic; executive vice presidents and battalion chiefs appeared alongside food handlers and janitors. Each profile was roughly 200 words.

"The peculiar genius of it was to put a human face on numbers that are unimaginable to most of us," said Kenneth T. Jackson, a professor of history at Columbia and director of the New-York Historical Society. He said the society hoped to borrow from the concept in developing a major exhibition on the disaster.

"As you read those individual portraits about love affairs or kissing children goodbye or coaching soccer and buying a dream home," he said, "it's so obvious that every one of them was a person who deserved to live a full and successful and happy life. You see what was lost."

Television and radio stations around the world broadcast reports on the project. A psychologist at the University of Michigan assigned the profiles as required reading for students and therapy groups. Readers approached The Times to offer the families everything from college scholarships to $300,000 in cash.

One reader, a lawyer in Manhattan, called reading the profiles "my act of Kaddish." Some said they found the stories uplifting, a guide to how to live a better life. Susan Sontag, the writer, said in an e-mail message, "I read the 'Portraits of Grief,' every last word, every single day. I was tremendously moved. I had tears in my eyes every morning."

Not everyone was happy. A small number of family members complained, saying certain profiles had failed to capture the people they knew.

In Portland, editors of The Oregonian obtained the profiles from The Times and began printing them on Page A2 in mid-September. In October, the paper published a column in which its ombudsman, Dan Hortsch, raised the question of when The Oregonian should stop. When he checked his voice mail that afternoon, he found 68 messages. Hundreds followed. The gist, he said, was: Don't stop.

THE VICTIMS

The Chaplain's Embrace, the Sergeant's Songs, and More Than One Parent's Devotion

Here are glimpses of some of the victims of the Sept. 11 attack on the World Trade Center.

MYCHAL JUDGE

Where He Was Needed

The Rev. Mychal Judge never shut his door at the Midtown Franciscan friary, literally or emotionally. Anybody with the slightest need for the contents inside — be it a warm jacket or his attentive ear — was welcome.

Not that Father Judge was often in. As chaplain to the New York Fire Department, Father Judge, 68, could be found joking or comforting firefighters or driving hellbent to emergencies. When a boatload of Chinese refugees were shipwrecked in the Rockaways, he was one of the first there, "handing out blankets and coffee and telling them jokes," said Peter Johnson, a friend. "They didn't know English, but he was doing pantomime and they were laughing."

He had "movie-star looks and a tremendous ability to speak and sing," said Mr. Johnson. "And that was tempered by his absolute consistent devotion to being a priest." He wore his friar's robes to soup kitchens, to Gracie Mansion, to the White House, to countless baptisms and funerals.

He had no use — none — for physical things, said Steven McDonald, the police officer paralyzed by a gunshot who accompanied Father Judge on peace trips to Belfast. Give the father a cashmere sweater, he said, and it would wind up on the back of a homeless person. Go to him with a troubled soul and he would listen intently for as long as it took. He went where he was needed. On Sept. 11, he faced the inferno with the firefighters.

GEORGE LLANES

A Poet of Bensonhurst

George Llanes was a sensitive, studious child, the kind that classmates often teased. His mother, Eugenia, wanted him to have an outlet, a safe place to express himself, so as he approached the painful years of adolescence, she bought him a journal and encouraged him to "unburden yourself."

From that modest beginning, a writer was born. A few years back, after Mr. Llanes began working as a clerk at Carr Futures, he gave his mother a bound volume of his poetry. After his death, when Mr. Llanes's parents cleaned out his apartment in Bensonhurst, Brooklyn, near their own, they found his poems everywhere.

Mr. Llanes, who would have turned 34 on Sept. 13, lived with his parents until recently. He was their only child and did not leave the nest until he took up smoking and decided to get a dog, both of which gave his mother allergy attacks. When he went apartment hunting and found one he liked, he told the landlady, "I have to talk to my mother first." The landlady repeated the exchange to Mrs. Llanes, saying, "That's when I knew he was a good boy."

Mr. Llanes's devotion to the dog, a pug named Mae Mae, persuaded him to rejigger his work schedule. He switched to a schedule of 7 a.m. to 3 p.m. from an ordinary one of 9 a.m. to 5 p.m., despite a lifelong aversion to getting up early.

Had he been on his old schedule, she noted, "We wouldn't be having this conversation now."

LUKE NEE

Bronx in His Blood

As a boy, Luke Nee played all the games that a Bronx sidewalk offered to kids on Minerva Place, just off the Grand Concourse: stickball, of course, and off-the-point and street hockey.

Right out of Cardinal Hayes High School, he answered a help-wanted advertisement for people with math skills and landed a job at Drexel Burnham Lambert. Before long, a half-dozen guys from the block followed. It was a small world, he would say, but he would not want to paint it.

At Drexel, he met Irene Lavelle, and they were married Sept. 11, 1982. After he had shifted to Cantor Fitzgerald, he would chew through a couple of novels a week on the train ride from Stony Point, N.Y., said his brother, John Nee. His Bronx roots showed: he shared a ticket plan for Friday night Yankee games with boyhood friends from St. Philip Neri School.

Mr. Nee, 44, made the simple pleasures glow. "He treasured Irene and loved bringing their son, Patrick, to ballgames," said his brother. On summer weekends, he, Irene and Patrick would jump in the car, pick up a few relatives and head for the beach. And on Sept. 11, he made a final call of farewell and love to his family.

"Luke was just a friendly, kind, peaceful, and unaffected guy," said Mr. Nee. "Meatball heroes, watch a movie with Patrick — that was a Saturday night."

LINDA OLIVA

Taking Charge With a Smile

She was a take-charge woman, but she did so with the upbeat fervor of a cheerleader, which she was in high school. Linda Oliva would march into her mother's home a few times a week, cook meals, shop, organize and fuss sweetly over her brother Frankie, who has special needs.

Ms. Oliva, 44, was like that at work, too. Temp agencies would send her to a job and she would have things running so smoothly that positions would open for this suddenly indispensable woman. She had been executive assistant to the president of the New York office of Carr Futures.

She succeeded not only because she was capable, but because she exuded joy: she would dance happily to Rod Stewart or Tony Bennett, her laughter bubbling forth without prompting. "I knew she had a great sense of humor because she thought everything I said was hilarious," said another brother, Chuck Oliva, whose young daughter, Alexandra, adored her.

Divorced, Ms. Oliva, who lived in Staten Island, had begun dating a family friend, Tom Donovan, this summer.

On their first date, he recalled, "There she was in a beautiful cream-colored outfit. She wore her brown hair long, and she was a knockout. And I thought, I can't believe this girl is going out with me."

THOMAS J. KENNEDY

Last Wishes, First Steps

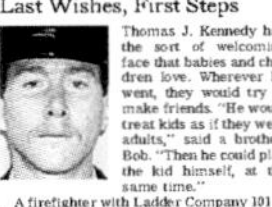

Thomas J. Kennedy had the sort of welcoming face that babies and children love. Wherever he went, they would try to make friends. "He would treat kids as if they were adults," said a brother, Bob. "Then he could play the kid himself, at the same time."

A firefighter with Ladder Company 101 in Brooklyn, Mr. Kennedy, 36, wanted five children of his own. He and his wife, Allison, had two children and planned to have another. Michael is 2, and James turned 1 on Nov. 17.

As a father, Mr. Kennedy cherished his children's bedtime rituals, administering evening baths and reading "Goodnight Moon." He and Michael would drop coins into a piggy bank, because the father was teaching the son the value of saving. This winter, Mr. Kennedy had hoped to take Michael skiing and ice skating, and to see James walk. On Sept. 14, the baby took his first steps. "Now he runs and climbs," said Mrs. Kennedy. "Tom would have loved that."

CATHERINE A. NARDELLA

Someone to Lean On

On Sept. 10, with her parents about to return home from a senior citizens' bus outing to Atlantic City, Catherine A. Nardella stopped by their home in Lincoln Park, N.J., to the make sure everything was in order. She knew it was their habit to have a cup of coffee as soon as they got in the door, but the electricity was temporarily out. So she went to a Dunkin' Donuts for a carafe of hot coffee, and had it waiting for them.

That's the way she was about her large Italian-American family. "Cathy always thought of others," said her sister Grace Samek. Another sister, Lavinia Wilson, said Miss Nardella "was the kind of person that just gave and didn't think she was going to get anything in return."

Miss Nardella, 40, was an insurance consultant at Aon Corp. Single, she owned her own house in Bloomfield, N.J., and was active in her local parish. She was a member of the choir and a regular lector, distinguished by her professional manner of dressing and speaking, and by a certain gentle kindness.

"Every Sunday after Mass she'd wait for this old man to come out and she'd help him walk down the steps of the church," said Msgr. William Hatcher, pastor of St. Thomas the Apostle.

MARY ALICE WAHLSTROM

Unstoppable 78

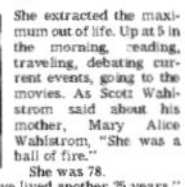

She extracted the maximum out of life. Up at 5 in the morning, reading, traveling, debating current events, going to the movies. As Scott Wahlstrom said about his mother, Mary Alice Wahlstrom, "She was a ball of fire."

She was 78.

"She could have lived another 25 years," he said. "I have no doubt about it."

Mrs. Wahlstrom, a retired loan officer, lived in Kaysville, Utah, with her husband, Norman. She loved to travel, but had been reluctant to leave home because he was recovering from a heart attack. Still, she had gone with her daughter, Carolyn Beug, to help settle Mrs. Beug's twin daughters into the Rhode Island School of Design. Mrs. Wahlstrom and Mrs. Beug were returning to Los Angeles, where Mrs. Beug lived, via American Airlines Flight 11.

The energized matriarch of a family of five children and 16 grandchildren, Mrs. Wahlstrom subscribed to about 20 magazines. She read books that she then sent off to her children, and still occasionally played golf. She might never have broken 100, but she did score two holes in one.

KATHLEEN HUNT-CASEY

A Friend, a Sister

Kathleen Hunt-Casey was a careful friend, who listened and acted on what she heard. "She would call me at least three or four times a day, and then she'd have to get off the phone because of work, but when she called back she would continue talking where she left off," said Virginia Lemmerman, who knew Ms. Hunt-Casey since she was 10. "If I was feeling down, going through hard times or rocky days, she always tried to make me feel better about myself."

And if someone mentioned they had had a baby and needed, say, a picture frame, she would find one, and never take anything in return, Ms. Lemmerman said.

Ms. Hunt-Casey, 43, worked on the trading desk at Sandler O'Neill & Partners, and lived in Middletown, N.J., with her husband, Kevin, and son Matthew, 14. She was a devoted mother, Ms. Lemmerman said: "He was her life."

Ms. Lemmerman said, "I didn't just lose my best friend, I lost a sister."

SEAN LYNCH

Red Sox and Best Friends

Sean Lynch was the uncle with the cool cars.

The fourth of five siblings, Mr. Lynch, 34, took joy in watching his nephews' soccer games and playing tic-tac-toe with his nieces. Then he would be off, often taking trips to other cities with friends to attend sporting events. One year it was the Super Bowl, another year the Final Four.

Mr. Lynch went to college in Boston. A devoted Red Sox fan, he counted among his accomplishments converting his best friend at Cantor Fitzgerald, a lifelong Yankee fan, to a Red Sox fan.

Mr. Lynch had known since high school that he wanted to be a stockbroker, and shortly before Sept. 11 he was promoted to senior vice president for equity trading. "He used to say he was paid to hang out with his friends," said his older brother, Mike. "He loved it."

At Pier 94 in Manhattan, where a assistance center has been helping the families of World Trade Center attack victims, a blocklong wall has come to resemble a memorial. The wall is dotted with missing posters depicting the faces of hundreds of lost loved ones.

James Estrin/The New York Times

KARLETON FYFE

'Really Living It'

Karleton Fyfe's mother had to be bedridden for the six months before he was born; he seemed to be in a hurry to get into the world.

There was so much to be excited about. Take the birth of his own son. He and his wife made it a group project. They sent family and close friends a video titled "It's a. . . ." showing them going for the sonogram, and at the end opening an envelope in which the doctor had written "boy." When Jackson turned 1, they asked the same group to write something and seal it for him to open when he turned 18.

Then, because Mr. Fyfe heard that the terrible 2's were caused by frustration at not being able to communicate, he taught his son sign language. "He was really living it," said Tristin Laughter a longtime friend of the couple.

Mr. Fyfe, 31, really lived everything, applying the same boyishness and determination whether he was mastering Steve Martin routines or the curveball as a kid, or tackling projects as a senior analyst at John Hancock — the job for which he was traveling on American Airlines Flight 11.

FRANK V. MOCCIA SR.

Laughter, Win or Lose

Frank V. Moccia Sr. was content to come away even. On a recent trip to Las Vegas with his wife, Elaine, and on countless trips to the Foxwoods Resort Casino in Connecticut, it suited him just fine.

In fact, it didn't even matter much to Mr. Moccia if he lost — as he often did to his son and golf partner, Frank Moccia Jr., a police officer.

"Whether he won, lost, broke even, it didn't matter," said Officer Moccia. "Whatever he did, he had a good time."

Mr. Moccia was a big believer in doing things for only as long as they were enjoyable, which is why he spent 26 years working for Washington Group International, as a facility planner in the World Trade Center.

It's also why Mr. Moccia would not consider a retirement away from his home in Hauppauge, N.Y., which was near his daughter, Donna Marie Velazquiz, and her children.

His wife described her husband as "a big teddy bear" and Mr. Moccia was just that to his grandchildren.

The weekend before Sept. 11, for a granddaughter's seventh birthday, Mr. Moccia took the family on a trip to Six Flags Great Adventure.

Unexpectedly, Mrs. Moccia decided to accompany her husband on one of the scarier roller coasters.

"I said the Lord's Prayer from the minute the ride started," Mrs. Moccia remembered about that day. "I squeezed his hand so tight, but he was laughing for the whole ride."

Mr. Moccia would have turned 58 tomorrow.

JACK CHARLES ARON

A Salt Baron's True Riches

After 24 years with the telephone company, Jack Charles Aron found himself with a few months off between jobs and was never happier. Staying at home meant he could spend all day taking care of his son, Timothy, which was especially important for Mr. Aron because his own childhood had been very unhappy.

It was also important because he and his wife had been forced to wait years before having their son.

More recently, Mr. Aron, 52, worked in information technology at Marsh & McLennan, leaving before dawn and traveling by car, train and ferry so he could be home in Bergenfield, N.J., in time to coach his son's Little League and basketball games.

Although he was often so dour at home that his wife Evelyn referred to him as "Mr. Grumpy," he was very easygoing on the ballfield or the court, she said.

Four years ago, the couple bought some land in the Philippines, where Mrs. Aron is from, and developed a salt farm. They called it Jet Farm (using the first letters of Jack, Evelyn and Timothy), and Mr. Aron told people he might like to live there after he retired.

The investment earned Mr. Aron a new nickname at work: Jack Aron the Salt Baron.

VICTOR J. SARACINI

Making Moments Count

As a veteran pilot for United Airlines, Victor J. Saracini placed great stock in paying attention to time. But as a father to his two daughters, the concept of time — or rather, maximizing the limited amount of it he had — took on an almost transcendent meaning.

Thank goodness, then, that Mr. Saracini, 51, a former Navy pilot, was about the most reliable person you could ever meet, and always thinking of his daughters, Kirsten, 13, and Brielle, 10, according to his in-laws, Bernard F. and Bernadette G. Hildebrand. "He taught them computers even before they could count, basically," Mrs. Hildebrand said about Mr. Saracini, who was the pilot of United Airlines Flight 175.

Once, Kirsten used her allowance money to buy a souvenir in Pennsylvania. After she paid for the item, she counted the change. Satisfied, she said, "Thank you," and picked up the package. "What kid would do that?" Mrs. Hildebrand said.

Mr. Saracini beamed, too, when his daughters did practice flight plans with him, or learned to read a compass. "He was very thorough with everything," Mr. Hildebrand said. "One time, he called to say, 'You won't have to worry about a thing if anything ever happens to me. The girls will be taken care of.' "

Portraits of Grief continues on the next page.

14

AFTER THE ATTACKS: Portraits of Grief

Snapshots of Their Lives, Told With the Pain of Those Who Loved Them

15

A NATION CHALLENGED: Those Who Answered the Call

Honoring the Rescuers

Günter Karl Bose has an autodidactic approach to graphic design. He never attended one of those universities or academies with a department of graphic design—those institutions that succeeded the Bauhaus and now proliferate around the world. Bose studied something decent: German philology, art history, and political science in the beautiful city of Freiburg, located at the edge of the Black Forest. Perfectly armed with a knowledge of the origins of language, especially German and its early literature, Bose settled down in West Berlin, a sort of no-man's-land in the divided Germany of the time. •• Bose is a refined man of culture but at the same time a secretive fighter for the cause, a man of convictions, a "zoon politicon." Tellingly, he didn't try to impose his ideas and visions on others, but instead preferred to found his own publishing house. Under the imprint of Brinckmann & Bose he releases titles dedicated to philosophy and literature, as well as film, art, and typography. In the process he has discovered a particular passion for the subtle typographic elements that express an intellectual culture, something not revealed in the decorative surface of an interface, but rather rooted in Marshall McLuhan's *The Gutenberg Galaxy*. •• In 1987 Bose republished Jan Tschichold's famous book *The New Typography*, which had first appeared in 1928; in 1991 this was followed by Tschichold's *Writings 1925–1974*. Two years later Bose became a professor at Leipzig's historic university of applied arts. In 2000 he not only opened his lmn-studio in Berlin, but also was made a member of the Alliance Graphique Internationale (AGI). •• Simultaneously with his work as a publisher and teacher he has designed a number of books and posters for the Deutsche Oper Berlin, the Oper Leipzig, Musica Viva (of the Bavarian Radio), and the Literaturhaus Berlin. These works are unique in their conceptual grasp and sensitive typographic translation of the subject matter. They are not superficially loud or catchy when the task is to announce a concert or an opera. •• Bose's approach is quiet, yet his typographic experiments are unmistakable. They are manifestos of cultural experience. In his work, ubiquitous, almost invisible elements are staged in a new and surprisingly contemporary way. •• Uwe Loesch ••

1 Musica Viva concert poster / Musica Viva / Germany / 1997
2 Poster for *Industriegebiet der Intelligenz* exhibition on cultural life in West Berlin during the 1920s and 1930s / Literaturhaus Berlin / 1988
3 Poster for *Protest! Literatur um 1968* exhibition on the literature influenced by the student uprisings of 1968 / Literaturhaus Berlin / 1999
4 Poster announcing change and reform efforts at the Academy of Visual Arts, Leipzig / Hochschule für Grafik und Buchkunst, Leipzig / Germany / 1999
5–6 Posters for premieres of the operas *Jenufa*, by Leos Janácek and *Semiramide*, by Gioacchino Rossini / Deutsche Oper Berlin / 2002–2003

Günter Karl Bose

Berlin

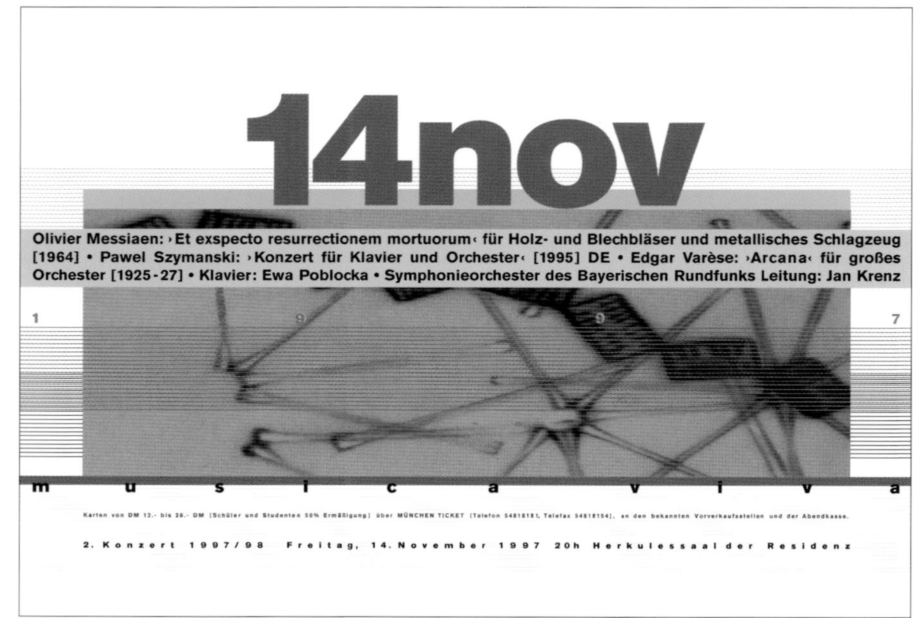

1

2

3

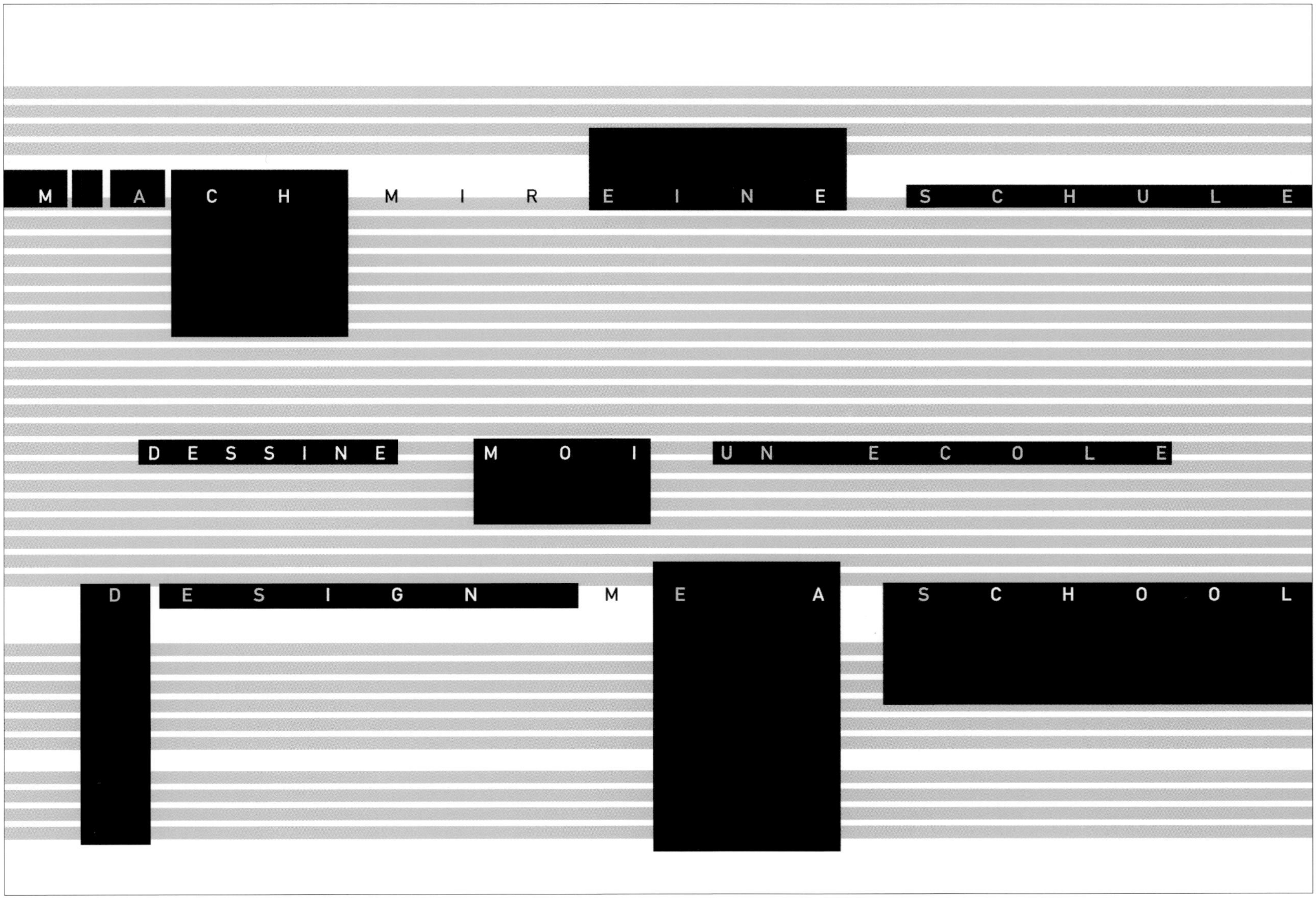

M A C H M I R E I N E S C H U L E

4 D E S S I N E M O I U N E C O L E

D E S I G N M E A S C H O O L

5 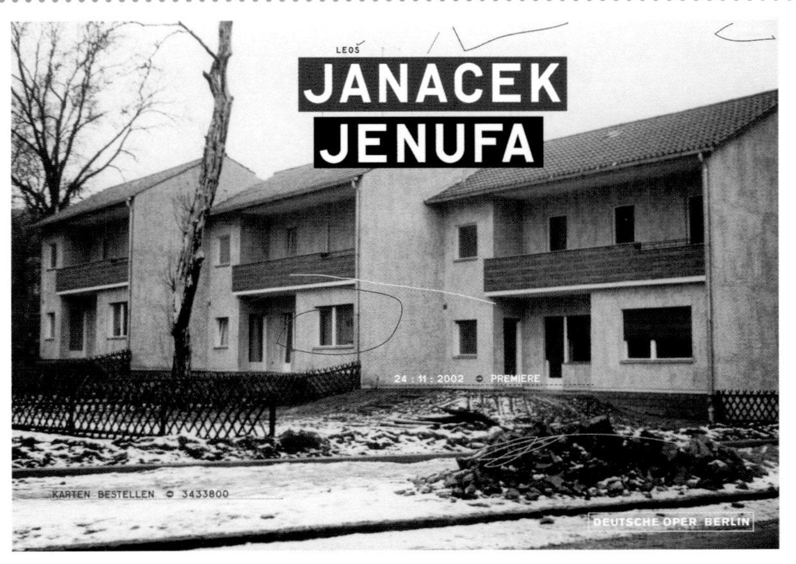

6 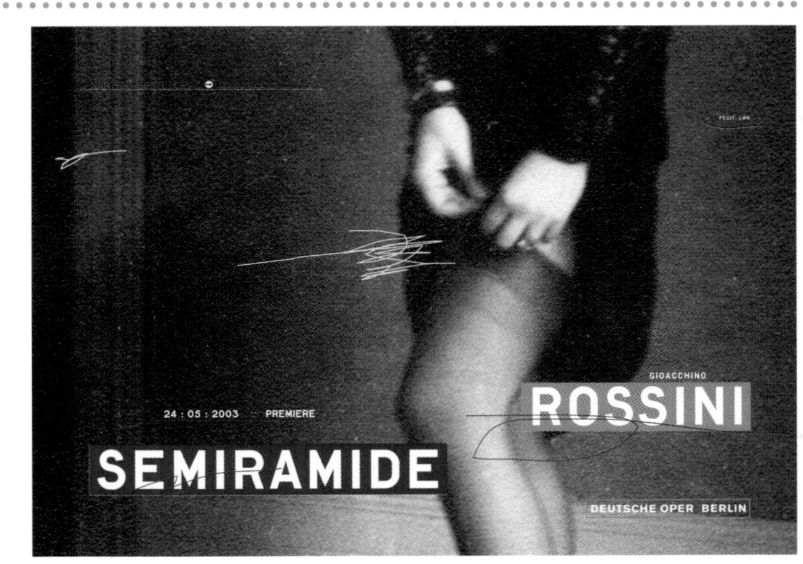

⑦

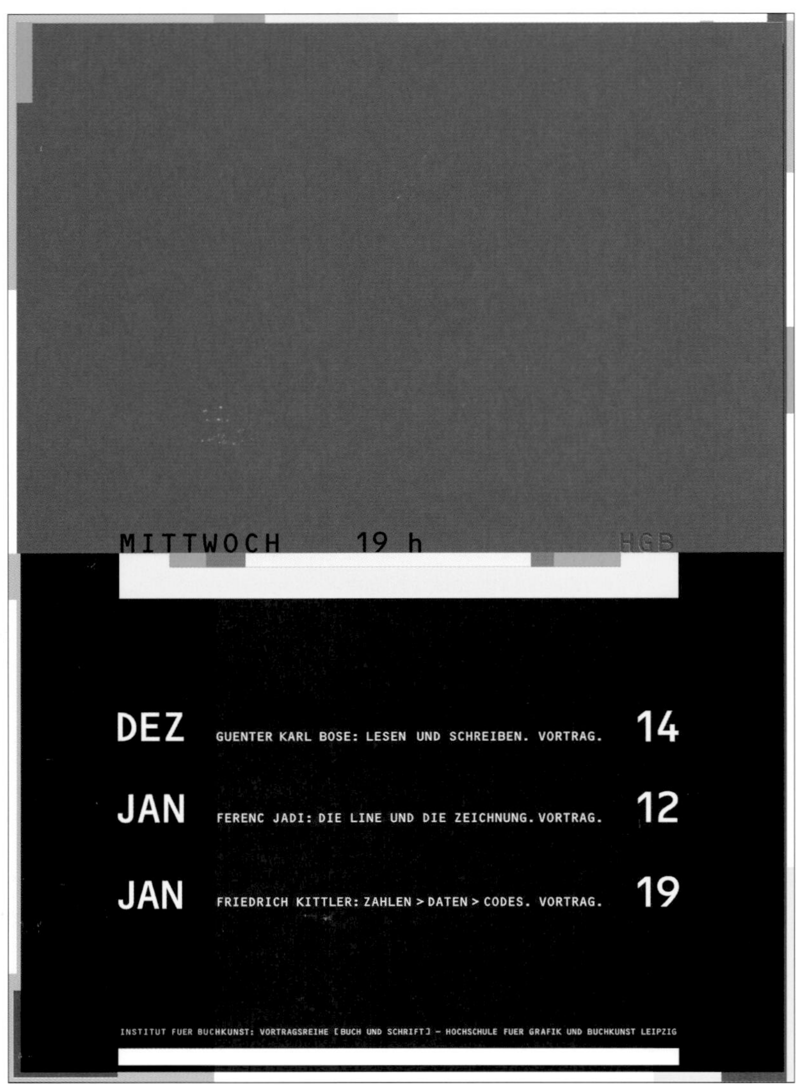

⑧

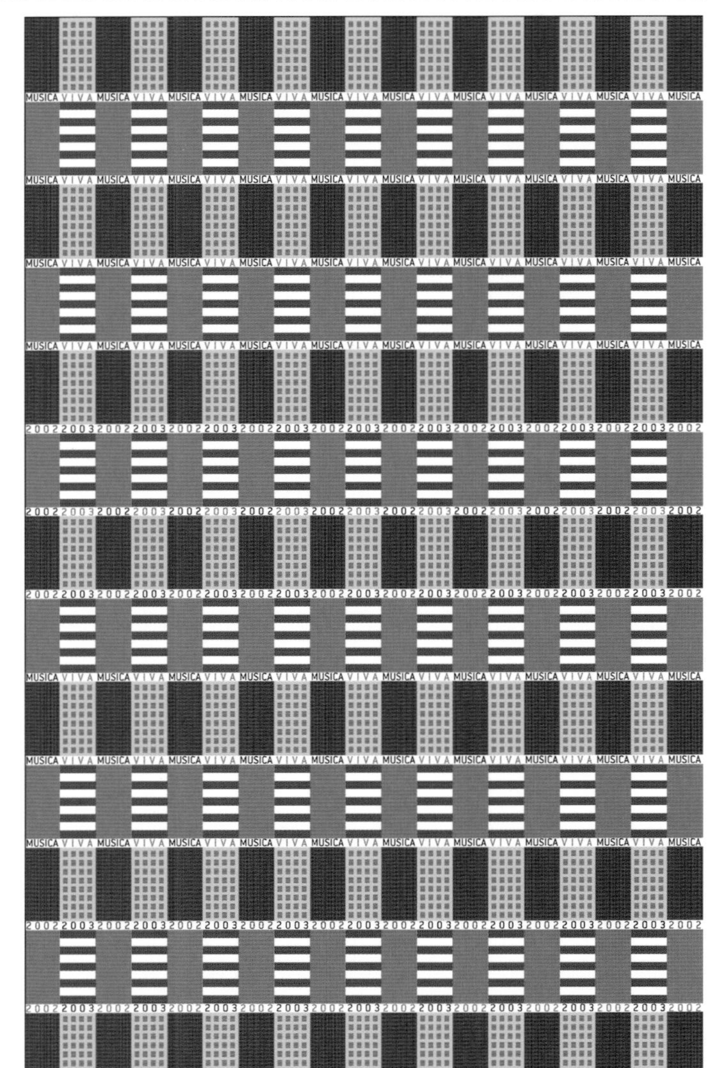

7 Poster for lecture series at the Academy of Visual Arts, Leipzig / Institut für Buchkunst, Hochschule für Grafik und Buchkunst, Leipzig / Germany / 1998
8 Cover, Musica Viva concert program for the season 2002–2003 / Musica Viva / Germany / 2002
9 Poster for Musica Viva concert dedicated to compositions by John Cage / Musica Viva / Germany / 2002
10 Poster for Musica Viva concert dedicated to the works of various contemporary composers / Musica Viva / Germany / 2002
11 Poster for premiere of the opera *Dmitri oder Der Künstler und die Macht*, by Luca Lombardi / Oper Leipzig / 2000
12 Poster for premiere of Musica Viva concert "Voiceless Voice in Hiroshima," by Toshio Hosokawa / Musica Viva / Germany / 2001

Günter Karl Bose

9

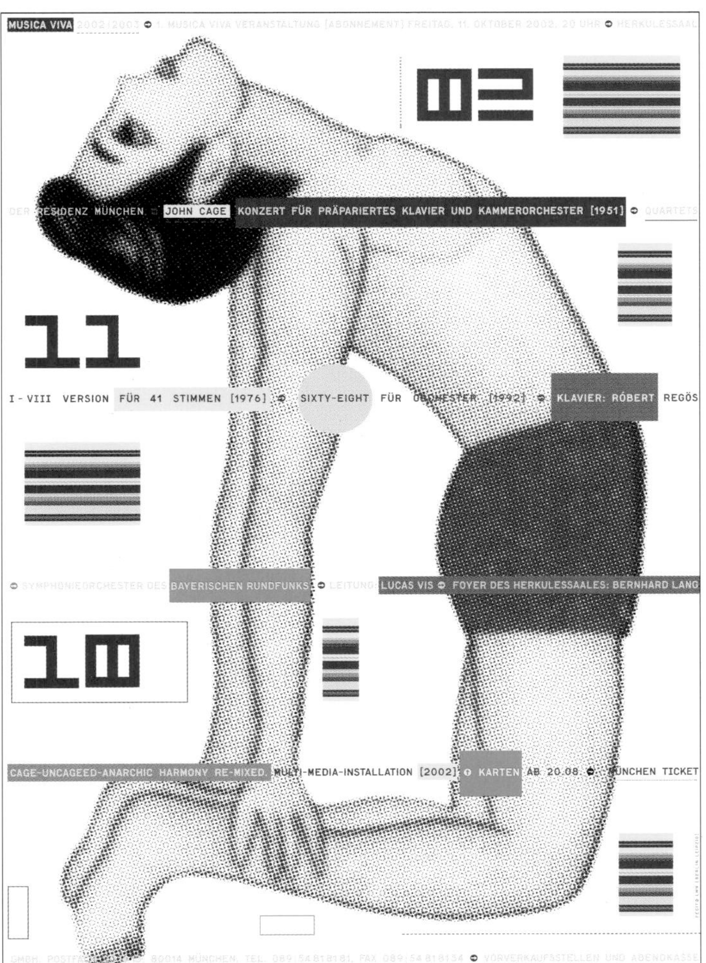

10

11

12

040501

040501

040501

040501

040501

0 4 0 5 0 1
H E R K U L E S S A A L D E R R E S I D E N Z
VIERTES KONZERT DER MUSICA VIVA 2000/2001
FREITAG/4. MAI 2001/20 UHR/
MUSICA VIVA PREIS DER ARD UND BMW AG/
PREISTRAEGERKONZERT/
DER MILLENNIUMSAUSSCHREIBUNG/2000/2001/
DES BMW KOMPOSITIONSPREISES/
DER MUSICA VIVA/
TOSHIO HOSOKAWA/VOICELESS VOICE
IN HIROSHIMA [2000/2001]
FUER SOLISTEN SPRECHER/CHOR
UND GROSSES ORCHESTER/
CHOR UND SYMPHONIEORCHESTER/
DES BAYERISCHEN RUNDFUNKS/
LEITUNG / SYLVAIN CAMBRELING/

040501

The feeling of a bag filled with soft feathers slowly sinking toward the bottom of the soul. A full, dark sound developing. The CD cover resonates in my eyes and in my mind. Munich's ECM Records has been using Mayo Bucher's strong paintings for selected new CD covers for several years now. Someone wrote that Bucher's images stand "at the end point of reduction," at the "threshold to self-dissolution." I believe that in reduction he has found a stillness that allows me to pause and breathe deeply. There might be something quietly holy, a tinge of the other, in Bucher's work. Central to his opus is the conceptual relationship he explores at the intersection of painting, graphic design, architecture, and music. Bucher has the courage to wander about where others burn their fingers, even their faces. For him visual arts, which he studied, are the entrance to graphic design. As a discoverer and creator of images he concentrates everything around and in him. He masters the visual language completely, he doesn't make any spelling mistakes, his sentences are always intelligible. Bucher speaks perfect Visual. Therefore no fissure opens between his graphic work and his two- and three-dimensional artistic works. He bridges obvious critical spots with words. His letters force their shape on me before I am able to grasp their meaning. Forms turn to letters turn to words turn to forms. Bucher is a language talent, because he knows how to delineate and enrich the delineated—and he leaves me alone. Perhaps it is the strength mentioned at the beginning that makes me stand there, the deliberate, space-taking vacuum, this one full, dark sound surrounding his work. He does it on purpose. Bucher is an artist, and he has given me as a present a piece of the universe. Werner Jeker

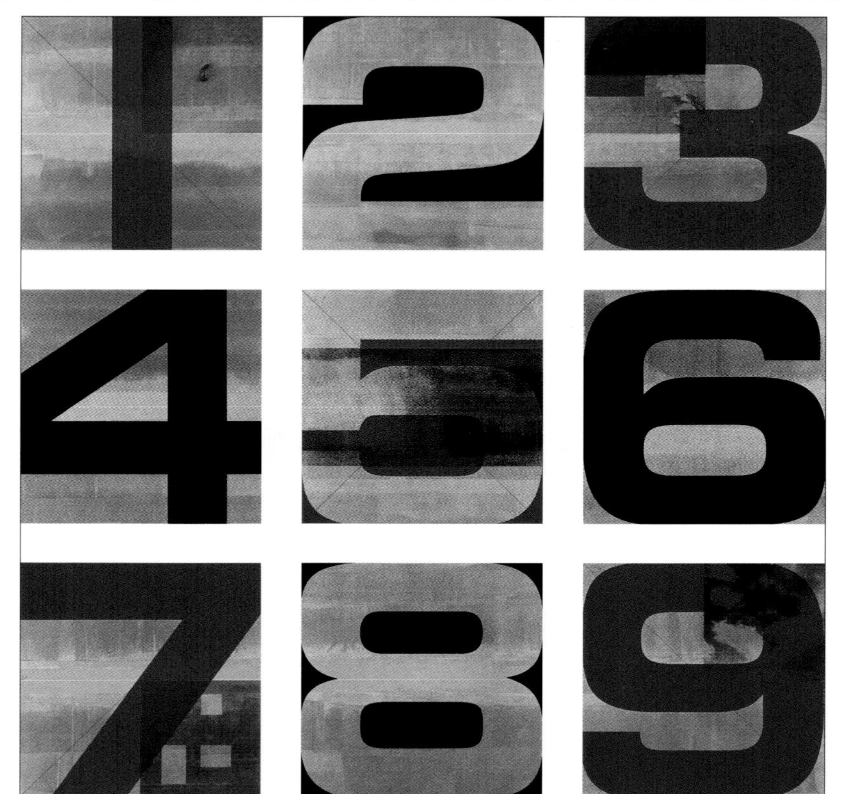

1

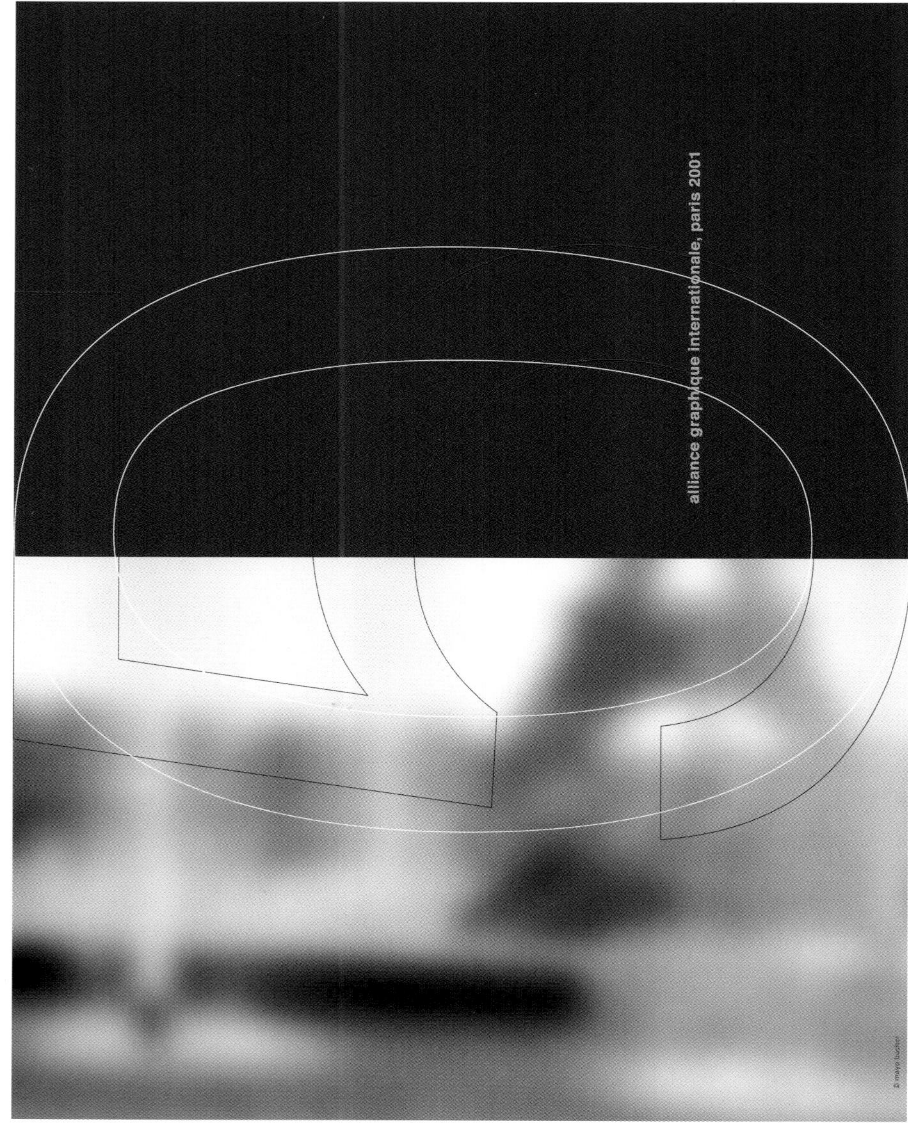

2

1 Self-commissioned piece "Figures 1 to 9" / Switzerland / 2001
2 Poster for fiftieth anniversary of the Alliance Graphique Internationale (AGI) / France / 2001
3 Facade concept in collaboration with Lussi & Halter Architects for a building in Emmenbrücke / Migros Genossenschaftsbund / Switzerland / 2002
4 Entrance-hall mural and light installation in collaboration with Burkhalter & Sumi Architects for Sulzer headquarters in Winterthur / Switzerland / 2003
5 Project study for a facade concept in collaboration with DGJ Architects / Museum Deutsche Bücherei, Leipzig / Germany / 2002

Mayo Bucher

Zurich

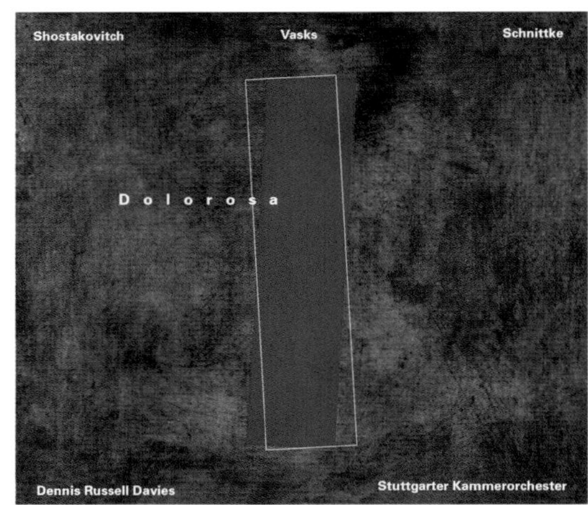

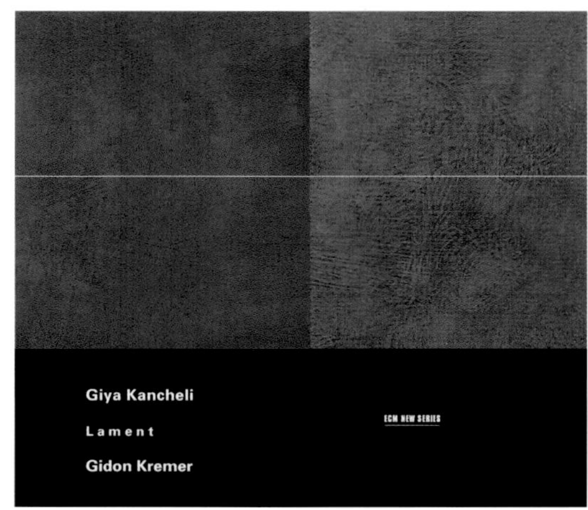

6–9 Cover and section dividers for publication accompanying a McKinsey international corporate conference (with Mifflin-Schmid Designers, Zurich) / Switzerland / 1999
10 CD cover, Keith Jarret at La Scala / ECM / Germany / 1995
11 CD cover, *Dolorosa*, pieces by Shostakovich, Vasks, and Schnittke / ECM / Germany / 1997
12 CD cover, *Trio Sonatas*, by Jan Dismas Zelenka / ECM / Germany / 1999
13 CD cover, *Lament*, by Giya Kancheli / ECM / Germany / 2000
14 Poster for *Mayo Bucher: OPEN SIGN in progress* exhibition / Academy of Visual Arts, Leipzig / Germany / 2002
15–16 "EINSZWEIDREIVIER" and "ZEROZERO" floor installations for *Mayo Bucher: OPEN SIGN in progress* exhibition / Academy of Visual Arts, Leipzig / Germany / 2002

Mayo Bucher

14

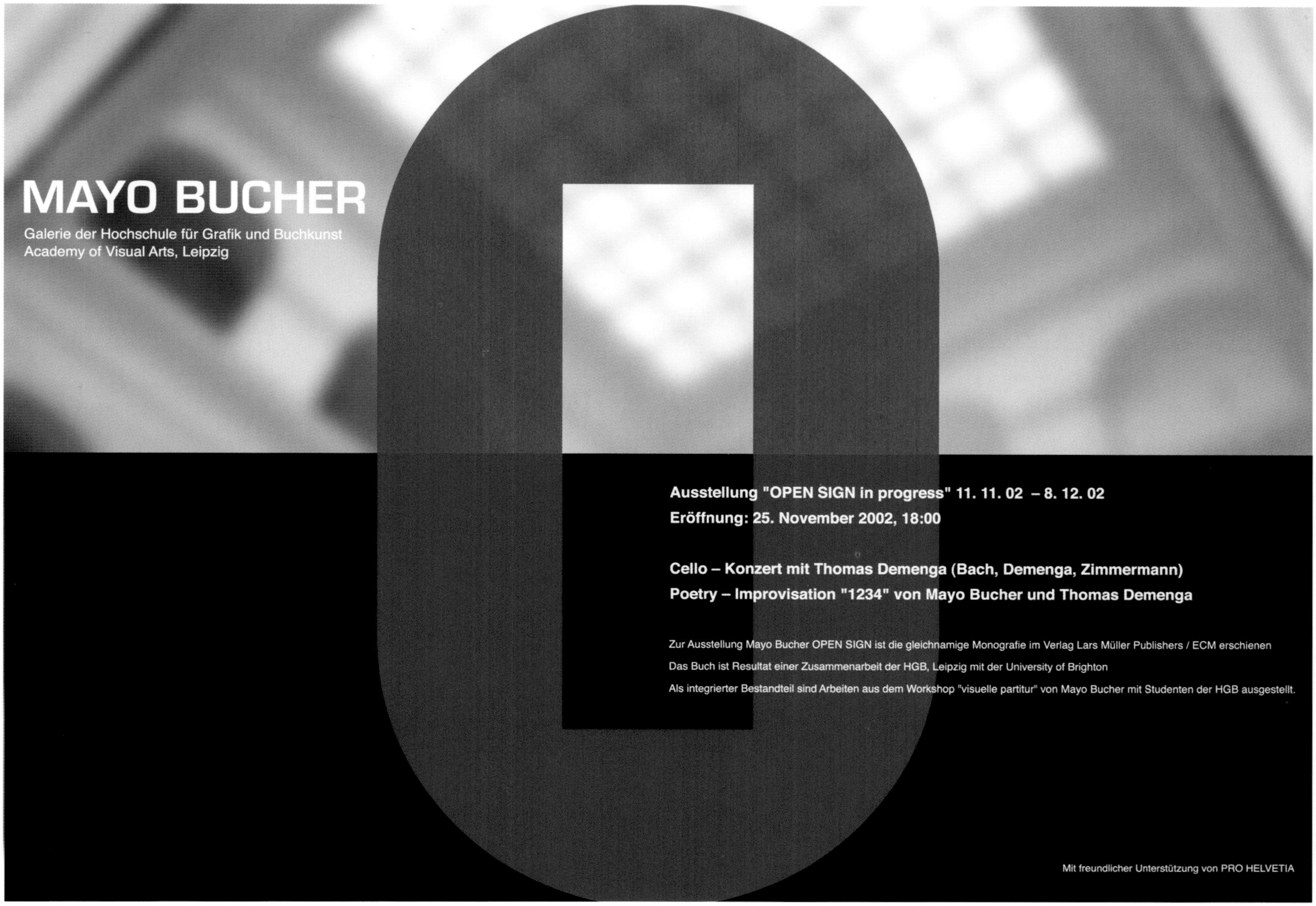

MAYO BUCHER

Galerie der Hochschule für Grafik und Buchkunst
Academy of Visual Arts, Leipzig

Ausstellung "OPEN SIGN in progress" 11. 11. 02 – 8. 12. 02
Eröffnung: 25. November 2002, 18:00

Cello – Konzert mit Thomas Demenga (Bach, Demenga, Zimmermann)
Poetry – Improvisation "1234" von Mayo Bucher und Thomas Demenga

Zur Ausstellung Mayo Bucher OPEN SIGN ist die gleichnamige Monografie im Verlag Lars Müller Publishers / ECM erschienen
Das Buch ist Resultat einer Zusammenarbeit der HGB, Leipzig mit der University of Brighton
Als integrierter Bestandteil sind Arbeiten aus dem Workshop "visuelle partitur" von Mayo Bucher mit Studenten der HGB ausgestellt.

Mit freundlicher Unterstützung von PRO HELVETIA

15–16

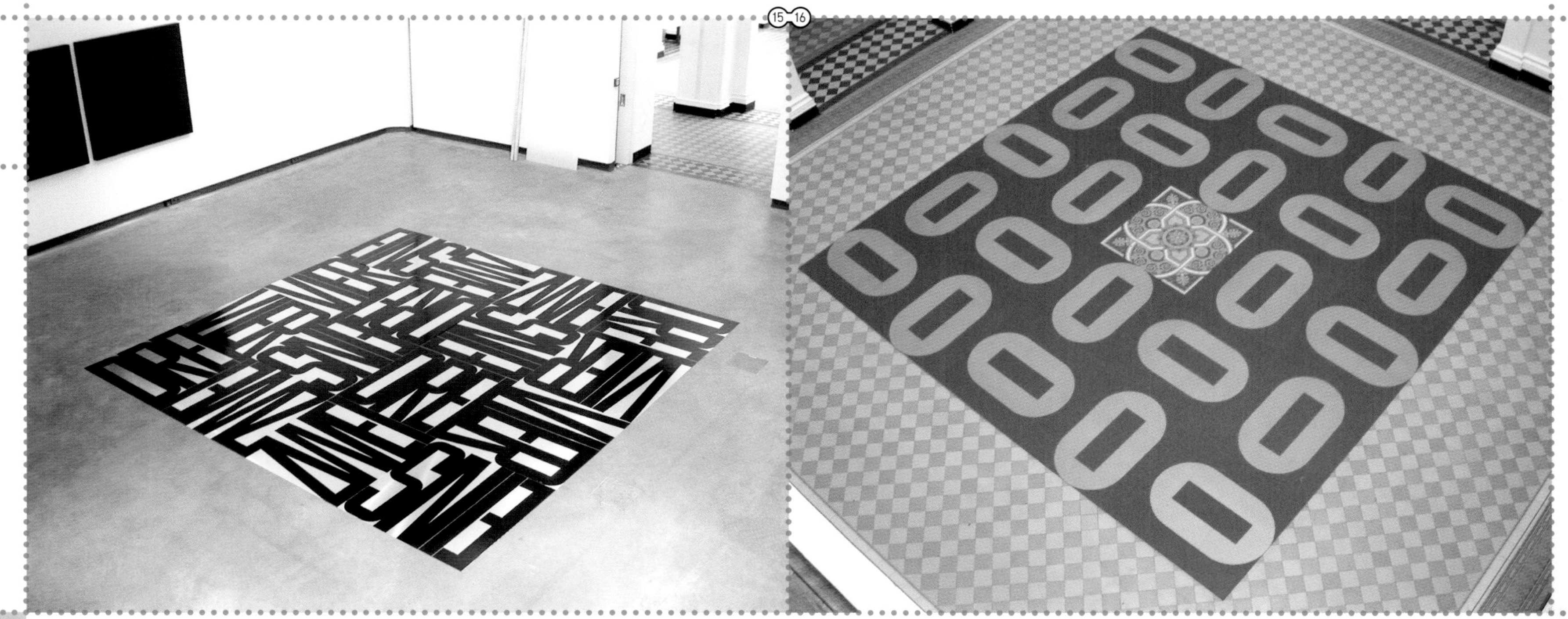

Some people are literally fated to be famous. Vladimir Chaika's last name in Russian means "seagull," an unimpeded sea bird, a symbol of freedom. And his ascent in the profession was bright and swift. • • Chaika dreamed of being a well-known designer while he was still a student at Strogonov University, and he became famous in Russia very early, in the mid-1980s. He became a bridge between the old Soviet school of graphic design and the new professional generation. For the new generation of designers he became a symbol of design itself. One can say, with a little exaggeration, that he bore this new generation, having shown the path to glory and fame to his only slightly younger comrades, who strove to imitate him in every way, right up to his hairstyle and dress. • • I had a moniker for this generation of young designers, who appeared in Russia in the late 1980s: "Chaika's younger brothers." Alexander Gelman, now a famous New York designer, as well as Andrey Logvin and Yuri Surkov were all part of this circle. This was still in the 1980s, in what was, for Russia, the precomputer era. • • In 1990, Chaika spent half a year in New York, in the studio of Massimo Vinelli, who became his idol. Chaika became a fan of Swiss minimalism and decided to become more Swiss than the Swiss themselves. In the mid-1990s Chaika gained wide international popularity. Many top designers who know him personally adore him for his charm and cheerfulness. • • I most value the work Chaika himself calls "HE-story," history of "him," a character made up of four little lines, short strokes, suggesting the outline of a face. He started drawing these lines, or finding them in the surrounding environment and photographing them, and turning them into posters or magazine covers in the late 1980s. In the past fifteen years one could come across these well-known strokes in different and sometimes the most unexpected of places throughout Russia and eventually the whole world. • • Who is this mysterious "HE"? Chaika's personal symbol? His mantra? A way of comprehending reality? A game? An omnipresent guardian angel? Or the soul of all things? I don't know. But if you see these lines somewhere high in the Himalayas or in unpopulated Mongolia, know this: Chaika was here, designer from Moscow. • • Serge Serov • •

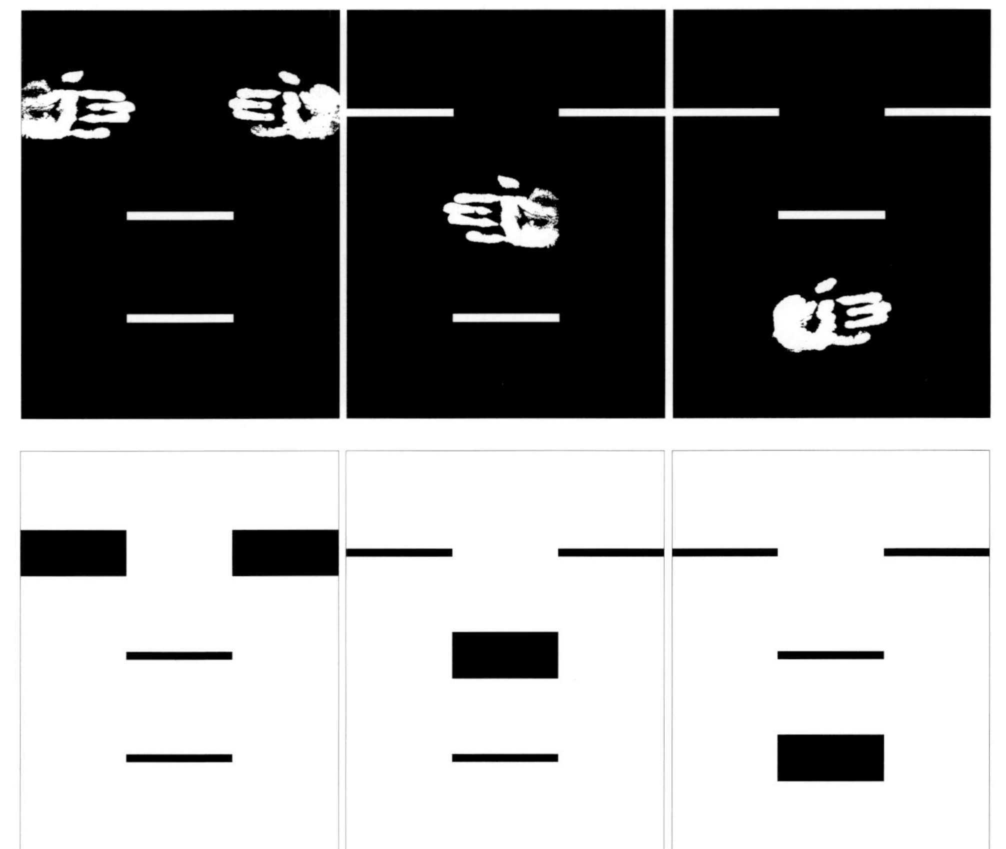

1

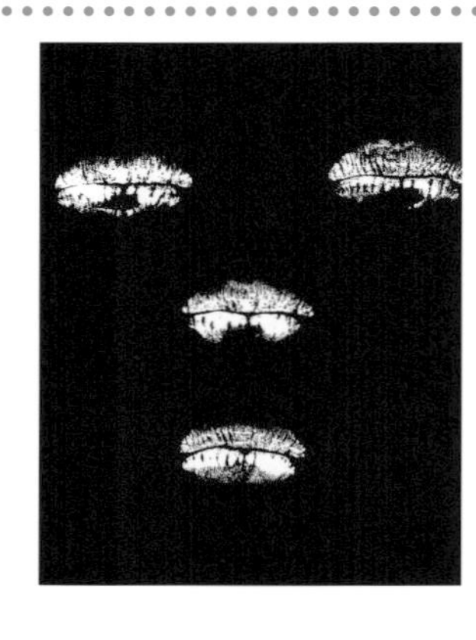

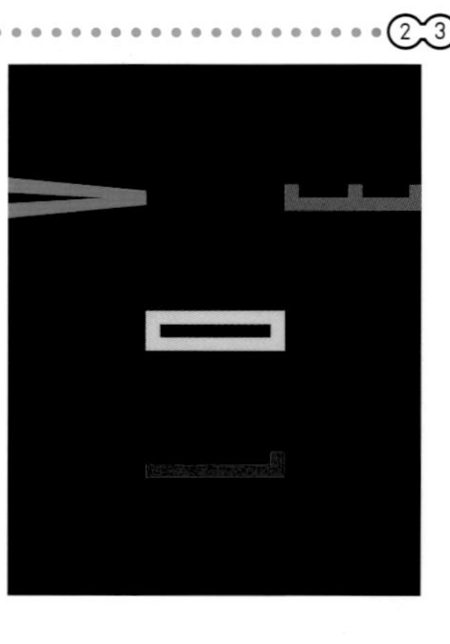

2 3 4

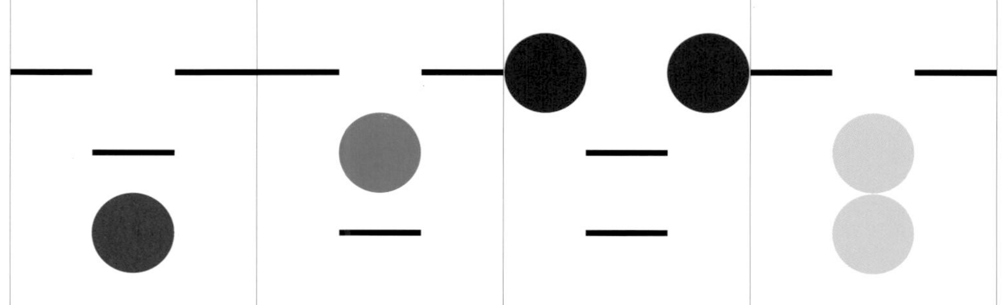

5

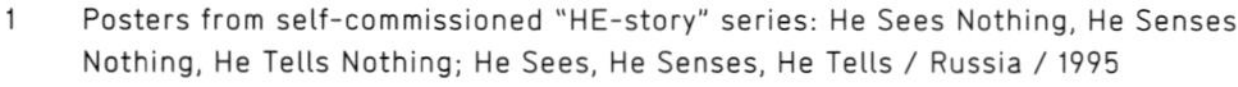

1 Posters from self-commissioned "HE-story" series: He Sees Nothing, He Senses Nothing, He Tells Nothing; He Sees, He Senses, He Tells / Russia / 1995
2–4 Kiss, Smile of EUROpe, and Love, from "HE-story" poster series / Russia / 2000–2002
5 Four Seasons, from "HE-story" poster series / Russia / 1996
6 He Is Here, from "HE-story" poster series / Russia / 1995
7 Poster dedicated to memory of Ikko Tanaka, from "HE-story" series / Russia / 2002
8 "HE," personal symbol of Vladimir Chaika / Russia / 1988

Vladimir Chaika

Moscow

6

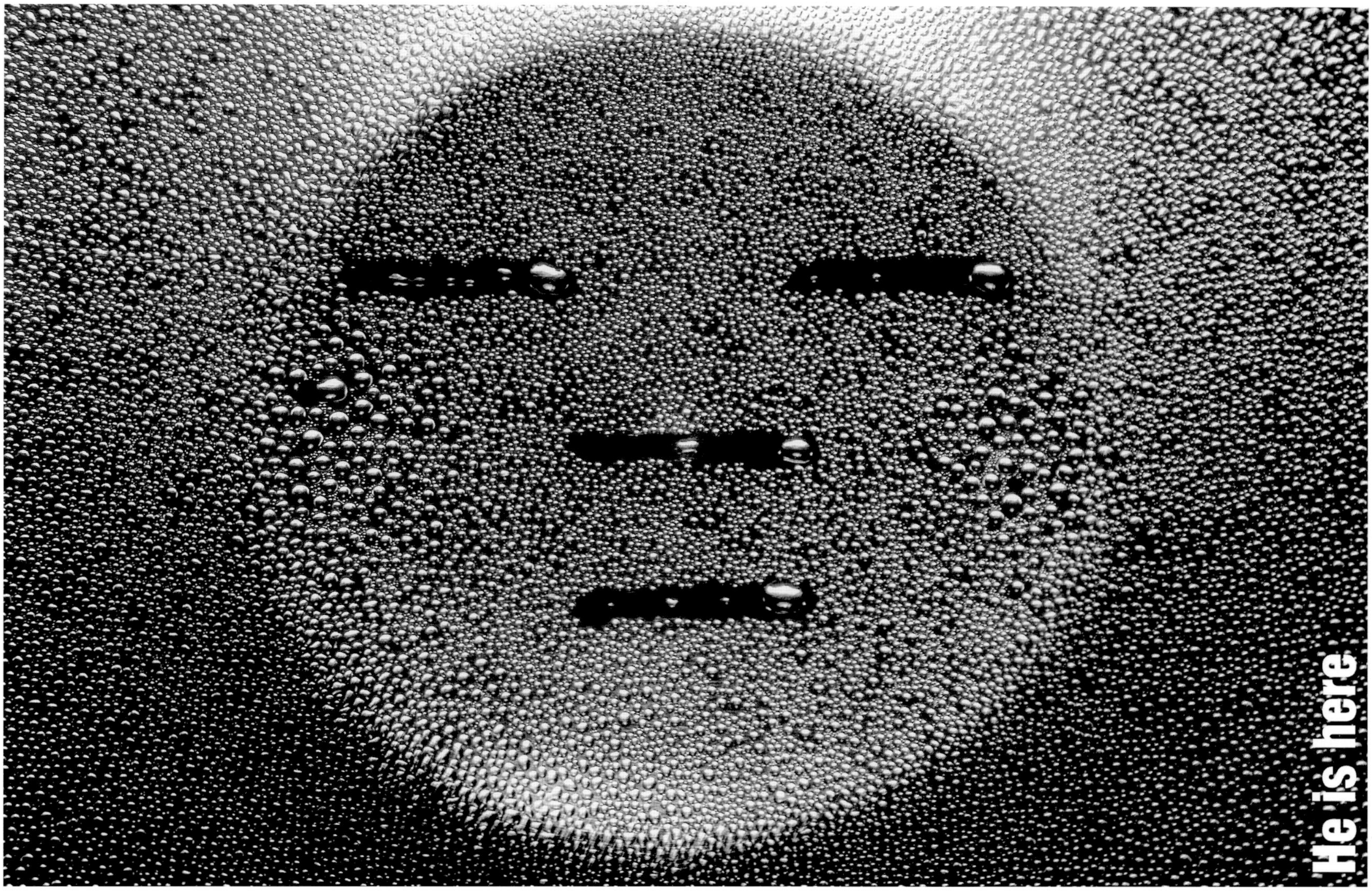

He is here

7

8

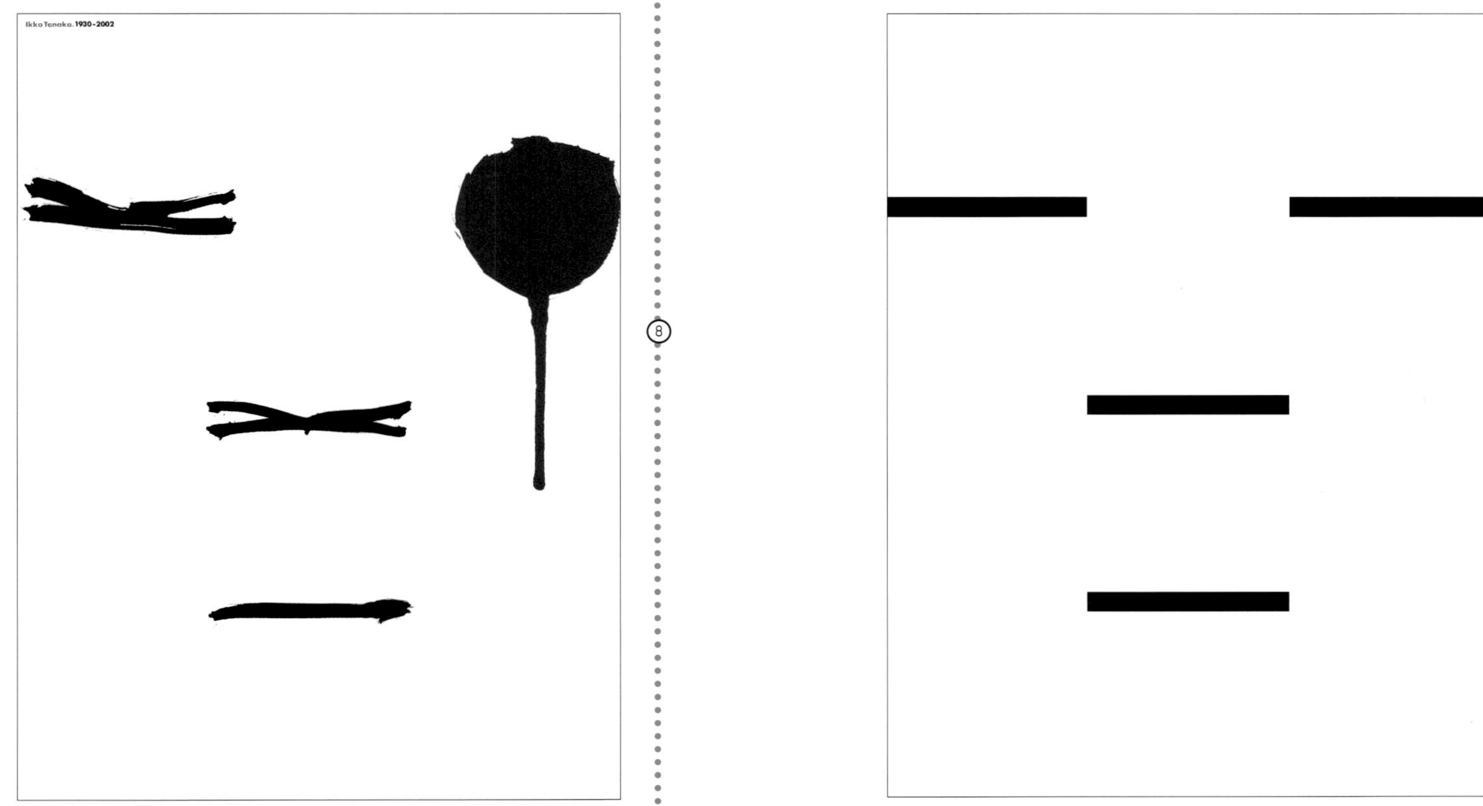

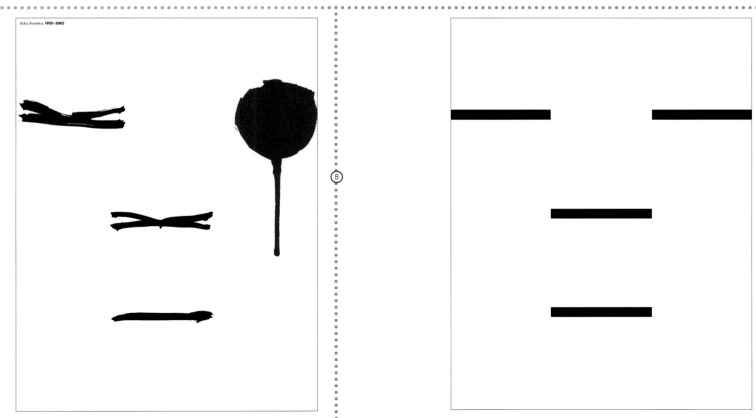

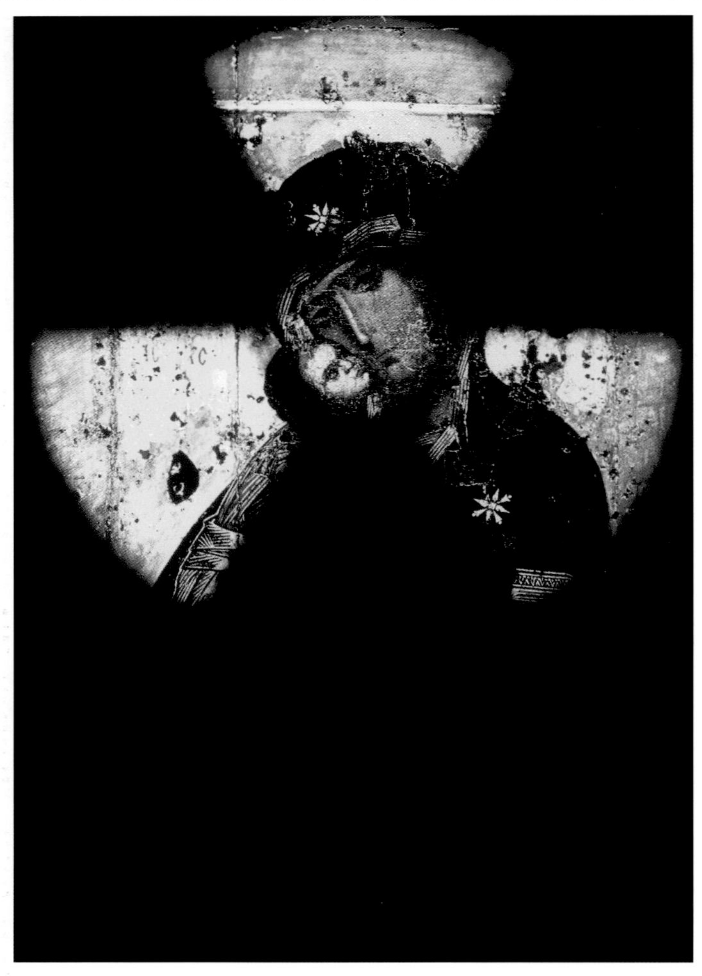

9

10

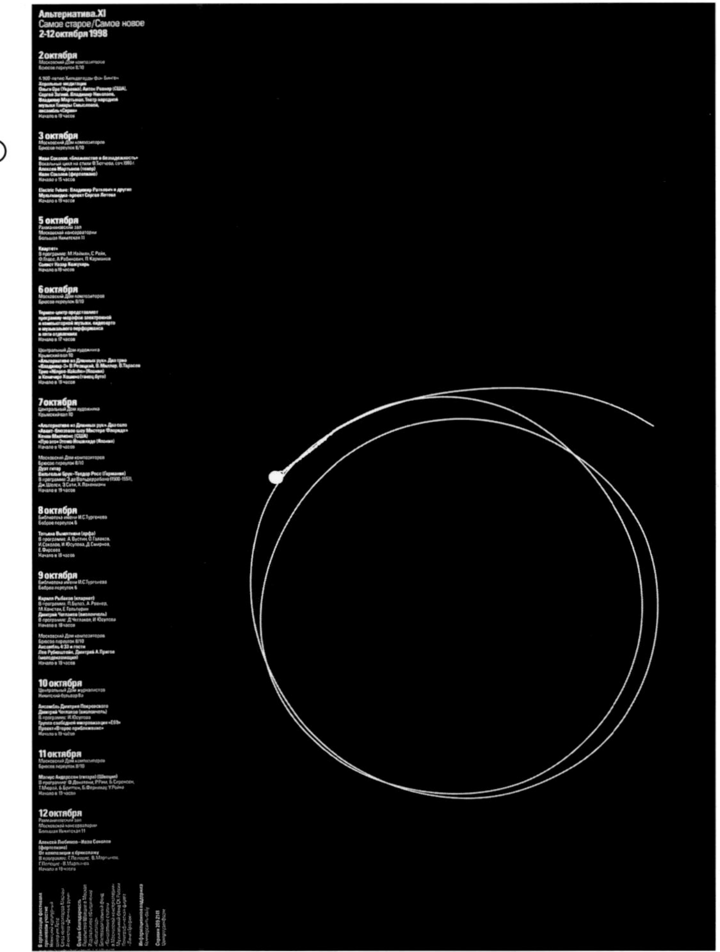

11

9 Self-commissioned Radioactive Mother of God poster dedicated to the victims of the Chernobyl radiation disaster / Russia / 1996
10 Poster for Alternative Music Festival in Moscow / Alternative Festival Organization / Russia / 1998
11 Dialogue of Other Worlds poster for Moscow International Festival of Visual Anthropology / Russia / 2002
12 Logo and pictograms for first World Youth Games held in Moscow / World Youth Games Organizational Committee / Russia / 1997
13–14 Logo and logo application / Oriol Avia Airlines / Russia / 1991
15 Logo / International Cultural Collaboration Art-Ark / Russia / 1991
16 Logo for *Go* graphic-design magazine / Go / Russia / 1992

Vladimir Chaika

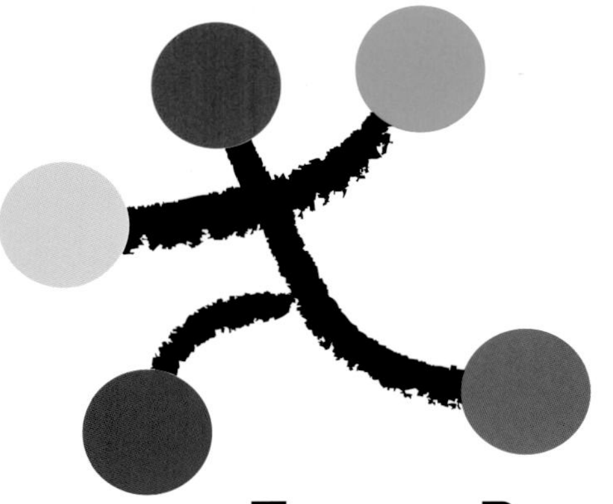

12

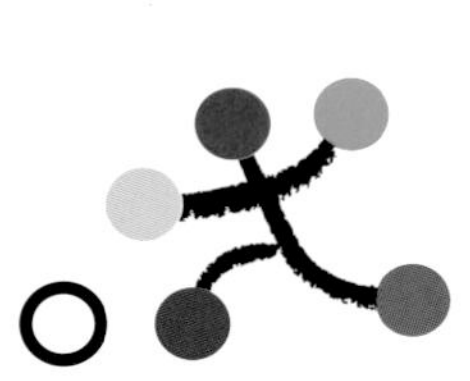

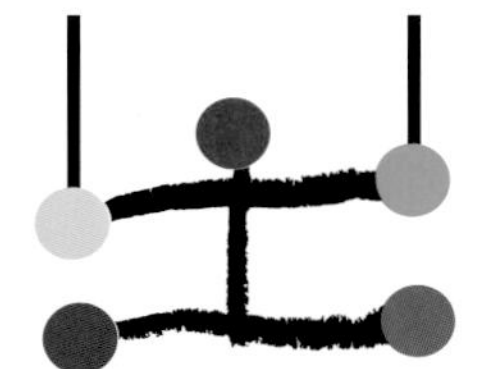

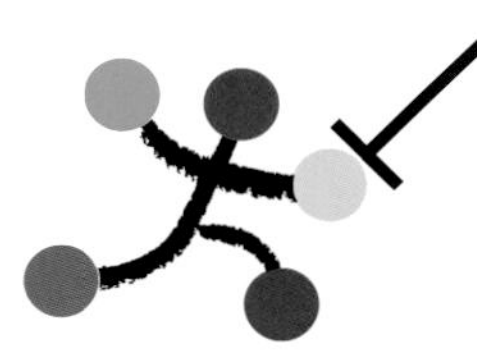

13
14

15

16

Marcel Hermans is a former student of mine, from the Rietveld Academy in Amsterdam, and he worked for about three years in my studio. Then he took off to the United States, with his Swiss girlfriend, Cornelia Blatter, and now they live between Amsterdam and New York. Their shared firm is COMA. Blatter, originally an artist, brought in her own background. I think COMA's work is thoroughly Swiss-Dutch, fiercely analytical and organized and at the same time adventurous and experimental. They work mainly for museums and publishers, and they art-direct the Dutch design magazine *Frame*. ••COMA continually thinks of new ways to formally organize the material they present in order to arrive at its essence. They make gorgeous catalogues in which they employ any typographic and visual means necessary to structure the work. With Swiss precision and Dutch playfulness, they unravel the artist's work and use it to make their own visual statement. Their choice of work is, in a sense, uncompromising: they stick to their own points of departure. They can work for clients around the world by virtue of the Internet, which makes it easier to exchange high-quality artwork and comps.••For each issue of *Frame* magazine, they choose a different typographic approach, giving each issue its own character. They redefine their position vis-à-vis the publication according to the contents at hand. Matching type and art is often complicated with a magazine: a potpourri of visual material lands on your desk, and you have to massage that into a coherent whole. COMA does that by devising a new—strong and inventive—mold for each issue. Clear, transparent, and imaginative within a rigidly researched concept. Their choice of scrutinizing a design to arrive at a personal statement, an individual interpretation, is very close to my own view on design.••Anthon Beeke••

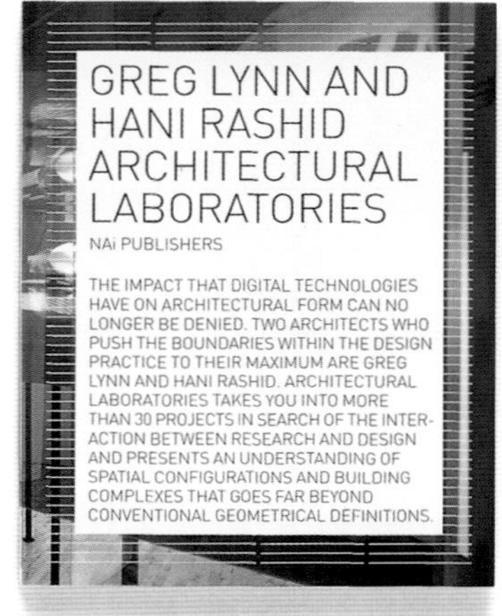
GREG LYNN AND HANI RASHID ARCHITECTURAL LABORATORIES

NAi PUBLISHERS

THE IMPACT THAT DIGITAL TECHNOLOGIES HAVE ON ARCHITECTURAL FORM CAN NO LONGER BE DENIED. TWO ARCHITECTS WHO PUSH THE BOUNDARIES WITHIN THE DESIGN PRACTICE TO THEIR MAXIMUM ARE GREG LYNN AND HANI RASHID. ARCHITECTURAL LABORATORIES TAKES YOU INTO MORE THAN 30 PROJECTS IN SEARCH OF THE INTERACTION BETWEEN RESEARCH AND DESIGN AND PRESENTS AN UNDERSTANDING OF SPATIAL CONFIGURATIONS AND BUILDING COMPLEXES THAT GOES FAR BEYOND CONVENTIONAL GEOMETRICAL DEFINITIONS.

1
2
3
4

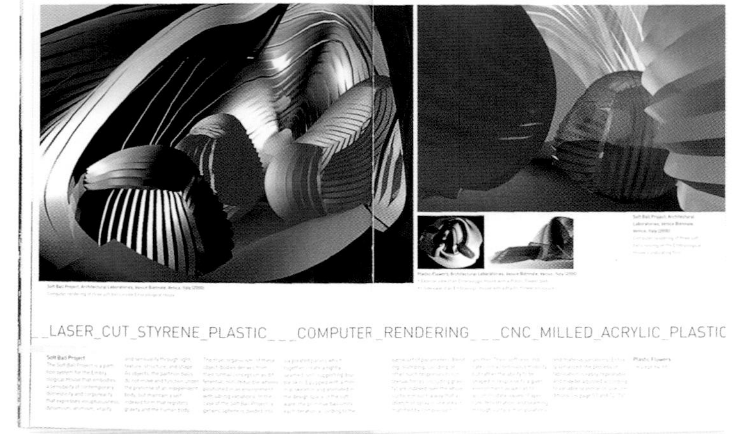

1–4 Cover and spreads, *Greg Lynn and Hani Rashid: Architectural Laboratories* / NAi Publishers / Netherlands / 2002 / The book showcases projects from a four-week workshop for architectural discourse at the 2000 Venice Biennale.
5–8 Cover and spreads, *Peter Halley–Maintain Speed* / Distributed Art Publishers (D.A.P.) / USA / 2000
9–12 Cover and spreads, *The Hugo Boss Prize 2002* / Solomon R. Guggenheim Museum New York / USA / 2002 / Publication accompanying Guggenheim Museum's fourth biennial Hugo Boss prize competition for contemporary art.

COMA

New York/Amsterdam

THE HUGO BOSS PRIZE 2002

Francis Alÿs
Olafur Eliasson
Hachiya Kazuhiko
Pierre Huyghe
Koo Jeong-a
Anri Sala

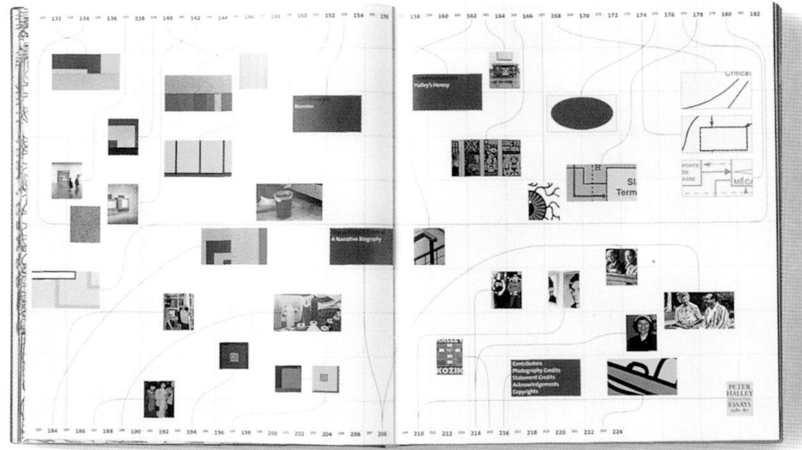

5 6 7 8

THE HUGO BOSS PRIZE 2002

Francis Alÿs
Olafur Eliasson
Hachiya Kazuhiko
Pierre Huyghe
Koo Jeong-a
Anri Sala

9 10 11 12

Introduction

Susan Cross

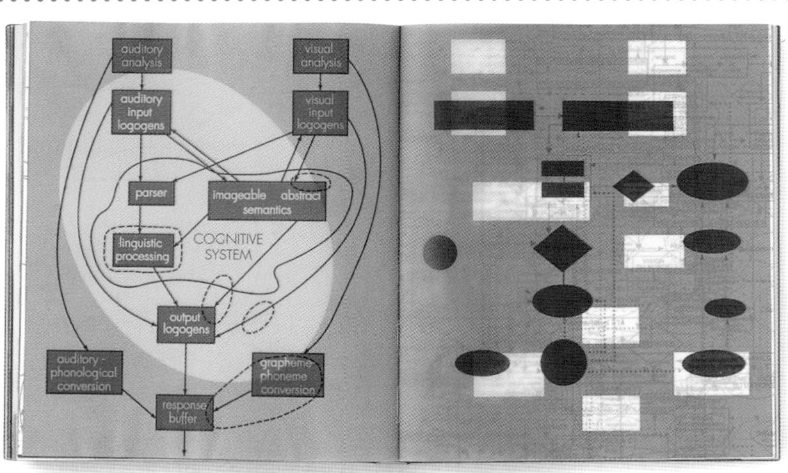

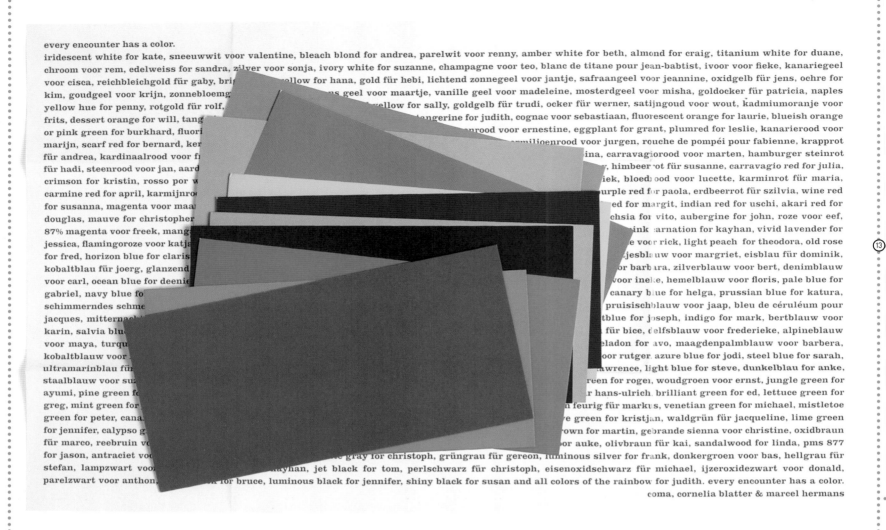

every encounter has a color.
iridescent white for kate, sneeuwwit voor valentine, bleach blond for andrea, parelwit voor renny, amber white for beth, almond for craig, titanium white for duane,
chroom voor rem, edelweiss for sandra, zilver voor sonja, ivory white for suzanne, champagne voor teo, blanc de titane pour jean-babtist, ivoor voor fieke, kanariegeel
voor cisca, reichbleichgold für gaby, bri ... yellow for hana, gold für hebi, lichtend zonnegeel voor jantje, safraangeel voor jeannine, oxidgelb für jens, ochre for
kim, goudgeel voor krijn, zonnebloemg ... ns geel voor maartje, vanille geel voor madeleine, mosterdgeel voor misha, goldocker für patricia, naples
yellow hue for penny, rotgold für rolf, ... yellow for sally, goldgelb für trudi, ocker für werner, satijngoud voor wout, kadmiumoranje voor
frits, dessert orange for will, tang ... tangerine for judith, cognac voor sebastiaan, fluorescent orange for laurie, blueish orange
or pink green for burkhard, fluori ... nrood voor ernestine, eggplant for grant, plumred for leslie, kanarierood voor
marijn, scarf red for bernard, ker ... rmilioenrood voor jurgen, rouche de pompéi pour fabienne, krapprot
für andrea, kardinaalrood voor f ... ina, carravagiorood voor marten, hamburger steinrot
für hadi, steenrood voor jan, aard ... , himbeerrot für susanne, carravagio red for julia,
crimson for kristin, rosso por w ... iek, bloedrood voor lucette, karminrot für maria,
carmine red for april, karmijnro ... urple red for paola, erdbeerrot für szilvia, wine red
for susanna, magenta voor maa ... ed for margit, indian red for uschi, akari red for
douglas, mauve for christopher ... chsia for vito, aubergine for john, roze voor eef,
87% magenta voor freek, mang ... ink carnation for kayhan, vivid lavender for
jessica, flamingoroze voor katj ... e voor rick, light peach for theodora, old rose
for fred, horizon blue for claris ... jesblauw voor margriet, eisblau für dominik,
kobaltblau für joerg, glanzend ... or barbara, zilverblauw voor bert, denimblauw
voor carl, ocean blue for deeni ... voor ineke, hemelblauw voor floris, pale blue for
gabriel, navy blue fo ... canary blue for helga, prussian blue for katura,
schimmerndes schme ... pruisischblauw voor jaap, bleu de céruléum pour
jacques, mittern ... tblue for joseph, indigo for mark, bertblauw voor
karin, salvia blu ... für bice, delfsblauw voor frederieke, alpineblauw
voor maya, turqu ... eladon for avo, maagdenpalmblauw voor barbera,
kobaltblauw voor ... oor rutger, azure blue for jodi, steel blue for sarah,
ultramarinblau für ... awrence, light blue for steve, dunkelblau for anke,
staalblauw voor su ... een for roger, woudgroen voor ernst, jungle green for
ayumi, pine green f ... r hans-ulrich, brilliant green for ed, lettuce green for
greg, mint green for ... n feurig für markus, venetian green for michael, mistletoe
green for peter, cana ... e green for kristjan, waldgrün für jacqueline, lime green
for jennifer, calypso g ... rown for martin, gebrande sienna voor christine, oxidbraun
für marco, reebruin vo ... or auke, olivbraun für kai, sandalwood for linda, pms 877
for jason, antraciet vo ... gray for christoph, grüngrau für gereon, luminous silver for frank, donkergroen voor bas, hellgrau für
stefan, lampzwart voo ... kayhan, jet black for tom, perlschwarz für christoph, eisenoxidschwarz für michael, ijzeroxidezwart voor donald,
parelzwart voor anthon ... k for bruce, luminous black for jennifer, shiny black for susan and all colors of the rainbow for judith. every encounter has a color.
coma, cornelia blatter & marcel hermans

13

14 15 16

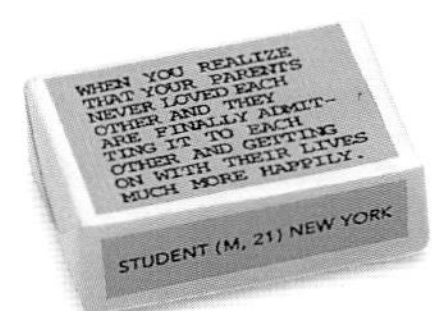

13 Self-commissioned project "Every Encounter Has A Color" / Netherlands and USA / 2001 / The project comprises ten color cards, a folded envelope, and an essay by Anna Blume. The inside of the envelope lists the names of all the people COMA encountered in 2001. Each person was given a color name in the language of the encounter. The color name, cards, and essay served as a present for friends and clients.
14–16 Self-commissioned project "Describe Something Sweet" / Netherlands and USA / 1998 / People of different ages, nationalities, and professions were asked to "describe something sweet." Each response was told on sugar-cube wrappers in the handwriting of the person asked.
17–18 Cover and spread, *Index* magazine, April–May 2000 / Peter Halley / USA / 2000
19–20 Cover and spread, *Frame* magazine, January–February 2003 / Frame / Netherlands / 2003
21–24 Cover and spreads, *Nanoarchitecture–a New Species of Architecture–John M. Johansen* / Princeton Architectural Press / USA / 2002

COMA

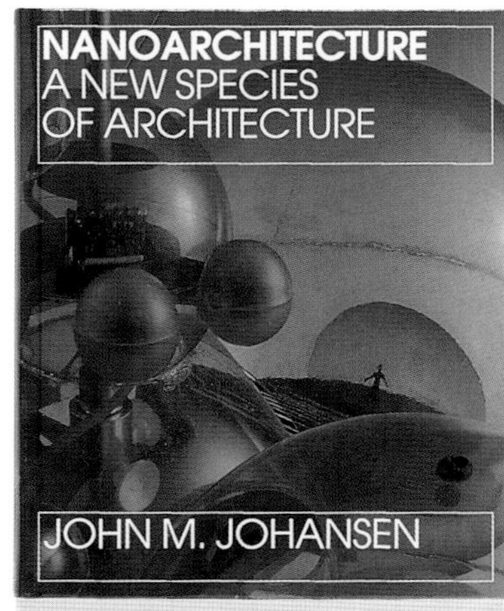

17
18

BIJOU PHILLIPS the veritable holy terror of page 6

For anyone with even a casual relationship with the delicious Page Six, *The New York Post*'s gossip column, "Bijou" should already be somewhat of a household word. In fact, Bijou Phillips, who will turn twenty in the year 2000, has been the veritable holy terror of Page Six for the past four or five years now. She's today's Tuesday, the new Drew, a wild child who, through fate and circumstance, was somehow allowed to partake of New York's nebulous nightlife at an age traditionally more suited to playing with dolls – that is, of the non-pharmaceutical variety.

with Bruce LaBruce
photographed by Terry Richardson

21
22
23
24

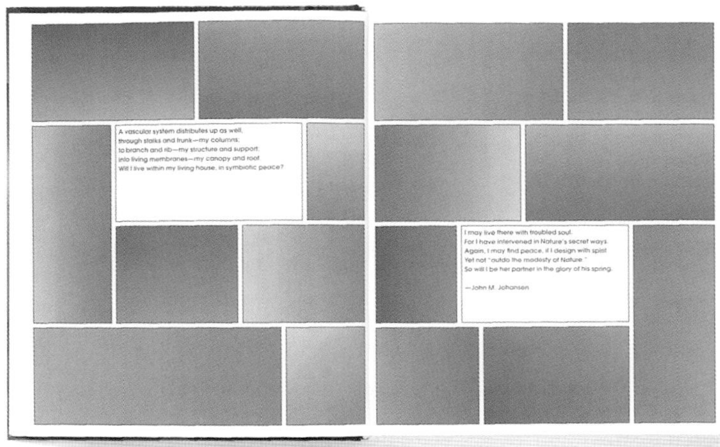

A vascular system distributes up as well,
through stalks and trunk—my columns;
to branch and rib—my structure and support;
into living membranes—my canopy and root.
Will I live within my living house, in symbiotic peace?

I may live there with troubled soul.
For I have intervened in Nature's secret ways.
Again, I may find peace, if I design with spirit
Yet not "outdo the modesty of Nature."
So will I be her partner in the glory of his spring.

—John M. Johansen

FRAME
THE INTERNATIONAL MAGAZINE OF INTERIOR ARCHITECTURE AND DESIGN > JAN/FEB 2001
Pick 'n' Mix
Sample Your Surroundings

19
20

textiles

CROSSING BORDERS

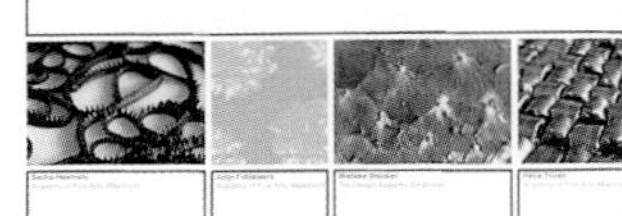

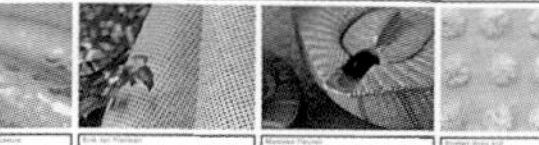

Graduation projects by Dutch design students indicate that textile and product designers are pushing the envelope of their profession as never before. A selection from the rich harvest of new designs discovered at academies in Arnhem, Eindhoven, The Hague and Maastricht not only reveals the specific properties of various textiles, but also shows the degree to which textile design touches on other disciplines. Young designers are crossing borders, giving 'old' a new coat and dressing 'new' in old clothes. They are aiming tactility, for instance, at target groups marked by a highly developed sense of touch, such as blind people and small children. Materials cleverly couched in a new context pull the wool over our eyes, making us chuckle. Patterns used in a new construction take on a different meaning and an extra dimension. The students whose projects are featured here approached the challenge of reconciling extremes and contrasts with eyes wide open. A series of photographs paints a picture of their experiments, their statements of social involvement and their prototypes for series production, while summarising the creative content of a new generation of designers.

I can't help it. Whenever I read the name Das Haus Rüegger und Albisetti (The House of Rüegger and Albisetti), I begin to imagine this house. Judith Rüegger and Anna Albisetti hereby suggest a kind of home, something intimate, for the house defines personality, manifests a style. Its site is of no importance, since their house materializes as their work, which is printed material. The two women live and work in their house. They maintain it in optimal condition. No project leaves the house through the back door, in shame. One of the women might very well work alone on occasion, but if a project is large enough for both of them, they work together, sometimes with one of them starting and the other finishing the project. This sounds symbiotic, like an intact world, like cowbells and chocolate, because the strategy is of utmost simplicity.•• Rüegger and Albisetti have known each other since their first days of training as graphic artists. Both follow the tradition of the craft, which the Schule für Gestaltung (School for Graphic Design) in Biel, Switzerland, so rapturously awakens in its students. Biel has a reputation for offering an easy-going education with an unusually strong emphasis on drawing for our time. This foundation may have generated the playful, sketchy, and collagelike element that forms the basis of Rüegger and Albisetti's work. The design process remains visible in all of their creations, they are among the few designers who are really apt at using the computer as a tool.•• Back to the "House of Symbiosis." They take their clients seriously. They become absorbed in the client's expectations. The layering of their streams of thought, allowing ideas to live next to one another, the juxtaposition of expectation, color, material, are mastered by Das Haus Rüegger und Albisetti with an enviable lightness. I would like to be a guest in such a house.•• Werner Jeker••

1 2 3

4 5 6

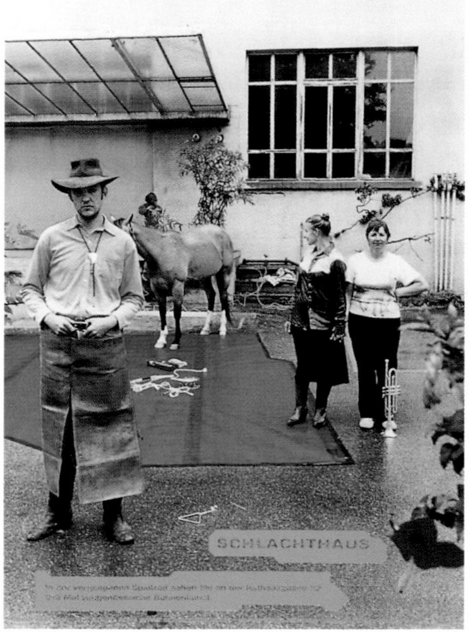

1–2 Posters for Ja'salâm! festival celebrating contemporary Arab culture in Bern / Pro Helvetia / Switzerland / 2002
3 Cover, Ja'salâm! festival program / 2002
4–6 Poster series *Gruppenbild* (Group Picture) announcing the theatrical program for the season 2000–2001 (3 of 6) / Schlachthaus Theater Bern / Switzerland / 2000–2001 / The series is based on a photograph incorporating elements of all plays to be shown during the season. The individual posters are created by covering different areas of the surface. The season finale-poster reveals the photograph in its entirety.
7–10 Poster series *Kürzest Dialoge* (Shortest Dialogues) advertising the Schlachthaus Theater Bern (4 of 7) / 1998–1999

Das Haus Rüegger + Albisetti

Bern

⑦

auch
im Winter
net
SCHLACHTHAUS
Theater | Rathausgasse 20/22 | CH-3011 Bern | Tel/Fax ++41 (0)31 312 96 47 | www.schlachthaus.ch
Der Bund
BERNERWOCHE
MÜNSTERGASS BUCHHANDLUNG
DreamLab

⑧

Kling
Kong
Am 31. Oktober '98 heisst es zum ersten Mal KNIRPS. KNIRPS ist der Anfang einer ziemlich scharfen Reihe von Konzerten für kurze Menschen und deren lange Begleitung. Nicht verpassen.
SCHLACHTHAUS
Theater | Rathausgasse 20/22 | CH-3011 Bern | Tel/Fax ++41 (0)31 312 96 47 | www.schlachthaus.ch
Der Bund
BERNERWOCHE
MÜNSTERGASS BUCHHANDLUNG
KROMPHOLZ

⑨

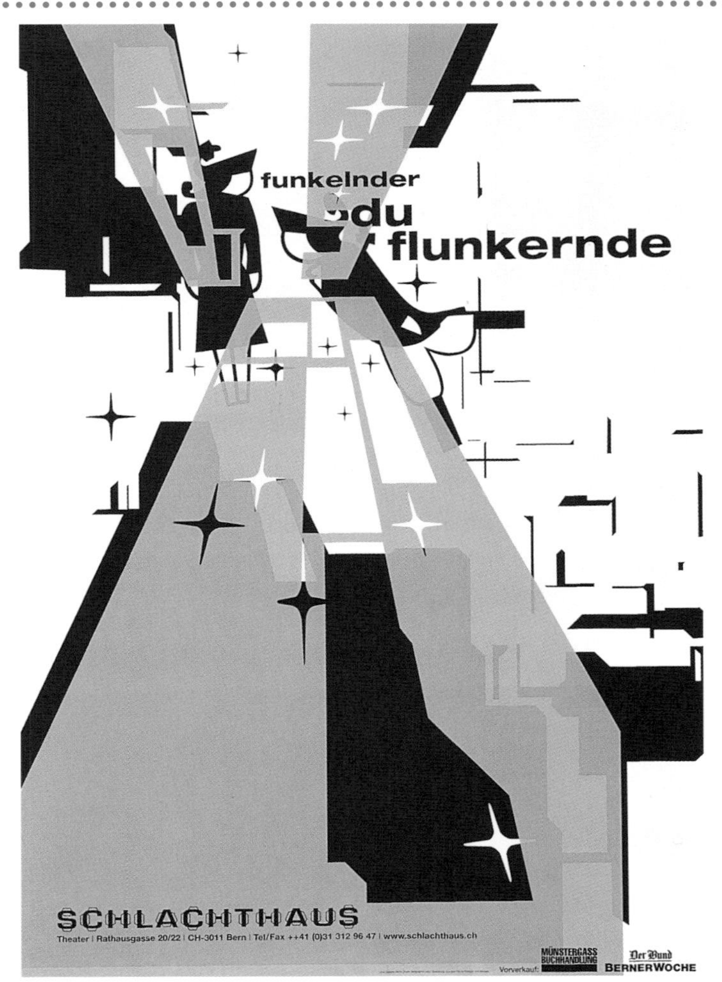
funkelnder
du
flunkernde
SCHLACHTHAUS
Theater | Rathausgasse 20/22 | CH-3011 Bern | Tel/Fax ++41 (0)31 312 96 47 | www.schlachthaus.ch
Vorverkauf:
MÜNSTERGASS BUCHHANDLUNG
Der Bund
BERNERWOCHE

⑩

bös
artig
SCHLACHTHAUS
Theater | Rathausgasse 20/22 | CH-3011 Bern | Tel/Fax ++41 (0)31 312 96 47 | www.schlachthaus.ch
Der Bund
BERNERWOCHE
MÜNSTERGASS BUCHHANDLUNG

11

12

13

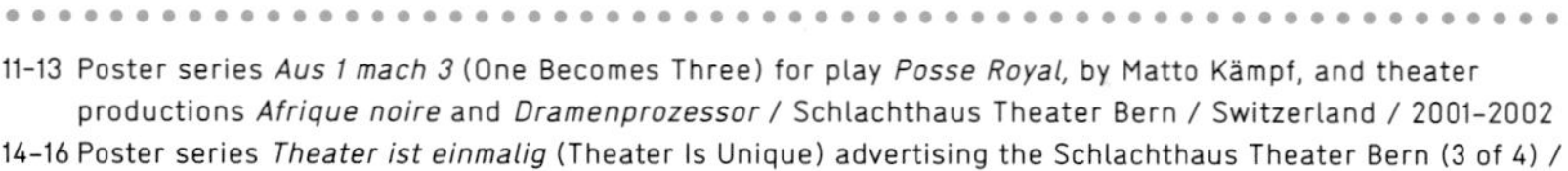

11–13 Poster series *Aus 1 mach 3* (One Becomes Three) for play *Posse Royal*, by Matto Kämpf, and theater productions *Afrique noire* and *Dramenprozessor* / Schlachthaus Theater Bern / Switzerland / 2001–2002
14–16 Poster series *Theater ist einmalig* (Theater Is Unique) advertising the Schlachthaus Theater Bern (3 of 4) / 1998–1999
17 Poster celebrating the fifth anniversary of the Schlachthaus Theater Bern / 2003

14

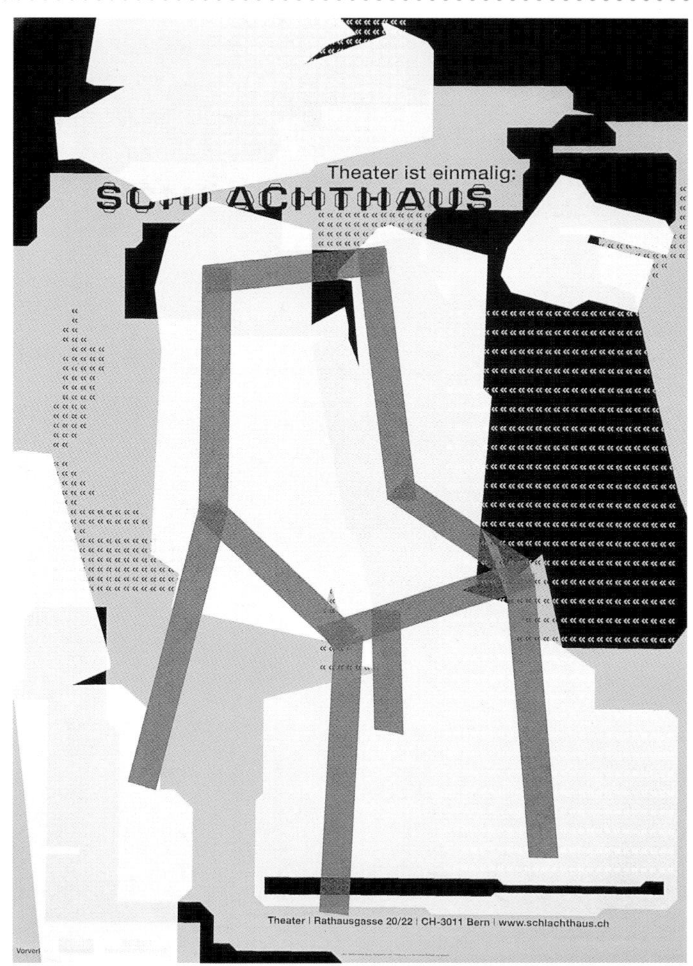
Theater ist einmalig:
SCHLACHTHAUS
Theater | Rathausgasse 20/22 | CH-3011 Bern | www.schlachthaus.ch

15

Theater ist einmalig:
SCHLACHTHAUS
Theater | Rathausgasse 20/22 | CH-3011 Bern | www.schlachthaus.ch
Vorverkauf:
BERNERWOCHE

16

Theater ist einmalig:
SCHLACHTHAUS
Theater | Rathausgasse 20/22 | CH-3011 Bern | www.schlachthaus.ch
Vorverkauf:
BERNERWOCHE

17

das Schlachthaus wird fünf!
Theater
SCHLACHTHAUS
Reservationen: 031 312 60 60 oder www.schlachthaus.ch - Vorverkauf: Münstergass-Buchhandlung

When Richard van der Laak entered our studio as an apprentice, he made a point of not being intimidated—he more or less took over the entire studio, not forgetting to bring his dog along. I soon noticed his remarkable ability to see things in perspective, a trait that also characterizes the work he and his partners at De Designpolitie produce. I think the name is an allusion to the battle over illegal software and fonts on the Internet—a bit ironic with a laddish bravado that has become second nature to them. They are rather original with a high visual intelligence, supported by a thorough knowledge of visual culture. They are typical representatives of a young rank of image mavericks, a generation that, perhaps unwittingly, has been trained by Dick Bruna. Bruna's priceless gift to visual culture has been to demonstrate to very young kids that images are "readable." This visual language, which the partners at De Designpolitie must have been familiar with at a tender age, made quite an impression. Like Bruna, De Designpolitie knows how to make an intelligent visual statement with the sparsest of means. They are also a bit Swiss, in their tight typography and the rigorous organization of their images. In the circles for the 1997 annual report for the Raad van Cultuur (Dutch State Council for Culture), for instance, they evoke info-architecture in their interpretation of the council's work and context. Precise and cheerful, they are still not easy to intimidate.•• Anthon Beeke••

1-4 Invitations/murals for various events and exhibitions at W139 art gallery in Amsterdam / W139 / Netherlands / 2002 / The invitations were first manually painted on blank walls in Amsterdam, then photographed and printed.
5-6 Posters for Springdance art and dance festival / Springdance Festival 1998 / Netherlands / 1998
7-8 Poster and cover for annual report of the Dutch State Council for Culture / Raad van Cultuur / Netherlands / 1998 / The poster folds around the book to serve as a dustjacket.

De Designpolitie

Amsterdam

SPRINGDANCE
13-25 APRIL 1999 UTRECHT

SPRINGDANCE
13-25 APRIL 1999 UTRECHT

5 6

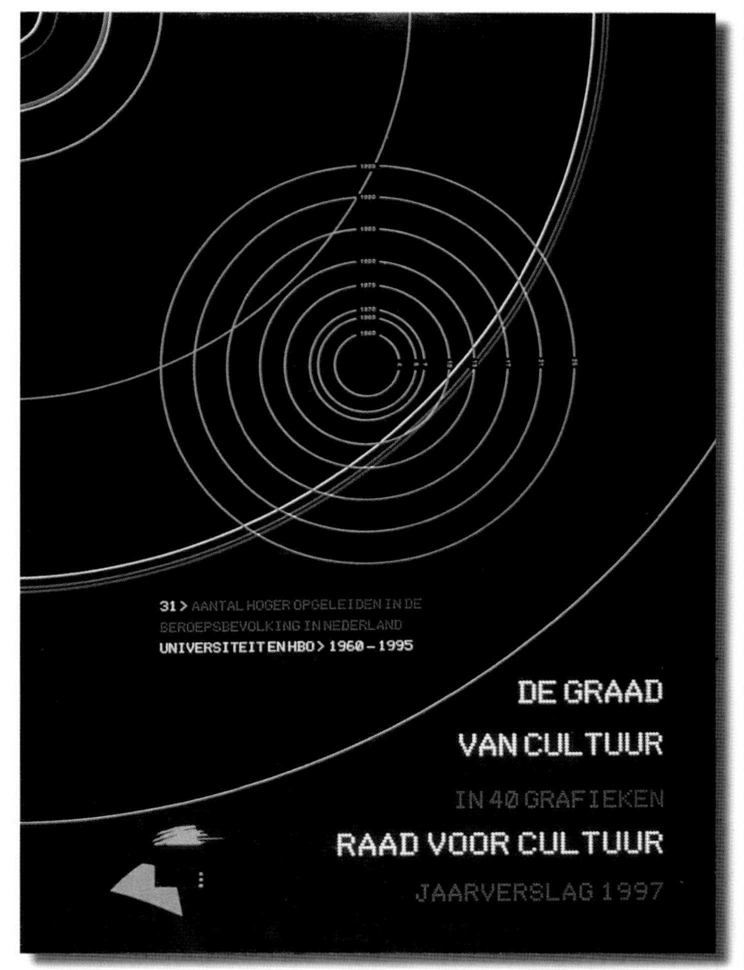
31 > AANTAL HOGER OPGELEIDEN IN DE
BEROEPSBEVOLKING IN NEDERLAND
UNIVERSITEITEN HBO > 1960 – 1995
DE GRAAD
VAN CULTUUR
IN 40 GRAFIEKEN
RAAD VOOR CULTUUR
JAARVERSLAG 1997

7 8

9

10 11 12 13

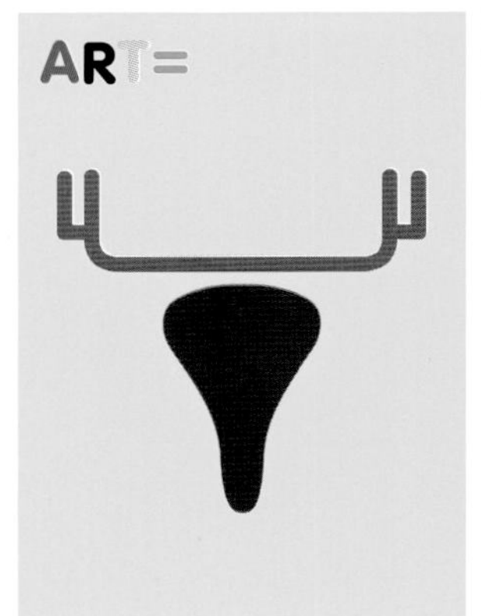

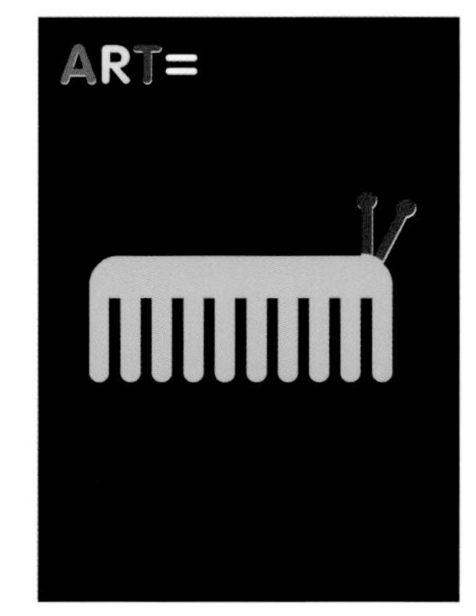

De Designpolitie

9 Poster for fashion show at Utrecht School of the Arts (HKU) / HKU / Netherlands / 1994

10–13 Poster campaign promoting the Amsterdam zoo Artis / FHV/BBDO / Netherlands / 1999 / The zoo's motto is *Natura Artis Magistra* (nature is the teacher of art).

14 Self-commissioned antiwar poster / Netherlands / 2003

15–16 Page and cover, informational brochure for Utrecht School of the Arts / HKU / Netherlands / 2003

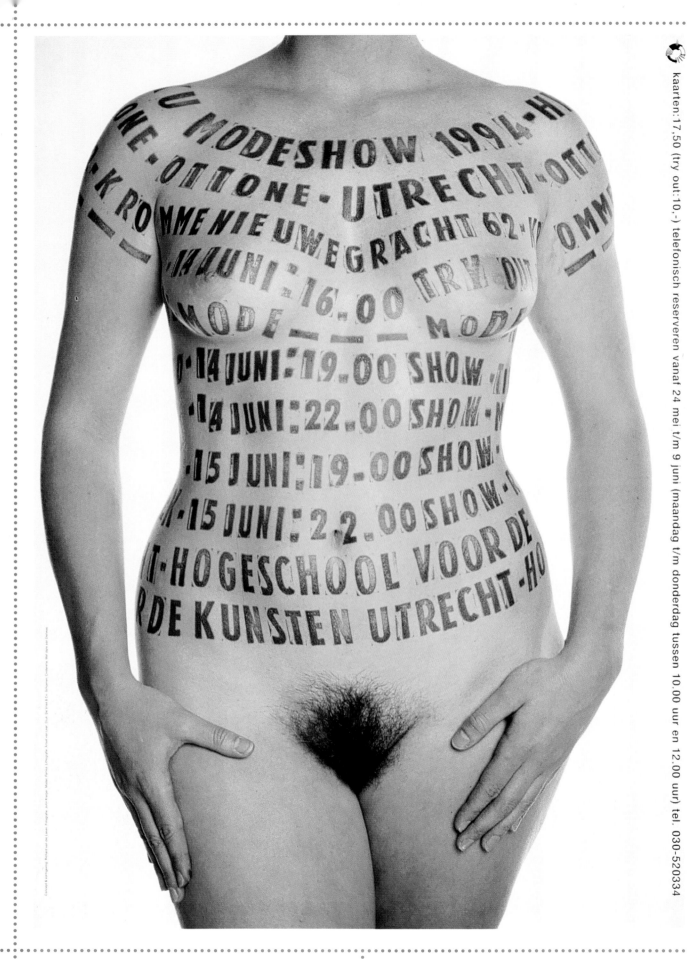

14

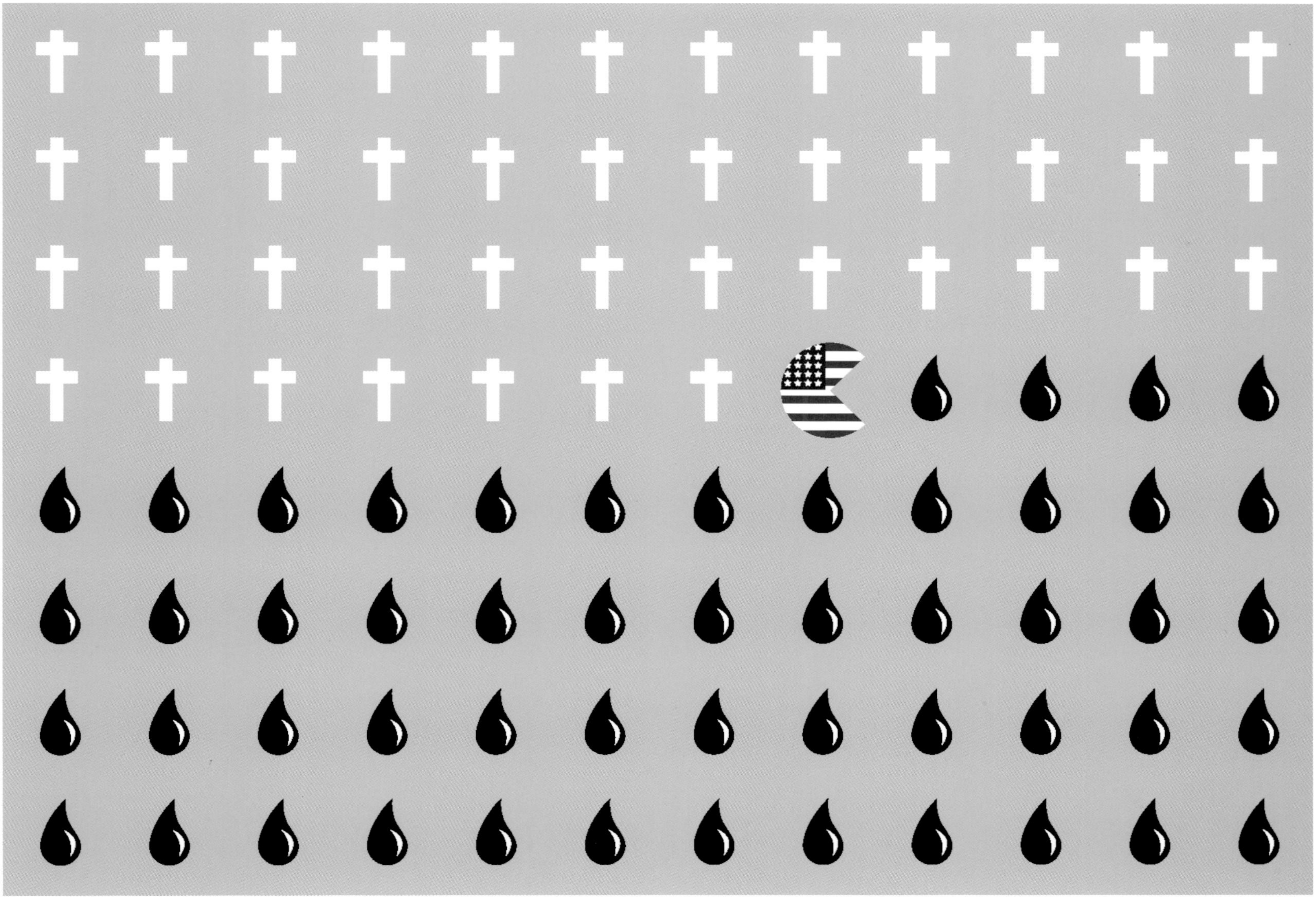

15

16

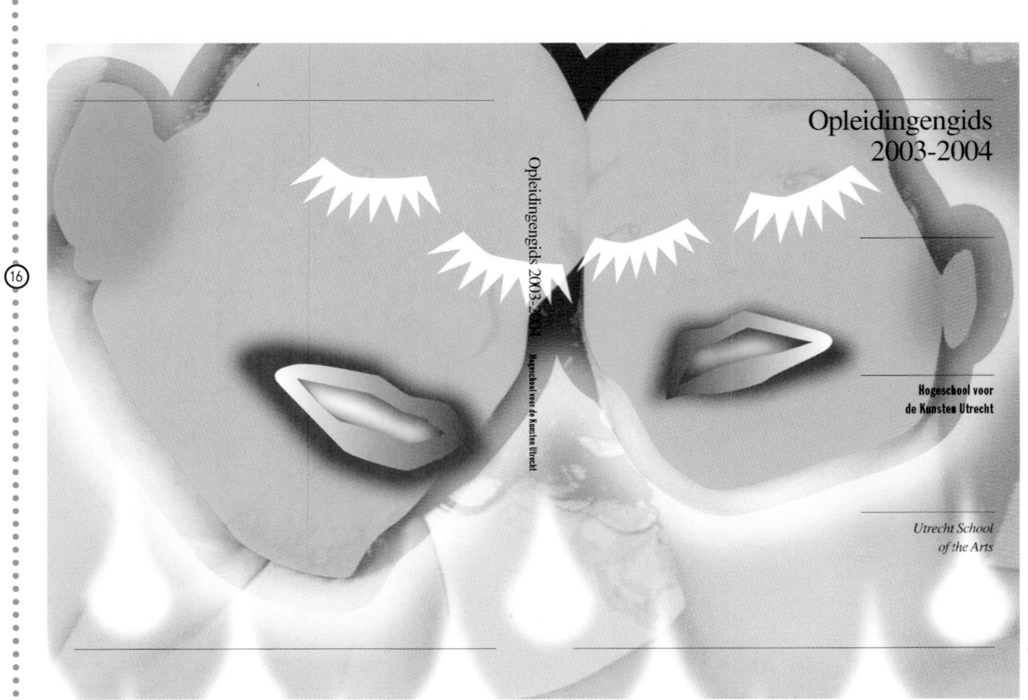
Opleidingengids
2003-2004
Opleidingengids 2003-2004
Hogeschool voor de Kunsten Utrecht
Hogeschool voor
de Kunsten Utrecht
Utrecht School
of the Arts

Delaware means Masato Samata, Aya Honda, Morihiro Tajiri, and Yoshiki Watanabe. Delaware comes from Japan, from rock 'n' roll, personal computers, mobile phones, and bitmaps. Delaware takes inspiration from Western-world artists like James Brown, the Beatles, Kraftwerk, Stanley Kubrick, and Roy Lichtenstein but most of all from the Japanese artist Hajime Tachibana, former member of the Plastics. • •Very few artists have fused graphic design, music, performance, and life as originally and organically as these four Japanese, who have worked mainly on CDs, magazines, T-shirts, commercials, websites, and live performances since 1993. Truly extraordinary is the total elimination of boundaries between the disciplines they endeavor in. Sound, surface, and action create one strong and vital communication experience whose only stated goals are fun, inner peace, and the search for the "future feeling." No self-indulgence in torturing social or philosophical theories here, just self-conscious day-to-day "rockin' the house" blended with introspective dialogue. This might risk superficiality, but most of the work goes deep. Pieces like Dokuro, Umbrella, Nice to Meet You, We Are Alone, Check Yourself, You Will be Soon Born—You Will be Soon Dead, and Walking in the Forest convey both intimate and social expressions of contemporary uncertainty, solitude, and concern. Other images might make us wonder what they are all about, but when the visual treat is so astounding, should we care? • •However indivisible this mix is, Delaware's graphic-design output is outstanding. Masato Samata, the only member who doesn't play an instrument, is the graphics wizard behind the curtain conceiving their trendsetting style. He is a source of true renewal in the world where change often comes only from software updates. Delaware's iconic dimensions are developed through an instinctive and often accidental mix of cultures, music, computers, internet, and cellphones. Delaware is content and form for the future of today. • •Omar Vulpinari • •

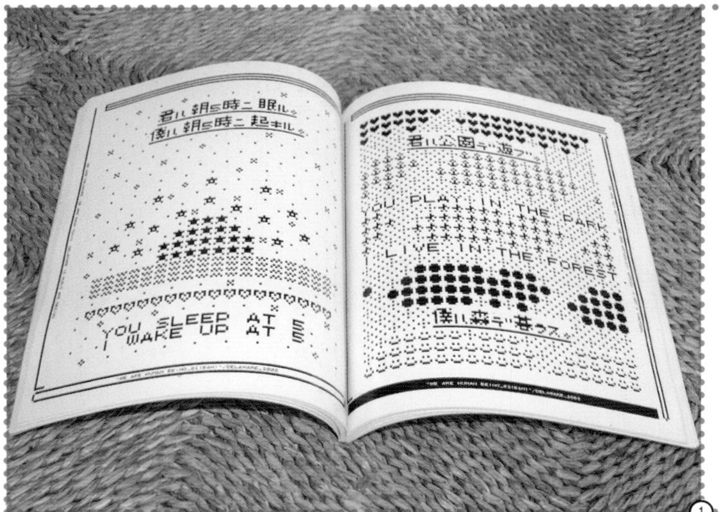

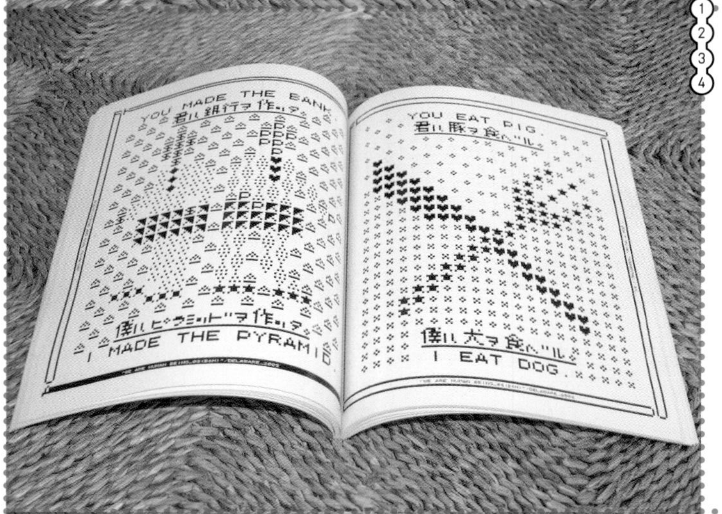

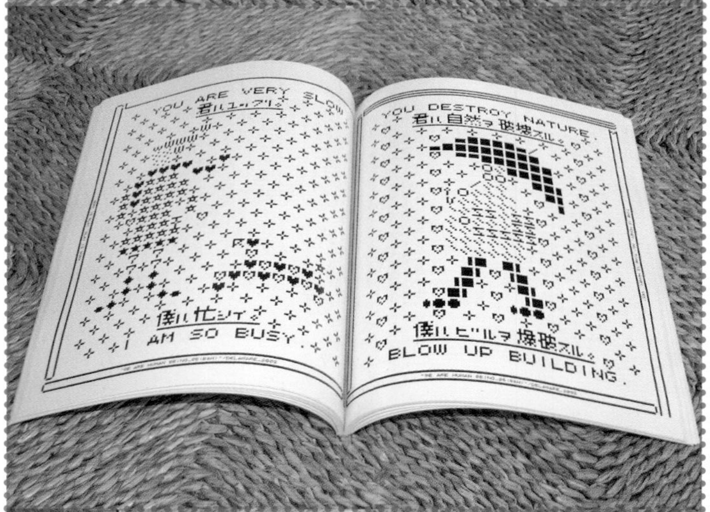

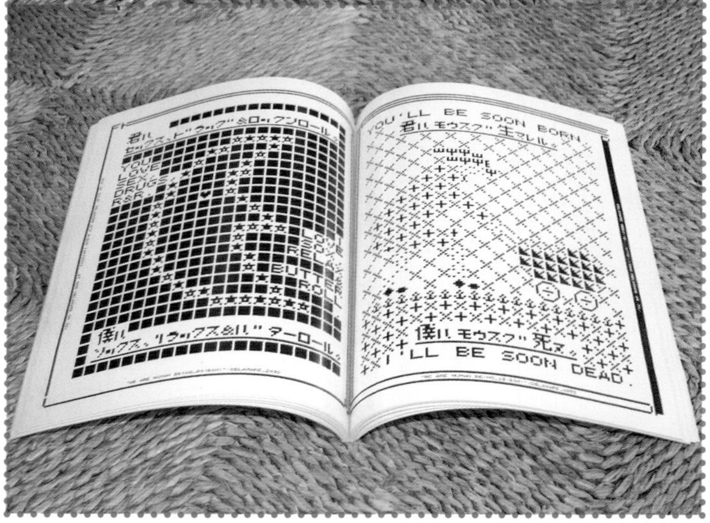

1–4 Spreads from *Textfield Magazine* 1.01 / Textfield Magazine / USA / 2003
5 Skull poster created for *I love to meet you–New graphic design* exhibition held at Palazzo Fortuny in Venice / Italy / 2002
6 Delaware design for the Pitti Uomo men's-fashion trade fair in Florence / Italy / 2003

Delaware

Tokyo

5

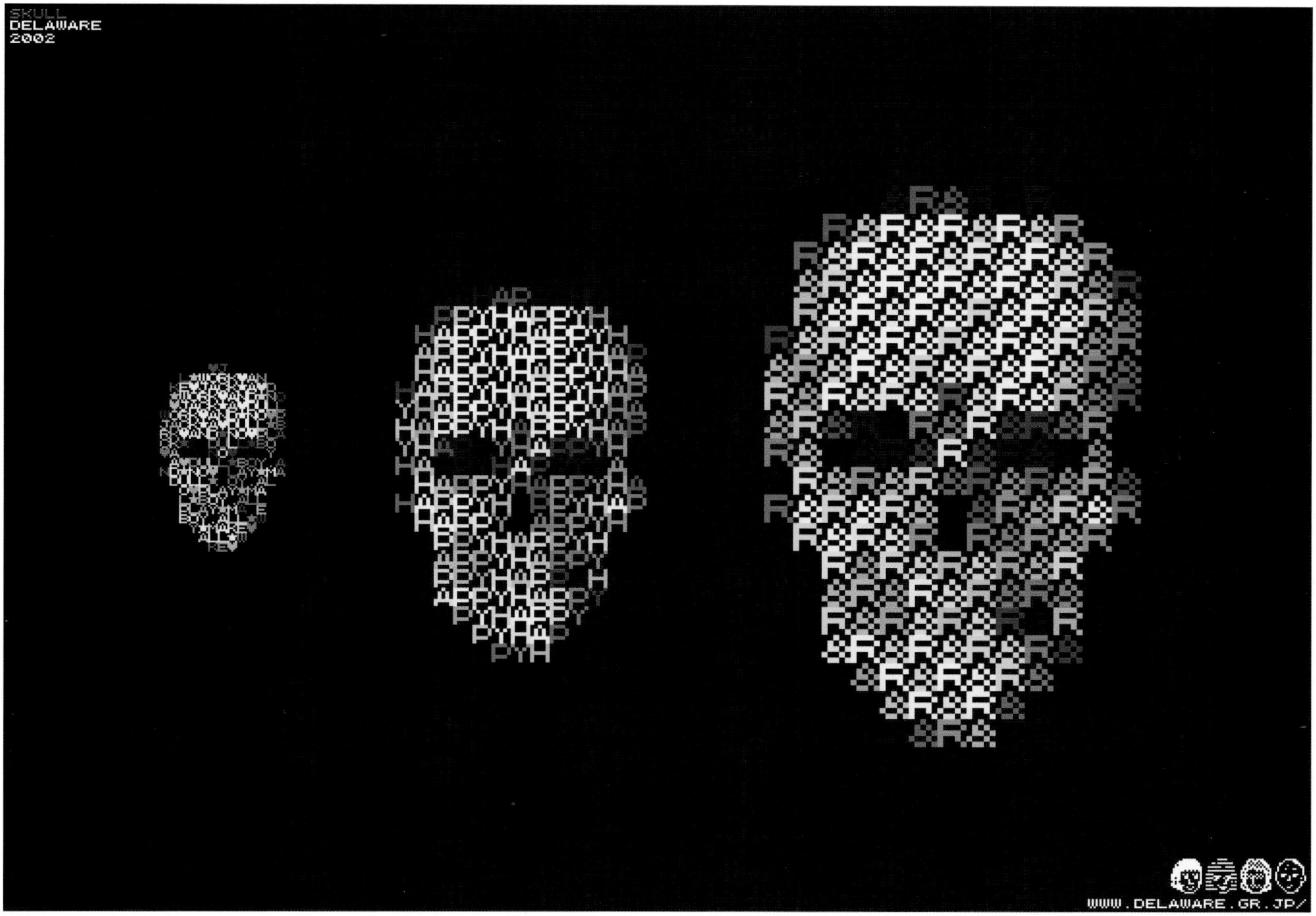

SKULL
DELAWARE
2002

WWW.DELAWARE.GR.JP/

6

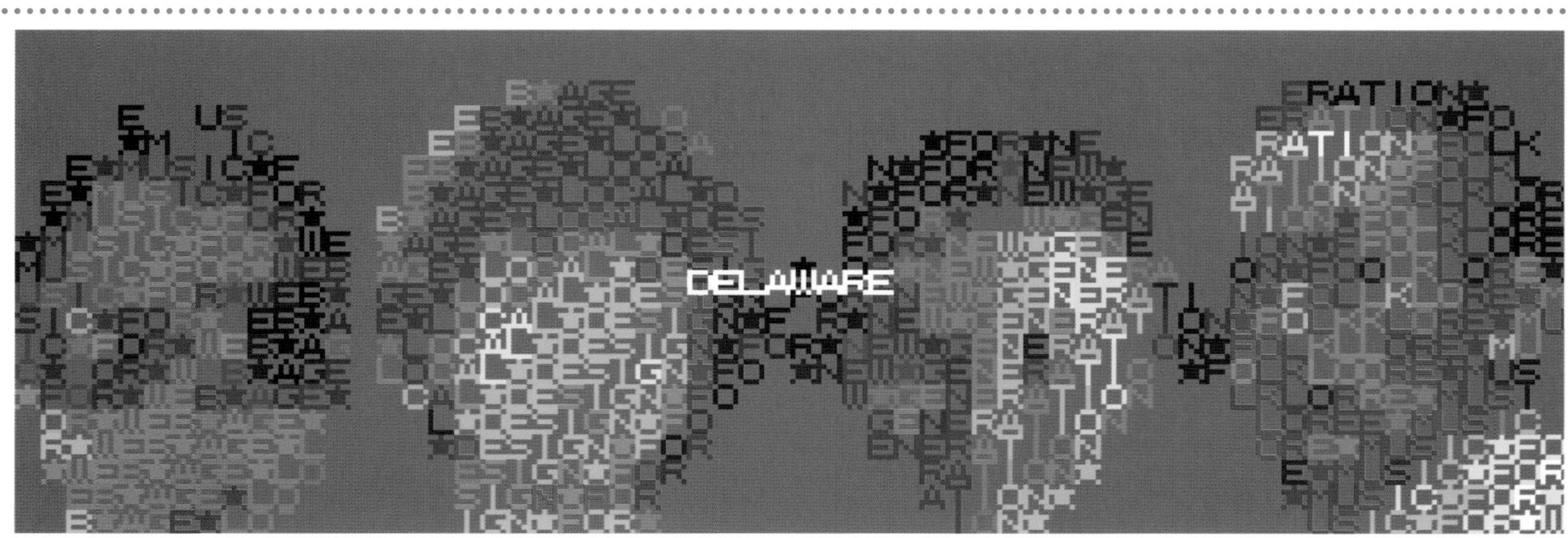

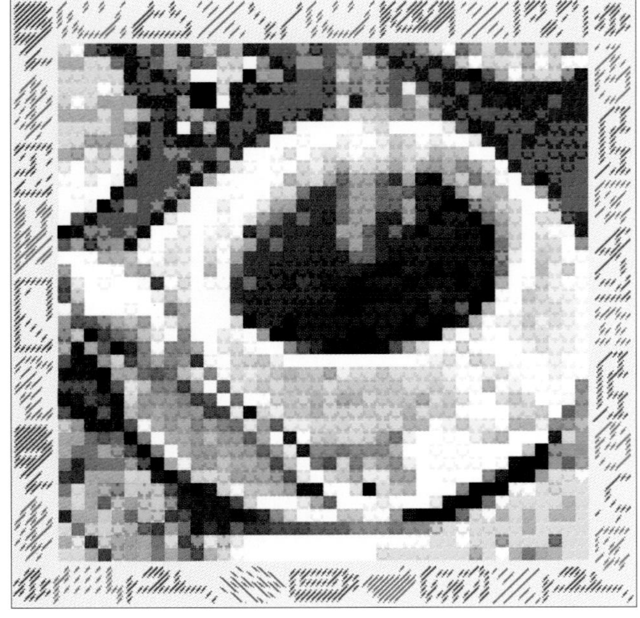

7 8

9 10

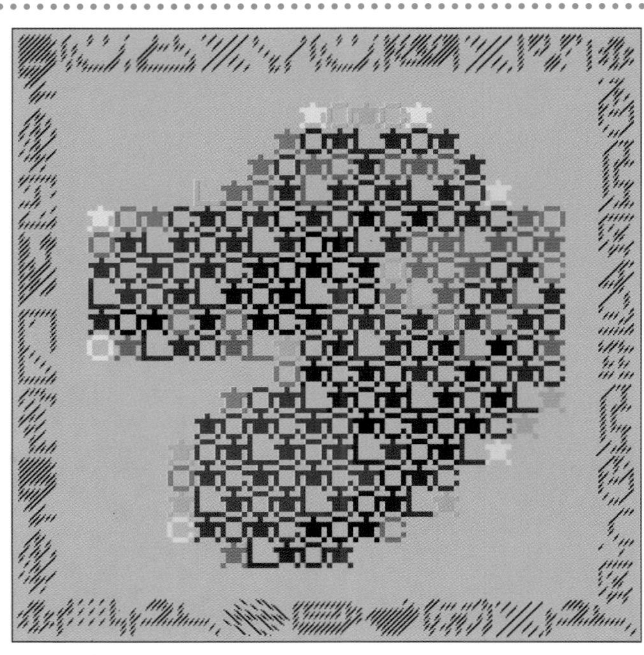

7 Have a Break design (unreleased) / Japan / 2003
8 We are Alone cross-stitched design for *Buzz Club: News from Japan* exhibition held at P.S. 1 Contemporary Art Center, New York / USA / 2001
9 Nice to Meet You poster for *JaPan Graphics* exhibition held at RAS gallery and FAD Capella dels Angels, Barcelona / Spain / 2002
10 You'll be Soon Born–You'll be Soon Dead design for "My Favorite Conference" organized by *IdN Magazine* in Hong Kong / IdN Magazine / Hong Kong / 2002
11 Work Shoes design (unreleased) / Japan / 2003
12–14 Dokuro, Umbrella, and Cool Cat projection and mural designs for Pitti Uomo men's-fashion trade fair in Florence / Italy / 2003
15–17 Views of Stairway to Heaven mural design at Pitti Uomo men's-fashion trade fair in Florence / Italy / 2003

11

12

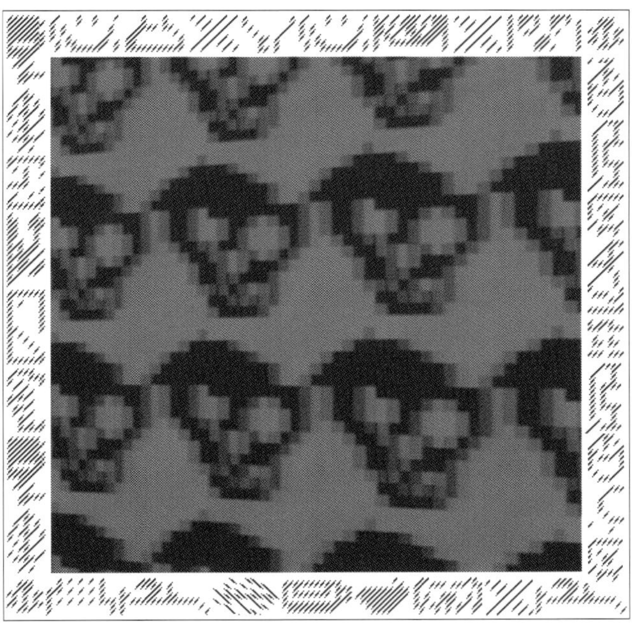

13

14

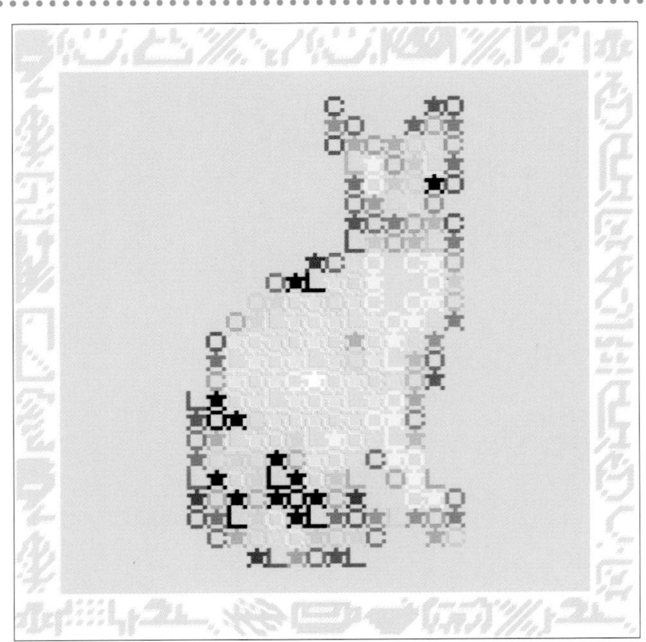

15
16
17

Chris Dixon has been working in editorial design since the mid-1990s and has created quite a name for himself. He is perhaps best known for his work on *Adbusters* magazine, which he redesigned in 1996 (and where he subsequently stayed for a further four years as art director). *Adbusters*' new look had a considerable impact on the world of editorial design and is regarded as one of the most ground-breaking publications in recent years. • • *Adbusters* requires a visual language that immediately grabs the attention of its target audience. It deals with issues of consumerism, the environment, and the mass media, with a subversive edge. As an international publication, it also demands universal appeal. Dixon's striking solution was incredibly successful: Not only did it look great—with consistently inventive covers and spreads, great image-sourcing and picture editing—it also communicated its message with impact and clarity. • • *Adbusters* provided Dixon with relative freedom and a chance to flex his muscles as an editorial designer with a seemingly endless number of ideas that always seemed appropriate to the content. He made the magazine more accessible, in a manner that retained its integrity. Circulation rose from 25,000 to 95,000 during his tenure as art director, and in terms of design, the results speak for themselves. • • Dixon's success at *Adbusters* led to other equally challenging projects, such as *rd*, a concept magazine developed for Microsoft's research and development division. Microsoft has not yet decided to go with it, which is a shame, as Dixon's initial concepts suggest a dynamism rarely found in corporate magazines. His work for *The New York Times Magazine* revealed his willingness to explore more classical forms. The spreads and covers he created for the magazine recall editorial design of the 1940s and '50s, albeit with a redefined sense of elegance and sophistication that is entirely relevant and contemporary. • • He recently designed and art directed a special anniversary magazine for the American edition of the *Financial Times*, created to suggest the *FT*'s growing popularity in the U.S. The design had to be simple and sophisticated in order to reflect the personality of the paper and the *FT* brand. Dixon succeeded: The magazine feels professional, confident, and authoritative. His versatility and prowess as a designer becomes more apparent with each project. • • Fernando Gutiérrez • •

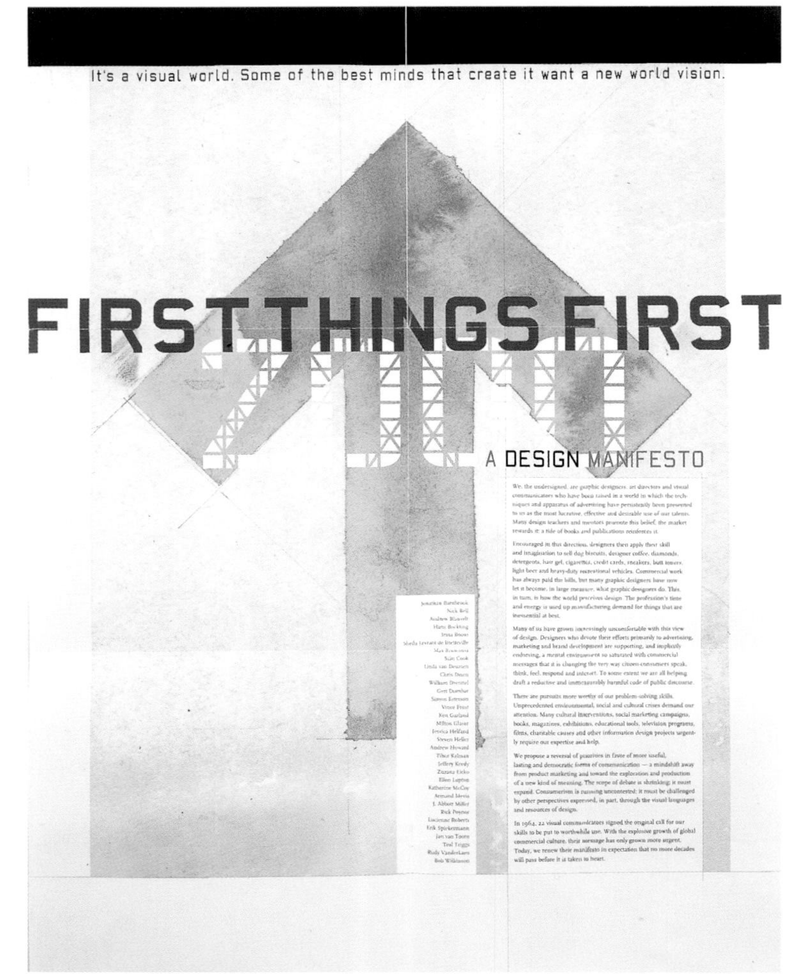

1
2

FIRST THINGS FIRST 1964-2000

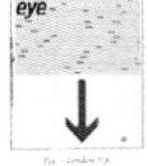

DESIGN ANARCHY

1–2 Front and back of poster launching the First Things First 2000 manifesto / The Media Foundation / Canada / 2000
3–4 Prototype covers, *rd* magazine / RD, Microsoft / USA / 2002
5–6 Covers, *Whiplash and Other Useful Illnesses*, by Andrew Malleson, and *Detemining Boundaries*, by Suzanne Lalonde / McGill-Queens Press / Canada / 2002

Chris Dixon

New York

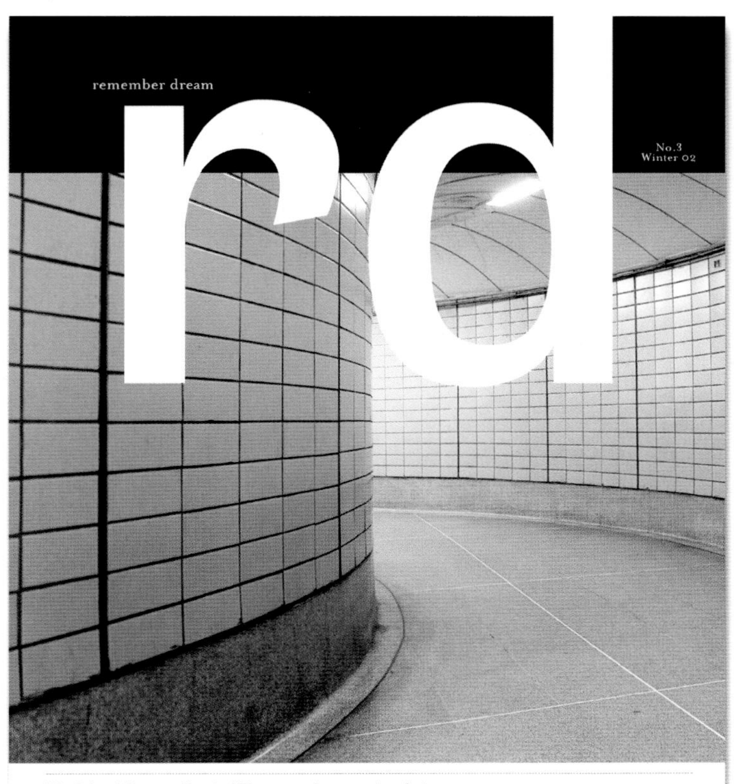
remember dream
rd
No.3
Winter 02
The Other Side
By John Williamson
Following the option gets you when you've not already been. A story about good lawyers.
Chemical Three
By Brian Rau
The best way to approach the problem is to see what the formula is.
Interpect Ananlysis
By Cathy Dempster
The guitar makes sense used where it was developed. What about the music that is done without sound?

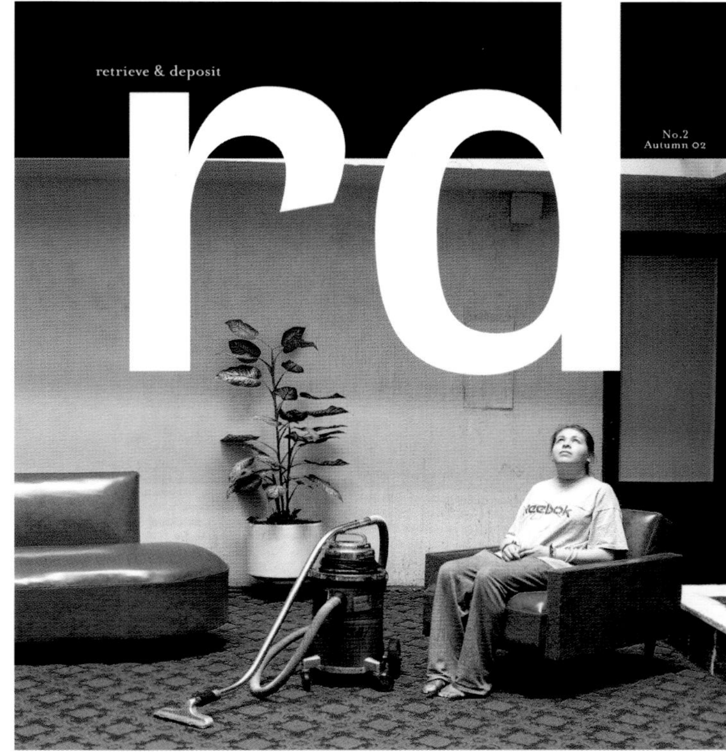
retrieve & deposit
rd
No.2
Autumn 02
Running Off Water
By John Williamson
Following the option gets you when you've not already been. A story about good lawyers who know science now.
Music Analogy
By Brian Rau
The best way to approach the problem is to see what the formula is.
Dominant Gene
By Cathy Dempster
The guitar makes sense used where it was developed. What about the music that is done?

3 4

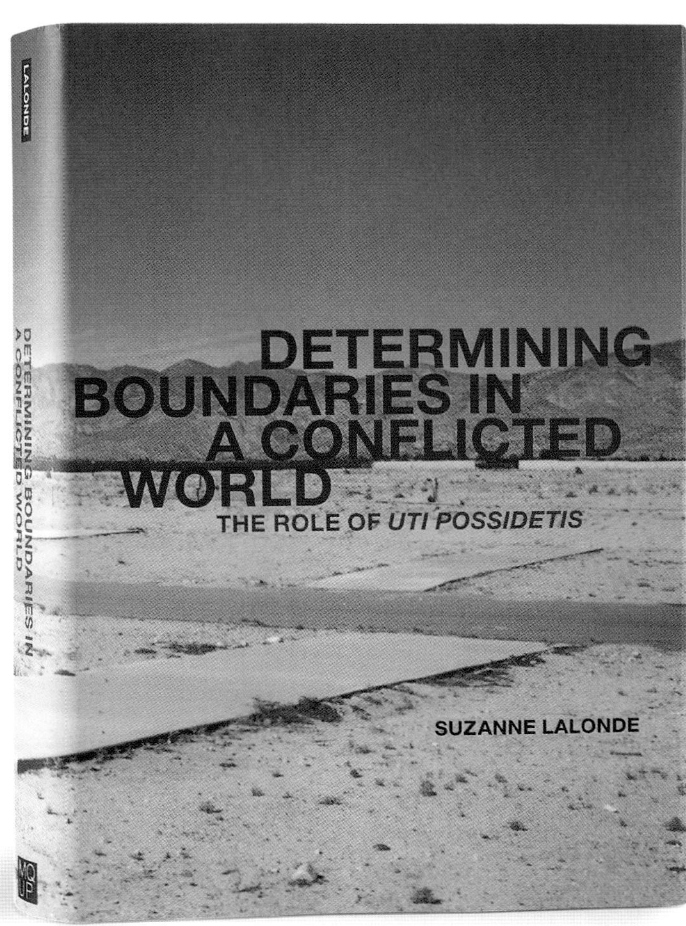
LALONDE
DETERMINING BOUNDARIES IN A CONFLICTED WORLD
THE ROLE OF UTI POSSIDETIS
SUZANNE LALONDE
MQUP

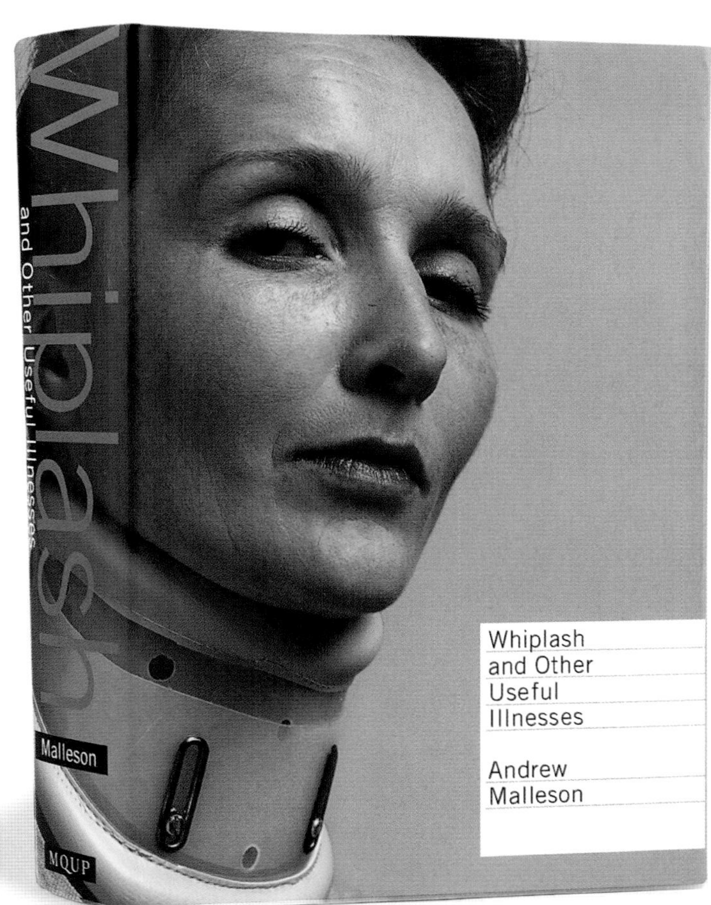
Whiplash
and Other Useful Illnesses
Malleson
MQUP
Whiplash and Other Useful Illnesses
Andrew Malleson

5 6

⑦

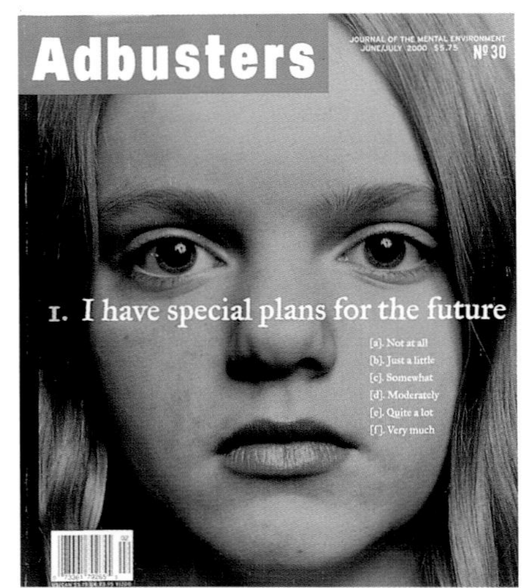

⑧

⑨

⑩

7–8 Covers, *Adbusters* magazine nos. 28 and 30 / The Media Foundation / Canada / 2000
9–11 Spreads, *Adbusters* magazine nos. 28, 27, and 29 / The Media Foundation / Canada / 1999–2000
12–13 Spreads, *The New York Times Magazine*, 20 August 2000 and 16 June 2002 / The New York Times / USA / 2000 and 2002
14 Cover, *Women at the Intersection*, edited by Rita Raj / Center for Women's Global Leadership-Rutgers University / USA / 2002
15–17 Cover and spreads, *Financial Times* special anniversary magazine, November 2002 / Financial Times, U.S. Edition / USA / 2002

⑪

Chris Dixon

The View From the Bridge
In Kosovo, in the city of Mitrovica, the Ibar River maintains a fragile peace — keeping Serbs and Albanians from each other's throats.
Photographs by Paolo Pellegrin Text by Guy Lawson

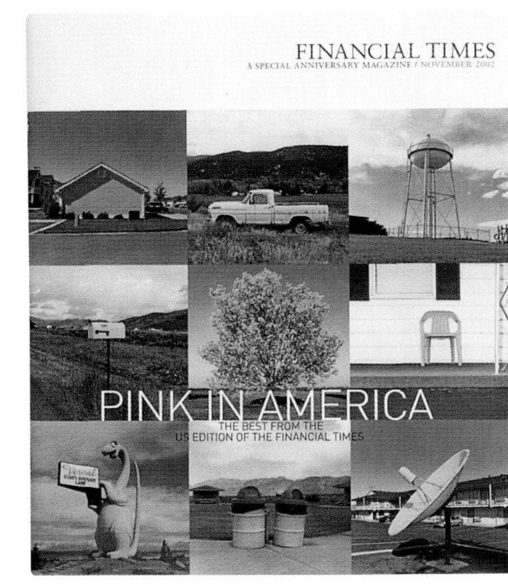

FINANCIAL TIMES
A SPECIAL ANNIVERSARY MAGAZINE / NOVEMBER 2002
PINK IN AMERICA
THE BEST FROM THE US EDITION OF THE FINANCIAL TIMES

12
13

15
16
17

Insert a Single Spider Gene into a Female Goat. Milk Regularly.
Got Silk.
By Lawrence Osborne
Photographs by Mackenzie Stroh

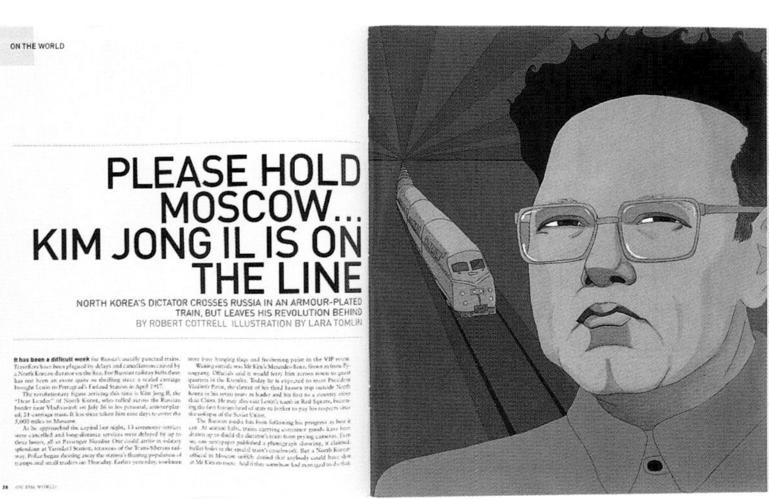

ON THE WORLD
PLEASE HOLD MOSCOW... KIM JONG IL IS ON THE LINE
NORTH KOREA'S DICTATOR CROSSES RUSSIA IN AN ARMOUR-PLATED TRAIN, BUT LEAVES HIS REVOLUTION BEHIND
BY ROBERT COTTRELL ILLUSTRATION BY LARA TOMLIN

14

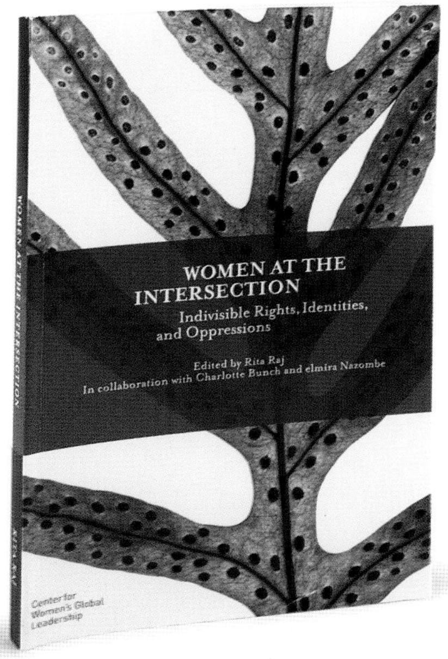

WOMEN AT THE INTERSECTION
Indivisible Rights, Identities, and Oppressions
Edited by Rita Raj
In collaboration with Charlotte Bunch and elmira Nazombe
Center for Women's Global Leadership

For Daniel Eatock, personal work is as important as commercial work. Each one informs the other, and with architect Sam Solhaug, Eatock has set up Foundation 33, a studio that caters specifically to that process. • • If you venture into the bathroom at Foundation 33, you'll find the Big Brother Mandate, created as a guide to their working process. It says a lot about their approach to design: "DON'T DESIGN, start: crude and radical, finish: considered and radical." • • There is certainly a radical quality to Eatock's work, a subversive edge communicated with the utilitarian, everyday veneer of his visual vocabulary that provides an antidote to ostentation. On the surface, it is a disciplined language, with a deadpan delivery that, when you consider the content, is very tongue-in-cheek. It constantly challenges our expectations. • • Foundation 33 are doing exactly that with the billboards they are creating for British television's Channel Four, utilizing a powerful communications medium to maximum effect. For the TV drama series *Shackleton*, the warning "Danger: Ice" appears in heavy white text on a red ground: very clear, very direct. A site-specific version of the billboard (on Cromwell Road in west London) featured actual blocks of ice in front of the poster, a potent stop-and-stare solution. Challenging our expectations. • • The World's Largest Signed and Numbered Limited Edition Artwork—created in 2002 for Channel Four's *The Art Show*—had an edition of a million and ran with the tagline: "This artwork is exclusive for a milion people. *The Art Show* is inclusive for everybody." Inclusive for everybody. Like E-mail, a postcard that allows people to send e-mails without a computer, or Peace Chart, a pie chart of world religions designed to resemble the CND logo. Both subversive in their own way, both simple and direct. Eatock's calling card is a sticker of used chewing gum, which he leaves under tables wherever he goes. • • Eatock and Solhaug first collaborated on a series of plywood furniture, designed and manufactured so that every piece of wood was an integral component of the finished piece. Just like Foundation 33's graphic oeuvre: no waste, no trimmings. Considered and radical. • • Fernando Gutiérrez • •

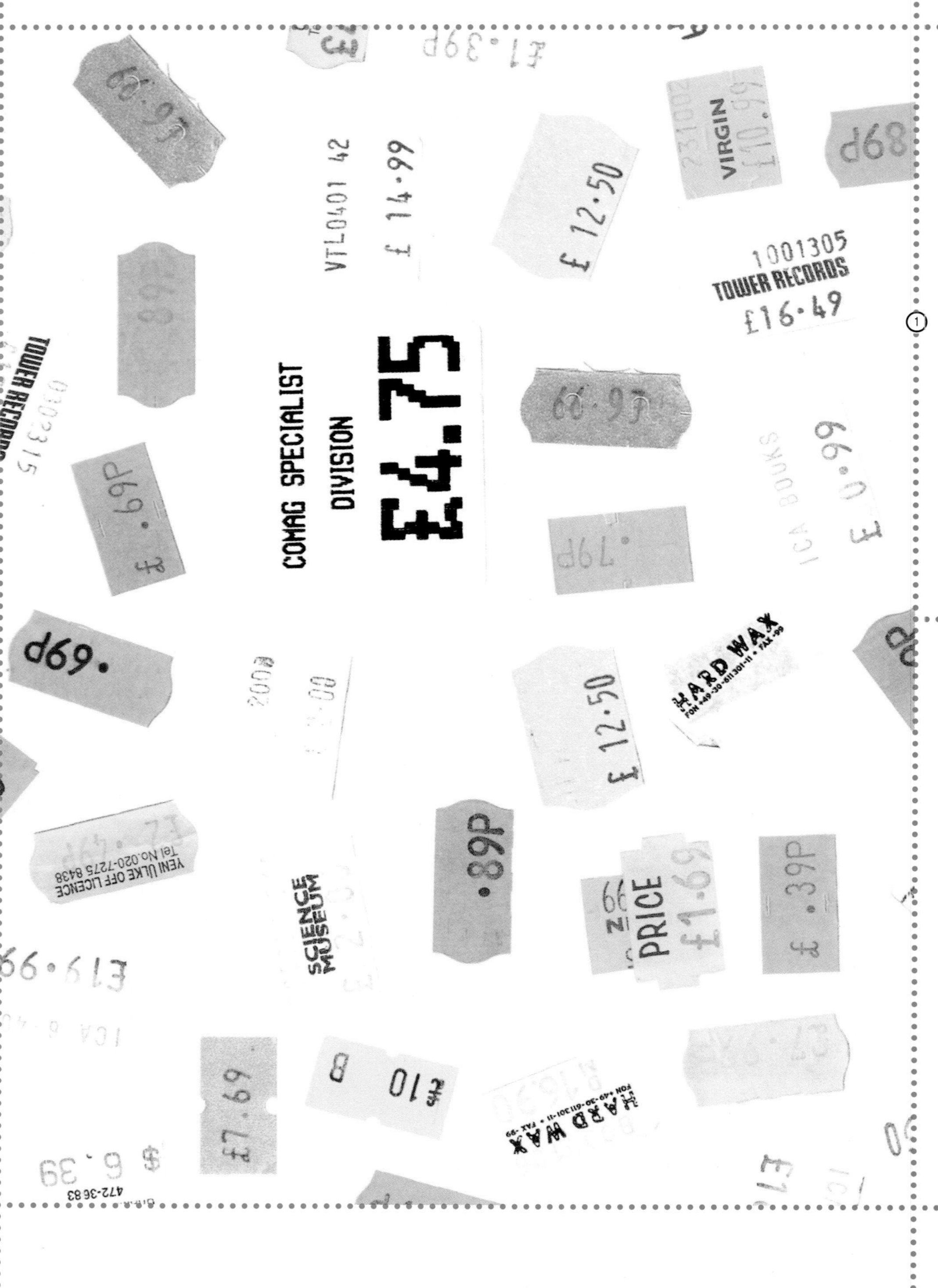

1

2

1 Pricing Labels wrapping paper / Foundation 33 / United Kingdom / 2003
2 Used chewing-gum sticker / Foundation 33 / United Kingdom / 2003
3 Utilitarian Greeting Cards / Foundation 33 / Untited Kingdom / 2003 / The sender must appropriate each card for its recipient.
4–5 Sun Light and Aerial View postcards (photography by Daniel Eatock) / Foundation 33 / United Kingdom / 2003
6–7 The World's Largest Signed and Numbered Limited Edition Artwork hosted by Whitechapel Art Gallery, London / Channel Four Television / United Kingdom / 2002 / Project announcing Channel Four's program *The Art Show* on contemporary art, design, and culture, in which one million "artworks" were distributed for free. The project was carefully recorded and is in the process of being submitted to the Guinness World Records.

Daniel Eatock/Foundation 33

London

3

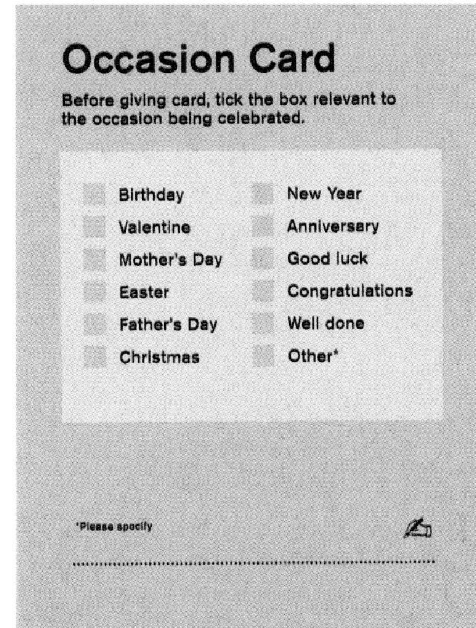
Occasion Card
Before giving card, tick the box relevant to the occasion being celebrated.
Birthday
Valentine
Mother's Day
Easter
Father's Day
Christmas
New Year
Anniversary
Good luck
Congratulations
Well done
Other*
*Please specify

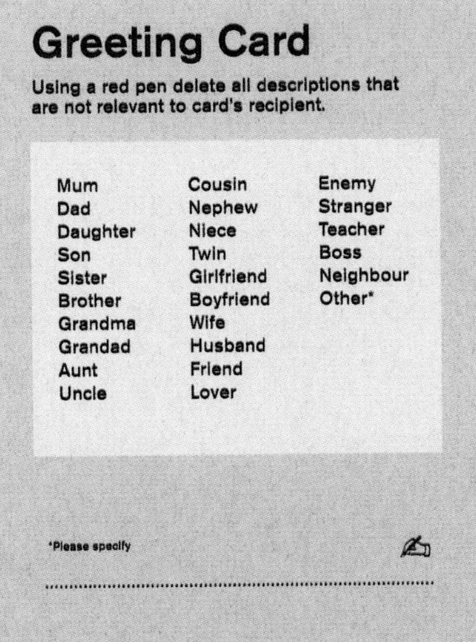
Greeting Card
Using a red pen delete all descriptions that are not relevant to card's recipient.
Mum
Dad
Daughter
Son
Sister
Brother
Grandma
Grandad
Aunt
Uncle
Cousin
Nephew
Niece
Twin
Girlfriend
Boyfriend
Wife
Husband
Friend
Lover
Enemy
Stranger
Teacher
Boss
Neighbour
Other*
*Please specify

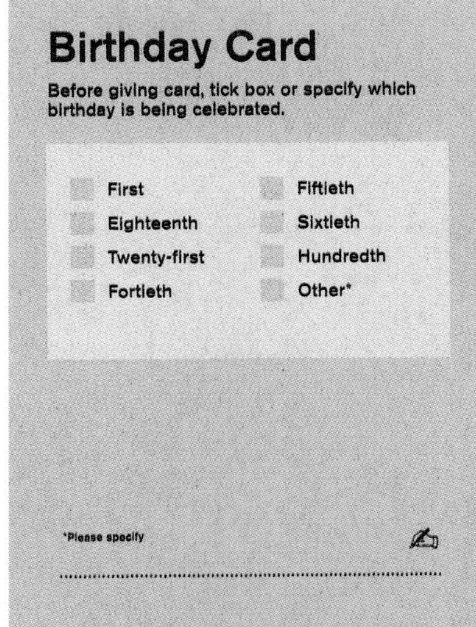
Birthday Card
Before giving card, tick box or specify which birthday is being celebrated.
First
Eighteenth
Twenty-first
Fortieth
Fiftieth
Sixtieth
Hundredth
Other*
*Please specify

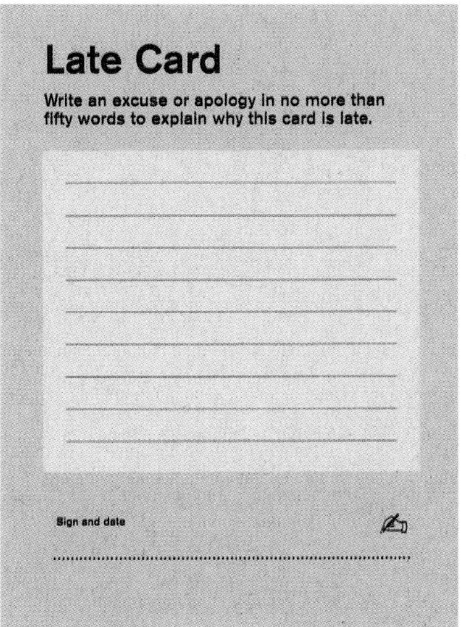
Late Card
Write an excuse or apology in no more than fifty words to explain why this card is late.
Sign and date

4

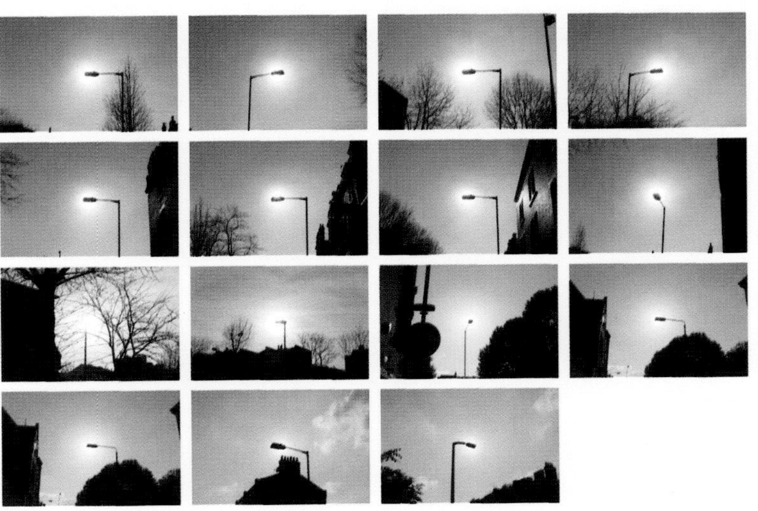

5

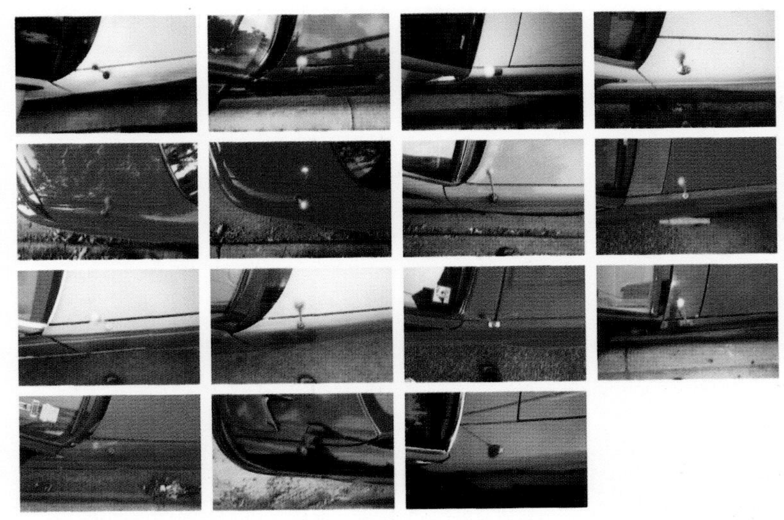

6 7

The world's largest
signed and numbered
limited edition artwork

The world's largest
signed and numbered
limited edition artwork
Authorised signatory
Daniel Eatock, Sam Solhaug, Hanna Werning, Lyn Winter, Flávia Müller Medeiros, Mark Hopkins, Soo Hong, Milos Covic, Naoko Sato, Kirsty Carter
Your number is
94000
/ One million

8 Billboard announcing Channel Four coverage of the World Rally Championship 2002 / Channel Four Television / United Kingdom / 2001
9 Billboard announcing live broadcast of Turner Prize award ceremony from Tate Britain / Channel Four Television / United Kingdom / 2001
10 Billboard for reality TV show *Big Brother* / Channel Four Television / United Kingdom / 2001–2002
11 Update of previous year's billboard campaign for *Big Brother* / Channel Four Television / United Kingdom / 2002
12 Billboard announcing MOBO (Music of Black Origin) awards / Channel Four Television / United Kingdom / 2001
13 Untitled Beatles poster / Foundation 33 / United Kingdom / 2000 / Poster is made up of all the lyrics of every Beatles song.

Daniel Eatock/Foundation 33

13

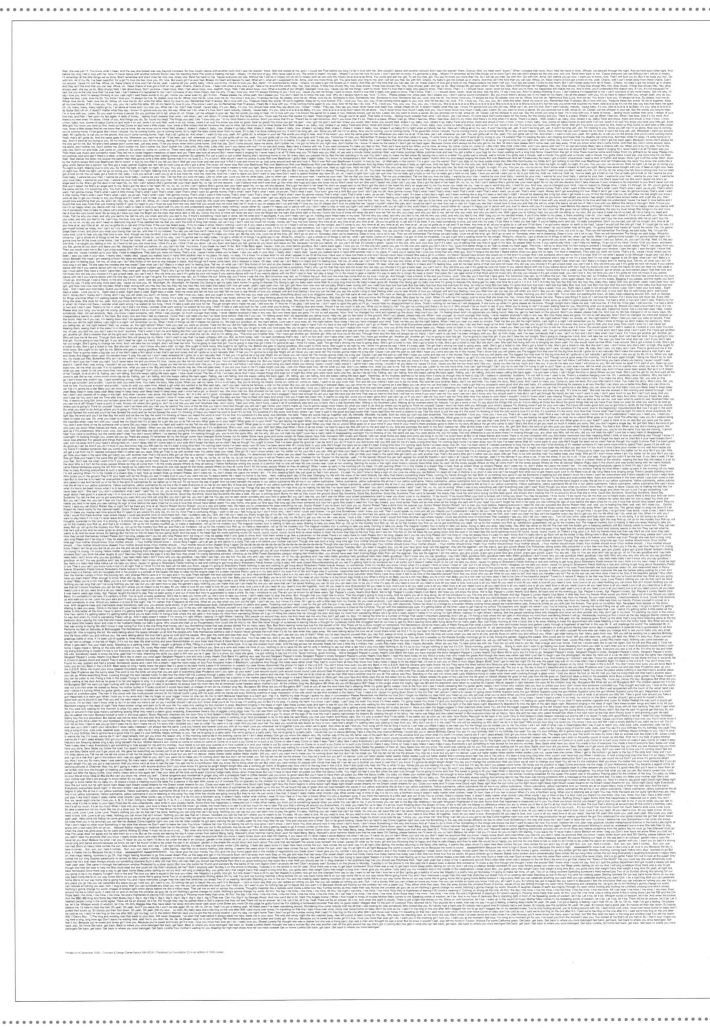
Printed on 8 December 2000 / Concept & Design Daniel Eatock MA (RCA) / Published by Foundation 33 in an edition of 1000 copies

Eboy is a design squad of four crew-cut look-alike fun-lovers who from their bases in Berlin and New York are spreading digital art worldwide. • • E-dudes, e-chicks, e-robots, and e-guns. E-cars, e-games, e-superstars, and e-dreams: a true boy's world that every man would want to play in, as the Eboy partners state. Images of contemporary urban youth culture that recall both ancient Byzantine mosaics and vernacular patchwork. Constructed often, like in their imaginary "eCities" project, by all four minds and eight hands of the members. Icons born for a digital, internet-connected realm but intensely speculating about today's life patterns. • • Steffen Sauerteig, Svend Smital, Peter Stemmler, and Kai Vermehr draw inspiration from the society they live in, the schools where they studied, the streets they played on, and the beaches where they went on girl hunts. Very often the four artists are among the actors of their fantasy scenarios—an attentive viewer can spot the Eboys themselves protesting, shooting, driving, and fighting on the streets and rooftops of their life-bubbling landscapes. • • Consumerism, MTV, supermarkets, street fashion, entertainment, sex, and violence give life to Photoshop pixel nightmares and Bézier curve dreams. A micro-to-macro investigation into environments populated by Lego- and Playskool-inspired characters exaggerate juvenile itches and desires. Pixels become subversive, beautiful, powerful, and easy to handle, while vector lines assume a seductive, intimate, and nasty allure. Eboy searches for unfettered human essentials where technology is seen as evolution, not danger. Their cities, robots, and weapons are often dark and scary because pain and fear are also part of the human spectrum. • • Research with humor and irony is the main engine of the group. Most commissions come from clients who come across Eboy's experimental, fun-driven projects on their website. Here visitors can become the authors of unseen creatures. The firm's Peecol modular system enables anyone to build body-part typefaces and schizophrenic virtual characters—a bit of help to rediscover the little e-boy/e-girl inside all of us. • • Omar Vulpinari • •

1 Poster for exhibition celebrating the inauguration of luxury apartment building in Singapore / Brazen Communications / Singapore / 2002
2 Cover illustration for *IdN Magazine* (not realized) / IdN Magazine / Hong Kong / 2002
3 Picture for Eboy exhibition at J-10 clothing store / Hong Kong / 2002
4 Detail of illustration for *Arena* magazine (not realized) / Arena / United Kingdom / 2001
5 Self-commissioned In Memory camouflage graffiti / Germany / 2001
6 Illustration for energy company / Harpen AG / Germany / 2001

Eboy

Berlin/New York

1

2

3

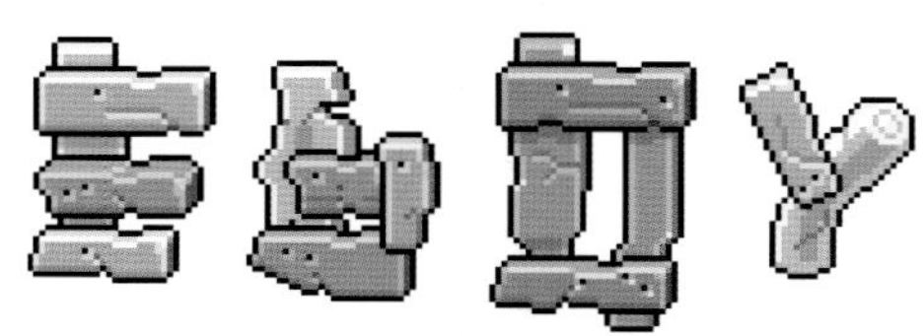

4

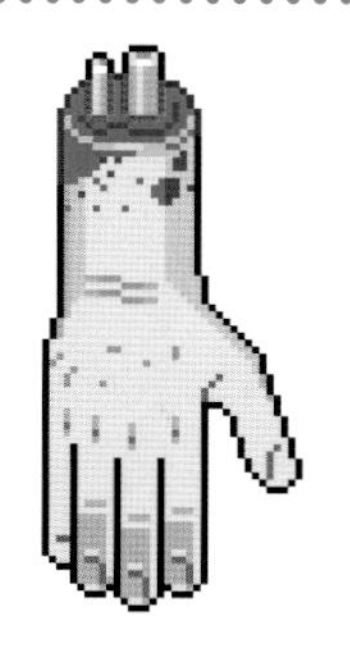

5

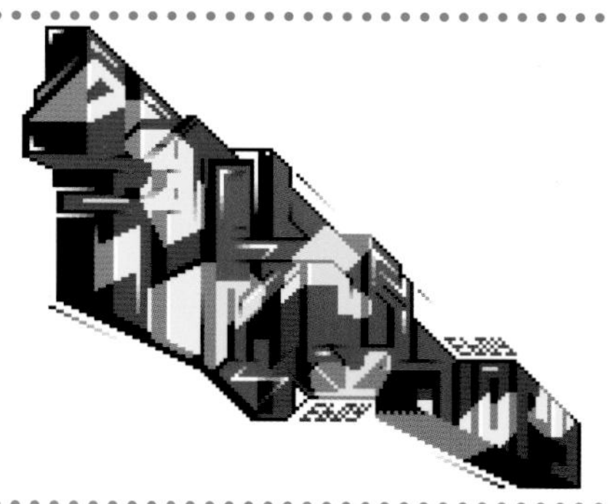

6

7

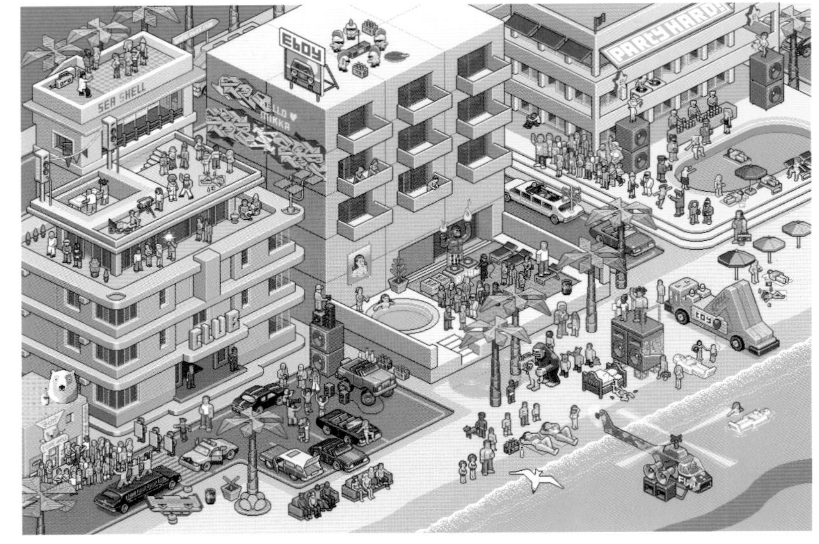

8

9

10

7 Illustration for *Electronic Gaming Monthly* magazine / Electronic Gaming Monthly / USA / 2002
8 Spread illustration for *The Face* magazine / The Face / United Kingdom / 2002
9 Self-commissioned Venice poster from "eCities" project / Germany / 2002
10 Spread illustration for *Mass Appeal Magazine* / Mass Appeal Magazine / USA / 2002
11 Adidas print advertisement / Leagas Delaney / United Kingdom / 2001
12 Pixel portraits of the four Eboys / Germany / 2002
13 Contribution to book *Disruptive Pattern Material* / Maharishi / United Kingdom / 2002
14 Print advertisement for gamer website powerplay.de / D-office / Germany / 2000

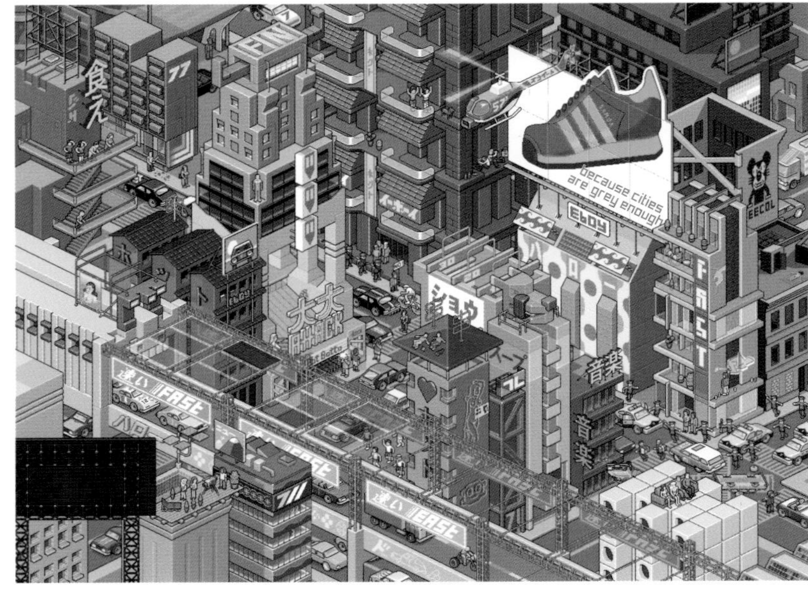

11

Eboy

12

13

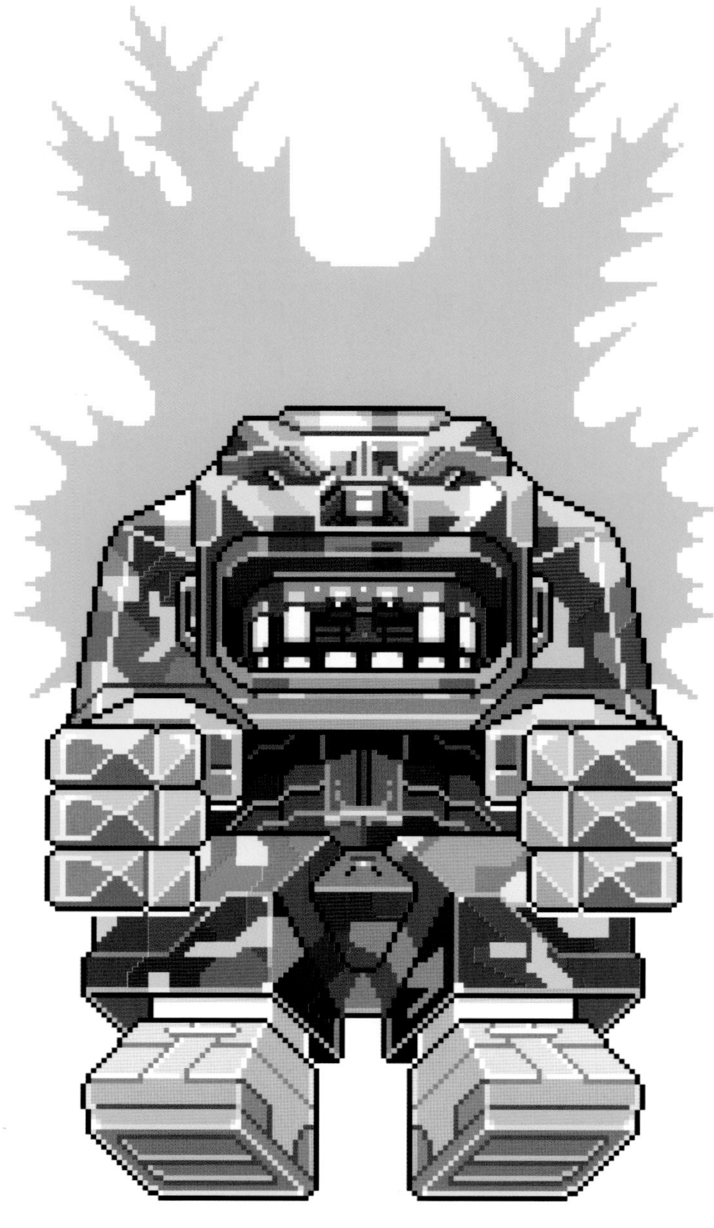

14

A billboard ad has only to hook you momentarily. It has worked if you have noticed it. No scrutiny necessary, as blanket coverage will ensure that a thousand fleeting interruptions in your day laminate into an awareness that perhaps you'd rather not have. Whereas a piece of graphic design like, say, a company brochure or a book has to hold your attention long enough to remain in your hands in order to function. It has to bear scrutiny, deliver on the promises its form makes. ••The self-deprecating design work of writer and publisher Dave Eggers taunts you with the prospect of boredom. For issue 3 of the cult literary journal *McSweeney's*, an obsessively meticulous yet clumsily assembled wheel of words and phrases is squeezed onto the cover and crowded by tiny, crude line drawings and minuscule marginalia. Words he has set in the wheel mock his own publishing effort: "Form as decoy," "All this: Cryptic, intriguing . . . or just kind of stupid?," "Yes, but remember we did not promise," "Come winter, much of this will make sense." Anyone who had already read issue 2 would have been familiar with Eggers's humor. That cover tempts readers with a conservatively centered list of announcements set in Garamond caps and italics that includes: "Welcoming: all comers, provided they're not going anywhere." Beside that, another wheel of letters tempers expectations once you can make out that they spell "sorry already." ••Designers more in awe than Eggers of inherited laws about what makes typography and layout tasteful will view his distinctive design work as compromised by its content. Form and content seem out of kilter. Yet it seems the more compromised his design is by verbiage, the more the content seems to promise. Eggers's use of writing as form-making gives him a completely different perspective on design. In *McSweeney's* no. 2 he asks, "And how often are formal innovations masking one's insecurity with the text?" His cover design for his second novel, *You Shall Know Our Velocity*, shows no such fear as that is where the text starts; the first paragraph unadorned, set justified to fill the space. While not a match for his first book, *A Heartbreaking Work of Staggering Genius*, it is nonetheless one that will remain in your hands for quite a while. ••Nick Bell••

1–3 Cover with bellyband and spreads, *The New Sins*, by David Byrne / McSweeney's Publishing / USA / 2001
4 Cover, *McSweeney's* no.9 / McSweeney's Publishing / USA / 2002
5 Cover, *McSweeney's* no.3, "Timothy McSweeney's Windfall Republic" / McSweeney's Publishing / USA / 1999
6 Spread, *McSweeney's* no.3
7 Page from "A Note About the Type," *McSweeney's* no.3

Dave Eggers

San Francisco

1

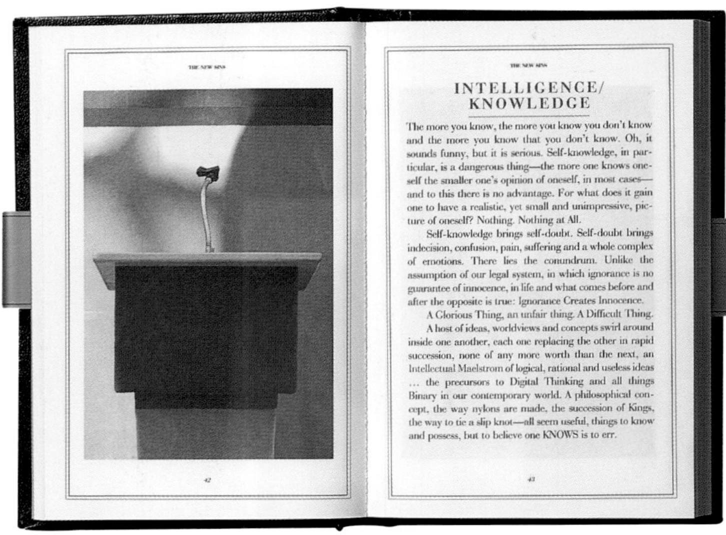

2

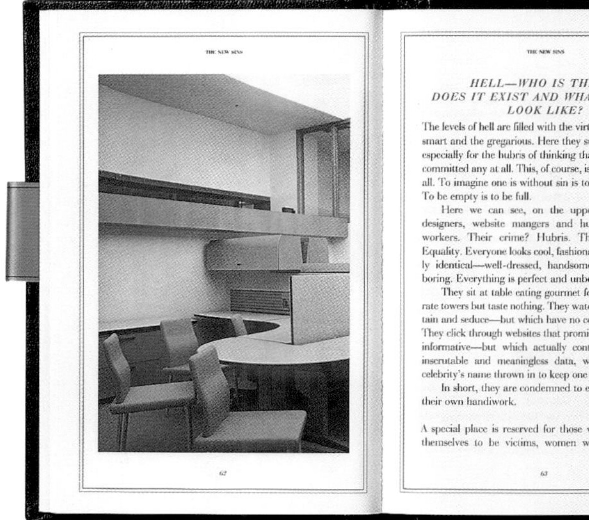

3

4

5

6

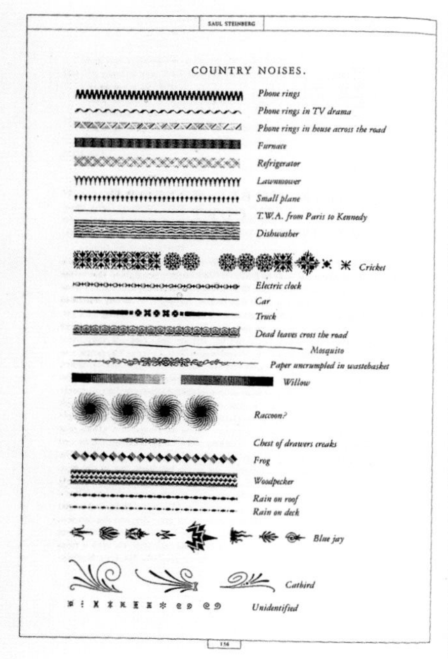

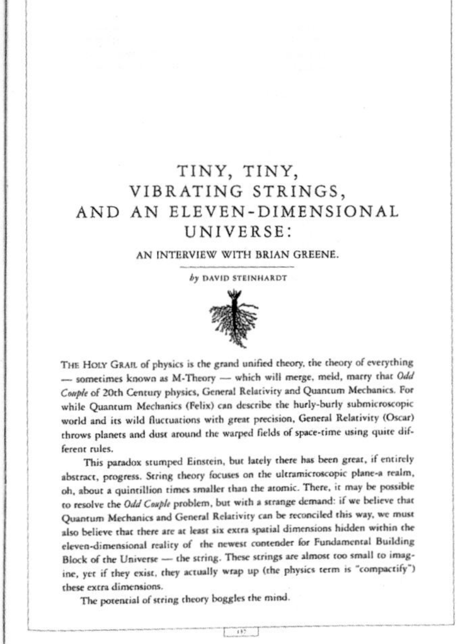

FOLKS LIKE SCIENCE

TINY, TINY, VIBRATING STRINGS, AND AN ELEVEN-DIMENSIONAL UNIVERSE:

AN INTERVIEW WITH BRIAN GREENE.

by DAVID STEINHARDT

THE HOLY GRAIL of physics is the grand unified theory, the theory of everything — sometimes known as M-Theory — which will merge, meld, marry that *Odd Couple* of 20th Century physics, General Relativity and Quantum Mechanics. For while Quantum Mechanics (Felix) can describe the hurly-burly submicroscopic world and its wild fluctuations with great precision, General Relativity (Oscar) throws planets and dust around the warped fields of space-time using quite different rules.

This paradox stumped Einstein, but lately there has been great, if entirely abstract, progress. String theory focuses on the ultramicroscopic plane-a realm, oh, about a quintillion times smaller than the atomic. There, it may be possible to resolve the *Odd Couple* problem, but with a strange demand: if we believe that Quantum Mechanics and General Relativity can be reconciled this way, we must also believe that there are at least six extra spatial dimensions hidden within the eleven-dimensional reality of the newest contender for Fundamental Building Block of the Universe — the string. These strings are almost too small to imagine, yet if they exist, they actually wrap up (the physics term is "compactify") these extra dimensions.

The potential of string theory boggles the mind.

7

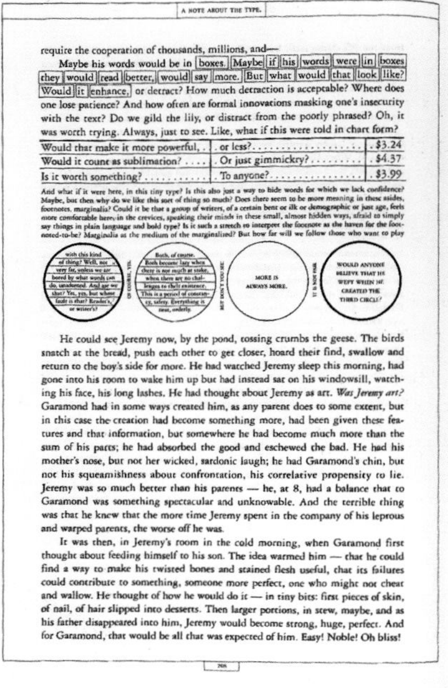

A NOTE ABOUT THE TYPE.

require the cooperation of thousands, millions, and—

Maybe his words would be in boxes. Maybe if his words were in boxes they would read better, would say more. But what would that look like? Would it enhance, or detract? How much detraction is acceptable? Where does one lose patience? And how often are formal innovations masking one's insecurity with the text? Do we gild the lily, or distract from the poorly phrased? Oh, it was worth trying. Always, just to see. Like, what if this were told in chart form?

Would that make it more powerful, . .	. or less?	. $3.24
Would it count as sublimation?	. Or just gimmickry?	. $4.37
Is it worth something?	. To anyone?	. $3.99

And what if it were here, in this tiny type? Is this also just a way to hide words for which we lack confidence? Maybe, but then why do we like this sort of thing so much? Does there seem to be more meaning in these asides, footnotes, marginalia? Could it be that a group of writers, of a certain bent or ilk or demographic or just age, feels more comfortable here, in the crevices, speaking their minds in these small, almost hidden ways, afraid to simply say things in plain language and bold type? Is it such a stretch to interpret the footnote as the haven for the footnoted-to-be? Marginalia as the medium of the marginalized? But how far will we follow those who want to play

with this kind of thing? Well, not very far, unless we are bored by what words can do, unadorned. And are we that? Yes, yes, but whose fault is that? Reader's, or writer's?

OF COURSE, YES.

Both, of course. Both become lazy when there is not much at stake, when there are no challenges to their existence. This is a period of constancy, safety. Everything is neat, orderly.

BUT DON'T YOU SEE

MORE IS ALWAYS MORE.

IT IS NOT FAIR

WOULD ANYONE BELIEVE THAT HE WEPT WHEN HE CREATED THE THIRD CIRCLE?

He could see Jeremy now, by the pond, tossing crumbs the geese. The birds snatch at the bread, push each other to get closer, hoard their find, swallow and return to the boy's side for more. He had watched Jeremy sleep this morning, had gone into his room to wake him up but had instead sat on his windowsill, watching his face, his long lashes. He had thought about Jeremy as art. *Was Jeremy art?* Garamond had in some ways created him, as any parent does to some extent, but in this case the creation had become something more, had been given these features and that information, but somewhere he had become much more than the sum of his parts; he had absorbed the good and eschewed the bad. He had his mother's nose, but not her wicked, sardonic laugh; he had Garamond's chin, but not his squeamishness about confrontation, his correlative propensity to lie. Jeremy was so much better than his parents — he, at 8, had a balance that to Garamond was something spectacular and unknowable. And the terrible thing was that he knew that the more time Jeremy spent in the company of his leprous and warped parents, the worse off he was.

It was then, in Jeremy's room in the cold morning, when Garamond first thought about feeding himself to his son. The idea warmed him — that he could find a way to make his twisted bones and stained flesh useful, that its failures could contribute to something, someone more perfect, one who might not cheat and wallow. He thought of how he would do it — in tiny bits: first pieces of skin, of nail, of hair slipped into desserts. Then larger portions, in stew, maybe, and as his father disappeared into him, Jeremy would become strong, huge, perfect. And for Garamond, that would be all that was expected of him. Easy! Noble! Oh bliss!

8

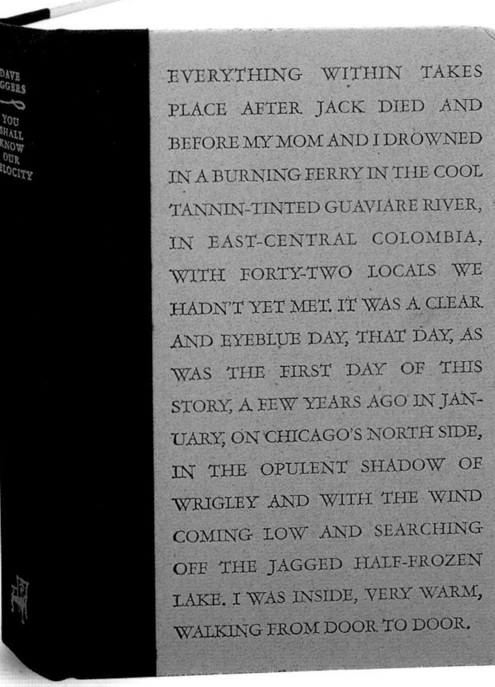

12

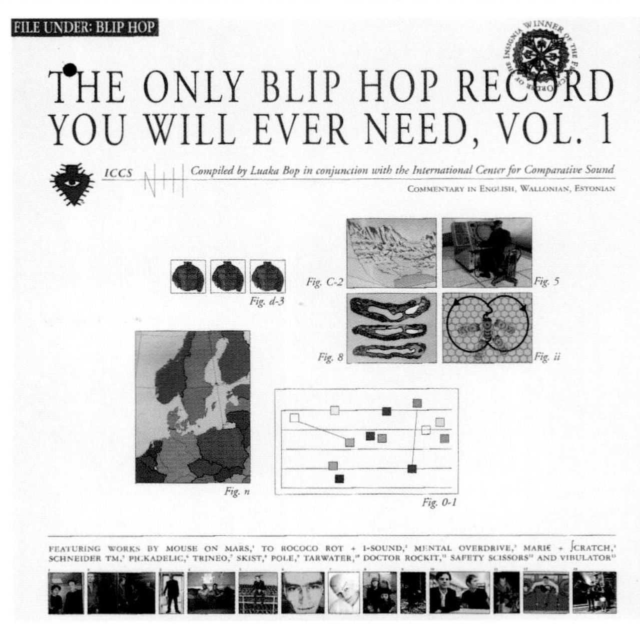

8 Cover, *You Shall Know Our Velocity*, by Dave Eggers / McSweeney's Publishing / USA / 2002
9–11 Spreads from *You Shall Know Our Velocity* / The blank spread appears in the middle of the sentence "...and the pause between when we became airborne [blank spread] and WHACK when we landed..."
12 Vinyl cover, *The Only Blip Hop Record You Will Ever Need* vol. 1 (with Danielle Spencer) / Luka Bop Inc. / USA / 2002
13 Back cover, *A Heartbreaking Work of Staggering Genius*, by Dave Eggers / Vintage Books / USA / 2000
14 Cover, *Timothy McSweeney's Blues-Jazz Odyssey* / McSweeney's Publishing / USA / 1999
15–16 Cover and inside booklets, *McSweeney's* no.7 (booklets with Elizabeth Kairys) / McSweeney's Publishing / USA / 2001

Dave Eggers

9

"Hold on," Hand said, jumping from the car.

He spoke to the group for a second, and one man directed him down the beach to an older man, painting a large white sign protruding from the beach. They discussed something, and Hand walked back to the car.

"We're going for a ride," he said. "Quick, but it'll be nice."

Hand had contracted this man, Thione, to take us up and down the coast for half an hour. We had to see things from this side, he said, and there was no speed, he said, like water speed.

We set off from the beach, helping with two other men to push the boat off a narrow sandbar near the shore. I sat at the front, Hand in the middle. A teenager jumped on just before we took off. He was the navigator.

We were in a small white motorboat-watertaxi steered by an older man and guided by a teenager who stood on the bow as the boat bounced, holding a rope tied to the point, standing as if riding a white and featherheaded circus horse. At our feet, the water sloshing to and fro. I leaned over the boat's edge, watched the same point as the froth blurred by, white and blue—and I wanted to have my arm in the water. To have it lazily running through the water, like I did that day, with Helen Peters, at Phelps Lake, on that boat, both of us naked— But here it wouldn't really be water like that, not here so fast, this wouldn't feel like water at all but more like fast-moving pavement. The foliage went right to the water and then went up, furry and dense, squiggly with dementia.

The sea was not smooth, the ride was thunderous, as if the boat had been thrown and was skipping along the surface. Tick-tick-tick—*WHAP!* When the boat jumped and its flat bottom struck the hard water, my spine compressed, briefly, between expectations of flight and the boat's great desire to come down and pound the surface, to slap it like you slap a shoe on a summit table—*WHACK*—and it rose and struck again, and the water blurred by and I saw it all, the white beaches, the small cottages along the

160

shore, the miles of rocky beach, and then I knew that all I wanted evermore was *WHAP!WHAP!* The boat was skipping and then there would be a larger wave, or we would hit a regular wave a certain way, and the pause between when we became airborne

161

10

11

and *WHACK* when we landed we landed like a cannon and I clenched my teeth—*BAMBAMBAM*—for the aftershocks and I looked to Hand and the old man for a commiserative glance—*what the fu-fu-fuck?*—but no one wanted to share. They were busy, devoting their attentions to traveling, to watching the progress of the boat—instrumental in traveling is the participation in it, the belief in progress, the witnessing of passage. And I was traveling, too, I was serious about it. In a low hard motorboat one had to be serious. *WHAP!* There was urgency about a boat like this, riding the coast, banging against the surface—three little waves coming: *BAPPITY!* We were going somewhere. And not just moving, but moving quickly—past things that were moving slowly or not moving at all. *WHAP!* The only motion I knew was relative motion, the only speed that truly felt like speed was when I was speeding past things. *WHAP! WHAP!* A sudden veering of the boat.

—Hand you've saved me today, but what about later?

—I will continue to move us.

—What about tomorrow?

—I'll move us tomorrow.

We sped through the savannah and suburbs—we'd tipped the boat man and boat boy like kings—and made it to the airport by eleven. We dropped the car in front of the rental office, gave the keys and a $50 tip to the attendant, and ran into the airport. At

164

the Air Afrique desk, the three stunning queens, again splendid in blue and yellow and green, wanted $400, in cash, for each of the tickets to Casablanca, so I put my name on more travelers checks at the money-change desk—*me! me! swoop! swoop!*—and came back and presented the money, two inches thick, to the eldest of the three.

"Ah, so you the big boss?" she asked.

"The what?" I said.

"The big boss! You!" she repeated.

"Yes, the big boss, this one!" said another of the women.

"But it was you who wanted of the cash," I said, in Handspeak. I was confused. I didn't want to be the big boss.

"Some man hit the big boss," said the third, gesturing at her face with loose fists.

Then they all laughed. For a long time.

Two hours in the air. I was in one row and Hand was across the way. We were both in the exit row, which he'd requested. "Extra legroom," he'd said to me and the queens, "and if anything big happens, we're right where the action is." My row was empty but Hand was sitting next to a young couple, maybe Senegalese. I had the idea that I'd try to sleep—with the ambient sounds of the cabin I figured I had a chance of rest with some kind of peace—and so set my head back and closed my eyes. But Hand was in an inquisitive mood and I couldn't avoid hearing the whole thing.

"You speak the English?" he asked.

"I do," the woman next to him said.

I opened my eyes briefly to take a look. She looked like royalty, as did her companion, who might have been her brother. They both looked like models, skin like polished teak. I closed my eyes.

"Where're you going?" Hand asked.

"Marrakesh. For medical school."

165

13

14

PEOPLE, PEOPLE—STOP BLAMING YOURSELVES! HAVE YOU FORGOTTEN:

TIMOTHY

McSWEENEY'S

BLUES/JAZZ ODYSSEY?

(FOR SHORT SAY "McSWEENEY'S.")

KNOWN ALSO AS:

"POLLYANNA'S
BOOTLESS ERRAND."

NOW FIX YOUR COLLAR—TODAY COULD BE YOUR DAY!

We say:

MARFA, TEXAS	*makes good readin'*	ALSO PLEASE FIND: *fire:*	FEATURING THESE BIG-NAME WRITERS:		Y E S
LOVE WITH LEMONS	*makes good readin'*	*giraffes: murder: cursing:*			E E E
SNAKES WHO BAKE	*makes good readin'*	*Tom Brokaw: deep feelings.*			S E E
19TH C. ASTRONOMY HOAXES	*are v. interesting*			*Show us a Spanish galleon, said the teeming hordes. A Spanish galleon yes, sure, we said. Then we said, um.*	*Have faith.*
FLYING FAT LADIES	*makes good readin'*				
ORNERY PIRATES	*makes good readin'*				

First of all know this:

WHEN THINGS SPILL
THEY DON'T MAKE A SOUND.

And please also acknowledge:

QUARTERS ARE EASIER TO PICK UP WHEN SPINNING;
THE ONLY REMEDY TO FRAUDULENCE IS DEATH.

and

TREES ALSO COME IN RED.

HURRAY FOR OUR HOVEL!

TAKE OFF YOUR SHOES, PULL OVER A BEANBAG AND — WHO, US? WELL, OKAY... AHEM:

Welcoming: ALL COMERS, PROVIDED THEY'RE NOT GOING ANYWHERE;
Realizing: PRECIOUS IS AS PRECIOUS DOES;
Still confused by: JUST HOW MUSIC IS MADE WHEN A NEEDLE TOUCHES A GROOVE CARVED IN VINYL;
Dearly wishing for: A BANANA THAT DOES NOT BRUISE;
Dedicated to: PUNCHING A HOLE THROUGH THE EASTERN FRONT; *and*
CREATED *in honor of and named for*

Mr. T. McSwy (19?-19?)
who was nuts, sure, but in the most endearing way.

OUR NEW MOTTO:

"HAVE PITY."

CONCEIVED WITH LOVE BY FAITHLESS DUMMIES.
PRINTED IN ICELAND.
1999

IF WORDS ARE *to* BE USED *as* DESIGN ELEMENTS *then* LET DESIGNERS WRITE THEM.

To fibbing →
To outright lying →
To a kind of humidity →
To the roof →

15–16

If you are the type of person who judges people on appearances, then you may well be misled by your first impressions of Jonathan Ellery. An ex–Rugby Union player with a fondness for sharply tailored suits, he can appear to be quite an imposing character. In reality he is a sensitive, refined type, with a very good eye and a keen understanding of aesthetics, qualities that have enabled him to develop an accomplished and well-rounded body of work. • • When we discussed how best to present his work, we decided upon a selection of recent posters. Posters are arguably the most direct medium of communication available to graphic designers, and even though most (if not all) of Ellery's posters belong to wider promotional print programs, the direct simplicity required for poster design is apparent throughout his portfolio. • • Ellery's work is characterized by its distinctive Britishness. The image of Tower Bridge on the cover of the book *Browns: A Walk Through Books* (2003), which contains examples of the studio's publishing design, is indicative of this British spirit that frequently informs Ellery's vocabulary. It hints at the heritage of London and stereotypical notions of Britain, while the context suggests something more modern. • • When Ellery's work references the past, it does so in a way that feels contemporary, and always in a manner appropriate to the project. In 2001 Ellery designed the book *Coney Island*—featuring the photography of Bruce Gilden—with a typographical language that recalls letterpress posters and ads for carnivals, circuses, and theaters from the early twentieth century. Back then, New York's Coney Island would have been awash with such examples. Elsewhere, he references the tradition of postcards with loose, scratchy, handwritten lettering. • • Above all, Ellery's work is about solving problems, with an approach that is driven by communication and simplicity of expression. It sounds simple enough, and that is the point. That is what graphic design is all about. • • Fernando Gutiérrez • •

1 Poster promoting Love and Peace agenda 2003 / Artic Papers - Trebruk / United Kingdom / 2002
2 Poster promoting Extreme agenda 2002 / Arctic Papers - Trebruk / United Kingdom / 2001
3 Poster for Grant Scott photography exhibition *Crash Happy* / Grant Scott / United Kingdom / 2002
4 Poster for D&AD–Nesta Product Design and Innovation Student Awards / D&AD and Nesta / United Kingdom / 2003
5 Poster for seminar at Falmouth College of Arts / Falmouth College of Art / United Kingdom / 1999
6 Poster for international "Pure Football. Pure Hope." campaign (1 of 10) / FIFA and UNICEF / 1999
7 Poster for D&AD–Nesta Product Design and Innovation Student Awards / D&AD and Nesta / United Kingdom / 2002

Jonathan Ellery

London

The Agenda 2003
70 Magnum Photographers
Published by Arctic Papers
Design by Browns/London
Available October 2002
www.arcticpapers.com
Price £15.00 €20.00 $20.00

1

2

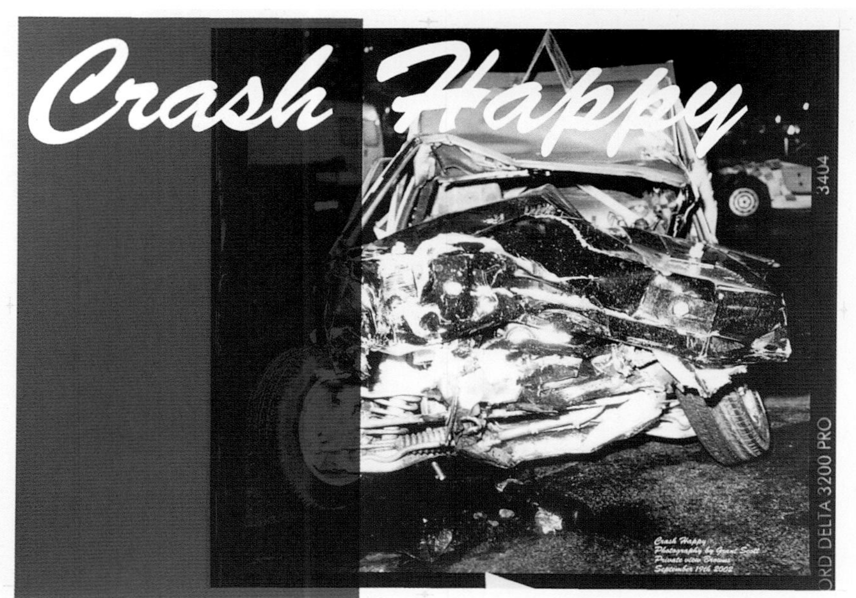

3

4

FLANGE
esa
CONRAN&PARTNERS
Design Council
nesta

5

make sense of it all
a browns perspective
jonathan ellery
falmouth college of arts
main lecture theatre
friday 21st may
2.00pm 1999
atelierbrownscdtdesig
nhouseergofarrowgra
phicthoughtfacilityhg
vimaginationjannuzzi
smithkaye(tony)lambi
enairnmufnorthomnifi
cpentagramquay(davi
d)randsastomatounav
incefrostwolffolinsxya
mamotozigguratmake
senseofitall★⊙➔✲!@?

6

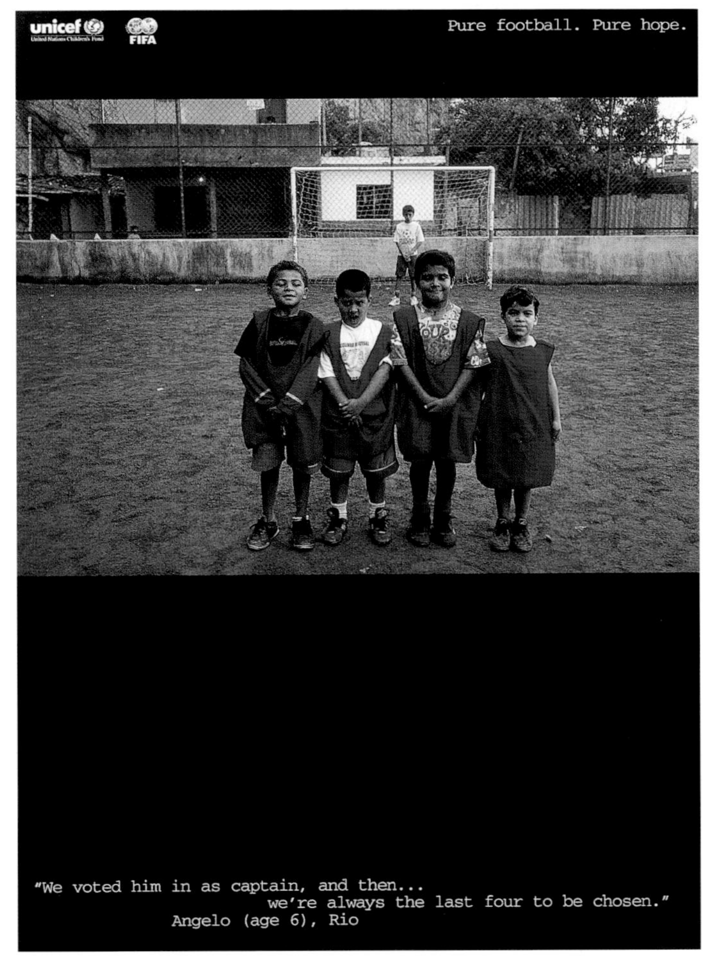
unicef
United Nations Children's Fund
FIFA
Pure football. Pure hope.
"We voted him in as captain, and then...
we're always the last four to be chosen."
Angelo (age 6), Rio

7

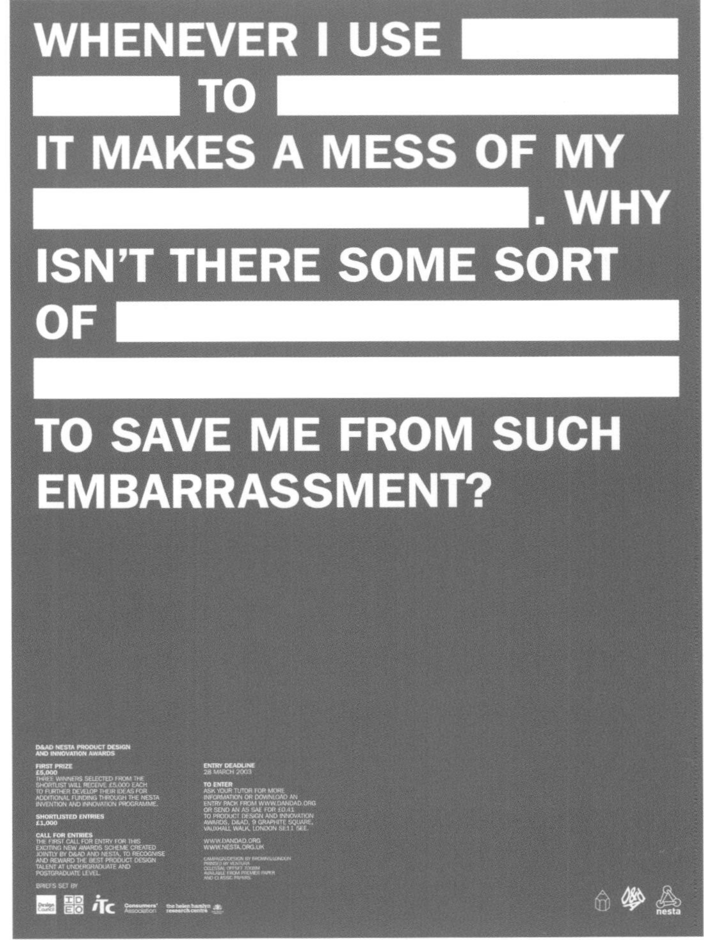
WHENEVER I USE
TO
IT MAKES A MESS OF MY
. WHY
ISN'T THERE SOME SORT
OF
TO SAVE ME FROM SUCH
EMBARRASSMENT?
nesta

8

9

23/09 '02 MON 09:29 FAX 0207 793 7579 BRITISH DESIGN & ART DIR 002

HOW FAR WOULD
YOU GO?
FAX +44 (0)20
7407 9075
BEST RESPONSES
PRINTED IN THE
D&AD STUDENT AWARDS
ANNUAL 2003
WWW.DANDAD.ORG

D&AD STUDENT AWARDS 2003
CALL FOR ENTRIES

FOR THE BEST IN STUDENT DESIGN, ADVERTISING AND COMMUNICATIONS.

ENTRY DEADLINE 28 MARCH 2003

PRIZES
FIRST PRIZE £1,000
SECOND £400
COMMENDATION £250
WPP BURSARIES
TWO ADDITIONAL £5,000 BURSARIES

SELECTED WORK IS PUBLISHED IN THE PRESTIGIOUS STUDENT AWARDS ANNUAL WHICH IS MAILED TO CREATIVES WORLDWIDE.

FIRST AND SECOND PRIZE WINNERS ALSO RECEIVE THE COVETED 'BABY' YELLOW PENCIL PRIZE AND THEIR WORK IS SHOWCASED ON THE D&AD GETTY IMAGES BLOODBANK WEBSITE.

TO ENTER
ASK YOUR TUTOR FOR MORE INFORMATION OR DOWNLOAD AN ENTRY PACK FROM WWW.DANDAD.ORG OR SEND AN A4 SAE FOR £0.66 SECOND CLASS OR £0.84 FIRST CLASS MARKED STUDENT AWARDS TO D&AD, 9 GRAPHITE SQUARE, VAUXHALL WALK, LONDON SE11 5EE.

CATEGORIES THIS YEAR
ADVERTISING – POSTCARD MEDIA, ADVERTISING – TRANSPORT MEDIA, ADVERTISING CAMPAIGN – OPEN BRIEF, AMBIENT MEDIA, BRAND IDENTITY, CORUS STEEL PACKAGING, DIRECT MAIL, DIRECT RESPONSE, ENVIRONMENTAL DESIGN, GRAPHIC DESIGN, ILLUSTRATION, INFORMATION DESIGN, INTERACTIVE DESIGN, MIXED MEDIA, PHOTOGRAPHY, POSTER ADVERTISING, PRESS ADVERTISING, PRODUCT DESIGN, RADIO, STREAMING, TV GRAPHICS, TV SHORT, TYPOGRAPHY, WEBSITE DESIGN, WRITING.

FAX BACK
THE QUESTION POSED ABOVE IS NOT A BRIEF OR CATEGORY IN THE 2003 STUDENT AWARDS. WE'RE HAVING A BIT OF FUN WITH THIS YEAR'S STUDENT AWARDS PRINT CAMPAIGN. THE MOST INTERESTING REPLIES WILL APPEAR ON THE CATEGORY DIVIDER PAGES IN THE STUDENT ANNUAL. REPLIES MUST INCLUDE YOUR NAME, COURSE AND COLLEGE.

8 Poster promoting *Pandora's Box*, by Susan Meiselas (1 of 3) / Trebruk / United Kingdom / 2001
9 Call for Entries poster for 2003 D&AD Student Awards / D&AD / United Kingdom / 2002
10 Poster promoting *Go*, by Bruce Gilden / Arctic Paper and Trebruk / United Kingdom / 2000
11–12 Posters promoting *Coney Island*, by Bruce Gilden (2 of 5) / Arctic Paper and Trebruk / United Kingdom / 2001
13 Poster promoting European Clichés agenda 2000 (1 of 5) / Munkedals-Trebruk / United Kingdom / 2000
14 Briefing Day poster for 2001 D&AD Student Awards / D&AD / United Kingdom / 2000

Jonathan Ellery

10

11

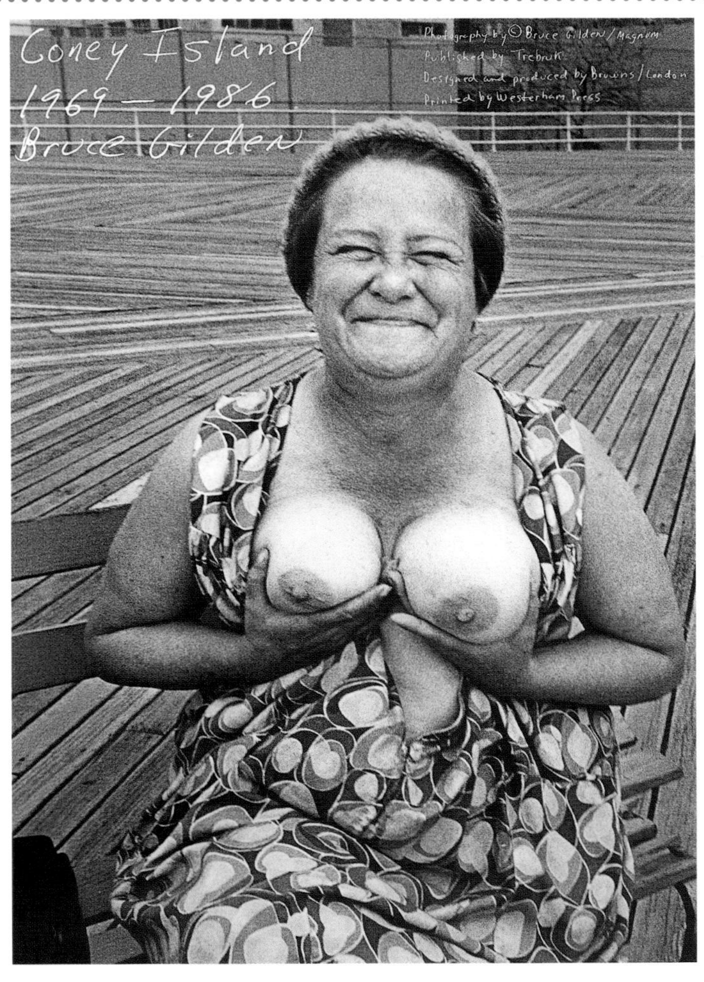
Coney Island
1969 — 1986
Bruce Gilden
Photography by © Bruce Gilden / Magnum
Published by Trebruk
Designed and produced by Browns / London
Printed by Westerham Press

12

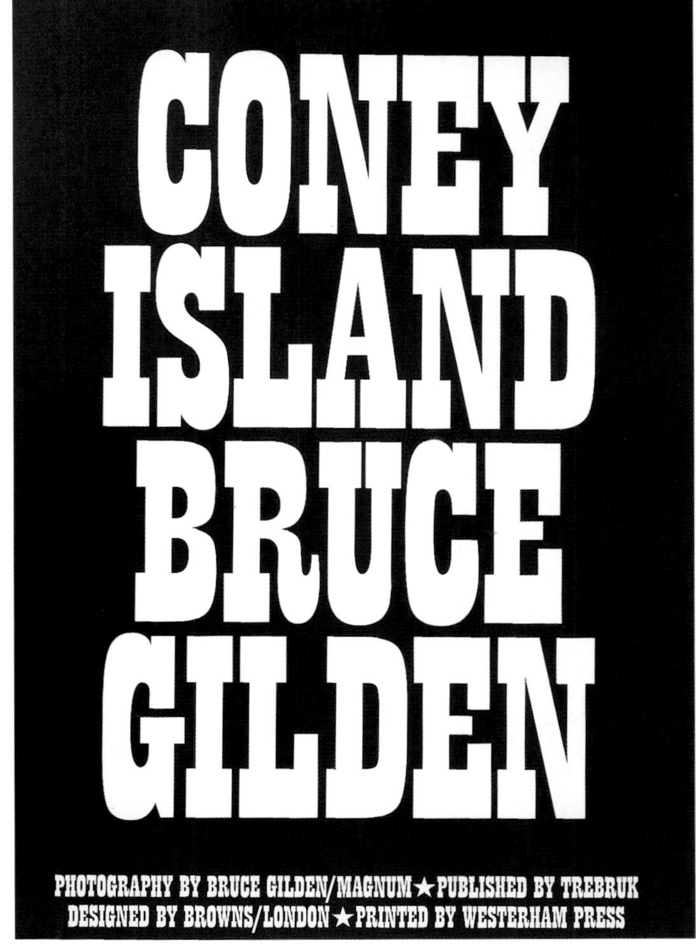
CONEY
ISLAND
BRUCE
GILDEN
PHOTOGRAPHY BY BRUCE GILDEN/MAGNUM★PUBLISHED BY TREBRUK
DESIGNED BY BROWNS/LONDON★PRINTED BY WESTERHAM PRESS

13

European clichés 2000
Munken Agenda, photography by Martin Parr/Magnum
Available at www.munkedals.se
Designed by Browns/London. Printed on Munken Lynx 170gsm. Printed by Westerham Press.

14

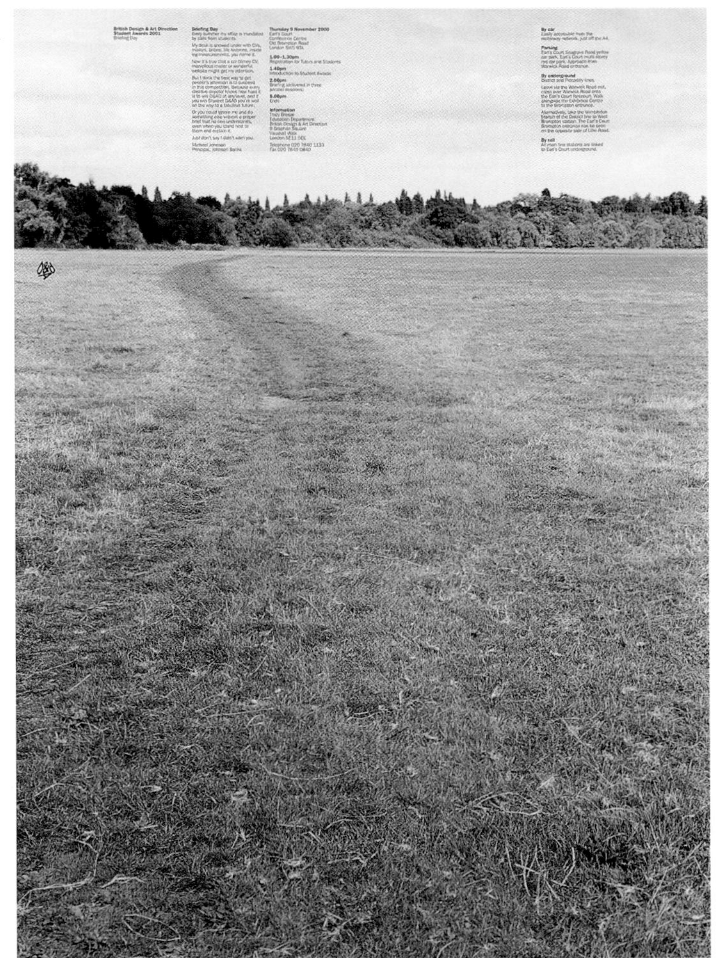
British Design & Art Direction
Student Awards 2001
Briefing Day
Thursday 9 November 2000
1.00–1.30pm
1.40pm
2.00pm
5.00pm
Information
By car
Parking
By underground
By rail

Experimental Jetset have a recurring nightmare, and it goes something like this: Your entire experience is fed to you by an image-based consumer culture that is second-guessing where you would like to go today. Marketing—it's everywhere, and it keeps EJ awake at night. • • EJ live with the vain hope that it is possible to design objects that are autonomous, free in their internal logic from the recommendations of the focus group, and immune to predictions of the trend forecaster. EJ want to be taken seriously. With Maureen Mooren and Daniel van der Velden they share the same desire to engage with individuals before groups. They wish to rescue communication design from mere representation. For them, the material, physical, tactility of design-as-object will prevent design from slipping into the swamp of mass information, where the primary motive of design is to imitate audience values. EJ want to stop you in your tracks with objects that exist only in relation to themselves and are not representations of the idea, that you may have in your head, of wanting to come across objects that exist only in relation to themselves. • • EJ use the visual language associated with modernism. They can't help it, it's their inheritance. Helvetica has become a signature for them, meant not as a sign of their admiration of modernist typography, but as their way of using neutrality to avoid metaphor—the use of visual effects that make associations with something other than the design object itself; for instance, the use of a rounded, friendly typeface because research has indicated that your audience is put off by things that look serious. • • The EJ manifesto is "to create designs that function as a part of reality instead of as a representation of reality." But then, on seeing the December stamps EJ designed for the Dutch PTT, I thought, illustration—representation surely! The portrayal of generic people enjoying a kind of generic landscape looked not so far away from pictures one might find in one of the gargantuan stock-photo catalogues. But then I had to hand it to them: The December snow draws attention to the whiteness of the paper—it is the paper (materiality)—and the happy people are reduced to silhouettes in microns of metallic gold ink (materiality again). • • Nick Bell • •

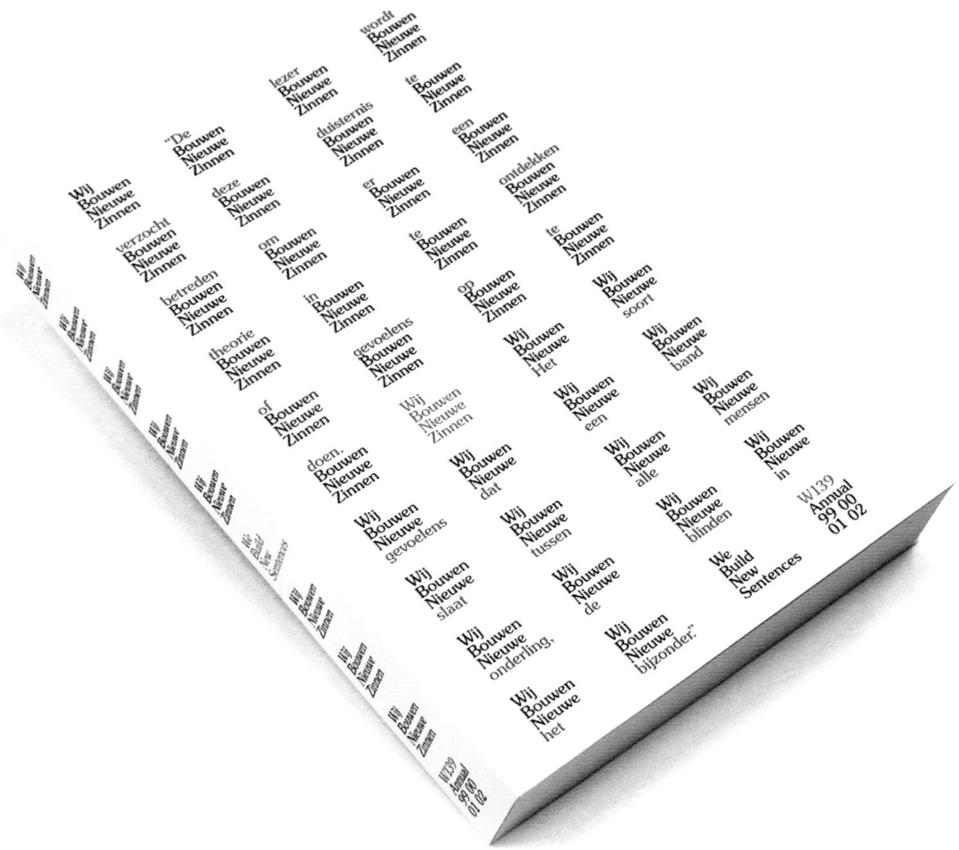

1–2 Cover and spread, *Wij Bouwen Nieuwe Zinnen* (We Build New Sentences) quadrennial for exhibition space W139 / W139 / Netherlands / 2002

3–6 Cover and spreads, *Elysian Fields* exhibition catalogue / Centre Georges Pompidou and Purple Institute / France / 2000

7–9 Catalogue and intsallation, *Kelly 1:1–A cover version by Experimental Jetset* solo exhibition / Casco Projects and Editions / Netherlands / 2002 / An actual size reproduction of Elsworth Kelly's painting *Blue, Green, Yellow, Orange, Red* mapped in sheets of A4 paper. The dismantled and bound artwork itself makes up the exhibition catalogue.

Experimental Jetset

Amsterdam

Elysian
Fields
EF

3 4 5 6

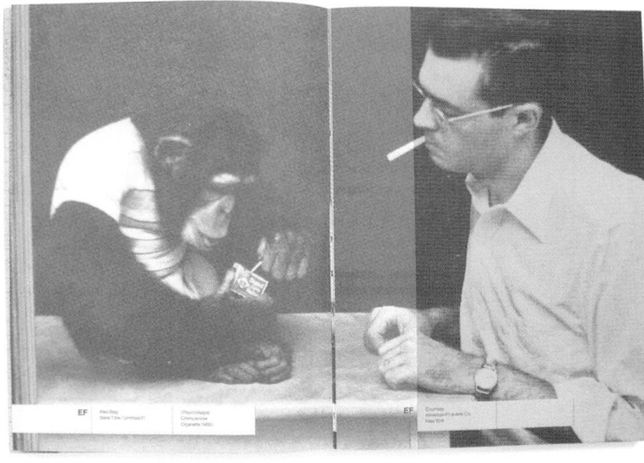

Kelly 1:1
A cover version by
Experimental Jetset
Casco Editions
An interpretation of
Ellsworth Kelly's Blue,
Green, Yellow, Orange,
Red. 1966 Actual size

7 8 9

CASCO
KELLY 1:1

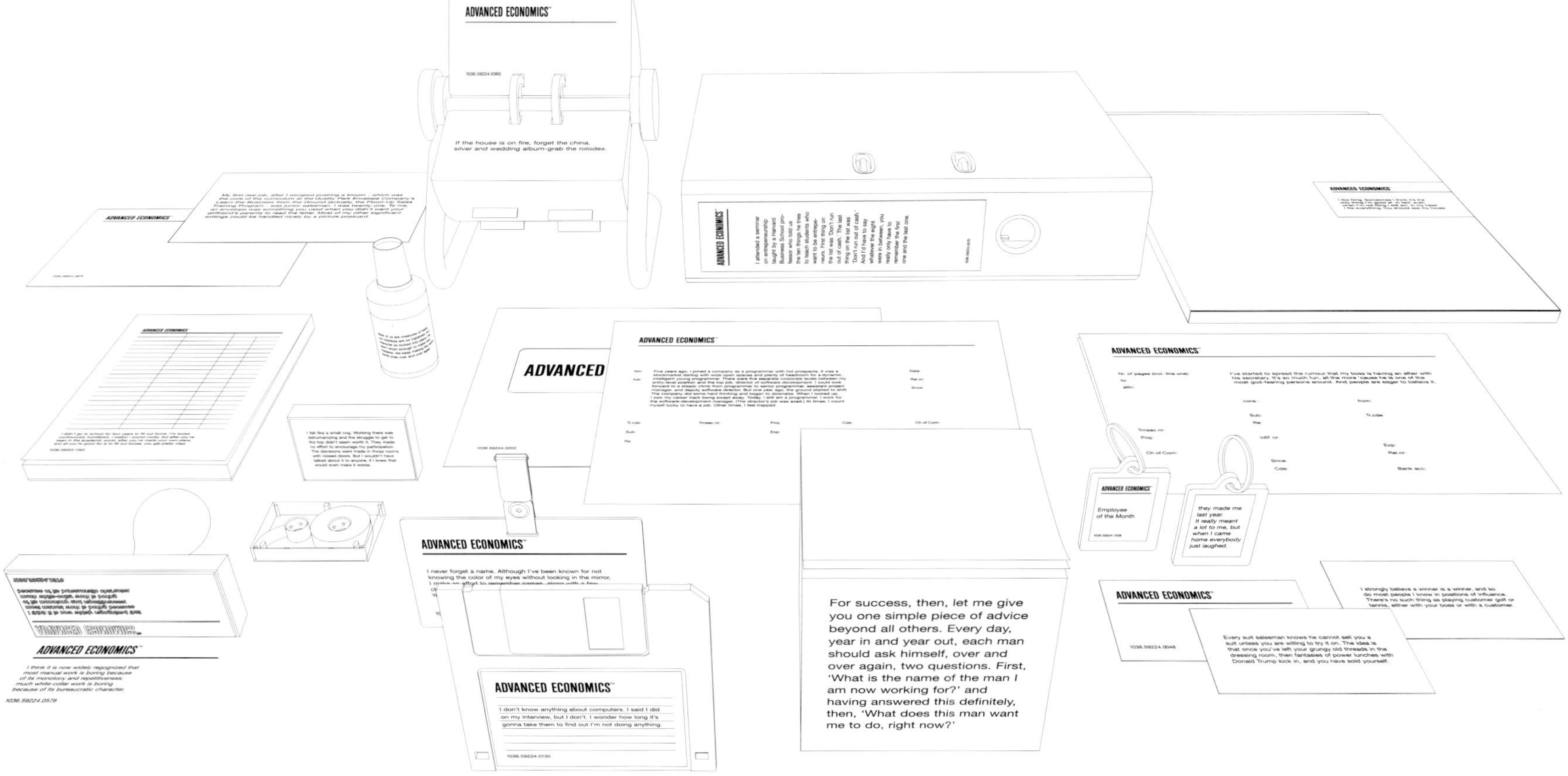

ADVANCED ECONOMICS™

If the house is on fire, forget the china, silver and wedding album-grab the rolodex.

ADVANCED

Employee of the Month

they made me last year. It really meant a lot to me, but when I came home everybody just laughed.

I never forget a name. Although I've been known for not knowing the color of my eyes without looking in the mirror,

I don't know anything about computers. I said I did on my interview, but I don't. I wonder how long it's gonna take them to find out I'm not doing anything.

For success, then, let me give you one simple piece of advice beyond all others. Every day, year in and year out, each man should ask himself, over and over again, two questions. First, 'What is the name of the man I am now working for?' and having answered this definitely, then, 'What does this man want me to do, right now?'

I think it is now widely recognized that most manual work is boring because of its monotony and repetitiveness, much white-collar work is boring because of its bureaucratic character.

10

11

10–11 Advanced Economics project, designed and published in limited edition by Experimental Jetset / Netherlands / 1998 / The project appears to be a complete corporate-identity program. Closer reading reveals a darker undertone, as every single item contains a story of corporate misery.
12 *Decembergedacheten* (December thoughts) stamps / Royal Dutch Mail / Netherlands / 2002
13–14 Covers, *The People's Art–A Arte do Povo* exhibition catalogue / Witte de With / Netherlands / 2001 / The catalogue featured twenty different dust jackets wrapped on top of each other.
15–17 Catalogue and exhibition design, *Display* exhibition on contemporary jewelry design / Stedelijk Museum / Netherlands / 2002

Experimental Jetset

12

13 14

15 16 17

Sara Fanelli creates the children's books that all designers wish they'd owned in their formative years. Her illustrations are wonderfully rich. More like paintings. The visual landscape is there to be explored. What seems initially quite simple in structure is full of content and information. Her layered and collage-style illustration is full of graphic surprises. Each element is rich with unique characteristics that provide individual and collective messages. Her illustrative techniques combine the traditional mediums of painting, drawing, and printmaking. While her work is all about ideas, the interpretation is highly personal. Her commercial projects have clearly benefited from the lessons of her self-initiated projects, where she has had the freedom to experiment and explore more creatively rewarding territory—areas that under the pressure of deadlines would be seen as dangerous. The combination of typography and image is seamless; often the text is the image. ••Born in Florence, Italy, Fanelli arrived in London to study design and illustration. Since her graduation from the Royal College of Art in 1995 she has worked as a freelance illustrator. She has also written and illustrated several award-winning children's books, including *Dear Diary*, *First Flight*, and *Mythological Monsters*. While Fanelli's work has reached great heights in its development, one senses the best is still to come. ••Ken Cato••

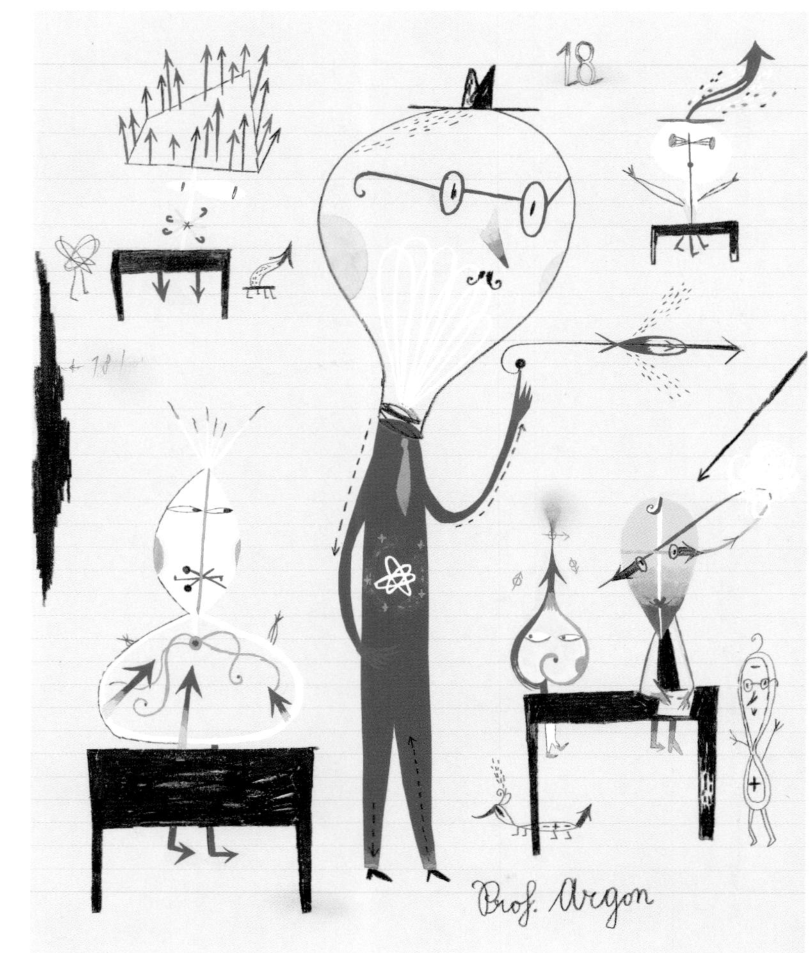

1

2

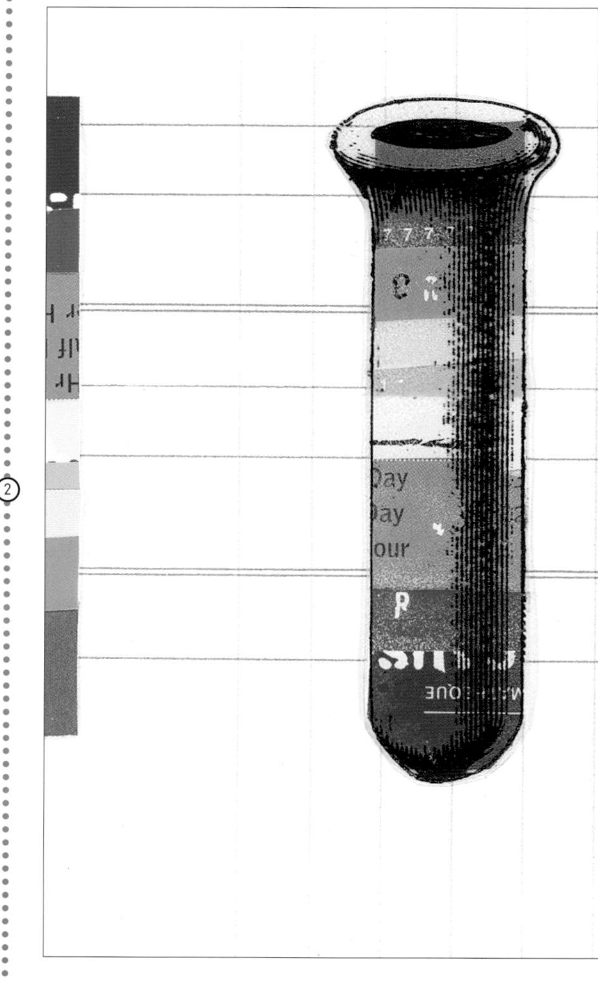

3

1–3 Illustrations for annual report of Swedish chemistry board Kemikontoret / Bark Design / Sweden / 2001
4 Cover and spreads from *Dear Diary*, written, illustrated, and designed by Sara Fanelli / Walker Books / United Kingdom / 2000
5 Spreads from *Mythological Monsters*, written, illustrated, and designed by Sara Fanelli / Walker Books / United Kingdom / 2002

Sara Fanelli

London

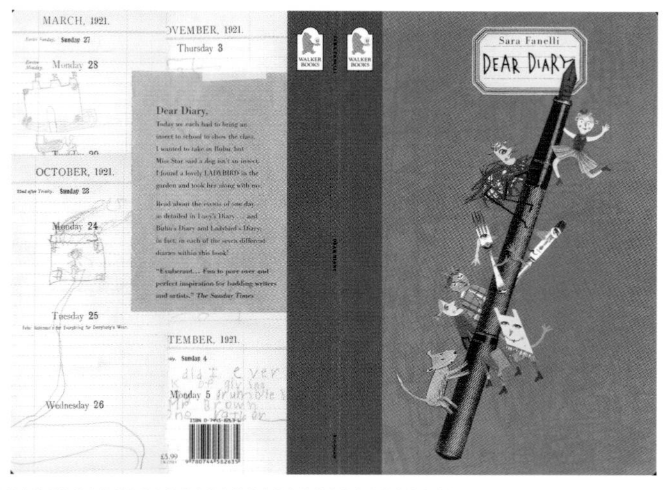

Sara Fanelli
DEAR DIARY
WALKER BOOKS
MARCH, 1921.
OCTOBER, 1921.
Dear Diary,

④

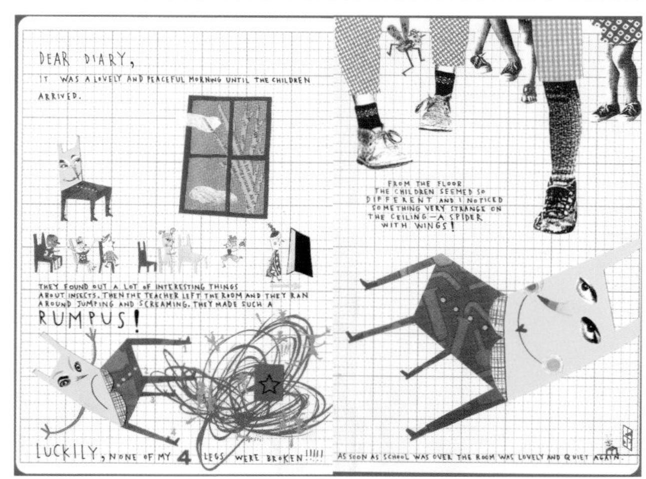

DEAR DIARY,
IT WAS A LOVELY AND PEACEFUL MORNING UNTIL THE CHILDREN ARRIVED.
FROM THE FLOOR THE CHILDREN SEEMED SO DIFFERENT AND I NOTICED SOMETHING VERY STRANGE ON THE CEILING — A SPIDER WITH WINGS!
THEY FOUND OUT A LOT OF INTERESTING THINGS ABOUT INSECTS. THEN THE TEACHER LEFT THE ROOM AND THEY RAN AROUND JUMPING AND SCREAMING. THEY MADE SUCH A RUMPUS!
LUCKILY, NONE OF MY 4 LEGS WERE BROKEN!!!!!
AS SOON AS SCHOOL WAS OVER THE ROOM WAS LOVELY AND QUIET AGAIN.

THE PARTY itself — well, what a SURPRISE!
All of my friends looked so ....
DIFFERENT

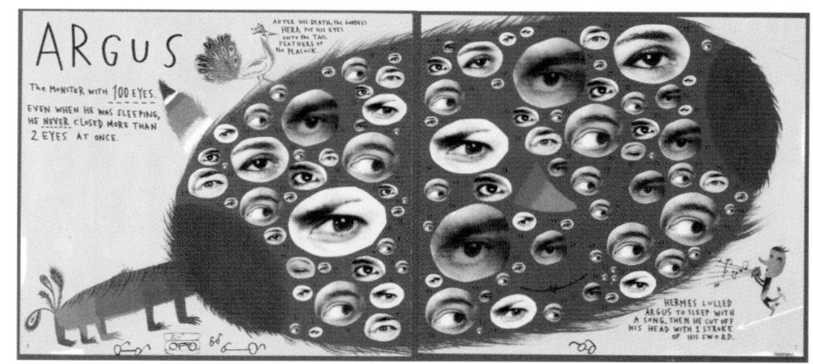

ARGUS
THE MONSTER WITH 100 EYES.
EVEN WHEN HE WAS SLEEPING, HE NEVER CLOSED MORE THAN 2 EYES AT ONCE.
HERMES LULLED ARGUS TO SLEEP WITH A SONG, THEN HE CUT OFF HIS HEAD WITH 1 STROKE OF HIS SWORD.

⑤

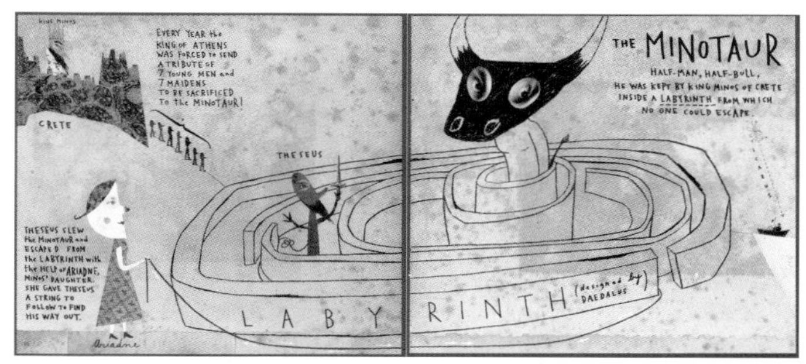

EVERY YEAR THE KING OF ATHENS WAS FORCED TO SEND A TRIBUTE OF 7 YOUNG MEN AND 7 MAIDENS TO BE SACRIFICED TO THE MINOTAUR!
CRETE
THESEUS
THE MINOTAUR
HALF-MAN, HALF-BULL,
HE WAS KEPT BY KING MINOS OF CRETE INSIDE A LABYRINTH FROM WHICH NO ONE COULD ESCAPE.
THESEUS SLEW THE MINOTAUR AND ESCAPED FROM THE LABYRINTH WITH THE HELP OF ARIADNE, MINOS' DAUGHTER. SHE GAVE THESEUS A STRING TO FOLLOW TO FIND HIS WAY OUT.
LABYRINTH (designed by DAEDALUS)

HER HUSBAND,
TYPHON
the 3 GORGONS
ECHIDNA
AND HER MONSTROUS CHILDREN!
the HYDRA
CERBERUS
HALF-WOMAN, HALF-SERPENT

BAD BREATH
THE HARPIES
SHRIEKING, GREEDY BIRDS WITH WOMEN'S HEADS
THE SIRENS HALF-WOMEN, HALF-VULTURES

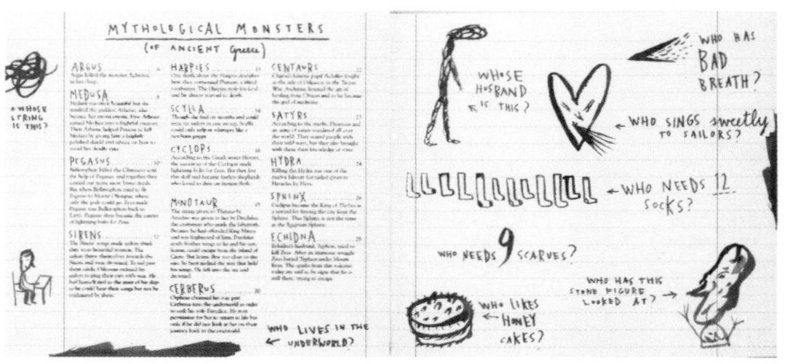

MYTHOLOGICAL MONSTERS
(of ANCIENT Greece)
ARGUS
MEDUSA
PEGASUS
SIRENS
CERBERUS
HARPIES
SCYLLA
CYCLOPS
MINOTAUR
CENTAURS
SATYRS
HYDRA
SPHINX
ECHIDNA
WHO LIVES IN THE UNDERWORLD?
WHOSE HUSBAND IS THIS?
WHO HAS BAD BREATH?
WHO SINGS sweetly TO SAILORS?
WHO NEEDS 12 SOCKS?
WHO NEEDS 9 SCARVES?
WHO LIKES HONEY CAKES?
WHO HAS THIS STONE FIGURE LOOKED AT?

6

7

8

9

10

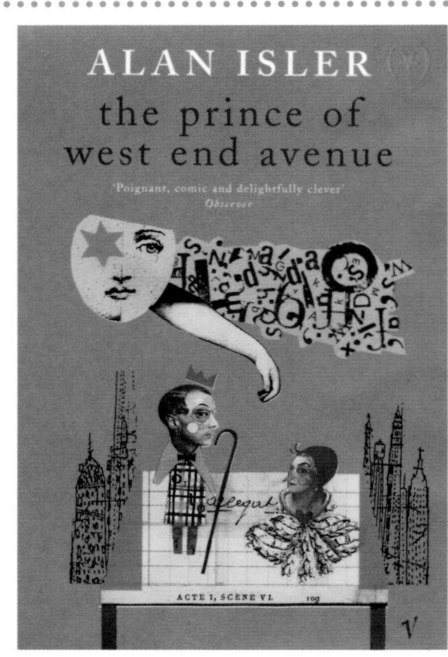

11

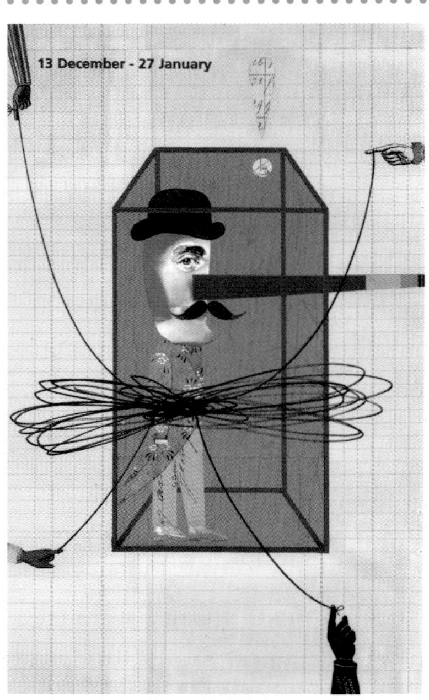

6 Cover, *The New Faber Book of Childeren's Verse*, edited by Matthew Sweeney / Faber and Faber / United Kingdom / 2001
7 Cover, *Kraven Images*, by Alan Isler / Vintage / United Kingdom / 1998
8 First-class stamp celebrating the emancipation of woman through the invention of the bicycle / Royal Mail / United Kingdom / 1999
9 Cover, *Where Are You, Robert?*, by Hans Magnus Enzensberger / Hamish Hamilton / Untited Kingdom / 2000
10 Cover, *The Prince of West End Avenue*, by Alan Isler / Vintage / United Kingdom / 1996
11 Poster for play *The Magistrate*, by A. Wing Pinero / Royal Exchange Theatre, Manchester / United Kingdom / 2001
12 "Airport" personal piece / 2000
13 Page from *A Dog's Life*, written, illustrated, and designed by Sara Fanelli / Heinemann Young Books / United Kingdom / 1998
14 "Six Characters in Search of an Author" personal piece / 2002
15 Print advertisement for Nat West bank air-miles program / Nat West / United Kingdom / 1999

Sara Fanelli

12

MINISTERO DELLE COMUNICAZIONI
FERROVIE DELLO STATO
SERVIZIO MATERIALE E TRAZIONE
AiRport

13

DOGS
Greyhound
BULLDOG (French)
As the proverb goes:
dogs are like to their mistresses
PLATO

14

uN povero DIAVOLO
6 characters in search of an AUTHOR
1
2
3
4
5
6

15

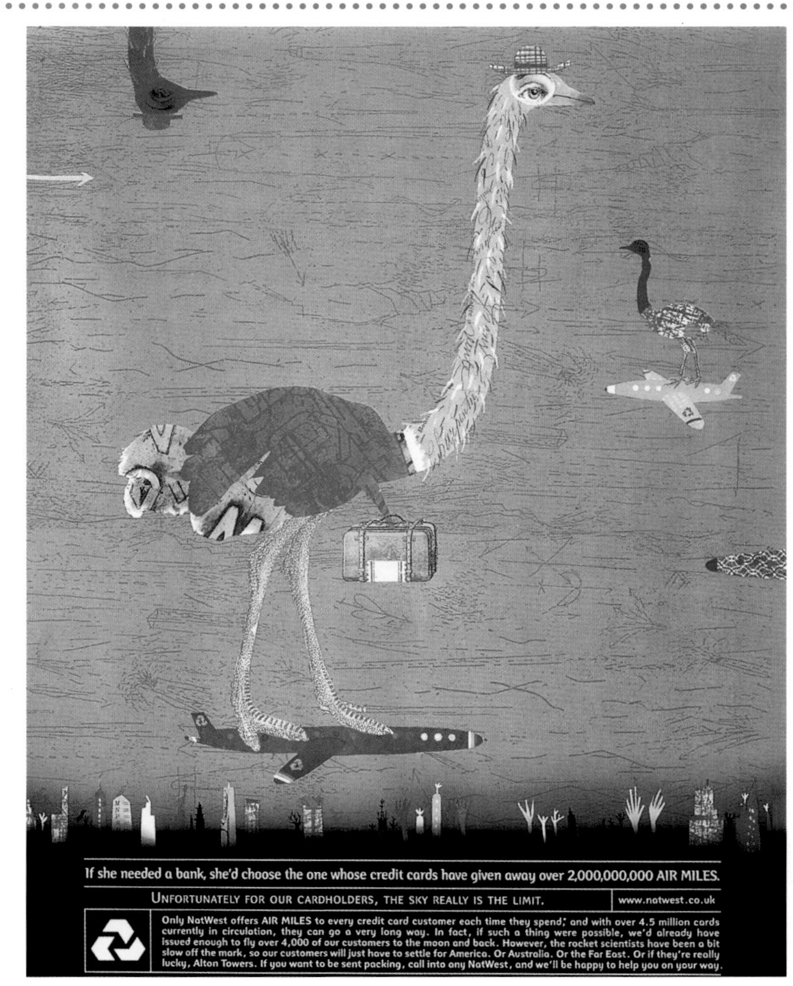
If she needed a bank, she'd choose the one whose credit cards have given away over 2,000,000,000 AIR MILES.
UNFORTUNATELY FOR OUR CARDHOLDERS, THE SKY REALLY IS THE LIMIT.
www.natwest.co.uk
Only NatWest offers AIR MILES to every credit card customer each time they spend;* and with over 4.5 million cards currently in circulation, they can go a very long way. In fact, if such a thing were possible, we'd already have issued enough to fly over 4,000 of our customers to the moon and back. However, the rocket scientists have been a bit slow off the mark, so our customers will just have to settle for America. Or Australia. Or the Far East. Or if they're really lucky, Alton Towers. If you want to be sent packing, call into any NatWest, and we'll be happy to help you on your way.

The first clue about Isidro Ferrer is his own personal symbol: a sharpened pencil bound by string to a triangular section of wood. The combination of elements creates the form of a gun, menacing and ready for action. It is so appropriate for someone who communicates so simply and so spontaneously and who is ready for the next opportunity and the next solution. His work is full of information, often combining found items with simple graphic elements. The solutions are eclectic, whimsical, and diverse. •• Born in Madrid in 1963, Ferrer initially studied drama. Somewhere between completing his acting studies and starting his design studio, he developed his illustrational craft in the workshop of graphic designer Peret in Barcelona. And then in partnership with three other designers he founded the Studio Camaleon in Zaragoza. Since 1996 he has run his own studio in Huesca where he applies his talents to a diverse range of projects. Editorial design, animation, artistic direction, exhibition design, comics, and work for television leave him with a broad spectrum of graphic design-solutions. To date he has had seventeen books published, in France, Portugal, and Spain. His work has been the subject of numerous national and international exhibitions. In the year 2000 he was inducted into the Alliance Graphique Internationale (AGI). To my mind he is one of a rare breed of graphic designer who has the ability to dramatically communicate a message and at the same time bring a smile to those who encounter his works. •• Ken Cato ••

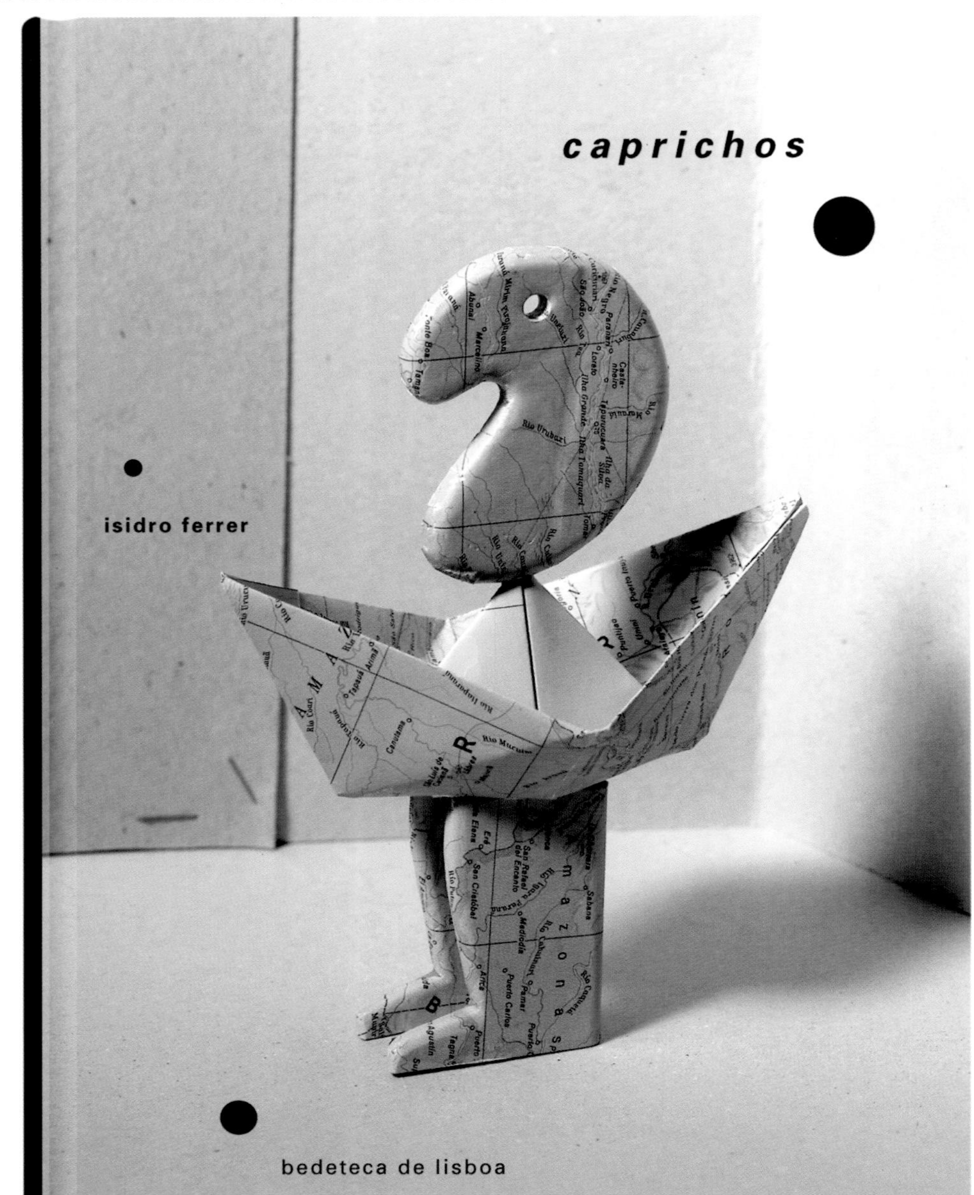

1

1 Cover, *Caprichos*, by Isidro Ferrer / Bedeteca de Lisboa / Portugal / 2000 /
2 *Lapiz* (pencil) personal image / Spain / 2000
3 Poster for celebration of Luis Buñuel's centennial / Government of Aragon / Spain / 2001
4 Cover, *Sociedad General de Autores y Editores* (General Society of Editors and Authors) annual / SGAE / Spain / 2002
5 Poster for play *Walter Negro, el asesino casual*, by José Luis Esteban / El Figurante / Spain / 2001
6 Poster for the international promotion of Spanish cinema / Ministry of Foreign Affairs / Spain / 2002

2

Isidro Ferrer

Huesca, Spain

3

NORTE
1900-2000
Luis Buñuel

4

'02
anuario
sgae
2002
de
las
artes
escénicas,
musicales
y
audiovisuales
sgae
sgae
2002
42

5

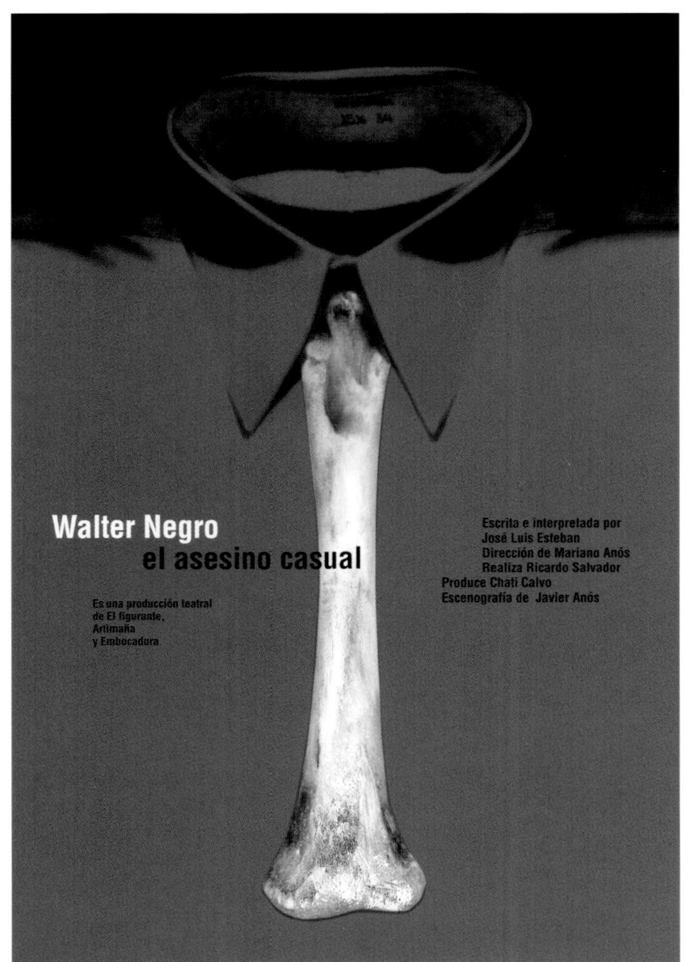
Walter Negro
el asesino casual
Es una producción teatral
de El figurante,
Artimaña
y Embocadura
Escrita e interpretada por
José Luis Esteban
Dirección de Mariano Anós
Realiza Ricardo Salvador
Produce Chati Calvo
Escenografía de Javier Anós

6

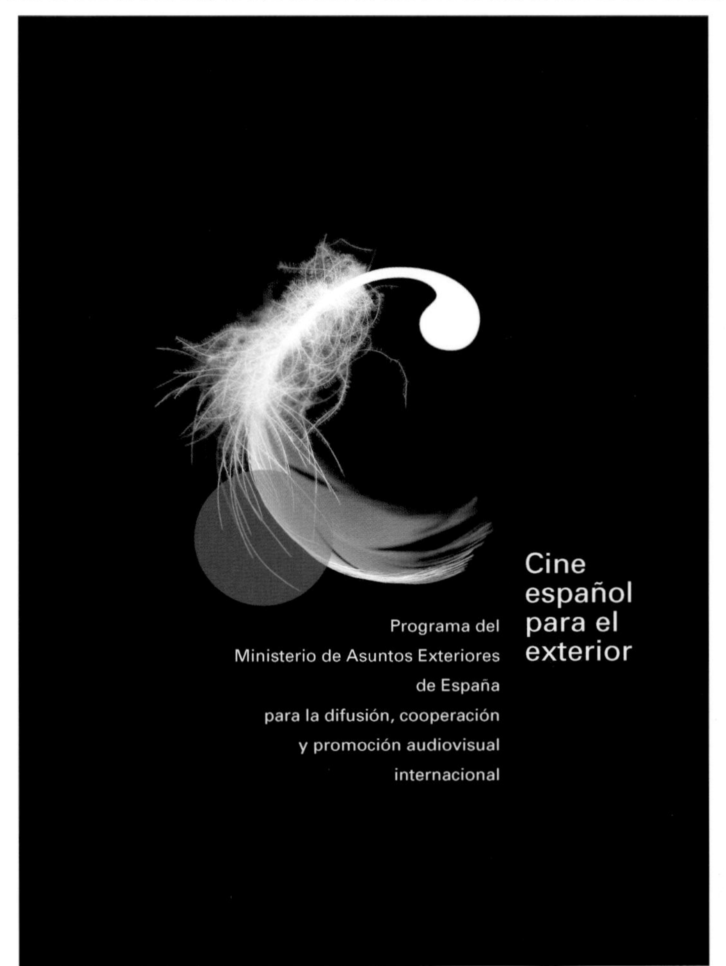
Cine
español
para el
exterior
Programa del
Ministerio de Asuntos Exteriores
de España
para la difusión, cooperación
y promoción audiovisual
internacional

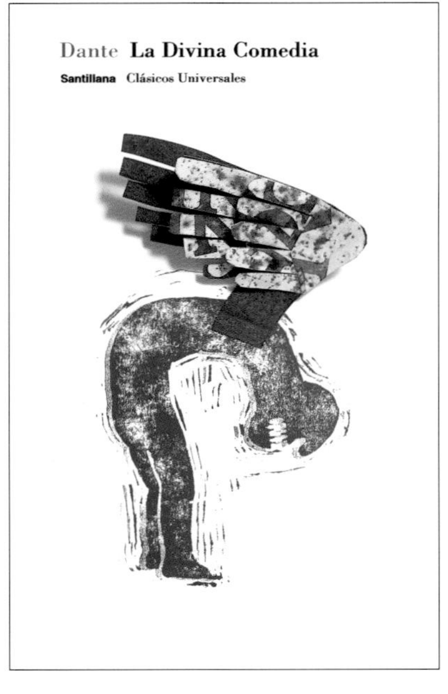

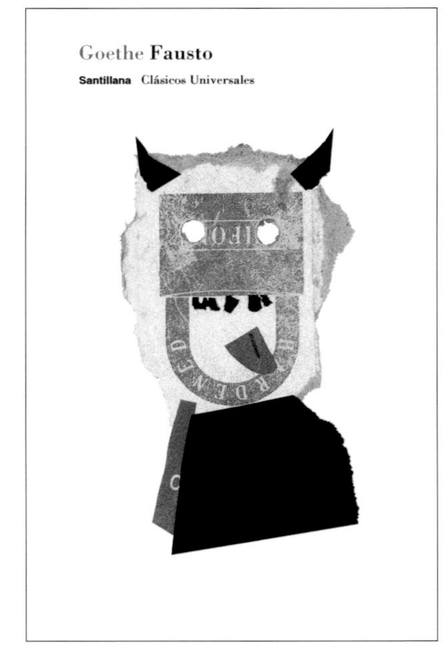

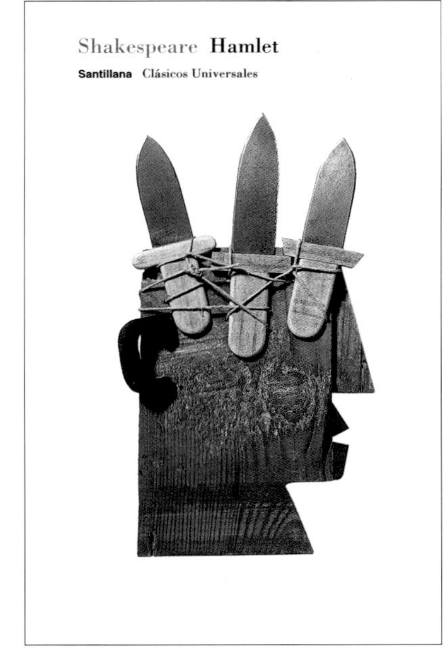

7 8 9

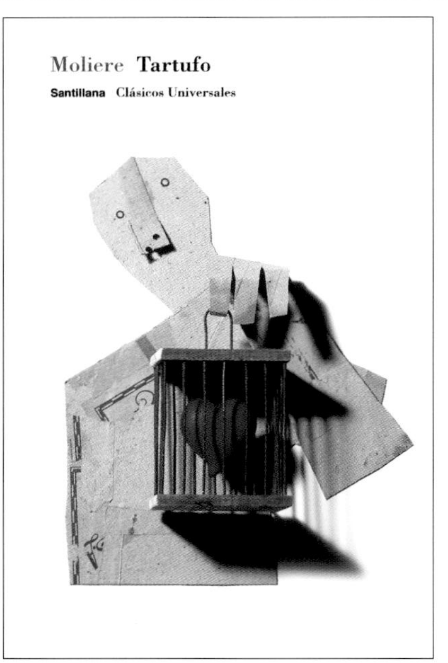

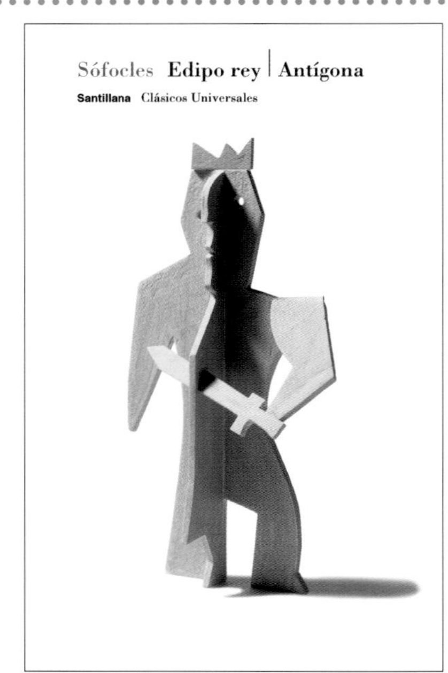

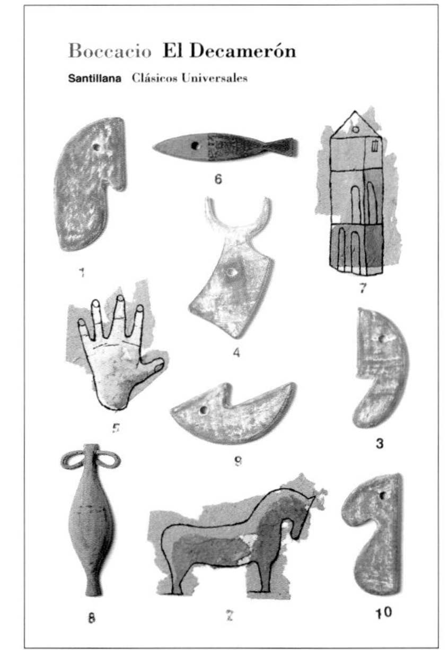

10 11 12

7–12 Book covers for Clásicos Universales paperback collection / Editorial Santillana / Spain / 1999–2000
13 Poster for paper-recycling festival in Zaragoza / Fundación ecología y desarrollo / Spain / 2000
14 Poster for South Pyrenees music festival / Diputación Provincial de Huesca / 1999
15 Poster for Jeanne d'Arc festival in Rouen / Municipality of Rouen / France / 2002
16 Poster for 12th theater festival in Aragon / Government of Aragon / Spain / 1998
17 Poster homage for Toulouse-Lautrec's centennial / Nouveau Salon des Cent / France / 2001
18 Poster for play *Ubu Rey*, by Alfred Jarry / University of Zaragoza / Spain / 1996
19 Poster for bullfighting festival / DDI-AEPD / Spain / 2002
20 Cover, *La illustración* magazine / Asociación Española de Ilustradores Profesionales / Spain / 1998
21 Antiwar poster / Instituto Europeo de Design / Spain / 2001
22 Poster for exhibition on Spanish graphic design in Berlin / DDI-SEACEX / Germany / 2002
23 Poster for exhibition of Isidro Ferrer's work / Universidad Nacional a Distancia / Spain / 2003

Isidro Ferrer

13 14

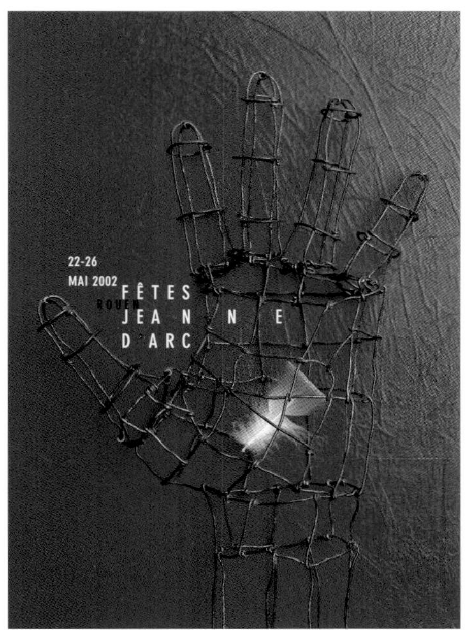

22-26
MAI 2002
ROUEN
FÊTES
JEANNE
D'ARC

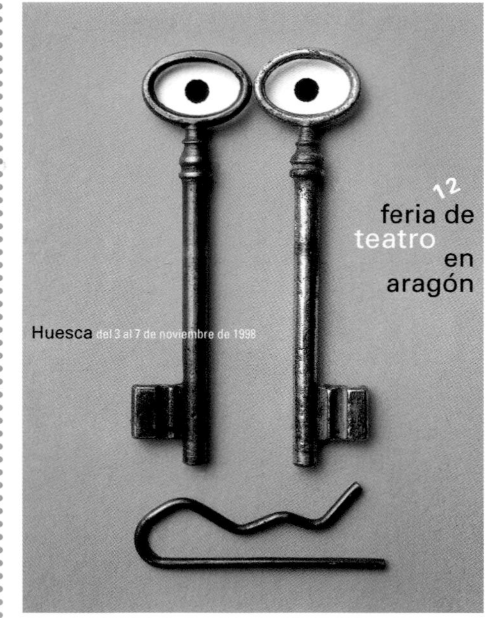

12
feria de
teatro
en
aragón
Huesca del 3 al 7 de noviembre de 1998

NOUVEAU SALON DES CENT EXPOSITION INTERNATIONALE D'AFFICHES.
HOMMAGE À TOULOUSSE-LAUTREC

15 16 17

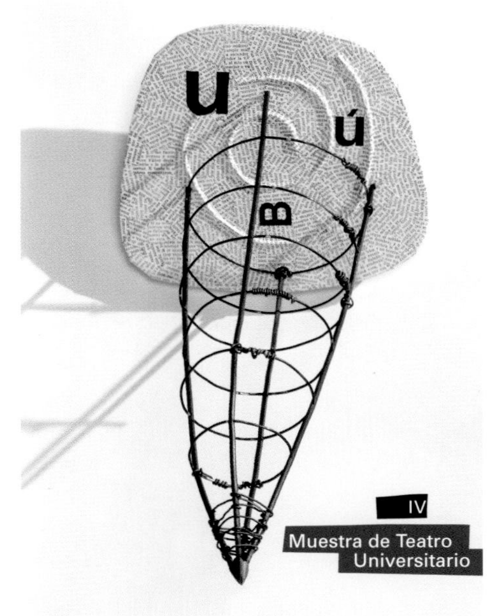

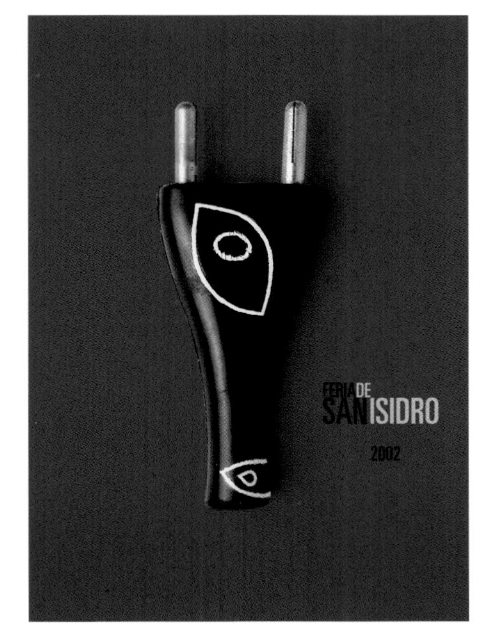

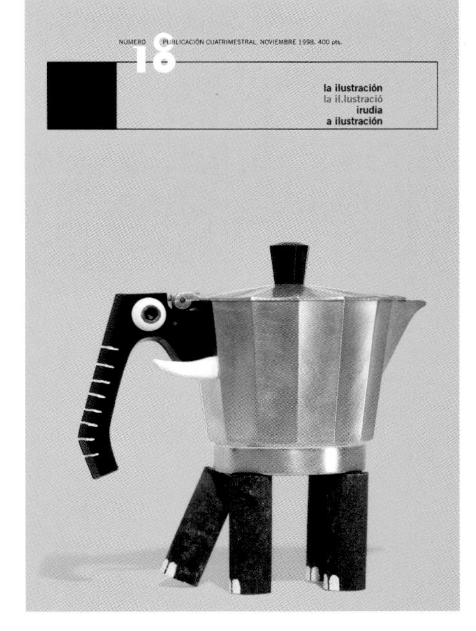

NÚMERO 18 PUBLICACIÓN CUATRIMESTRAL. NOVIEMBRE 1998. 400 pts.
la ilustración
la il.lustració
irudia
a ilustración

18 19 20

sala de exposiciones
de la UNED, argensola
55, barbastro
PAISAJE
DIARIO
isidro ferrer
del 15 de noviembre
al 12 de diciembre
UNED
FUNDACIÓN "RAMON J. SENDER"
BARBASTRO

21 22 23

Laurent Fétis developed an original visual language informed by vector art, photography, graffiti, airbrush, and Kippenberger. (Martin Kippenberger is quoted prominently in *ABC+*, Fétis's new monograph: "*Jetzt geh ich in den Birkenwald, denn meine Pillen wirken bald*" [Now I'll head for the birch forest as my pills will be taking effect soon].) ••Producing work for all the magazines a young designer wants to be featured in (*Dazed and Confused*, *The Face*, etc.) and working for all the clients a young designer would like to be associated with (Beck, Björk, etc.), he sits at that interestingly blurred border where design and art meet. ••Fétis sees tight analogies between design and pop music: "Each has its codes, its skeleton, its format, and finds itself in a situation of permanent research. One radically transformed the twentieth-century music scene. However, if you open a general encyclopedia of music, it takes up only a few lines. For its part, graphic design—more so than art—has transformed the visual scene of the past twenty years, yet it remains excluded from the history of art and is for this reason decontextualized." ••One of his most striking pieces is a poster for Audiolab, a daring typographic tour de force synthesizing different stylistic and formal questions into an organic whole. "I am led only by the idea of making the things I wish to see exist at a given time. It remains very intuitive. I am far from being a formalist, to my regret, moreover, as everything would be so much more simple." ••Stefan Sagmeister••

1
2
3

1–3 CD packaging, *Rocker's Delight* compilation (with Elisabeth Arkhipoff) / Quatermass / Belgium / 2002
4–6 Cover and spreads, *ABC+* by Laurent Fétis / Die Gestalten Verlag / Germany / 2002
7–10 Cover and spreads, *Ronan et Erwan Bouroullec–Catalogue de raison*, by Laurent Le Bon / Editions Ceo and Editions Images Modernes / Paris / 2002

Laurent Fétis

Paris

abc+
Laurent Fétis
EXTRA
DEBILE
GENIAL
COOL
SUPER

7
8
9
10

Ronan et Erwan
Bouroullec
Catalogue de raison

4
5
6

zones of behaviour,
sensation, information:
design and a few
of its paradoxes.'

2001
1991
1996
1998
1992
1997
1993
1994
1995
1999
2000

11

12

13

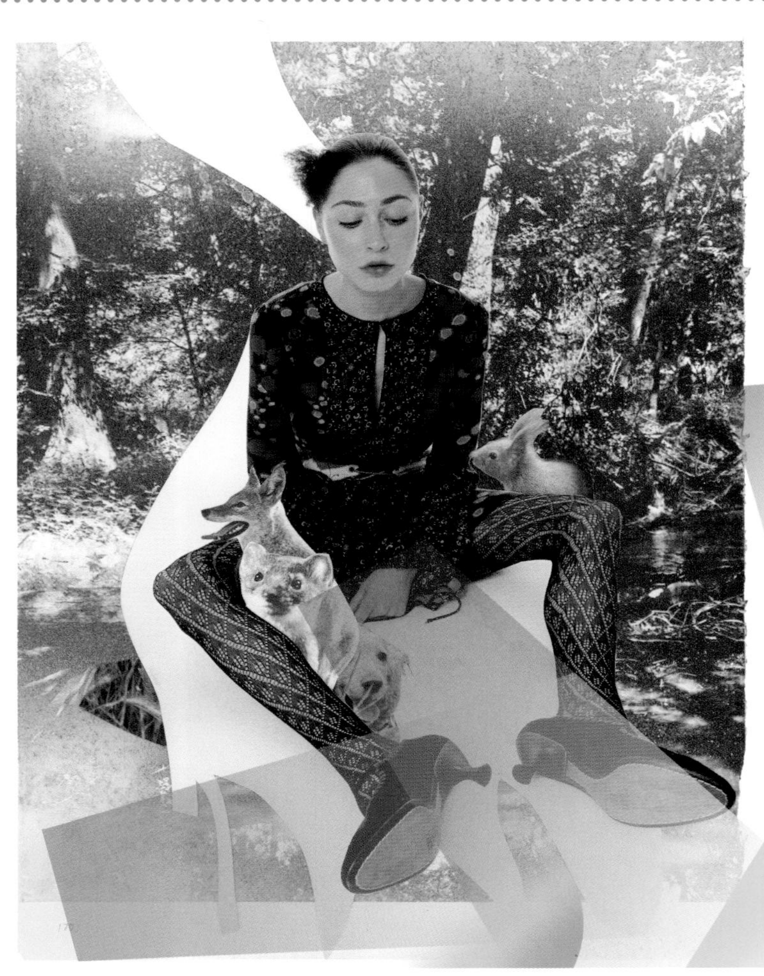

14

11 Poster for Beck's "Sea Change" tour 2002-2003 / USA / 2002
12 Poster project for film *Dancer in the Dark* / Liberator and Zentropa Entertainment / France and Germany / 2000
13 Visual identity, *Into You* magazine / Into you / 2001 / Every issue is published in different place and format.
14 Page from *Vogue Nippon* with clothes by Anna Sui (with Elisabeth Arkhipoff) / Vogue Nippon / Japan / 2002
15 Maxi-vinyl design, *Instant Love*, by Mellow / East-West / United kingdom / 1999
16 Visual identity for a sonic programmation project Audiolab / Caisse des dépôts et consignation / France / 2000

Laurent Fétis

15

mellow
instant love

/500

mellow
instant love

EW206T 3984-29060-0 EW231

This Side
1/Original Version
2/Andy Votel remix

Other Side
3/Nick Mc Cabe remix

16

Field Study came to my attention through an eccentric self-promotional mailer that landed on my desk last summer: an old-fashioned buff board document folder containing a pleasingly motley collection of printed papers and photographs fastened upon two metal binding prongs. The cover carried a text printed in brown and promoted the simple virtue of knowing your subject. This modest piece of softsell projected the aura of a school classroom; items gathered on a field trip and presented for inspection. Inside were two business cards; a sixteen-page leaflet folding down to the size of a postcard emblazoned with the word *Study*; two color photographs, one of stuffed llamas, the other of stuffed ibex; and, visible underneath that, an off-white cotton-fiber letterhead, rubber-stamped in silver at the top left corner and laser-printed with a letter addressed to UNA from someone called Roy Brooks who claimed to know me. He said he had participated in a workshop I held at North Carolina State University more than six years before. In fact his name was familiar, but for a different reason. It turns out this was the same Roy Brooks whose design assistance was credited on a significant number of J. Abbott Miller projects we had just laid out for the "Reputations" interview in *Eye* no. 45, which had been sent to press just days before. • • Through this mailer, Brooks was informing me that he had set up his own company with fellow NC State grad Matthew Peterson. Here he was reporting in with the evidence of original research gathered from his and his partner's formative graphic-designing experience so far. It was impressive. It turns out that Peterson has had an equally challenging, rewarding, and enviable apprenticeship to write home about; he worked under Andrew Blauvelt at the Walker Art Center in Minneapolis. With that in mind, we should all be expecting a hell of a lot from them. • • The Field Study mailer seems to emerge out of a documentary ethos, from a gentler age, free of spin. It's a dialect in which design is more about the articulation of contents (fragments of raw material) that speak through being unmodified, remaining in their original, unadulterated form, rather than becoming subsumed by the rules of an aesthetic system susceptible to valuing only uniformity. For Field Study, it's the pure, untutored charm of formats unalloyed with the prevailing design canon that hold their attention. • • Nick Bell • •

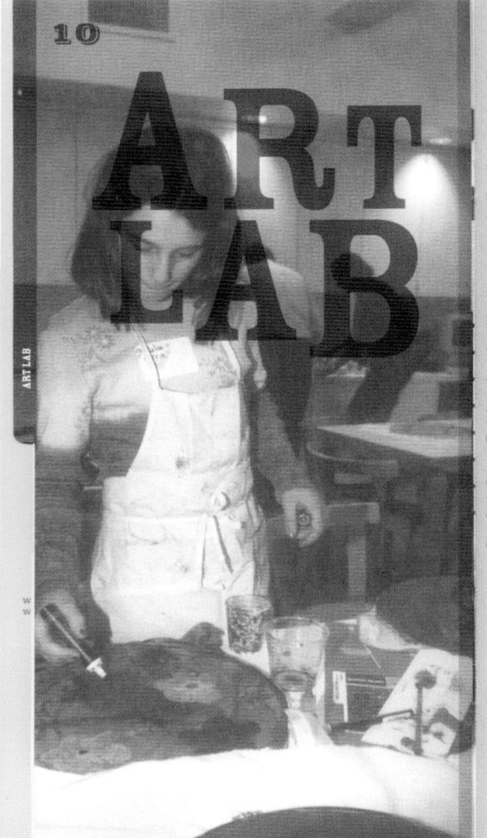

10
11
ART LAB
A HANDS-ON, CREATIVE WAY TO ENHANCE YOUR TOUR
Available in conjunction with a guided tour of the galleries or the Minneapolis Sculpture Garden, the Art Lab offers hands-on learning activities for students of all ages. Projects are designed to help students further explore the ideas and themes covered during their tour. An Art Lab lasts 45–60 minutes in addition to a tour. The fee is $1 per student. For availability, call 612.375.7609. For information on scheduling a tour, see page 9.
new this year!
Art Lab Installation: OPEN FACE by Ta-Coumba Aiken
ON VIEW THROUGH MARCH 3, 2001
CLASSROOM MATERIALS
MUSEUM INFORMATION

1
2

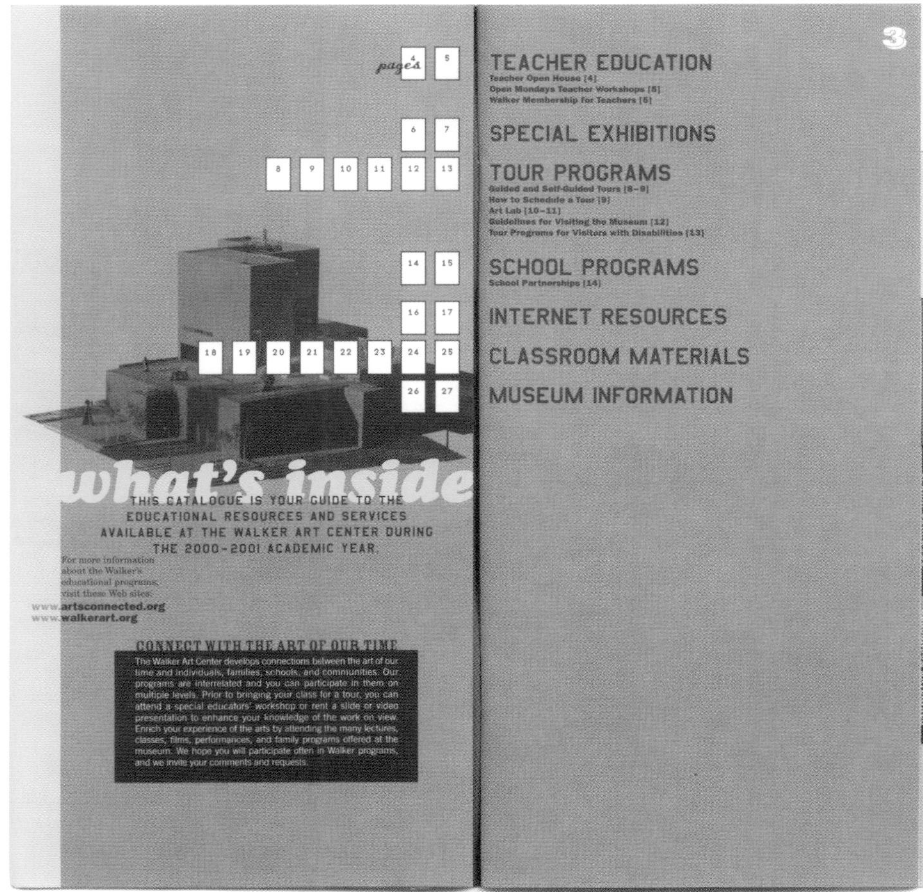

3
pages
TEACHER EDUCATION
SPECIAL EXHIBITIONS
TOUR PROGRAMS
SCHOOL PROGRAMS
INTERNET RESOURCES
CLASSROOM MATERIALS
MUSEUM INFORMATION
what's inside
THIS CATALOGUE IS YOUR GUIDE TO THE EDUCATIONAL RESOURCES AND SERVICES AVAILABLE AT THE WALKER ART CENTER DURING THE 2000–2001 ACADEMIC YEAR.
www.artsconnected.org
www.walkerart.org
CONNECT WITH THE ART OF OUR TIME

1–2 Spreads from Walker Art Center 2000–2001 education catalogue (with Andrew Blauvelt) / Walker Art Center / USA / 2000
3 Poster for the GraficEurope:Pan-European Graphic Design Conference / Spain / 2003
4–6 Poster and CD packaging, *Lullaby for Sue*, by Clogs / Brassland Records / USA / 2003

Field Study

Chicago

③

④

"Clogs consist of four classically trained instrumentalists who work eerie, looping folk melodies through a vortex of delicately bowed and struck strings to beautiful 'lost at sea' effect."

The Wire

"Fans of Sigur Rós, Rachel's, and other post-rock ensembles who know how to listen in respectful silence to a live performance will have no trouble appreciating the softly evocative compositions."

The New Yorker

"Few new CDs in any genre will do as much to challenge the way you listen to music."

Philadelphia City Paper

"Great band names of our time: what d'ya call yr contemporary classical outfit with pretensions to be Satie, Stravinsky, Sigur Rós, and a more approachable Godspeed? Clogs. Sweet."

Careless Talk Costs Lives

LULLABY FOR SUE

CLOGS

IN STORES NOW

OFFICIAL SITE:
www.clogsmusic.com

Brassland

WWW.BRASSLAND.ORG info@brassland.org

Manufactured & Distributed in Europe by Southern Records WWW.SOUTHERN.NET info@southern.net

NOW ON TOUR

⑤⑥

Assuming risk in hope of gain

Meditating on or pondering a subject

Suggesting, testing and examining

Curiosity and questioning

Theorizing vs. demonstrating

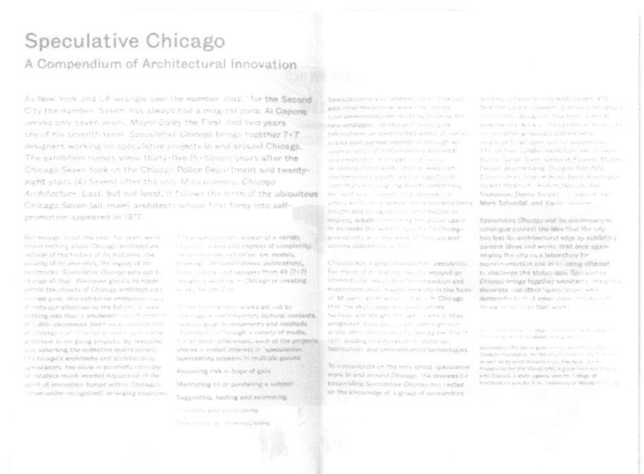

GALLERY 400
Speculative
Chicago
A Compendium of Architectural Innovation
FEBRUARY 25 – MARCH 29 2003
Including works and projects by 49 architects, designers, theorists and other 'speculators' working in Chicago or building projects in Chicago, the exhibition argues that innovation concerning the built environment continues to thrive in the 'city that works.'
OPENING RECEPTION
Wednesday, February 26 4–7 pm
Gallery 400, 1240 West Harrison Street
PANEL DISCUSSION
Moderator and 5–6 exhibitors
Thursday, March 27 6 pm
Gallery 400, 1240 West Harrison Street

7 Poster for concert by The National / Brassland Records / USA / 2002
8–10 Unfoldable invitation/poster for *Speculative Chicago* exhibition / Gallery 400–University of Illinois at Chicago / USA / 2002
11–12 Field Study self-promotional package / 2002
13–14 Front and back of opening announcement mailing with detachable business cards / Geotrack, Inc. / USA / 2003

In beginning a study of the trees the student should be careful to confine himself to well-established facts. Once started he should proceed slowly, assimilating each new discovery before seeking another. He should begin with the trees nearest home, and, as he gradually grows to know these in all their aspects, should extend his trips afield. Not only should he be able to name the trees when they are fully clothed in their summer dress, but he should know as readily these same trees when the leaves have fallen and only the bare branches stand silhouetted against the sky. Then, and only then, will he derive the utmost satisfaction from his efforts.

From "Michigan Trees," by Charles Herbert Otis

11
12

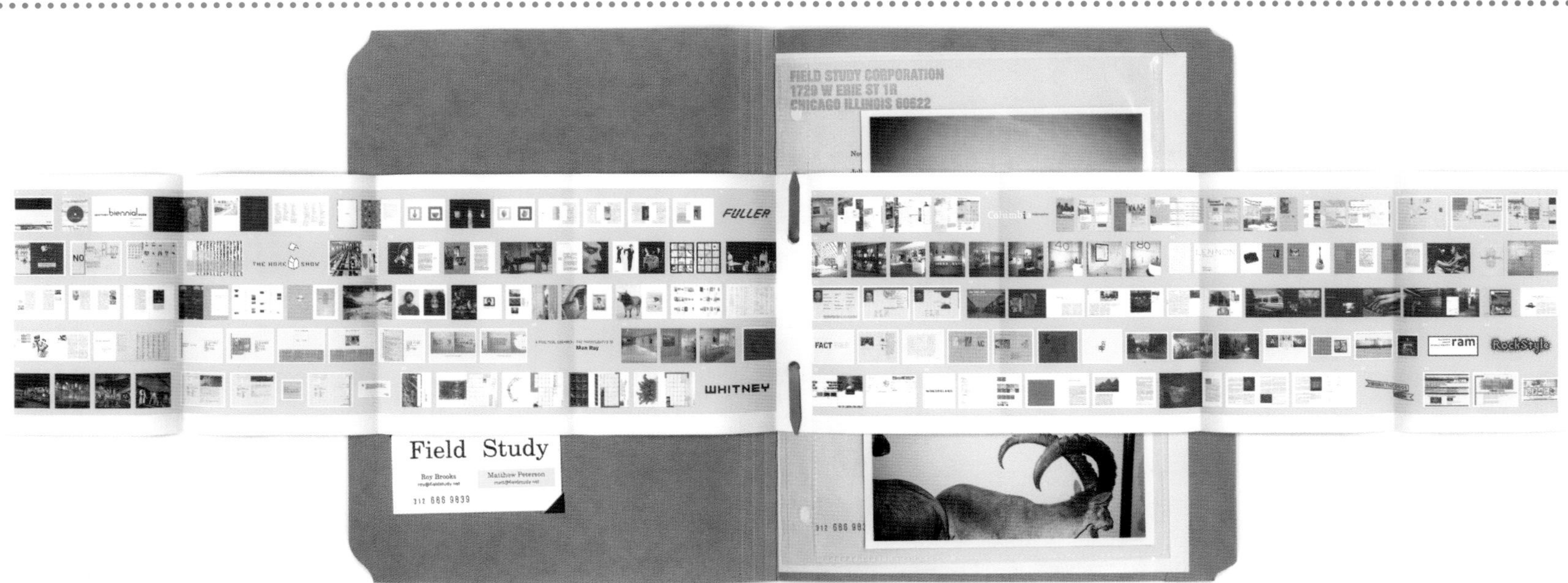

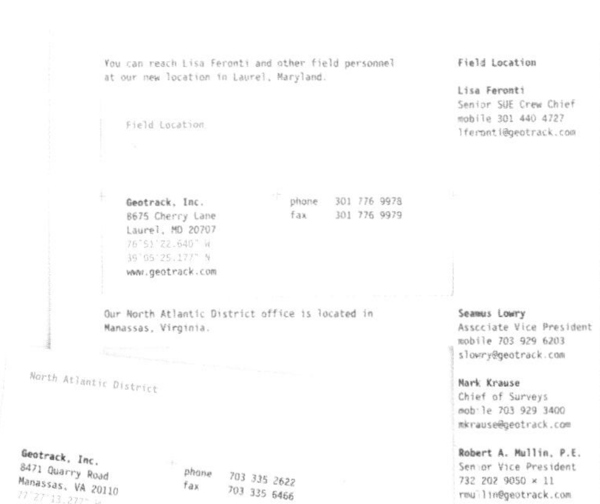

You can reach Lisa Feronti and other field personnel at our new location in Laurel, Maryland.
Field Location
Geotrack, Inc.
8675 Cherry Lane
Laurel, MD 20707
76°51'22.640" W
39°05'25.177" N
www.geotrack.com
phone 301 776 9978
fax 301 776 9979
Our North Atlantic District office is located in Manassas, Virginia.
North Atlantic District
Geotrack, Inc.
8471 Quarry Road
Manassas, VA 20110
www.geotrack.com
phone 703 335 2622
fax 703 335 6466
Field Location
Lisa Feronti
Senior SUE Crew Chief
mobile 301 440 4727
lferonti@geotrack.com
Seamus Lowry
Associate Vice President
mobile 703 929 6203
slowry@geotrack.com
Mark Krause
Chief of Surveys
mobile 703 929 3400
mkrause@geotrack.com
Robert A. Mullin, P.E.
Senior Vice President
732 202 9050 x 11
rmullin@geotrack.com
+geotrack
Geotrack, Inc.
1325 Tri-State Parkway
Suite 375
Gurnee, IL 60031

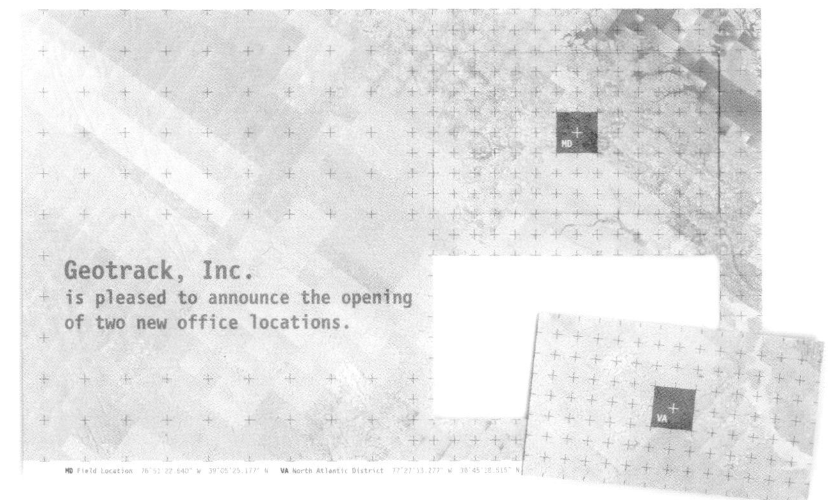

Geotrack, Inc.
is pleased to announce the opening
of two new office locations.
MD
VA

13 14

Like most designers today, Lizzie Finn does not work without a computer, but the first tools she uses are pencil and paper, followed by needle, thread, and sewing machine. Finn has long loved the century-old history of traditional household crafts but was further inspired by 1970s feminists who adopted domestic stitching in their protest signs for equal rights. Sewing became a symbol the oppressed domestic female used to fight male dominance. A certain subversiveness in Finn's work is evident, but her passion for sewing, do-it-yourself, and the handmade would last and strive far beyond all sex battles.•• Finn's unique interest emerged in 2000 with a CD cover for the British house band Moloko. A beautiful cross-stitched logo on top of a dense group shot of about thirty colorful rag-doll animals. The title she proposed with the design was "Things to Make and Do," which is also the title of her favorite do-it-yourself magazine. The group loved both design and title. The inside CD booklet corresponds to the cover language and is equally surprising. In typical do-it-yourself style, Finn gives instructions for cutting and sewing one of the rag cats on the cover. Later, a few of the animals were used as solo primary subjects for promotional singles.•• "Things to make and do" became Finn's working philosophy. The nature of her work naturally attracted the international clothing and textile industries that commission both communication and product design. Editorial illustrations for cutting-edge trend and fashion magazines were another source of work. Technique and form seem to deeply influence the content of her output.•• In her recent "Eye Spy" pages for *Dazed and Confused* she brilliantly pushed further in her effort to discover new speculative dimensions by combining sewing, patchwork, and erotic imagery. In considering Finn's provocations the question to ask could be, Design by woman or woman by design?•• Omar Vulpinari••

1

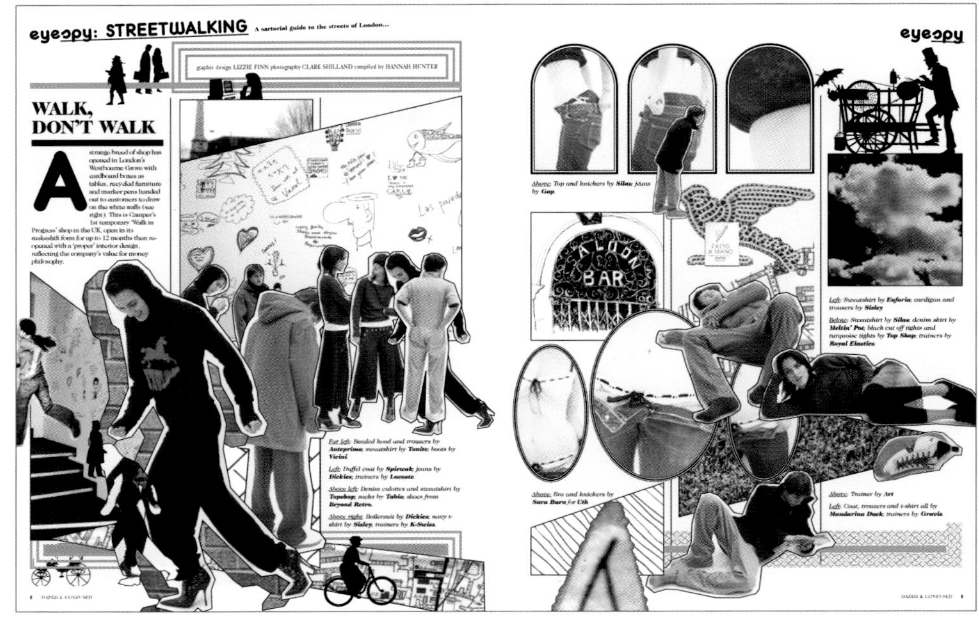

2

3

1–3 "Eye Spy" spreads, *Dazed and Confused* magazine (photography Clare Shilland) / Dazed and Confused / United Kingdom / 2003

4–9 CD packaging and design, *Things to Make and Do* album and singles "Indigo" and "Pure Pleasure Seeker" by Moloko / The Echo Label-Chrysalis / United Kingdom / 2000

Lizzie Finn

London

MOLOKO
THINGS
TO MAKE
AND DO

4
5
6

7
8
9

MOLOKO
INDIGO

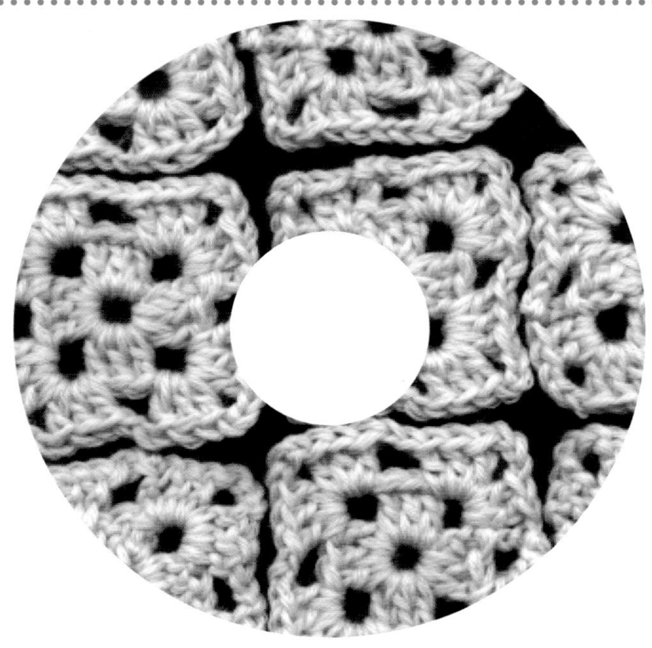

MOLOKO
PURE
PLEASURE
SEEKER

10

11 12

Lizzie Finn

10 Illustration for *150 B&T*, book published by printer Butler and Tanner in celebration of their 150th anniversary / Butler and Tanner / United Kingdom / 2001
11–12 "Sit back & Relax" stitch and spread for *Relax Magazine* / Relax Magazine / Japan / 2002
13–14 Stitch and opening spread on UK fashion brand Silas for *Relax Magazine* / Relax Magazine / Japan / 2001
15 Front and back cover and spreads from Silas promotional catalogue, autumn/winter 1999–2000 / Silas / United Kingdom / 1999

SILAS & MARIA

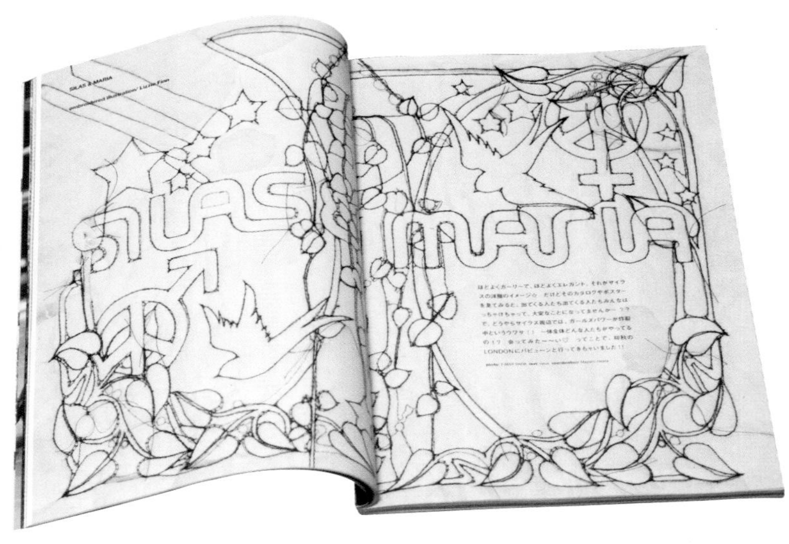

SILAS & MARIA

13 14

The festivities went on till the sun rose the next morn. The princesses together, laughed and jested and everything was happy ever after ...
LET ME BITE YOUR APPLE LUV. HEH ..HEH.. HEH
YOU'RE LOOKING WELL DESPITE YOUR TENDENCY TO DRIBBLE
OH HONESTLY OSRIC! - EATING FROM THE SWORD IS SO COMMON!
YEAH!
WOW!
YOU DRUNK IT ALL DIDN'T YOU, YOU FIKEY BASTARD
THE CHEF HAS SURPASSED HIMSELF WITH THIS ROAST WILD BOAR
THE END
But wait! ... Can you spot the evil Hobbit-Wizard dancing his evil jig yet again!?
16
SILAS
A/W
99/00
♥ PHOTO STORY! ♥
♥ Fun! ♥
Love!
Fighting!

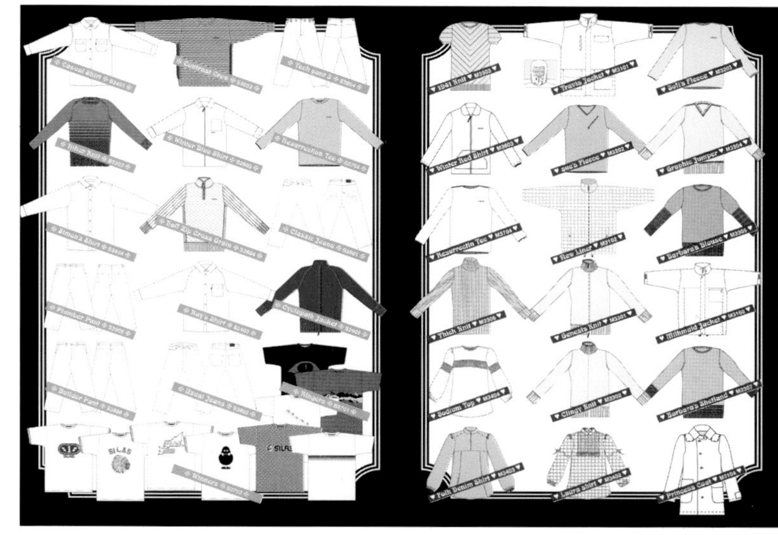

15

At the Fayre the villagers partook of the traditional activities: Apple swallowing ...
... Sword swallowing ...
... the Dance of the evil Goat ...
... Tug o' war ...
... ??? ...
... and the Handsome Princes favourite sport ... Pony wrestling
I'D SNAG HIM!
... Unbeknown to the Handsome Prince both princesses had fallen for his manly ways.
HE'S SO HANDSOME – I'D DANCE THE NIGHT AWAY WITH HIM!
A romance soon blossomed ...
I'M SO HAPPY I COULD JUST DIE!
YEAH. ME TOO.
With both princesses! ... The prince was playing a dangerous game
FOOL
LOOK AT THAT BEAUTIFUL SUNSET!
Unbeknown to the young lovers, the devious evil Hobbit-Wizard had witnessed his double-dating. He saw an opportunity for mischief.
Overcome by joy at the prospect of spreading misery he danced his evil jig to summon the evil Goat-demon
The story continues on page 17 ...

The Good Queen
The Bad King
The Handsome Prince
The Good Princess
The Bad Princess
The Evil Hobbit-wizard
The Good Army
The Bad Army
Love at First Fight!
A FAIRY TALE OF HONOUR, LUST AND EVIL DANCES
ONCE UPON A TIME IN A LAND FAR AWAY THERE WAS A KING AND QUEEN WHO HATED EACH OTHER SO THEY EACH WENT TO LIVE IN CASTLES ON OPPOSITE SIDES OF THE KINGDOM. THEY HAD TWO BEAUTIFUL DAUGHTERS WHO WERE BITTER RIVALS.
THE GOOD PRINCESS LIVED WITH THE QUEEN AND THE BAD PRINCESS LIVED WITH THE KING. BOTH SPENT THEIR DAYS WORKING ON THE LATEST TAPESTRY STITCHES AND DREAMING OF HANDSOME PRINCES ...
WITH A HEY NONNY-NOH, TODAY IS SPRING!
GOTCHA! - YOU SMALL FURRY BASTARD.

Amy Franceschini comes from a paradoxical Californian background. Her father was a corporate farmer (owner of a pesticide company), and her mother left him to embrace the worlds of organic farming and New Age philosophy. "I grew up bouncing between these conflicting logics," she recalls. "I spent half of my childhood with my father, cultivating 3,000 acres of irrigated farmlands, and the other half with my mother cultivating our consciousness through ideologies derivative of Rudolf Steiner, Sai Baba, Permaculture, and the like." • • In her design/art practice Franceschini thinks of herself as a biodynamic farmer. "Biodynamic farming is a model that speaks to a philosophy of mind, body, and spirit that I would like to employ into whatever I do: [It] involves restoring to the soil a balanced living condition through the application and use of the completely digested form of crude organic matter known as stabilized humus." She named her studio Futurefarmers and titled the anthology of their work published in 2002 *Harvest*. • • Another project, Games for the Masses, reveals a strong interest in social interaction. "Games for the Masses was an experiment in social interaction [...] I placed this fake game in the gallery and started it with a simple set of rules but told the players they could make up rules as they pleased. Over the course of one night the game evolved from a purely fantastical game played with seven kids to a complex gambling game played by four adults." • • In the project Holding Pattern, Franceschini combines social interaction with her innate concern for nature. "Holding Pattern addressed environmental problems suffered by wetlands and migratory birds as a result of population growth and economic expansion." Through her love for the intricate systems of nature, Franceschini works to create an awareness about the fragility of these systems. • • In her most recent work Franceschini has been trying to find the simplest way to get people to play together. "I recently made a 14-inch seesaw in a gallery show. A seesaw is really the simplest interactive architecture. It involves a certain amount of immediate cooperation and trust. • • Technology is an important factor in her work, but her relationship with it definitely remains love/hate. "On one hand I am completely fascinated and excited about new technologies, and on the other hand I want to run back to the forest. A piece of work should begin with an idea or a feeling about something. This idea should dictate the form and technology. A pencil is still a very powerful tool." • • Omar Vulpinari • •

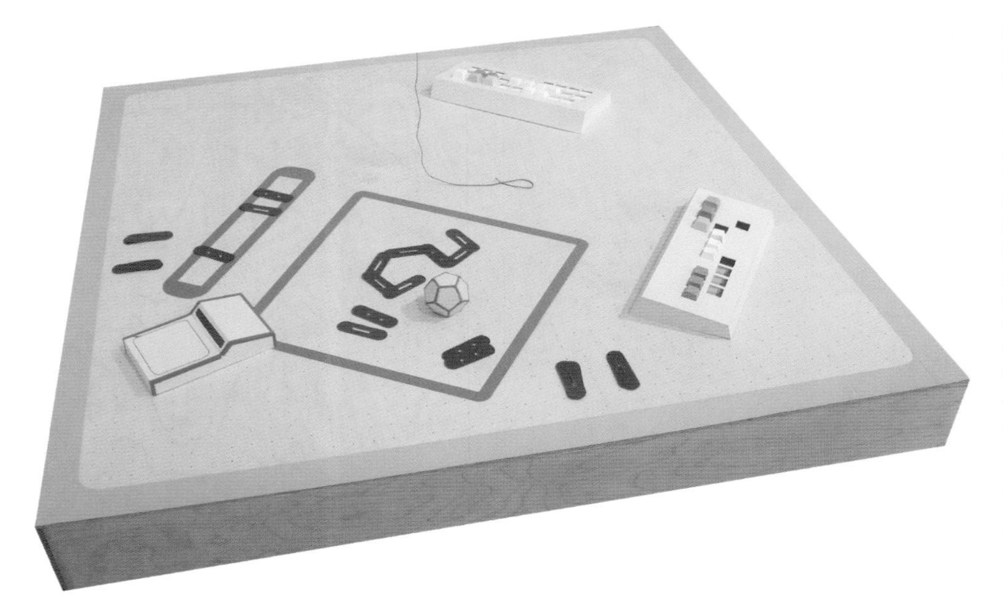

1

1 Games for the Masses at Jack Hanley Gallery, San Francisco / USA / 2003 / The game begins with three "open" rules that change while playing, allowing it to evolve at random to increasing intricacy.
2 Poster for *Communication What* exhibition, Venice / Italy / 2002
3 Logo for Amy Franceschini's design studio Futurefarmers / USA / 2002
4 "Seeds of Inspiration" poster for *Communication What* exhibition / Italy / 2002

Amy Franceschini

San Francisco

2

SEEDLINGS

SEEDS ARE THE MEMORY BANK OF NATURE

CONSERVE THE GENETIC DIVERSITY FOR THE FUTURE.

Seeds are magical: given proper stewardship, they will acclimate to specific areas over time. By growing them out, we weave the stories of our lives and seeds into an unending chain of community, tradition, and history.

3

4

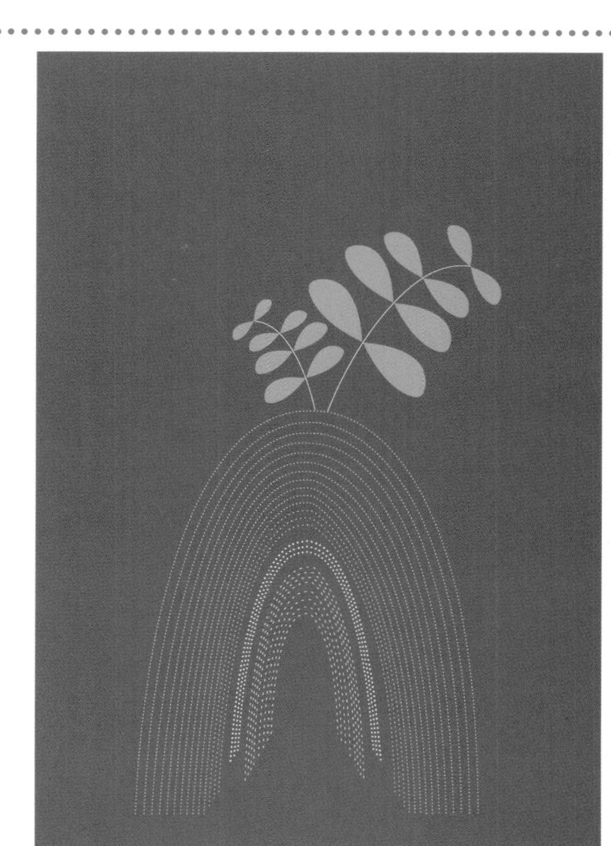

5

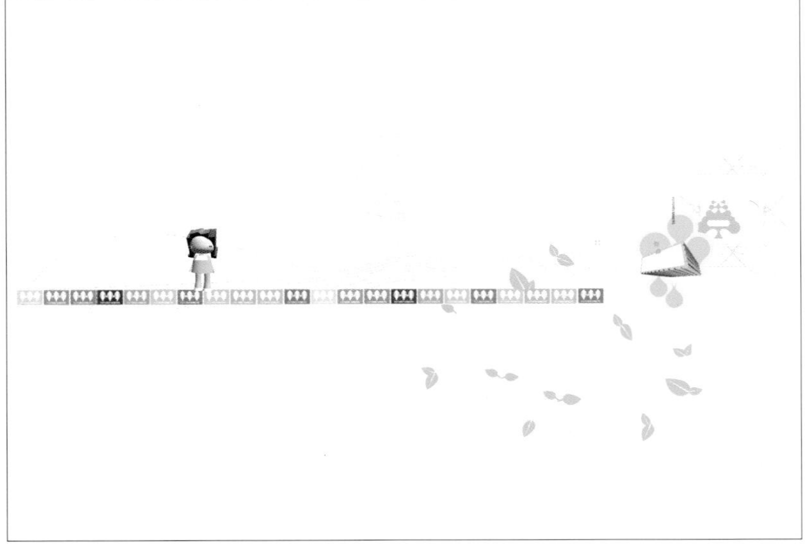

9

6 7 8

5 Cover illustration for *Design Plex* magazine / Design Plex / Japan / 2002 / The illustration is a portrait of Amy Franceschini, Josh On, Sascha Merg, and Michael Swaine, all members of Futurefarmers.
6–8 "Hydrogen" poster series for *Communication What* exhibition, Venice / Italy / 2002
9 "T(h)ree" illustration, study for Futurefarmers logo / USA / 2002
10 Cover and spreads from *Harvest* / Futurefarmers and IdN / USA and Hong Kong / 2002 / The book is an anthology of Futurefarmers projects from 1995 to 2002. It includes a CD-ROM and the toy "Pinga."

Amy Franceschini

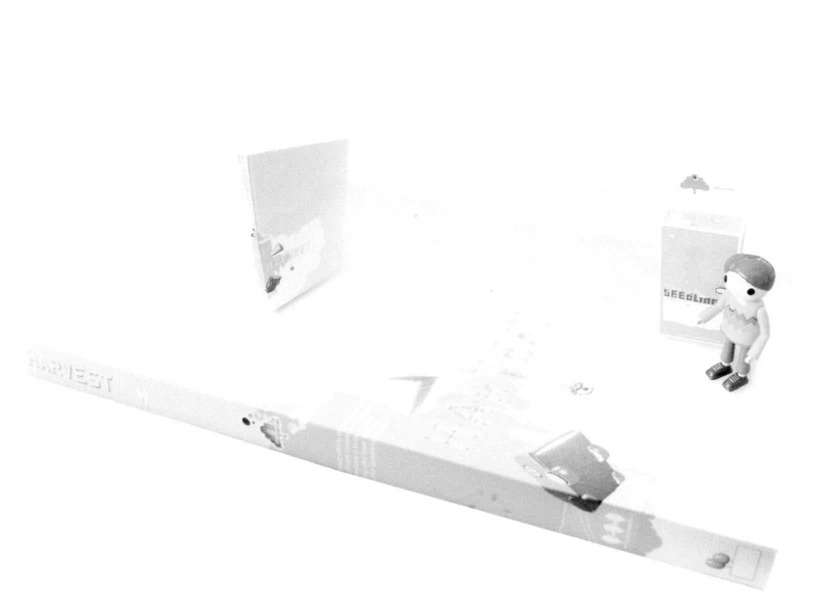

10

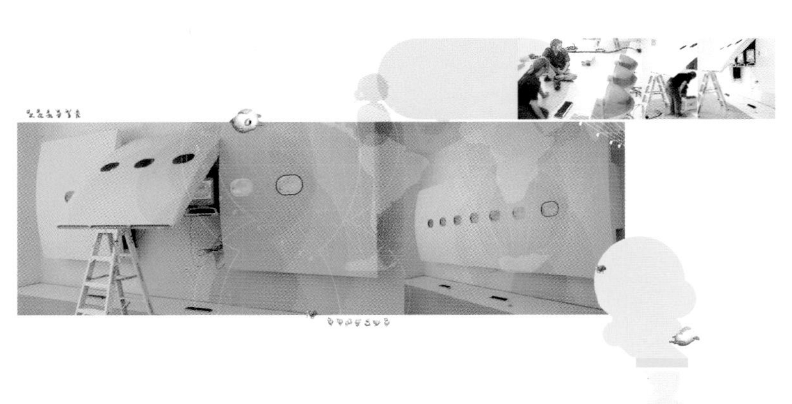

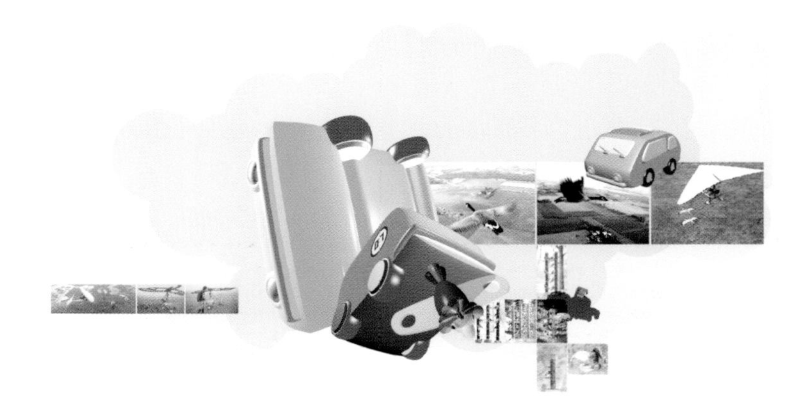

Born in Brighton, England, Vince Frost was educated in graphic design at West Sussex College of Design. After working freelance for some time, he joined Pentagram in 1989 but returned to private practice and started his own London-based design consultancy, Frost Design, in 1994. In independent practice, Frost's work attracted attention due to its innovative use of photographic images combined with clean, crisp typographic elements. He has gained international recognition through his editorial work for *P Magazine*, a Polaroid publication aimed at professional photographers, and further in *Big Magazine*, a dual-language publication. This work led to the opportunity to design the *Saturday Independent Magazine*. His publication work continues through numerous publishing houses around the world.•• Like so many before him, Frost believes the profession is not just about making money. He realized at an early age that it was about making the most of every opportunity that came his way. Clearly he has done this. Strong ideas, well executed, resulting in highly effective pieces of communication: a formula that can lead only to success.•• During his development as a designer he has worked on a diverse spectrum of projects including stamps for the Royal Mail, television advertising, the development of signage systems, and corporate identity and promotional programs. Frost is also a very active member of the design community, lecturing at conferences around the world, conducting design workshops, and participating as a judge at international design competitions and exhibitions. Frost is a designer of influence, now and for the future. ••Ken Cato••

1

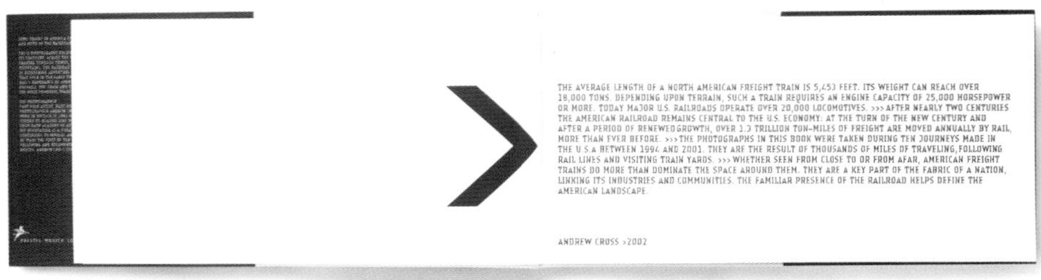

1 Cover and spreads, *Some Trains in America*, by Andrew Cross / Prestel / United Kingdom / 2002
2 Cover and spreads, *D&AD Annual Report* (illustration Marion Deuchars) / D&AD / United Kingdom / 2002
3 Cover and spreads, D&AD magazine *Ampersand* (with Matt Willey) / D&AD / United Kingdom / 2002

Vince Frost

London

2

D&AD
WHAT'S THE POINT?

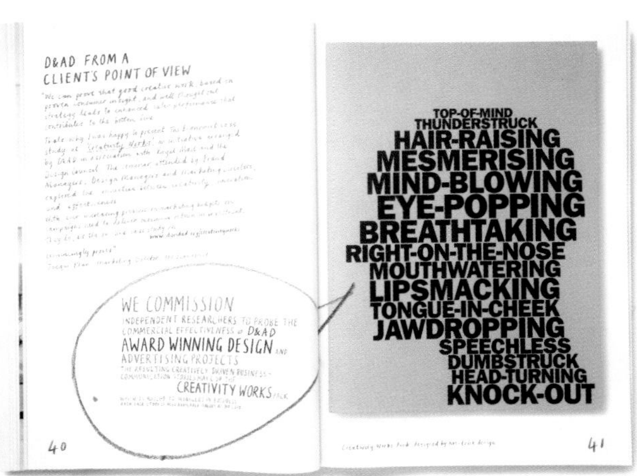

D&AD FROM A CLIENTS POINT OF VIEW
WE COMMISSION
AWARD WINNING DESIGN
CREATIVITY WORKS
TOP-OF-MIND
THUNDERSTRUCK
HAIR-RAISING
MESMERISING
MIND-BLOWING
EYE-POPPING
BREATHTAKING
RIGHT-ON-THE-NOSE
MOUTHWATERING
LIPSMACKING
TONGUE-IN-CHEEK
JAWDROPPING
SPEECHLESS
DUMBSTRUCK
HEAD-TURNING
KNOCK-OUT
40
41

OUR MISSION:
TO SET CREATIVE STANDARDS
IN DESIGN AND ADVERTISING.
TO EDUCATE
AND NURTURE THE NEXT CREATIVE
GENERATION.
TO COMMUNICATE
TO BUSINESS THE IMPORTANCE OF
GOOD DESIGN
AND ADVERTISING
6
7

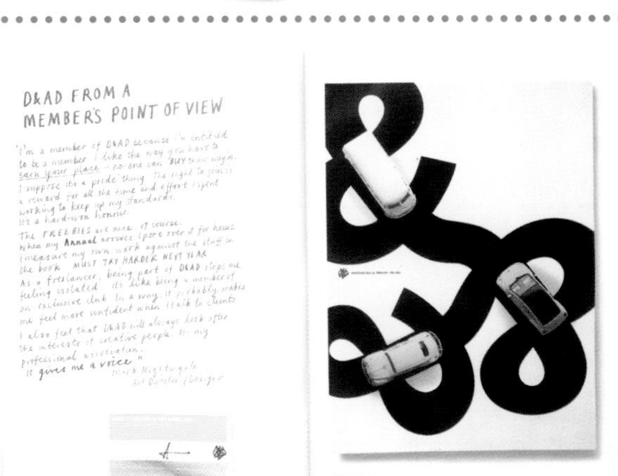

D&AD FROM A MEMBER'S POINT OF VIEW
12
13

3

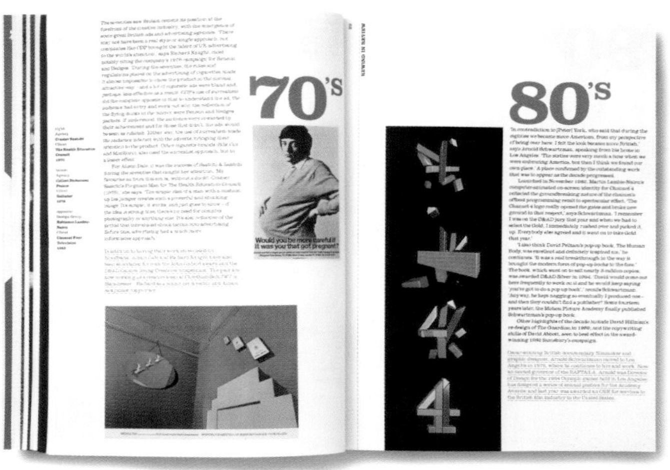

70's
80's

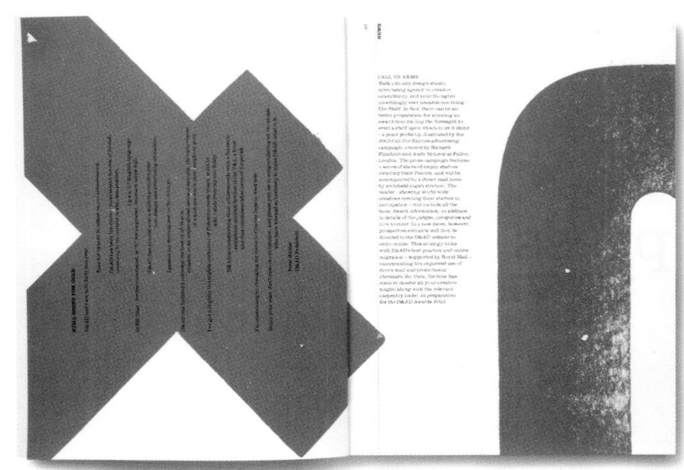

rewind review
To celebrate the publication of our 40-year review of legendary design and advertising, Lakshmi Bhaskaran invited a handful of creatives to pick their personal favourites
60's
IBM

Vince Frost

4–5 Advertising posters for ING Barings bank / Ogilvy / United Kingdom / 2001
6 Cover and spreads, publisher's catalogue for 1996–1997 / Fourth Estate / United Kingdom / 1996
7–8 "Clapperbox" poster and award, Nike Young Directors Awards / Nike / United Kingdom / 2002
9 Cover and spreads, publisher's catalogue for 2003 (illustration Marion Deuchars) / Fourth Estate / United Kingdom / 2003
10 Cover and spreads, publisher's catalogue for 2002 (illustration Marion Deuchars) / Fourth Estate / United Kingdom / 2002

⑨

Fourth Estate
January – June 2003

New Fiction
Giving Up the Ghost
Hilary Mantel

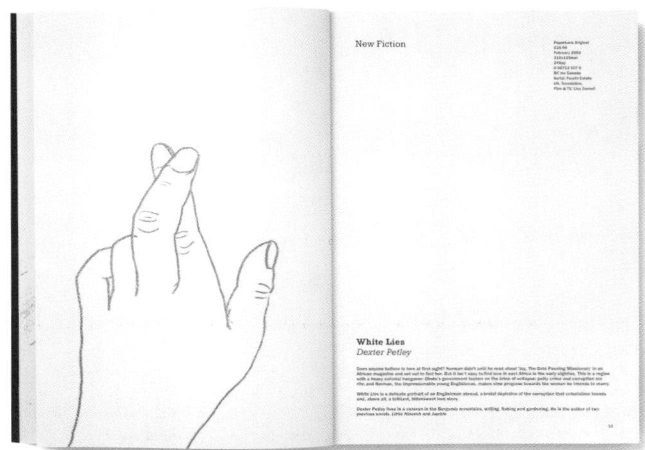
New Fiction
White Lies
Dexter Petley

⑩

Fourth Estate
July–December 2002

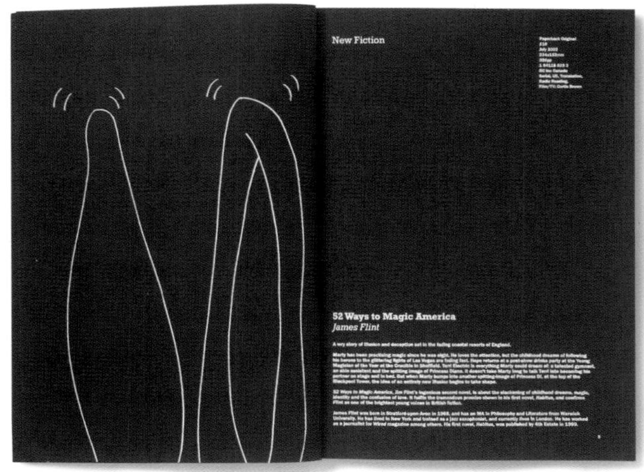
New Fiction
52 Ways to Magic America
James Flint

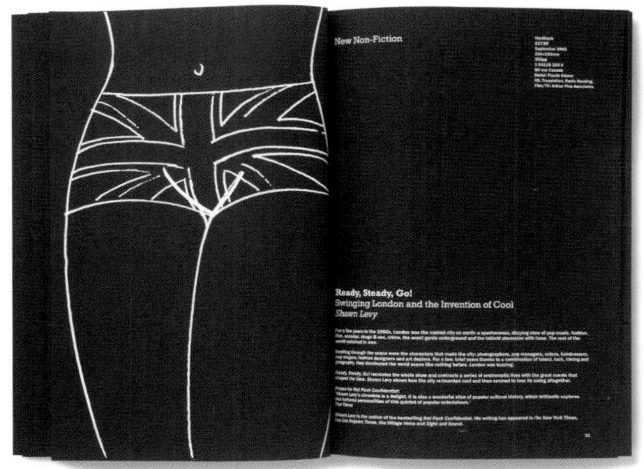
New Non-Fiction
Ready, Steady, Go!
Swinging London and the Invention of Cool
Shawn Levy

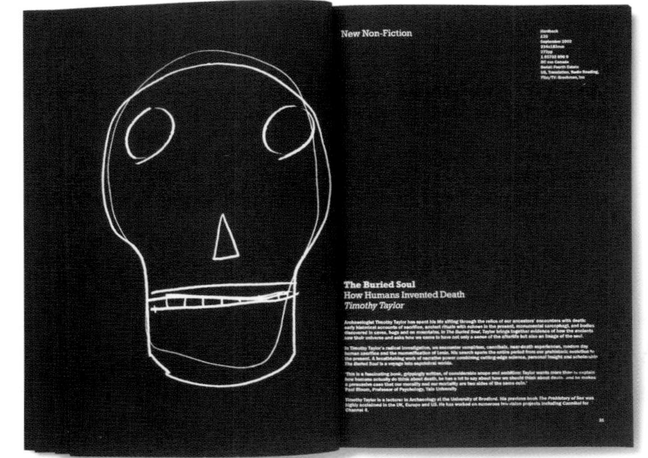
New Non-Fiction
The Buried Soul
How Humans Invented Death
Timothy Taylor

Tom Gauld's work belongs to a long and rich tradition, yet his approach to that tradition is remarkably refreshing. His commercial work includes projects for *The Guardian*, *WISH* magazine, and publishers such as Penguin and HarperCollins. However, it's work such as Move to the City—a comic strip that appears weekly in the London edition of *Time Out*—and the work he publishes via his own company, Cabanon Press, that provides Gauld with the ideal medium for his eccentric vision. • • Gauld is a wonderful storyteller. Stories like "Outside," for example, in which an explorer falls just short of what could be the promised land because the safety rope is not quite long enough; stories where warrior robots discuss the possibility of doing something other than fight or where two wrestlers kill time before a match by visiting a park and feeding stale muffins to ducks. Often, the joke requires only one frame, one image, one gesture, and a small amount of text to work. In one piece, two astronauts on the surface of a distant planet have had an argument. All we have—and it's all we need—is one line: "Oh come on...I was joking." • • Gauld's work never fails to bring a smile to your face. He has a less-is-more approach that, on the surface at least, often appears quite surreal, but all you have to do is scratch that surface to realize that the humor comes from the everyday. He engages his audience by presenting not a world a million miles away, but our own. • • As a draftsman his style is direct and honest, presenting his stories and characters in a straightforward manner that echoes the economy and deadpan delivery of his comedic vocabulary. Comprising predominantly black-and-white line drawings, his work has veered well clear of technological advances. Maybe it would be easy to skim the surface and regard Gauld's style as pedestrian; but all you have to do is look a little closer. • • Fernando Gutiérrez • •

1

2

1 "Dante's Inferno," illustration for *The Guardian* newspaper / The Guardian / United Kingdom / 2002
2 Hilltop handkerchief design for Japanese retail brand / United Arrows / Japan / 2002
3-4 Pages 1 and 2 of 6-page comic strip "Cat, Bear and Ghost" in *Sturgeon White Moss* magazine / Sturgeon White Moss / United Kingdom / 2003
5 "Seven Robots Go to the Shops" illustration for *Graphics International Diary* (unpublished) / Graphics International / United Kingdom / 2002
6 Billboard, Happiness in Brockley project / United Kingdom / 2001 / Project organized by artist Simone Lia for which artists produced cheerful billboard pieces to be displayed in Brockley, South London.

Tom Gauld

London

CAT, BEAR AND GHOST
BY TOM GAULD
GHOST
HEY! GHOST! WAKE UP!
OH, HELLO CAT

3

4

ARE YOU READY?
UM..
WE'RE SUPPOSED TO MEET BEAR TONIGHT, REMEMBER?
OH YEAH, JUST A SEC...
OKAY, LET'S GO
...CAT, REMIND ME WHY WE'RE MEETING BEAR
GHOST, YOU MUST HAVE THE WORST MEMORY IN THE WORLD, HE SAID HE HAD SOMETHING TO SHOW US
OOOH MYSTER-IOUS

5

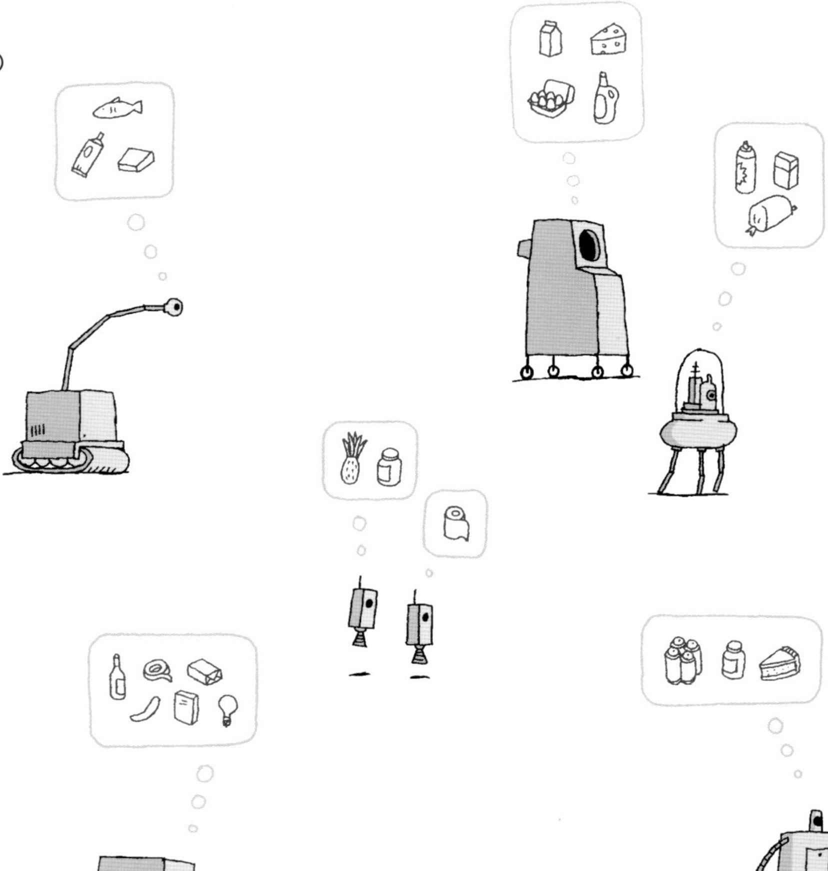
SEVEN ROBOTS GOING TO THE SHOPS

6

562801
hello
HAPPINESS IN BROCKLEY
MAIDEN

7

8

9

10

7–8 "Collectors' and "Libraries" illustrations for *The Guardian* newspaper / The Guardian / United Kingdom / 2002
9–10 Pages from comic magazine *Second* / Cabanon Press / United Kingdom / 2001
11 "Characters from an Epic Tale," personal postcard project / United Kingdom / 2001
12 Poster for comic-magazine publisher / There Goes Tokyo / United Kingdom / 2002
13 Page from comic magazine *Second* / Cabanon Press / United Kingdom / 2001
14 "Theatre Previewer" illustration for *Time Out* magazine / Time Out / United Kingdom / 2001

Tom Gauld

11

CHARACTERS FOR AN EPIC TALE
THE HERO
THE PIRATE
THE THREE WITCHES
THE MESSENGER
THE WRESTLERS
THE OLD MAN
THE GIRL
THE MONKEY
THE MIDGET
THE TWINS
THE CONVICT
THE HERMIT
THE KING
THE PRIEST
THE ESCAPIST
THE RINGMASTER
THE CORPSE
THE DANCING BEAR
THE INVALID
THE NURSE
THE QUEEN
THE APPARITION
THE WANDERERS
THE HEADLESS MAN
THE GIANT
THE GENIUS
THE MINOTAUR
THE BIRD MAN
THE VISITORS
THE KNIGHT
THE FLOATING SKULL
THE FREAKS
THE INNKEEPER
THE URCHINS
THE GOLEM
THE PROPHET OF DOOM
THE MAGIC COW
THE SNIPER
THE HAIRY BEAST
THE LOVER
THE NUDIST
THE SKELETON
THE NECRO-MANCER
THE DANDY
THE HUSBAND
THE GIANT CAT
THE GUARDS
THE DEVIL
THE BOY
THE TART
THE METAL MAN
THE SCARECROW

12

THERE GOES TOKYO
WWW.TGTOKYO.COM
SMALL PRESS
BIG MONSTERS

13

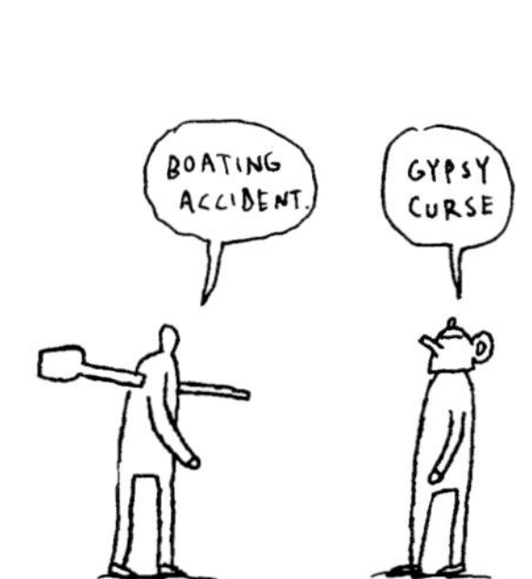
BOATING ACCIDENT.
GYPSY CURSE

14

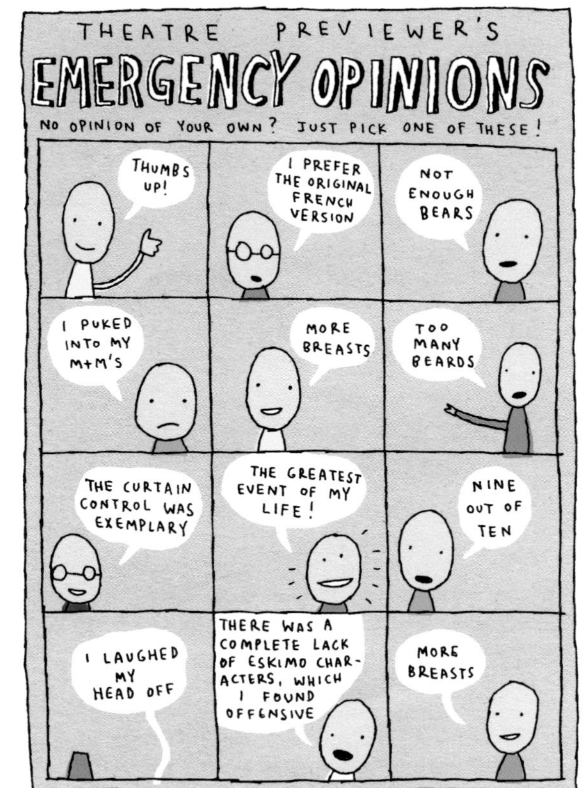
THEATRE PREVIEWER'S
EMERGENCY OPINIONS
NO OPINION OF YOUR OWN? JUST PICK ONE OF THESE!
THUMBS UP!
I PREFER THE ORIGINAL FRENCH VERSION
NOT ENOUGH BEARS
I PUKED INTO MY M+M'S
MORE BREASTS
TOO MANY BEARDS
THE CURTAIN CONTROL WAS EXEMPLARY
THE GREATEST EVENT OF MY LIFE!
NINE OUT OF TEN
I LAUGHED MY HEAD OFF
THERE WAS A COMPLETE LACK OF ESKIMO CHAR-ACTERS, WHICH I FOUND OFFENSIVE
MORE BREASTS

Juli Gudehus's little calendar *Mindestens Haltbar bis* 31.12.1999 (Best Before 12/31/1999) is one of the smartest time lines I've ever seen: The countdown of the last year of the millennium using nothing but expiration dates of food products. • • A different product goes bad on every calendar sheet on every day. Some of the products, shown in tight crops in order to transform the date itself into the hero, are still recognizable: On 14 February the mousse au chocolat is fresh no more, on 23 April butter cookies turn stale, the white bread gets moldy on 5 January, and Windsor Tea is off by 5 August. • • The typographic diversity and the variation of application techniques are also incredible: embossed, tampon-printed, stamped, offset-printed, letterpressed, flexi-printed, ink-jetted, and debossed expiration dates are included. Gudehus painstakingly collected all the items, products she likely would have never bought were it not for that missing date in her collection. • • The resulting round-cornered calendar, ordinary everyday designs put into a different context and shrinkwrapped into a green foamcore tray, is simply breathtaking in its simplicity. It fulfills the requirements for good design: an original idea well executed. • • Or take her smart and hilarious retelling of Genesis: She retells God's creation of the earth and the skies using only corporate logos, directional icons, and pictograms. Gudehus is probably the purest conceptual designer I know. • • Stefan Sagmeister • •

1

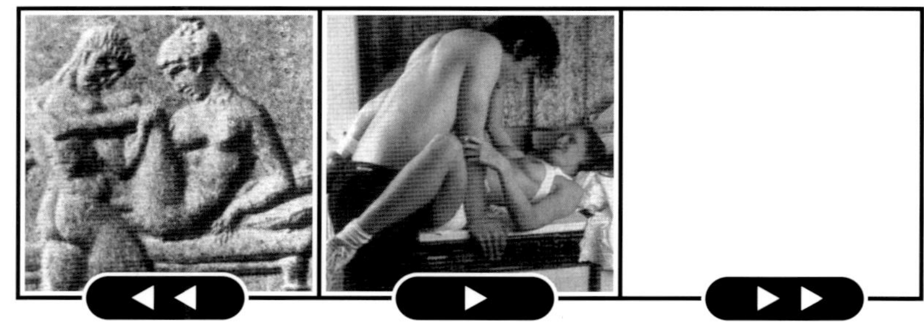

1 *Gestern War Heute Morgen* (Yesterday Was Today Tomorrow) project for *Die Zeit* newspaper / Die Zeit / Germany / 1999 / Commentary on the millennium and what it holds for the future.

2–4 Cover and spreads, *Genesis*, by Juli Gudehus / Lars Mueller Publishers / Switzerland / 1997 / The biblical story of the Creation told in modern hieroglyphics.

Juli Gudehus

Berlin

2

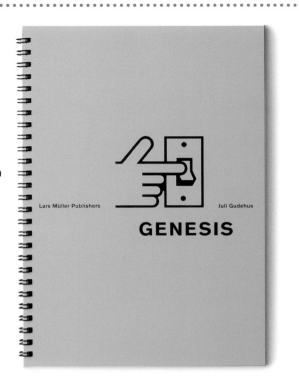

Lars Müller Publishers

Juli Gudehus

GENESIS

3

and said, "Be fruitful
und sprach: »Seid fruchtbar
et dit: «Soyez féconds,
dicendo: «Crescete
diciendo: Fructificaos

and increase in number."
und mehret euch!»
multipliez!»
e moltiplicatevi.»
y multiplicaos.

And after the evening and morning there came the fifth day.
Da ward aus Abend und Morgen der fünfte Tag.
Il y eut un soir et il y eut un matin: cinquième jour.
Fu sera, poi fu mattina: quinto giorno.
Y fue la tarde y la mañana el dia quinto.

And God said: "Let the land produce living creatures."
Und Gott sprach: »Die Erde bringe hervor lebendiges Getier.»
Dieu dit: «Que la terre produise des êtres vivants.»
Poi Dio disse: «Produca la terra animali viventi.»
Luego dijo Dios: Produzca la tierra seres vivientes.

And it was so.
Und es geschah so.
Et il en fut ainsi.
E così fu.
Y fue asi.

God made the wild animals,
Und Gott machte die Tiere des Feldes
Dieu fit les bêtes sauvages selon leur espèce,
Dio fece gli animali selvatici della terra,
E hizo Dios animales de la tierra

the livestock and all the creatures that move along the ground according to their kinds.
und das Vieh und alles Gewürm, ein jedes nach seiner Art.
les bestiaux selon leur espèce et toutes les bestioles du sol selon leur espèce.
il bestiame e tutti i rettili della terra secondo le loro specie
y ganado y todo animal que se arrastra sobre la tierra según su especie.

And God saw that it was good.
Und Gott sah, dass es gut war.
Et Dieu vit que cela était bon.
Dio vide che questo era buono.
Y vio Dios que era bueno.

4

The Creation
Die Schöpfung
La création
La creazione
La creación

In the beginning God created heaven and earth.
Am Anfang schuf Gott Himmel und Erde.
Au commencement, Dieu créa les cieux et la terre.
Nel principio Dio creò i cieli e la terra.
En el principio creó Dios los cielos y la tierra.

And the earth was without form and void
Und die Erde war wüst und leer,
Or la terre était vide et vague,
La terra era informe e vuota,
Y la tierra estaba desordenada y vacía

and the deep was covered in darkness
und es war finster in der Tiefe,
les ténèbres couvraient l'abîme
le tenebre coprivano la faccia dell'abisso
y las tinieblas estaban sobre la faz del abismo

and the Spirit of God was hovering over the waters.
und der Geist Gottes schwebte auf dem Wasser.
un vent de Dieu tournoyait sur les eaux.
e lo Spirito di Dio aleggiava sulla superficie delle acque.
y el Espiritu de Dios flotaba sobre la faz de las aguas.

And God said "Let there be light,"
Und Gott sprach »Es werde Licht.«
Dieu dit: «Que la lumière soit.»
Dio disse: «Sia luce!»
Y dijo Dios: Sea la luz;

and there was light.
Und es ward Licht.
Et la lumière fut.
E luce fu.
y fue la luz.

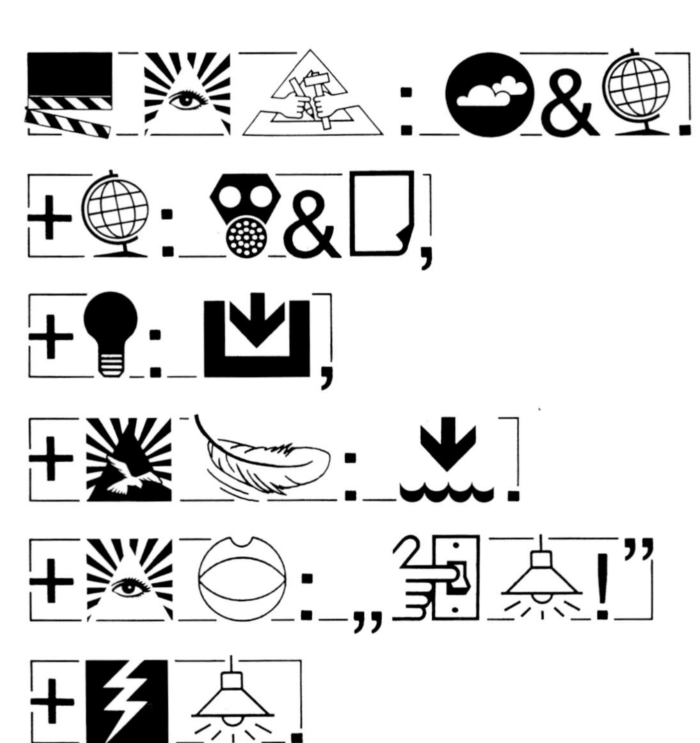

⑤

⑥

cheerful T

crest-fallen T

T

well-balanced T

Juli Gudehus

5 Christmas card for printer and publisher / Druck- und Verlagshaus Wienand / Germany / 1997 / The card lists 453 variations of the key colors white, blue, yellow, red, and black.

6 *Aus dem Leben des T* (From the Life of T) project for *100 T-Variationen*, book on the letter T / Verlag Hermann Schmidt / Germany / 2000

7 *Mindestens Haltbar bis* 31.12.99 (Best Before 12/31/99) calendar / Verlag Hermann Schmidt / Germany / 1998 / Each day of the year is represented by the expiry date taken from package of a general household product.

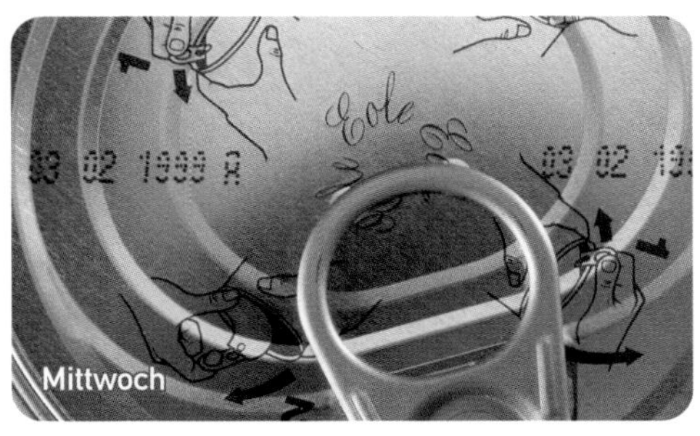
Mittwoch

Mousse au Chocolat
Volume net:
15 cl e
14. 02
Sonntag Valentinstag

7

mindestens haltbar bis:
31.12.1999
ein Kalender von Juli Gudehus im Verlag Hermann Schmidt Mainz

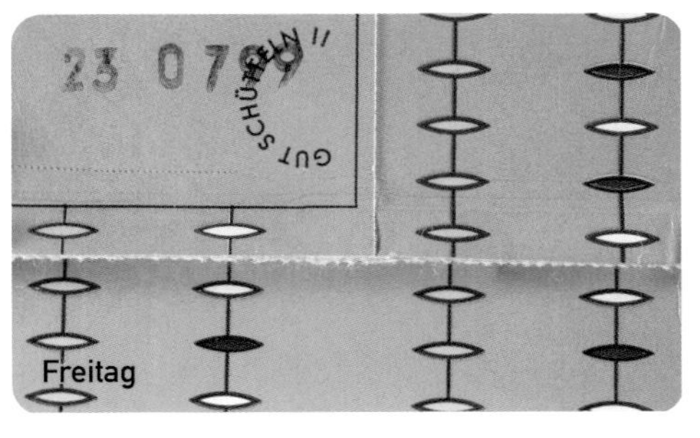
GUT SCHÜHELN
Freitag

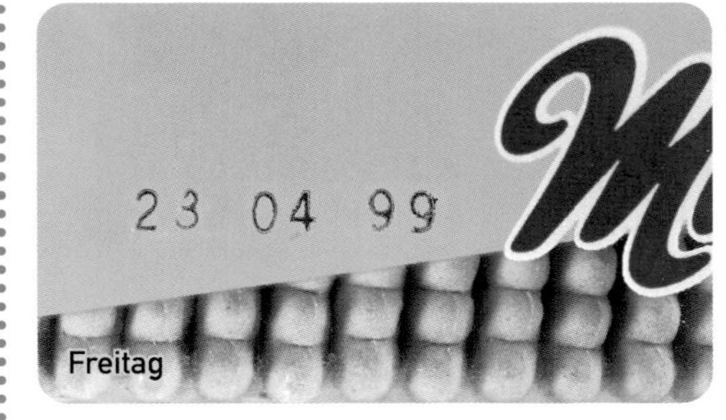
23 04 99
Freitag

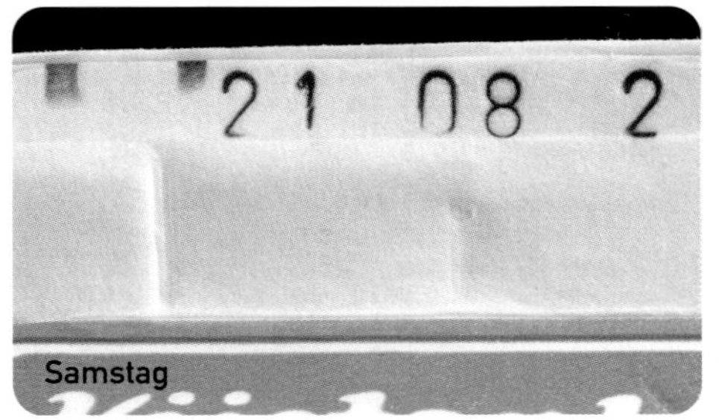
21 08 2
Samstag

Mindestens haltbar bis: 24.03.99
Da consumarsi preferibilmente entro:
Mittwoch

GUT BILLIG
Sonntag

05.01.
Dienstag

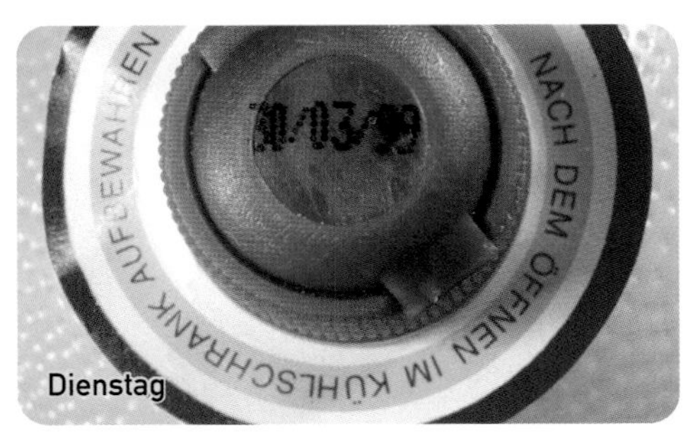
NACH DEM ÖFFNEN IM KÜHLSCHRANK AUFBEWAHREN
Dienstag

PREIS 2.60 DM
VERKAUFEN BIS
22 11 99
MINDESTENS
HALTBAR BIS
29 11 99
Montag

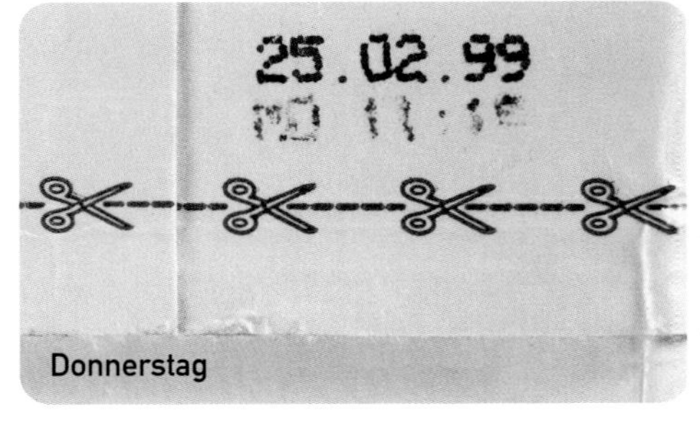
25.02.99
Donnerstag

05.06.1999-1
Samstag

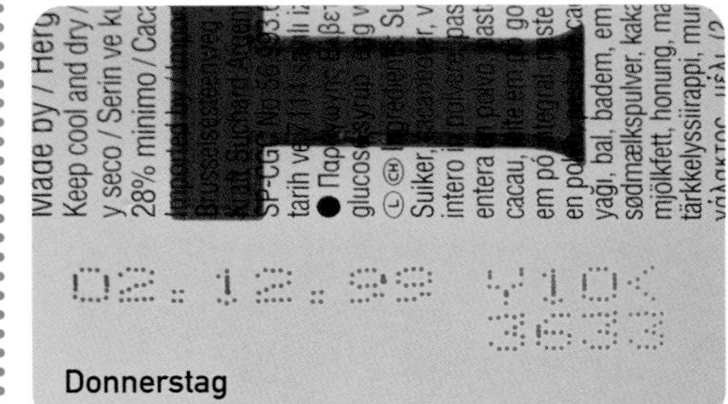
02.12.99
Donnerstag

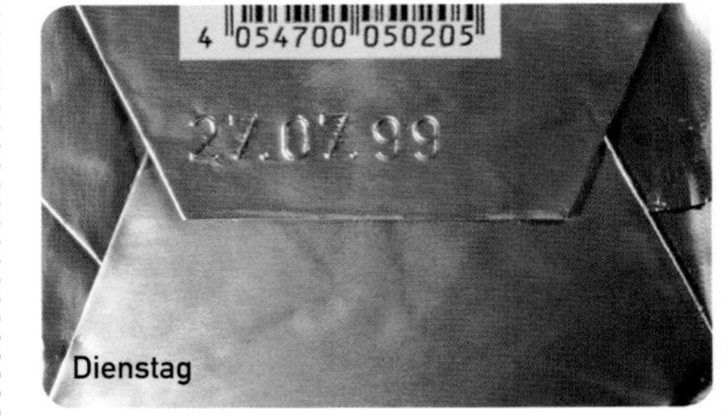
4 054700 050205
27.07.99
Dienstag

During Soviet times, there was not much design in the USSR, yet there were many designers. New times came with black humor: Design now exists, but there seem to be no designers. Yuri Gulitov is one of the few masters who refuses to fit into this gloomy paradox. He is a professional and observable personage with his own creative position. ••In the Russia of the 1990s, graphic design suddenly became a popular and prestigious profession. It woke up famous, propelled into the limelight by the favorable conditions of the growing market economy. To satisfy the needs of the advertising boom, huge quantities of graphic design were generated from nothing. Unfortunately, the design required in commercial advertising is one that sells fast, that indulges the wild tastes of the client, not design as a culture-preserving and culture-creating profession. ••In the midst of all this, Gulitov continues to defend the honor of graphic design. He fights for the trade's right to play an independent cultural role. His typefaces, posters, logos, advertising booklets, journals, and newspaper layouts are never limited simply to a series of decisions pertaining to the piece's problems and functionality. He is always in search of something greater. Each work is an artistic experiment, one more opportunity to "foster the idea." ••This "idea" is about the particularities of national design; about core archetypes of visual culture and the Russian field being shaped by graphic design; about the unsolved specificity of our Slavo-Greco-Latin Cyrillic alphabet. Gulitov is interested in the character and nature of the Russian "inside-outness" that begins with the mirror-image appearance of letters in our alphabet. Font is a model of national cosmos. ••The graphic particularities he embraces were born in the street and can be traced back to his native Sebastopol, in Crimea. The specific, widespread style of graffiti that exists in this southern city made a lasting impression on him. Like street graphics, Gulitov's designs breed energy and are characterized by a dynamic and unpredictable nature. They have a touching naiveté, sincerity, and credulity and break down the barriers between the author and the audience. They are saturated with an atmosphere of real freedom. This deeply personal inspiration places Gulitov's designs in the context of not only "predesign era" Russian visual culture, but also today's postmodern design concepts, which embrace regionalisms. As a result, his quest is more relevant than ever. ••Serve Serov••

①

ACADEMIA ROSSICA
(ВЕЛИКОБРИТАНИЯ)
И ГОСУДАРСТВЕННАЯ
ТРЕТЬЯКОВСКАЯ ГАЛЕРЕЯ
ПРЕДСТАВЛЯЮТ:
СЕРГЕЙ
РАХМАНИНОВ
ВСЕНОЩНОЕ
БДЕНИЕ
КОНЦЕРТ ПАМЯТИ Е.Ф.СВЕТЛАНОВА
ЧЕТВЕРГ 19 СЕНТЯБРЯ 2002
БОЛЬШОЙ ЗАЛ КОНСЕРВАТОРИИ
СВЯТО-НИКОЛЬСКИЙ ХОР ТРЕТЬЯКОВСКОЙ ГАЛЕРЕИ
АНТОН ВИСКОВ ВОКАЛИЗ
ДИРИЖЕР АЛЕКСЕЙ ПУЗАКОВ
НАЧАЛО КОНЦЕРТА В 19 ЧАСОВ
Б.НИКИТСКАЯ 13
БИЛЕТЫ ПРОДАЮТСЯ В КАССЕ БОЛЬШОГО ЗАЛА
ПО ТЕЛЕФОНУ И НА САЙТЕ

②

③

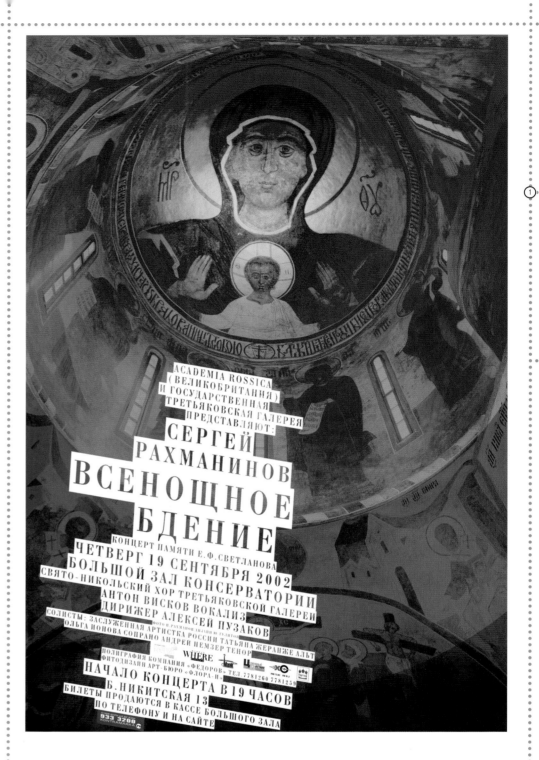

1 Poster for concert, *Vespers* by Sergei Rachmaninov / St. Nikolai Church Choir of the State Tretyakov Gallery / Russia / 2002
2–3 Logos for art gallery ST-ART and advertising agency ODA / Russia / 1995–96
4 Front and back of invitation and poster for the *Russian Design 99* competition and exhibition / Design Union of Russia / 1999
5 Poster for solo exhibition *Yuri Gulitov–Beach Pictures* / Russia / 2001

Yuri Gulitov

Moscow

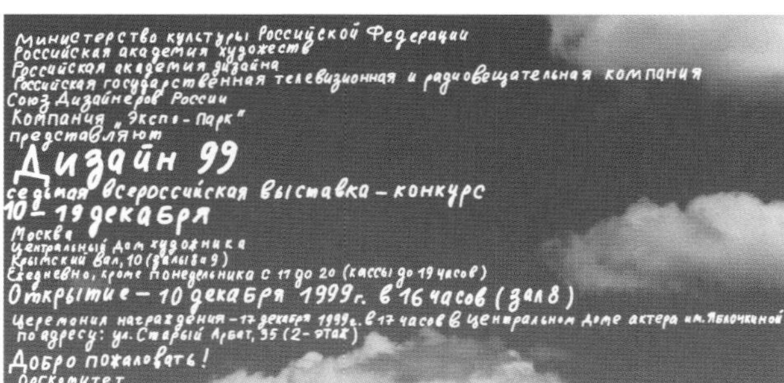

④

⑤

Выставка
Юрий Гуликов
«Пляжные картинки»
16–23 марта 2001
в редакции журнала «Пинакотека»
ул. Малая Бронная, 32, кв. 2
полиграфическая поддержка «Линия Графика»
Гуликов

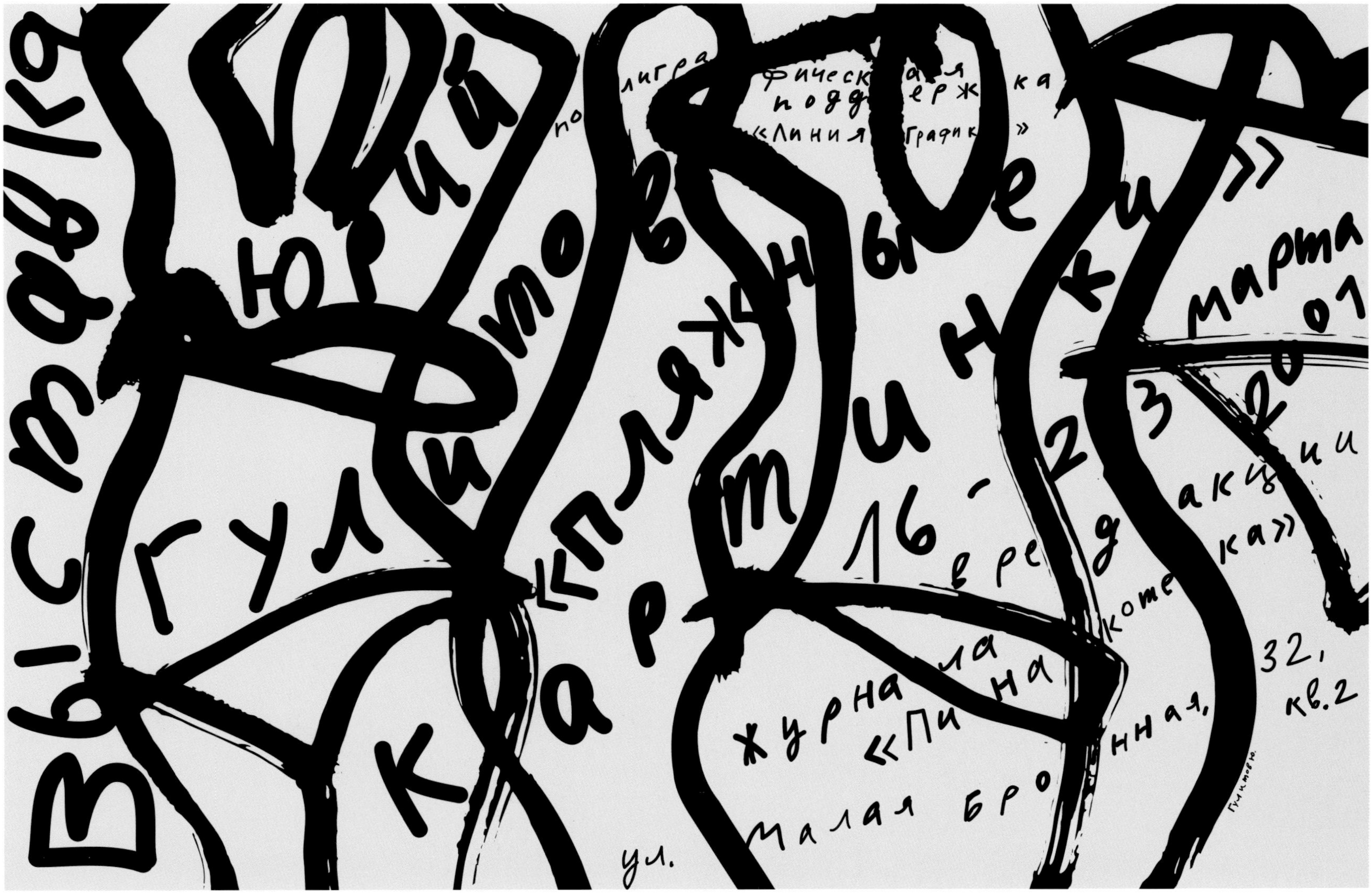

6

7

АБВГДЕЖЗИЙ
КЛМНОПРСТУ
ФХЦЧШЩЪЫЬ
ЭЮЯ1234567
890!?<>:;,.

8

АБВГДЕЖЗИЙ
КЛМНОПРСТУ
ФХЦЧШЩЪЫЬ
ЭЮЯ1234567
890!?<>:;,.

9

АБВГДЕЖЗИ
ЙКЛМНОПРС
ТУФХЦЧШЩ
ЪЫЬЭЮЯ123
4567890

6 Typeface Calligraphic / Russia / 1995
7 Typeface *Uleechnaya 1* (Street 1) / Russia / 1997
8 Typeface *Uleechnaya 2* (Street 2) / Russia / 1997
9 Typeface *Studencheskaya* (Students) / Russia / 1999
10 Poster for solo exhibition *Yuri Gulitov–Typeface* / Dom Cultural Center / Russia / 2000
11 Happy New Year poster / Linea Graphic / Russia / 1996
12 Poster for Christmas concert *Lestvica* / St. Nikolai Church Choir of the State Tretyakov Gallery / 2002
13 Poster for concert, *Matthaeus-Passion*, by Johann Sebastian Bach / St. Nikolai Church Choir of the State Tretyakov Gallery / 2003

Yuri Gulitov

10 
Юрий
Гулитов
3–7 мая 2000
Центр „Дом"
Большой Овчинниковский пер.,
дом 24, строение 4
Шрифт
персональная
выставка

11 

12 
14 ДЕКАБРЯ
БОЛЬШОЙ ЗАЛ
МОСКОВСКОЙ
КОНСЕРВАТОРИИ
ПРЕДРОЖДЕСТВЕНСКИЙ
КОНЦЕРТ-МИСТЕРИЯ
АННА АХМАТОВА
МАРИНА ЦВЕТАЕВА
БОРИС ПАСТЕРНАК
ИОСИФ БРОДСКИЙ
ЧИТАЕТ
АЛЛА ДЕМИДОВА
ИОГАНН СЕБАСТЬЯН БАХ
ОЛИВЬЕ МЕССИАН
И СОВРЕМЕННАЯ
МУЗЫКА
СВЯТО-НИКОЛЬСКИЙ ХОР
ТРЕТЬЯКОВСКОЙ ГАЛЕРЕИ
ПОД УПРАВЛЕНИЕМ
АЛЕКСЕЯ ПУЗАКОВА
ФЕДОР СТРОГАНОВ ОРГАН
БИЛЕТЫ В КАССЕ
КОНСЕРВАТОРИИ
ПО ТЕЛЕФОНУ И НА САЙТЕ
НАЧАЛО В 19 ЧАСОВ
БОЛЬШАЯ НИКИТСКАЯ 13
933 3200
KONTRAMARKA

13 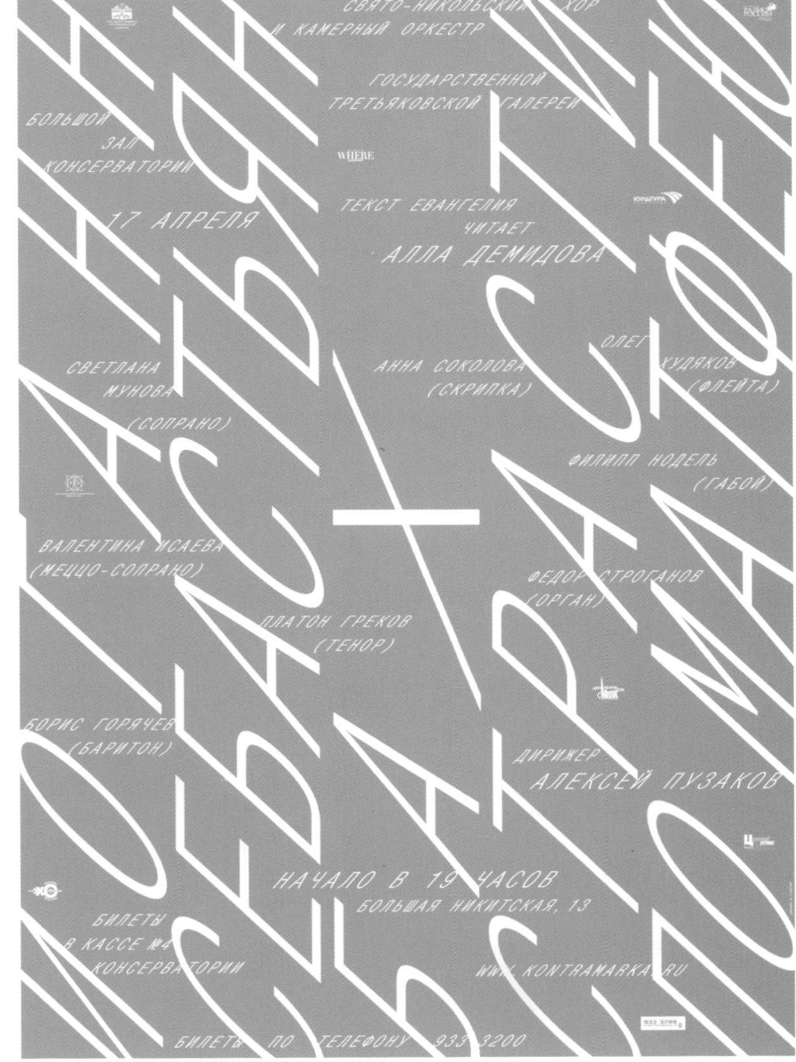
СВЯТО-НИКОЛЬСКИЙ ХОР
И КАМЕРНЫЙ ОРКЕСТР
ГОСУДАРСТВЕННОЙ
ТРЕТЬЯКОВСКОЙ ГАЛЕРЕИ
БОЛЬШОЙ
ЗАЛ
КОНСЕРВАТОРИИ
17 АПРЕЛЯ
ТЕКСТ ЕВАНГЕЛИЯ
ЧИТАЕТ
АЛЛА ДЕМИДОВА
СВЕТЛАНА
МУНОВА
(СОПРАНО)
АННА СОКОЛОВА
(СКРИПКА)
ОЛЕГ ХУДЯКОВ
(ФЛЕЙТА)
ФИЛИПП НОДЕЛЬ
(ГАБОЙ)
ВАЛЕНТИНА ИСАЕВА
(МЕЦЦО-СОПРАНО)
ФЕДОР СТРОГАНОВ
(ОРГАН)
ПЛАТОН ГРЕКОВ
(ТЕНОР)
БОРИС ГОРЯЧЕВ
(БАРИТОН)
ДИРИЖЕР
АЛЕКСЕЙ ПУЗАКОВ
НАЧАЛО В 19 ЧАСОВ
БОЛЬШАЯ НИКИТСКАЯ, 13
БИЛЕТЫ
В КАССЕ №4
КОНСЕРВАТОРИИ
WWW.KONTRAMARKA.RU
БИЛЕТЫ ПО ТЕЛЕФОНУ 933 3200

Julia, the wondergirl in New York with the perfectly English-sounding name Hasting can be found in a high-rise building in Manhattan, where, for some years now, she has been designing appallingly beautiful books for a publisher with the lyrical name Phaidon.••Phaidon was a pupil of Socrates. Four hundred years before Christ, Phaidon founded his own philosophy school in Elis. Plato named his dialogue on the immortality of the soul after him.••Hasting was a pupil of Gunter Rambow. She began her studies at the famous art university in Kassel (Kasseler Schule) in 1990 and in 1992 followed Rambow to the newly founded university for design (HfG) in Karlsruhe. After receiving her diploma in 1997, she emancipated herself from her master and developed her own forms of expression.••Hasting was successful right from the start. Her particular love for typographic detail becomes clear in all of her work. The same can be said for the surprising way she stages text and image. While still a student, she designed an excellent corporate identity for the EIKK (European Film Institute Karlsruhe), which was soon decorated with an award.••In fact, there are very few projects of Hasting's that have not been awarded prizes and received corresponding international publicity. Perfectly equipped with the recognition of the design scene, she quickly landed a job at the number-one publishing address for art and design: Phaidon in London—where else?••The "master" Rambow soon remembered his pupil, who had by now become Phaidon's art director in the newly opened New York office. In the role of a "godfather," he nominated her to be a member of the Alliance Graphique Internationale (AGI). Chance had it that I was then part of the AGI jury. She was unanimously voted in and became the youngest member of the Alliance. ••Since 2001, Hasting has had her own students. She teaches Publication Design at the renowned Cooper Union School of Art in New York. And she naturally continues to make beautiful books, conscious of the immortality of her typographic soul.••Uwe Loesch••

1 Poster for door-handle manufacturer FSB / FSB / Germany / 1993
2 Book and packaging, *Cream–Contemporary Art in Culture* / Phaidon Press / United Kingdom and USA / 1998
3 Book, *10x10–10 Critics, 100 Architects* / Phaidon Press / United Kingdom and USA / 2000
4 Book, *Vitamin P–New Perspectives in Painting* / Phaidon Press / United Kingdom and USA / 2002
5 Book, *Magnum°* / Phaidon Press / United Kingdom and USA / 1999
6 Book, *Gordon Matta-Clark* / Phaidon Press / United Kingdom and USA / 2003
7 Inflatable point-of-sale and book, *Fresh Cream–Contemporary Art in Culture* / Phaidon Press / United Kingdom and USA / 2000
8 Book, *Robert Capa–The Definitive Collection* / Phaidon Press / United Kingdom and USA / 2001

Julia Hasting

New York

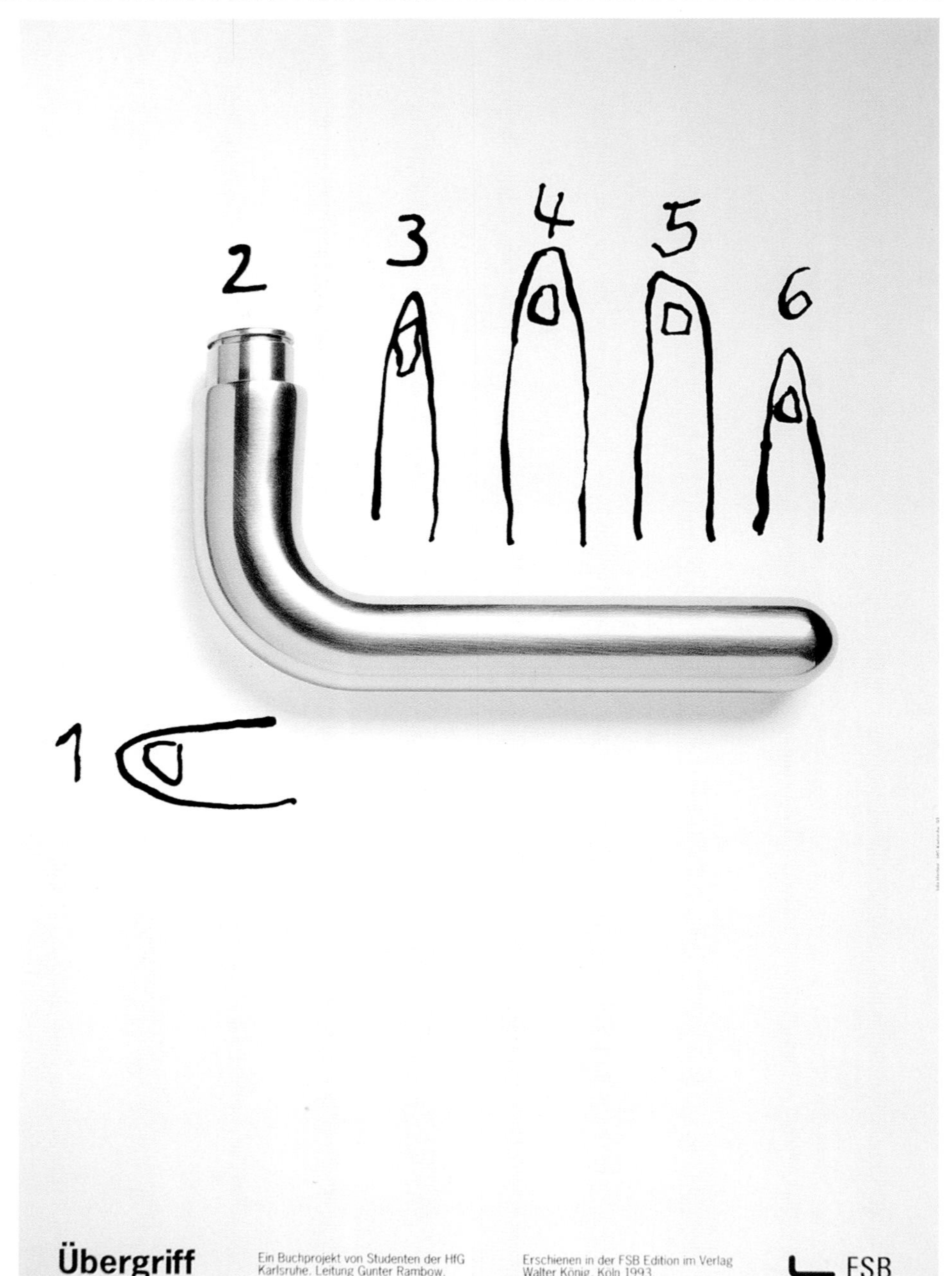

1

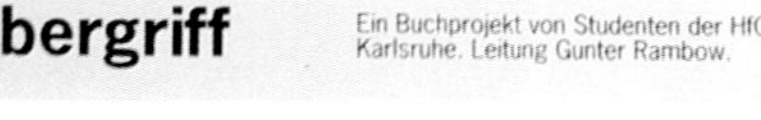

Übergriff
Ein Buchprojekt von Studenten der HfG Karlsruhe. Leitung Gunter Rambow.
Erschienen in der FSB Edition im Verlag Walther König, Köln 1993.
FSB

2

3

10 critics
10 x 10
100 architects
PHAIDON

4

VITAMIN P
NEW PERSPECTIVES IN PAINTING
PHAIDON

5

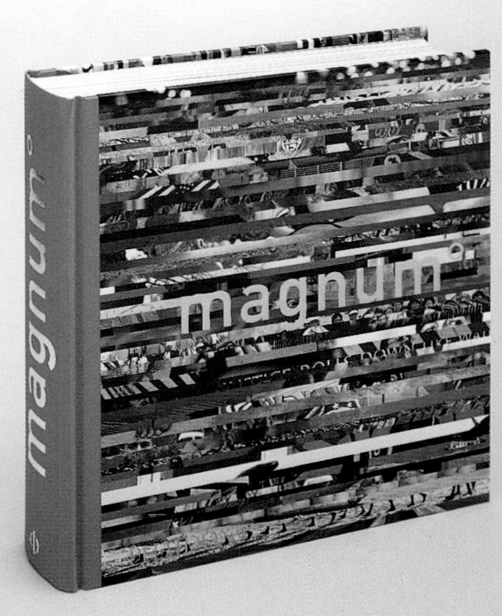
magnum°
magnum°

6

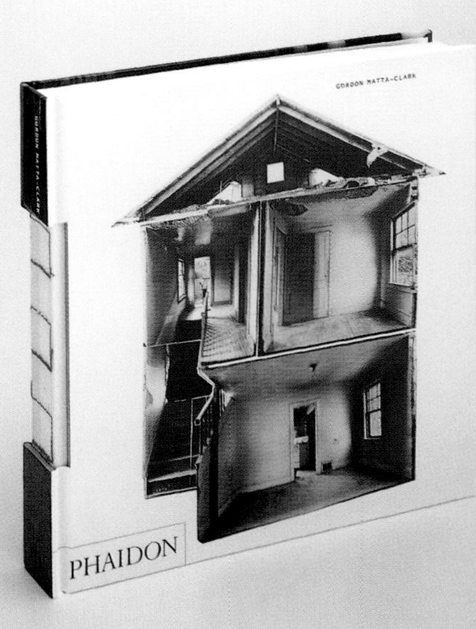
GORDON MATTA-CLARK
PHAIDON

7

8

PHAIDON

9
10
11
12

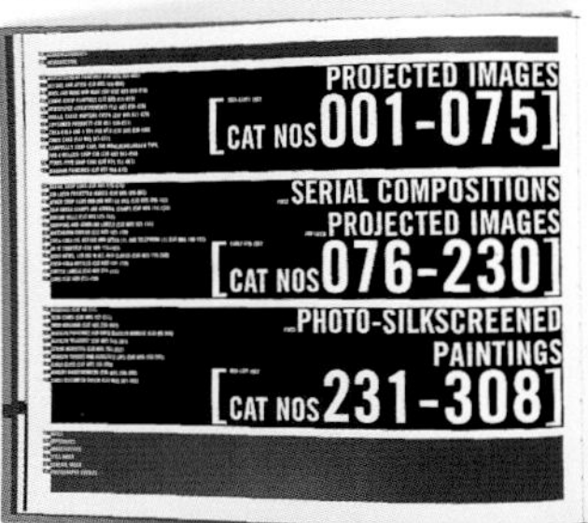

13
14
15
16

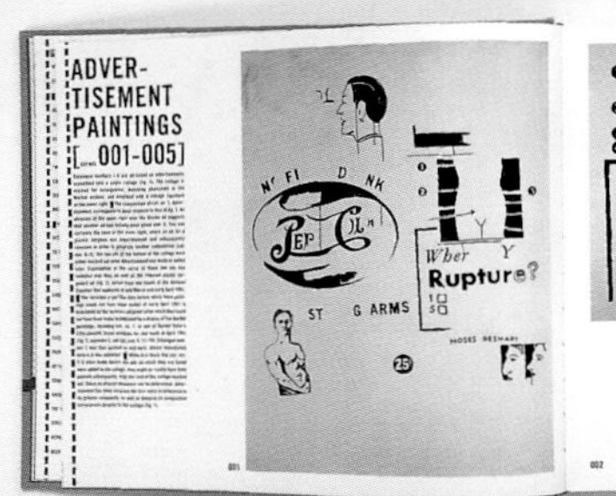

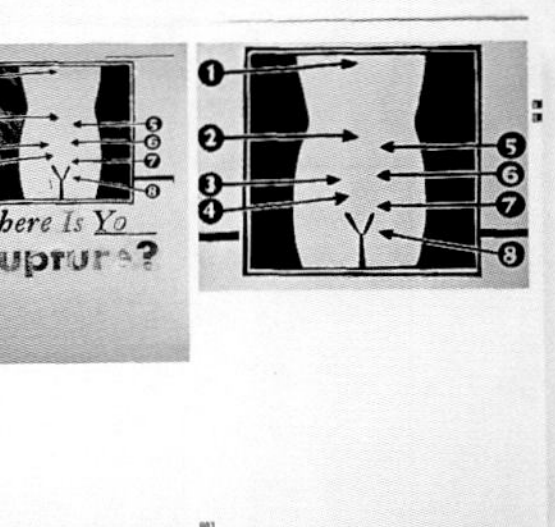

Julia Hasting

9–12 Cover and spreads, *Andy Warhol Catalogue Raisonné–Volume I: Painting and Sculpture, 1961–1963* / Phaidon Press / United Kingdom and USA / 2002

13–16 Cover and spreads, *Blink. 100 Photographers, 10 Curators, 10 Writers* / Phaidon Press / United Kingdom and USA / 2002

17–19 Poster series for exhibition *Die 100 Plakate des Jahres 1994* (The best 100 posters of 1994), Berlin / Germany / 1994

20–22 Poster series for student ball at design academy Hochschule für Gestaltung Karlsruhe (with Thomas Mayfried) / Hochschule für Gestaltung Karlsruhe / Germany / 1998

23–25 Posters and catalogue, part of corporate identity for the European Film Institute Karlsruhe (EIKK) / EIKK / Germany / 1998

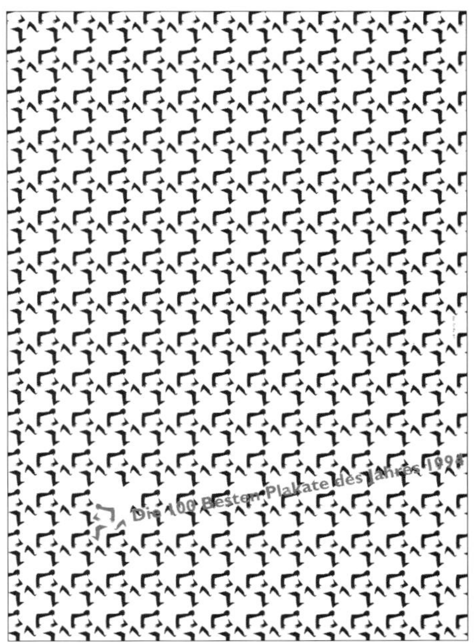

17 18 19

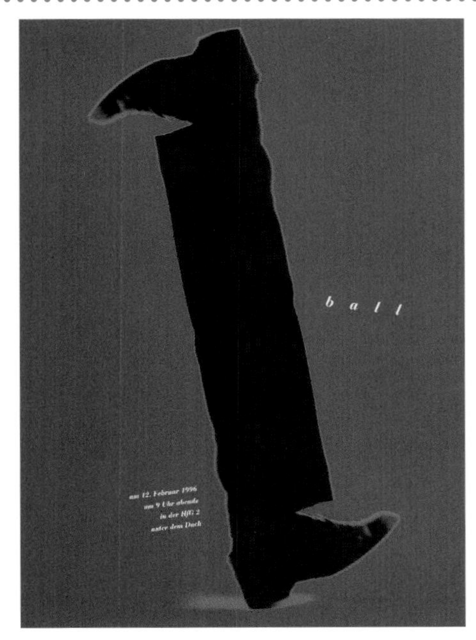

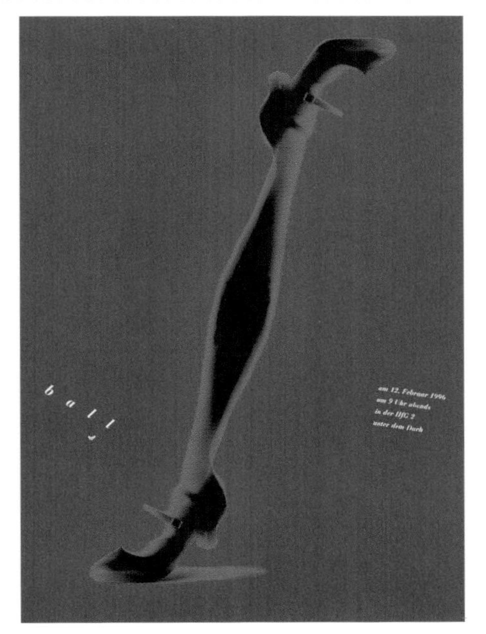

20 21 22

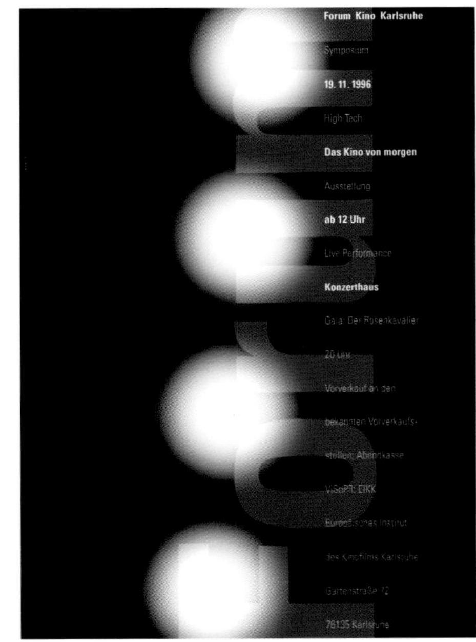

23 24 25

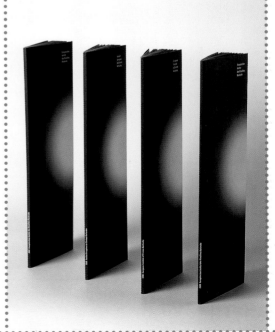

Fons Hickmann appeared one day in my seminar at Wupperthal University, although he had already received a degree from the excellent university in Düsseldorf. Hickmann didn't just want to learn something, he also wanted to shake things up, so it didn't come as a surprise that I was soon correcting the typography of a poster he had designed for Bazon Brock, a professor in the school's department of aesthetics. One year later he was on the move again. In his luggage he had a fantastic poster series for the silent-movie festival in Graz, which was soon awarded gold medals around the world. • • Hickmann wore a T-shirt on which was written "Fons." Small wonder that he has now become a professor himself, teaching at the University of Applied Arts in Vienna and running its institute for design. He is not only an excellent designer with the ability to create a *Gesamtkunstwerk*, but also an admirable communicator. In his biography he writes: "Fons M. Hickmann was born somewhere among the coal heaps of the Ruhr area. Afflicted by bouts of typographic fever, after falling into a bowl of alphabet soup as a child. 1972: beginning of school career spent on soccer pitches between Dortmund and Schalke. Travels in distant lands. 1987: start of attempts at studying philosophy, Germanic philology, photography, art and design, leading to a diploma in graphic design. In 1991, crowned as 'Guaredisch the First' by the Düsseldorf Typographic Society and dubbed Typographic Knight for Life. Established design offices in Düsseldorf and Berlin, with virtual stations in Dortmund and Essen. Currently 'Fons Hickmann m23' in Berlin [...] 1997: appointments as a lecturer and professor at various universities, lecture tours, participation in juries, numerous publications. Received innumerable design awards and honours...." • • He who so confidently and unconventionally reflects on his designer life with such critical and ironic distance must be able to present work that is up to the highest standard. Hickmann does this! What's more, his output in poster and corporate design is increasingly living up to his aspirations. His work has been represented at biennials and exhibitions around the world, and in 2002 he won the prestigious corporate design commission for the Kieler Woche, Europe's most important sailing regatta. • • Hickmann now lives in Berlin and Vienna with the illustrator Gesine Grotrian-Steinweg and a small Fontissima with the lovely name Uma Malina. And when one meets him, one always has the impression that he is just at the beginning. • • Uwe Loesch • •

1–3 Poster series for Kieler Woche sailing regatta / Festival Kieler Woche / Germany / 2002
4–6 Poster series for concerts, *St John Passion*, by Johann Sebastian Bach, *Messiah*, by Georg Friedrich Haendel, and *Requiem*, by Giuseppe Verdi (photography Wolfgang Bellwinkel) / Johanneskantorei / Germany / 2001–2002
7 *Als Augen noch sprechen konnten* (When Eyes Could Still Speak) poster series for silent-film festival in Graz, Austria / Stummfilm Tage Graz / Austria / 1996

Fons Hickmann

Berlin/Vienna

①

④

②

⑤

③

⑥

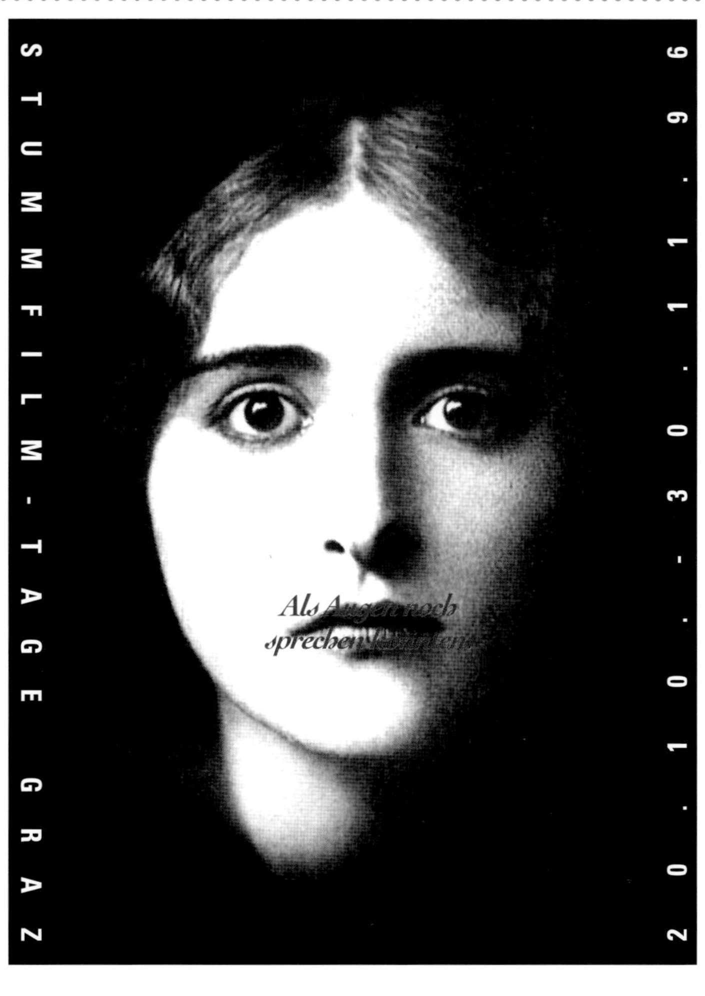
STUMMFILM-TAGE GRAZ
20.10.-30.11.96
Als Augen noch
sprechen

STUMMF .TAGE G
20.10 .11.

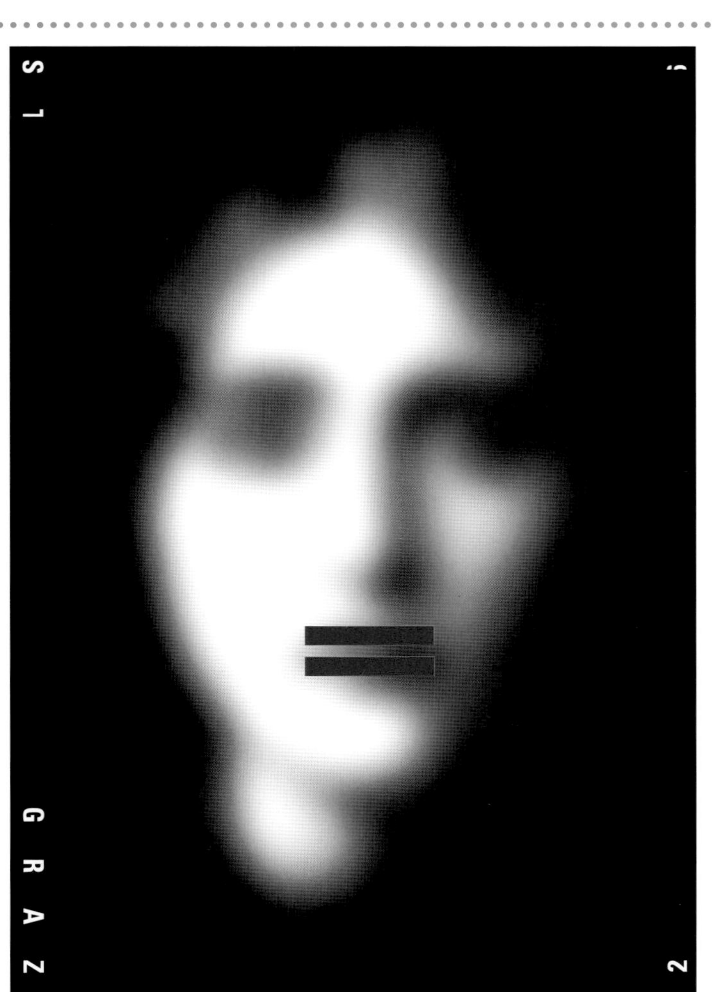
GRAZ

FILM-

8 9 10

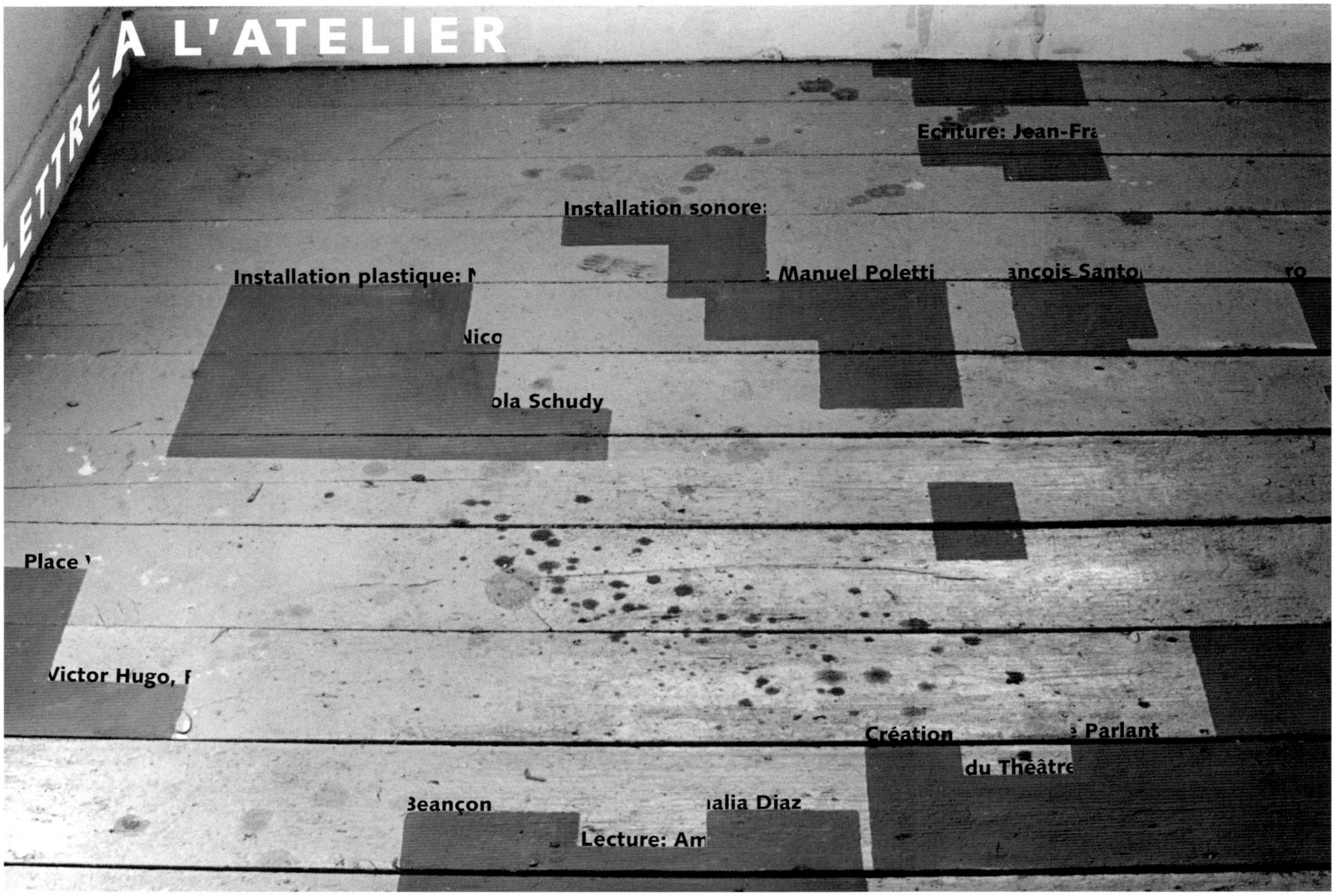

11

Fons Hickmann

8–10 *Anonyme Idylle* (Anonymous Idyll) poster series for open-air concerts at the Freibad Rheinstadion, Düsseldorf / B8 / Germany / 2000
11 Poster for *Lettre à l'atelier* exhibition of the Franco-German artist group Théâtre Parlant / Théâtre Parlant / France / 1998
12 Poster for Hickmann lecture in Beijing (illustration Gesine Grotrian-Steinweg) / Central University of Fine Arts, Bejing / China / 2002
13 Poster for lecture by Hickmann at the Hochschule für Gestaltung Offentbach / Hochschule für Gestaltung Offentbach / Germany / 2002
14 Poster announcing Hickmann's website (photography Simon Gallus) / www.fonshickmann.com / Germany / 2002
15–20 Posters for exhibitions, concerts, and lectures in Düsseldorf / Labor für Soziale und Ästhetische Entwicklungen / Germany / 1999–2002

12 13 14

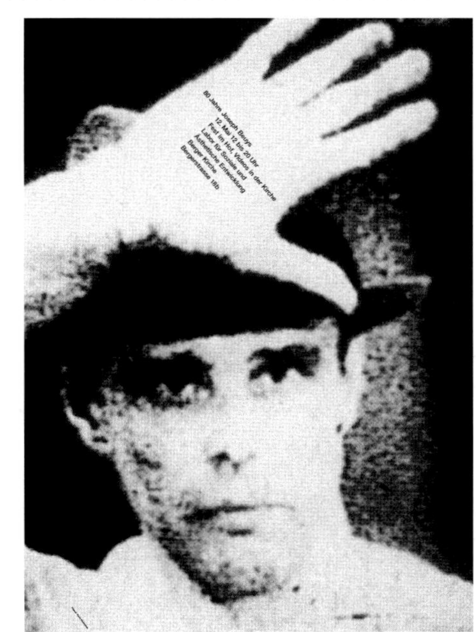

15 16 17

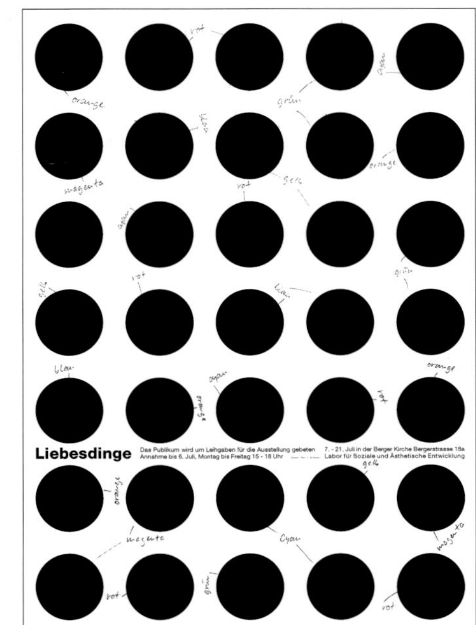

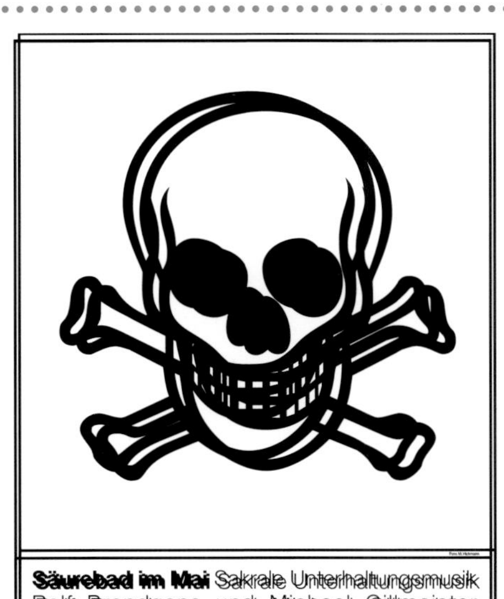

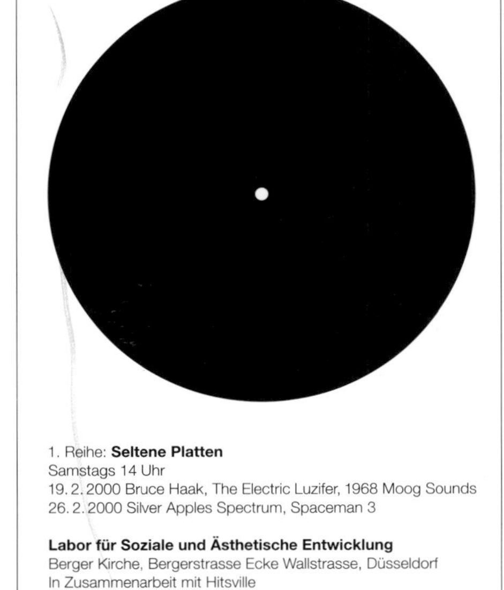

18 19 20

I first saw Kim Hiorthøy's work when I gave a workshop in Bergen, Norway, and asked which young designers were now the Norwegian graphic trailblazers. From between the fjords, Kim arose, a young designer who is in his element in the country's music scene. At his tender age he has already published a book on his work, which suggests a similarly defiant feel for self-promotion as David Carson's did: it talks to its own audience, in codes that can be recognized and unraveled by that audience. • • Kim's designs are completely incompatible with my own musical background of Blue Note (Reid Miles) and Verve (David Stone Martin), with their brilliant record sleeves, but Kim's style is certainly his own, especially in the case of covers that he draws in wispy lines or conceives with the sparsest of colored planes. He may not be unique, but he is a good representative of the "Bruna generation": young designers who use the most minimal of means to make something "readable." In this case, readable means recognizable by people who know and appreciate the music and who will immediately comprehend the visual codes on Kim's covers. Apart from that, he is an excellent draftsman, who, in his best works, maintains a sense of space in his drawings, preventing them from becoming clogged. He represents a somewhat peripheral culture, which through travel, the Internet, and publications still manages to keep track of the rest of the world—and feeds back to it through the same channels. And the fact that Kim has found a client (Rune Grammofon) who lets him do what he wants—that, of course, is spectacular! • • Anthon Beeke • •

1

2

3

4

Kim Hiorthøy

Oslo

1–4 Wall designs for restaurant in Roppongi, Tokyo / Thisisrealart and Peter Smith / Japan / 2002 / The designs are mounted on a "Venetian blind"-like billboard that rotates every fifteen minutes displaying the different flower designs.
5 CD cover, *Genetic Engineering*, by Phonophani / Rune Grammofon / Norway / 2001
6 CD cover, *Duck-Rabbit*, by Alog / Rune Grammofon / Norway / 2001
7 CD cover, *Den øverste toppen på en blåmalt flaggstang*, by Spunk / Rune Grammofon / Norway / 2002
8 CD cover, *Veggie*, by Food / Rune Grammofon / Norway / 2002
9 CD cover, *Scorch Trio*, by Björkenheim/Flaten/Nilssen-Love / Rune Grammofon / Norway / 2002
10 CD cover, *Free Music*, by Monolight / Rune Grammofon / Norway / 2002

5

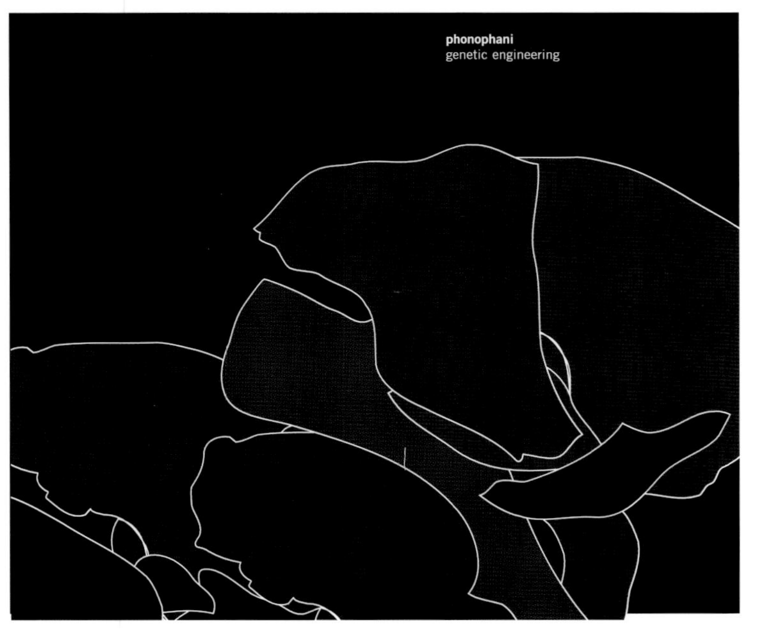

phonophani
genetic engineering

6

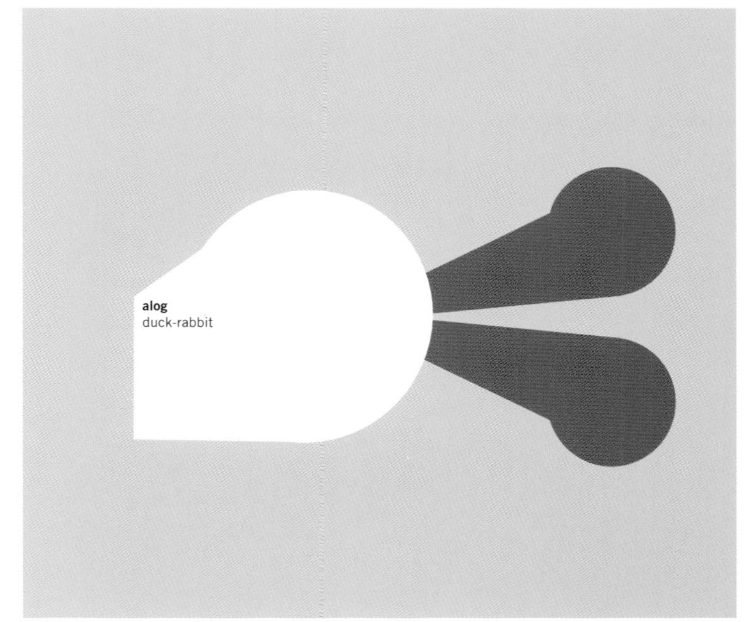

alog
duck-rabbit

7

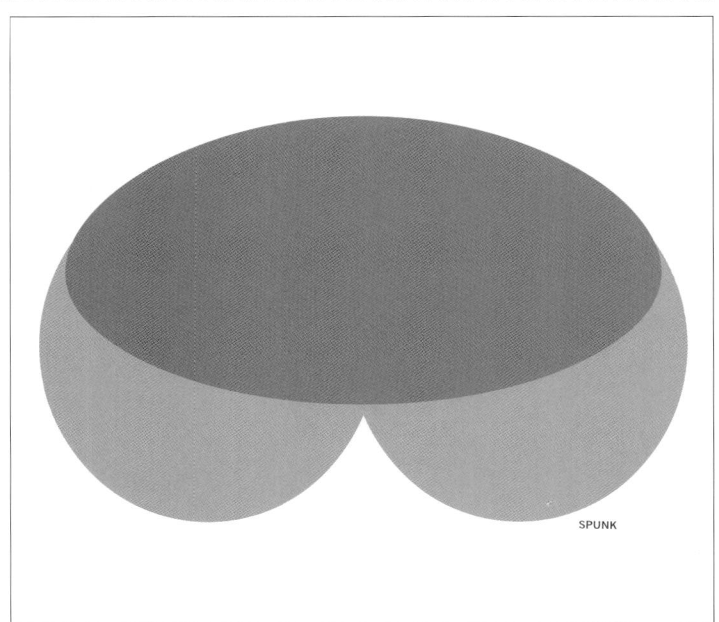

SPUNK

8

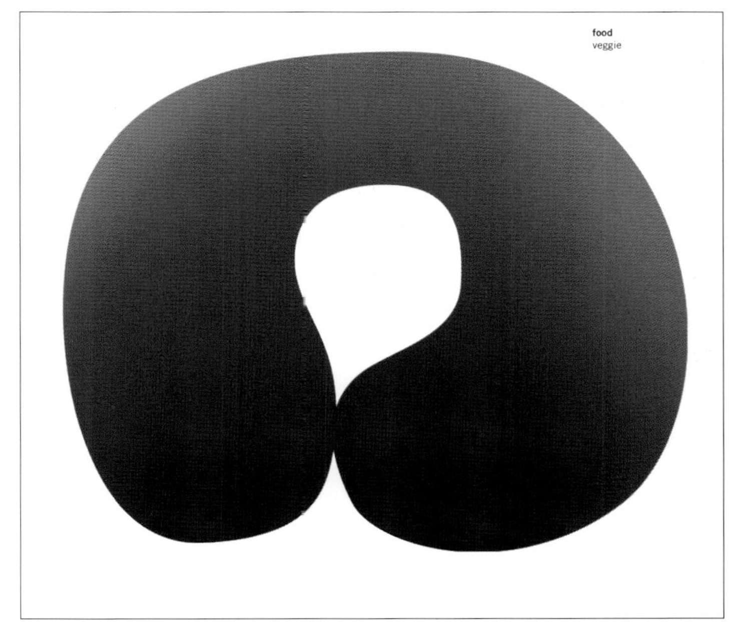

food
veggie

9

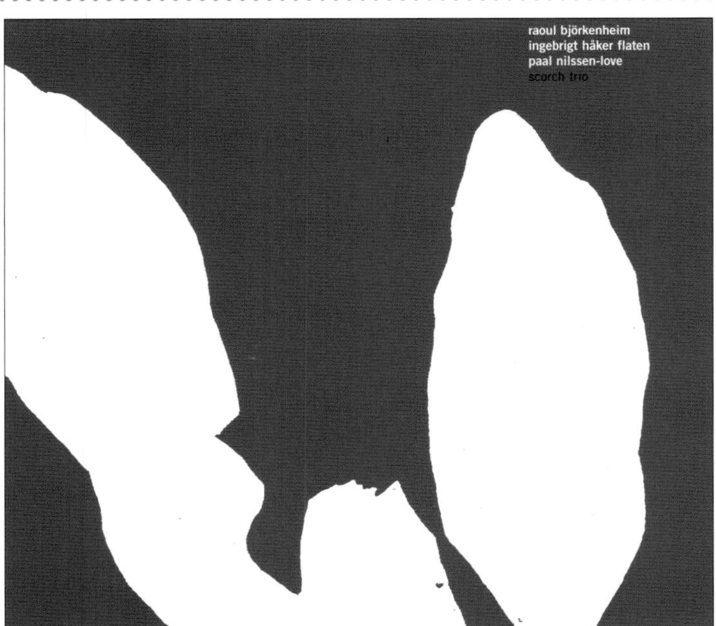

raoul björkenheim
ingebrigt håker flaten
paal nilssen-love
scorch trio

10

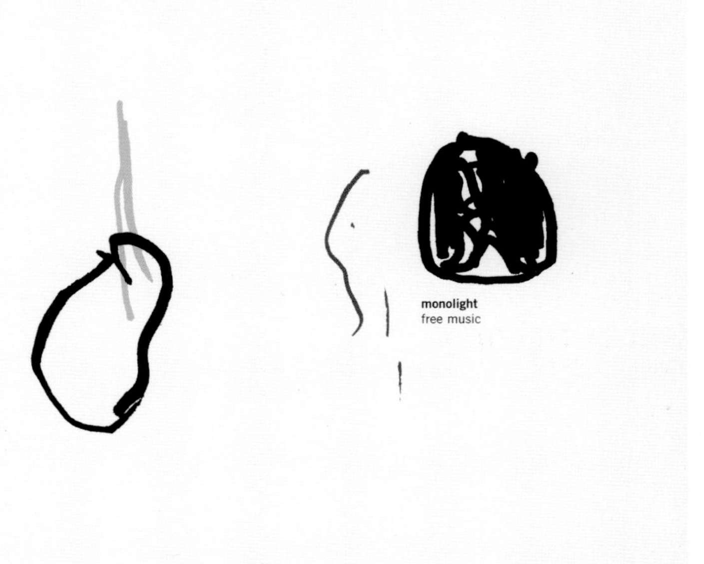

monolight
free music

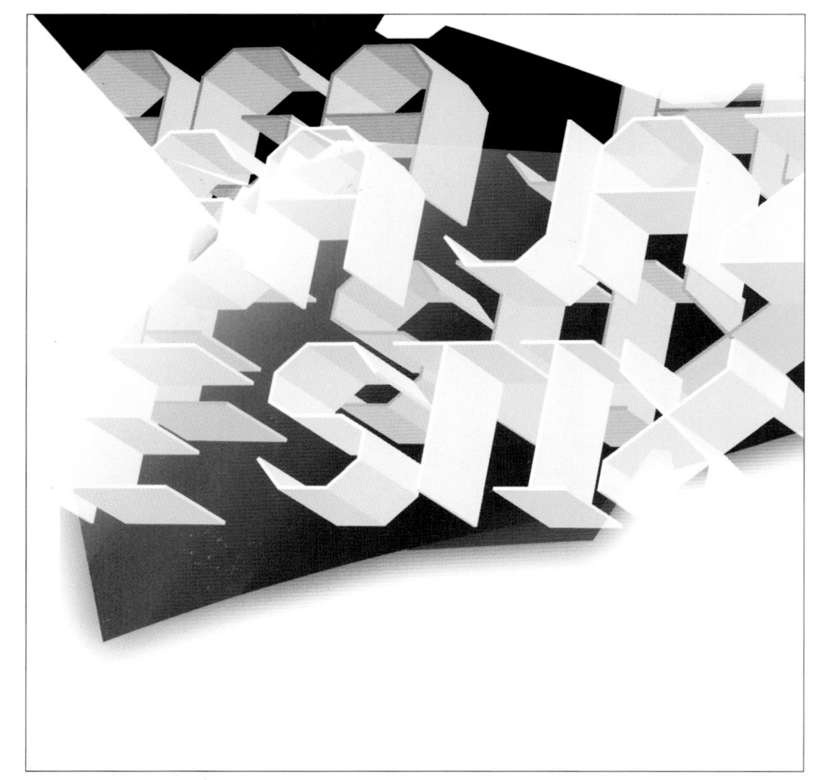

11

12

13

14

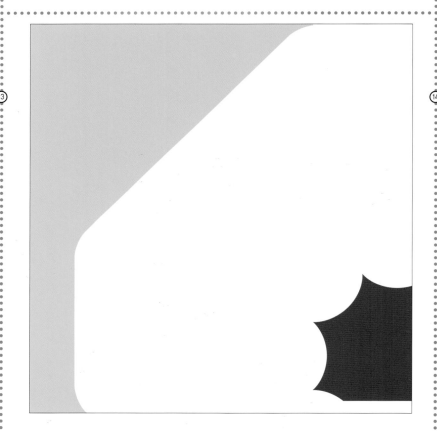

Kim Hiorthøy

11 Early version of CD cover for *The Stix*, by Jaga Jazzist / Smalltown Supersound and Ninja Tune / Norway / 2003
12 CD cover, *Various Artists: The Smalltown Supersampler* / Smalltown Supersound / Norway / 2002
13 CD cover, *Voice*, by Maja Ratkje / Rune Grammofon / Norway / 2002
14 Cover illustration, *2001 D&AD Award Winners* booklet / Creative Review / United Kingdom / 2001
15–16 Illustrations for March/April and July/August programs of the Oslo Cinematheque / Oslo Cinematheque / Norway / 2002
17 Poster for exhibition *Jeg er nesten alltid redd* at the Photographers' Gallery, Oslo / Norway / 2003
18 Promotional poster for album *Hei*, by Kim Hiorthøy / Smalltown Supersound / Norway / 2000

15

16

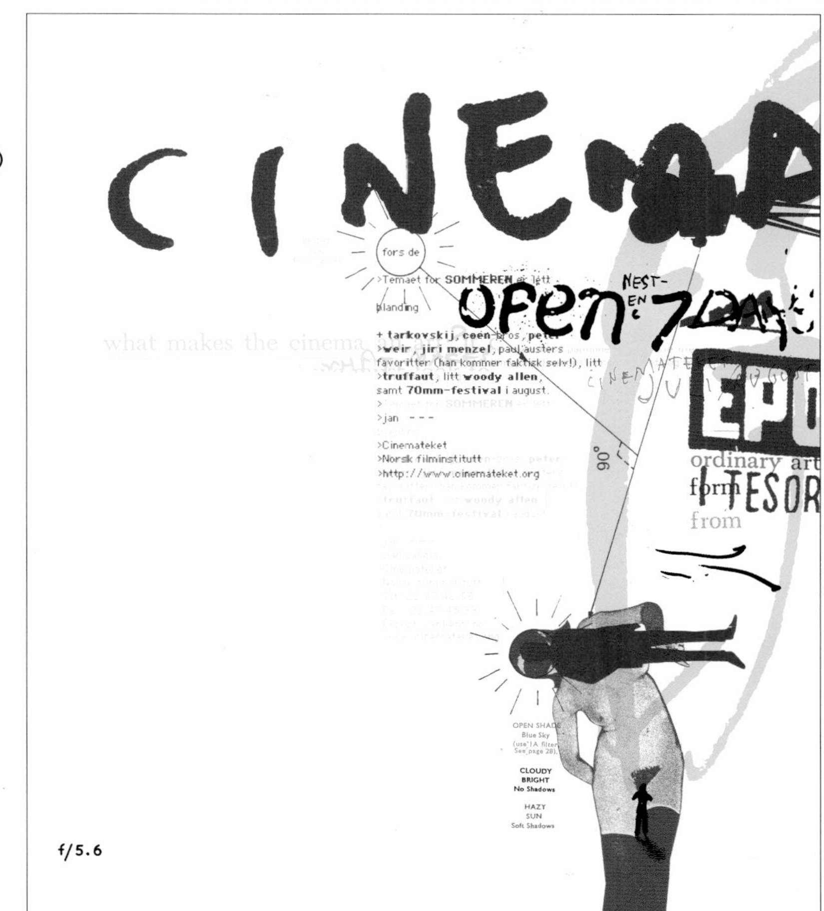
fors de
>Temaet for SOMMEREN er lett
blanding
+ tarkovskij, coen-bros, peter
>weir, jiri menzel, paul austers
favoritter (han kommer faktisk selv!), litt
>truffaut, litt woody allen,
samt 70mm-festival i august.
>jan ---
>Cinemateket
>Norsk filminstitutt
>http://www.cinemateket.org
what makes the cinema
ordinary art
form
from
90°
OPEN SHADE
Blue Sky
CLOUDY
BRIGHT
No Shadows
HAZY
SUN
Soft Shadows
f/5.6

17

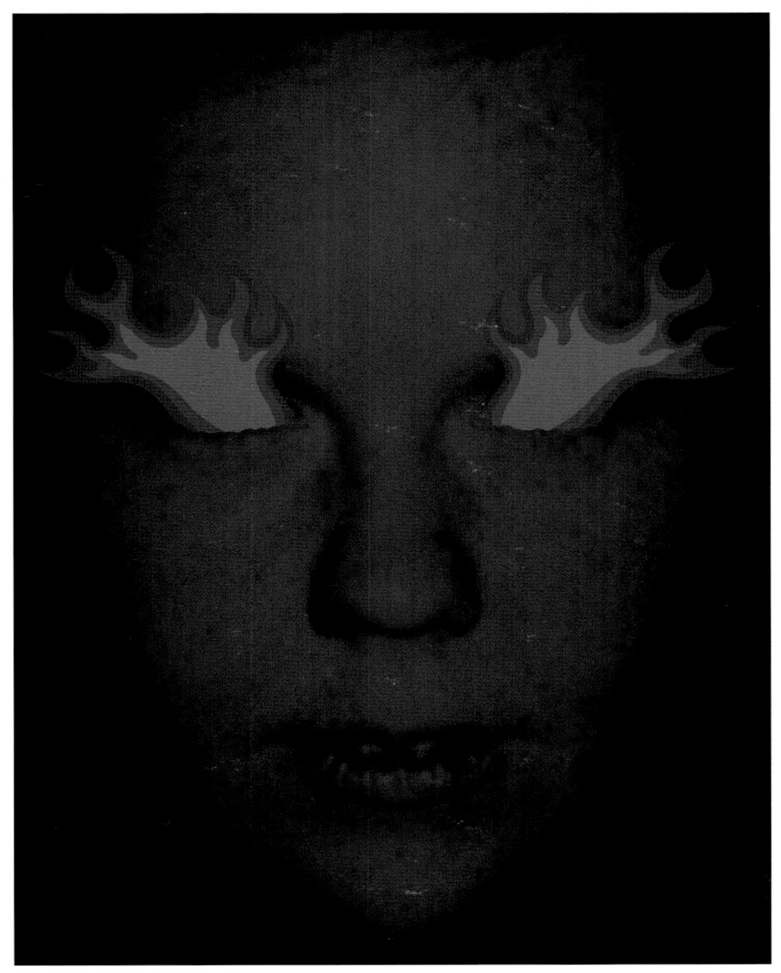

18

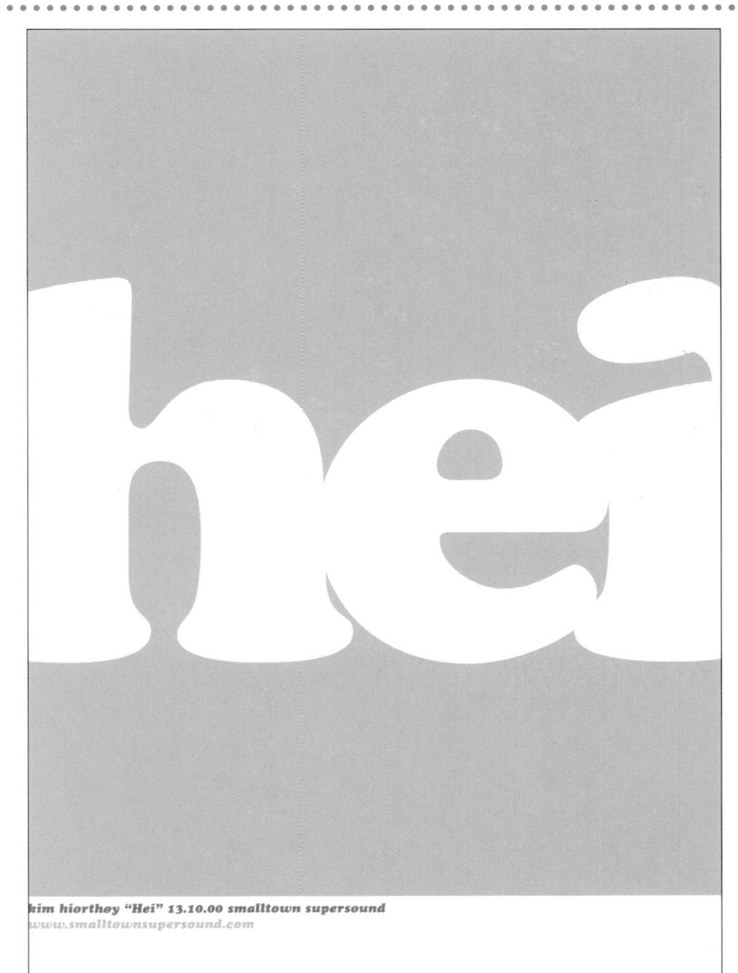
hei
kim hiorthøy "Hei" 13.10.00 smalltown supersound
www.smalltownsupersound.com

On a cold winter morning, a thin, clear film of ice forms in the shallow flower basin in the garden. When I try to scoop the fragile ice with my hands, it melts away in my palm. Keiko Hirano's works do not by any means melt away. They have a firm presence with their delicate but deep, penetrating colors. Are they the colors of the surface of the sea when a mermaid looks up from the depth of the ocean? Are they the colors of the universe when an angel casts a glance from atop a cloud? They are strange, clear colors. • •Hirano's graphic designs, packaging designs using varied materials, and display spaces all transcend the idea conceived on the designer's worktable. Their abstract composition, which may appear too clean, and their delicate construction result in great works that seem to firmly reflect a strong creative ideology. • •In the noisy and flashy advertising business of Japan's declining economy, Hirano's designs have a gentle, soft touch that appeals to the heart. They make us recall the long-forgotten virtue of good style and grace. • •Her ability is demonstrated in the logo of the National Museum of Modern Art, Tokyo and the overall art direction for Qiora cosmetic products . She is one of the new powers who will change the direction of graphic design in Japan. • •Shigeo Fukuda• •

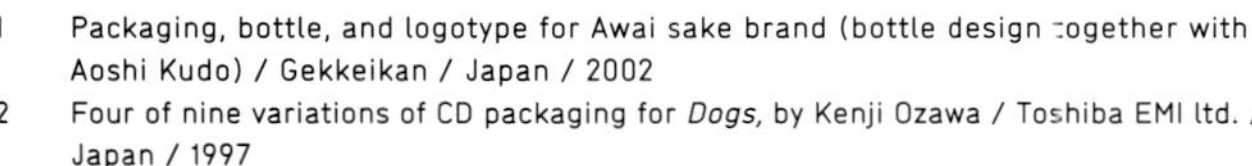

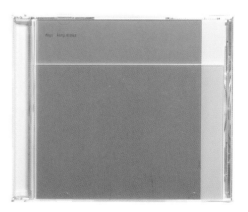

1 Packaging, bottle, and logotype for Awai sake brand (bottle design together with Aoshi Kudo) / Gekkeikan / Japan / 2002
2 Four of nine variations of CD packaging for *Dogs*, by Kenji Ozawa / Toshiba EMI ltd. / Japan / 1997
3 Logo, invitation cards, vinyl bags, and banner for National Museum of Modern Art, Tokyo / Japan / 2002

Keiko Hirano

Tokyo

The National Museum of Modern Art, Tokyo

The National Museum

of Modern Art, Tokyo

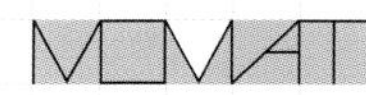

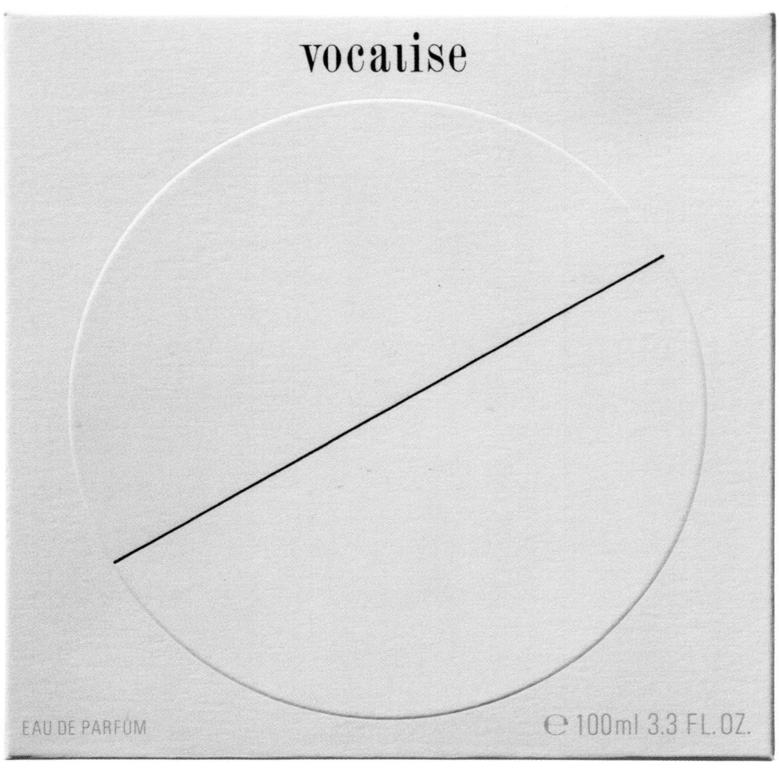

4
5

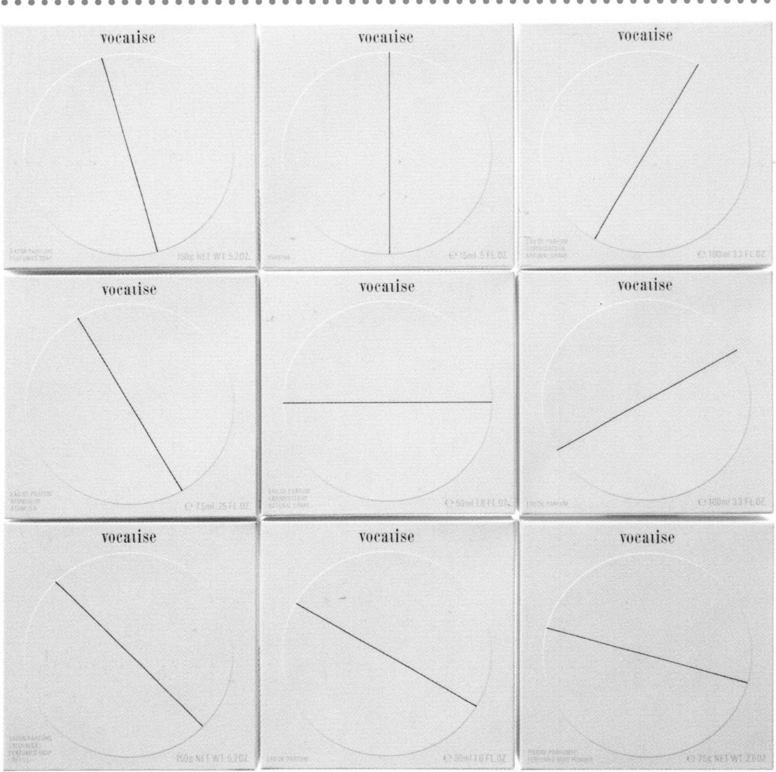

6
7

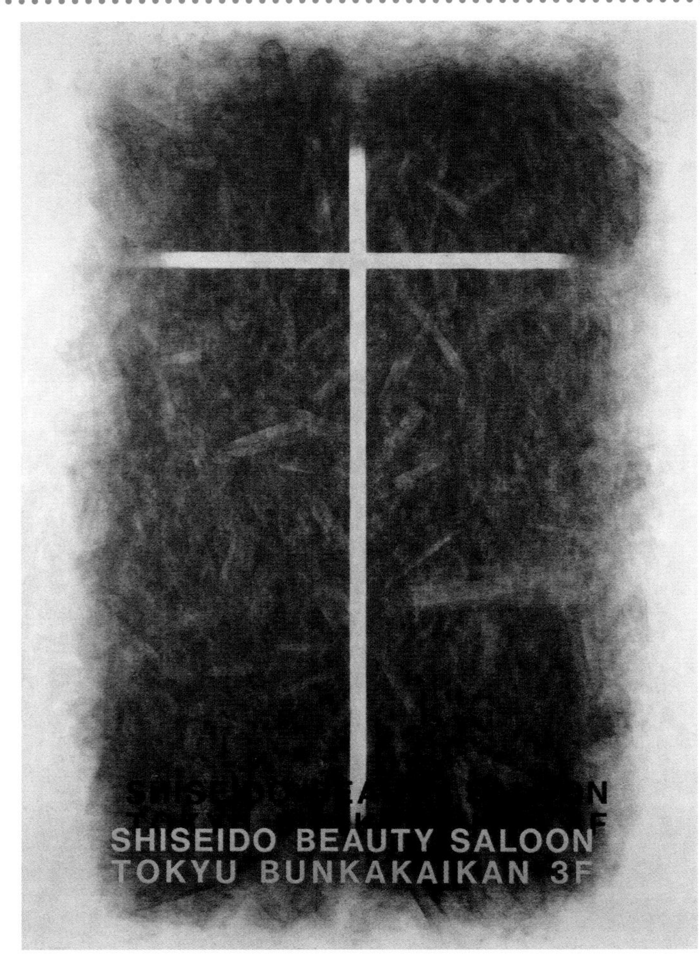

4–5 Logo and packaging for Vocalise perfume / Shiseido / Japan / 1997
6–7 Poster series for beauty salon / Shiseido Beauty Saloon / Japan / 1994
8–9 Poster, banner, and flyer for *Graphic Wave 1998* exhibition at Ginza Graphic Gallery / Dai Nippon Printing / Japan / 1998
10–13 Visual identity including logo, stationery, shop facade, and display-unit system for cosmetic brand Qiora / Shiseido / Japan / 2000–2001

Keiko Hirano

ギンザ・グラフィック・ギャラリー第148回企画展
Graphic Wave 1998
蝦名龍郎 平野敬子 三木健

10
11
12
13

qiora

8
9

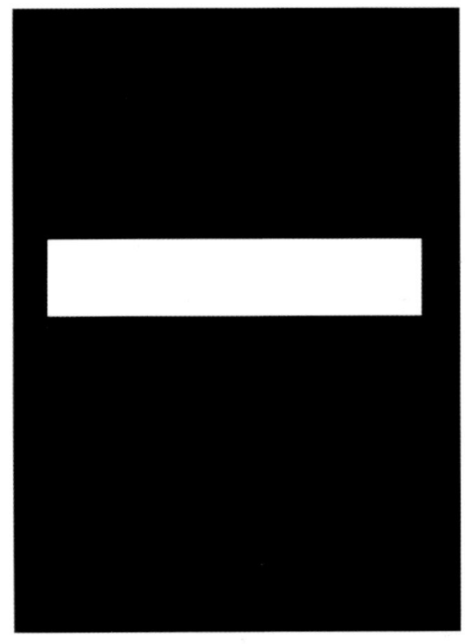
ギンザ・グラフィック・ギャラリー第148回企画展
Graphic Wave 1998
蝦名龍郎 平野敬子 三木健
1998年9月1日(火)–9月26日(土)
ggg
DAI NIPPON PRINTING

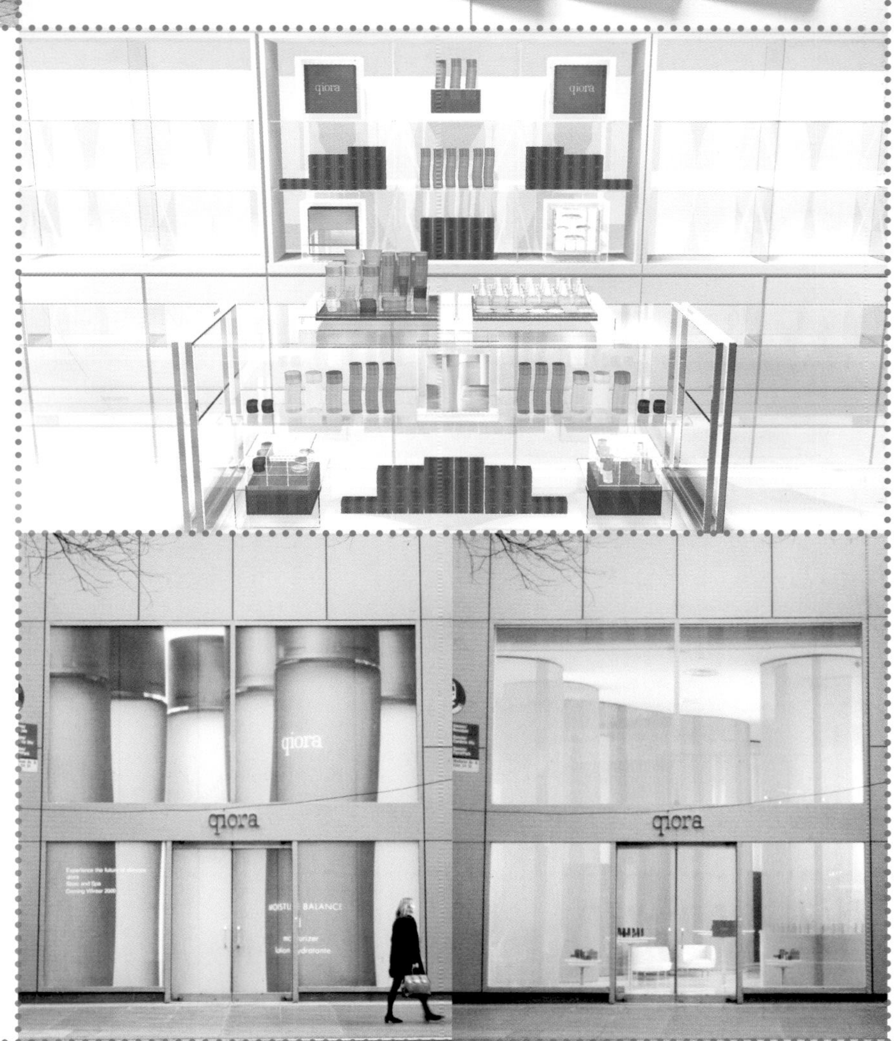
qiora
qiora
qiora

Graphic designers are engaged in works that represent the entire culture of their society. Their works cover areas from business communications to leisure activities with no boundary in applications. Thus, a designer faces an extremely difficult task to satisfy all the needs of different objectives. He must have a good understanding of his client's needs, he must have a good grasp of the society at large, and above all he must possess the unyielding spirit of an avant-gardist with full command of the techniques of the formal arts. • • Hon Bing-wah has overcome all these difficulties. I have full confidence that he is one of those creators who will bravely deal with new challenges in the future. He has demonstrated his talent in such areas as figurative illustration, abstract photography, creative typography, and three-dimensional design. • • In Hong Kong, where the design business is fiercely competitive, Hon has successfully demonstrated his broad vision combining the tradition of Asia with a modern sensitivity. We learn from his passionate works that graphic design transcends the business world to the culture of a city, country, and society. • • Shigeo Fukuda • •

1

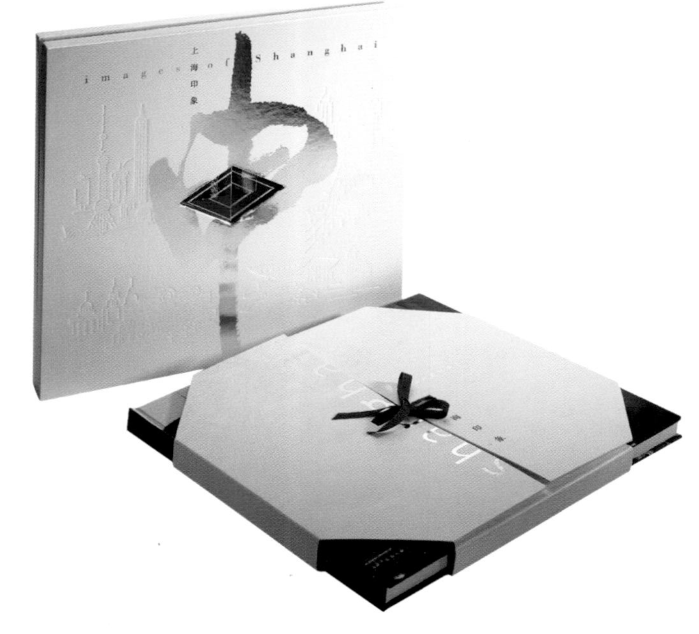

2 3 4 5

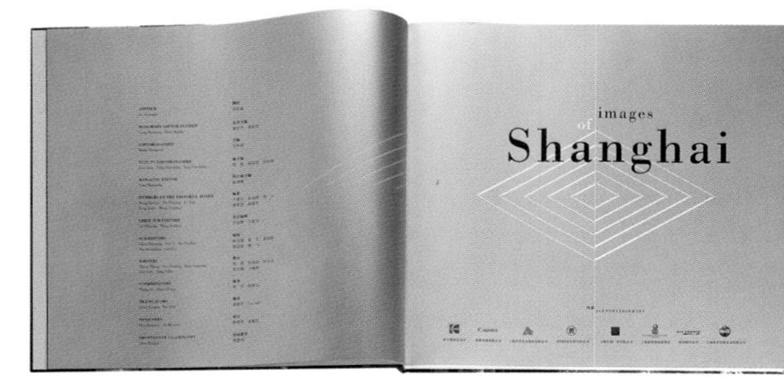

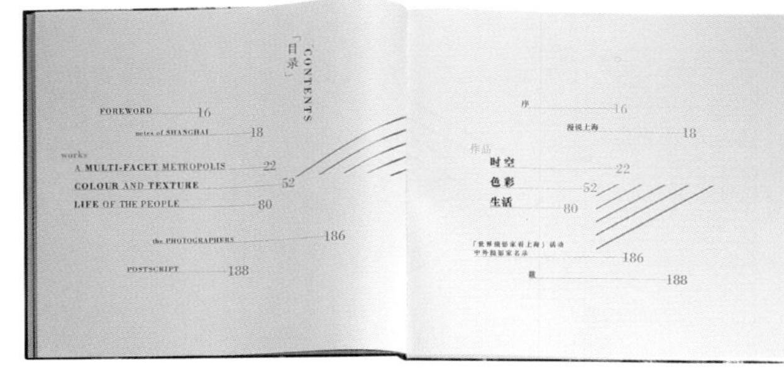

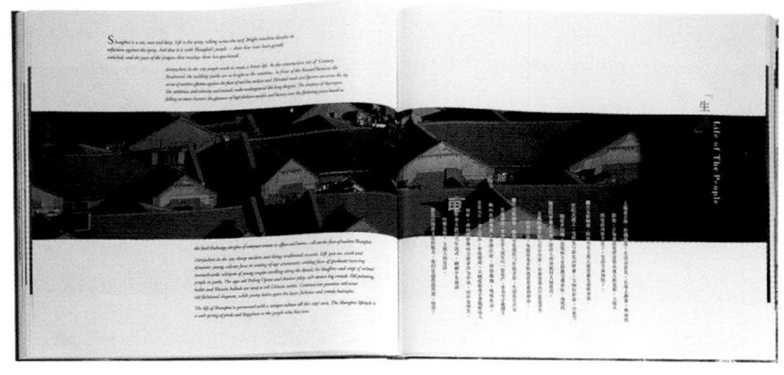

1–5 Cover and spreads, *Image of Shanghai* / Information Office of Shanghai Municipal People's Government / China / 1999 / The book was part of the campaign Shanghai in the Eyes of the World's Top Photographers, which celebrated the fiftieth anniversary of the liberation of Shanghai.
6 Kiss or Kill poster for *Peace Poster Exhibition 2001, Taiwan* / Taiwan Poster Design Association / Taiwan / 2001
7 Profession of Perfection poster for *10th Hong Kong Awards Poster Exhibition* / Heidelberg Printing Machine Co. / Hong Kong / 1998
8 Poster for *Suzhou Image Poster Exhibition* / Suzhou Graphic Designers Association / China / 2000
9 Redeeming Culture poster for *Living Heritage* exhibition / Hong Kong Heritage Museum / Hong Kong / 2001

Hon Bing-wah

Hong Kong

6

Kiss OR Kill

7

PRINTING..
The 10th Hong Kong Print Awards Poster Exhibition
PROFESSION of PERFECTION
HEIDELBERG

8

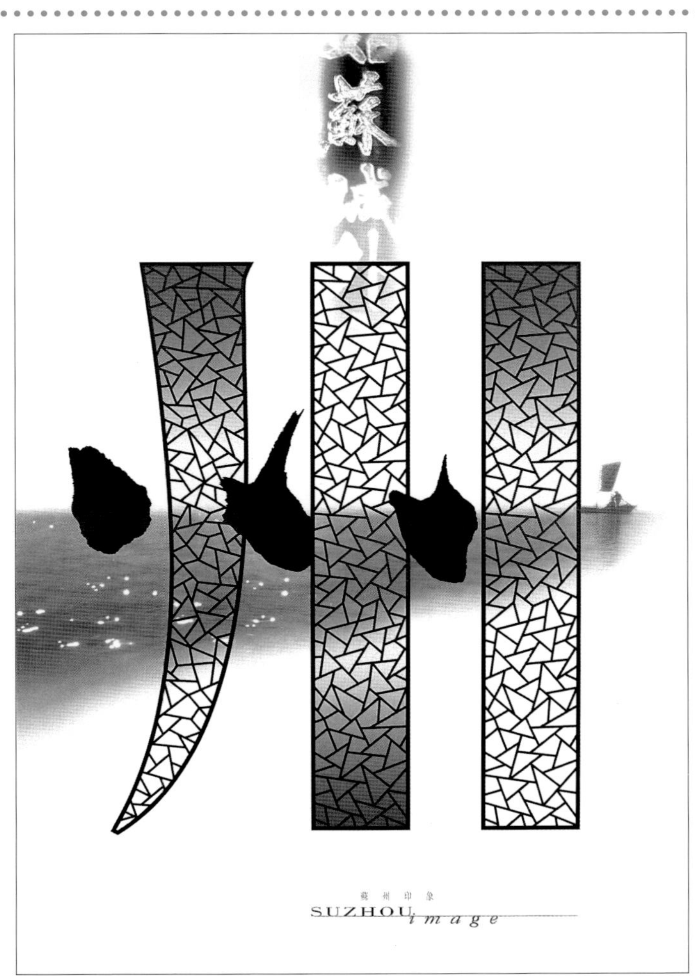
蘇州
蘇州印象
SUZHOU image

9

文化
囍
香港
押
Cultural value

10

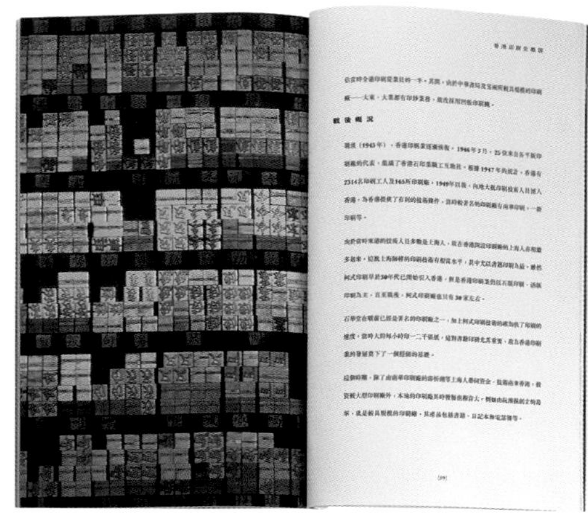

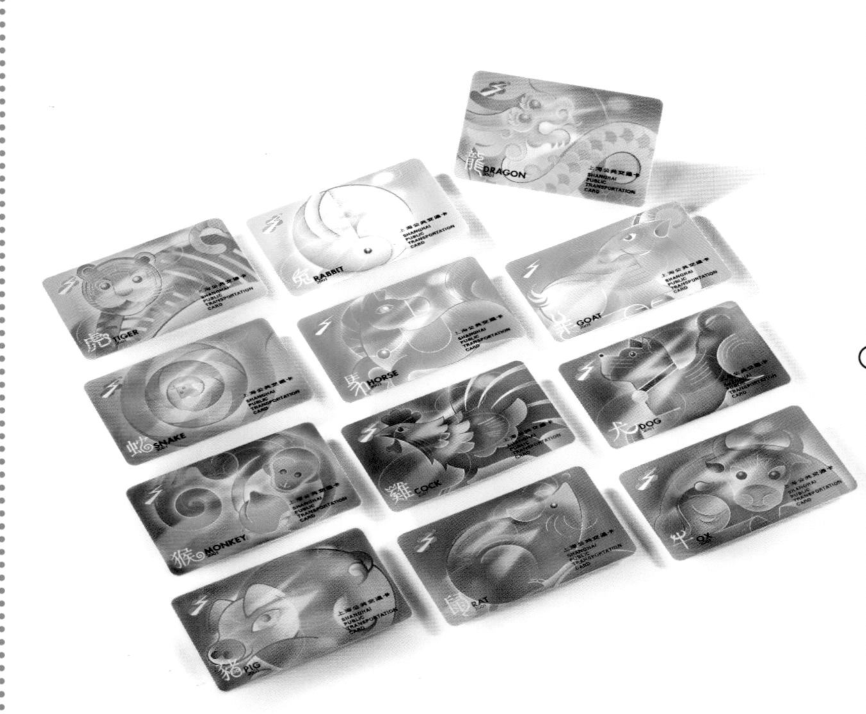

11

10 Slipcase, cover, and spreads, 60th Anniversary commemorative brochure / Hong Kong Printers Association / Hong Kong / 1999
11 Set of transportation cards with Chinese zodiac theme / Shanghai Public Transportation Card Co. Ltd. / China / 2000 / The set was designed for the first anniversary of the Shanghai Public Transportation Card System.
12 Cover and spreads, information brochure to promote Shanghai's bidding for the World Expo 2010 / Expo 2010 Shanghai China Bidding Office / China / 2002

Hon Bing-wah

SHANGHAI CHINA

CHINA

12

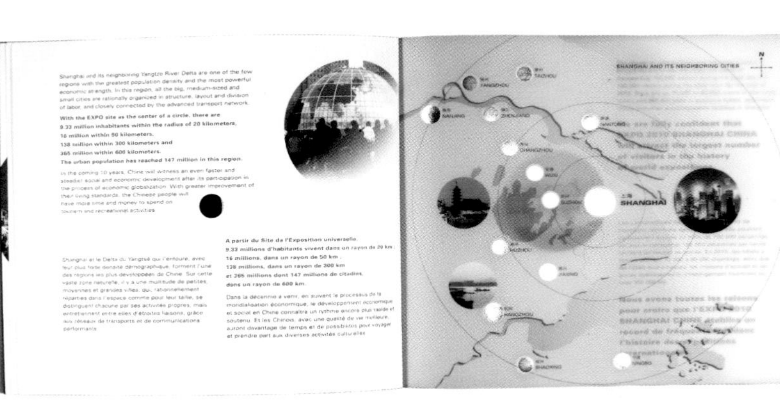
SHANGHAI AND ITS NEIGHBORING CITIES

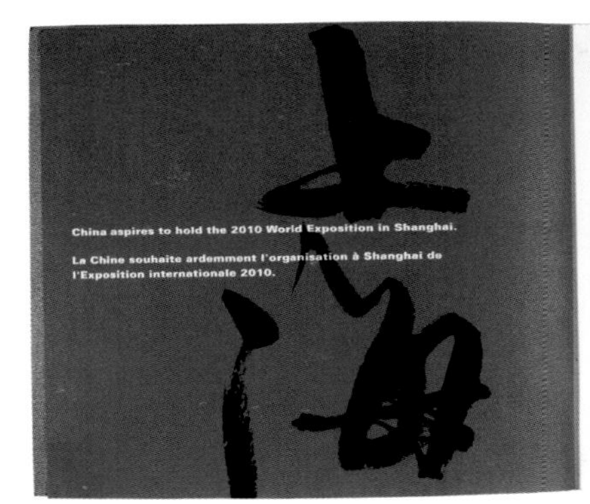
China aspires to hold the 2010 World Exposition in Shanghai.
La Chine souhaite ardemment l'organisation à Shanghai de l'Exposition internationale 2010.

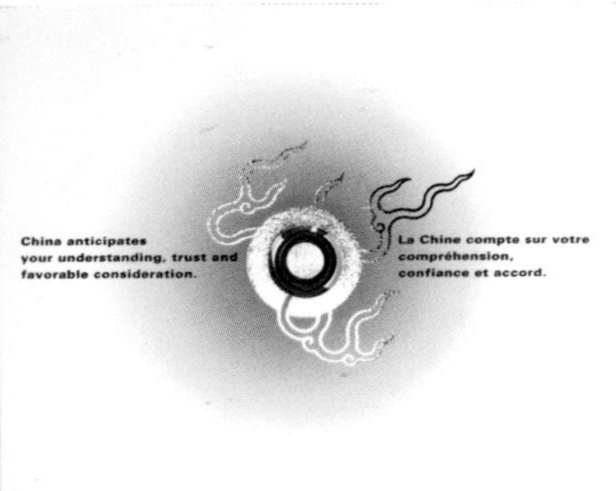
China anticipates your understanding, trust and favorable consideration.
La Chine compte sur votre compréhension, confiance et accord.

China will make EXPO 2010 SHANGHAI CHINA a memorable world exposition.

La Chine fera de l'EXPO 2010 SHANGHAI CHINE une exposition mémorable.
US$ 100 MILLION
A special assistance fund of 100 million US dollars is established.

China will make EXPO 2010 SHANGHAI CHINA a successful world exposition.

La Chine fera de l'EXPO 2010 SHANGHAI une exposition parfaitement réussie.

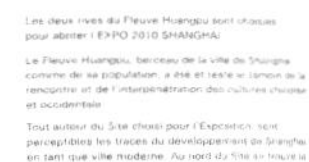

SHANGHAI 2010

China will make EXPO 2010 SHANGHAI CHINA a wonderful world exposition.

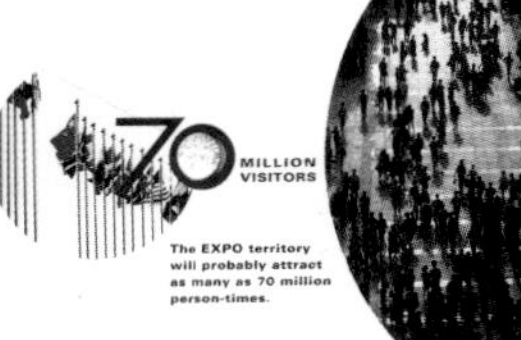
70 MILLION VISITORS
The EXPO territory will probably attract as many as 70 million person-times.

La Chine fera de l'EXPO 2010 SHANGHAI une exposition des plus éclatantes.

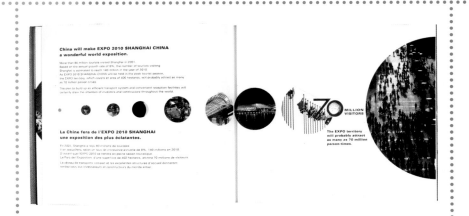

Inkahoots began as a government-assisted community screenprinting workshop and was founded as a public-access poster collective in 1990 by three self-taught graphic designers—Chris Stannard, Geoff Heller, and Robyn McDonald—during a chronic housing shortage in Brisbane. For five years the posters designed for, with, and by local community groups were characterized by an often crude yet vibrant and raw immediacy that reflected the urgency of their messages and Inkahoots's passionate, card-carrying commitment to addressing social inequalities. Their active participation in protest and debate about aboriginal land rights, gay rights, women's rights, labor issues, war, housing, and ecological matters gives real substance to the tagline they use to describe themselves, "direct design action". At a time when anthologies of the "new typography" were showing how a new generation of designers questioned the polite modernist principle of service by foregrounding artistic self-expression, Inkahoots had already rejected the service principle. While proponents of postmodernism engineered opportunity for their own aesthetic obsessions, this band of Australian idealists created a platform for their political beliefs.••The arrival of Inkahoots's first college-trained graphic designer, Jason Grant, followed the enforcement of Brisbane's anti-bill-posting laws in 1994. Out of the grassroots poster collective had emerged a graphic-design practice free of the binds of state funding and able to tackle broader communication problems. Grant brought with him ideologically compatible professional design values that enabled Inkahoots to bring to their social work a highly sophisticated visual language. This was a combination powerful enough to provoke right-wing extremists into action; their studio was burned down in 1998. More recently with the addition of young graduates Lucas Surtie, Ben Mangan, and Joel Booy, the practice places increasing importance on the use of design as a seductive tool. With new graphic approaches married to an informed use of irony and biting wit, Inkahoots have proved that a critical stance need not be a didactic one. They understand how best to engage an audience, what American activist David Solnit calls "show, don't tell."••Nick Bell••

1

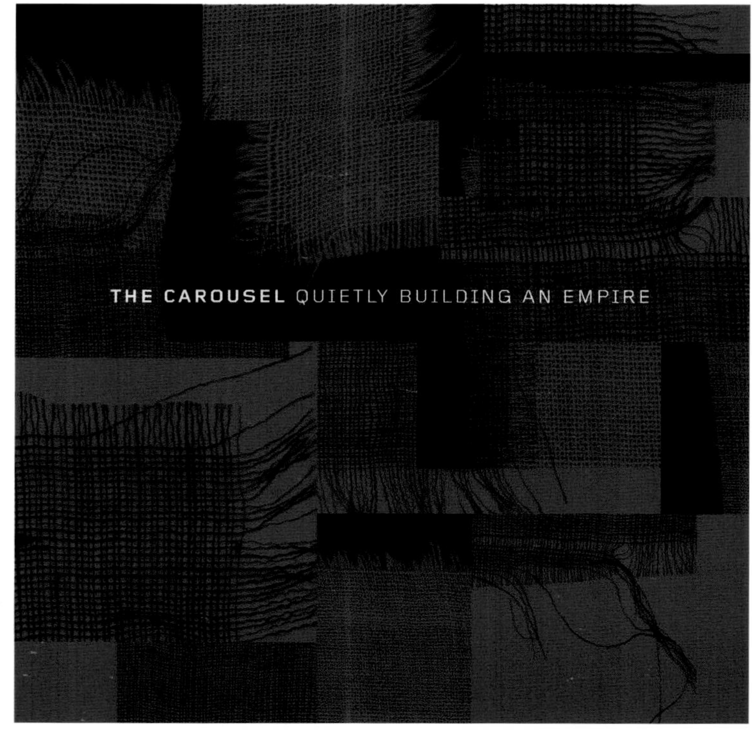

2

1 Poster protesting the harassment of the homeless by local authorities / Inner Brisbane Housing Network / Australia / 2000
2 CD packaging, *Quietly Building an Empire*, by The Carousel / The Carousel / Australia / 2001
3 Visual identity/promotional poster for company planning Australia's first zero-emission residential community / Ecodomo / Australia / 2001
4 Visual identity/promotional poster for Australia's oldest ethical investment institution / Foresters ANA Friendly Society / Australia / 2000
5 Cover, annual report for group organizing emergency accommodations for migrant women / MWESS / Australia / 2002
6 Spread from booklet promoting resources for young parents / Young Mothers for Young Women / Australia / 2002

Inkahoots

Brisbane, Australia

3

NATURAL LIVING
PASSIVE DESIGN PRINCIPLES | RENEWABLE ENERGY | WATER CONSERVATION | COMMUNITY, EMPLOYMENT & SOCIAL INTEGRATION | SENSITIVE LAND MANAGEMENT
ECODOMO ecological developments
ecodomo™

4

FORESTERS ANA
FRIENDLY SOCIETY
real ethical investment since 1890
ethical investing community development mutual aid
ETHICAL INVESTING
MUTUAL AID
COMMUNITY DEVELOPMENT
ESTERS ANA

5

MIGRANT WOMEN'S EMERGENCY SUPPORT SERVICE INC

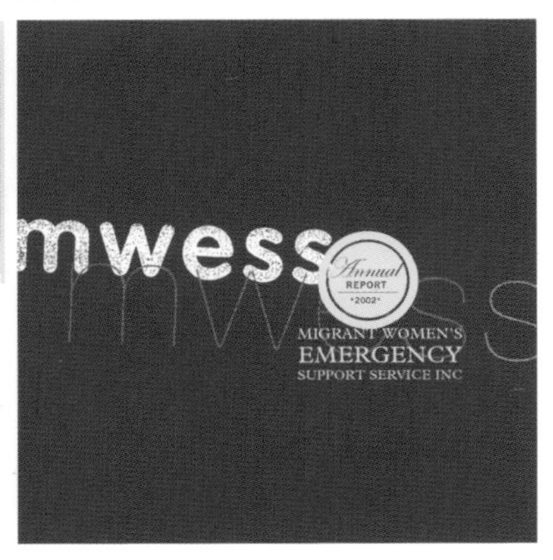
mwess
Annual REPORT 2003
MIGRANT WOMEN'S EMERGENCY SUPPORT SERVICE INC

6

a fair & inclusive SOCIETY
Healthy Relationships
(early intervention and prevention)
MULTI-FUNCTIONAL SPACE

PRISON AND DEBT

The findings of the Prison and Debt Project

by Anne Stringer FOR THE PRISONERS' LEGAL SERVICE

Funded by The National Consumer Trust Fund.

THE PRISONERS' LEGAL SERVICE INC. QUEENSLAND

7

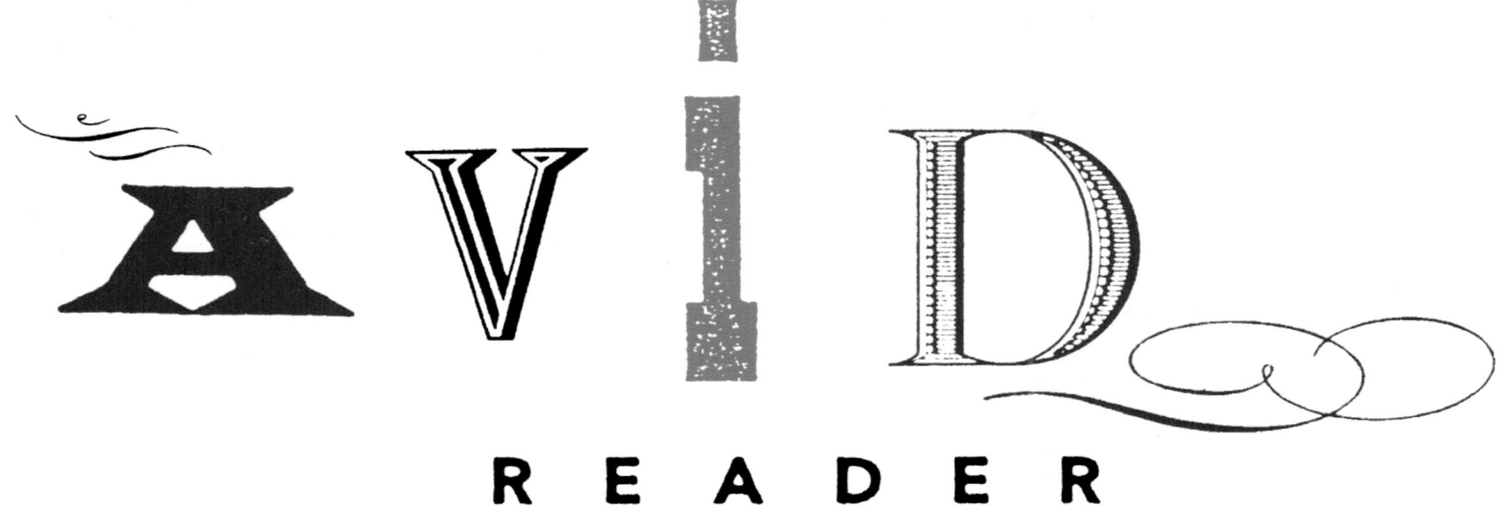

8

Inkahoots

7 Cover, report on the effect of imprisonment on debt of prisoners / Prisoners' Legal Service / Australia / 1998
8 Visual identity for independent bookstore in Brisbane / Avid Reader / Australia / 1997
9 Poster promoting street festival in Brisbane / West End Traders Association / Australia / 2002
10 Street poster satirizing a local politician's official campaign / Australia / 1991
11 Street poster posted on the eve of the Gulf War / Australia / 1991
12 Street poster promoting a national anticapitalism protest / M1 Alliance / Australia / 2001

9

THE 15th ANNUAL
Westend
Festival
CELEBRATING WESTEND'S WILDLIFE
Sunday 13th October 12noon to 10pm
FIVE STAGES, CINEMA, KIDS AREA, STREET ENTERTAINERS, UNDERGROUND ART LOUNGE, YUMMY FOOD, BARS, FANCY GOODS
Afro Dizzi Act, Hot Rubber Glove, Superfluid, La Gran Salsa, Freaky Lou, Cloudland, Pty Ltd, Xta'Chi, Margret Roadknight, Swingin Miss B and the Brand New Sweeties, Spankinhide, Intercooler, Asa Broomhall, Zimbira, Das Rumpus, The Naked Apes, Kafka, Kleinzeit, The Tides, The Limes, The Verge, Spicer Drake, Elysia Humphries, Alf, The Soul Retrievers, Chris Maver and friends, Miss Kate, Multicultural Street Dance Demos, Alive'n'Swingin, Wakka Wakka Dance Troupe, Gravity Warriors, Rio Rhythmics, Book Launch – Craig Bolland's: I Knit Water,
Festival Entry $5, Children under 16 Free
XXXX
inkahoots
SSI
D·N·Y

10

Help! Joh!
JOH
QUEENSLAND
Queensland is the greatest country on Earth. Joh helped make it that way. Now he needs your help to defend his honour.
For just $15 including packing and posting, you can own a brilliant 4 colour copy of the original 1983 Joh Campaign Poster. Size is 90cms × 60cms on top quality art paper ideal for framing or putting on the wall. Order yours now!

11

don't do it!

12

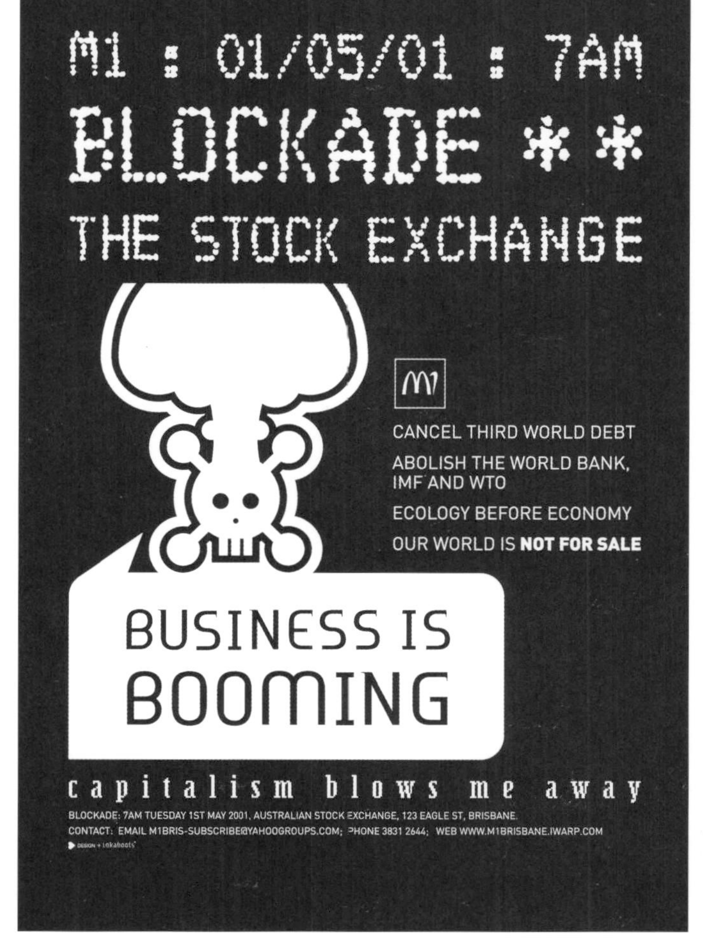
M1 : 01/05/01 : 7AM
BLOCKADE **
THE STOCK EXCHANGE
M1
CANCEL THIRD WORLD DEBT
ABOLISH THE WORLD BANK, IMF AND WTO
ECOLOGY BEFORE ECONOMY
OUR WORLD IS NOT FOR SALE
BUSINESS IS BOOMING
capitalism blows me away
BLOCKADE: 7AM TUESDAY 1ST MAY 2001, AUSTRALIAN STOCK EXCHANGE, 123 EAGLE ST, BRISBANE.
CONTACT: EMAIL M1BRIS-SUBSCRIBE@YAHOOGROUPS.COM; PHONE 3831 2644; WEB WWW.M1BRISBANE.IWARP.COM
DESIGN + inkahoots

What do you get when two young designers, one Icelandic and one German, get together and set up a graphic-design studio in Manhattan? The answer: Karlssonwilker Inc. In order to introduce their new studio in late 2000, Hjalti Karlsson and Jan Wilker distributed a rather interesting mailing. Printed on newsprint, it featured a portrait of the two designers—stiff as boards, all very Gilbert and George—and an animated diagram with layer upon layer of information (including contact details, sound bites, and illustrations) on the reverse. It captured the studio's eclectic personality to a T and brought a number of jobs to their door.••A glance at their well-rounded portfolio reflects the convergence of cultural backgrounds, the European aesthetics, and the myriad stimuli of Manhattan's voracious cultural landscape. It is a recipe that encourages eclecticism and makes it impossible to pigeonhole their work. They aren't afraid to try a new direction, so long as it will achieve the most appropriate and relevant solution for the client, and for themselves.•• The CD covers and promotional program they developed for the Vines have taken their work into a huge arena. Karlssonwilker created an appropriate graphic language, with shaky hand-drawn typography suggesting the edgy, postpunk ethic of the band. One of the CDs was shrinkwrapped in plastic that was printed in three colors. To spend time, effort, and resources on an element of the packaging that will end up in most people's wastebaskets says a lot about Karlssonwilker.••The firm's solution for a collection of live recordings by the psychedelic rock-jazz cult band Kraan is particularly appropriate. The graphic language suggests contemporary "psychedelic rock-jazz" without resorting to stereotypical psychedelic graphics. *Curious Boym*—a book designed for industrial-design studio Boym & Partners—has a die-cut cover, and the waste circle from that cut was subsequently used as an invite/coaster for the book's launch party. A fun, practical, and cost-effective solution.•• Are they space cadets or just plain, run-of-the-mill eccentrics? In 2001, they were invited to design a lamp for auction as part of an annual design benefit to fund scholarships for disadvantaged students. They created Doglamp, which is...a dog in a lamp, or rather a dog with a protective shade on its head, turned into a lamp. You have to admire that. There is no grand gesture involved, no pseudo-intellectual crap; just good, clean, twisted fun. ••Fernando Gutiérrez••

1–4 Promotional poster and CD packaging, *Live 2001*, by Kraan / Kraan and Bassball Records / USA / 2001
5–8 Book, cover, spreads, and promotional party invitation/coaster, *Curious Boym* by Studio Boym & Partners, New York / Princeton Architectural Press / USA / 2002 / The invitation/coaster is the cutout of the die-cut cover.

Karlssonwilker

New York

1

2

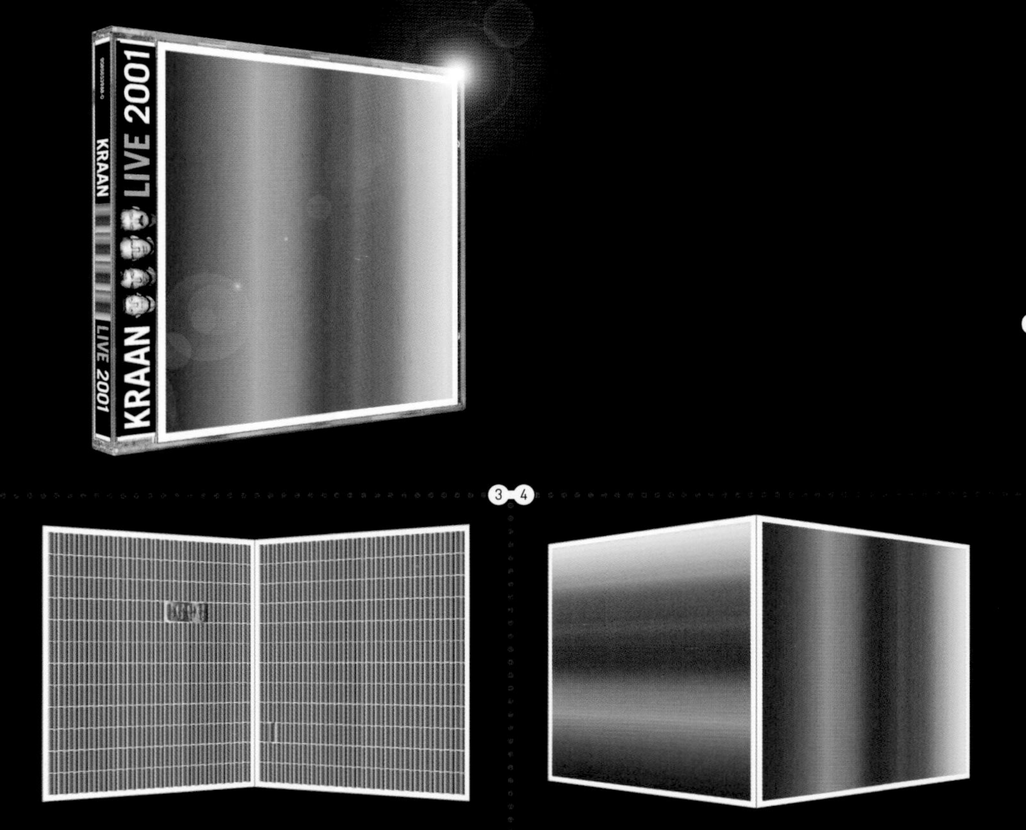

3 4

5

6

Curious
BOYM
coaster

7

Curious
BOYM
Curious BOYM
PRINCETON ARCHITECTURAL PRESS

DESIGN WORKS

RE-
DECORATION

8

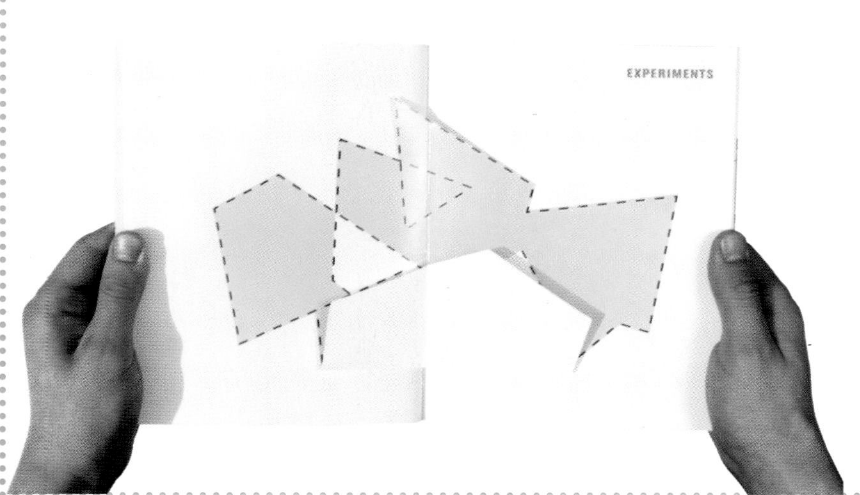
EXPERIMENTS

SONY

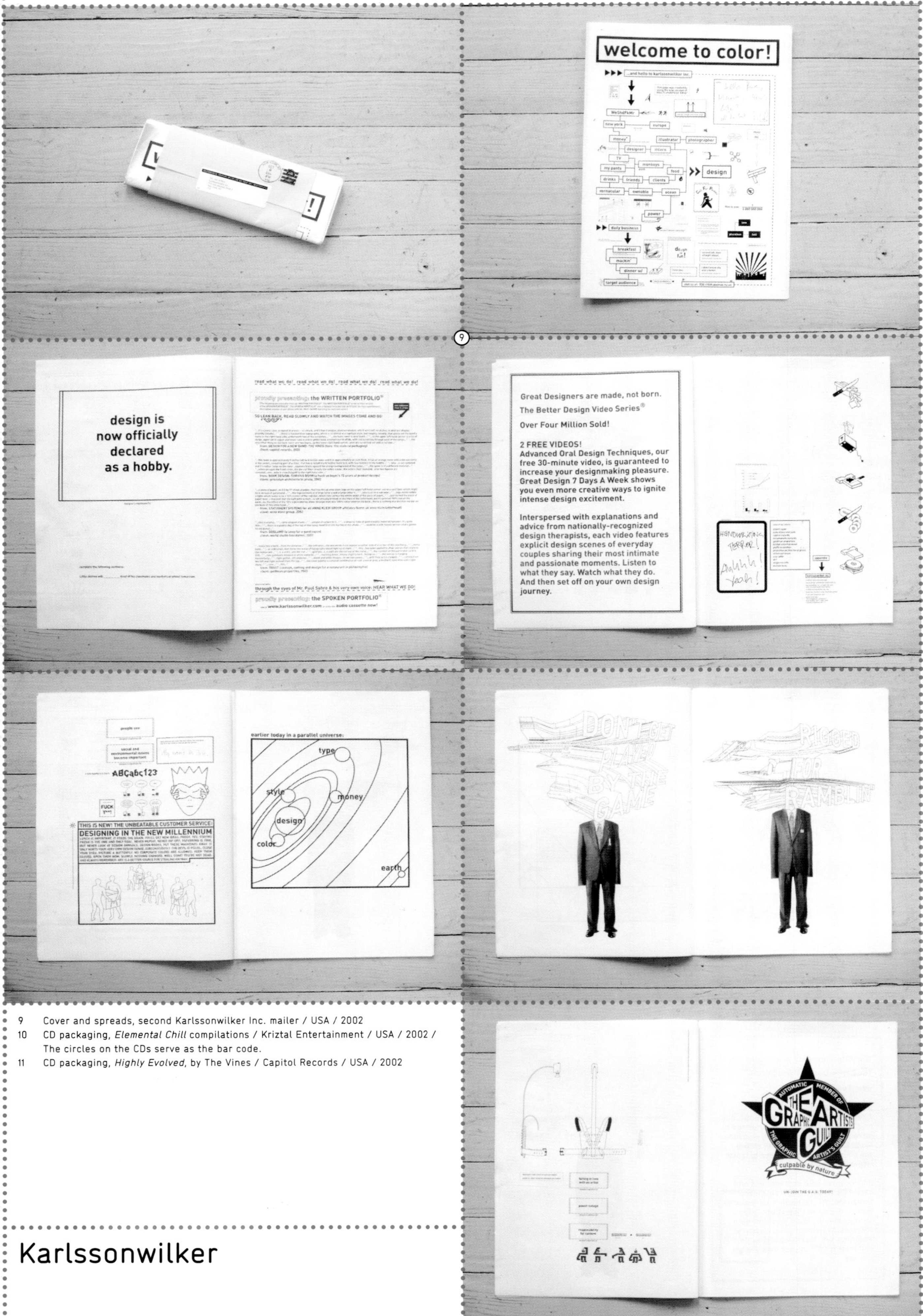

9 Cover and spreads, second Karlssonwilker Inc. mailer / USA / 2002
10 CD packaging, *Elemental Chill* compilations / Kriztal Entertainment / USA / 2002 / The circles on the CDs serve as the bar code.
11 CD packaging, *Highly Evolved*, by The Vines / Capitol Records / USA / 2002

Karlssonwilker

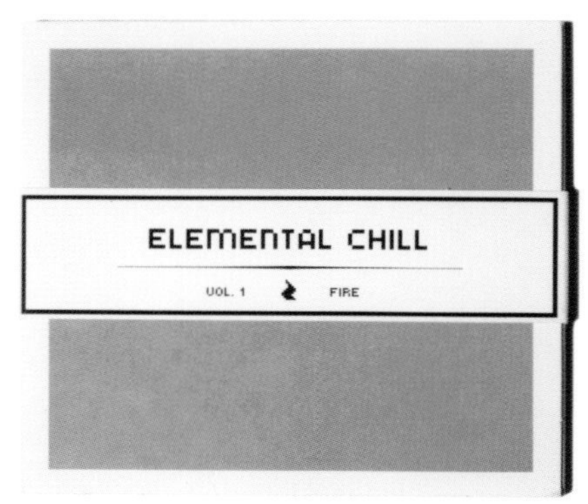
ELEMENTAL CHILL
VOL. 1
FIRE

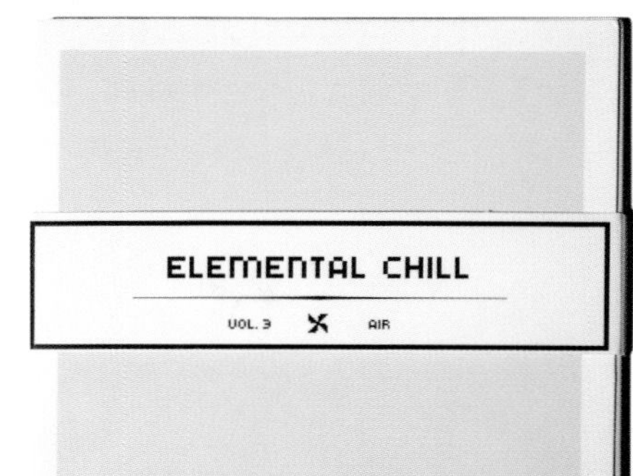
ELEMENTAL CHILL
VOL. 3
AIR

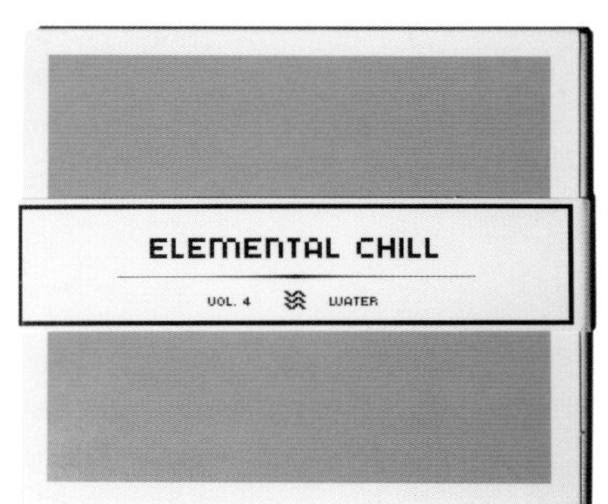
ELEMENTAL CHILL
VOL. 4
WATER

10

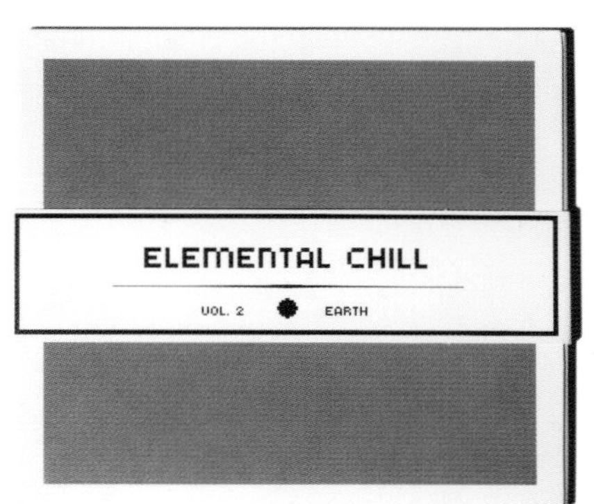
ELEMENTAL CHILL
VOL. 2
EARTH

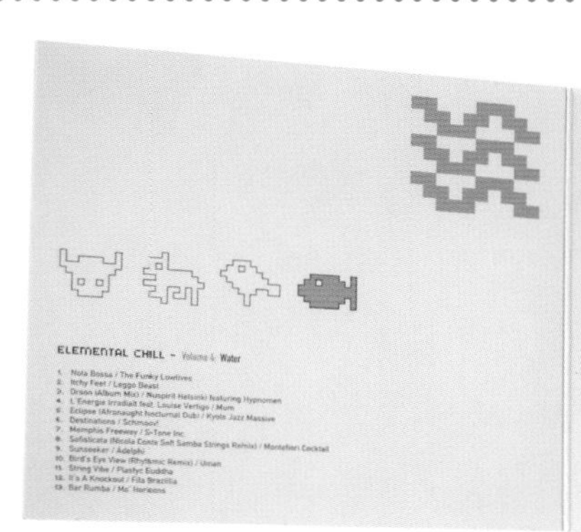
ELEMENTAL CHILL – Volume 4: Water

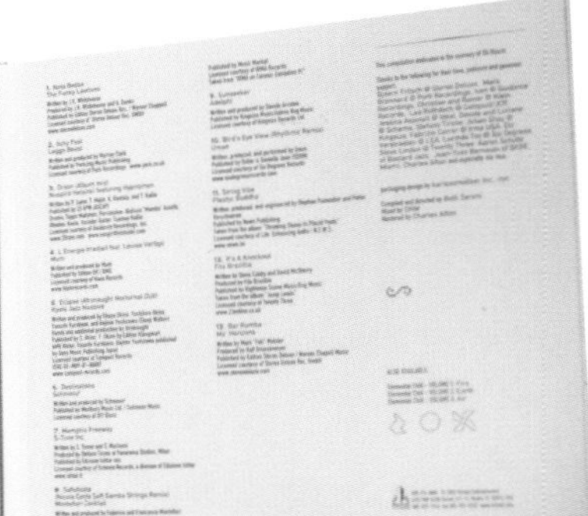

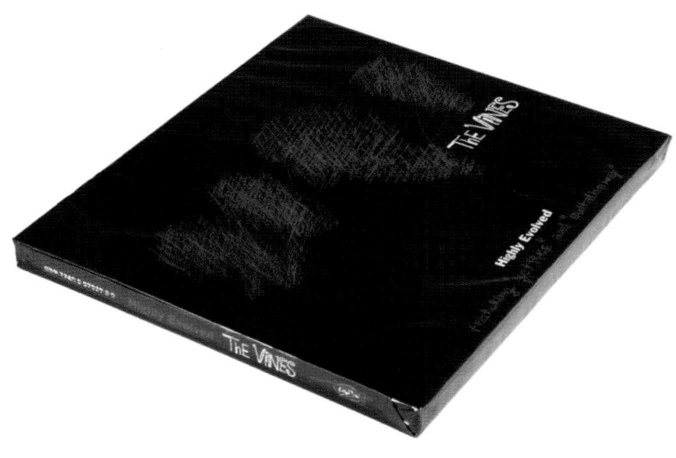
THE VINES
Highly Evolved

11

THE VINES

2002 CAPITOL RECORDS, INC. MANUFACTURED BY CAPITOL RECORDS, INC. ALL RIGHTS RESERVED. UNAUTHORIZED DUPLICATION IS A VIOLATION OF APPLICABLE LAWS. PRINTED IN U.S.A.
PROMOTIONAL USE ONLY/NOT FOR SALE
DPRO 7087 6 16919 2 4

Maverick! Siobhan Keaney has been described as a lone woman pioneer in London. She prides herself on the ability to remain independent and her knowledge that creative freedom is more important than just making money. This complete freedom from restrictions on her creativity allows her to approach each project in a distinctive way. She believes her route forward should be experimental. Keaney describes her method of working as "steering well clear of the mainstream." Whatever her approach, the resulting work is powerful and direct. Very now. The numerous awards, exhibitions of her work, and invitations to speak nationally and internationally stand testament to a consistent quality of work and a commitment to its standards. She also has strong links to design education, having lectured at the Royal College of Art in London and consulted for Leeds University and Bath Spa University. She also currently tutors at the University of Brighton. In 1997 she became a member of Alliance Graphique Internationale (AGI). Keaney is a designer who continues to reemerge, and her road of experimentation should establish her as one of design's innovative and influential forces in years to come.

Ken Cato

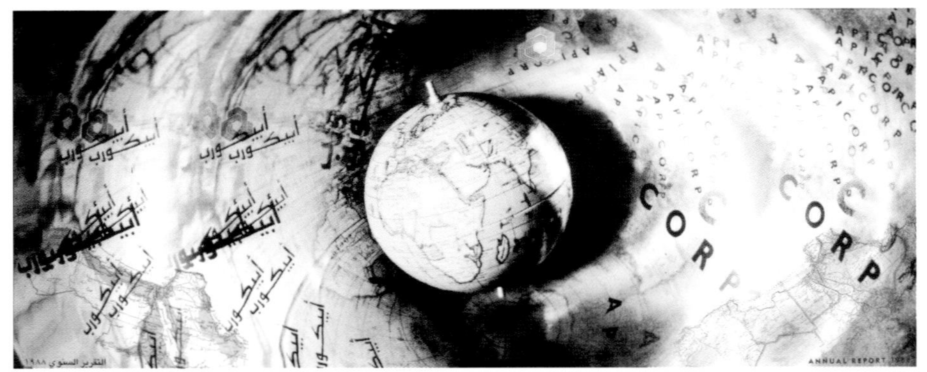

1 2

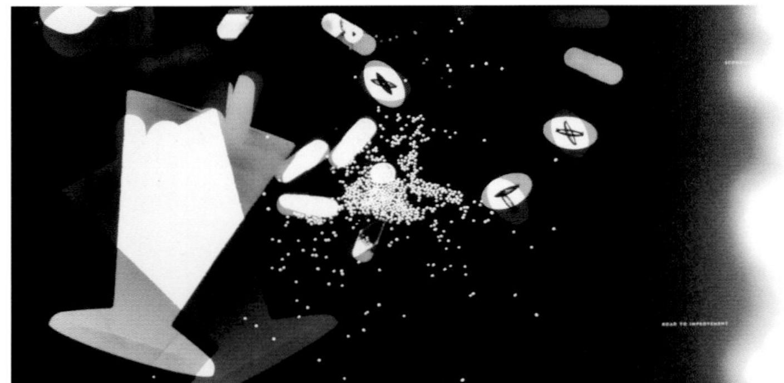

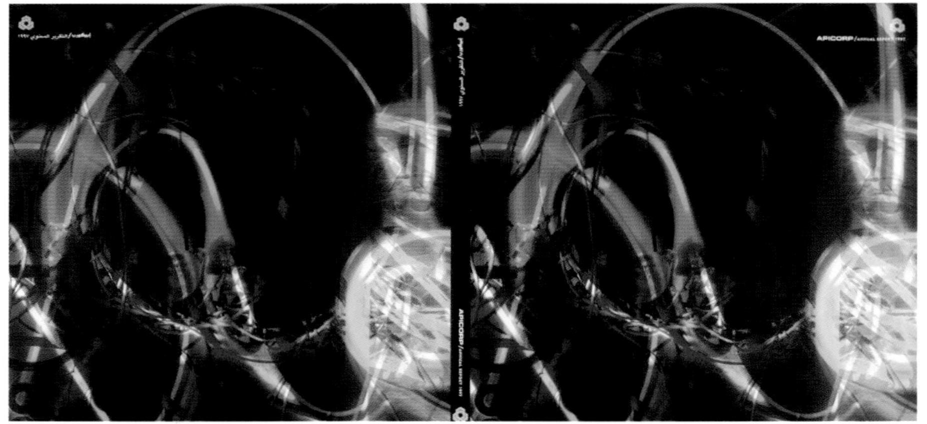

3 4

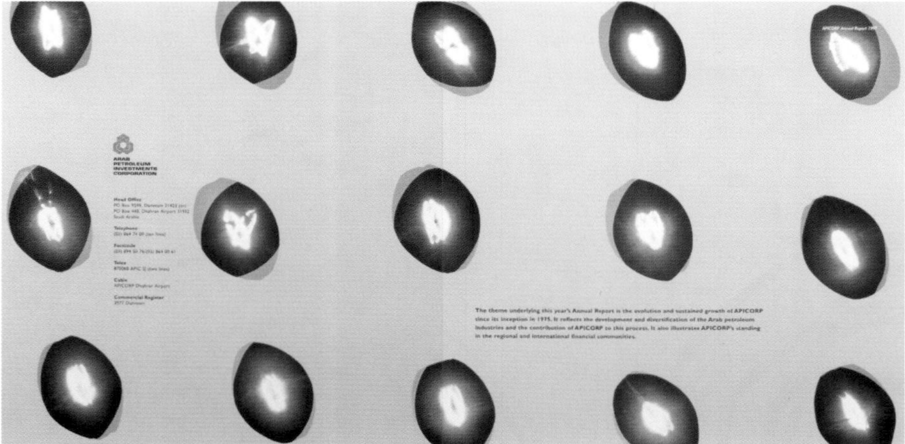

1–2 Cover and spread, 1988 annual report for international investment firm Apicorp / Apicorp (Arab Petrolium Investments Corporation) / United Kingdom / 1988
3–4 Cover and spread, 1997 annual report for Apicorp
5–6 Inside and outside, Royal Mail yearpack folder featuring all the special-edition stamps of the year / Royal Mail / United Kingdom / 2002

Siobhan Keaney

London

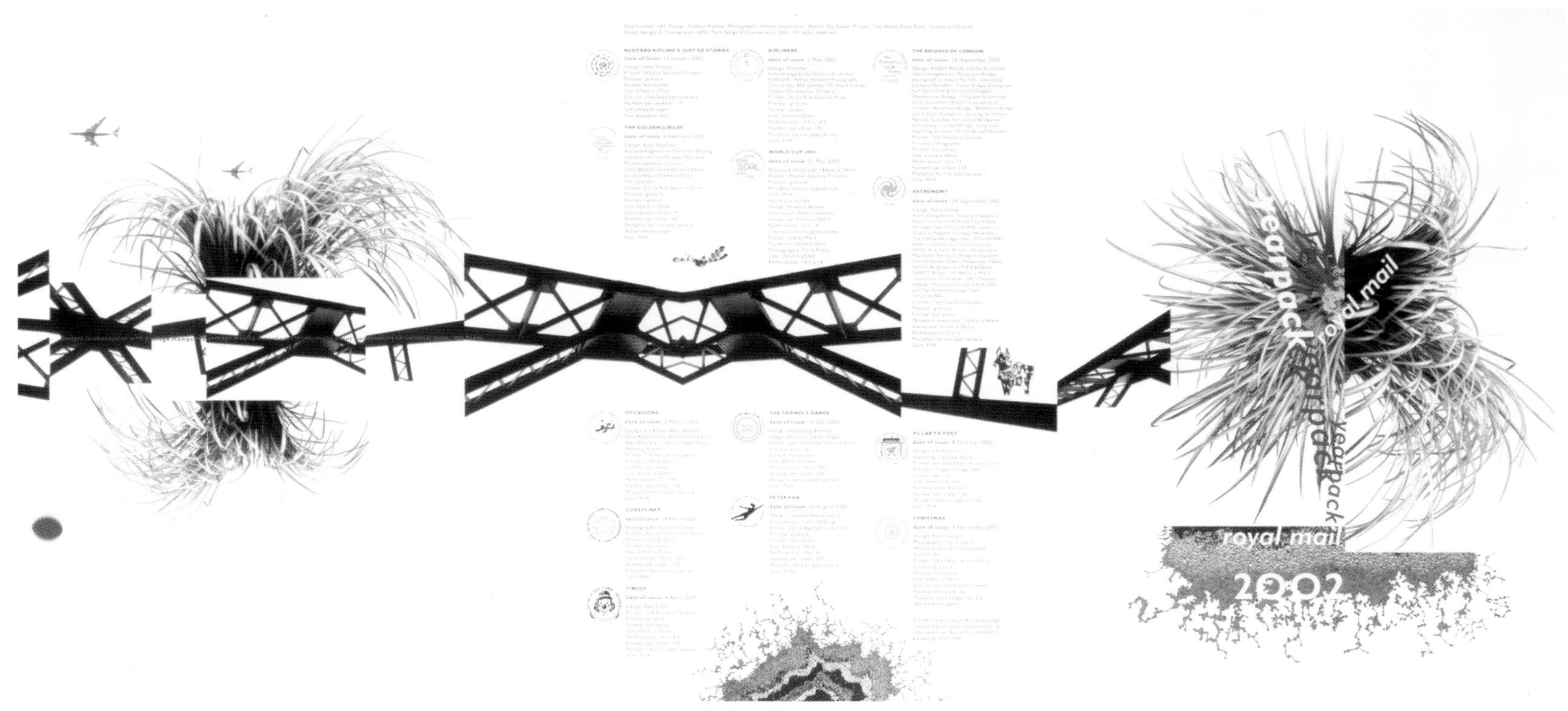

royal mail
yearpack
2002

5
6

royal mail
2002
RUDYARD KIPLING'S JUST SO STORIES
THE GOLDEN JUBILEE
OCCASIONS
COASTLINES
CIRCUS
AIRLINERS
WORLD CUP 2002
THE FRIENDLY GAMES
PETER PAN
THE BRIDGES OF LONDON
ASTRONOMY
PILLAR TO POST
CHRISTMAS

7

8

9

Siobhan Keaney

7 Postcards aimed at communicating the value of intangible assets and their importance in building a successful business / Design Council / United Kingdom / 2001
8 Self-promotional poster / United Kingdom / 1999
9 Print advertisment for postproduction company / The Mill / United Kingdom / 1997
10–12 Millennium poster and images produced for Millennium Dome brochure / New Millennium Experience Company / United Kingdom / 1999

10

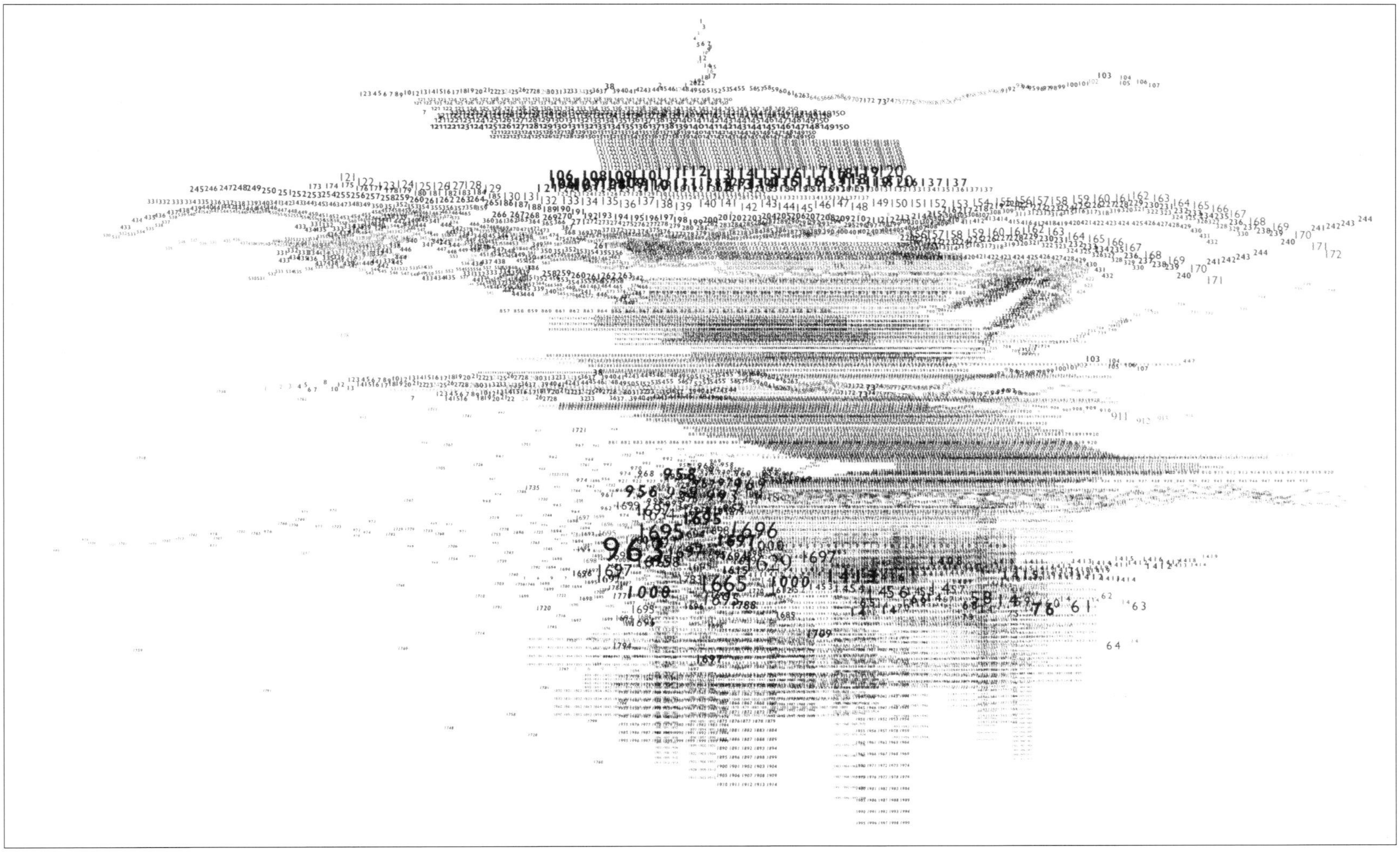

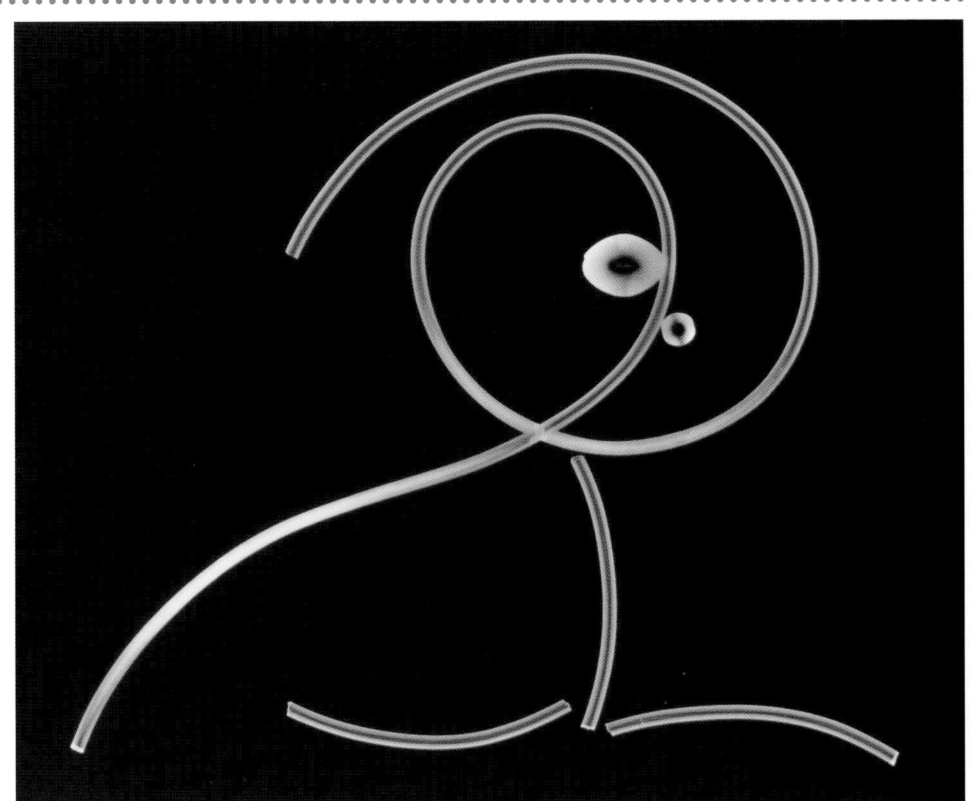

11 12

There is something particularly nostalgic about the work of London-based duo Frith Kerr and Amelia Noble, but to describe it as old-fashioned would be way off the mark. Their work shows a willingness to experiment and reinvent traditional elements of graphic design in order to achieve the most appropriate and relevant solution. They certainly aren't afraid of mixing the myriad elements that inform their visual vocabulary. • • A prime example of this is the map/guide they designed for British Television's Channel Four riverboat trip in 1999, which utilizes typography to create the shape of the River Thames as it flows through London. It is a basic concept that has been explored before, but you'd struggle to find an example that feels as fresh. • • The riverboat trip map/guide is an elegant, understated example of print design that openly suggests a nostalgia entirely appropriate for content of this nature. The Thames reeks of history, which is why Kerr/Noble sourced a poem—"A Description of London," written in 1738 by John Bancks—and set the poem in the shape of the river in a variety of classic serif typefaces. You can't help but sense the history; then again, you can't look at a piece like this without feeling refreshed. • • Typography plays an important role in the way Kerr/Noble communicate information, personality, and content. Take, for example, the cover of *Accommodating Change*, a book designed to accompany an Architecture Foundation exhibition of the same name. Rather than adorn the cover with one project, the team opted for a democratic solution that communicates the diverse nature of the work in the exhibition. The name of each firm is set in a different typeface—ranging from clean sans serifs to more rounded, psychedelic typefaces—which suggests the individual personalities and qualities of each company as well as the diverse nature of the exhibition. All communicated with a sense of wit and clarity that can be found time and time again in Kerr/Noble's work. • • Fernando Gutiérrez • •

1

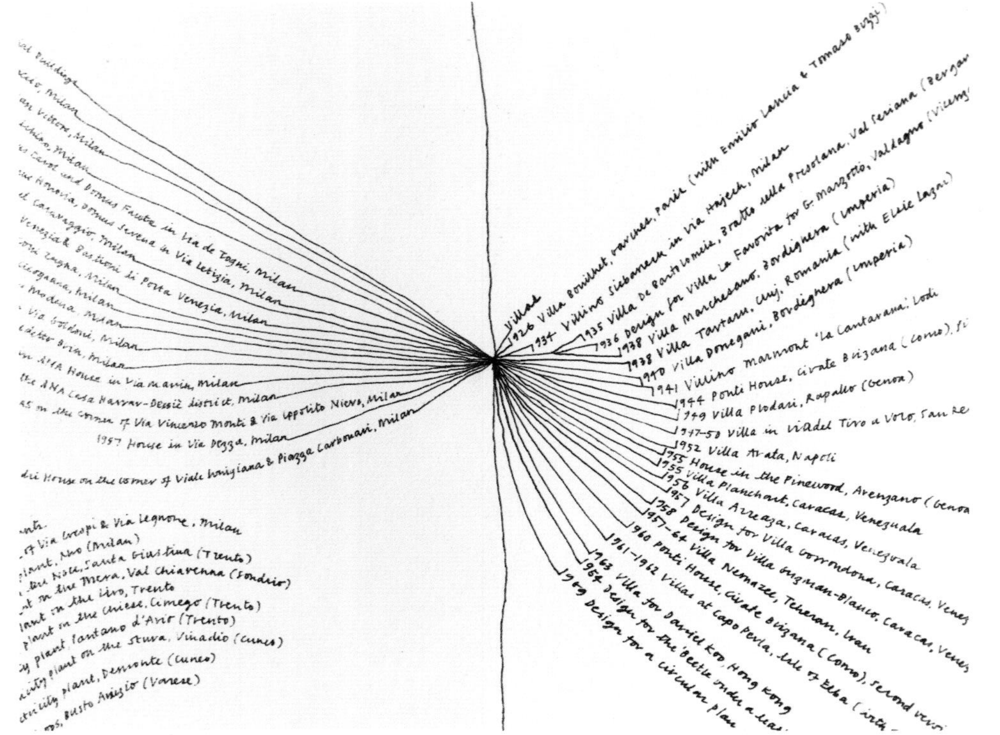

2 3

1 Hand-drawn mural for *Gio Ponti–A World* exhibition / Design Museum, London / United Kingdom / 2002 / The "tree" is a register of Ponti's works, detailing every project he worked on, in the style of his own handwriting.

2–3 Title wall designs for *Gio Ponti–A World* exhibition / The leaf is taken from Ponti's 1974 "Facade with Leaves" on a building in Hong Kong.

4 Front of *Accommodating Change: Innovation in Housing* exhibition guide / Architecture Foundation / United Kingdom / 2002

5 Short-film viewing aperture made of translucent cast resin, part of exhibition design for *Accommodating Change: Innovation in Housing* / Architecture Foundation / United Kingdom / 2002

6 Opening spread, *No More Rules–Graphic Design and Postmodernism*, by Rick Poynor (illustration Edward Fella) / Laurence King Publishing / United Kingdom / 2003 / Kerr/Noble's Modified Pop typeface featured in the book was based on Neville Brody's Pop font and created especially for the project.

Kerr/Noble

London

④

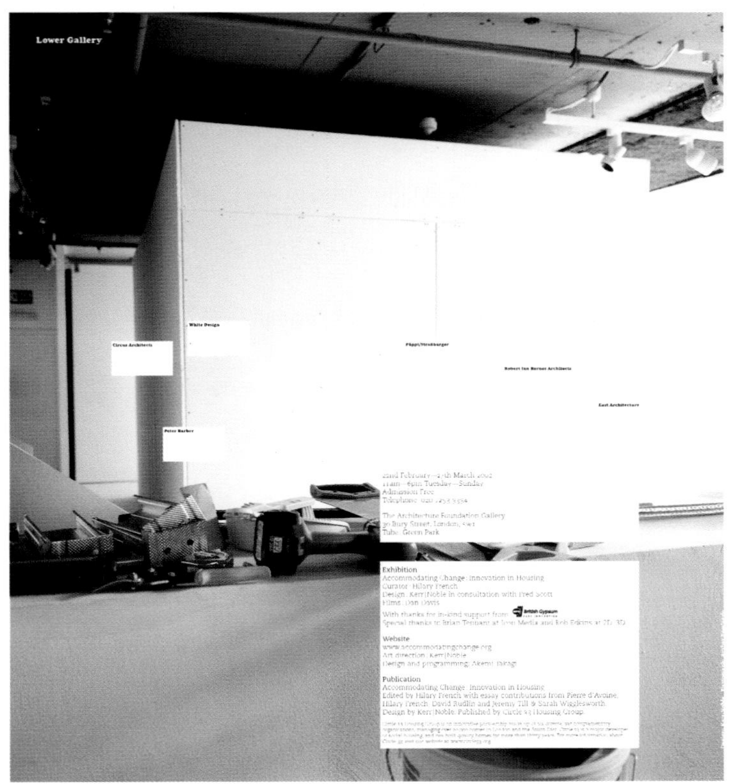

⑤

⑥

No
More
Rules

Graphic Design and Postmodernism

Rick Poynor

Laurence King Publishing

7

8

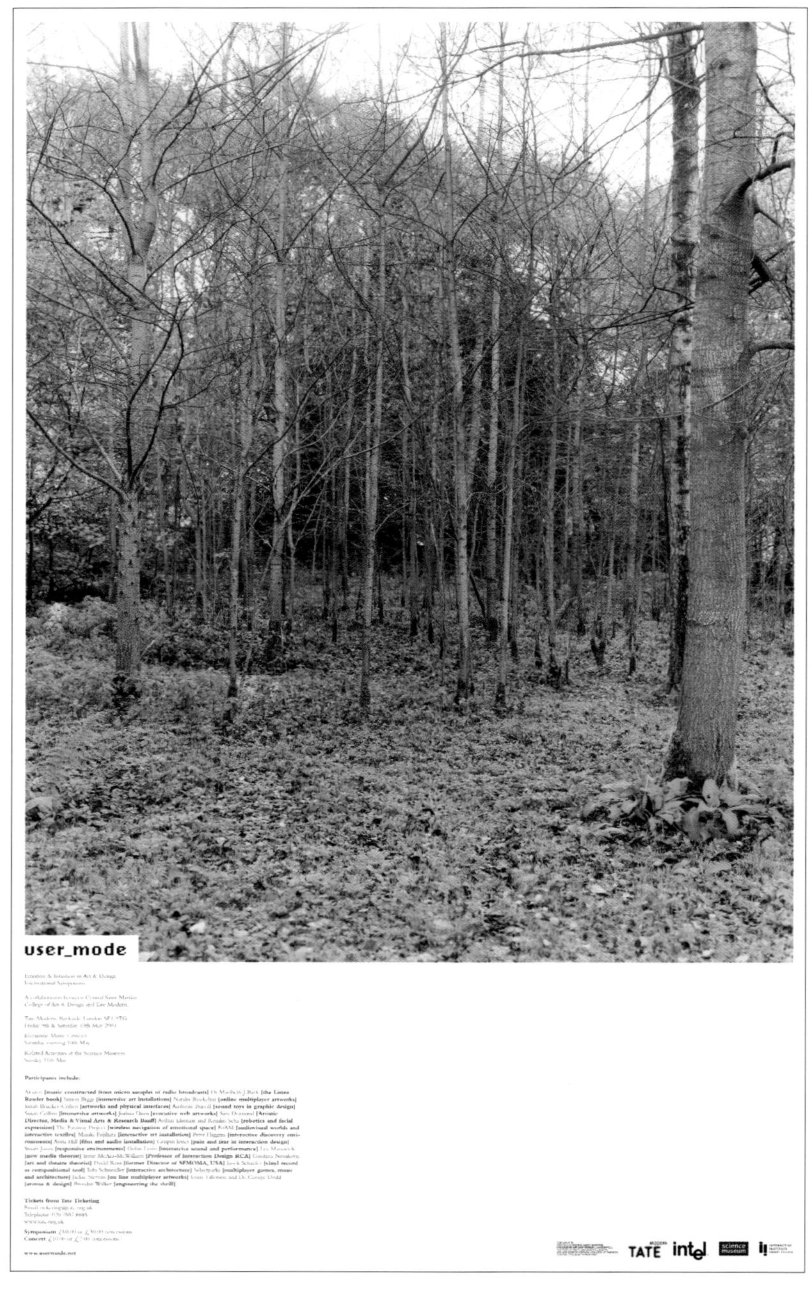

9

7 Foldout souvenir for riverboat trip on the Thames / Channel Four Television / United Kingdom / 1999 / The foldout features the poem "A Description of London," by John Bancks (1738).

8 Poster for open gig of film director Tony Kaye's rock band K at Cannes Film Festival (with Ian Wright) / Tony Kaye / United Kingdom / 2001

9 Poster for international symposium on emotion and intuition in art and design (photography Amber Rowlands) / Central Saint Martins College of Art & Design and Tate Modern / United Kingdom / 2003

10–12 Spreads and front and back cover, self-published magazine *Lost But Not Forgotten* (photography Clare Shilland) / Kerr/Noble / United Kingdom / 2002 / Kerr/Noble designed a special font for the magazine, which was inspired by a day trip to London's Highgate Cemetery. The title of the magazine is revealed to the reader throughout the publication.

Kerr/Noble

10

11

12

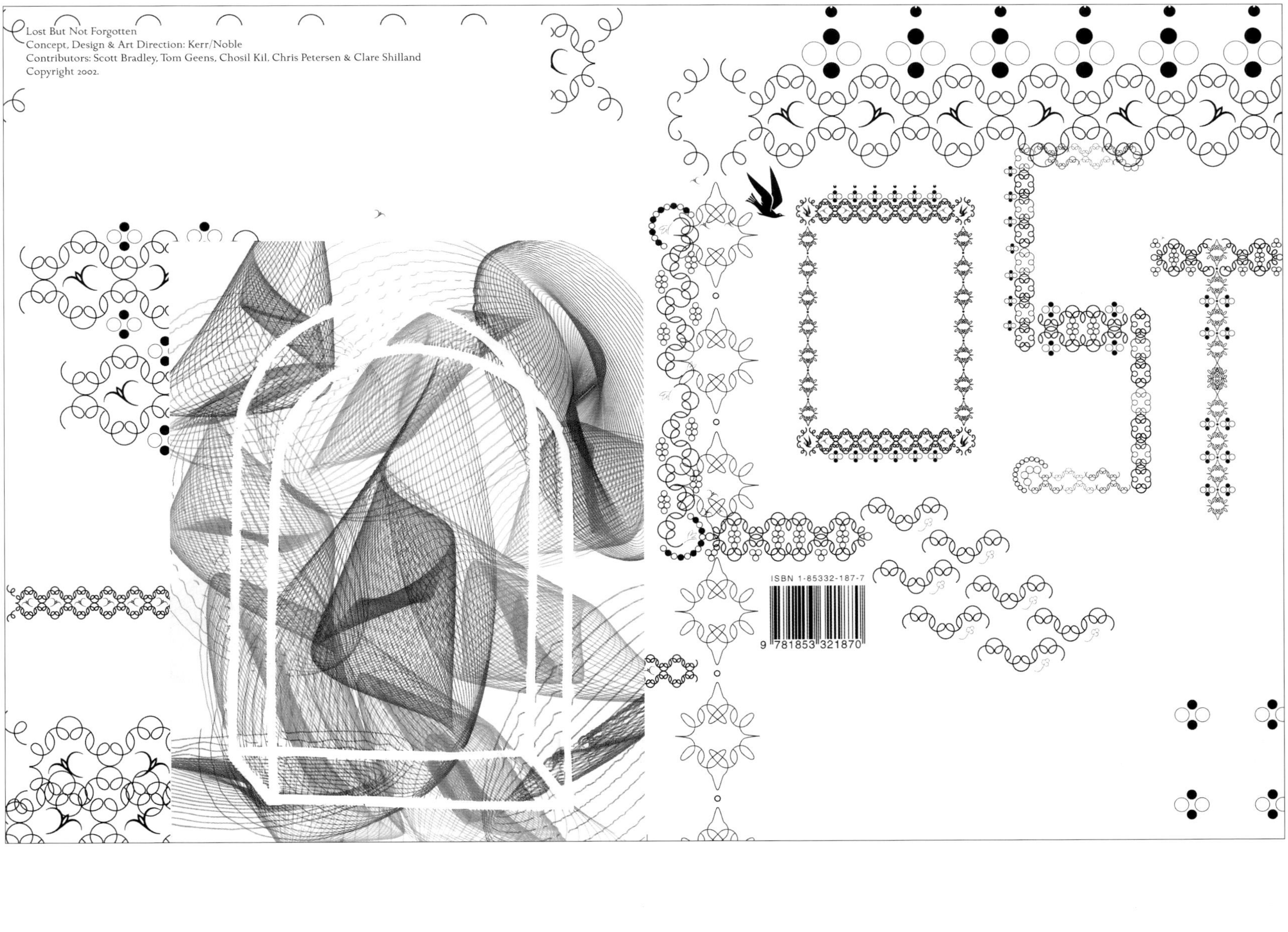

Lost But Not Forgotten
Concept, Design & Art Direction: Kerr/Noble
Contributors: Scott Bradley, Tom Geens, Chosil Kil, Chris Petersen & Clare Shilland
Copyright 2002.

ISBN 1-85332-187-7
9 781853 321870

The first thing Rene Knip did, within half an hour of entering my studio as an apprentice, was blow up the only computer we had. He thought that would get him fired on the spot, but I didn't care that much. I hadn't hired him for his computer skills, but for his typographic talent, which he engaged for us for over three years. René exemplifies a new generation of designers. His theme is the architecture of letters—he is deeply fascinated with letters as three-dimensional objects. Today we have slightly forgotten about the way letters used to be employed on buildings in the 1930s, and in reclaiming the field of spatial typography, Knip revives an old craft. He polishes as long as it takes to find the right form. • • His point of departure as a designer is handwriting; he writes beautifully and is an ardent correspondent. But in the end, that handwriting results in very precisely constructed typography, with a very peculiar sensibility for color. • • Knip is a bit brainy, but also someone who embraces modern life to the fullest—he loves sailing, good cooking, is a social guy and an excellent host. He is one of those rare people who knows how to share. • • Like so many intelligent people, Knip is also a bit lazy. He knows exactly what he wants and hates wasting time with nonsense or, in other words, working for clients or projects he doesn't believe in. Knip is not a career planner. He might just decide to go sailing around the world for a year or to pick up studying again. He once said that if he could start over, he would become an architect. This feeling for architecture, for space, is superbly expressed in a calendar he made, a cube, exactly 12 x 12 x 12 centimeters—the matrix of the months. He researched paper stock until he found the weight to get exactly 12 centimeters of height with 365 pages. The year 2003 has been cut out in the sides of the block and each month has a different diecut in the middle of the page, so that almost every day has a different form. Typographically, it's a beauty as well: a masterpiece! I'm glad that—besides being his good friend—I am working with Knip again, now as a teacher in my communication department at the Design Academy in Eindhoven. • • Anthon Beeke • •

① ②

ABCDEFGHIJKLM
NOPQRSTUVWXYZ
123789
LAUNDRY SANS

③

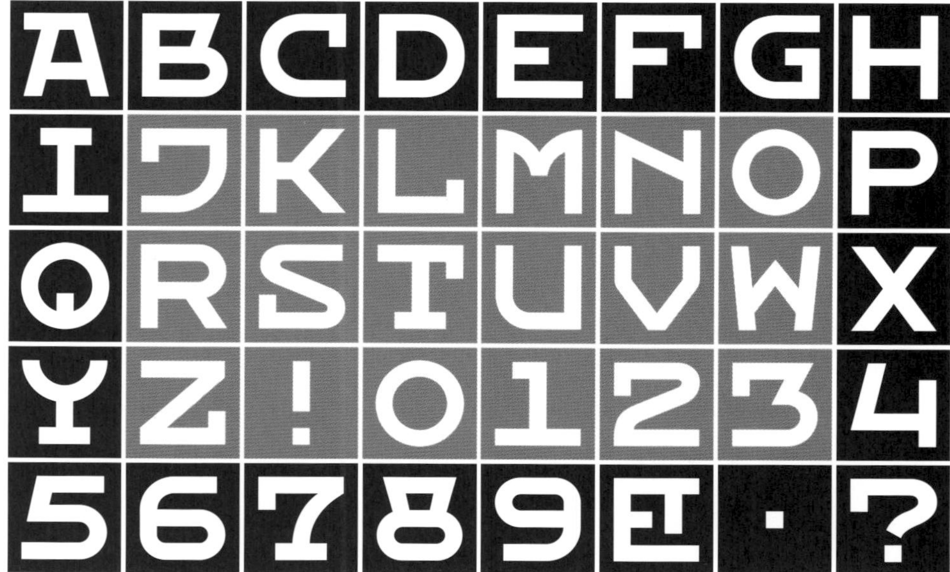

④

1, 3 Hanging typeface Laundry Sans used for *Mooi Maar Goed* exhibition on graphic design at Stedelijk Museum, Amsterdam / Stedelijk Museum / Netherlands / 1999
2, 4 Terra-cotta tile typeface HEMA used by Merkx + Girod Architects for restaurants in HEMA department stores / Merkx + Girod Architecten / Netherlands / 1998
5 Self-commissioned project "Firebasket" (with Edgar Knip) / Netherlands / 2002 / Laser-cut steel basket composed of words: zinc, moss, silence, dust, bone, moon, etc.

Rene Knip

Amsterdam

5

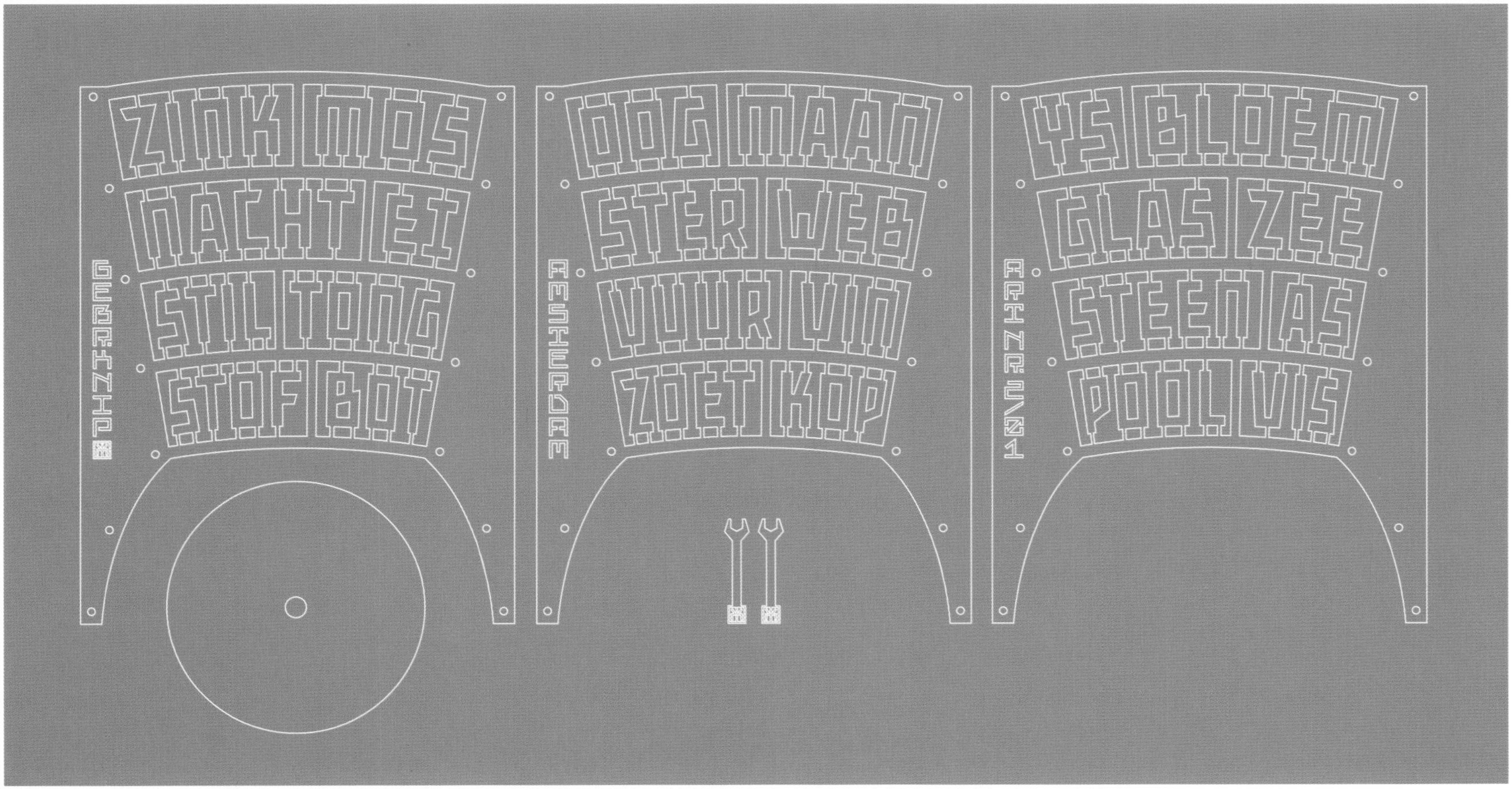

6

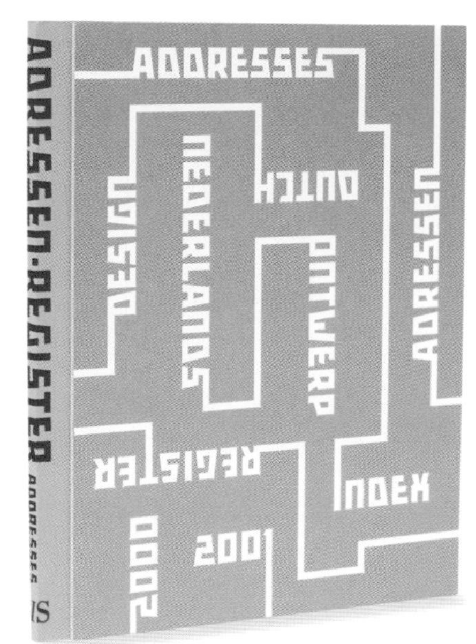

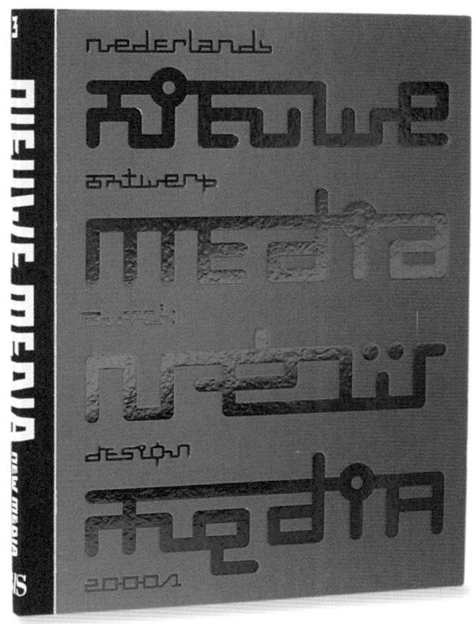

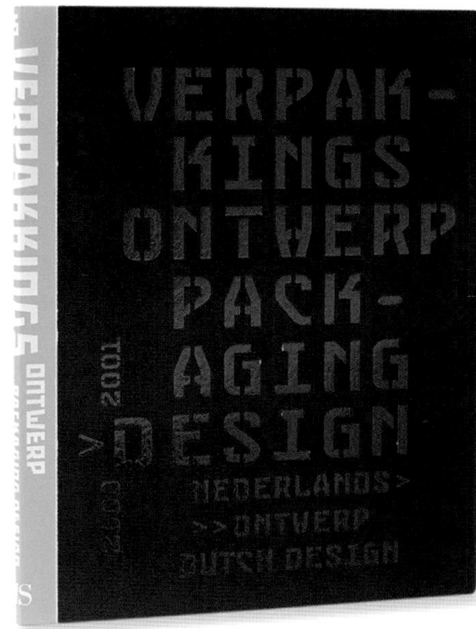

6 Six-volume set with slipcase, "Dutch Design 2000–2001" / BIS publishers and the Association of Dutch Designers (BNO) / Netherlands / 2001 / The set comprises of individual books on graphic design, environmental design, industrial design, packaging design, illustration, new media. Knip specifically developed a different "illustrative" typeface for each book.

7 Calender cube designed for Dutch printers Calff & Meischke / Calff & Meischke / Netherlands / 2003 / Every month is cut in a different form.

8 Aluminium house-number design developed for Merkx + Girod Architects as a gift for clients in celebration of their fifteenth anniversary / Merkx + Girod Architecten / Netherlands / 1999

Rene Knip

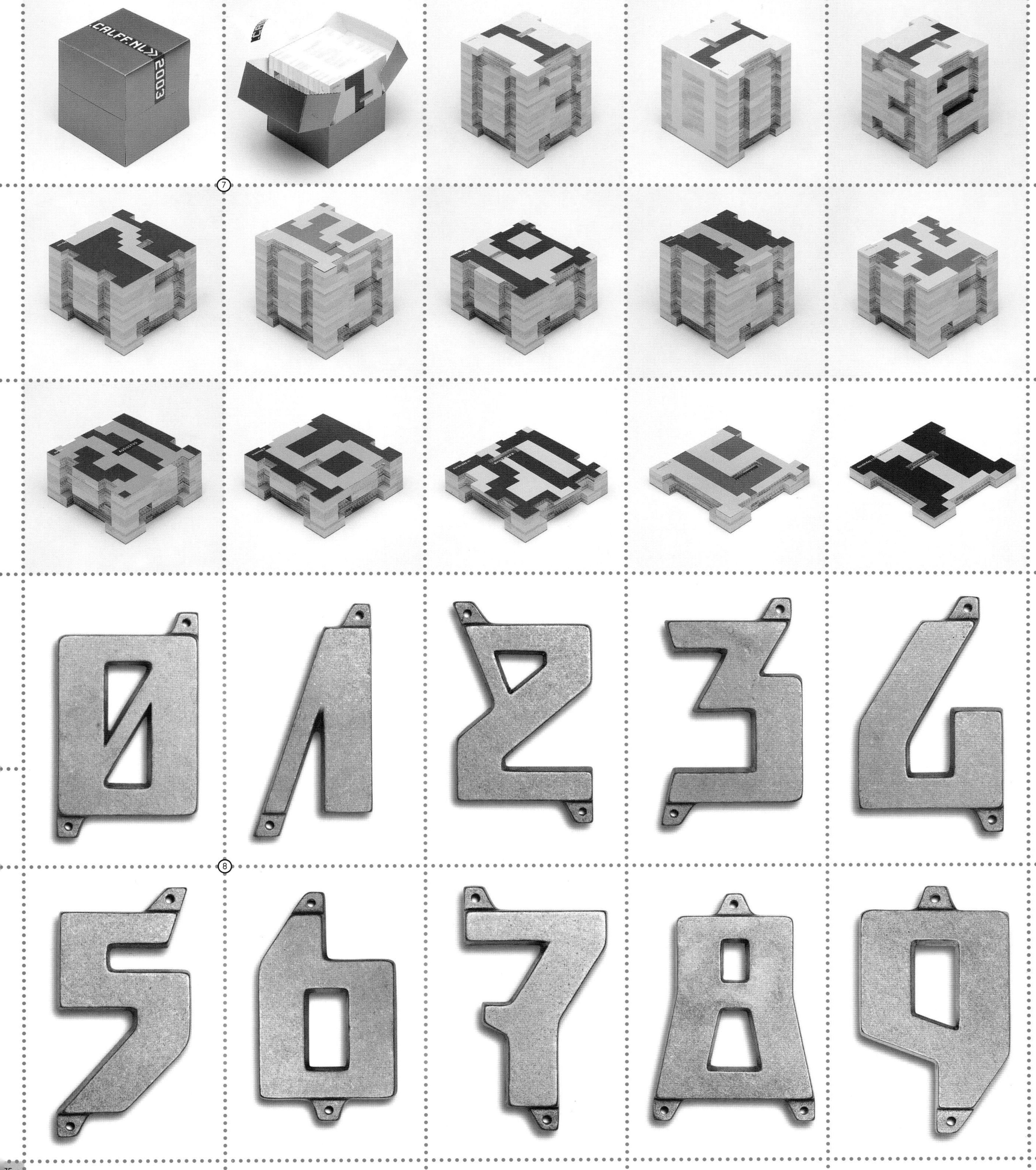
.CALFF.NL>>
2003
7
8

Since the use of a hip typeface or the application of a new Photoshop filter is often misinterpreted as innovation, it is becoming increasingly rare for a piece of graphic design to be truly exciting. • • The mysteriously dark blue Musik Box Elisabeth Kopf designed for the Vienna Art Orchestra is one of those very few pieces that blew me away: It not only packages music beautifully, but performs music itself, thereby creating a conversation between design and content I have nowhere else experienced so elegantly. Kopf commissioned thirty short compositions, ten relating to Vienna, ten to art, and ten to orchestra. Each piece is performed on an ingenious harmonica system when one of the limited-edition CD packages is opened. The musicians of the Vienna Art Orchestra produced a live music piece utilizing the packaging as instruments, a conceptual loop that blurs the borders not only between art and design, and between content and packaging, but also between music and object. This *is* innovation. • • Many of Kopf's less lavishly conceived and produced packages are also little performance pieces, graphics that not only visualize the music perfectly but expand on it. • • While working on the exhibition design for the *Arbeitersamariterbund*, a small Austrian version of the Red Cross, she learned from the client that in situations requiring first aid, many people are willing to help but afraid to do the wrong thing; that first-aid course was a while back, after all. All those booklets containing first-aid rules did little to reduce that fear. The rules must be reiterated all the time to make people aware of them. Kopf's response was to print a different first-aid rule on each and every graphic-design piece her studio produces, be it a CD cover, a theater poster, or a lecture invitation. If a client refuses to have the rule printed on their project, they have to donate to the *Arbeitersamariterbund* to remain one of her clients. • • I am very tempted to steal that idea. • • Stefan Sagmeister • •

1

2

1 CD packaging, *Segmente*, by Peter Herbert and David Tronzo (with Werner Korn) / Aziza Music / USA / 1999 / The cover print consists of two images placed on top of each other. The hidden image can be revealed by scratching off the top layer.
2 Four pieces from personal project "Scratch Gallery," collection of scratched *Segmente* CD covers by friends and colleagues / 1999-present
3 CD packaging, *Peter Herbert & Aktionstheater Ensemble 2000* / Aziza Music and Aktionstheater Ensemble / USA / 2000 / In this packaging for a CD of theater music, the wide black curtain revealed inside the unfolded hardcover contains a booklet. When one flips through it, the curtain gradually opens and shows a one-act theater scene. The curtain is also a bar code saying, "It's art when you can't add and you can't reduce anymore little theater for music by elisabeth kopf for peter herbert."

Elisabeth Kopf

Vienna

3

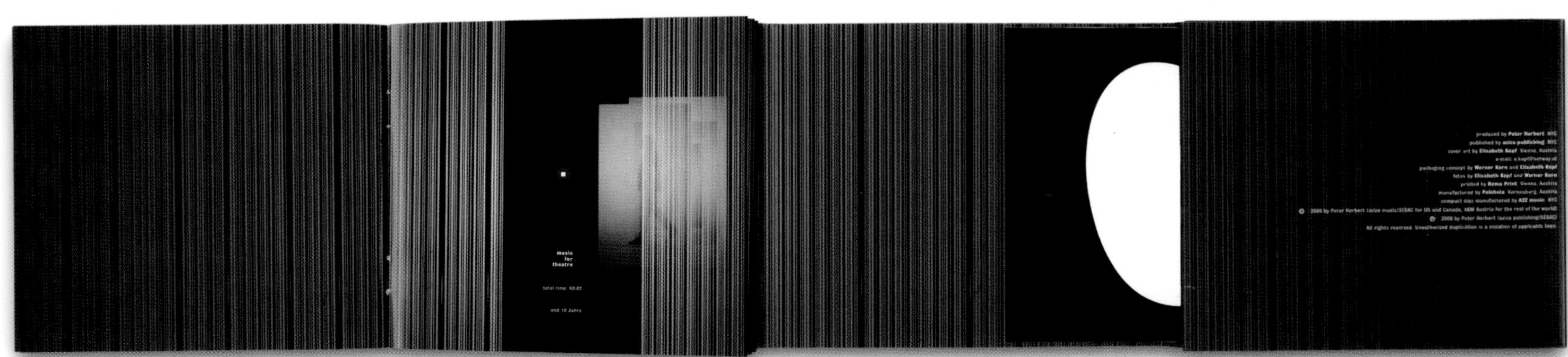

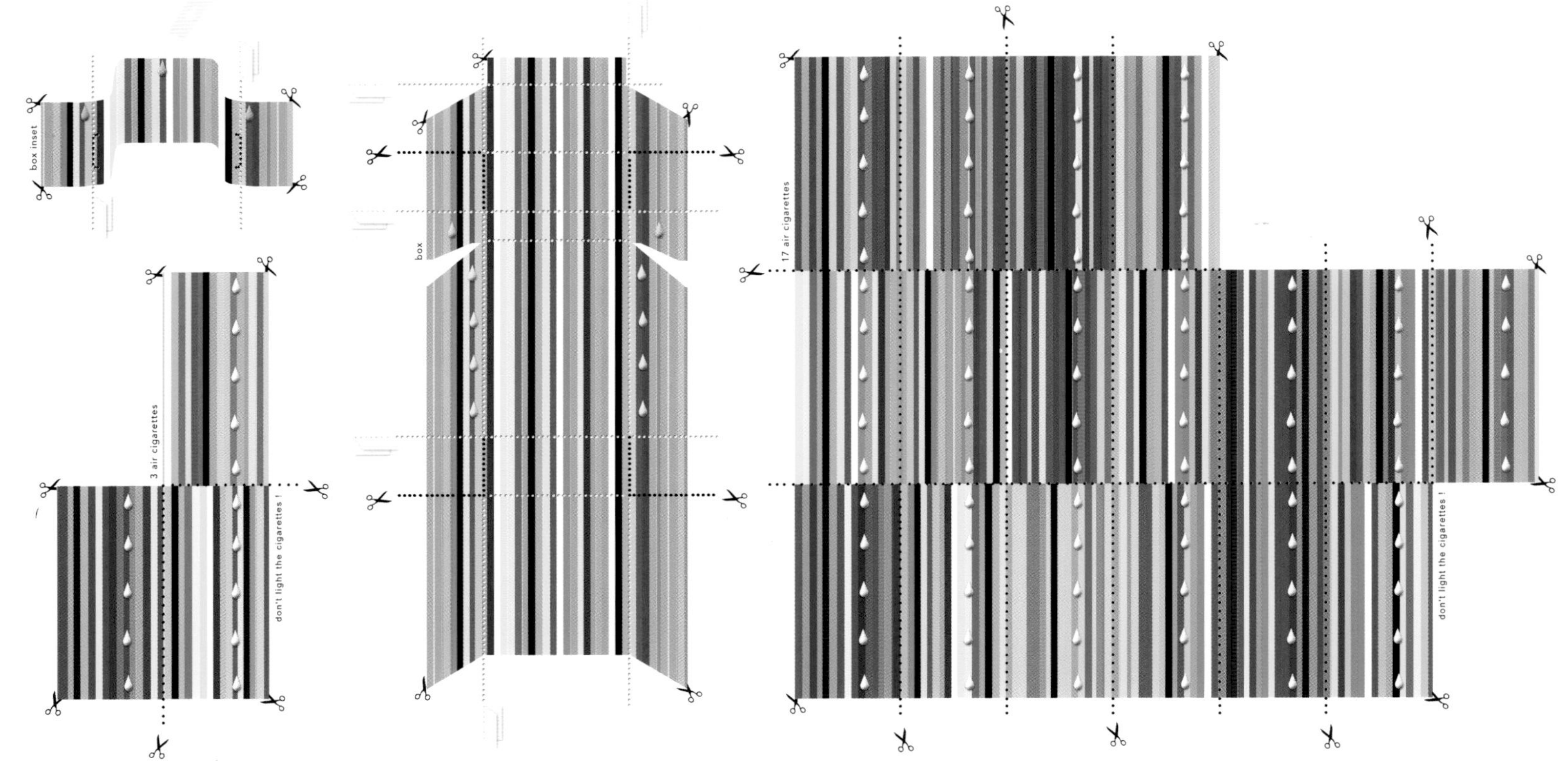

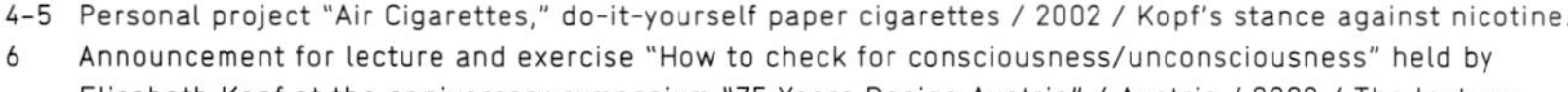

4–5 Personal project "Air Cigarettes," do-it-yourself paper cigarettes / 2002 / Kopf's stance against nicotine.

6 Announcement for lecture and exercise "How to check for consciousness/unconsciousness" held by Elisabeth Kopf at the anniversary symposium "75 Years Design Austria" / Austria / 2002 / The lecture formed part of Kopf's personal "First Aid" project.

7 "Little Orchestra" CD packaging, unique edition of thirty handmade CD cases (with Werner Korn) / Vienna Art Orchestra / Austria / 1997 / Created for the twentieth anniversary of the Vienna Art Orchestra, the CD packaging itself makes music by using the air flow produced through opening and closing. Each case plays its own tune, the complete collection creating a full orchestral composition. The orchestra performed live with the musical CD boxes during its Anniversary World Tour.

8 Packaging for CD featuring performances of the Little Orchestra musical CD boxes / Austria / 1997

Elisabeth Kopf

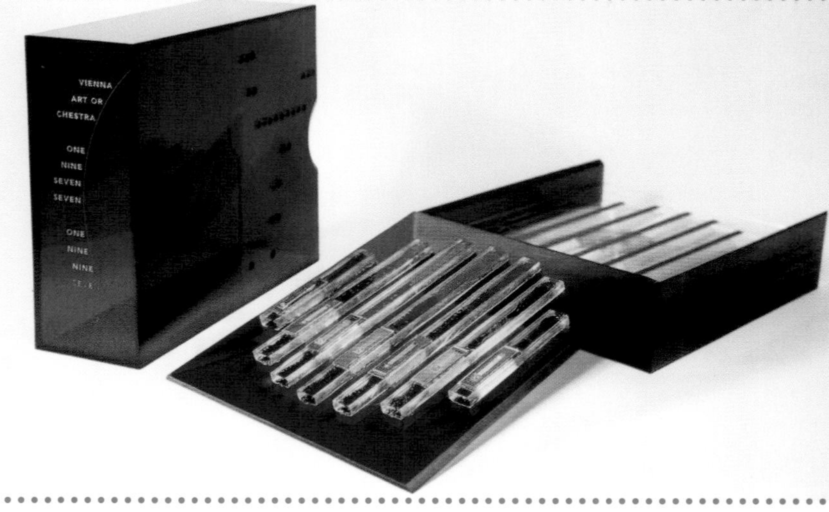
VIENNA
ART OR
CHESTRA
ONE
NINE
SEVEN
SEVEN
ONE
NINE
NINE

7

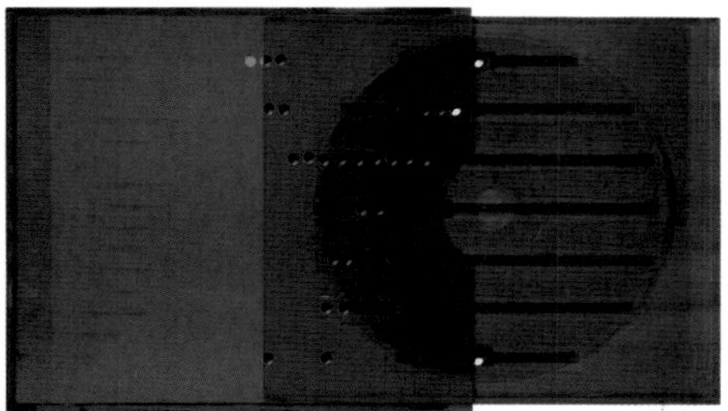
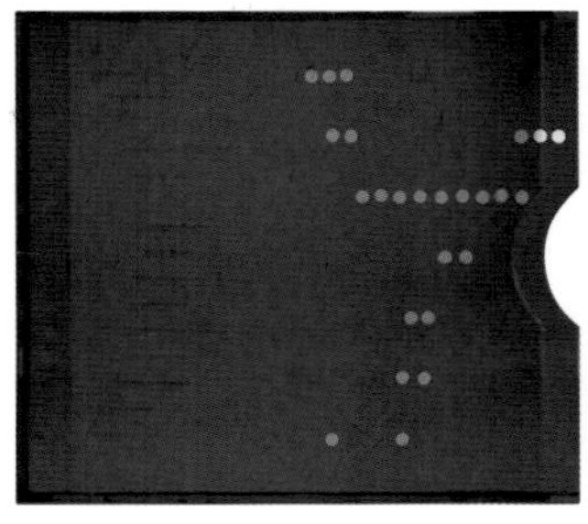
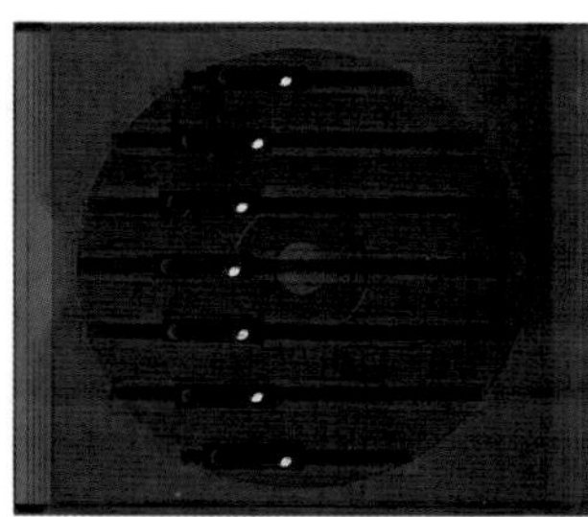
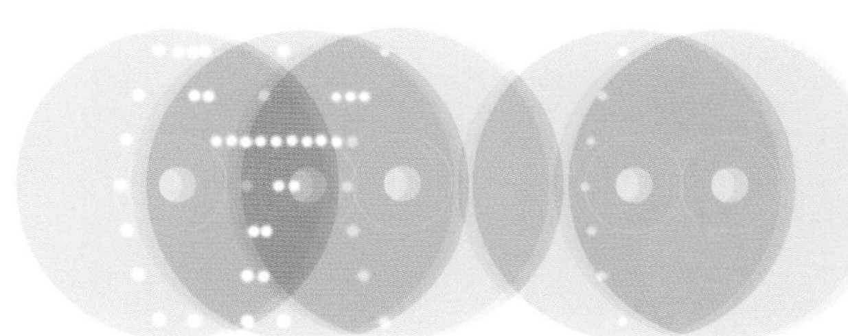

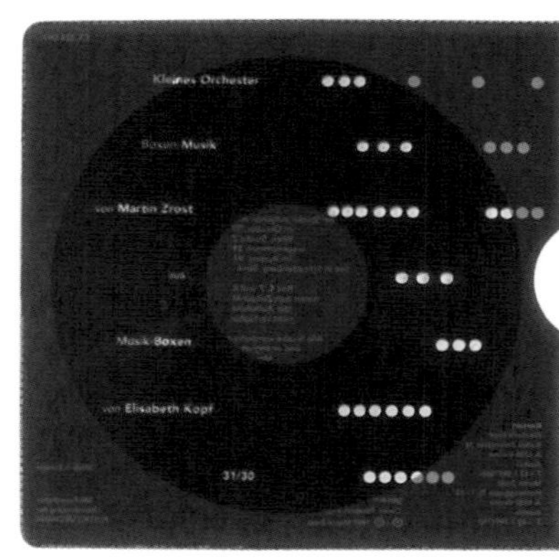
Kleines Orchester
Musik
von Martin Zrost
Musik-Boxen
von Elisabeth Kopf

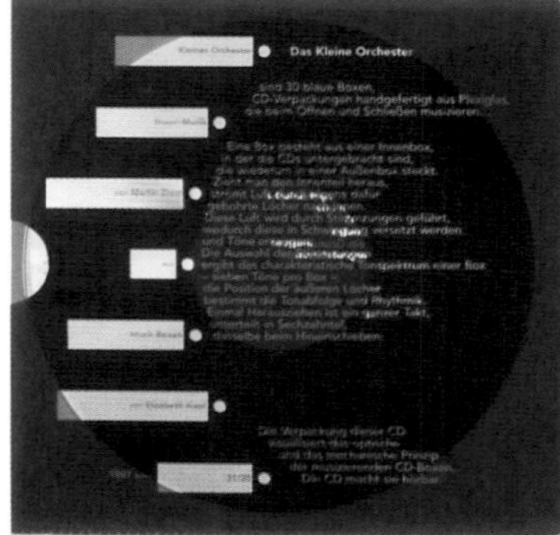
Das Kleine Orchester

Das Kleine Orchester
Vienna Art Orchestra
20th Anniversary

8

Ji Lee took it upon himself to produce and pay for the production of 15,000 speech-bubble stickers, large and small. He glues them everywhere he goes but mostly on posters around town that feature people, thus giving those flat heads a voice and transforming a one-way communication into a dialogue. Everybody wins: The advertiser gets more people to look at its (now personalized) posters, the public finally gets a chance to talk back to the advertisers, and the rest of us are able to enjoy these little jolts of joy by seeing and reading the transformed posters. • •And how much more interesting they become. Take a regular record-release poster, the likes of which hang around New York City by the hundreds, announcing that the new CD by Glenn Lewis will be available on March 19. Whoever wrote the text in Lewis's (really Lee's) speech bubble, "I am concerned that my CD will not sell more than 200,000 units and that, as a result, my recoupable advance from my label will be taken away from me, after which my contract will be canceled and I'll be back doing Journey covers on Bleecker Street," transformed a dull promotion into an apt comment on the music industry. • •Lee uses every medium available to him. One moment he dedicates himself fully to developing a revolving alphabet that invites viewers to decode it in three dimensions; the next he is busy inventing the Abstractor, basically a TV whose screen is covered with two black cardboards leaving only a small slit visible, thus transforming any dull program into "a beautiful and pleasant experience at any time with any channel." You have to see it to believe it. • •Lee has a day job as an art director for one of the big advertising conglomerates where he produces fine but less remarkable work. In a way the speech-bubble campaign can be seen as a nightly atonement for sins committed during the day. • •Stefan Sagmeister • •

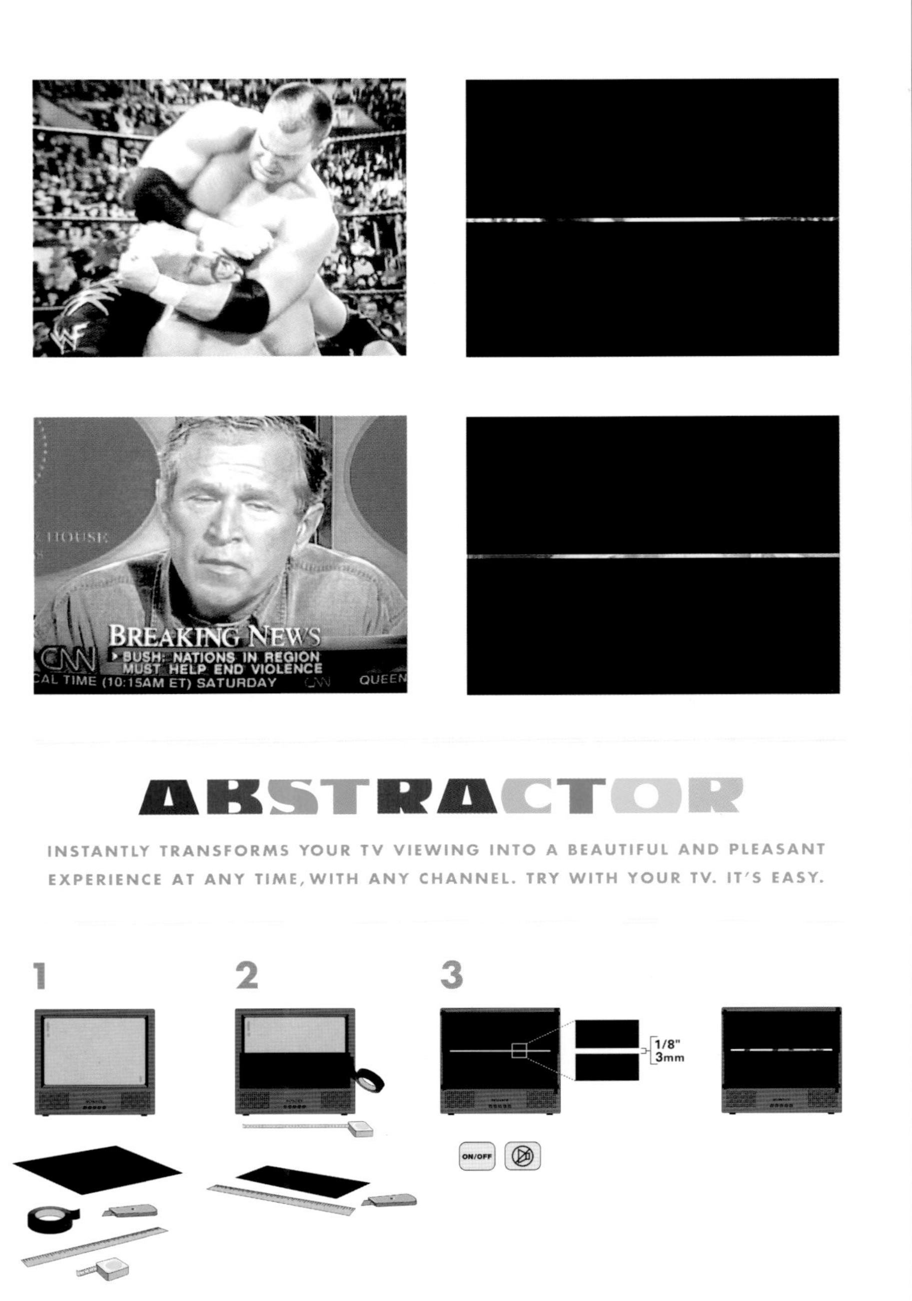

1

Ji Lee
writetojilee@hotmail.com

Where did I meet him? How do I know him?
Age group: Profession: Marital Status: ☐ M ☐ S ☐ D
What can I get from him?
☐ PROF. HELP ☐ SEX ☐ DRUGS ☐ NOTHING ☐ OTHER:
What does he seem to want from me?
☐ PROF. HELP ☐ SEX ☐ DRUGS ☐ NOTHING ☐ OTHER:
Sex appeal (circle one): 1 2 3 4 5 6 7 8 9 10
Intelligence: 1 2 3 4 5 6 7 8 9 10
Financial/Social status: 1 2 3 4 5 6 7 8 9 10
When to contact him: ☐ TOMORROW ☐ IN 2 DAYS ☐ WAIT ☐ NEVER

2

Ji Lee

New York

1 Abstractor project / USA / 2002 / "An easy way to transform TV viewing into a beautiful and pleasant experience."
2 Ji Lee's business card / USA / 2002
3 Speech-bubble sticker project in New York City / USA / 2002-present / Blank speech-bubble stickers placed on posters, ads, public signs, etc. throughout the city invite passersby to fill them with comments.

New York City
Public Telephone Co.
MN 1280 R
NO STANDING 4PM-7PM
NO PARKING ANYTIME

No WAR ON IRAQ Nov 20th UNION SQUARE 1pm
Robert De
Billy Crys
analy

MARCH 19
GLENN LEWIS
WORLD OUTSIDE MY WINDOW
I am concerned that my C.D. will not sell more than 200,000 units and that, as a result, my recoupable advance from my label will be taken from me, after which my contract will be cancelled, and I'll be back singing Journey covers on Bleecker Street.
Love, Glenn, Lewis

I used to Smoke KRAK on the 6 train
maid in manhatta
REVOLUTION STUDIOS PRESENTS A RED OM FILMS PRODUCTION A FILM BY WAYNE WANG STARRING JENNIFER LOPEZ RALPH FIENNES 'MAID IN M

③

④

⑤

⑥

⑦

Ji Lee

4 Print advertisement, Head & Shoulders Refresh campaign targeting teenagers / Head & Shoulders / USA / 2001
5 Three-dimensional chessboard visualizing the territorial hierarchy of the game / USA / 2003
6 Print advertisement, "Tylenol–no headache" / Tylenol / USA / 2002
7 "Thinking Ahead 'Waatchi,'" promotional watch and clock / Saatchi & Saatchi / USA / 2001
8–11 Univers Revolved 3-dimensional alphabet (formation of the letter A, full alphabet, and applications: *A Dog and A Shadow* fable by Aesop and "wake up") / USA / 1999 / The letters are formed by being rotated on themselves.

⑧

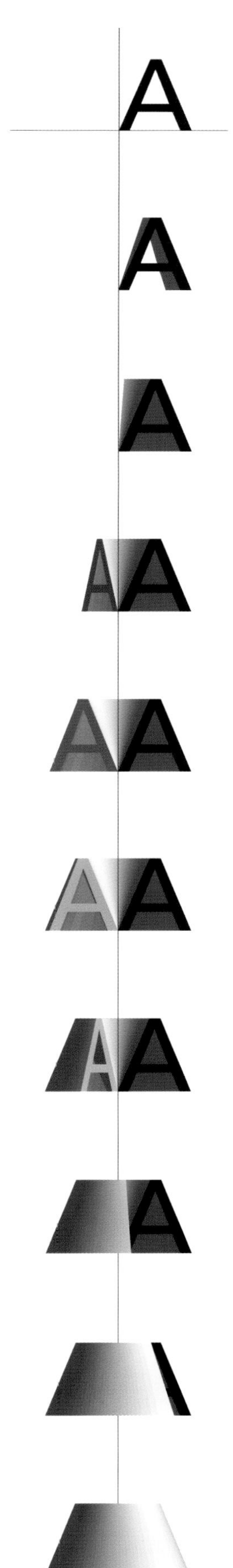

⑨

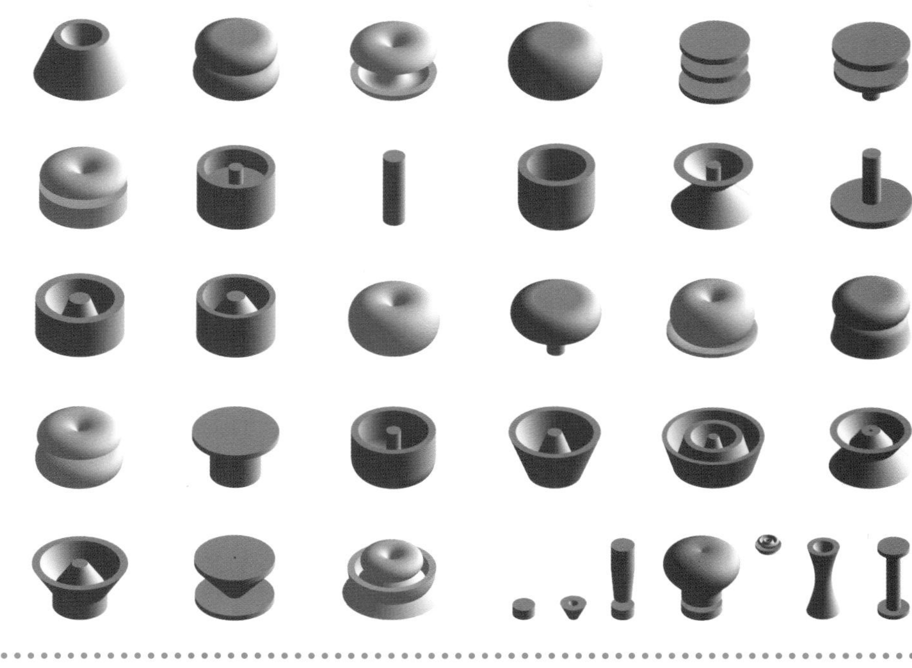

⑩

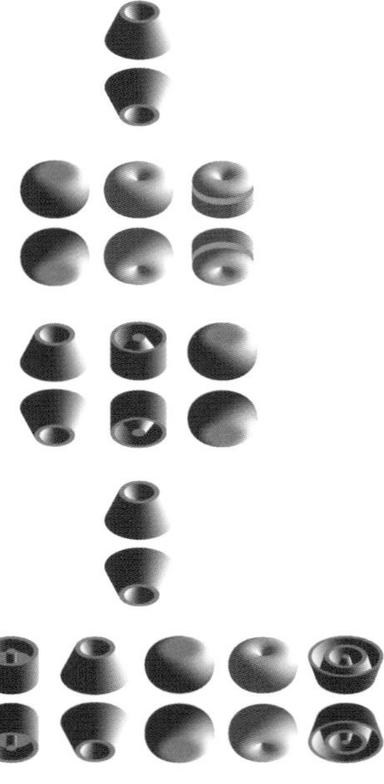

⑪

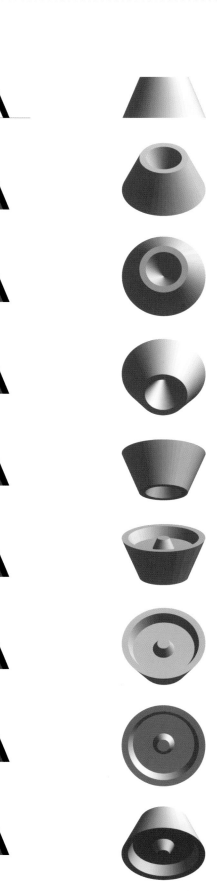

There is no national boundary in human emotion (joy, anger, sadness, and pleasure), and humor can be one of the most important elements in visual communication. Graphic designers throughout the world attempt to deliver messages in a humorous manner. However, it is difficult to incorporate humor in a single poster. Humor can be delivered through concrete expression, and success depends on the wisdom and ability of a designer in upending the common sense and anticipation of the audience.•• Ken-Tsai Lee has been concentrating on this area throughout his career. He can courageously shut out colors and sideline words in order to achieve the desired effect. Look at, for instance, the simple and clear visual messages he created for his client, E+E (Earth and Environment) Paper. One of the posters shows a leaf composed of empty bottles and cans of chemical products in black. The tip of the leaf is contaminated and shown in red. In another poster, the veins and nerves of the human body are connected to a blue plant growing out of the top of the figure's head. Lee's youthful sensitivity is on display in these works.•• In our global era saturated with the influence of all-purpose computers, I am not the only one to have great expectations for Lee and his creative, humorous philosophy.•• Shigeo Fukuda••

1

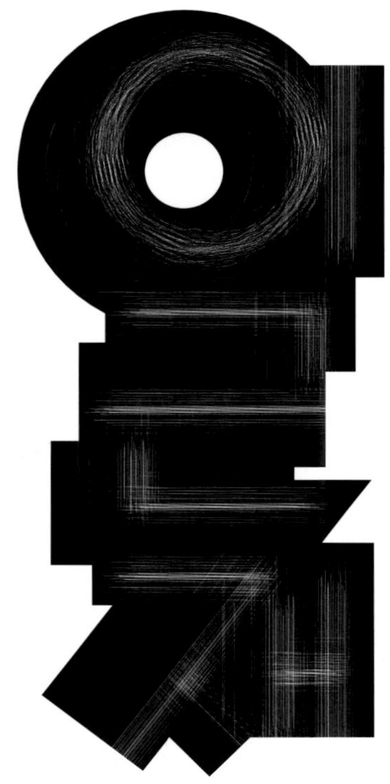

2

3

1 Logo / Ken-Tsai Lee Design Studio / Taiwan / 2001
2–3 Two posters from "My Name is Ken-Tsai" Lee street-poster series / USA / 2003 / Self-promotional effort during three-month stay in New York City. Every week Lee hung posters all over the city with designs of his name written in the native tongue of the people he had met. Here in Korean and Bangladeshi.
4 Network Snake poster for poster-design exhibition / Taiwan Poster Design Association / Taiwan / 2001

Ken-Tsai Lee

Taipei

5 

6 

7

8

Ken-Tsai Lee

5–8 Posters for public Chinese AIDS-prevention campaign / Chinese Society of Preventive Medicine-Living with Hope Organization / Taiwan / 2001
9–10 "Peace-China and Taiwan" and "War-China and Taiwan" posters for poster-design exhibition / Taiwan Poster Design Association / Taiwan / 2001
11–12 Posters promoting recycled E+E (Earth and Environment) Paper / Fonso Enterprise / Taiwan / 2001

9

10

11

12

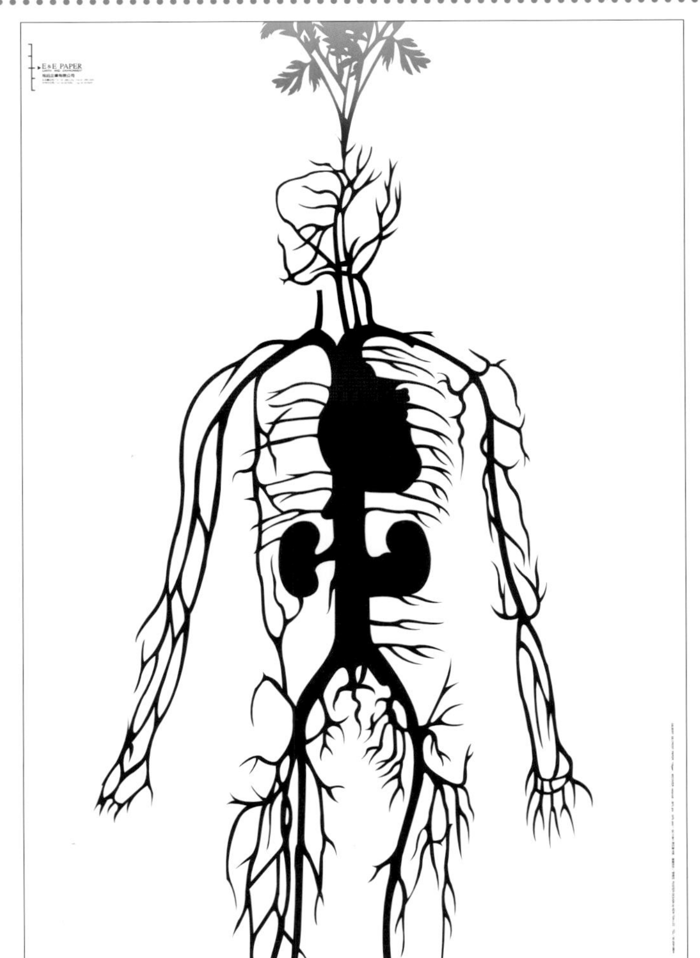

Anette Lenz is an insider's secret. Since she has been living in Paris for more than a decade now, she could nearly pass for being French. But in reality, she is a legal alien in the city of lights. • • Her biography is as impressive as her work. After finishing her visual communication studies in Munich, Lenz began her career as a graphic designer for a Munich-based design agency. In 1989 she moved to Paris, where she first worked for Grapus with Alexander Jordan and then cofounded Nous Travaillons Ensemble. For three years she worked within this graphic-design collective and played an important role designing books, posters, and corporate identities for cities and cultural institutions. Finally, in 1993, she set up her own studio in Paris. Her list of clients included the town of Blanc-Mesnil, for which she created a poster series for the exhibition *Approches* that was seen in Chaumont, Paris, and many other European cities. Thanks to this exposure, numerous cultural institutions became aware of her work, and she began collaborating with new clients. For AFAA (the foreign ministry) she embarked on a yearlong campaign for the Saison Culturelle du Maroc, and for the city of Chaumont Lenz developed a corporate identity and a set of graphic guidelines. From 1998 to 2001 she designed the communication materials of the Théâtre de Rungis, a job that, in 2002, earned her a gold medal at the international graphic-design biennial in Brno. Since 2000 she has been working for Radio France, and in 2001 she joined forces with Vincent Perrottet for the Théâtre d'Angoulême. Together with Hervé Binet, with whom she shares an interest in literature and poetry, she established "editions 23," a collaborative effort focusing on book projects that combine typography, poetry, and text. Lenz joined the Alliance Graphique Internationale (AGI) in 1999. • • She is special because she is truly her own person. Headstrong, she developed her own style, hardly revealing her influences. On the one hand, I discover in her work typically German forms of expression, especially in her handling of typography. On the other hand, I find her work very French. Sometimes I wonder whether she would have had the same opportunities and acclaim in Germany or whether it is precisely the symbiosis of French delicatessens and German wine that is the secret to her success. • • Throughout her career Lenz has done so many notable projects that I find it difficult to select my favorites. I would even go so far as to say that I am jealous of her beautiful, intelligent posters. • • Uwe Loesch • •

1-2 Poster series for Radio France concerts for the 2000-2001 season (2 of 9) / Radio France / France / 2001
3 Poster announcing the 2000-2001 theatrical season / Théâtre de Rungis / France / 2000
4-8 Poster series announcing individual plays for the 2000-2001 theatrical season (5 of 17) / Théâtre de Rungis / France / 2000

Anette Lenz

Paris

(1)

(2)

③

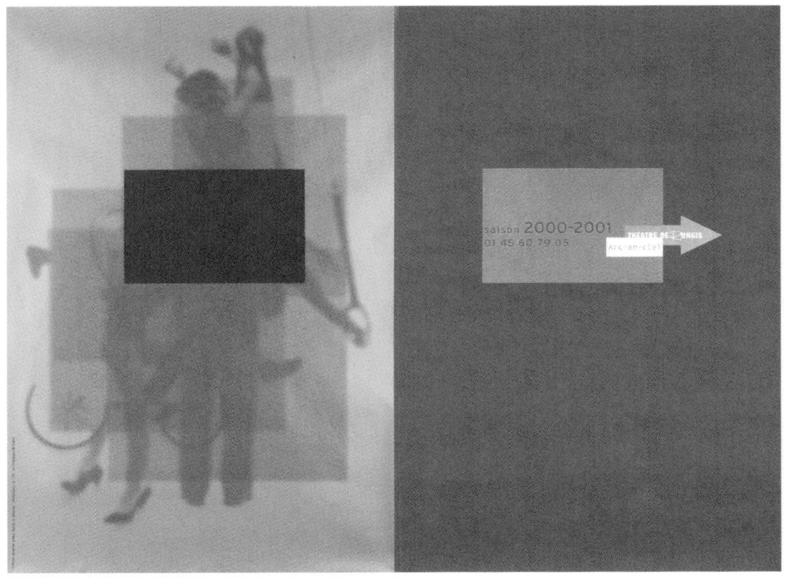

saison 2000-2001
01 45 60 79 05
Arc-en-ciel

④

Arc-en-ciel
DOM JUAN
OU LE FESTIN
DE PIERRE
de Molière
Mise en scène Gilbert Rouvière
vendredi 9 février 2001 à 21 h
→ 1, place du Général-de-Gaulle 94150 Rungis
Location 01 45 60 79 05

⑤

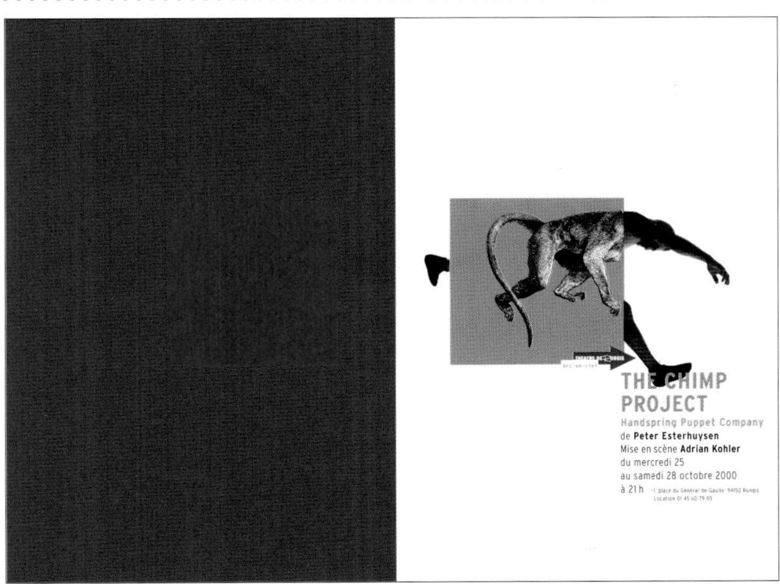

THE CHIMP
PROJECT
Handspring Puppet Company
de Peter Esterhuysen
Mise en scène Adrian Kohler
du mercredi 25
au samedi 28 octobre 2000
à 21 h

⑥

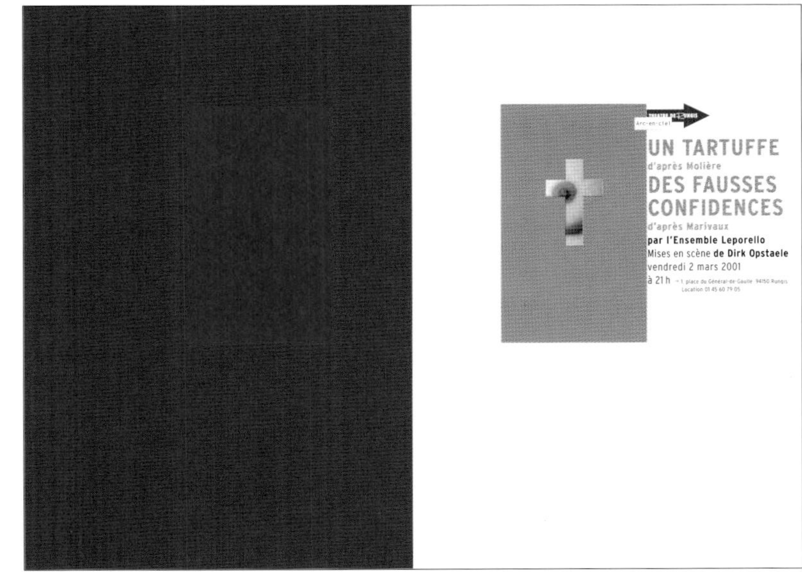

UN TARTUFFE
d'après Molière
DES FAUSSES
CONFIDENCES
d'après Marivaux
par l'Ensemble Leporello
Mises en scène de Dirk Opstaele
vendredi 2 mars 2001
à 21 h

⑦

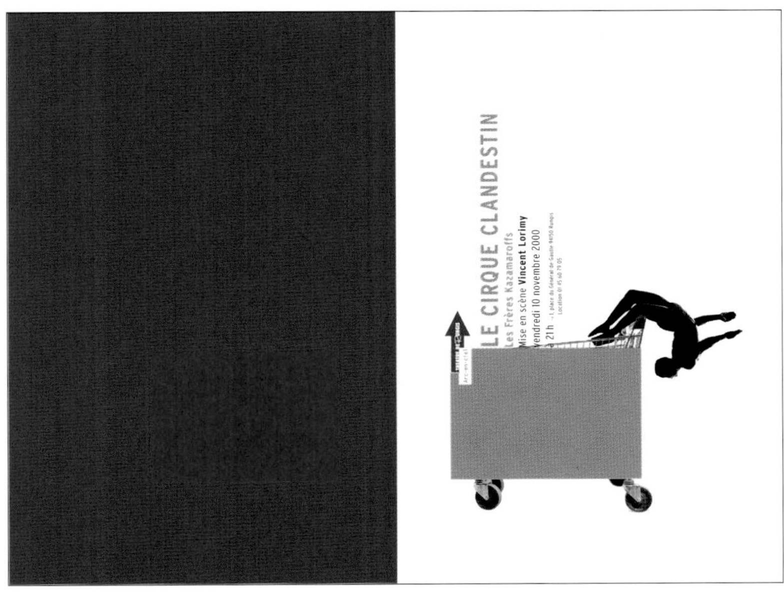

LE CIRQUE CLANDESTIN
Les Frères Kazamaroffs
Mise en scène Vincent Lorimy
vendredi 10 novembre 2000
à 21 h
→ 1, place du Général-de-Gaulle 94150 Rungis
Location 01 45 60 79 05
Arc-en-ciel

⑧

GAD ELMALEH
La Vie normale
Mise en scène Isabelle Nanty
vendredi 13 octobre 2000
à 21 h

9

10

11

9 Poster submission for the Kieler Woche sailing regatta / Festival Kieler Woche / Germany / 2002
10 Poster and invitation for 2002–2003 theatrical season (with Vincent Perrottet, photography Myr Muratet) / Théâtre d'Angoulême / France / 2002
11 Poster announcing the 2002–2003 Radio France concert season / Radio France / France / 2002
12 Cover and spreads, 2002–2003 theatrical-season brochure (with Vincent Perrottet, photography Myr Muratet) / Théâtre d'Angoulême / France / 2002

Théâtre
d'Angoulême
saison 2002–2003

12

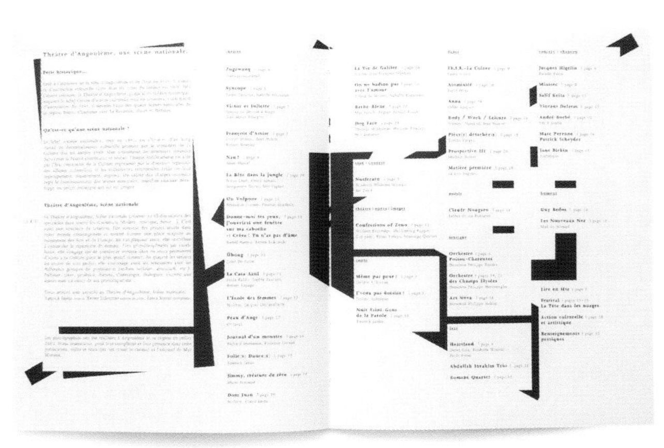

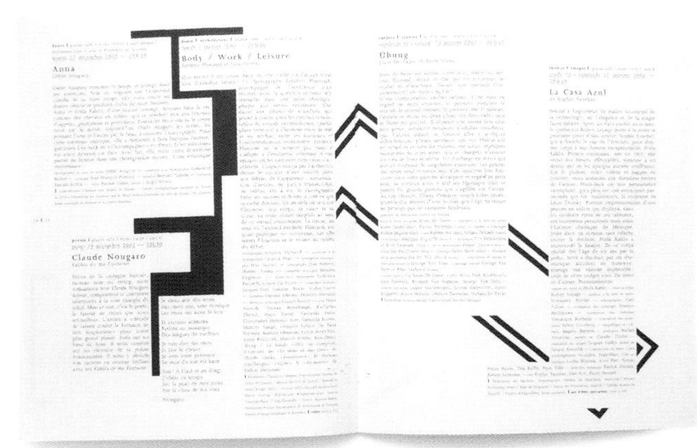
Body / Work / Leisure
Claude Nougaro

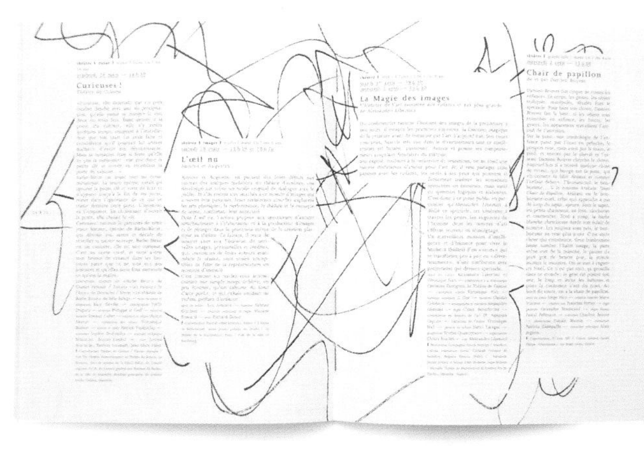

Auchan

You cannot cut a giant tree with a sickle, and you cannot reap rice plants with a saw. Experts must choose their tools and deliberate their means. The tasks imposed on a graphic designer are various and diverse, almost limitless. Sometimes a designer is asked to deliver a message visually to many people in a beautiful manner without words, and sometimes this means struggling with his or her own creative ideology as a graphic designer. • • Apex Lin is one of those praiseworthy people endowed with common sense, sensitivity, and the capacity to tackle these difficult tasks. He has a natural understanding of how to communicate with a given target audience. One can observe this ability for persuasion in the way he switches the meaning of characters on his posters. He demonstrated his creative wisdom by giving the middle letter *A* of PEACE a sense of eternal future though his use of perspective. Equally impressive is the exquisite red cross formed by the combination of *F* and *E* in LIFE. • • The era of communication to limited audiences is already history for graphic design. It is now plunging into communication on a global scale. Lin's philosophy of fine arts will enable him to develop his creativity in the new vortex. • • Shigeo Fukuda • •

①

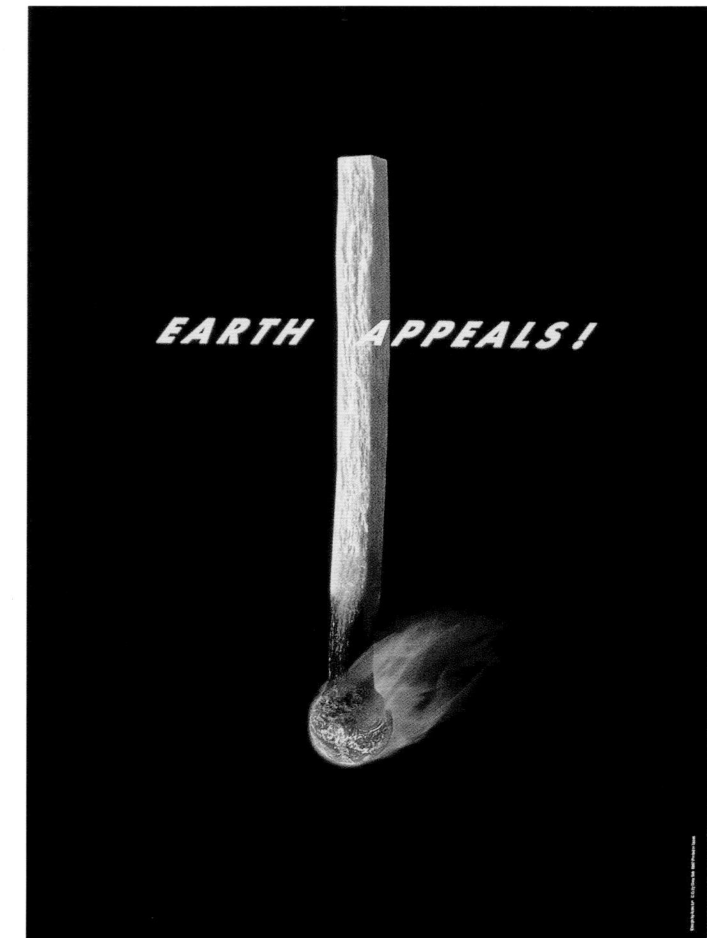

②

1 Poster commemorating victims of Taiwan's 21 September 1999 earthquake / Taiwan 921 Earthquake Reconstruction Committee / Taiwan / 2001
2 Earth Appeals poster / Apex Design Consultant Corporation / Taiwan / 1997
3–6 Formosa? Republic of Casino, Illusion of Taiwan, Green & Life, and Levitating Taiwan posters from "Taiwan" series / Taiwan Image Poster Design Association / Taiwan / 1993–96

Apex Lin

Taipei

③

臺灣印象
FORMOSA
C

④

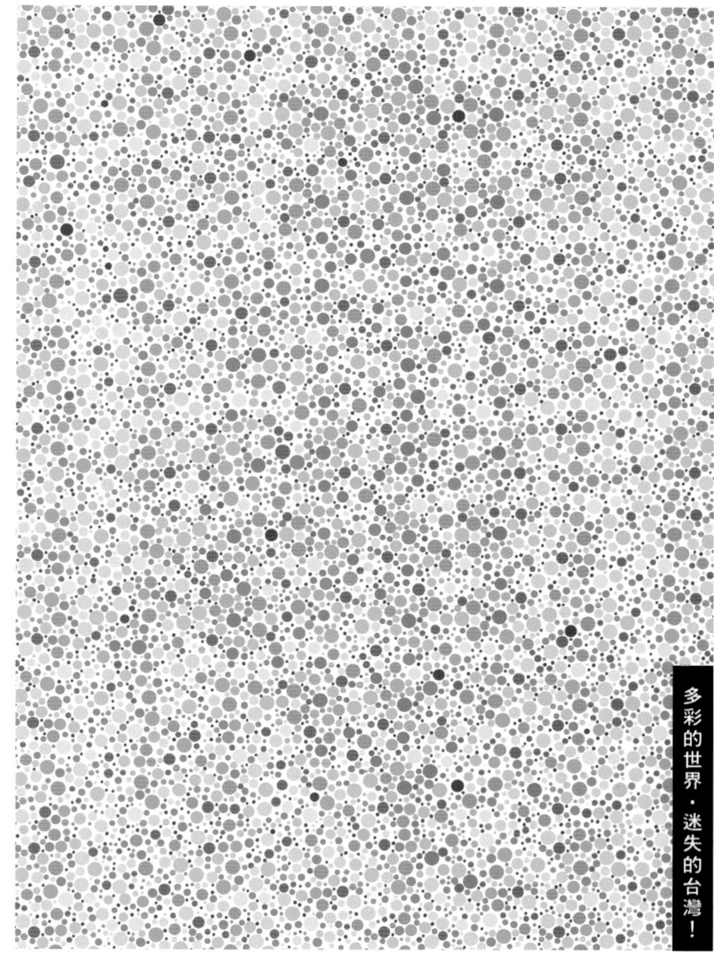

多彩的世界・迷失的台灣！

⑤

1994
TAIWAN
IMAGE
It's Green, It's Life. 珍惜綠色生命 永保台灣活命.

⑥

臺灣印象

SHANGHAI
CITY
EXPO 2010 SHANGHAI,CHINA

7

8

9

10

7 Poster for Shanghai's bid to host the World Expo 2010 / Expo 2010 Shanghai Committee / China / 2002
8 Promotional poster for NACPES / National College of Physical Education and Sports / Taiwan / 1989
9 Logo / Greatwall Oil Corporation / China / 1996
10 Discover Asia, Discover Taipei poster / Taiwan Poster Design Association / Taiwan / 2002
11 Life poster / Apex Design Consultant Corporation / Taiwan / 1998
12 Poster for Apex Lin exhibition in Macau / UNESCO Center of Macau / Macau / 1999
13 Green in Your Heart poster / Apex Design Consultant Corporation / Taiwan / 2001
14 Peace-One Way of the World poster / Taiwan Poster Design Association / Taiwan / 2001

Apex Lin

11

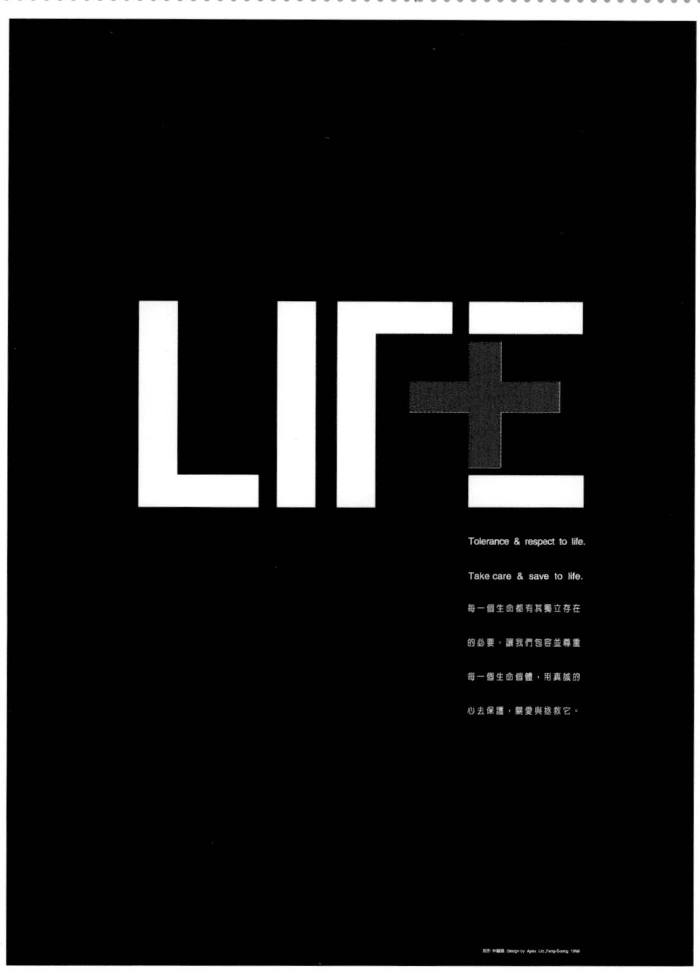
LIFE
Tolerance & respect to life.
Take care & save to life.
每一個生命都有其獨立存在
的必要，讓我們包容並尊重
每一個生命個體，用真誠的
心去保護，關愛與拯救它。

12

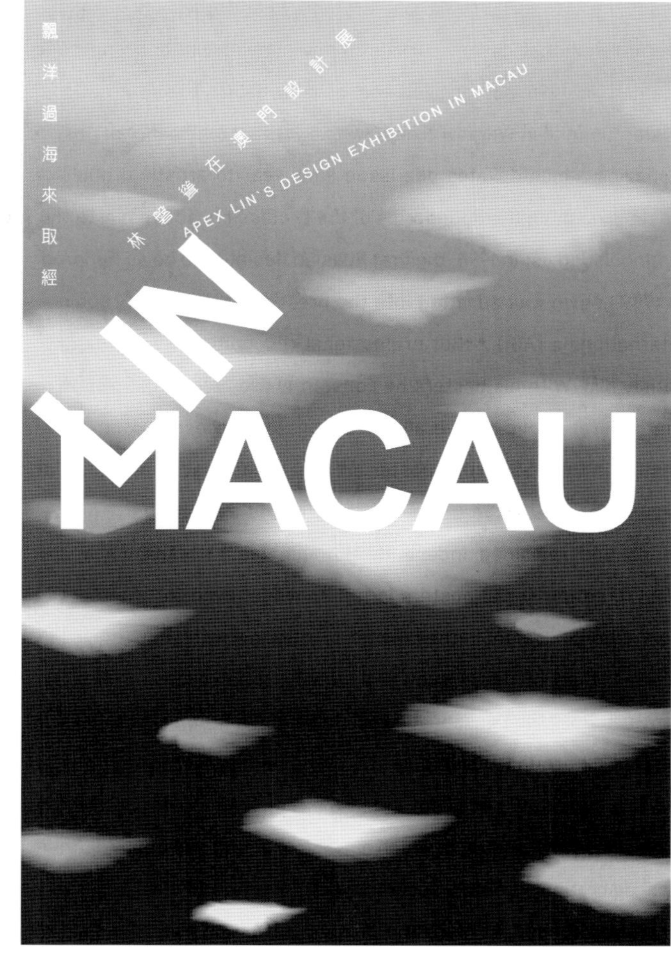
飄洋過海來取經
林磐聳在澳門設計展
APEX LIN'S DESIGN EXHIBITION IN MACAU
IN
MACAU

13

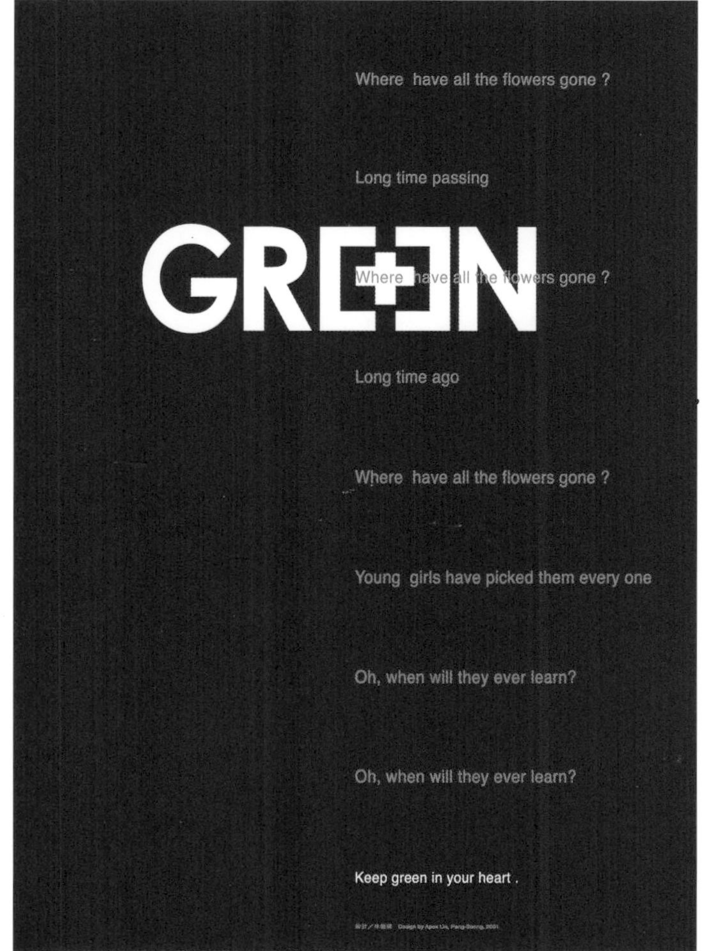
Where have all the flowers gone ?
Long time passing
GREEN
Where have all the flowers gone ?
Long time ago
Where have all the flowers gone ?
Young girls have picked them every one
Oh, when will they ever learn?
Oh, when will they ever learn?
Keep green in your heart .

14

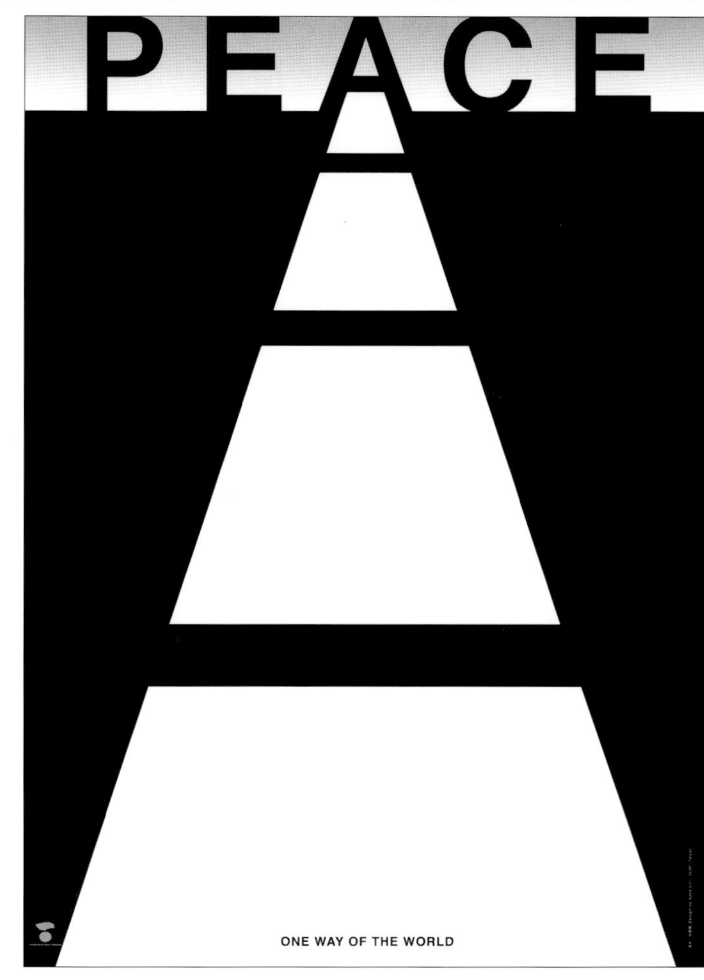
PEACE
ONE WAY OF THE WORLD

In the late 1990s, Moscow designer Andrey Logvin became famous in the international design community for his witty, bright, energetic posters. In 1996 he received the gold medal at the international poster biennial in Warsaw. The New York journal *International Design Magazine*, which devotes one issue each year to artistic profiles of masters pushing the boundaries of the profession, added him to this distinguished list in 1998, the first Russian designer to be so honored. In 1999 Logvin was admitted into the prestigious Alliance Graphique Internationale (AGI). ••But professional recognition alone does not satisfy him. With his posters he constantly tries to break through to the general public. Above all, he dreams of success for the social poster. In the USSR, such poster art was called "sociopolitical." For decent designers, the genre was discredited as communist propaganda and remained indecently untouchable. ••Meanwhile in the West, creating social posters is not shameful even for the stars of international design. In the fall of 1994, during a workshop offered by jury members of the Moscow Golden Bee graphic-design biennial, Logvin's idol, Uwe Loesch, showed slides of his green environmental posters all around Düsseldorf. Thus Logvin discovered that poster art is a means of mass, not elitist, communication. He started the project Moscow-poster, in which a group of young designers, at their own discretion, created sociopolitical posters and the young firm LiniaGrafik funded, printed, and plastered two hundred of them. But Moscow is not Düsseldorf. Two hundred posters are not enough to blanket a capital. ••In another campaign, seven national and seven international design celebrities visually interpreted the fiftieth anniversary of the victory in World War II. This time the posters didn't even make it to the field. Moscow authorities did not allow their posting, afraid that they would not be "understood by the people." ••Recently Logvin participated in the large-scale poster project "I don't want to hate." His contribution showed Christ, Muhammad, and Buddha sharing a meal. The poster was displayed in various Russian cities, but religious orthodoxy organized pickets against it. ••Logvin is not discouraged. He still believes that his efforts will fuel a rebirth of the visually and socially active street poster. ••Serge Serov••

1

2

3

1 Poster for *Russian Design 95* competition and exhibition / Design Union of Russia / Russia / 1995
2 Self-commissioned Life Was Successful poster / Russia / 1996 / The phrase written in caviar ironically refers to a Russian idiom on success in life.
3 The Best in the World poster for caviar retailer / Russian Alaska Company / Russia / 1997
4 Poster for artist Stas Ishenko's *In the Cube* exhibition / Stas Ishenko / Russia / 1999
5 Poster for international poster project "10 Graphic Designers for Human Rights" / Ministère de l'Éducation nationale / France / 2001
6 It's Sad Without a Label poster for *The Label 95* exhibition organized by printing company LiniaGrafic / LiniaGrafic / Russia / 1995
7 Bear Up, Egory poster celebrating Moscow's 850th anniversary / LiniaGrafic / Russia / 1998 / Egory is Moscow's patron saint.

Andrey Logvin

Moscow

4

В КУБЕ
ЗНАКИ ЗЕМЛИ
И МИРОВЫЕ СИМВОЛЫ
ОБЪЕКТЫ СТАСА ИЩЕНКО
ЗВЕРЕВСКИЙ ЦЕНТР СОВРЕМЕННОГО ИСКУССТВА 10-13 МАРТА 1999

5

Déclaration Universelle des Droits de l'Homme
Article 5
ne sera soumis à la torture, ni à des peines
ou traitements cruels, inhumains ou dégradants.

6

LiniaGrafic!
ФИРМА «ЛИНИЯ ГРАФИК»: ЭТИКЕТКИ, ЯРЛЫКИ, КОЛЬЕРЕТКИ ЛЮБОГО ФОРМАТА И КОНФИГУРАЦИИ НА БУМАГЕ ВСЕХ СОРТОВ,
МАЛОФОРМАТНАЯ УПАКОВКА ОФСЕТОМ И ШЕЛКОГРАФИЕЙ С ИСПОЛЬЗОВАНИЕМ КОНГРЕВА, ТИСНЕНИЯ, ЛАКИРОВКИ, ВЫРУБКИ, ВЫСЕЧКИ
БЕЗ ЭТИКЕТКИ
ГРУСТНО!
РОССИЯ 109382 МОСКВА, СОВХОЗНАЯ 2, «ЛИНИЯ ГРАФИК», ТЕЛЕФОН: (095)351-9655, (095)230-0169, (095)204-1190, ТЕЛЕФАКС: (095)351-9726

7

Держись, Егорий!

8

9
10
11

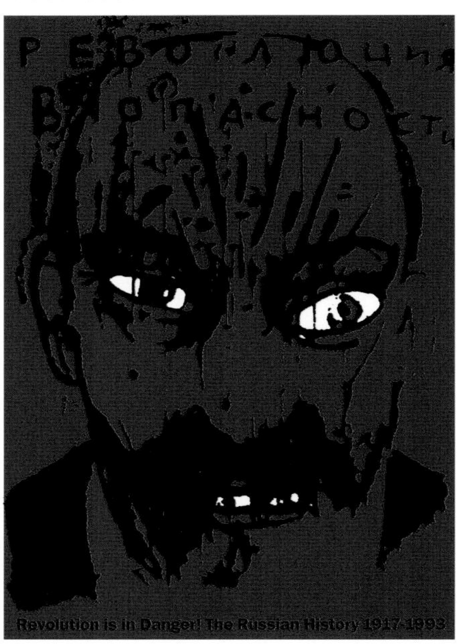

8 Poster advertising workshops offered by jury members during 5th Moscow Golden Bee poster biennial / Golden Bee Committee / 2000
9 Poster for puppet show *Cowboy Story* / Saratov Puppet Theatre / Russia / 1991
10 Poster for *Revolution Is in Danger! The Russian History 1917–1993* exhibition / National Center for Contemporary Art / Russia / 1995
11 Poster for *Fauna* exhibition / National Center for Contemporary Art / Russia / 1998
12 Poster for concert by the band Mouse Trap / Mouse Trap / Russia / 2002
13 Poster for festival celebrating the 100th anniversary of Vladimir Mayakovski / futurism.ru / Russia / 2002
14 Poster for Swiss-Russian art project Supremus / Supremus Foundation / Russia and Switzerland / 2002
15 Poster for *Serials* exhibition / National Center for Contemporary Art / Russia / 2000

Andrey Logvin

12

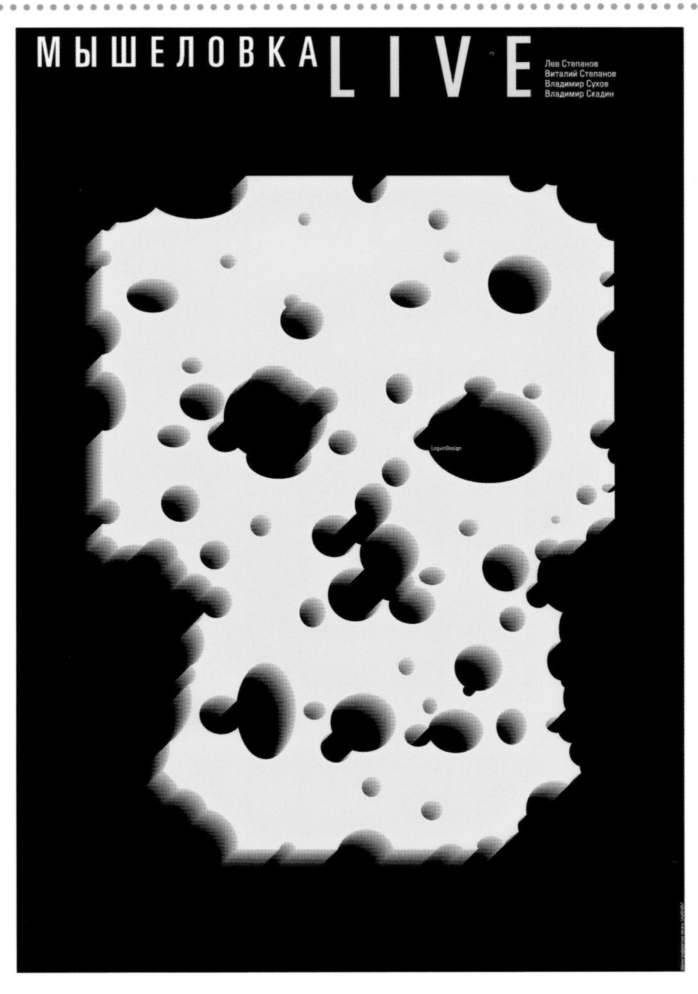
МЫШЕЛОВКА LIVE
Лев Степанов
Виталий Степанов
Владимир Сухов
Владимир Скадин

13

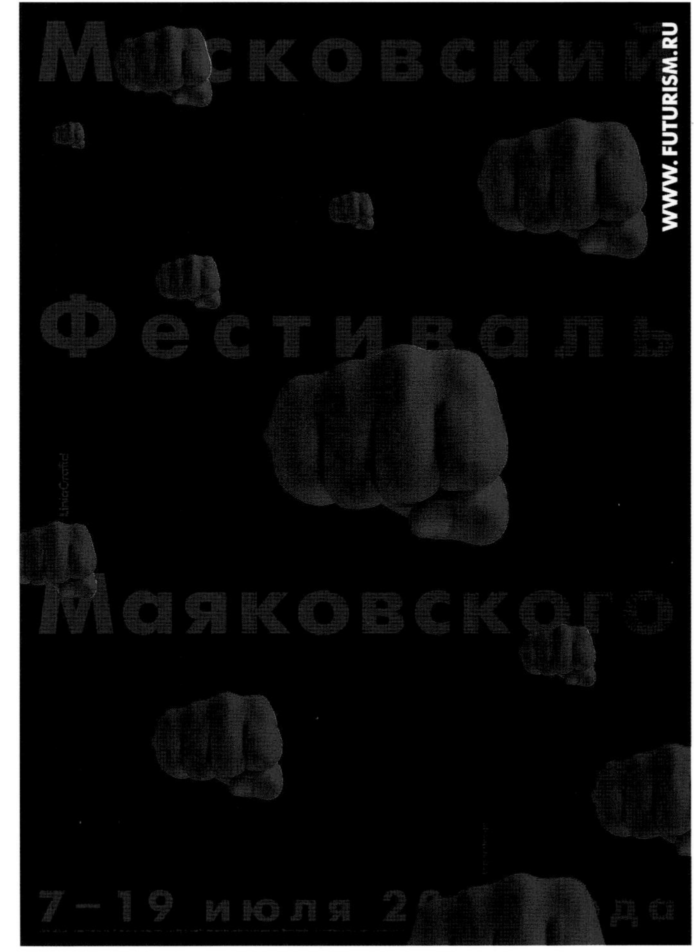
WWW.FUTURISM.RU
Фестиваль
Маяковского
7–19 июля 2

14

Москва-Пустынь-Zurich
SUPREMUS
ORGASMUS
TOTALIS
МИФОЛОГИЯ И ПРАКТИКА СОВРЕМЕННОГО ИСКУССТВА

15

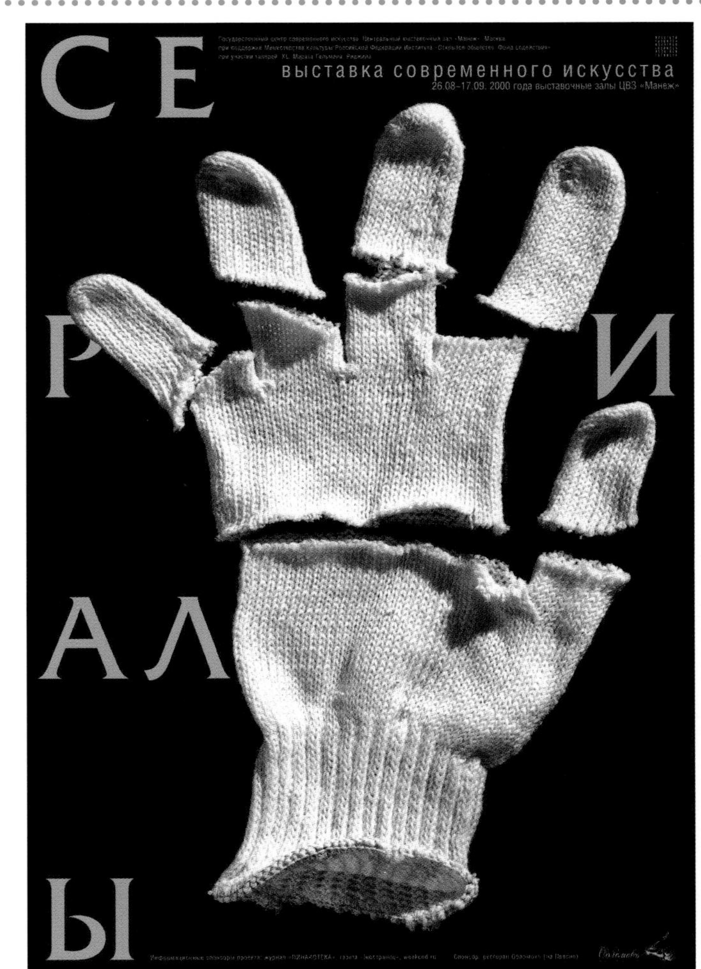
СЕ
Р
И
АЛ
Ы
выставка современного искусства
26.08–17.09. 2000 года выставочные залы ЦВЗ «Манеж»

Most graphic design strives to balance the views of society and a general sense of beauty, but Victor Hugo Marreiros's design is an exception. Many of his works demonstrate a magic that reminds us of watching a circus performance. They are pleasant, humorous, and at the same time bewitching. The poster in the series created for the 12th Macao Arts Festival is a masterpiece. It looks like both a face and an instrument, and amazingly you can visualize music from the rhythmically composed surface. The well-controlled variations of a string instrument, a piano, melody, and dance are truly exquisite. The new talent of this exceptional designer is likewise demonstrated in his poster for the Macao Youth Musician Contest and in the series of posters for the Luís de Matos magic show. • • Marreiros is one of the most precious and most dangerous and interesting designers in the global graphic-design world, like a creature from another planet. His designs do not require many words or explanation. They should be savored silently, just like listening to music. • • Shigeo Fukuda • •

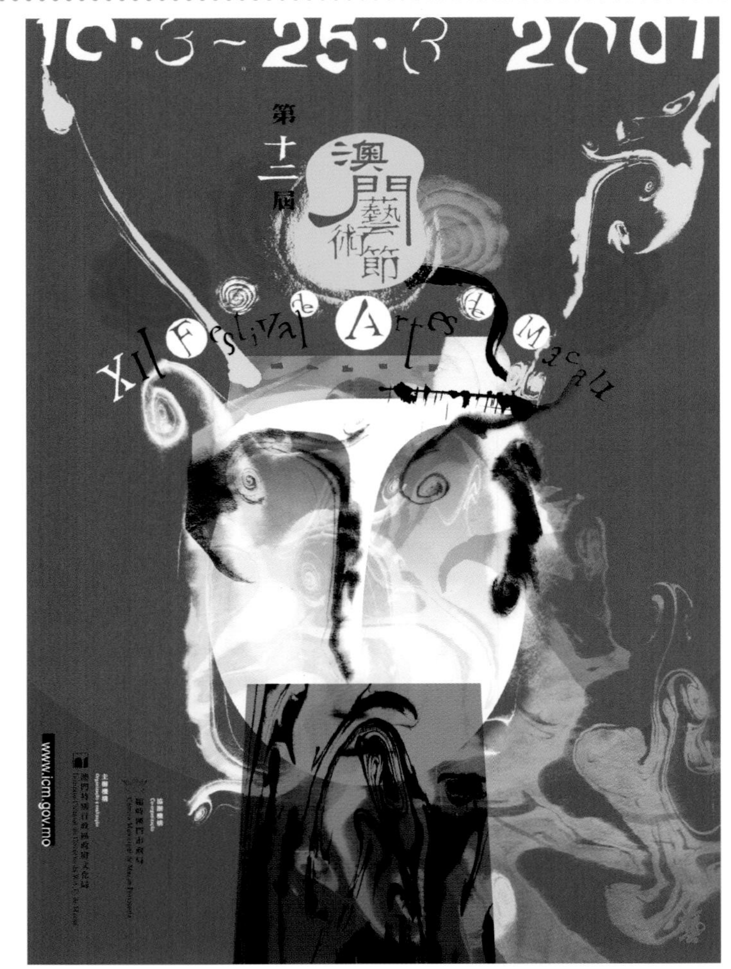

1

2

1 Poster for XII Macao Arts Festival / Macao Cultural Institute / China / 2001
2 Cover illustration for *Oriente Occidente–East West* magazine no. 4 / International Institute of Macao / China / 2001
3 Poster series for fourth Chinese Drama Festival in Macao / Macao Cultural Institute / China / 2002

Victor Hugo Marreiros

Macao, China

第四屆
IV Festival
de Teatro Chinês
Macau · 2002
The 4th Chinese Drama Festival (Macao · 2002)
23 ~ 29 / 11
澳門 · 2002

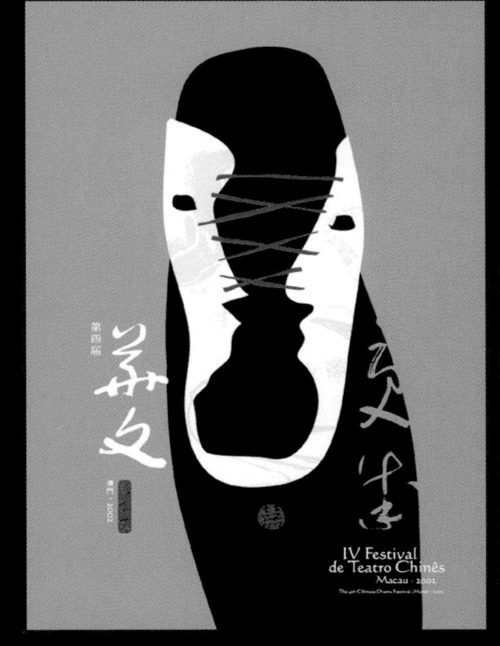
第四屆
IV Festival
de Teatro Chinês
Macau · 2002

IV Festival
de Teatro Chinês
Macau · 2002
第四屆

3

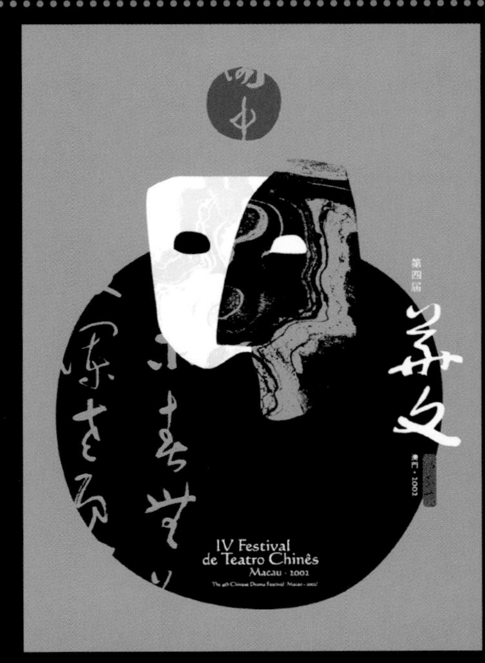
第四屆
IV Festival
de Teatro Chinês
Macau · 2002

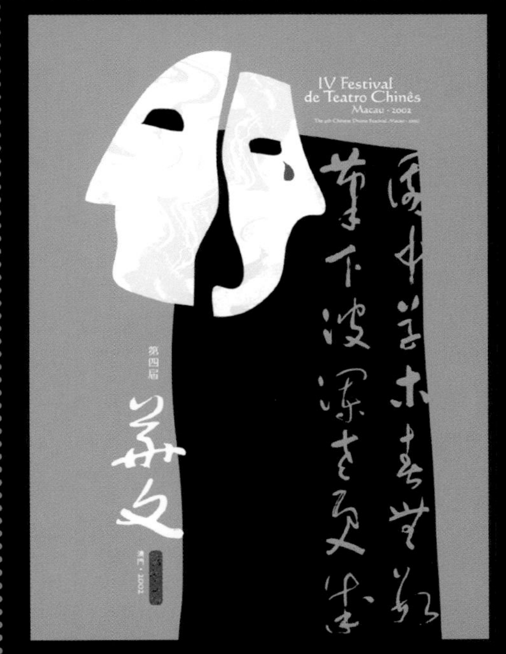
IV Festival
de Teatro Chinês
Macau · 2002
第四屆

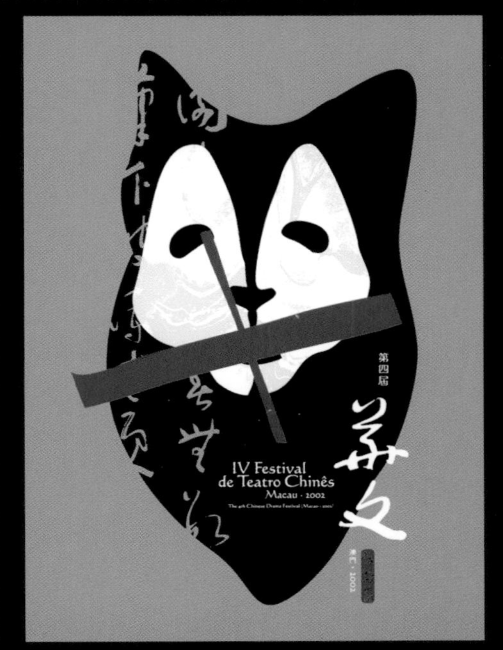
第四屆
IV Festival
de Teatro Chinês
Macau · 2002

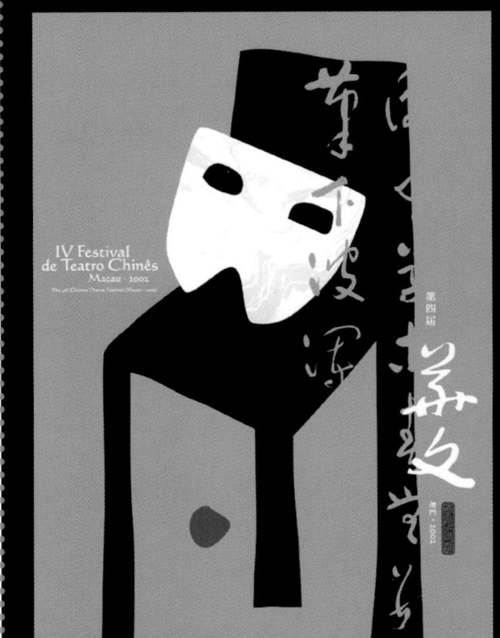
IV Festival
de Teatro Chinês
Macau · 2002
第四屆

IV Festival
de Teatro Chinês
Macau · 2002
第四屆

第四屆
IV Festival
de Teatro Chinês
Macau · 2002

4

5
6

4 Poster for nineteenth Macao Youth Musician Contest / Macao Cultural Institute / China / 2001
5–6 Program covers for nineteenth Macao Youth Musician Contest / Macao Cultural Institute / China / 2001
7 Poster for Portugese Movies Fortnight in Macao / Instituto Português do Oriente / China / 2001
8 September 11, 2001, poster, contribution to sixteenth Asian Art Exhibition / China / 2001
9 Poster for Luís de Matos magic show / Macao Cultural Institute / China / 1999
10–12 Posters for XIII, XV, and XVI Macao International Music Festival / Macao Cultural Institute / China / 1999–2002
13 Poster for International Painting Prize in Macao / International Institute of Macao / China / 2000
14 Poster for exhibition *Design 2000, Taipei International Poster Invitational Exhibition* / Taiwan / 1999
15 Poster for XIII Macao Arts Festival / Macao Cultural Institute / China / 2002

Victor Hugo Marreiros

7

8

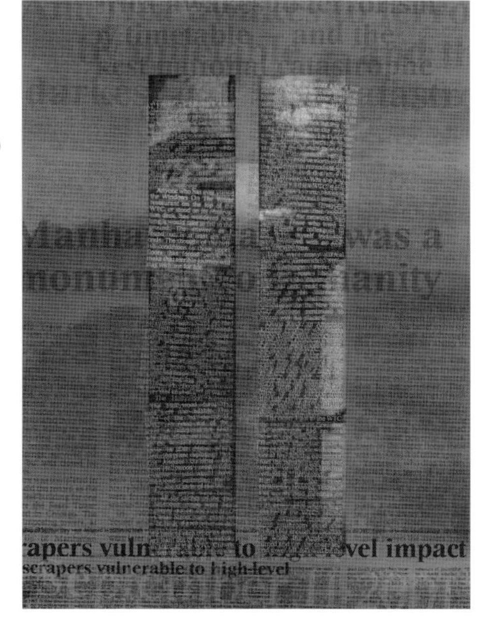

9

10

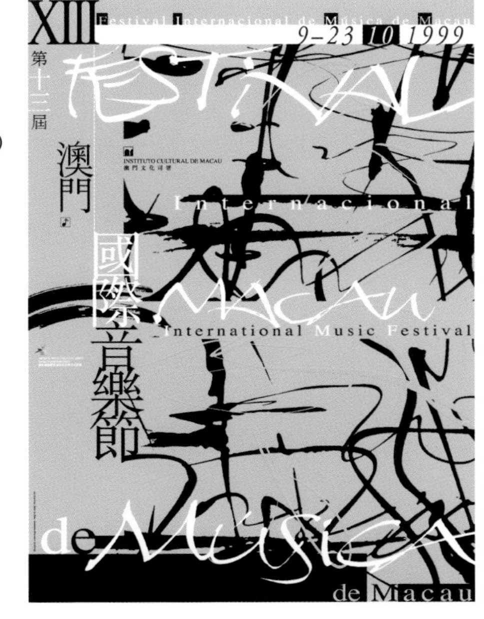

11

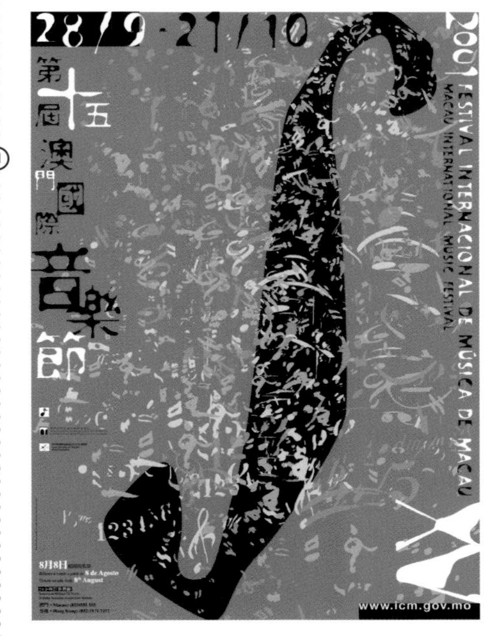

12

13

14

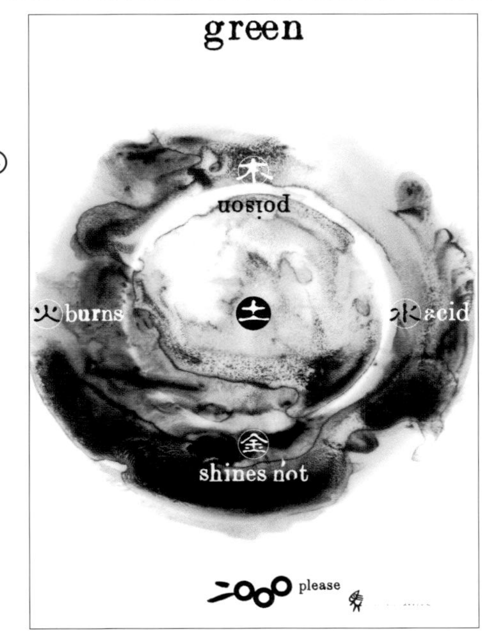

15

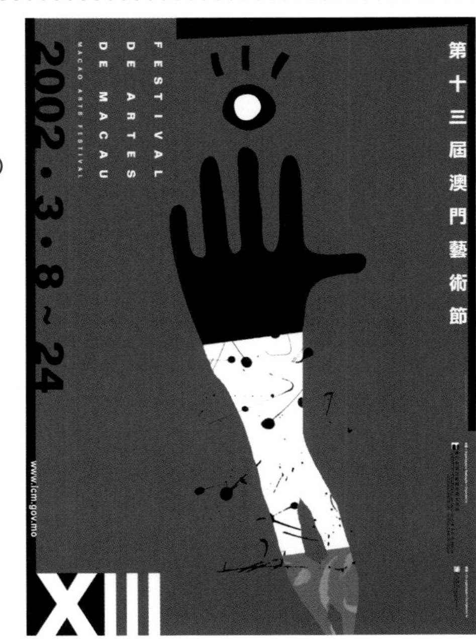

I met Malte Martin during the preparations for my exhibition *Zwischenkieferknochen (Os Intermaxilliare)* at the Galerie Anatome in Paris. When speaking he switched effortlessly between perfect French and German, making it difficult for me to figure out where he was really from. He soon hinted that once upon a time, long ago, he had come to Paris without any intention of staying and had never left. I was even more impressed when he handed me a literary journal that he publishes himself, self-designed, of course, with every typographic subtlety. • • Later, we bumped into each other again in the small city of Chaumont in the French heartland. Chaumont has dedicated itself to the art of postermaking and once a year hosts an international poster festival. Martin was standing on a ladder surrounded by many helping hands: a large-scale poster-mounting operation, a sort of typographic manifesto, that spread over the entire city. The posters and banners were poetry for the eye. This type of operation is typical of Martin. • • In his graphic design studio he devotes himself to contemporary theater, dance, and music. In a permanent dialogue with his clients he conceives new signs and images, always developing his preference for experimentation and new technologies, such as digital picture processing. At the same time, he does not shy away from using traditional techniques like photograms. • • Another project to which Martin dedicates himself is the Agrafmobile, a sort of mobile visual theater that creates and organizes artistic processes and prefers forms of expression that work well in public spaces. Martin, often in collaboration with other artists, such as sound designers, composers, writers, dancers, and performers, provides the visual concepts. With this "visual theater" he hopes to win back public areas as "agoras"—creative spaces for the people who live around them. • • Uwe Loesch • •

1 Installation *Quoi de neuf Denis*, Chaumont, France / Agrafmobile / France / 2002 / One of several installations distributed throughout Chaumont showing a young citizen's face accompanied by a quote from philosopher Denis Diderot.

2 Installation *Takalefaire*, Chaumont, France / Agrafmobile / France / 2001 / Installation in front of the town hall for the centenary celebration of the law on associations, which established freedom of association in France.

3–6 Program spreads, poster, and bus design for 2002–2003 theatrical season (with Stéphanie Schuller) / La Comédie de Reims / France / 2002

7–8 Poster/program cover and spread for theater festival *La mousson d'été* (spread image Julien Cochin) / La maison européenne des écritures contemporaines / France / 2001

Malte Martin

Paris

le diable
en partage
Fabrice Melquiot
Emmanuel Demarcy-Mota
création. En diptyque avec "l'inattendu"

Une machine à broyer les corps et les âmes, une famille prise dans le désert de leur rêve. Un théâtre du vertige.

(3)
(4)
(5)
(6)

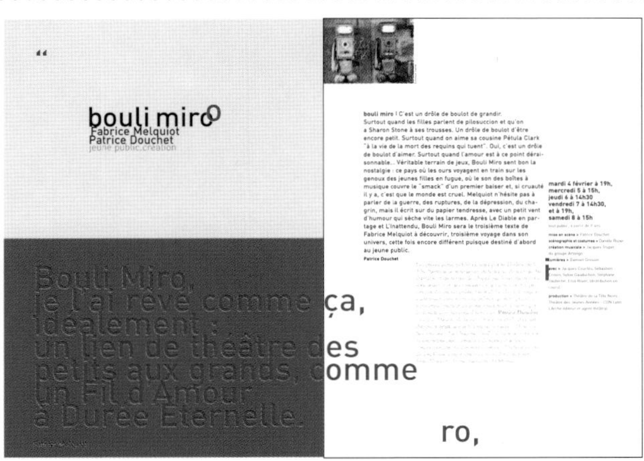

bouli miro
Fabrice Melquiot
Patrice Douchet
jeune public, création
Bouli Miro,
je l'ai rêvé comme ça,
idéalement :
un lien de théâtre des
petits aux grands, comme
un Fil d'Amour
à Durée Éternelle.
ro,

la suspension
du plongeur
Lionel Spycher
création

La Suspension du plongeur : natation, politique, affaires et champagne !

la Comédie
de Reims
vous invite à l'envol
de la saison 02/03
que le rega
et des idée
théâtre
la Coméd
un conflit famil
des blague

la maison européenne
des écritures contemporaines
présente
la mousson d'été
écrire le théâtre d'aujourd'hui
du 23 au 29 août 2001
à l'Abbaye des Prémontrés
les auteurs français et d'Europe du Sud
Université d'été à Pont-à-Mousson,
Lorraine.

(7)
(8)

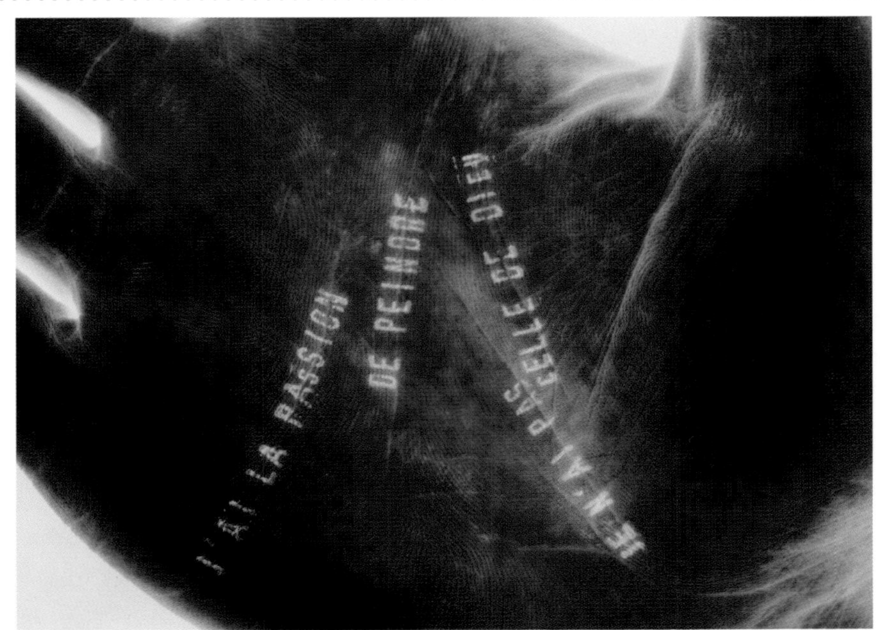

LA PASSION
DE PEINDRE
JE N'AI PAS CELLE DE DIEU

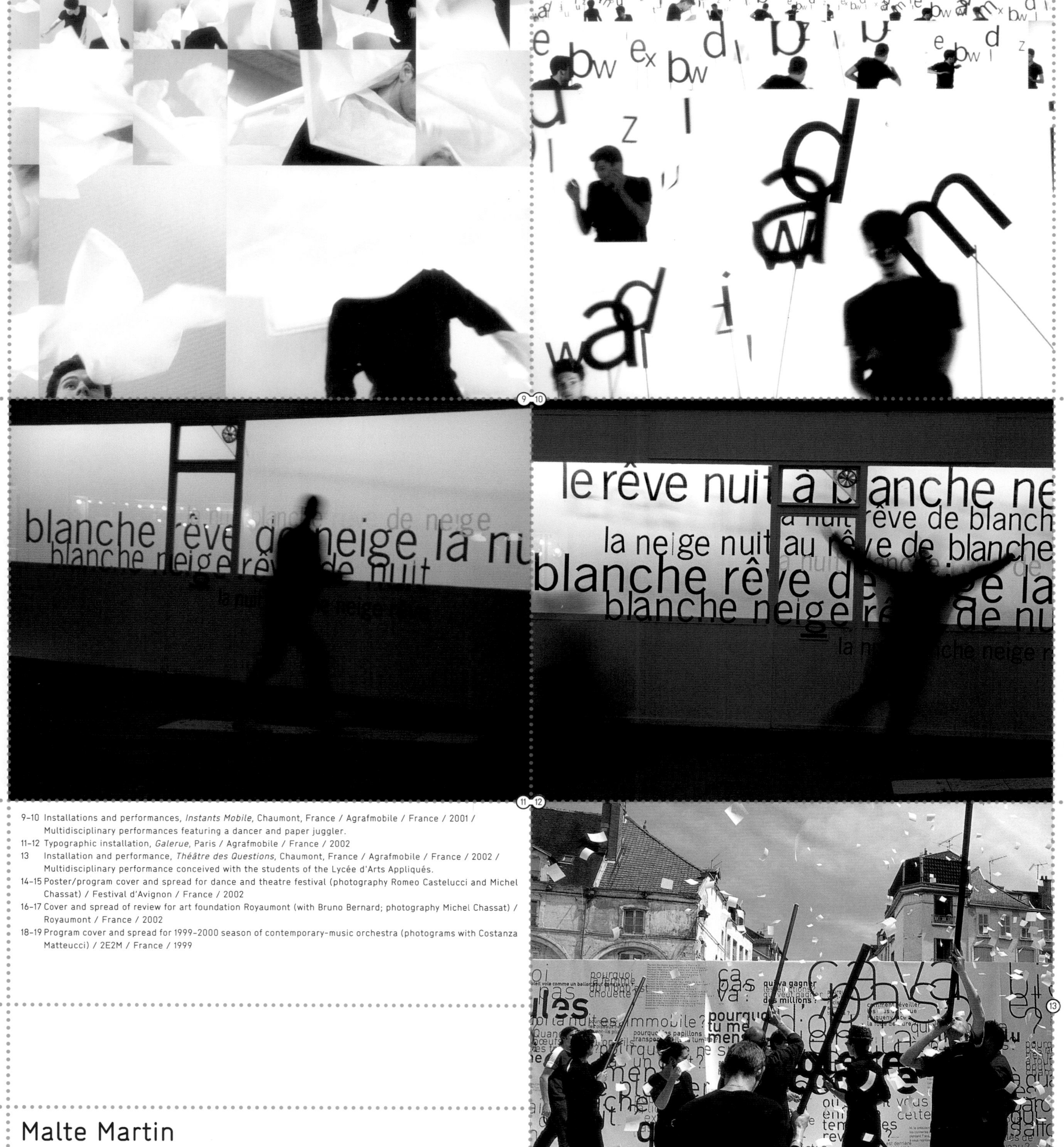

9–10 Installations and performances, *Instants Mobile*, Chaumont, France / Agrafmobile / France / 2001 / Multidisciplinary performances featuring a dancer and paper juggler.
11–12 Typographic installation, *Galerue*, Paris / Agrafmobile / France / 2002
13 Installation and performance, *Théâtre des Questions*, Chaumont, France / Agrafmobile / France / 2002 / Multidisciplinary performance conceived with the students of the Lycée d'Arts Appliqués.
14–15 Poster/program cover and spread for dance and theatre festival (photography Romeo Castelucci and Michel Chassat) / Festival d'Avignon / France / 2002
16–17 Cover and spread of review for art foundation Royaumont (with Bruno Bernard; photography Michel Chassat) / Royaumont / France / 2002
18–19 Program cover and spread for 1999–2000 season of contemporary-music orchestra (photograms with Costanza Matteucci) / 2E2M / France / 1999

Malte Martin

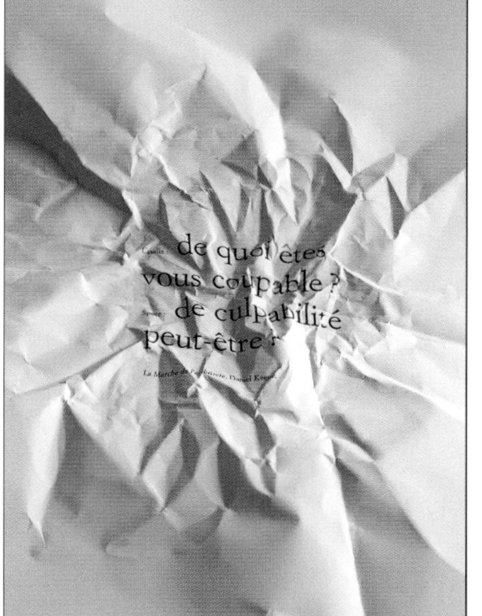

théâtre création | Cloître des Célestins | 22h | durée estimée 1h20

la marche de l'architecte

de **Daniel Keene** mise en scène **Renaud Cojo**
avec **Bruno Blairet**, **Emmanuel Burgen** et **Gabriel Coin** (en alternance),
Maurice Deschamps, **Frédéric Leidgens**, **Michel Peyrelon**
traduction **Séverine Magois** musique **Michael Smetanin** direction musicale
Patrick Marco scénographie **Claude Chestier** création lumière **Éric Blosse**
création son **Nicolas Barillot** création des vêtements **Pascale Robin**
directeur de chant **Patrick Marco** assistante à la mise en scène **Miren Lassus-Olasagasti**
Coproduction Ouvre le Chien, Espace Malraux Scène Nationale Chambéry Savoie,
Festival d'Avignon, Théâtre National de Bordeaux Aquitaine [en préfiguration]
Avec la participation artistique du Jeune Théâtre national avec le soutien de la Maîtrise de Paris,
de l'IDDAC, ce l'OARA, de l'aide à la création d'œuvres dramatiques du ministère de la Culture
et du Conseil régional d'Aquitaine En compagnie de l'**ADAMI** Texte publié aux éditions Théâtrales

5 6 7 8 9 10 11 12 13 14 15 16 17 18 19 20 21 22 23 24 25 26 27

Jugé à Nuremberg, où il plaida coupable, le nazi Albert Speer, architecte d'Adolf Hitler, fut condamné à vingt ans de réclusion à la prison de Spandau. C'est là que nous le rejoignons, mis à nu par l'auteur australien, Daniel Keene. Loin d'être une biographie, la pièce plonge au plus profond d'une conscience vide de remords et tente d'explorer la folie d'un homme qui se déroba, jusqu'au bout, à la responsabilité de ses actes. Sans jamais franchir les murs de l'enceinte, Speer ne cesse de s'évader mentalement. Il marche dans le jardin, il marche, sans fin, et rallie les extrêmes du globe. Lorsqu'il discute avec ses compagnons, Hess, l'autre nazi, ou Casalis, pasteur aumônier, il déploie la même capacité à se soustraire à l'émotion. Mécanique fascinante que Daniel Keene observe et restitue en dialogues elliptiques, entrelacés de poèmes de Paul Celan, qui fut l'un des témoins essentiels de l'holocauste. Le chant et le conte tracent, ainsi, à la lisière de l'histoire, un récit poétique. Renaud Cojo le donne à entendre comme un oratorio. Le monstre gît dans son mensonge. Pour le metteur en scène, il ne fait aucun doute que la bête qui nous fait face, sur le plateau, est tapie, silencieuse, en chacun d'entre nous. Tout cela est affaire de conscience et le théâtre, en l'occurrence, est le plus sûr chemin menant vers la lucidité.

31

14–15

Longtemps focalisée sur sa propre histoire, la musique occidentale savante s'ouvre aux traditions extra-européennes. Elle y redécouvre des instruments qui sont les ancêtres des nôtres, et une immense richesse de timbres, modes, techniques d'interprétation. La fusion ne pourra se faire qu'en cherchant un équilibre entre la musique écrite et la pratique orale, dans le respect des traditions de chacun.

* Comparé à la richesse des instruments du monde entier, nous en avons relativement peu. En outre, la plupart proviennent du Proche-Orient où ils existent encore dans leurs formes ancestrales avec une extraordinaire variété. Le oud, par exemple – considéré dans le monde arabe comme l'instrument roi – s'est répandu à l'Est comme à l'Ouest : luth, et plus tard guitare en Espagne, pipa si typique en Chine, biwa au Japon. Le nay (flûte orientale), le kamanche (viole de gambe, puis violon chez nous, erhu en Chine) ont connu une histoire similaire. À seulement considérer les cultures musicales vivantes de la Turquie au Japon, on y découvre un inépuisable trésor de déclinaisons locales pour chaque instrument.

Bien qu'elle ait sans cesse exploré de nouveaux territoires, la musique contemporaine est plutôt restée tournée vers elle-même. Le dodécaphonisme, qui a certes cassé et remplacé le système tonal, n'a pas brisé l'échelle chromatique tempérée ; l'emploi du microton dans la musique d'aujourd'hui n'étant en somme qu'une subdivision du chromatisme, bien différente de l'usage raffiné des micro-intervalles dans les musiques non-occidentales.

Tout se passe comme si l'électronique, l'informatique musicale, et les recherches de nouveaux modes de jeux sur les instruments de l'orchestre avaient satisfait notre soif de timbres nouveaux. Malgré un souci permanent d'innovation, notre musique savante a toujours le Stradivarius pour parangon. Seule une poignée d'esprits aventureux comme Harry Partch ou Leon Theremin ont inventé de nouveaux instruments, mais cela reste marginal.

rendez-vous
- Concert Hosokawa, Harvey, Xu Shuya, Loevendie, Rijnvos Nieuw Ensemble d'Amsterdam le 21 septembre à 20h45.
- Concert: 15 créations de la session de composition le 28 septembre à 15h45 et 17h45.

un nouveau monde de sons **a new sound WOrld**

paroles

n°4 07 › 12 2002 page 2

l'influence extra-européenne

les pièges du folklore à la Russe

tempéraments et modes

édito

À l'heure où nous bouclons ces *Nouvelles* commence le rush vers les routes. Désir de vacances, dépaysement, ailleurs, ne pas bronzer idiot. S'amorce le long parcours du combattant pour accéder à la culture avec l'impossible choix dans le labyrinthe des festivals. Aujourd'hui, la rentrée s'organise, restent les souvenirs, ils nous aident à penser que cette année tout sera différent. Mais septembre n'est pas forcément toujours prédisposé à nous laisser le sourire aux lèvres et la tête dans les nuages. Alors, si tout simplement on passait quelques heures à Royaumont, à entendre toutes ces propositions de métissage et de découverte et peut-être se dire que finalement, à coté, juste à côté de chez nous, il existe d'autres « ailleurs » possibles.

Véronique Barcelo

n°4 07 › 12 2002 page 3

16–17

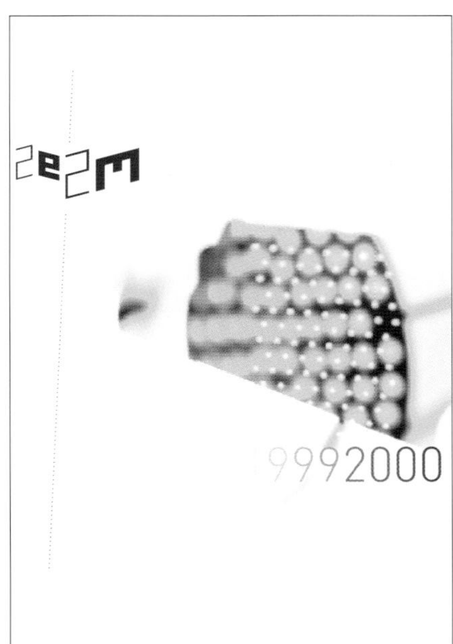

Présences Radio France

Paul Méfano	Micromégas – Scène 3 – Voyager
Aurel Stroë	Concerto pour violon
Octavio Lopez	Bunterblitz
Anne-Sophie Duprel	soprano
Amy Flammer	violon
Renato Rivolta	direction
Igor Ballereau	Cent sales mouches ★ ★
Yassen Vodenitcharov	Golden Drops III ★ ★
Frédéric Martin	Scherzo Erotico
Jean-Baptiste Devillers	O. Yu ★ ★
Pascale Criton	La ritournelle et le galop
Régis Campo	Dance
Thierry Blondeau	Ici et là II
Pierre Roullier	flûte
Didier Aschour	guitare
Jacqueline Méfano	piano
Sona Khochafian	violon
David Simpson	violoncelle

Le programme complet du Festival Présences et les horaires des concerts seront disponibles à partir de décembre 1999.

les **19 et 20 février** 2000
Paris
Radio-France
Festival Présences

entrée libre

renseignements
Ensemble 2e2m
01 47 06 17 76

coproduction
Ensemble 2e2m
Radio France

18–19

Kei Matsushita seeks the root of graphic design in Japan among the ukiyo-e works of the Edo era. Ukiyo-e use only outlines of plane figures, and it is in this unique world that Matsushita pursues his graphic activities and finds his ideological inspiration. He is a new breed of designer and rejects perspective-drawing techniques. He accomplishes three-dimensional images by using a two-dimensional technique. • • In the history of graphic design, the most difficult tasks are faced during a chaotic economic slump. In this environment, Matsushita has been delivering all sorts of fresh messages. He cleverly chooses ordinary houses, rooms, and furniture, which attract the interest of ordinary citizens, and at the same time he exercises his wisdom of realizing his two-dimensional expression. No other designer is so committed to using living space as the basis of his works, and no other work gives us such joy in appreciating the skillful renderings of that space. Here is the lesson of the importance of having a theme in creative work. In the cheerfully colored spaces created in Matsushita's work, one can see a four-dimensional pleasure beyond the scope of three dimensions. Matsushita's creative activities may represent the future direction of visual communication. • • Shigeo Fukuda • •

①

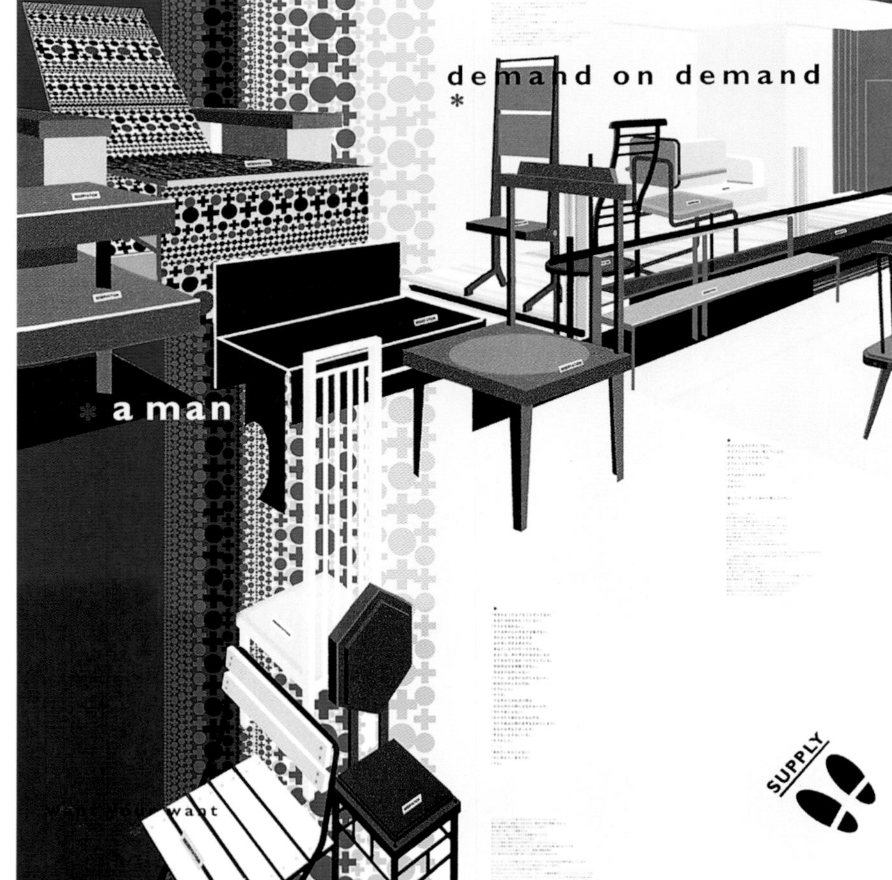

②

1–2 Promotional leaflets for paper-processing company PCM Takeo / PCM Takeo / Japan / 1997
3–4 Posters advertising the entertainment robot AIBO / Sony Creative Products Inc. / Japan / 2001
5–6 Posters for the *30x100* meeting and architecture exhibition / Japan Institute of Architects / Japan / 1997 / The *30x100* events focus around the work of 100 architects in their thirties.

Kei Matsushita

Tokyo

③

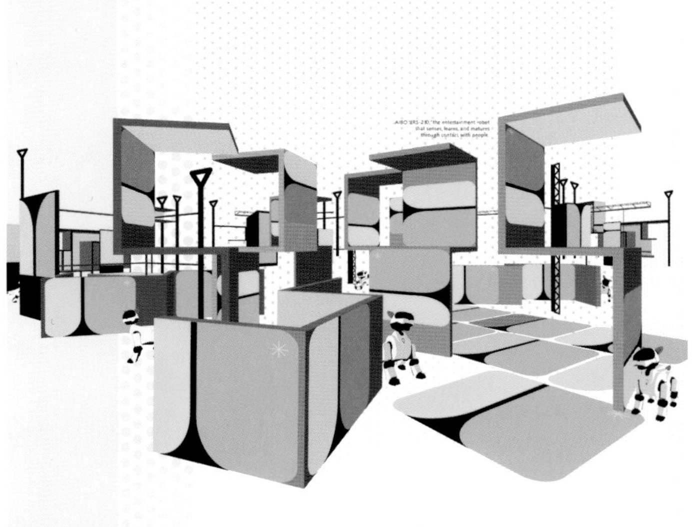

④

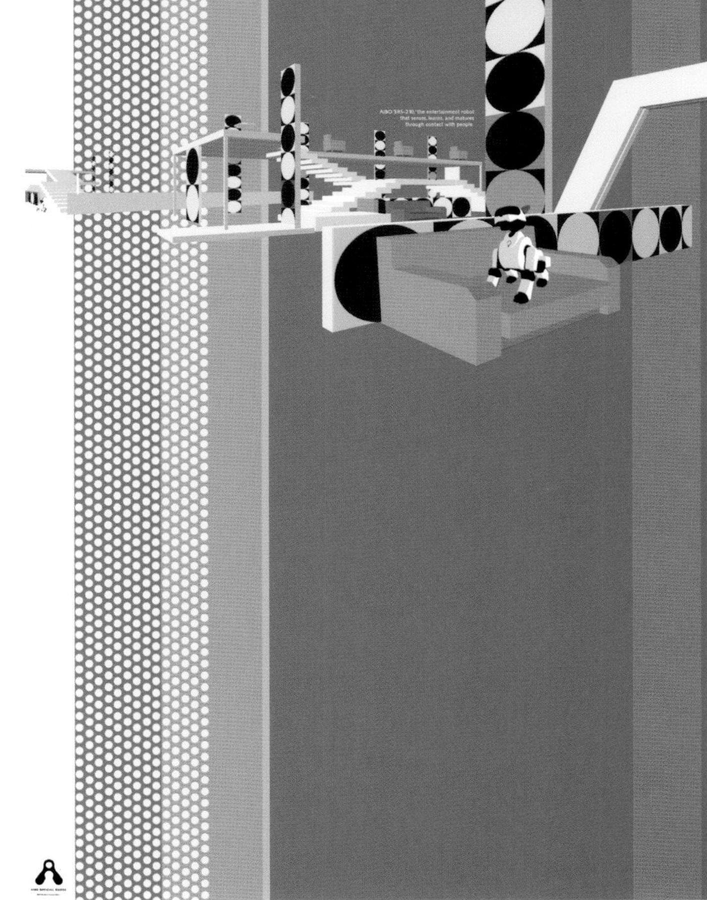

⑤

THIRTY by HUNDRED meeting

30×100
meeting

30代建築家100人会議

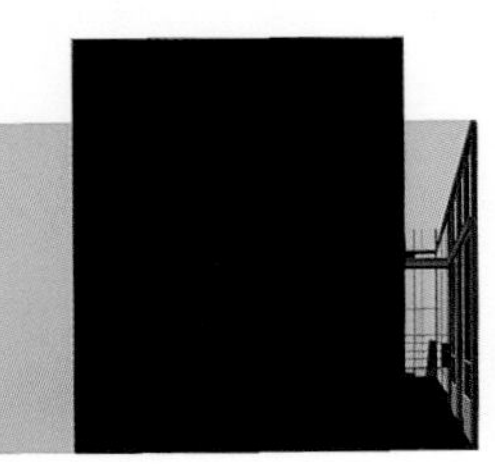

⑥

30代 建築家100人展

30×100architects展は30×100meetingでの言葉を空間に置き換えたものです。
30代の視座から切り取られた風景を100個の定点で観測する場です。
その各定点に意味を生じさせるのはわれわれにあると考えます。

1997年11月6日木→12日水

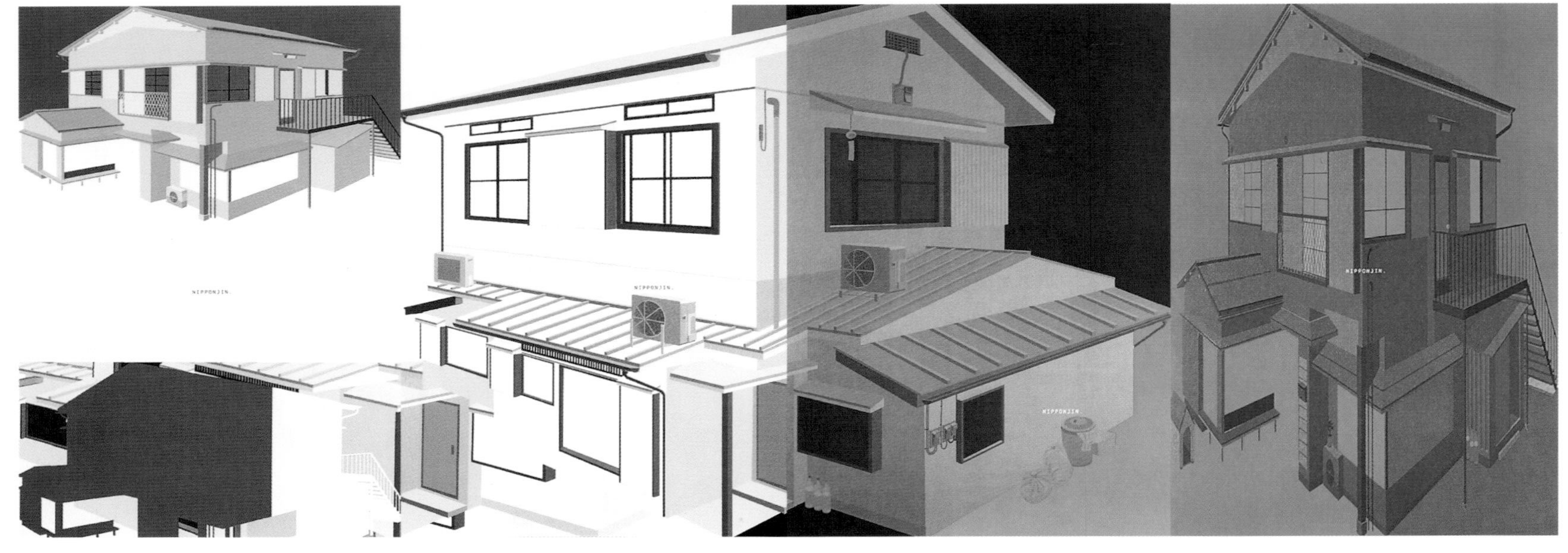

(7)(8)(9)(10)

(11)

(12)

7–10 Poster series "Nipponjin" for the exhibition *Close-up of Japan*, Museu de Arte de São Paulo / Mitsui Public Relations Committee / Japan / 1995

11 Calendar conceived for the Takeo Paper Show / Takeo Co. / Japan / 2001

12 Poster for *The Doraemon* exhibition, Suntory Museum, Osaka (© Fujiko-pro and Kei Matsushita) / Executive Committee for *The Doraemon* Exhibition / Japan / 2002 / Doraemon is an animation character that has been highly popular in Japan since the 1970s.

13–15 Posters for Kei Matsushita exhibition *DI+VISION* at the Ginza Matsuya Design Gallery, Tokyo / Japan Design Committee / Japan / 2002

Kei Matsushita

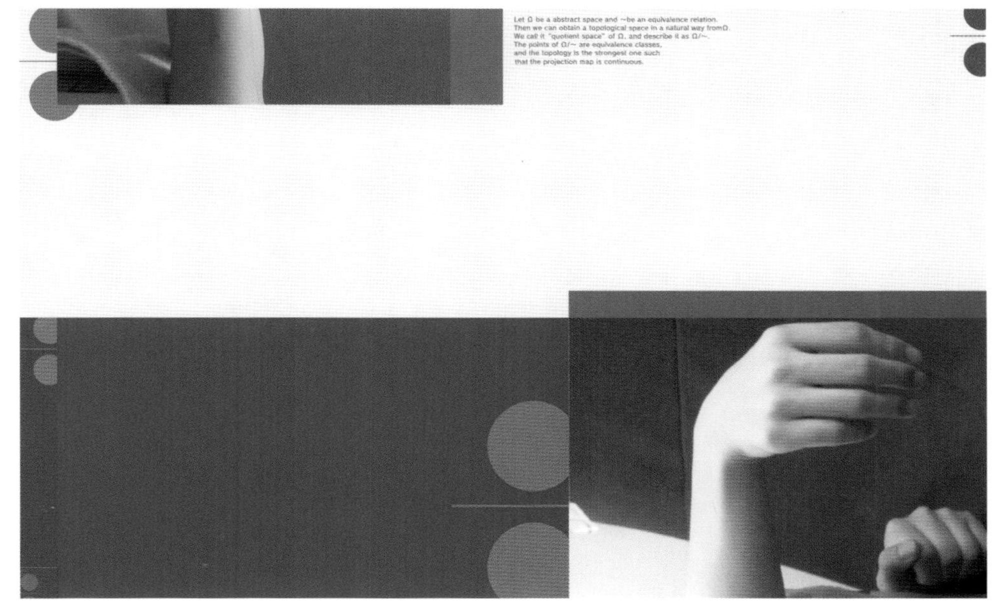
Let Ω be a abstract space and ~be an equivalence relation.
Then we can obtain a topological space in a natural way fromΩ.
We call it "quotient space" of Ω, and describe it as Ω/~.
The points of Ω/~ are equivalence classes,
and the topology is the strongest one such
that the projection map is continuous.

13 14 15

+ACCELERATION

BOOKS+HANDS+TASTE

As I leafed through books and magazines over the years, my eye often stopped at the work of Chaz Maviyane-Davies from Zimbabwe. Each time I was struck by his powerful, intriguing images. Early in 2001, I asked Maviyane-Davies to contribute to an exhibition and book celebrating the hundredth anniversary of the death of Henri de Toulouse-Lautrec, and he happily agreed. • •Although I regrettably have yet to meet him, we have developed a bond that deepened when in 2002 he started his "Portal of Truth" campaign. For one month, we and others around the world received a new poster each day via E-mail. Each day a new indictment against Robert Mugabe's ZANU-PF party in Zimbabwe, and a call to Maviyane-Davies's fellow countrymen to go out and vote. Each morning, that day's poster was printed out at our studio and discussed with all collaborators. My admiration for Maviyane-Davies's one-man guerrilla campaign grew with each new poster; day in, day out, he succeeded in engaging us with the elections in his country. In the end, it didn't have the political effect he wished it would, but not for lack of effort! • •Maviyane-Davies combines a great knowledge of craft with a deep insight in the power of words and images. And he knows how to use the Internet to reach a lot of people. With these skills he is one of the rare voices speaking out on the deplorable political situation in Zimbabwe. He demonstrates that graphic design can be fatally dangerous—because to be openly critical in Zimbabwe can get you killed. Against this background, Maviyane-Davies wisely moved to the United States; he now teaches at Massachusetts College of Art in Boston. • •In January 2003, I learned that I played a role in Maviyane-Davies's life long before our first acquaintance. He sent me a photo of his studio in Harare as it was back in 1983, and on the wall was a copy of my Leonce en Lena poster, from 1979. I was moved by the sight of my poster on a twenty-year-old photo from a faraway country. Now I feel even more like we have known each other for a long time, and I want more than ever to meet Maviyane-Davies in the flesh. • •Anthon Beeke • •

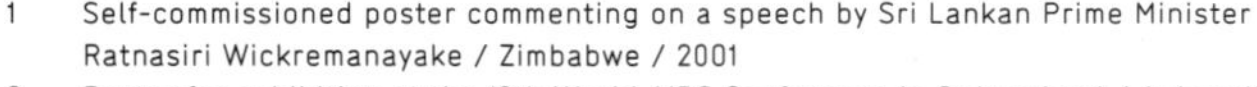

1 Self-commissioned poster commenting on a speech by Sri Lankan Prime Minister Ratnasiri Wickremanayake / Zimbabwe / 2001
2 Poster for exhibition at the 12th World AIDS Conference in Switzerland / Aujourd'hui pour demain / Switzerland / 1998
3–6 Self commissioned "Rights" poster series (4 of 12; photography Ian Murphy) / Zimbabwe / 1996 / The posters are based on the United Nations Articles on Human Rights as seen from an African perspective.

Chaz Maviyane-Davies

Boston/Harare, Zimbabwe

1

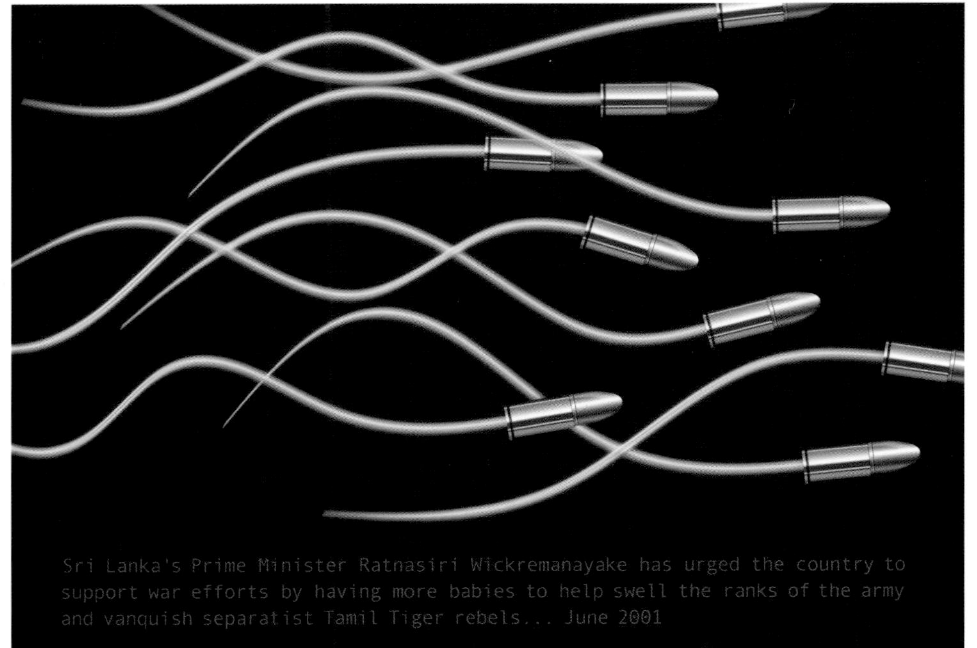

Sri Lanka's Prime Minister Ratnasiri Wickremanayake has urged the country to support war efforts by having more babies to help swell the ranks of the army and vanquish separatist Tamil Tiger rebels... June 2001

2

③

Article
Rights 4
No one should be subjected to slavery or servitude
QUANTEL

④

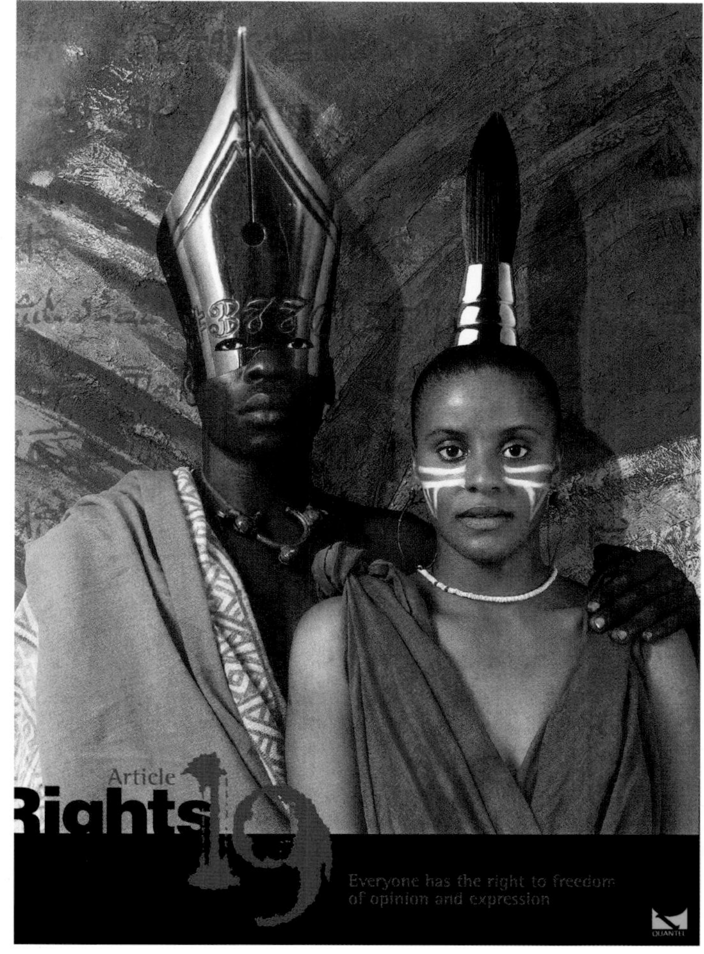
Article
Rights 19
Everyone has the right to freedom of opinion and expression
QUANTEL

⑤

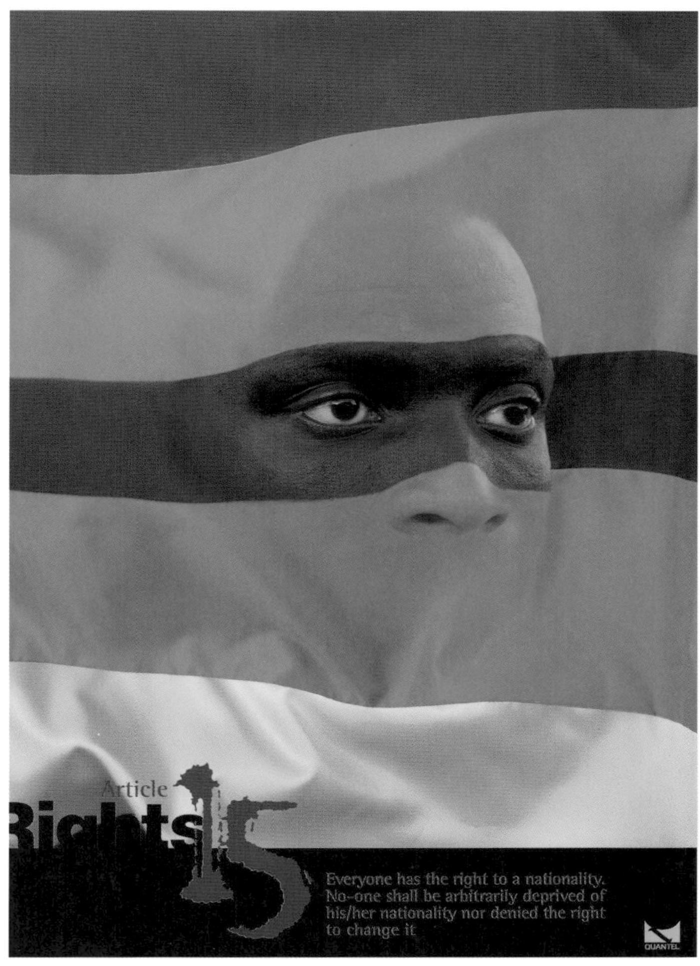
Article
Rights 15
Everyone has the right to a nationality. No-one shall be arbitrarily deprived of his/her nationality nor denied the right to change it
QUANTEL

⑥

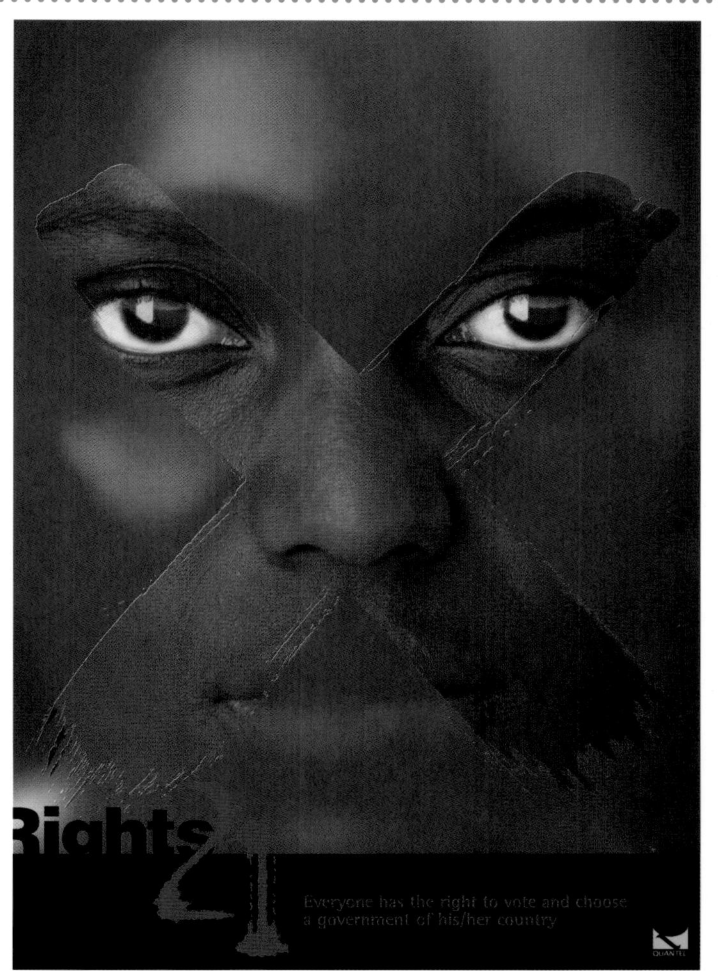
Rights 21
Everyone has the right to vote and choose a government of his/her country
QUANTEL

7

VOTE
®
the cure for impotency
Don't be intimidated
Use your vote
It's your secret weapon

8

"we have degrees in violence..."

take courage: VOTE

9

7–9 Self-commissioned posters from resistance campaigns "Graphic Commentary" and "Portal of Truth" / Zimbabwe / 2000 and 2002 / During the thirty days before the Zimbabwean parliamentary elections in 2000 and presidential elections in 2002, Maviyane-Davies created graphic commentaries on a daily basis. Due to lack of funding and fear of persecution, these posters were originally diffused through the Internet.

10 Cover, *Jacaranda* magazine / Nippon Club / Zimbabwe / 1997 / *Jacaranda* is the publication of a Japanese social group in Zimbabwe.

11 Poster homage for Toulouse-Lautrec's centennial (photography Steve Hammon) / Nouveau Salon des Cent / France / 2001

12 Illustration for university journal *Rhodes Review* special edition created for race summit in South Africa / Rhodes Review / Zimbabawe / 2001

Chaz Maviyane-Davies

10

じゃからんだ
SAHARA
AFRICA
ANGOLA
PLAIN
Kalahari
Desert
Cape Town
NATAL
MASCARENE

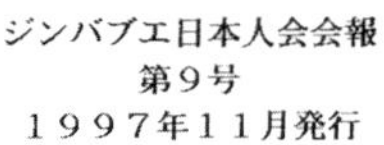

ジンバブエ日本人会会報
第９号
１９９７年１１月発行

11

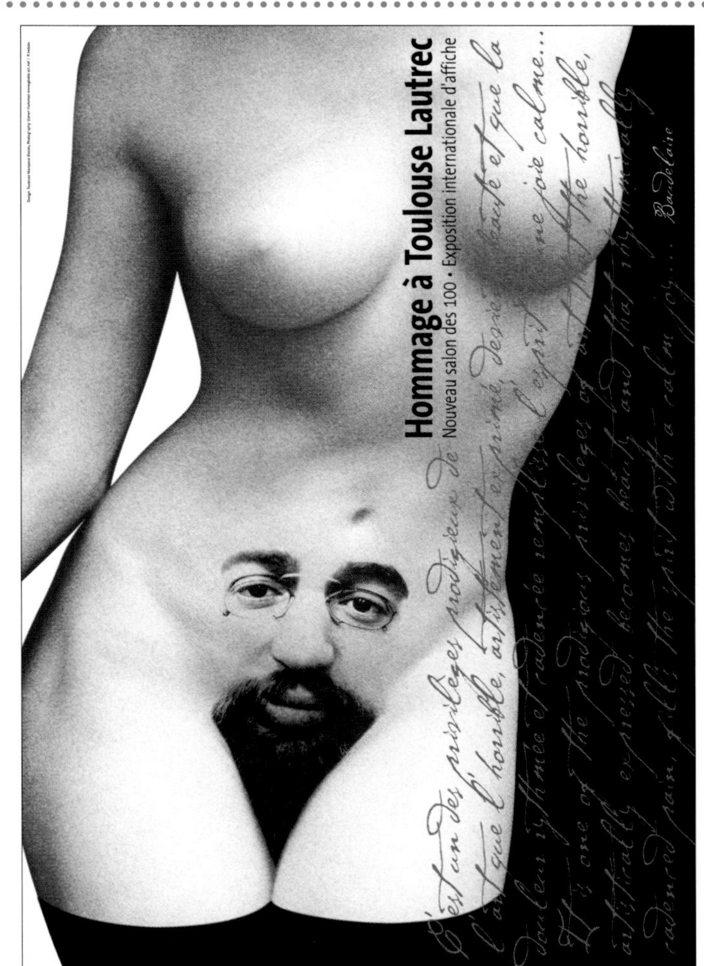

Hommage à Toulouse Lautrec
Nouveau salon des 100 · Exposition internationale d'affiche

12

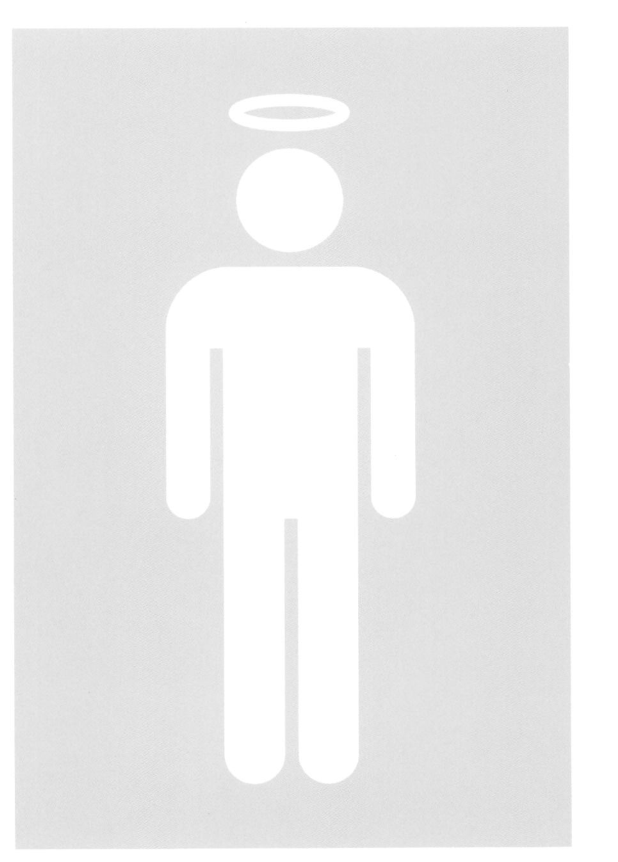

It is very rare that the highly-cultivated techniques used in artistic sketches can be applied to graphic design to successfully deliver messages. Instead, the established means of illustration, typography, and layout are considered the integral tools of the trade. The work of Ung Vai Meng makes for a wonderful exception. Although he clearly masters all of the more conventional graphic-design techniques, his beautiful, fresh posters live in a world quite far from the established concepts. The artistic strokes of his pen run through half-concrete and half-abstract shadow, and letters float up into two-dimensional space. I have seldom seen posters that can convey a feeling of such free joy. •• Moreover, it is impressive that these unique posters are done for such public organizations as the Macao Cultural Institute, the Macao Museum of Art, and the Cultural Foundation for Music. •• The stance Meng takes by confronting us with works of such hand-drawn beauty must be appreciated in a design field where the artificial technicians that are computers are commonly employed to guide creative endeavors. True originality remains an essential element within the culture of graphic design and Meng's works will surely leave an enduring mark in the global history of posters. •• Shigeo Fukuda ••

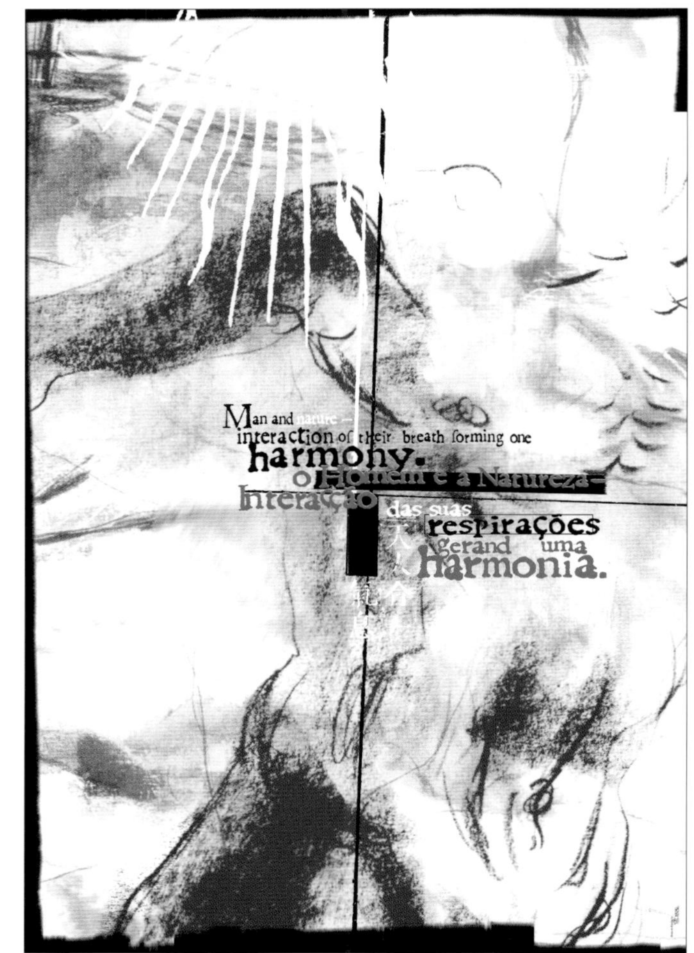

1

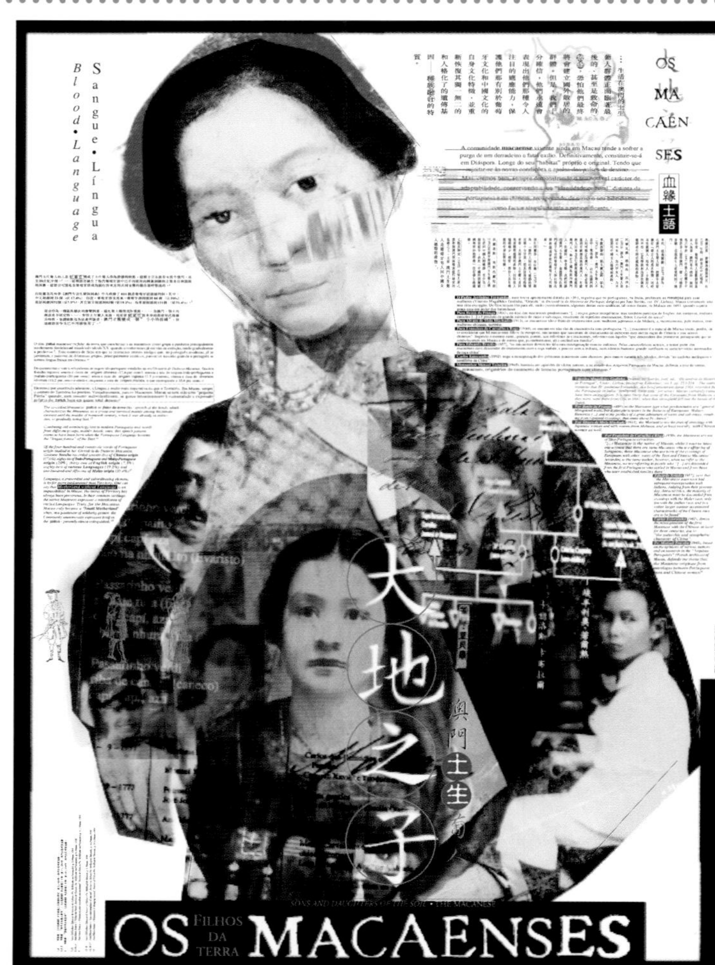

2

1 Self-commissioned Man and Nature poster / China / 1999
2 The Macanese-Blood/Language poster conceived for the 3rd International Macanese Congress / Leal Senado do Macau / China / 1999 / The poster was designed as a tribute to the unique culture in Macao and was given to the participants of the congress.
3 Poster for XII Macao International Music Festival / Macao Cultural Institute / China / 1998
4 Poster for performances by the Macao Chinese Orchestra / Macao Cultural Institute / China / 1998
5 Cultural Epicenter poster promoting the Museum of Macao / Museum of Macao / China / 1998
6 Self-commissioned Macau poster / China / 2002

Ung Vai Meng

Macao, China

3

24/10-8/11
1998
DE MÚSICA
de MACAU
Instituto Cultural de Macau
INTERNACIONAL
XIII MACAO
INTERNATIONAL
MUSIC FESTIVAL
XII
FEST IVAL
第十二屆澳門國際音樂節

4

DIGRESSÃO a PORTUGAL
一九九八年
澳門文化司署
INSTITUTO CULTURAL DE MACAU
葡萄牙巡迴演出
澳門中樂團
ORQUESTRA
CHINESA
DE
MACAU
六 七月
22 de JUNHO a
2 de JULHO de 1998

5

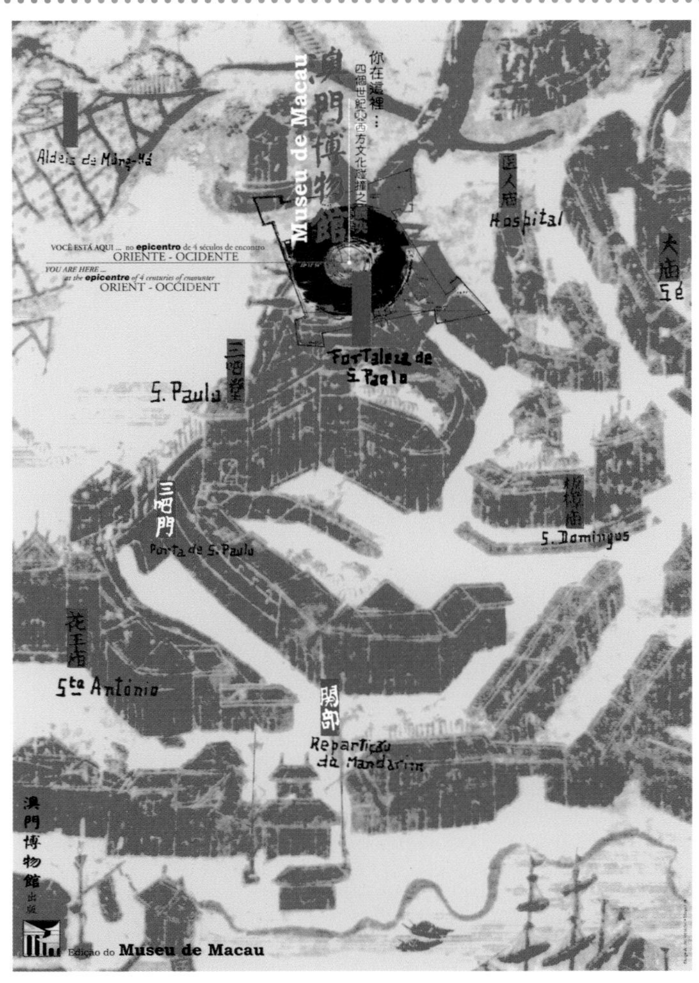

Museu de Macau
澳門博物館
Aldeia da Mong-Há
醫人廟
Hospital
大廟
Sé
VOCÊ ESTÁ AQUI ... no epicentro de 4 séculos de encontro
ORIENTE - OCIDENTE
YOU ARE HERE ... at the epicentre of 4 centuries of encounter
ORIENT - OCCIDENT
Fortaleza de S. Paulo
S. Paulo
三巴門
Porta de S. Paulo
S. Domingos
Sto António
關部
Repartição do Mandarim
澳門博物館
Edição do Museu de Macau

6

m a c a u

7

Ung Vai Meng

7 Self-commissioned Godfather poster / China / 1999
8, 10 Posters for the for 2008 Olympic Games in Beijing / Beijing Organizing Committee for the Games of the XXIX Olympiad / China / 2001
9 Poster for exhibition of works from Macao's fourth Design Biennial / Macao Museum of Art / China / 2001
11 Poster for *Tequila-Sangría* cinematic series featuring films from Mexico and Spain / Macao Museum of Art / China / 2001

8

新北京
綠色新奧运
GREEN BEIJING ◦ GREAT OLYMPICS

9

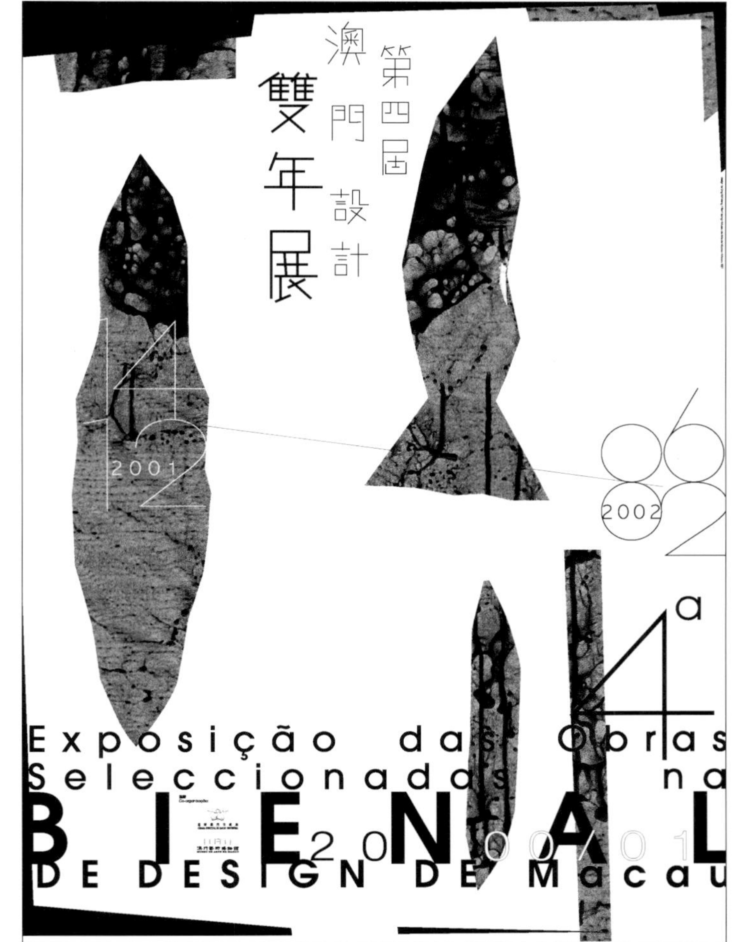
第四屆
澳門設計
雙年展
14
12
2001
06
08
2002
4a
Exposição das Obras
Seleccionadas na
BIENAL 2000/01
DE DESIGN DE Macau

10

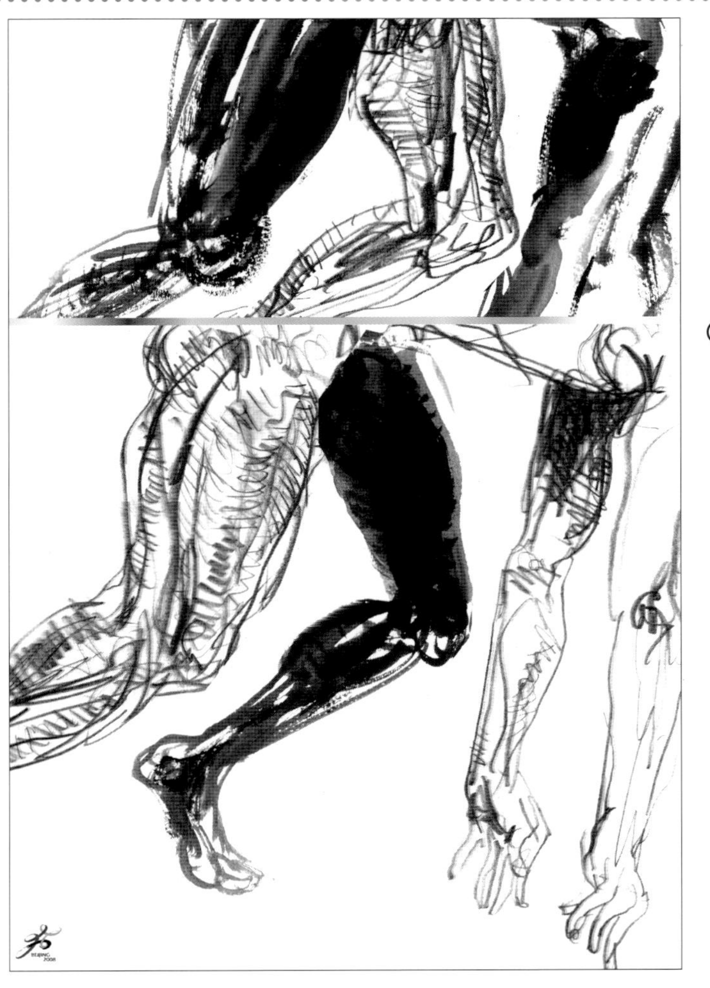

11

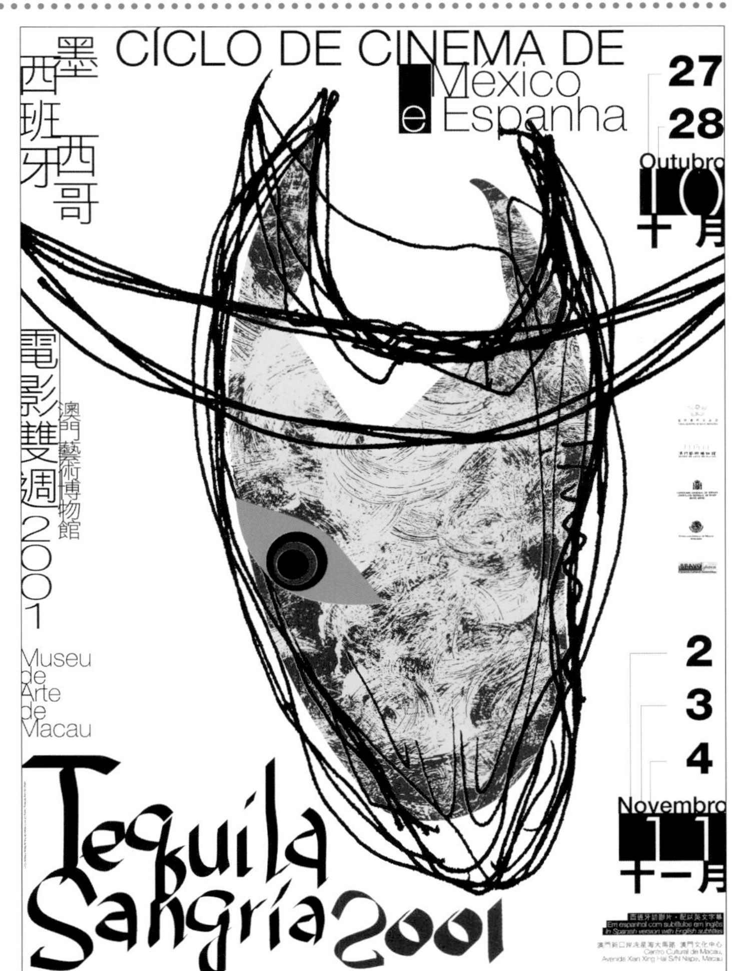
CÍCLO DE CINEMA DE
México
e Espanha
墨西哥
西班牙
27
28
Outubro
10
十月
電影雙週2001
澳門藝術博物館
Museu de Arte de Macau
Tequila
Sangría 2001
2
3
4
Novembro
11
十一月
Em espanhol com subtítulos em inglês
In Spanish version with English subtitles
Centro Cultural de Macau

Every year, the small French town of Échirolles, a ski resort along the Swiss border, organizes a poster festival. In 2002 French graphic designer and guest curator Alain Le Quernec invited a number of designers from Iran for the exhibition *Le graphisme en Iran*. The work by Saed Meshki in the exhibition was, in my view, representative of graphic work now emanating from Iran: romantic, poetic, craft-inspired. In Meshki's work one sees, apart from a few obvious Western influences, a personality formed outside the reach of the Dutch, the Polish, the Swiss, and the American designers that have defined the trade of graphic design worldwide. Meshki's subjects are painterly. Some look like they were made a thousand years ago and just excavated; others seem to be sampled from abandoned scraps, left next to the copying machine; and sometimes they look like watercolors.• • Apart from being poetic, Meshki's work is also of its time. Everything is made on the computer from scanned elements. Despite the obvious limitations of clients and technology, this is vital work that demands to be seen far beyond the borders of Iran.• • Meshki is a kind man and an honest designer, just like his colleagues in the exhibition, who all demonstrated exceptional qualities and who, in France, were on a mission to another world. They were glad to be in contact with associates from quite different cultures and in return offered their gift of a graceful spirituality. I hope to be able to visit them in their own country soon.• • Anthon Beeke• •

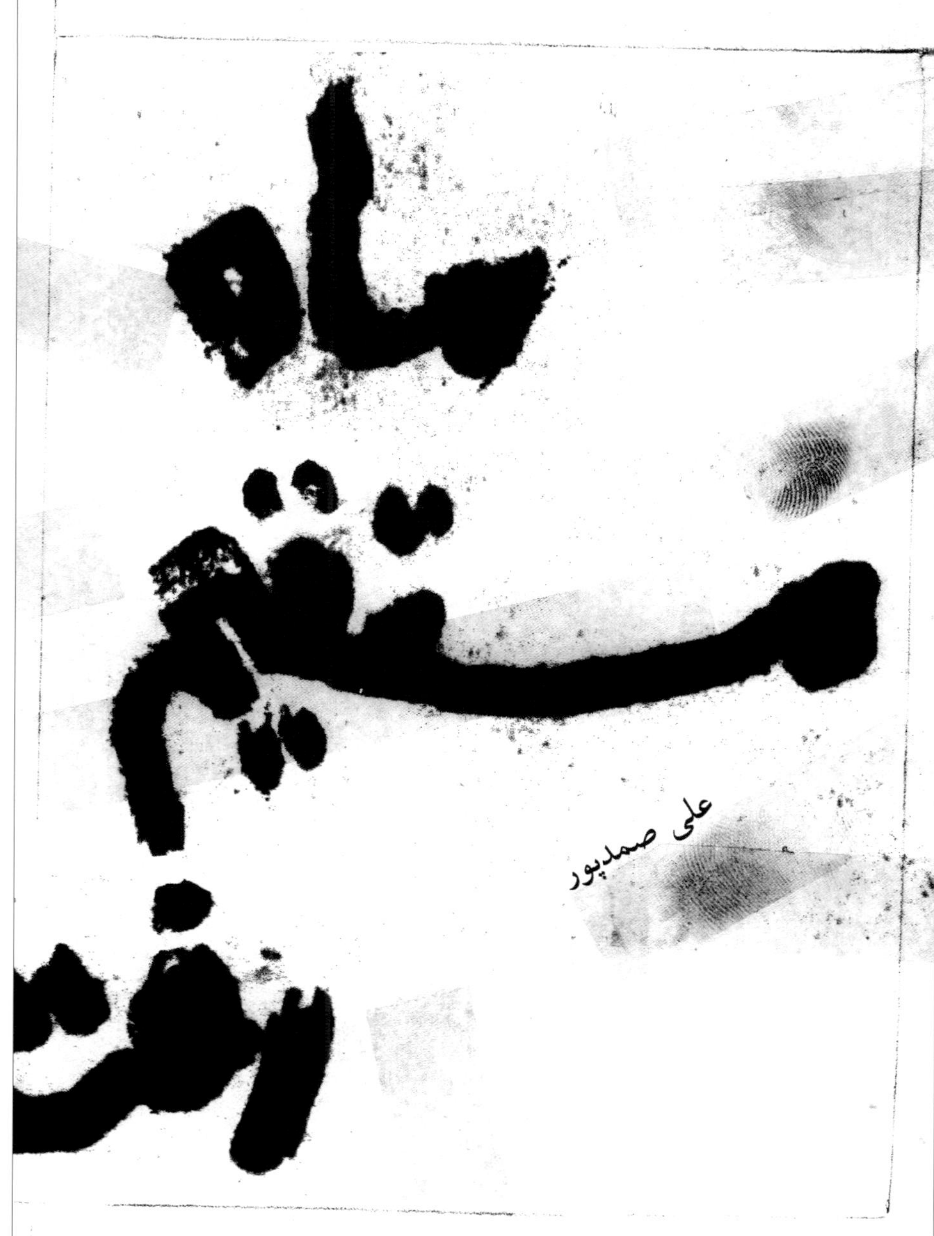

1 Book cover, *Lost Paradises*, poems by Jorge Luis Borges / Mahriz Publications / Iran / 2002
2 Book cover, *Mah mostaghim raft* (The Moon Went Directly), by Ali Samadpour / Mahriz Publications / Iran / 2002
3 Book cover, *Vahemehaye bi nam o neshan* (Imaginations Without Any Name and Trace), by G. H. Saedi / Mahriz Publications / Iran / 2001
4 Book cover, *Bi Eshgh, Ma Sang, Ma hich* (Without Love, We Are Stone, We Are Anything), by Bahman Rafei / Goftman Publications / Iran / 2001
5 Book cover, *Yek Manzoomeye Diryab dar Barf o Barab yaft shod* (A Rare Poem Was Found in the Rain and Snow), by A. R. Ahmadi / Mahriz Publications / Iran / 2002
6 Book cover, *Agar in Mahian rangi naboodand* (If These Fishes Weren't Colored), by Bahman Rafei / Goftman Publications / Iran / 2002

Saed Meshki

Tehran

3

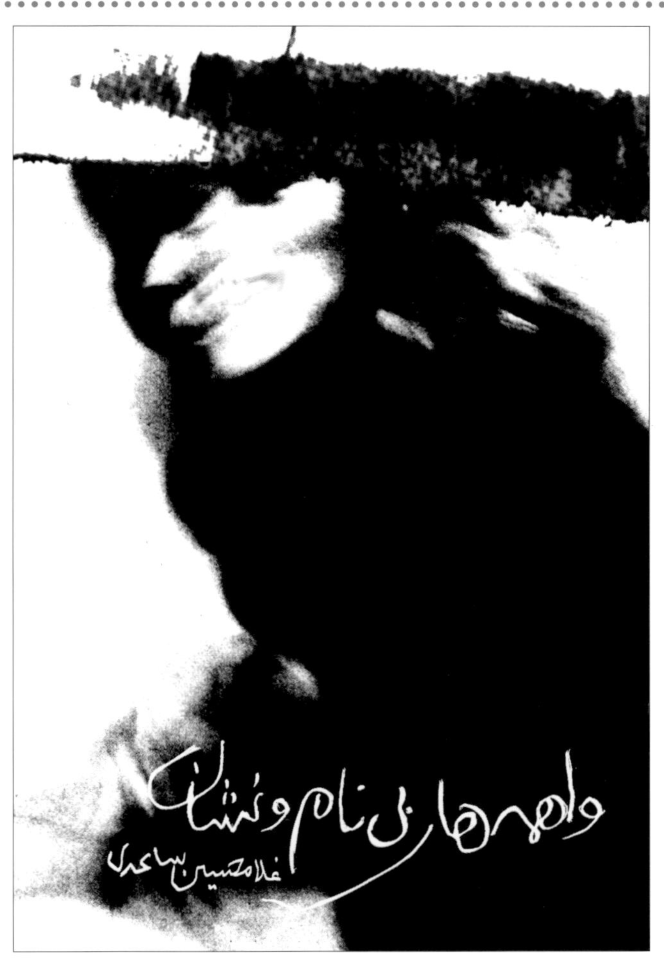
واهمه های بی نام و نشان
غلامحسین ساعدی

4

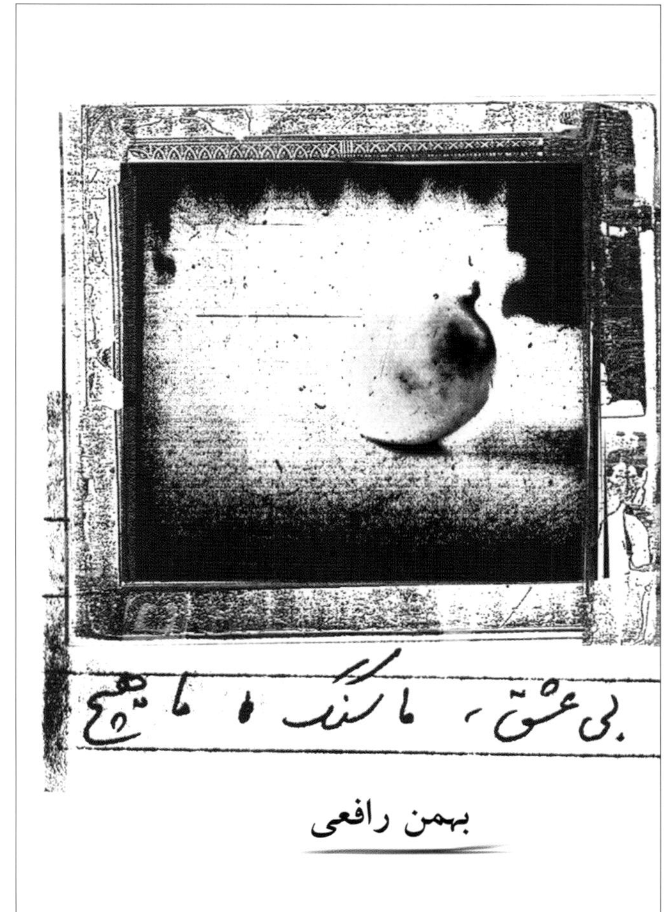
بی عشق، ما سنگ، ما هیچ
بهمن رافعی

5

احمدرضا احمدی
۱۳۸۱

6

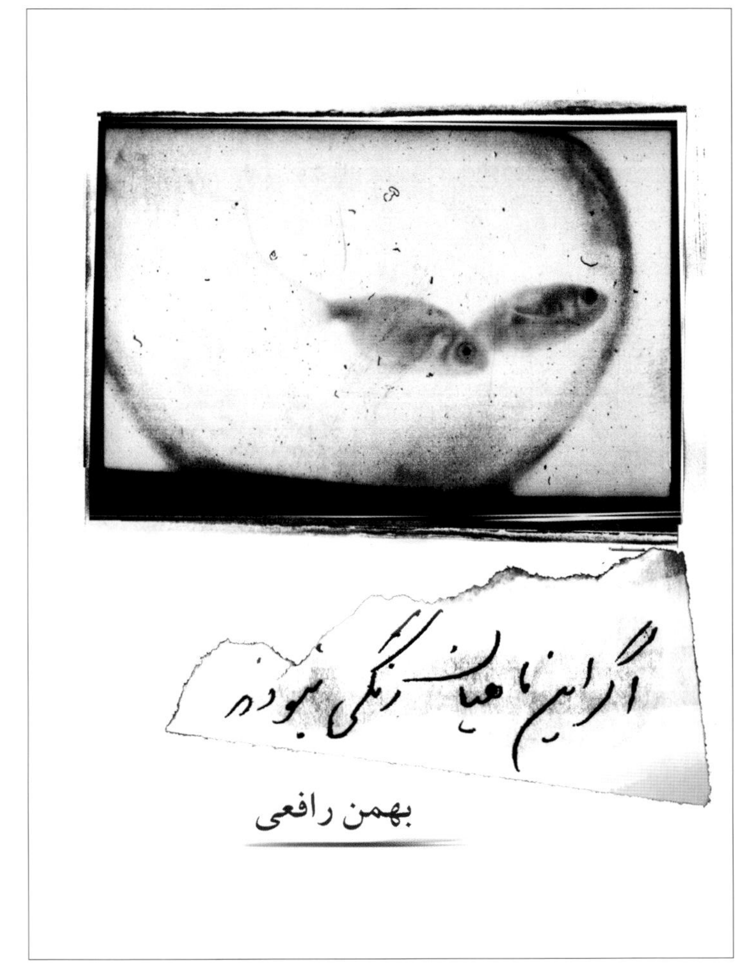
اگر این ماهیان رنگی نبودند
بهمن رافعی

7

8

9

10

11

7 Logo / Apple and Mirror Film Studio / Iran / 1999
8 Logo / Theatre Festival of Iranzamin / Iran / 2000
9 Logo / Roozgar Publishing / Iran / 1999
10 Logo / Avay-e-Doost Cultural Center / Iran / 2001
11 Logo / Sunlight magazine / Iran / 1999
12 Poster for movie *LEYLI bahaneye nagozir* / Farabi Cinema Foundation / Iran / 2001
13 Poster for 3rd International Theatre Festival of Iranzamin / Theatre Festival of Iranzamin / Iran / 2001
14 Poster for Abadan Film Festival / Iranian Ministry of Culture / Iran / 1999
15 Poster for 3rd Kish Documentary Film Festival / Kish Documentary Film Festival / Iran / 2002

Saed Meshki

12 

لیلی بهانه ناگزیر

13 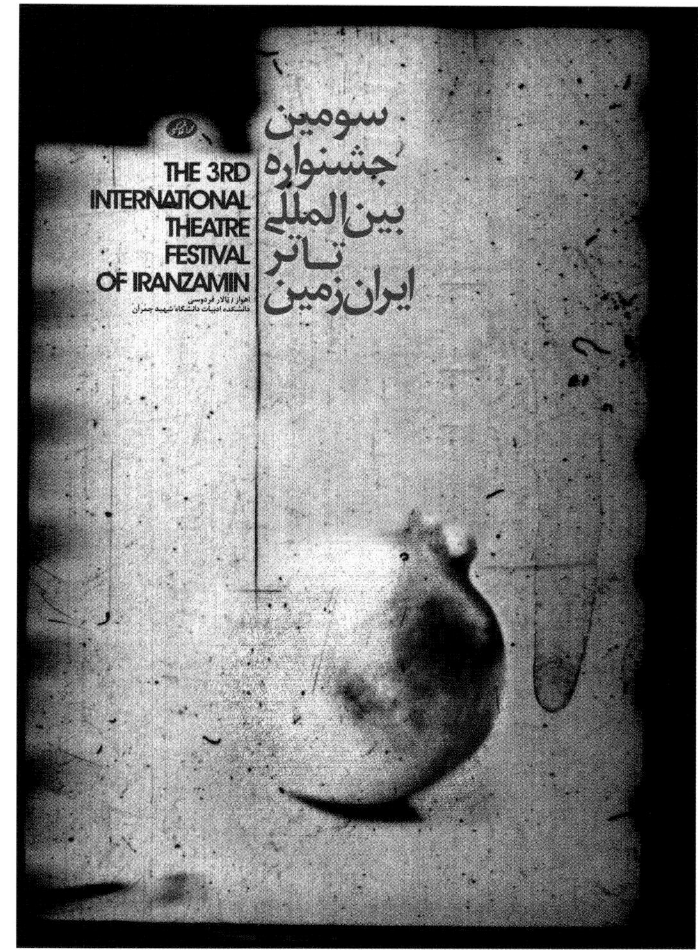

سومین
جشنواره
بین المللی
تئاتر
ایران زمین
THE 3RD
INTERNATIONAL
THEATRE
FESTIVAL
OF IRANZAMIN
اهواز / تالار فردوسی
دانشکده ادبیات دانشگاه شهید چمران

14 

سومین
جشنواره
فیلم آبادان
سینمای اجتماعی ایران و جهان
۱۲ تا ۱۶ اسفند ۱۳۸۰

15 

سومین جشنواره سینمای مستند کیش
3RD KISH DOCUMENTARY FILM FESTIVAL
10-13 MARCH 2002 , KISH ISLAND
۱۹ تا ۲۲ اسفند ۱۳۸۰، جزیره کیش

No one is interrogating modern graphic design quite like Maureen Mooren and Daniel van der Velden. In fact they are torturing it. This is nothing for them to feel queasy about, since they see graphic design as comatose anyway. By trampling on it, poking fun at it, tearing it apart, and reassembling it in new and formidably grotesque mutations, Mooren and van der Velden shoot a million volts through the veins of its twitching body. This crazy experiment will, they hope, help catapult their visual communication beyond the generic, the hackneyed, and the merely representative toward what they call a "new and immediate personal communicative relevance."••Person-to-person messaging is the ideal they apply in their design. Mooren and van der Velden are greatly concerned with the "personal space in between design and its user" at a time when, with the help of the Internet, "the status of information, and therewith, the information object, has degraded to something close to trash." They confront the user of their design with a multitude of possibilities for interaction (see *Archis* magazine). The invitation to interact is skewed by the appropriated design convention that is employed as the information carrier. Sound confusing? It is. I'll try to simplify.••First of all, it is important to point out that Mooren and van der Velden, conceptually driven designer/writers that they are, have managed to liberate themselves from the inhibitions of good taste. It's like they believe that design conventions, together with their respective information objects (for example, signage, newspapers, posters, and books), are now so familiar as information carriers that they have become impotent, or at least they don't engage us in the vital way Mooren and van der Velden would like. In response they have chosen to mess with this accepted duality by altering the context within which design conventions and their concomitant information objects are usually found. For instance, a passport masquerades as a catalogue, an invented crossword puzzle carries the events program of an art gallery, a fax sheet operates as a poster, and an architecture magazine aspires to the form of a document file bursting with loose sheets of information. Transposing these formats into unfamiliar territory produces a clash that throws their associated conventions into relief. This makes the user question them and in so doing question the process of communication. The experience of the familiar in these unexpected realms is a form of poetry, one that Mooren and van der Velden call "fictional functionalism."••Nick Bell••

1

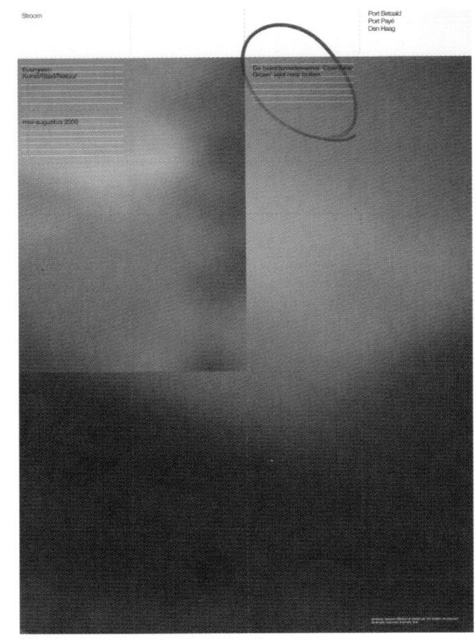

2

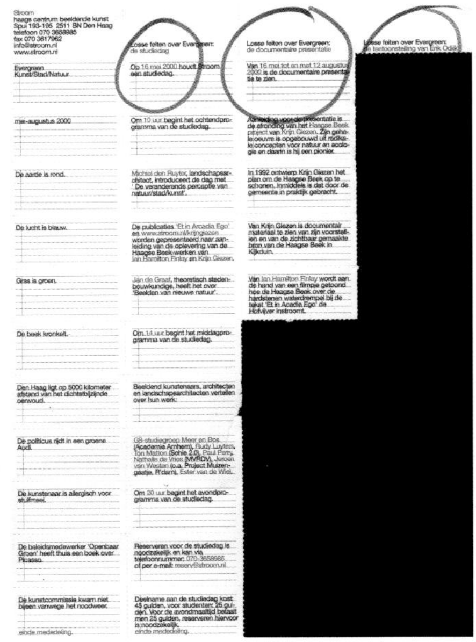

3

Mooren + van der Velden

1 Flyer for Rotterdam Design Prize 2001 events and exhibition at the Museum Boijmans Van Beuningen / Rotterdam Design Prize / Netherlands / 2001

2-3 Front and back of invitation for *Evergreen* conference and exhibition on public space and art in relation to nature / Evergreen / Netherlands / 2000 / The invitation is conceived as a perforated A4 card made up of smaller cards on which all information pertaining to the event is written.

4-6 Invitations for different events at the Maastricht-based art space Marres / Marres / Netherlands / 2002 / An A3 sheet of paper is folded down in different ways to create the various invitations. Functional information is provided in the crossword puzzle.

7-9 Informational publication accompanying Droog Design project for a small hotel presented at the Salone del Mobile, Milan / Droog Design / Italy

Amsterdam

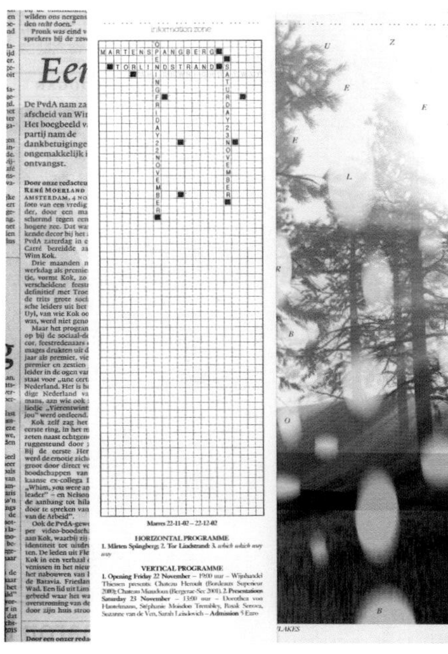

4
5
6

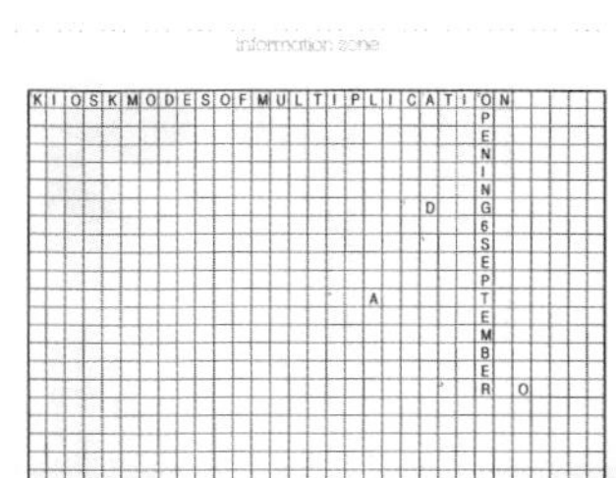

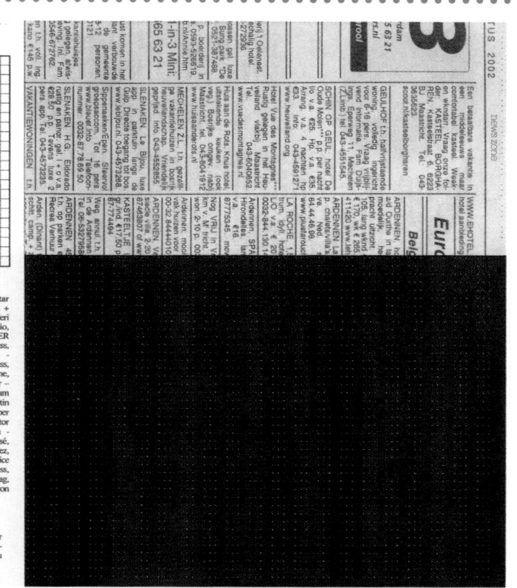

Marres 06-09-02–13-10-02

HORIZONTAL PROGRAMME:
1. KIOSK (VII): Modes of Multiplication: 100 Magazine, Zurich - Artimo, Amsterdam - b_books, Berlin - bdv / art-view, Paris - Because Tomorrow Comes, Cologne - Black Dog Publishing Limited, London - Blatt, blad - Boileau & Narcejac, Frankfurt/Main - Book Works, London - Bottrop Boy - EN/OF, Kleve - BQ, Cologne - The Breeder, Athens - Bruno Dorn Verlag, Berlin - Galerie Daniel Buchholz, Cologne - Butt, Amsterdam - Catalogue, Amsterdam - CCAB, Belgrade - Centre d'èdition contemporaine, Geneva - cneai, Paris - Galerie Ascan Crone, Hamburg - Der Wandel, Berlin - Finger, Frankfurt/Main - Die Gabe, Berlin - Gagarin, Waasmunster - Galerie für Landschaftskunst, Hamburg - Herzrasen, Karlsruhe - infection manifesto, Düsseldorf - Irrégulomadaire, Paris - Pork Salad Press, Copenhagen - JRP Editions, Geneva - Les presses du réel, Dijon - Lukas & Sternberg, Inc., Berlin - Memory/Cage Editions, Zurich - Metronome, London - Montage, Vienna - Morning Star Publications, Edinburgh - naiv hören + sehen, Stuttgart - Neid, Berlin - Galleri Nicolai Wallner, Copenhagen - Ohio, Cologne - OneStarPress, Paris - oVER Magazine, Bangkok - Permanent Press, Hamburg - Point d'Ironie, Paris - Pocketbooks, Edinburgh - Possible Press, Berlin - Purple, Paris - Re_Magazine, Amsterdam - Regina, Berlin - Revolver – Archiv für aktuelle Kunst, Frankfurt am Main - Salon-Verlag, Cologne - Martin Schmitz Verlag, Berlin - Silke Schreiber Verlag, Munich - Site, Düsseldorf - Spector cut+paste, Leipzig - Starship, Berlin - Super-Umbau, Hamburg - supposé, Cologne - tonschacht, Cologne - Valdez, Bogotá - Verbrecher Verlag, Berlin - Vice Versa Verlag, Berlin - Whatness, Frankfurt/Main - Wiens Laden und Verlag, Berlin - Work Web Art, Cologne - Yvon Lambert, Paris

VERTICAL PROGRAMME:
25. Opening Vrijdag 6 september - 16:00–17:00 lezing door Manuel Räder over de wisselwerking tussen ontwerp en editing - 17:00–18:00 lezing door Christoph Keller over vormen van distributie - 18:00–20:00 Corbières (Chateau Moulin) & Jupiler.

7
8
9

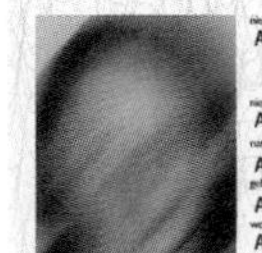

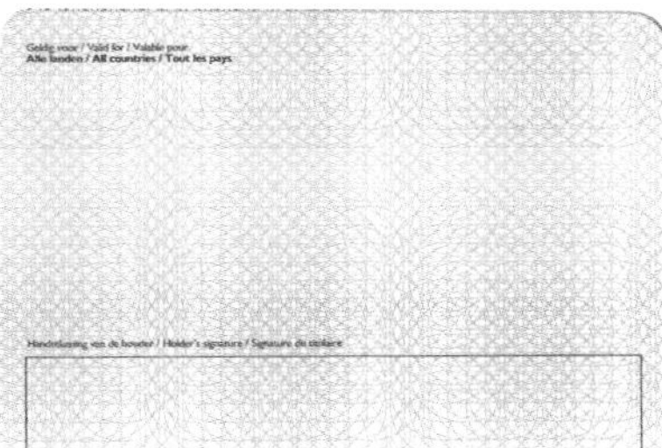

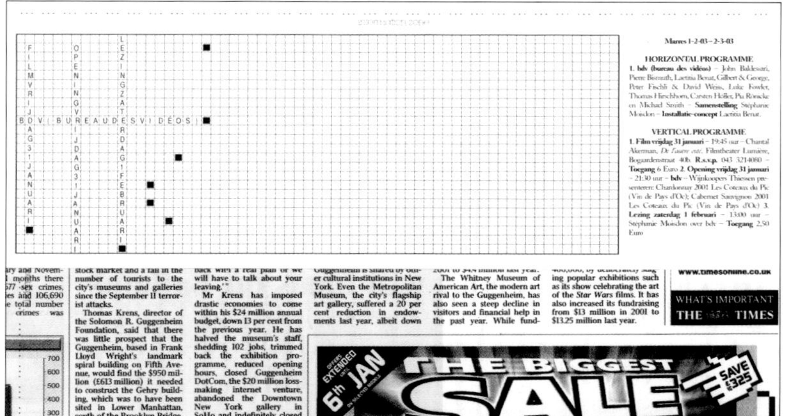

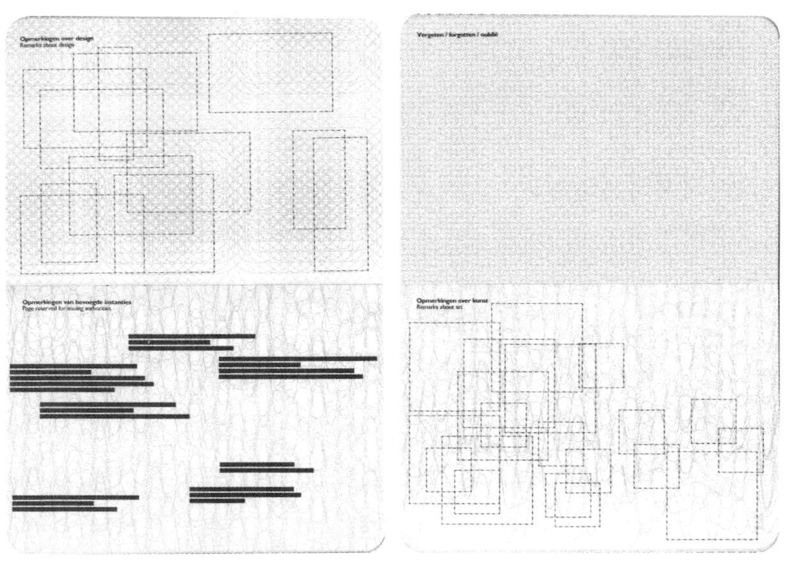

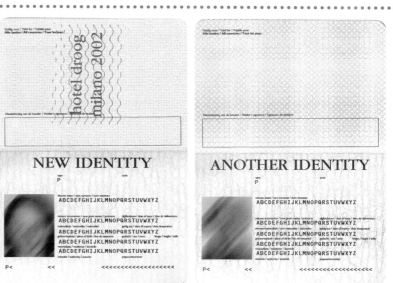

'OSCILLATIONS' -1

MANON DE BOER * ANNEMIEK DE HAAN * CHLOÉ MARTIN * MAUREEN MOOREN * DANIEL VAN DER VELDEN

everybody, forever

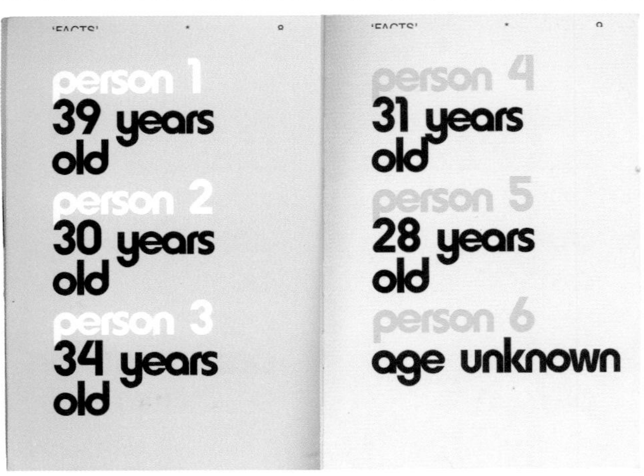

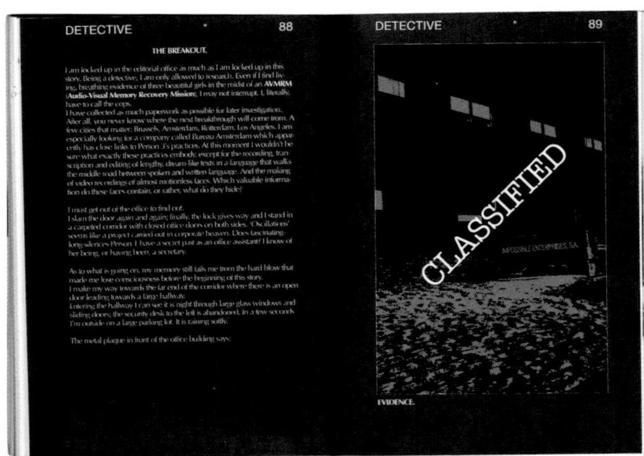
DETECTIVE 88

THE BREAKOUT

DETECTIVE 89

EVIDENCE

1, 2, 3

Numbers instead of months

From the familiar to the abstract

Sharon Lockhart, Untitled, 2000

1

Tentoonstelling Exposition 12/1–16/2

DOUG AITKEN

SHARON LOCKHART

Galerie Jan Mot

4, 5

12, 13

Passers-by think gallery already closed down

A conversation with Dora García

27 September 2002, opening of the new gallery's space, Antoine Dansaert Street 190 (photo: M. Coppers)

12

DORA GARCÍA

THE LOCKED ROOM

Galerie Jan Mot

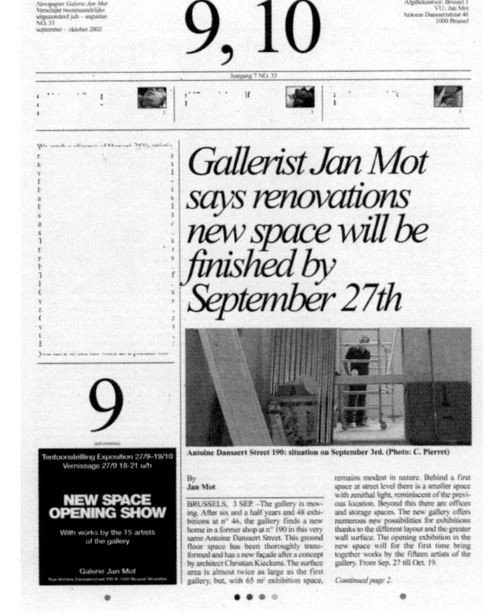
9, 10

Gallerist Jan Mot says renovations new space will be finished by September 27th

9

NEW SPACE OPENING SHOW

With works by the 15 artists of the gallery

Galerie Jan Mot

Antoine Dansaert Street 190: situation on September 3rd. (Photo: C. Pierret)

4 Newspaper Galerie Jan Mot — Essay — Nov, Dec

5 Newspaper Galerie Jan Mot — What to do with art? — Nov, Dec

Quatre questions à Herman Daled

BRUSSELS, SEP. 13, Opening Rineke Dijkstra, Galerie Jan Mot and restaurant Kasbah (video still: Manon de Boer)

10–12 Cover and spreads, *Oscillations*, by Manon de Boer, Annemiek de Haan, Chloé Martin, Maureen Mooren, and Daniel van der Velden / La Lettre Volée / Belgium / The book collects conversations between two friends. The starting point for the design and editorial approach, however, is not the content of the conversations, but the complex interplay between the book's five collaborators.

13–17 Covers and spread of newsletters for the Jan Mott Galerie, Brussels / Jan Mott Galerie / Belgium / 2001–present / The newsletter takes the form of a downsized newspaper.

18–20 Covers of architectural magazine *Archis*, issues 5, 2001, and 4, 5, 2002 / Archis / Netherlands / 2001–2002

21–23 Spreads from *Archis* magazine, issue 4 / Archis / Netherlands / 2002 / The publication is designed as a tear-out magazine focusing on the layering of interactive reading elements.

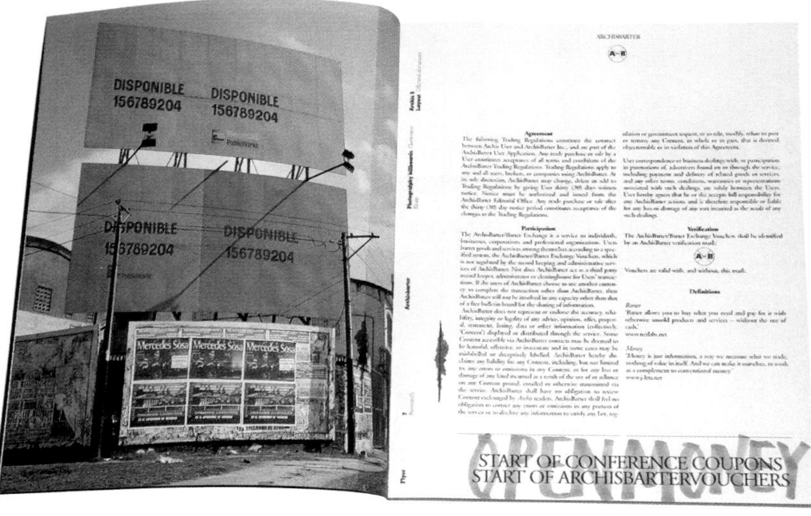

18
19
20

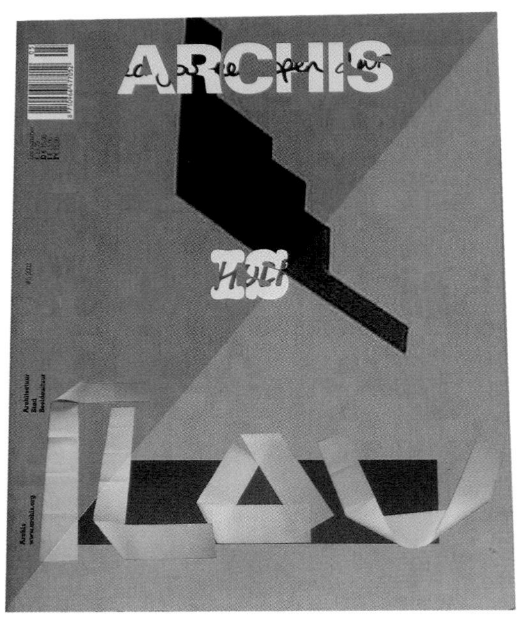

21
22
23

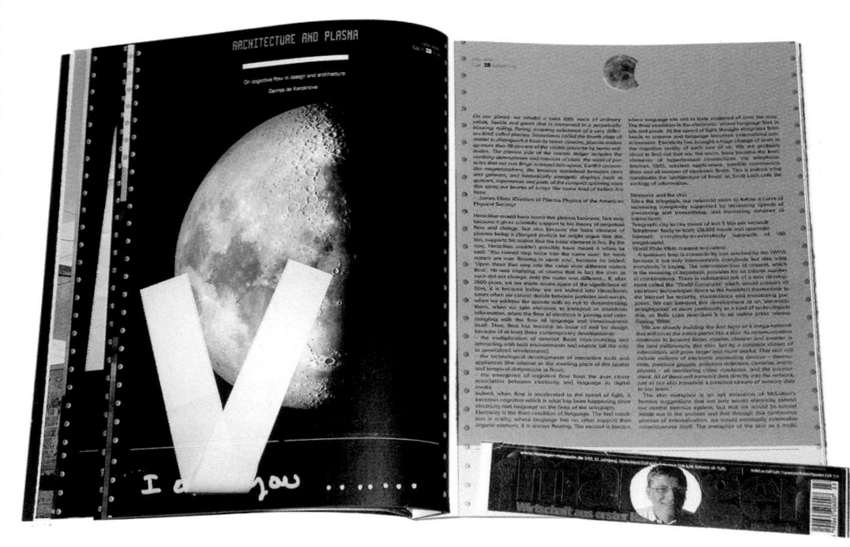

Good graphic design polarizes, and so does good theater. When Barbara Mundel became the new director of the Luzerner Theater, Lucerne began to boil. Her new concept surprised both actors and the subscription audience and put pressure on the town administration. She is a person who demands complexity and exhibits it. She is direct and without frills, and in this spirit commissioned the agency Velvet, and its principal Peter Moser, to develop a new corporate identity and campaign for the theater. Peter Moser's concept team sat down and got going. • •For the seasonal theme "homely, secretive, eerie," Velvet took the Lucerne telephone book, wrote down names of professions and associations from the area, visited them, took photos, and completed the posters. For the cycle "happy, the man of the future," Velvet took the actors, photographed them unclothed and without makeup, and produced another series of engaging posters. For the "money, power, nature" season, Velvet went onto the street and photographed people in the pose of Rodin's Thinker. • •Peter Moser is bold and provocative. Peter Moser tapes over his own posters (see *Tatort* project). Or, Peter Moser makes a poster, and therein the model wears a knit hat, and at the speed of light this absurdity becomes a cult object in Lucerne, and swiftly the clever people from Velvet bring multiple reproductions of the hat into circulation. Or, Peter Moser satirizes advertising clichés for a communications museum exhibition and turns a female butcher into a Claudia Schiffer double; rarely was a poster in Switzerland so widely discussed in the media. • •Peter Moser is somebody who balances the sharp directness of advertising with a tenderhearted and soulful graphic design and combines what sensibly should not be separated anyhow. He profits from his studio's internal distribution of work and the separation of profit and nonprofit segments. Thus large clients—by hiring Velvet—might well be supporting those who mock them, for indirectly they are supporting subculture, they are supporting theater. Velvet is a tremendously smart way to effect persistent influence. • •Werner Jeker • •

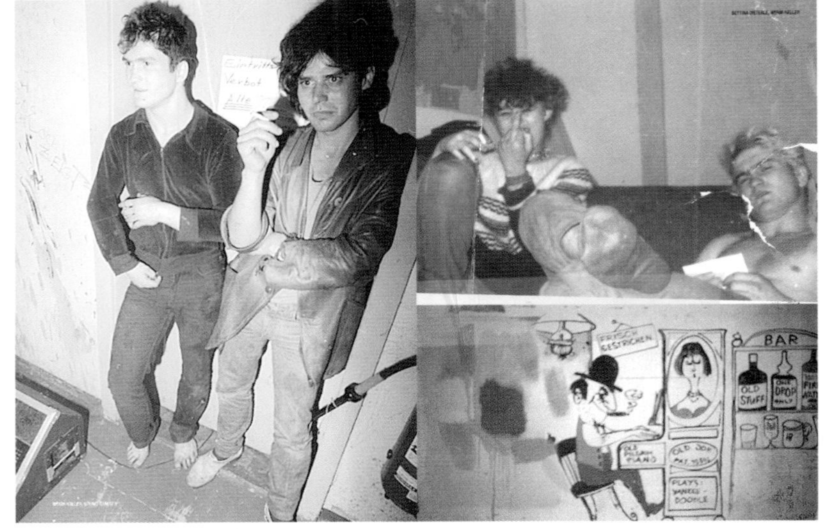

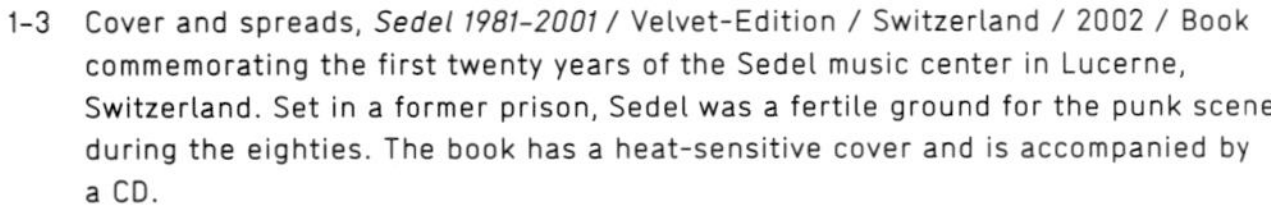

1–3 Cover and spreads, *Sedel 1981–2001* / Velvet-Edition / Switzerland / 2002 / Book commemorating the first twenty years of the Sedel music center in Lucerne, Switzerland. Set in a former prison, Sedel was a fertile ground for the punk scene during the eighties. The book has a heat-sensitive cover and is accompanied by a CD.

4 Poster for art event "Eros/" at the Plattform für Zeitgenössische Kunst (PZK), Lucerne / PZK / Switzerland / 2001

5 Poster for exhibition *Happy–Das Versprechen der Werbung* (Happy–The Promise of Advertising), Bern / Museum für Kommunikation / Switzerland / 2001

6 Poster for exhibition *Frankensteins Kinder–Film und Medizin* (Frankenstein's Children–Film and Medicine) / Museum für Gestaltung Zürich / Switzerland / 1997

7 Poster for exhibition *Ich & Du–Kommunikation und neue Medien* (Me & You–Communication and New Media) / Museum für Gestaltung Zürich / Switzerland / 1996

Peter Moser

Lucerne, Switzerland

4

PZK plattform für zeitgenössische kunst
27. januar – 11. februar 2001
mi – fr 15-19 uhr sa 11-17 uhr
eros/

5

Musée de la communication
Museum für Kommunikation
HAPPY
Das Versprechen der Werbung
La promesse de la publicité
07.09.01–28.07.02
MfK
www.mfk.ch

6

Museum für Gestaltung Zürich
8. März – 20. April 1997
Frankensteins Kinder
– Film und Medizin

7

MUSEUM FÜR GESTALTUNG ZÜRICH
6. MÄRZ · 28. APRIL 1996
ICH & DU
KOMMUNIKATION UND NEUE MEDIEN

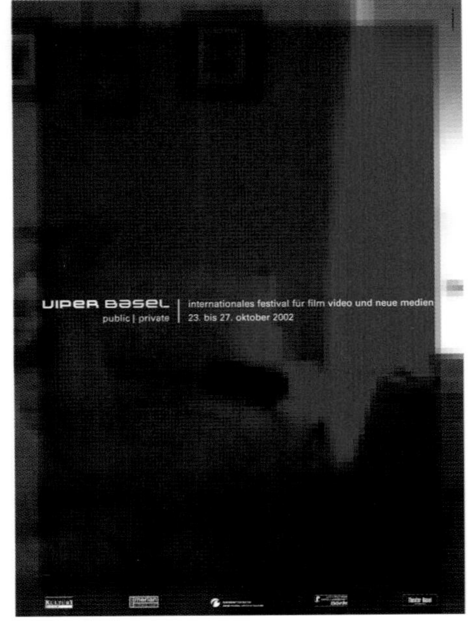

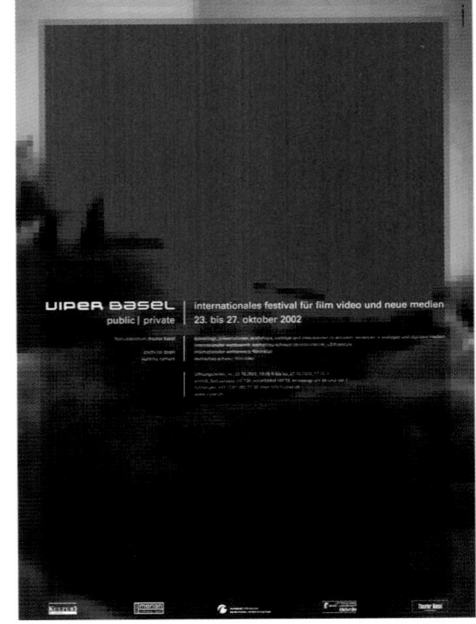

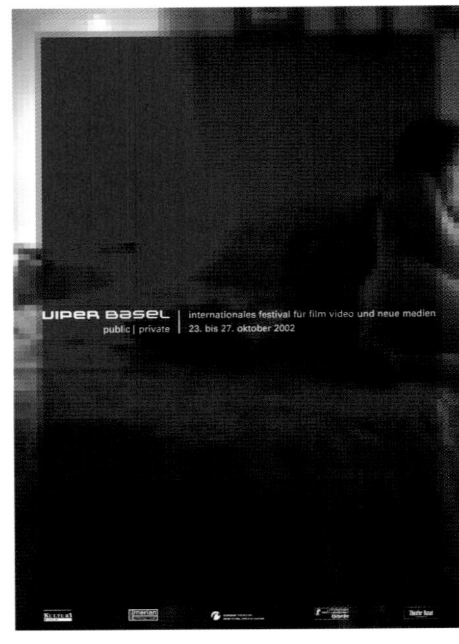

8 9 10

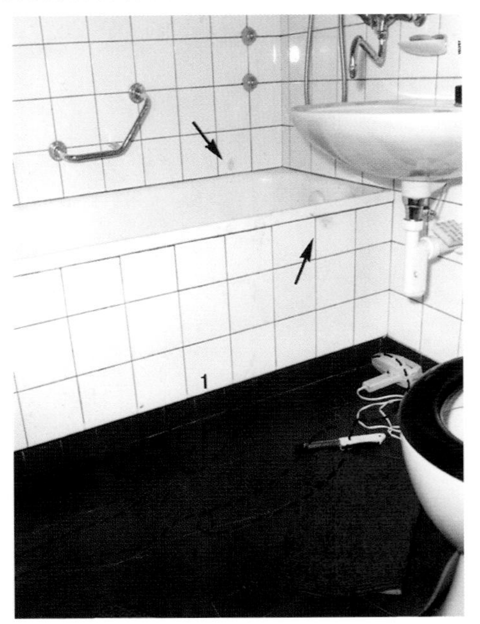

11

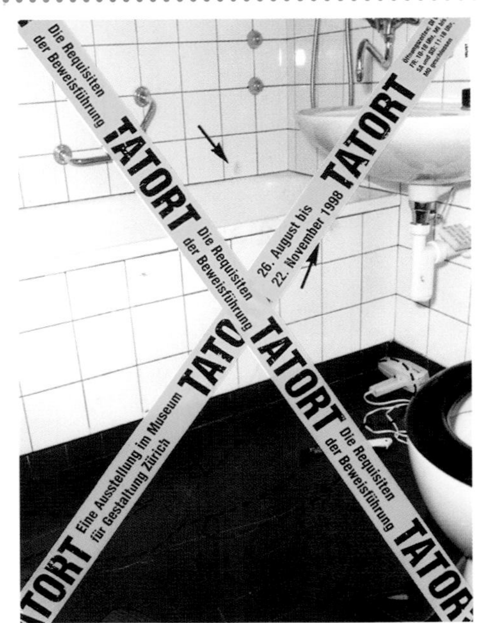

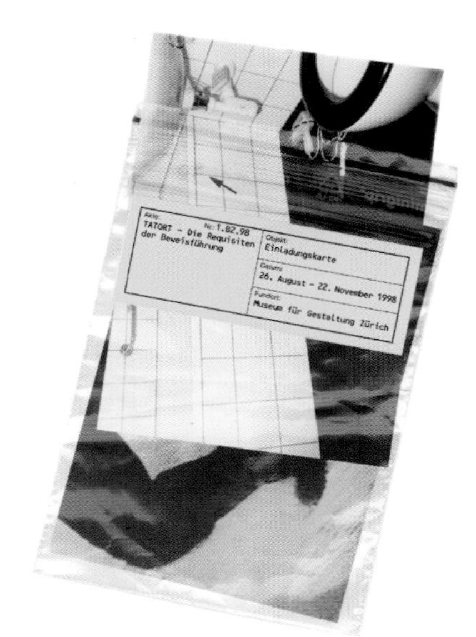

12

Peter Moser

8–10 Poster series for 2002 Viper Basel International Festival for Film Video and New Media / Viper / Switzerland / 2002

11–12 Posters and informational flyer for exhibition *Tatort* (Crime Scene) / Museum für Gestaltung Zürich / Switzerland / At first, only the simple poster showing a real crime-scene photo of the Zurich police was posted. Two days later, it was "cordoned off" with mock yellow police tape. The flyer is packaged in a plastic bag similar to the ones used for forensic evidence.

13–15 Poster series for performances at the Luzerner Theater under the 1999/2000 season theme, *heimatlich-heimlich-unheimlich* (homely-secretive-eerie) / Luzerner Theater / Switzerland / 1999

16–18 Poster series for performances at the Luzerner Theater under the 2001/2002 season theme, *geldmachtnatur* (money, power, nature) / Luzerner Theater / Switzerland / 2001

19–21 Poster series for performances at the Luzerner Theater under the 2002/2003 season theme, *transit* (transit) / Luzerner Theater / Switzerland / 2002

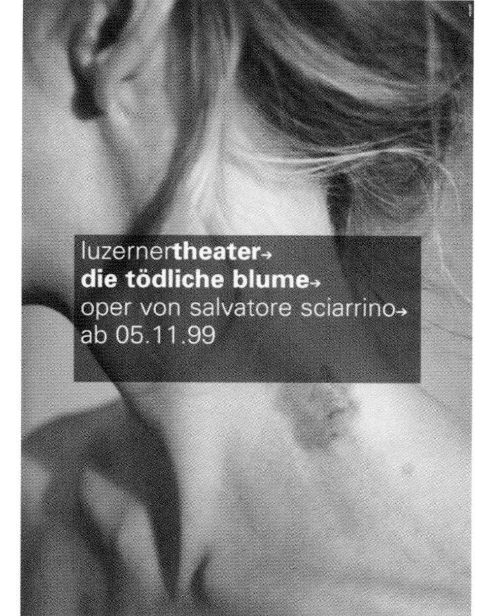

13 14 15

16 17 18

19 20 21

While Melanie Mues was studying at the Academy of Art in Bremen, one of her teachers, Peter Rea, advised her to relocate to London in order to "loosen up." It seems to have been sound advice. She graduated in 1995, spent a year freelancing in Berlin, and moved to London in 1996. Following five years of valuable experience in some of London's leading design studios, she decided to go freelance again. • • In recent years, she has worked on a variety of projects including book design, invitations, posters, promotional programs, and exhibitions. Her passion for the work and her resourcefulness have led her to some great projects. Recent projects for the V&A and, in particular, Tate Modern also allowed Melanie to develop her skills as an exhibition designer. • • She recently created an identity for a Tate exhibition of work by the sculptor Eva Hesse that recalls the light, transparent nature of the show's subject. She also designed the exhibition space, a guide, and an interpretation area, where visitors experience the materials used by the artist. The Hesse interpretation area is a fine example of how resourceful Melanie is: The boxes and display cases were made from Plexiglas left over from previous shows at the Tate. Her cost-effective solution reflected Hesse's aesthetic. The graphics at the entrance to the show continued the theme, with the artist's name built out of transparent Plexiglas. • • Melanie recently also entered the world of publishing design, with *Sanctuary: The Temples of Angkor*, a book she designed for Phaidon in 2002. *Sanctuary* features Steve McCurry's evocative photography of Buddhist temples in Angkor, Cambodia. Melanie's sensitive approach resulted in a landscape-format book that allows the quality of the photography to shine. • • When necessary, her work can be playful and often bears the influence of British design. Take, for example, the Garden Party invitation she designed for Omni Colour—a lawn-green card that opens to reveal a pink gingham tablecloth. Simple, playful, and very English. It seems as if Peter Rea's advice was perfect: living and working in London may have loosened her up a little. It has allowed her to grow as a designer and amass a body of work that clearly indicates her talent and potential.

• • Fernando Gutiérrez • •

1-3 Café type installation, reading-room type detail, and reading room with run-around type and specially designed furniture, as part of *Eija-Liisa Ahtila* exhibition design / Tate Modern / United Kingdom / 2002

4 Poster, print advertisment, exhibition guide and invitation, and signage, as part of *Eva Hesse* exhibition design / Tate Modern / United Kingdom / 2003

5-6 Classic Design Award voting wall at Victoria & Albert Museum, London / Victoria & Albert Museum / United Kingdom / 2003 / The voting wall is designed to allow V&A visitors to vote for "The People's Award" given away by the magazine *Homes and Gardens*.

Melanie Mues

London

MODERN
TATE
EVA HESSE
Until 9 March 03
Southwark/Blackfriars
'Vivacious... fabulous... tremendous and exhilarating.'
'Don't miss it.'
EVA HESSE
13 NOVEMBER 02 – 9 MARCH 03
HESSE
Vote for your favourite design to see it win the
BUGATTI CUTLERY
4
5 6

7

8
9

Melanie Mues

7 Mailer/unfoldable poster for Resource Room at Tate Modern, London / Tate Modern / United Kingdom / 2003
8–9 Spreads from chapter design, *Paul Smith: You Can Find Inspiration In Everything* (with Aboud Sedano) / Violette Publishing / United Kingdom / 2002
10–12 Cover and spreads, *Sanctuary: The Temples of Angkor*, by Steve McCurry / Phaidon Press / United Kingdom and USA / 2002
13 Invitation for picnic party organized by printers Omni Colour and K2 Screen in conjunction with the Serpentine Gallery, London / Omni Colour / United Kingdom / 2001
14 Membership mailing pack for future members of the National Art Collections Fund / National Art Collections Fund / United Kingdom / 2003
15 Poster for Richard Wilson's *Butterfly* installation at the Wapping Project, London / Wapping Project / United Kingdom / 2003

13

10
11
12

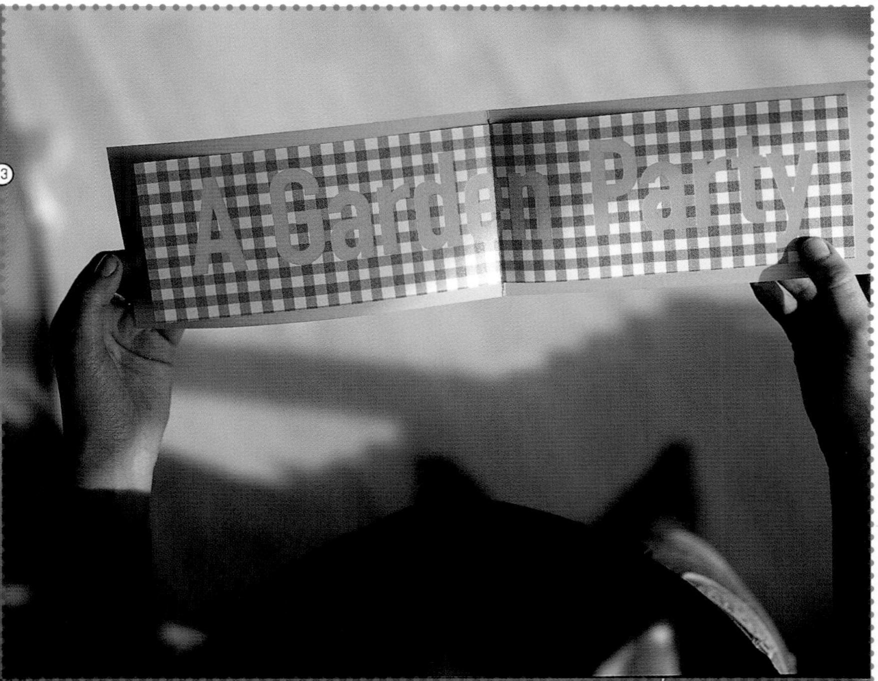

14

15

In Basel a distinct dialect of Swiss-German is spoken. Here syllables aren't swallowed like elsewhere.••Basel is home to one of the largest art fairs in the world, Art Basel. Basel, geographically situated in a basin, is committed to the chemical industry and about as endangered by an earthquake as Kobe, Japan. Basel has never been politically volatile, like, for example, Zurich in the 1980s and 1990s. Because Basel lies in close proximity to the borders with Germany and France, Basel is aware of the other, lives with the foreign. Basel knows no boundaries.••Müller + Hess are from Basel. Müller + Hess communicate in a precise, thoughtful, and traditional design language; they don't allow themselves any aesthetic shortcuts; they are independent and therefore better than other graphic artists. This was also noticed by Art Basel, which has used their talents for five years now. Others clients have followed suit and don't regret it. Müller + Hess, acknowledged with prizes, have also been honored with an exhibition at the Design Museum London. They are atop the Mount Olympus of graphic artists.••Beat Müller and Wendelin Hess are fabulous tailors of thoughts, images, colors—and above all typomaniacs through and through. "During our education we experienced a dedication to thoroughness and the beauty of the detail that continues to set the standard for our work today. Yet we are always exploring, in search of something new, never backward-looking," comment Müller + Hess in an interview on the occasion of their exhibition at the Design Museum. For these two, graphic design is a world circled by the sun, a world that provides and destroys meaning at the same time. Therefore, the most exacting customers are their favorite ones, those who work with them on the content, the ones who reject artifice. Their interest in debate- and process-oriented products have led—logically—to redesigns for no less than three prominent Swiss monthly and weekly magazines. It's the world in reduction, in the very precise reproduction of the now and today. Müller + Hess are relentless in their aestheticism—but they are also smart and have soul.••Werner Jeker••

1–3 Cover, spread, and book-launch invitation, *Art Directors Club Schweiz* yearbook 2001 (with Ludovic Balland) / Art Directors Club Switzerland / Switzerland / 2001
4–7 Poster and invitations for exhibition *Richard Paul Lohse-Konstruktive Gebrauchsgrafik* / Museum für Gestaltung Zürich / Switzerland / 1999
8 Poster and invitations/programs for 1996-97 exhibitions at the gallery Kaskadenkondesator, Basel / Kaskadenkondensator / Switzerland / 1996-97 / A year's worth of programs was printed initially featuring just the events of the first month. Some were relesed for immediate use. The remainder was overprinted on a monthly basis in a different color, each time adding the following month's events and crossing out what had already taken place.

Müller + Hess

Basel, Switzerland

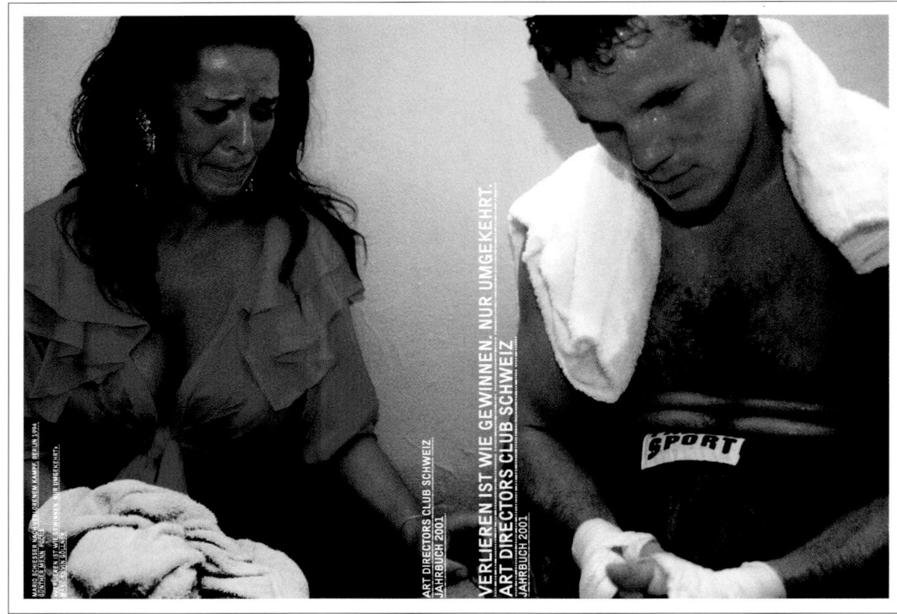

1

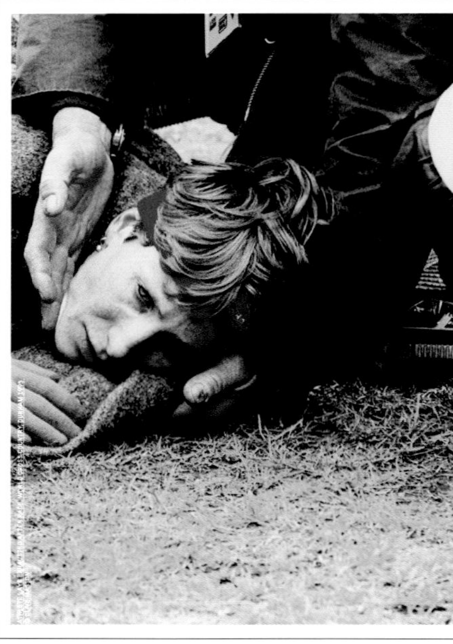

2

3

4

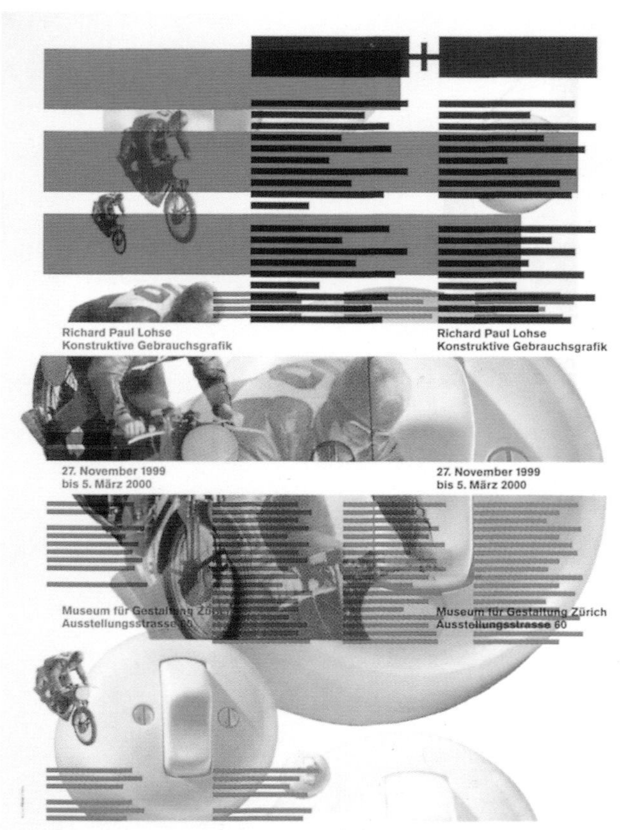

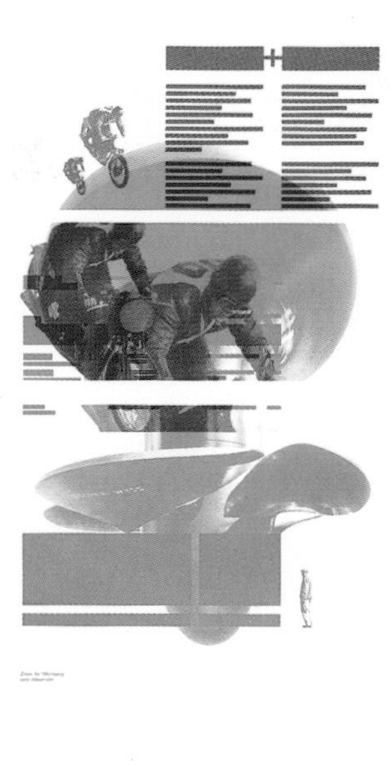

5 6 7

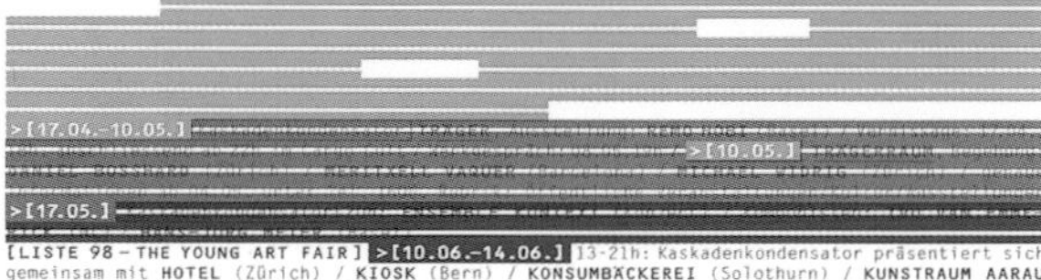

>[17.04.–10.05.]
>[10.05.]
>[17.05.]
[LISTE 98 – THE YOUNG ART FAIR] >[10.06.–14.06.] 13–21h: Kaskadenkondensator präsentiert sich gemeinsam mit HOTEL (Zürich) / KIOSK (Bern) / KONSUMBÄCKEREI (Solothurn) / KUNSTRAUM AARAU (Aarau) / Vernissage: 09.06., 16–22h

KASKADENKONDENSATOR | Warteck pp | Burgweg 7 | 4058 Basel | Tram Nr. 2 bis Wettsteinplatz |
>1 | VÉRONIQUE ZUSSAU | BLANC COMME NEIGE | 12.10.–03.11.96 | Vernissage: 11.10.96, 18 Uhr | Werkgespräch: 01.11.96, 19 Uhr | >2 | ARIANE EPARS | INS BLAUE HINEIN | 16.11.–08.12.96 | Vernissage: 15.11.96, 18 Uhr | >3 | POUR LE CLAVIER | JEAN-JACQUES DÜNKI (Klavier, Clavichord) in eigenen Werken | Matinée | So 24.11.96, 11 Uhr | >4 | SUSANNE FANKHAUSER | 14.12.96–05.01.97 | Vernissage: 13.12.96, 18 Uhr | Werkgespräch: Do 19.12.96, 19 Uhr, ab 16 Uhr geöffnet | geschlossen: 23.12.96–02.01.97 | >5 | HEINRICH LÜBER | DOWNLOAD | Performance | 14.01.97, 18–21 Uhr | >6 | ERNST THOMA | INSTANT SOUND NETWORK | Konzert | Do 16.01.97, 20.30 Uhr | >7 | PASCALE GRAU / SIMONE KURZ / ANDREA SAEMANN | LEIBLIED VARIATIONEN | 20.01.–02.02.97 | Vernissage: 19.01.97, 17 Uhr | Werkgespräch: 31.01.97, 19 Uhr | Finissage und Performance: 02.02.97, 17 Uhr | >8 | SIBYLLE HAUERT UND MUDA MATHIS | THE PLOT – DIE VERSCHWÖRUNG, HEY MARY JANE, WHERE ARE YOU GOING WITH THIS SCISSORS IN YOUR HAND | 22.02.–16.03.97, 18–21 Uhr | Vernissage: 21.02.97, 18 Uhr | Werkgespräch: 14.03.97, 19 Uhr | >9 | CHRISTOPH BÜCHEL | ZU VERMIETEN | 05.04.–20.04.97, Do–So 16–21 Uhr | Vernissage: 04.04.97, 18 Uhr | >10 | CHIARENZA & HAUSER & CROPTIER | HEUTE IST ES ÜBERALL SCHÖN | 02.05.–25.05.97 | Vernissage und CD-Taufe: 02.05.97, 19 Uhr | Kunst und Öffentlichkeit. Thematisches Werkgespräch mit Philip Ursprung (Zürich) und Gästen: 23.05.97, 19 Uhr |

Der Kaskadenkondensator wird unterstützt von: Migros Kulturprozent | Schweizerische National-Versicherungs-Gesellschaft, Basel | Stiftung für kulturelle, soziale und humanitäre Experimente, Binningen |
Öffnungszeiten: Fr–So | 16–19 Uhr | (wenn nicht anders vermerkt) | oder nach Vereinbarung T 061 693 26 40 | >3 | T 061 692 94 51 | >4 | T 061 322 19 26 | >5/6/7 | T 061 381 39 12 | >8 | T 061 691 86 24 | >9 | T 061 261 89 72 | >10 | T 061 261 89 72 |
Müller+Hess

8

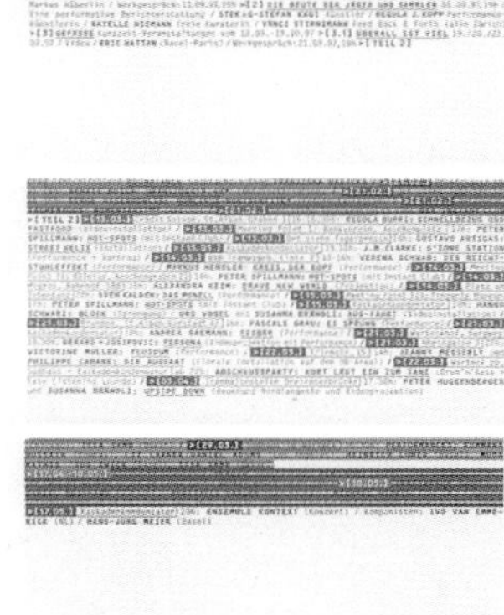

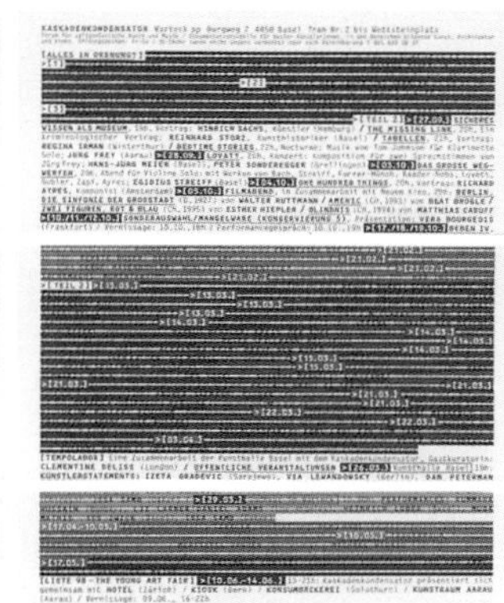

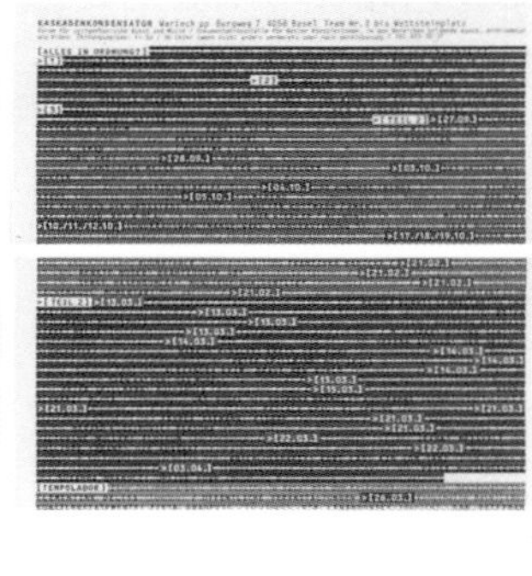

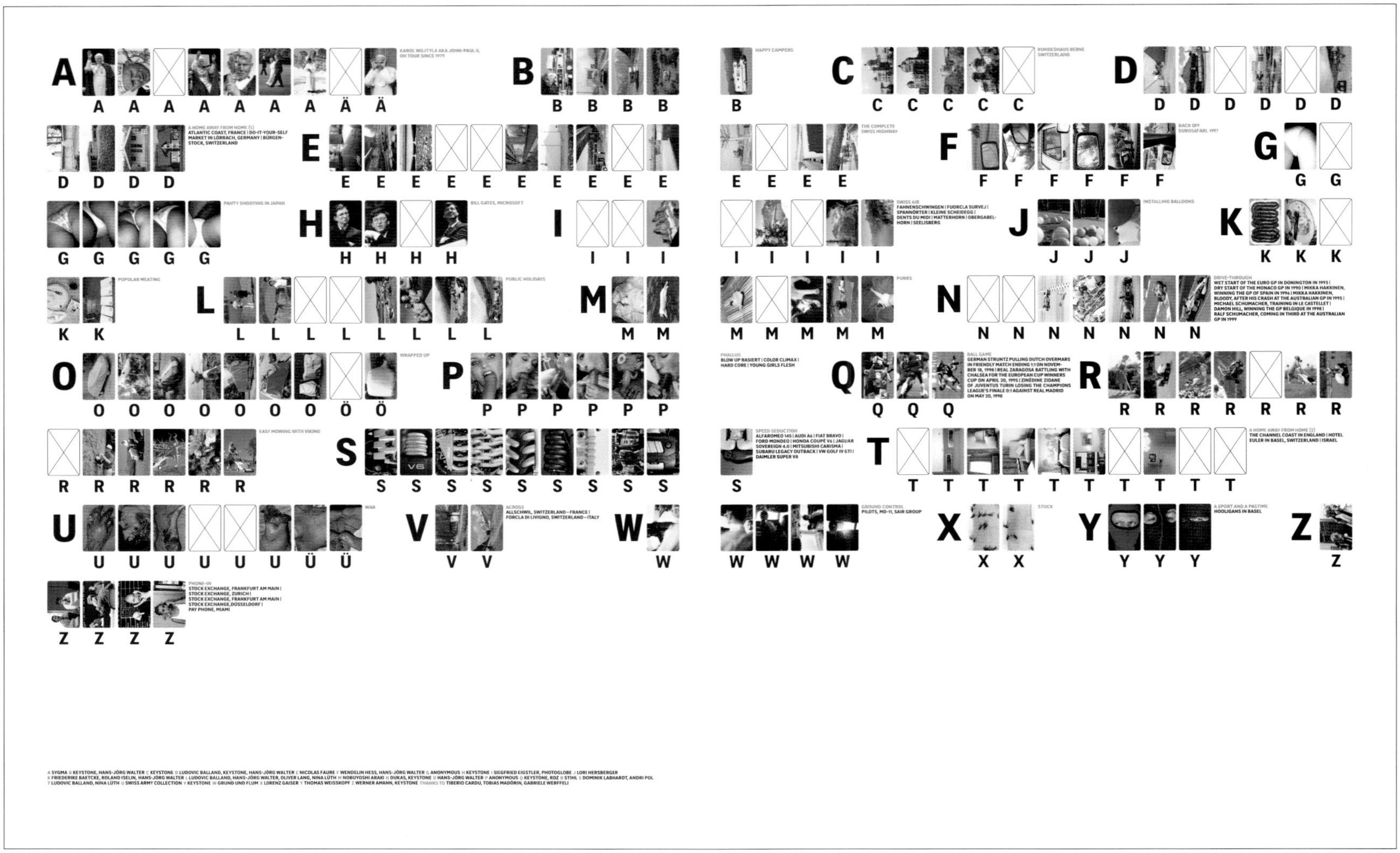

9

9 Spread from "Dismantling the Basel Principle," *Eye–The International Review of Graphic Design*, no. 32 / Eye–The International Review of Graphic Design / United Kingdom / 1999
10 Issues of *Das Magazin*, redesigned and art directed by Müller + Hess / Tamedia AG, Das Magazin / Switzerland / 1999–2002
11–13 Cover and spreads, *Grenzwert* magazine, no. 3 / Bar Grenzwert and Müller + Hess / Switzerland / 1998 / The magazine is wrapped in a protective plastic bag, which, together with the magazine, has a hand hole punched through it. The motto of the issue was "sex, crime, and violence."
14–16 Poster and program spreads for music festival Neue Musik Rümlingen / Neue Musik Rümlingen / Switzerland / 1997

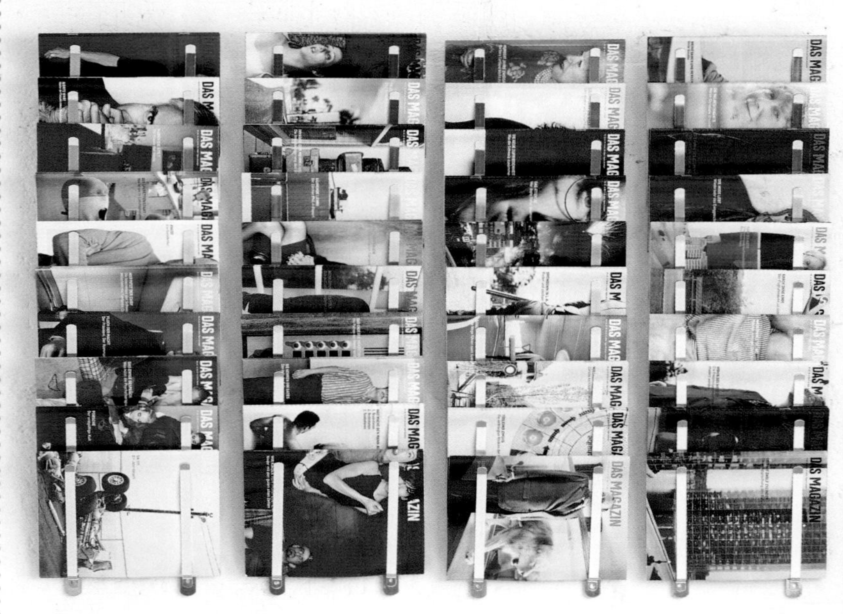

10

Müller + Hess

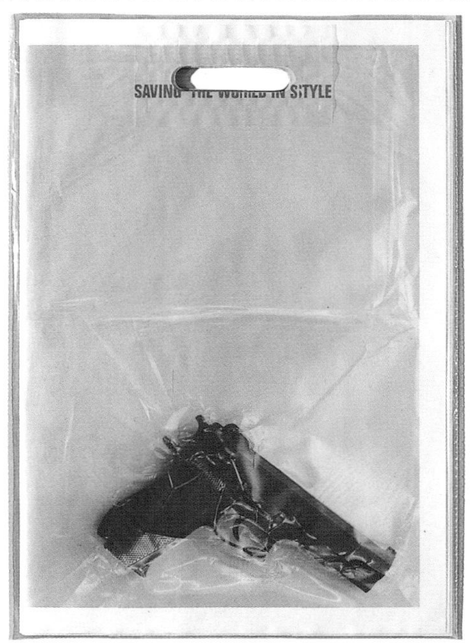

11
12
13

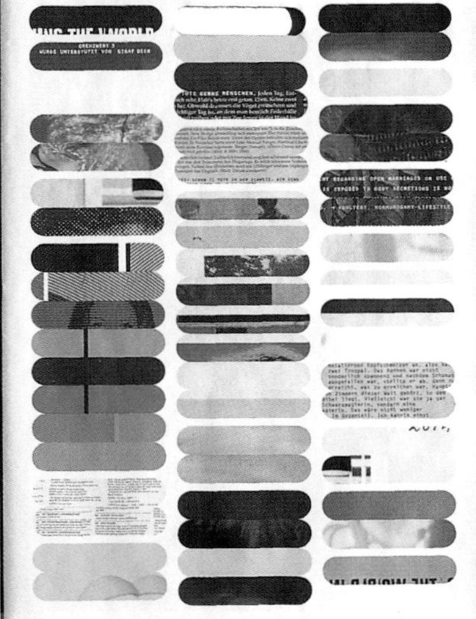

14
15
16

///SONNTAG/24/8/97

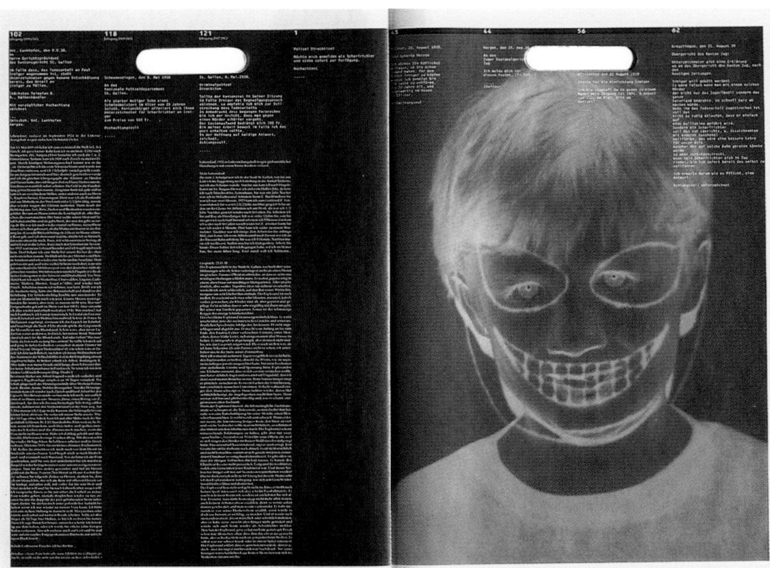

///SAMSTAG/23/8/97

The highly sophisticated design world of Japan nurtures many new design talents. Standing out in such a competitive environment, however, requires talent and determination. Something special. Hideki Nakajima has those qualities. In his view, new technology demands new means of expression and new ways of communicating—not just in graphic design, but in all fields of creative endeavor. He assigns himself the most difficult task of developing something that is truly unique. He searches for an orginal form, something that has not been seen before, that will endure and influence our visual vocabulary over the next decade. Clearly Nakajima seeks to lead and influence the designers of the world. He began his career at Misami Shimizu Design Office before establishing his own practice, Nakajima Design, in 1995. Since then his work has received national and international acclaim resulting in exhibitions and the publication of his work in numerous books and magazines. In 1999 he became involved in the Code group with Ryuichi Sakamoto, Shigeo Goto (editor), and Norika Sora (creative director). The Code group has been actively campaigning for the production of goods that put little or no strain on the earth's resources, foods without chemical additives, and experimental art books. In 2002 the group's first large-scale exhibition *Code: New Village* was held in Tokyo, Osaka, and Kyoto. •• In 2000, Nakajima became a member of Alliance Graphique Internationale (AGI). He strongly believes that design has many brand-new possibilities. He is a pioneer of the future we will watch with anticipation. ••Ken Cato••

①

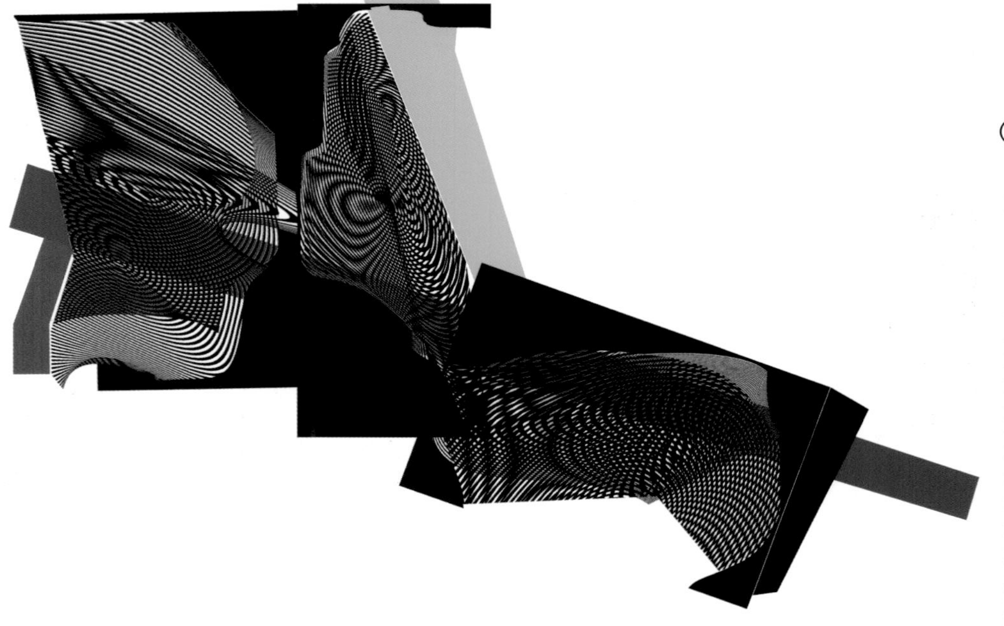

②

1–8 Cover and spreads, "Re-cycling," *IDEA* magazine no. 295 / IDEA / Japan / 2002 / The images are abstractions and mutations of previously created work.

Hideki Nakajima

Tokyo

③
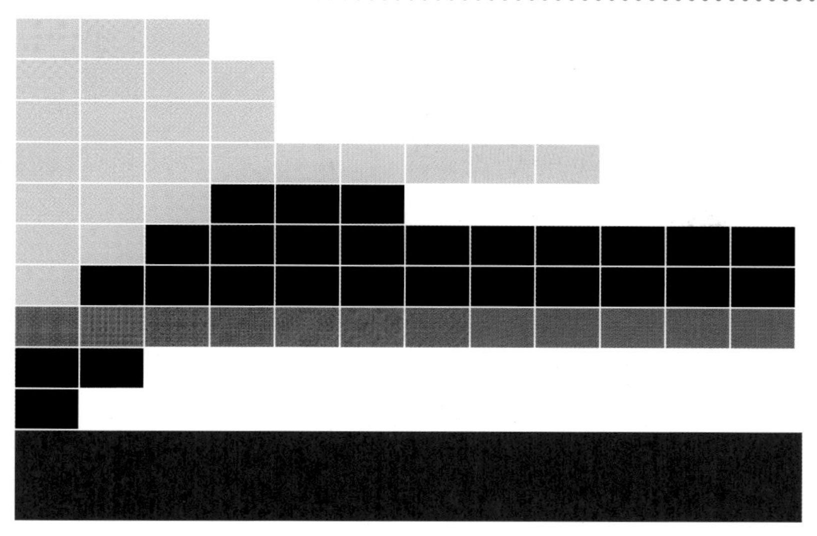

④
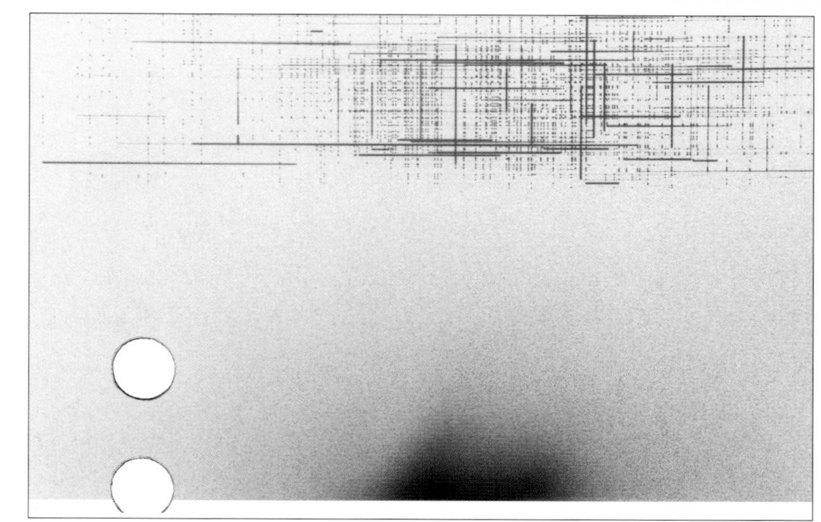

⑤
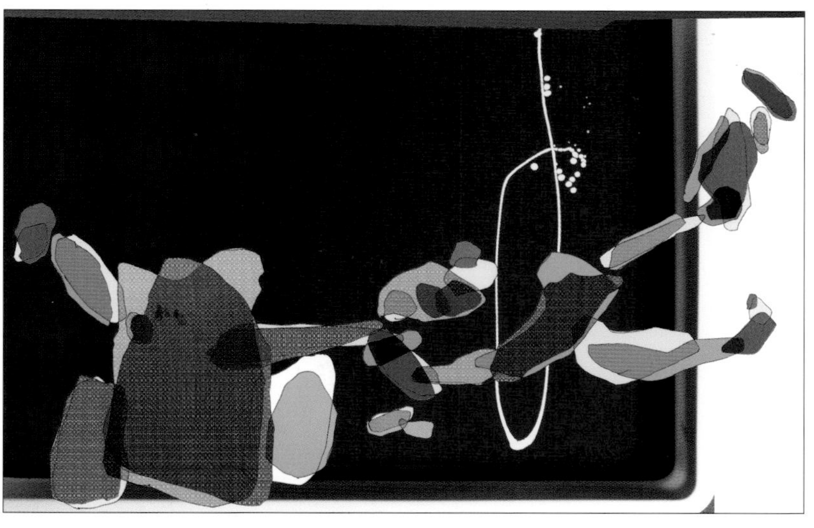

⑥
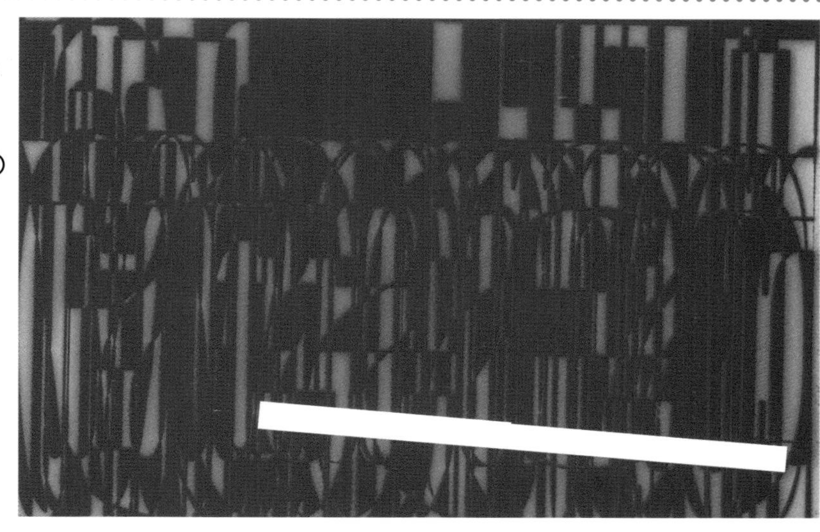

⑦

⑧
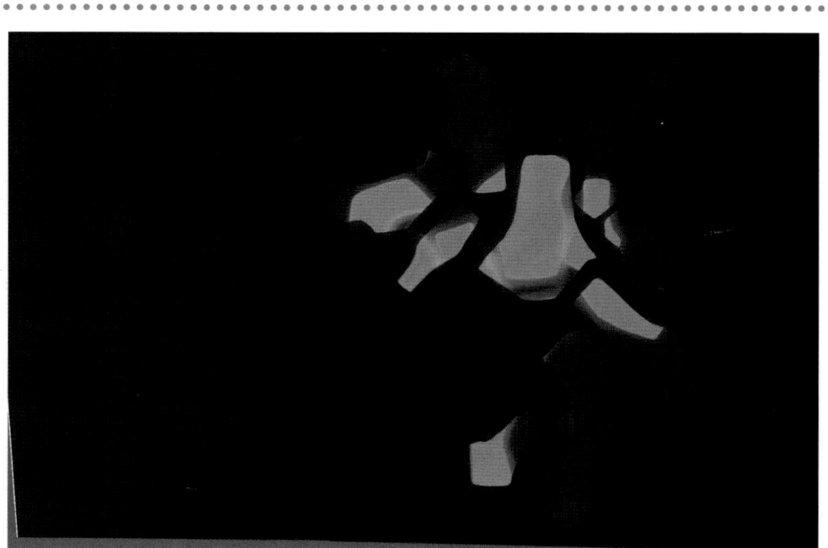

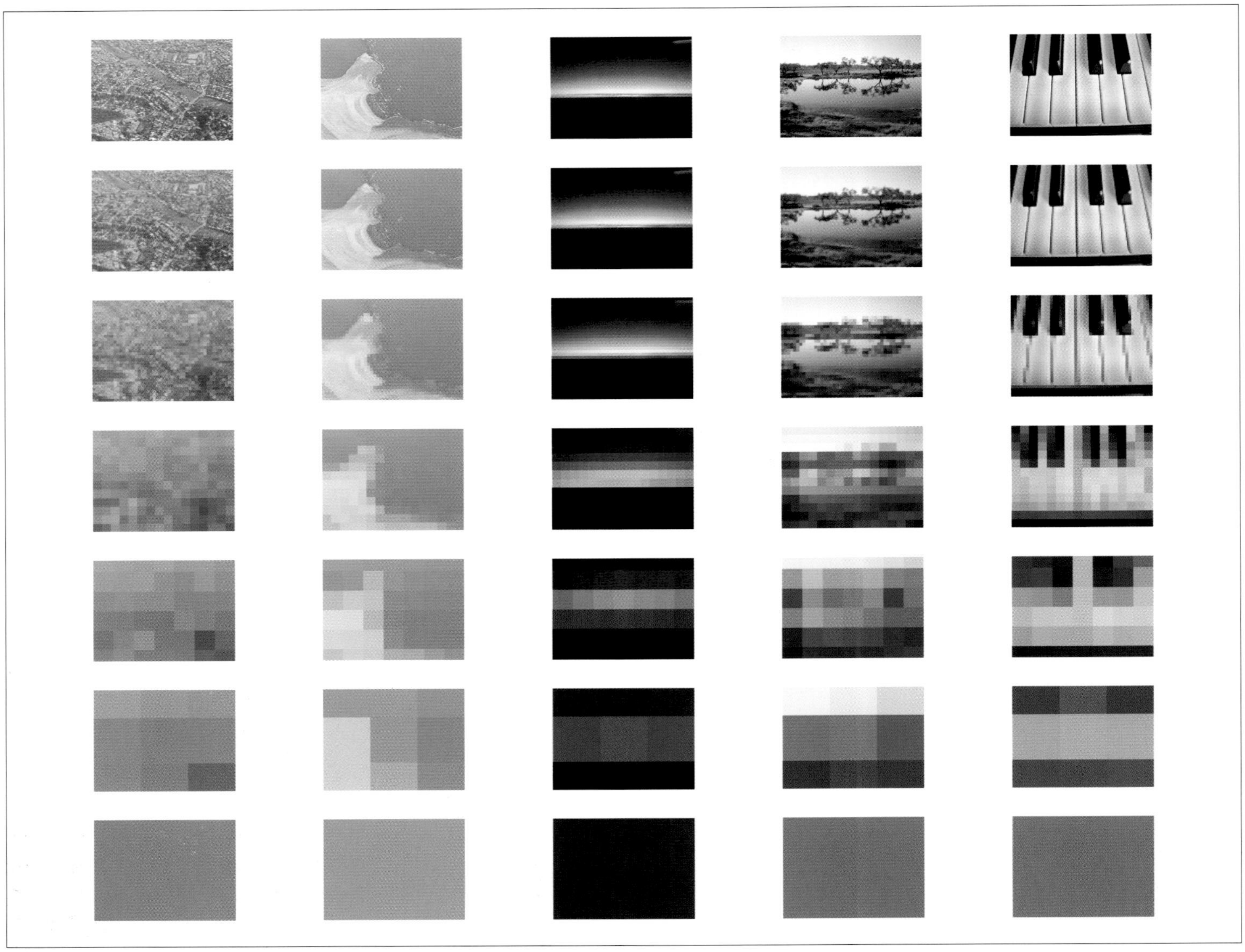

9

10

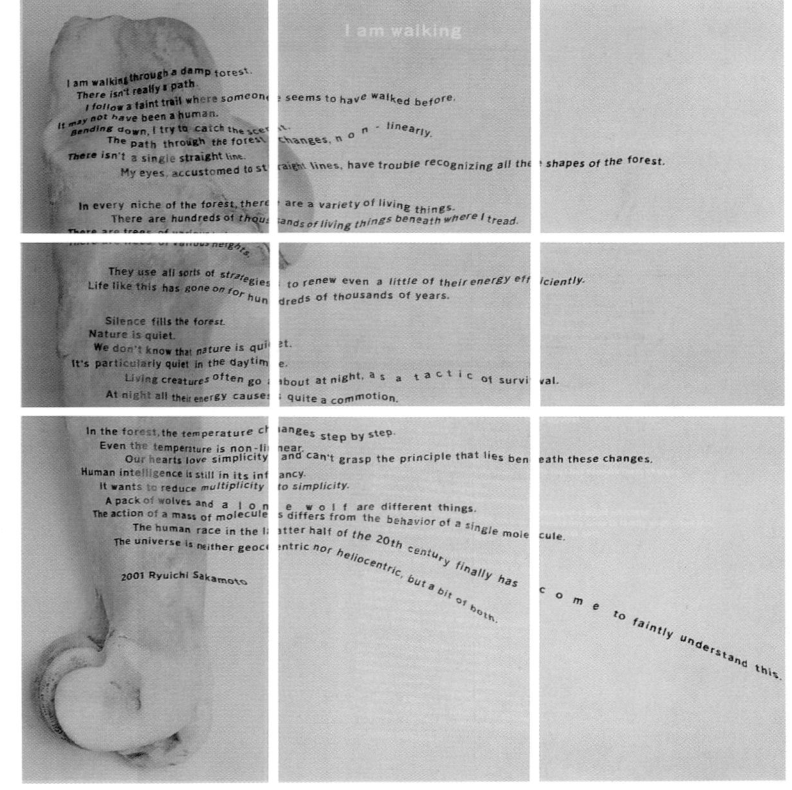

9 Poster from "S/N" series for *Code: New Village* exhibition held in Tokyo, Osaka, and Kyoto (with Ryuichi Sakamoto) / Code / Japan / 2002 / Code is a project established by Ryuichi Sakamoto, Shigeo Goto, Norika Sora, and Hideki Nakajima to organize and distribute a wide range of art forms in cooperation with people from different artistic fields.

10 I am Walking poster for exhibition organized by paper manufacturer Takeo (with Ryuichi Sakamoto) / Takeo Co. / Japan / 2001 / The poster is made up of nine different types of paper.

11–14 Posters from "S/N" series for *Code: New Village* exhibition held in Tokyo, Osaka, and Kyoto (with Ryuichi Sakamoto) / Code / Japan / 2002

Hideki Nakajima

11

Please

12

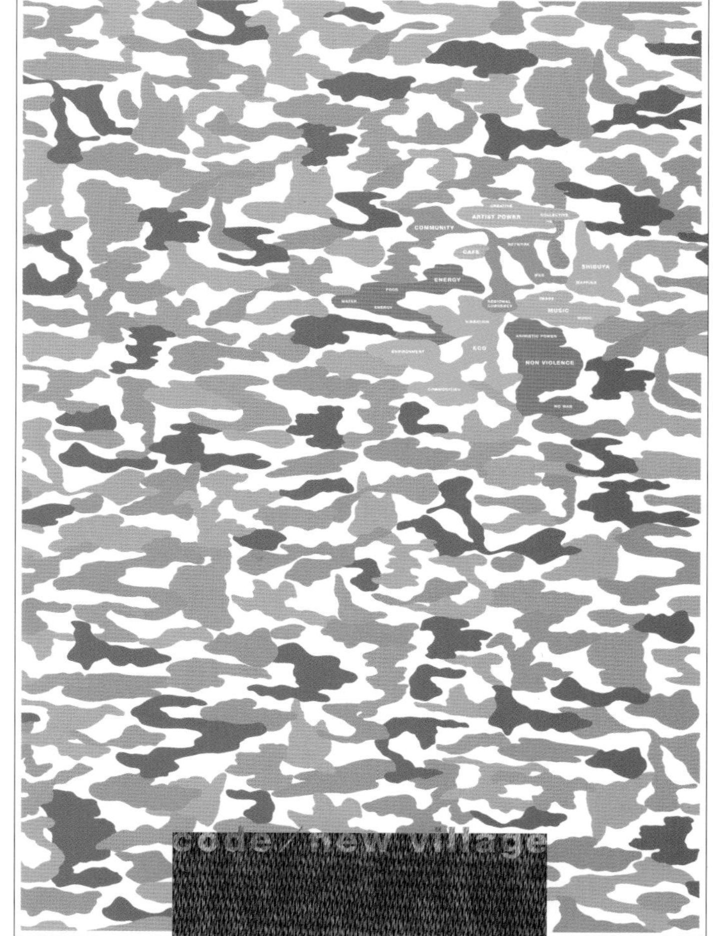
code: new village

13

environment
collective
web
energy
commodities
network
vibration
no war

14

S
N

Working, doing, and producing were fundamental tenets of Dylan Nelson's childhood in a small mill town. Son of a carpenter, Nelson grew up among rugged craftsmanship, wood, hammers, nails, and the sound of Metallica—the tools and environment of his father's trade that deeply influence his own life and work today. • • The Cranbrook Academy of Art is the other primary influence in his art and design, supplying him with new "tools." Mind-opening conceptual instruments that enabled him to "let loose" and create work untouched by complex theoretical bindings. Days and nights of thinking, making, and breathing work straight from the heart became natural and liberating. His attention expanded from two-dimensional design to writing, from furniture design to installation art. Nelson explores any realm where mind and body can be inspired and energized by "just doing." Life and work become one. • • In applying what he absorbed from Cranbrook, today his most original and personal creations come from the conscious materialization of his intimate contrasts from the past. Bright Disney-like wonderlands of wilderness and harmless fairy-tale animals that were distant during his restricted childhood are provocatively juxtaposed with carpentry tools, chains, studs, and stuffed deer heads. Professional practice becomes dream reality and introspective escape. • • But it's not only "what you see is what you get." Environmental concerns are also explicit. Many of his pieces carry a distinct pro-wildlife message. His cynical usage of hunting references raises questions and sparks debate. Through his idiosyncratic creations Nelson does not search for a prescribed reaction from his audience, but he wants people to understand and investigate. Behind both his commercial and research work the philosophy is, "Do it right for yourself, and you'll do it right for the world." • • Omar Vulpinari • •

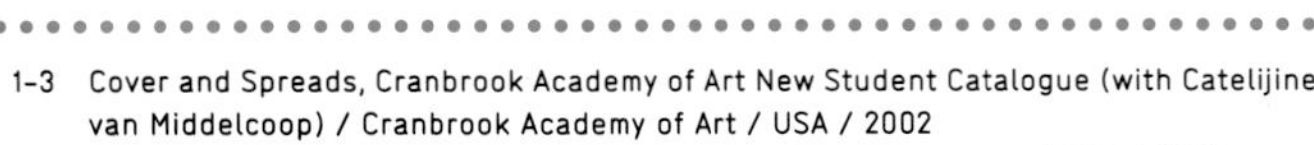

1-3 Cover and Spreads, Cranbrook Academy of Art New Student Catalogue (with Catelijine van Middelcoop) / Cranbrook Academy of Art / USA / 2002
4 Self-commissioned Wear dat Rusty Smile Like A Champion poster / USA / 2002
5 Self-commissioned Astro Twins poster / USA / 2002

Dylan Nelson

Portland, Oregon

4

WEAR DAT RUSTY SMILE LIKE A CHAMPION

HE STARTED OFF AS A PROSPECTIVE GOLD MINER BEFORE BECOMING A CARPENTER

ON THE WEEKENDS THEY WOULD GO CAMPING AT THE RESERVOIR. THEY USED A BLUE TARP WITH A LEAN TWO FOR THEIR TENT HAD BEEN TAKEN BY THE IRS.

MATERIALS. HE GREW GOODNESS FOR ALL THE YOUNG BOYZ AND GIRLZ.

SUNDAY EVENING CAME ABOUT. THE GROUP DECIDED TO GO FOR A FINAL STROLL IN THE CANOE. NO ONE IS EXACTLY SURE WHAT HAPPENED TO THEM THAT SUNDAY AFTERNOON, BUT THE GLISTENING OF THE RUSTY SMILE HAS BEEN SEEN OVER AND OVER AGAIN IN THE BRISK MORNING LIGHT THAT HOVERS ABOVE THE RESERVOIR.

5

ASTRO TWINS

5

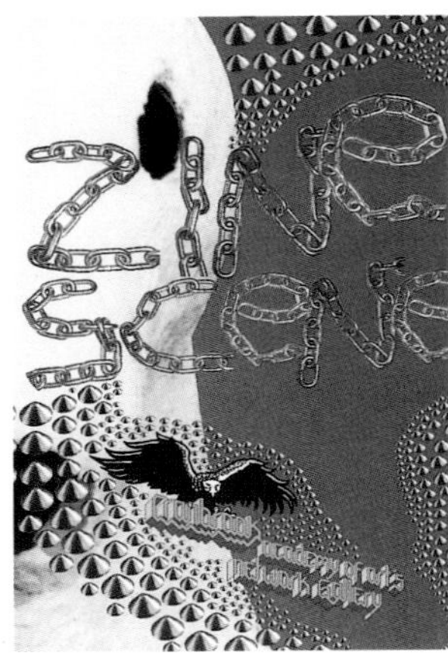

6 7 8 9

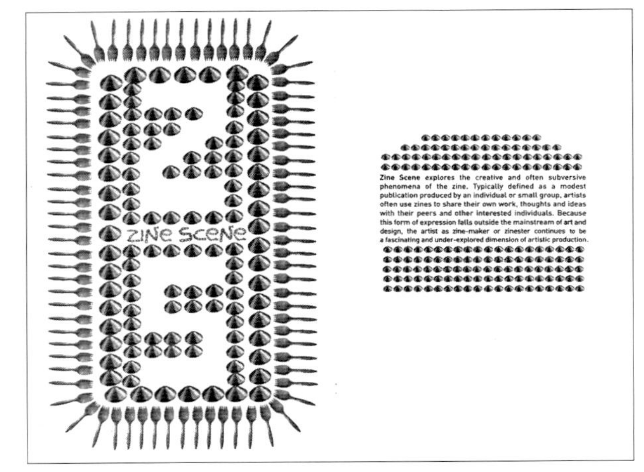

Zine Scene explores the creative and often subversive phenomena of the zine. Typically defined as a modest publication produced by an individual or small group, artists often use zines to share their own work, thoughts and ideas with their peers and other interested individuals. Because this form of expression falls outside the mainstream of art and design, the artist as zine-maker or zinester continues to be a fascinating and under-explored dimension of artistic production.

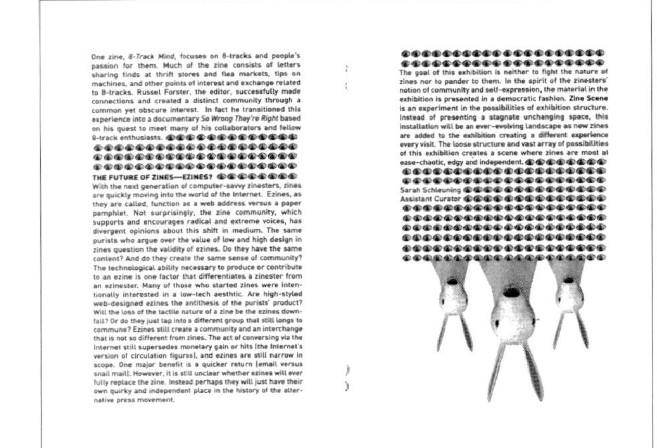

One zine, *8-Track Mind*, focuses on 8-tracks and people's passion for them. Much of the zine consists of letters sharing finds at thrift stores and flea markets, tips on machines, and other points of interest and exchange related to 8-tracks. Russel Forster, the editor, successfully made connections and created a distinct community through a common yet obscure interest. In fact he transitioned this experience into a documentary *So Wrong They're Right* based on his quest to meet many of his collaborators and fellow 8-track enthusiasts.

THE FUTURE OF ZINES—EZINES?

With the next generation of computer-savvy zinesters, zines are quickly moving into the world of the Internet. Ezines, as they are called, function as a web address versus a paper pamphlet. Not surprisingly, the zine community, which supports and encourages radical and extreme voices, has divergent opinions about this shift in medium. The same purists who argue over the value of low and high design in zines question the validity of ezines. Do they have the same content? And do they create the same sense of community? The technological ability necessary to produce or contribute to an ezine is one factor that differentiates a zinester from an ezinester. Many of those who started zines were intentionally interested in a low-tech aesthtic. Are high-styled web-designed ezines the antithesis of the purists' product? Will the loss of the tactile nature of a zine be the ezines downfall? Or do they just tap into a different group that still longs to commune? Ezines still create a community and an interchange that is not so different from zines. The act of conversing via the Internet still supersedes monetary gain or hits (the Internet's version of circulation figures), and ezines are still narrow in scope. One major benefit is a quicker return (email versus snail mail). However, it is still unclear whether ezines will ever fully replace the zine. Instead perhaps they will just have their own quirky and independent place in the history of the alternative press movement.

The goal of this exhibition is neither to fight the nature of zines nor to pander to them. In the spirit of the zinesters' notion of community and self-expression, the material in the exhibition is presented in a democratic fashion. **Zine Scene** is an experiment in the possibilities of exhibition structure. Instead of presenting a stagnate unchanging space, this installation will be an ever-evolving landscape as new zines are added to the exhibition creating a different experience every visit. The loose structure and vast array of possibilities of this exhibition creates a scene where zines are most at ease–chaotic, edgy and independent.

Sarah Schleuning
Assistant Curator

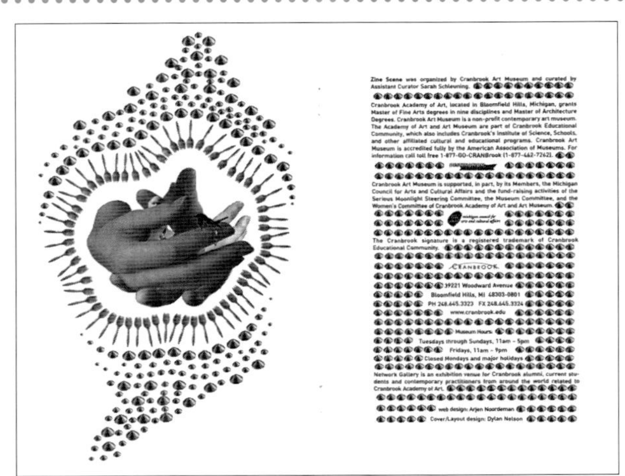

Zine Scene was organized by Cranbrook Art Museum and curated by Assistant Curator Sarah Schleuning.

Cranbrook Academy of Art, located in Bloomfield Hills, Michigan, grants Master of Fine Arts degrees in nine disciplines and Master of Architecture Degrees. Cranbrook Art Museum is a non-profit contemporary art museum. The Academy of Art and Art Museum are part of Cranbrook Educational Community, which also includes Cranbrook's Institute of Science, Schools, and other affiliated cultural and educational programs. Cranbrook Art Museum is accredited fully by the American Association of Museums. For information call toll free 1-877-GO-CRANBrook (1-877-462-7262).

Cranbrook Art Museum is supported, in part, by its Members, the Michigan Council for Arts and Cultural Affairs and the fund-raising activities of the Serious Moonlight Steering Committee, the Museum Committee, and the Women's Committee of Cranbrook Academy of Art and Art Museum.

The Cranbrook signature is a registered trademark of Cranbrook Educational Community.

Cranbrook

39221 Woodward Avenue
Bloomfield Hills, MI 48303-0801
PH 248.645.3323 FX 248.645.3324
www.cranbrook.edu

Museum Hours:
Tuesdays through Sundays, 11am – 5pm
Fridays, 11am – 9pm
Closed Mondays and major holidays

Network Gallery is an exhibition venue for Cranbrook alumni, current students and contemporary practitioners from around the world related to Cranbrook Academy of Art.

web design: Arjen Noordeman
Cover/Layout design: Dylan Nelson

5 Poster for *Zine Scene* exhibition at the Cranbrook Art Museum's Network Gallery / Cranbrook Art Museum / USA / 2002
6–9 Back and front cover and spreads, *Zine Scene* exhibition guide / USA / 2002
10–12 Self-commissioned pieces Untitled and Basketball Stylos and installation / USA / 2002

Dylan Nelson

10

11

12

When I look at certain images, I hear sounds. The messages of Yves Netzhammer's images are, however, mute. Looking at them, I feel alienated, as if a capsule were closing in on me and blocking out the outside world. In this sensory-deprivation tank, I am absorbed in pure contemplation. Results, realizations occur only through the reflection with my own world of experience. I am inside a dream. In this metaphysical dimension, the surprising connection of elements reveals simple processes or provides sudden insight into extremely complex occurences. Netzhammer is able to put into images that which causes us to stumble even when we try to put it in words. • • He asks these somnambulistic questions. He asks for meaning with such directness that it often seems embarrassingly naked. As soon as the observer gets somewhat used to this nakedness, however, he realizes with consternation that he has already been taken possession of. With the inquiries Netzhammer undertakes about the functioning of things and with his complete, plausible, linear answers to them, he stirrs up depths quietly rotting away in our society and ourselves. Netzhammer looks into his own backpack and therefore knows exactly what we others carry around with us. He looks, feels, smells, and thinks with accuracy, scientifically, clinically. He is someone who walks along the border, a storyteller who lovingly yet emphatically gives back to my heart things put away carelessly. He is someone who makes me think, and I like that. • • Werner Jeker • •

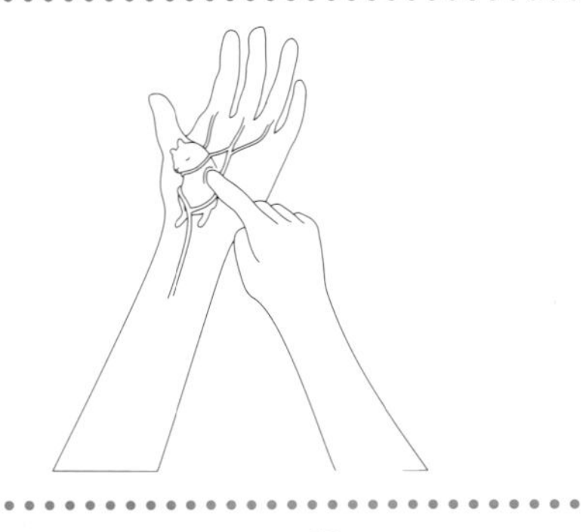

1

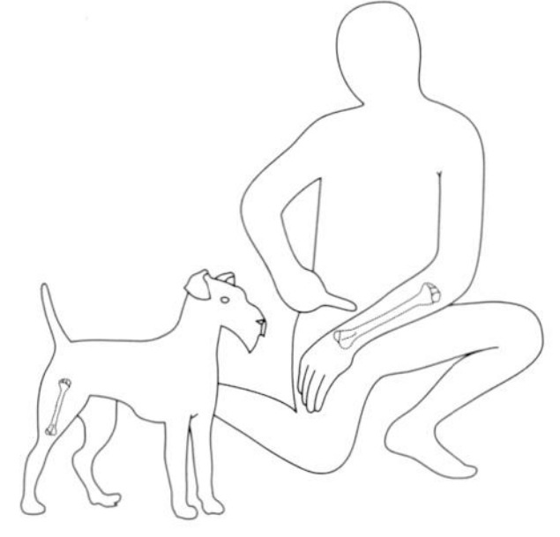

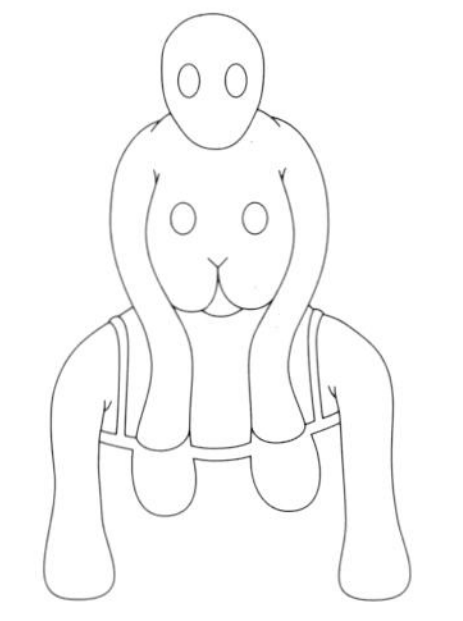

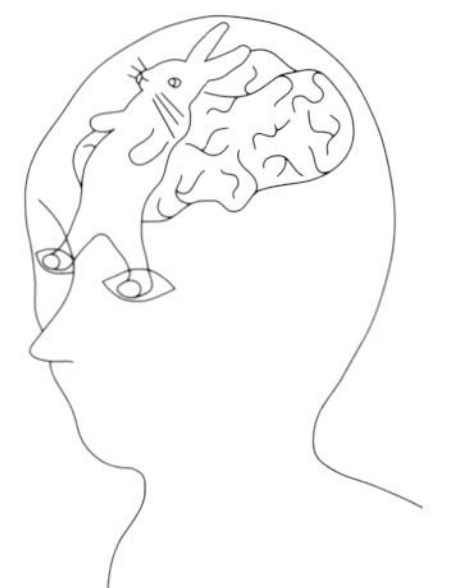

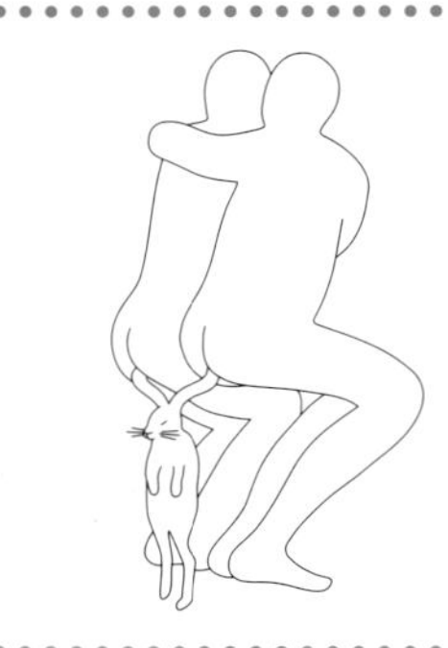

1 Illustrations from *Was sich erzählen lässt wird verbessert werden* (What Can Be Told Will Be Improved), by Yves Netzhammer / Verlag Ricco Bilger / Switzerland / 1997
2 Poster for 2001 international Frankfurt Book Fair / Frankfurt Book Fair / Germany / 2001
3–5 Poster and front and back of invitation for *Curators' Digest* exhibition at the Helmhaus, Zurich / Helmhaus Zürich / Switzerland / 1999
6 Poster for exhibition *Der Abgelenkte Blick–Malerei* (The Distracted View–Painting) at the Helmhaus Zürich / Helmhaus Zürich / Switzerland / 2000
7–9 Poster and front and back of invitation for Yves Netzhammer exhibition *Wenn man etwas gegen seine Eigenschaften benützt, muss man dafür einen anderen Namen finden* (If One Uses Something Against Its Characteristics, It Must Be Renamed) at the Museum zu Allerheiligen, Schaffhausen / Museum zu Allerheiligen / Switzerland / 1999

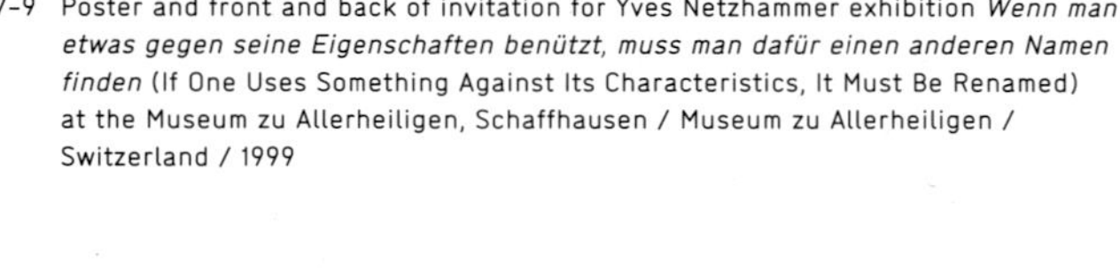

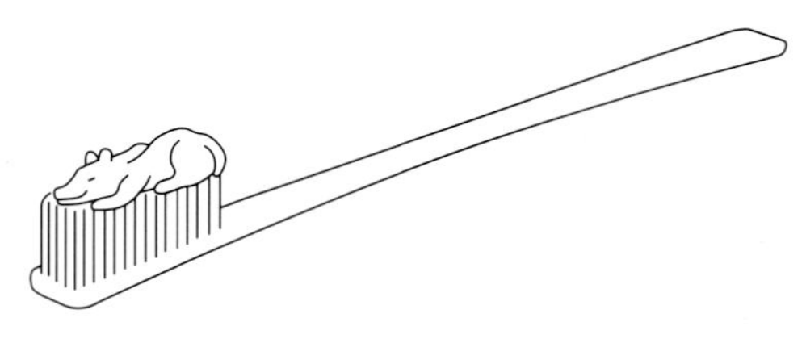

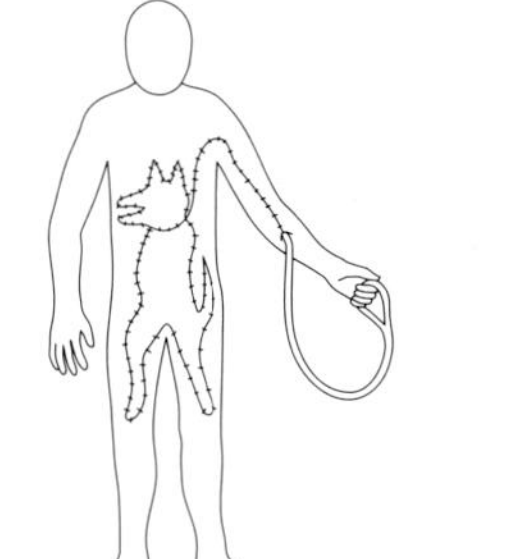

Yves Netzhammer

Zurich

2

Fachbesuchertage: 10.–15.Oktober 2001
Publikumstage: 13.–14.Oktober 2001
Öffnungszeiten
Täglich: 9–18.30 Uhr
Kassenschluss 18.00 Uhr
Montag: 9–14.00 Uhr
Kassenschluss 13.00 Uhr
53. Frankfurter Buchmesse · 10.–15. Oktober 2001 · Gastland Griechenland
www.buchmesse.de · www.frankfurt-book-fair.com
Buchmesse Frankfurt Book Fair

3

5. FEBRUAR BIS 21. MÄRZ 1999
CURATORS´ DIGEST

4

CURATORS DIGEST

5

6

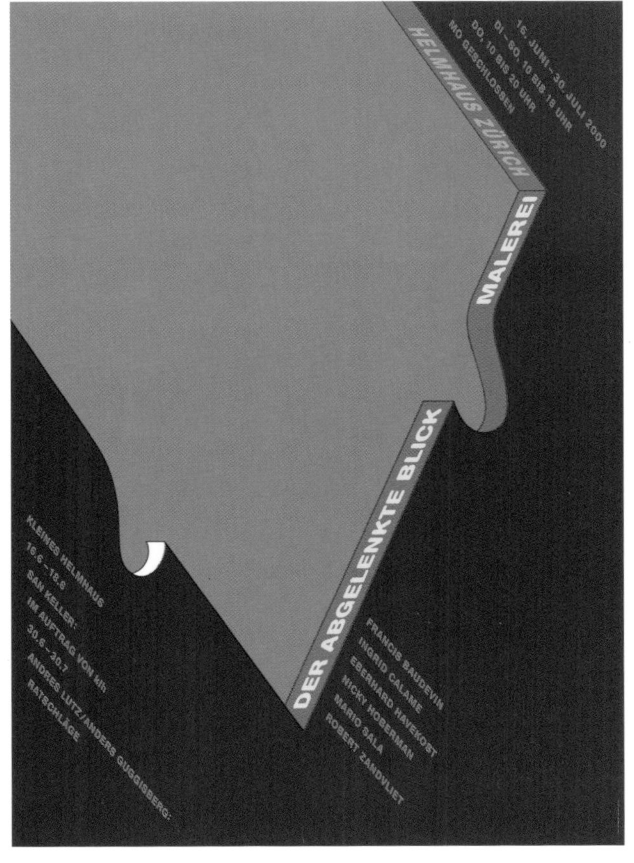
16. JUNI–30. JULI 2000
DI–SO, 10 BIS 18 UHR
DO, 10 BIS 20 UHR
MO GESCHLOSSEN
HELMHAUS ZÜRICH
MALEREI
DER ABGELENKTE BLICK
FRANCIS BAUDEVIN
INGRID CALAME
EBERHARD HAVEKOST
NICKY HOBERMAN
MARIO SALA
ROBERT ZANDVLIET
KLEINES HELMHAUS
16.6–18.6
SAN KELLER:
IM AUFTRAG VON kfh
30.6–30.7
ANDRES LUTZ/ANDERS GUGGISBERG:
RATSCHLÄGE

7

WENN MAN ETWAS GEGEN SEINE EIGENSCHAFTEN BENÜTZT
MUSS MAN DAFÜR EINEN ANDEREN NAMEN FINDEN

8

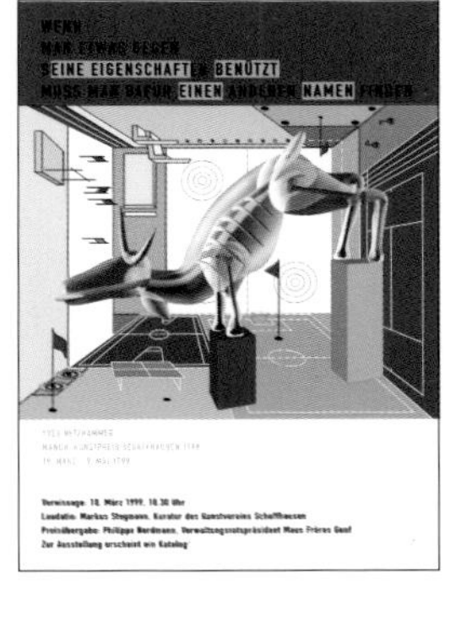

9

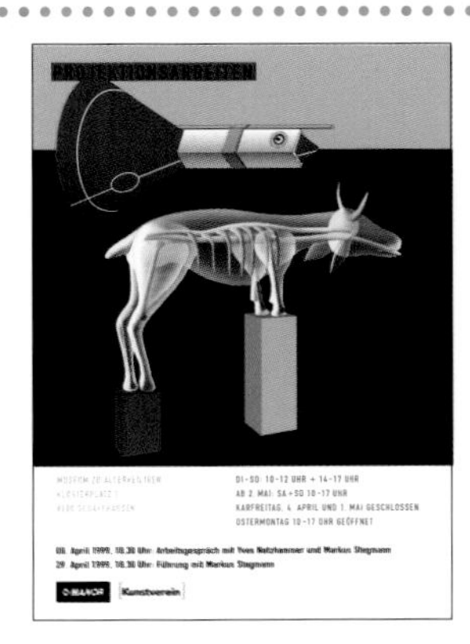

10

11

Yves Netzhammer

10 Special stamps conceived for the hundredth anniversary of the association of Swiss chocolate makers (with Ralph Schraivogel) / Swiss Post / Switzerland / 2001 / The stamps are chocolate-scented.

11 Projections from Yves Netzhammer exhibition *Die überraschende Verschiebung der Sollbruchstelle eines in optimalen verhältnissen aufgewachsenen Astes* (The Surpising Shift of the Predetermined Breaking Point of a Branch Raised in Optimal Conditions) at the Helmhaus Zürich / Helmhaus Zürich / Switzerland / 2003

12–15 Cover illustrations and pages, "*Die Zukunft*" (The Future) and "*Glaubenskrieg*" (War of Faith), *Das Magazin*, no. 47 and 51 / Tamedia AG and Das Magazin / Switzerland / 1999

(12)

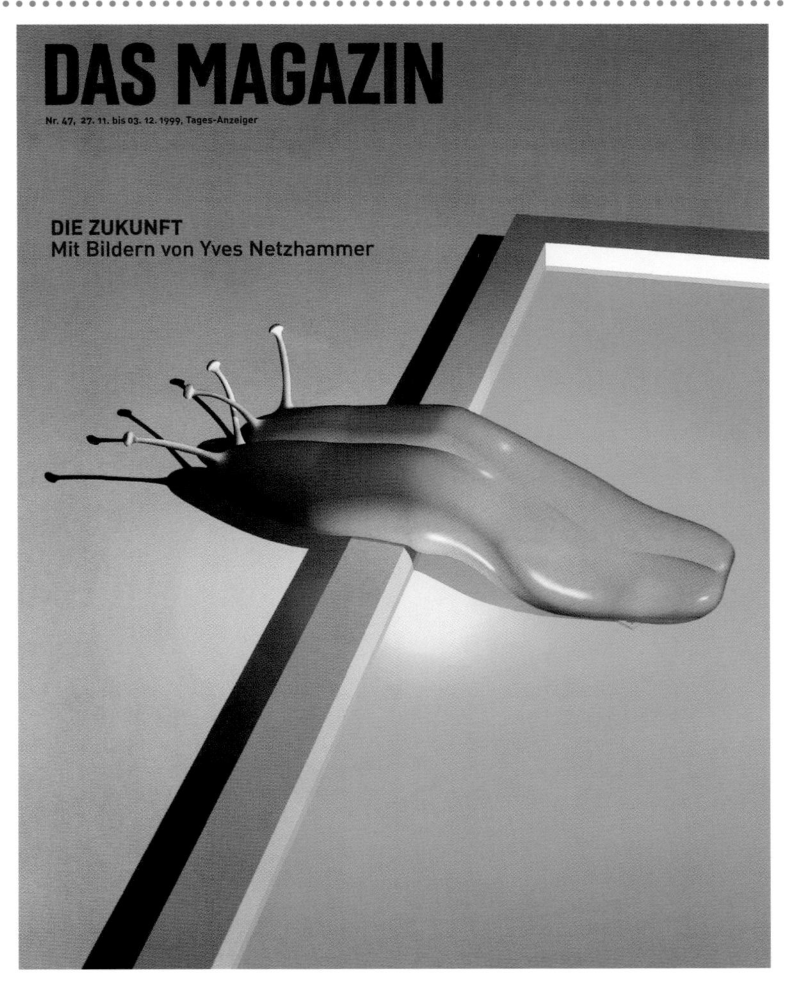
DAS MAGAZIN
Nr. 47, 27. 11. bis 03. 12. 1999, Tages-Anzeiger
DIE ZUKUNFT
Mit Bildern von Yves Netzhammer

(13)

DAS MAGAZIN
NR. 51 22. BIS 28. 12. 2001 TAGES-ANZEIGER
GLAUBENSKRIEG
Was schief läuft zwischen den Religionen

(14)

(15)

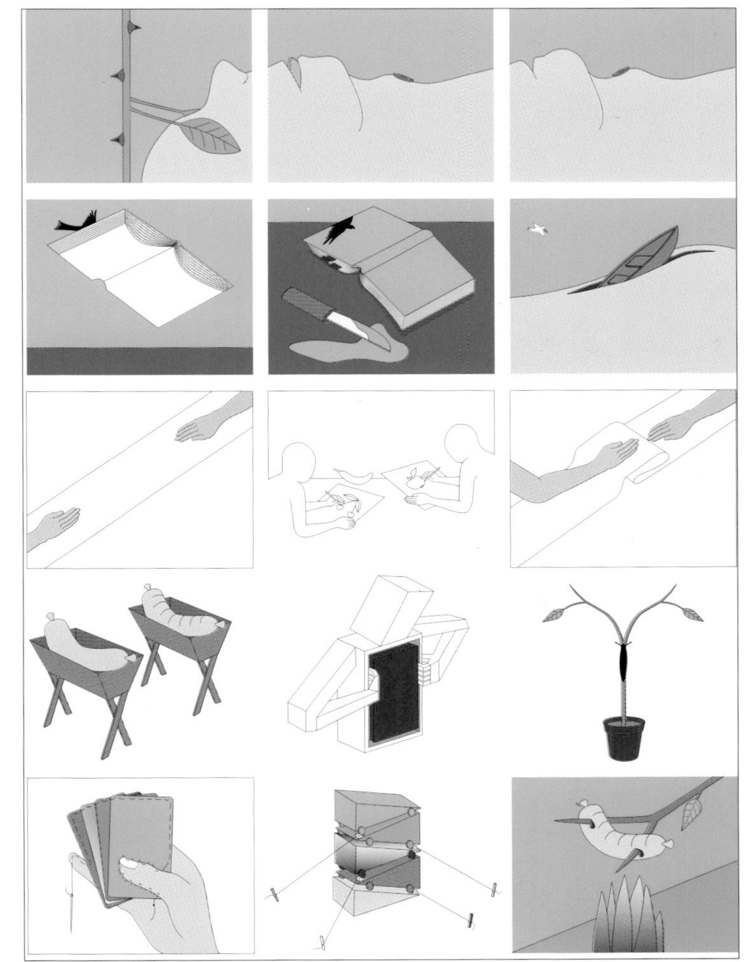

Ideas, ideas, ideas! For me Christoph Niemann was an easy selection. His talent and training guarantee the quality of his output. Heinz Edelmann, Paul Davis, and Paula Scher have all been his mentors. His illustrative approach to design is genuinely idea-driven. "I have always been a designer who has to solve problems with illustration," he says. He doesn't hold back. Be it political, satirical, humorous, it's always pointed. What's more, he is versatile enough to adopt an illustrative language best suited to make the idea even more potent. He has been described as a dedicated storyteller. The wonderful part of it is that he does it in his own way. His keen intelligence and respect for the traditions that have come before him allow him to constantly reinvigorate styles that have been forgotten in the computer-driven illustrative environment. ••Born and edu-cated in Stuttgart, Germany, he now lives and works in New York. He teaches a class in conceptual graphic design at the School of Visual Arts in New York, and in collaboration with Nicholas Blechman he publishes a series of limited-edition books entitled *100%*. It is a highly suitable and appropriate title given Niemann's tendency to squeeze every last drop out of an idea and pursue it relentlessly until he has found the ultimate graphic expression to make it work. ••Ken Cato••

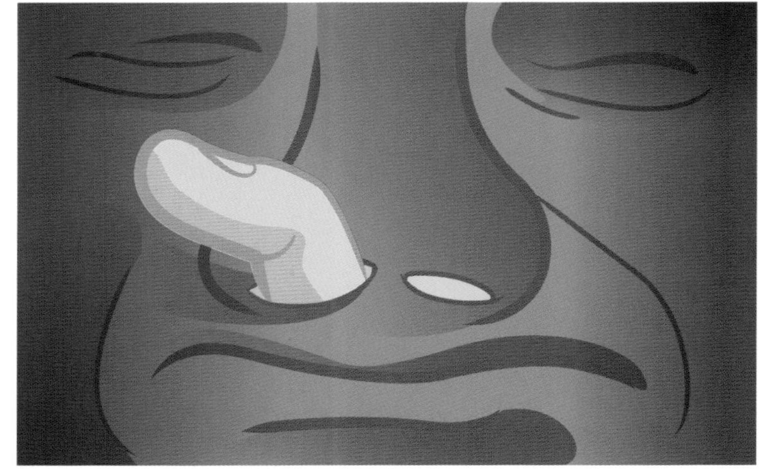

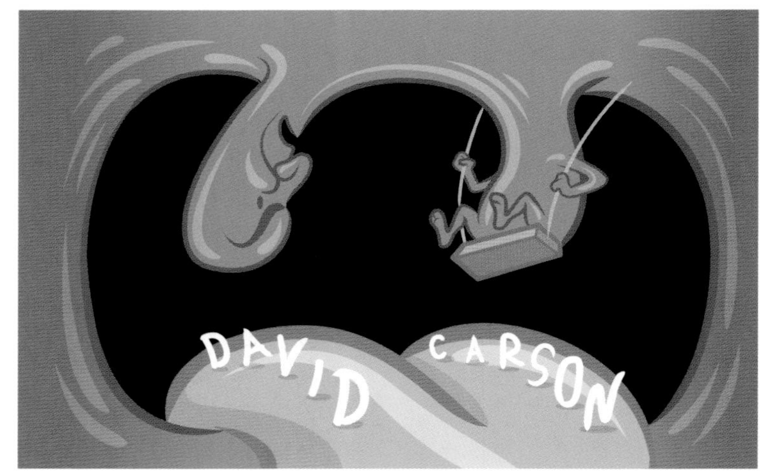

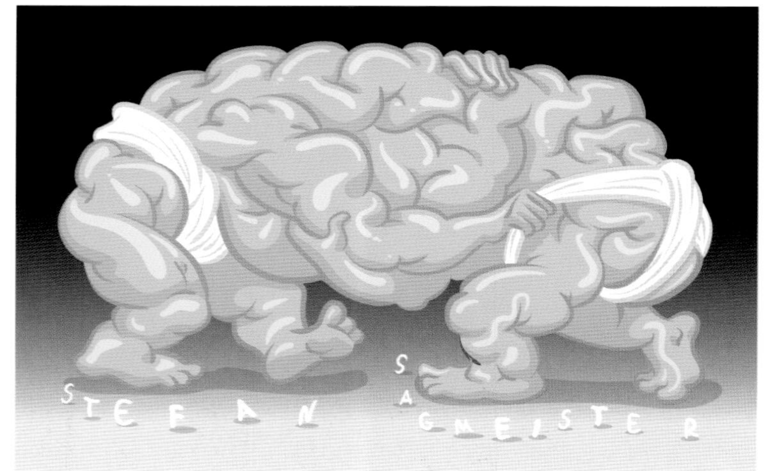

1–4 Chapter-opening illustrations, *F-Stop* / Font Shop International / Germany / 2003 / *F-Stop is* a stock-image catalogue designed by Stefan Sagmeister.
5 Illustration, *The New York Times Magazine*, 8 April 2001 / The New York Times / USA / 2001
6 Cover illustration, *The New York Times Book Review*, 25 April 1999 / The New York Times / USA / 1999
7 Poster for exhibition held on occasion of the 2001 Alliance Graphique Internationale (AGI) congress in Paris / AGI / France / 2001
8 Opening illustration for article on innovation, *Fortune Small Business* magazine, April 2001 / Fortune / USA / 2000
9 Cover illustration, *The New York Times Book Review*, 10 September 2000 / The New York Times / USA / 2000
10 Illustration for campaign advertising the Parsons School of Design's continuing-education program / Parsons School of Design / USA / 1999

Christoph Niemann

New York

1 2 3 4

⑤ 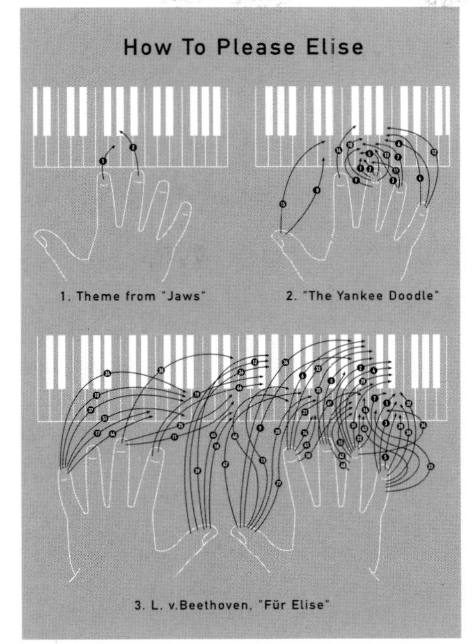
How To Please Elise
1. Theme from "Jaws"
2. "The Yankee Doodle"
3. L. v.Beethoven, "Für Elise"

⑥ 

⑦ 

⑧ 

⑨ 

⑩ 
Reconnect

11

12

13

14

11–12 Cover Illustrations, *The New Yorker* magazine, "Style Japan" issue, 18 March 2002 and "Independence Day" issue, 9 July 2001 / The New Yorker / USA / 2001–2002
13 Illustration for "Worst Websites Ever," *Rethinking Design* journal, "Subculture" issue / Mohawk Paper / USA / 2000
14 Cover Illustration *The New Yorker* magazine, "Down and Out" issue, 7 October 2002 / The New Yorker / USA / 2002
15 Wine label created on occasion of an Alliance Graphique Internationale (AGI) conference in San Francisco / AGI / France / 2002
16 Cover illustration, *The Nation*, "Bush Goes Nuclear" issue, 1 April 2002 / The Nation / USA / 2002
17–18 Illustrations for *American Illustration 20* annual / Amilus Inc. / USA / 2001

Christoph Niemann

15

16

17

18

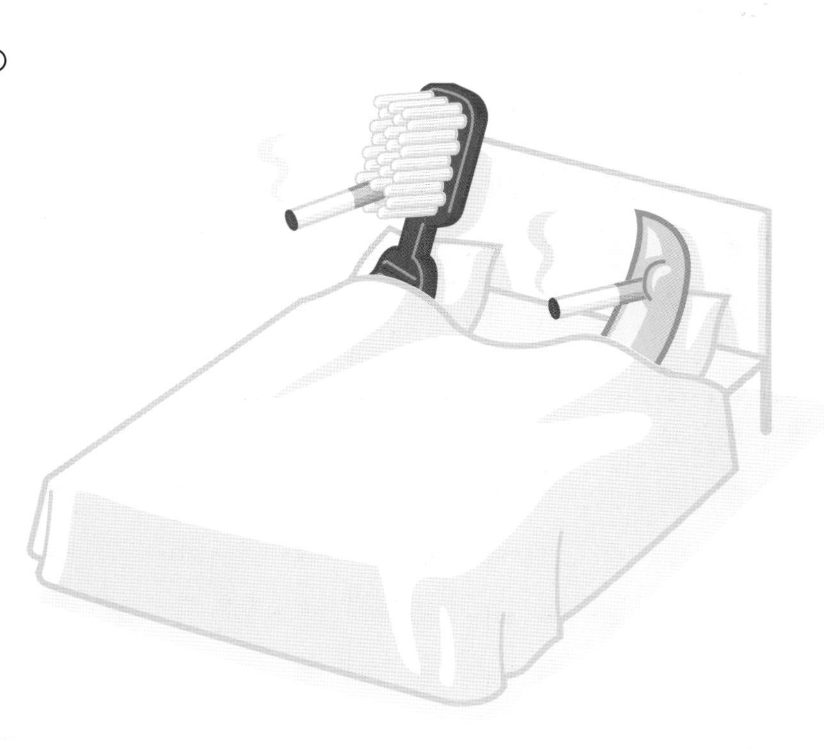

Nagi Noda is arguably the brightest new design star on the Tokyo design scene. In her late twenties, she is sparkling and funny and quirky, just like her work. • • Noda is able to mix small cultural projects with huge advertising campaigns. All the more surprising is that the large projects remain as quirky as the small stuff—a rarity in a world where the usual rule is, "The more money involved the blander the outcome." • • Her "I'm a Kaugirl" campaign for the Tokyo department store Laforet is built not only on a sweet wordplay (the Japanese word *Kau* means "shopping"), but also features a cowgirl twirling her three-meter braided lock of hair like a lasso. The whole scene is surrounded by beautifully braided custom typography. • • Her stylistic scope is remarkable: From the expert art direction of a Nike swimwear campaign (when was the last time you saw sports visualized in a truly original way while still showing hero shots of the product?) to her polka-dotted-Christmas-tree-Mexican-wrestler masks or the most elegant, heartfelt, hand-drawn typography on the Spring 2001 campaign for Laforet, she seems to get even the most outrageous formal compositions just right. How can you not like the typography entirely made out of sperm she created for the Sperm Palace project? • • Noda mixes her own idiosyncratic illustration with an idiosyncratic logo design into a remarkable program for Colorbar. And her Shungiku Uchida books featuring abundances of braided bookmarks leave me with only one wish: that I had thought of them myself. • • Stefan Sagmeister • •

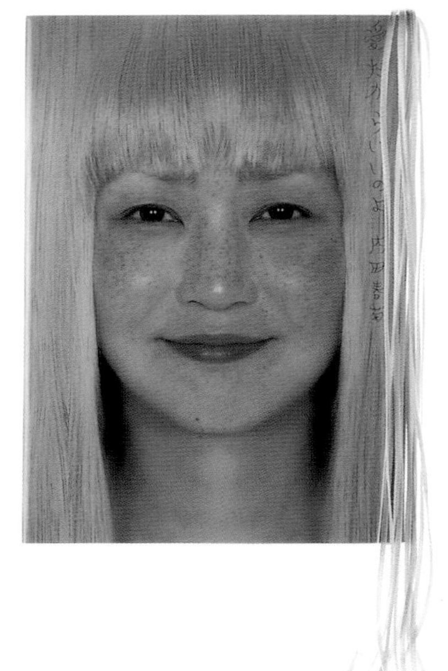

1

2 3

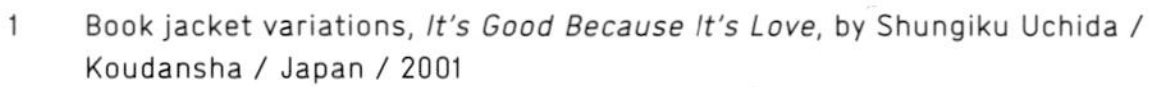

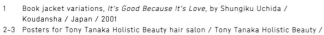

1 Book jacket variations, *It's Good Because It's Love*, by Shungiku Uchida / Koudansha / Japan / 2001
2–3 Posters for Tony Tanaka Holistic Beauty hair salon / Tony Tanaka Holistic Beauty / Japan / 2000
4 Poster for Japanese department store Laforet's spring season 2001 / Laforet Harajuku / Japan / 2001
5–6 Poster and packaging design for Colorbar beauty products / Colorbar / Japan / 2000

Nagi Noda

Tokyo

④

⑤

NEW OPEN!
hair face nail
COLORBAR

⑥

hairsoap
facecare milk
cleansing oil
lip gloss
mascara
mascara

The woman
with physical strength.
The way a beautiful woman
is seen seems to be changing.
Introducing, Nike swimwear.

The woman
with healthy appetite.
The way a beautiful woman
is seen seems to be changing.
Introducing, Nike swimwear.

7

The woman with vitality.
The way a beautiful woman
is seen seems to be changing.
Introducing, Nike swimwear.

The woman
whos not skinny.
The way a beautiful woman
is seen seems to be changing.
Introducing, Nike swimwear.

7 Poster series for Nike Japan's women's swimwear campaign / Nike / Japan / 2001
8 Poster for Japanese fashion brand Theatre PRODUCTS' opening fashion show / Theatre PRODUCTS / Japan / 2002
9–10 Poster series "I'm a Kaugirl" for Japanese department store Laforet's Autumn season 2001 / Laforet Harajuku / Japan / 2001
11 Poster for Japanese fashion department store Laforet's Christmas season 2001 / Laforet Harajuku / Japan / 2001

8

I'm 買うガール
LAFORET
AUTUMN

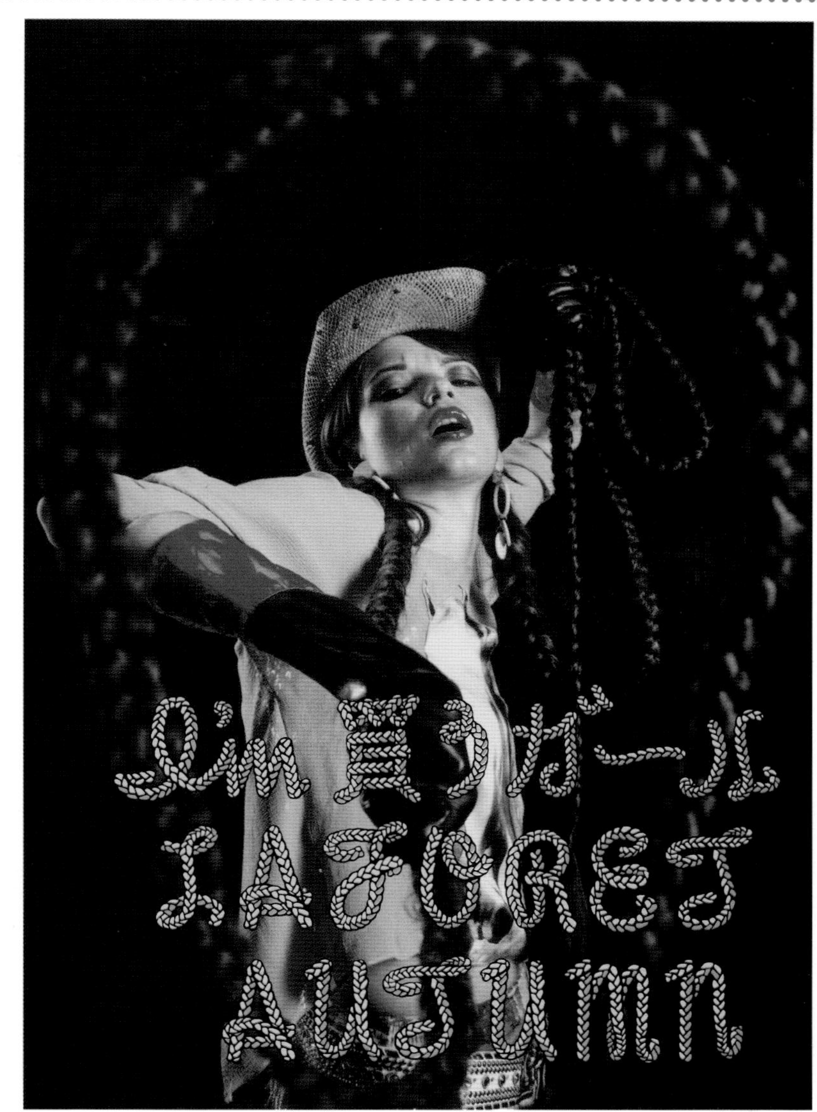
I'm 買うガール
LAFORET
AUTUMN

9 10

11

MERRY X'mask. LAFORET.

The work of the Swiss designers Dimitri Bruni and Manuel Krebs is definitely not "in the norm" as their studio name might make one think. Coming from a sound Swiss education with maximum respect for the days of Joseph Müller-Brockmann, they claim that the importance of structure, hierarchy, and readability is unquestionable but also that graphic design of the present cannot replicate that of the past. • •Their intentions are diverse and go from crystal-goblet information design to irritating, confusing, subversive, and mischievous speculation, depending on the nature of the effort. But whether it's public service work for an airport signage program or a self-initiated research project, their concern never focuses on formal matters like the mere choice of a typeface or specific image treatment. It will rather be toward a distinctive conceptual approach where visual clarity and attention to detail are fundamental ingredients. Never unifying, constantly diversifying. • •Norm started with *Introduction*, a specific research project but mainly a quest for freedom from the mainstream design they had done at the firms they worked for at the beginning of their careers. They craved a conceptual domain of their own where they could escape the conventional art-director-over-designer concept and finally set their own "norms." Being able to define the rules as they feel necessary gives them the liberty and power to play and (why not?) break the rules as they please. • •The recent prize-winning book *The Things* was written, designed, and published by Norm. It defines an eye-punching, mind-blowing visual analysis not only for the Latin alphabet but also for universal, everyday, three-dimensional objects. This project demonstrates how a system can be pushed very far and make solution finding automatic, doubtless, and surprising at the same time. It can become an operational mode capable of ironing out the decision-making process and possible errors. "The more restrictions we have," Norm tells us, "the happier we are." • •Omar Vulpinari • •

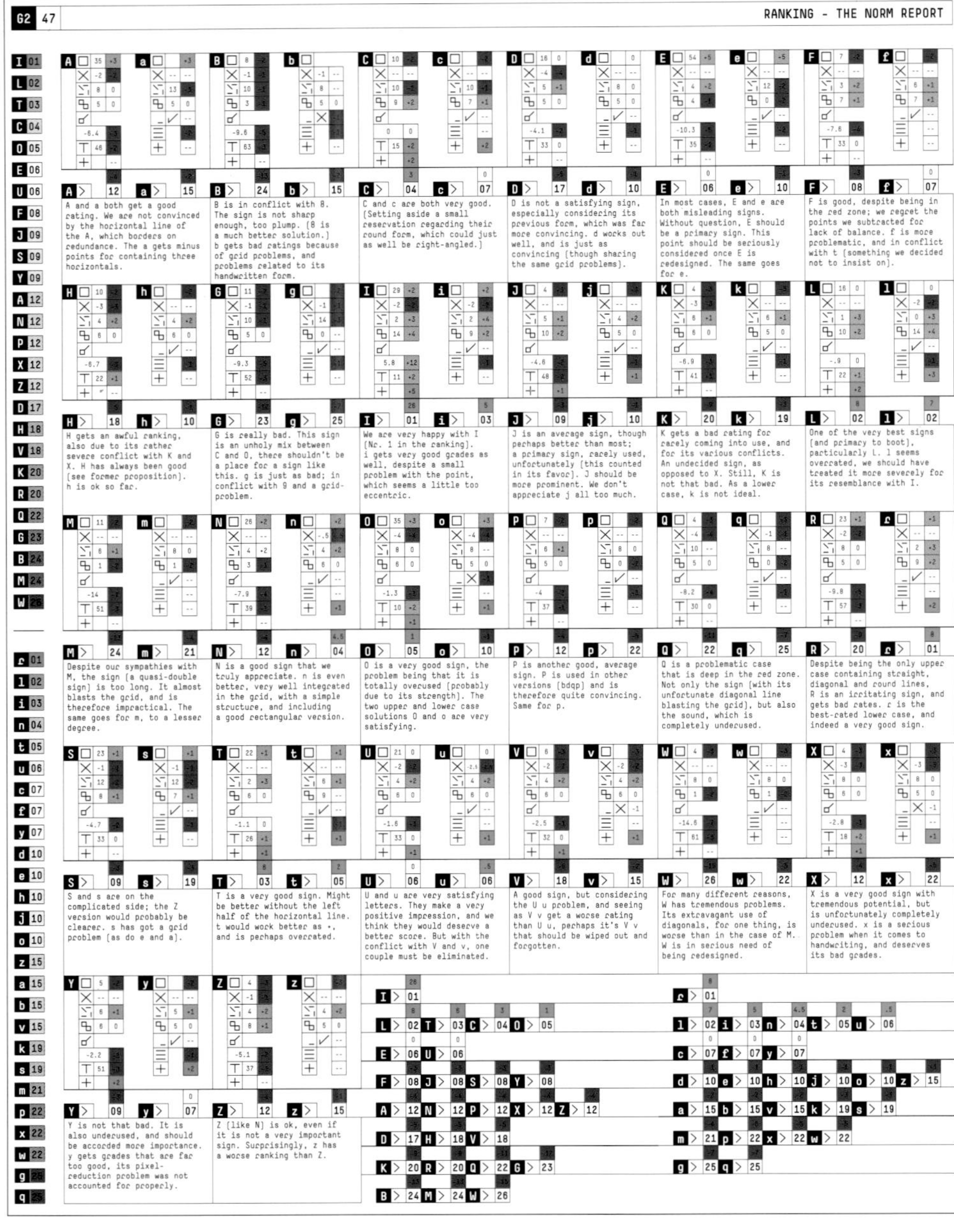
G2 47 RANKING - THE NORM REPORT

A and a both get a good rating. We are not convinced by the horizontal line of the A, which borders on redundance. The a gets minus points for containing three horizontals.

B is in conflict with 8. The sign is not sharp enough, too plump. (8 is a much better solution.) b gets bad ratings because of grid problems, and problems related to its handwritten form.

C and c are both very good. (Setting aside a small reservation regarding their round form, which could just as well be right-angled.)

D is not a satisfying sign, especially considering its previous form, which was far more convincing. d works out well, and is just as convincing (though sharing the same grid problems).

In most cases, E and e are both misleading signs. Without question, E should be a primary sign. This point should be seriously considered once E is redesigned. The same goes for e.

F is good, despite being in the red zone; we regret the points we subtracted for lack of balance. f is more problematic, and in conflict with t (something we decided not to insist on).

H gets an awful ranking, also due to its rather severe conflict with K and X. H has always been good (see former proposition). h is ok so far.

G is really bad. This sign is an unholy mix between C and O, there shouldn't be a place for a sign like this. g is just as bad; in conflict with 9 and a grid-problem.

We are very happy with I (Nr. 1 in the ranking). i gets very good grades as well, despite a small problem with the point, which seems a little too eccentric.

J is an average sign, though perhaps better than most; a primary sign, rarely used, unfortunately (this counted in its favor). J should be more prominent. We don't appreciate j all too much.

K gets a bad rating for rarely coming into use, and for its various conflicts. An undecided sign, as opposed to X. Still, K is not that bad. As a lower case, k is not ideal.

One of the very best signs (and primary to boot), particularly L. l seems overrated, we should have treated it more severely for its resemblance with I.

Despite our sympathies with M, the sign (a quasi-double sign) is too long. It almost blasts the grid, and is therefore impractical. The same goes for m, to a lesser degree.

N is a good sign that we truly appreciate. n is even better, very well integrated in the grid, with a simple structure, and including a good rectangular version.

O is a very good sign, the problem being that it is totally overused (probably due to its strength). The two upper and lower case solutions O and o are very satisfying.

P is another good, average sign. P is used in other versions (bdqp) and is therefore quite convincing. Same for p.

Q is a problematic case that is deep in the red zone. Not only the sign (with its unfortunate diagonal line blasting the grid), but also the sound, which is completely underused.

Despite being the only upper case containing straight, diagonal and round lines, R is an irritating sign, and gets bad rates. r is the best-rated lower case, and indeed a very good sign.

S and s are on the complicated side; the Z version would probably be clearer. s has got a grid problem (as do e and a).

T is a very good sign. Might be better without the left half of the horizontal line. t would work better as +, and is perhaps overrated.

U and u are very satisfying letters. They make a very positive impression, and we think they would deserve a better score. But with the conflict with V and v, one couple must be eliminated.

A good sign, but considering the U u problem, and seeing as V v get a worse rating than U u, perhaps it's V v that should be wiped out and forgotten.

For many different reasons, W has tremendous problems. Its extravagant use of diagonals, for one thing, is worse than in the case of M. W is in serious need of being redesigned.

X is a very good sign with tremendous potential, but is unfortunately completely underused. x is a serious problem when it comes to handwriting, and deserves its bad grades.

Y is not that bad. It is also underused, and should be accorded more importance. y gets grades that are far too good, its pixel-reduction problem was not accounted for properly.

Z (like N) is ok, even if it is not a very important sign. Surprisingly, z has a worse ranking than Z.

1–5 Pages from *The Things*, by Norm / Norm Publishers / Switzerland / 2002 / Pages taken from the "*Kritik*" part of the book, which analyzes and reviews the letters of the Latin alphabet.

Norm

Zurich

2

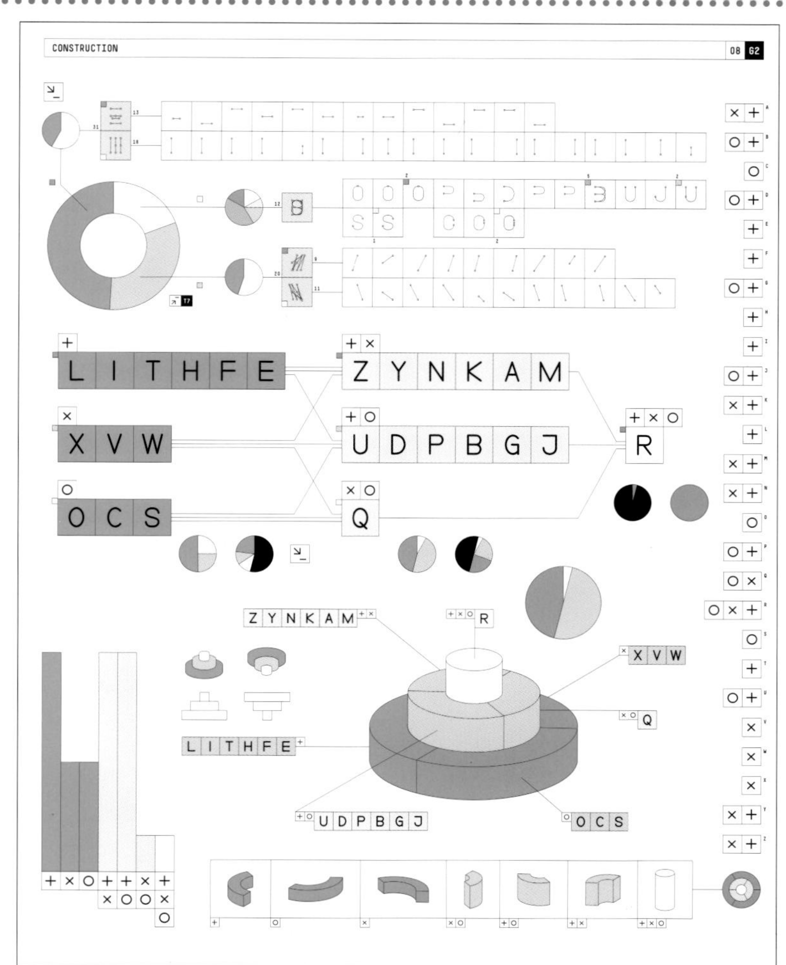

CONSTRUCTION 08 G2
LITHFE
ZYNKAM
XVW
UDPBGJ
R
OCS
Q

3

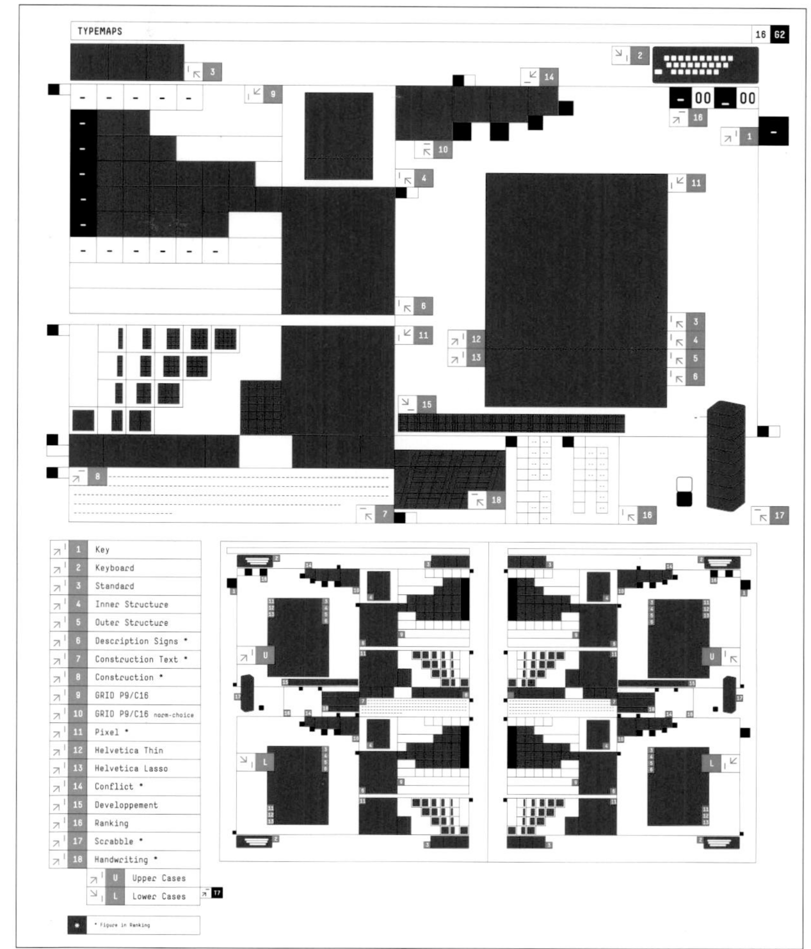

TYPEMAPS 16 G2
1 Key
2 Keyboard
3 Standard
4 Inner Structure
5 Outer Structure
6 Description Signs *
7 Construction Text *
8 Construction *
9 GRID P9/C16
10 GRID P9/C16 more-choice
11 Pixel *
12 Helvetica Thin
13 Helvetica Lasso
14 Conflict *
15 Developpement
16 Ranking
17 Scrabble *
18 Handwriting *
U Upper Cases
L Lower Cases
* Figure in Ranking

4

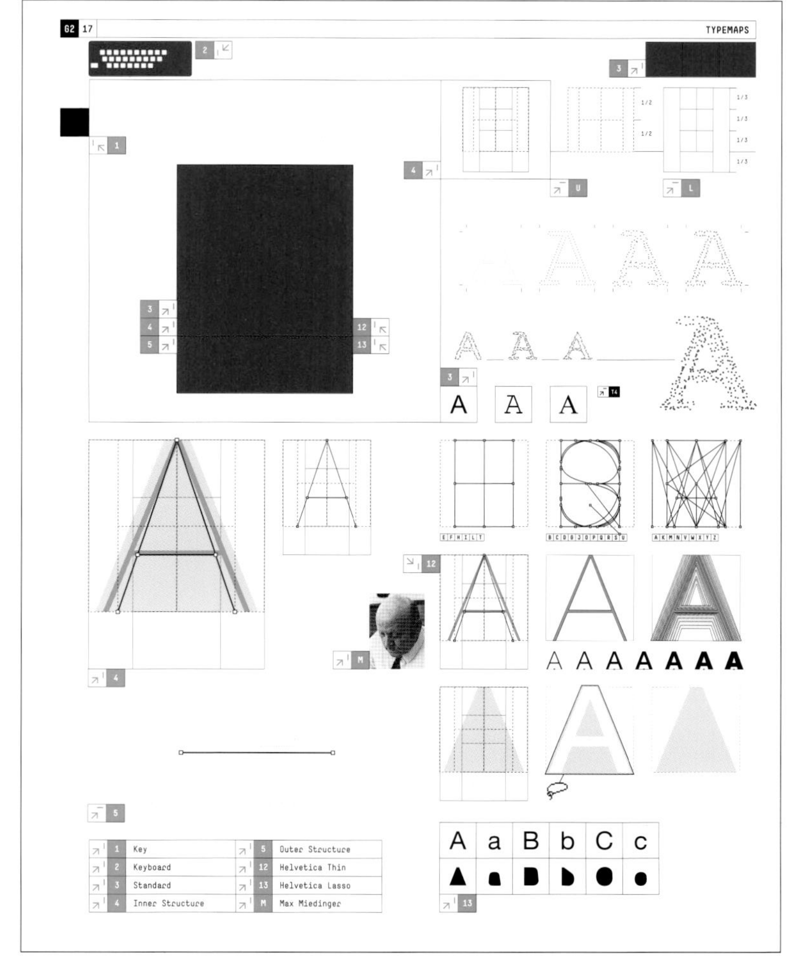

G2 17 TYPEMAPS
A A A
1 Key
2 Keyboard
3 Standard
4 Inner Structure
5 Outer Structure
12 Helvetica Thin
13 Helvetica Lasso
M Max Miedinger
A a B b C c

5

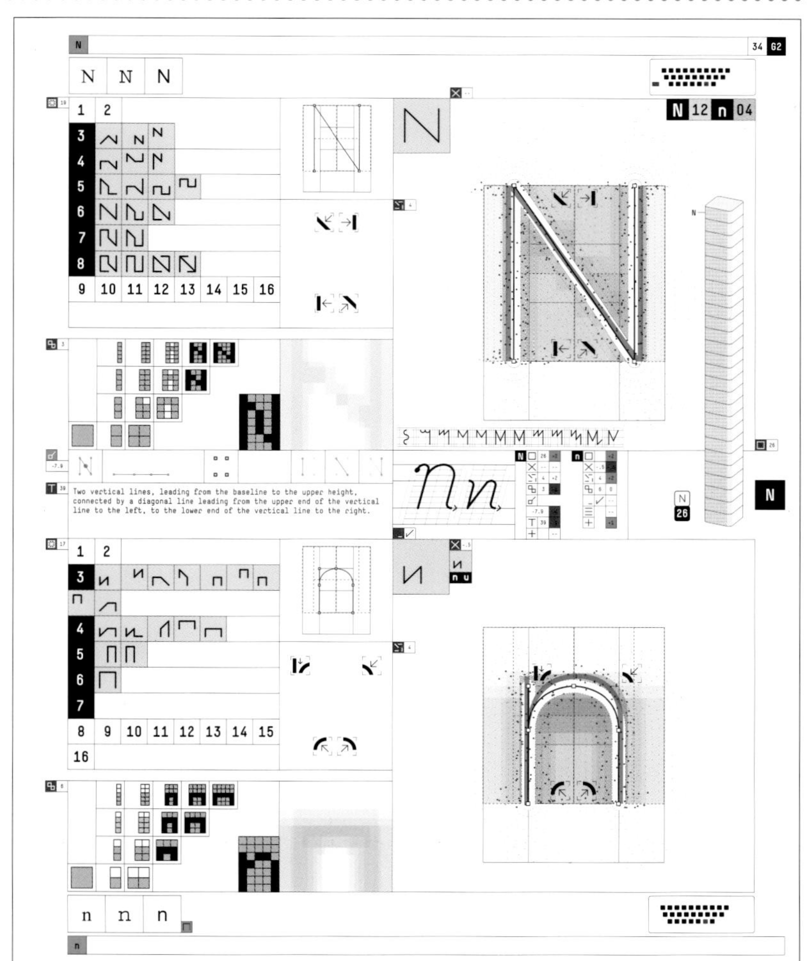

N 34 G2
N N N
N 12 n 04
Two vertical lines, leading from the baseline to the upper height, connected by a diagonal line leading from the upper end of the vertical line to the left, to the lower end of the vertical line to the right.
n n n

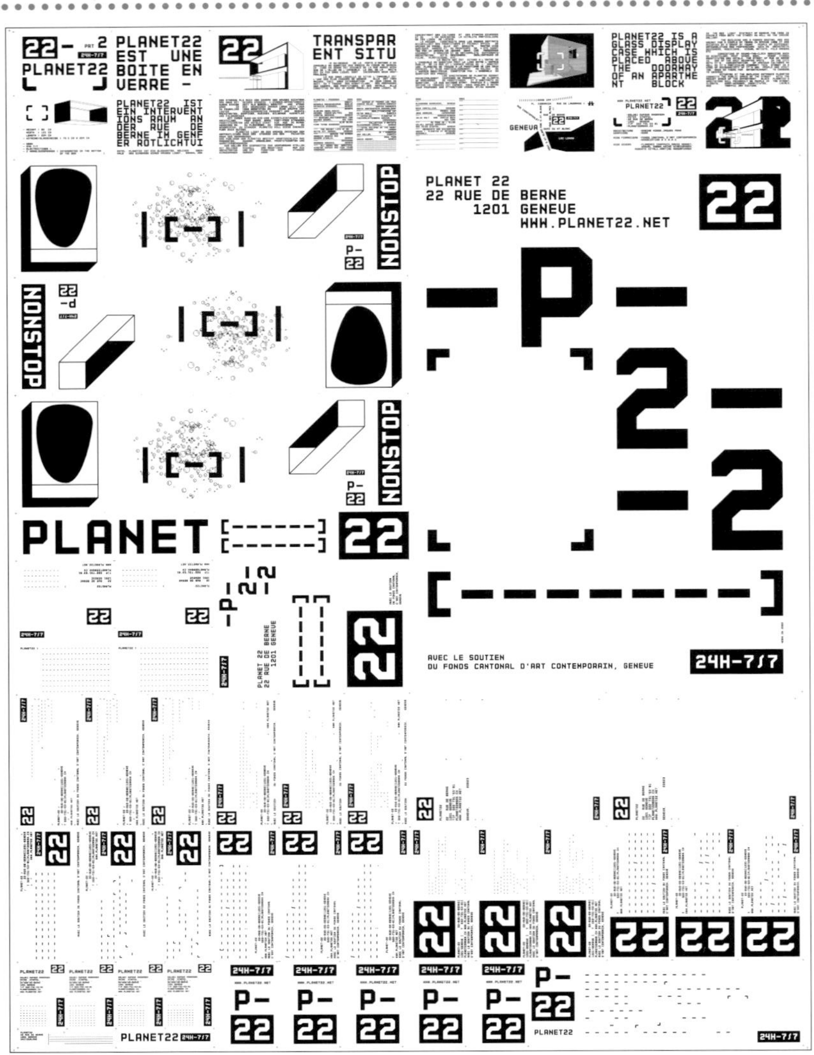

6

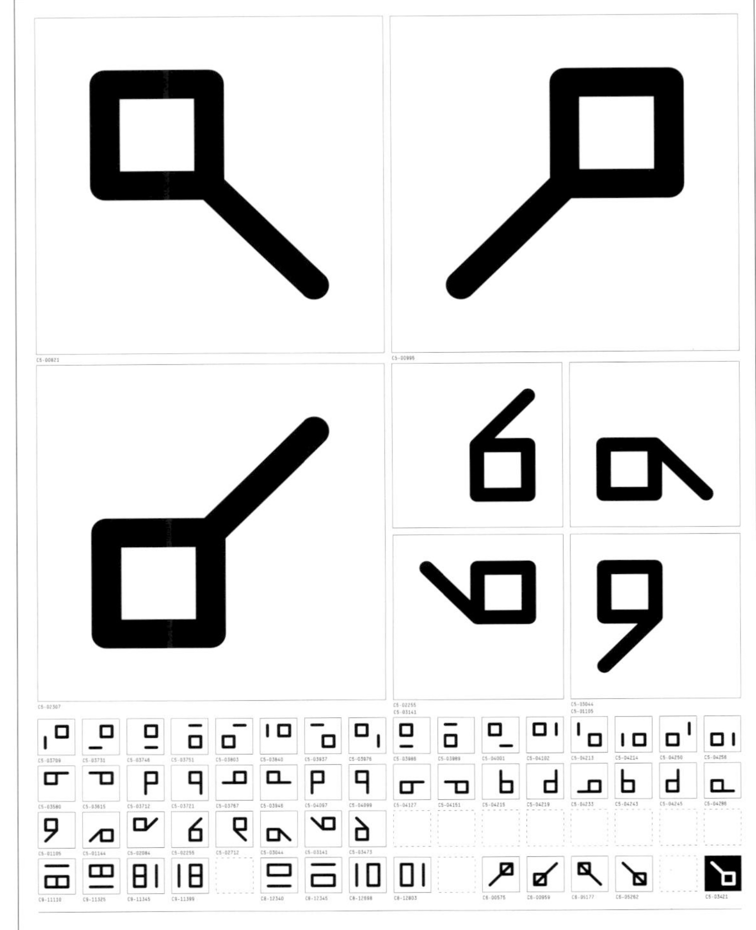

7

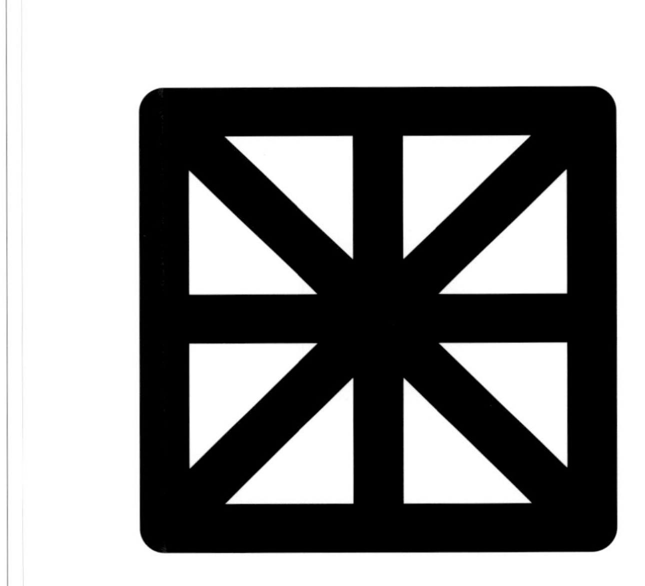

8

6 Poster for contemporary-art gallery Planet 22, Geneva / Planet 22 / Switzerland / 2002 / The poster can be divided up to create various smaller posters, flyers, and business cards.

7–8 Pages from *The Things*, by Norm / Norm Publishers / 2002 / After the analysis of the Latin alphabet, this part of the book presents collections of newly generated signs with high "letter" potential. The last sign has sixteen connections.

9 Poster for *Transmission02: Utopia* exhibition and publication / :phunk / Singapore / 2002

Norm

9

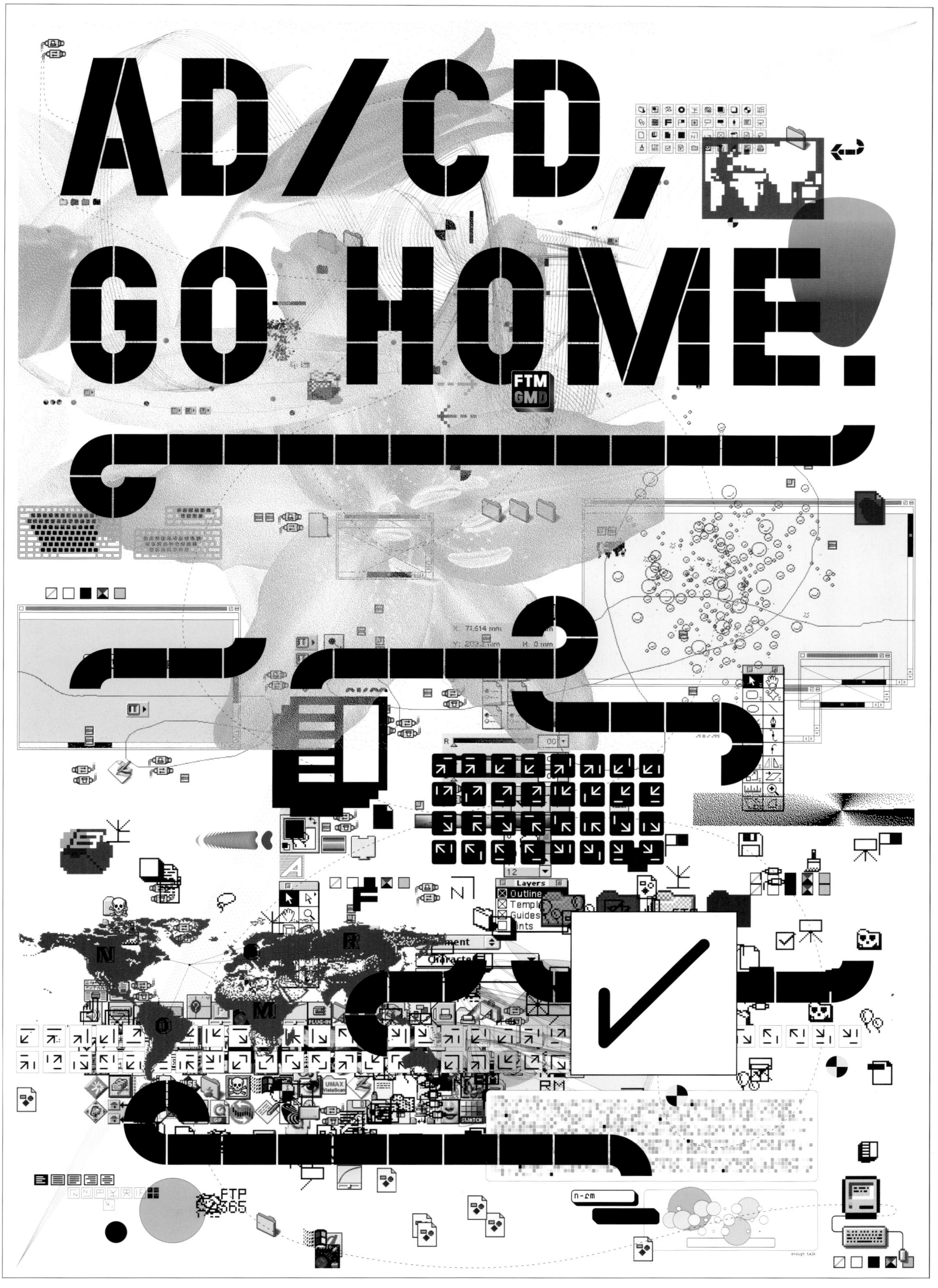

When at the end of the twentieth century Philip Teufel stumbled upon my former students Petra Knyrim and Stefan Nowak at the University of Applied Arts in Düsseldorf, I was already long gone and teaching at the university in Wupperthal. Teufel was the successor chosen to fill my empty chair in Düsseldorf. Within the design scene, this new Bermuda Triangle of communication—named Nowakteufelknyrim—soon became known for its exceptionally original concepts and creations for museums and exhibitions. I particularly remember the publicity material for an open house by Düsseldorf artists, as it stood out from the overload of bad information about cultural institutions. It was a blue folder full of white dots. Later I discovered the corresponding poster. Each dot represented an artist on the map of Düsseldorf, finely calculated and placed with cartographic and typographic precision.•• By now there is hardly a museum along the banks of the Rhine for which Nowakteufelknyrim has not designed a comprehensive exhibition and developed the communication materials. They also conceive special orientation systems. For the city of Dresden they created cultural maps and guides that use the pavement surface as informational space—a project that was immediately honored with the Josef Binder Award. And to finally come into some money without further detours, they designed a money museum and information center for the Deutsche Bundesbank.•• Equally notable and artful is their publication dedicated to their field of work: Entitled *Einszueines. Positionen zum Austellen* (One to One. Positions on Exhibiting), it is hard to make better publicity for oneself.•• The work that is shown here represents only a fraction of Nowakteufelknyrim's complex output. Their systematic approach, their deep understanding of the topic at hand and its graphic and typographic interpretation, cannot be displayed so succinctly. Therefore, there is only one solution: you must go to the next exhibition that Nowakteufelknyrim superbly conceives and designs—or at least order the catalogue! ••Uwe Loesch••

1 Poster for *Kunstpunkte* (Art Points) open-house event in which four hundred artists opened the doors of their ateliers to the public / Kulturamt Düsseldorf / Germany / 2000

2 Adhesive Flyers for *Miss.You.* exhibition featuring the works of eighteen female artists / Museum für Neue Kunst Freiburg / Germany / 2002

3–5 Spread from exhibition guide, train design (unrealized), and ground orientation guides for exhibition *Continental Shift* / Ludwig Forum Aachen, Bonnefantenmuseum Maastricht, Musée d'Art Moderne Liege, Stadsgalerij Heerlen / Germany, Netherlands, Belgium / 2000 / The exhibition focused on artists who came from other continents to work and live in Europe. It was shown at four museums in three different countries.

6–8 Posters for exhibition *Continental Shift* / 2000

Nowakteufelknyrim

Düsseldorf

1

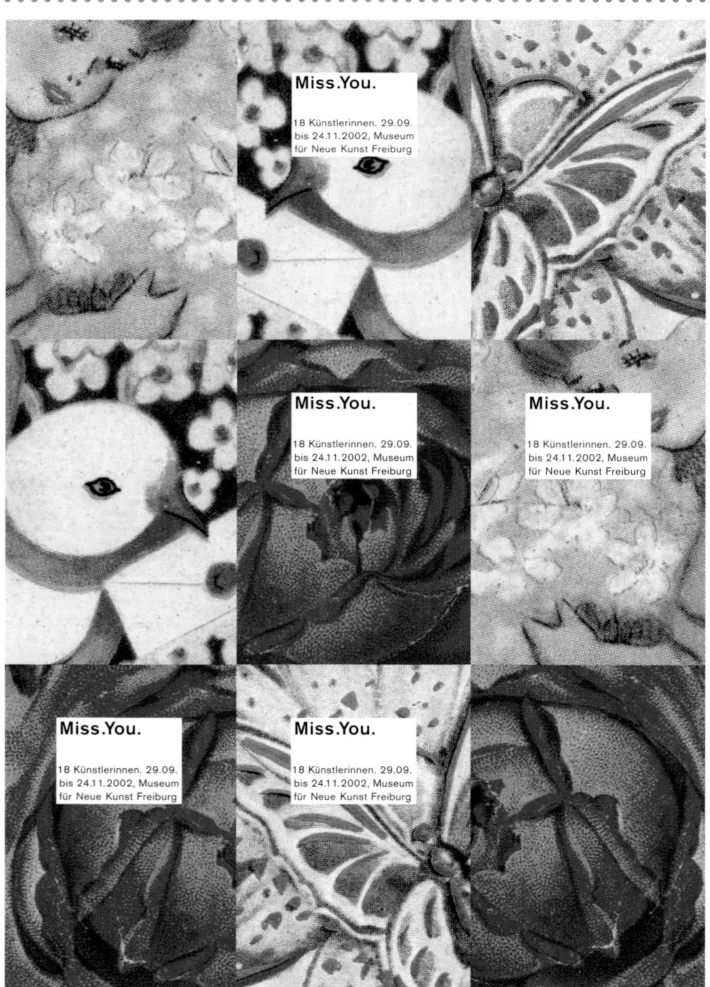

2

INHALT / INHOUD / TABLE ➽

AACHEN

AKASHI

CONTINENTAL SHIFT / 21 05–10 09 2000 / Ludwig Forum AACHEN / Eine Reise zwischen den Kulturen / JAPAN / KOREA / An Exhibition of Contemporary Art

Ludwig Forum AACHEN / Jülicher Straße 97–109 / D 52070 Aachen / Information +49 (0) 241 1807 0 / www.continentalshift.org / Design: grafikbüro / DANKE ➽

3
4
5

6
7
8

CONTINENTAL SHIFT 21 05 – 10 09 2000

A voyage between cultures / AACHEN / MAASTRICHT / HEERLEN / LIÈGE / An Exhibition of Contemporary Art

Eine Reise zwischen den Kulturen / Een reis tussen culturen / Un voyage entre les cultures / Ludwig Forum AACHEN / Bonnefantenmuseum MAASTRICHT / Stadsgalerij HEERLEN / Musée d'Art moderne LIÈGE / Information +49 (0) 241 1807 0 / www.continentalshift.org / Design: grafikbüro / DANKE ➽

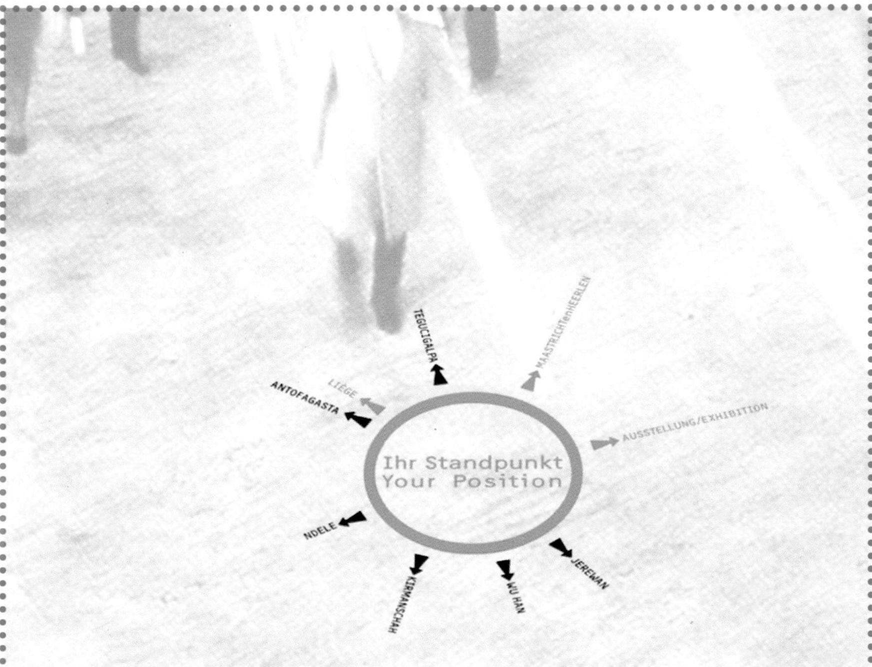

AACHEN

AZUL

CONTINENTAL SHIFT / 21 05–10 09 2000 / Ludwig Forum AACHEN / Eine Reise zwischen den Kulturen / LATEINAMERIKA / An Exhibition of Contemporary Art

Ludwig Forum AACHEN / Jülicher Straße 97–109 / D 52070 Aachen / Information +49 (0) 241 1807 0 / www.continentalshift.org / Design: grafikbüro / DANKE ➽

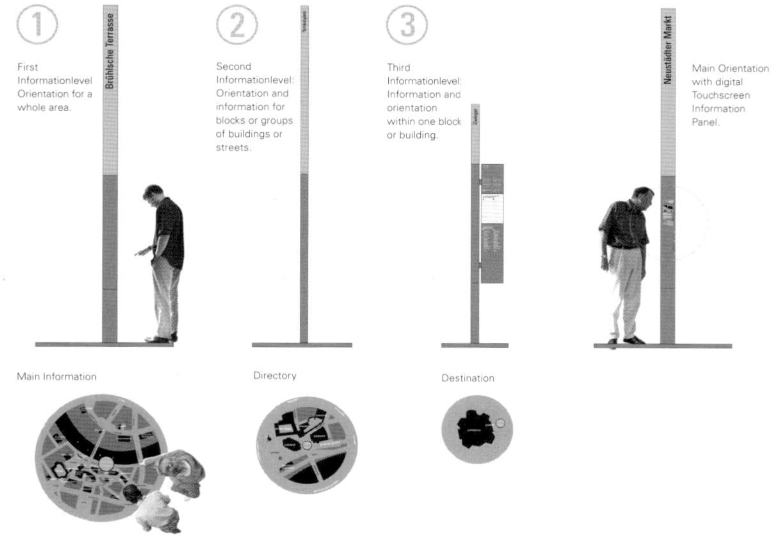

9 Pedestrian orientation system "Pylon" for the historic city-center of Dresden, Germany (unrealized) / Municipality of Dresden / Germany / 2001 / Three pylons are conceived to convey different specificity levels of orientational information. The pylons themselves also work on various levels, showing maps on the ground, written information in the middle, and the general location at the top.

10 Posters for different phases of *Totale 2000* exhibition / Museum für Neue Kunst Freiburg / Germany / 2000 / The exhibition showcased the museum's entire collection. Due to space limitations it was impossible to show all the works at once. Therefore, Nowakteufelknyrim conceived a system of hanging the artworks on top of each other. There were three layers, each representing a different period: 1900–40s, 1950s–1970s, and 1980s–1990s. One by one, at specific opening events, the layers were "peeled off."

Nowakteufelknyrim

TOTALE 01 02 03 5 Feb bis 7 Mai 00 27 Mai bis 10 Sep 00 30 Sep bis 31 Dez 00

Das Jahrhundert im Blick der Sammlung 00er 10er 20er 30er 40er Jahre 50er 60er 70er Jahre 80er 90er Jahre

Museum für Neue Kunst Freiburg Marienstrasse 10a www.mnk-freiburg.de/TOTALE

Städtische Museen Freiburg, Museum für Neue Kunst, Marienstrasse 10a, 79098 Freiburg, Tel 0761 2012581, Di bis So 10 bis 17 Uhr geöffnet. Einzelbesucher 8 DM, ermäßigt 5 DM, Dauerkarte 10 DM, Familienkarte 15 DM, Freier Eintritt für Mitglieder des Fördervereins und Besitzer des Oberrheinischen Museumspasses. Vielen Dank an Rhodia Acetow GmbH Freiburg, Partner des Museums für Neue Kunst. ©grafikbüro 2000

TOTALE 01 02 03 5 Feb bis 7 Mai 00 27 Mai bis 10 Sep 00 30 Sep bis 31 Dez 00

Das Jahrhundert im Blick der Sammlung 00er 10er 20er 30er 40er Jahre 50er 60er 70er Jahre 80er 90er Jahre

Museum für Neue Kunst Freiburg Marienstrasse 10a www.mnk-freiburg.de/TOTALE

Städtische Museen Freiburg, Museum für Neue Kunst, Marienstrasse 10a, 79098 Freiburg, Tel 0761 2012581, Di bis So 10 bis 17 Uhr geöffnet. Einzelbesucher 8 DM, ermäßigt 5 DM, Dauerkarte 10 DM, Familienkarte 15 DM, Freier Eintritt für Mitglieder des Fördervereins und Besitzer des Oberrheinischen Museumspasses. Vielen Dank an Rhodia Acetow GmbH Freiburg, Partner des Museums für Neue Kunst. ©grafikbüro 2000

10

TOTALE 01 02 03 5 Feb bis 7 Mai 00 27 Mai bis 10 Sep 00 30 Sep bis 31 Dez 00

Das Jahrhundert im Blick der Sammlung 00er 10er 20er 30er 40er Jahre 50er 60er 70er Jahre 80er 90er Jahre

Museum für Neue Kunst Freiburg Marienstrasse 10a www.mnk-freiburg.de/TOTALE

Städtische Museen Freiburg, Museum für Neue Kunst, Marienstrasse 10a, 79098 Freiburg, Tel 0761 2012581, Di bis So 10 bis 17 Uhr geöffnet. Einzelbesucher 8 DM, ermäßigt 5 DM, Dauerkarte 10 DM, Familienkarte 15 DM, Freier Eintritt für Mitglieder des Fördervereins und Besitzer des Oberrheinischen Museumspasses. Vielen Dank an Rhodia Acetow GmbH Freiburg, Partner des Museums für Neue Kunst. ©grafikbüro 2000

TOTALE 01 02 03 5 Feb bis 7 Mai 00 27 Mai bis 10 Sep 00 30 Sep bis 31 Dez 00

Das Jahrhundert im Blick der Sammlung 00er 10er 20er 30er 40er Jahre 50er 60er 70er Jahre 80er 90er Jahre

Museum für Neue Kunst Freiburg Marienstrasse 10a www.mnk-freiburg.de/TOTALE

Städtische Museen Freiburg, Museum für Neue Kunst, Marienstrasse 10a, 79098 Freiburg, Tel 0761 2012581, Di bis So 10 bis 17 Uhr geöffnet. Einzelbesucher 8 DM, ermäßigt 5 DM, Dauerkarte 10 DM, Familienkarte 15 DM, Freier Eintritt für Mitglieder des Fördervereins und Besitzer des Oberrheinischen Museumspasses. Vielen Dank an Rhodia Acetow GmbH Freiburg, Partner des Museums für Neue Kunst. ©grafikbüro 2000

Fabio Ongarato belongs to the emerging generation of designers from Down Under. As with so many of his predecessors, what really drives him is a passion for design. His work reflects a love of and belief in the power of contemporary photography and architecture. It is not difficult to detect the influence of Op Art and Kinetic Art. He is one of the new true collaborators, seeking input from those around him and remaining open to comment and new views that might influence the direction of the work. Through thoughtful and incisive art direction he eliminates the unnecessary. All that remains is that part of the communication that genuinely sends the message. Never losing sight of the content or the idea is essential. Analyzing the brief in search of the single idea is natural to his method. While he is very process-driven, there is an undeniable spark of intuition, a sensitivity to creative subtlety that invades his work. He speaks enthusiastically of a passion for the craft of design and the beauty of the printed medium. It is also evident that his work allows him to explore the alternative disciplines of design. The willingness to cross boundaries is innate.••Like so many designers in this publication, Ongarato is much honored locally and internationally. Most notable among his acclamations is his ISTD London award for the *Lineage* project and exhibition dedicated to the work of architect Daniel Libeskind. Ongarato's company, Fabio Ongarato Design, is based in Melbourne, Australia. Despite the geographic isolation, I am sure the impact of his work will be felt on more distant continents. ••Ken Cato••

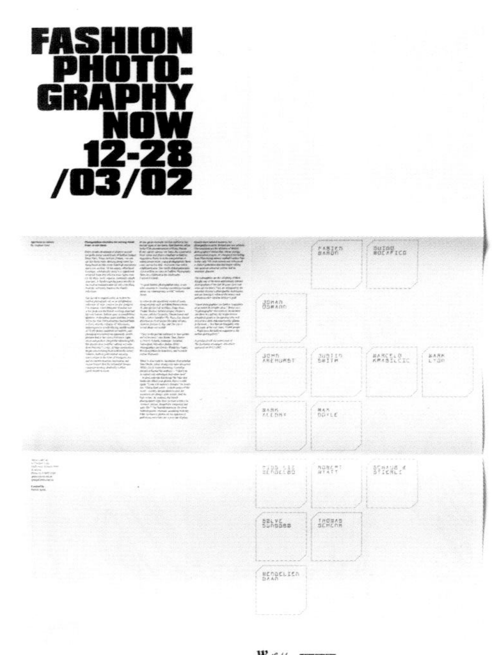

1–2

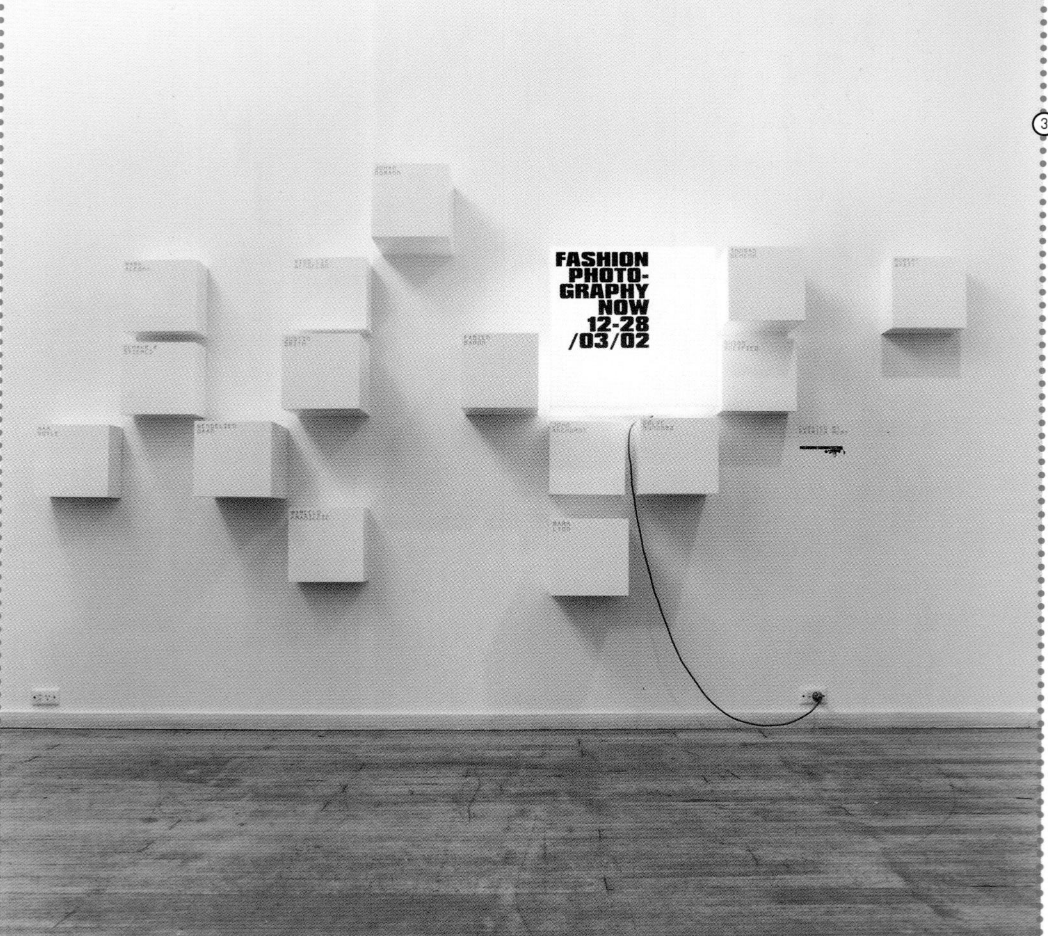

3

1–2 Front and back of foldout poster for *Fashion Photography Now* exhibition (photography Sølve Sunsbo) / Melbourne Fashion Festival / Australia / 2002
3 Signage for *Fashion Photography Now* exhibition / 2002
4 Poster for the Melbourne Art Fair 2002 / Melbourne Art Fair / Australia / 2002
5 Poster for the BMW Festival of German Cinema in Melbourne and Sydney / Goethe Institute / Australia / 2002
6 Cover, *Big Magazine* no. 44, "Australian issue" / Big Magazine / USA / 2002
7 Poster/corporate identity for architectural firm Elenberg Fraser / Elenberg Fraser / Australia / 2001

Fabio Ongarato

Melbourne

4

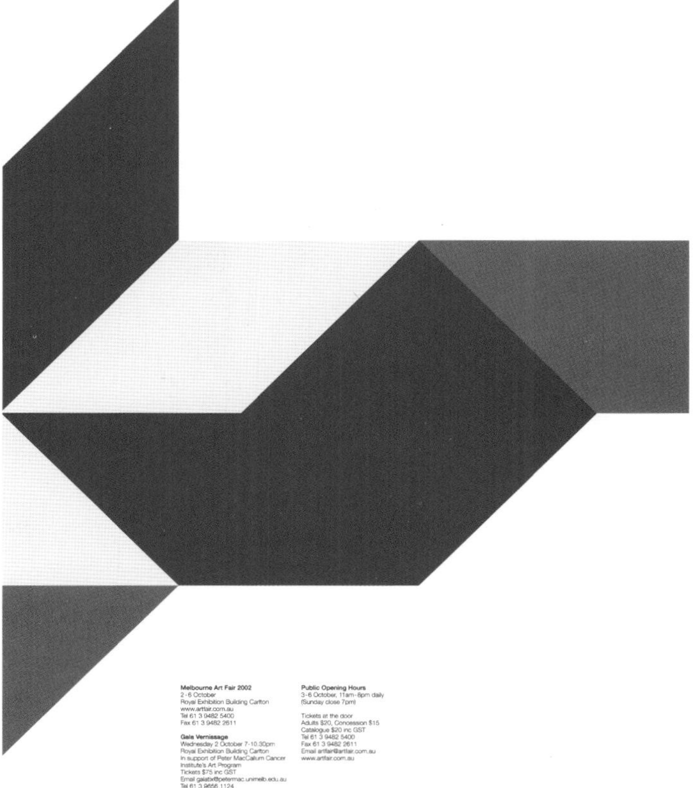
MELBOURNEARTFAIR2002
2-6 OCTOBER
Melbourne Art Fair 2002
2-6 October
Royal Exhibition Building Carlton
www.artfair.com.au
Tel 61 3 9482 5400
Fax 61 3 9482 2611
Gala Vernissage
Wednesday 2 October 7-10.30pm
Royal Exhibition Building Carlton
In support of Peter MacCallum Cancer Institute's Art Program
Tickets $75 inc GST
Email galatix@petermac.unimelb.edu.au
Tel 61 3 9656 1124
Fax 61 3 9656 1444
Public Opening Hours
3-6 October, 11am-6pm daily
(Sunday close 7pm)
Tickets at the door
Adults $20, Concession $15
Catalogue $20 inc GST
Tel 61 3 9482 5400
Fax 61 3 9482 2611
Email artfair@artfair.com.au
www.artfair.com.au

5

BMW
FESTIVAL
OF GERMAN
CINEMA
2002
Melbourne
September 12-22
Palace Como
Sydney
September 13-24
Palace Verona

6

Big
AUSTRALIA
WWW.BIGMAGAZINE.COM
Printed in Spain
US$15 Canada $20
42
0 74470 64573 3

7

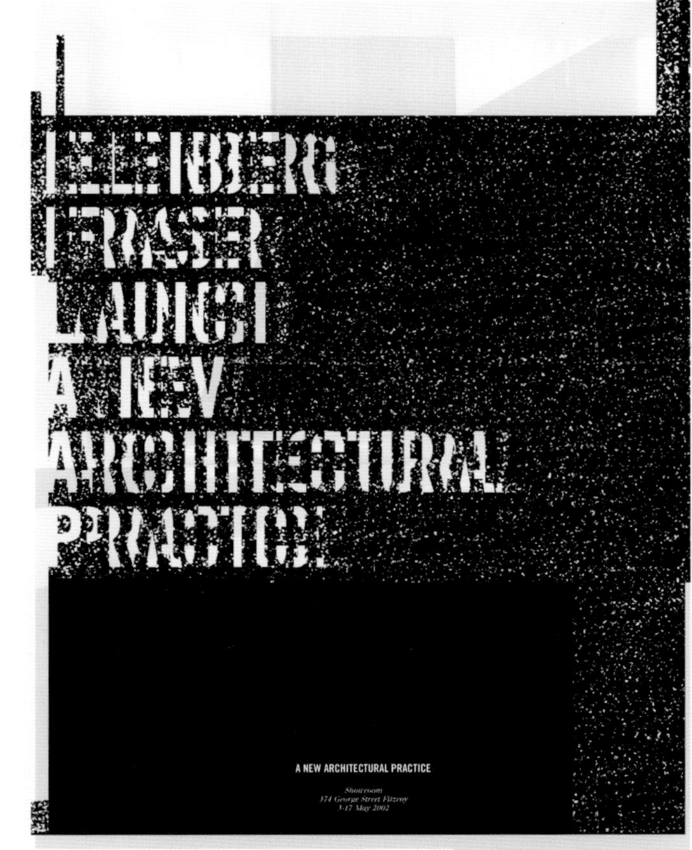
A NEW ARCHITECTURAL PRACTICE
Showroom
374 George Street Fitzroy
3-17 May 2002

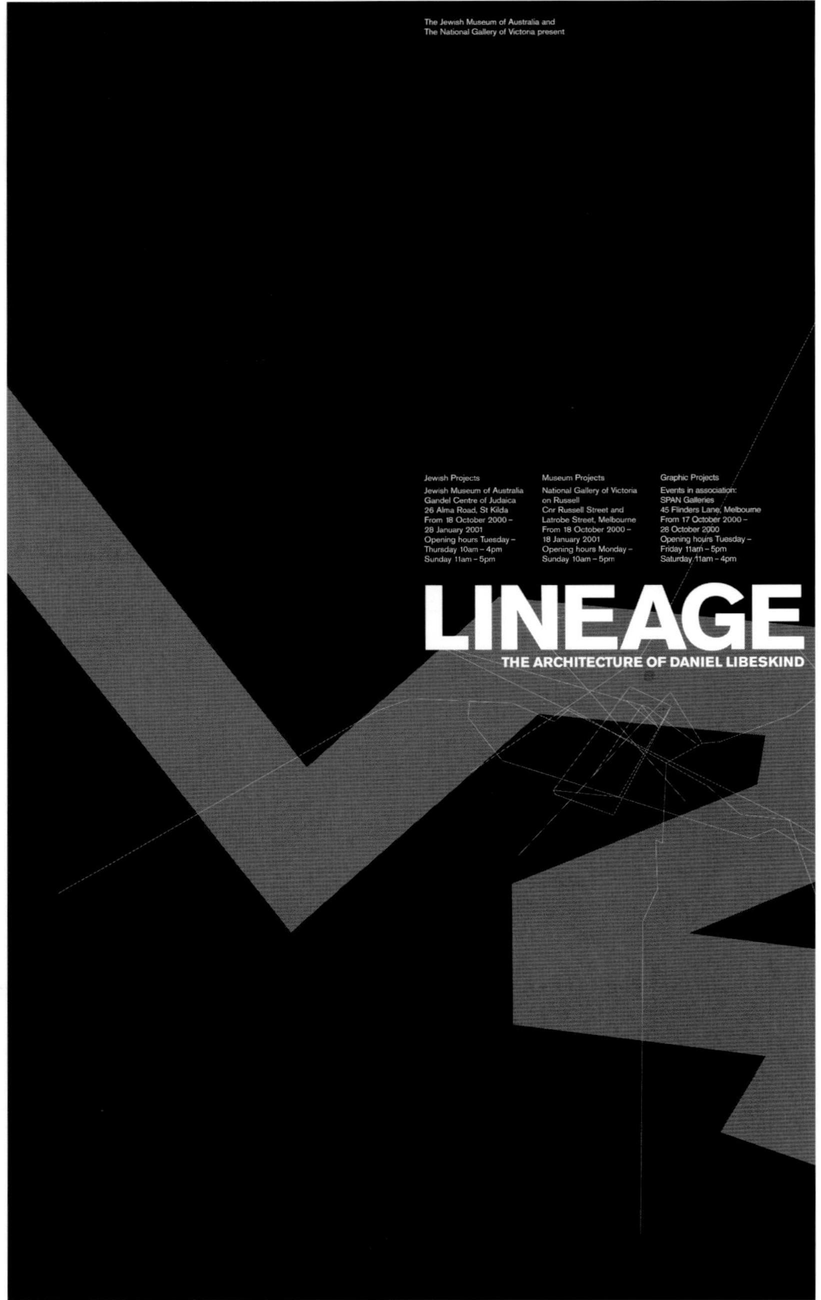

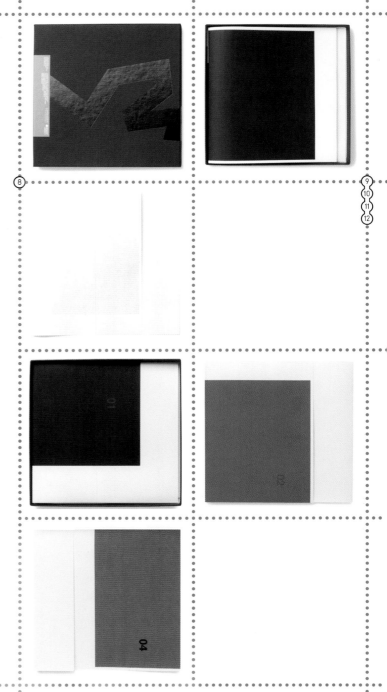

8

9
10
11
12

13

8 Poster for *Lineage: The Architecture of Daniel Libeskind* exhibition / Jewish Museum of Australia / Australia / 2000
9–12 Boxed-set exhibition catalogue with foldout posters, *Lineage: The Architecture of Daniel Libeskind* / 2000
13 Unfolded poster from exhibition catalogue *Lineage: The Architecture of Daniel Libeskind* / 2000
14–16 Book cover and spreads, *Red* / Australian Centre for Contemporary Art / Australia / 2001
17–19 Unfolded cover, spread with foldout, and individual pages from spring/summer catalogue of fashion designer Karen Walker / Karen Walker / New Zealand / 2001
20 Poster for Karen Walker Spring/Summer campaign / Karen Walker / New Zealand / 2001

Fabio Ongarato

17
18
19

14
15
16

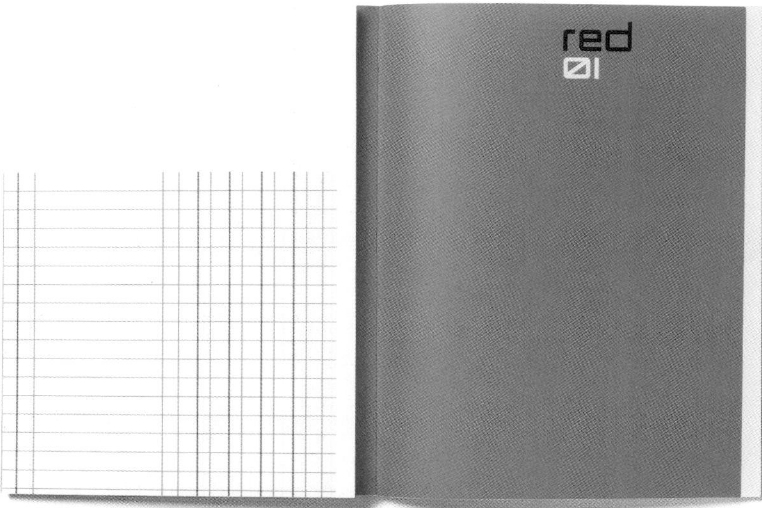

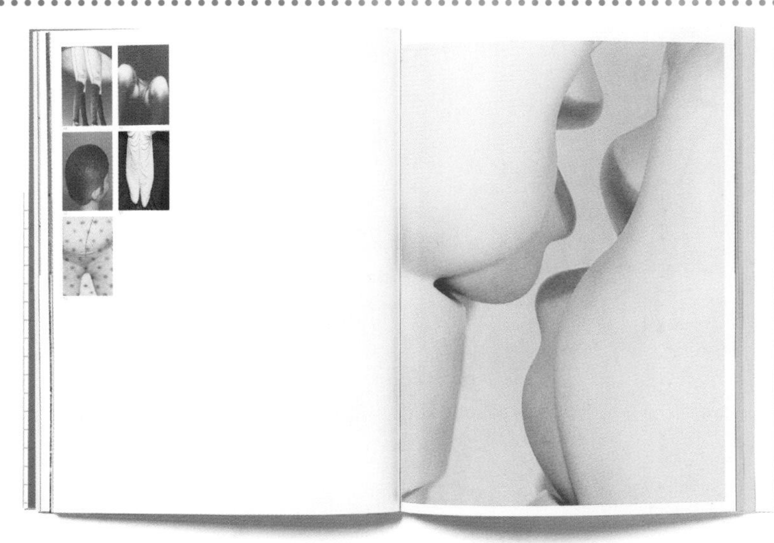

20

Switzerland is a special country for graphic design. It may seem that its moment in the sun came and went in the middle of a century now left in the past, when the Swiss school was synonymous with graphic design. But as the years go by and the world changes, what remains constant is that this small country continues to produce wonderful young talents.•• At the Moscow graphic design biennial Zolotaya Pchela (Golden Bee) I received a large series of silver-gray posters, covered with entrancing patterns, and I immediately noted this new name, Tania Prill, especially since it sounded so Russian. ••But Prill's posters are distinctly Swiss, even if at a brief glance they don't seem anything like the works of Müller-Brockmann or Armin Hofmann, or Ralph Shraivogel or Rudolph Lutz. Their origin is expressed not so much in the stylistic particularities and shapes of their composition, but in the special treatment of letters, lines, and text. I would call this approach typographical postulation, as if all the answers in this discipline were already provided by the Swiss themselves.•• The Swiss never seem to tire of marveling at the everyday miracle of a line connecting with a sheet of paper. For them, each time this union occurs is a question, and each time everything starts anew. Again and again, the text becomes a problem of composition and image. And typography, again and again, becomes the main hero of the poster. It is precisely this way in Prill's work.•• Moreover, her designs seem very fresh. The text creates a lush intellectual environment, a quivering, vibrating, living texture. Prill's lines fly and streams of information flow, forming the finest pulsating ether. Prill's posters and books are also permeated by the special charm of precise, careful work. They seem filled with a flickering light, quiet and warm.•• This delicate virtual ether, this environment, this light, this sound, this music delights me and seems extraordinarily pertinent to the developments in international design today.•• Serge Serov••

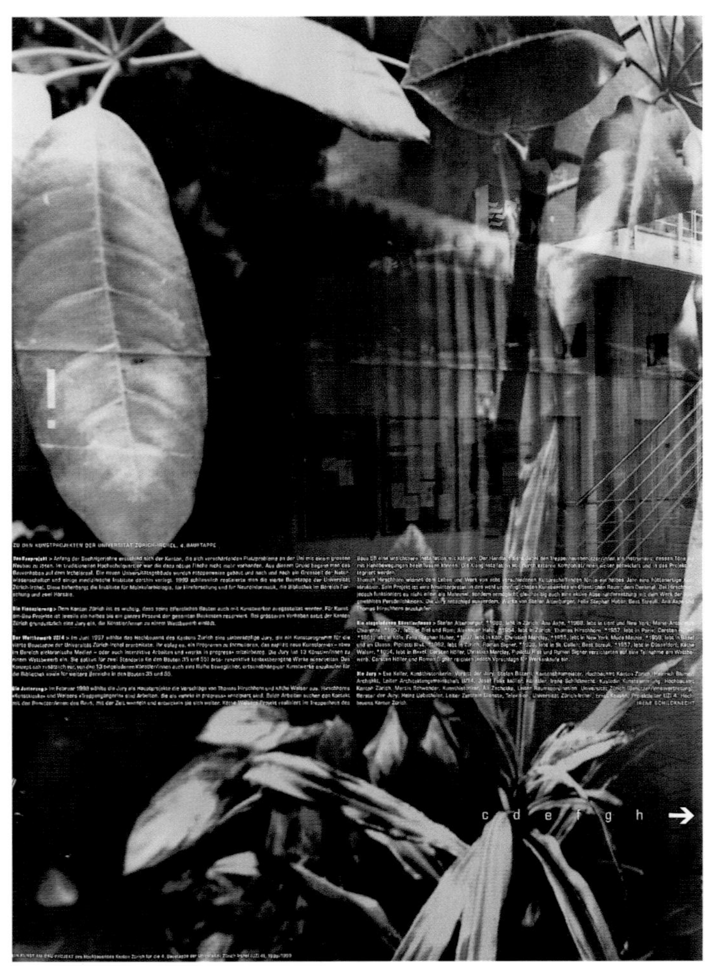

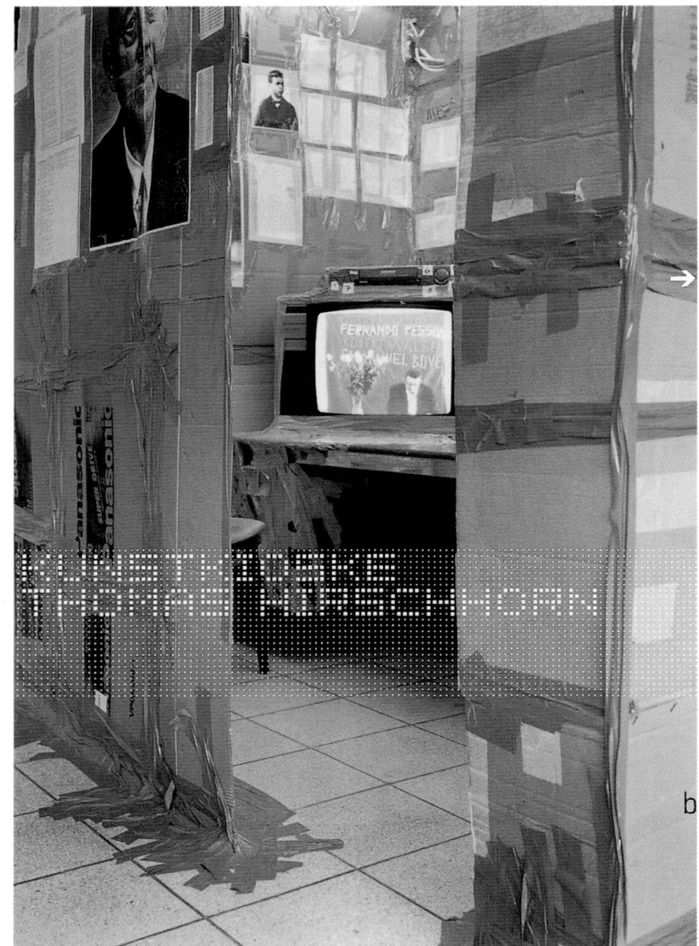

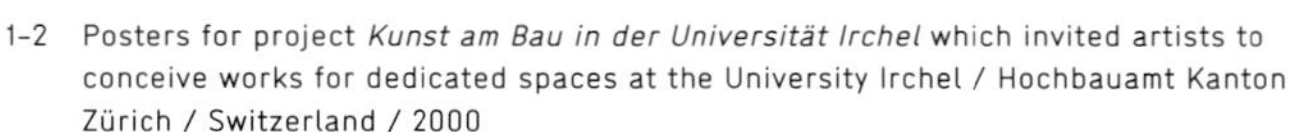

1–2 Posters for project *Kunst am Bau in der Universität Irchel* which invited artists to conceive works for dedicated spaces at the University Irchel / Hochbauamt Kanton Zürich / Switzerland / 2000

3–4 Pages and poster from All Blues! project (4 of 12) / Verein Schichtwechsel / Lichtenstein / 1999 / A visual translation of a twelve-part text by Norbert Haas, All Blues! is made up of twelve unbound pages and a poster in which all pages are featured. The project was commissioned by the cultural association Verein Schichtwechsel as a gift for its members.

Tania Prill

Zurich

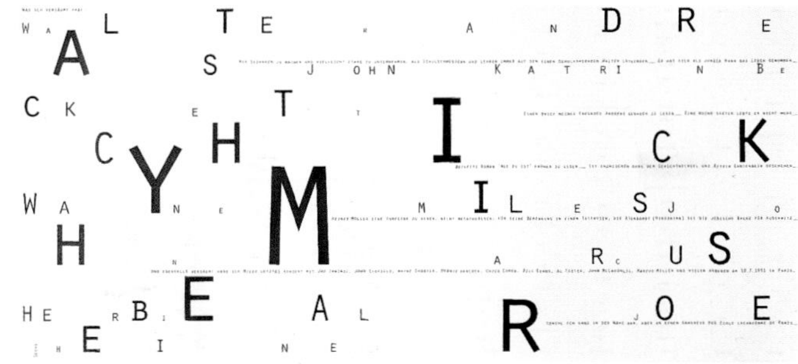

MEINE FREUNDIN UND

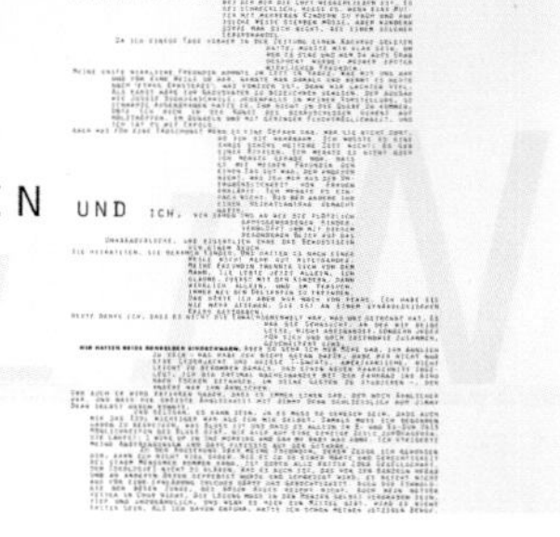

… gefallen. Wie kommt Ihr auf die Anführungszeichen bei Säuberungen? Was soll in diesem desaströsen Zusammenhang die linguistische Blödelei mit man/frau? Man hätte auch gelegentlich Mittel vorgesehen … Ja wer denn? Wer ist hier man? Es ist eben nicht nur oben, es ist auch unten passiert, und genaugenommen ist es Euch passiert, hier und jetzt in Euren unglaublichen Zeilen. Ist es die lange Geschichte der Verlogenheit revolutionärer Selbstdarstellung und Biographik, durch die die Jüngeren immer wieder dazu gebracht werden, noch die schmerzlichsten Brüche als Kontinuität, den Irrsinn als Sinn zu interpretieren? Wer immer den Atem der Geschichte eingebracht hat, wie es in Eurem Nachruf auf Amalie Pinkus heisst, der oder die hat es versäumt, die unter Umständen über das Leben entscheidende Information weiterzugeben, dass die Geschichte nicht einfach einen Atem hat, sondern den Jüngeren immer ins Gesicht hustet. "Wenn Ihr Euch schon mit [revolutionärer] Geschichte beschäftigt, dann tut es doch selber und lasst Euch dabei nicht führen. Denkt auf Eure eigenen Kosten. Denn wo es um biographische Eitelkeiten geht, lügen die Älteren alle. Amalie Pinkus kannte ich nicht, aber Theo Pinkus. Als ich ihn zusammen mit drei anderen Berlinern 1968 in Zürich besucht habe, versuchte er uns zu schocken, indem er gleich zu Beginn der Unterhaltung erklärte, er sei immer Stalinist gewesen und sei es bis zur genannten Entstalinisierung in der Aera Chruschtschew auch geblieben. Wir waren aber nicht geschockt, wir waren einfach stocksauer über eine solche Eröffnung. Irgendwie muss Theo gemerkt haben, dass ein Abchecken von Gesinnung damals nicht mehr lief, er begann zu reden wie ein Wasserfall, lauter Repertoire mit komischen Einlagen dazwischen. Wir standen nur da. Ich muss zugeben, dass ich irritiert war. Heute bin ich froh darüber, dass wir die Nerven hatten, eine Stunde lang nur da zu stehen und kein Wort zu sagen

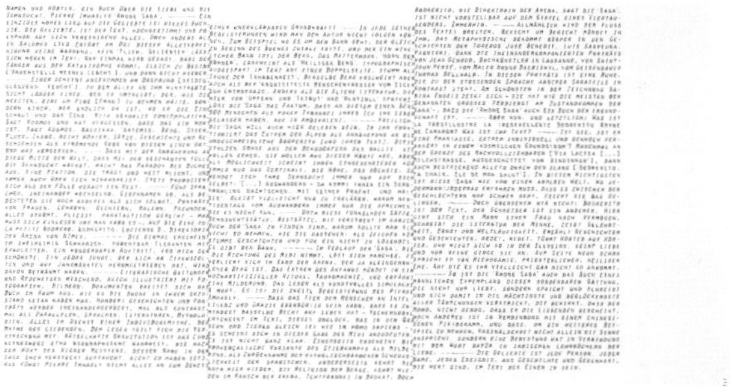

DISCOGRAFIE Was lief, während ich geschrieben habe

James Cotton with Joe Louis Walker and Charlie Haden
DEEP IN THE BLUES
1996 Gitanes/Verve

Detroit Gary Wiggins & Fabrice Eulry
PARIS JOOK
1996 Syncope

Cowboy Junkies
THE CAUTION HORSES
1990 BMG Music Canada Inc.

Holly Cole
TEMPTATION
1995 Metro Blue/Capitol Records

Original Funk
LE SON DE LA NOUVELLE ORLEANS
1996 Novapress

ALL BLUES!

Ein Text von Norbert Haas Herbst 1996

Marianne Faithfull
A SECRET LIFE
1995 Island Records

Miles Davis
GET UP WITH IT
1974 Coline Records

5

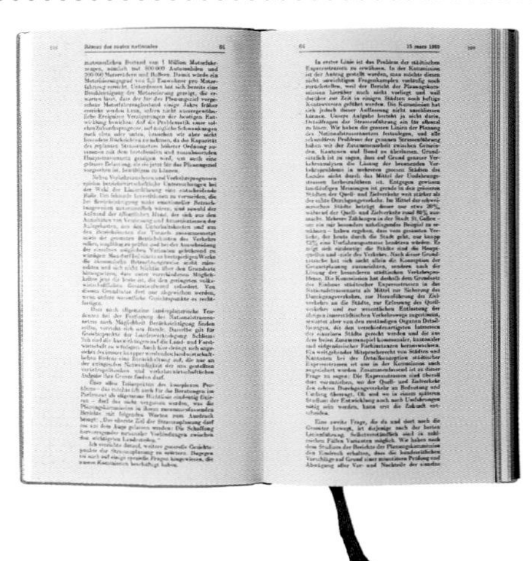

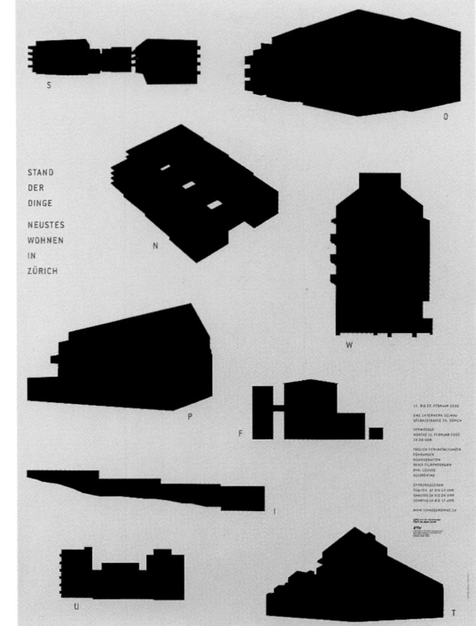

6
7
8

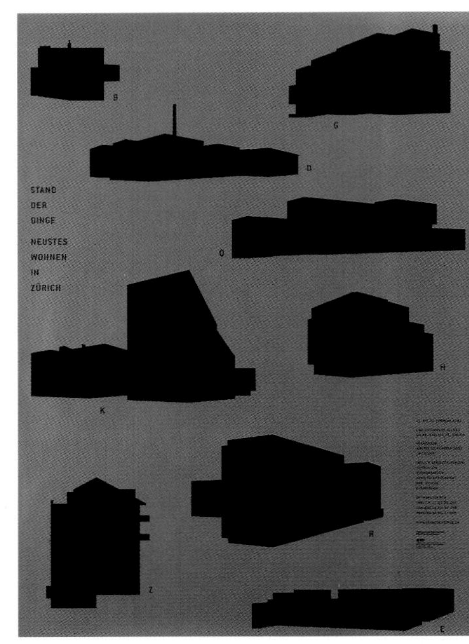

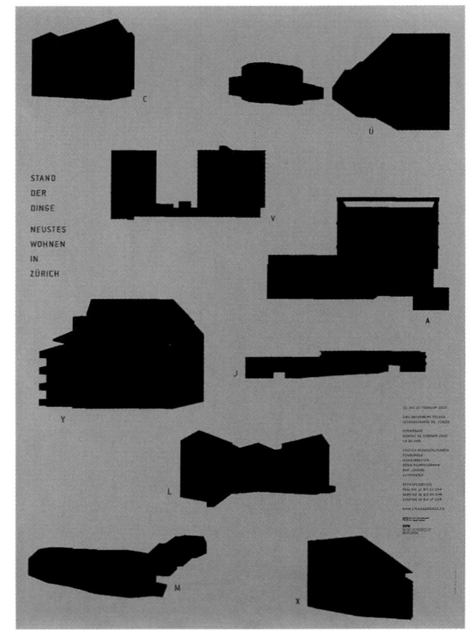

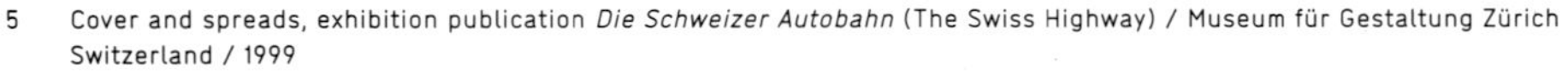

5 Cover and spreads, exhibition publication *Die Schweizer Autobahn* (The Swiss Highway) / Museum für Gestaltung Zürich / Switzerland / 1999

6–8 Posters for exhibition *Stand der Dinge: Neustes Wohnen in Zürich* (The State of Affairs: New Living in Zurich) / Hochbauamt Kanton Zürich / Switzerland / 2002

9 Self-commissioned poster Faxaction conceived in memory of Swiss typographer and teacher Hans-Rudolf Lutz / Switzerland / 2002 / In January 1998, while working on the conception of his exhibition *Werkschau Hans-Rudolf Lutz*, Hans-Rudolf Lutz passed away. His friends followed through with the exhibition, which took place in the Visosuisse Factory, Emmenbrücke, a few months later. A fax machine was installed in the exhibition space, allowing people from around the world to react to the loss. The faxes became part of the exhibition and a selection was used to make up this poster.

Tania Prill

FIVE
MORE
DAYS
COMEBACK!
Hans-Rudolf Lutz
Typografie als Passion
A CHAMPION AGAIN
LUTZ
OUR ENFANTS,
NOS,
SUMMER
VETEMENTS
ROPA PARA N
KINDERKLEID
ES WAR
SO
SCHÖN
dettagli
di
un
pugile
FINISSAGE
21.Juni 1998 ab 18.00
hier
LOTH,
GRÜSSE AUS
LUTZERN
so
crazy

Read from left to right, QWER are the first four letters on a standard keyboard. QWER is also the symbiosis of two graphic designers who communicated with one another until they had their own studio and a beautiful baby. The studio was founded in a day, when they won the commission for the corporate design for the Expo 2000 in Hannover. Their concept was as unusual as it was convincing. Instead of a logo they presented an optical impulse—not a conventional sign, but rather an ever-changing structure. This important success right at the beginning of their careers served as both an obligation and a motivation. It therefore comes as no surprise that their Cologne-based studio now takes on projects for reputable corporations and cultural institutions. ••Iris Utikal and Michael Gais studied communication design at the Academy for Applied Arts in Düsseldorf and received their diplomas in 1992 under my auspices. After this they worked in my studio for several years. Even their final-year projects were worth seeing: Among other things, Utikal directed a movie about the belly button, and Gais designed a razor-sharp book about the sociocultural meaning of shaving. During their studies they separately gathered experience in renowned design and advertising agencies from London to Tokyo. Since then both have become professors of typography and book design at Cologne's International School of Design. ••Their work has received numerous awards at national and international competitions—not least for its excellent typographic design. Particularly characteristic of them, however, is their ambition to understand even boring assignments as creative challenges. They are not afraid to embrace the consistent application of a design system: for example, the corporate design manual that they created for the Expo 2000 is heavy enough to bend your bookshelf. Since they are untiringly committed and active, I am already looking forward to their future work. ••Uwe Loesch••

1

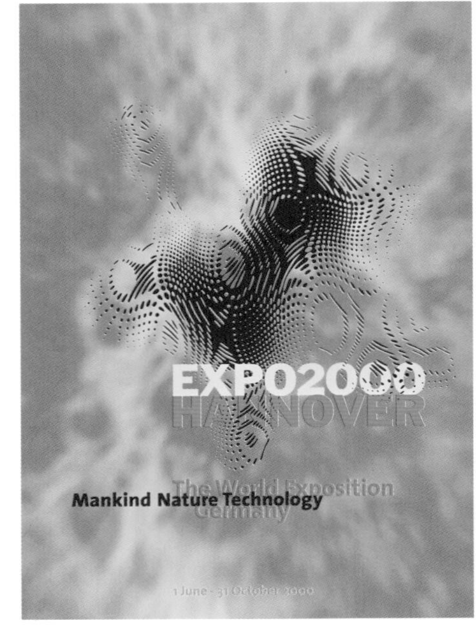

2

1–2 Airplane design and poster series for Expo 2000 Hannover World Exposition / Expo 2000 Hannover / Germany / 1996–2000
3 Logo detail, brochure, design for stationery, and invitations to various events of the *Stiftung Kulturregion Hannover* (Foundation of the Cultural Region Hannover) / Stiftung Kulturregion Hannover / Germany / 2001
4–5 Box set of paper-sample booklets and cover variations for paper company Zanders / Zanders Feinpapiere AG / Germany / 1997–present

QWER

Cologne, Germany

Kulturregion Hannover

Stiftung
Kulturregion Hannover

3

Einladung
2009 - die Welt, in der wir morgen leben
Einladung
Jugend denkt
Einladung
pro visio

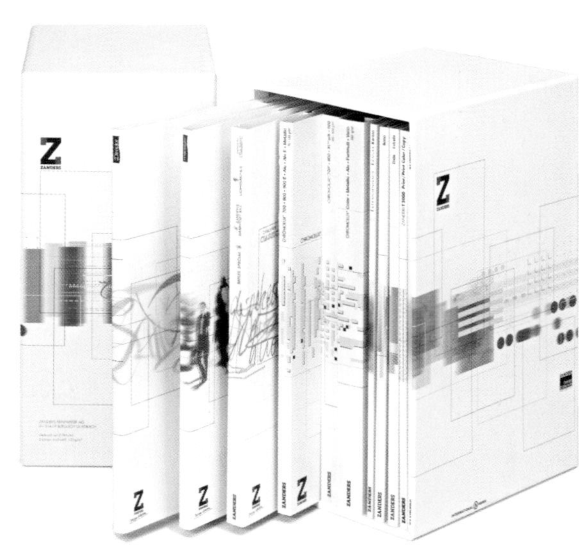

4

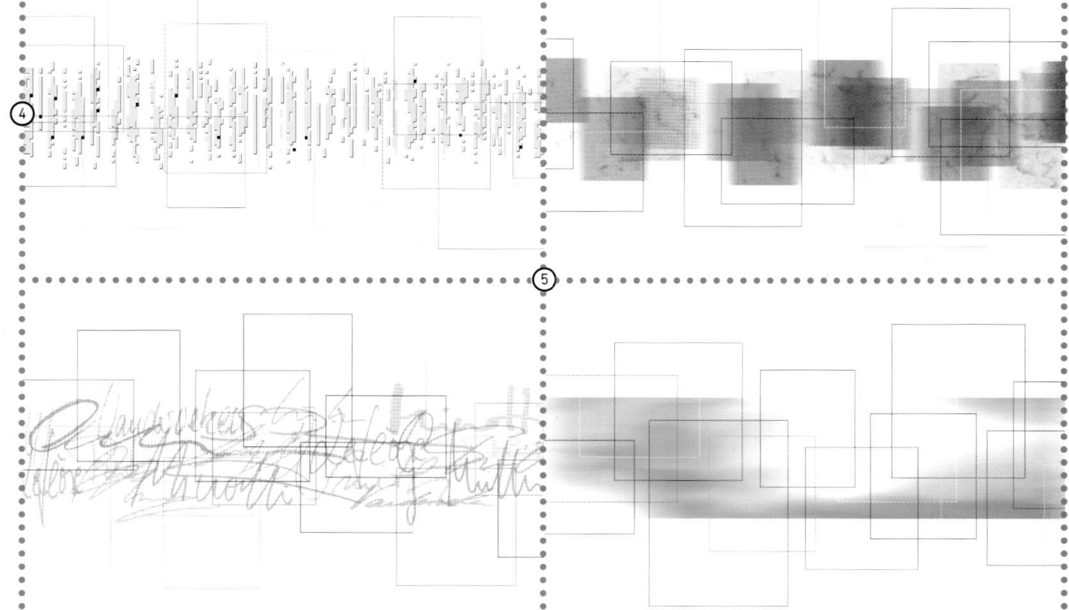

5

Stiftung
Wilhelm
Lehmbruck
Museum

Zentrum
Internationaler
Skulptur

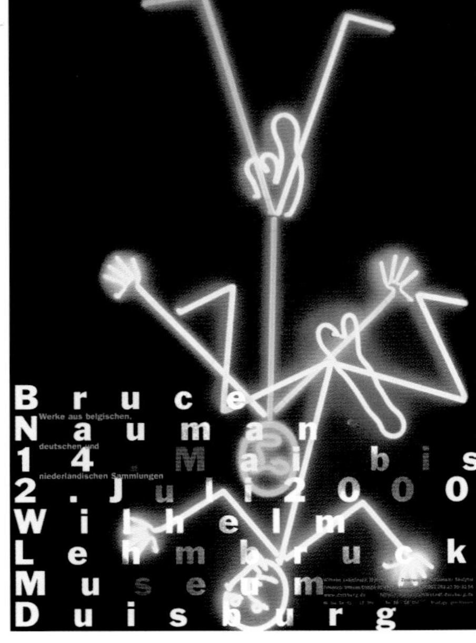

6 7 8

9 10 11

6–8 Logo and posters for exhibitions *Bruce Nauman* and *Alexander Rodtschenko und die Raumkonstruktion im 20. Jahrhundert*, Wilhelm Lembruck Museum, Duisburg / Stiftung Wilhelm Lembruck Museum / Germany / 2000–2002
9–11 Posters for exhibitions *Holub Ludens–Kunst für Kunst, Unter der Haut*, and *Nam June Paik–Fluxus und Videoskulptur* / Stiftung Wilhelm Lembruck Museum, Duisburg / Germany / 2001–2002
12 Logo application on facade of Wilhelm Lembruck Museum, Duisburg / 2000
13–14 Logo variations and street campaign for *Rotterdam 2001, Cultural Capital of Europe* (unrealized) / Rotterdam Cultural Capital 2001 / Netherlands / 2001
15–17 Poster, magazine cover, and spread for *Rotterdam 2001, Cultural Capital of Europe* campaign (unrealized) / 2001

12

QWER

rotterdam 2001
culturele hoofdstad van europa

rotterdam 2001
cultural capital of europe

rotterdam 2001
culturele hoofdstad van europa

13 14

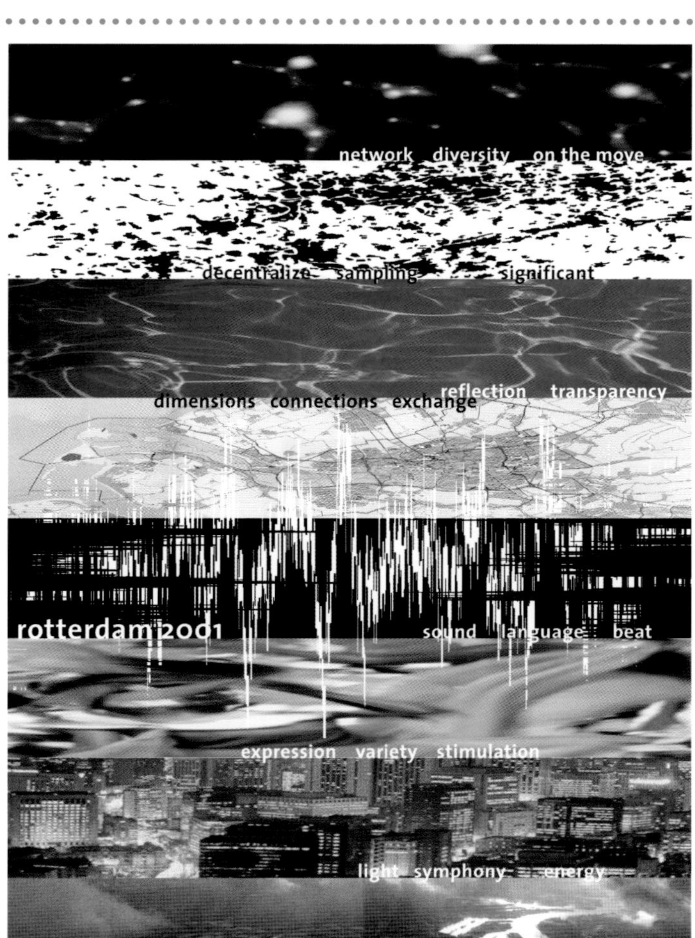

15

16 17

Samuel Nyholm and Jonas Williamson from Sweden, Laurent Benner from Switzerland: three middle-class western Europeans with a common sense of humor, knack for music, and passion for high and low culture. Federico Fellini blended Kafka and *piadina romagnola*; Reala do something similar with the *Tractatus Logicus Philosophicus* and Superman. Their inspiration emerges from their not-so-distant teenage days, art school, friends, and daily lives. Nyholm states, "Work becomes pretty playful, but with strict rules. We often pick up systems/objects from the backyards of human culture, as signifiers of different themes. We try relate to the subject, assignment, in the most obvious way. Trying not to be too clever. This point of view helps us to find the signfiers that later become a system around which we can build our work."••Reala are your friendly next-door-neighbor designers. They want to present information in a nice costume. "Like Limburger cheese," explains Williamson, "you may not like it at first, only to then realize that the taste is very complex, rich, and mature." They want to elicit strong emotional reactions (see "I love to meet you"), obviously not through market logic, but through sincere and instinctive human activities. Such as "sleeping, cooking, fixing your bike, phase shifts, listening to yet another pile of garbage from a son of a bush, stealing chairs, Gore Vidal, having a cup of tea, having a pint, rewinding, selecting, busting," in the words of Benner.••Omar Vulpinari••

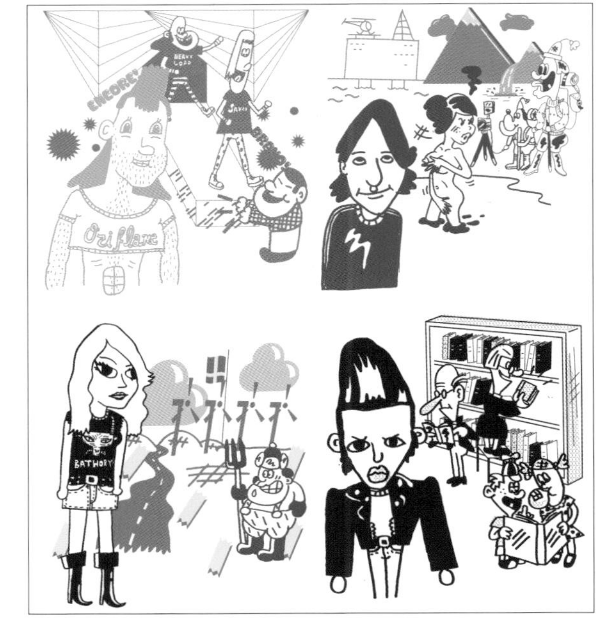

1

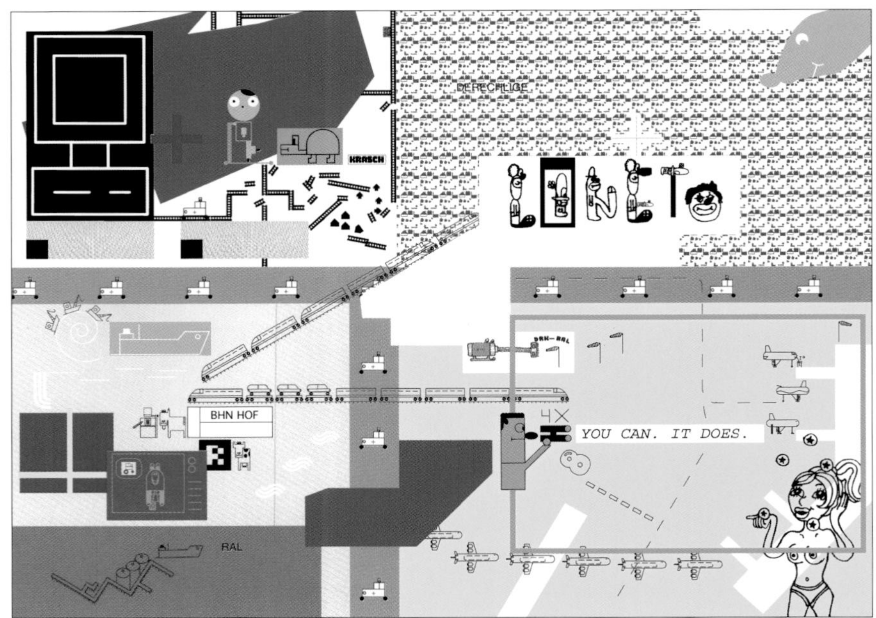

2

3

1 Portrait illustrations for weekly segment in the culture section of Swedish newspaper *Svenska Dagbladet* / Svenska Dagbladet / Sweden / 2002

2–3 Thematic spreads "global/regional/local," *Benzin-Young Swiss Graphic Design*, published by Lars Müller Publishers / Lineto.com / Switzerland / 2000

4–5 Posters for contemporary-art event "After Shopping," Kulturhuset, Stockholm / After Shopping / Sweden / 2002

6 Promotional poster for Japanese jeans company Edwin Jeans / Yotsugi Yasunori Incorporation and Edwin Jeans / Japan / 2002

7 Poster for short film *She is Dead*, by Henry Moore Selder and Sara Lundén / Pinguin Film / Sweden / 2002

Reala

London/Stockholm

6

Erst
After- Shopping
then
then
sedan
9–5
7=11
handla
igen och igen
I'M A REAL ARTIST

ORGANIZE
SELECT
INTERPRET
ART
BLOCKS
COLOR
CRAZY
JAZZY!
DENIM
HIKING
HOLIDAY
ICE-CREAM
System break-down?
15 LOVE
MEDIA
POLITICS
Post your vote
RUSH HOUR
SHOPPING
STOOPID

4
5

7

Joyeux Noel
10% FREE
After Shopping
BEFORE FRESHNESS?

SHE IS DEAD
HON ÄR DÖD
En film av Henry Moore Selder och Sara Lundén

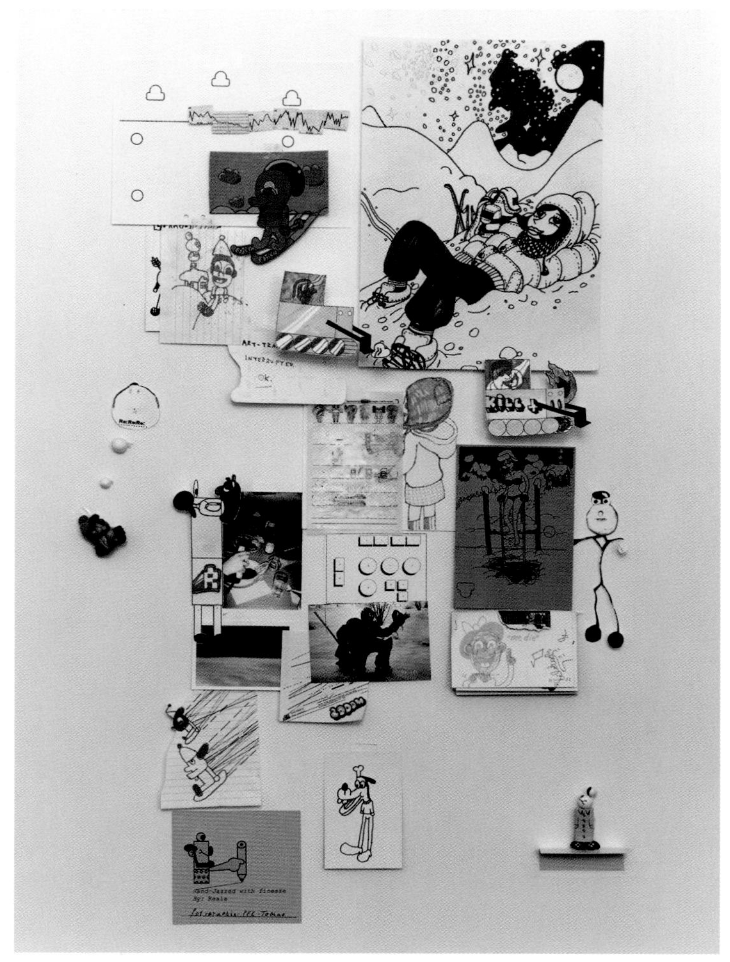

8

9

10

8–10 Cover illustrations for winter, summer, and autumn menus of the Lydmar Hotel restaurant / Lydmar Hotel / Sweden / 2000–2001
11–12 Posters for Payam Sharifi and Alan Clarke's exhibition and short film *Hall of Fame*, held and shown at Fanclub, Amersterdam, and the Stockholm Film Festival / Payam Sharifi / France / 2002
13 Official poster for exhibition *I love to meet you–New graphic design* held at Palazzo Fortuny in Venice / Studio Camuffo / Italy / 2002
14 Poster/calendar created as Reala's Christmas card / United Kingdom and Sweden / 2002

Reala

11

Tsunami/Bruise Presents
HALL
OF
FAME
Alan Clarke
Payam Sharifi
22–29 Apr 2002
Fanshop
Nieuwezijds
Voorburgwal
262B
AMSTER
DAM

12

Bruise, Kin & La Pac present
HALL
OF
FAME
Payam Sharifi
Alan Clarke
STOCKHOLM
FILM FESTIVAL
Premiere*
19th Nov 22h00
Skandia
20th Nov 15h15
Skandia
23th Nov 11h00
Polstjärnan

13
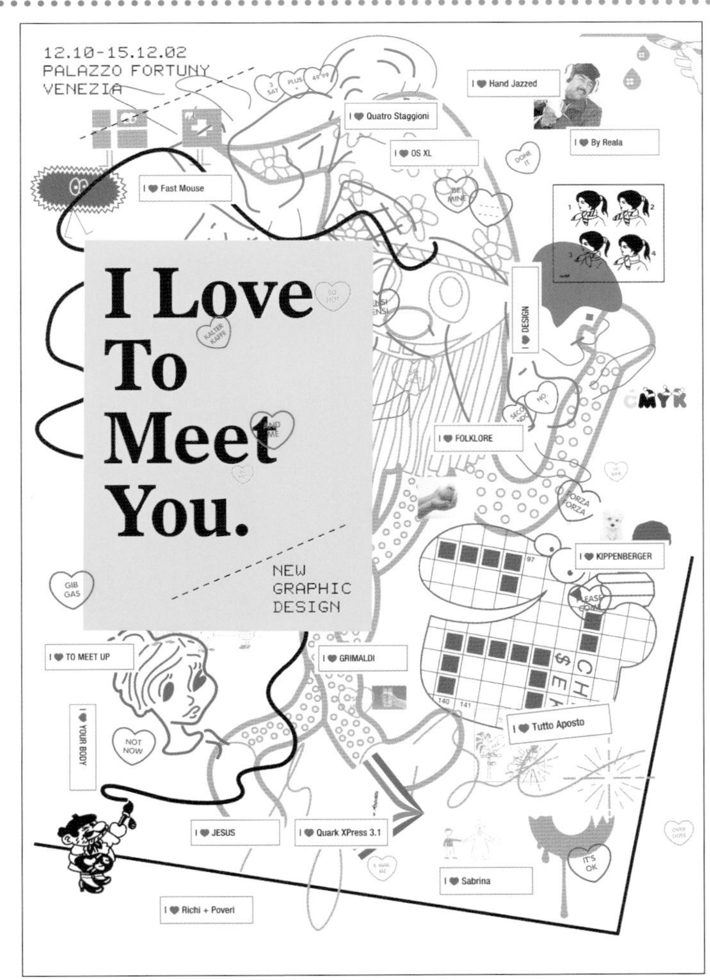
12.10–15.12.02
PALAZZO FORTUNY
VENEZIA
I Love
To
Meet
You.
NEW
GRAPHIC
DESIGN
I ♥ Hand Jazzed
I ♥ Quatro Staggioni
I ♥ OS XL
I ♥ By Reala
I ♥ Fast Mouse
I ♥ DESIGN
I ♥ FOLKLORE
I ♥ KIPPENBERGER
I ♥ TO MEET UP
I ♥ GRIMALDI
I ♥ YOUR BODY
I ♥ Tutto Aposto
I ♥ JESUS
I ♥ Quark XPress 3.1
I ♥ Sabrina
I ♥ Richi + Poveri
CMYK

14
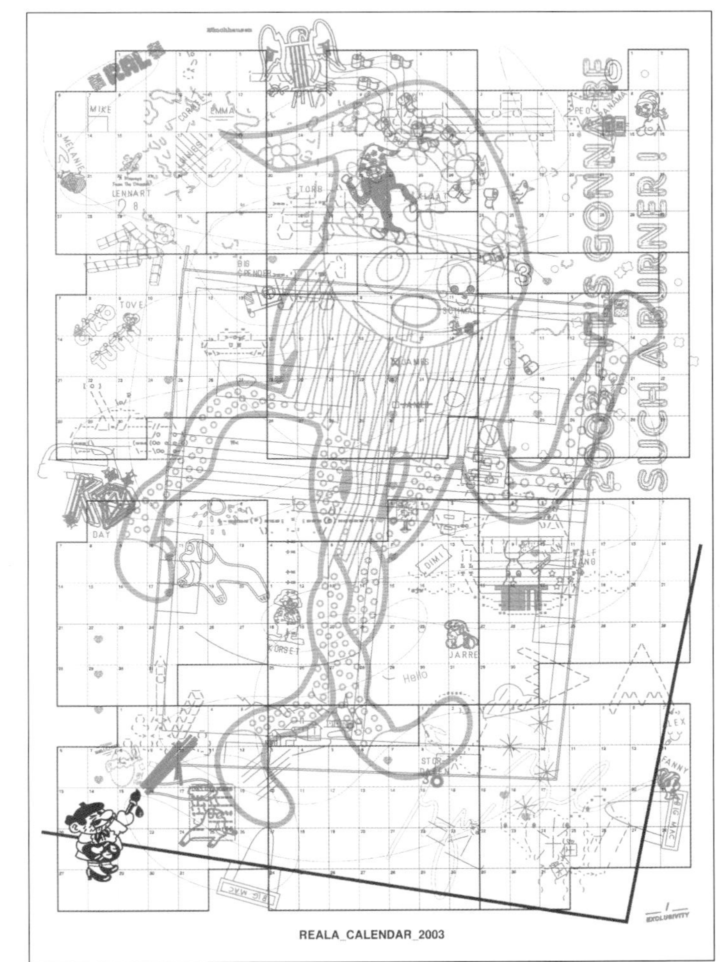
2003 IS GONNA BE
SUCH A BURNER!
REALA_CALENDAR_2003

Casey Reas's research examines abstractions of biological and natural systems by means of various digital media such as software art, print media, and animation. As a member of John Maeda's Aesthetics and Computation Group (ACG), he researches the conception and execution of intelligent, interactive, mobile sculpture (behavioral kinetic sculpture). He designs independently, and is a professor at the newly founded Interaction Design Institute in Ivrea, Italy. • • Reas is constantly looking for new forms. Every day he reacquaints himself and practices with the computer, with this illustration tool, which for many of us has very set limits. He peeks behind each byte, he tinkers with the zeros and ones, strums around on them. For him all barriers regarding the pure function of the computer have fallen completely, allowing him a fascinating ease and freedom with its applications. He knows how to work the machine, about its possibilities, the way the rest of us know paper and pencil. But he clearly goes even further: It is as if, in order to draw a line with a pencil, we were to start by hewing a tree or grinding lead. Listening to Reas talk about his research, I quickly understand that computers are open books, that computers are generated, natural systems, that computers are also just human beings. He is an addict, a maniac. His output is more than impressive. He is someone who *must* do research. He is a real explorer, because he works without a specific goal: He is not in a binding commitment to any company, no enterprise has bought him. • • Werner Jeker • •

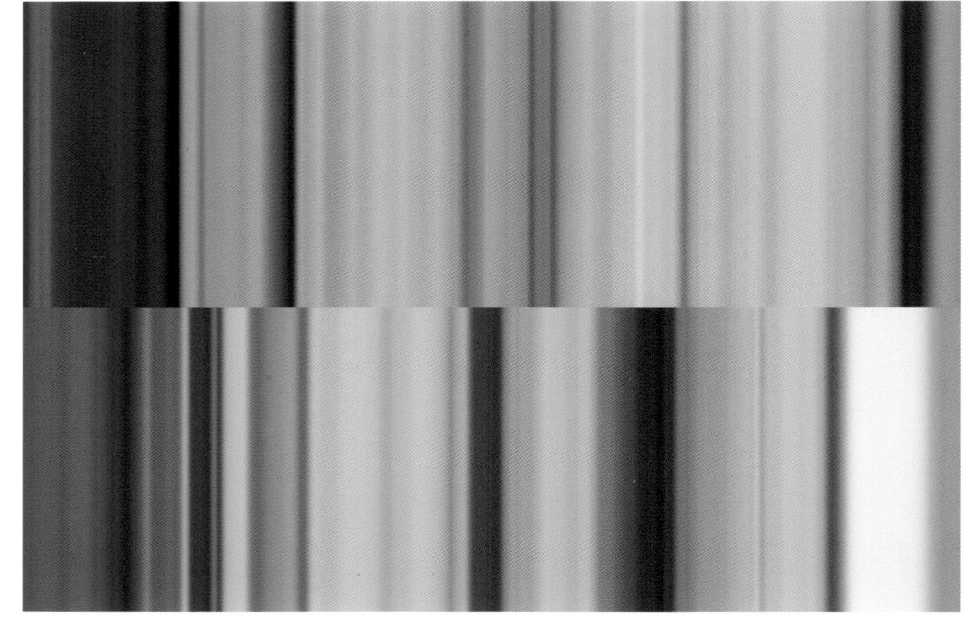

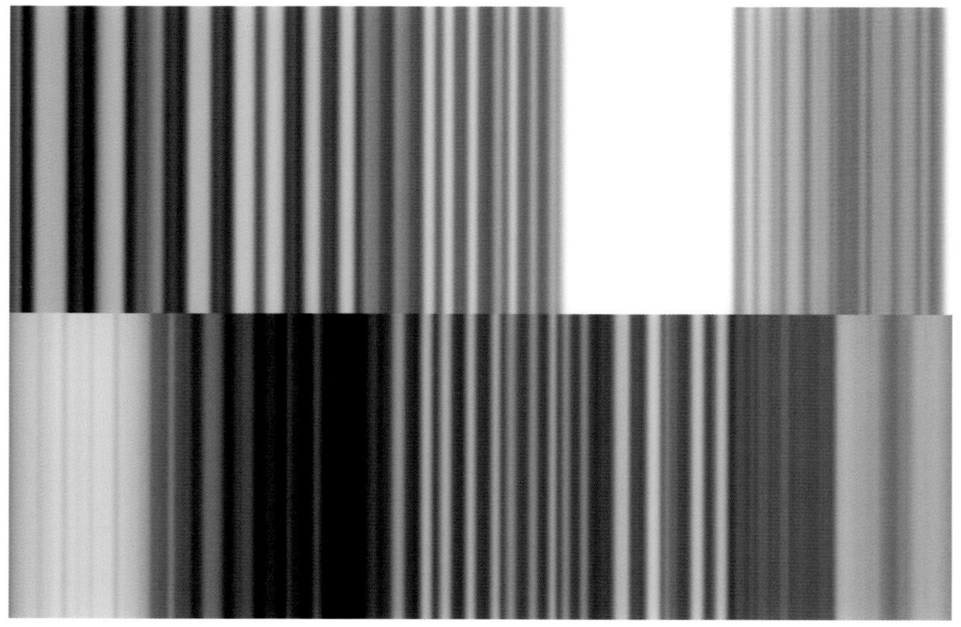

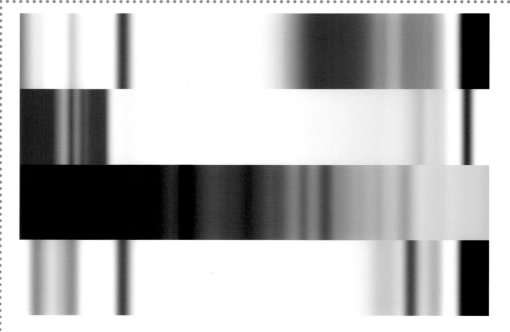

1–3 Print series "Mediation" / Group C / United States / 2002 / In this series the representational and symbolic content of a photograph is systematically obscured and replaced with an empty surface.
4–6 Print series "Path" / Group C / United States / 2001 / The prints explore the movement of four synthetic systems reacting to different stimuli. Each image is a frozen moment in time from this continually shifting ecology.

Casey Reas

Ivrea, Italy

1 2 3

4

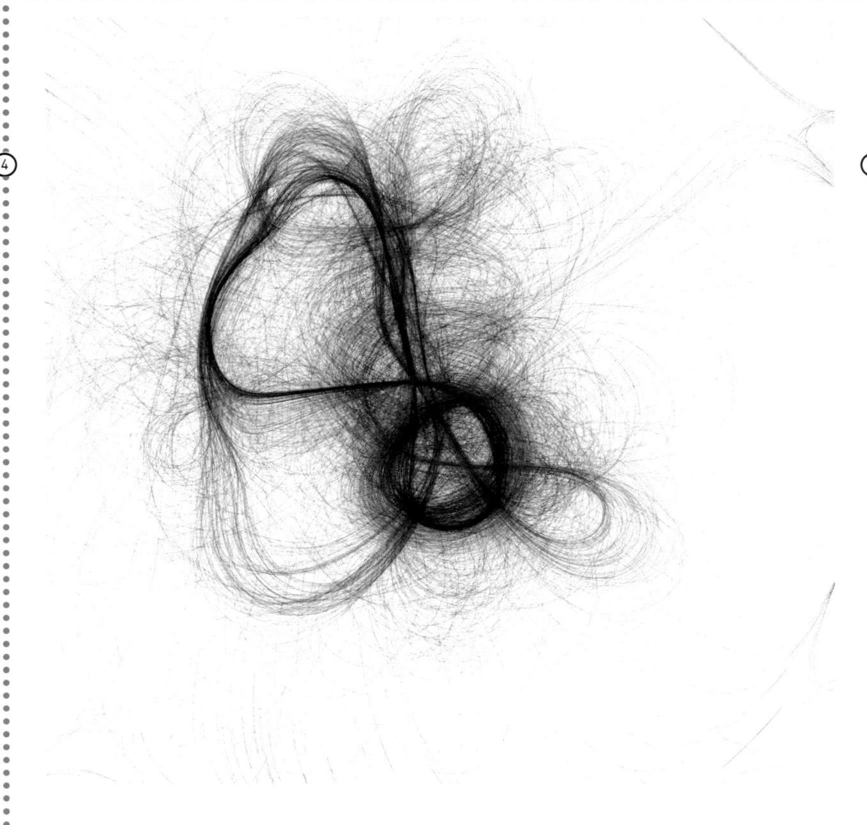

5

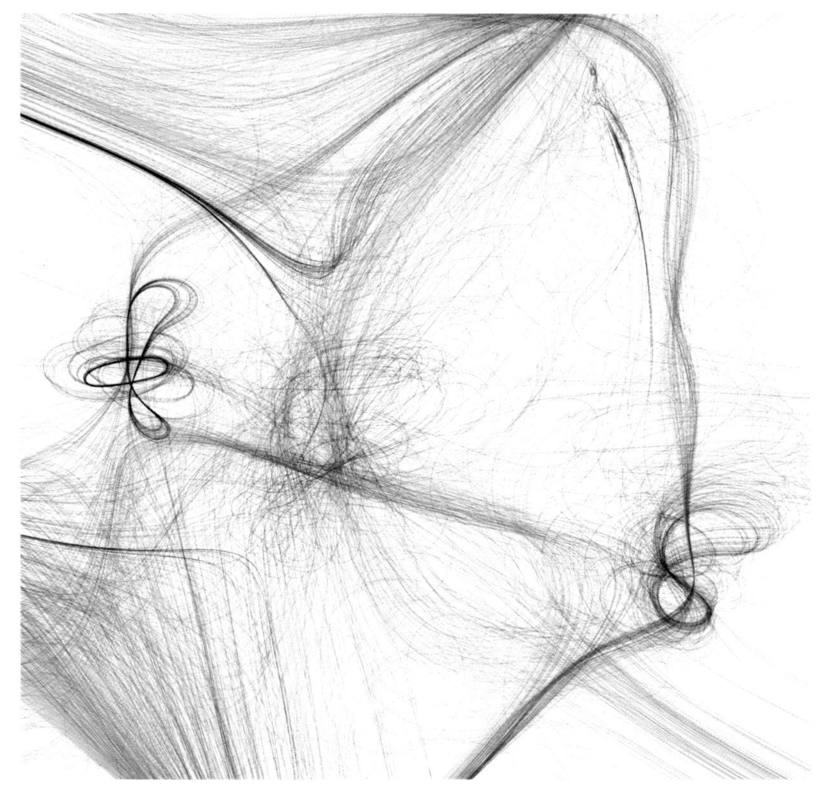

6

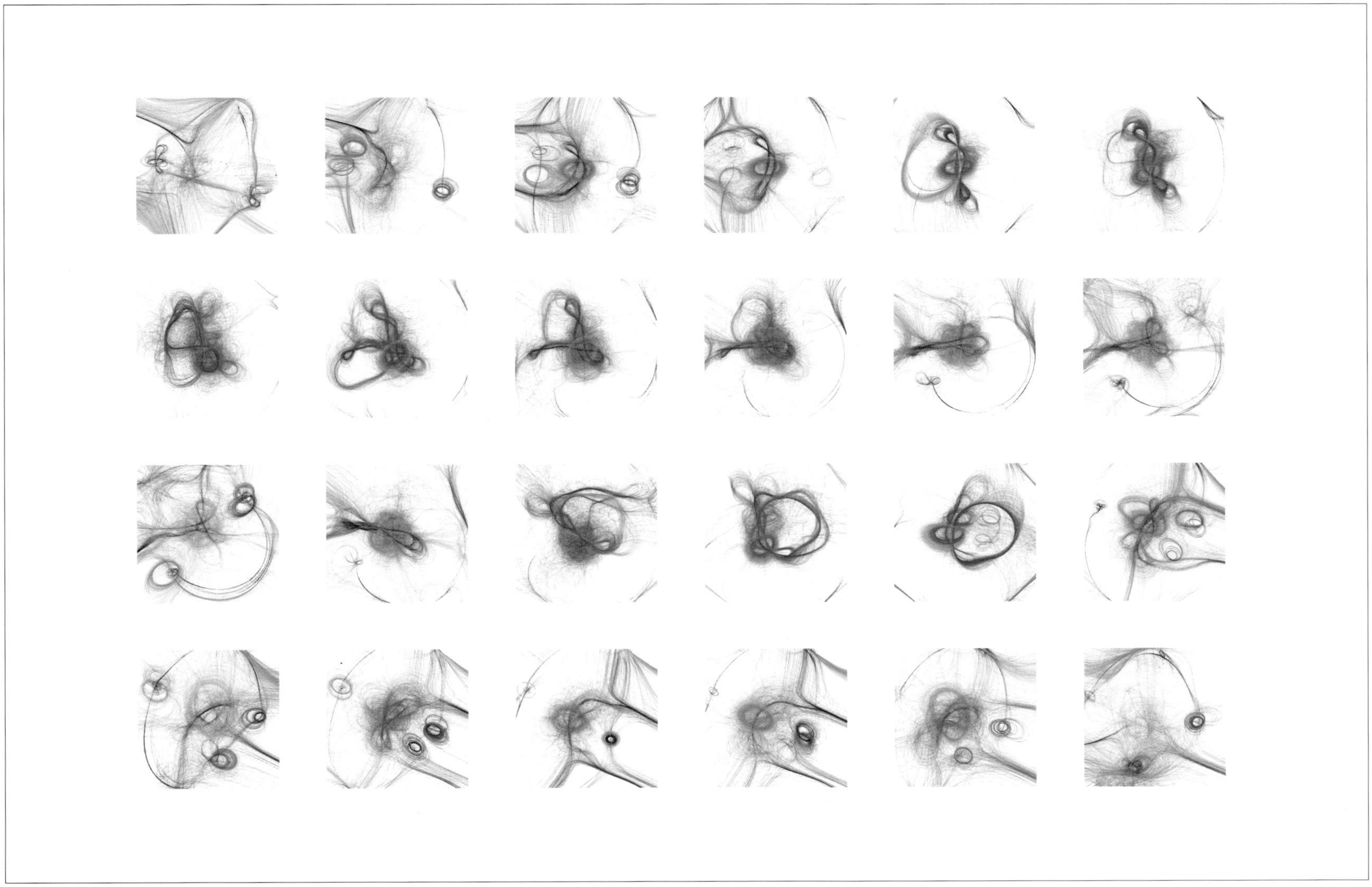

7

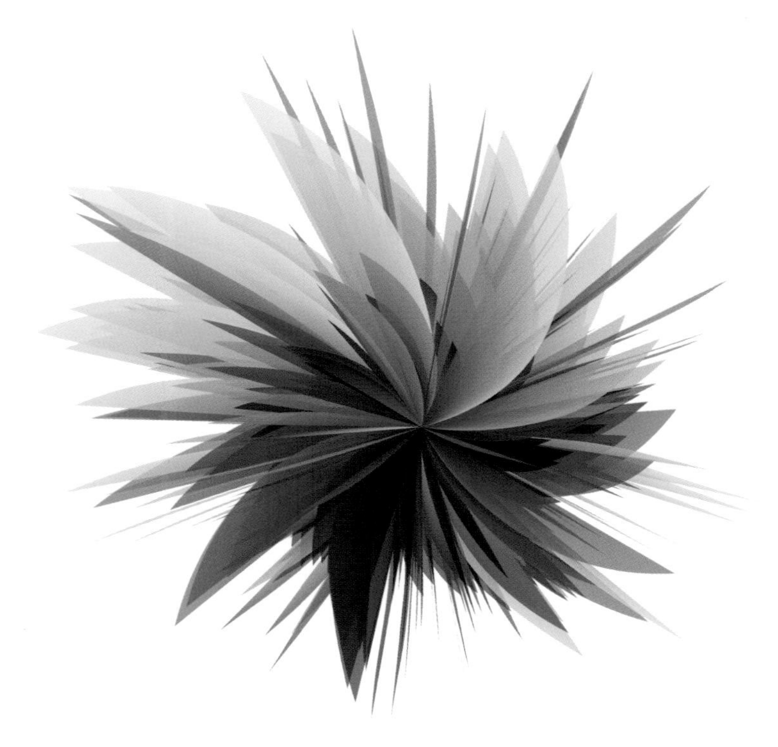

8

7–8 Print series "Seed" / Group C / United States / 2001 / Each image is the result of a synthetically cloned seed growing in a unique environment.
9–10 Prints from RPM project / IAMAS / Japan / 2001 / The prints represent kinetic forms created through manipulation of location, phase, speed, and transparency of the same moving object.

Casey Reas

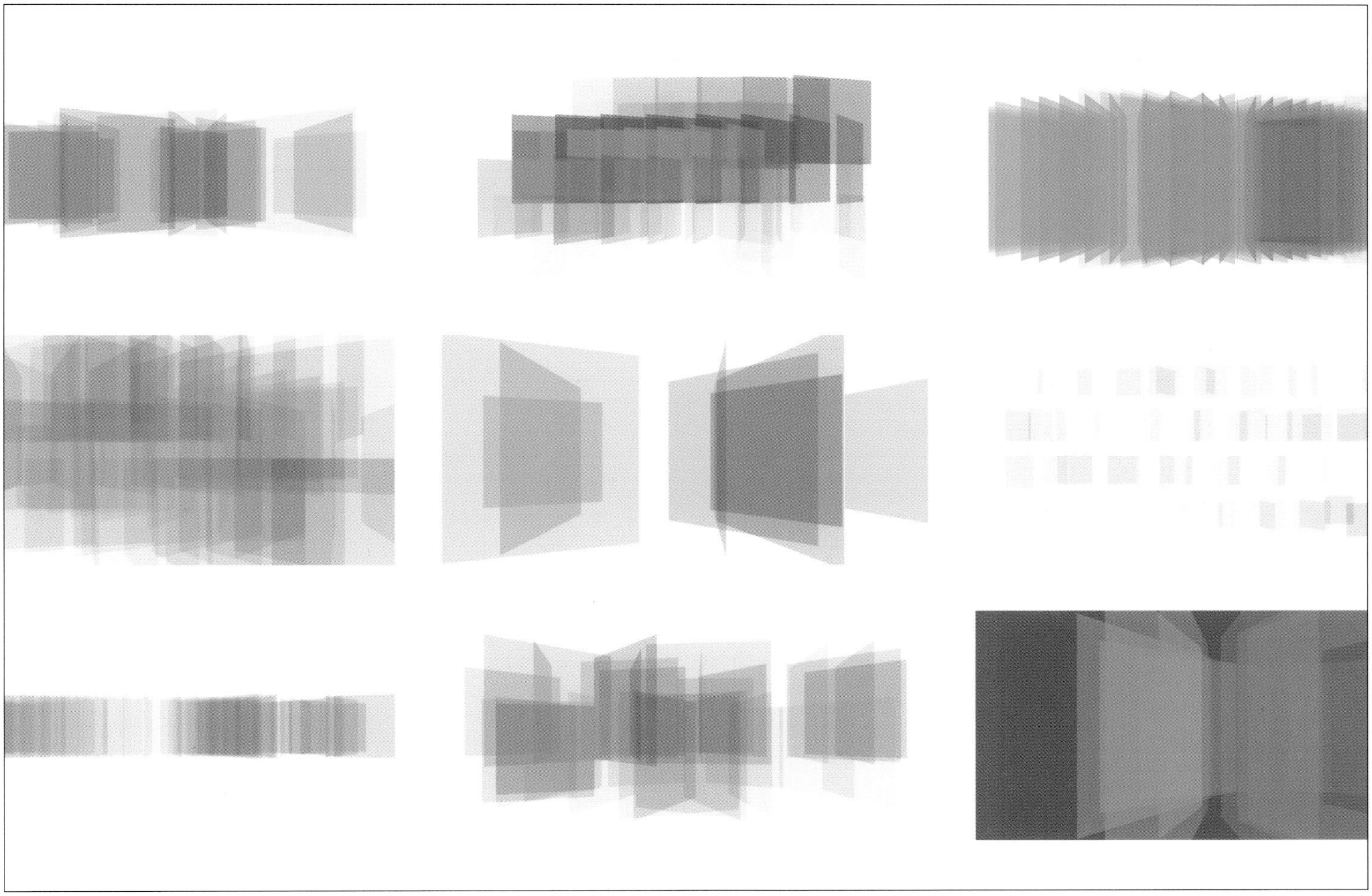

9
10

R Studio, David Richmond's graphic-design company, is currently based in a converted church near Camden. Introducing the company on their Web site, Richmond says that while this may be quite strange, they believe that "divine intervention on any project is always welcome." I've known Richmond since we were both students at the London College of Printing, and he's always had a dry, northern sense of humor. He has managed to filter that into his work, bringing a distinctive personality to the kinds of products that usually end up looking tired, bland, and faceless. • • His humor is evident in his work for the Food Doctor, which offers advice and information on all aspects of nutrition, and their own line of healthy food products. Richmond developed an identity and range of packaging that capture the essence of the brand. The identity is modern, approachable, and suggests authority, while the packaging is warm and friendly, bringing a distinctive personality to an area that is highly commercialized and increasingly competitive. Products were given breezy names such as "A Bit on the Side" mayonnaise, "Well Dressed" salad dressings, or "Good Morning" cereals. The humorous language acts as an icebreaker, giving the brand more appeal than other, more sober-looking health-food lines. • • He recently created a new look for the store-brand food packaging of the English department store Selfridges. With it, he hoped to challenge people's perceptions of how food should be packaged. He has truly succeeded, with an approach that engages the consumer and builds on the customer experience. No fancy food photography here, just bold, bright typography on a black ground—an audacious solution that is incredibly effective. • • His work extends beyond the world of brand packaging. His identities—such as those designed for Martin Pritchard (a dentist) and Sara Bruce (a food consultant)—display his ability to create warm, humorous solutions, with an approach that is consistently direct and human. The dentist's logotype transforms his name into a smiling mouth. It's as simple as that. No frills. Just a friendly identity that makes you smile. • • Fernando Gutiérrez • •

1

2

1 Identity for food consultant Sara Bruce / Sara Bruce / United Kingdom / 2002
2 Packaging for flavored olive oil brand Inventory Oils / Inventory Oils / United Kingdom and Spain / 1999
3 Branding and packaging for UK supermarket Selfridges's in house product range / Selfridges / United Kingdom / 2002

David Richmond

London

SELFRIDGES&Co
RUNNY
HONEY
WITH
HONEYCOMB

SELFRIDGES&Co
CLEAR
RUNNY
HONEY

SELFRIDGES&Co
CRANBERRY
& ORANGE
SAUCE

SELFRIDGES&Co
APPLE
& MINT
SAUCE

SELFRIDGES&Co
PURE
GROUND
KENYAN
GETHUMB-
WINI
COFFEE

SELFRIDGES&Co
PURE
GROUND
COLOMBIAN
EMERALD
MOUNTAIN
COFFEE

SELFRIDGES&Co
PURE
GREEN TEA
20 TEA BAGS
SELFRIDGES&Co
SINGLE ESTATE
DARJEELING TEA
20 TEA BAGS

SELFRIDGES&Co
CHRISTMAS
PUDDING
WITH
CHAMPAGNE
produce of England

(3)

SELFRIDGES&Co
CHARDONNAY
VIN DE PAYS D'OC
2001

SELFRIDGES&Co
HANDMADE
PANETTONE

4

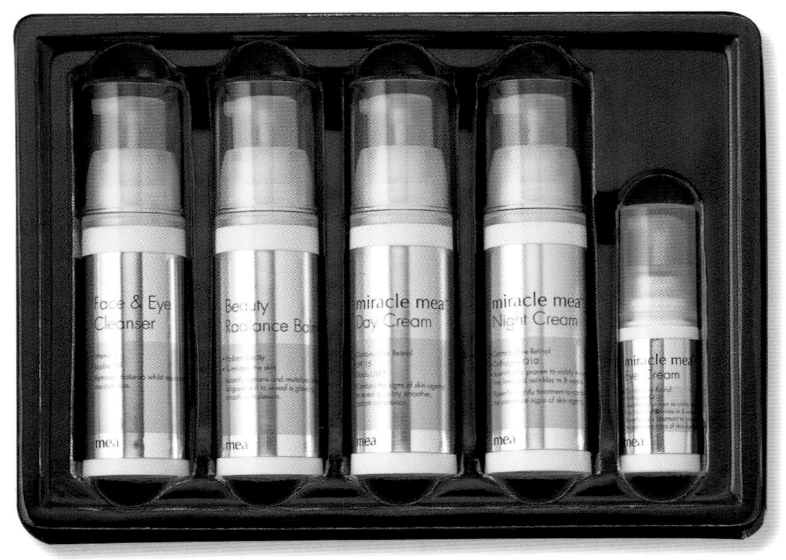

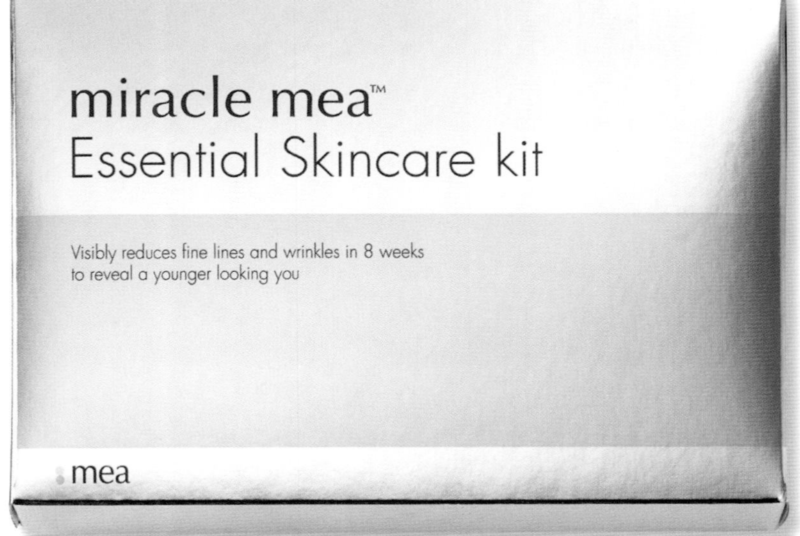

miracle mea™
Essential Skincare kit
Visibly reduces fine lines and wrinkles in 8 weeks
to reveal a younger looking you
mea

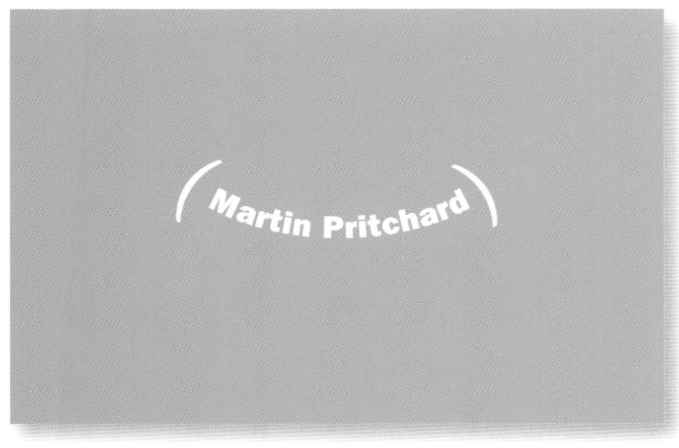

5

David Richmond

4 Identity and packaging for new range of Mea makeup and skincare products / Mea / United Kingdom / 2000
5 Identity/business card for Martin Prichard's dental pratice / Martin Prichard / United Kingdom / 2000
6 Identity, packaging, and posters for UK food brand The Food Doctor / The Food Doctor / United Kingdom / 2002

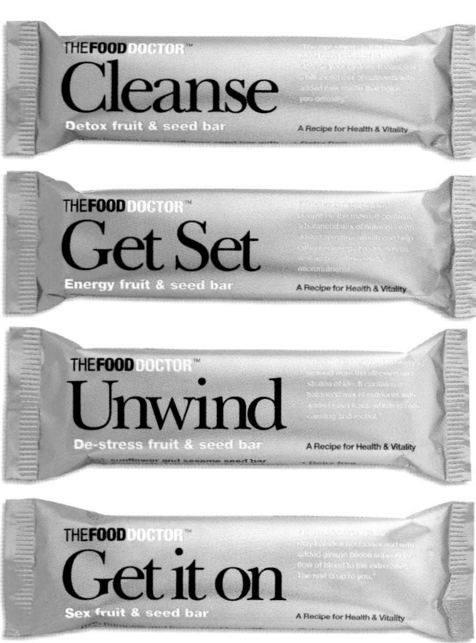

6

A fresh start

Feeling low? Your environment affects your immunity for which you need antioxidants on a daily basis. What you eat makes all the difference.

Find out how to get the most out of your life with a 'one-to-one' nutrition consultation. Please ask at reception for details.

THEFOODDOCTOR™
A Recipe for Health & Vitality

www.thefooddoctor.com

Is your food good to you?

Food intolerance testing available
You may love food, but does your food love you?
Few people actually have allergies, but many can react badly to the food they eat.

THEFOODDOCTOR™
A Recipe for Health & Vitality

www.thefooddoctor.com

Sanja Rocco. I came across this beautiful, rolling name—sounding Latin and Slavic at the same time—when two posters were received at the Moscow international graphic-design biennial Zolotaya Pchela (Golden Bee): a black one and a white one, produced for the Croatian Typhlology Museum. The text can only be seen when illuminated from an angle, because it's set in raised dots of braille. A poster for the blind! It was hard to imagine. A poster you can perceive by touch. I was very impressed. • •Graphic design often provokes both visual and tactile sensations: the heaviness of fine paper stock in a magazine or book, the textured cardboard of packaging, or the smoothness of an invitation card. These pleasures are grander than mere information by itself. • •In postmodernism this quality becomes one of the most relevant today. The fact that we are in contact with the whole world through mobile phones, faxes, electronic mail, and the Internet is more important than the information we receive through these channels. Connecting is more important than communicating. The Internet makes this fact obvious, felt by fingertips on a computer keyboard. • •Paradoxically, the key underpinnings of modernism and postmodernism—"grid" (modular grid) and "net" (Internet)—are almost synonyms. Meanwhile they belong to two different cultural epochs. • •The growing importance of tactile sensations and of subtle physical contact in postmodernism is visualized through such traditional concepts as "texture." In Sanja Rocco's work for the Jordan Catalogue, the texture of the canvas seeps through to the surface, demonstrating that painting is born on the resilient, animate base of this sort of organic "net" rather than the strict modular "grid" that fits the nature of graphics. • •It seems to me that this quality is part of feminine nature. And when Sanja Rocco allows this nature to spread its wings, "texture" and "painting" make her work privy to the actualities of postmodernism. On the Rundek CD cover, the hero has closed his eyes. This doesn't mean he doesn't see anything. It simply means that he's looking inside, into himself. • •Serge Serov • •

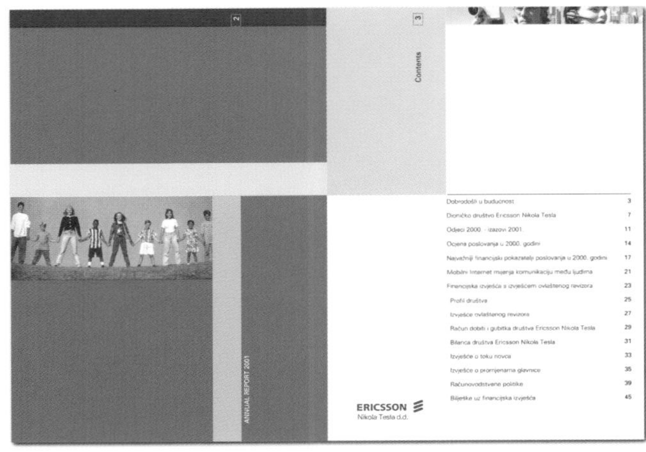

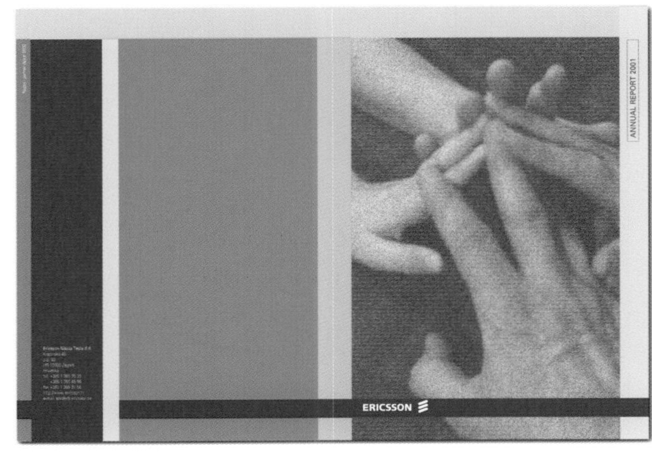

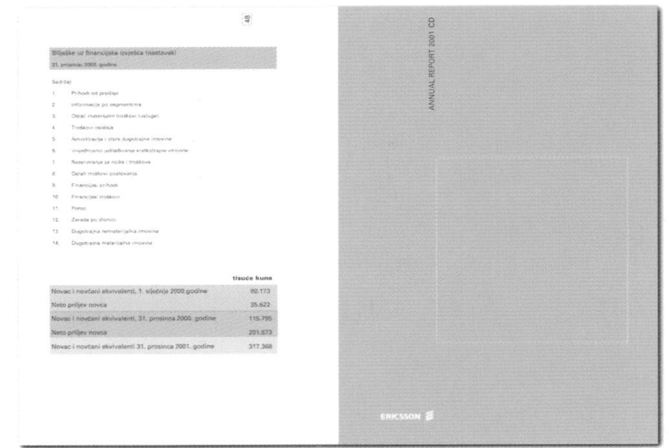

1–4 Annual report with CD-ROM for telecommunications company Ericsson / Ericsson Nikola Tesla Croatia / Croatia / 2002
5–6 Black and White posters for the Croatian Typhlology Museum / Croatian Typhology Museum / Croatia / 1991 / The braille type is embossed on the posters.

Sanja Rocco

Zagreb

1 2 3 4

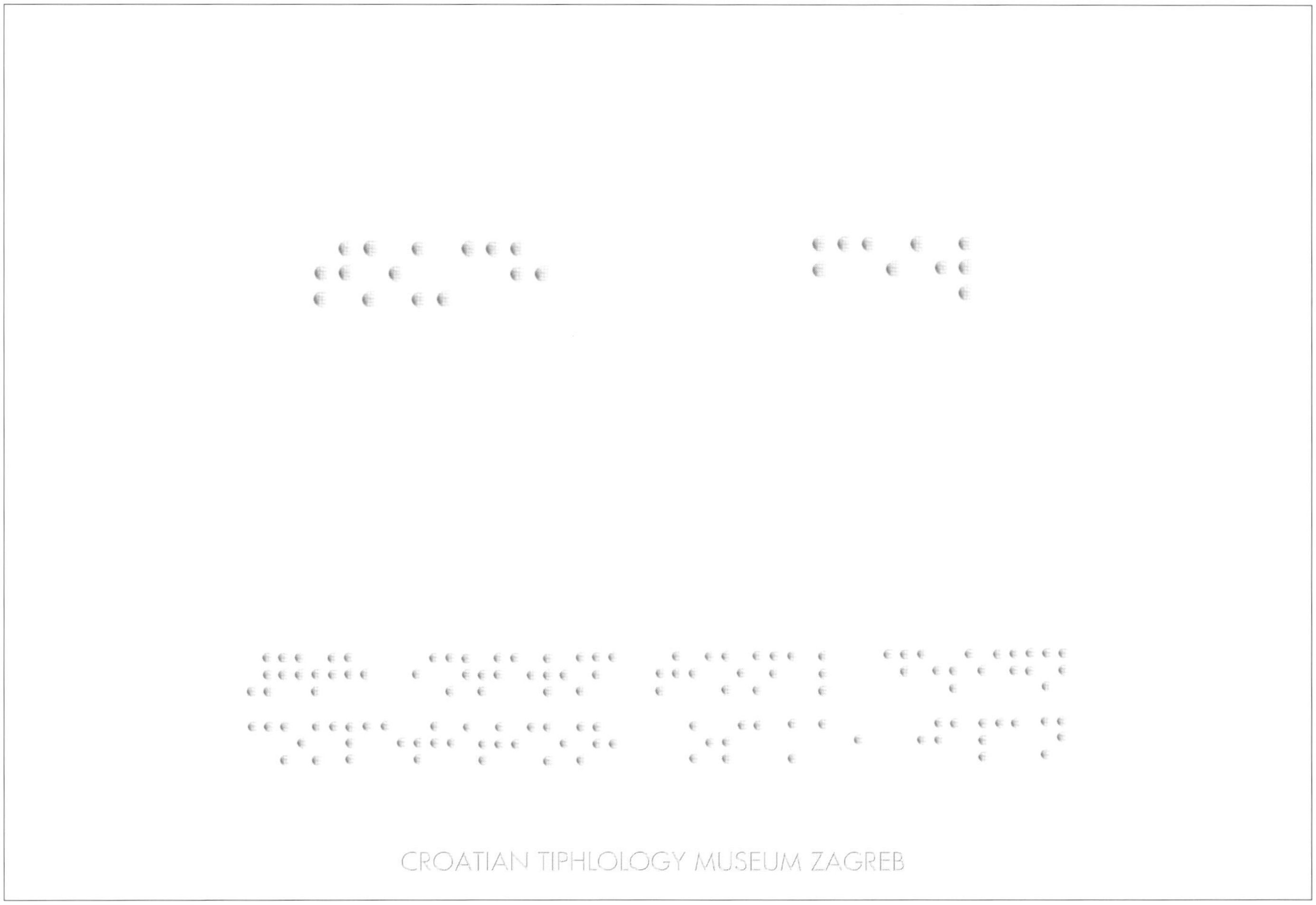

CROATIAN TIPHLOLOGY MUSEUM ZAGREB

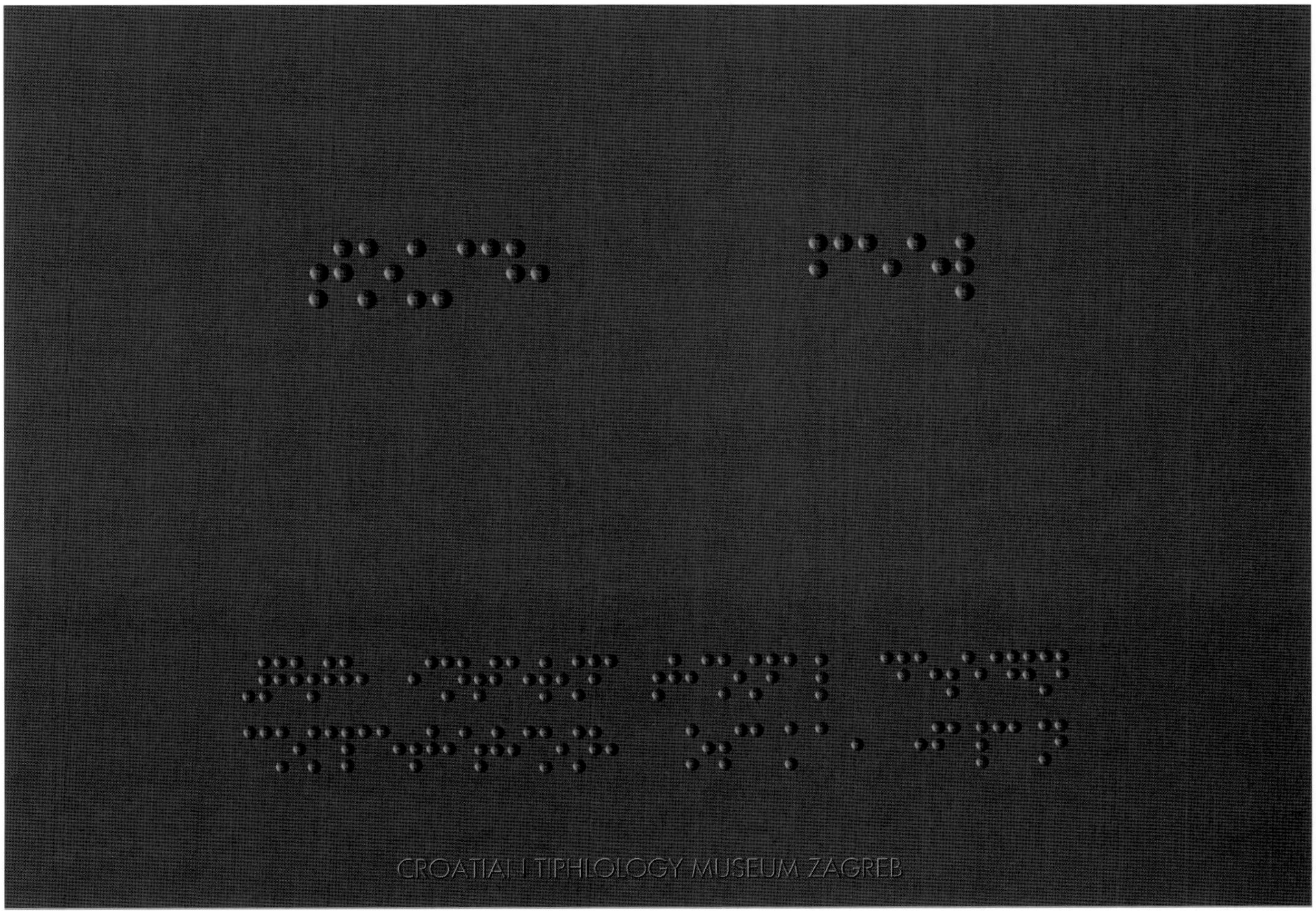

CROATIAN TIPHLOLOGY MUSEUM ZAGREB

7

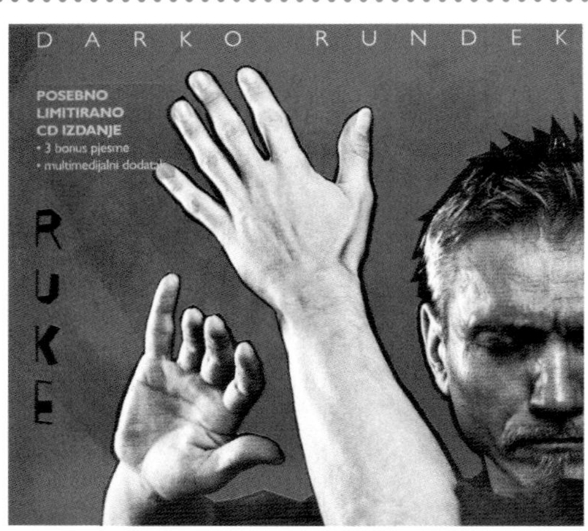

8

9

7 Poster for Radio Drama's Second International Festival of Radio Play and Documentary / Croatian Radio / Croatia / 1998
8 CD cover, *Ruke*, by Darko Rundek / Menart / Croatia / 2002
9 Poster for play *How the Other Half Lives*, by Alan Ayckbourn / National Theater of Varazdin / Croatia / 1997
10 Variations of the Raiffeisen Bank Smart Card / Raiffeisenbank Croatia / Coatia / 2001

Sanja Rocco

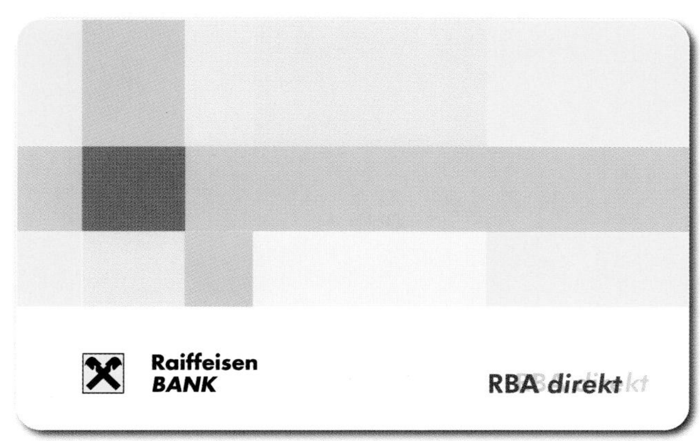
Raiffeisen
BANK
RBA direkt

0000000000
ActivCard®
www.activcard.com

Raiffeisen
BANK
RBA direkt

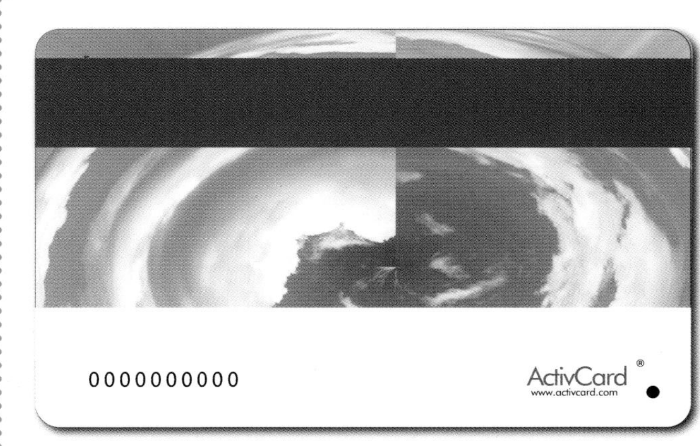
0000000000
ActivCard®
www.activcard.com

Raiffeisen
BANK

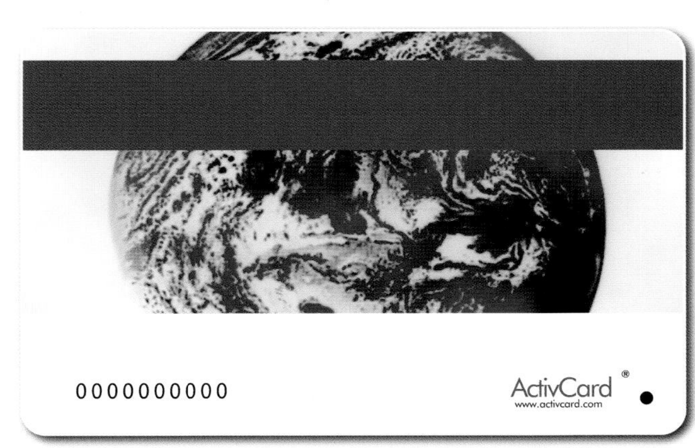
0000000000
ActivCard®
www.activcard.com

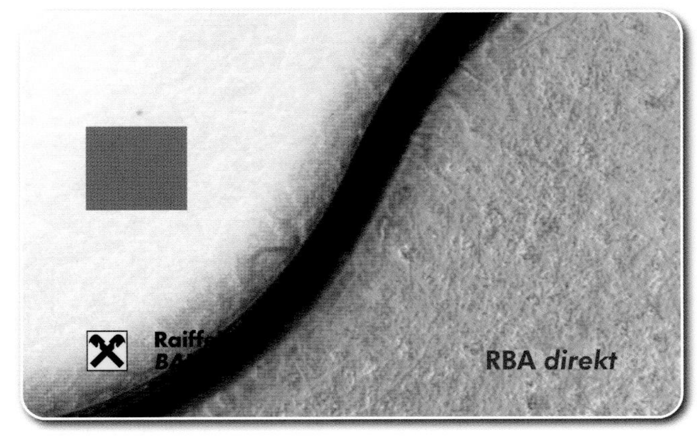
RBA direkt

0000000000
ActivCard®
www.activcard.com

10

Mexican-born graphic designer Gabriela Rodriguez comes from a land where the bold use of bright color is second nature. Yet her work also embraces the subtlety and refined use of colors outside the obvious local palette. While being proudly Mexican, she is a citizen of the world. She is a multitalented designer and artist. Following her graduation from design school, she worked mainly in the design of books, magazines, and assorted print material. While producing many excellent works, she was not content to be confined to the restrictions of the printed page. She has since moved on to produce bold, daring, and provocative posters for political and social issues—things that relate directly to her country. In executing these works she has not been afraid to use the tools of graphic design to confront her public. Her work is simple, strong, bold, and very much to the point. Beyond the surface there is an undercurrent of messages that revolve around carefully planned imagery relating to various aspects of the culture, the country, and the particulars of the project itself. • •More recently she has collaborated internationally on a number of projects, adding a cross-cultural element while exploring new areas such as architectural graphics and exhibitions. Opening up new horizons is something that she is very familiar with. She is constantly searching for the next lesson and the next big idea. She is continually involved in activities that promote and educate the practitioners and consumers of graphic design in Mexico. There is always a strong sense of history, achievement, and culture that often blends both the old and the new. Sometimes it is subtle, other times blatant, but always relevantly applied. She is a natural leader and champion of the profession in a country that is naturally graphically rich but naive to the more commercial aspects of the design profession. • •Ken Cato • •

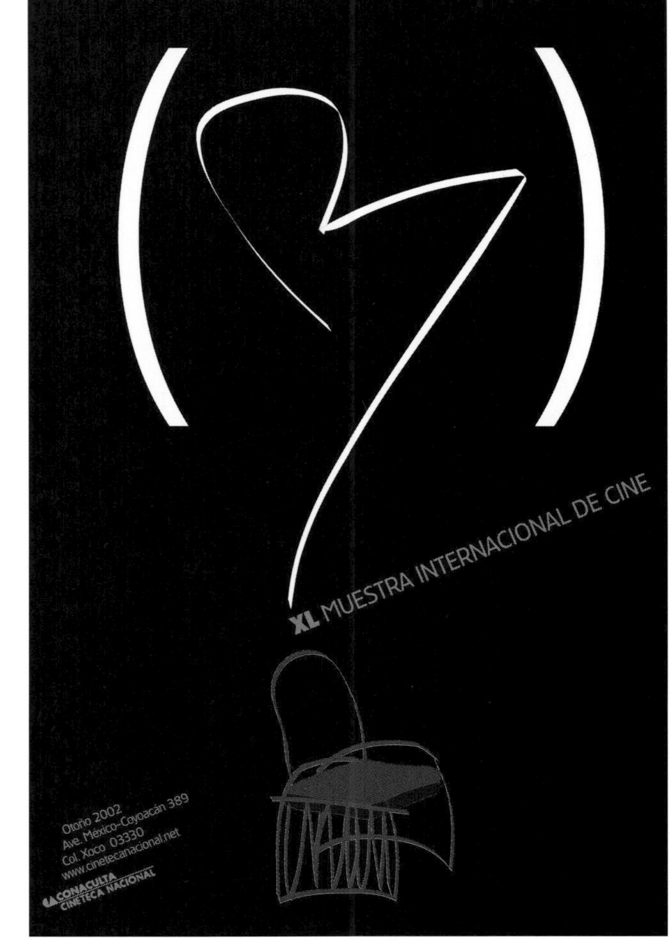

1

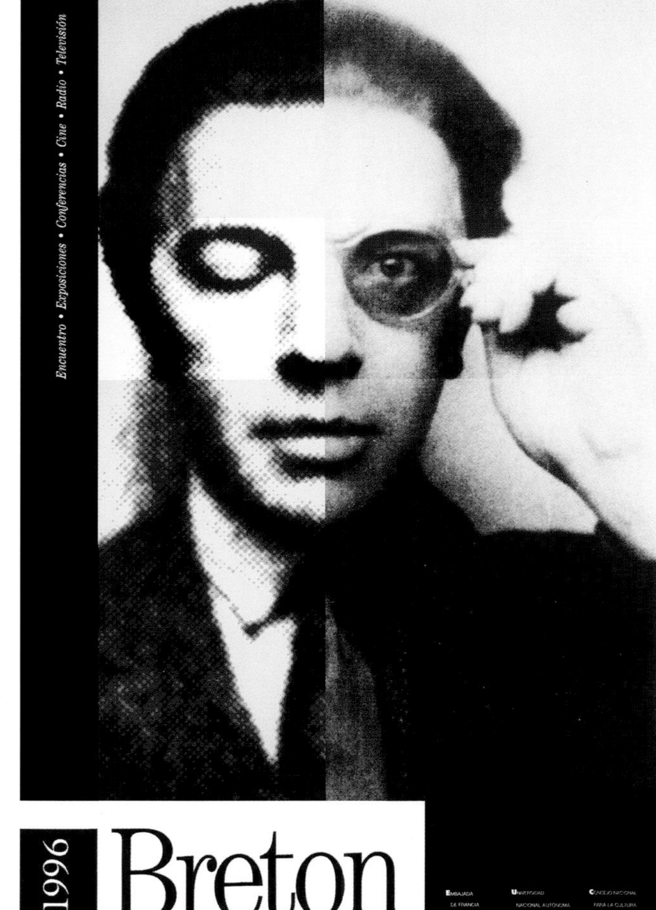

2

1 Poster for XL *Muestra Internacional de Cine* (International Film Festival), Mexico City / National Film Archive of Mexico / Mexico / 2002
2 Poster for festival on occasion of André Breton's centennial / National Council for Culture and Arts (CONACULTA) and the French Embassy / Mexico / 1996
3 Poster inviting young artists to apply for National Foundation of Culture and Arts (FONCA) scholarships / CONACULTA / Mexico / 1999
4 Poster for cultural-exchange project and exhibition *Goya Posada* / Mexican Ministry of Foreign Affairs and the Mexican Institute, Madrid / Mexico and Spain / 2002
5 Promotional poster for book *Miradas sobre el Aborto* (Views on Abortion) / Grupo de Información de Reproducción Elegida / Mexico / 2001
6 Poster homage for Toulouse-Lautrec's centennial / Nouveau Salon des Cents / France / 2001

Gabriela Rodriguez

Mexico City

3

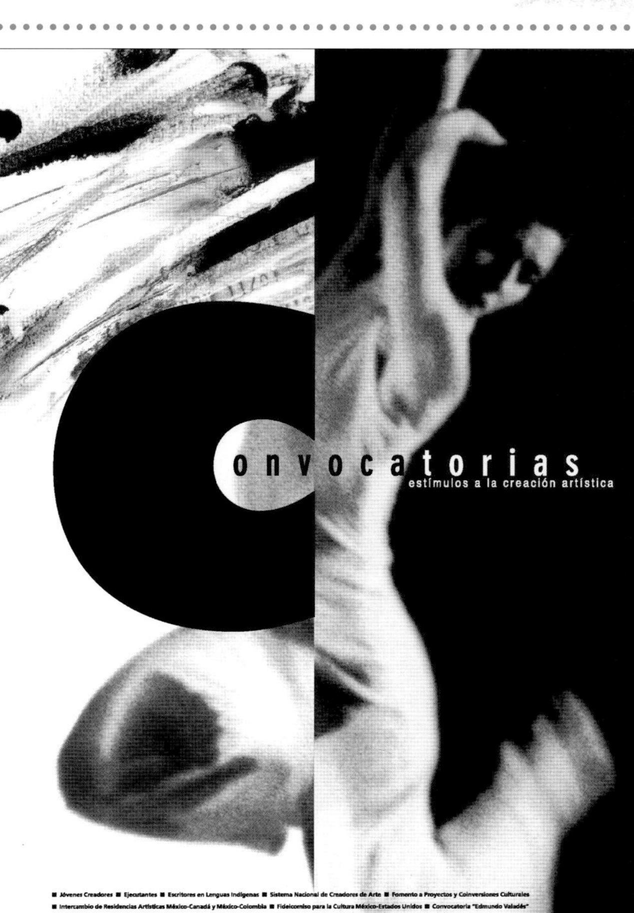
onvocatorias
estímulos a la creación artística
■ Jóvenes Creadores ■ Ejecutantes ■ Escritores en Lenguas Indígenas ■ Sistema Nacional de Creadores de Arte ■ Fomento a Proyectos y Coinversiones Culturales ■ Intercambio de Residencias Artísticas México-Canadá y México-Colombia ■ Fideicomiso para la Cultura México-Estados Unidos ■ Convocatoria "Edmundo Valadés" de apoyo a la edición de Revistas Independientes ■ Sistema Nacional para la producción de Programas de Televisión Cultural ■ Traducción Literaria ■ Premio "Vidas para leerlas" de apoyo a la Creación de Biografías ■ Premio Acer "Expresión de México en Multimedia" ■ Fondos Especiales ■ Teatros para la Comunidad Teatral ■ Fondo Nacional para la Cultura y las Artes (FONCA) ■ Av. México-Coyoacán 371, Col. Xoco. 03330, México, D.F. Tel. 56 05 54 32 y 56 05 73 81, Fax: 56 05 73 61, Ext. 162.
Correo electrónico: foncacel@iserve.net.mx / Internet: www.conaculta.gob.mx/cnca/fonca/
CONACULTA · FONCA

4

GOYA
PO
SA
DA

5

MIRADAS SOBRE EL ABORTO

6

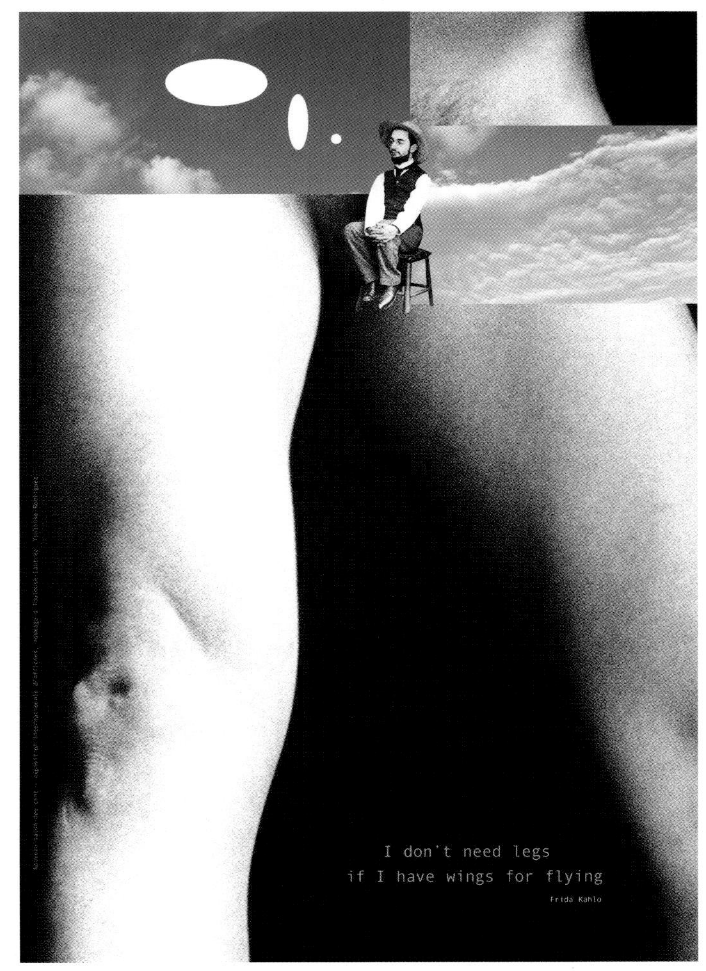
I don't need legs
if I have wings for flying
Frida Kahlo

7

9

8

7 Back and front cover, *I and My Circumstance* exhibition catalogue / CONACULTA and the Montreal Museum of Fine Arts / Mexico and Canada / 1999
8–9 Ceiling design and installation, Monterrey International Airport, Mexico (with Ken Cato) / Grupo Aeroportuario Centro Norte and Eduardo Terrazas / Mexico / 2001
10 Identity for *Festival Cinema Europa* 2002 / Delegation of the European Commission, Mexico / Mexico / 2002
11 Cover for brochure accompanying the 2000 Alliance Graphique Internationale (AGI) congress in Oaxaca, Mexico / AGI / France / 2000
12 Contribution to promotional calendar for Mexican paper company / Pochteca Group / Mexico / 1999
13 Cover, *Fronteras* magazine, spring 1997 / CONACULTA / Mexico / 1996 / *Fronteras* is a Mexican cultural magazine dedicated to the regions around the country's northern and southern borders.

Gabriela Rodriguez

10

FESTIVAL
CINEMA
EUROPA
2002

11

AGI

12

abril
Duchamp
1999

13

Revista de diálogo cultural
entre las FRONTERAS
de México
CIEN AÑOS CON PELLICER
Felipe Garrido, Samuel Gordon
Andrés González Pagés
Miguel A. Ruiz Magdonel
VIVIR LA FRONTERA SUR
Andrés Fábregas Puig
NUEVAS FRONTERAS, NUEVOS LENGUAJES
Federico Campbell
LITERATURA DE LAS
CALIFORNIAS MEXICANAS
Raúl Antonio Cota
PORTAFOLIOS
Guadalupe Velasco, Alejandra Platt
DOSSIER DE LITERATURA
Patricia Laurent, Cristina Leirana
NÚMERO 4 ■ AÑO 2 ■ VOLUMEN 2 ■ PRIMAVERA 1997 ■ ISSN 1405-39-18

Joe Sacco's comic books leave me thinking that news is overrated. Labeled with the words "Breaking News" or "LIVE," the world crisis du jour is being delivered instantly to our screens. Why is so much value pinned on the immediacy of news when so often it is later proved to be inaccurate or grossly misleading? Why are we glued to the thousands of bulletins of this saturated coverage when it is failing to stack up, form a bigger picture? When "official" phrases like the purposely vague *collateral damage* and the crazy *mutually assured destruction* start to be used on the major TV networks, it is even more important that self-respecting journalists like Joe Sacco manage to avoid the clichés and strive to employ a specific language that actually tells us what is happening. • •Sacco inhabits another time zone. Topicality is not one of his concerns despite his enthusiasm for placing himself in the thick of the world's hot spots; from Bosnia to Palestine to, most recently, Ingushetia. In 1993, Sacco spent two months in the Occupied Palestinian Territories holding interviews and taking reference photographs. Once this information—typically for Sacco, always a complexity of the extraordinary shot through with the mundane—was collected, he returned home to Portland, Oregon, and spent months meticulously drawing it up, carefully re-creating his experience for us all to share in a series of nine comics called *Palestine*. Only now, because all the comics have been brought together and published in a single book, is *Palestine* getting the attention it deserves—just as relevant now as it was ten years ago. • •Sacco choreographs your gaze across the frames of his pages like a film director in control of a lens. He achieves this by fragmenting commentary and dialogue text into short sentences that are carefully placed, so that as you read, the details he wants you to notice are dwelled upon in a lingering sequence he has complete mastery of—details such as the individualized faces of people in crowds, the particular texture and pattern of their clothes, the miserable state of the ground they walk on, and the precarious condition of the roofs that shelter them. • •Sacco is a cartoonist who became a journalist who favors "humanizing people who are broadly labeled 'terrorists' or 'victims.'" Sacco feels that while journalism's main aim is to inform, why should people care when so little of it is moving? Sacco's art is about redress—for peoples and places mis- and unrepresented by the mainstream media. It's ironic that Sacco has pulled it off in a medium often dismissed as kids' stuff. • •Nick Bell• •

1–3 Spreads, *Safe Area Gorazde–The War in Eastern Bosnia 1992–95*, by Joe Sacco / Fantagraphics Books / USA / 2000 / *Safe Area Gorazde* details Sacco's trips to the Bosnian town of Gorazde during the aftermath of the war.

4 Spread from *The War Crimes Trials*, a six-page story for *Details* magazine / Details / USA / 1998 / The story focuses on the Bosnian War Crimes Trials in the Hague.

Joe Sacco

New York

1 2 3

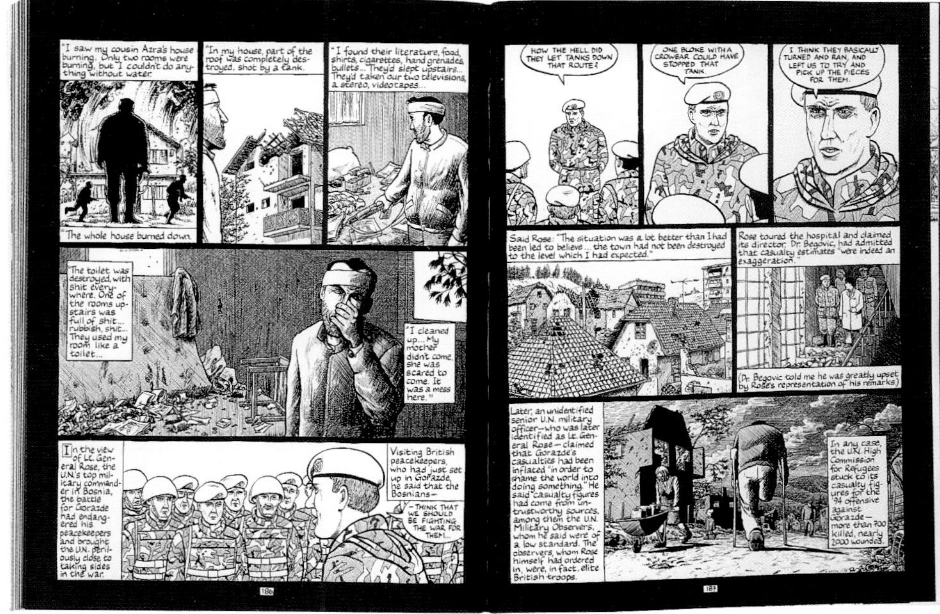

260 DETAILS • SEPTEMBER 1998

5

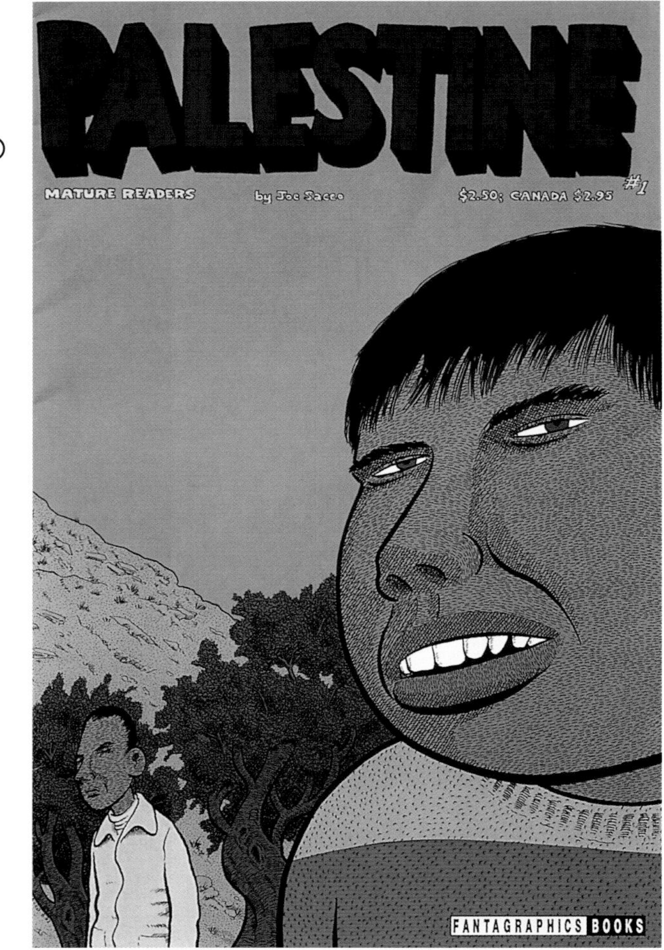

6

7

5–7 Covers, first three issues of nine-issue comic series *Palestine*, by Joe Sacco / Fantagraphics Books / USA / 1993–94 / *Palestine* details Sacco's two-month stay in the Palestinian occupied territories.

8–15 Cover and spreads, *Palestine*, by Joe Sacco / Fantagraphics Books / USA / 2001 / The book is a collection of all nine issues of the *Palestine* comic series.

Joe Sacco

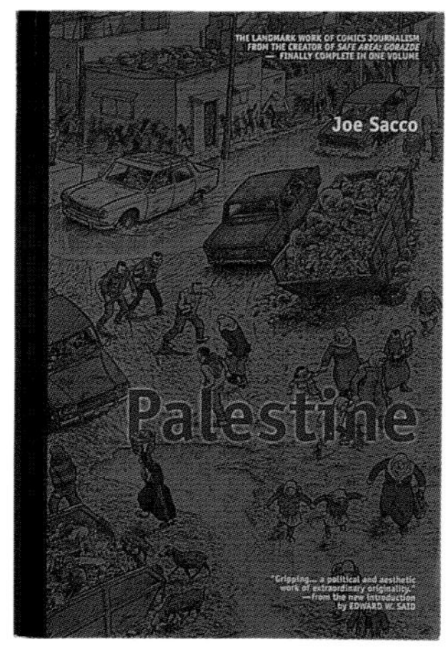

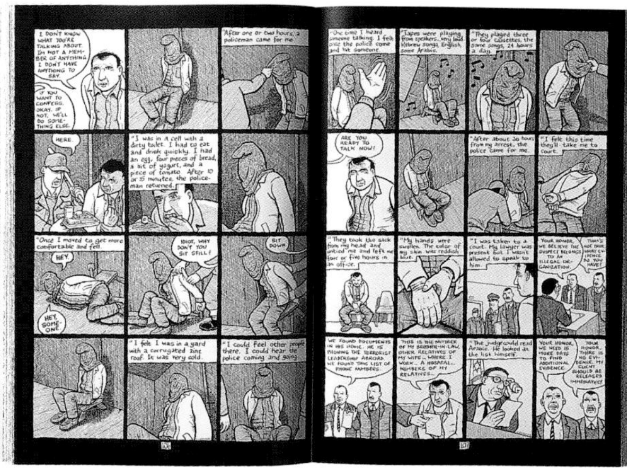

8
9
10
11

12
13
14
15

At the turn of the millennium, Korean designer Ahn Sang-Soo managed to coin a new word in international design: Oullim. • • Oullim suggests absolute harmony of nature, humanity, and technology; of the past, present, and future; east and west, north and south. But this simple word is not as empty or as favorable as may seem at first glance. Behind it hides a deep crisis through which our culture, civilization, and design are living. • • Twentieth-century design, according to Sang-Soo, developed from Bauhaus ideology, industrialization, and mass production. These developments took place in opposition to nature and in aesthetic terms can be described as having created "contrast." Such contrast, in the end, led to ecological destruction, increasing cruelty, and other frictions between man and his surroundings. As a result, we now find ourselves in search of new ideals, a new design paradigm for the twenty-first century. This new conception of design must be found in the delta of Eastern rather than Western philosophical traditions. The design of the new millennium must break the fetters of contrasts that bound it in the twentieth century and establish a balance between "all of you" and "me," between the society and the individual, between the skies and the earth. • • Sang-Soo tries to solve these difficult philosophical dilemmas within the framework of his main professional specialty—typeface design and typography. Or, rather, he constantly strives to step outside this framework in search of the cultural meaning of graphic design: His typographic experiments often include dance, architecture, sculpture, and music. Innovative and elegant, his works appear wise and bright, like Sang-Soo himself. They instill hope and appease. • • One of his latest experimental works is called "From Alpha to Huit." Huit is the last letter in hangul, the Korean alphabet. Thus, instead of the common expression "from alpha to omega," Sang-Soo offers an alternative and redirects Greco-Latin civilization eastward. • • In another project we see this idea as part of a live performance in which letters disappear and emerge again behind a semitransparent wall. We thus experience a work that speaks about itself and engages us in the intellectual and aesthetic process of its creation. • • Serge Serov • •

1–3 Typographic installation and performance "From Alpha to Hiut" held at the Rodin Gallery, Seoul / Korea / 2002 / Huit is the last character of the Korean hangul alphabet.
4 Black Planet poster for *Kyoto Environmental Poster Design Exhibition* on occasion of United Nations environmental summit in Kyoto, Japan / Korea / 1997
5 Poster for concert by saxophone player Kang Tae-Hwan / Kang Tae-Hwan / Korea / 1997
6 Poster series promoting Korean arts and culture magazine *bogoseo/bogoseo* / bogoseo/bogoseo / Korea / 2001 / *Bogoseo* is Korean for "report."
7–9 Poster series as part of advertising campaign for Korean fashion brand / Ssamzie / Korea / 1999

Ahn Sang-Soo

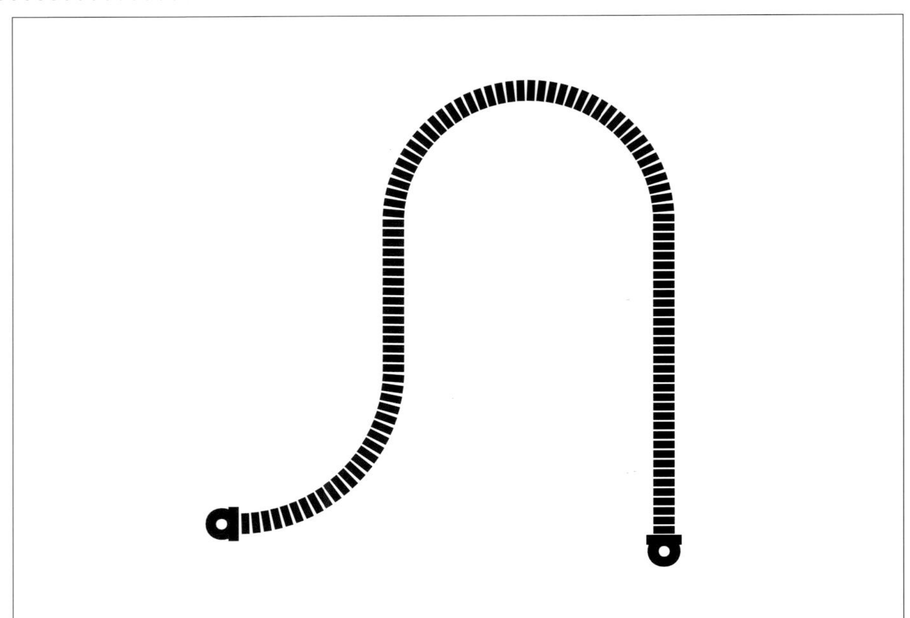

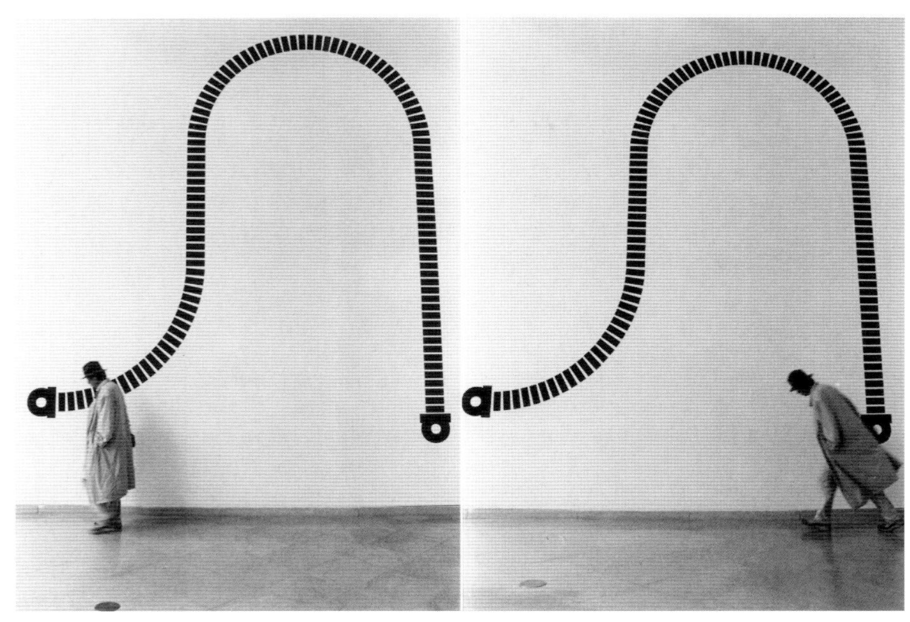

4

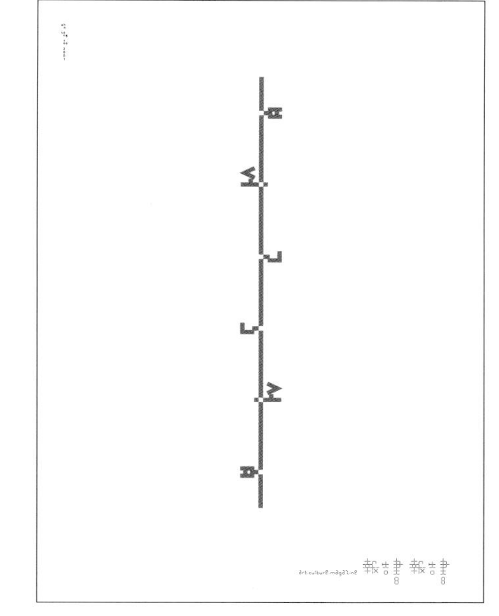

6

5

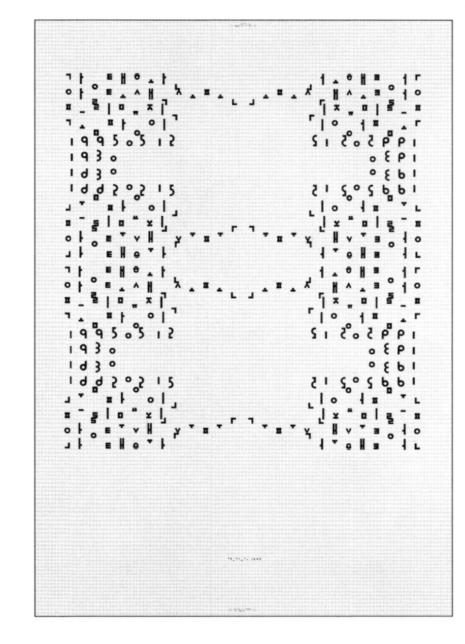

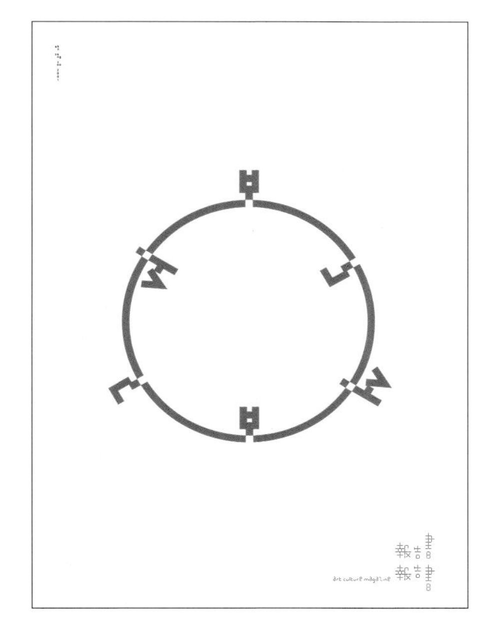

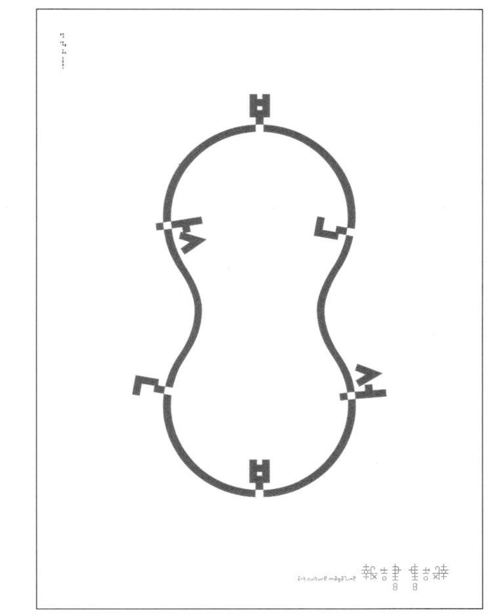

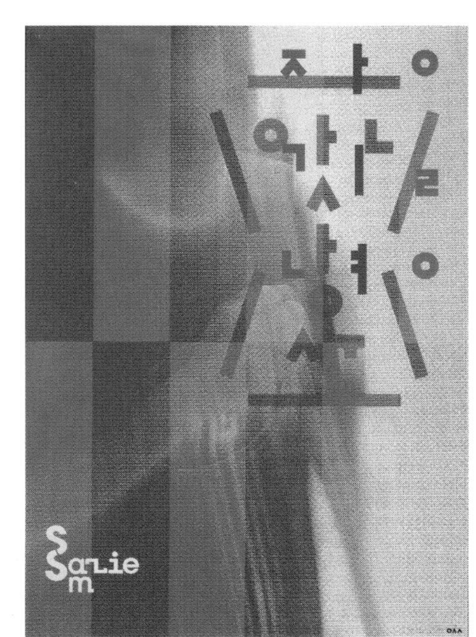

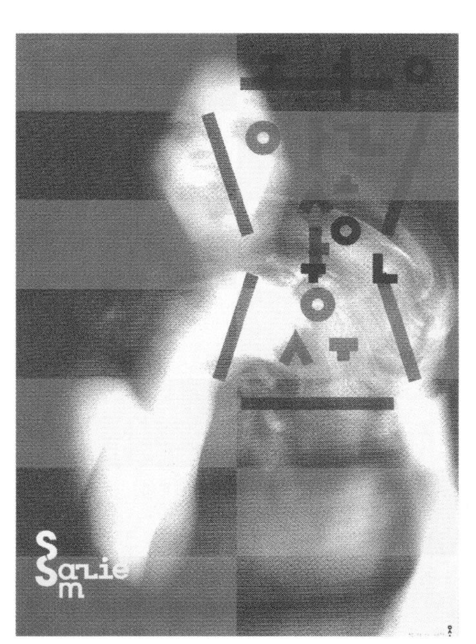

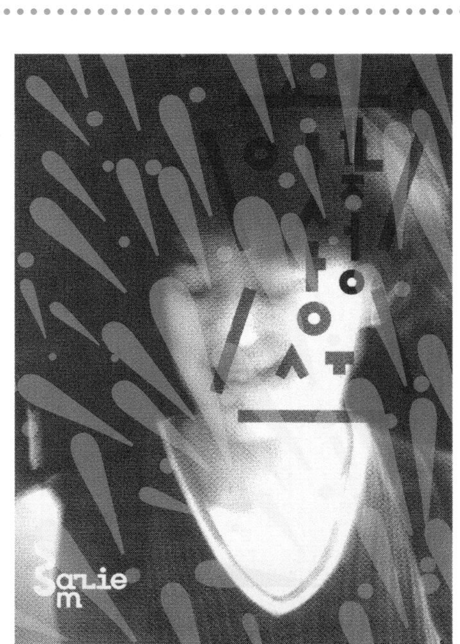

7 8 9

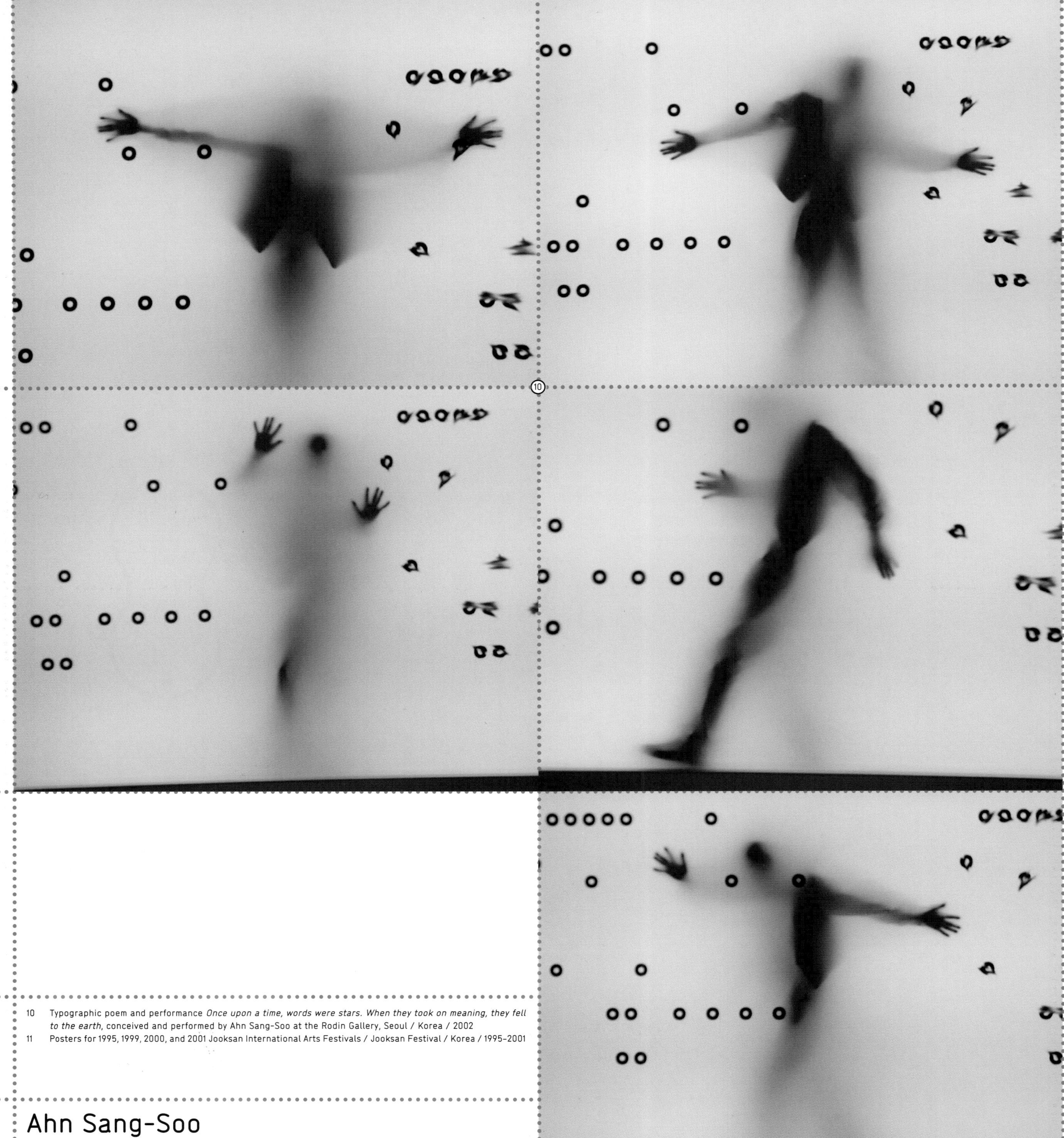

10 Typographic poem and performance *Once upon a time, words were stars. When they took on meaning, they fell to the earth*, conceived and performed by Ahn Sang-Soo at the Rodin Gallery, Seoul / Korea / 2002
11 Posters for 1995, 1999, 2000, and 2001 Jooksan International Arts Festivals / Jooksan Festival / Korea / 1995–2001

Ahn Sang-Soo

first jooksan arts
festival
1995 06 17 - 06 18
namiko kawamura
isadora duncan, dance
nam jeong-ho + kim dae-hwan
laughing stone
maida withers

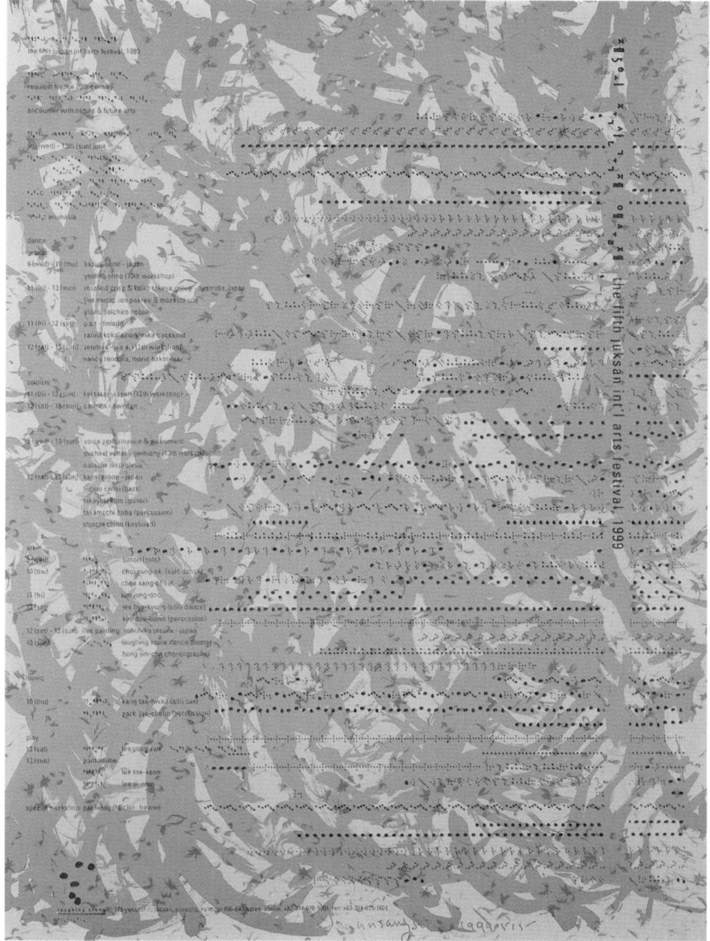
the fifth juksan int'l arts festival 1999

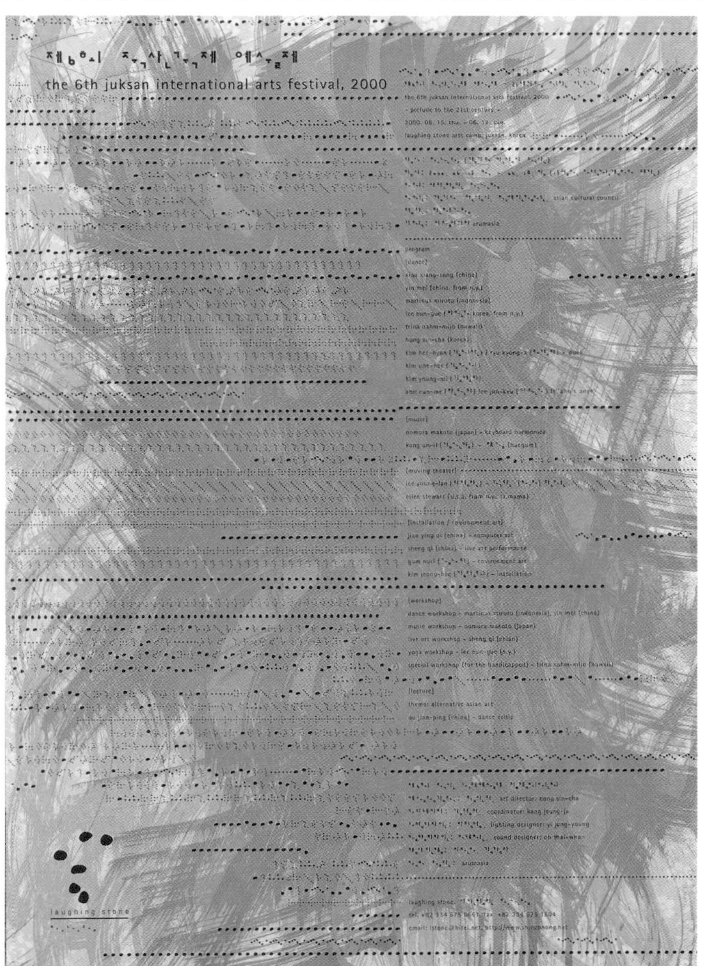
the 6th juksan international arts festival, 2000
laughing stone

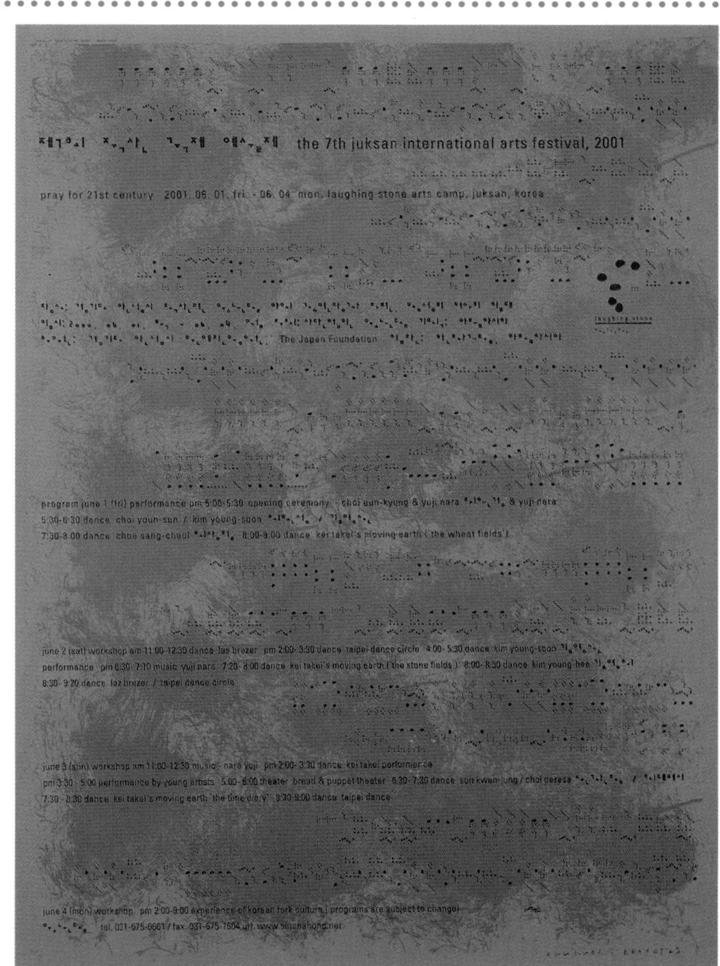
the 7th juksan international arts festival, 2001
pray for 21st century 2001. 06. 01. fri. - 06. 04. mon. laughing stone arts camp, juksan, korea
The Japan Foundation
laughing stone

In the Japanese martial arts of swordsmanship, kendo, there is a position called *gedan-no-kamae*. Instead of swinging the sword above one's head to slash it down, one dangles it low on the right side, inviting the opponent to attack. In the sphere of Japanese graphic design, Yasuhiro Sawada's style is unquestionably *gedan-no-kamae*. • •Sawada is a new talent who has consistently been demonstrating his unique sensitivity through his graphic creations. His works are based on ordinary forms such as circles, squares, rectangles, polka dots, and so forth, and he uses commonplace materials such as fabric and wood. Like the *gedan-no-kamae* position, they appear to be ordinary and harmless. In reality, however, Sawada's works create highly effective messages owing to their well-thought-out composition. • •There is a Japanese expression that describes the subtle relationship created between two people before embarking on a task they are going to undertake together. By observing each other closely, they don't have to speak to communicate. Just like a question-and-answer session of Zen priests that is beyond the comprehension of outsiders, Sawada's work communicates with the viewer while letting him or her feel and think freely. • •I imagine Sawada stepping onto a stage. One of his works fills the space around him, forming the set. "I cannot find anything new," our hero declares. I would like to say to him, "Why, you yourself are the new material." • •Shigeo Fukuda • •

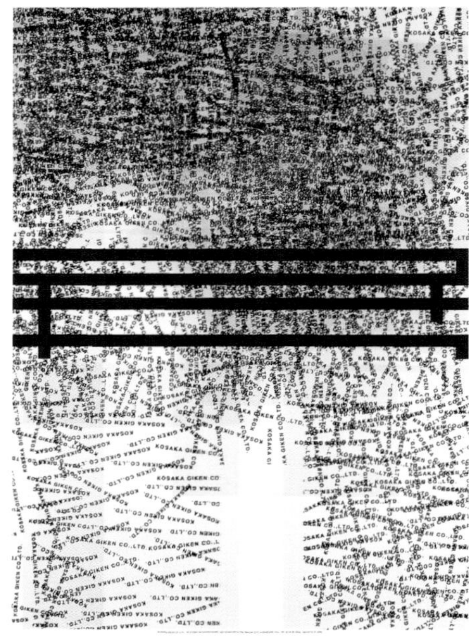

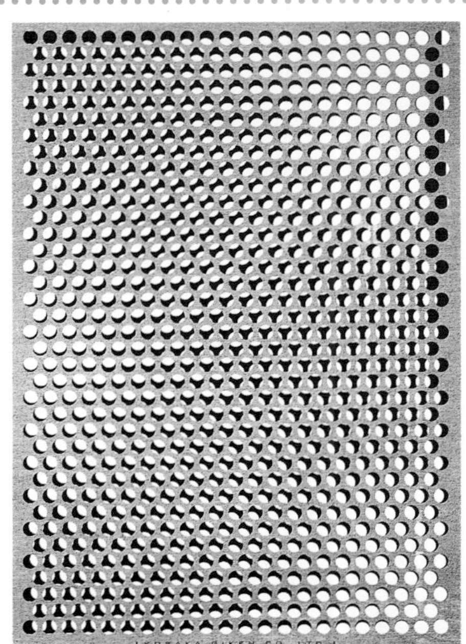

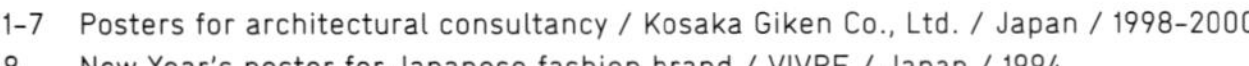

1–7 Posters for architectural consultancy / Kosaka Giken Co., Ltd. / Japan / 1998–2000
8 New Year's poster for Japanese fashion brand / VIVRE / Japan / 1994
9–10 Posters for exhibition *4 from Tokyo* held at the Art Directors Club Gallery, New York / Art Directors Club New York / USA / 1997

Yasuhiro Sawada

Tokyo

⑦

KOSAKA GIKEN CO.,LTD.

⑧

ベスト。

あなたと、
あなたの愛するすべての、
ベストになりたい。
平成五年一月一日
VIVRE

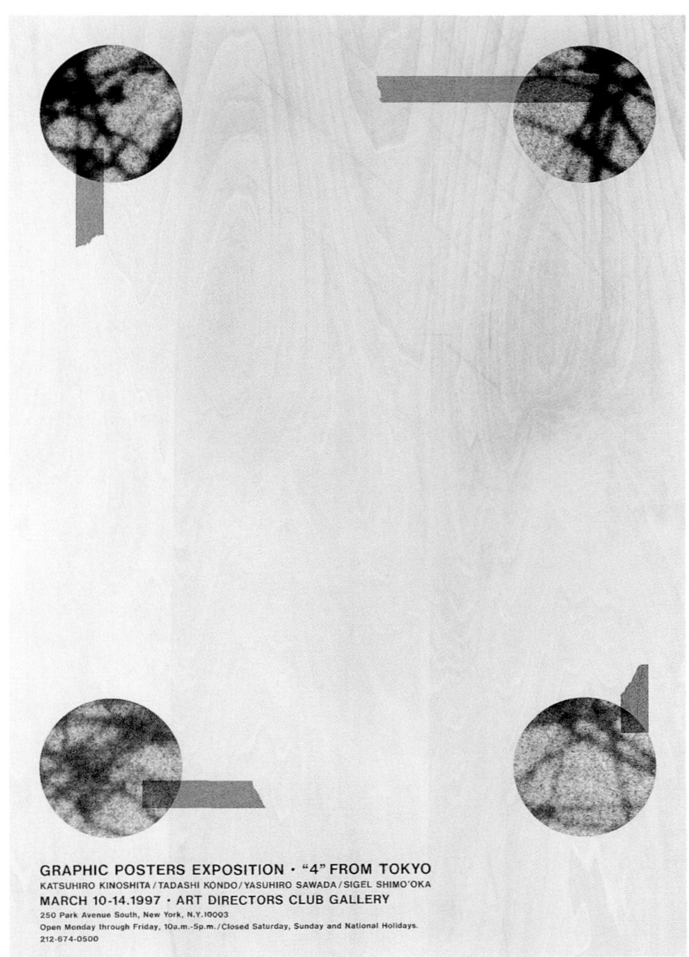
GRAPHIC POSTERS EXPOSITION · "4" FROM TOKYO
KATSUHIRO KINOSHITA / TADASHI KONDO / YASUHIRO SAWADA / SIGEL SHIMO'OKA
MARCH 10-14.1997 · ART DIRECTORS CLUB GALLERY
250 Park Avenue South, New York, N.Y.10003
Open Monday through Friday, 10a.m.-5p.m./Closed Saturday, Sunday and National Holidays.
212-674-0500

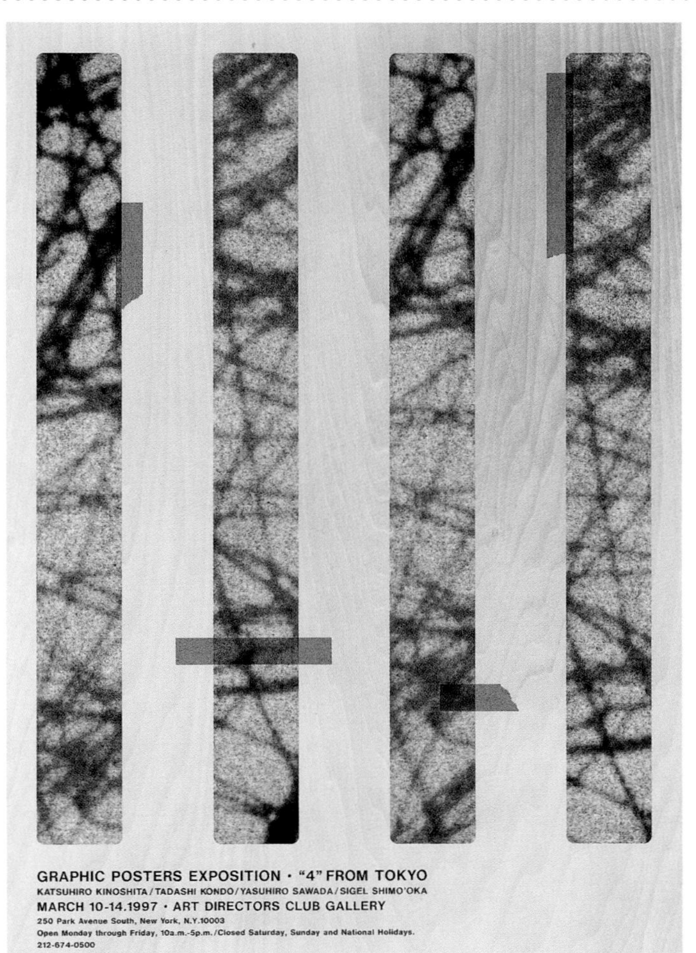
GRAPHIC POSTERS EXPOSITION · "4" FROM TOKYO
KATSUHIRO KINOSHITA / TADASHI KONDO / YASUHIRO SAWADA / SIGEL SHIMO'OKA
MARCH 10-14.1997 · ART DIRECTORS CLUB GALLERY
250 Park Avenue South, New York, N.Y.10003
Open Monday through Friday, 10a.m.-5p.m./Closed Saturday, Sunday and National Holidays.
212-674-0500

⑨⑩

11

12

13

11 Poster for exhibition celebrating the two hundredth birthday of Japanese ukiyo-e artist Sharaku held at the Shibuya Parco Gallery, Tokyo / Mainichi Newspapers / Japan / 1994

12 Poster for exhibition *The Design Spirit of Japan* held at the University Art Museum, Tokyo / Tokyo National University of Fine Arts and Music / Japan / 2001

13 Poster designed to be sold at fund-raising event organized by the International Commissioner for the Protection of Fundamental Human Rights / Amnesty International / Japan / 1991

14–15 Poster series "Trimming" for *Graphic Wave 2002* exhibition held at the Ginza Graphic Gallery, Tokyo / Japan / 2002

16–17 Pages from catalogue for Yohji Yamamoto's fashion brand Y's for men / Y's for men / Japan / 1989

Yasuhiro Sawada

Graphic Wave 2002
Ginza Graphic Gallery
September 4(Wed.)-30(Mon.)

Graphic Wave 2002
Ginza Graphic Gallery
September 4(Wed.)-30(Mon.)

14 15

PEA COAT/WF-J09-129/¥32,000/ •MOCHA •DARK BROWN •BLACK

THIS COLOR IS MOCHA

JEANS/WF-P06-054/¥9,000/ •BLUE •BLACK

THIS COLOR IS BLUE

16 17

The term personal computer implies that the computer is personal rather than impersonal, more human than machine. "Personal computer" means "humanist technology." Indeed, the arrival of the PC coincided with a mental evolutionary jump. Technology that delivers an end result in no time, eliminating the slow and methodical progression of ideas from prologue to epilogue, changes the thought process itself. ●● Throughout the twentieth century—a century in which the Swiss school formed an important apex of graphic design—technology attempted to demystify the world and turn it into a machine to serve life. At the threshold of the twenty-first century, however, technology opened the window to the magical world of the virtual, showing us its inexhaustible depths and spellbinding mystery. ●● Claudia Schmauder is a designer whose work clearly demonstrates this development. With the Swiss design school at her core, she extracts and creates images of modernity—or, more correctly, of postmodernity, images of the new computer age. ●● The American "new wave" that started mastering digital images in the 1980s saw that what was most important was the background's openness, its context, its medium. The Swiss graphic designer Schraivogel in the 1990s increased the depth of field and discovered the astonishing density and richness of light spaces. Claudia Schmauder continues this journey, advancing postmodernism and pushing the boundaries of the paradigm. ●● At the same time, Schmauder is a typical representative of the Swiss graphic school. In the depths of the chaos of her works, strict Swiss composition is always visible; at the core of the magical effects is a rational framework. What can you do? The personal computer is, after all, a machine. ●● Serge Serov ●●

1
2

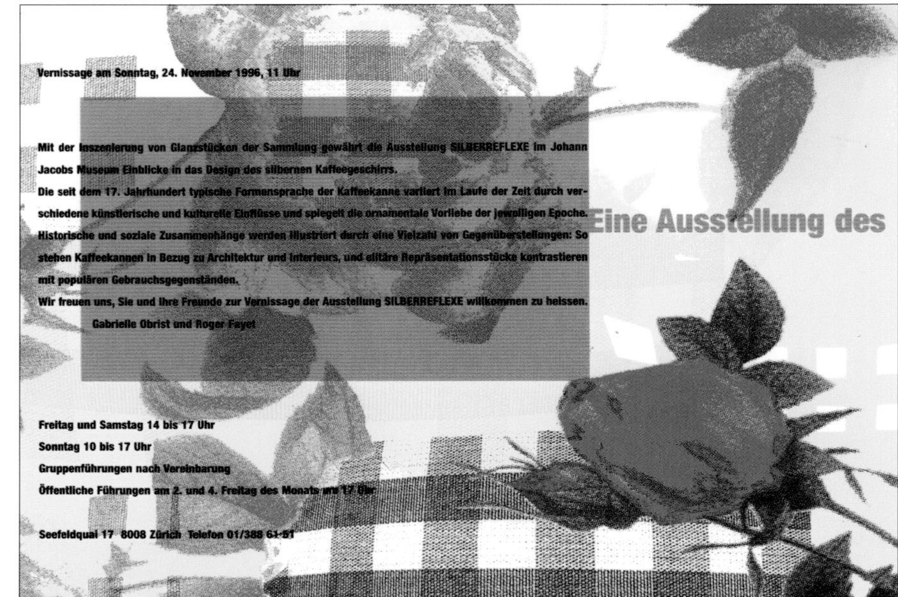

1–2 Front and back of invitation for exhibition *Silberreflexe* (Silver Reflexes) / Johann Jacobs Museum, Zurich / Switzerland / 1996
3–4 Shopping-bag designs from personal project "Food Culture" / Switzerland / 1997
5 Poster for exhibition *Silberreflexe* (Silver Reflexes) / Johann Jacobs Museum, Zurich / Switzerland / 1996
6 Poster for exhibition *Am Limit–Kaffeegenuss als Grenzerfahrung* (At the Limit–Coffee as a Border Experience) / Johann Jacobs Museum, Zurich / Switzerland / 2001
7 Poster for exhibition *Café Mundo* / Johann Jacobs Museum, Zurich / Switzerland / 2000
8 Perforated invitation/unfoldable poster for open-air contemporary-art exhibition *Passagen* on the half-island Au / Au Konsortium / Switzerland / 2001

Claudia Schmauder

Zurich

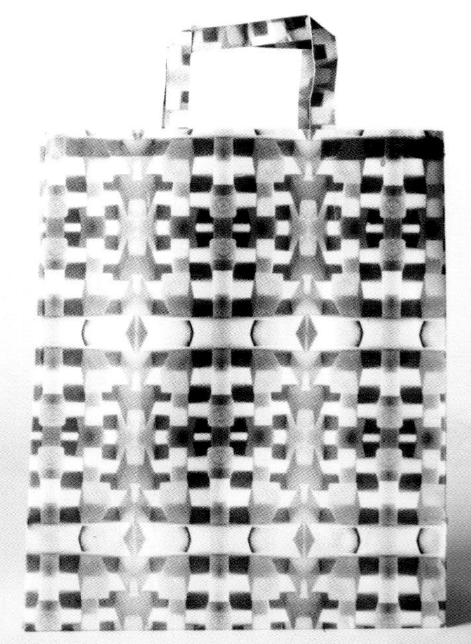

3 4

5

24.11.1996–26.10.1997
SILBER
REFLEXE
Johann Jacobs Museum
Sammlung zur Kulturgeschichte des Kaffees
Kaffeekanne und Design – Eine Entdeckungsreise

6

KAFFEEGENUSS ALS GRENZERFAHRUNG
AM LIMIT
SEEFELDQUAI 17 CH-8008 ZÜRICH
++41/1/388 61 51 WWW.JOHANN-JACOBS-MUSEUM.CH
FR 14 BIS 19 UHR, SA 14 BIS 17 UHR, SO 10 BIS 17 UHR
GRUPPENFÜHRUNGEN NACH VEREINBARUNG
ÖFFENTLICHE FÜHRUNGEN GEMÄSS ANKÜNDIGUNG
VOM 18.11.01 JOHANN JACOBS MUSEUM
BIS 20.10.02 SAMMLUNG ZUR KULTURGESCHICHTE DES KAFFEES

7

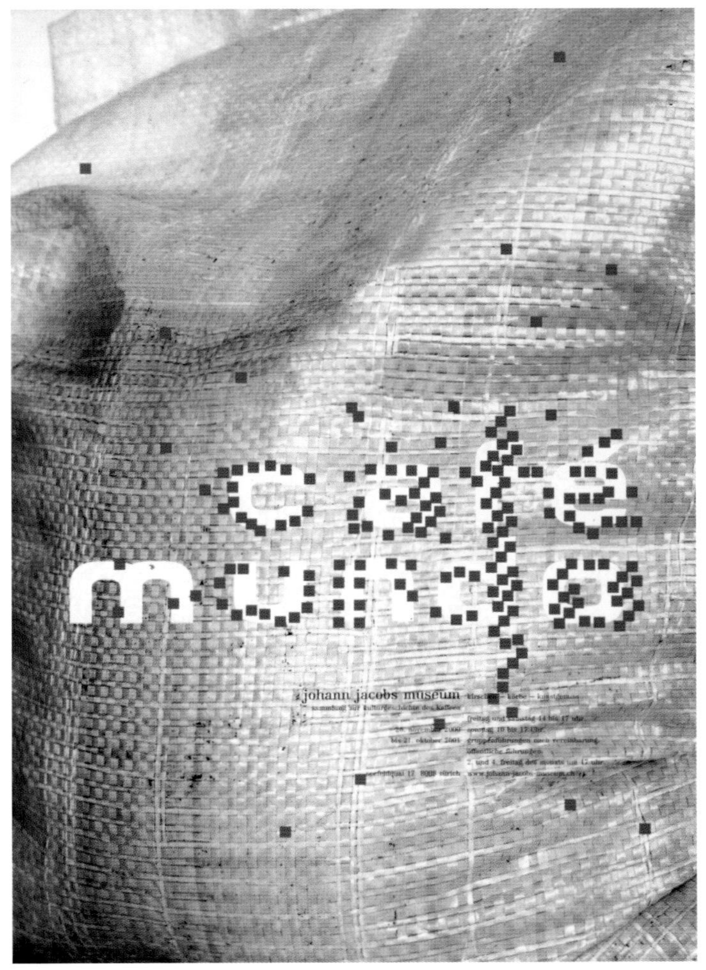
café
mundo
johann jacobs museum

8

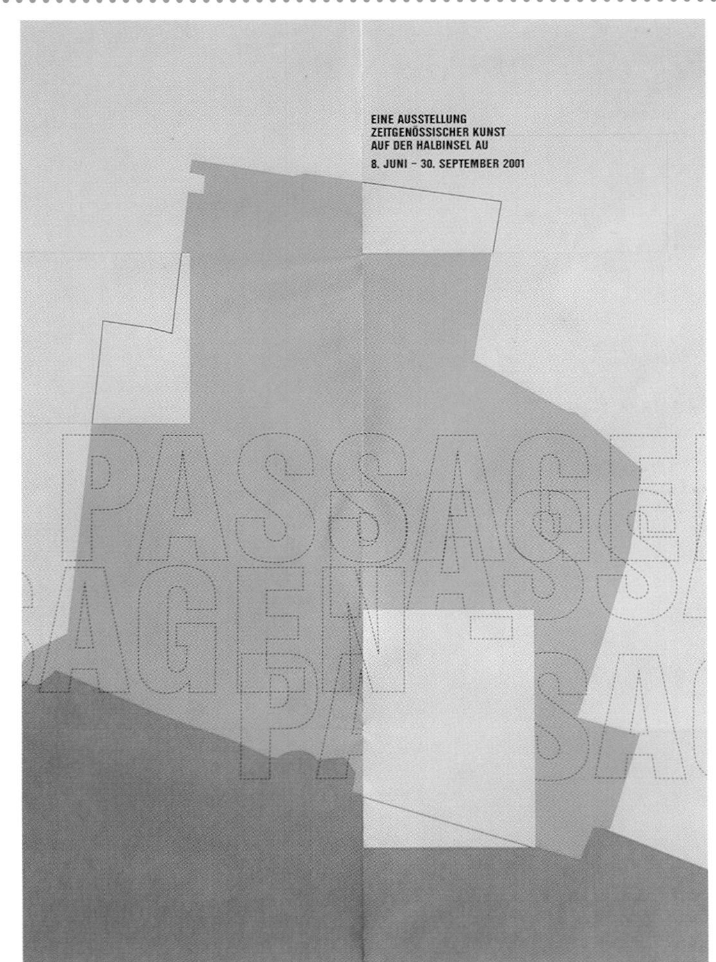
EINE AUSSTELLUNG
ZEITGENÖSSISCHER KUNST
AUF DER HALBINSEL AU
8. JUNI – 30. SEPTEMBER 2001
PASSAGEN

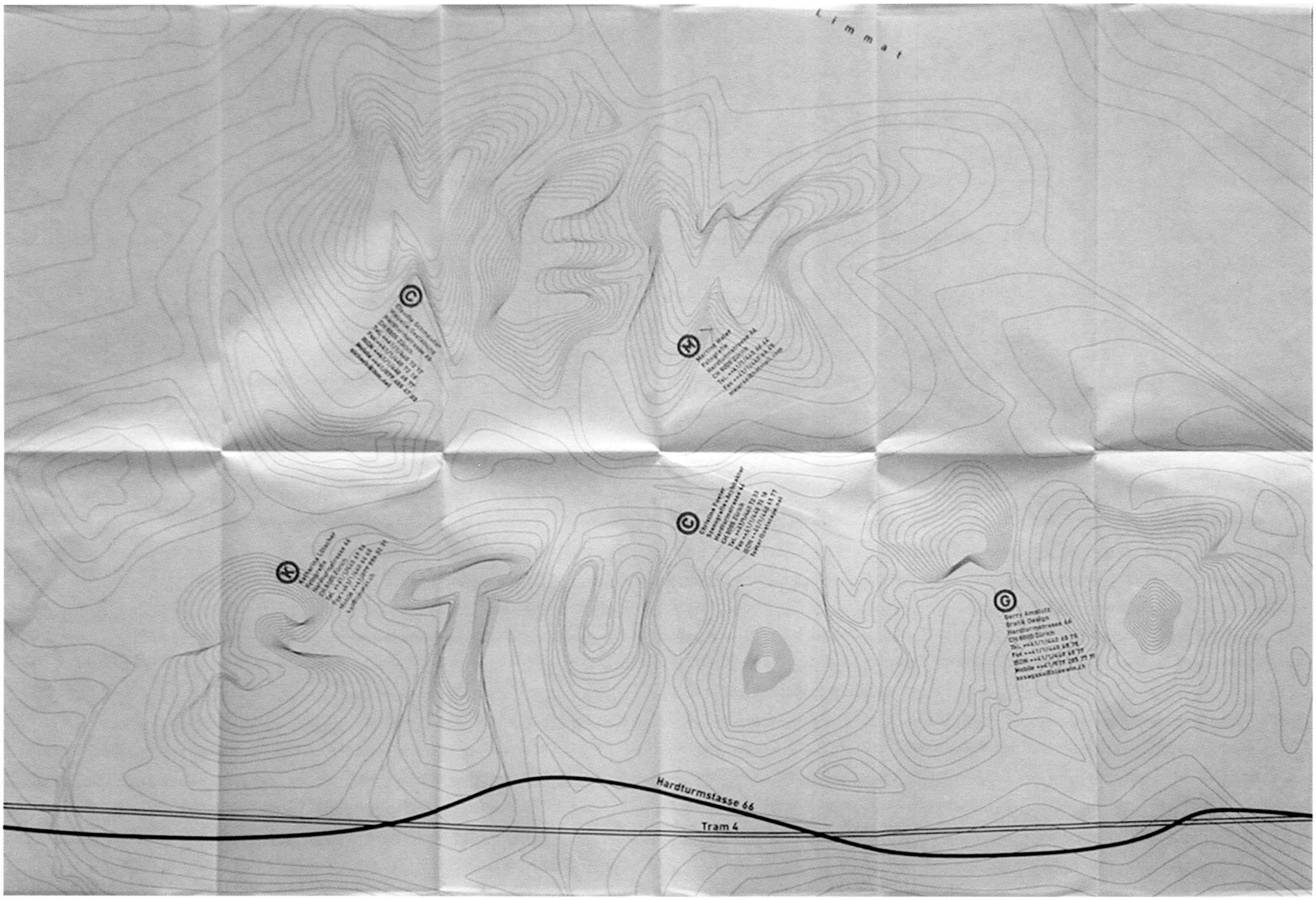

Limmat

Hardturmstasse 66

Tram 4

9

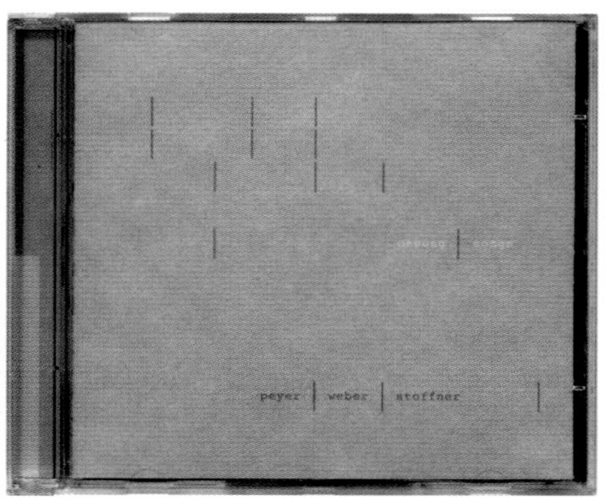

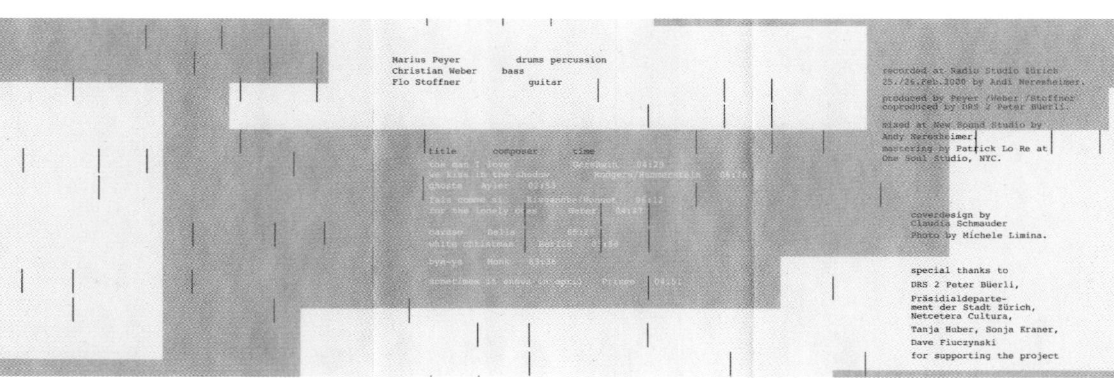

10 11

Claudia Schmauder

9 Mailer/unfoldable poster announcing Claudia Schmauder's new studio location / Switzerland / 1999

10–11 CD cover and booklet for *Unsung Songs* by jazz trio Peyer, Weber, Stoffner / Peyer, Weber, Stoffner and Unit Records / Switzerland / 2000

12 Front and back of invitation and poster for exhibition *Das Kaffeetrinken und der Blick der Kunst* (The Drinking of Coffee and the Eye of Art) / Johann Jacobs Museum, Zurich / Switzerland / 1997

13 Front and back of invitation and poster for exhibition *Coffee Talks* / Johann Jacobs Museum, Zurich / Switzerland / 1999

DAS KAFFEETRINKEN &
DER BLICK DER KUNST
EINE AUSSTELLUNG DES JOHANN JACOBS MUSEUM
SAMMLUNG ZUR KULTURGESCHICHTE DES KAFFEES
EINLADUNG ZUR VERNISSAGE
SONNTAG 23. NOVEMBER 11 UHR
AUSSTELLUNGSDAUER: 23. NOV. 1997 BIS 25. OKT. 1998
FREITAG UND SAMSTAG 14 BIS 17 UHR
SONNTAG 10 BIS 17 UHR
GRUPPENFÜHRUNGEN NACH VEREINBARUNG
ÖFFENTLICHE FüHRUNGEN JEDEN
2. UND 4. FREITAG DES MONATS UM 17 UHR
SEEFELDQUAI 17 8008 ZÜRICH TEL. 01 388 61 51

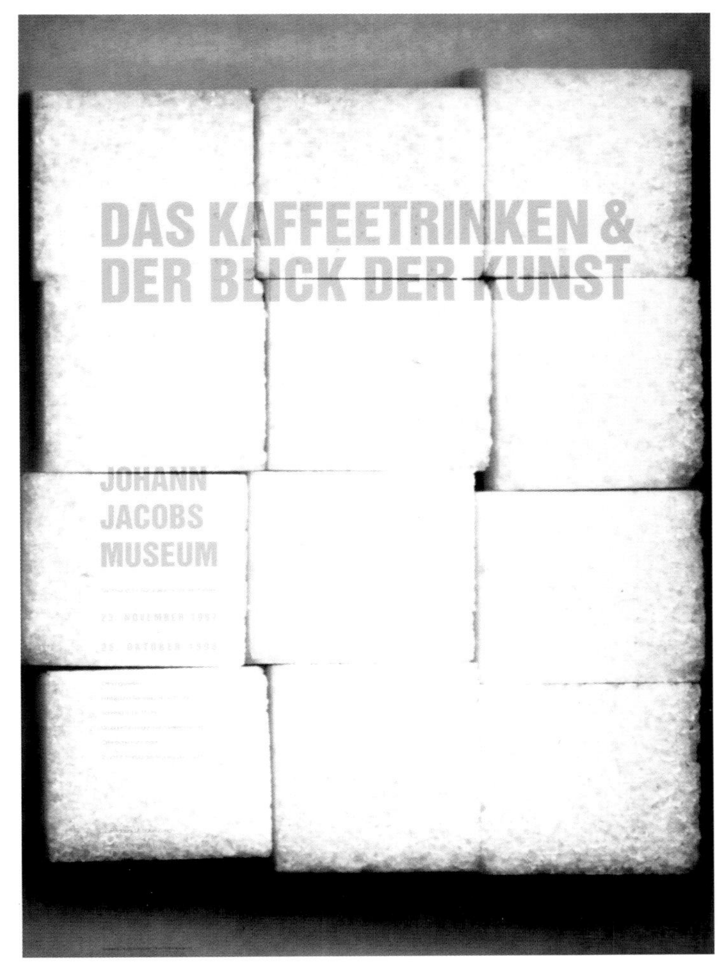

12

13

coffee talks/vom tête-à-tête zum internet/eine ausstellung des johann jacobs museums/sammlung zur kulturgeschichte des kaffees/ 21.11.1999--------22.10.2000/fr.sa 14 ---17 uhr. so 10-----17 uhr/oeffentliche fuehrungen jeden 2./4. fr des monats um 17 uhr/gruppenfuehrungen nach vereinbarung/seefeldquai 17/ch-8008 zuerich/telefon ++41/1/388 61 51/jjm@tic.ch/www.johann-jacobs-museum.ch

Coffee Talks! Ist Kaffee ein Kommunikator?

Dass Wein die Zunge löst und den Redefluss begünstigt, ist gemeinhin bekannt. Dass dem Kaffee gleichermassen das Etikett des Gesprächsanimators verliehen werden kann, dies deklamiert die neue Ausstellung im Johann Jacobs Museum. Vom Tête-à-Tête zum Internet-Café ist der Bogen gespannt. Vom Monolog über das Zwiegespräch bis hin zur Redeschlacht sind die unterschiedlichsten Formen des wortreichen Austausches beim Kaffeetrinken kommentiert. Sie als Besucherinnen und Besucher sind eingeladen, interaktiv mit der Ausstellung ins Gespräch zu kommen, indem Sie Ihren eigenen Kaffeekommunikationstypus eruieren. Welcher Art diese Analyse vonstatten geht, sei hier nicht verraten. Weitere Formen der Kommunikation können Sie beim Lesen des Kaffeesatzes praktizieren oder beim Einklinken in die globale Vernetzung in unserem Internet-Café. Wir heissen Sie und Ihre Freunde willkommen im Netz und laden Sie am 21. November, 11 Uhr herzlich ein zu unserer Vernissage am See.

Gabrielle Obrist und Fredi Bischoff

gest.ch/sch

Nico Schweizer lives inside a colossal beast, in an abyss of infinite variety. Here, nothing is impossible, except, perhaps, for smoking. He lives and works in New York. New York is the excess of options, a giant Moloch, a monster, and also the old world. New York compels, focuses, splits open, caresses, polishes, curses, dances, grinds its teeth, and laughs. New York lives. Boundless impressions perish, a multitude of ideas emerge, the cold facts of life set boundaries. Schweizer sits in this billowing giant entity and works. • • Schweizer incorporates, his detailed creative observations draw from analyses of actual visual conditions. These transformations and adaptations take well-known paths. For instance, when he turns to the redesign of common commercial typefaces, they gain a contemporary relevance, the aesthetic of which yields substantial successes; *Wallpaper* magazine uses his fonts exclusively. • • The previously mentioned "known paths" are certainly not to be misunderstood as the beaten track, as the highways of a generally preferred taste. Schweizer confronts and builds on his Swiss roots as a graphic designer and illustrator and likes to orient himself therein when constructing his work. This discrete yet persistent self-reliance, which is strongest in his interpretations that break new ground, forms one aspect of his mode of working; his elegant, sober executions, the carefully thought-out color choices, and the weighting of tactile moments form the other, slightly more playful side. Schweizer's works are convincing because they employ such well-rounded—at times trendy—forms and always look and feel so wonderfully rich and complete. • • Werner Jeker • •

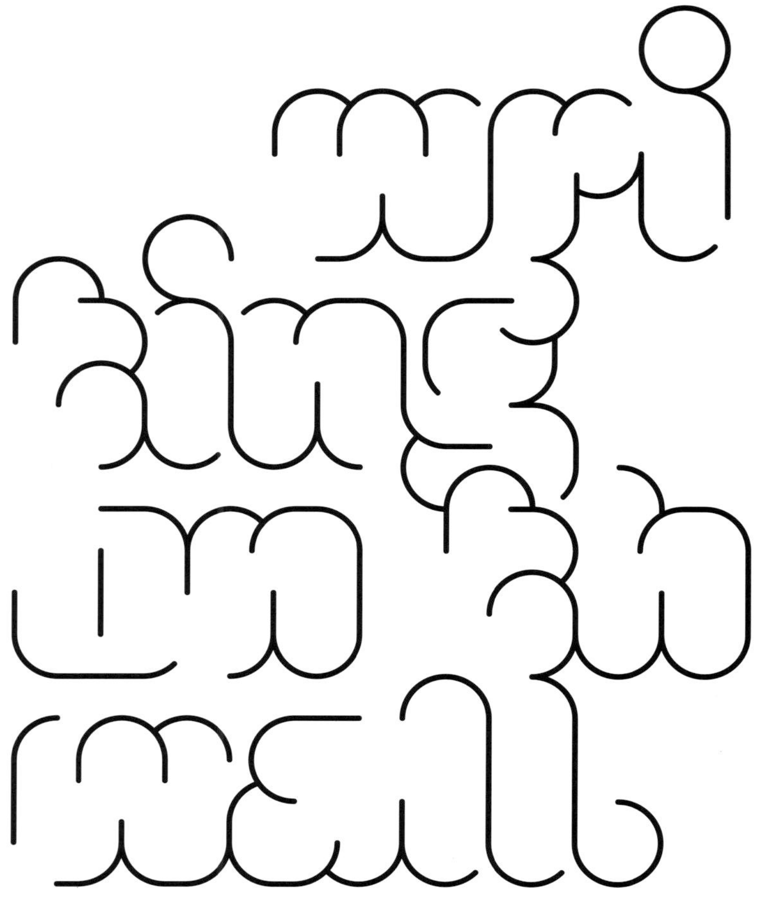

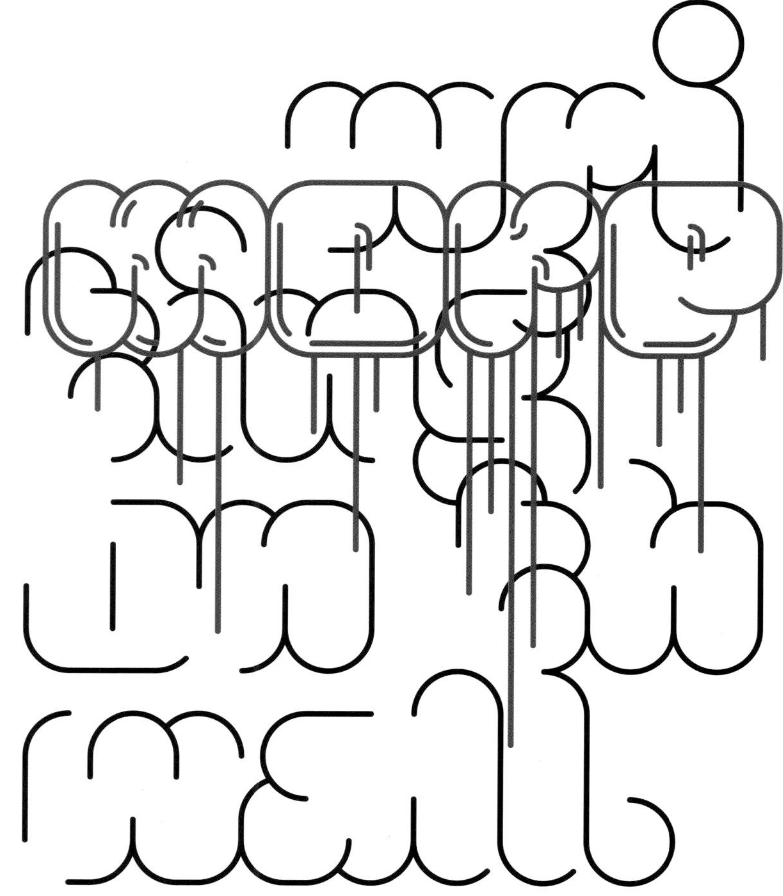

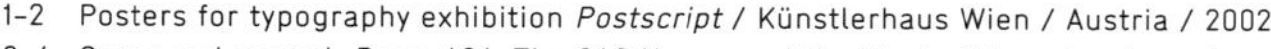

1–2 Posters for typography exhibition *Postscript* / Künstlerhaus Wien / Austria / 2002
3–4 Cover and spread, *Room 606–The SAS House and the Work of Arne Jacobsen*, by Michael Sheridan / Phaidon Press / United Kingdom and USA / 2003
5 Record cover, *Kamaal/The Abstract*, by Q-Tip (unrealized) / Arista Records / USA / 2002
6 Invitation for presentation of Hugo Boss Eyewear collection at the Fiera di Milano / Hugo Boss / Germany / 2000
7 Record cover, *Kamaal/The Abstract*, by Q-Tip / Arista Records / USA / 2002
8 Record cover, *Young Lawyer*, by French Kicks / Startime Records / USA / 2001

Nico Schweizer

New York

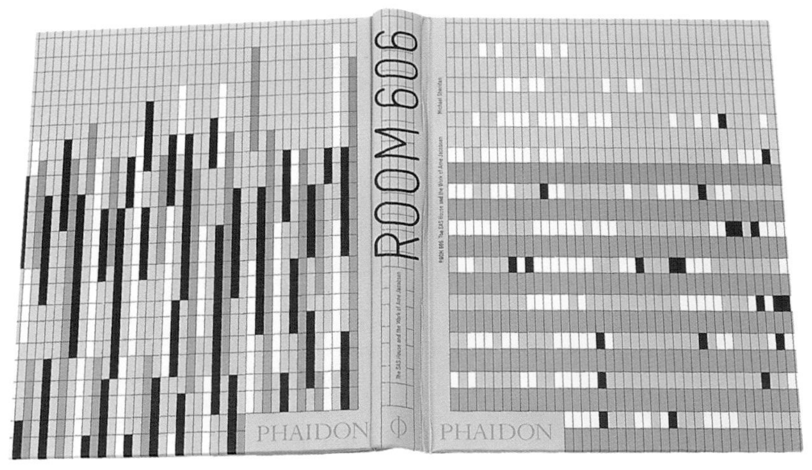
ROOM 606
PHAIDON
PHAIDON

3 4

5

Q-Tip

6

FIERA D E
CXD WOULD LI KE T O I NVITE

7

Q-Tip
Kamaal/The Abstract

8

ST-001
FRENCHKICKS
YOUNG LAWYER

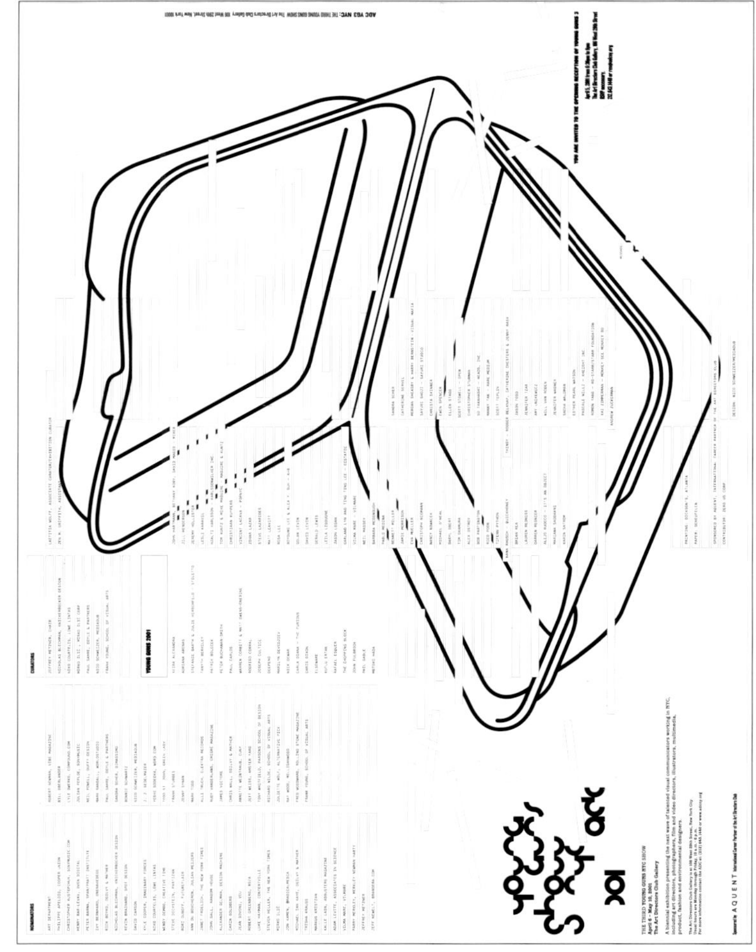

9 10

11

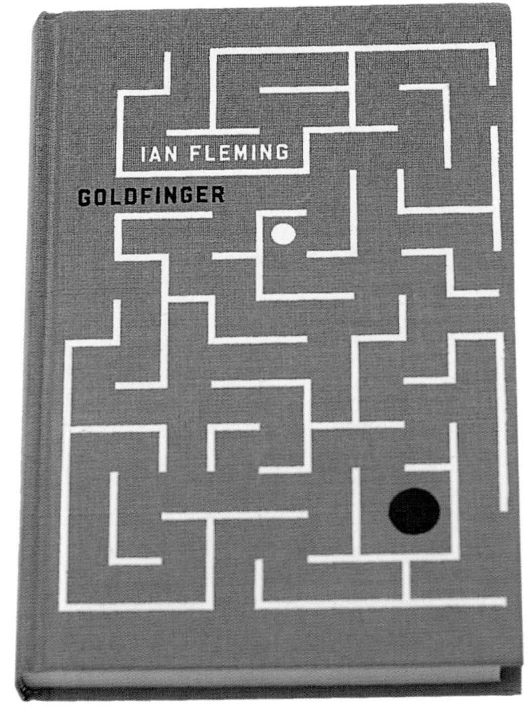

12

9–11 Front and back of poster and catalogue cover, *Young Guns 3* design exhibition / Art Directors Club New York / USA / 2001
12 Book cover, *Goldfinger*, by Ian Fleming / Flagstick Publications / USA / 2000
13 Type specimen, Typ 1441 Stencil / Mediadub.com / USA / 2001
14 Type specimen, LeCorbusier Bold / Mediadub.com / USA / 2002
15 Type specimen, Deluxe Script / Lineto.com / Switzerland / 1999–2003
16 Type specimen, Typ 1451, Typ 1441, Typ 1461 / Lineto.com and Mediadub.com / USA / 1995–2002

Nico Schweizer

13

SCHWEIZER SCHRIFTEN
Designed by Nico Schweizer for Mediadub/New York
letteracte.
ABCDEFGHIJKLMNOPQRSTUVWXYZŒ
abcdefghijklmnopqrstuvwxyzfiflßæœ 1234567890
Monocoque
FORCE OUVRIÈRE Isopode
Critical Mass WE CYCLE
Critical Mass is NOT AN ORGANIZATION, it's an unorganized coincidence
Alpha BRIONVEGA
Call: (201) 386.0337
IAN SAYS: "DO IT YOURSELF"
I ♥ Passion Bait Komed
RiverKeepers
NEW STENCIL FONT EXCLUSIVELY SOLD THROUGH MEDIADUB TYPE FOUNDRY
(BUY) ARCHITECTURAL STENCIL DRAWN IN 2000 FOR INTERIORS MAGAZINE/NYC

14

SCHWEIZER SCHRIFTEN
Designed by Nico Schweizer for Mediadub/New York
letteracte.
ABCDEFGHIJKLMNOPQRSTUVWXYZÆŒ
abcdefghijklmnopqrstuvwxyzfiflßæœ 1234567890
*LeCorbusier Antiqua Stencil
Jeanneret, Edouard
(Halston Gucci Fiorucci McQueen Chloé Mooks)
Wonderful!
creative camera
123456789
LeCorbusier Antiqua. Available through Lineto. Contact nico@mediadub.com for more Info.
Autechre Confield WARP
I Love My SUV!
THAT'S SPORTS UTILITY VEHICLE
£

15

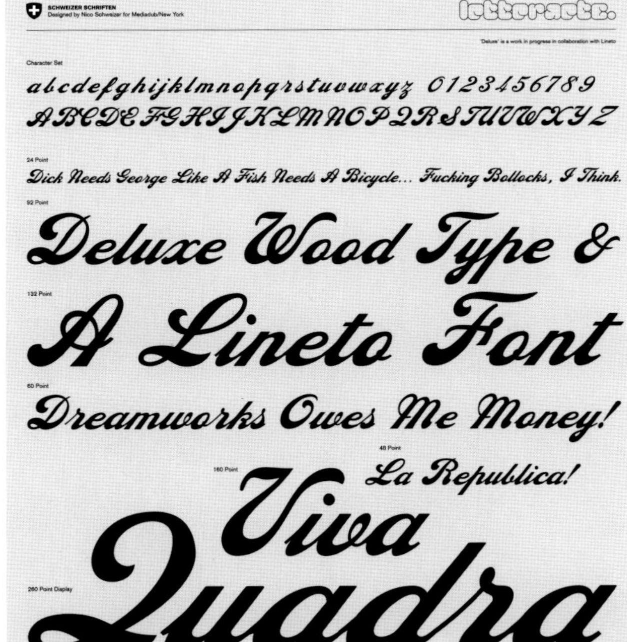

SCHWEIZER SCHRIFTEN
Designed by Nico Schweizer for Mediadub/New York
letteracte.
abcdefghijklmnopqrstuvwxyz 0123456789
ABCDEFGHIJKLMNOPQRSTUVWXYZ
Dick Needs George Like A Fish Needs A Bicycle... Fucking Bollocks, I Think.
Deluxe Wood Type &
A Lineto Font
Dreamworks Owes Me Money!
La Republica!
Viva
Quadra
Considering All Options
Andy Warhol Catalogue Raisonne Volume
The Worlds Largest Ketchup

16

SCHWEIZER SCHRIFTEN
Designed by Nico Schweizer for Mediadub/New York

letteracte.

Two New Stencil Fonts For The Consumer

Quagmire, Inc.

Embedded Character Incl.

Awe! ABCabcde

TYP 1451 / 1461 – Available Soon At Your Local Store.

To Ella Grace

Four Delightful New Weights Available Now!

TYP1451A

Hand Made in Switzerland

NEW STENCIL TECHNOLOGY EXCLUSIVELY SOLD THROUGH LINETO.COM

AAAA NEOQUIDQUOPRO

MEDIADUB TYPE FOUNDRY 1036 Garden Street, Unit 1 Hoboken 07030-4324, New Jersey U.S.A Tel. ++ 201.386.0337 http://www.mediadub.com

Emerging countries must ultimately breed emerging designers. Twenty years ago in China there was virtually no such thing as graphic design. In the period that has followed, a graphic design community has rapidly come to life and developed. Highly influenced by the aesthetics of the trade's more evolved and design-conscious communities, however, the output of this young group has not always been characterized by originality. • •Shaohua is aware of this, and his refreshing work comes as a welcome exception. His goal is to find direct and rapid mechanisms to communicate while searching for a new, inspring visual language. • •Through his commitment and creativity, Shaohua has become one of the leaders of the new Chinese design community. He understands that design and business are partners·and that designers have a role in helping the Chinese business community find a place in the international arena. Shaohua's work seeks to provide innovative identities for corporations, organizations, and branded products in an environment that previously disregarded such things. The 1980s Cultural Revolution in China changed this and significantly influenced Shaohua's career path. In 1987, discarding thoughts of engineering and science, he entered the Central Academy of Crafts and Art, Beijing, where he first encountered modern graphic design. At the beginning of the 1990s he moved to Shenzhen to pursue his chosen career. One senses that for Shaohua and for China, the journey has just begun. • •Ken Cato • •

①

②

③

1 Poster promoting traffic safety in Shenzhen / Advertising Association, Shenzhen Bureau of Industry and Commerce / China / 1997
2 Logo series for publication *China Annual Graphic Design* / Shenzhen CIS Type Association / China / 2002
3 Stamps designed on occasion of Fourth United Nations World Conference on Women, held in Beijing / Stamp Printing Bureau / China / 1995
4 Poster for first congress of the Shenzhen Graphic Designers' Association / Shenzhen Graphic Designers' Association / China / 1995
5 Poster for *Communication* invitational exhibition, Shenzhen / Shenzhen Graphic Designers' Association / China / 1996
6 Poster for *Graphic Design in China* exhibition, Shenzhen / China Industry Design Association and Package & Printing Magazine / China / 1992
7 Poster for the seventieth anniversary of the China Academy of Art / China Academy of Art / China / 1998

Chen Shaohua

Beijing/Shenzhen, China

4

深圳市平面设计协会第一届会员大会
First Congress of Shenzhen Graphic Designers' Association

5

COMMUNICATION
"沟通"
海报邀请展
"COMMUNICATION"
INVITATIONAL
POSTER
EXHIBITION'96

6

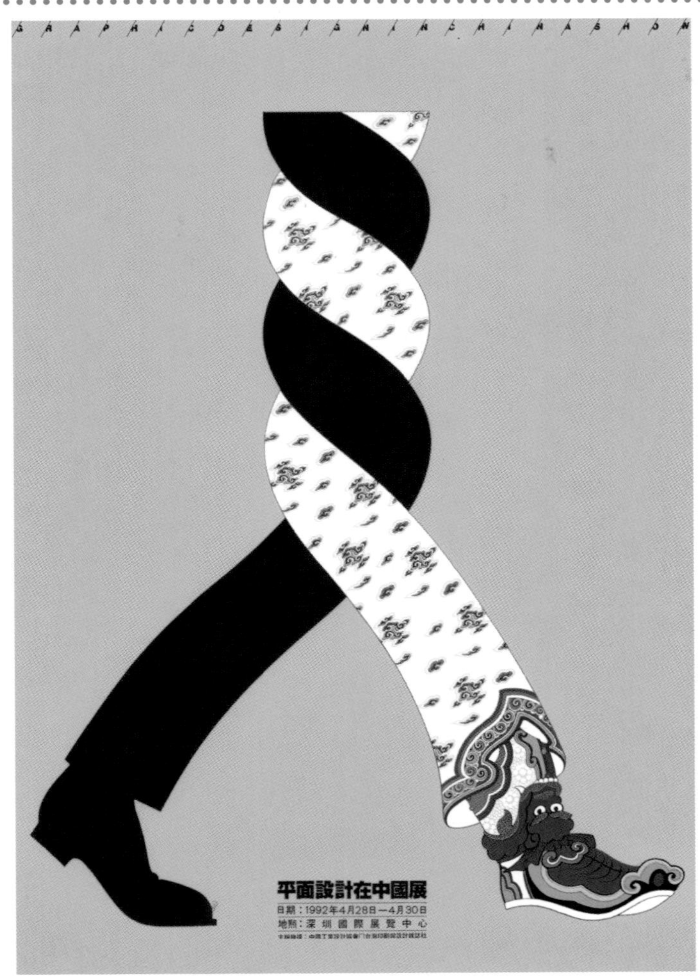
平面設計在中國展
日期：1992年4月28日—4月30日
地點：深圳國際展覽中心

7

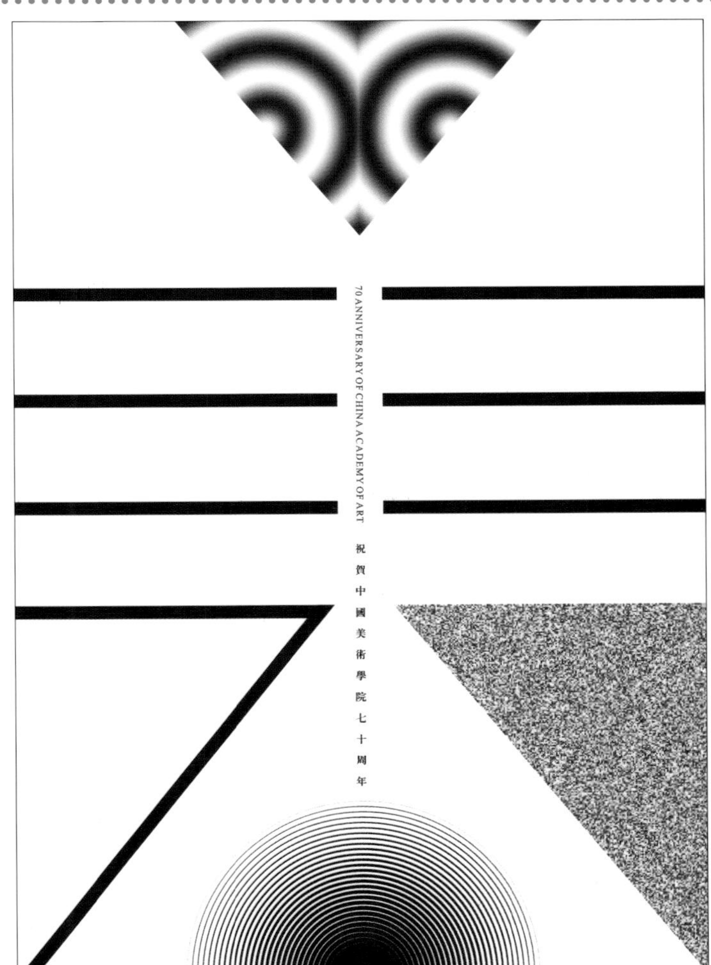
70 ANNIVERSARY OF CHINA ACADEMY OF ART
祝賀中國美術學院七十周年

8

9

10

11

12

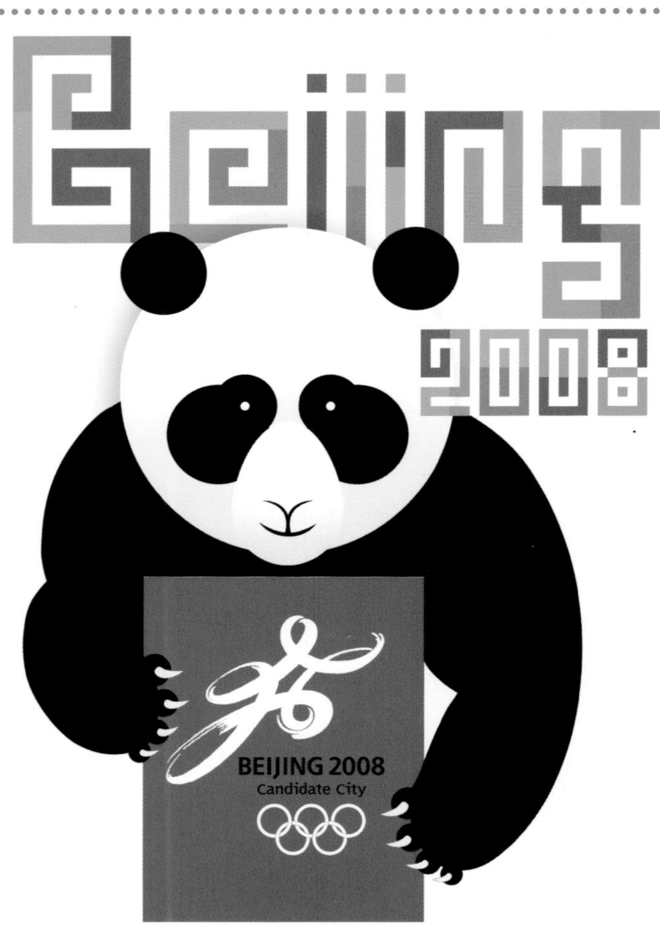

8 Logo for Asian Development Bank meeting in Shanghai / Asian Development Bank / China / 2002
9 Poster for *9/11* invitational exhibition / Japanese Poster Museum, Tokyo / Japan / 2002
10 Logo / Shenzhen Commercial Bank / China / 2000
11–12 Logo and poster for 2008 Olympic Games in Beijing / Beijing Organizing Committee for the Games of the XXIX Olympiad / 2002
13 Self-commissioned poster protesting NATO's bombing of Yugoslavia / China / 1999
14 Poster for *01* invitational exhibition, Beijing / Beijing Poster Academy / China / 2001
15 Poster for Alliance Graphique Internationale (AGI) invitational exhibition / AGI / France / 2000
16 Poster celebrating the tenth anniversary of Chen Shaohua's design studio / Chen Shaohua Design / China / 2002

Chen Shaohua

⑬

New version of Humanitarism

⑭

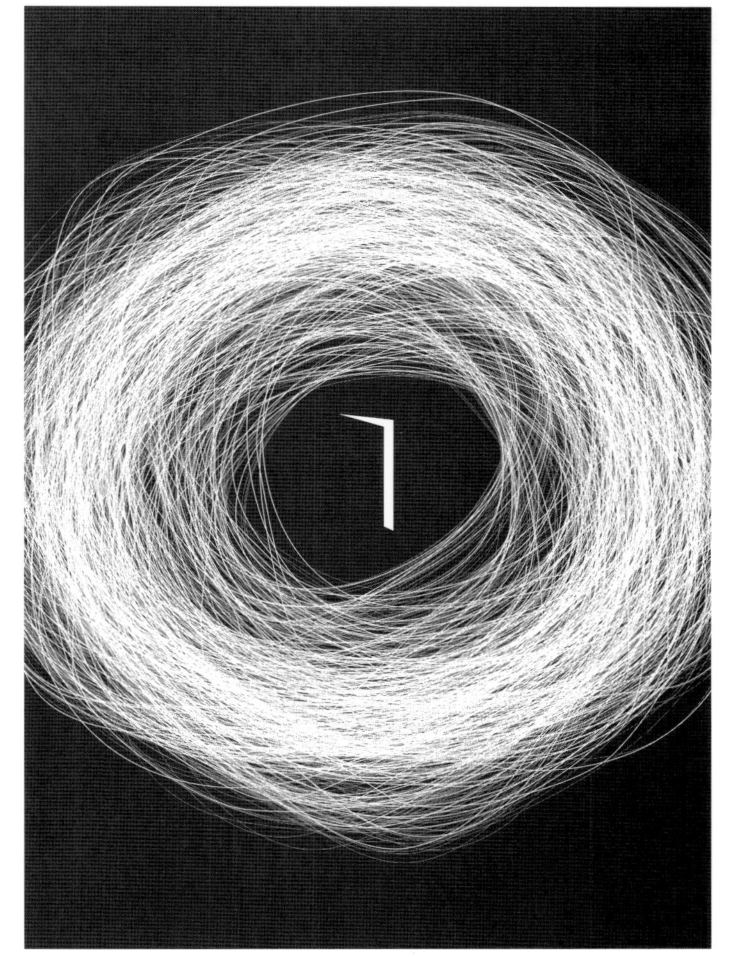

⑮

Childhood
is not chid's
play

⑯

陈绍华设计十年

There is an old saying, "Those who fail to describe what they see cannot possibly express what is in their minds." It is my belief that drawing a picture is the very base of creativity, and, at the same time, through the course of continued drawing, one's individuality is cultivated. In graphic design, however, if one limits one's creative activities to this specific form of expression, one risks being confined to the field of illustration. Despite her talent and initial education as a painter, So Man-yee's creativity knows no such restriction. ••The graphic worlds So creates are based on the lyricism of pictures and transparent colors. Traditionally, communication in the visual arts aims at an appeal of strength, of boldness. So, by contrast, is a great talent who has developed a unique graphic world through an appeal of depth and softness. ••Her love of the trade is evident in the delightful tension she subtly instills in her numerous packaging designs, small graphic pieces, and calendars. Her graphic activities, which are supported by her delicate illustration techniques, represent a stone cast gently in today's loud communication world which runs at full speed on a global scale. ••Shigeo Fukuda••

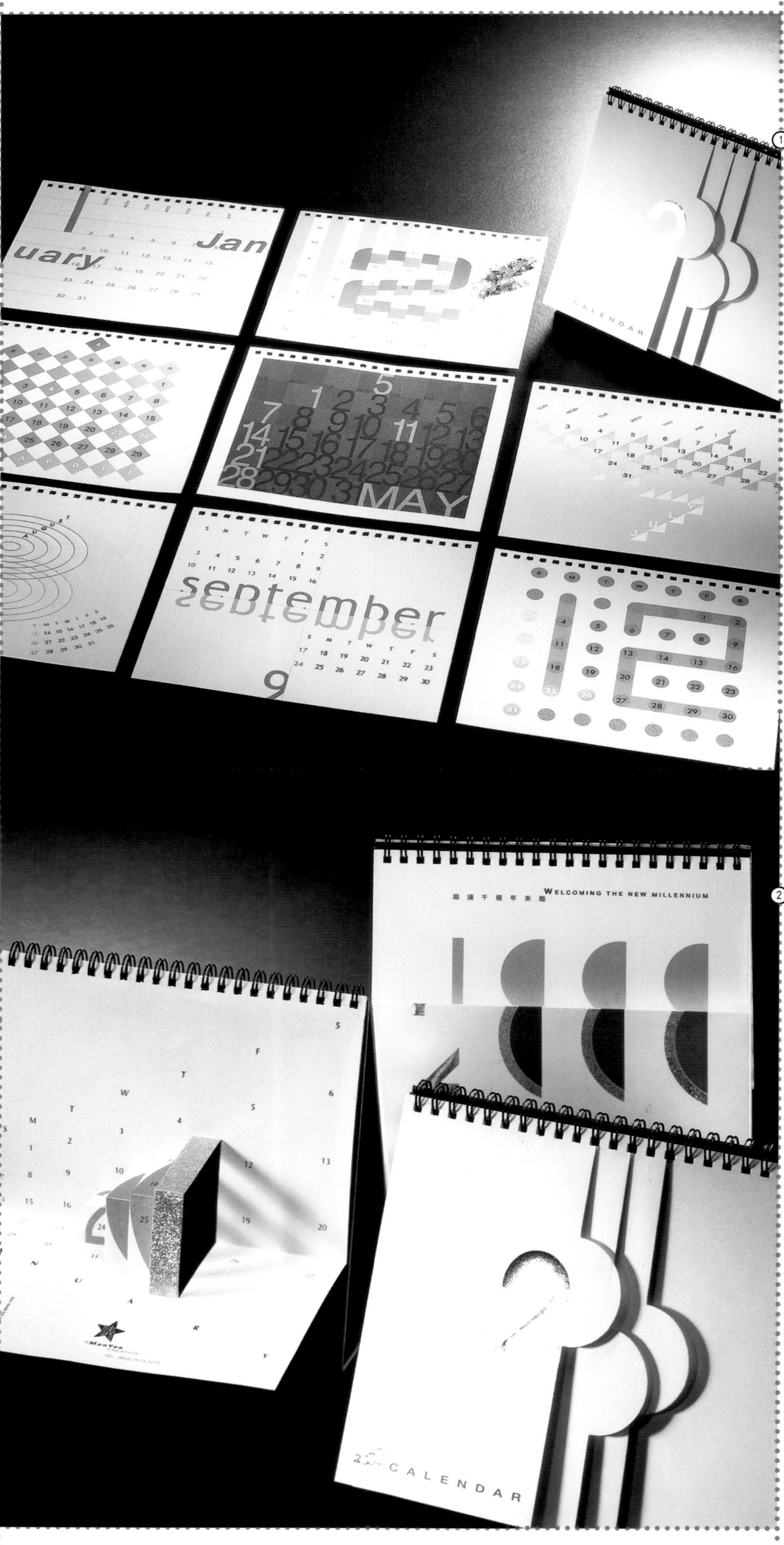

1–2 Promotional calendar for paper company / Tai Tak Takeo Fine Paper Co. Ltd. / Hong Kong / 2000

3 Poster to promote the importance of environmental consciousness in the new millennium / Hong Kong Designers Association / Hong Kong / 2000

4 Poster for *Discover Asia International Poster Exhibition* in Taipei / Taiwan Poster Design Association / Taiwan / 2002

5 Poster in celebration of the reunification of Macao with China / Macao Designers Association / China / 1999

So Man-yee

Hong Kong

3

environment 2000

環 保 千 千 年

展望 designers' eyes on hongkong

4

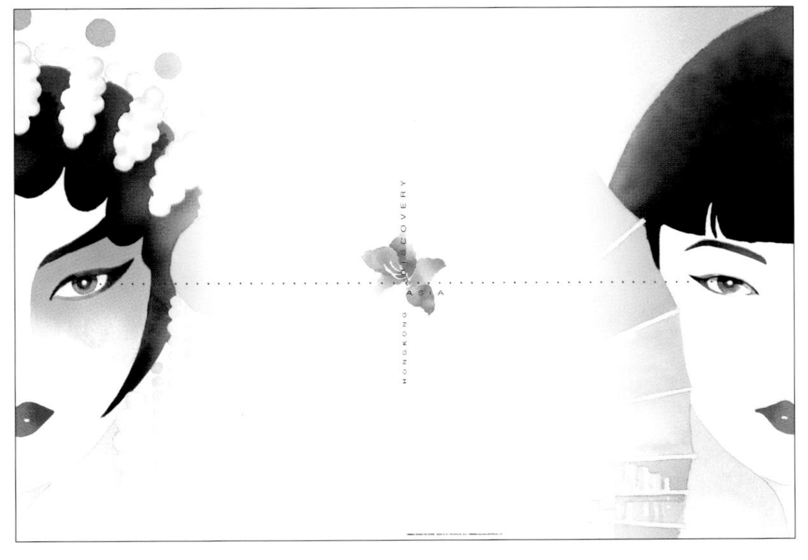

5

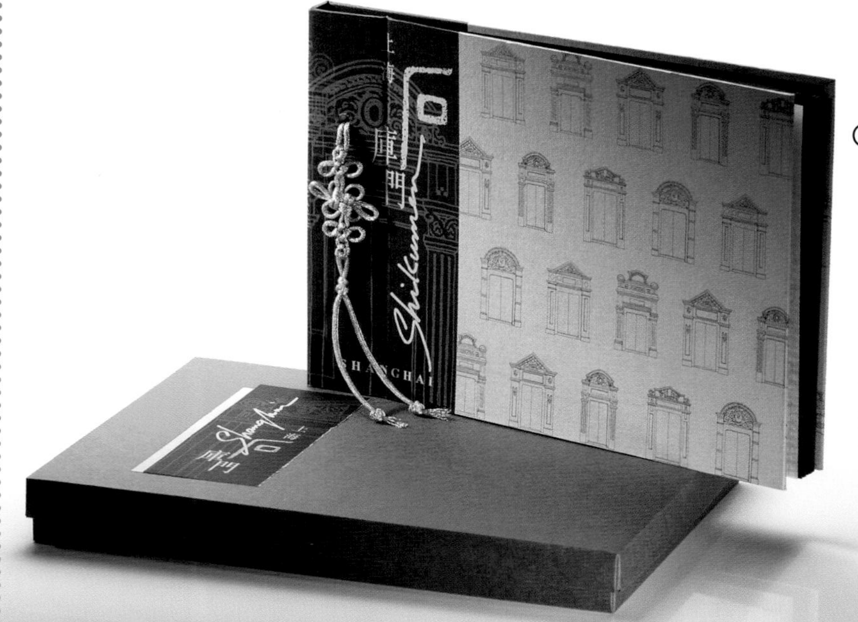

6 Poster for International Fashion Festival held in Ningbo, China / Ningbo International Fashion Festival Organization / China / 1999
7 Promotional calendar / Tai Tak Takeo Fine Paper Co. Ltd. / Hong Kong / 2002
8–9 Photo album and address book / H+S Gallery / China / 2002 / These items were designed for the gift shop of a traditional Shikumen house, a popular tourist desination in Shanghai.
10 Packaging for Blossom Garden Fine Tea / The Blossom Garden / United Kingdom / 2000

So Man-yee

10

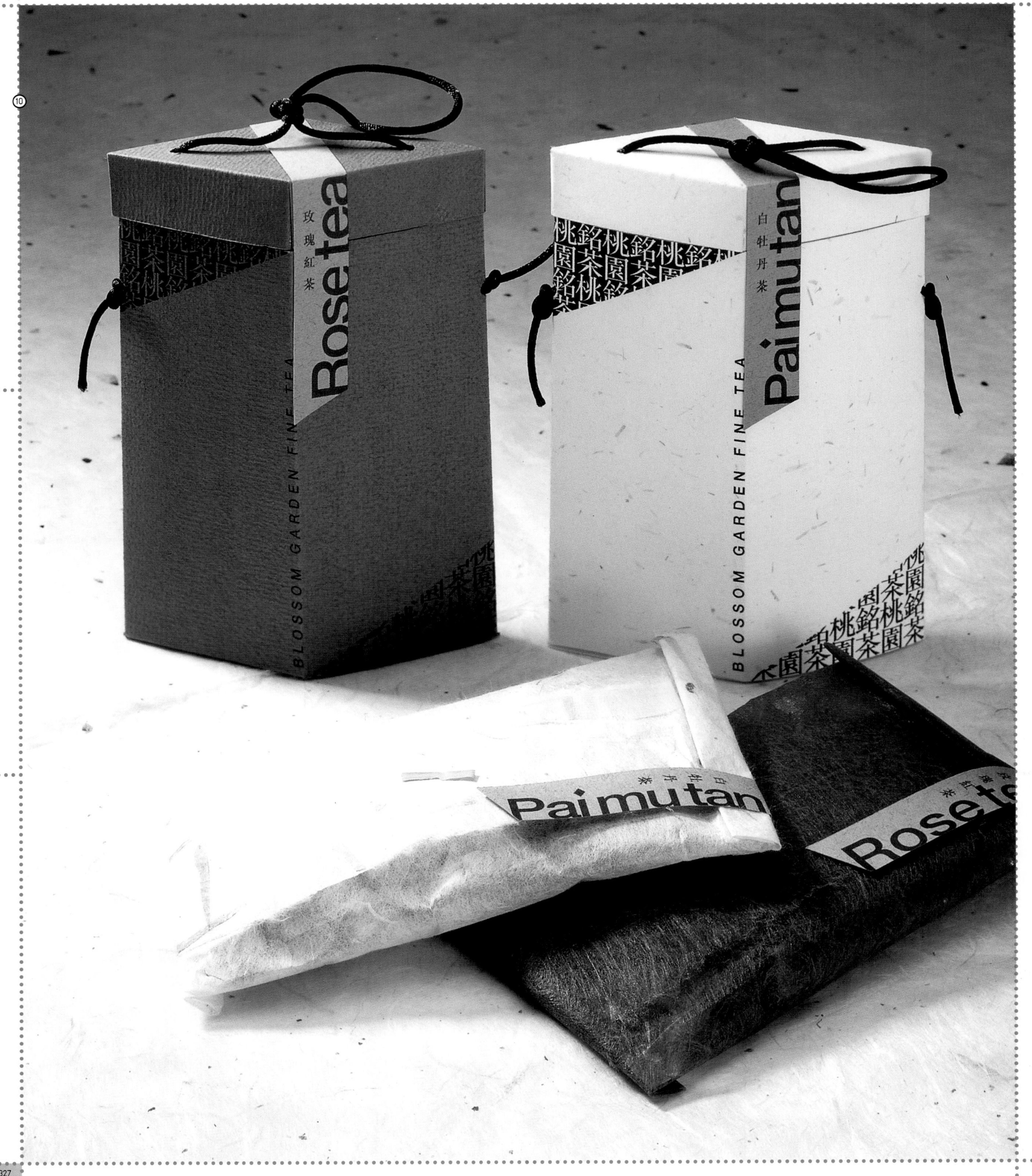
Rose tea
玫瑰紅茶
BLOSSOM GARDEN FINE TEA
Pai mu tan
白牡丹茶
BLOSSOM GARDEN FINE TEA
Pai mu tan
白牡丹茶
Rose te

I discovered Leonardo Sonnoli one fine day, because he had discovered me and sent some of his recent work. At the international poster triennial in Toyama, Japan, I came across him again: after the jury decoded his Alphabeto Palindromo, the poster was awarded the silver medal. We finally met in person at a restaurant in Venice eating with Giorgio Camuffo, also a graphic designer, and Sergio Polano, a philosopher and sharp critic of the Italian design scene. The conversation was as inspirational as the food—a revelation! ••Unfortunately you cannot eat Sonnoli's work, but you can admire it. It arises from an unusual intellect seldom found in the world of design. To be raised in "bella Italia," to live and work there, represents a special pleasure yet also a commitment, since both Italian graphic designers and Italian universities for communication design have seen better days. ••Sonnoli found international acclaim primarily through his "manifestos." Appropriately, *manifesto* is the Italian word for "poster." Impossible to better convey the communication assignment of a rectangular surface of paper! Sonnoli's posters are indeed manifestos. They are message-conscious, stimulating attacks on our visual perception and understanding of language. ••Sonnoli was born in Trieste, a city that before the First World War was still part of the Austro-Hungarian Empire, equally influenced by German and Italian culture. Demonstratively and relentlessly implementing the influences of twentieth-century German typography, he reflects this particular cultural background in his work. He likes to call this "remixing—like a DJ." Existing typographic concepts, such as Jan Tschichold's *New Typography*, are not just mechanically imitated, but instead cited and rearranged in an original way. ••Sonnoli's passion for experimentation, his enthusiastic love of typography, and, last but not least, his unconventional use of text and image are remarkable. Beyond this, I share his fondness for "black on white." ••Uwe Loesch••

1 Poster for Teatro Contatto theatrical season (with Pierpaolo Vetta) / CSS Udine / Italy / 2001
2 Poster for presentation of experimental typeface Palindrome / Italy / 1998
3 Poster for exhibition on local archeological discoveries / Municipality of Pesaro / Italy / 1998
4 Poster for lecture by philosopher Massimo Cacciari on the origin of the word / Municipality of Pesaro / Italy / 1997
5 Poster for photographic exhibition on the Bosnian war / Municipality of Pesaro / Italy / 1998
6 Poster for congress on immigrant's rights / Don Gaudiano Foundation / Italy / 1996
7 Poster for conference on Mediterranean design / Municipality of Pesaro / Italy / 1998
8 Poster for conference on the rights and obligations of the people / Don Gaudiano Foundation / Italy / 1997
9 Poster for lecture series on children's literature / Municipality of Pesaro / Italy / 1998
10 Poster for presentation of the book *La Discarica*, by Paolo Teobaldi / Municipality of Pesaro / Italy /1998.
11 Poster for lecture on tolerance and respect / Don Gaudiano Foundation / Italy / 1996

Leonardo Sonnoli

Rimini, Italy

1

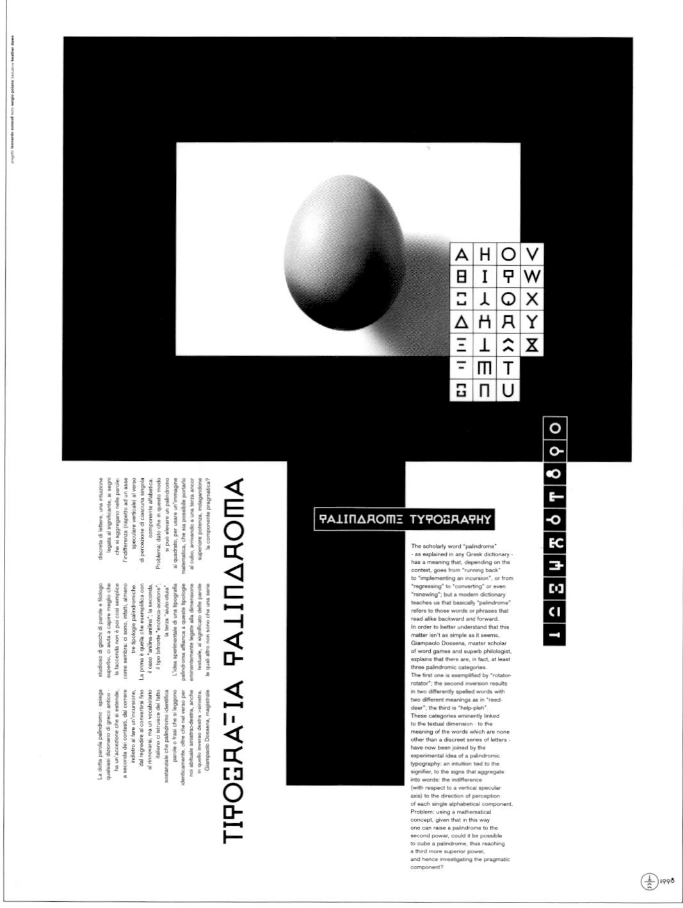

2

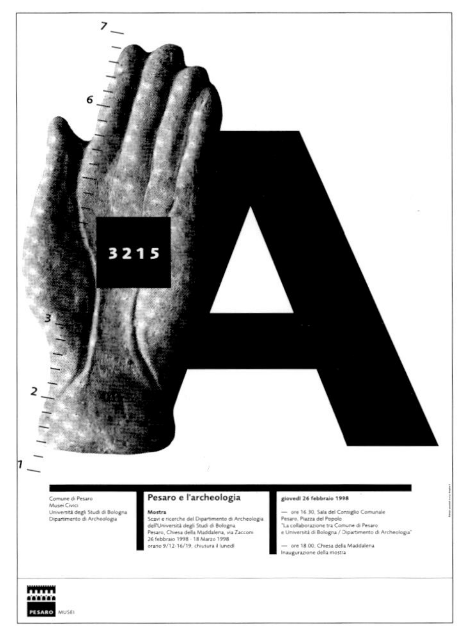

3 4 5

6 7 8

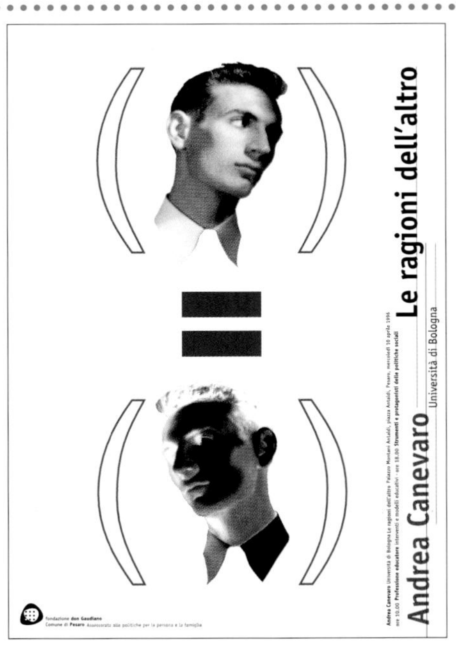

9 10 11

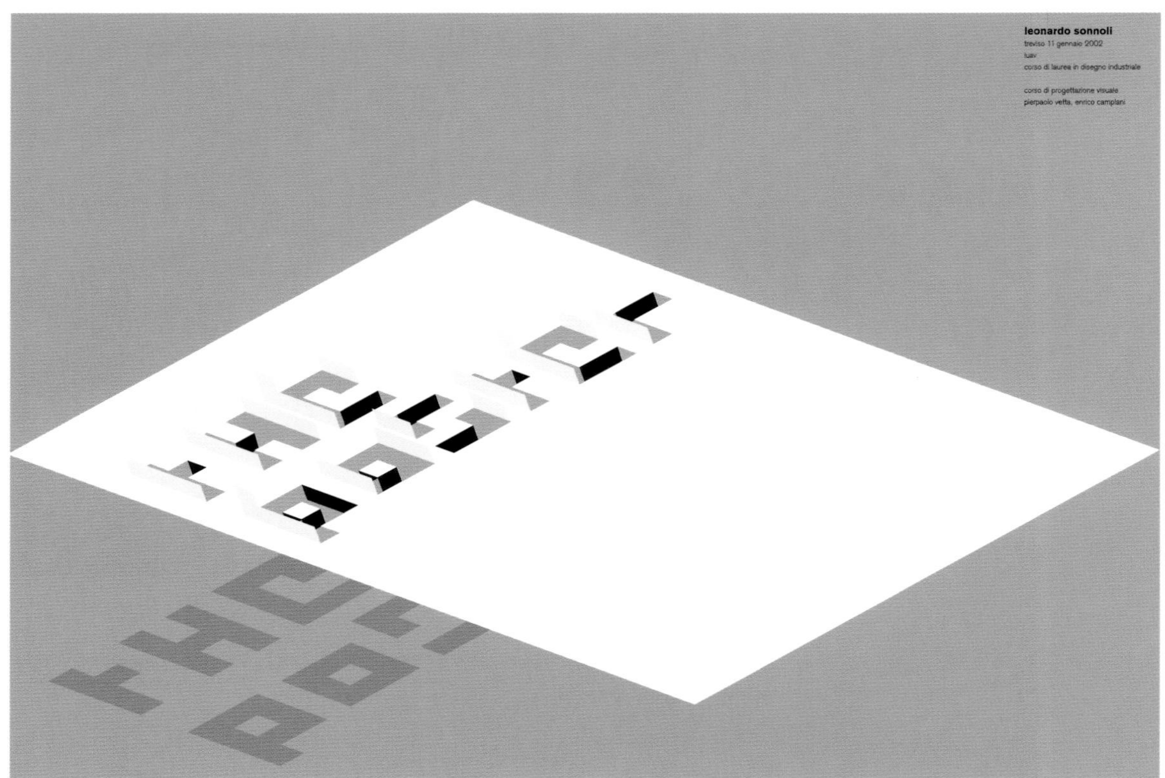

12

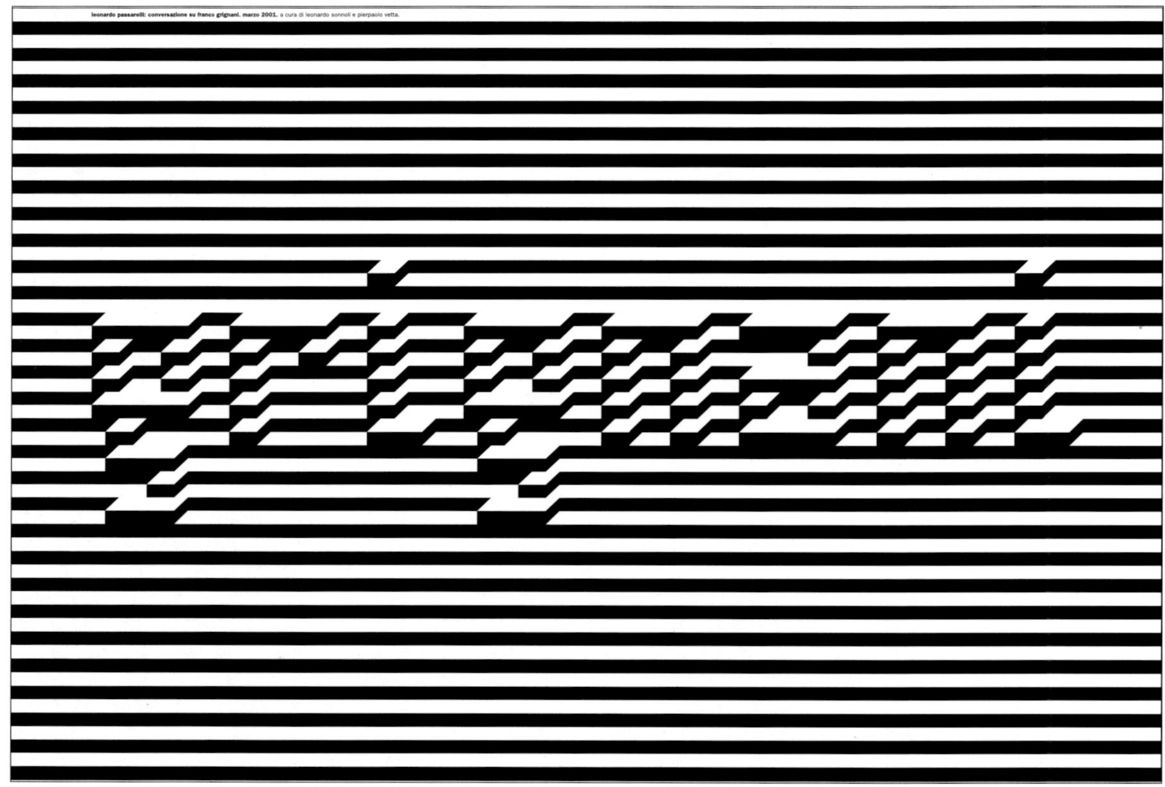

13

Leonardo Sonnoli

12 Poster for lecture by Leonardo Sonnoli at the University of Architecture in Venice (IUAV)/ IUAV / Italy / 2002
13 Poster for open lecture on Italian graphic designer Gianfranco Grignani at Leonardo Sonnoli's studio (with Pierpaolo Vetta) / Italy / 2001
14 Poster for *Lonely Living* architectural exhibition at the Venice Biennale (with Pierpaolo Vetta) / AldA–La Biennale di Venezia / Italy / 2002
15 Poster to announce the seventeenth issue the architectural magazine *D'Architettura* / Federico Motta Editore / Italy / 2002
16 Poster for opening of academic year of the University of Architecture in Venice (IUAV) / IUAV / Italy / 2002
17 Front and back of poster designed on occasion of University of Architecture in Venice (IUAV) student trip to Albe Steiner retrospective exhibition in Bolzano, Italy (with Pierpaolo Vetta) / Italy / 2002
18 Poster for lecture by Leonardo Sonnoli at the High Institute for Design, Naples / High Institute for Design / Italy / 2000
19 Poster for lecture by German design group Grappa Blotto at Leonardo Sonnoli's studio (with Pierpaolo Vetta) / Italy / 2001

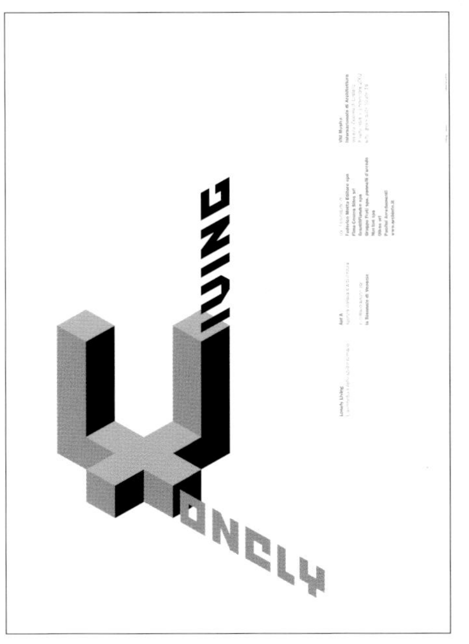

ciarlo
garofalo+miura
rizzi
sàito
abdr
cspe, di franco,
ipostudio
archea, gambogi,
pellegrini,
portoghesi, zucchi
d'Architettura
ISSN 0394-0055

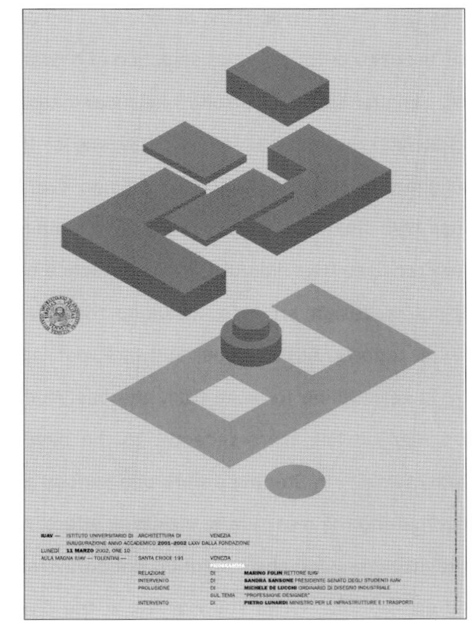

15 16

17

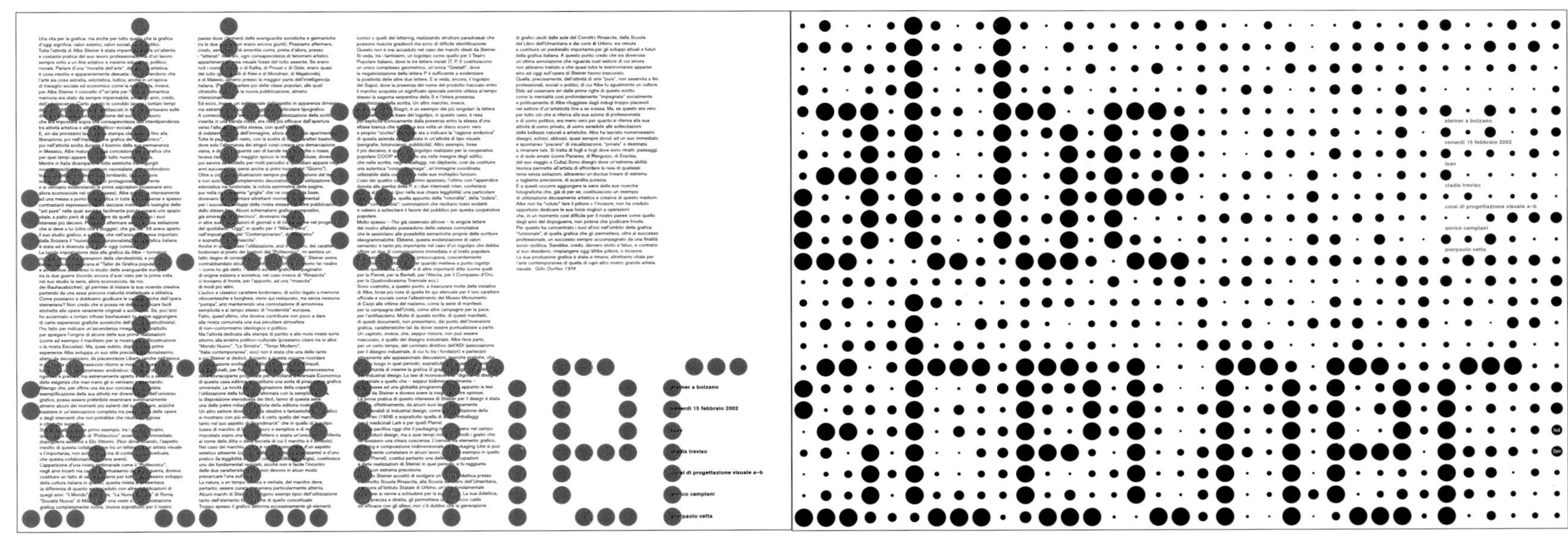

steiner a bolzano
venerdì 15 febbraio 2002
iuav
cladia treviso
corsi di progettazione visuale a–b
enrico camplani
pierpaolo vetta

18

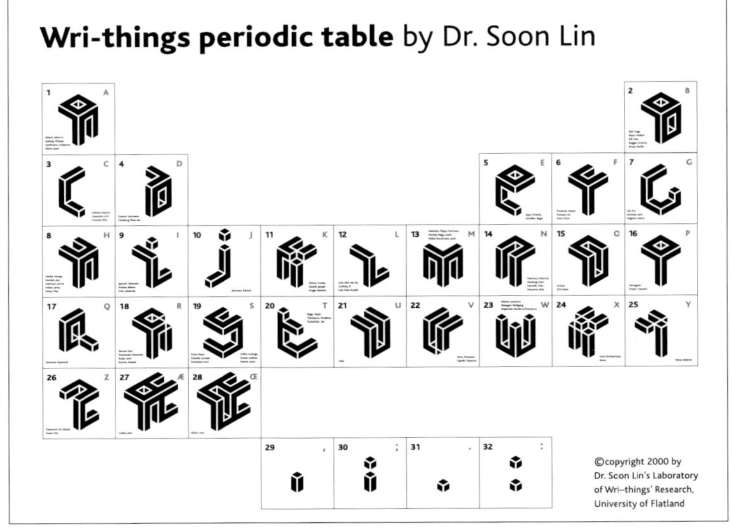

Wri-things periodic table by Dr. Soon Lin
©copyright 2000 by
Dr. Soon Lin's Laboratory
of Wri–things' Research,
University of Flatland

19

Ideas and the ability to think beyond graphic design were two of my self-imposed criteria for the selection of designers for this publication. Jennifer Sterling's strongly held views, together with her design excellence, demand her inclusion as one of the recently emerged designers who will influence the design scene in years to come. Since 1995 she has been the principal of Jennifer Sterling Design in San Fransisco. Her multidisciplinary practice has worked on a wide variety of design projects, including the development of brands, annual reports, publications, software, packaging, and Web sites. She is very willing to move from one design discipline to another. This has led her, more recently, to the development of her own product line. • • In Sterling's work one senses a pragmatic approach of conveying the message to maximum effect. At the same time, her graphic expression and execution are always stylish, contemporary, and appropriate. While she marvels at the diversity of design, she carries a concern that, in the current climate, it is in great danger of devaluation. She believes that graphic design has lost much of its ability to persuade clients to develop long-lasting or highly cherished items. Not the "us wealthy, you not so wealthy" kind, but the variety that could be created in an environment where design partners with smart technology to find wonderful new solutions that enrich our lives at an affordable cost. High ideals indeed. Sterling also believes that the excessive "branding" of items has demanded more accountability of designers. The increased branding has become the "blanding" of graphic design. • • While Sterling is highly idealistic, she is also accountable. Among her numerous achievements, Sterling serves on the San Fransisco Museum of Modern Art's Architecture and Design Accessions board, and in 2000 was invited to become a member of the national registry of "Who's Who in America." In 2000 she was elected to the Alliance Graphique Internationale (AGI). More recently, the San Francisco Museum of Modern Art hosted a three-month solo exhibition of her work. • • Ken Cato • •

1 Poster for performance by Wim Vandekeybus and Ultima Vez at Yerba Buena gardens / San Francisco Performances / USA / 1999
2 Poster for performance by Eiko and Koma and the Kronos Quartet at Yerba Buena Gardens / San Francisco Performances / USA / 1999
3 Stationery system for Sterling Design featuring microperforations, blind debossing, and stainless-steel business cards / USA / 1996–present
4 Five promotional brochures showcasing the work of Sterling Design enclosed in a metal mesh portfolio case / USA / 1996–present
5 CD packaging, *Trust Me*, by Bhoss / Bhoss and Actionpatch Music / USA / 1998 / A metal bolt holds together the CD and letterpressed, disc-shaped coasters featuring individual song lyrics.
6 Promotional catalogue for work of photographer David Maisel / Maisel Studios / USA / 2001

Jennifer Sterling

San Francisco

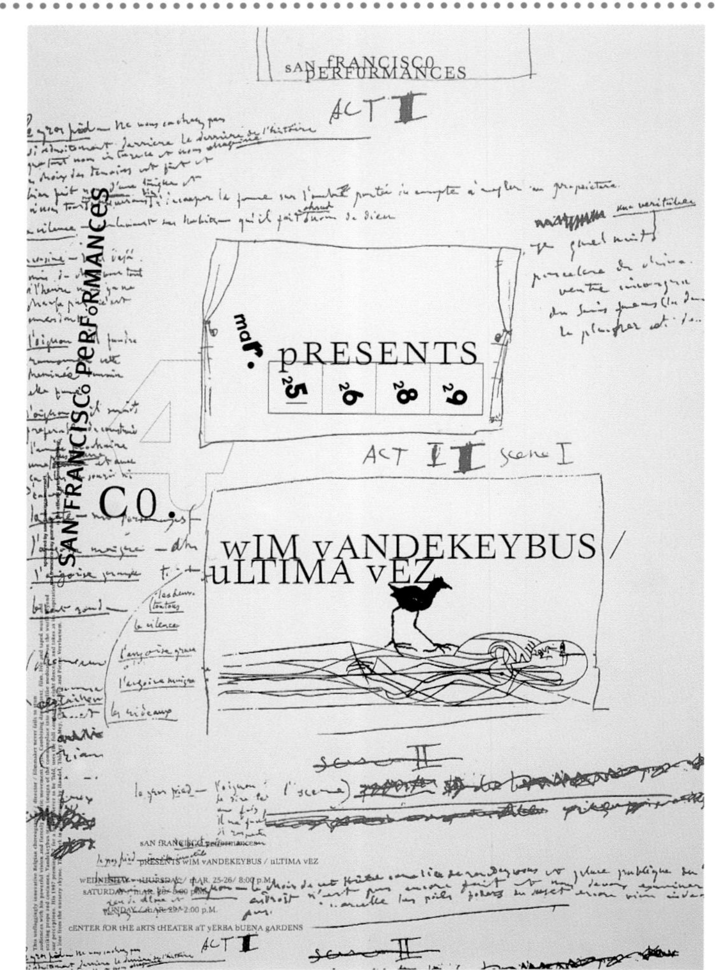

1
2

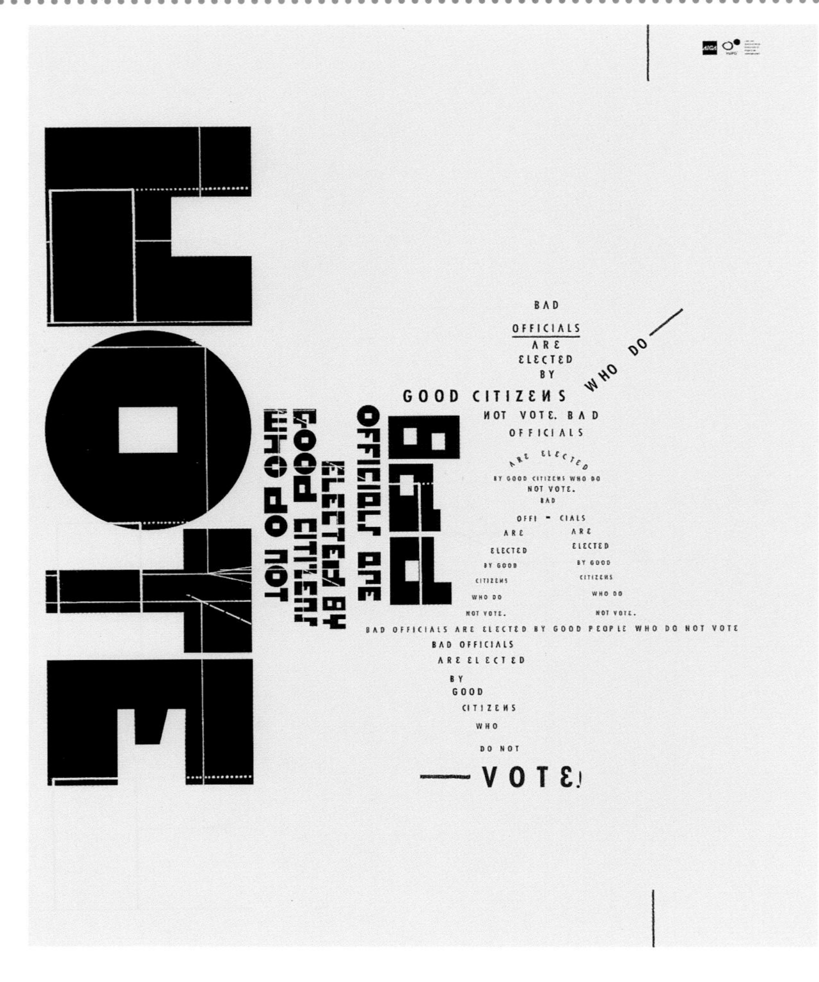

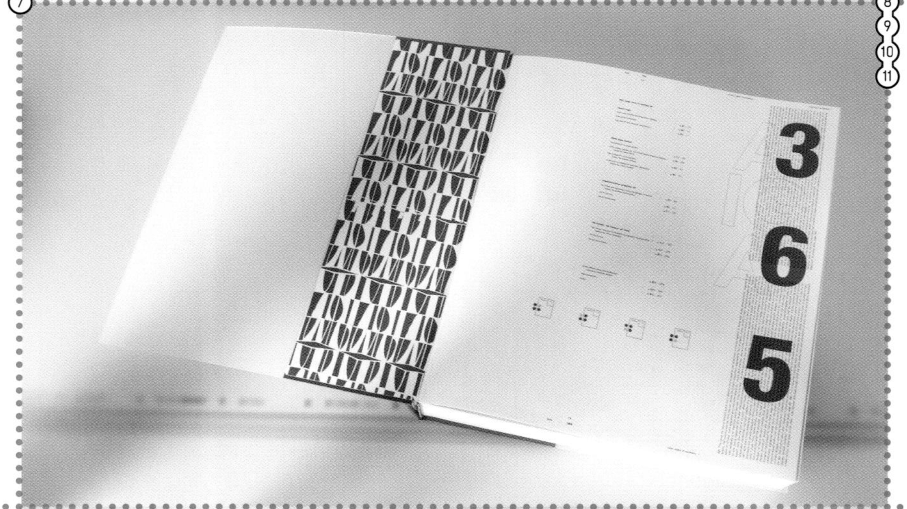

7 Poster for American Institute of Graphic Arts (AIGA) "Get out the Vote" campaign to encourage voter turnout in 2000 US presidential election / AIGA and Yupo / USA / 2000

8–11 Cover and spreads, *365: AIGA Year in Review* / AIGA / USA / 2001

12 Poster for spring lecture series offered at the Southern California Institute of Architecture (SCI-Arc) / SCI-Arc / USA / 1999

Jennifer Sterling

12

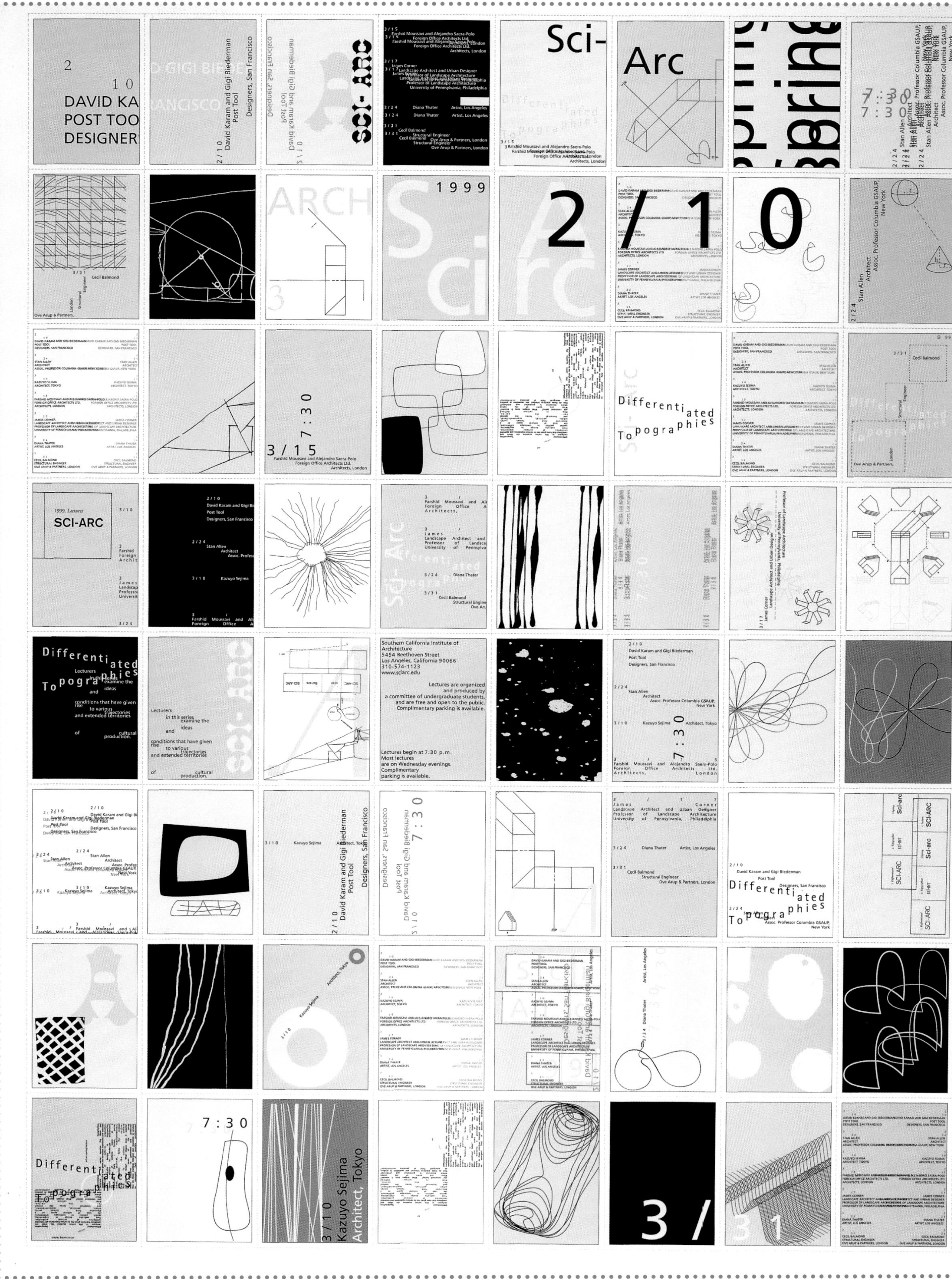

2 / 10
DAVID KARAM AND GIGI BIEDERMAN
POST TOOL
DESIGNERS, SAN FRANCISCO
David Karam and Gigi Biederman
Post Tool
Designers, San Francisco
SCI-ARC
3/15 Farshid Moussavi and Alejandro Saera-Polo
Foreign Office Architects Ltd.
Architects, London
3/17 James Corner
Landscape Architect and Urban Designer
Professor of Landscape Architecture
University of Pennsylvania, Philadelphia
3/24 Diana Thater
Artist, Los Angeles
3/31 Cecil Balmond
Structural Engineer
Ove Arup & Partners, London
Sci-
Arc
Differentiated Topographies
7:30
2/24 Stan Allen
Architect
Assoc. Professor Columbia GSAUP, New York
1999
2/10
3/15
3/10
Kazuyo Sejima
Architect, Tokyo
1999. Lectures
SCI-ARC
Lecturers in this series examine the ideas and conditions that have given rise to various trajectories and extended territories of cultural production.
Southern California Institute of Architecture
5454 Beethoven Street
Los Angeles, California 90066
310-574-1123
www.sciarc.edu
Lectures are organized and produced by a committee of undergraduate students, and are free and open to the public. Complimentary parking is available.
Lectures begin at 7:30 p.m.
Most lectures are on Wednesday evenings.
Complimentary parking is available.
3 / 31

I would like to suggest that, from now on, we call the practice of graphic design "stolking," derived from the surname of my friend and colleague Swip Stolk.•• Why? Over many years, I have seen Stolk work frantically: not to get rich, but to make the "things" that he had in mind. He has designed books, posters, houses, packaging, calendars, and sets—far too much to list. Everything is done with the same dedication to high quality and has substance that lives up to the design. The current project always comes first and always remains above compromise. Stolk dreams graphic design in all colors and formats, eats typography in every conceivable font and size, drinks printing techniques, paper types, and binding. As a "craftsman," he has undertaken much technical research, which prompts many colleagues, when they study his work, to call out, "How on earth did he do that?" In other words, Stolk is not a graphic designer, he *is* graphic design. This attitude has enabled him to put together a sublime portfolio that measures up to the greatest in our profession. In the best of worlds, a graphic designer is a "stolker": A professional who unites passion, vision, skill, and artistry into a form of "visual intelligence."•• On my first visit to Stolk's tiny studio, he was busy with a design that involved lines made from complex curves. He drew the lines—with the aid of templates, a pen, and poster paint—by hand on thin transparent paper. Nothing special at the time, but what took my breath away was the fact that where those lines met, the intersection was completely invisible. My admiration grew when I realized that while his hand was clearly damp, there was not a trace of moisture on the extremely sensitive tracing paper. Most amazing, however, was that this display of technical virtuosity provided only a minor contribution to the stunning overall piece. Wonderful: he was barely twenty years old and already a master.•• It is striking that Stolk maintains very long-term relationships with both the companies he works with (lithographers, printers, etc.) and his clients. His collaboration with art historian and former museum director Frans Haks is one of the most beautiful. Together they put the Groninger Museum in the Netherlands on the map. You can only be grateful for something like that. Swip, you are rightly a "master forever."•• Anthon Beeke••

1 Entrance tickets for the Groninger Museum (illustration Atelier Mendini) / Groninger Museum / Netherlands / 1995
2 Poster for *Peiling 4–Hollandse Nieuwe!* exhibition (illustration Micha Klein) / Groninger Museum / Netherlands / 1995
3 Corporate identity for Studio Swip Stolk / Studio Swip Stolk / Netherlands / 1998
4 Poster for *Mingei* exhibition / Groninger Museum / Netherlands / 1999
5 Poster for "Week of the Book," a promotional event to encourage reading (with Erwin Olaf) / CNPB / Netherlands / 2000

1

Swip Stolk

Zaandam, Netherlands

2

PEILING 4
HOLLANDSE NIEUWE!
PARADISE
GRONINGER MUSEUM
02 APR
MUSEUMEILAND 1, GRONINGEN
POSTBUS 90, 9700 ME GRONINGEN
INFO 06-8212132 FAX 050-3120815 TEL 050-3666555
OPENINGSTIJDEN
DINSDAG T/M ZONDAG: 10.00-17.00 FEESTDAGEN
GESLOTEN: 'S MAANDAGS, 1 JANUARI, 28 AUGUSTUS, 25 DECEMBER
T/M 1995
21 MEI

3

SSS
1ST LINE
SSS
2ND USE
©oll

4

20 DEC 1998 T/M 07 MRT 1999
Paint it Red
05 28
Schilderijen
16e-20e eeuw
05 28
Quik & Co
12 14
De Montgomery collectie van Japanse volkskunst
MINGEI
GRONINGER MUSEUM

5

15
25
03

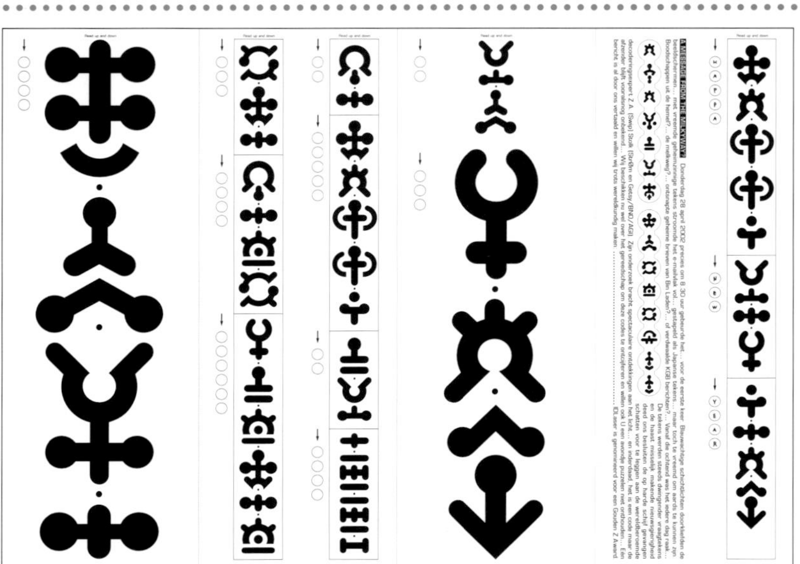

6

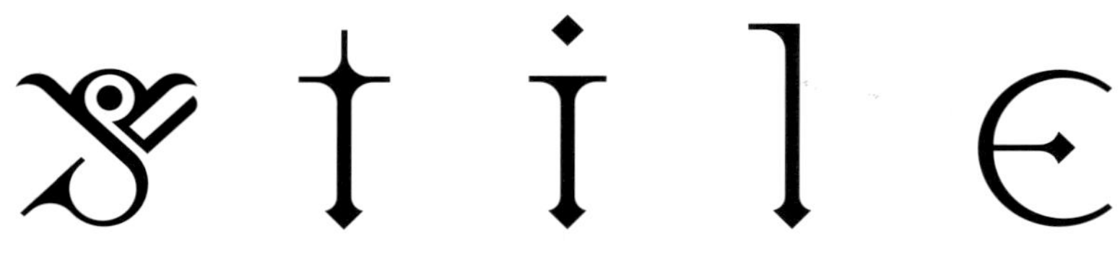

7

8

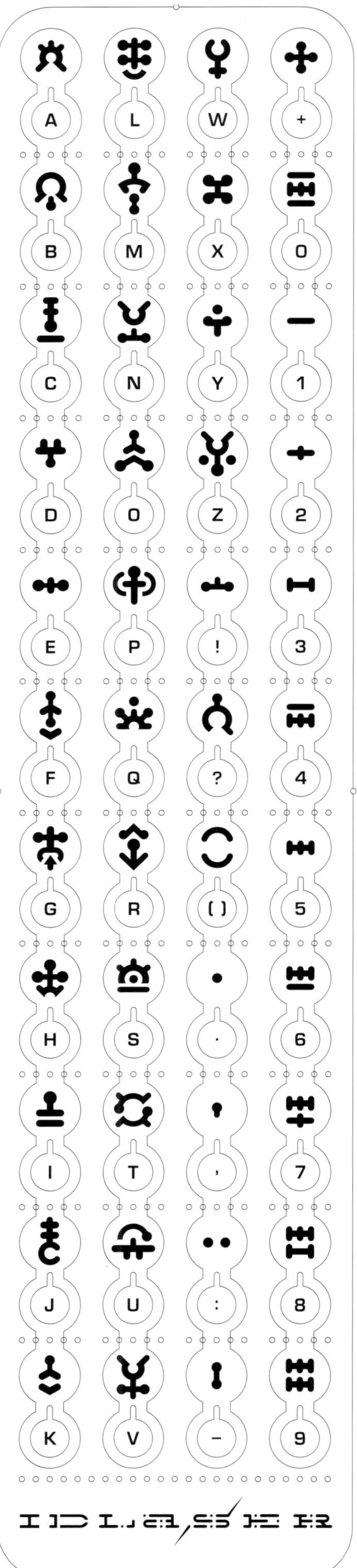

9

6, 9 Encoded flyer and decoder card as part of the Code-Encode project presented in *Stile* magazine no. 4 / IDlaser / Netherlands / 2002
7 Logo / Stile Magazine / Italy / 2002
8 Logo / Gallery Flatland / Netherlands / 2000 / The logo was made into a poster for the Swip Stolk exhibition *2nd Use* held at the Flatland Gallery, Utrecht.
10–12 Logo and covers, *Dutch Magazine*, nos. 19, 26, and 28 (photography Cometti) / Dutch Magazine / Netherlands and France / 1998–2000
13 Logo and cover, *Chiq–Navigator for Women* magazine no. 1 / Chiq / Netherlands / 1999

Swip Stolk

10

DUTCH
#19
1998
DUTCH

11

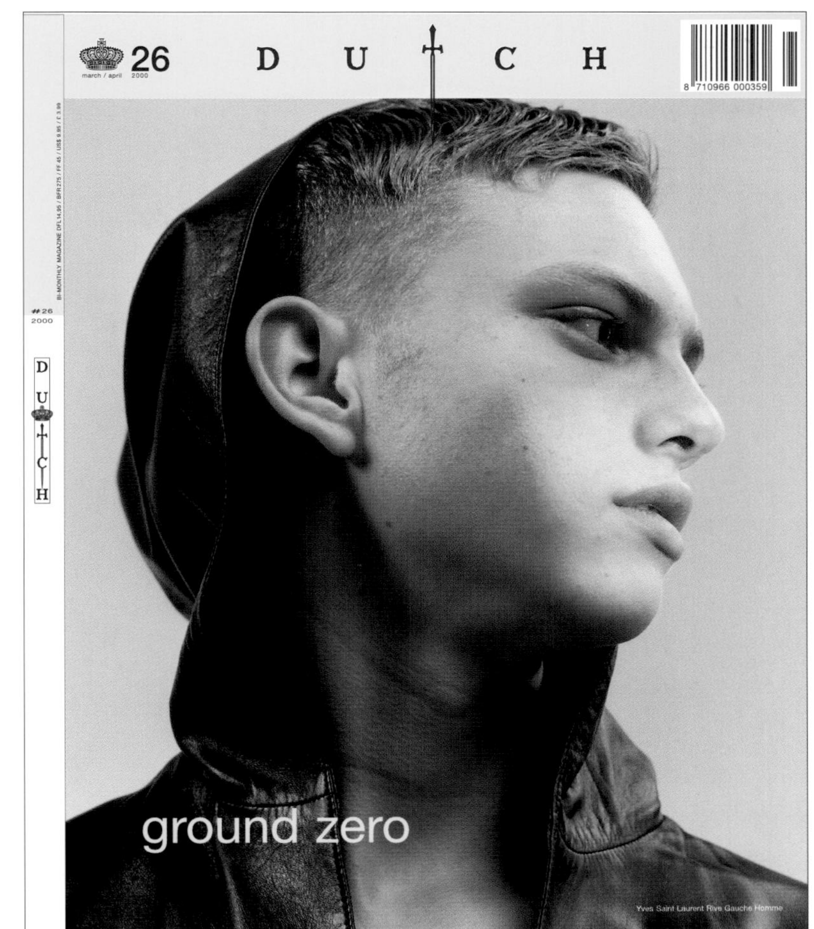
26
march / april 2000
DUTCH
#26
2000
ground zero
Yves Saint Laurent Rive Gauche Homme

12

28
july / august 2000
DUTCH
8 710966 000359
Master Forever

13

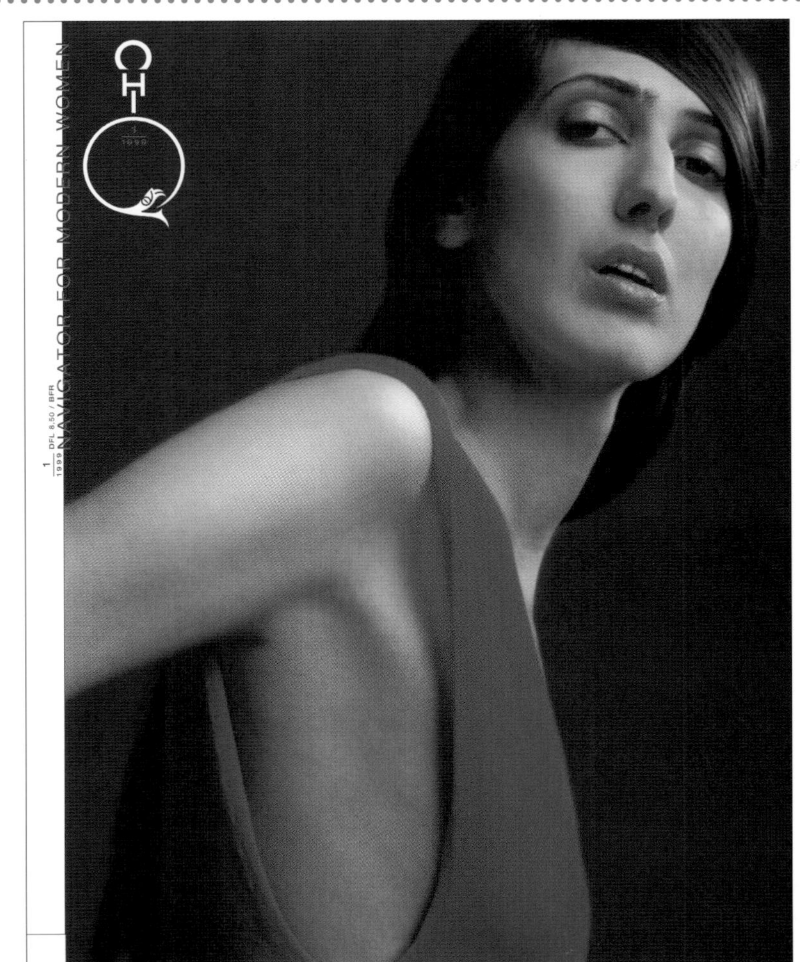
CHIO
NAVIGATOR FOR MODERN WOMEN
1
1999

Remo Stoller appears to be of a new breed, a mutation of the canonical Swiss designer. When he was a student, the massive wave of new technology distracted his attention from the classic Swiss graphic design heroes and their theories on graphic systems and legibility. Today much of that seems to be popular again under an advanced form, but as Stoller missed out on the original school, he finds it difficult to understand what in these recent years has often been referred to as the neo-Swiss trend. • •His total elimination of typography makes him even more awkward in the land of the masters. His playful experimentation goes wild on photographic imagery of daily objects and human body parts. Manipulation, subtraction, addition, and crossbreeding are his tools. In his work, he says, "the element of play fits in mostly in the way the fragments are designed. I'm like a gardener starting to grow a plant, influencing its growth by crossing, combining, and putting together, being influenced myself by unexpected results and shapes. I cut off unliked branches, go back to an older fork, and start again till it seems right to me and growth stops." • •Stoller is a discreet artist, with a rich inner dialogue. His imagination concentrates on creating parallel realms of two-dimensional characters, each with his own role under the spotlight where Stoller is at the same time writer, director, and costume designer. He suggests, "they could be a collection of actors on the stage of an imaginary world, the result of trying to reproduce our world, trying to find structures, constants, and variables, to group things and produce versions. They could be fragments of possible stories or instructions on how to fill up the empty spaces in between, through my imagination. They could be exercise pieces to find out how to give shape to a fantasy without freezing it." Or perhaps a search for an undiscovered realm of life to better understand its terrestrial counterpart. • •Stoller knows his work cannot be divided without pain and loss of integrity. "It's not one particular piece. It's their accumulation, because in accumulation a piece or fragment creates another fragment again, and a new piece is shaped on a higher level. Every level brings it closer to what I want it to be." • •Omar Vulpinari • •

1

Remo Stoller

Bern

1 Self-commissioned, untitled work / Switzerland / 2003
2 Self-commissioned, untitled work / Switzerland / 1999–2001

②

Remo Stoller

3 Self-commissioned, untitled work / Switzerland / 1997–2001
4 Self-commissioned, untitled work / Switzerland / 1999–2001

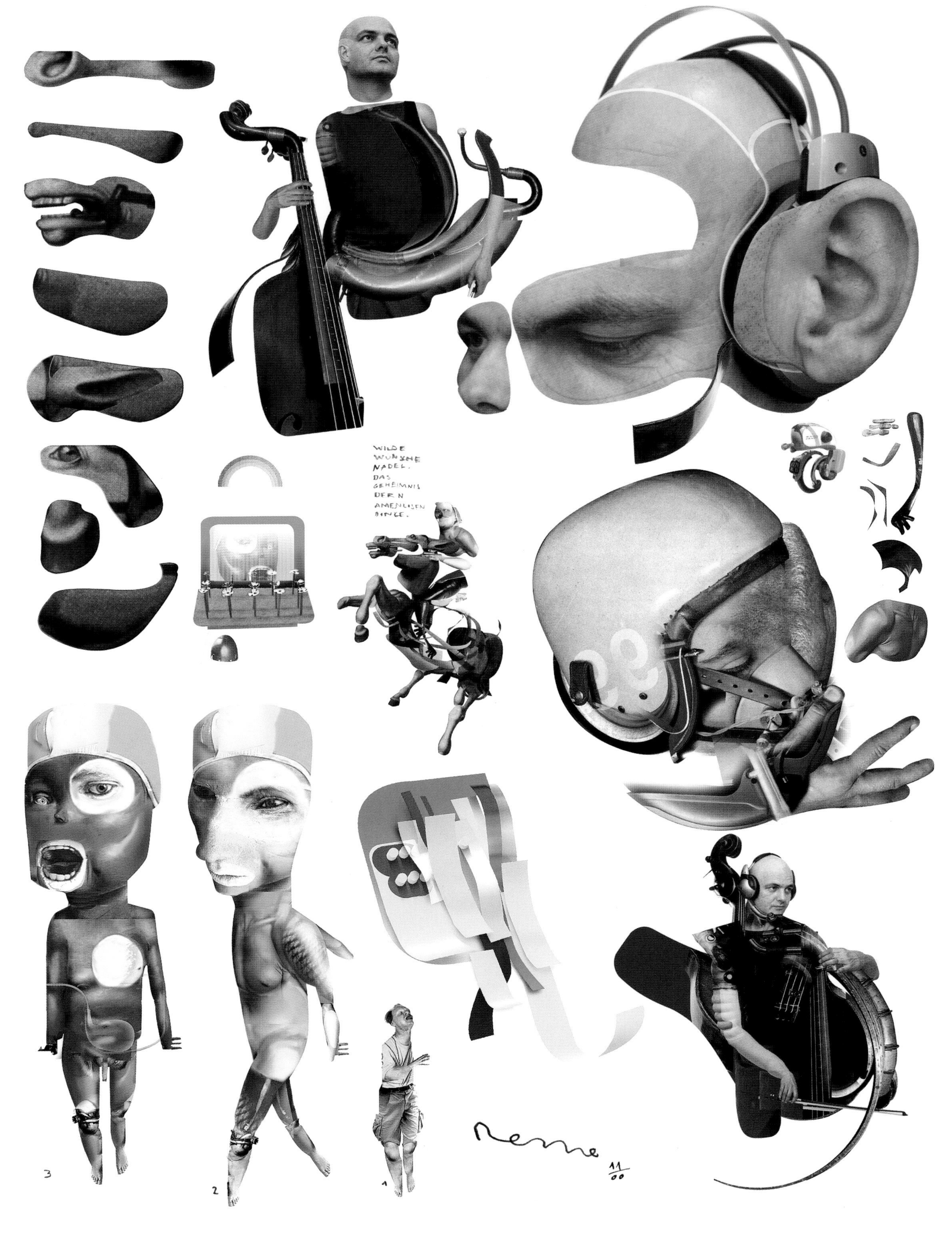
4
WILDE
WUNSCHE
NADEL.
DAS
GEHEIMNIS
DER N
AMENLOSEN
DINGE.
3
2
1
11/00

Kosta Stratigos tries to be a good man to run into on the street or to deal with in business or personal matters. He will hold the door for you. He will meet his obligations how and when he says he will meet them. He will buy his mother flowers for Valentine's Day and pay her a visit. But his design pieces Scrambler, Dirty Whore Megastore, and The Representatives evidence a craze for rock 'n' roll, consumerism, girls, guns, and gears. "How right you are!" he exclaims. "Growing up and living in the Detroit area, I have been absolutely surrounded and immersed in industry. My father is an engineer and an electrician, so there were always electrical parts and devices all over the house when I was a kid. I guess the fascination begins there. In my practice as a designer now, I approach design as a sort of mechanical problem solving whereby certain elements are needed on a page and my job is to figure out how they fit and work together, like the parts of a machine. Soviet Constructivism has been a big deal to me in that regard....The consumerism piece stems largely from my reluctant relationship with progress and globalization....Now in the U.S., all of these little towns are being slowly absorbed in the suburban sprawl of the larger cities, and locally owned businesses are being driven out by national and international concerns. This upsets me."•• "Play" assumes a very interesting meaning in Stratigos's work. He explains, "My father introduced me to another use of the term 'play' when I was younger. He described the way that the steering wheel on my mother's car could be turned a bit before the wheels themselves would actually turn as the steering wheel having some 'play' in it. As this relates to design and the design process, I find it hugely beneficial to approach any design project with a bit of 'play.' By this I mean that when I start a new project, I think it's great to start working without having every little parameter mapped out and every move planned and every inch of the page designed in my mind. Previously, I've tried to work where I try to plan everything in advance and nothing ever gets done; now I try to just get to work and let the piece take shape on its own."••For Stratigos, design is a personal playground, a place to indulge and investigate the connections that occur when people interact with one another face to face, the hazards of progress, the power of music, neurosis, and the strange ways that people deal with things.••Omar Vulpinari••

1 Promotional flyer for fashion show and exhibition *Composite* held at the Brooklyn 2000 Gallery, Detroit / Detroit Bitter / USA / 2000
2 Self-commissioned Elbow Grease poster, featuring Kosta Stratigos's typeface Heft / USA / 2000
3-4 Self-commissioned Scrambler and Howard Hughes posters / USA / 2001 / The posters represent an investigation into physical and cerebral lifestyles.

Kosta Stratigos

Detroit, Michigan

1

2

3

TO HAVE A CLOSET FULL OF SUITS
INSTEAD OF A DUFFEL BAG AND A PAIR OF BOOTS

4

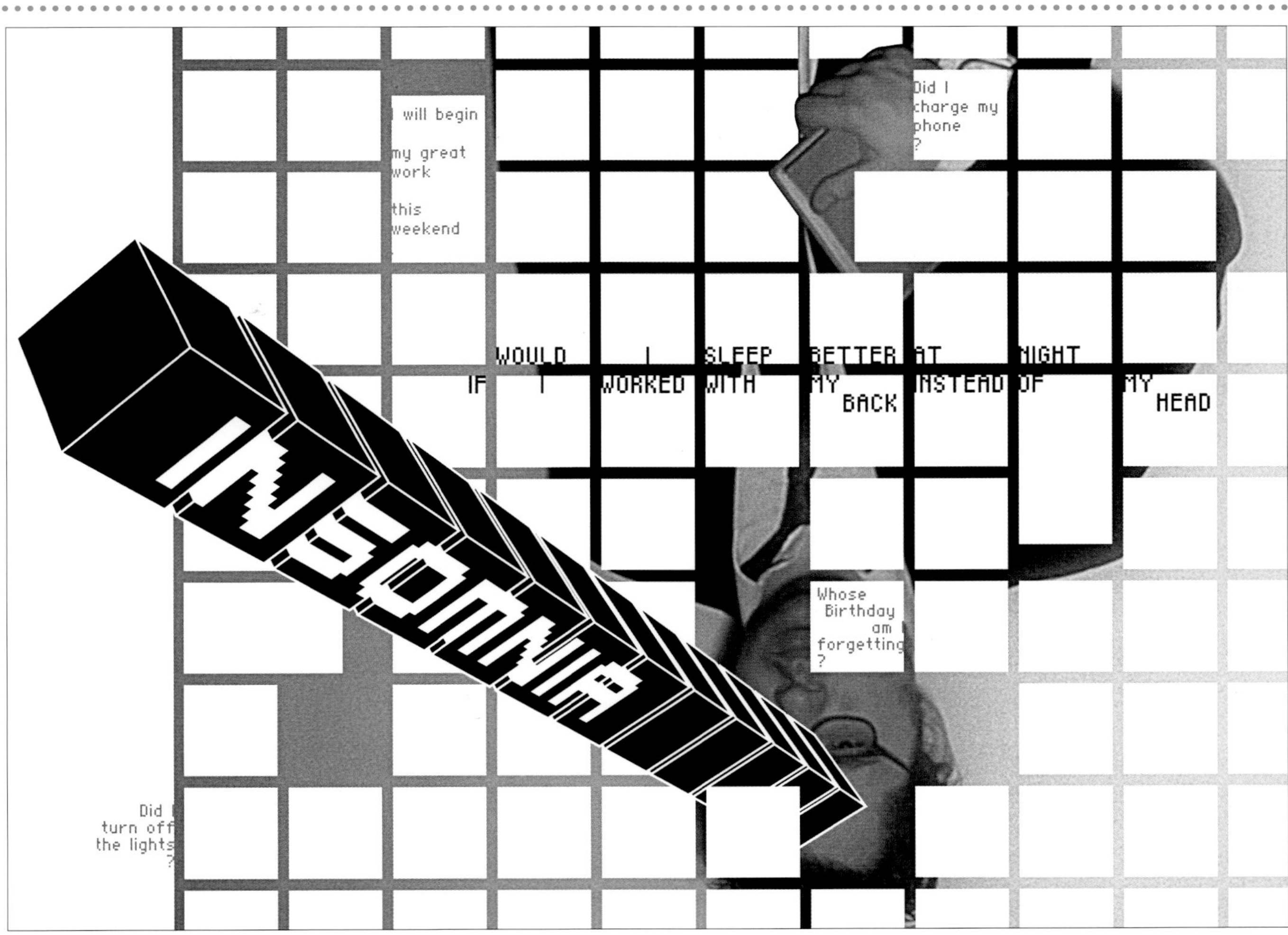
I will begin
my great work
this weekend
Did I charge my phone ?
WOULD I SLEEP BETTER AT NIGHT
IF I WORKED WITH MY BACK INSTEAD OF MY HEAD
INSOMNIA
Whose Birthday am I forgetting ?
Did I turn off the lights ?

⑤

MICHAEL GEIGER
MIKE HUCKABY
2 HEADS
ARE BETTER THAN ONE

⑥

LECTURE
WEDNEDAY
MARCH 7
DESALLE
12:30
FROM THE NEW
INTERMEDIA CENT
HOCHSCHULE FUR
KUNSTE BREMEN,
GERMANY

⑦

Kosta Stratigos

5–6 CD covers for self-released house mixes by DJs Michael Geiger and Mike Huckaby / USA / 2003
7 Poster for lecture by Peter Rea at the Cranbrook Academy of Art / Cranbrook Academy of Art / USA / 2001
8 Poster for exhibition *The Representatives* held at the Cranbrook Academy of Art / Katrayna Randall, Moonjoo Lee, and Megan Mcginnis / USA / 2002
9–11 Cover and spreads, *Dirty Whore Megastore* zine / Medialuxe / USA / 2002 / The publication focuses on the death of locally owned businesses in suburban America.

8

REPRESENTATIVES
COMING
SOON
THREE GIRLS & THEIR GUNS

9

DIRTY WHORE MEGASTORE
THE SEDUCTION OF CONVENIENCE AND THE DEATH OF COMMUNITY
Fresh Squeezed Orange Juice 1/2 gal.
56 SIZE!

BUT SO ARE WHORES
GOOD.
FIRE WORKS
I'D RATHER HAVE CANDY THAN CIGARETTES ANY DAY.

10 11

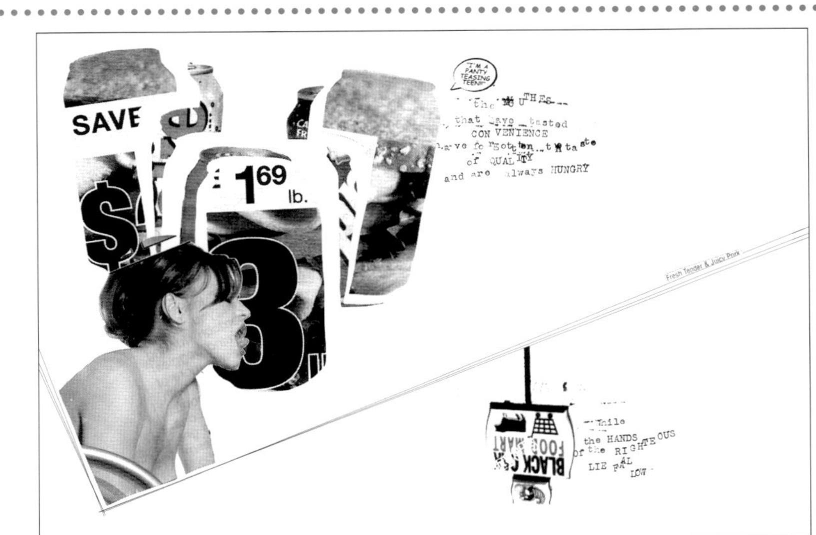

SAVE
1.69 lb.
CON VENIENCE
and are always HUNGRY
the HANDS

Yuri Surkov—or, as the signature on his works goes, "Suric"—is one of the prophets of Russian graphic design, which is enjoying an unprecedented commercial boom.•• The prophet goes his own way. Suric is one of the few who continues to revere design as a demiurgical craft, a mystery. For him, design is labor of the mind, the means to understanding the world. It is the path, the truth, not just an ordinary profession for quirky characters. He wants to work for the glory of life, not for the glory of the client. He knows that the designer who indulges the caprices of a crude client is also raising the level of crudeness in life.•• As a result, Suric doesn't have that many works—where do you find a customer whose purpose, like yours, is eternity? That's why a significant part of his posters are limited-edition esoteric investigations, free exercises, experiments for himself. These experiments have become possible thanks to the support of a handful of enthusiasts, such as the Moscow-based printing company LiniaGrafic, which printed collector's editions of a whole series of his posters.•• A contemplative attitude in life and ethical priorities in art led Suric, rather organically, to such a burning issue as the environment. The theme permeates his work of recent years. During Soviet times, propaganda posters for protection of the environment, or for world peace, most often invoked a struggle against an outside enemy. Our peace dove was, so to speak, a bird of prey. Suric, on the other hand, sees the enemy within—in the depths of the human conscience and subconscious.•• Suric's posters are marked by artistic erudition, by attention to the inner life of words, allowing him to extract unexpected visual effects from a literal foundation. Suric's artistic language has a propensity for minimalism. A minimum of color, a minimum of shape. Constructivist rhythms, actively working with contrasts. In Rodchenko's and Lissitsky's homeland, Suric is one of the very few who can be considered an heir to the Russian Constructivists.•• But his is a slightly different type of minimalism, a different type of Constructivism—not so sober and realistic, but rather slightly mystical and virtual. In any case, his approach is different enough for his works to be considered as part of the future, not of the past.•• Serge Serov••

1 Poster for international poster exhibition on occasion of Bertolt Brecht's hundredth birthday / Berliner Ensemble and Verband der Grafik-Designer e.V. / Germany / 1998
2 Poster for Moscow Film Festival / IMA Press-Print / Russia / 1992
3 Poster for exhibition on occasion of the Vladimir Mayakovski Festival, Moscow / Academy of Graphic Design / Russia / 2002
4 Poster promoting ecological awareness for the World Wildlife Fund for Nature (WWF) / WWF / Russia / 1995
5 Poster for exhibition celebrating of the fiftieth anniversary of the ending of the "Great Patriotic War" (1941–45), Moscow / Academy of Design / Russia / 1995
6 Poster contribution to exhibition on the importance and preservation of water / Association pour une banque d'images: l'eau pour l'humanité / France / 2000
7 Self-commissioned ecological poster series "Signature" / Russia / 1997

Yuri Surkov

Moscow

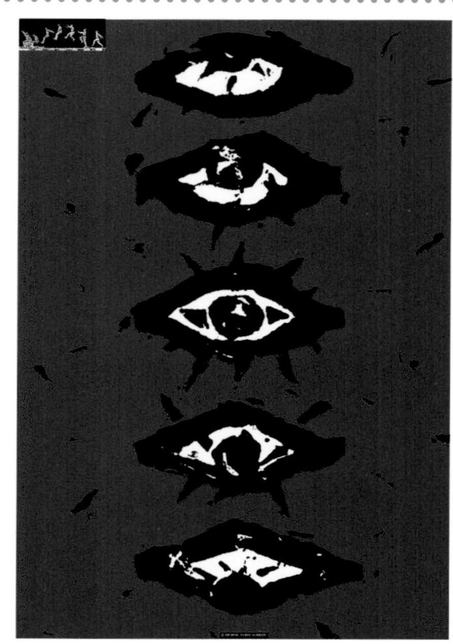

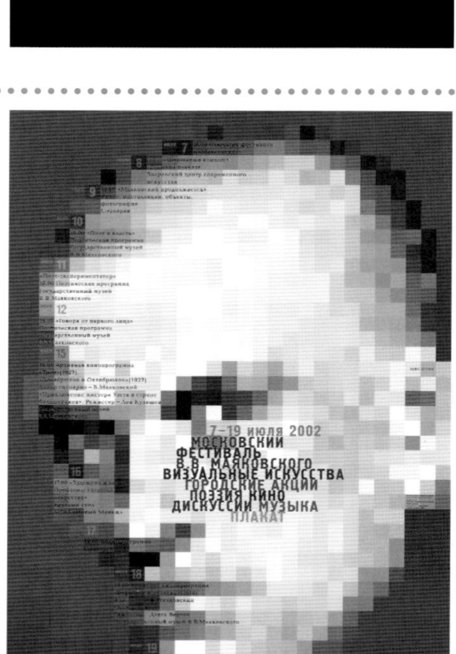

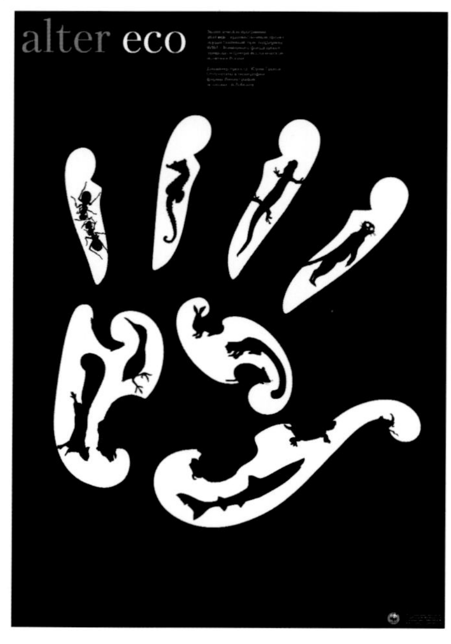

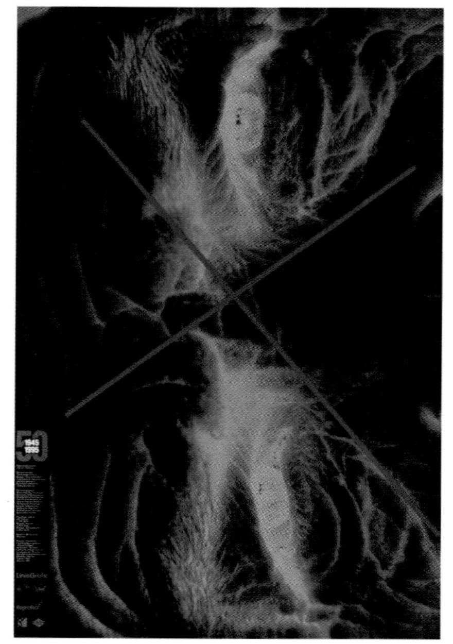

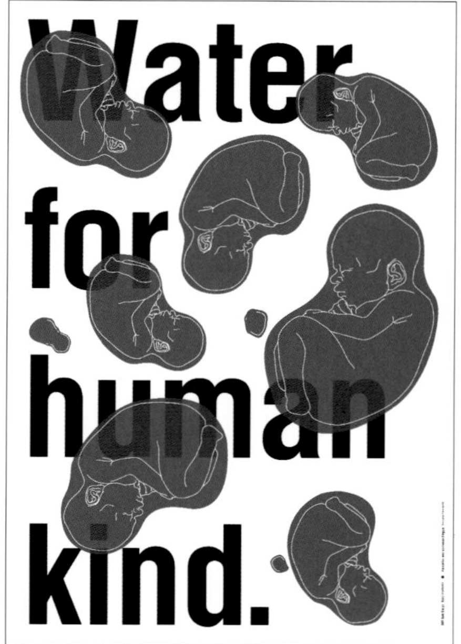

SIGNNATURE

SIGNNATURE

SIGNNATURE

SIGNNATURE

(8)

Yuri Surkov

8 Poster for international exhibition organized by the Museum on the Seam, Jerusalem / Museum on the Seam / Israel / 2000
9–10 Idea and Form posters for exhibition at the MAR'S Gallery, Moscow / Russia / 2000
11 Self-commissioned poster for exhibition at the Golden Bee V, Moscow International Biennale of Graphic Design / Russia / 2000
12 Self-commissioned Nature Morte poster for the tenth anniversary of the Chernobyl radiation disaster / Russia / 1996

9
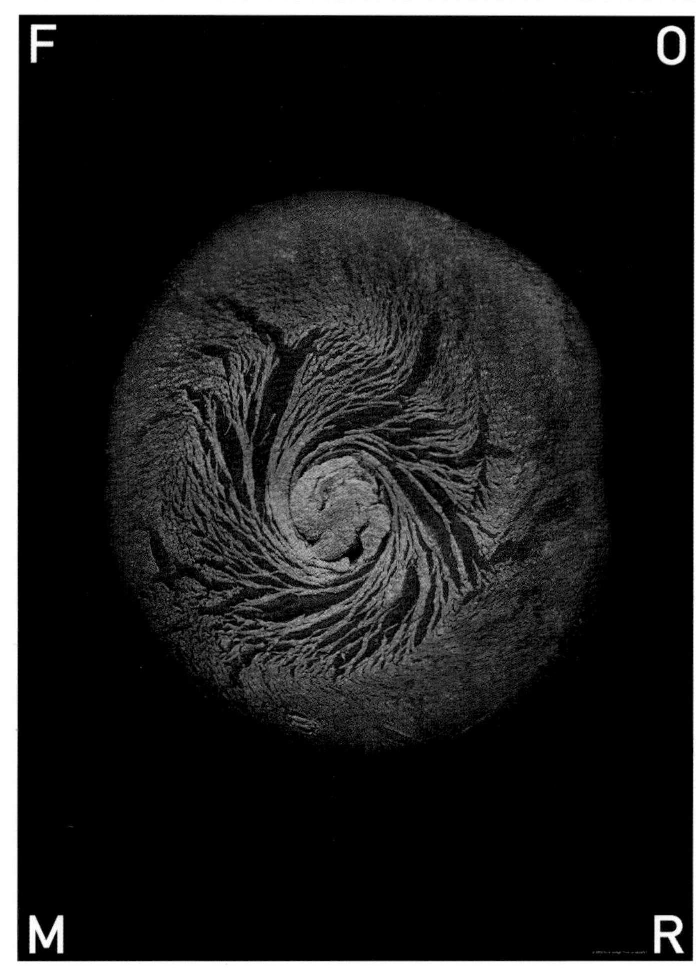
F
O
M
R

10
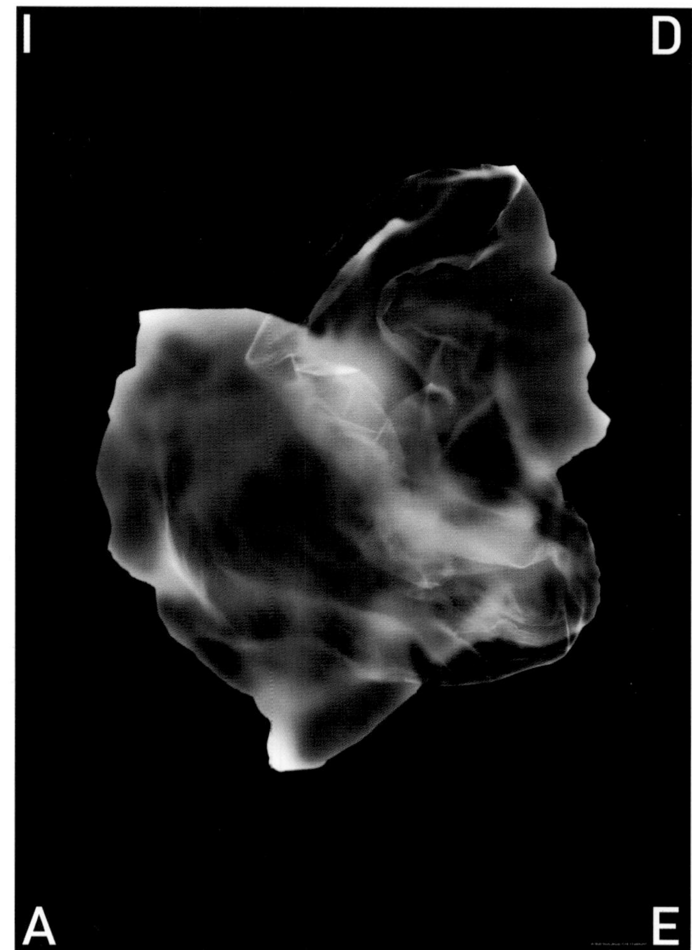
I
D
A
E

11

Золотая Пчела 2000 Международная Биеннале Графического Дизайна
Golden Bee 2000 Moscow International Biennale of Graphic Design
Let it Bee!

12

still life
nature morte
stilleben
чернобыль

If there's one Dutch designer who deserves to be put on the world map, it's Dick Bruna. His designs and illustrations radiate order, purity, and clarity on all sides. Bruna's telltale style is principally one-dimensional: one typeface, Helvetica; four "proper" colors plus a bit of black for the lines; and a standard page format of 15.5 x 15.5 centimeters. Bruna is a "brand" in the best sense of the word. When I asked him if he had finally finished his illustrated children's character Miffy—after over a hundred versions of the rabbit—and if it was not time to slaughter the little creature, Bruna answered, "Oh no, there's still development—I'm still simplifying it!" • • But I digress—this was to be about Thonik. Thomas Widdershoven and Nikki Gonnissen look a bit like Bruna—in their work, that is. They have appropriated his generic modus operandi. They, too, prefer standardized formats, one typeface (Avenir), and a limited range of colors. But that's where the comparison ends, because Bruna's cuddly simplicity—read and understood by millions of toddlers around the world, mind you!—transforms into a style front in the hands of Thonik, a cheerful cover for a message that tells the passerby exactly what the client wants to communicate. • • I first noticed Widdershoven years ago because of the experimental and witty forms he devised for the irregular poetry magazine *De Zingende Zaag* (The Singing Saw). Sometimes packed in cigar boxes with loose pages and funny objects, sometimes a strange printed object—always with a taste of dry poetic humor that often surpassed the quality of the published poems. That dry sense of poetry is characteristic of Thonik, the studio Widdershoven and his partner, Gonnissen, run. Their fearlessness with regard to controversy is evident from their explosively orange studio in Amsterdam, designed by cutting-edge Dutch architecture firm MVRDV, which has provoked much dispute. For a younger generation, Thonik is a source of inspiration, which makes them one of the more influential design studios in the Netherlands today. • • Anthon Beeke • •

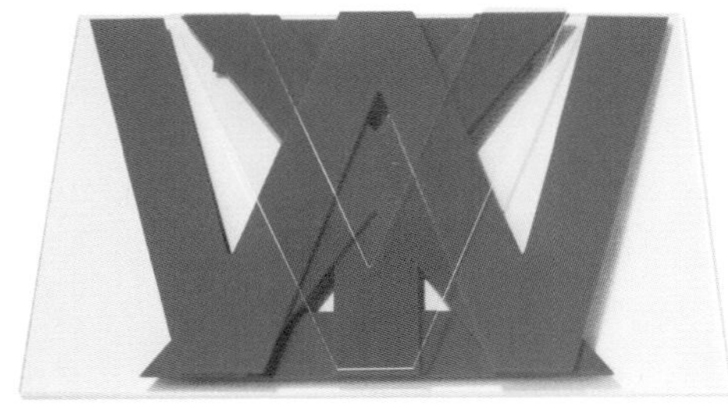

1

2

1 Three-dimensional manuscript for Vedute project / Vedute / Netherlands / 2001 / The Vedute project invites designers and architects to express their views on space in a "three-dimensional manuscript" that must fit in a 44 x 32 x 7 centimeter area. Thonik's entry employs the twenty-six letters of the alphabet. All letters are orange, except for those that make up the name of the employed font, Avenir.

2 Poster forming part of campaign for exhibition *Over The Edges* in Ghent / S.M.A.K. / Netherlands / 2000 / The exhibition invited fifty-two artists to create works of art on the street corners of Ghent, the Netherlands.

3 Book, *Apples & Oranges 2001*, a yearbook of graphic design in the Netherlands / BIS Publishers / Netherlands / 2001

4 Book, *Eternally Yours–Visions on Product Endurance* / 010 Publishers / Netherlands / 1997

5 Book, *Thonik–New Dutch Graphic Design*, part of a series of monographs dedicated to young Dutch design groups / BIS Publishers / Netherlands / 2001

6 *Narcisse Tordoir* exhibition catalogue (with De Designpolitie) / Centraal Museum, Utrecht / Netherlands / 1997

7–10 Cover and spreads, *Less+More–Droog Design in Context* / 010 Publishers / Netherlands / 2002

Thonik

Amsterdam

3

APPLES & ORANGES
01

4

eternally yours
visions on product endurance
eternally yours

5

From the start thonik have been at the forefront of a new generation of graphic designers. The designer as director, as conceptual artist, as strategist, as media expert and as obstinate busybody – thonik* cover all these roles with gusto. And with results. Ineke Schwartz – new Dutch graphic design. BIS Publishers

6

N.T.
Z.T.

7
8
9
10

Droog Design in context
Less
More
Renny Ramakers
010 Publishers

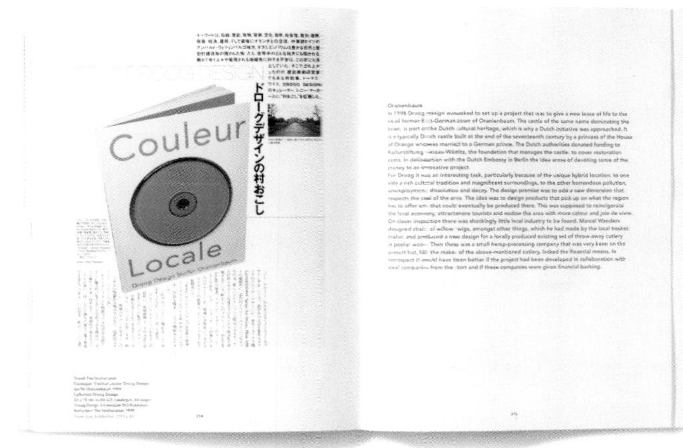
Couleur
Locale

de Architect

注目するのか?
Vitra Design Museumが
スタルクの次にミニチュア化したのは
この椅子でした
Vitra Design Museum
Miniatures Collection

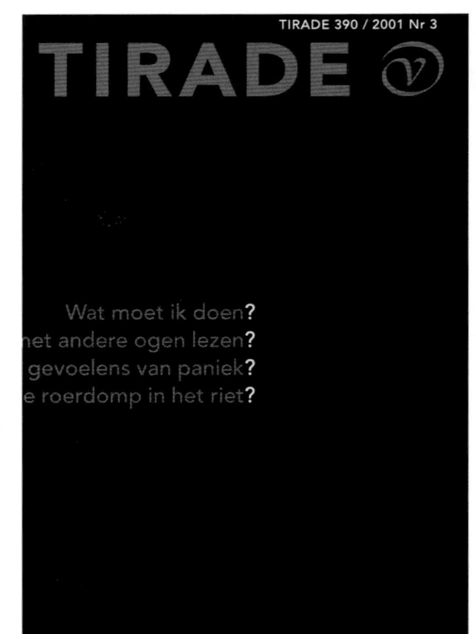

TIRADE 390 / 2001 Nr 3
TIRADE
Wat moet ik doen?
net andere ogen lezen?
gevoelens van paniek?
e roerdomp in het riet?

11 12 13

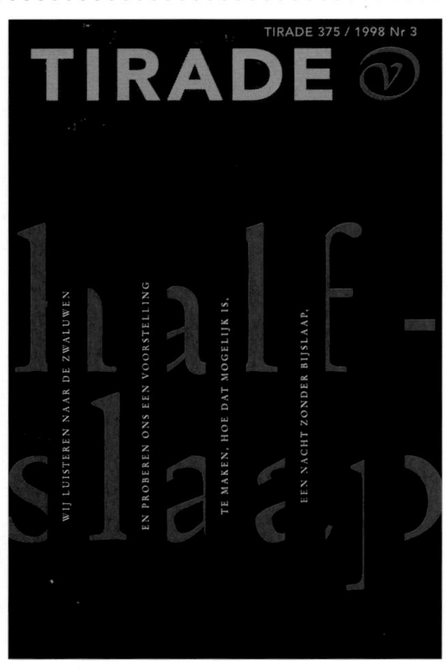

TIRADE 375 / 1998 Nr 3
TIRADE
WIJ LUISTEREN NAAR DE ZWALUWEN
EN PROBEREN ONS EEN VOORSTELLING
TE MAKEN, HOE DAT MOGELIJK IS,
EEN NACHT ZONDER BIJSLAAP.

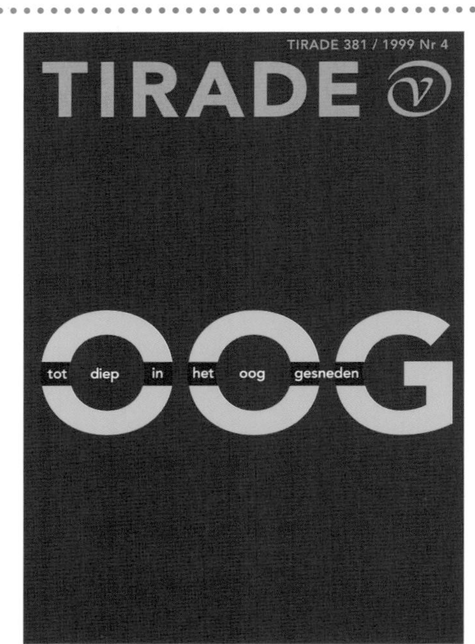

TIRADE 381 / 1999 Nr 4
TIRADE
OOG
tot diep in het oog gesneden

TIRADE 385 / 2000 Nr 3
TIRADE
als een vogel die een vogel gehaald wordt en weer teruggezet

14 15 16

Thonik

11–16 Covers for Dutch literary magazine *Tirade*, issues 389, 390, 370, 375, 381, and 385 / Tirade / Netherlands / 1997–2001

17 Identity, exhibition and event posters, invitations, and newspaper / Centraal Museum, Utrecht / Netherlands / 1996–present / In order to increase the overall recognizability of the Centraal Museum's relatively autonomous five collections (old masters, modern art, local city history, costume, and design) a new identity was conceived. This identity program is modified and adapted to accommodate the museum's various events and promotional items.

centraal museum krant
Open, open!!
Panorama 2000
Ronald Giphart
GRATIS
made in japan

centraal museum krant
Licht
Familie
Solo
GRATIS
caravaggisten
meesters van het licht

centraal museum krant
Open, open!!
Ingmar Heytze
Erich Wichman
GRATIS
OPEN
OPEN
OPEN
Open, open open open open, open!

17

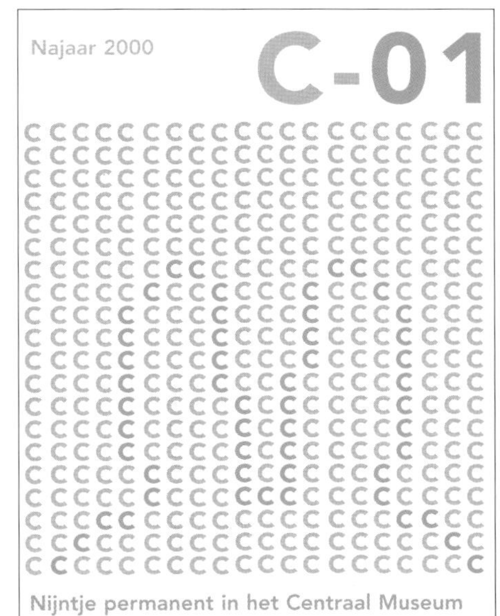
Najaar 2000
C-01
Nijntje permanent in het Centraal Museum
Saenredam Relatiearrangement

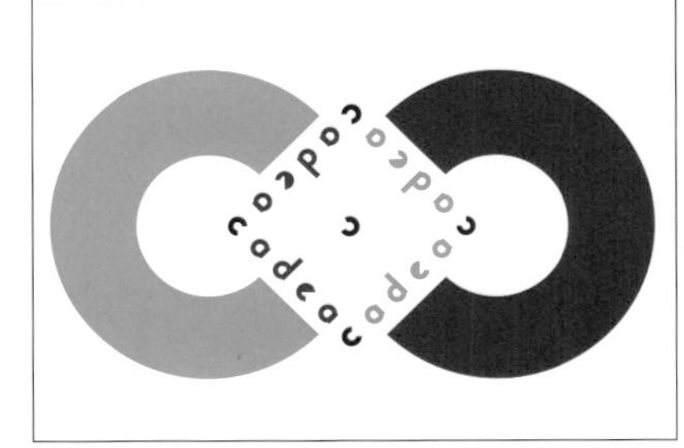

Utrechts Gouden Eeuw
De topwerken van de Meesters van het Licht
29 juni - 23 september 2001

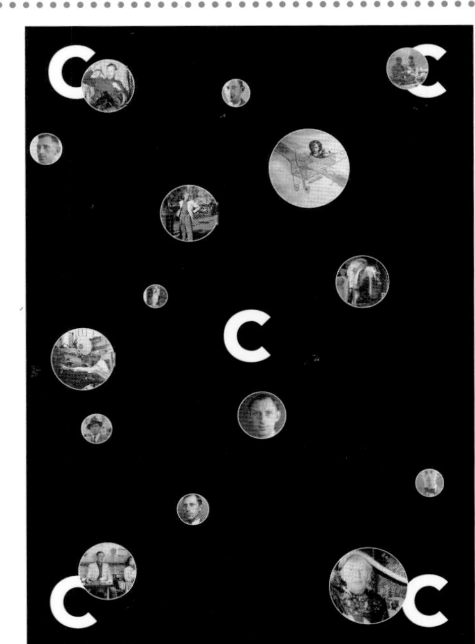

centraal museum
Op vertoon van deze kaart krijgen cmbusiness
clubleden gratis toegang tot het museum,
kortingen in de museumwinkel. Deze kaart is
geldig tot 31-12-2001.
busi
ness
club

centraal museum

Among all the fluff that is available out there, it is rare for a design project to touch my heart. TRUE has managed this unlikely and incredibly difficult feat a couple of times. • •One is a project that took place within the New York subway. As in most public transport systems, the NY subway has a slew of official signs and stickers to tell you what you should and should not do. TRUE printed up a range of additional stickers imitating the look of the official ones but designed his to be rather more philosophical in content. • •The reason they touched me was their location: riding on a train, staring in the air, being bored, looking at but not reading a directional sign, slowly realizing the message is different from the one expected, enjoying the content, happily anticipating others' reactions. I might have been able to come up with an idea like that, but I would have made the content cynical, critical of the mayor's office or the Metropolitan Transit Authority. It is a testament to TRUE's genius to have opted for unfashionable optimism. People I know mentioned that when they saw his "Strive to be Happy" sign, it actually made them feel better. • •For the campaign, TRUE met every Wednesday at midnight with fifteen to twenty friends at the same subway stop, and they divided up the different subway lines among them. One group would do the A line, another the F, and so on. Being a true humanitarian he also equipped all of his helpers with fake Transit Authority IDs and even made up fake authorization letters so his friends would not get arrested. None did. • •For another piece, he changed the wording of the "Walk/Don't Walk" pedestrian signs at specific sites all over New York. After he was through, the one in front St. Patrick's Cathedral said "Sin" and then started blinking "Repent." On Malcolm X Boulevard in Harlem it said "Strive" and "No Limits." • •The power of these urban postings comes directly out of their anonymous, non-corporate heritage. They were produced selflessly, with little but the joy of the process to be gained for TRUE. A Nike logo on those subway stickers would have ruined the entire campaign. • •Stefan Sagmeister • •

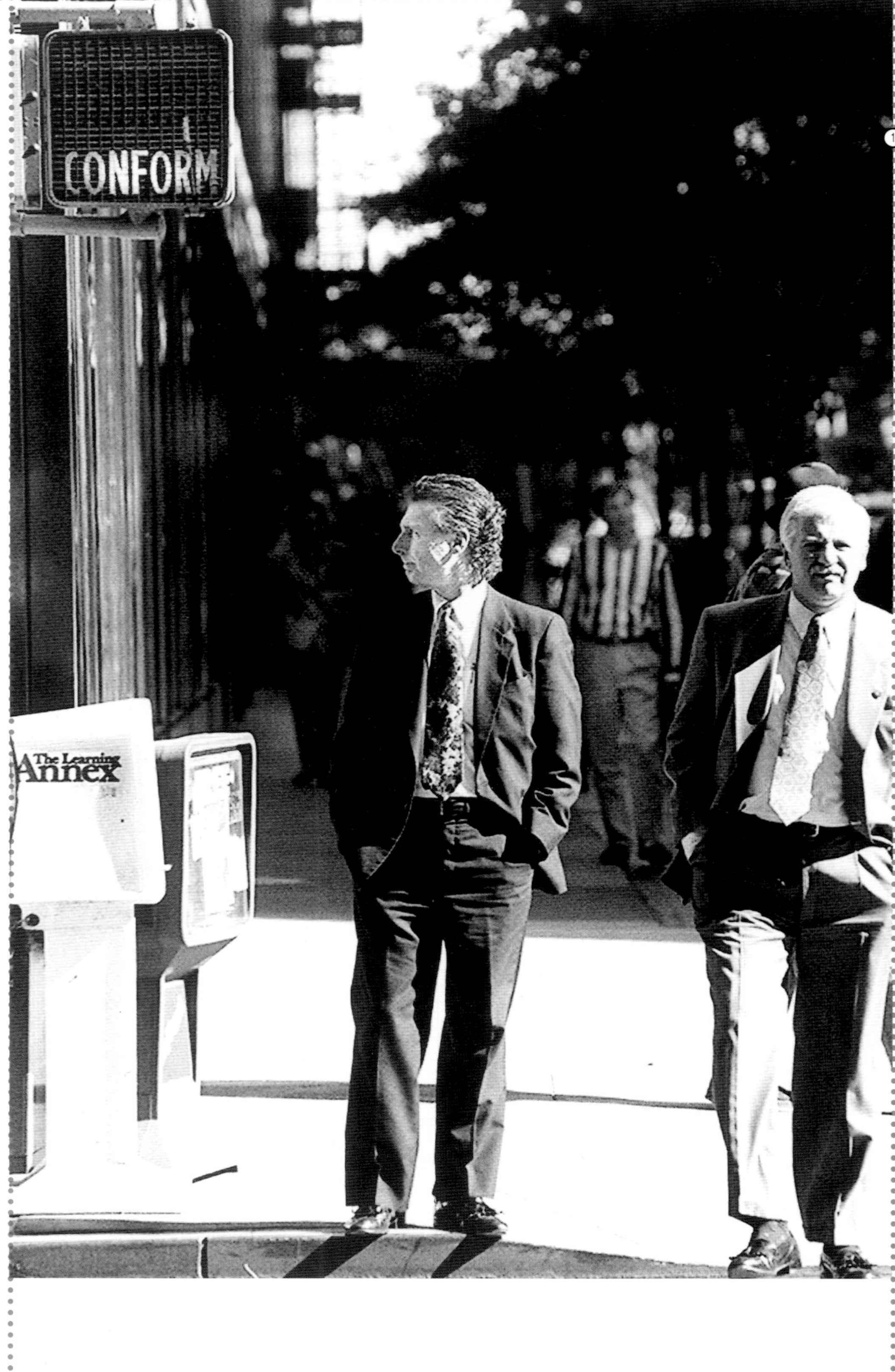

1

TRUE

New York

1 Self-commissioned Consume/Conform project / USA / 1993 / A pedestrian traffic sign in front of Gap store in midtown Manhattan was altered to read "Consume/Conform" rather than "Walk/Don't Walk."

2 Self-commissioned No Limits/Strive project / USA / 1993 / A pedestrian traffic sign on the corner of Malcolm X and Martin Luther King Jr. Boulevards in Harlem was altered to read "No Limits/Strive."

2

3

4

Do not hold grudges

5

Karma Conditioned Car
Please watch what you do

6

7

Officially Authorized

8

ATTENTION:
This sign has been commissioned by
The Department of Cultural Affairs in cooperation
with the City of New York and The New York Department
of Transportation. To remain until further notice.
DO NOT REMOVE
DOT

9

Riding with despair prohibited
Keep hopes up

3–6 Adhesive subway signage created for self-commissioned New York Subway Sticker project / USA / 1994 / Designed to look like conventional Metropolitan Transit Authority (MTA) signage, these stickers were applied in subway cars throughout New York.
7 Laminated MTA volunteer card created for participants in the Subway Sticker project as protection against MTA officials / 1994
8 Sticker created to avoid immediate removal of the new subway signage / 1994
9 Adhesive subway signage created for New York Subway Sticker project / 1994
10–11 TRUE and his friends applying new signage in a New York subway / 1994

Life Instructions
Have fun
Do not hurt people
Do not accept defeat

10
11

2x4 is a design group. That might sound like an obvious statement but consider for a moment that many other design groups aren't. A group, that is. Instead, many, like Pentagram for instance, are a collection of individuals who remain as separate principals running several groups within one. 2x4, on the other hand, is a studio of creative directors, writers, designers, and programmers who through collaboration claim to have managed "to a certain extent" to "erase personality and expression" from their work. This is not 2x4 riding the backlash against the insular, self-indulgent design that characterized the 1990s. 2x4 wants to be known as much for the organizational process they employ on projects as the fruits that result from them. They want to "make process the product" because this makes collaboration with big companies like Rem Koolhaas's Office of Metropolitan Architecture much easier. "Often our role is laying out the diagram of the project that is often filled in by the other people working alongside us." • • 2x4 represent a new model for a design group, one where design ideology has been replaced by what they call a "sensibility." On the evidence of their portfolio, this seems to give them a greater elasticity of response to the challenges that their mainly cultural clients place before them. The gamut is wide, from the understated yet simultaneously bold layout of *Charrette* (a book for OMA/MoMA) to the frenetic detail on the covers of the Any book series to the dramatic, kaleidoscopic environmental graphics for both Prada and Vitra. The key to 2x4's approach, their resistance to design dogma, has something to do with the founders' unorthodox paths to becoming graphic designers; Michael Rock via a humanities degree and later as a design critic, Susan Sellers as a cultural critic, and Georgie Stout via furniture design. This background, says Rock, has given them a healthy skepticism that "informs everything we do." The distance they maintain from design prevents it from overshadowing the content they are asked to communicate. And that's fortunate, since they have an enviable list of clients who have interesting things to say. • • Nick Bell • •

1 Wallpaper designs for Prada boutique in New York / Prada / USA / 2001 / The wallpaper is changed every season.

2 Identity system and Mies van der Rohe elevation as part of environmental design for the Illinois Institute of Technology McCormick Tribune Building (with the Office of Metropolitan Architecture and Petra Blaisse) / Illinois Institute of Technology / USA / 2003

2x4

New York

2

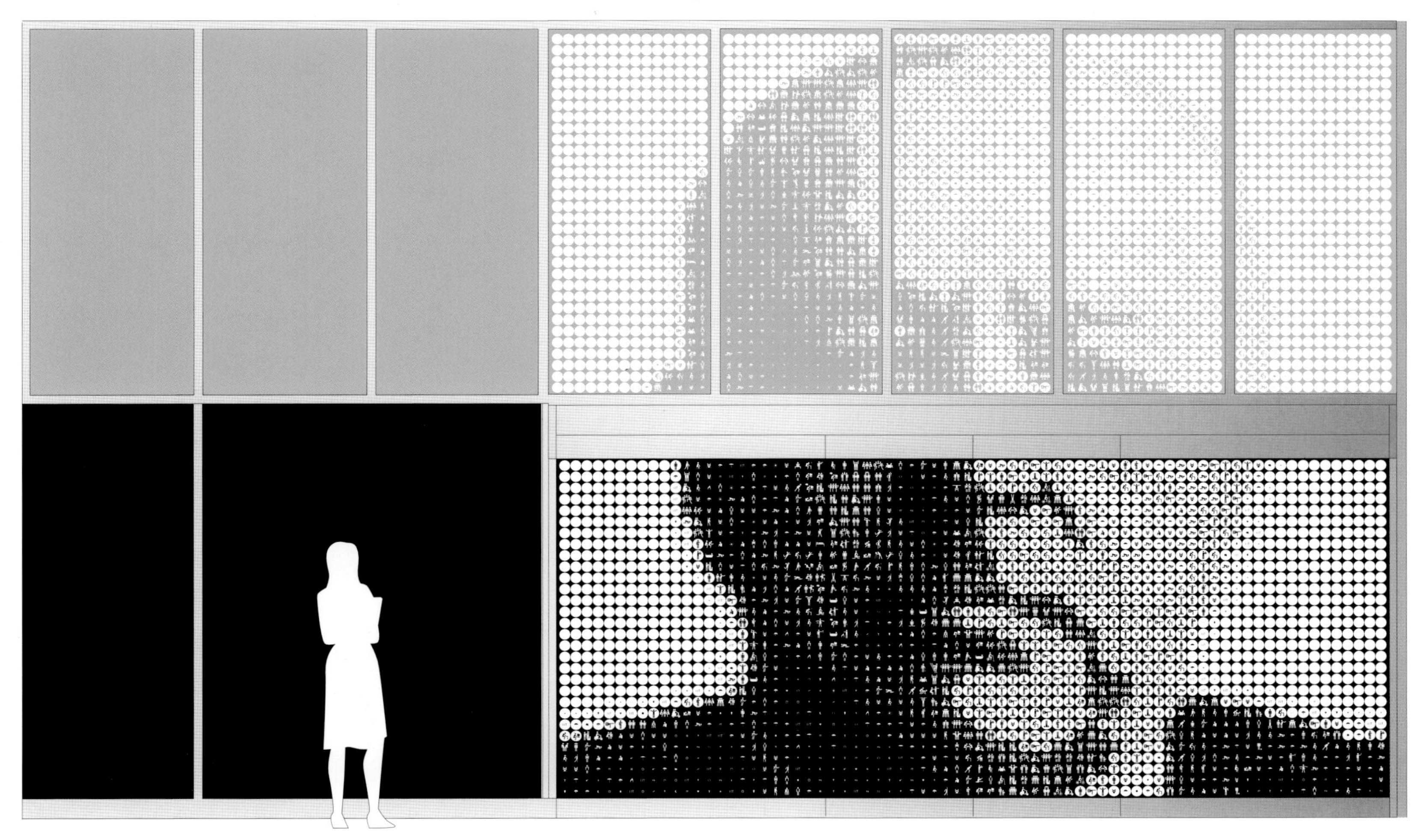

3 4 5

The Classics 58

Vitra Herbarium

20th-Century Blossoms

The Classics 59

6

7

3–5 Installations in design store Vitra's showroom, Los Angeles / Vitra / Switzerland / 2002
6 Spread, Vitra publication *Workspirit* no. 8 / Vitra / Switzerland / 2003
7 Installation in design store Vitra's showroom, Los Angeles / 2002
8–11 Cover, wraparound jacket and spreads, *Philip Johnson's Glasshouse* / YKK and Tadahiro Yishida / Japan / 1998
12–13 Covers, architectural magazine *Any* no. 18, "Public Fear," and no. 20, "The Virtual House" / Any / USA / 1997
14 Book cover, *Anything* / Any / USA / 2001 / The book documents the "Anything" conference of contemporary architecture and urbanism held in New York, 2000.

8
9
10
11

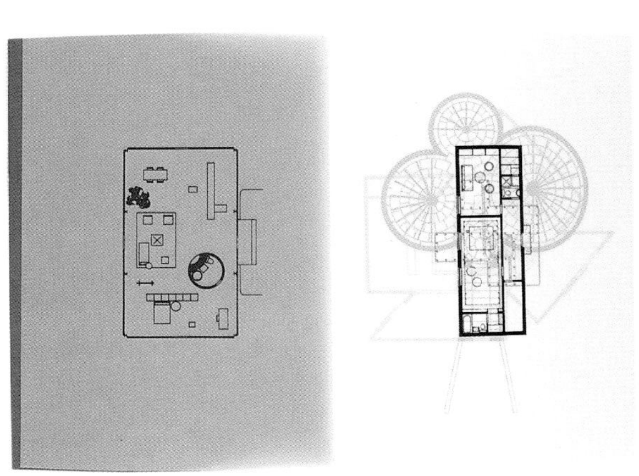

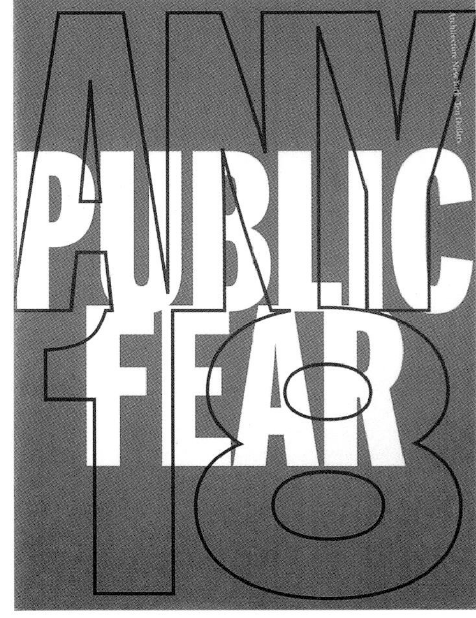

12
13
14

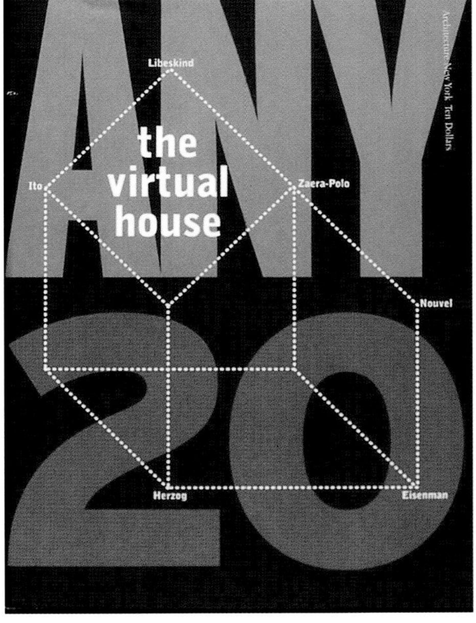

When Yuichi Miyashi and Naoyuki Suzuki cofounded Tycoon Graphics in the early 1990s, they were one of the first graphic-design groups to initiate their own experimental projects on a regular basis. They decided to become graphic authors before the term became ubiquitous. Who could ever forget the photographs of two of their members in the Tokyo subway system dressed up in American football uniforms carrying signs stating, "No more bad design"? ••While you can draw slight connections to Fluxus, Dada, and even Deconstructivism, the work does not seem to be directly influenced by any precedent in design or art. It really does inform itself. From the magically realistic photographic paintings for the Gokujo Hybrid CD cover to the TyGun vending machine, Tycoon often chooses to go down their own individual road.••There is an innocent fun about much of their work, a lovely sincerity that differentiates itself beautifully from all the staid professionalism so prevalent in graphic design today.••Stefan Sagmeister••

1

Tycoon Graphics

Tokyo

1 Poster contribution to exhibition *VERSUS EXHIBITION 02* at the Parco Museum, Tokyo / Japan / 2002
2–5 Lucky Strike advertising campaign including cigarette packaging, posters, ashtrays, lighters, picture books, and other promotional items / British American Tobacco Japan / Japan / 2002
6 CD packaging, *Gojuko Hybrid*, by Bird / Sony Music Associated Records / Japan / 2002

②

③

④

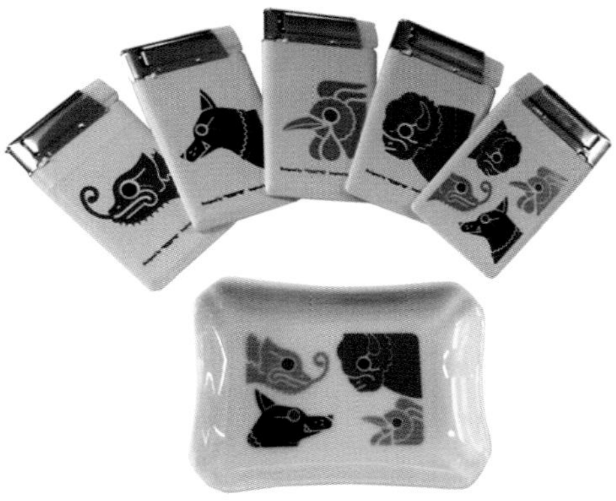

⑤

⑥

7

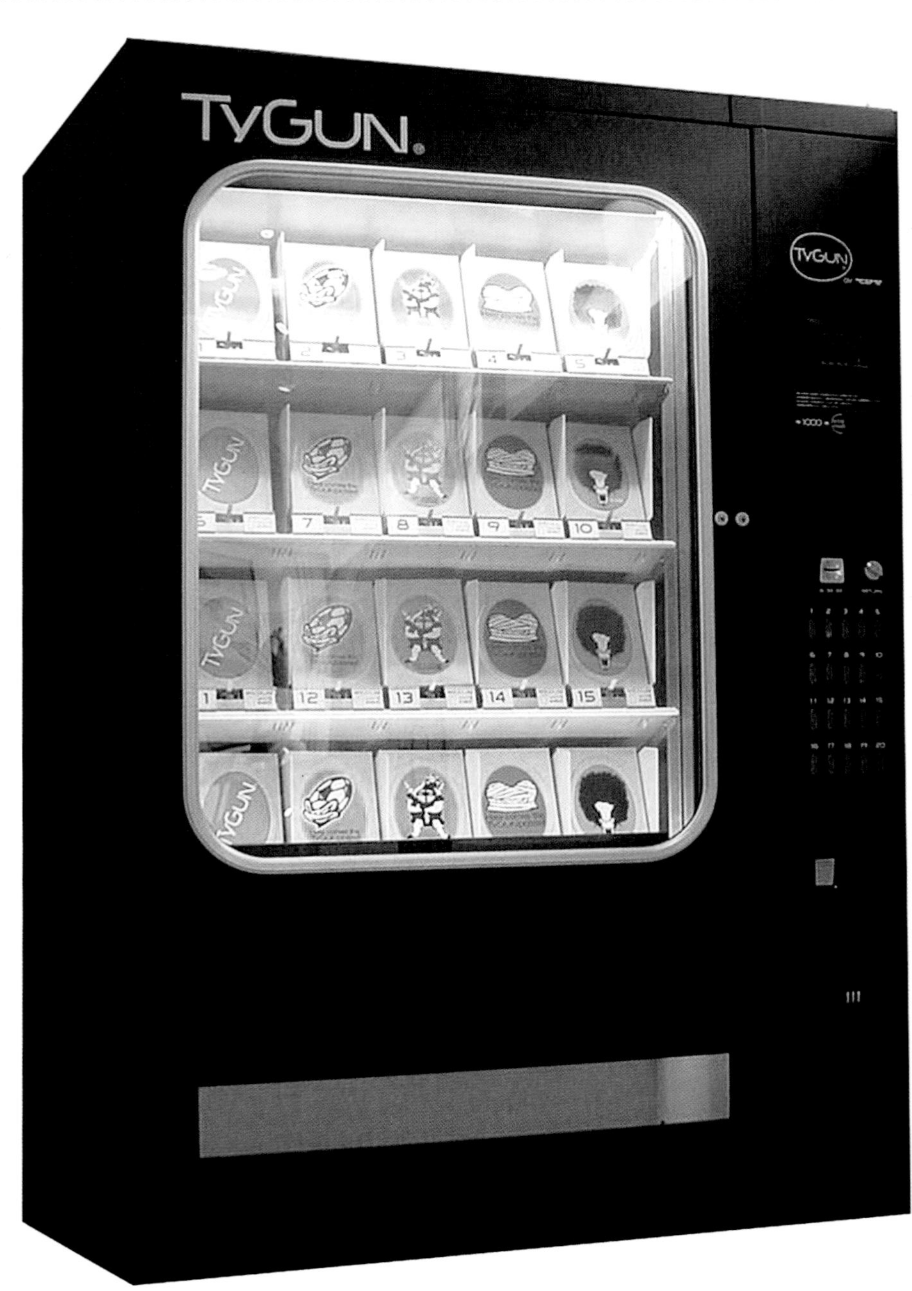

7 Tygun paper bags, book, and vending machine / Tycoon Graphics / Japan / 2002 / Tygun is a brand created by Tycoon Graphics, featuring a group of illustrated comic characters that appear in monthly Tygun publications and on various media such as bags, stickers, and T-shirts. In addition to being distributed at Tokyo cafés and book and record stores, Tygun items are sold through a special vending machine installed in Tokyo's modern-furniture store Daikanyama.

8–10 Print advertisment and posters for the Atehaca Home Appliances Project / Toshiba Corporation and United Arrows / Japan / 2002 / The Atehaca Home Appliances Project, together with the Intentionallies architectural design office, focuses on creating a new line of attractive home appliances that harmonize with Japanese gastronomic culture.

Tycoon Graphics

8

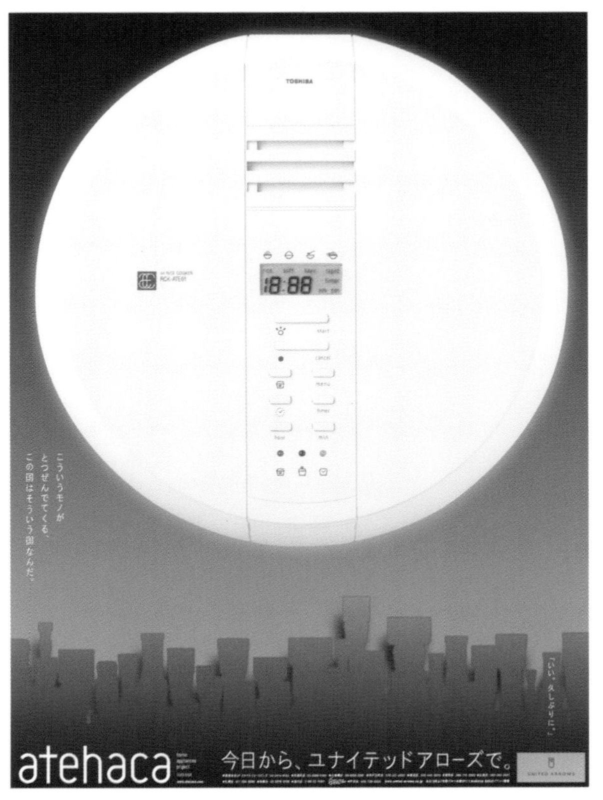

TOSHIBA
こういうモノが
とつぜんでてくる。
この国はそういう国なんだ。
atehaca
今日から、ユナイテッドアローズで。

9

atehaca
2002
02.16
debut
TOSHIBA

10

Design, like pop music (but unlike, say, architecture), is a young person's profession. Many talented professionals create their best, breakthrough work before they are forty and spend the second half of their careers either managing other designers or producing competent but ultimately irrelevant work. • •One of the very few designers who is experimenting at fifty and pushing at all the corners is Rick Valicenti. While it is exhausting to work on the edge for a couple of years, it requires a different kind of stamina altogether to keep going and going for decades: Rick = our very own Energizer bunny. • •His four-letter-word magazine has a forever-changing title (*FINK*, *WANT*, *MYTH*, etc.) and a constant mixture of content you have not experienced before with formal treatments you have not seen before. • •Some animations he developed for trade-show presentations are formally and technically so inventive that I felt sorry they were stuck inside a trade-show screen. You would have hoped for them coming alive at MoMA. • •For a talk in New York organized by the American Institute of Graphic Arts (AIGA), he designed a video in which he asked a woman on a porn Web site to form all the letters of the alphabet with her body. While she was contorting into A, B, and C, he took screen shots and later animated them into one of the freshest and most daring pieces of typography to come along in some time. Large parts of the audience were outraged and left without applauding. • •Stefan Sagmeister • •

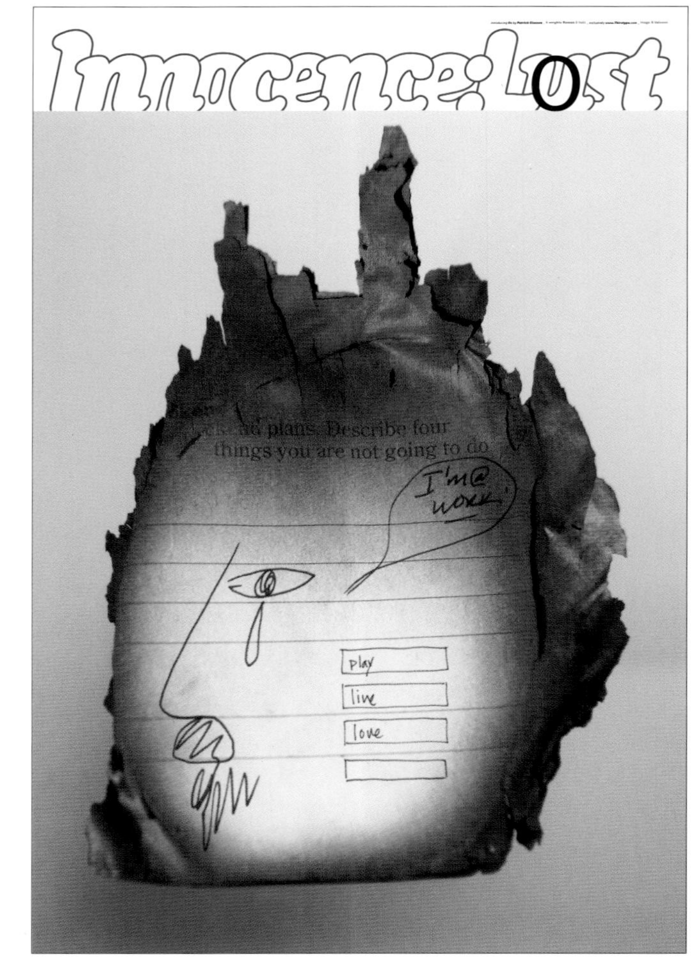

1

2

1 Poster introducing font design Oz, by Patrick Giasson / Thirstype / USA / 2000 / The font is based on Oswald Cooper's Cooper Font Family.
2 Poster to commemorate the introduction of North Star Printing's eight-color press / North Star Printing / USA / 1993
3–4 Spread illustrations from *FINK*, second issue of the "**** (four letter word)" magazine series / Thirstype / USA / 1997
5 Poster for lecture series organized by paper manufacturer Gilbert Paper / Gilbert Paper / USA / 1994

Rick Valicenti

Chicago

3

Heaven's Gate: America

4

5

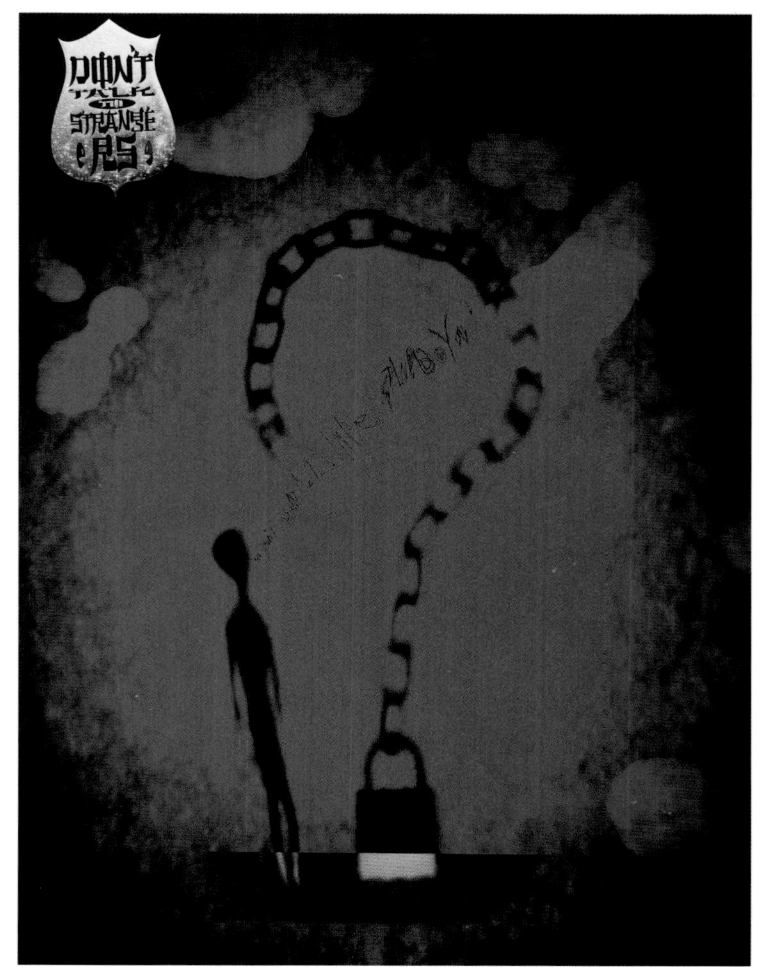

⑥

⑦

⑧

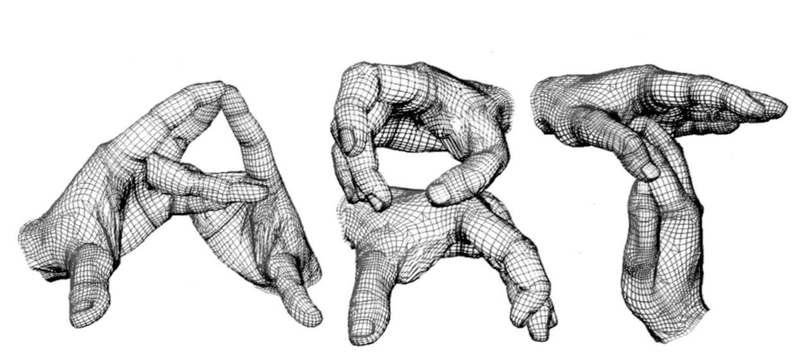

⑨

Rick Valicenti

6 Page from press kit for *Ray Gun* and *Bikini* magazines / Ray Gun Publishing / USA / 1998
7 Illustration commenting on sexism for MTV Music Awards catalogue / MTV / USA / 1993
8 Typeface design Handsome (with Brian McMullen) / Thirstype / USA / 2000
9 Logo for teen fashion brand (with Chad Johnston) / Wonderboy / Japan / 2003
10 Illustration for *ESPN The Magazine* (with Matt Dally) / ESPN / USA / 1998
11 Filmstill-based typography Just My Type for AIGA conference in New York (with Gregg Brokaw) / USA / 1999

10

11

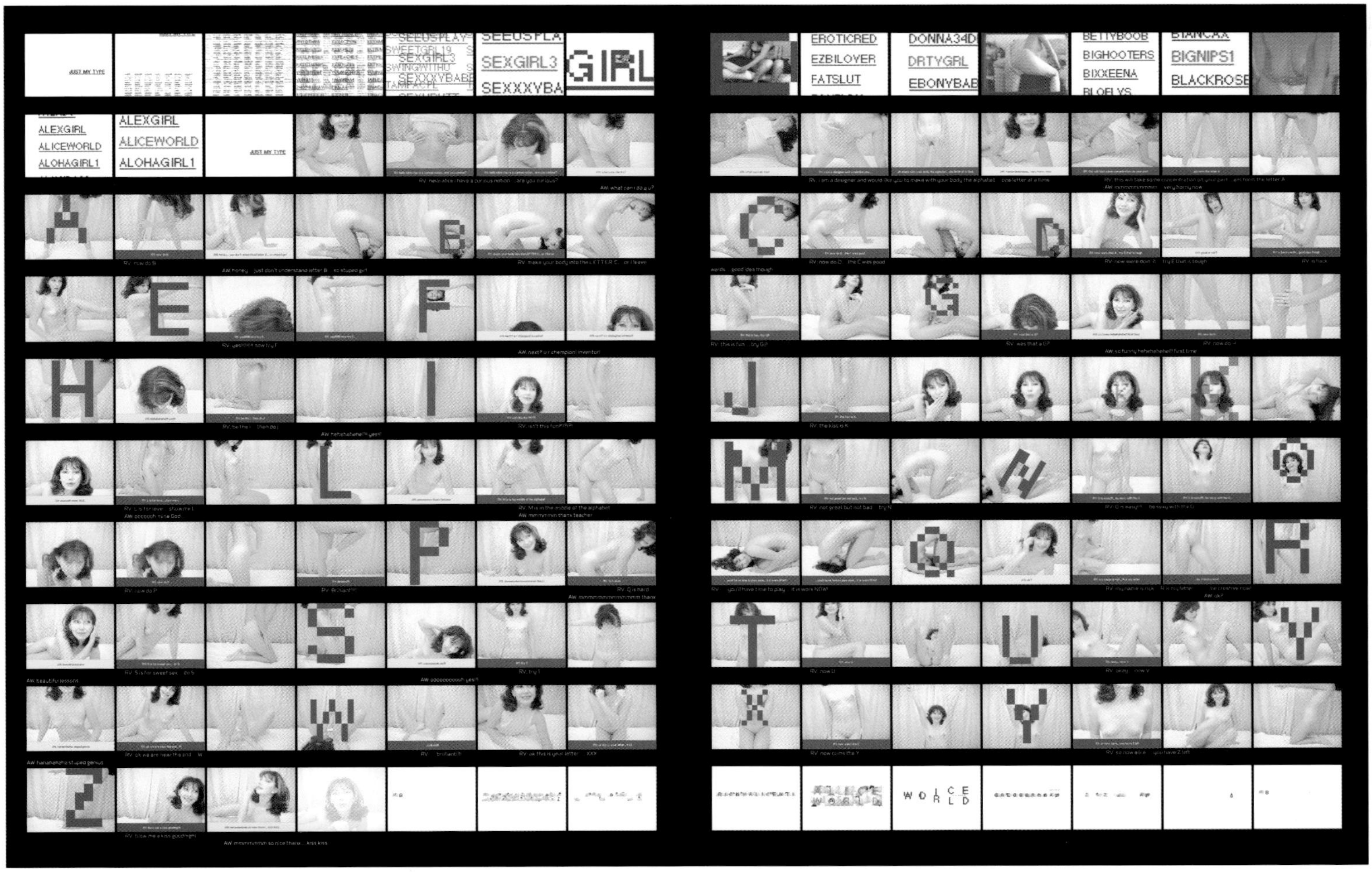

Seemingly few people know Alberto Vieceli's name, but the wonderfully discreet and quiet books he designs keep winning prizes. Vieceli always puts himself completely at the service of his projects, bringing out everything he has to offer in order to provide a book's content with its optimal form. He interprets each assignment carefully, seriously, without encroaching on the subject matter, but with an intuition that speaks volumes.••It might be appropriate to compare Vieceli to an accomplished pastry chef. Not just any pastry chef, of course, and certainly not one who deals with ready-made products. He studied his profession seriously and thoroughly—all the beautiful ingredients, colors, forms, as well as the care and respect for the material. This knowledge allows him to bake beautiful little cakes. These "book cakes" have the advantage that they can be picked up, their texture can be felt, they can be smelled and read over and over again. Vieceli likes variation in his recipes, not in order to create overly rich artifices—he is careful with his use of butter, cream, and sugar—but to approach every project's content with new, subtle flavors. Without much fuss and with an enviable consistency, he seems to imbue one book design after the next with higher blessings.••Vieceli has been collaborating with Tania Prill for more than a year now. Together they have already won several graphic-design competitions, created an award-winning poster, and made an award-winning book. Still waters run deep.••Werner Jeker••

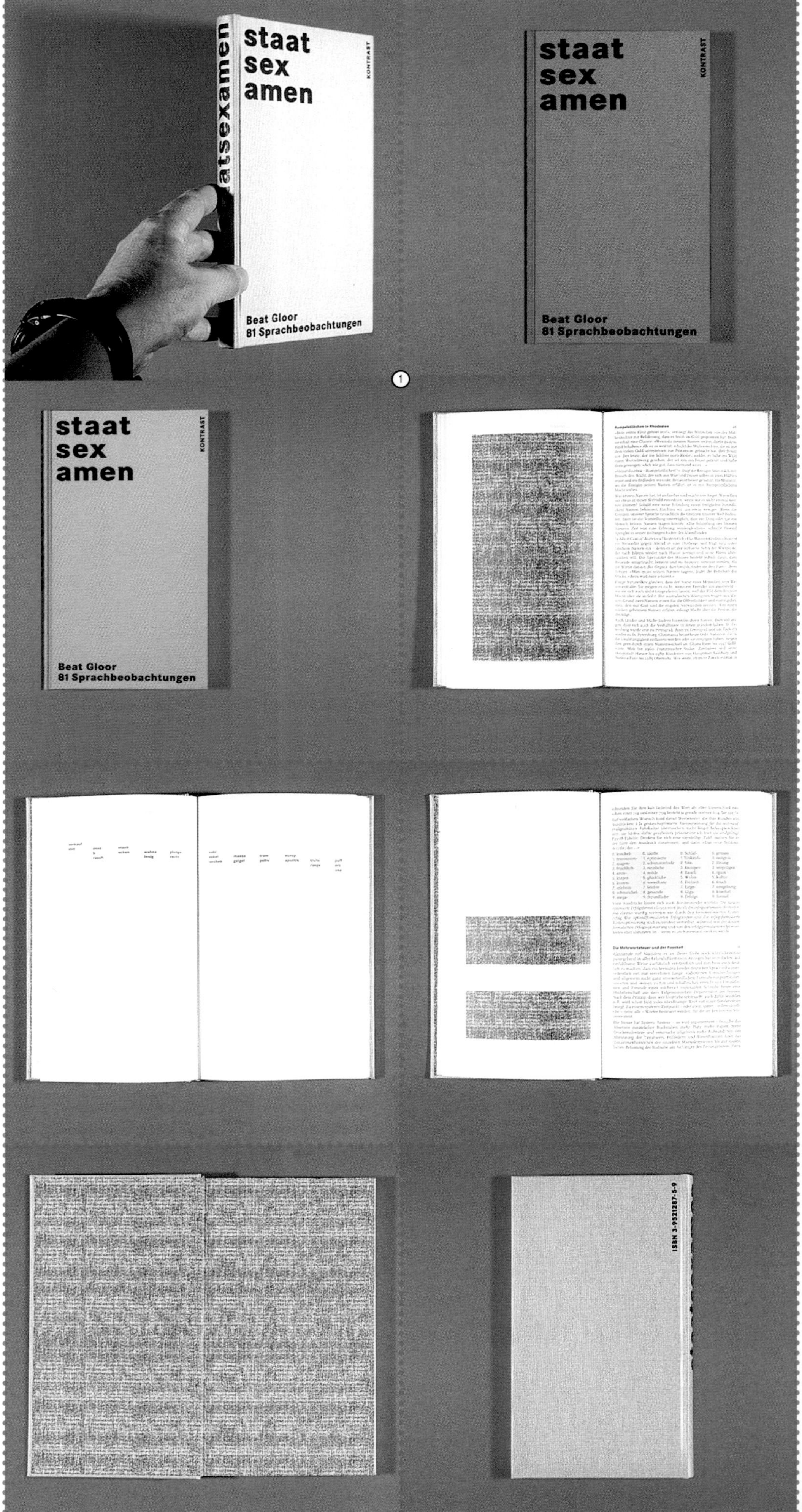

1 Silver, copper, and gold edition covers and spreads, *Staatsexamen–81 Sprachbeobachtungen* (State Examination–81 Linguistic Observations), by Beat Gloor / Kontast Publishing / Switzerland / 1999–2001

2–5 Cover, spreads, and back cover, *Die Tage gehen vorüber und klopfen mir nur noch nachlässig auf die Schulter–365 Tage Buch* (The Days Go By and Pat Me Only Indifferently on the Shoulder–365-Day Book), by Beat Gloor / Kontrast Publishing / Switzerland / 2002

6–9 Back and front cover and spreads, *Khadi–Textile of India*, by Manuel Bauer and Berard Imhasly (with Tania Prill) / Kontrast Publishing / Switzerland / 2002

Alberto Vieceli

Zurich

Beat Gloor
Die Tage gehen vorüber und klopfen mir nur noch nachlässig auf die Schulter.
8
Juni
KHADI–TEXTILE OF INDIA
2
3
4
5
6
7
8
9
16
3
4
29
17

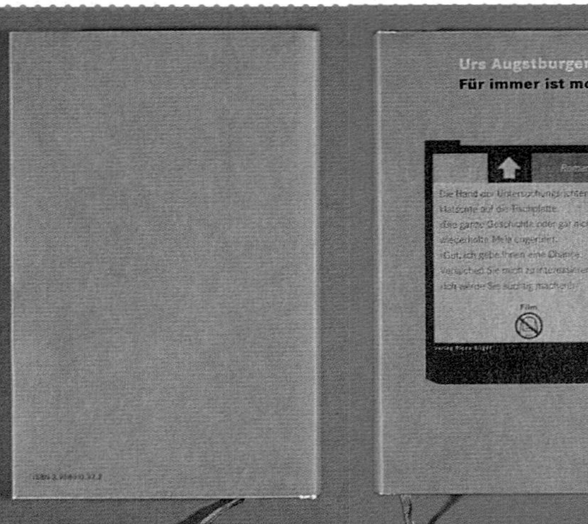

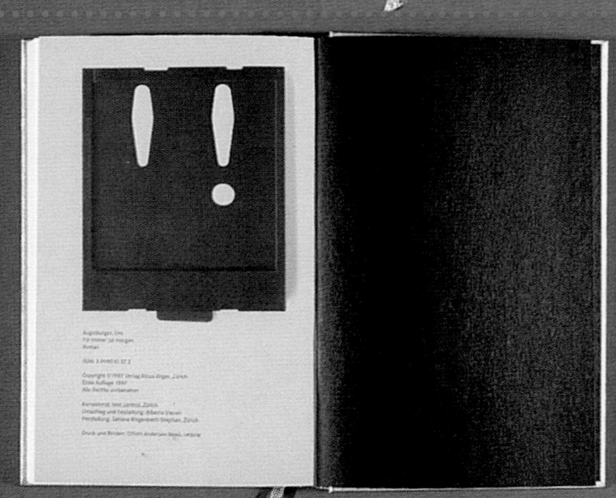

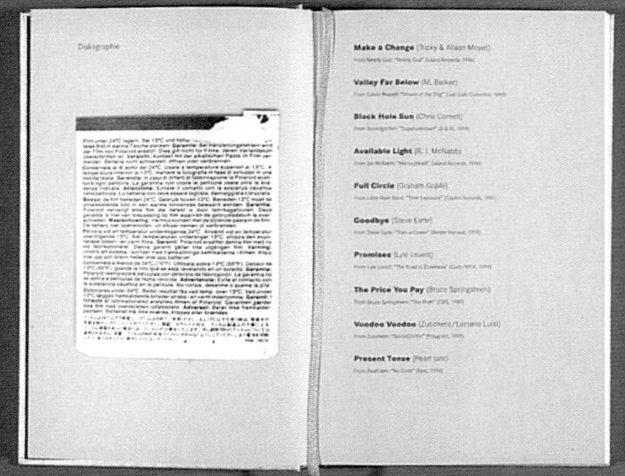

10
11
12

13
14
15
16

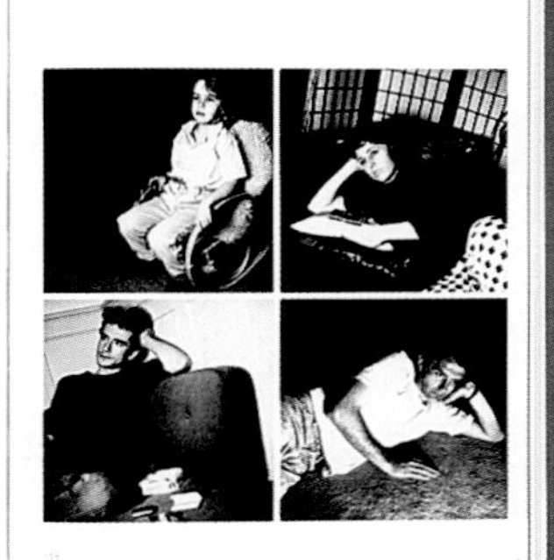

10–12 Back and front cover and spreads, *Für Immer ist Morgen* (Forever is Tomorrow), by Urs Augstburger / Ricco Bilger Publishing / Switzerland / 1999
13–16 Back and front cover and spreads, *Von Dingen und Menschen* (Of Things and People), by Yvonne Griss / Kontrast Publishing / Switzerland / 1999
17–20 Back and front cover and spreads, *Das Beste kommt noch–Theater Neumarkt 1993–1999* (The Best is Yet to Come–Theater Neumarkt 1993–1999) / Kontrast Publishing / Switzerland / 1999
21–24 Back and front cover and spreads, *Top Dogs, Entstehung–Hintergründe–Materialien* (Top Dogs, Origins–Backgrounds–Materials) / Kontrast Publishing / Switzerland / 1999

Alberto Vieceli

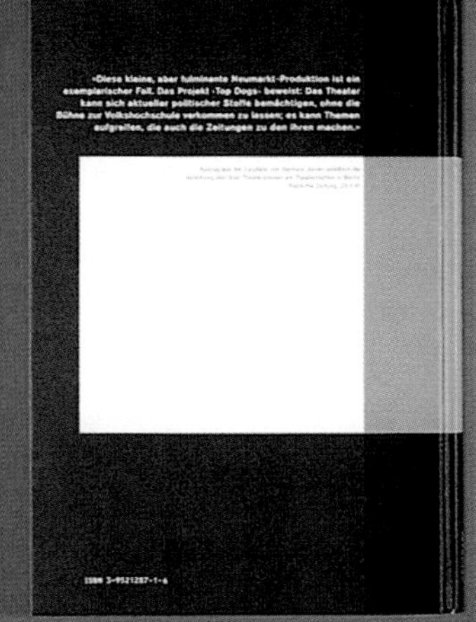

17
18
19
20

21
22
23
24

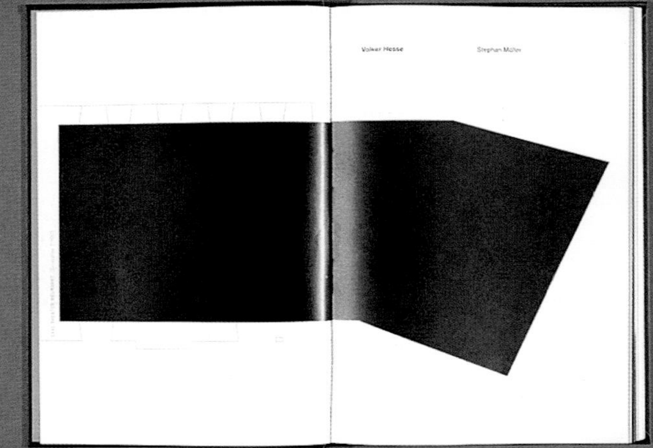

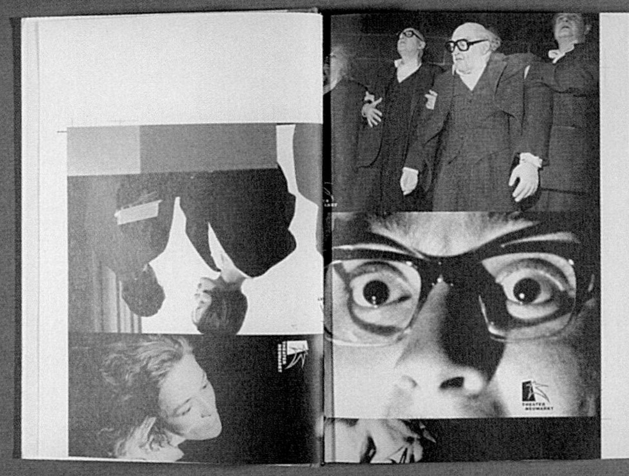

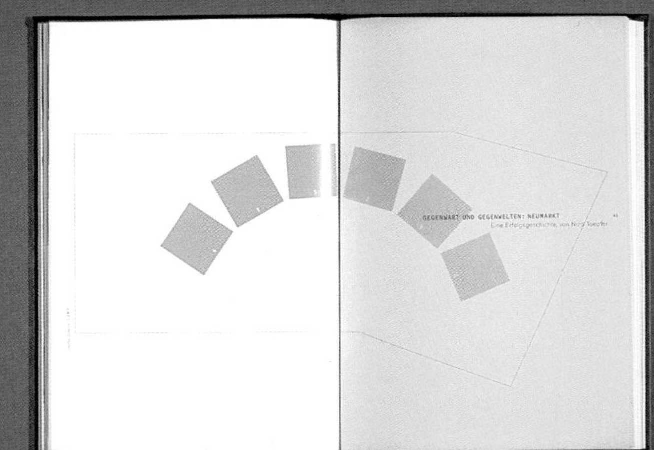

I first met Garth Walker at the annual International Design Indaba in Capetown, South Africa. I had seen his irregular magazine *i-jusi* before and became fascinated by the work he presented at the conference: a series of images of cemeteries and richly decorated graves, set within a context of his own typography and locally inspired visual signals. The work suggested that he is reinventing the craft of graphic design. • • Walker's medium for doing this is the aforementioned magazine *i-jusi*, a publication replete with extraordinary visual and typographic experiments, based on southern Africa's enormous wealth of visual cultures. Often it has published excerpts from Walker's growing collection of images from these cultures, images featuring everything from traditional decorative patterns to hand-lettering on shabby cardboard announcements in townships and rural communities. Walker's work, and that of his colleagues, is streetwise, primitive, and direct but also subtle, intelligent, and visually literate—and definitively South African. • • You can't upset Walker more than by suggesting (as some do) that he, as a white guy, colonializes the cultural heritage of the indigenous black peoples of South Africa. He'll retort, emotionally, "I was born and raised as a South African. This *is* my culture!" He is also an important supporter of young South African typographic designers (both black and white) who show and distribute their work in *i-jusi* and other, often Web-based places. He is a stone in the water over there, making a splash that you hope will result in a new graphic style. Maybe this will happen, despite the enormous pressure in South African design to follow the established Western European and American models. • • Anthon Beeke • •

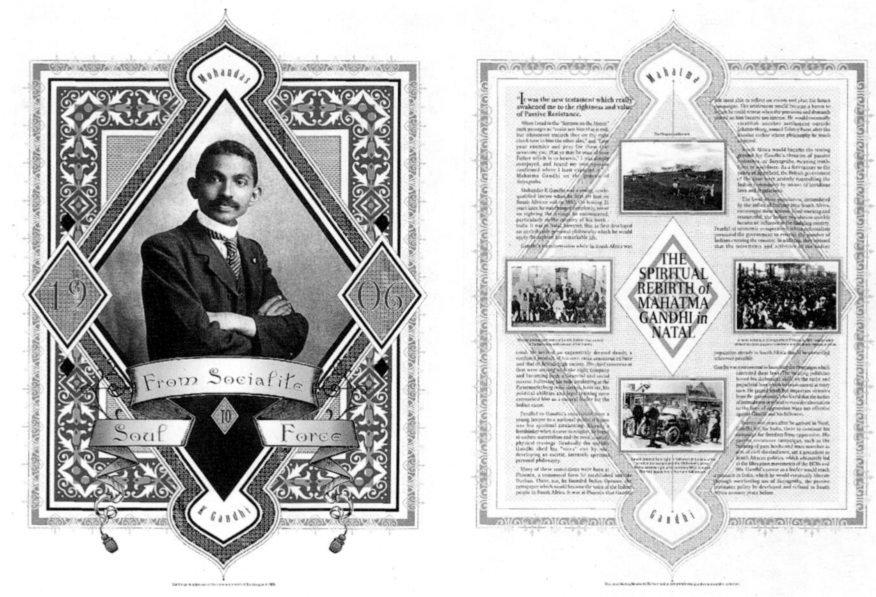

1

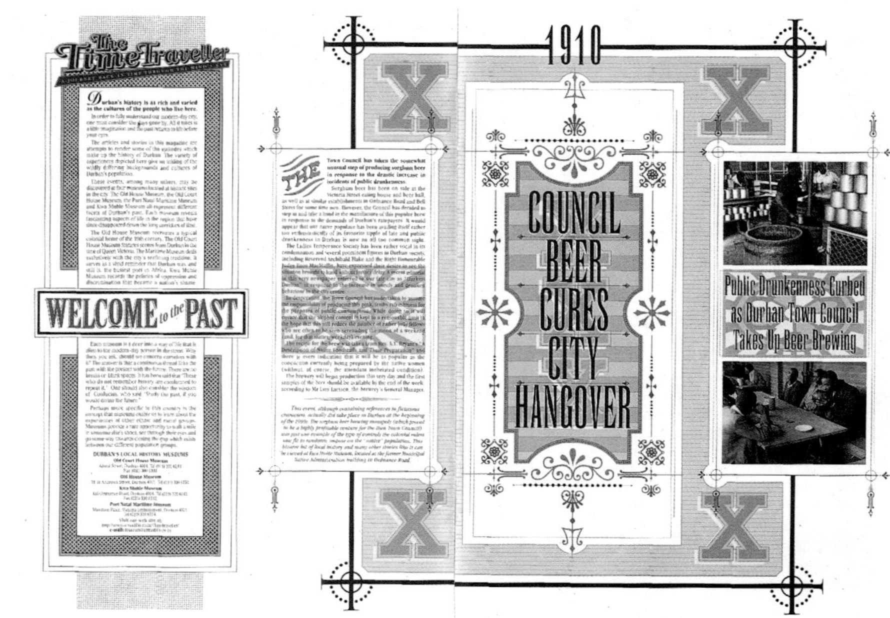

2

Garth Walker

Durban, South Africa

1–2 Spreads, *The Time Traveller–A Journey Back in Time Through the Mind's Eye*, a publication of Durban's local history museums / Local History Museums of Durban / South Africa / 1996
3–4 Cover and spread, *i-jusi* magazine no. 14, "A–Z issue" / Orange Juice Design / South Africa / 2001
5–6 Cover and spread, *i-jusi* magazine no. 6, "Power issue" / Orange Juice Design / South Africa / 1997
7–8 Cover and spread, *i-jusi* magazine no. 10, "Street Style issue" / Orange Juice Design / South Africa / 1999

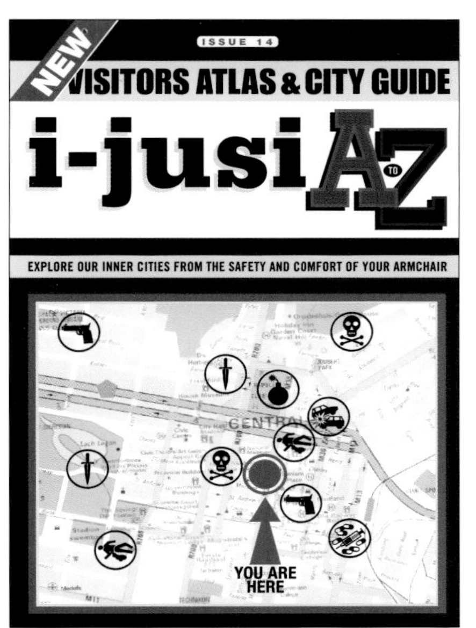
ISSUE 14
NEW
VISITORS ATLAS & CITY GUIDE
i-jusi A TO Z
EXPLORE OUR INNER CITIES FROM THE SAFETY AND COMFORT OF YOUR ARMCHAIR
YOU ARE HERE

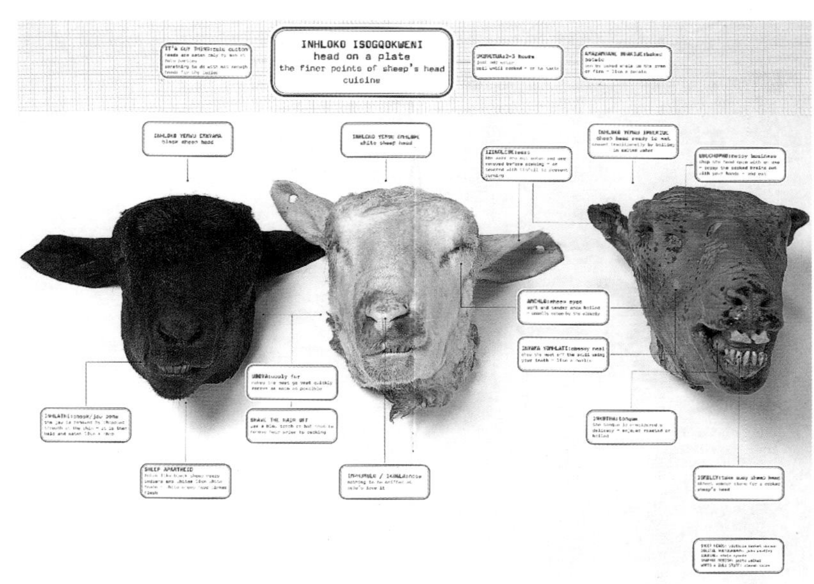
INHLOKO ISOGQOKWENI
head on a plate
the finer points of sheep's head cuisine

3 4

i-jusi
6ix
NOW WITH 8 POWER

HAIR CUT
Boyz II men

Five slain in night of bloodshed

5 6

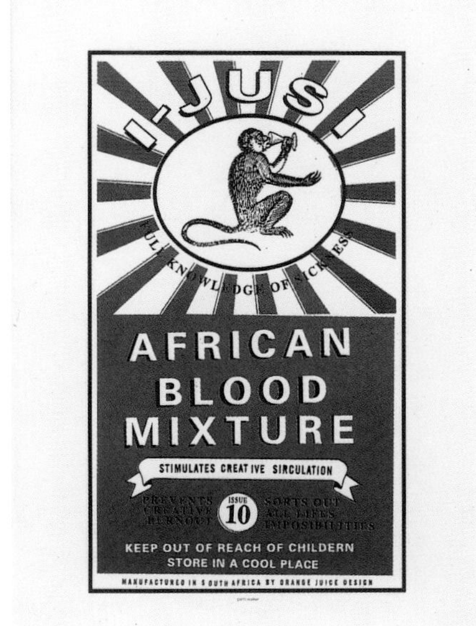
I-JUSI
AFRICAN BLOOD MIXTURE
STIMULATES CREATIVE SIRCULATION
ISSUE 10
KEEP OUT OF REACH OF CHILDERN
STORE IN A COOL PLACE
MANUFACTURED IN SOUTH AFRICA BY ORANGE JUICE DESIGN

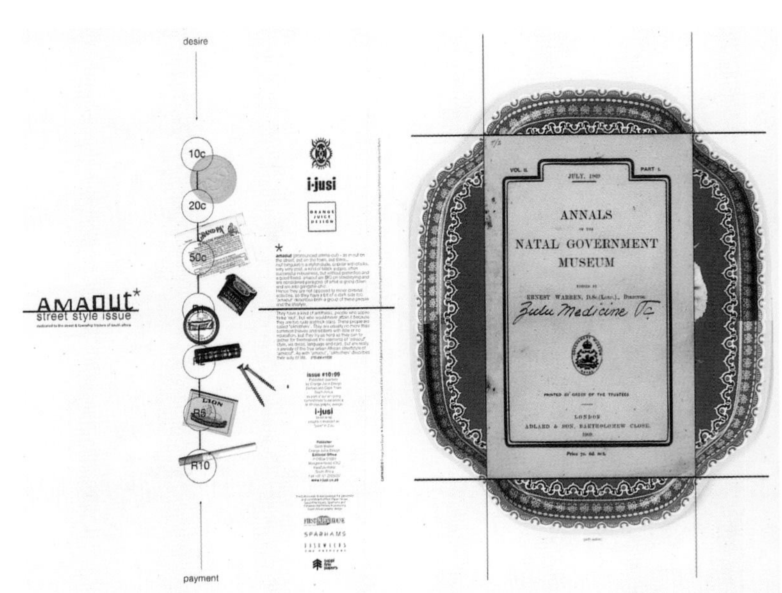
desire
10c
20c
50c
R10
payment
AMANDUT*
street style issue
i-jusi
ANNALS
OF THE
NATAL GOVERNMENT
MUSEUM
Zulu Medicine

7 8

9

10

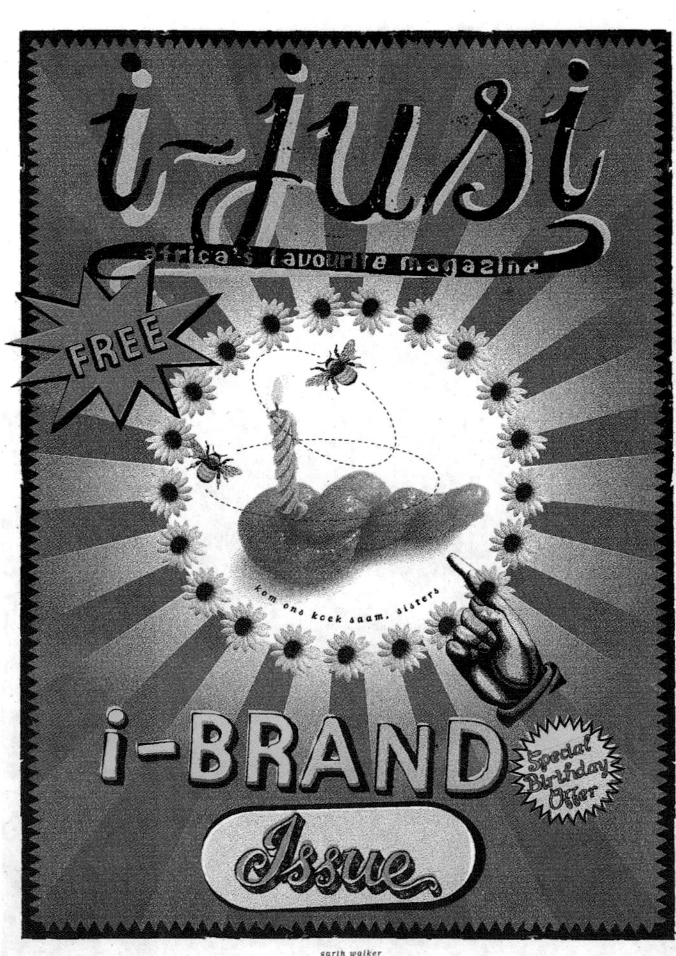

11

9 Cover, *i-jusi* magazine no. 2, "Durban issue" / Orange Juice Design / South Africa / 2001
10 Cover, *i-jusi* magazine no 12, "Death issue" / Orange Juice Design / South Africa / 2001
11 Cover, *i-jusi* magazine, special "i-Brand" issue celebrating advertising agency Ogilvy & Mather's fiftieth anniversary / Orange Juice Design / South Africa / 2001
12 Spread presenting Winky typeface by Garth Walker, *i-jusi* magazine no. 15, "Porn issue" / Orange Juice Design / South Africa / 2001
13 Spread presenting Vassie Naidoo typeface by Garth Walker, *i-jusi* magazine no. 17, "Typography issue" / Orange Juice Design / South Africa / 2002

Garth Walker

12

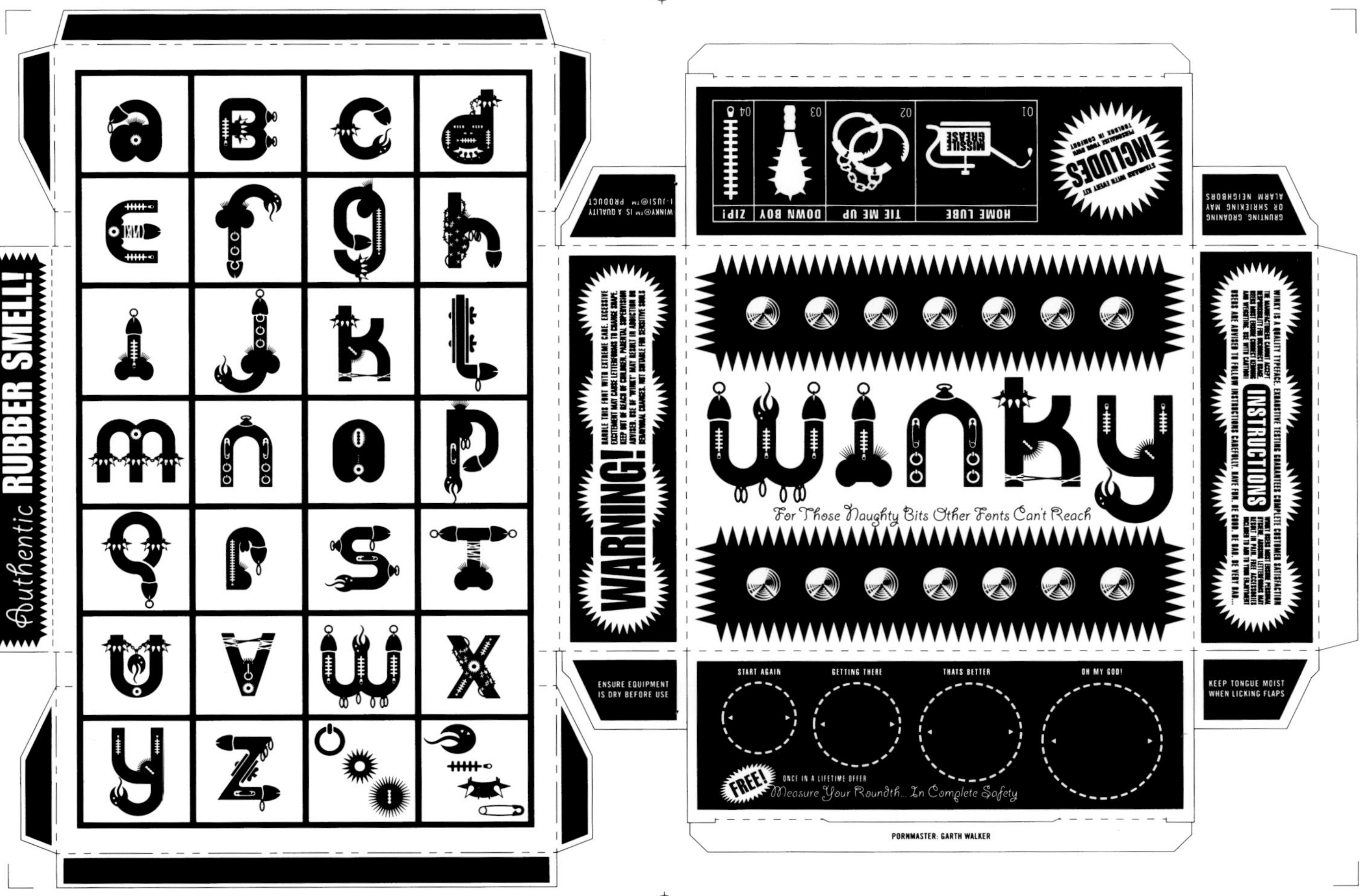

Authentic RUBBER SMELL!

WARNING!

winky

For Those Naughty Bits Other Fonts Can't Reach

INCLUDES

01 HOME LUBE

02 TIE ME UP

03 DOWN BOY

04 ZIP!

WINKY™ IS A QUALITY I-JUSI™ PRODUCT

GRUNTING, GROANING OR SHRIEKING MAY ALARM NEIGHBORS

INSTRUCTIONS

ENSURE EQUIPMENT IS DRY BEFORE USE

KEEP TONGUE MOIST WHEN LICKING FLAPS

START AGAIN

GETTING THERE

THATS BETTER

OH MY GOD!

FREE! ONCE IN A LIFETIME OFFER

Measure Your Roundth... In Complete Safety

PORNMASTER: GARTH WALKER

13

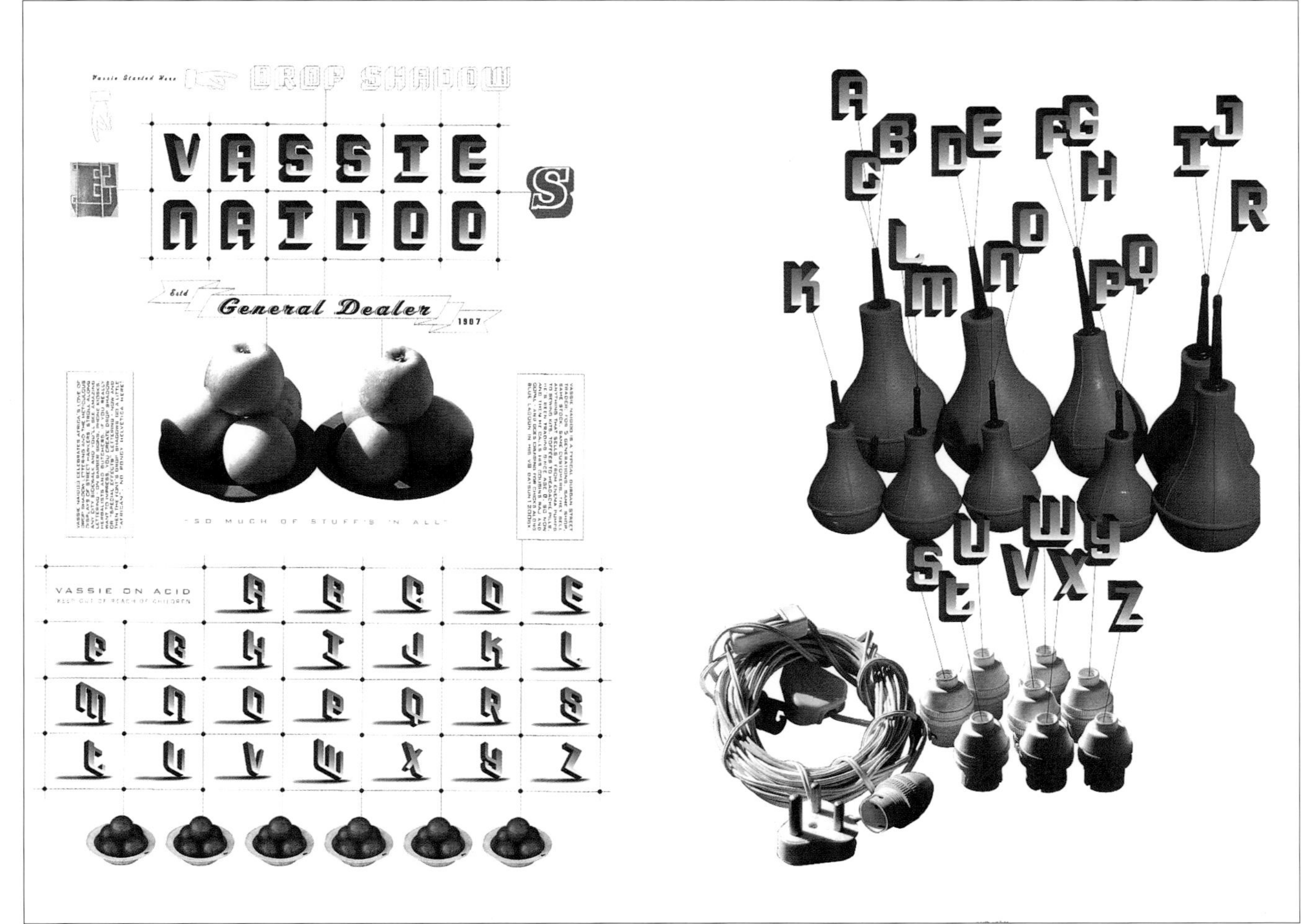

Some graphic designers were beginning to think that the conventions of design were constricting their capacity to surprise. There was concern that audiences had become accustomed to codes. Sometimes design itself seemed to be getting in the way. This led many designers to experiment with less designed approaches. Attentions turned toward a nostalgic aesthetic of the everyday that carried comfort in the amateur, the homemade, the uncrafted, and obsolete technology. It was not long, however, before laggards followed the early adopters and this aesthetic—the pinnacle of fashion for a while—had itself become yet another design convention. Although the trend has now blown over, it has left remnants of an austerity that can still be detected while the pendulum swings back the other way.•• Thankfully, comic artist Chris Ware obsesses over unrepentantly luscious forms. Present in his work is much that is now missing in graphic design, probably as a result of his being completely oblivious to the trend mentioned above. If you are a graphic designer and suspect that your medium has lost its facility to engage, take a look at a few pages of *Jimmy Corrigan, The Smartest Kid on Earth* and you'll be left feeling that you're not trying hard enough. Once you've picked yourself up off the floor, consider for a moment what makes these pages so effective. There is the lovingly crafted typography, hand-drawn in a broad range of late-nineteenth- and early-twentieth-century commercial-display styles. There is the quirky yet meticulous illustration style that, as its creator explains, is "more like typography, a mechanical sort of picture lettering." And, of course, there is the wonderfully subtle and sophisticated use of color, the carefully proportioned and controlled page layout, and the studied composition of frames hung off a grid so versatile you would be forgiven for thinking that it was created by the staunchly modernist studio Eight Five Zero. Within the frames, there are stunning changes of scale as we are hurled forward to inspect a detail, held there for several counts, pulled back to view the action in silhouette, shown a plan view, and then, in the next frame, the lights are turned off.••Ware might be a comic artist, but he demonstrates what graphic design can be...just in case you had forgotten.••Nick Bell••

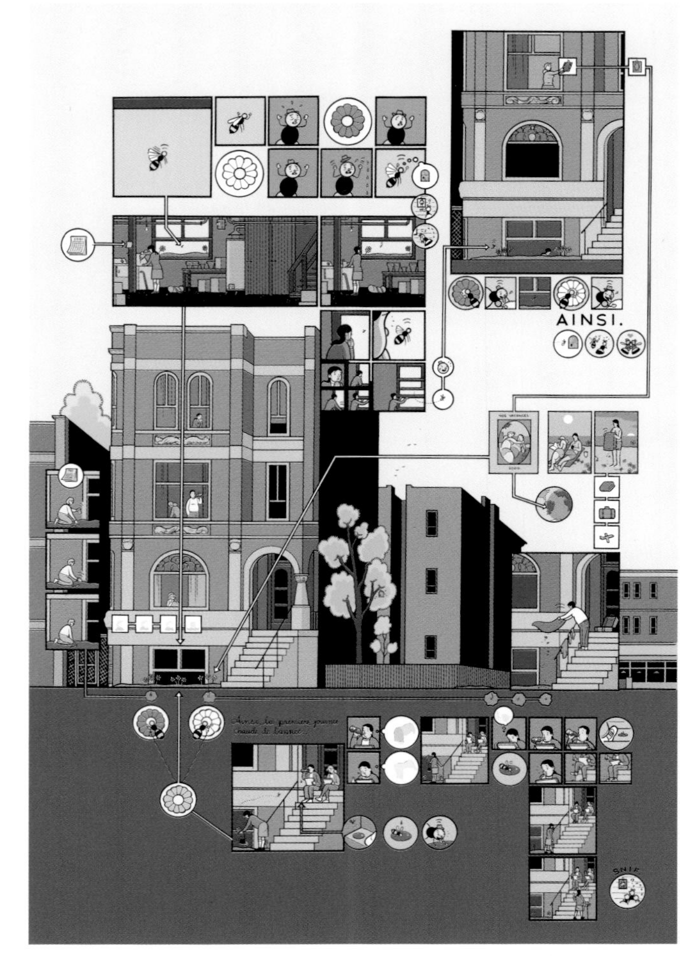

1

2

1–2 Comic strips *Building Story* and *Branford Bee*, featured in *The Acme Novelty Library*, by Chris Ware / Fantagraphics Books / USA / 2001–2002
3 Cover, *The Acme Novelty Library* no. 15, by Chris Ware / Fantagraphics Books / USA / 2001
4 Cover, *Untold Tales of Kavalier and Clay*, by Michael Chabon, featured in *McSweeney's* no. 7 / Michael Chabon and McSweeney's Publishing / USA / 2001
5 Exterior signage design for Quimby's bookstore, Chicago / Quimby's / USA / 1997

Chris Ware

Chicago

3

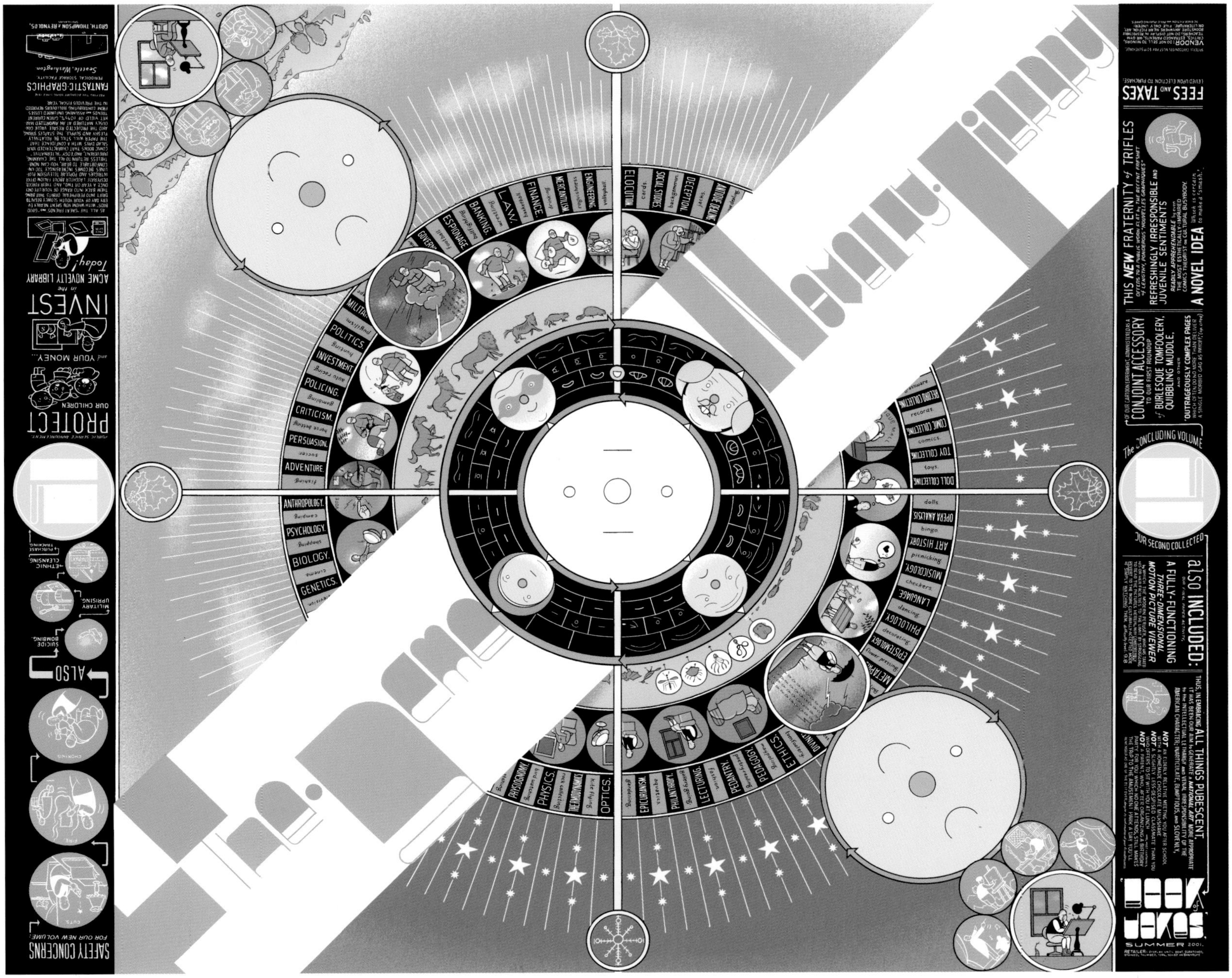

4

UN-TOLD TALES
of KAVALIER & CLAY
WINTER · NUMBER
POST-WAR 10¢ THRILLS
ALL NEW!
14 EXCITING PAGES
Featuring – THE RETURN OF THE AMAZING CAVALIER!

5

QUIMBY'S
LEFT HALF
RIGHT HALF
'QUIMBY'S' BOOKSTORE · SIGNAGE SKETCHES.~
PROBABLY BEST TO FASHION 'DONUT' SHAPE FROM LAMINATED SEGMENTS of PLYWOOD — SHOULD BE ABOUT 2" THICK WHEN FINISHED, OR EVEN SLIGHTLY THICKER. 'LEGS' of MICE ARE DOWELS WHICH MATE WITH CORRESPONDING HOLES IN INNER PERIMETER of 'DONUT.' NOTE THAT MOUSE HEADS ARE SORT of AT A "COCKED" ANGLE ~ SORRY I CAN'T MEASURE THAT.
IN ALL QUESTIONS of SCALE, REFER TO 3-DIMENSIONAL MOCK-UP.

6

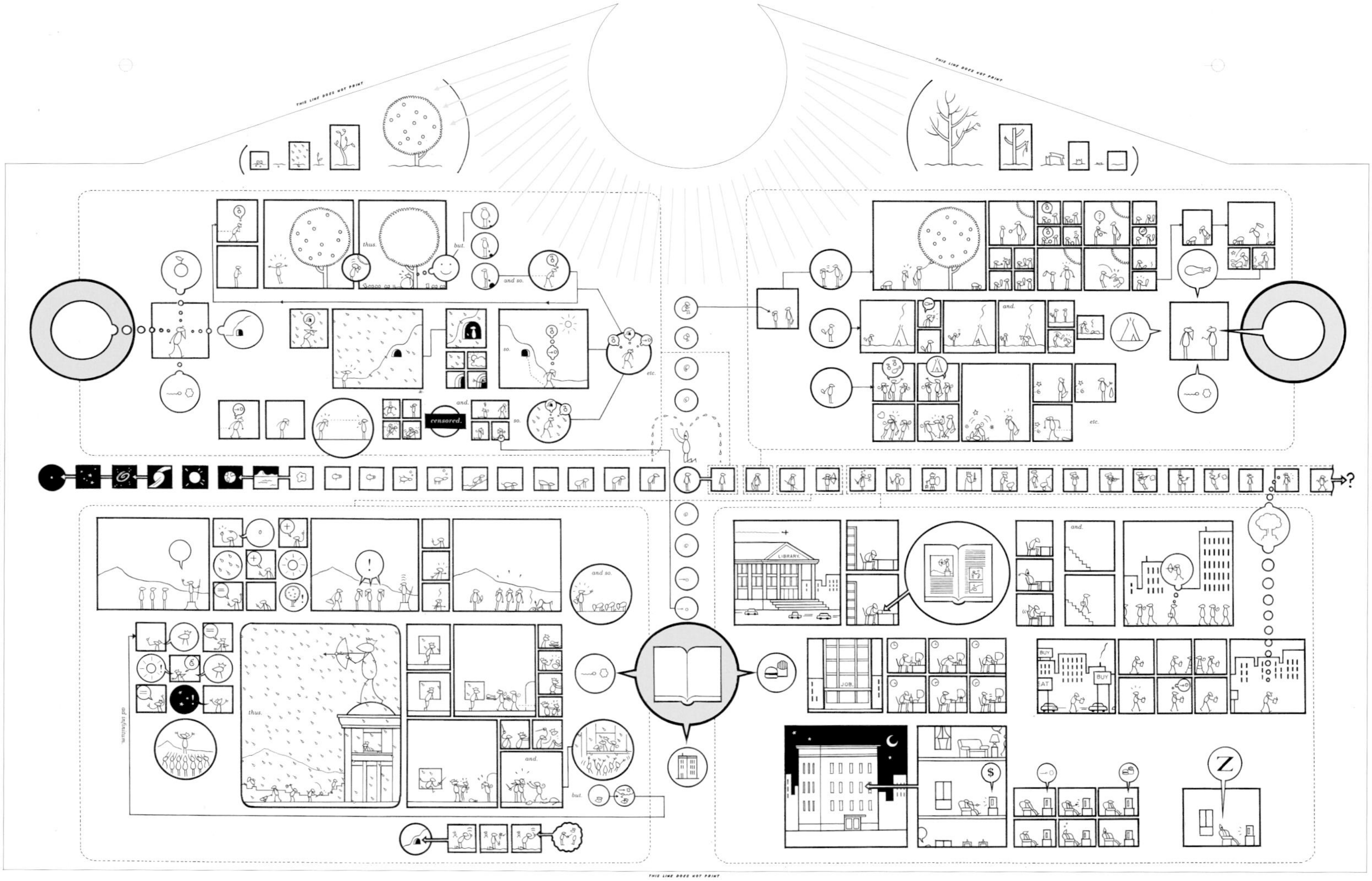

7

Chris Ware

6 Cover for paperback edition, *Jimmy Corrigan, The Smartest Kid on Earth*, by Chris Ware / Pantheon Books / USA / 2003
7 Quimby the Mouse mural design for McSweeney's building, San Francisco / McSweeney's / USA / 2002
8 Cover, *The Comics Journal* no. 200 / Fantagraphics Books / USA / 1997

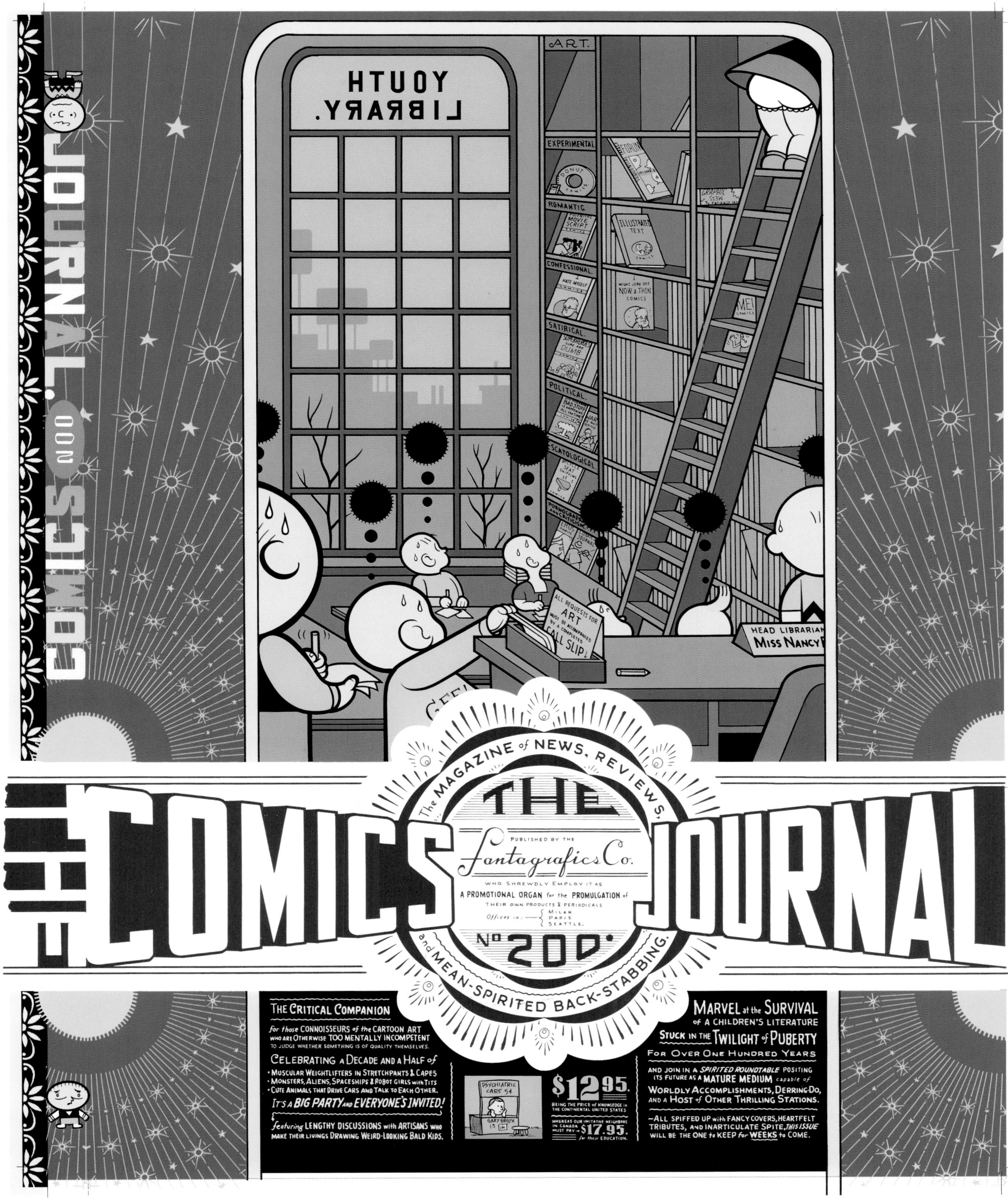

COMICS JOURNAL, 200

THE COMICS JOURNAL

The MAGAZINE of NEWS, REVIEWS, and MEAN-SPIRITED BACK-STABBING.

THE

PUBLISHED BY THE
Fantagrafics Co.
WHO SHREWDLY EMPLOY IT AS
A PROMOTIONAL ORGAN for the PROMULGATION of
THEIR OWN PRODUCTS & PERIODICALS
Offices in: MILAN, PARIS, SEATTLE.

Nº 200.

THE CRITICAL COMPANION

for those CONNOISSEURS of the CARTOON ART WHO ARE OTHERWISE TOO MENTALLY INCOMPETENT TO JUDGE WHETHER SOMETHING IS OF QUALITY THEMSELVES.

CELEBRATING A DECADE AND A HALF of

- MUSCULAR WEIGHTLIFTERS IN STRETCHPANTS & CAPES
- MONSTERS, ALIENS, SPACESHIPS & ROBOT GIRLS with TITS
- CUTE ANIMALS THAT DRIVE CARS AND TALK TO EACH OTHER.

IT'S A BIG PARTY AND EVERYONE'S INVITED!

featuring LENGTHY DISCUSSIONS with ARTISANS WHO MAKE THEIR LIVINGS DRAWING WEIRD-LOOKING BALD KIDS.

$12.95.
BEING THE PRICE of KNOWLEDGE in THE CONTINENTAL UNITED STATES

WHEREAS OUR IMITATIVE NEIGHBORS IN CANADA MUST PAY → $17.95. for their EDUCATION.

MARVEL at the SURVIVAL of A CHILDREN'S LITERATURE STUCK IN THE TWILIGHT of PUBERTY FOR OVER ONE HUNDRED YEARS

AND JOIN IN A SPIRITED ROUNDTABLE POSITING ITS FUTURE AS A MATURE MEDIUM capable of WORLDLY ACCOMPLISHMENTS, DERRING-DO, AND A HOST of OTHER THRILLING STATIONS.

—ALL SPIFFED UP with FANCY COVERS, HEARTFELT TRIBUTES, AND INARTICULATE SPITE, THIS ISSUE WILL BE THE ONE to KEEP for WEEKS to COME.

Martin Woodtli is perhaps the most accomplished representative of the new design scene in Switzerland, where the joy of the design process (as opposed to monetary reward) seems to determine the direction of the studios. Swiss designers would rather work for small cultural projects to which they are often connected personally than to fall into the trap of large advertising conglomerates. While at first glance this may seem to be a complete break with all traditions of the famed Swiss International Style, the roots of the new generation are still firmly grounded in the world of Brockmann and Bill. • • Woodtli does not subscribe to the silly adage circulated by many of his colleagues about the computer being just a tool; he sees it simply as a process. He is also the only person I know who can actually think with the keyboard. His proficiency in various programs is such that he sketches with the keyboard as quickly and uninhibitedly as with pencil and paper. • • Having worked with many artists within the art market, he has no interest in following them but happily remains in the design world. He considers graphic design a "wonderful medium in which you can create friction within the existing world." To work within that world, to intervene and throw it just slightly out of balance, is his biggest challenge. • • Woodtli is obsessive. He seems to have taken to heart that line from Brian Eno's diary that a good way to create something original is to do something so incredibly painstaking and time-consuming that nobody else bothers. Woodtli notes, "Sixteen-square-foot black paintings made with a very fine (6H) pencil would qualify." Woodtli's black squares manifest themselves in complex typographic plays and manically layered, dense patterns of everyday objects produced in perplexingly exact silk screens. • • After spending a couple of months as an intern in my New York studio, he returned to Switzerland, buried himself in a two-year excess of work, and created a beautifully conceived monograph. He also became the youngest member of Alliance Graphique Internationale (AGI), that most venerable group of the international design establishment. • • I knew I was old when our intern became an AGI member. • • Stefan Sagmeister • •

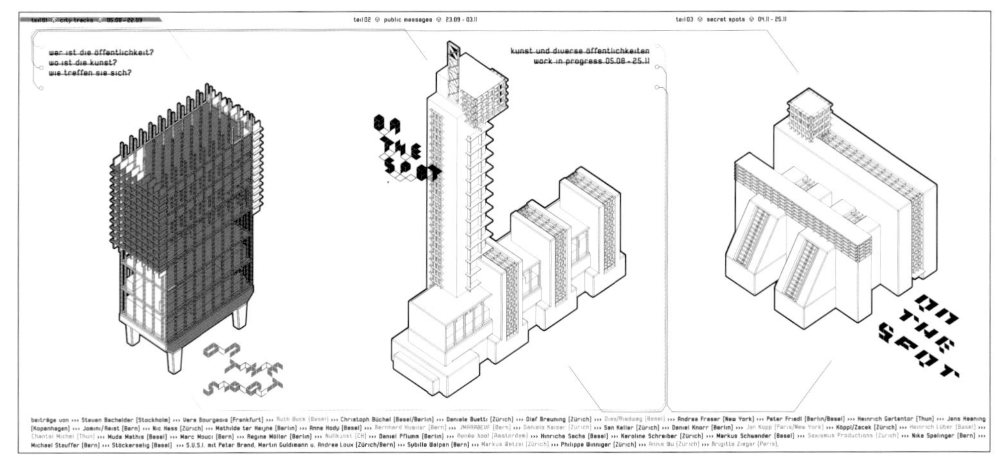

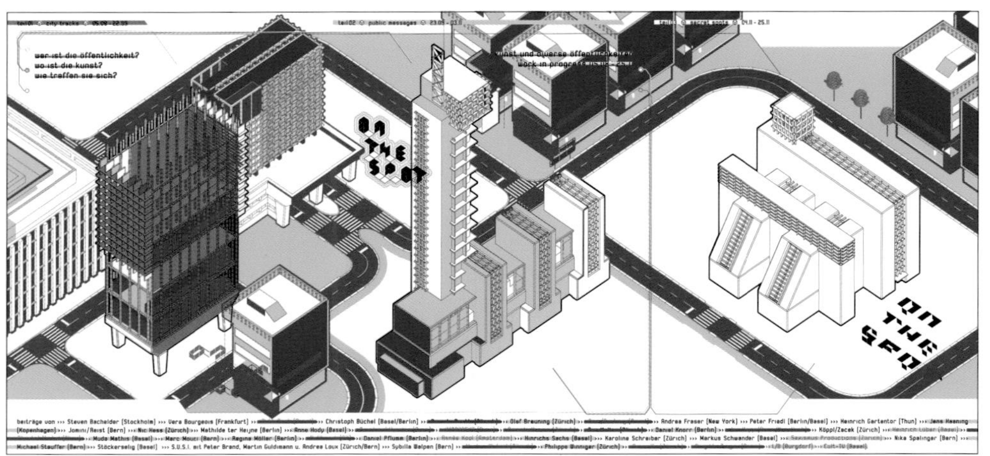

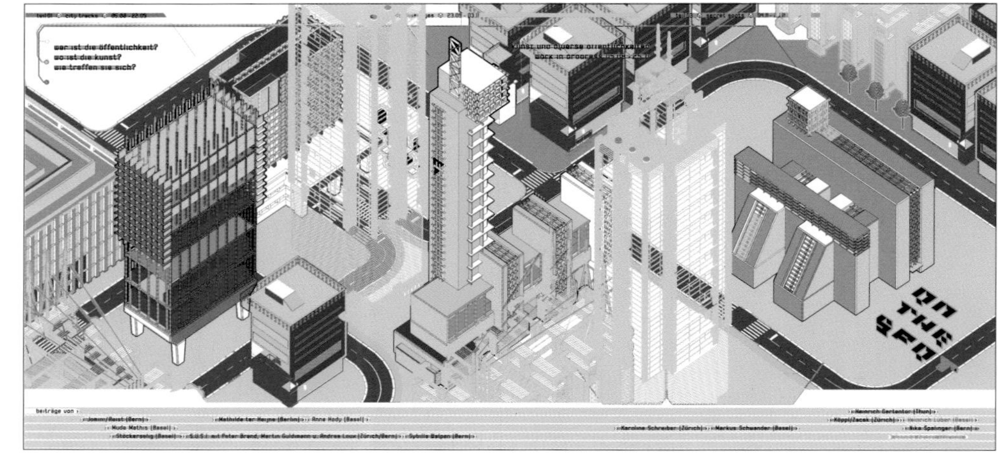

1
2
3

Martin Woodtli

Zurich

1–3 Informational flyers for contemporary-art event *On The Spot*, Bern / Kiosk and Stadtgalerie Bern / Switzerland / 2000
4 Back and front cover and spreads, *Soda Magazin* no. 11 / Soda Magazin / Switzerland / 1999 / The spreads form part of the Martin Woodtli special feature "Millennium Starter Kit (MSK)."

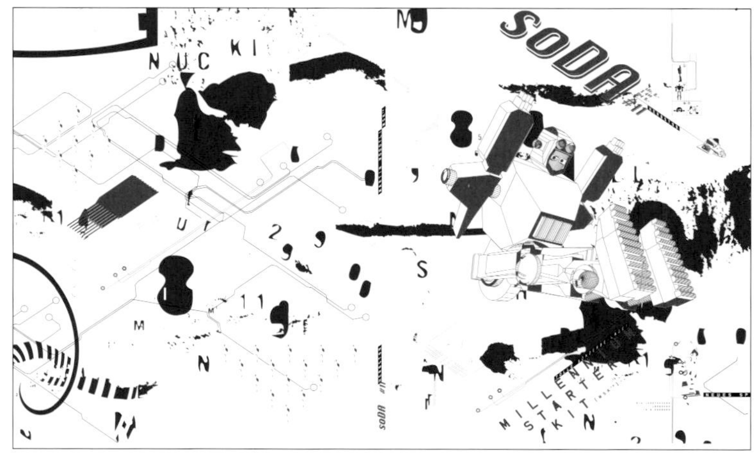
SoDA

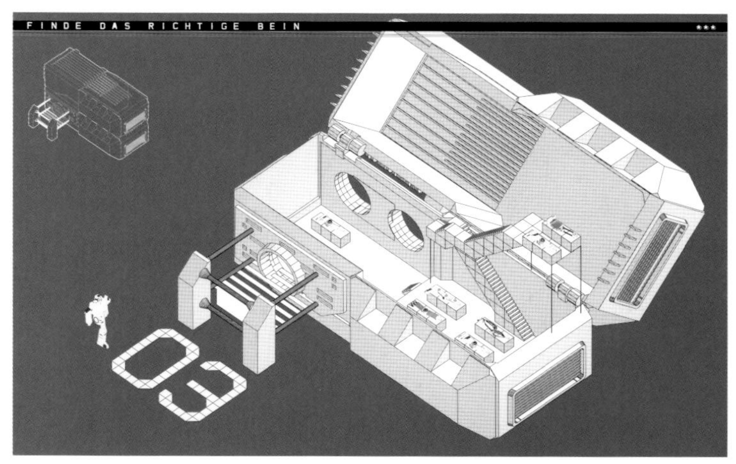
FINDE DAS RICHTIGE BEIN
03

TRAINIER-KAMMER

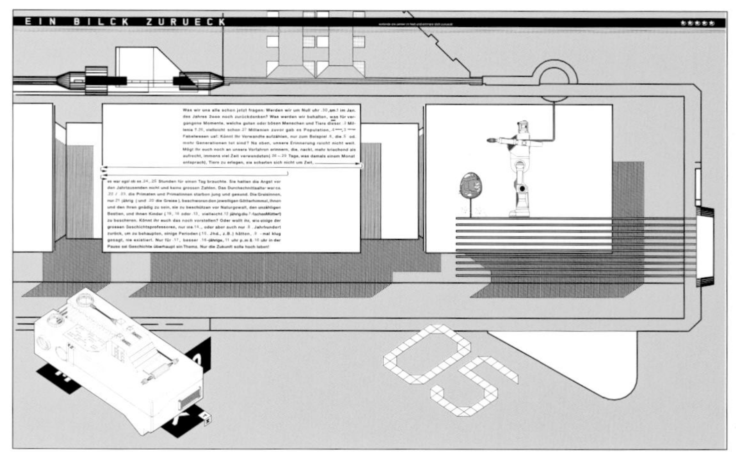
EIN BILCK ZURUECK
05

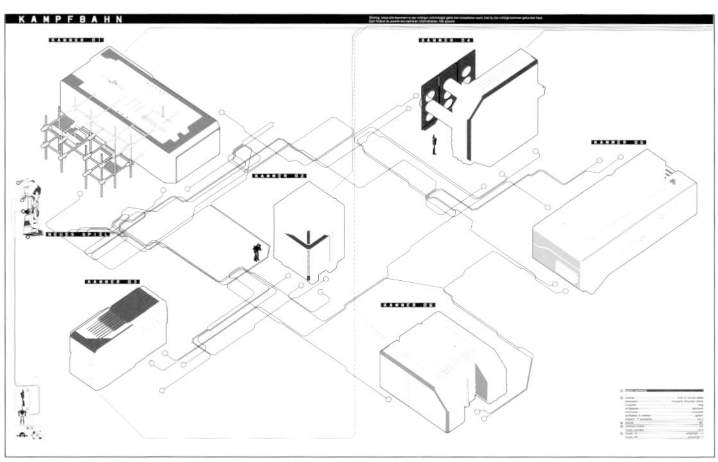
KAMPFBAHN

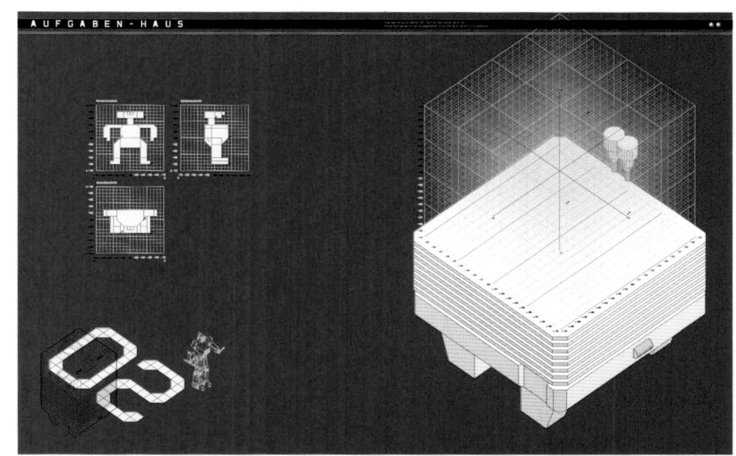
AUFGABEN-HAUS
02

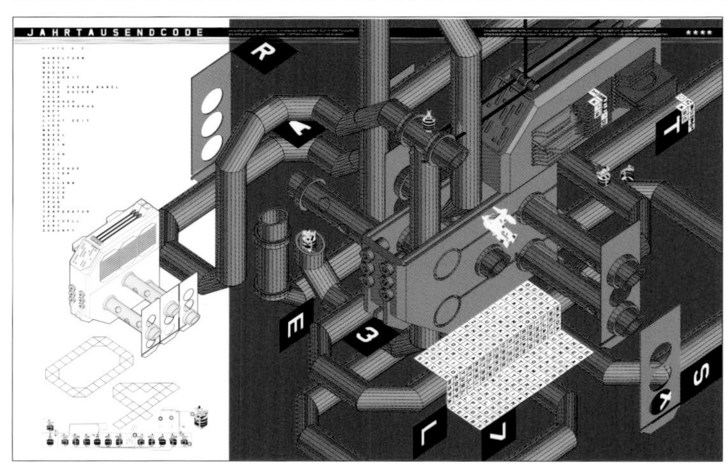
JAHRTAUSENDCODE

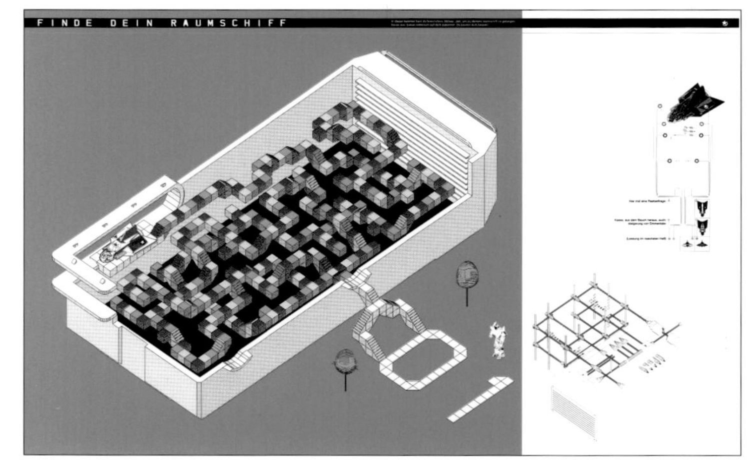
FINDE DEIN RAUMSCHIFF
01

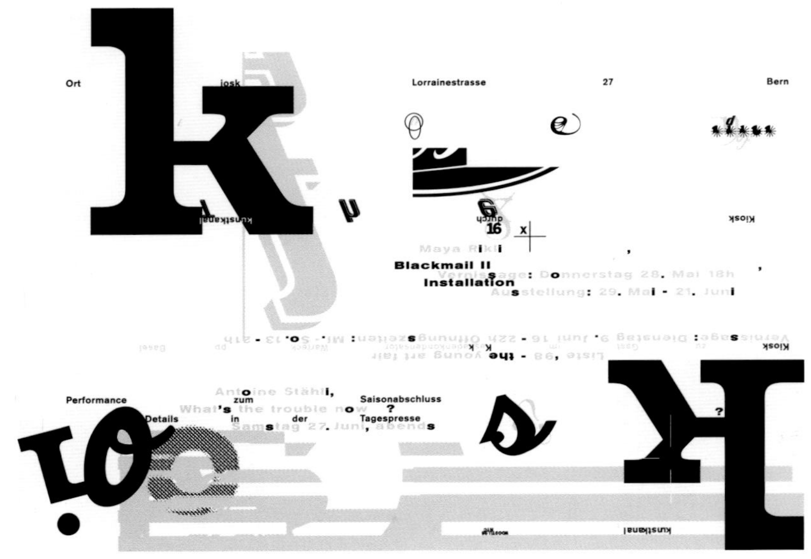

5

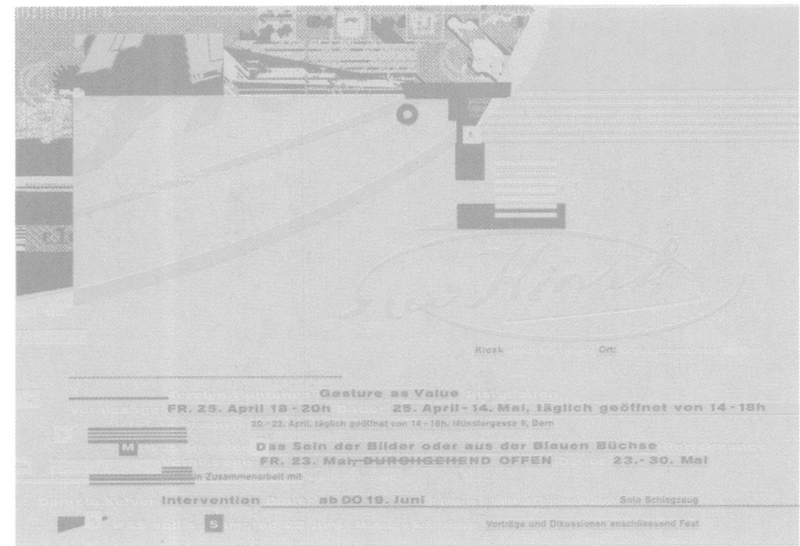

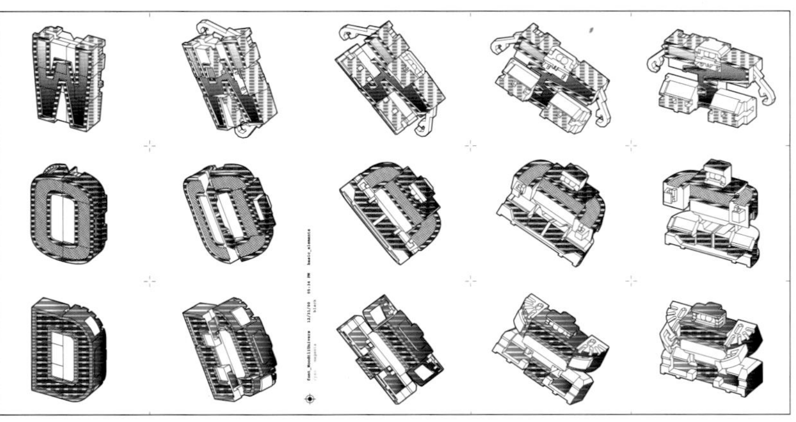

6

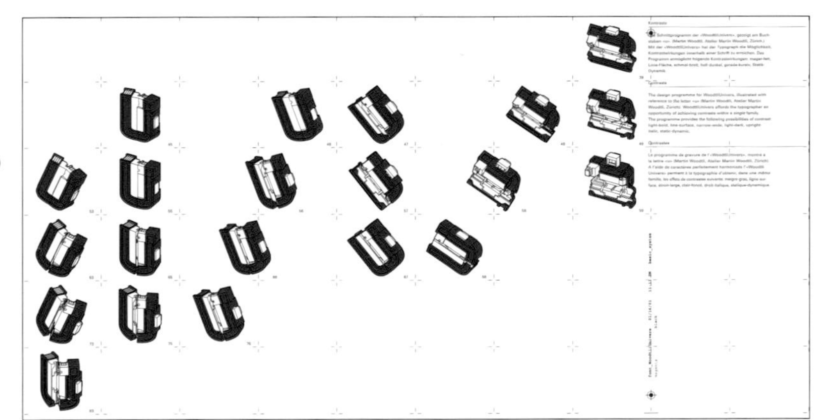

Martin Woodtli

5 Flyers for various vernissages and exhibitions at the art gallery Kiosk, Bern / Kiosk durch Kunstkanal / Switzerland / 1996–99
6 Demonstrations of the font design WoodtliUnivers / USA / 2001
7 Poster for the font design WoodtliUnivers / USA / 2001

7

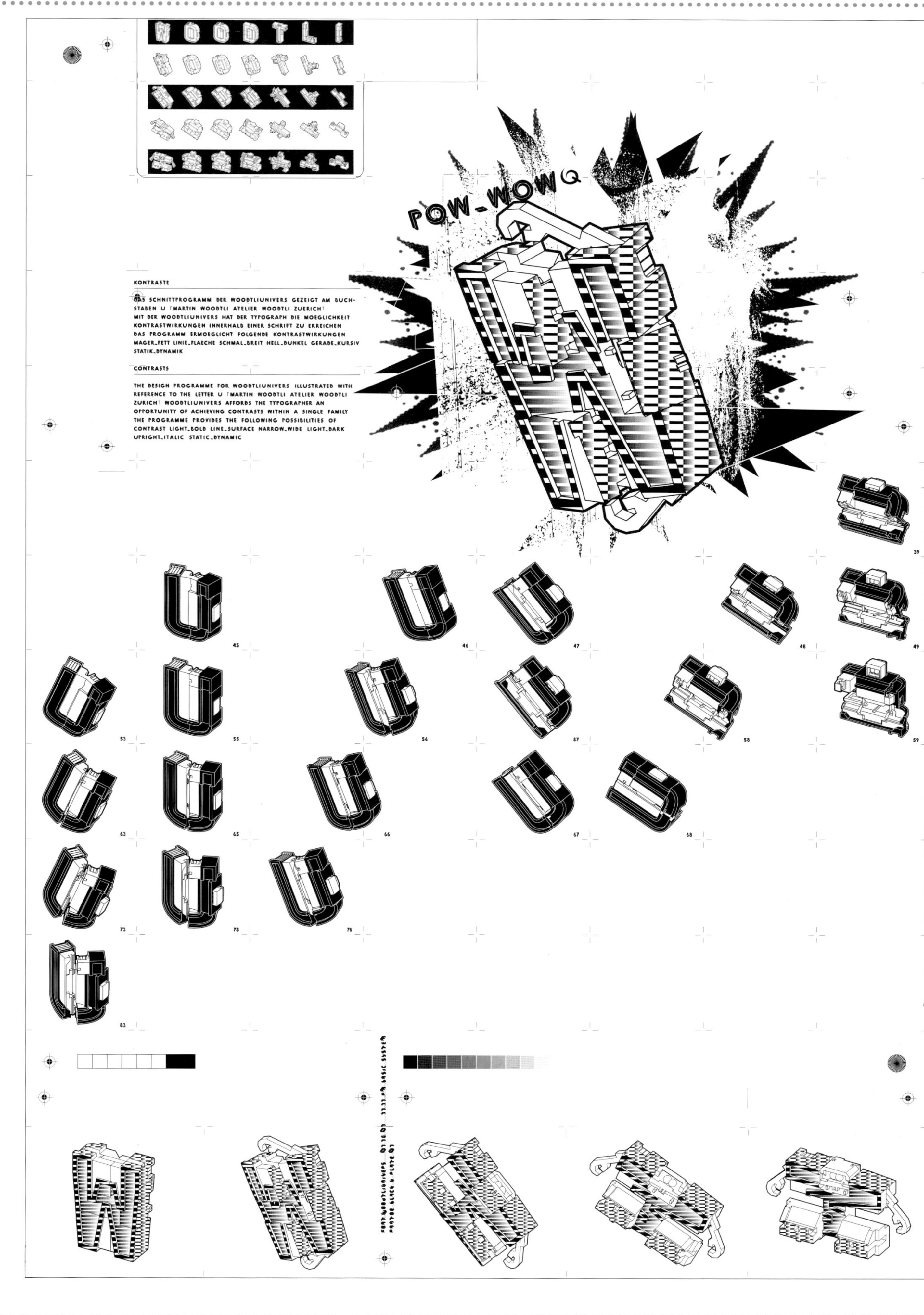
WOODTLI
POW-WOWQ
KONTRASTE
DAS SCHNITTPROGRAMM DER WOODTLIUNIVERS GEZEIGT AM BUCH-
STABEN U ⌈MARTIN WOODTLI ATELIER WOODTLI ZUERICH⌉
MIT DER WOODTLIUNIVERS HAT DER TYPOGRAPH DIE MOEGLICHKEIT
KONTRASTWIRKUNGEN INNERHALB EINER SCHRIFT ZU ERREICHEN
DAS PROGRAMM ERMOEGLICHT FOLGENDE KONTRASTWIRKUNGEN
MAGER_FETT LINIE_FLAECHE SCHMAL_BREIT HELL_DUNKEL GERADE_KURSIV
STATIK_DYNAMIK
CONTRASTS
THE DESIGN PROGRAMME FOR WOODTLIUNIVERS ILLUSTRATED WITH
REFERENCE TO THE LETTER U ⌈MARTIN WOODTLI ATELIER WOODTLI
ZURICH⌉ WOODTLIUNIVERS AFFORDS THE TYPOGRAPHER AN
OPPORTUNITY OF ACHIEVING CONTRASTS WITHIN A SINGLE FAMILY
THE PROGRAMME PROVIDES THE FOLLOWING POSSIBILITIES OF
CONTRAST LIGHT_BOLD LINE_SURFACE NARROW_WIDE LIGHT_DARK
UPRIGHT_ITALIC STATIC_DYNAMIC
39
45
46
47
48
49
53
55
56
57
58
59
63
65
66
67
68
73
75
76
83

There was a time when Michael Worthington's own brand of practice might have led a writer to call him an artist and then launch into some interminable debate about the difference between art and design. Over the last fifteen years graphic-design criticism has learned to deal with designers like Worthington. Receiving commissions from companies and organizations much like any other designer, he is particularly good at finding ways to secrete his own personal voice—be it a judgment on the content he is asked to deliver or, more commonly, the spice of his own aesthetic concerns—into a client's message. His work is conceptually driven, not in compensation for any insecurity with form, but always through joyful experimentation with it. In fact, irrespective of context, his impetus always seems to come from his restless desire to make things. Before starting on the Lyrics project (made possible by a grant from the City of Los Angeles), for instance, he wrote, "I knew I wanted to make something purely typographic." • •Worthington is very much a graphic designer and one who wants to forge a new form of graphic-design criticism. "Personal Modernism," his eight-page contribution to the book *Restart*, is a recent example of his critical methodology. Contrary to the journalistic ideal of distance, Worthington is, in his own words, "trying to use design to talk about design" and "to create designs that do what they are talking about." We would all like to see more designers participating in critical debates. "Personal Modernism" is a critique on the style fetish of modernist methods of systematizing, a crutch for so many of us. Worthington does not dismiss modernism for this, but develops a visual argument for ways in which what he calls the "generic" can be personalized. "Stylistic individuality," he writes, "exists within a system consisting of preformed components, only when the concept is thoroughly considered." • •In the West, brought about by our desire for economy and convenience, we live in a highly mediated, shrinking world saturated with representation, with fake images of people we supposedly would like to be. Taking refuge in our personal imagination to ponder alternatives could make life a bit more interesting, especially if our personal armory of visual devices, ideas, and approaches were as amazingly rich as Worthington's. His response to all his commissions is specific, beautiful, and original every time. Considering half his studio time is eaten up by teaching, that is quite a feat. • •Nick Bell • •

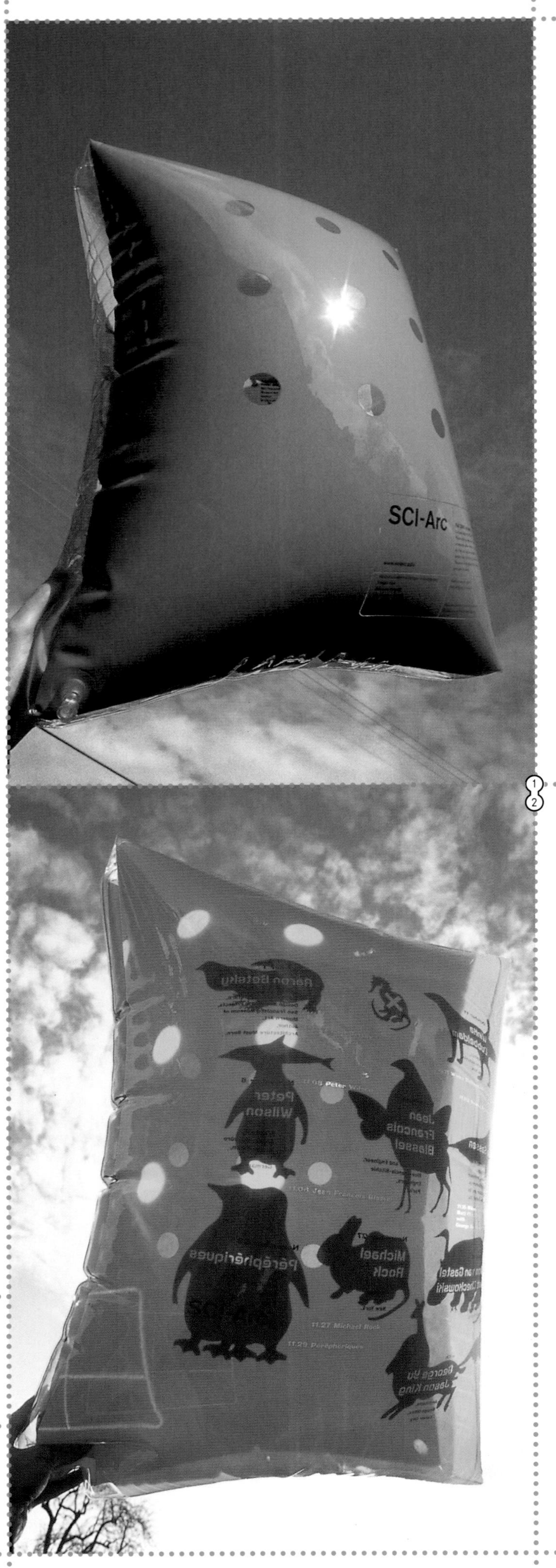

1–2 Front and back of inflatable poster for fall lecture series at the Southern California Institute of Architecture (SCI-Arc) / SCI-Arc / USA / 2000

3–5 Back and front covers, *X-TRA* magazine 2, no. 3, "Beauty and Criticism" (illustration Brad Spence); no. 2, "Gardens" (illustration Patrick Nickell); no. 1, "Lost and Found" / X-TRA / USA / 1998–99

Michael Worthington

Los Angeles

X-TRA

Volume II. Issue Number 3. Spring 1999.

3

4

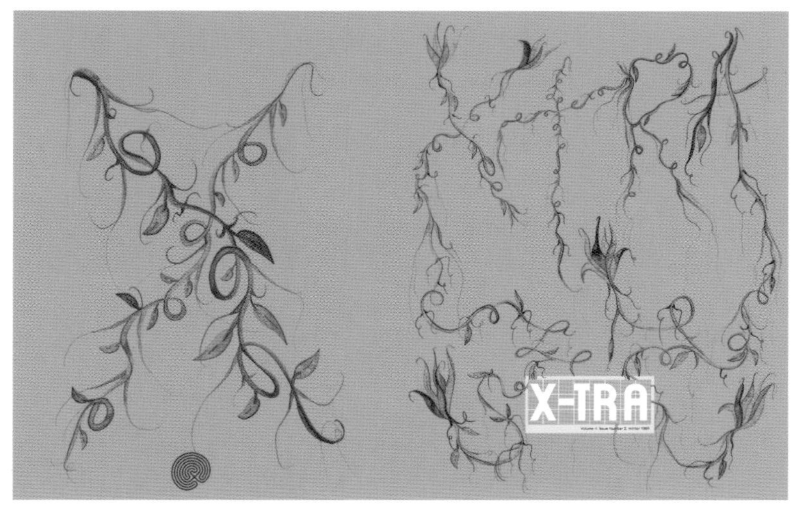

5

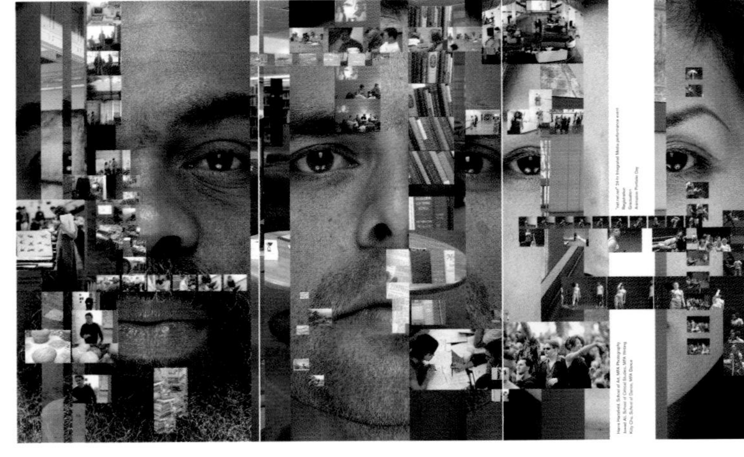

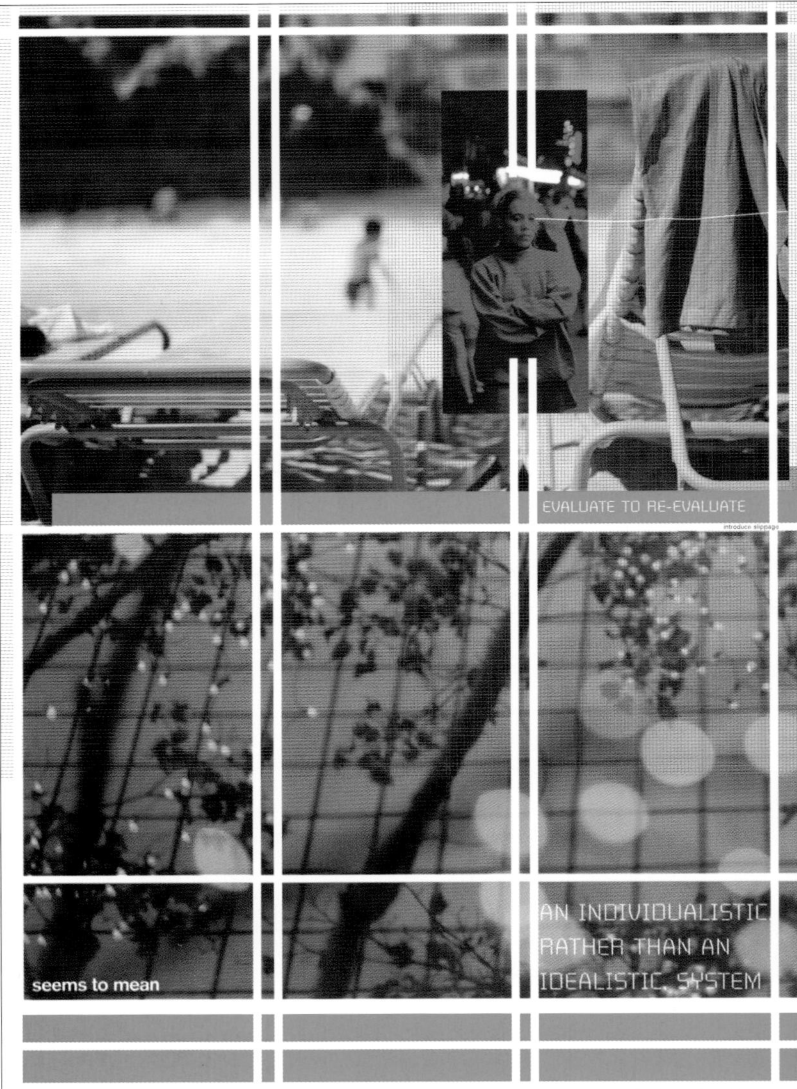

EVALUATE TO RE-EVALUATE
Simplification.
Looks good,
seems to mean
A training system
which beyond a
certain point is
AN INDIVIDUALISTIC
RATHER THAN AN
IDEALISTIC SYSTEM

Their system was

Now your system

Michael Worthington

6–7 Back and front cover and spread, California Institute of the Arts bulletin (type design Jon Notaro) / California Institute of the Arts / USA / 2001

8 Spread from "Personal Modernism" book feature, *Restart: New Systems in Graphic Design* (type design Lee Schultz) / Thames & Hudson / United Kingdom / 2001

9–11 Posters from Lyrics project for exhibition at the Japanese American National Museum, Los Angeles (made possible by a grant from the City of Los Angeles) / USA / 2002

12–13 Exterior and interior of record sleeve for *Landscape Number 2*, part of the multidisciplinary art project Song Poems (type design Jon Notaro) / USA / 2001

9

10

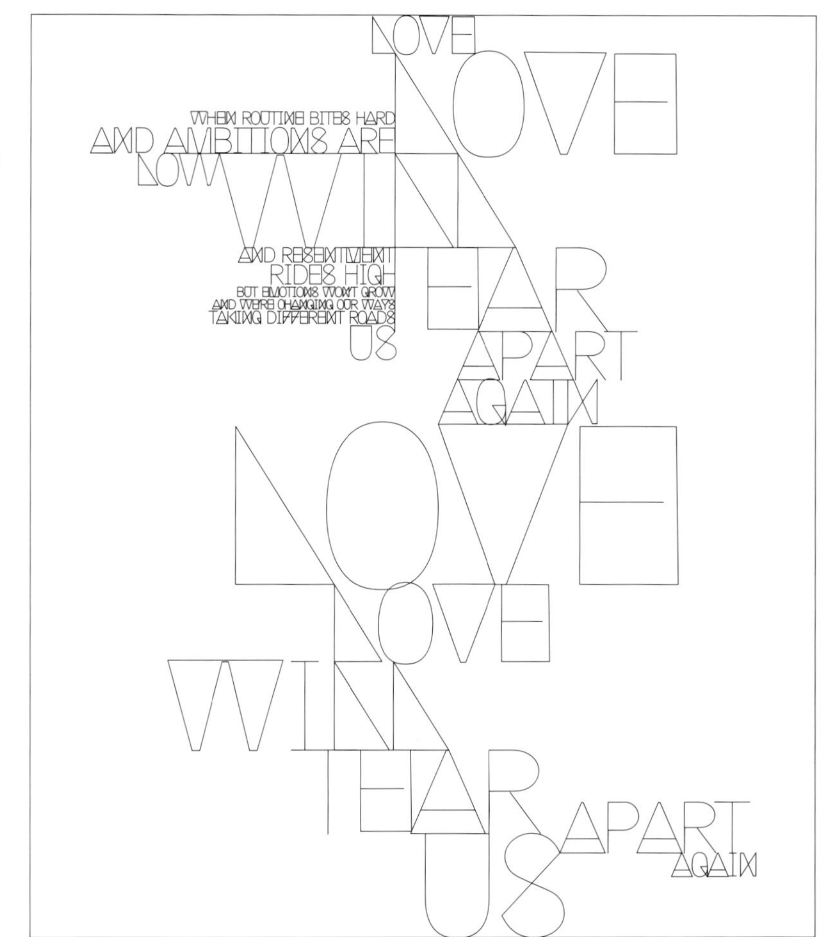

11

12
13

SCAPE LANDS
LANDSCAPE
NUMBE
NUMBER.2.

INSIDE IS
THE SAME PAINTING

You're always somewhere strange
The changing view unnoticed
green and gray The same blue
pavement Of sky, grass and
Speeding in a blur
the reflection of your eyes
miliar The scene is dense and fa
ust passed Places resemble ones ju
and ones just ahead.

Looking at the works of Chinese designer Wang Xu is like staring at a freshly washed window. Behind it opens a different dimension. It's clean and airy, with lots of transparent light and a steady breeze. Using the stamp of truism, one can say that this is light from the East, wind from the East. • • It seems as if Xu has been offered the highest truth, which God hid from the wise and gave instead to children and people with simple and pure hearts. Those who know him personally will no doubt forever remember that booming silver laughter that reveals his inner harmony and happiness. • • His delicate, elegant works seem very Eastern, Chinese, I would even say ancient Chinese. And at the same time they're absolutely Western, stylish, acutely modern. In them, organic nature stridently joins with the techno-genetic civilization. • • How does the designer achieve such a union? It's a mystery. But I think it is no coincidence that the journal that Xu published, edited, and laid out was called *Design Exchange*. That excellent, oversized magazine was the window to the world for Chinese designers, uniting West and East. • • Spilling from behind the Great Wall of China, which for a long time acted as an iron curtain, Chinese design was the last to join the ranks of world design. It spread quickly, calmly, without fuss. It seems the Chinese, as did the Russians in their time, feel themselves "laborers of the eleventh hour" as in the evangelical parable, workers who appear last on the world stage but stand next to the first, awarded not for merits but by the grace of God. I'm not sure whether the Chinese are aware of the parable, but they hold themselves with undeniable dignity. • • Chinese design succeeds also thanks to its sensitivity to different kinds of breezes and winds, to its openness and readiness for different cultural inflows. With the conviction of "laborers of the eleventh hour," Chinese design reaps where it didn't sow and, as a result, appears as a kind of weathervane of cultural interests in the new epoch—the epoch that chose as its slogan the combination of the uncombinable. When all of this falls on a pure heart, the result turns out organic and harmonious. • • Serge Serov • •

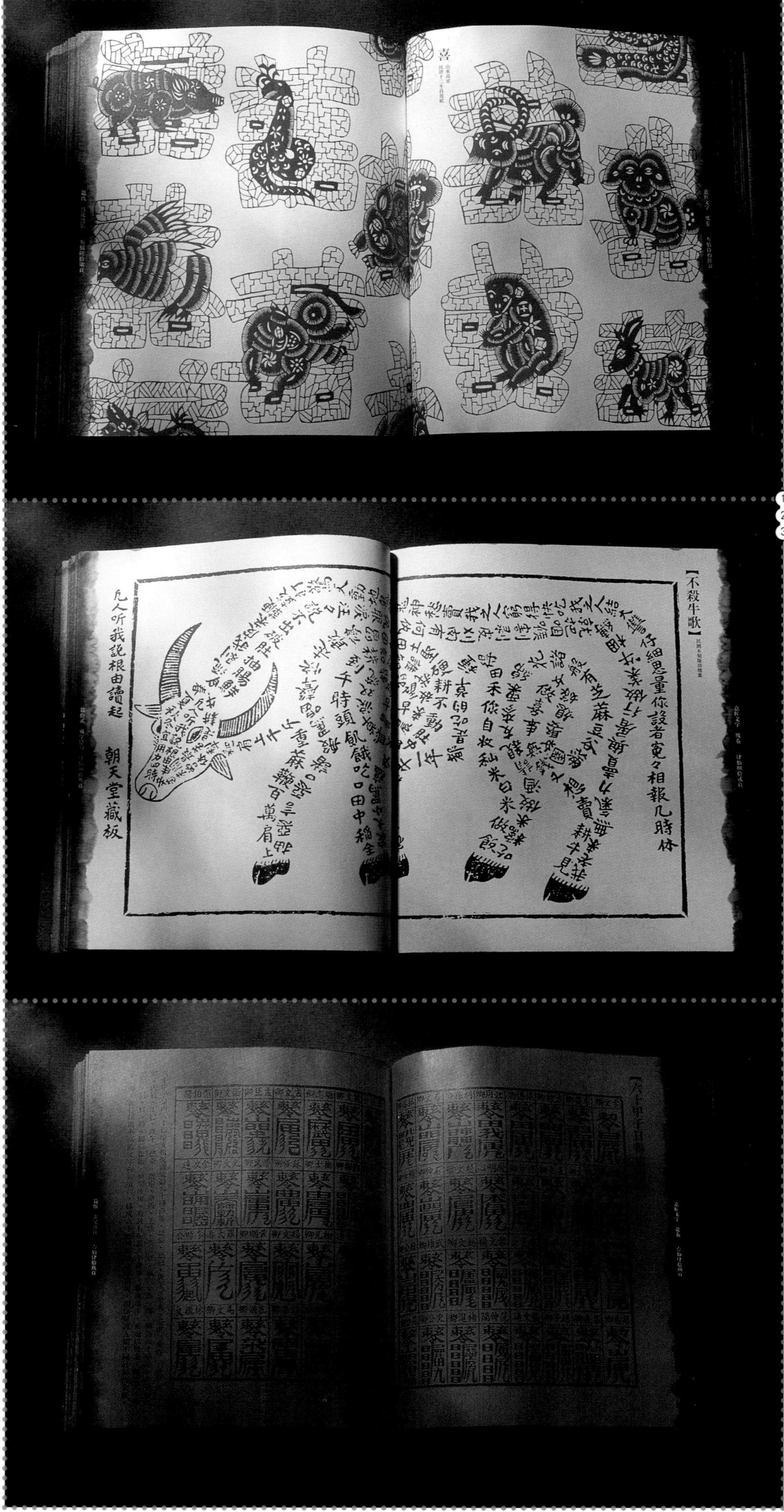

1–3 Spreads, *Artistic Conception Writing* / China Youth Press / China / 2000 / The book is dedicated to the characters of the Chinese alphabet and all of its cultural facets.
4–9 Promotional poster series for the book *Artistic Conception Writing* / China / 2000
10–12 Poster series for *Ambiguity* exhibition and book launch, Beijing (illustration Quan Zi) / Now Design Club / China / 2003

Wang Xu

Beijing/Guangzhou, China

15

4 5 6

7 8 9

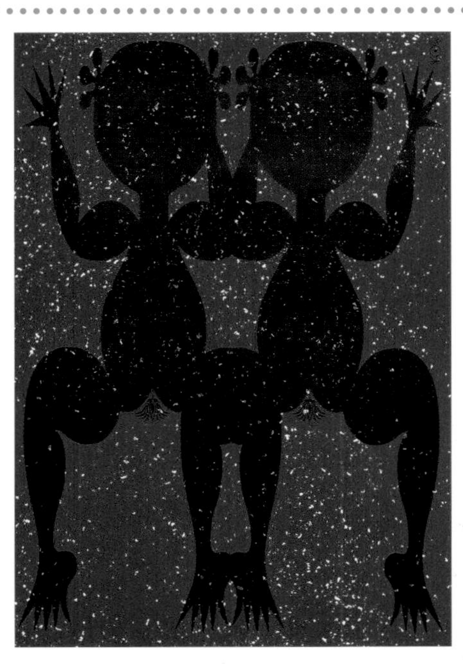

10 11 12

No. 15

13
14
15

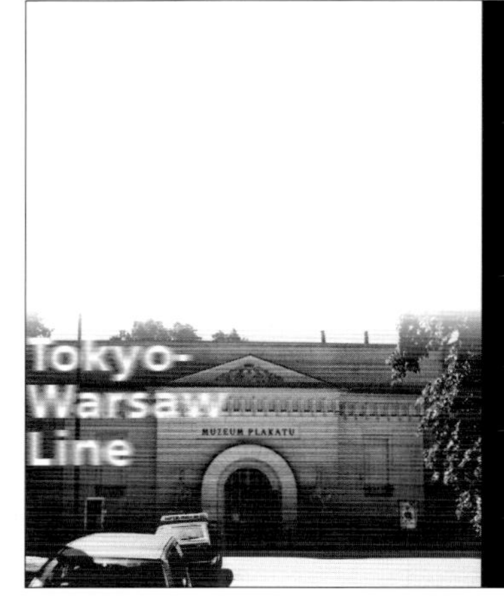

Tokyo-
Warsaw
Line
MUZEUM PLAKATU
The 1994 edition of the International Poster Biennale in Warsaw has presented a larger number of Japanese graphic artists compared to their Polish counterparts. At the same time the Warsaw Academy of Fine Arts has granted the honoris causa doctorate to Yusaku Kamekura and the National Museum of Poznan has dedicated an important retrospective to the history of the Japanese poster. Meeting with Yusaku Kamekura and Lech Majewski, I ask them the meaning of the encounter between two visual cultures that may appear far apart.

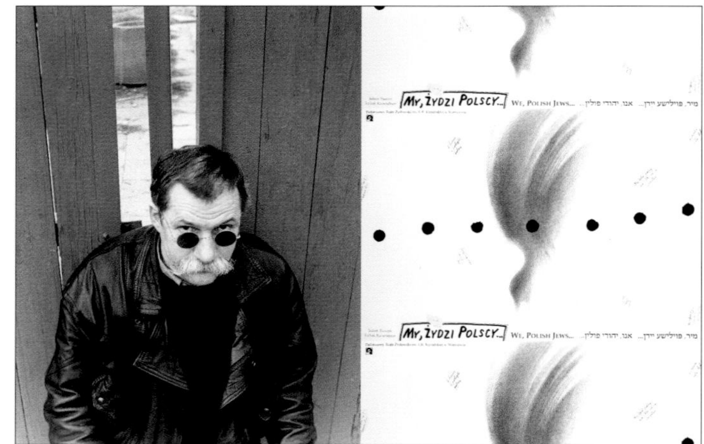

MY, ŻYDZI POLSCY...
WE, POLISH JEWS...

16
17
18

Wang Xu

13–15 Cover and spreads, new edition of *Design Exchange* magazine no. 15 / China Youth Press / China / 2000
16–18 Cover and spreads, new edition of *Design Exchange* magazine no. 12 / China Youth Press / China / 1997
19 Poster for thematic workshop "Water" / Shanghai Graphic Designers Association / China / 2000
20 Poster for *Chinese Character* exhibition, Taipei / Taiwan Poster Design Association / Taiwan / 1995
21 Poster for *Paper* exhibition, Taipei / Taiwan Poster Design Association / Taiwan / 2001
22 Poster for Second International Ink Painting Biennial of Shenzhen / China / 2000

19

when the
well is dry
we know
the worth
of water

20

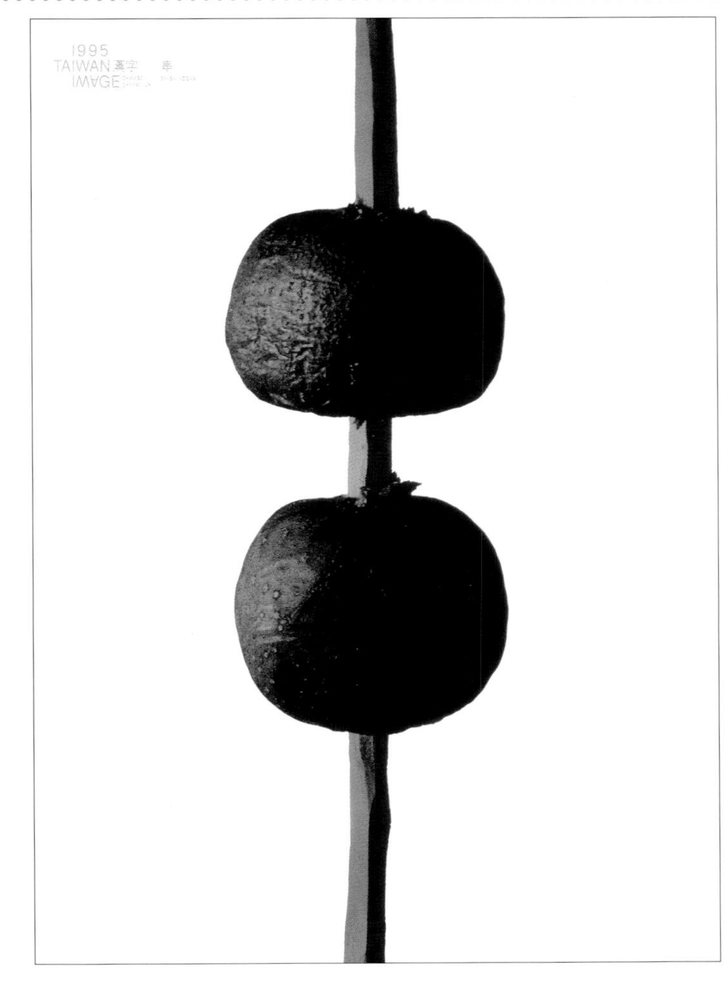

21

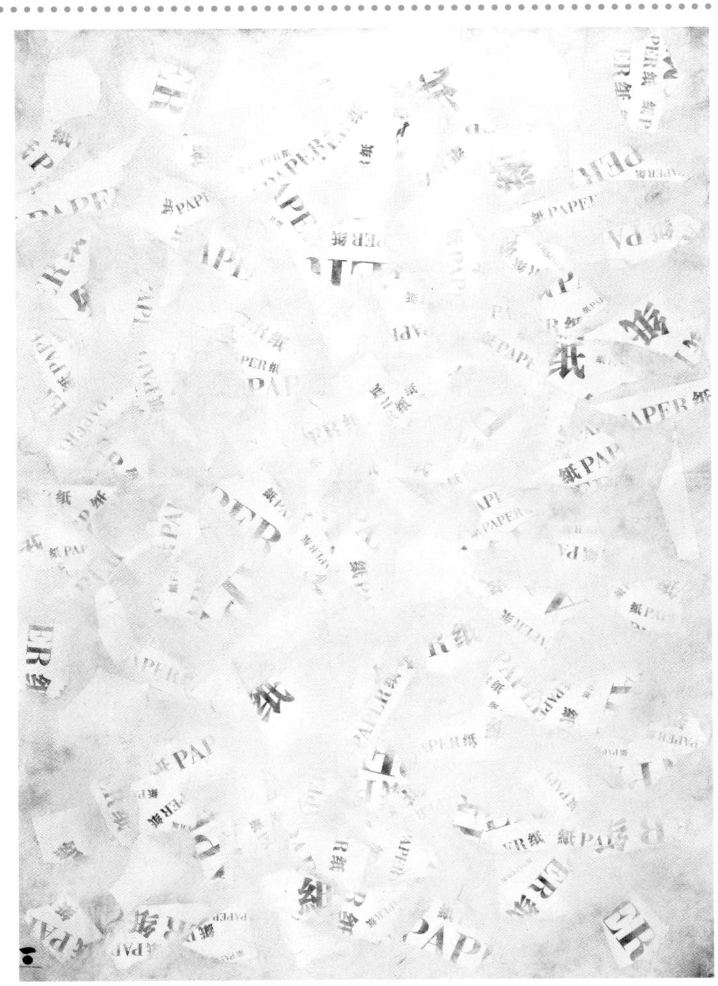

22

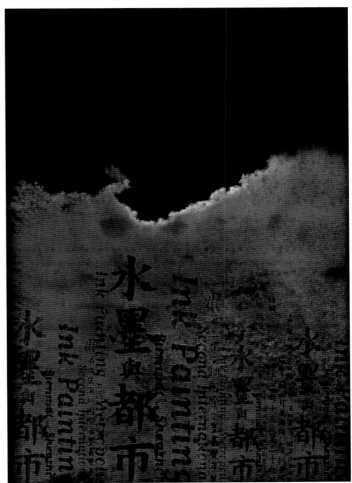

It is always a pleasure to spend time with Catherine Zask—be it in her atelier on the Rue du Faubourg-Saint-Martin in Paris, where her fantastic posters hang from the ceiling, drying like washing in Naples, or at a symposium at the other end of the world, where she never fails to impress the audience with her intelligent typographic experiments. • • To truly understand her work, however, one must have seen her dance or watched how she rolls herself a perfect cigarette with great ease. In short, I am a big fan of Zask, her work, her way of being. She is a one-woman show. She is a master of playfully using letters and words to interpret the world. Some of her work even borders on witchcraft. In the Middle Ages she would have surely been burned at the stake: like every artist, she is independent and free in her work and bound only to herself. • • Zask clearly knows how to defend herself with much élan and energy against the superficial premise of graphic design, against the small-minded requirements of the marketing world or even the unimaginative desires of some clients. Her work is the expression of a mentality that is uninterested in decorative sensationalism. Through her generous use of the surface she demonstrates the possesive claim for space that characterizes words. With her sophisticated trimming and cutting of the individual letters she creates a unique sign language. Even the breathing time, the space between the words, is an object of her creativity. • • Her current client roster reads like a "who's who" in the administration of intellectual interests in France: L'Hippodrome, scène nationale de Douai, Université de Franche-Comté, Ministère de la Culture, the list goes on and on. • • One of her best poster series was awarded the 2002 Grand Prix at the international poster biennial in Brno, Czech Republic. To everybody's delight, she flew in right away, because parties must be celebrated as and when they occur. À la prochaine, ma chère Catherine! • • Uwe Loesch • •

1 Poster for play *Macbeth*, by William Shakespeare / L'Hippodrome, scène nationale de Douai / France / 2001
2 Poster for dance performance *Rain*, by Anne Teresa de Keersmaeker / L'Hippodrome, scène nationale de Douai / France / 2001
3 Poster for musical juggling performance *Le chant des balles*, by Rémi Balagué / L'Hippodrome, scène nationale de Douai / France / 2001
4 Poster for play *Tête d'or*, by Paul Claudel / L'Hippodrome, scène nationale de Douai / France / 2001
5 Poster for dance performance *La tribu Iota*, by Francesca Lattuada / L'Hippodrome, scène nationale de Douai / France / 2002
6 Poster for Merce Cunningham Dance Company performance / L'Hippodrome, scène nationale de Douai / France / 2002

Catherine Zask

Paris

1

2

3

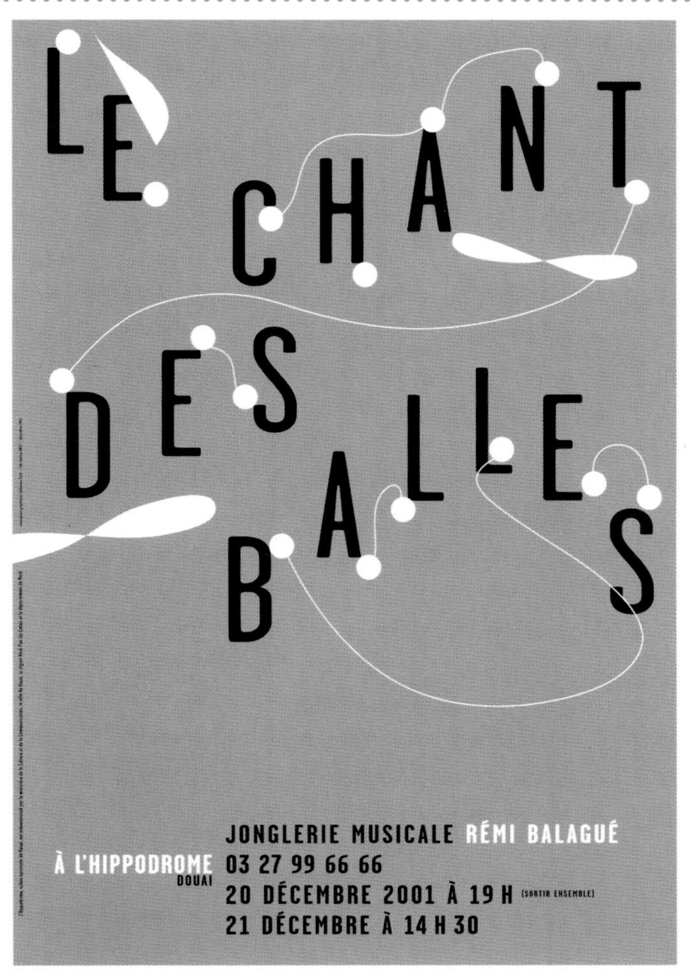
LE CHANT DES BALLES
JONGLERIE MUSICALE RÉMI BALAGUÉ
À L'HIPPODROME DOUAI
03 27 99 66 66
20 DÉCEMBRE 2001 À 19 H (SORTIR ENSEMBLE)
21 DÉCEMBRE À 14 H 30

4

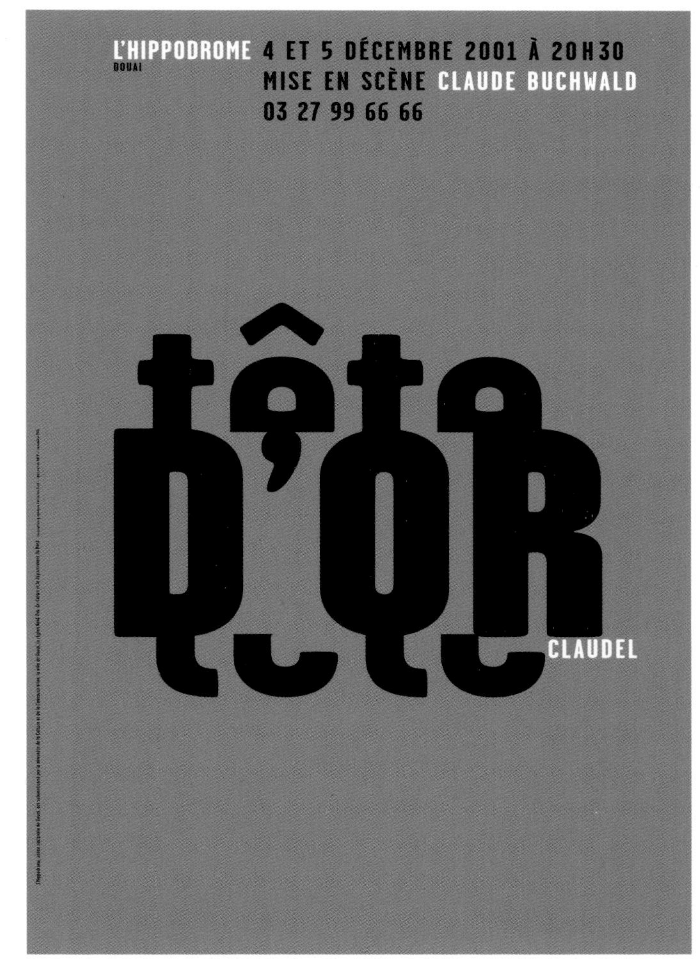
L'HIPPODROME DOUAI
4 ET 5 DÉCEMBRE 2001 À 20H30
MISE EN SCÈNE CLAUDE BUCHWALD
03 27 99 66 66
tête d'OR
CLAUDEL

5

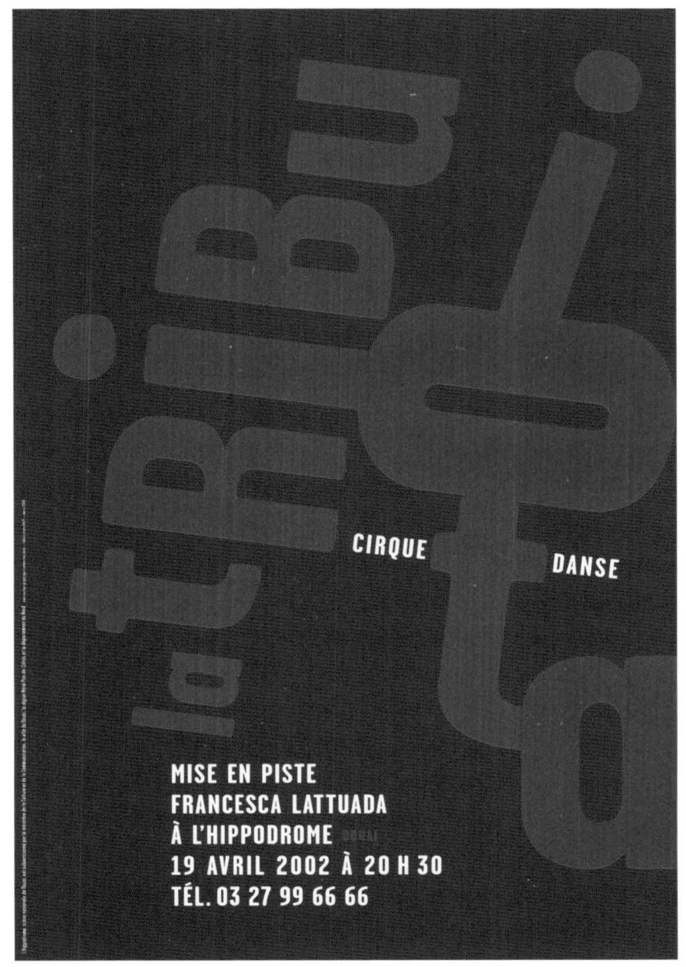
la tribu iota
CIRQUE
DANSE
MISE EN PISTE
FRANCESCA LATTUADA
À L'HIPPODROME DOUAI
19 AVRIL 2002 À 20 H 30
TÉL. 03 27 99 66 66

6

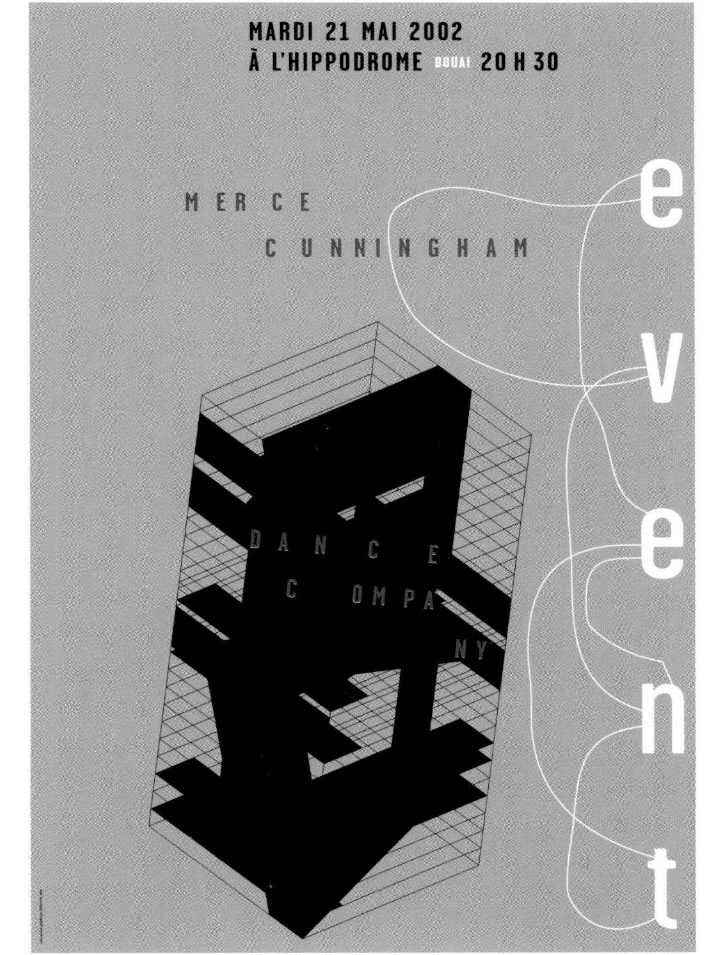
MARDI 21 MAI 2002
À L'HIPPODROME DOUAI 20 H 30
MERCE CUNNINGHAM
DANCE COMPANY
event

⑦

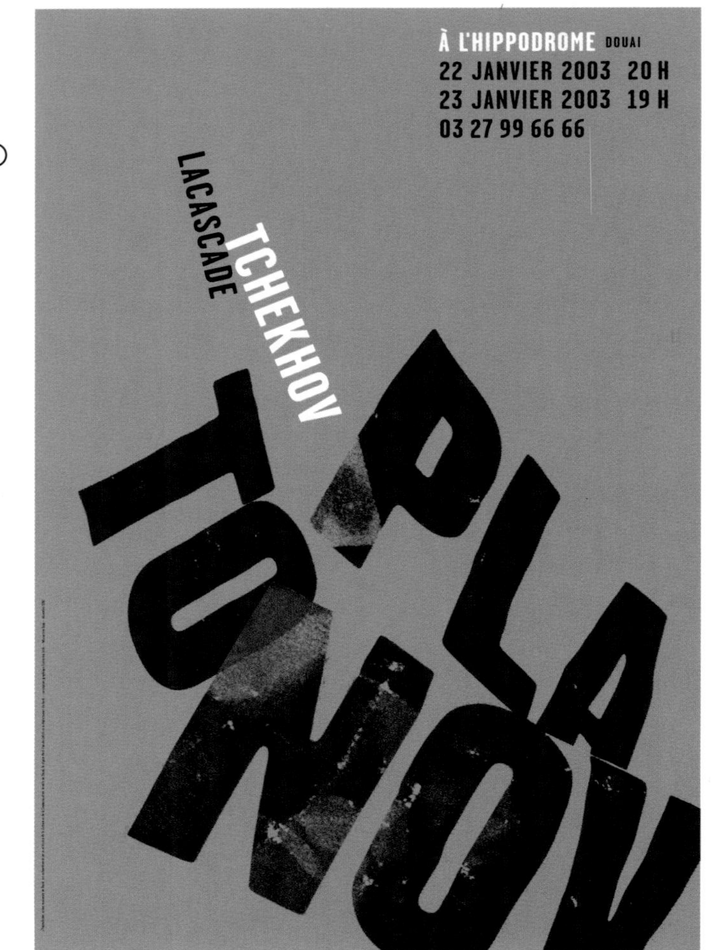

⑧

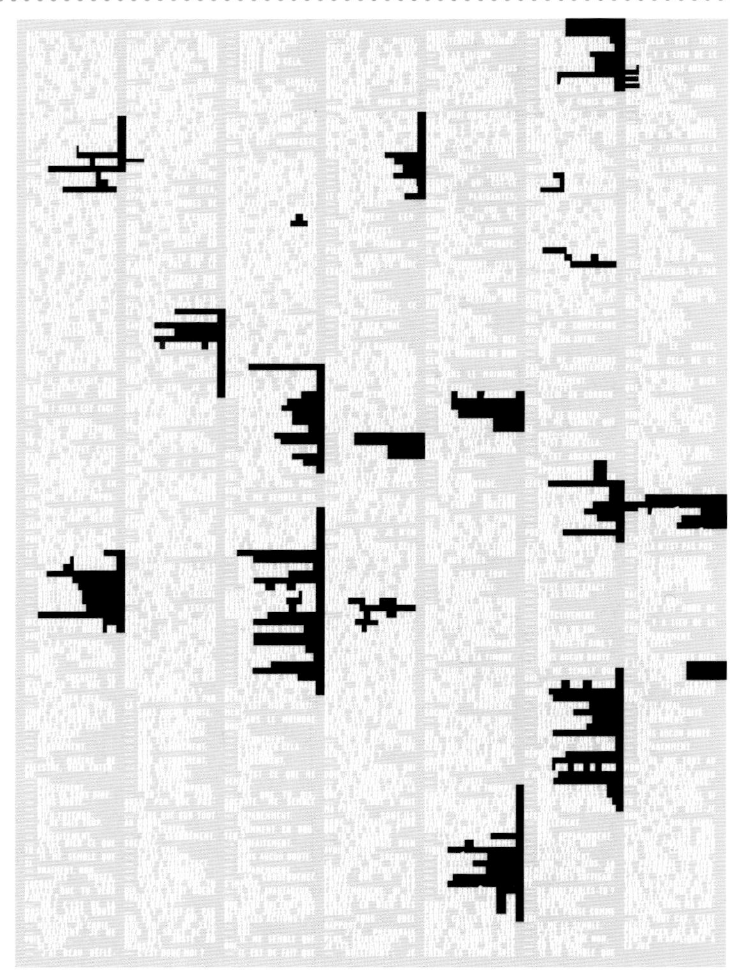

⑨

7 Poster for performance by the Philharmonic Orchestra of Strasbourg / L'Hippodrome, scène nationale de Douai / France / 2002
8 Poster for play *Platonov*, by Anton Chekhov / L'Hippodrome, scene nationale de Douai / France / 2002
9 Self-commissioned Alcibiade au téléphone poster / France / 2000
10 Spreads from various programs for the Société civile des auteurs multimedia (Scam) / Scam / France / 2001–2002

Catherine Zask

VIR-
TUAL
LIFE
ART

mardi 2 et lundi 8 octobre de 19 h à 22 h 30
vernissages – entrée libre

La vie en transparence. Exposition Rodolphe Gombergh et Albert Castro. Imaginons qu'un nouveau pinceau soit subitement apparu dans la main de l'homme. Imaginons que ce nouveau pinceau ne reproduise plus seulement une image formée par la lumière, mais permette de traduire une image formée d'autres ondes... Médecins radiologues et plasticiens, Rodolphe Gombergh et Albert Castro jouent de la transparence des hommes et des objets, transforment les images médicales pour en faire des œuvres d'art. Exposition et mur d'images vidéo du 2 octobre au 30 novembre 2001. Entrée libre du lundi au vendredi de 9 h à 18 h.

2 3

JEAN NOUVEL

ARCHITECTURE. URBANISME ET REGARD DOCUMENTAIRE

10

RÉVOLUTION DU REGARD SUR LE LYCÉE

DU LIEU MENAÇANT AU LIEU MENACÉ

24

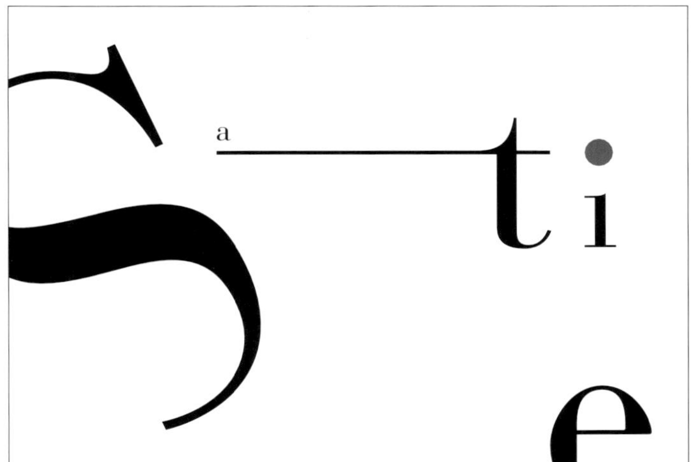

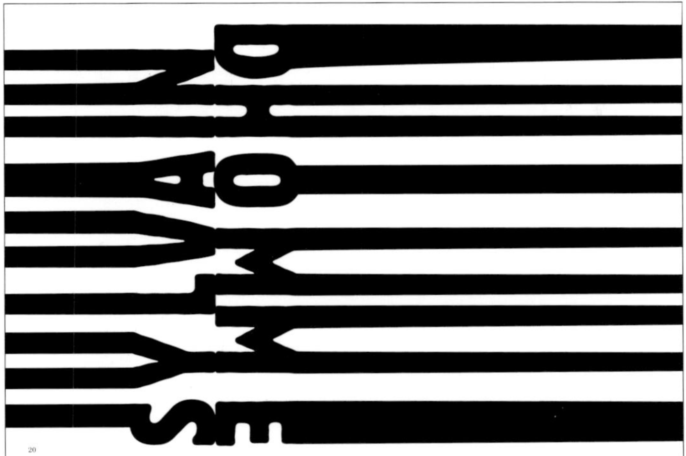

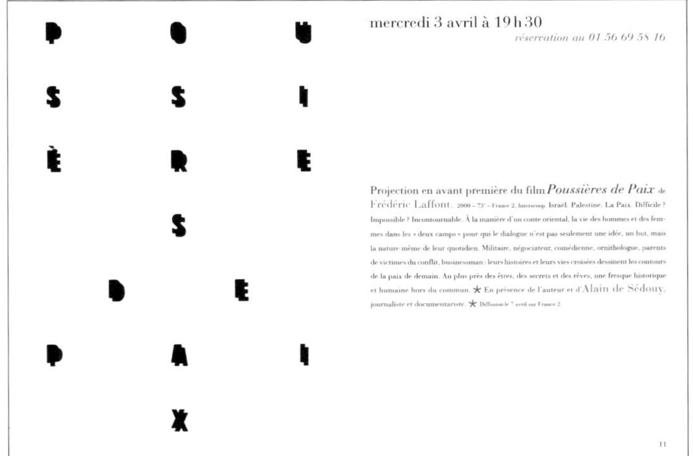

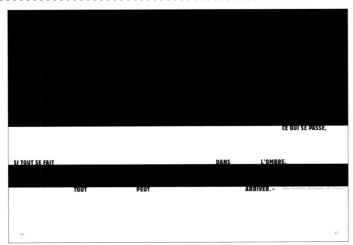

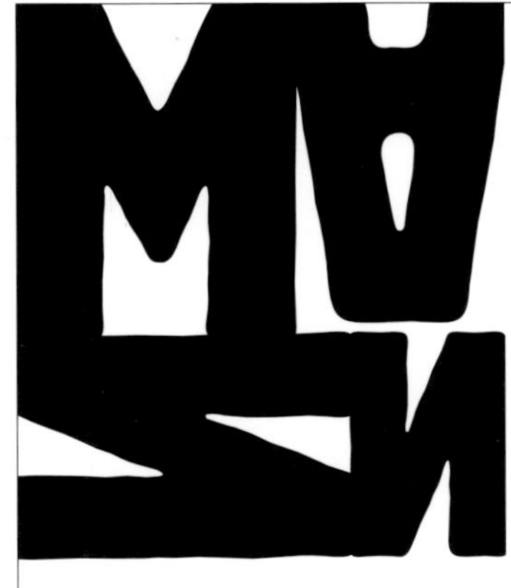

mercredi 14 novembre à 19 heures
réservation au 01 55 00 73 14

Documentaire-fiction

Projection, en avant-première, des deux premiers épisodes de la série *Thomas Mann et les siens* de Heinrich Breloer. Interprété par Armin Mueller-Stahl, Monica Bleibtreu, Jürgen Heursch, Veronica Ferres. 2001 – 3 x 90' – Bavaria, WDR, NDR, BR, Arte. Pierre-André Boutang, conseiller du président d'Arte France, animera un débat en présence de l'auteur, sur le thème littérature et histoire à la télévision. Ce documentaire fiction est l'œuvre originale de l'un des plus grands réalisateurs de télévision allemands dont l'écriture mêle archives, interviews et scènes jouées, en alternance subtile. Sur un arrière-plan politique et social, ce documentaire-fiction retrace les heures de gloire et les sombres périodes de la vie d'une illustre famille d'écrivains allemands du XXe siècle, la famille Mann. ★ Diffusion sur Arte les 5, 6 et 7 décembre 2001 à 20 h 45.

14 15

032c is a groundbreaking magazine designed, edited, and art directed by the 032c workshop, an "office for creative direction" based in Berlin. The name derives from the Pantone reference for the studio's house color, the only color other than black and white to grace the pages of *032c*. It is a confident editorial approach, understated but honest and direct. The standard of photography is high, as is the quality and relevance of the writing, and even when the subject matter lies in the past, it is somehow relevant to the here and now. • • The first three issues of *032c* were tabloid format, printed on newsprint-quality paper, each with more or less the same cover: heavy black sans serif type on a white ground, with a large off-center red square covering almost three quarters of the cover's surface; it is incredibly striking. The tabloid format and inexpensive paper suggest the ephemeral, reflecting the fast-moving nature of contemporary culture, a subject at the heart of *032c*. Issue 4 is a rather different proposition. It has a glossy cover and includes several full-color, full-bleed ads for brands such as Lee jeans and Camper. However, it is a sideways move into the commercial world that hasn't affected the quality of the design or content, nor blunted its subversive edge. • • Each issue concerns itself with one "umbrella" theme. Issue 4, for example, asks readers to "Embrace Instability," and if the modern world can be summed up in one word, then instability wouldn't be far from the mark. The themes of earlier issues, such as "Destruction" (issue 2) and "What's Next?" (issue 3), suggest the ethos of *032c*. It communicates the way in which contemporary culture is in a constant state of flux. • • *032c* is a document of our times. More specifically, it is a declaration of how a new creative spirit is placing Berlin at the forefront of contemporary culture. Many of the photo stories and essays represent the viewpoints of young Berliners and the new opportunities that are opening up for them. It will be interesting to see where *032c* magazine goes next and how that informs the commercial work of the 032c workshop. If the exceptional standard maintained over their first five issues continues, then there's an awful lot to look forward to. • • Fernando Gutierrez • •

1–4 Cover and spreads, *032c*, issue 1, "Professionalism" / 032c / Germany / 2000
5–8 Cover and spreads, *032c*, issue 2, "Destruction" / 032c / Germany / 2001
9–12 Cover and spreads, *032c*, issue 3, "What's Next?" / 032c / Germany / 2001

032c

Berlin

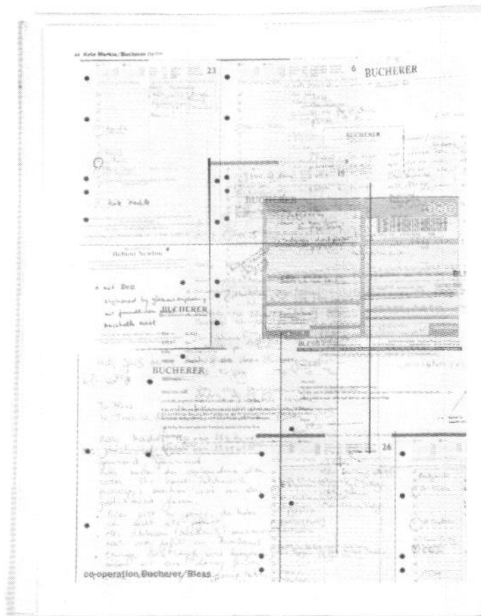

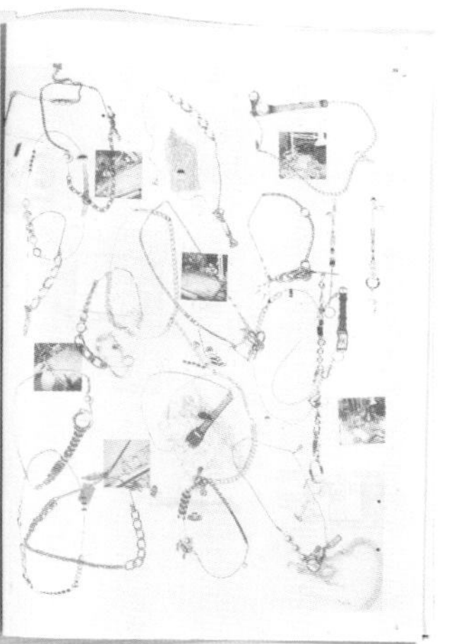

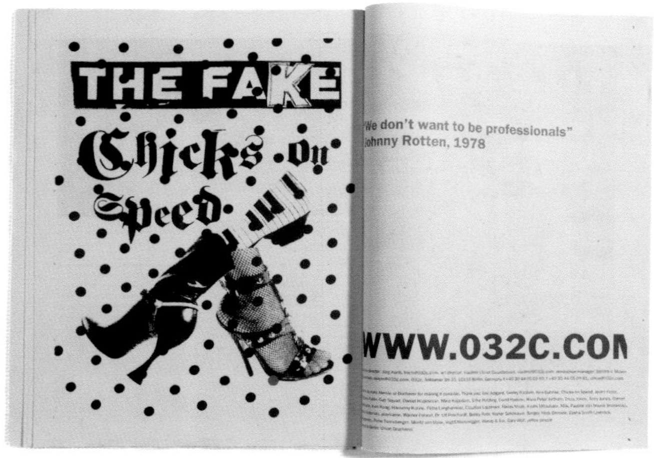

1
2
3
4

5
6
7
8

9
10
11
12

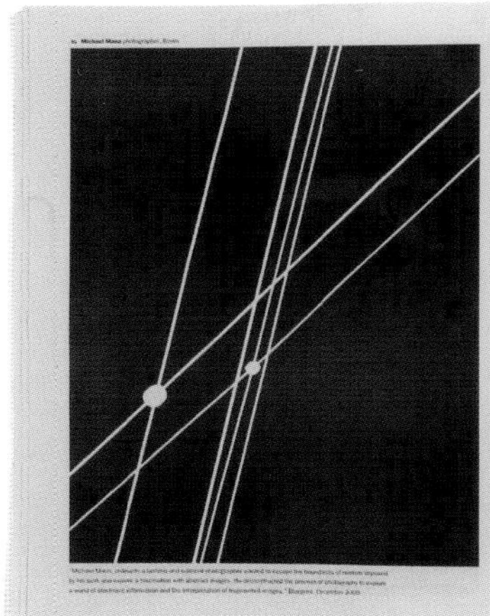

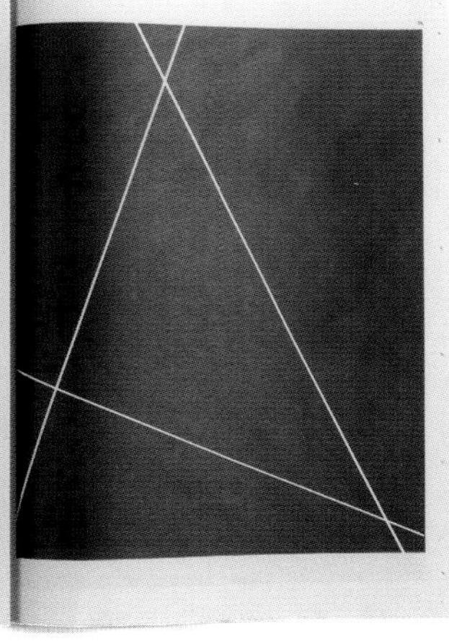

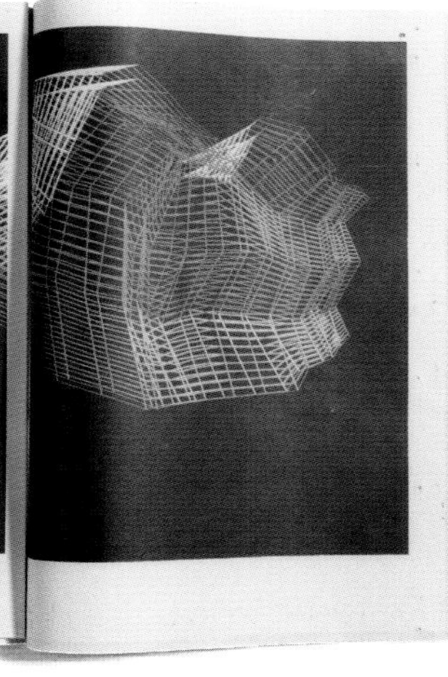

THE SEARCHING STAYS WITH YOU

INTERVIEW WITH HELMUT LANG

032c

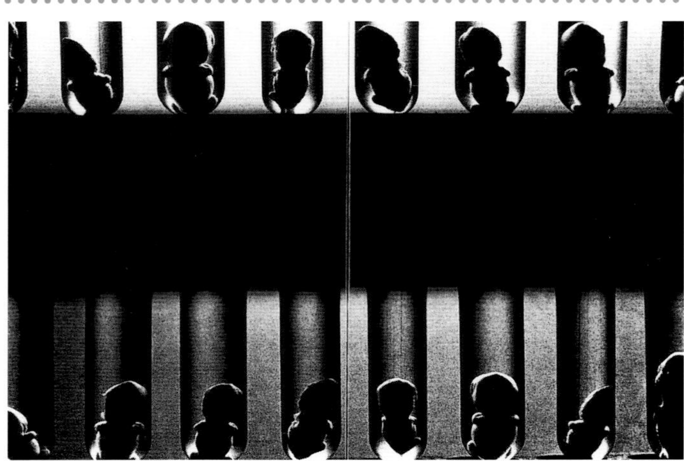

13

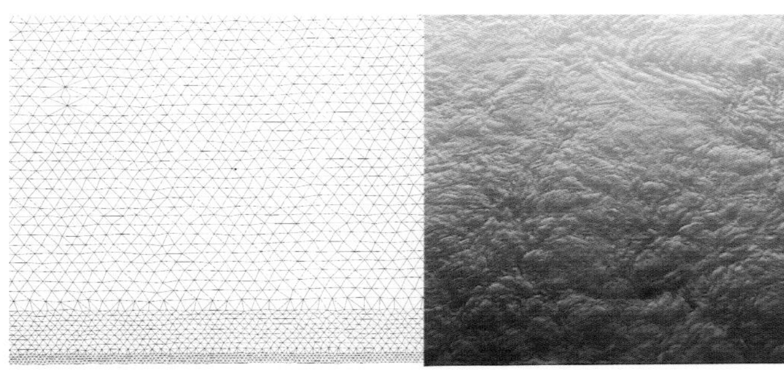

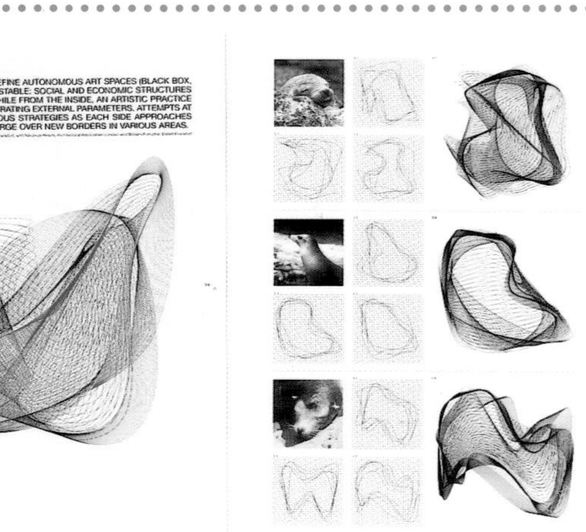
FRANKFURT 2002
SEAL NOTATIONS THE LINES THAT DEFINE AUTONOMOUS ART SPACES (BLACK BOX, WHITE CUBE) ARE BECOMING UNSTABLE: SOCIAL AND ECONOMIC STRUCTURES PRESS IN FROM THE OUTSIDE, WHILE FROM THE INSIDE, AN ARTISTIC PRACTICE ARISES, TRANSLATING AND INTEGRATING EXTERNAL PARAMETERS. ATTEMPTS AT DESCRIPTION LEAD TO PRECARIOUS STRATEGIES AS EACH SIDE APPROACHES THE OTHER AND CONFLICTS EMERGE OVER NEW BORDERS IN VARIOUS AREAS.

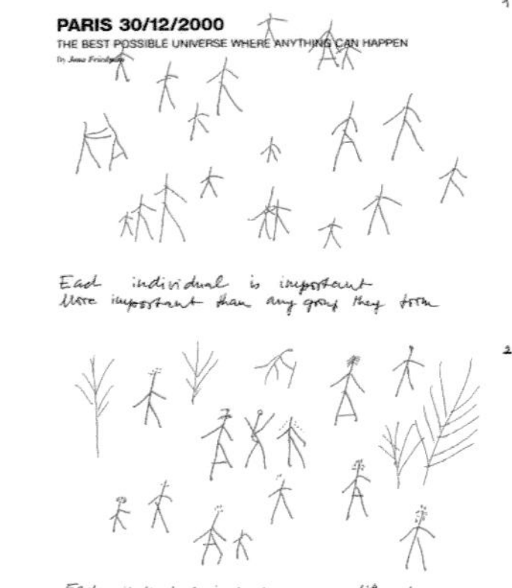
PARIS 30/12/2000
THE BEST POSSIBLE UNIVERSE WHERE ANYTHING CAN HAPPEN

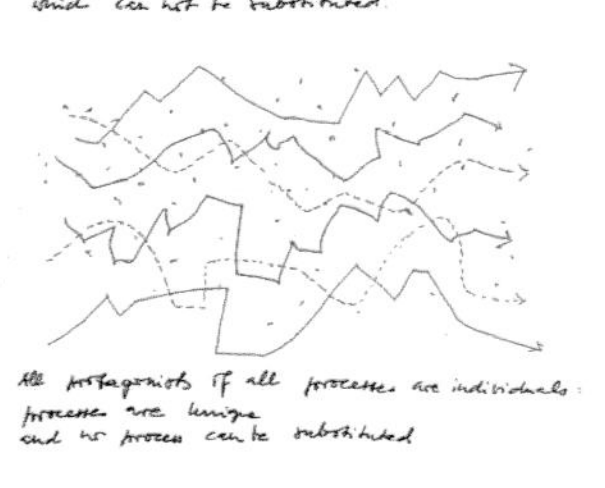

13 Cover and spreads, *032c*, issue 4, "Embrace Instability" / 032c / Germany / 2002

14 Cover and spreads, *032c*, issue 5, "Shanghai Desire" / 032c / Germany / 2003

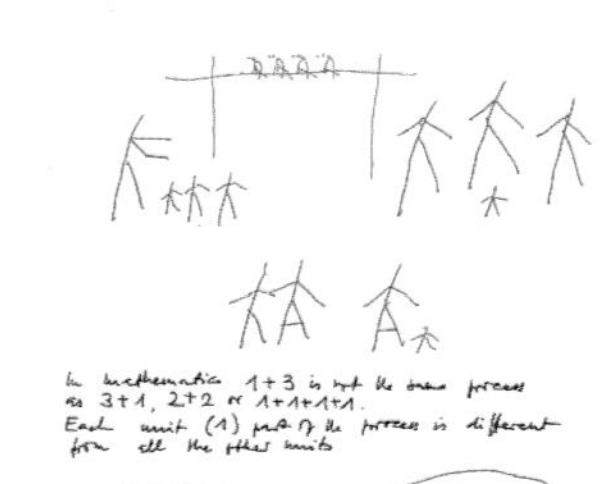

032c

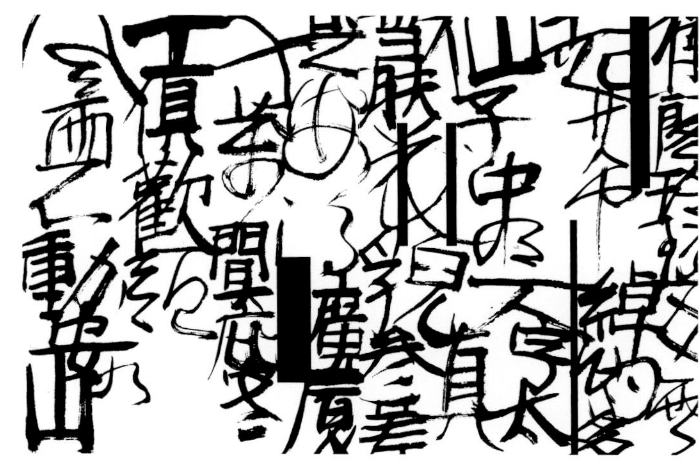

14

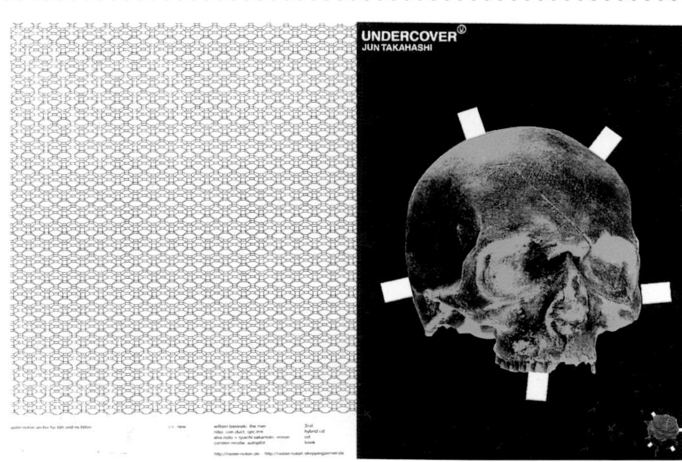
UNDERCOVER
JUN TAKAHASHI

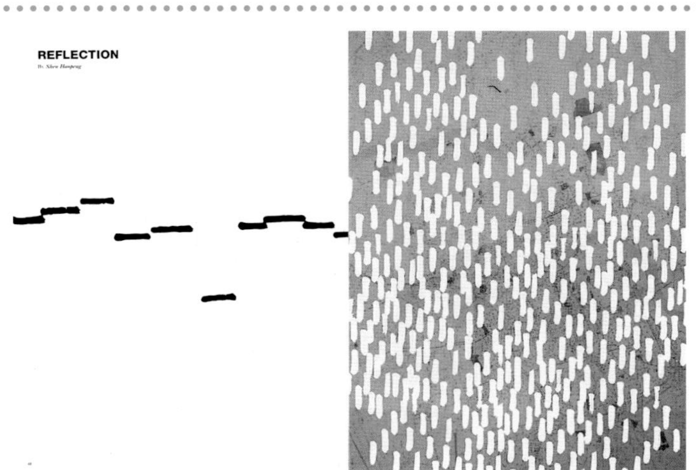
REFLECTION

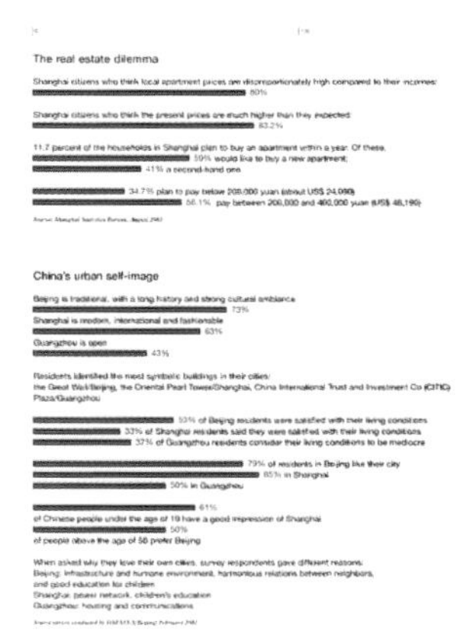
The real estate dilemma
China's urban self-image

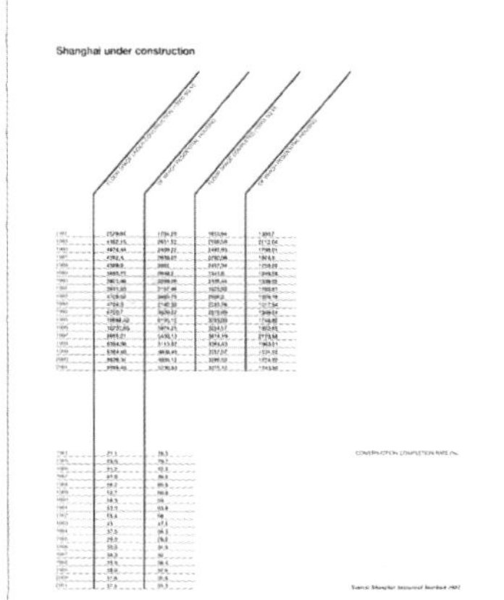
Shanghai under construction

Ms. Viola Zimmermann is a speedy woman, for the pulse of the times races inside her. Her career is full of sophistication, but with just enough edge to keep it from being predictable. She is wide awake and for me something like a "She-J" of the graphic possibilities of everyday life, which, unfortunately, sounds so extremely dry—and inadequate—that I will have to start right at the beginning. • •When it was still customary to spend a career in one single profession, when too many changes of employment were considered a sign of indecision or immaturity, when popular wisdom said that successful people find their place by the age of thirty—already then Zimmermann was working according to her searching, active spirit, hopping from agency to agency, from party to party. • •Since then quite a few things have changed. The commissions she receives have become as diverse as the expectations are high. All this might not seem to be that unique, but someone who, with these opportunities, with this specific set of instruments, manages to create an innovative, beautiful, even intelligent song, sparks something inside of me. Zimmermann's compositions are multitonal and contemporary. Her designs concentrate on the everyday, on all the "designed communications" that life may require. • •Zimmermann got her start with parties and all that they entail: She has built up more than just one trendy music club DJ-ing, cooking, creating posters and flyers, and animating her environment with her serious bravado. Zimmermann is able to bring a project to life, accompany it, and then let it go like few others • •Today her concerns are taking the new, interesting, and edgy direction of political awareness. She has courage. Nothing is less sexy in our profession than becoming politically active as a designer. Clients want the moldable, happy designer, the clean-cut designer, in short, the polished mirror in which their interests are sure to be perfectly understood and reflected. Clients sometimes forget that independent thinking and responsible action make graphic designers so much more exciting. • •Werner Jeker • •

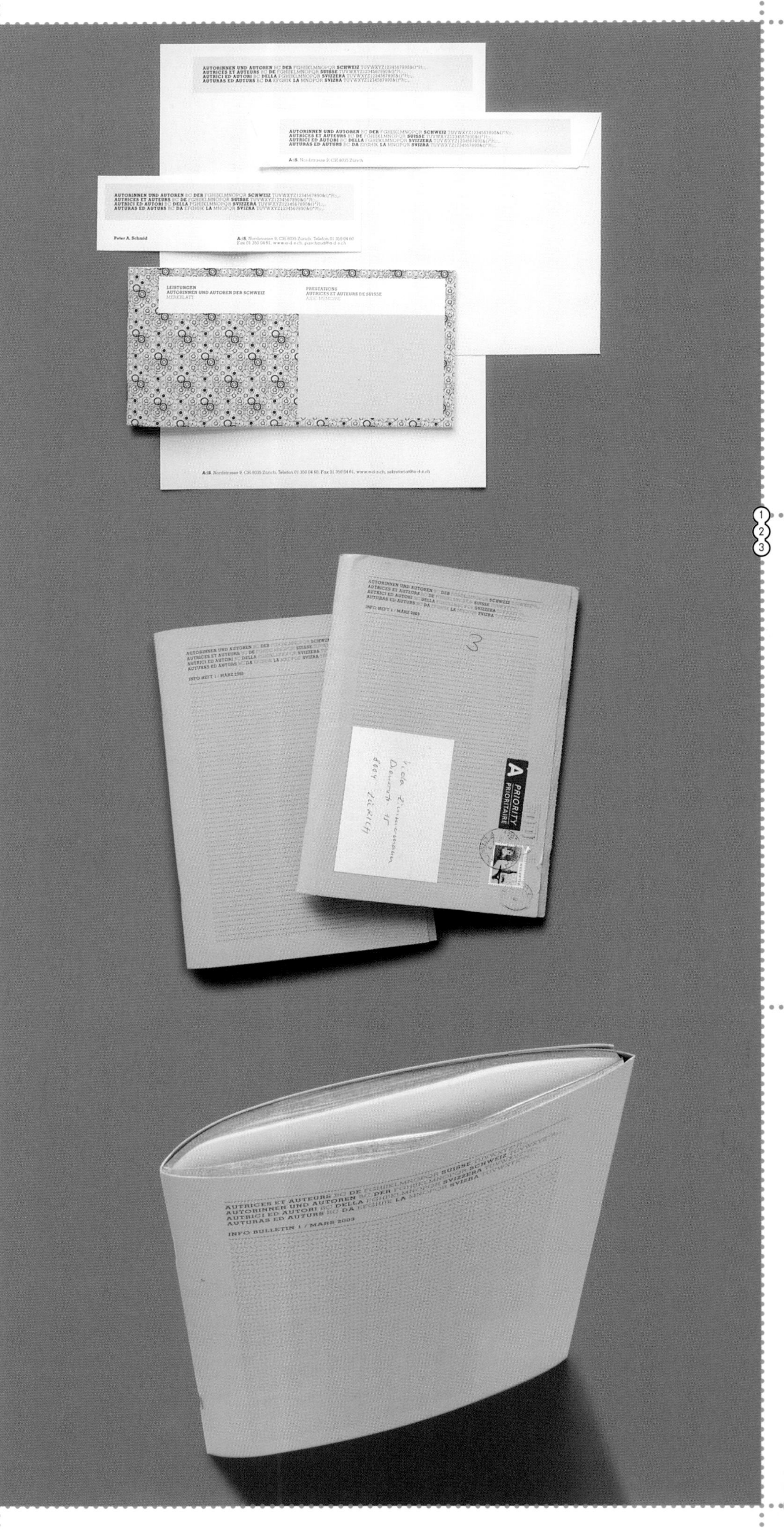

1 2 3

1-3 Corporate design and informational bulletin for organization Authors of Switzerland / Autorinnen und Autoren der Schweiz (AdS) / Switzerland / 2002-2003
4-5 Entrance ticket and T-shirt for Zurich drum 'n' bass club SNOT / SNOT / Switzerland / 1997
6 Skateboard designs / Airflow Skateboards / Switzerland / 2002-2003

Viola Zimmermann

Zurich

4

'N'
Schweizergasse 22
Sonntag 20-01 h
24. A

5

'N'
ONESNOTSTOP
WHAT?

6

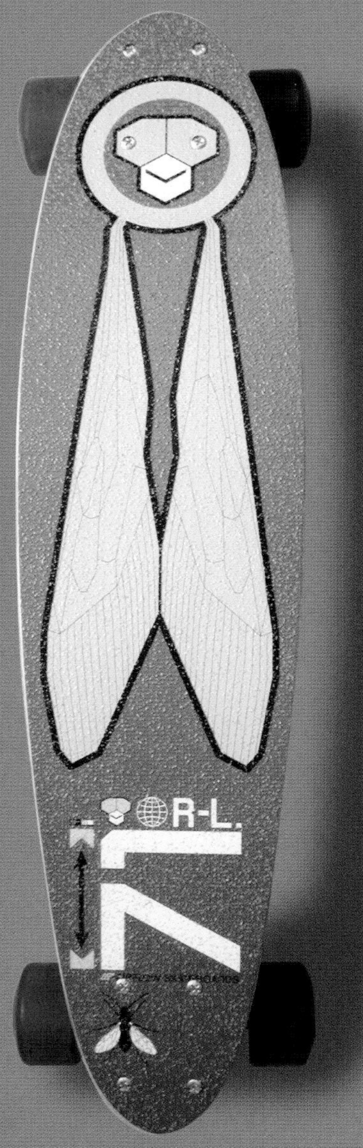
R-L.
71

R-L.
71

71
AIRFLOW
AIRFLOW SKATEBOARDS

7

8 
9 
10

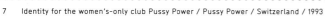

7 Identity for the women's-only club Pussy Power / Pussy Power / Switzerland / 1993
8–10 Packaging and design for card game Chuko / Inka Druck / Switzerland / 2000
11–14 Covers and spreads, *Outlet-Interventionen im Stadtteil VI, Bern Bümpliz* and *Outlet-Interventionen in der MesseStadt München Riem* / Hochschule für Gestaltung, Kunst und Konservierung (HGKK) / Switzerland / 2002–2003 / The publication accompanies an exchange project between students of the HGKK, Bern, and the Academy of Fine Arts, Munich, dedicated to artistic interventions in both cities.
15–18 Promotional postcards for short-story and poetry competition organized by Zurich's Department of Public Transport / Verkersbetrieb Zürich (VBZ) / Switzerland / 2002

Viola Zimmermann

11
12
13
14

15
16
17
18

When I was a boy of about sixteen, I went on a holiday to France with a friend of mine. I drove a bike pieced together from a dozen other bicycles, with a three-speed Sturmy Acer gear, two side bags, and a tent. Armed with a huge cap (I didn't have money for sunglasses), I cruised France with my mate, along country roads and through small villages. In every town or village there would be a couple of blind walls, and without exception these walls would be covered with a gigantic painted advertisement. Colorful images, monumental lettering—the kind of brazen sales pitch one wouldn't see in Holland. The most fascinating of those images looked like they were fragments of an even larger whole: mysterious parts of messages that, on these enormous surfaces, contrasted sharply with the expansive landscape. I was so impressed that I started to look out for these strange emblems. I had no idea what they meant. Sometimes you saw only letters—"Saint," or "aël"—other times just a stylized waiter, sometimes a fat, short one, sometimes thin and tall. It completely escaped me. But I did recognize they belonged together. You never got the whole picture, but you knew it was something special. I tried to memorize the parts and imagine how they would fit together, but didn't succeed. Until I came across an enameled announcement, in Paris, that for the first time revealed the complete image: two little waiters, each with a tray held at shoulder height on which sat a stylized glass. On top of that, the brand name: Saint-Raphaël. Three colors—black, red, white—and that characteristic hand-painted French lettering...I thought it was marvelous! I had no idea of the existence of a craft named graphic design or typography, but I was fascinated by these bold, graphic signs in the landscape. I thought it must have something to do with Cubist art—a kind of street version of Picasso, about whom I had read something somewhere. I still have an ashtray and a clock at home with that splendid logo of the two waiters and those beautiful letters, but I have never tried the drink. I'm afraid that its taste could spoil the illusion of the image and, with that, the experience of one of the most beautiful and intriguing pieces of public graphics I have ever come across. To this day I don't know who made these superb images, but whoever it may be, he still inspires me. Thank you!

St. Raphaël Quinquina

by Charles Loupot

Anthon Beeke

Transport, a typeface designed by Jock Kinneir and Margaret Calvert, was introduced in 1965 as part of their firm's design program for British road signs. It exists in two weights—Heavy, for use in dark colors on white backgrounds, and Medium, for reversal out of dark backgrounds in light colors—which appear of equal weight when in use. The font's purpose was to remain legible to drivers who were by now traveling at faster speeds on a modern road network. According to a contemporaneous report on roadway signage, signs needed to be "clear at a glance so that the driver's attention is not distracted from the task of driving." That these signs still work and look fresh and modern some forty years later is testament to their logical layout and simple color coding, but especially to their skillfully drawn, thoroughly detailed, "invisible" yet distinctive typeface. •• Transport is a rare example of a typeface that is both functional and humane. By "humane" I mean the letterforms exhibit an aesthetic sensibility that is skeptical of the overrationalized and which therefore tempers the coldness of their inherent structural geometry. Achieving this balance requires highly skilled drawing. Transport is very warm for a sans serif typeface and, as Phil Baines said of it recently, well ahead of its time. Baines wrote, "mainstream typefaces following this 'softer' approach such as Lucida and Meta were not produced until 1985 and 1991 respectively." •• To understand the particular character of Transport's letterforms it helps to compare them with other typefaces. Beside Akzidenz Grotesk, Transport's lowercase letters are narrower yet surprisingly softer and more open. The circular dot over the *i*, the curl at the foot of the *l*, and the curving tail of the *a* lend the font a childlike, youthful, and friendly appearance. Compared with cold Helvetica, it has a monolinear naïveté and makes Helvetica counters look oversize and clumsily attached to their verticals. Interstate (the face for road signs in the U.S. and closest in appearance to Transport) looks self-consciously mannered with its diagonally sliced terminals and tall x-height. The German Din, beside Transport, looks like the result of a dogmatic adherence to a system, ugly and compromised by its predetermined mechanical structure. The design of Transport has captured within it the history of Britain's own diffident courtship of modernism. It reflects how designers in postwar Britain received modernism with a healthy measure of doubt and suspicion, but also diehard conservatism. •• Nevertheless, today in Britain many graphic designers are fascinated by modernism—well, at least by the glittering sheen of functionalism, now that the ideology has been stripped away over the years. Today, functionalism seems merely the adaptation of form to create the *appearance* of purpose as if in compensation for the fact that so much of the information that is thrown at us has no urgent need (unless you are a shareholder benefiting from a company chalking up its quota of media appearances every day on the back of it, that is). Despite that, various intriguing mutations of modernism crop up in my choice of ten graphic-design practices from around the world: personal (Michael Worthington), fictional (Mooren & van der Velden), neutral (Experimental Jetset), skeptical (2x4), and as if it hadn't happened yet (Field Study). All ten understand the difference between purpose and mere function as exemplified here by this choice of design classic.

Transport

by Kinneir Calvert

Nick Bell

There have been numerous works in each generation of graphic design that influence, inspire, and are the beacons of our profession. To choose one is a near-impossible assignment. Thinking back to the beginnings of my career, there were several works that made me pause, assess my own work and understand my shortcomings, and impelled me to more inventive solutions. My choice of real influence, however, comes from a designer I was fortunate to meet in the early 1970s, when the piece in question had already been done. Through this work I discovered that type wasn't simply the vehicle for writing the words. With thought, interpretation, and the craft of typography, words could come to life and impart emotion and meaning way beyond an assembly of letters. •• Herb Lubalin was a true master. For me his work throughout the 1960s and 1970s was particularly influential. I could have chosen many of his creations as my favorite piece, but his identity for a never published magazine stands out: it not only states the magazine's name, but graphically interprets the message and enhances its meaning. *Mother & Child* is a simple enough and universally understood concept. When I first saw it, the words leaped off the page. The inspired use of the ampersand as an implied fetus form inserted into the letter *o* spoke fondly and dramatically about the closeness of the relationship. The significance of this work is profound. •• In the computer age, when the convenience of technology so often overrides the culture of the typographer's craft, this work serves as a timely reminder that our profession is largely about communication and the designer's obligation to deliver the message in a far more potent way. I also love the work for its simplicity and clarity of message. In stark contrast to the more prevalent overlaid images being generated by many of today's practicing designers, this work delivers instantly. •• It was always meant to be. Its ability to communicate across cultures and language barriers justifies its position as an outstanding global work and demands inclusion as one of the best works of any generation. The only hesitation in regard to its selection was the fact that the magazine was never really produced. I have often commented and lamented that the graphic-design profession is all too ready to dispense awards to works that are not, in a sense, real projects. The award shows are full of them. A lot of self-congratulations for what are essentially our own projects. Despite not being published, this work has generated numerous awards and been included in the permanent collection of the Museum of Modern Art. •• After struggling to write these inadequate words, ultimately I think the work has to speak for itself. Like all great design, it really doesn't need explanation or justification. It's quite simply "great."

Mother & Child

by Herb Lubalin

Ken Cato

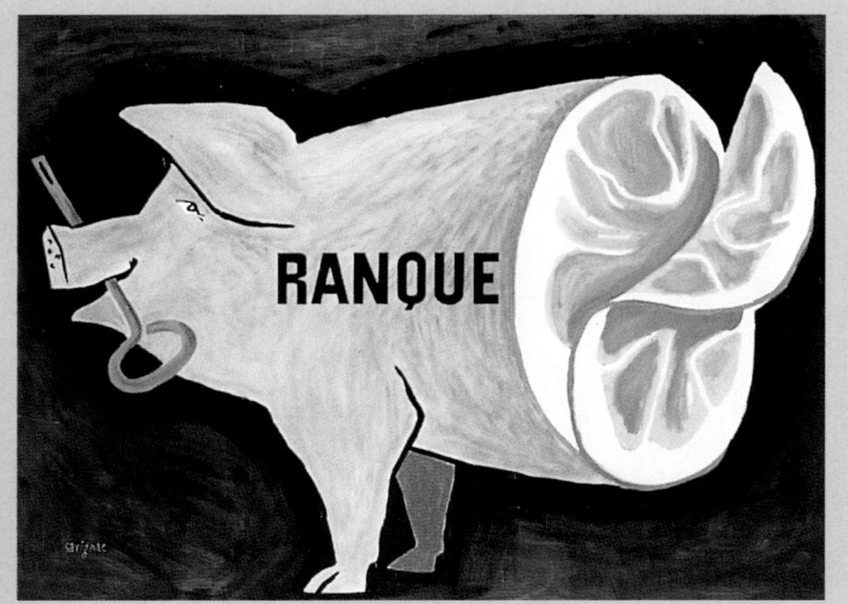

In the 1950s posters and advertisements of superb quality created by American and European designers were introduced to Japan through design and trade magazines and shocked and stimulated the Japanese design field. During this era, organizations such as the Tokyo Art Directors Club and the Foundation of Advertisement and Arts were established, and numerous design magazines were launched. It was a trying period for me, as I, a student, was attempting to express humor in designs, although the prevailing philosophy was to emphasize beauty. • • It is then that I came across an article on an exhibition of illustrations for advertising posters by Bernard Villemot and Raymond Savignac held in Paris in 1949. It was quite a shock to me. Most shocking was Savignac's powerfully humorous poster titled Cochon, in which the belly of a hog is sliced into ham. The hog wears an incredibly humorous expression. I told myself that the creative spirit behind this work was the very one I should pursue. • • "A design should be as free and interesting as this work": This belief has been the backbone of my creative activities for the past fifty years.

Cochon

by Raymond Savignac

Shigeo Fukuda

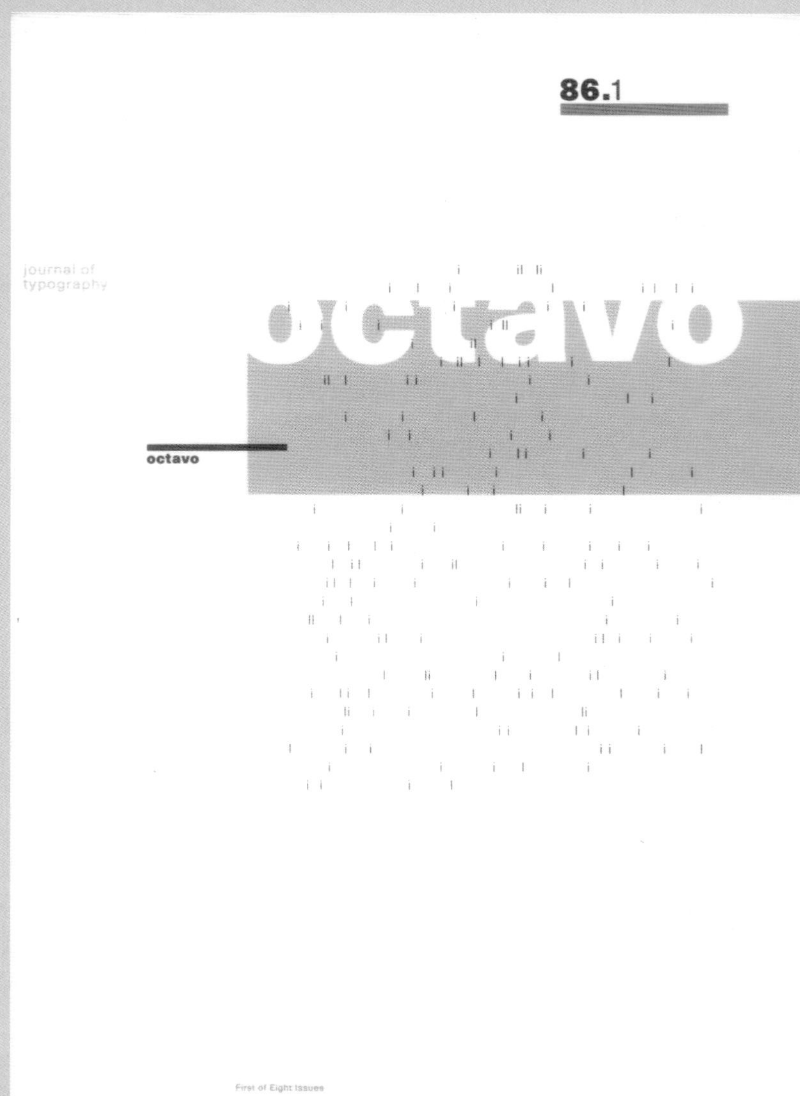

86.1
journal of
typography
octavo
octavo
First of Eight Issues

When the first issue of *Octavo* was published in 1986, it was way ahead of its time. *The Face* magazine was seen more as the epitome of 1980s editorial design, but for me, everything changed when *Octavo* appeared. If Neville Brody's graphic language for *The Face* reflected the loud, brash, futuristic elements of the 1980s, then *Octavo* provided the perfect antidote. • • The standard of *Octavo*'s content was incredibly high: the first issue featured essays on Anthony Froshaug, Richard Long, groundbreaking computer-generated type by April Greiman, and a page of monograms belonging to twentieth-century artists and designers. The design, with its subtle visual poetry and attention to detail, reflected the exceptional quality of the content. • • *Octavo* was designed and published by Eight Five Zero (Simon Johnston, Mark Holt, Michael Burke, and Hamish Muir) as a "serious forum for the discussion of matters, both contemporary and historical, relating to typographic design." *Octavo*'s life span was limited to just eight issues, with a print run of three thousand per issue. Each issue retained the same format but differed in design according to its content. • • I first found *Octavo* in the library at the London College of Printing, and it really leaped off the shelf. Compared with it, the other publications looked tired and conventional. It presented an elegance and clarity lacking in 1980s editorial design that tended to be quite decorative, ostentatious even. *Octavo* went completely against that trend, referencing the ordered grids and visual vocabularies of European modernist design. The type was exclusively sans serif, while the color palette was restricted to black, gray, red, and white, an approach that gave the content an understated, authoritative tone. It recalled the work of designers such as Anthony Froshaug and made typographers such as Tschichold relevant again, breathing life into figures who had been consigned to the history books. • • Perhaps the most eye-opening spread from the first issue is the one featuring several quotations from leading typographers/designers such as Tschichold, Froshaug, Weingart, Bill, and Moholy-Nagy. The layout is rational yet animated, and the type is set in a variety of weights of Helvetica in black and gray (with notes in red) on a white ground that has been divided into sections, subtly defined by different varnishes. The use of sans serif typography and large, unbroken areas of white space was incredibly radical. • • *Octavo* was a breath of fresh air and still stands out as a true design classic.

Octavo Journal of Typography by Eight Five Zero

Fernando Gutiérrez

Political Street Flyers

anonymous

Graphic designers are filtering systems with hearts. •• They absorb unbelievable quantities of informational particles, sort through them, divide them up, put some in small piles, others in large piles, keep what they want, and dump large quantities back into the primordial soup. Graphic designers store things you and I don't think, don't see, don't hear, smell, and at times don't even feel. Good graphic designers are better people than you and me. Yes. •• More important, graphic design is a high-tech regulative force in today's industrialized world. Its visual channels build media empires and influence our way of thinking. Graphic design is an instrument that yields power. •• A profession that has such a diverse sphere of action, with fingers in so many pies, must assume a special ethical responsibility.

Werner Jeker

The author of my classic lived on another planet. Born in Philadelphia in 1928, he spent his life on both sides of the Atlantic but primarily in Paris. He was one of the all-around geniuses of the twentieth century, the conjurer of Dada, the protagonist of Surrealism. With boundless imagination, he was a master of ironic ambiguity in painting, collage, film, and poetry. Photography in particular owes him many of its decisive creative impulses: With the obsession of an alchemist he invented the Rayogramme, a self-named new form of expression—photography without a camera. • • He was also an excellent typographer and a highly talented poster designer, but I only discovered this in 1988 during the legendary Museum of Modern Art exhibition *The Modern Poster* in New York. His Keeps London Going poster from 1932 anticipates nearly all the design principles valid today, some of which I even temporarily believed I had invented myself! • • The unconventional use of the poster surface alone is astounding: It is cut on two sides, thereby pointing toward an "event space" outside the picture. The illustrations on the inside are also placed in a rather unexpected way, following the "principle of optical disappointment." The connection between illustration and meaning, between image and text, is unmistakable. The prefixed dash in the subhead prompts the viewer to complete the beginning of the sentence by free association, for example, "The Heavenly Underground —KEEPS LONDON GOING." • • The uncovering of a formal relationship between the logo of the London Underground and the representation of the planet Saturn is a stroke of genius. Both images presuppose motion. Their symbolic content opens the gates to a fantasy world that stimulates our imagination with both poetry and irony. The axes of these planet meet outside the format in eternity. • • Above all, however, the poster's minimalist use of "sign language" is extremely striking to the eye—even without the text. In this sense, it is a nonverbal poster, timeless in its virtue. Regardless, its designer remains immortal. • • Who was this six-letter man?

Keeps London Going

by Man Ray

Uwe Loesch

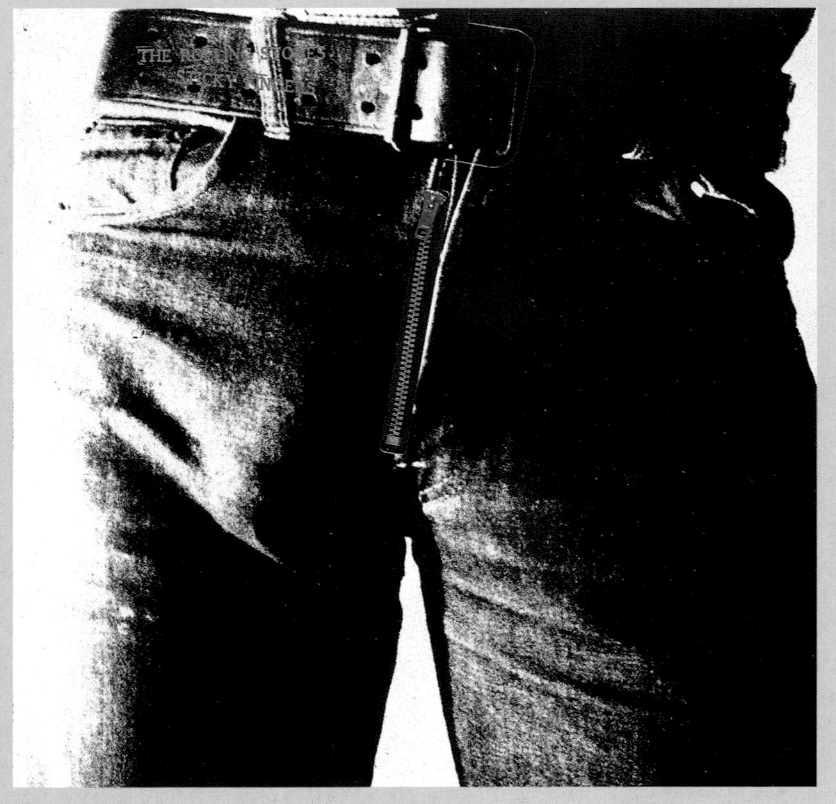

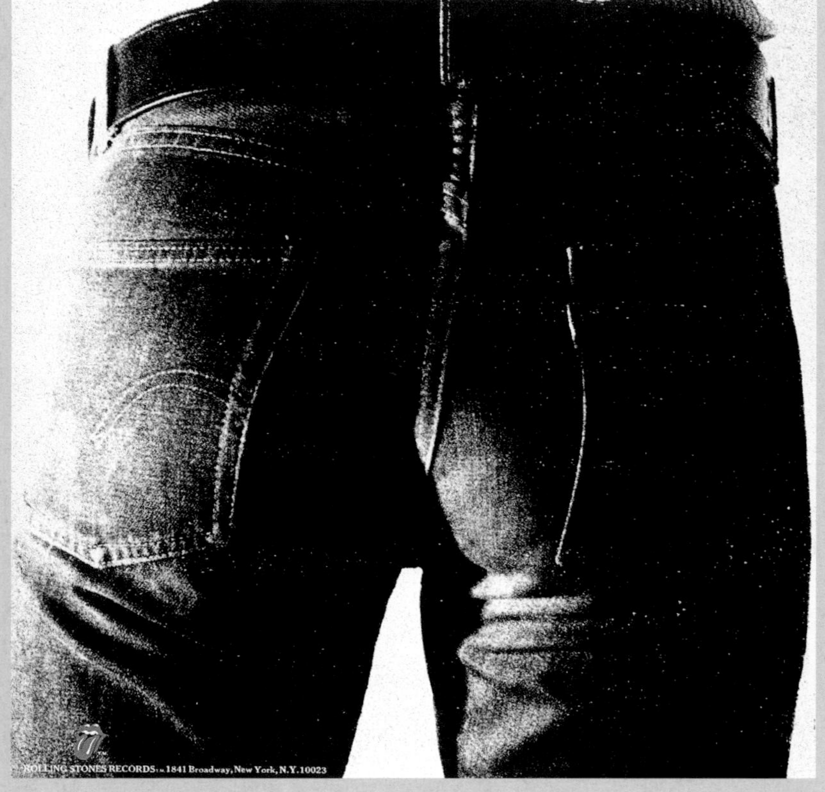

I picked the *Sticky Fingers* album design for the Rolling Stones by Andy Warhol and Craig Brown for many reasons: First, it uses the album-cover format to its best advantage, a twelve-inch sleeve with an innovative front, back, and inner sleeve—a site-specific design. Second, I admire the obvious trouble the designers, the band, and the record company were willing to go through to affix that actual zipper to the front cover. And it took a lot of determination to keep that zipper in regular production for decades, unlike the "limited edition" designs nowadays that are mostly produced as a promotional item for radio DJs and journalists.

The zipper wound up scratching other albums in people's record collections, a fact that likely was not part of the concept but worked—not only with the Stones' abrasive bad-boy image of the time, but also with the rough and grating sound of the music.

This memorable* cover left many questions open: Are these really Mick's jeans, is that actually his body underneath, and most important, will we see his privates when we open that zipper? (Sorry, no.) The fact that the music is thought of by many as the greatest album by the world's greatest rock 'n' roll band did not hurt either. Katherine McCoy's adage that design can never rise above its content is all the more true in the music industry: If the music is crap, the best cover won't make a difference.

Questions about content are now at the forefront of graphic design. While we were busy in the 1980s talking about layouts and lifestyles, lived through the 1990s discussing readability, layering, and money (!), there is now finally time to think about what we do and for whom we do it. This not only is evident in the enormous impact of the First Things First manifesto, which in 2000 urged designers to redirect their creative efforts away from promoting unfettered consumerism, but is also underlined by luminaries such as Peter Saville bemoaning our "monthly culture" and proclaiming the "crisis of the unnecessary."

The first sentence in Victor Papanek's influential book *Design for the Real World* is as true today as it was when he wrote it twenty years ago: "In persuading people to buy things they don't need, with money they don't have, in order to impress others that don't care, advertising design is probably the phoniest field in existence today."

There are people in this book who try to do something about that.

* Not everybody thought this design so memorable. Twenty-five years later my studio designed a CD cover for the Stones. In an initial meeting, Mick Jagger answered my question about his three favorite Stones album covers with "*Exile on Main Street*, *Some Girls*, and *Sticky Fingers*." Charlie Watts leaned over to Jagger and whispered, "What's ON *Sticky Fingers*?"

"Oh, you know, the one with the zipper, the one that Andy did."

Sticky Fingers

by Andy Warhol + Craig Brown

Stefan Sagmeister

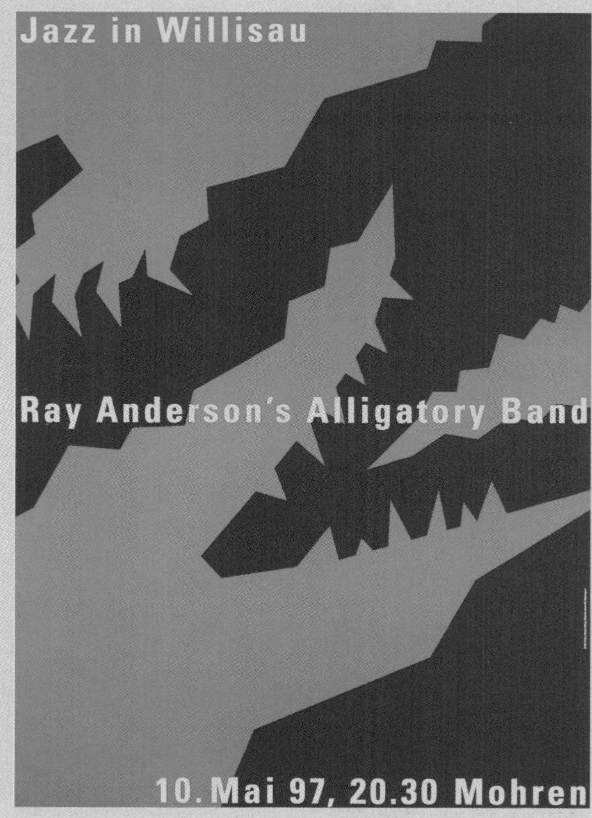

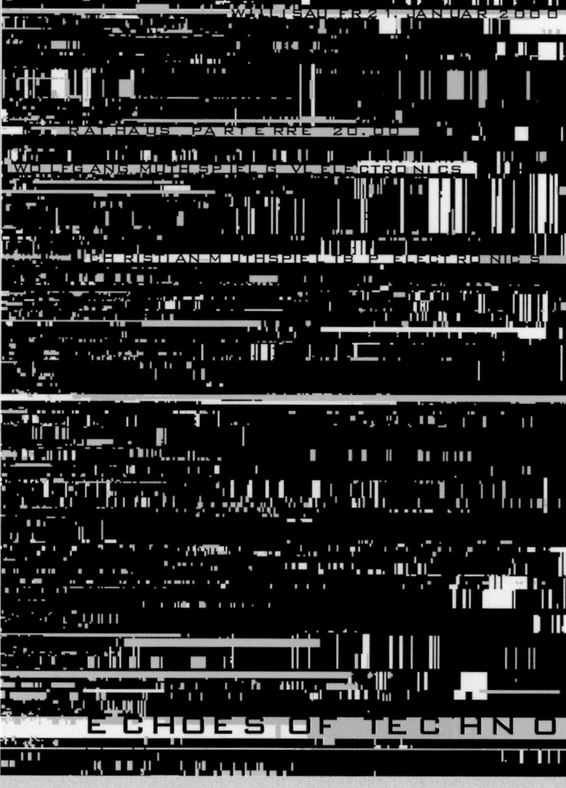

Why did I decide to present a series of jazz posters by the Swiss designer Niklaus Troxler as a classic work of international graphic design? There are three reasons. First, because Troxler works with the fundamental basis of twentieth-century graphic-design language. All his life, only this: the bare outlines, the essence, the distilled dots and lines that make up an expression, form a face. Troxler is in love with pure graphics, with points and lines, and he's unafraid to tell everyone about this love. Decades of visual exploration of expressive possibilities in elementary geometry; precise, functional decisions; subjectivity that accurately hits the target each time: For thirty-five continuous years, Troxler has not only organized the annual jazz festival in his native Willisau, he has also designed the posters for it. The works form a legitimate artistic dissertation, dedicated to the instruction of graphic design. Troxler's minimalism is never boring. What else, it would seem, could one do with a line? But his virtuoso inventiveness is overwhelming. It seems to know no limits. Second, because Troxler, remaining true to himself, reflects in this series, which encompasses many years, the changing times. Each new work is fresh and timely. Postmodern multilayers and articulation of meaning in the background, qualities that are seemingly the exact opposite of classical design composition, have both organically entered his works. During his first visit to Moscow in 1998, I managed to interview him. "How is this possible?" I asked, about this fusion of modernism and postmodernism. "I don't know," answered the maestro. "I rely more on spontaneity than logic." Third, and this is the most important reason, I next asked Troxler about what he thought most important in design. "The heart." And then he added, "I only do that which my heart dictates. I never take on a project if my heart is not with it." Swiss precision? We know the watches. Swiss quality? Exactly, Swiss knives. Swiss dependability? Right, the banking. But Swiss tenderness of the heart...Never heard of anything like that before. But what else do Troxler's dazzling posters represent if not genuine cardiograms? Broken, flexible, pulsating lines. His posters are alive with open color and light, radiating energy and purity. Where does it come from, this lightness, this sincerity, this artistry, this absolute organity? Clearly, from a pure heart.

Jazz Festival Willisau by Niklaus Troxler

Serge Serov

Tarot cards arrived from India, from China, or from Spain, where they were introduced by the Arabs. They were imported by the Crusaders, or perhaps they were found in the only book that survived the dispersion of the Egyptian libraries, delivered to our day through the pythagoreans, the agnostics, and the alchemists. The origins of tarot cards are obscure, but what really matters is that the images they carry correspond with the symbols of the cosmogonies and the oldest antique mythologies of all humankind. Their roots lie deep in the timeless collective unconscious. Tarot cards attract me because they tell stories, which is what communication is all about. One tarot figure intrigues me particularly and guided me in my selection of ten designers for this book. That figure is the Fool. I curiously detect that this character personifies the necessary essentials that will influence the creativity and graphic design of the future. The Fool I'm presenting belongs to the set conceived by Arthur Edward Waite, drawn by Pamela Coleman Smith, and published for the first time in London in 1910 by Rider & Co. This set is so open and direct to our contemporary sensibility that it is one of the most popular today. The Fool is central. The Fool is all and none. He is the projector, the director, the screen, and the spectator. He is the beginning, the end, the alpha, and the omega. The Fool is the Salt Man of the Buddhist tradition who wanted to see what the ocean was made of. He dove into it and never emerged again. Contrary to the more conventional card sets that depict the Fool as ugly with a dog or cat or lynx tearing at his trousers and exposing his rump, Waite gives a positive interpretation to the madness of the Fool, expressing clearly his sublime duality of madman and enlightened sage. The Fool, with his one foot over a cliff, reminds me of a famous Zen story: A man walking along a path encountered a tiger. He started running, chased by the tiger. Reaching a cliff, he grasped the root of a wild vine and let himself hang over the edge. The tiger smelled him from above. The man looked down trembling. At the bottom of the drop another tiger was waiting to devour him. Only the vine was holding him. Two mice started nibbling the vine little by little. The man discovered next to him a magnificent strawberry. Clasping the vine with only one hand, with the other hand he picked the strawberry. How sweet it was! At the beginning of the game the Fool is the unconscious conscience, at the end he is the conscious unconsciousness. The controlled madness of Casteneda's Don Juan. The Fool stands on a cliff with one foot over. He is suspended, and he is not aware of it. He is watching the stars and is happy. His head is full of dreams. He is carrying four sacred symbols on his shoulders but does not even know that they are there, nor what they are. They are the jungle, the forest, the garden and the home. Hindu symbols for the four stages of research and truth. Behind him unreachable peaks. The Fool becomes searcher of truth, meditating in isolation from the world that considers him mad and idiotic. His only friend is a joyful little dog that runs alongside him, representing instinct and animal nature. His clothes are green. They recall the mysterious influences of springtime, related to purity, innocence, and the freshness of a new beginning, a new cycle and also play and irresponsibility (April Fools). I am a designer to be a Fool.

The Fool

from a deck of tarot cards

Omar Vulpinari

biographies

Majid Abbasi Born Tehran, Iran, 1965. Lives and works in Tehran **education** 1992–96 B.A., Graphic Design, Fine Arts Faculty of Tehran University **practice** 1998–present Web Site Assistant and Web Designer, Iranian Graphic Designers Society (IGDS) • •1989–present Art Director, Did Graphics Inc., Tehran • •2003 Professor of Graphic Design, Fine Arts Faculty, Tehran University • •2002 Member of editorial board of *Neshan* quarterly, Iranian graphic-design magazine • •1998 Assistant Professor of Basic Design, Fine Arts Faculty, Tehran University • •1986–89 Freelance graphic designer **selected projects** 2001 Art direction and design, *Graphic Design Iran 1*, Iranian Graphic Designers Society (IGDS), Tehran • •2000 Official Web site of Iranian Graphic Designers Society (IGDS), graphiciran.com, Iranian Graphic Designers Society (IGDS), Tehran • •1996 Identity and promotional campaign, Behrizan door-handle company, Isfahan, Iran • •1996 Campaign for Cheshmak facial tissue, Pars Crepe Company, Tehran • •1996 Identity campaign, Yazd Tire Company, Tehran • •1995 Identity and packaging design for Varian lubricants, Guilan Oil Refining Company, Tehran **selected bibliography** 2002 *Graphic Design Iran 1*, Iranian Graphic Designers Society, Tehran • •2002 *7th Biennial of Iranian Graphic Designers*, Iranian Graphic Designers Society, Tehran • •2002 "*Graphisme en Iran*," *Création Numérique* magazine, Paris • •2002 "*Réveil Iranien*," *Étapes Graphiques* magazine 87, Paris **selected exhibitions** 2002 18th International Poster Biennale Warsaw, Poster Museum Wilanow, Warsaw • •2002 20th International Biennale of Graphic Design Brno • •2002 *Un cri persan*, Echirolles Visual Communication Center, Echirolles, France • •2000 6th Biennial of Iranian Graphic Designers, Tehran Museum of Contemporary Art, Tehran **awards** 2000 Advertising and Packaging Design awards, 6th Biennial of Iranian Graphic Designers, Tehran **memberships** 1998 Iranian Graphic Designers Society (IGDS)

Reza Abedini Born Tehran, Iran, 1967. Lives and works in Tehran **education** 1987–92 B.A., Painting, Tehran Art University **practice** 1989–present Freelance graphic designer • •2003 Professor for Poster Design, Tehran University • •1998–2001 Professor of Printmaking (1998), Graphic Design (1999), and Poster Design (2000–2001), Faculty of Art and Architecture, Azad University • •1996–97 Professor of Graphic design & Visual Design, Fine Arts School, Tehran **selected projects** 2001 Poster for *Wisdom and Philosophy of Art*, Tehran Museum of Contemporary Art • •2000 Book design, *A Tale of Dwarfs and Linker*, Nai Publications, Tehran • •1999 Book design, Tehran University Press • •1999 Mowlana poster, Marc Bloch University, Strasbourg • •1993/1995 Posters for 11th & 13th Fajr International Film Festivals (FIFF), FIFF, Tehran **selected bibliography** 2002 "*Réveil Iranien*," *Étapes Graphiques* magazine 87, Paris • •2001 *AutoBioGraphic*, Rouzaneh Publications, Tehran **selected exhibitions** 2002 Essen Poster Museum, Germany • •2002 *Answer?* poster exhibition, Iranian Artists House, Tehran • •2002 20th International Biennale of Graphic Design Brno • •2002 Korea International Poster Competition, Seoul • •2002 *Un cri persan*, Echirolles Visual Communication Center, Echirolles, France **awards** 1999 Special Award for Creativity, Iranian Graphic Designers Society, Tehran • •1999 Poster Award, 6th Biennial of Iranian Graphic Designers, Tehran • •1993/1996 Honorary Diploma for best film poster, FIFF, Tehran • •1994 Crystal Simorq award for best film, FIFF, Tehran **memberships** 2001 Alliance Graphique Internationale (AGI) • •1997 Iranian Graphic Designers Society (IGDS)

Aficionado Born Buenos Aires, Argentina, 1977. Lives and works in London **education** 1997–2000 Graphic Design, Central Saint Martins College of Art and Design, London **practice** 2002–present Operating under the name Aficionado • •2000–present Lecturer, Graphic Design, Central Saint Martins College of Art and Design, London • •1998–2002 Partner, Praline, London • •2000–2001 Designer, Jannuzzi Smith, London • •2000 Intern, Omnific, London **selected projects** 2003–present *Graphic Magazine*, BIS Publishers, Amsterdam • •2003 Civilian™, self-published T-shirt, London • •2002 Interactive Surfaces, Harper Mackay Architects, London • •2001 *Chat and Business*, by Ikara Colt, Fantastic Plastic Records, London • •2001 *The Mobile Effect*, by Sadie Plant, Milk Projects / Motorola, London • •2000 Visions de futur, Channel N-4, Barcelona **selected bibliography** 2002 "Campos' guide to etiquette & modern manners," *Dot dot dot* magazine, Amsterdam • •2001–02 *Lab Magazine* 3 and 4, London • •2001 *Transmission 002—Utopia*, :phunk, Singapore **selected exhibitions** 2003 *Graficas Ocultas*, FAD, Barcelona • •2002 *Graphic Britain*, Magma Bookshop, London • •2002 *The Book Corner*, British Council, London / Milan • •1999 *Conversations*, Galeria Visions, Barcelona **awards** 2000 First Prize, Environmental Design, D&AD, United Kingdom **memberships** 2000–02 British Design & Art Direction (D&AD)

Kum Nam Baik Born Seoul, Korea, 1948. Lives and works in Seoul **education** 2000 Ph.D. course work, History of Korean Arts, Dong-Kuk University, Seoul • •1992 M.F.A., Advertising & Public Relations, Chung-Ang University, Seoul • •1981 M.F.A., Fine Arts, Kyung-Hee University, Seoul • •1974 M.F.A., Art , Hong-Ik University, Seoul • •1969 B.F.A., Art, Hong-Ik University, Seoul **practice** 1976–2003 Professor, College of Art, Sungkyunkwan University, Seoul • •2002 Member of Design Committee, Metropolitan City of Seoul • •2002 Chairman of Executive Committee, Korean International Poster Biennale • •1998–2002 Chairman of Design Committee, Korean Organizing Committee for 2002 FIFA World Cup, Korea **selected projects** 2002 Posters for Gahoe Museum Opening • •2002 Posters for Haein-Sa Museum Opening • •2001 Poster, Korean Contemporary Poster Exhibition • •2001 Poster, Seoul International Fax Art Exhibition **selected bibliography** 2002 *Impress Graphic Design Magazine*, Seoul • •2002 *Design Net* magazine, Seoul • •2001 *Travel & Culture* magazine, Seoul **selected exhibitions** 2002 Korea International Poster Biennale, Seoul • •2002 France International Poster Salon, Paris • •2001 Chaumont International Poster Exhibition, Chaumont • •2001 International Poster Biennale Warsaw, Poster Museum Wilanow, Warsaw **awards** 2002 Diploma of Excellence, 6th International Graphic Annual, Stockholm • •2001 The Most Innovative Artist Award, 5th International Graphic Annual, Stockholm **memberships** 2002–03 Member of Special Committee, Visual Information Design Association of Korea, Seoul • •2000–2003 Member of Advisory Committee, Korean Society for Experimentation in Contemporary Design, Seoul • •1976–2003 Invited artist and member of Jury and Executive Committee, Korean National Design Exhibition

André Baldinger Born Zurich, Switzerland, 1963. Lives and works in Paris and Lausanne **education** 1994 Postgraduate studies, Visual Communication (specialization typography and type design), Atelier National de Recherche Typographique, Paris •• 1992 Diploma in Typography, Kunstgewerbeschule Zürich **practice** 2001–present Guest Professor, Atélier Nationale de Recherche Typographique, Nancy •• 1995–present Independent graphic designer •• 1995–present Professor, Faculty of Visual Communication, Graphic Design and Typography, University of Art and Design, Lausanne •• 1990–1992 Freelance designer for graphic-design agencies such as Eclat, GGK, Aebi and ASGS/BBDO •• 1988–1990 First coworker of design agency Eclat **selected projects** 2001 Conception of an interactive typeface for Integral Ruedi Bauer, Paris •• 1996 Conception and realization of visual identity for winter Olympic candidature of Sion 2006, Switzerland •• 1997 Design and realization of two stamps for the Swiss Post •• 1995 Book design, Editions de la Bibliothèque Nationale de France •• 1995 Redesign and extension of corporate typeface for the Centre Georges Pompidou (with assistance of H.J. Hunziker), Paris •• 2000 Lettering and mural, Librairie Pacifique, Geneva **bibliography** 2002 *Étapes Graphiques* 76, Paris •• 2001 *Type Directors Club Annual 2001*, Nippon Books, Tokyo •• 2001 *Swiss Typographic Monthly*, Zurich •• 1999 *1+2 color graphics*, P.I.E Books,Tokyo •• 1995 *Typographics*, Duncan Baird Publishers, London **selected exhibitions** 2002 *Toit du Monde*, Centre Culturel Suisse, Paris •• 2001 *Graphisme(s), 1997–2001*, Bibliothèque Nationale, Paris •• 2000 17th International Poster Biennale Warsaw, Poster Museum Wilanow •• 1996 Federal Design Competition, Museum Neuhaus, Biel, Switzerland **awards** 2001 Tokyo TDC Award (Type Directors Club) •• 1996 Winner of annual Swiss federal design competition •• 1993 Postgraduate student grant from French Ministry of Culture **memberships** 2002 Alliance Graphique Internationale (AGI)

Jop van Bennekom Born Scherpenzeel, Netherlands, 1970. Lives and works in Amsterdam **education** 1995–97, M.A. Design, Jan van Eyck Akademie, Maastricht •• 1990–94 Graphic Design, Hogeschool voor de kunsten, Arnhem **practice** 2001–present Editor/Designer, *BUTT* magazine, Amsterdam •• 2000–present Editor/Designer *Re-Magazine*, Amsterdam •• 2000–present Teacher, Graphic Design, Rietveld Academy, Amsterdam •• 1997–present Freelance graphic designer/art director •• 2000–2002 Art Director, fashion brand SO by Alexander van Slobbe, Amsterdam •• 1998–2000 Editor/Designer, *Forum* Magazine, Amsterdam •• 1998–99 Art Director, *Blvd. Magazine*, Amsterdam **selected projects** 2003 Exhibition catalogue, *Reality Machines—Mirroring The Everyday in Dutch Design*, NAi Publishers, Rotterdam •• 2001 Invitations for Droog Design, Amsterdam •• 2000 Invitations for fashion brand SO by Alexander van Slobbe, Amsterdam **selected bibliography** 2003 *Graphic Design for the 21st Century*, Taschen, London •• 2003 *Reality Machines—Mirroring the Everyday in Dutch Design*, exhibition catalogue, NAi Publishers, Rotterdam •• 2002 "Butt and Kutt, Who's got the crack?," *The Face*, April issue, London •• 2002 "Re-Magazine," *NRC Handelsblad* newspaper, April 15, Netherlands **selected exhibitions** 2003 *Magasin*, Marres Gallery, Maastricht •• 2003 *Reality Machines—Mirroring The Everyday in Dutch Design*, Netherlands Architecture Institute (NAi), Rotterdam •• 2002 *Commitment*, Las Palmas Gallery, Rotterdam •• 2001 *Play-Use*, Witte de With, Rotterdam **awards** 2003 Charlotte Köhler Prize, Prince Bernhard Foundation, Netherlands •• 2001 Rotterdam Design Prize, Netherlands •• 2000 Mercur Award, Art Director of the Year, Netherlands

Andrew Blauvelt Born West Point, New York, USA, 1964. Lives and works in Minneapolis, Minnesota **education** 1986–88 M.F.A., Design, Cranbrook Academy of Art, Bloomfield Hills, Michigan •• 1982–86 B.F.A., Visual Communications, Herron School of Art, Indianapolis, Indiana **practice** 1998–present Design Director, Walker Art Center, Minneapolis, Minnesota •• 1997–98 Department Head, Associate Professor of Graphic Design, School of Design, North Carolina State University •• 1996–97 Director of Graduate Studies, Graphic Design, School of Design, North Carolina State University •• 1995–97 Visiting Lecturer, Design Department, Jan van Eyck Akademie, Maastricht •• 1991–96 Assistant Professor of Graphic Design, School of Design, North Carolina State University •• 1995 Designer in Residence, 2D Design Department, Cranbrook Academy of Art, Bloomfield Hills, Michigan •• 1989–91 Assistant Professor, Visual Communications, Herron School of Art, Indianapolis, Indiana **selected projects** 2002–05 Media Communications and Wayfinding Program (with Lisa Strausfeld of Pentagram, New York), Walker Art Center, Minneapolis •• 2001–05 Experience Design Planning (with Steve Dietz and Sarah Schultz), Walker Art Center, Minneapolis •• 2003 *Strangely Familiar: Design and Everyday Life*, Walker Art Center, Minneapolis •• 2003 *LOT—EK: Mobile Dwelling Unit*, Distributed Art Publishers, New York •• 2002 Student Recruitment and Membership Materials, American Institute of Graphic Arts, New York •• 2001 *The Indexical Archive, 100 Show of Excellence*, American Center for Design, Chicago **selected bibliography** 2002 *Metropolis Magazine*, January, New York •• 2000 *Eye* magazine, Spring issue, London •• 1996 *Typography Now 2*, Booth-Clibborn Editions, London •• 1994 *Emigre Magazine* 31, Sacramento, California **selected exhibitions** 2002 *Design Now: Graphics*, Design Museum, London •• 2001 *100 Show of Excellence*, American Center for Design, Chicago •• 1997 *Mixing Messages: Graphic Design in Contemporary Culture*, Cooper-Hewitt National Design Museum, Smithsonian Institution, New York •• 1990 *Cranbrook Design: The New Discourse*, Cranbrook Art Museum, Bloomfield Hills, Michigan; IBM Gallery, New York; Axis Gallery, Tokyo **awards** 2001 Nominee, Chrysler Award for Design Innovation, Daimler-Chrysler Inc., USA •• 2001 Nominee, National Design Award, Cooper-Hewitt National Design Museum, USA •• 2000 Design Distinction Award, *I.D. Magazine*, USA •• 1995 Young Educator Award, Graphic Design Education Association, USA **memberships** 1996 American Institute of Graphic Arts (AIGA) •• 1993 American Center for Design

Blue Source Alice Cowling, born London, United Kingdom, 1971; Simon Earith, born Manchester, United Kingdom, 1973; Andrew Flack, born Bury St. Edmunds, 1971; Seb Marling, born Hull, United Kingdom, 1969; Pete Richardson, born Whitehaven, United Kingdom, 1978; and Mark Tappin, born Exeter, United Kingdom, 1973. Live and work in London **practice** 1995 Established Blue Source **education** 1997–2000 (Hons), Graphic Arts, Liverpool School of Art, Liverpool •• B.A. 1992–95 B.A. (Hons), Visual Communication Design, Middlesex University, London •• 1991–94 B.A. (Hons), Visual Communication Design, Middlesex University, London •• 1990–93 B.A.

(Hons), Fine Art, Bath Academy of Art, Bath selected projects 2002–03 Consultancy and Art Direction, Zakee Shariff Limited, London••2002–03 Brand consultancy including identity design, on-screen graphics, and marketing campaign for launch of music television channel The Amp, BSkyB, London••2002–03 Identity and typography design for Contemporary Art Gallery, Modern Art, London••2001–02 Music packaging and campaign art direction, Chemical Brothers, Virgin Records, London••2000–01 Design and art direction of print advertising campaign, Adidas, Amsterdam selected bibliography 2003 *This End Up—Original Approaches To Packaging Design*, London••2002 *Gas Book 08—Blue Source*, Tokyo••2002 *Soon—Brands Of Tomorrow*, London••2001 Blue Source Special Feature, *IDEA* magazine, Tokyo selected exhibitions 2001–03 *Great Expectations: New British Design Stories*, international touring exhibition••2002 *Remix: Contemporary Art and Pop Music*, Tate Liverpool••1999–2000 *Ultravision*, touring exhibition organized by the British Council••1996 *Jam: Style, Music and Media*, Barbican Art Gallery, London awards 2002 Best Design Team, Music Week: Creative and Design Awards, London••2002 Best Visual Effects and Graphic Design, BAFTA: Television Craft Awards, London••2000 Best Design Team, Music Week: Creative and Design Awards, London

Tom Bodkin Born New York, USA, 1953. Lives and works in New York education 1973 School of Visual Arts, New York••1973 Columbia University, New York••1971–73 Brown University, Providence, Rhode Island practice 2000–present Assistant Managing Editor and Design Director, *The New York Times*••1987–2000 Design Director, *The New York Times*••1980–87 Section Art Director, *The New York Times*••1978–80 Art Director, *Us Magazine*••1977–78 Designer, CBS Broadcast Group••1974–77 Creative Director, Avant-Garde Media selected exhibitions 2004 *New York Times Op-Ed Illustration*, Society of Illustrators, New York••2003 *Picturing the Times—Eastern European Illustrators at The New York Times*, School of Visual Arts, New York••1999 *New York Times Magazine*, Art Directors Club, New York awards 1988 Design Leadership Award, American Institute of Graphic Arts, New York••2002 Best of Show, Society of News Design, USA••2002 Special Achievement Award for Design in the Public Interest, American Institute of Graphic Arts, New York memberships 1990 Society of Publication Design••1986 Society of News Design••1985 American Institute of Graphic Arts (AIGA)

Günter Karl Bose Born Debstedt, Wesermünde, Germany, 1951. Lives and works in Berlin and Leipzig education 1970–76 German Studies, Art History, and Politics, University of Freiburg, Germany practice 2000–present lmn-studio, Berlin••1998–present Head of Typography Department, Institute for Book Design, Hochschule für Grafik und Buchkunst, Leipzig••1993–present Professor of Typography, Hochschule für Grafik und Buchkunst, Leipzig••1980–96 Publisher, Brinckmann & Bose, Berlin selected projects 1997–present Posters for Musica Viva, Bayerischer Rundfunk, Munich••1986–present Posters for Literaturhaus Berlin••2002 Posters for Kunststiftung Nordrhein-Westfalen, Düsseldorf••2001 Posters for the Deutsche Oper Berlin••1997–99 Posters for the Oper Leipzig selected bibliography 2002 "German Graphic Design," *IDEA* magazine 292, Tokyo••2001 *Design 271*, Seoul••1998 *Typography. Typographie. Typographie*, Könemann, Cologne••1997 *Lesemaschine. Buchgestaltung im 20. Jahrhundert*, Stiftung Buchkunst, Frankfurt selected exhibitions 2003 *Summit. The Best Posters at the End of the 20th Century*, PAN Kunstforum, Emmerich, Germany••2002 *Plakate aus Berlin*, Deutsches Plakat Museum, Essen••1997 *In Augenhöhe. Günter Karl Bose Graphik Design*, Hochschule für Grafik und Buchkunst, Leipzig awards 1999 Bronze Medal, The Most Beautiful Books in the World, Stiftung Buchkunst, Germany••1990–present The 100 Best Posters, German Design Associations AGD/BDG memberships 2000 Alliance Graphique Internationale (AGI)

Mayo Bucher Born Zurich, Switzerland, 1963. Lives and works in Zurich education 1981–86 Graphic Design, Hochschule für Kunst und Gestaltung Zürich practice 1990 Beginning of collaboration with artist/designer Seraina Feuerstein••1986–present Artist and graphic designer selected projects 2002 Exhibition and poetry performance, *Mayo Bucher: OPEN SIGN in progress*, Academy of Visual Arts, Leipzig••2002 Art and architecture project *BUCH & SCHRIFT* (with DGJ architects), Museum Deutsche Bücherei, Leipzig••2000 Facade-design concept for public building in Emmenbrücke, Switzerland••1998 CD design for Keith Jarrett at La Scala, ECM, Munich selected bibliography 2002 Mayo Bucher monograph *OPEN SIGN*, Lars Müller Publishers / ECM, Munich selected exhibitions 2002 *Mayo Bucher: OPEN SIGN in progress*, Academy of Visual Arts (HGB), Leipzig••2002 *Le nouveau salon des cent*, international touring exhibition••1999 *ECM: Selected Signs*, Gallery of the University of Brighton, UK awards 1994 Federal grant for applied arts, Switzerland••1991 Award of recognition, city and canton of Lucerne memberships 1995–2000 Executive Board, Schweizerischer Werkbund (SWB), Zurich••1998 Alliance Graphique Internationale (AGI)

Vladimir Chaika Born Kapustin Yar, Astrakhan Region, Russia, 1955. Lives and works in Moscow education 1977–82 Stroganov Higher School of Arts and Crafts, Moscow••1968–72 Art School 1, Moscow practice 1982–present Freelance graphic designer selected projects 1988–present Personal project "HE-story"••2002 Poster for Moscow International Festival of Visual Anthropology••1997 Logo for World Youth Games, Moscow••1991 Logo for International Cultural Collaboration Art-Ark, Moscow selected bibliography 1995 *Best Signs and Logo 1990–1995*, Linia Graphic Publishers, Moscow••1993 *Greatis* magazine 3, Moscow••1992 *New Russian Design*, Rizzoli, New York selected exhibitions 2000 International Biennale of Graphic Design Brno, Czech Republic ••2000 Golden Bee Moscow International Biennale of Graphic Design••2000 International Poster Festival, Chaumont, France••1998 *Troika: Three Dimensions of Russian Graphic Design*, DDD Gallery, Osaka••1997 Solo exhibition as part of IX Colorado International Invitational Poster Exhibition, Lincoln Centre, Fort Collins, USA selected awards 2000 Golden Bee Award, 5th Moscow International Biennale of Graphic Design••1999 Excellence Award, International Exhibition of Graphic Design Zgraf 8, Zagreb, Croatia••1998 Grand Prix, *Best Sign* national exhibition/competition, Moscow••1997 Second Prize, *Football. Culture of the Twentieth*

Century international poster exhibition/competition, Pantin, France memberships 1999 Alliance Graphique Internationale (AGI)••1998 Honorary member, International Biennale of Graphic Design Brno, Czech Republic••1993 International Academy of Graphic Design, Moscow

COMA Cornelia Blatter, born Aarau, Switzerland, 1960; Marcel Hermans, born Utrecht, Netherlands, 1961. Live and work in Amsterdam and New York education 1986–88 Painting, Yale University School of Art, New Haven, Connecticut (CB)••1986 (summer), Multimedia, Skowhegan School of Painting and Sculpture, Skowhegan, Maine (CB)••1985–90 Graphic Design, Rietveld Academie, School of Art and Design, Amsterdam (MH)••1984–86 Multimedia, School of the Museum of Fine Arts, Boston, Massachusetts (CB)••1980–84 Printing Techniques, Grafische MTS, Amsterdam (MH)••1976–81 Sculpture and Education, Hochschule für Gestaltung und Kunst, Zurich (CB) practice 2002 Guest Lecturers, Minneapolis College of Art and Design, Minneapolis, Minnesota••2000 Guest Lecturers, International Center of Photography, New York••1997 Guest Lecturer, Rhode Island College, Providence (CB)••1996–present Cofounders of COMA interdisciplinary art & design studio••1996 Lecturer, Hoge School voor de Kunsten, Utrecht (MH)••1995 Guest Lecturer, Merz Akademie, Stuttgart, Germany (CB)••1993–95 Guest Lecturer, Merz Akademie, Stuttgart, Germany (MH)••1990–95 Adjunct Lecturer, State University of New York, Purchase (CB)••1989–91 Visiting Assistant Professor, Pratt Institute, New York (CB)••1988–96 Practicing artist (CB)••1986–89 Head Designer, Studio Anthon Beeke, Amsterdam (MH) selected projects 2003 Art Direction, *FRAME* Magazine, Amsterdam••2003 Book design, *Hella Jongerius*, by Louise Schouwenburg, Phaidon Press, London and New York••2003 Exhibition design, *John M. Johansen*, STROOM, The Hague's center for visual arts••2002 Book design, *Architectural Laboratories: Greg Lynn & Hani Rashid*, NAi Publishers, Rotterdam••2002 Book design, *The Hugo Boss Prize 2002*, Solomon R. Guggenheim Museum, New York selected bibliography 2001 "*Coma een open retour Zeeburg-Brooklyn*," *ITEMS*, Amsterdam ••2000 "*Topvorm-De Nuchtere Vorm van COMA*," Het Parool, Amsterdam••2000 "Speed Reading," *I.D. Magazine*, New York••1998 *Visible*, Graphische Sammlung der Schweizerischen Landesbibliothek, Bundesamt für Kultur, Bern selected exhibitions 2002 *Roadshow: Dutch Graphic Design*, American Institute of Graphic Arts, New York••2001 *Designprijs Rotterdam 2001*, Museum Boijmans Van Beuningen, Rotterdam••2000 *10 Letters from Furka Pass*, Sandra Gering Gallery, New York••2001 *The Best Dutch Book Design*, Stedelijk Museum, Amsterdam awards 2002 *AIGA 50 Books/50 Covers*, American Institute of Graphic Arts, New York••2001 Nominated for Rotterdam Design Prize, Rotterdam ••2000 *I.D. Magazine* Design Review winner, New York••2001 *The Best Dutch Book Designs of 2000*, Stichting De Best Verzorgde Boeken, Amsterdam memberships 1998 American Institute of Graphic Arts (AIGA)

Das Haus Rüegger + Albisetti Judith Rüegger, born Solothurn, Switzerland, 1973; Anna Albisetti, born Bern, Switzerland, 1969. Live and work Bern and Zurich education 1991–95 Graphic design, Kantonale Schule für Gestaltung, Biel (JR+AA) practice 1998–present Self-employed graphic designers selected projects 2003 Glückwunsch poster, Schlachthaus Theater Bern••2002 Poster series for Ja'salâm! festival, Pro Helvetia, Bern••2001–02 Poster series "*aus 1 mach 3*," Schlachthaus Theater Bern••2000–2001 Poster series "*Gruppenbild*," Schlachthaus Theater Bern••1998–99 Poster series "*Unikate*," Schlachthaus Theater Bern••1998–99 Poster series "*Kürzest-Dialoge*," Schlachthaus Theater Bern selected bibliography 2000 *Benzin–Young Swiss Graphic Design*, Lars Müller Publishers, Baden, Switzerland•• 1999 *Trigger*, Die Gestalten Verlag, Berlin

De Designpolitie Richard van der Laken, born Amstelveen, Netherlands, 1970; Pepijn Zurburg, born Amsterdam, Netherlands, 1971; Alexander Clay, born Lørenskog, Norway, 1974; Karin van den Brandt, born Blerick, Netherlands, 1975; Roel Stavorinus, born Zwolle, Netherlands, 1971; Gaelle Rivet, born Laval, France, 1972. Live and work in Amsterdam education 1997–2000 Dance education, Arnhem school of the Arts, Arnhem (GR)••1996–97 Postgraduate studies, Graphic Design, Sandberg Institute, Amsterdam (RvdL+PZ)••1996–2000 Graphic Design, Arnhem school of the Arts, Arnhem (KvdB+AC)••1995–96 Communication Management, Utrecht University, Utrecht (RS)••1992–96 Commercial and Presentation Techniques, St. Lucas, Boxtel (KvdB)••1993–95 Graphic Design School, Oslo (AC)••1991–95 Design and Communication, Ichthus College, Rotterdam (RS)••1989–95 Graphic Design, Utrecht School of the Arts, Utrecht (RvdL+PZ) practice 2002–present Project Manager, De Designpolitie (RS)••2001–present Graphic Designer, De Designpolitie (KvdB)••2001–present Office Manager, De Designpolitie (GR)••2000–present Graphic Designer, De Designpolitie (AC)•• 1995–present Founder and Graphic Designer, De Designpolitie (RvdL+PZ)••1999–2002 Project Manager, Funcke designers (RS) ••1998–99 Communication Adviser, Informatiebeheergroep, Netherlands (RS) ••1998–99 Teacher, Graphic Design, Academy St. Joost, Breda (RvdL)••1997–98 Teacher, Graphic Design, Utrecht School of the Arts (RvdL)••1996–98 Marketing Coordinator, Wolters-Noordhoff publishers (RS)••1996–97 Teacher, Graphic Design, Arnhem school of the Arts (RvdL) selected projects 2002–present Illustrations for *De Volkskrant* newspaper, Amsterdam••2001 Social annual report, KPN Telecom, The Hague••2000 Corporate identity, Novib, Oxfam Netherlands, The Hague••1995–2000 Art direction, *MillenniuM* magazine, Amsterdam••1998 Annual report, Raad van Cultuur, The Hague••1997–98 Art direction, *Blvd. Magazine*, Amsterdam selected bibliography 2001 *New Design: Amsterdam*, Rockport, Gloucester, Massachusetts••2001 *Apples & Oranges: Best Dutch Graphic Design*, BIS Publishers, Amsterdam selected exhibitions 2000 18th International Biennale of Graphic Design Brno, Czech Republic••1999 *Mooi maar Goed*, Stedelijk Museum, Amsterdam••1998 *Do Normal*, San Francisco Museum of Modern Art awards 2003 Nominations, Dutch Art Directors Club, Netherlands ••1999 Selection, Rotterdam Design Prize, Rotterdam••1998 Dutch Art Directors Club Award, Netherlands••1997 Selection, Best Book Design, Netherlands memberships 1995–present Dutch Designers Association (BNO)••1998–2002 Art Directors Club Netherlands (ADCN)

Delaware Masato Samata, born Gunma, Japan, 1959; Aya Honda, born Kanagawa, Japan, 1969; Morihiro Tajiri, born Kumamoto, Japan, 1970; Yoshiki Watanabe, born Tokyo, Japan, 1972. Live and work in Tokyo education Self-educated practice 1993–present Graphic-design and music group Delaware selected projects 2003 Graphic design and music for Pitti Uomo Trade Fair, Florence••2001 Music for e-Kawasemi television commercial, Tokyo••1998 Audio-visual live show for Mac Expo '98, Japan••1996 Music and motion graphics for Iwata-ya television commercial, Fukuoka, Japan selected bibliography 2002 *The Face* magazine 68, London••2001 Fourth CD, *Artoon*••2001 *IDEA* magazine 285, Tokyo••1999 Third CD, *with the delaware*••1997 Second CD and CD-ROM, *Surfin' USSR*••1996 First CD, *Private CD* selected exhibitions 2002 *JaPan Graphics*, FAD Convent Dels Angeles, Barcelona ••2002 *Motion Graphic Art*, Wild Cat Gallery, London••2001 *Mobile Gallery*, Japanese mobile phone web••2001 *Artoon at P.S. 1*, P.S. 1 Contemporary Art Center, New York

Chris Dixon Born Regina, Saskatchewan, Canada, 1968. Lives and works in New York education 1993–96 Communication Design, Emily Carr Institute, Vancouver, Canada••1990–93 Psychology, University of Saskatchewan, Canada practice 2002–present Art Director, Studio Plural, New York••2002–03 Design faculty, New York University••2002–03 Design faculty, Parsons School of Design, New York••2000–2002 Editorial Designer, *New York Times Magazine*••1996–2000 Art Director, *Adbusters* magazine selected projects 2002 Book cover, *Women at The Intersection*, Rutgers University, New York••2002 In-house magazine *rd*, RD/Microsoft, Seattle••2002 *Financial Times* special anniversary issue, Financial Times, U.S. Edition, New York••2000 Poster to launch First Things First 2000 manifesto, The Media Foundation, Vancouver selected bibliography 2002 *Eye* magazine, London••2001 *Azure* magazine, Toronto••2001 *Digital Lab—Editorial Design*, Rotovision, London••2001 *Issues: New Magazine Design*, Ginko Press, California••1999 *Emigre Magazine* 49, Sacramento, California selected exhibitions 2001 *Young Guns New York*, Art Directors Club, New York••2000 Society of Publication Design Exhibit, Parsons School of Design, New York awards 2000 Gold medal, Magazine of the Year, National Magazine Awards, Canada••2000 Selected, 100 Show Award, American Center for Design, Chicago••2000 Gold Medal, Judges Choice Award, Graphex: Society of Graphic Designers of Canada••1999 Magazine of the Year finalist, Society of Publication Design, USA memberships 2002 Board member, American Institute of Graphic Arts (AIGA), New York

Daniel Eatock/Foundation 33 Born Manchester, United Kingdom, 1975. Lives and works in London education 1996–98 M.A., Graphic Design, Royal College of Art, London••1993–96 B.A., Communication Design, Ravensbourne College of Design and Communication, London practice 2001–present Lecturer, Graphic Design, University of Brighton••2000–present Cofounder and Graphic-Design Director, Foundation 33 (Foundation 33 is Sam Solhaug, Architectural-Design Director, Hanna Werning, Graphic Designer, Sara de Bondt, Graphic Designer)••1998–99 Graphic Design Intern, Walker Art Center, Minneapolis selected projects 2001–03 Self-commissioned Sun Light photographs/postcards••2002 *Big Brother* identity, Channel 4, London••2001 MOBO 96 sheet billboard, Channel 4, London••2002 The world's largest signed and numbered limited edition artwork, Channel 4, London••2000 Self-commissioned Untitled Beatles poster selected bibliography 2003 *The New Handmade Graphics, Beyond Digital Design*, Rotovision, London••2002 *GB: Graphic Britain*, Laurence King Publishing, London••2002 *No Brief, Graphic Designers' Personal Projects*, Rotovision, London••2001 *Specials*, Booth-Clibborn Editions, London selected exhibitions 2002 *Infotecture*, Artist Space, New York••2001 *Design Now: London*, Design Museum, London••2001 *16.8/10.2/8.4*, Pentagram Gallery, London••1998 *Creative Review Creative Futures*, Kings Cross Gallery, London awards 2000 *I.D. Magazine* Award, Top Forty Designers Under Thirty••1998–1999 100 Show Award, American Center for Design, Chicago••1997 Energy Efficiency Award, first prize, Royal College of Art, London

Eboy Kai Vermehr, born Caracas, Venezuela, 1964; Steffen Sauerteig, born Prenzlau, Germany, 1967; Peter Stemmler, born Berlin, Gemany, 1966; Svend Smital, born Berlin, Germany, 1967. Live and work in Berlin and New York education Kunsthochschule Berlin (PS)••Hochschule der Künste Berlin (SS+SS) practice 1995–present Freelance designers••1998 Founded eboy selected projects 2002 Book *eboy hello*, by eboy, Laurence King Publishing, London selected bibliography 2000 *72 dpi*, Die Gestalten Verlag, Berlin••2000 *The Face* magazine 36, London••1999 *Reload*, Laurence King Publishing, London••1999 *Trigger*, Die Gestalten Verlag, Berlin••1998 *IMS 100*, Auras, Tokyo selected exhibitions 2002 *eboy hello*, Magma Books, London••2002 *I love to meet you*, Palazzo Fortuny, Venice

Dave Eggers Born Boston, Massachusetts, USA, 1970. Lives and works in San Francisco education 1988–92, Journalism/Painting, University of Illinois, Champaign-Urbana practice 2003–present Art Director, *The Believer* magazine, Brooklin, Maine••2002–present Founder/Teacher, 826 Valencia, San Francisco••1998–present Founder/Editor/Designer, *McSweeney's*, New York and San Francisco••1998 Editor at Large, *Esquire* magazine, New York••1993–1997 Founder/Designer, Gigantic Design, San Francisco••1994–1997 Founder/Editor/Designer, *Might* magazine, San Francisco selected projects 2002 Vinyl design, *The Only Blip Hop Record You Will Ever Need* vol. 1, Luka Bop, USA••2001 Book design, *The New Sins*, by David Byrne, McSweeney's Publishing, San Francisco••1998–present Design/editorial, *McSweeney's* literary journal, New York and San Francisco selected bibliography 2002 Editor, *The Best American Nonrequired Reading*, Houghton-Mifflin, Boston••2002 *You Shall Know Our Velocity*, by Dave Eggers, McSweeney's Books, San Francisco••2000 *A Heartbreaking Work of Staggering Genius*, by Dave Eggers, Simon & Schuster, New York••1998 Editor, *Shiny Adidas Tracksuits and the Death of Camp*, Penguin/Putnam, New York selected exhibitions 2003 National Design Triennial, Smithsonian Cooper-Hewitt National Design Museum, New York awards 2002 50 Books Award/365 Illustration Award, American Institute of Graphic Arts••2002 *Print* Design Regional Award, USA

Jonathan Ellery Born Welwyn Garden City, United Kingdom, 1964. Lives and works in London education 1982–84 Falmouth College of Arts & Design••1986–89 Bournemouth and Poole College of Art & Design practice

1998–present Founding Partner, Browns, London • • 1989–98 Sampson Tyrrell, Addison, Design House, London **selected projects** 1999 Pure Football. Pure Hope. poster campaign, FIFA/UNICEF • • 2000 European Clichés poster campaign, Trebruk, United Kingdom • • 2001 Coney Island poster campaign, Trebruk, United Kingdom • • 2002 Crash Happy exhibition poster, Grant Scott, London **selected bibliography** 2003 *Browns: A Walk Through Books*, GCE Publishing, London • • 1999–2002 D&AD Annuals • • 2002 *No Brief: Graphic Designers Personal Projects*, RotoVision, London • • 2002 *Branding: From Brief to Finish Solution*, RotoVision, London • • 2002 *100 Graphics International*, Graphics International, London • • 2001 *Graphis Design Annual*, *Graphis* magazine, New York **awards** 2002 Best Annual Report, Investor Relations Awards, London • • 2002 Silver Nomination: Poster Campaign, D&AD, London • • 2002 Graphic Design: Posters, Crafts, and Corporate Identity, D&AD, London • • 2002 Merit Award, Art Directors Club, New York • • 2000 Best Business to Business Advertising Campaign, Marketing Week Advertising Excellence Awards, United Kingdom **memberships** 1995–present D&AD, London • • 1998–2000 The Typographic Circle, London

Experimental Jetset

Erwin Brinkers, born Rotterdam, Netherlands, 1973; Danny van den Dungen, born Rotterdam, Netherlands, 1971; Marieke Stolk, born Amsterdam, Netherlands, 1967. Live and work in Amsterdam **education** 1993–97 Graphic design, Gerrit Rietveld Academy, Amsterdam **practice** 1997–present Experimental Jetset • • 2000–present Teachers, Graphic Design, Gerrit Rietveld Academy • • 2001–03 Lectures/workshops at Fabrica, Italy, CCS Detroit Art Academy, University of Western Michigan, and GraficEurope, Barcelona **selected projects** 2002 Catalogue and exhibition design, *Display*, Stedelijk Museum, Amsterdam • • 2002 Christmas stamps "DecemberThoughts," Royal Dutch Mail (PTT/TPG), The Hague • • 2001 Guest-editing and graphic design, "Lost Formats Preservation Society," *Emigre Magazine* 57, Sacramento • • 2000 Catalogue for group exhibition *Elysian Fields*, Centre Georges Pompidou/Purple Institute, Paris • • 2000 Set of three plastic wristbands "Been There/Done That," Purple Institute, Paris • • 1999 Stamps "I Love Stamps/Stamps Love Me," Royal Dutch Mail (PTT/TPG), The Hague **selected exhibitions** 2002 Solo exhibition *Kelly 1:1*, Casco Gallery, Utrecht • • 1999 Installation *Modular Meaning*, group exhibition *AEX*, Stedelijk Museum, Amsterdam • • 1999 *31 Flavours of Doom*, solo exhibition, De Gele Rijder, Arnhem • • 1998 Installation *Black Metal Machine*, group exhibition *SuperNova*, Bureau Amsterdam **selected bibliography** 2002 *What is Graphic Design?*, Rotovision, London • • 2002 *No Brief, Graphic Designers' Personal Projects*, RotoVision, London • • 2001 *IDEA* magazine 287, Tokyo • • 2000 *Eye* magazine 38, London

Sara Fanelli

Born Florence, Italy, 1969. Lives and works in London **education** 1993–95 M.A., Illustration, Royal College of Art, London • • 1990–93 B.A. (Hons), Graphic Design, Camberwell College of Arts, London • • 1989–90 Foundation Course Diploma, City and Guilds of London Art School, London **practice** 1993–present Independent graphic designer, writer, and illustrator **selected projects** 2002–03 Invitations for Ron Arad at the Salone del Mobile, Milan • • 2002 Design, writing, and illustrations, *First Flight*, Jonathan Cape, London • • 2001–02 Invitations for Alessi's London showroom and Issey Miyake's London A-POC presentation • • 2001 Images for "Family and Events" brochure, Tate Modern and Tate Britain, London **selected exhibitions** 2001–03 *A Baker's Dozen*, touring exhibition • • 2002 *The Magic Pencil*, British Library, London • • 2000 *Peter Blake—About Collage*, Tate Liverpool • • 1995 *Hidden Treasures—An Adventure in Contemporary, Innovative, Children's Book Illustration*, Djangoli Art Gallery, Nottingham **selected bibliography** 2002 *The Graphics Book*, Mastercraft Series, D&AD, London • • 2002 *Originals—Designers Who Work Beyond the Brief*, RotoVision, London • • 2001 *Print* magazine, March/April issue, New York **awards** 2001/2003 Honorable Mention, Bologna Ragazzi, Italy • • 2000 National Art Library Illustration Award, Victoria & Albert Museum, London • • 2000 Silver Award, D&AD, London • • 1999 Kall-Kwik Award, Images 24, Association of Illustrators, London **memberships** 2001 Alliance Graphique Nationale (AGI)

Isidro Ferrer

Born Madrid, Spain, 1963. Lives and works in Huesca, Spain **education** 1986 Mime, Mouvement Théatre, École Jacques Lecoq, Paris • • 1982–85 Drama, Escuela de Teatro, Zaragoza **practice** 1996 Establishment of own studio in Huesca • • 1995 Conceived storyboards for animation production company Tijuana Films, Valencia • • 1990–95 Part of the studio Camaleón, Zaragoza • • 1989 One-year internship in Peret's graphic-design studio, Barcelona **selected projects** 2000 Television advertisement for Volkswagen's New Beetle, Spain • • 1999 Cover designs for publishers Alfaguara y Santillana • • 1999 Designs for television station Canal Plus, Paris • • 1997 Illustrations for daily newspaper *El País*, Madrid **selected bibliography** 2002 *El sentido de lo dicho se consume en los silencios*, Mores Ediciones, Spain • • 2001 *Caprichos*, Bedeteca de Lisboa, Portugal • • 1999 *La voz ajena*, Diputación Provincial de Huesca, Spain • • 1999 *Exils*, AMOK editions, France • • 1994 *Te leo*, Ediciones Ambiguas, Spain **selected exhibitions** 2002 *Ojo por hoja*, Museo de Arquitectura, Universidad Nacional, Bogotá • • 2001 *La palabra dibujada*, Centro de Cultura Antiguo Instituto, Gijón, Spain • • 2001 *Impresiones*, Insula Galérie, Paris • • 2000 *Isidro Ferrer*, Armazém 7, Lisbon • • 2000 *Exils*, Les Index, Rouen, France • • 1995 Biennale Mladih, Mali Salon, Rijeka, Croatia **awards** 2002 National Design Prize, Spain • • 2001 Award, 12th International Poster Festival Chaumont, France • • 2000 PROMAX Gold Award for animation, Canada • • 1996 Gold Award for Illustration, Spain **memberships** 2000 Alliance Graphique Internationale (AGI)

Laurent Fétis

Born Orsay, France, 1970. Lives and works in Paris **education** 1994–99 Ecole Nationale Supérieure des Arts Décoratifs • • 1991–93 Ecole d'Architecture de Versailles **practice** 1999–present Independent graphic designer • • 2000–present Guest Lecturer, Reims Superior Design School, France **selected projects** 2002 Poster for Beck's "Sea Change" tour, Geffen, USA • • 2002 CD packaging, *Rocker's Delight*, Quatermass, Belgium (With Elisabeth Arkhipoff) • • 2001 Book, *ABC+*, by Laurent Fétis, Die Gestalten Verlag, Germany • • 2001 "Anna Sui" insert for *Vogue Nippon* (with Elisabeth Arkhipoff) **selected bibliography** 2002 *ABC+*, by Laurent Fétis, Die Gestalten Verlag, Germany • • 2002 "Laurent Fetis," *IdN* 9, no. 1, Hong Kong • • 2001 *Specials*, Booth-Clibborn Editions, United Kingdom • • 2001 Centerfold in *Creative Review*, July issue, London **selected exhibitions** 2002 *13*, London

Underground, London••2001 *Signes, The New Generation of Graphic Design*, Centre Georges Pompidou, Paris••2001 *Idea about a Place*, Transmission Gallery, Glasgow••2000 Solo exhibition, Gallery Kreo, Paris

Field Study Roy Brooks, born Stanfield, North Carolina, USA, 1975; Matthew Peterson, born Cary, North Carolina, USA, 1975. Live and work in Chicago education 1994–98 Graphic Design, North Carolina State University School of Design, Raleigh, North Carolina (MP)••1993–97 Graphic Design, North Carolina State University School of Design, Raleigh, North Carolina (RB) practice 2002–present Field Study••2001–02 Freelance designer (MP)••1999–2002 Senior Designer, Pentagram, New York (RB)••1999–2000 Design Intern, Walker Art Center, Minneapolis, Minnesota (MP)••1998–99 Graphic Designer, Whitney Museum of American Art, New York (RB)••1998–99 Graphic Designer, x Design Group, Raleigh, North Carolina (MP) selected projects 2003 Corporate identity, Geotrack, Inc.••2003 CD design, *Lullaby for Sue*, by Clogs, Brassland Records••2003 Exhibition-catalogue design, *Speculative Chicago*, Gallery 400, University of Illinois at Chicago••2002 Website design for Vincent Whitehurst selected exhibitions 2003 *GraficEurope*, Barcelona memberships 2003 American Institute of Graphic Arts (AIGA)

Lizzie Finn Born London, United Kingdom, 1973. Lives and works in London education 1993–96 B.A. (Hons.), Graphic Design, Central Saint Martins College of Art and Design, London••1992–93 Foundation in Art & Design, Central Saint Martins College of Art and Design, London practice 1998–present Freelance graphic designer••2002–2003 Visiting Lecturer, Surrey Institute of Art & Design, Epsom ••2001–2002 Visiting Lecturer, Camberwell College of Art & Design, London ••1996–98 Junior Designer, Blue Source, London selected projects 1998–present Art direction, fabric repeat, embroidery, and T-shirt designs, SILAS, London••2003 Album-sleeve image for *Songbird*, single by Oasis, Big Brother Recordings, London••2002–03 Graphic design, "Eye Spy" fashion special (four issues), *Dazed & Confused* magazine, London••2002–03 Fashion illustration (four issues), British *Vogue*, London••2000 Promotional material, Hysteric Glamour UK, London••2000 Album-sleeve design, *Things to make and do*, by Moloko, The Echo Label, London selected bibliography 2002 *GB: Graphic Britain*, Laurence King Publishing, London••2001 *Specials*, Booth-Clibborn Editions, London••2001 *Annual*, Vision On, London••1998 *20th Century Type*, Laurence King Publishing, London selected exhibitions 2002 *I Love to Meet You*, Palazzo Fortuny, Venice••2001 *Annual*, Dazed & Confused Gallery, London•• 2000 *Product 250 "t-shirts,"* Artomatic Gallery, London••2000 Poster show, Gavin Brown's Enterprise, New York awards 2002 Creative Future for Illustration, Creative Review Awards, United Kingdom••2001 Nominated for Best Designer, CAD Music Week Awards, United Kingdom

Amy Franceschini Born Patterson, California, USA, 1970. Lives and works in San Francisco and Gent, Belgium education 2000–2002 Art, Stanford University, Palo Alto, California••1988–92 Art, San Francisco State University, San Francisco practice 2002–present Visiting Faculty, Stanford University Art Department, Palo Alto, California••1995–present Founder, Futurefarmers, San Francisco••1994–present Interaction designer, illustrator, and artist selected projects 2002 Stanford University Art Department Web site••2002 Poster for *Communication What?* exhibition, Venice••2002 Cell-phone graphics for MTV Japan selected bibliography 2002 *Harvest, Futurefarmers Anthology*, Futurefarmers/IdN Publication, San Francisco••2002 *Pictoplasma*, Die Gestalten Verlag, Berlin••2002 "Exlibris," *Page Magazine*, Berlin••2002 "3d Characters," *Eye Magazine*, London••2001 "Silicon Valley Issue," *National Geographic Magazine* selected exhibitions 2004 *Gaming Show*, Yerba Buena Center for the Arts, San Francisco••2003 National Design Triennial, Cooper-Hewitt, NationalDesign Museum, Smithsonian Institution, New York••2002 *Vasi Communicanti*, Palazzo Fortuny, Venice awards 2002 Net Excellence Award, Arts Electronica, Austria••2001 DNA Prize, Die Kulturinitiative von Videor Technical, Rödermark, Germany

Vince Frost Born Brighton, United Kingdom, 1964. Lives and works in London education 1985–87 Graphic Design, West Sussex College of Design, Worthing practice 1994–present Frost Design, London••1987–98 Design Assistant to Howard Brown, London••1993–94 Associate Partner, Pentagram Design, London••1989–93 Junior to Senior Designer, Pentagram Design, London selected projects 2003 Redesign of identity for Rüshlikon Center for Global Dialogue, Zurich••2001–02 Art direction of Laurence King Publishing••2000 Redesign launch of Laurence King Publishing••2000 Album design, *Forever*, by the Spice Girls••1998 Stamp design, Royal Mail, United Kingdom••1998 Design of *Financial Times, The Business Magazine*, London••1995 Redesign of the *Independent* magazine, London selected bibliography 2003 *Creative Review Annual*, United Kingdom••2003 *Making and Breaking the Grid*, Rockport Publishers, Gloucester, Massachusetts••2002 *Rewind: Fourty Years of Design and Advertising*, Phaidon Press, London and New York••2001 *Graphis* magazine, New York selected exhibitions 2002 *Rewind*, Victoria & Albert Museum, London••2002 Design Council traveling exhibition••2002 Book exhibition, British Council, London awards 2003 Silver nominations, D&AD, London••2003 Best Annual Report, Design Week Awards, London••2003 Silver, Art Directors Club, New York memberships 2002 Alliance Graphique Internationale (AGI)••2001 International Society of Typographic Designers (ISTD)••1994 British Design & Art Direction (D&AD)

Tom Gauld Born Aberdeen, Scotland, 1976. Lives and works in London education 1999–2001 M.A., Communication Art and Design, Royal College of Art, London••1995–99 B.A., Illustration, Edinburgh College of Art, Edinburgh practice 2001–present Copublisher (with Simone Lia), Cabanon Press ••2000–present Freelance illustrator selected projects 2003 Illustrations for members' brochure, Royal Society of Arts, London••2002–03 Designed watches and prints, United Arrows, Tokyo••2002–03 *Move to the City*, weekly comic strip, *Time Out*, London••2002 *The Moving Finger*, series of Illustrations for the *Guardian*, London••2001 Billboard design, Happiness in Brockley Project, London selected bibliography 2003 *Both* (with Simone Lia), Bloomsbury, London••2002 *Second* (with Simone Lia), Cabanon Press, London••2001

Guardians of the Kingdom, Cabanon Press, London • • 2001 *First* (with Simone Lia), Cabanon Press, London selected exhibitions 2002 *Wedding or Funeral?*, District Gallery, Tokyo • • 2001 *Between the Lines*, Pumphouse Gallery, London • • 2000 *Folio Society Illustration Awards*, RCA, London • • 2000 *The Instruction Manual*, Blue Room, London awards 2002 Pentagram Illustration Award • • 2001 Deutsche Bank Pyramid Award

Juli Gudehus Born Hamburg, Germany, 1968. Lives and works in Berlin education 1990–96 Visual Communication, University of Applied Arts, Düsseldorf • • 1994 Omnific Studios, London • • 1994 Internships, Alan Kitching, Pentagram, and Phaidon Press, London • • 1987–90 Apprenticeship, Wienand, Cologne practice 1996–present Freelance graphic designer and visual consultant • • 1999–2000 Lecturer, Graphic Design Department, University of Applied Arts, Düsseldorf • • 1996–2000 Design studio with friends • • 1996 Freelance work for Birnbach Design, Bonn selected projects 2000–present Design for various publications, exhibitions, and events of the German Parliament, Berlin • • 1999 *Gestern war heute morgen*, project for newspaper *Die Zeit*, Zeit Verlag, Hamburg • • 1998 *Mindestens haltbar bis*, calendar, Verlag Hermann Schmidt, Mainz, Germany • • 1996 Showroom design, Bayer Corporation, Leverkusen, Germany • • 1992 *Genesis*, by Juli Gudehus, Lars Müller Publishers, Baden, Switzerland selected bibliography 2003 *Type & Typography*, Laurence King Publishing, London • • 1999 *Art Directors Club (ADC) Yearbook*, Verlag Hermann Schmidt, Germany • • 1999 *Zoo Book*, Zoo, London • • 1996 *Typoundso*, Verlag Hans-Rudolf Lutz, Zurich selected exhibitions 1999 *Type Directors Show*, traveling exhibition • • 1999 *Wie Zeit vergeht*, Kölnisches Stadtmuseum, Cologne • • 1996 *13 Forum Typografie*, Düsseldorf • • 1993 *Mediale*, Museum für Kunst und Gewerbe, Hamburg awards 1999 Gold Award, Art Directors Club, Germany • • 1999 Gold Award, Art Directors Club, Europe • • 1999 Award for Typographic Excellence, Type Directors Club, New York

Yuri Gulitov Born Sevastopol, Crimea, Ukraine, 1964. Lives and works in Moscow education 1986–91 Graphic design, Art Industrial Institute, Kharkov, Ukraine • • 1980–84 Art College, Samokish, Simpheropol, Ukraine practice 2002–present Art Director of design studio Rocolor, Moscow • • 2001–present Professor, High Academic School of Graphic Design, Moscow College of Applied Arts • • 1998–2001 Freelance graphic designer • • 1996–98 Art Director, *Kommersant*, Moscow • • 1993–95 Art Director, Oda, Sevastopol, Ukraine • • 1991–93 Art Director, Zerkalo, Sevastopol, Ukraine selected projects 2002 *Ladies' Night* identity, packaging, and poster, Rocolor and Independent Theatrical Project, Moscow • • 2002 Poster, Sergei Rachmaninov *Vespers*, St. Nikolai Church Choir of the State Tretyakov Gallery, Moscow • • 2002 Poster, Christmas Concert mystery *Lestvica*, St. Nikolai Church Choir of the State Tretyakov Gallery, Moscow • • 2002 Book design, *Sotheby's Russian Art on Auction 1990–2000*, Artlibris, Moscow • • 2002 Series of booklets for French Cultural Center, Embassy of France, Moscow • • 1999 Poster and invitation for all-Russian competition/exhibition *Design '99*, Society of Russian Designers, Moscow selected bibliography 2002 "Outside of Road Signs," *Design Illustrated*, Moscow • • 2001 "Yuri Gulitov," *Novum World of Graphic Design* magazine, Munich • • 2000 "No modern urgency of Yuri Gulitov," *Kak*, Moscow • • 1999 "Yuri Gulitov," *Fusion 2002 International*, Tokyo selected exhibitions 2001 *Yuri Gulitov. Beach Pictures*, Gallerie Pinacotheke, Moscow • • 2000 *Yuri Gulitov. Typeface*, Art Industrial Institute, Kharkov and Gallerie Dom, Moscow • • 2000 6th International Poster Triennial, Toyama awards 2001 Association Typographique Internationale (ATypI) Award, Bukva:Raz!, Moscow • • 2000 Golden Bee Award, poster category, Moscow International Biennale of Graphic Design • • 1998 Silver Diploma , Best Calendar Design of Russia Exhibition, Moscow • • 1996 Grand Prix, logo category, and Golden Bee Award, typeface category, Golden Bee Moscow International Biennale of Graphic Design memberships 1994 Society of Designers of Russia • • 1992 Union of Ukrainian Artists

Julia Hasting Born Bremen, Germany, 1970. Lives and works in New York education 1992–97 Graphic Design, Staatliche Hochschule für Gestaltung Karlsruhe, Germany • • 1990–92 Visual Communications, Gesamthochschule Kassel, Germany practice 2000–present Art Director, Phaidon Press, New York • • 2000–present Professor, Design Faculty, Cooper Union School of Art, New York • • 1998 Designer, Phaidon Press, London • • 1993–98 Freelance designer, Karlsruhe, Germany selected projects 1998–2003 Book design, *Cream, Magnum°, Breuer Houses, Acta Est, Annunciation, Descent, Crucifixion, Last Supper, 10x10, Chaos, Fresh Cream*, Phaidon 55 photography series, *Robert Capa, The Sound I Saw, The Andy Warhol Catalogue Raisonné: Volume I, Blink., Vitamin P, Gordon Matta-Clark, Red-Color News Soldier*, Phaidon Press, London and New York • • 1997 Corporate identity, European Institute of Cinema, Karlsruhe (EIKK) • • 1997 Corporate identity, Central Education Institute (ZFP) of television and radio stations ARD/ZDF, Cologne • • 1995 Participant in official logo competition EXPO 2000 Hannover • • 1994 Corporate identity and books *Camera Silens, Mienenspiele, buna 4*, Media Museum—Zentrum für Kunst und Medientechnologie (ZKM), Karlsruhe • • 1993 Catalogue for the architects COOP Himmelb(l)au, Erich Schelling Architecture Foundation, Karlsruhe, Germany • • 1993 Posters, invitations, and catalogue for exhibition *Bühnenbild heute, Bühnenbild der Zukunft*, Zentrum für Kunst und Technology (ZKM) and Cantz Verlag, Stuttgart selected bibliography 2003 *First Choice—Leading international designers select the very best of their work*, edited by Ken Cato, Images, Australia • • 2003 D&AD Annual, London • • 2003 *50 Books/50 Covers*, American Institute of Graphic Arts, New York • • 2002–03 "Regional Design Annual," *Print* magazine, Cincinnati, Ohio • • 2002 Type Directors Club Annual, New York • • 1999–2001 "I.D. Annual Design Review", *I.D. Magazine*, New York • • 1997 *form* magazine 158, Germany • • 1997 *Rambow Studenten*, Cantz Verlag, Stuttgart selected exhibitions 2001 *AGI—Graphisme(s)*, Bibliothèque Nationale de France, Paris • • 2000 19th International Biennale of Graphic Design Brno, Czech Republic • • 1998 International Poster Triennial, Toyama, Japan • • 1995 *The Nicest Books 1995*, Book Fair Frankfurt and Leipzig • • 1994 *The 100 Best Posters*, Berlin • • 1993 *The Best Posters 1990–1993*, 7th Triennale, German Poster Museum, Essen awards 2003 Gold Medal, Art Directors Club, New York • • 2003 Silver Award Nomination, D&AD, London • • 2002 First Prize, *Print* magazine's A–Z Competition, New York • • 2000 25th Kodak Fotobuchpreis, Stuttgart • • 1999 Certificate of Typographic Excellence, Type Directors Club, New York • • 1993 Henri de Toulouse-Lautrec Gold Medal, 7th Triennale, German Poster Museum, Essen memberships 2003 International Jury, 21st International

Biennale of Graphic Design Brno, Czech Republic, 2004••2001 American Institute of Graphic Arts (AIGA)••2000 Alliance Graphique Internationale (AGI)••2000 Art Directors Club, New York

Fons Hickmann Born Hamm, Germany, 1966. Lives and works in Berlin and Vienna education 1988–93 Philosophy, Creative Writing, Photography, Art, and Design, Universities of Düsseldorf and Wuppertal, Germany practice 1999–present Design studio Fons Hickmann m23, Berlin••1995–2002 Lecturer in Essen, Dortmund, London, and Beijing••2001 Professor of Graphic Design, New Media, and Applied Football, University of Applied Art Vienna, Austria••1993–96 Artist group "kairos," Düsseldorf selected projects 2001–02 Posters for classical concerts, Johanneskantorei, Düsseldorf••1999–2002 Posters for the Labor für Soziale und Ästhetische Entwicklungen, Düsseldorf••1996 Posters for silent film festival, Graz, Austria••2002 Fons Goes China poster for lecture in Beijing••2002 Posters for sailing regatta Kieler Woche 2002, Kiel, Germany••2000 Poster series "Anonyme Idylle" for music concerts, B8, Düsseldorf selected bibliography 1996–2003 *The Annual of the Type Directors Club*, HBI, New York selected exhibitions 2000 Golden Bee International Biennale of Graphic Design, Moscow••2001 Poster Biennial Ningbo, China••2002 Heiligenkreuzer Hof, Vienna••1998 International Stage Poster Triennial, Sofia awards 2002–2003 Excellence Award, Type Directors Club, New York••1999–2003 100 Best Posters, Berlin••2002 Joseph Binder Award for Multimedia Design, Design Austria••2001 Excellence Award, Poster Biennial Ningbo, China••2000 Golden Bee Award, Golden Bee International Biennale of Graphic Design, Moscow••1997 Silver Cube, Art Directors Club, New York memberships 1999 Art Directors Club, Germany••1996 Type Directors Club, New York

Kim Hiorthøy Born Trondheim, Norway, 1973. Lives and works in Oslo education 1999–2001 Royal Academy of Fine Art, Copenhagen••1991–96 Fine Art, Kunstakademiet i Trondheum, Trondheim, Norway••1994–95 Film, School of Visual Arts, New York selected projects 2003 Book design, *Money Will Ruin all Good Things*, Rune Grammofon, Oslo••2003 Album sleeve, *Jaga Jazzist: The Stix*, Ninja Tune, London••2003 *Jeg er nesten alltid redd*, 7 films, The Photographers' Gallery, Oslo••2002 *Flowers*, mural design, Thisisrealart Associates/Peter Smith, Tokyo selected bibliography 2003 *Graphic Design in the 21st Century*, Taschen, Cologne••2001 *Pen&Mouse*, Laurence King Publishing, London••2000 *Tree Weekend*, Die Gestalten Verlag, Berlin••2000 *Sampler2*, Laurence King Publishing, London selected exhibitions 2003 *Kim Hiorthøy: Jeg er nesten alltid redd*, The Photographers' Gallery, Oslo••2001 *Generation X: Young Nordic Design*, Scandinavian House, New York••2000 *Kim Hiorthøy: Tegninger for en hundrings*, Tegner-forbundet, Oslo

Keiko Hirano Born Himeji city, Hyogo Prefecture, Japan, 1959. Lives and works in Tokyo education self-educated professional 1986–present Independent Graphic Designer, founder of Hirano Studio selected projects 2002 Package design, Awai sake, Gekkeikan••2001 Visual Identity, The National Museum of Modern Art, Tokyo••2000 Art direction for brand image for qiora, Shiseido, Tokyo••1999 Package design for Carita Le Visage, Cartita, France••1998 Packaging and logotype design for Vocalise perfume, Shiseido, Tokyo••1997 CD jacket design for *Dogs*, by Kenji Ozawa, Toshiba EMI, Tokyo selected bibliography 2003 *Axis* magazine 104, Tokyo••2000 "Design X2000 pt.01," *IDEA* 280, revised edition, Tokyo selected exhibitions 2002 *What is qiora's creation?*, Hirano Studio, Tokyo••1995 *Today's Japan—Design*, Harbor Front Center, Canada••1994 *Keiko Hirano Graphic Works*, Matsuya Ginza Design Gallery, Tokyo••1986 *The Portrait of Light and Shadow*, INAX Gallery, Tokyo awards 2001 Mainichi Design Award, Mainichi Newspapers Co., Japan••1998 Gold Prize, 77th Annual Art Directors Award, Art Directors Club, New York••1998 ADC Award ,Tokyo Art Directors Club, Japan••1996 New Designer Award, Japan Graphic Designers Association memberships 2002 Japan Design Committee••1999 Tokyo Art Directors Club••1996 Japan Graphic Designers Association (JAGDA)

Hon Bing-wah Born Guangzhou, China, 1949. Lives and works in Hong Kong education 1973 Graphic Design, Extramural Studies of the Chinese University of Hong Kong practice 2000–present Partner, H + S Design, Hong Kong••2000–present Visiting Professor, University of Shanghai••1998–present Museum Honorary Adviser, Leisure and Cultural Services Department, Hong Kong••2002 Juror, China Star, Red-Cross International Poster Contest, China; Biennale in Design, Macau; and Taiwan Design Biennale••1998–99 Chairman, Hong Kong Designers Association••1988–90 Judging panel, Regional Flag and Emblem of the Hong Kong Special Administration Region selected projects 2002 Poster, information brochure, and gift-packaging design for the bidding of World Expo, 2010 Shanghai China, Expo 2010 Shanghai China Bidding Office••1999 Book design, *Image of Shanghai*, Information Office of Shanghai Municipal People's Government, Shanghai••1999 Corporate Identity design for Shanghai Public Transportation Card, Shanghai Public Traffic Card Co. Ltd., Shanghai••1997 Environmental graphic and signage design for Riverside Point Singapore, Far East Organization, Singapore••1997 Mascot design for the celebration of reunification of Hong Kong with China, Hong Kong Special Administrative Government, Hong Kong selected bibliography 2002 *Package & Design*, Guangzhou, China••2000 *Graphis Poster Annual*, USA••1998 *Monthly Design*, Korea••1998 *New Logo and Trademark Design*, Japan selected exhibitions 2002 *Art & Design Exhibition*, Xintiandi Shanghai, China;••2001 *Hon Bing-wah Poster & Corporate Identity Design Exhibition*, Shanghai International Convention Centre, Shanghai, China••1997 *Back to Nature, Artworks by Hon Bing-wah*, Hong Kong••1986 *The Poster Works of Hon Bing-wah*, Landmark Central, Hong Kong awards 2002 Gold Award, China Corporate Identity System Award, Beijing••1998 Gold Award, Signage System Design, Hong Kong Designers Association, Hong Kong••1997 Gold Medal of Publication Design, Creativity Annual, USA••1992 Designer of the Year Award, Hong Kong Artist Guide, Hong Kong memberships 2001 Adviser, Hong Kong Designers Association ••1998–2000 Chairman, Hong Kong Designers Association

Inkahoots Robyn McDonald, born Melbourne, Australia, 1958; Jason Grant, born Blenheim, New Zealand, 1971; Ben Mangan, born Ballarat, Australia, 1976; Lucas Surtie, born Sydney, Australia, 1980; Joel Booÿ, born Brisbane, Australia, 1981. Live and work in Brisbane education 2001 Graphic Design, Queensland College of Art, Brisbane (JB)••2001 Graphic Design, Queensland College of Art, Brisbane (LS)••1990–92 Graphic Design, Queensland College of Art, Brisbane (JG)••1989 Visual Arts, BCAE, Brisbane (JG)••1989 University of Ballarat, Ballarat (BM)••1980–87 Bachelor of Arts, Art History and Philosophy, Queensland University (RM)••1984–86 Diploma of Illustration, Queensland Art College (RM) practice 1990 Establishment of Inkahoots selected projects 2001 CD artwork, *Quietly Building an Empire*, by The Carousel, Australia••2001 Visual identity and promotional material, Ecodomo, Australia••2000 Visual identity and promotional material, Foresters ANA Friendly Society, Australia••1997 Logo for independent bookstore Avid Reader, Australia selected bibliography 2003 *Graphic Design for the 21st Century*, Taschen, Cologne••2002 *Eye* magazine 46, London

Karlssonwilker

Hjalti Karlsson, born Reykjavik, Iceland, 1967; Jan Wilker, born Marl, Germany, 1972. Live and work in New York education 1996–2001 Communication Design, State Academy of Fine Arts, Stuttgart (JW)••1989–92 Graphic Design, Parsons School of Design, New York (HK)••1984–88 Design, Menntaskolinn I Reykjavik, Iceland (HK) practice 2000–present karlssonwilker Inc., New York••1996–2000 Sagmeister Inc., New York (HK) selected projects 2002 Book design, *Curious Boym*, by Studio Boym & Partners, Princeton Architectural Press, New York••2002 CD packaging, *Highly Evolved*, by the Vines, Capitol Records, New York••2001 Poster and CD packaging, *Live 2001*, by Kraan, Kraan and Bassball Records, Germany••2001 "Doglamp" design, Worldstudio Foundation, New York selected bibliography 2003 *tellmewhy –the first 24 months of karlssonwilker inc.*, Princeton Architectural Press, New York••2003 *ID Magazine*, USA••2002 *Coast to Coast—Contemporary American Graphic Design*, Die Gestalten Verlag, Berlin••2002 *55 Degrees North*, Laurence King Publishing, London selected exhibitions 2003 *designIS*, Berlin••2002 *Soundblast*, American Institute of Graphic Arts, Los Angeles••2001 *Young Guns 3*, Art Directors Club, New York

Siobhan Keaney

Born London, United Kingdom, 1959. Lives and works in London education 1978–82 B.A. (Hons.), Graphic Design, London College of Printing, London practice 1985–present Independent designer and consultant••2002–present Year Tutor, School of Arts & Communication, University of Brighton••2000–present External Assessor, B.A. (Hons.) Art & Design Communication course, Bath Spa University College••1999–present External Assessor, B.A. (Hons.) Art & Design Communication course, Leeds Metropolitan University ••1998–2001 External Assessor, M.A. Communication Design course, Manchester Metropolitan University ••1995–98 Visiting Lecturer, Royal College of Art, London••1995–98 External Assessor, B.A. (Hons.) Graphic Design course, Central St. Martin's, London selected projects 2002 Yearpack 2002, The Royal Mail, London ••2000 Film promoting the United Kingdom, Foreign & Commonwealth Office, London••1990–97 Identity program, The Mill, London••1997, 1991, 1989, 1988 Apicorp Annual Reports, Apicorp, London••1995 "Science Fiction" special edition stamps, first-day cover and presentation pack, The Royal Mail, London selected bibliography 2002 *Rewind: 40 Years of Design and Advertising*, Phaidon Press, London and New York••1998 *Design Without Boundaries: Visual Communication in the Nineties*, Booth-Clibborn Editions, London••1993 *International Women in Design*, USA selected exhibitions 2002–2003 *Rewind: 40 Years of Design & Advertising from the D&AD Awards*, Victoria & Albert Museum, London••1996–98 *Work from London*, international traveling exhibition••1995 *Siobhan Keaney*, Hochschule fur Gestaltung Offenbach, Germany••1994 *British Design*, Maison du Livre de l'Image et du Son, Villeurbanne, France awards 1990 Silver Award, Most Outstanding Annual Report, D&AD, London••1990 Silver Award, Most Outstanding Brochure, D&AD, London••1987 Gold Award, Most Outstanding Brochure, United Kingdom memberships 1997–2002 Alliance Graphique Internationale (AGI)

Kerr/Noble

Frith Kerr, born Surrey, United KIngdom, 1973; Amelia Noble, born London, United Kingdom, 1973. Live and work in London education 1995–97 Royal College of Art, London (FK+AN)••1992–95 Camberwell College of Arts, London (FK)••1992–95 Central Saint Martins College of Art and Design, London (AN) practice 1997–present Kerr/Noble (FK+AN)••1997–present Visiting Lecturer, Camberwell College of Arts, London (FK)••1997–present Visiting Lecturer, Central Saint Martins College of Art and Design, London (AN) selected projects 2003 Modified Pop, typeface created for *No More Rules—Graphic Design & Postmodernism*, by Rick Poynor, Laurence King Publishing, London••2003 Identity and publicity material for *user_mode*, Central Saint Martins College of Art and Design and Tate Modern, London••2002 Printed material and exhibition graphics, *Gio Ponti—A World*, Design Museum, London••2002 *Lost But Not Forgotten*, self-published magazine, London••2002 *Accommodating Change: Innovation in Housing*, Architecture Foundation, London••1999 Fold-out souvenir for Channel Four riverboat trip, London selected bibliography 2003 "Art & Craft—Awards," *Graphics International* 103, London••2002 "Freed from Technology's Spell," *IDEA* 295. Tokyo••2002 "The Top Brass," The Sunday *Independent*, London••2001 *Specials*, Booth-Clibborn Editions, London selected exhibitions 2003 *The Arts Foundation's 10th Anniversary Exhibition*, Pentagram Gallery••2002 *The Book Corner*, British Council, Milan and London••2002 *Creative Futures 2002*, Creative Review, London awards 2003 Arts Foundation Award for Graphic Design••2002 Creative Futures Award for Editorial Design, Creative Review••2002 Best of Show, Design Week Awards••1997 Chris Garnham Award, Royal College of Art, London

Rene Knip

Born Hoorn, Netherlands, 1963. Lives and works in Amsterdam education 1985–90 Graphic and Type Design, Saint Joost Academy of Fine Arts, Breda••1984–85 Painting, Royal Academy, The Hague practice 1996–present Atelier Rene Knip, Amsterdam••1992–95 Assistant to Anthon Beeke, Studio Anthon Beeke, Amsterdam; part-time designer, Studio Lidewij Edelkoort, Paris selected projects 2003 Calender, Calff & Meischke, Amsterdam ••2002 Self-commissioned Firebasket (with Edgar Knip), Amsterdam••2001 *Dutch Design 2000–2001*, BNO and BIS Publishers, Amsterdam••1999 Laundry Sans typeface, (used for exhibition *Mooi Maar Goed)*, Amsterdam••1999 Housenumber design, Merkx+Girod Architects, Amsterdam selected bibliography 2003 *Fontshop* magazine, April, Belgium••2002 "Rene Knip, Unconventional Spatial Typography," *Designer's Workshop* magazine 121, Tokyo••2001 *Apples + Oranges—Best*

Dutch Graphic Design, BIS Publishers, Amsterdam •• 2001 "Rene Knip, Ideas that can't wait," *Graphis* magazine 333, New York •• 1999 *Items* magazine 1, Amsterdam **memberships** 2001 Association of Dutch Designers (BNO)

Elisabeth Kopf Born Vorarlberg, Austria, 1963. Lives and works in Vienna **education** 1996–present Personal studies in graphic design and visual concepts •• 1989–present Personal studies in photography •• 1981–84 Psychology, History, and Philosophy, University of Vienna **practice** 1996–present Freelance graphic designer and photographer •• 1992–96 Assistant in a graphic-design studio •• 1989–91 Freelance photographer, Hong Kong **selected projects** 2002 Self-commisioned Air Cigarettes Project, Vienna and Beijing •• 2002 Baustelle First Aid Project, Lesson 9: The Recovery Position •• 2000 Little Theatre project, *Peter Herbert & Aktionstheater Ensemble 2000*, Aziza Music, New York and Vienna •• 1999-present Scratch Gallery, Peter Herbert & David Tronzo: *Segmente*, Aziza Music and Peter Herbert, New York •• 1997 Little Orchestra project, Vienna Art Orchestra, Vienna **selected bibliography** 2003 *This End Up: Original Approaches to Packaging Design*, RotoVision, London •• 2002 *Lighter* magazine, Beijing •• 2002 *PAGE*, Hamburg •• 2001 *Print: European Design Annual 2001*, New York **selected exhibitions** 2002 *Hans Koller Music Awards Exhibition*, Vienna •• 2000–2001 Joseph Binder Awards touring exhibition, Austria, Switzerland, Germany •• 1999 Limites—Festival for Contemporary Music and Art, VHS Stöbergasse, Vienna •• 1997 Vienna Art Orchestra Anniversary World Tour, Brucknerhaus, Linz and Vienna **awards** 2001 Gustav Klimt Award, Cultural Department of the City of Vienna and GEWISTA, Austria •• 2000 Joseph Binder Award, Design Austria •• 2000 79th Annual Award, Art Directors Club, New York •• 2000 Certificate of Excellence, European Design Annual 5, USA and United Kingdom **memberships** 2001 Design Austria

Ji Lee Born Seoul, Korea, 1971. Lives and works in New York **education** 1995 B.F.A., Communication Design, Parsons School of Design, New York **practice** 1999–present Art Director, Saatchi & Saatchi, New York •• 2001–02 Instructor, Graphic Design, Parsons School of Design, New York •• 1996–97 Graphic Designer, Tsang Seymour Design, New York •• 1995–96 Graphic Designer, Frankfurt Balkind, New York **selected projects** 2003 3-D Chess Board, New York •• 2002 Speech-bubbles sticker project, New York •• 2002 Abstractor, New York •• 2002 Nonnumeric Calendar, New York •• 1997 Universe Revolved, a 3-D alphabet, New York **selected bibliography** 1997 *New York Times Magazine*, special issue on technology, New York •• 1996 *Dimensional Typography*, by J. Abbott Miller, Princeton Architectural Press, New York **awards** 1998 Finalist, Innovation in Communication Award, Saatchi & Saatchi, USA

Ken-Tsai Lee Born Taipei, Taiwan, 1968. Lives and works in Taipei **education** 1999–2001 Graduate Degree, Design, National Taiwan Normal University, Taipei •• 1988–91 Department of Applied Art, Shih Chien University, Taipei **practice** 2001–02 Lecturer for Visual Communication, Mingchi Institute of Technology, Taipei •• 1996–present Ken-Tsai Lee Design Studio, Taipei **selected projects** 1996–2002 Visual design, poster, and advertising for Chinese Society of Preventive Medicine—Living with Hope Organization, Taipei •• 1997–99 Poster design for Soho Cosmetic Accessories Co., Taipei •• 1998 Visual design, poster, and advertising, Fonso Enterprise Co., Taipei •• 1997 Cover Design for Japan Design Foundation booklet, Osaka **selected bibliography** 2003 *Communication Arts* magazine, USA •• 2002 *Graphis Poster 2002*, USA •• 2002 *P.I.E Book*, Japan •• 2002 *International Graphis Design Annual*, Germany **selected exhibitions** 2003 Colorado International Invitational Poster Exhibition, Colorado, USA •• 2002 Howon University Invitational International Design Exhibition, Seoul, Korea •• 2001 *Das AvantgardePlakat aus China*, Hochschule der Künste, Berlin •• 2001 *Chinese Graphic Design towards the International Sphere*, Lubalin Study Center of Design and Typography, Cooper Union School of Art, New York **awards** 2001–02 Two-time winner, Red Dot Award, Red Dot Communication Design Competition, Germany •• 2000 Two Gold Awards, Hong Kong Designers Association •• 1999 Best of Printed Design Award, *IdN Magazine* , Hong Kong •• 1999 Taiwan National Design Award

Anette Lenz Born Esslingen am Neckar, Germany, 1964. Lives and works in Paris **education** 1984–88 Communication Design, Fachhochschule München **practice** 1993–present Independent Designer, Atelier Anette Lenz, Paris •• 1991–93 Founding Member, Nous Travaillons Ensemble, Paris •• 1990 Grapus, Paris •• 1988–89 AWG, Munich **selected projects** 2002 Season poster and brochure, Théâtre d'Angoulême, France •• 2001 Poster series, "The Concerts of Radio France," Paris •• 2000 Poster series, Théâtre de Rungis, Paris **selected bibliography** 2002 *Etapes Graphiques* 89, Paris •• 2002 "European Design Annual," *Print* magazine, New York •• 2000 *Le 20ème siècle s'affiche*, Éditions Larousse, Paris •• 1996 "Young Graphic Creation in France," *Signes* 15/16, Paris **selected exhibitions** 2002 International Biennale of Graphic Design Brno, Czech Republic •• 2001 Graphic-design exhibition, Bibliothèque Nationale de France, Paris •• 2001 *La Fête de la Musique*, Centre Georges Pompidou, Paris •• 1996 *Approche*, international traveling exhibition of 10 young graphic-design studios in France **awards** 2002 Gold Medal for Corporate Identity, International Biennale of Graphic Design Brno, Czech Republic **memberships** 1999 Alliance Graphique Internationale (AGI) •• 1996 Verband der Grafik Designer, Berlin

Apex Lin Born Pintung, Taiwan, 1957. Lives and works in Taipei, Macao, and Singapore **education** 1981–84 Master of Fine Arts, National Taiwan Normal University, Taipei •• 1976–80 Bachelor of Fine Arts, National Taiwan Normal University, Taipei **practice** 1996–present Managing Director, Graphic Design Association, Taipei •• 1986–present Professor, Graduate School of Fine Arts, National Taiwan Normal University, Taipei •• 2002–04 President, Taiwan Poster Design Association, Taipei •• 1988–2004 Consultant, Macao Designers Association, Macau •• 2001–03 Treasurer, International Council of Graphic Design Association (ICOGRADA), Brussels •• 1989–2002 Consultant, Apex Design Consultant Corporation, Taipei •• 1990–96 Founder and President, Taiwan Image Poster Design Association, Taipei **selected projects** 2002 Curator of international touring exhibition *Discover Asia International Touring Exhibition*, Taipei and Kaoshiung, Taiwan; Singapore; Kuala Lumpur, Malaysia •• 2001 Curator, *The Trio of Asia Poster Exhibition* (Japan, Korea, Taiwan), Taipei •• 2000 Curator, *Say Good-Bye to the 20th Century* design exhibition, Taipei and Beijing ••1997 Corporate identity, Chunghwa Telcom Corporation & Taiwan Stock Exchange Corporation, Taipei ••1996 Corporate identity, Vantone Corporation & Greatwall Oil Corporation, Beijing ••1989 Corporate identity, Taiwan Sugar Corporation, Taipei **selected exhibitions** 2000 *Apex Lin in Macau*, Macao UNESCO Center ••1997 *Taiwan Image Poster Design*, Taiwan Cultural Center, New York and Paris ••1997 *The Design World of Apex Lin*, China Fine Art Academy, HangZhou; Beijing Design Museum, Beijing ••1995 *The Design World of Apex Lin*, NTNU Gallery, Taipei **awards** 2002 ICOGRADA Achievement Award, Taiwan **memberships** 2002–present Jury Member, 2008 Beijing Olympic Design Competition Committee ••1999 ICOGRADA ••1990 Taiwan Poster Design Association ••1989 Graphic Design Association, Taiwan

Andrey Logvin Born Ipatovo, Russia, 1964. Lives and works in Moscow **education** 1984–87 Graphic Design, Moscow 1905 Art School ••1981–82 Graphic Design, Moscow 1905 Art School **practice** 1997 Established virtual design group LOGVINDESIGN ••1992–97 Freelance graphic designer ••1989–92 Art Director, IMA-Press publishers, Moscow ••1987 Graphic Designer, Studio of the Russian Artists Union, Moscow **selected projects** 2002 Packaging for Hennessy GQ Reserve, Condé Nast, Moscow ••2001 Poster for international project "10 Graphic Designers for Human Rights," French Ministry of Education, Paris ••1999 Advertising campaign, Bosch kitchen systems, Moscow ••1987 Poster for Moscow Marathon of Peace, Russian Ministry of Sport, Moscow **selected bibliography** 2001 *The Russian Poster. 100 Masterpieces from 100 Years*, Kontakt-Kultyra, Moscow ••2000 *Graphistes Autour Du Monde*, Les Éditions Textuel, Paris ••1998 "Pin-up Boy," *I.D. Magazine* 40, New York ••1994 *Who's Who In Graphic Design*, Benteli-Werd Verlag AG, Zurich **selected exhibitions** 2002 *Logvin, Peret, Pluta, Tartakover*, Warsaw ••2001 *5 Grafist*, MSU Tophane i Amire Cultural Center Art Gallery, Istanbul ••2000 *Graphistes Autour Du Monde*, Échirolles, France ••1998 *Troyka. Kitajeva, Logvin, Chaika*, DDD Gallery, Osaka **awards** 2001 Russian State Prize for Art ••1996 Gold Medal, 15th Warsaw Poster Biennale ••1994 Critics Award, 16th International Biennale of Graphic Design Brno, Czech Republic ••1992 Grand-Prix, First Golden Bee International Biennale of Graphic Design, Moscow **memberships** 2002 Russian Academy of Graphic Design ••1999 Alliance Graphique Internationale (AGI)

Victor Hugo Marreiros Born Macao, China, 1960. Lives and work in Macao **education** 1986 Painting and Printmaking, Escola Superior de Belas Artes do Porto, Porto, Portugal **practice** 1990–present Head of the Graphic Department, Macao Cultural Institute; Art Director, *Revista da Cultura* ••1998 Founded Victor Hugo Design ••1990 Founded MARR Design ••1984–88 Art Director, Macao Television, Teledifusão de Macau (TDM) **selected projects** 2002 Poster series for fourth Chinese Drama Festival in Macao, Macao Cultural Institute ••2001 Poster for XII Macao Arts Festival, Macao Cultural Institute ••2001 Poster for Portuguese Movies Fortnight in Macao, Instituto Português do Oriente, Macao ••1998 Artistic Director, *Presença de Macau na Expo 98*, World Expo 98, Lisbon **selected exhibitions** 2002 *Discover Asia* international poster exhibition, Taipei ••2001 *Chinese Graphic Design Towards the International Sphere*, Lubalin Study Center of Design and Typography, Cooper Union School of Art, New York ••2001 *Das AvantgardePlakat Aus China*, Hochschule der Künste, Berlin ••1999 *Victor Hugo Marreiros—Design*, Casa Garden Gallery, Orient Foundation, Macao ••1999 *Victor Hugo Marreiros & Ung Vai Meng*, DDD Gallery, Osaka ••1998 International Art Fair of Guangzhou, Guangzhou, China **awards** 2002 Two Bronze and Thirteen Excellence Awards, HKDA Design Show, Hong Kong ••2001 Distinction Award, Prémio Bienal de Design de Macau 00/01, Macao ••2000 Nominated, International Designers Network Design Awards, Hong Kong ••1999 Medal of Professional Merit, Government of Macao **memberships** 1986 Design Association of Macao ••1986 Founding Member, Círculo dos Amigos da Cultura (CAC) de Macau

Malte Martin Born Berlin, Germany, 1958. Lives and works in Paris **education** 1978–86 Graphic Design and History of Art, Akademie für Bildende Kunst, Stuttgart ••1980–81 Graphics and Painting, Ecole Supérieure des Beaux Arts, Paris **practice** 1995–2000 Professor of Graphic Design and Image Concepts, ECV (École de Communication Visuelle) ••1996–present Cofounder, Agrafmobile ••1996 Establishment of Malte Martin, Atelier Graphique ••1989–1996 Freelance graphic designer **selected projects** 2002 Typographic installation *Galerue*, Agrafmobile, Paris ••2002 Installation and performance, *Théâtre des Questions*, Agrafmobile, Chaumont, France ••2002 Corporate identity, Festival d'Avignon, France ••2002 Program, Fondation Royaumont, Paris ••2001 Installations and performances *Instants Mobiles*, Agrafmobile, Chaumont, France ••1999 Program, 2E2M Orchestra, Paris **selected bibliography** 2003 "Malte Martin," *Design and Designers*, Éditions Pyramid, Paris ••2000 *New Design Paris*, Rockport Publishers, Gloucester, Massachusetts ••1998 *Cent Affiches Francaises*, SNG, Paris ••1995 *Signes*, Paris **selected exhibitions** 2000–2002 Visual Installations, Festival of Graphic Arts, Chaumont, France ••2000 Bibliothèque François Mitterrand, Paris ••1998 Galerie Vivienne, Paris **memberships** 2003 Alliance Française des Designers (AFD) ••2000 Association Typographique Internationale (ATypI), France ••1995 Syndicat National des Graphistes (SNG), France

Kei Matsushita Born Yokohama, Japan, 1961. Lives and works in Tokyo **education** 1987 M.A., Visual Design, Tokyo University of Fine Arts and Music, Tokyo ••1985 General Design, Tokyo University of Fine Arts and Music, Tokyo ••1981–85 Fine Arts General Design Course, Tokyo National University of Fine Arts and Music (GEI-DAI—Tokyo Geijutsu Daigaku) **practice** 1999–present Part-time Lecturer, General Design Course, Tokyo National University of Fine Arts and Music ••1995–98 Part-time Lecturer, Department of Arts and Design, Faculty of Humanities and Culture, Tokai University ••1990 Founded Kei Matsushita Design Office **selected projects** 2000 Brochure for Japan Team at Venice Biennale, 30x100 Committee, Tokyo ••2000 AIBO, Poster for development of AIBO entertainment robot, Sony Creative Products, Tokyo ••1999 Signage and logo plan for Japan Pavilion, Hannover International EXPO, Japan External Trade Organization, Tokyo ••1997–99 Poster Designs, 100x30 congress and exhibitions, Japan Institute of Architects, Tokyo ••Poster for exhibition of 30 Residential Areas by 100 Architects in their Thirties, Japan Institute of Architects, Tokyo ••1998 CD booklet design *Islands & Continents*

600MHz, by Ken Ishii, Sony Music Entertainment (Japan), Tokyo••1997 Demand on Demand, posters and leaflets for sales promotion, PCM TAKEO, Tokyo••Poster series "Nipponjin" (for *Close-up on Japan* exhibition), Tokyo selected bibliography 2002 *Sendendaigi*, Tokyo••1999 *Illustration*, Genko-Sha Publishing Co., Tokyo••1999 *Graphic Wave: Mamoru Suzuki, Kei Matsushita, Hiroshi Yonemura*, TransArt, Tokyo••1998 *i Magazine*, Amana Inc., Tokyo selected exhibitions 2002 *The Doraemon*, Suntory Museum, Osaka••2002 *DI+VISION*, Ginza Matsuya Design Gallery, Tokyo••1999 *Graphic Wave*, Ginza Graphic Gallery, Tokyo••1995 *Close-up of Japan*, Museo de Arte de São Paulo, São Paulo, Brazil awards 1997 Tokyo ADC Prize, Tokyo Art Directors Club, Tokyo••1997 JAGDA New Designer Award, Japan Graphic Designers Association, Tokyo••1991 Tokyo TDC Bronze Prize, Tokyo Type Directors Club, Japan••1986 Mainichi Design Awards First Advertisement Prize, Mainichi Shinbun-Sha, Japan memberships 1996 Japan Graphic Designers Association (JAGDA)

Chaz Maviyane-Davies Born Harare, Zimbabwe, 1952. Lives and works in Boston education 1990–91 Advanced Diploma, Filmmaking, Central Saint Martins College of Art and Design, London••1980–81 M.A., Central School of Art & Design, London••1976–80 B.A., Middlesex University, London practice 2001–present Associate Professor, Massachusetts College of Art, Boston••1983–2000 Principal, The Maviyane-Project, Harare selected projects 2002 Poster, Circle of Hell, American Institute of Graphic Design, USA••2001 Homage to Lautrec, Nouveau salon des Cent, France••1996 Rights Article 4 poster, Zimbabwe••1998 Disease poster, Aujourd' hui pour demain, Switzerland ••1996 Rights Article 21 poster, Zimbabwe••1996 Rights Article 19 poster, Zimbabwe ••1996 Rights Article 15 poster, Zimbabwe selected bibliography 1998 "ID Forty," *I.D. Magazine*••1996 *Who's Who in Graphic Design*, Benteli-Werd Verlag, Switzerland, 2nd edition••1996 *First Choice: Leading International Designers*, Craftsman House, Australia, 2nd edition••1993 *Graphic Agitation*, Phaidon Press, London and New York selected exhibitions 2002 *Human Rights Human Lives: The Graphic Design of Chaz Maviyane-Davies*, Massachusetts College of Art, Boston••2001 Toulouse Lautrec, *Nouveau Salon des Cents* traveling exhibition••1999 *Dignity: The World of Chaz Maviyane-Davies*, Dai Nippon Gallery, Osaka, Japan••1997 "Rights," series of 13 posters, more than 25 countries worldwide awards 2003 "Yet with a Steady Beat" Award, Museum of Fine Arts, Boston••1993 Poster Award Ekoplagat, Gbel'any, Slovakia••1993 Best Director, Southern African Film Festival, Harare, Zimbabwe••1984 Bronze Medal, 11th International Biennale of Graphic Design Brno, Czech Republic memberships 2003 American Institute of Graphic Design (AIGA)••1985 Graphics Association of Zimbabwe

Ung Vai Meng Born Macao, China, 1958. Lives and works in Macao education 1999–2002 Master studies, Theory of Chinese Painting, Academy of Fine Art of Guangzhou, Guangzhou, China••1991–92 Fine Art, ArCo, Lisbon, Portugal practice 1999–present Director, Macao Museum of Art••1985–98 Designer, Instituto Cultural de Macau selected projects 2001 Green Beijing, Great Olympics poster, Beijing Organizing Committee for the Games of the XXIX Olympiad, Beijing••1999 The Macanese poster, Leal Senado de Macau••1998 Orquestra Chinesa de Macao poster, Instituto Cultural de Macau••1998 Poster design for XII Macao Internacional Music Festival, Instituto Cultural de Macau selected bibliography 2002 *Discover Asia International Poster Exhibition*, International Council of Graphic Design Associations (ICOGRADA) and Taiwan Poster Design Association••2002 *Korea International Poster Exhibition*, CDAK Communication Design Association of Korea, Seoul••1999 *China Design Yearbook 1998–99*, Jiu Zhou Books Publishing House, Beijing••1996 *HKDA Design 96 Show*, Hong Kong Designers Association, Hong Kong selected exhibitions 1998 *Traços sobre Macau*, World Trade Center, Macao••1998 *Tales of two cities*, Gallery of First Institute of Art & Design, Hong Kong••1993 *Works by Ung Vai Meng*, Zen Gallery, Oporto, Portugal••1992 *Landscapes of Body*, Macanese Mission in Lisbon awards 1997 Best of Visual Images, IdN Design Awards, Hong Kong••1996 Judge's Award, HKDA Design 96 Show, Hong Kong••1995 Distinction Award in the 1st Macao Design Contest, Macao••1989 1st prize for mural design, Central Library of Macau memberships 1987 Founding Member, Circulo dos Amigos de Cultura (CAC) de Macao

Saed Meshki Born Gonabad, Iran, 1964. Lives and works in Tehran education 1988–93 Graphics, Faculty of Arts, Tehran University, Tehran••1986–88 Art, Teacher Training Faculty, Tehran practice 1989–present Freelance graphic designer selected projects 2002 Art director and graphic designer, 4th International Theatre Festival of Iranzamin, Ahvaz••2002 Design for the Constantinople, Constantinople music group, Montreal••2001 Art director and graphic designer, 3rd Abadan Film Festival, Abadan••2000 Organizer, *A Remarkable Event* exhibition, Tehran••1999 Art Director and Graphic Designer, EYE collection, Mahriz Publications, Tehran selected bibliography 2003 *World Graphic Design*, Merrill Publishing, London••2002 *Étapes Graphiques*, Paris selected exhibitions 2003 *Boof-e-Koor Iranian Typography*, Seyhoon Gallery, Tehran••2002 *Un cri persan*, Échirolles, France••2002 *Solidarity*, Galerie Bratri Capku, Prague••2002 *First stone*, Iranian Artist's house, Tehran awards 1997 Silver Medal for Book Cover Design, 6th Biennial of Iranian Graphic Designers, Tehran••1997 Creativity and Innovation Award, 6th Biennial of Iranian Graphic designers, Tehran••2002 Gold Medal for Book Cover Design, 7th Biennial of Iranian Graphic designers, Tehran memberships 2002 Alliance Graphique Internationale (AGI)••1997 Iranian Graphic Designers Society (IGDS)

Mooren + van der Velden Maureen Mooren, born Dordrecht, Netherlands, 1969; Daniel van der Velden, born Rotterdam, Netherlands, 1971. Live and work in Amsterdam education 1996–98 Postgraduate Design, Jan van Eyck Academy, Maastricht (DvdV)••1990–96 Graphic Design, Rotterdam Academy of Arts (MM)••1992–96 Graphic Design, Rotterdam Academy of Arts (DvdV) practice 1998–present Freelance graphic designers••2001–present Guest Lecturers, Arnhem Academy of Arts••2000–present Guest Lecturers, Willem de Kooning Academy, Rotterdam••2001 Guest Lecturers, Gerrit Rietveld Academy, Amsterdam••2001 Guest Lecturers, Maryland Institute School of Arts, Baltimore selected projects 2001–04 *Archis* magazine, Artimo Foundation, Amsterdam••1999–2003 Invitations, ROOM art space, Rotterdam••2001 Informational beer cups in cooperation with Fanclub, Lowlands Festival, Amsterdam••2001 Intersubjective novel *Oscillations*, La Lettre Volée, Brussels••1998 Invitations, Marres art space, Maastricht selected bibliography 2003 *Democratic Design: The Lectures*, Casco Projects, Utrecht••2003 *Reality Machines*, NAi Publishers, Rotterdam••2002 "File under Archis," *Eye* magazine 45, London selected exhibitions 2003 *Reality Machines*, Netherlands Architecture Institute, Rotterdam ••2003 *Rotterdam Design Prize 2003*, Museum Boijmans van Beuningen, Rotterdam••2000 International Biennale of Graphic Design Brno, Czech Republic ••1999 *Mode(s) d' Emploi*, Foundation for Visual Arts, Design and Architecture, Amsterdam awards 2003 Honorable Mention, Rotterdam Design Prize

Peter Moser Born Lucerne, Switzerland, 1962. Lives and works in Lucerne education 1978–83 Graphic Design, Schule für Gestaltung, Lucerne practice 1995–present Partner, Velvet Creative Office, Lucerne ••1984–95 Personal studios in Zurich and Lucerne selected projects 2002 *Sedel 1981–2001*, Velvet-Edition, Lucerne••2002 Poster series for Viper Basel International Festival for Film Video and New Media••2001 Poster for exhibition *Happy—Das Versprechen der Werbung*, Museum für Kommunikation, Bern••2001 Book design, *Suggestions*, Architekturgalerie Luzern••1997 Poster for exhibition *Frankensteins Kinder—Film und Medizin*, Museum für Gestaltung Zurich••1989 Poster series for Viper Lucerne International Festival for Film Video and New Media awards 2002 Most Beautiful Swiss Books, Federal Office for Culture, Switzerland••2002 100 Best Posters Award, Berlin••2001 Bronze Poster Award, Art Directors Club, Switzerland••1999 Poster of the Year, APG and Eidgenössisches Departement des Innern, Switzerland memberships 2001 Alliance Graphique Internationale (AGI)

Melanie Mues Born Bielefeld, Germany, 1970. Lives and works in London education 1991–95 Communication Design, Academy of Art, Bremen practice 2001–present Freelance designer, London••1997–2001 Designer, Frost Design, London••1996–97 Designer, Meta Design, London••1995–96 Freelance designer, Berlin selected projects 2003 Poster design for resource room, Tate Modern, London••2003 Exhibition design, *Eva Hesse*, Tate Modern, London••2003 Poster design for *Butterfly* installation by Richard Wilson, The Wapping Project, London••2003 Installation for the Classic Design Awards, Victoria & Albert Museum, London••2002 Exhibition design, *Eija-Liisa Ahtila*, Tate Modern, London••2002 *Sanctuary*, by Steve McCurry, Phaidon Press, London and New York••2001 Invitation, Omni Colour, London

Müller + Hess Beat Müller, born Basel, Switzerland, 1965; Wendelin Hess, born Basel, Switzerland, 1968. Live and work in Basel and Zurich education 1986–92 Graphic Design, Schule für Gestaltung, Basel (WH)••1986–91 Graphic Design, Schule für Gestaltung, Basel (BM) practice 1995–present Müller + Hess••1994–present Various teaching jobs in design schools, Basel, Lucerne, Zurich••1993 Started Hoch drei design studio selected projects 2001 Art Directors Club Switzerland Yearbook 2001 (with Ludovic Balland), ADC, Switzerland••1999 Poster and invitations for exhibition *Richard Paul Lohse—Konstruktive Gebrauchsgrafik*, Museum für Gestaltung Zürich••1999–2002 Redesign and art direction of *Das Magazin*, Tamedia AG, Zurich••1997 Poster and program for music festival Neue Musik Rümlingen, Switzerland selected bibliography 2000 *Swiss Graphic Design*, Die Gestalten Verlag, Berlin••2000 *Benzin: Young Swiss Graphic Design*, Lars Müller Publishers, Baden, Switzerland••1999 "Dismantling the Basel Principle," *Eye* magazine 32, London selected exhibitions 2002 *Design Now*, Design Museum, London awards 1998 Jan Tschichold Award, Switzerland

Hideki Nakajima Born Saitama, Japan, 1961. Lives and works in Tokyo education No specific education for graphic design practice 1999–present Member of creative unit Code••1995–present Director, Nakajima Design••1992–95 Art director, Rockin' on, Tokyo••1988–91 Senior Designer, Masami Shimizu Design Office, Tokyo selected projects 1992–present Art direction, *CUT* magazine, Rockin' on, Tokyo••1996–present Art direction and design for Ryuichi Sakamoto's CDs and LPs, Warner Music Japan and For Life Records, Tokyo••2002 Cover design, *Argentine Hag*, by Banana Yoshimoto, Rockin' on, Tokyo••1999 Promotional posters for Tag Heuer, Switzerland••1999 "Sampled Life" art box for Ryuichi Sakamoto's opera *LIFE*, Code, Tokyo selected bibliography 2002 *IDEA* magazine 295, Tokyo••2001 "Artist, Designer and Director Hideki Nakajima," *Scan #13*, Rikuyosha Publishing, Tokyo••1999 *Revival*, Rockin' on, Tokyo selected exhibitions 2002 *Code exhibition: new village*, Tokyo, Osaka, and Kyoto••2001 *AGI—Graphisme(s)*, Bibliothèque Nationale de France, Paris••2001 *032c / The searching stays with you*, vonRot and The Pineal Eye, Berlin and London••2000 *Graphic wave 5* , Ginza Graphic Gallery, Tokyo awards 2001 Chicago Athenaeum's Good Design Award••2000 Best Design Award, 19th International Biennale of Graphic Design Brno, Czech Republic••1995–2000 Five Gold and seven Silver Awards, Art Directors Club, New York••1999 Tokyo Art Directors Club Award memberships 2002 Art Directors Club, Tokyo••2002 Type Directors Club, Tokyo••1998 Alliance Graphique Internationale (AGI)••1997 Art Directors Club, New York

Dylan Nelson Born Albany, Oregon, USA, 1977. Lives and works in Portland education 2000–2002 M.F.A., Graphic Design, Cranbrook Academy of Art, Bloomfield Hills, Michigan••1995–99 B.F.A., Graphic Design, Oregon State University, Corvallis, Oregon practice 1997–present Co-Owner/Creative Director, Spare Parts, Portland, Oregon••2002–present Art direction/motion design, Nike, Beaverton, Oregon••2000–2002 Designer, Cranbrook Academy of Art/Museum, Bloomfield Hills, Michigan••1999–2000 Designer, Wieden + Kennedy, Portland, Oregon selected projects 2003 Print campaign, Nike Cycling Patch Kit, TREK, Wisconsin••2002 Broadcast campaign Yellow, Nike, Beaverton, Oregon••2002 Book design, Cranbrook Academy of Art catalogue, Cranbrook Academy of Art, Bloomfield Hills, Michigan••2002 *Zine Scene* identity, Cranbrook Art Museum, Bloomfield Hills, Michigan••2002 Self-promotional mixed-media installation *Don't Stop Living in the Red* ••2001 Self-promotional poster, Albany, OR 97321 selected bibliography 2003 Art Directors Club Yearbook, New York••2003 Nederlandse Designselectie Yearbook, Netherlands••2003 "Design Competition

Winner," *CMYK* Magazine••2002 "New Talent Design," *Graphis* magazine **selected exhibitions** 2002 *Walk on Water*, Basil Hallward Art Gallery, Portland, Oregon••2002 *Zine Scene*, Cranbrook Art Museum, Bloomfield Hills, Michigan••2001 *GM Design Exhibition*, General Motors, Detroit, Michigan••2001 *Exhibit of Evidence*, Center for Creative Studies, Detroit, Michigan **awards** 2003 Typography of Distinction Winner, New York Type Directors Club••2003 Design Competition Winner, *CMYK* Magazine••2002 Featured Talent, Blood Bank••1998 AIGA Harvest Award, Portland, Oregon

Yves Netzhammer Born Schaffhausen, Switzerland, 1970. Lives and works in Zurich **education** 1990–95 Graphic Design, Hochschule für Gestaltung und Kunst, Zurich••1986–90 Studies in architectural drawing, Schaffhausen **professional** 1995–present Independent artist and graphic designer **selected projects** 2003 Exhibition project including film, installation, book, poster, and invitation, Helmhaus Zürich••2002 Theater production, *Die Stelle im Park*, Theater Neumarkt, Zurich••2001 "Chocolate" stamp design for Swiss Post (with Ralph Schraivogel)••2000 Exhibition works and catalogue with CD-ROM, "Statements"••1999 Concept and imagery, *Das Magazin no. 47*, Tamedia AG, Zurich **selected bibliography** 2003 *Die überraschende Verschiebung der Sollbruchstelle eines in optimalen Verhältnissen aufgewachsenen Astes*, by Yves Netzhammer, Verlag für Moderne Kunst, Nuremberg••1999/2003 *Wenn man etwas gegen seine Eigenschaften benützt, muss man dafür einen anderen Namen finden*, by Yves Netzhammer, Verlag für Moderne Kunst, Nuremberg••2000 *Grosse Spiegel werden verloren: Informationen von Abwesenheit, damit Anwesenheit entstehen kann*, Statements IV catalogue and CD-ROM••1997 *Was sich erzählen lässt, wird verbessert werden*, by Yves Netzhammer, Verlag Ricco Bilger, Zurich **selected exhibitions** 2003 *Die überraschende Verschiebung der Sollbruchstelle eines in optimalen Verhältnissen aufgewachsenen Astes*, solo exhibition, Helmhaus Zürich••2001 *Body As Bite*, Neues Kunstmuseum, Lucerne••2000 *Statements*, solo exhibition, Kunst-Werke Berlin••1999 Manor-Kunstpreis solo exhibition, Museum zu Allerheiligen, Schaffhausen **awards** 2002 One-year "Atelier" grant from City of Zurich to work in New York••2001 Most Beautiful Swiss Books Award, Federal Office for Culture, Switzerland••2000 Most Beautiful Swiss Posters Award, Federal Office for Culture, Switzerland••1998 Most Beautiful Swiss Books Award, Federal Office for Culture, Switzerland

Christoph Niemann Born Waiblingen, Germany, 1970. Lives and works in New York **education** 1991–97 Graphic Design, State Academy of Fine Arts, Stuttgart, Germany **practice** 1999–present Teacher, Conceptual Design, School of Visual Arts, New York••1995–present Freelance designer/illustrator for magazines, newspapers, and corporate clients **selected projects** 2003 F-Stop Catalogue for Font-Shop Berlin (art director Stefan Sagmeister)••2001 Cover, *American Illustration Annual XX* (art director Robert Priest) **selected bibliography** 2002 *D&AD Graphics Book*, RotoVision, London••1999 *Fresh Dialogue 1*, with Nicholas Blechman and Paul Sahre, Princeton Architectural Press, New York••1998 *The Good Portrait*, Maro Verlag, Germany **selected exhibitions** 2003 National Design Triennal, Cooper-Hewitt, National Design Museum, Smithsonian Institution, New York••2002–03 Young Guns I & II, Art Directors Club, New York **awards** 2001 American Illustration Award••2000 ADC Award, Art Directors Club, New York••1998 Student Talent Award, Art Directors Club, Germany **memberships** 1999 Alliance Graphique Internationale (AGI) ••1997 American Institute of Graphic Arts (AIGA)

Nagi Noda Born Tokyo, Japan, 1973. Lives and works in Tokyo **education** 1991–95 Graphic, Product and Interior Design, Women's College of Fine Arts, Tokyo **practice** 2003–present Founder, Uchu Country, Tokyo••1997–2003 Designer, Sun-AD, Tokyo••1995–97 Designer, I & S Onuki Design, Tokyo **selected projects** 2002 Poster and TV commercials for Japanese fashion brand Theatre PRODUCTS', Theatre PRODUCTS', Tokyo••2002 Poster and music video for Yuki, Epic Records, Japan••2001 Book covers, *It's Good Because It's Love*, by Shungiku Uchida, Koudansha, Tokyo••2001–02 Posters and TV campaign for department store Laforet, Laforet Harajuku, Tokyo••2001 Poster campaign for Nike women's swimwear, Nike, Japan **selected bibliography** 2002 *New Blood*, rikuyou-sha, Japan **selected exhibitions** 2003 *Graphic Wave 2003*, Ginza Graphic Gallery, Tokyo **awards** 2002–03 TDC Prize, Tokyo Type Directors Club••2002 Silver Award, Art Directors Club, New York••2001 ADC Prize, Tokyo Art Directors Club••1999 Gold Prize, Tokyo Type Directors Club **memberships** 2001 Tokyo Type Directors Club••2001 Japan Graphic Designers Association (JAGDA)

Norm Dimitri Bruni, born Biel, Switzerland, 1970; Manuel Krebs, born Bern, Switzerland, 1970. Live and work in Zurich **education** 1991–96 Graphic Design, Kantonale Schule für Gestaltung, Biel (DB+MK) **practice** 2000–present Professors of Graphic Design, École Cantonale d'Art de Lausanne••1999–present Norm **selected projects** 2002 *Norm: The Things*, Norm, Zurich••2001 Typeface Simple, Lineto, Zurich and Berlin••2000 *Norm: Introduction*, Norm, Zurich••1999 Typeface Normetica, Lineto, Zurich and Berlin **selected bibliography** 2002 *Super–Welcome to Graphic Wonderland*, Zurich••2001 *Restart: New Systems in Graphic Design*, Thames & Hudson, London••2000 *Swiss Graphic Design*, Die Gestalten, Berlin••2000 *Benzin: Young Swiss Graphic Design*, Lars Müller Publishers, Baden, Switzerland **selected exhibitions** 2002 *Postscript*, Künstlerhaus Wien, Vienna••2002 *We love to meet you*, Palazzo Fortuny, Venice••2002 *Swiss Design Awards*, Museum für Gestaltung, Zurich••2001 *Swiss Design Awards*, Museum Bellerive, Zurich **awards** 2003 Jan Tschichold Prize, Switzerland••2002 Swiss Design Award, Switzerland••2001 Swiss Design Award, Switzerland••1999 Swiss Design Award, Switzerland

Nowakteufelknyrim Stefan Nowak, born Hoexter, Germany, 1964; Philipp Teufel, born Altshausen, Germany, 1958; Petra Knyrim, born Wermelskirchen, Germany, 1967. Live and work in Düsseldorf **education** 1989–92 Visual Communication, University of Applied Arts, Düsseldorf (PK+SN)••1986–89 Communication Design, University of Applied Arts, Darmstadt, Germany (PK+SN)••1980–85 Visual Communication, Hochschule für Gestaltung, Schwäbisch Gmünd, Germany (PT) **practice** 1995–present Partner, Nowakteufelknyrim (PT) ••1992–present

Founding Partners, Nowakteufelknyrim (PK+SN)••1994–present Professor of Communication Design, University of Applied Arts, Düsseldorf (PT)••1995–2001 Lecturer, University of Applied Arts, Düsseldorf (SN)••1993–95 Lecturer, University of Applied Arts, Dortmund (SN)••1985–94 Concept Design, Illner & Teufel, Frankfurt (PT) selected projects 2003 Corporate and exhibition design, Museum Römerkastell, Monheim, Germany••2002 Orientation System for Pedestrians, Düsseldorf, Germany ••2001 Pilon, Orientation System for Dresden••2000 Corporate design, *Continental Shift—A Voyage Between Cultures* exhibition, Bonnefanten Museum Maastricht, Belgium••2000 Communication design, *Totale* exhibition, Museum für Neue Kunst Freiburg, Germany ••1996–99 Corporate and exhibition design, Geldmuseum Frankfurt, German Federal Bank selected bibliography 2003 *Sushi* magazine, HfG Offenbach, Germany••2001 *Museografie und Ausstellungsdesign*, avedition, Ludwigsburg, Germany••1999 *Einszueins—Positionen zum ausstellen*, Nowakteufelknyrim, Düsseldorf••1997 *Design Ausstellen—Austellungsdesign*, Lars Müller Publishers, Baden, Switzerland selected exhibitions 2002 International Poster Biennale, Seoul••2001 International Design Exhibition, Osaka••2000 German Award for Communication Design exhibition, Essen awards 2001 Grand Prize, Prime Ministers Prize, International Design Competition, Osaka••2001 Society of Typographic Design Award, London••2002 Joseph Binder Award, Silver, Vienna••2000 German Award for Communication Design, Design Zentrum, Essen memberships 2002 Art Directors Club (ADC), Germany (PK+SN+PT)••2000 2id, Founding Member, Institute for Interdisciplinary Design, Leipzig (PT)

Fabio Ongarato Born Melbourne, Australia, 1971. Lives and works in Melbourne education 1987–91 Visual Communication, Royal Melbourne Institute of Technology, Melbourne practice 1992–present Creative Director, Fabio Ongarato Design selected projects 2002 Identity, Australian Centre for Contemporary Art, Melbourne••2001 Event and catalogue design, *Lineage—The Architecture of Daniel Libeskind*, Jewish Museum, Melbourne••2000–2001 Event identity, Melbourne Festival Australia••1997 Winter fashion campaign featuring artist Bill Henson, Scanlan & Theodore, Melbourne••2002 Editorial design, *BIG* magazine, New York••2001 Summer fashion campaign, Karen Walker, Auckland, New Zealand selected bibliography 2003 *I.D. Magazine*, New York••2003 "Melbourne Drawing on Culture," *Composite* Magazine, Tokyo••2002 Australian Special Issue, *Eye* magazine, London••2001 *Graphics International*, London awards 2002 Distinction, Australian Graphic Design Association (AGDA)••2001 Major Award, International Society of Typographic Designers (ISTD), London••2000 Judge's Prize, Australian Graphic Design Association (AGDA)••1999 Silver Award Nomination, Design & Art Direction (D&AD), London memberships 2000 International Society of Typographic Designers (ISTD), London••1999 Design Institute of Australia (DIA)••1998 Design & Art Directors (D&AD), London••1997 Australian Graphic Design Association (AGDA)

Tania Prill Born Hamburg, Germany, 1969. Lives and works in Zurich education 1990–96 Visual Communication, University of Fine Arts, Bremen, Germany••1993–95 Visual Communication, University of Art and Design, Zurich practice 2001–present Lecturer, Lucerne School of Arts of Design, Lucerne••2001 Cooperation with Alberto Vieceli, Zurich••2000 Lecturer, School for Art and Media Design, Zurich••1996–2000 Lecturer, School for New Media, Karlsruhe, Germany••1998 Founding of the GmbH für visuelle Gestaltung, Zurich••1997 Professional Designer, Zintzmeyer & Lux, Zurich, and running own studio, Zurich selected projects 2003 Book Design, *Inchoate: An Experiment in Architectural Education*, ETH, Zurich, and ACTAR, Barcelona••2002 Posters for *Stand der Dinge: Neustes Wohnen in Zürich* (with Alberto Vieceli), Federal Building Department of Zurich••1999 Book project, *Die Schweizer Autobahn*, Museum für Gestaltung, Zurich••1998 *Werkschau Hans-Rudolf Lutz*, exhibition of the work of the Swiss typographer, author, publisher, and teacher Hans-Rudolf Lutz, Emmenbrücke, Lucerne selected bibliography 2001 *KAK* magazine, January issue, Moscow••2001 "Swiss Design Now," *KAK* magazine, February issue, Moscow ••2000 *Benzin: Young Swiss Graphic Design*, Lars Müller Publishers, Baden••1996 *Typoundso*,Verlag Hans-Rudolf Lutz, Zurich selected exhibitions 2003 *Die schönsten Schweizer Bücher*, Museum für Gestaltung, Zurich ••2001 2nd International Poster Exhibition, Ningbo, China••2000 19th International Biennale of Graphic Design Brno, Czech Republic awards 2003 Most Beautiful Swiss Books (with Alberto Vieceli), Federal Office for Culture, Switzerland

QWER Iris Utikal, born Kassel, Germany, 1966; Michael Gais, born Hagen, Germany, 1965. Live and work in Cologne education 1986–92 Graphic Design, University of Applied Arts, Düsseldorf (IU+MG) practice 2002–present Professors of Typography and Book Design, Cologne International School of Design (IU +MG)••1994–present Founding Partners, QWER, since 1995 in Cologne••1991–94 Assistance in the Arbeitsgemeinschaft Loesch, Düsseldorf (IU+MG)••1988–90 Internships in London, Helsinki, and Turku (MG)••1985–90 Internships in London, New York, Paris, Zurich, Madrid, and Tokyo (IU) selected projects 1997–present Graphic design, Zanders Feinpapiere, Bergisch Gladbach, Germany••2001 Corporate Design, Kommunalverband Ruhrgebiet, Essen••2001 Corporate and communication design, Kulturregion Hannover••2001 Corporate and communication design, Niedersächsische Sparkassenstiftung, Hannover•• 1994–2000 Corporate identity and Web design, World EXPO 2000 Hannover••2000 Corporate and communication design, Wilhelm Lehmbruck Museum, Duisburg selected exhibitions 2000 *Corporate Design der Stadt Frankfurt am Main*, Frankfurt••1998 *Brecht 100 Plakate*, Berlin••1996 German Award for Communication Design exhibition, Essen••1994 Triennial of the German Poster Museum, Essen••1994 International Poster Festival Chaumont, France••1994 14th International Poster Biennial, Warsaw, Poland selected bibliography 2003 *QWER*, Floating Design, Beijing••1998 *Typographie Wann Wer Wie*, Könemann, Cologne••1997 *Corporate Identity und Corporate Design*, avedition, Ludwigsburg••1997 *form* magazine, January, Germany awards 2002 Second Prize, Kalenderschau, Stuttgart••2001 Art Directors Club Award, Berlin••2001 100 Best Posters Award, German Design Associations, Berlin••2001 Merit Award, Art Directors Club, New York••1999 Winner, Pro Carton CMA Carton Award Competition, Belgium

Reala Laurent Benner, born Langenthal, Switzerland, 1975; Samuel Nyholm born Lund, Sweden, 1973; Jonas Wlliamson, born Umeå, Sweden, 1973. Live and work in

London (LB) and Stockholm (SN+JW) education 1998–2000 M.A., Royal College of Art, London (LB)••1995–99 M.F.A., Konstfack University College of Art, Stockholm (SN+JW)••1995–98 B.A. (Hons.), Central Saint Martins College of Art and Design, London (LB)••1998 Central Saint Martins College of Art and Design, London (SN)••1997 Parsons School of Design, New York (JW) practice 1998–present Founders and Principals, Reala••1996–present Freelance graphic design, illustration, animation••2002 Professors, Beijing Institute of Art and Design••2002 Professors, Brighton University••2000–2002 Professors, Konstfack University, College of Arts, Craft and Design, Stockholm••2001 Professors, École Cantonale d'Art de Lausanne (ECAL)••2000 Professors, Beckman's School of Design, Stockholm selected projects 2003 Design Concept, "Perfect Performance," Performance Festival, Stockholm••1998–2003 Graphic Design, Lydmar Hotel, Stockholm••2002 Music Video, Garbage, Harry Nash, London••2001–02 Research project and motion graphics, Konstfack, Stockholm••2001–02 Graphic concept and motion graphics, Swedish National Television selected bibliography 2003 *Super–Welcome to Graphic Wonderland*, Zurich••2003 *Reala* DVD, GAS, Tokyo••2000 *01+81*, Tokyo••2000 *Benzin:Young Swiss Graphic Design*, Lars Müller Publishers, Baden selected exhibitions 2003 *From Sweden with Love*, Museum für Gestaltung, Zurich••2002 *I Love To Meet You*, Palazzo Fortuny, Venice••2001 *Stealing Eyeballs*, K-Haus, Vienna awards 2000 Winner of the Swiss Federal Design Competition••2000 Company of the Year, Konstfack••1999 Ung Svensk Form, Sweden

Casey Reas Born Troy, Ohio, USA, 1972. Lives and works in Ivrea, Italy education 1999–2001 Media Arts and Sciences, Aesthetics + Computation Group, MIT Media Laboratory, Cambridge, Massachusetts••1991–96 Graphic Design, School of Design, Architecture, Art, and Planning, University of Cincinnati practice 2001–03 Associate Professor, Interaction Design Institute, Ivrea, Italy••1999–2001 Research Assistant, Aesthetics + Computation Group, MIT Media Laboratory, Cambridge, Massachusetts••1997–99 Design Director/Designer, I/O 360° Digital Design, New York selected projects 2003 Processing, Interaction Design Institute Ivrea, Italy••2002 HairyRed, GroupC, Troy, Ohio••2002 Tissue, GroupC, Troy, Ohio••2001 Path, GroupC, Troy, Ohio••2001 RPM, IAMAS, Ogaki, Japan••2000 Dakadaka, Ars Electronica Center, Linz, Austria selected bibliography 2003 *Ubersee #2*, Die Gestalten Verlag, Berlin••2002 *The Graphics Book*, D&AD, London••2002 "Behavioral Kinetic Sculpture," *The Art of Programming*, Sonic Acts Press, Amsterdam••2002 "New Visual Artists Review: 20 Under 30," *Print* magazine, New York selected exhibitions 2002 *Casey Reas/Golan Levin*, Bitforms Gallery, New York••2001 *Animations*, P.S. 1 Contemporary Art Center, New York••2001 *Interaction '01, Dialog with Expanded Images*, IAMAS, Ogaki, Japan••2001 *Workspheres*, Museum of Modern Art, New York awards 2001 Silver Medal, 80th Annual Art Directors Club Awards, New York••2000 Honorable Mention, Tokyo Type Directors Club••1999 Communication Graphics 20 Award, American Institute of Graphic Arts, New York••1998 Web 100 Show, American Center for Design, Chicago

David Richmond Born Manchester, United Kingdom, 1964. Lives and works in London education 1983–86 Graphic Design, London School of Printing practice 2000–present R Design, London (with Iain Dobson, Steve Sheffield, Helen Brewer, Beverly Cook, Lindsey Webb, Janey Barrett)••1991–92 David Richmond Associates, London••1990–91 Michael Abramson, New York••1986–90 Smith & Milton, London selected projects 2001 Branding, packaging, and advertising, The Food Doctor, London••2003 Packaging, Selfridges, London••2000 Identity and packaging, Mea Cosmetics, London••1996 Packaging, Inventory Olive Oil, London••2003 Identity, Sara Bruce Food Consultant, London••2001 Identity, Martin Pritchard Dentist, London selected bibliography 1996 *British Packaging 1996*, BC Editions, London••1990 *Power Packaging 1990*, USA memberships 1998 D&AD••1998 Design Business Association

Sanja Rocco Born Zagreb, Croatia, 1955. Lives and works in Zagreb education 2003 Marketing, Faculty of Economics, University of Zagreb••1982 M.A., Architecture, Faculty of Architecture, University of Zagreb practice 2000–present Art Director and Manager, Rocco & Partner••1990–2000 Freelance designer working in team with T. Bratelj at Castelvenere design studio••1984–90 Designer, Zagreb Publishing House••1983–84 Graffiti design studio selected projects 2002–03 Visual identity, Rocco & Partner Music Production Label, Zagreb••1996–2003 Visual identity and promotion, Sobota Art Gallery, Zagreb••1998–2000 Package redesign project, Pik Vrbovec meat industry, Vrbovec••1998–99 Visual identity, Radio Drama International Festival, Croatian Radio and Television, Zagreb••1991–96 Visual identity and promotion, Croatian Union for the Blind, Zagreb selected bibliography 2000 *European Design Annual*, RotoVision, London••2000 *Print* magazine 54, no. 2, New York••1999 *78th Art Directors Club Annual*, New York••1996 *BIO 15*, Biennial of Industrial Design catalogue, Ljubljana selected exhibitions 2000 19th International Biennale of Graphic Design Brno, Czech Republic••1998 ZGRAF 8, Zagreb••1996 BIO 15, Ljubljana••1995 UNESCO, Paris••1995 Golden Bee Biennale of Graphic Design, Moscow awards 1999 Merit Award, 78th Art Directors Club Annual Design Competition, New York••1996 Golden Award, Third Crane European Letterhead Competition, London and Amsterdam••1996 Silver Bell, 3rd Festo Croatian Advertising Festival, Croatia••1992 1st Prize, Visual Identity Competition, Croatian National and University Library, Croatia memberships 2001 Friends of ICOGRADA••1991 ICOGRADA••1984 Croatian Association of Applied Arts Artists (ULUPUH)

Gabriela Rodriguez Born Mexico City, 1956. Lives and works in Mexico City education 1981–83 Fine Art, San Carlos Academy, Mexico City••1976–81 Graphic Design, National School of Fine Arts, Mexico City practice 2001–present Working in collaboration with Ken Cato on various design projects••1993–present Principal, own studio, Mexico City••1983–present Freelance graphic designer, Mexico City••1981–83 Director of Graphic Design Department, National Institute of Education for Adults, Mexico City selected projects 2002 Channel Eleven Identities, Canal Once, Mexico City••2002 "Greece: Women, Eroticism & Poetry," Agipinu Restaurant, Mexico City••2001 Monterrey Airport ceiling design, Grupo Aeroportuario Centro Norte, Monterrey••1996 Homage to Breton, Embassy of France/CONACULTA/UNAM, Mexico City••1993 Spanish Textbooks, Public Education Ministry, Mexico City••1986 Values of Democracy posters, Federal Electoral

Institute, Mexico City **selected bibliography** 2003 *Eye* magazine, London •• 2003 *Package & Design*, Beijing •• 2002 *A! Diseño*, Mexico City •• 2000 *Étapes Graphiques*, Paris **selected exhibitions** 2003 *Mexican Design*, Milan Biennale •• 2001 *Homage to Toulouse-Lautrec*, international touring exhibition •• 2000 *Traces of Light*, Museo Santa Domingo, Oaxaca •• 1997 *10 Mexican Graphic Designers*, DNP Duo Dojima, Osaka and Ginza Graphic Gallery, Tokyo **awards** 2003 Creative Consulting, DVA Platinum Total Package Design, Los Angeles •• 1998 Gold Award, Political Graphics, Fifth International Biennial of the Poster in Mexico, Mexico City •• 1996 Silver Award, Cultural Graphics, Fourth International Biennial of the Poster in Mexico, Mexico City •• 1992 and 1993 Textbook Design, Public Education Ministry, Mexico City **memberships** 1998 Alliance Graphique Internationale (AGI)

Joe Sacco Born Kirkop, Malta, 1960. Based in New York **education** 1978–81 B.A., Journalism, University of Oregon, Eugene **practice** 1981–present Independent cartoonist/journalist •• 2000 Lecturer, School of Visual Arts, New York •• 1986 Editor, *The Comics Journal*, Los Angeles •• 1985–86 Coeditor and copublisher, Portland Permanent Press **selected bibliography** 2002 *Eye* magazine 44, London •• 2000 *Safe Area Gorazde*, by Joe Sacco, Fantagraphics Books, Seattle •• 1998 *Details* magazine, September issue, New York •• 1993–96 *Palestine*, by Joe Sacco, Fantagraphics Books, Seattle **selected exhibitions** 2001 *Joe Sacco a Ravenna*, Museo d'Arte della Citta, Ravenna, Italy •• 2000 State University of New York, Buffalo **awards** 2002 VPRO Grand Prix, Haarlem, Netherlands •• 2001 Will Eisner Award for Best Original Graphic Novel, USA •• 2001 Guggenheim Fellowship

Ahn Sang-Soo Born Chungju, Korea, 1952. Lives and works in Seoul **education** 2001 Hon. Doctor of Design, Kingston University, London •• 1995 Ph.D., Hanyang University, Seoul •• 1981 M.F.A., Graphic Design, Hongik University, Seoul •• 1977 M.A., Graphic Design, Hongik University, Seoul **practice** 1991–present Graphic Designer and Professor, Hongik University, Seoul •• 1985–91 President, Ahn Graphics •• 1981–85 Art Director, *Madang Magazine* **selected projects** 1985–present Design for magazine *Bogoseo/Bogoseo* •• 1995–present Poster designs for the Jooksan International Art Festival •• 1995–present Ahn Graphics Calendar Design •• 2001 Seoul TypaoJanchi Symbol Design •• 2000 ICOGRADA Millennium Congress, *Oullim* symbol design •• 1999 Ssamzie Art Book Project **selected bibliography** 2002 *Graphis* 327, New York •• 2002 *Baseline* magazine, United Kingdom •• 1999 *Hangul Design*, Ahn Graphics, Seoul **selected exhibitions** 1990 *Front DMZ Cultural Arts Movement Exhibition*, Seoul City Museum •• 2001 *Hangul Exhibition*, GGG Gallery, Tokyo; Osaka DDD Gallery, Japan •• 2002 Solo exhibition, Rodin Gallery, Seoul •• 2002 *Works*, Rhode Island School of Design, Providence **awards** 1999 Grand Prix, Zgraf, Croatia **memberships** 1999 Alliance Graphique Internationale (AGI) •• 1990 Visual Designers' Association of Korea (VIDAK)

Yasuhiro Sawada Born Tokyo, Japan, 1961. Lives and works in Tokyo **education** 1981–85 Graphic Design, Tokyo University of Fine Arts and Music, Tokyo **practice** 1994–present Assistant Professor, Department of Graphic Design, Tama Art University •• 1989–present Sawada Yasuhiro Design Studio •• 1985–89 Art Director, Creative Department, Suntory, Japan **selected projects** 1998–2000 Posters for architectural consultancy, Kosaka Giken, Tokyo •• 1994 Poster for hundredth birthday of Sharaku, Mainichi Newspapers, Tokyo •• 1991 Poster for Amnesty International event, Tokyo •• 1989 Catalogue, Y's for men, Yohji Yamamoto, Tokyo **selected exhibitions** 1997 *4 From Tokyo*, New York Art Directors Club Gallery, New York •• 1997 *100 Japan Plakat 20 Tevezotol*, Decsi Galerie, Budapest •• 1995 *Close-up of Japan*, São Paolo Art Museum •• 1999 *Graphic Message for Ecology*, Ginza Graphic Gallery, Tokyo •• 1996 International Poster Triennial, Toyama •• 1991 Solo exhibition *P2*, Ginza Graphic Gallery, Tokyo **awards** 1994 Bronze Prize, International Poster Triennial, Toyama •• 1993 New Designer Award, Japan Graphic Designers Association, Tokyo •• 1991 Silver Prize, Tokyo Type Directors Club **selected bibliography** 2002 *Graphic Wave 7*, Ginza Graphic Gallery, Tokyo •• 1999 *Sawada Yasuhiro, No Graphic Design*, Kohoku Art Publishers, Tokyo **memberships** 2001 Alliance Graphique Internationale (AGI) •• 1992 Japan Graphic Designers Association •• 1992 Tokyo Type Directors Club

Claudia Schmauder Born Zurich, Switzerland, 1967. Lives and works in Zurich **education** 1992–97 Visual Communication, Schule für Gestaltung, Zurich **practice** 1998–present Freelance graphic designer •• 1998–99 Research Projects, Schule für Gestaltung, Zurich **selected projects** 2001 Illustrations for in-flight magazine, *Swissair Gazette*, Swissair •• 1996–2001 Posters and book designs, Johann Jacobs Museum, Zurich •• 2000 Cover illustration, Trucks calendar 2001, Daimler-Benz (Mercedes) •• 1999 Research project for Blister Packaging, Schule für Gestaltung, Zurich **selected bibliography** 1998 "Claudia Schmauder," *IDEA* magazine 271, Tokyo **selected exhibitions** 2002 Poster exhibition, *Swiss Posters: Collection of the National Museum*, Poznan, Poland •• 1999 *Type Directors Exhibition*, New York •• 1998 18th International Biennale of Graphic Design Brno, Czech Republic **awards** 2000 Tokyo Type Directors Club Award •• 1999 Diploma for Typographic Excellence, Type Directors Club, New York •• 1998 18th International Biennale of Graphic Design Brno, Czech Republic •• 1996 Swiss Posters of the Year

Nico Schweizer Born Zurich, Switzerland, 1969. Lives and works in New York **education** 1992-94 School of Visual Arts, New York •• 1990-92 Art Center College of Design, Montreux, Switzerland **practice** 2003–present Art Director, *I.D. Magazine*, New York •• 2000–present Professor, Typography and Design, Cooper Union School of Design, New York •• 1997–98 Collaborated with J. Abbott Miller, Design/Writing/Research, New York •• 1997 Collaborated with Cornel Windlin, Switzerland •• 1994 Collaborated with Jonathan Hoefler, The Hoefler Type Foundry, New York **selected projects** 2003 Book design, *Room 606—The SAS House and the Work of Arne Jacobsen*, by Michael Sheridan, Phaidon Press, London and New York •• 2002 Record cover, *Kamaal/The Abstract*, by Q-Tip, Arista Records, USA •• 2002 Typeface, LeCorbusier Bold, Mediadub.com, New York •• 2001 Record cover, *Young Lawyers*, by French Kicks, Startime Records, USA •• 2000 Book cover, *Goldfinger*, by Ian Fleming, Flagstick Publications, USA **selected bibliography** 2001 *Young Guns 3*, Art Directors Club, New York **selected exhibitions** 2002

Postscript, Künstlerhaus Wien, Vienna ••2001 *Young Guns 3* design exhibition, Art Directors Club, New York

Chen Shaohua Born Zhejiang, China, 1954. Lives and works in Shenzhen and Beijing **education** 1982 Graduated from Tingshua University, Academy of Art and Design, Beijing ••1978 Graduated from Central Academy of Craftwork and Art, Beijing ••1975 Graduated from Central Academy of Arts & Design, Xi'an, China **practice** 2001 Established Beijing Chen Shaohua Design ••1992 Established Shenzhen Chen Shaohua Design ••1988 Engaged in advertising and design in Shenzhen ••1982–88 Professor, Xi'an Academy of Art, Xi'an, China **selected projects** 2002 Logo, Beijing Foreign Studies University, Beijing ••2002 Logo, China Development Bank ••2001 Logo, Beijing 2008 Olympic Games Bid Committee ••2001 Logo, Asian Development Bank 35th annual meeting, Shanghai ••1995 Stamp design for Fourth United Nations World Conference on Women, Stamp Printing Bureau, China **selected exhibitions** 1998 16th International Poster Biennale, Warsaw ••1998 *L'affiche Chinoise* exhibition and lecture, Centre Georges Pompidou, Paris ••1997 Included in the *Asia-Pacific Poster Exhibition*, Hong Kong ••1997 5th Best Advertising Exhibition of China **awards** 1998 Chairman's Prize, 18th International Graphic Design Biennale Brno, Czech Republic ••1996 Judge's Award and silver prize for poster design, *Graphic Design in China* exhibition ••1992 Silver Prize, Poster Design, *Graphic Design in China* exhibition ••1984 Gold Prize, 6th Exhibition of Fine Art of China ••1984 Gold Rooster Award, Fine Art Direction of Chinese film **memberships** 1999 Alliance Graphic International (AGI) ••1984 China Association of Artists

So Man-yee Born Hong Kong, 1953. Lives and works in Hong Kong **education** 1973 Graphic Design, First Institute of Art and Design, Hong Kong ••1972 Western Painting, Hong Kong Ninghoi Arts School, Hong Kong **prac-tice** 2000–present Partner, H + S Design, Hong Kong ••2000–present Visiting Professor, University of Shanghai ••2000–present Adviser, Shanghai Hong Kong Culture Exchange Association ••1996–present Chairperson, Hong Kong Female Contemporary Art Association ••1994–present Board of Directors, Hong Kong Chingying Institute of Visual Arts **selected projects** 2002 Gift-pack design, Expo 2010 Shanghai China Bidding Office, Shanghai ••2000 Calendar design 2002, Tai Tak Takeo Fine Paper, Hong Kong ••2002 Product and packaging design, H + S Gallery, Shanghai ••1999 Book design, *Image of Shanghai*, Information Office, Shanghai Municipal People's Government, Shanghai ••1999 Poster design, Macau Return to China, Macao Designers Association, Macao ••1998 Book Design, *Colours of Macau*, Society of Worldwide Ethnic Chinese Photographers, China **selected bibliography** 2002, 1999, 1998 *Package & Design*, Guangzhou, China ••1998 *Monthly Design*, Korea ••1981 *Graphic Design*, Japan ••1981 *Asian Designers*, Taiwan **selected exhibitions** 2002 *Art & Design Exhibition*, Xintiandi, Shanghai ••1998 *Century Woman Art Exhibition*, Beijing ••1996 *Hong Kong Artist Series*, Hong Kong Museum of Art ••1981 *Design Now Hong Kong*, Japan **awards** 2002 Gold Award, Packaging Design, China Star, China ••1998–2002 Award of Distinction, Creativity Annual, USA ••1998 Publication Gold Award, Hong Kong Designers Association Show ••1982 Professional Gold Award, Conqueror Corporate Identity Design Competition, Hong Kong **memberships** 1980 Hong Kong Designers Association

Leonardo Sonnoli Born Trieste, Italy, 1962. Lives and works in Rimini and Trieste **education** 1982–87 Graphic Design, High Institute for Applied Arts (ISIA), Urbino **practice** 2002–present Cofounder and Partner, CODEsign ••1989–2002 Creative Director, Dolcini Associati **selected projects** 2003 Venice Biennale, International Art Exposition ••2000–2003 Posters for University of Architecture in Venice (IUAV) ••2000–2003 Corporate identity, Province of Rimini ••2002 Calendar 2003, Scheufelen Paper Company, Stuttgart ••1996–2002 Corporate posters for cultural events, Don Gaudiano Foundation, Pesaro ••1998–99 Corporate posters for cultural events, City of Pesaro **selected bibli-ography** 2002 *Up Against the Wall*, Mies, Switzerland ••2002 *New AGI Members*, China ••2002 *Images du Monde, Monde des Images*, Chaumont, France ••2000 *Type Graphics*, Rockport Publishers, Gloucester, Massachusetts ••2000 *4:3-50 Years of Italian and German Design*, Bonn **selected exhibi-tions** 2002 *AGI Poster Exhibition*, California College of Arts and Crafts, San Francisco ••2002 *Images du Monde, Monde des Images*, Chaumont Poster Festival, France ••2001 *Graphisme(s)*, Bibliothèque Nationale de France, Paris ••2001 *Leonardo Sonnoli and the City of Pesaro*, Chaumont, France **awards** 2002 Merit Award, Art Directors Club, New York ••2001 Honorable Mention, XIX Compasso d'Oro, Italy ••2000 Silver Medal, 6th International Poster Triennal, Toyama, Japan ••1998 Golden Bee poster award, Golden Bee Internationale Biennale of Graphic Design, Moscow **memberships** 2000 Alliance Graphique Internationale (AGI)

Jennifer Sterling Born Miami, USA, 1964. Lives and works in San Francisco **practice** 1997–present Professor, Typography and Graphic Design, California College of Arts and Crafts, San Francisco ••1995–present Principal, Sterling Design, San Francisco **selected projects** 2003 Book design, Sterling Design Monograph, Ginko Press, California ••2001 Yahoo! Interactive Instant Messenger Design, San Francisco ••2000 Branding design for a coalition under the direction of Hillary Clinton and Madeline Albright, New York ••2000 Poster design, San Francisco Museum of Modern Art **selected exhibitions** 2001 Solo exhibition, San Francisco Museum of Modern Art ••2001 National Design Triennial, Cooper-Hewitt, National Design Museum, Smithsonian Institution, New York ••Part of the permanent collections of the Library of Congress, Cooper-Hewitt, National Design Museum, Museum für Kunst und Gewerbe Hamburg, San Francisco Museum of Modern Art, and Bibliothèque Nationale de France **awards** 2002 Communication Arts award for book design, American Institute of Graphic Arts (AIGA) ••2000 *ID* Design Review Award for interactive video ••1999 and 2000 Walter Landor Award for Design, San Francisco ••1999, 2000 Best of Show, San Francisco Advertising Association ••1999, 2000 Marget Larson Award, San Francisco Advertising Association ••1998 *Graphis* Magazine, voted one of the top 12 gobal design firms **memberships** 2000 Alliance Graphique Internationale (AGI) ••2000 Architecture and Design Accessions Board, San Francisco Museum of Modern Art ••2000 Who's Who in America ••1995 Type Directors Club ••1995 American Center for Design ••1993 American Institute of Graphic Arts (AIGA)

Swip Stolk Born Zaandam, Netherlands, 1944. Lives and works in Zaandam **education** self-educated **practice** 1965–present Freelance graphic designer••2003 Designer, Visionair, 2D-3D, Netherlands••1996–2000 Art Director/Designer, Rembrandt House museum, Amsterdam••1980–87 Professor, Graphic Design, Illustration, and Miixed Media, Gerrit Rietveld Academy, Amsterdam••1977–79 Art director, VARA Television, Netherlands••1974–79 Professor, Graphic Design, Aki (Academy of Art and Industry), Enschede, Netherlands **selected projects** 2003 Corporate identity, *D Magazine*, Berlin••2002 Code—Uncode project, ID Laser, Netherlands••2001 Shop design for shoe designer Jan Jansen, Amsterdam••2001 Corporate Indentity, *Chiq* magazine, Amsterdam••1987–2000 Corporate Indentity, New Groninger Museum, Groningen (with Allesandro Mendini, Philppe Starck and Coop Himmelb(l)au) **selected bibliography** 2003 "A –Z," by Swip Stolk and Valerio Spada, *Stile* magazine no. 4, Italy••2002 "Radically Swip Stolk," *Graphis* magazine 340, New York••2000 *Swip Stolk—Master Forever*, by Han Steenbruggen and Frans Haks, Groninger Museum, Netherlands ••2000 "Swift Swift Swip," *Dutch* magazine, Netherlands **selected exhibitions** 2001 Solo exhibition *106 Poster Designs*, Groninger Museum, Netherlands••2000 *Rembrandt Series*, Gallery Flatland, Utrecht and Paris••2000 Swip Stolk retrospective exhibition, Groninger Museum, Netherlands **awards** 1998–2003 Best Dutch Book Design Award, BNO, Netherlands••1990 H.N.Werkman Award, City of Amsterdam••1969 Frans Duwaer prize for Typography, City of Amsterdam ••1968–1974 Several awards from the Art Directors Club, Netherlands **memberships** 2001 Alliance Graphique Internationale (AGI)••1996 Dutch Designers Association (BNO)

Remo Stoller Born Thun, Switzerland, 1977. Lives and works in Bern **education** 1993–98 Graphic Design, Schule für Gestaltung, Bern **practice** 1998–present Independent graphic designer **selected bibliography** 2001 *Benzin, Young Swiss Graphic Design*, Lars Müller Publishers, Baden, Switzerland••2000 *Swiss Graphic Design*, Die Gestalten Verlag, Berlin **awards** 1998 SGV Förderpreis, Design Network, Switzerland **memberships** 2000 Rainbow, Switzerland

Kosta Stratigos Born Ann Arbor, Michigan, USA, 1974. Lives and works in Metro-Detroit **education** 2002 M.F.A., 2D Design, Cranbrook Academy of Art, Bloomfield Hills, Michigan••1997 B.A., Film and Video Studies, University of Michigan, Ann Arbor, Michigan **practice** 2001–present Principal, MEDIA-LUXE••2002–03 Adjunct Faculty, School of Art and Design, University of Michigan, Ann Arbor, Michigan••2001-02 Instructor, Digital Media and Animation, College for Creative Studies, Detroit••1999–2000 Production Artist, Organic, Inc., Bloomfield Hills, Michigan••1998–99 Traffic Coordinator, Ross Roy Communications, Inc., Bloomfield Hills, Michigan••1992–98 Worked in a record store **selected projects** 2002 Miss Thunder National, Rock and Roll Music and Packaging, Bloomfield Hills, Michigan••2002 Dirty Whore Megastore, Zine, Bloomfield Hills, Michigan••2001 Insomniac's Handbook, Narrative Cycle, Illustrations and Binding, Bloomfield Hills, Michigan••2000 Composite event flyer, Detroit Bitter, Detroit, Michigan **selected bibliography** 2002 Insomniac's Handbook, Cranbrook Academy of Art Catalogue••2002 Fairy Tale, Cranbrook Academy of Art Catalogue **selected exhibitions** 2003 *Zine Scene*, Orange County Art Museum, Costa Mesa, California••2002 Cranbrook Academy of Art Student Degree Show, Bloomfield Hills, Michigan••2002 Cranbrook Academy of Art Student Video Show, Cranbrook Art Museum, Bloomfield Hills, Michigan••1999 New York International Film and Video Festival, New York••1997 University of Michigan Student Film Show, Ann Arbor, Michigan

Yuri Surkov Born Moscow, Russia, 1961. Lives and works in Moscow **education** 1986–90 Graphic Design, 1905 Art School, Moscow **practice** 1992–present Freelance graphic designer **selected projects** 2000 Coexistence poster for international invitational poster action, Museum on the Seam, Jerusalem••2000 Poster for Golden Bee 5, Moscow International Biennale of Graphic Design••2000 Water for human kind poster for international poster action, Association pour une Banque d'Images, Paris••1998 Brecht 100 poster for International Invitational Poster Action, Berliner Ensemble, Verband der Grafik-Designer (VGD), Berlin **selected bibliography** 2000 "Yuri Surkov," *Design Exchange*, China Youth Press, China••1999 "Born a Survivor," *Graphis* 320, New York••1999 *Fusion 2002 International*, Fusion Art Institute, Tokyo••1996, 1994 *Graphis Poster*, Zurich and New York **selected exhibitions** 1995–2002 International poster biennials and triennials in Chaumont, Helsinki, Mons, Moscow, Toyama, and Warsaw••2000, 1998, 1996 Ogaki International Invitational Poster Exhibition, Japan••1999, 1997 Colorado International Invitational Poster Exhibition, Colorado State University Gallery, Fort Collins••1998 International poster exhibition on the occasion of Bertolt Brecht's hundredth birthday, Deutsches Plakat Museum, Essen, Germany **awards** 2002 Bronze Medal, 18th International Poster Biennale, Warsaw••2000, 1997 Gold Medals, "Fourth Block" International Ecological Graphics and Poster Trienniale, Kharkiv, Ukraine••1998, 1996, 1994 Golden Bee Awards, Golden Bee International Biennale of Graphic Design, Moscow••1995 Encouraging Diploma, *ZGRAF 7*, International Exhibition of Graphic Design in Zagreb **memberships** 2000 Alliance Graphique Internationale (AGI)••1999 Academy of Graphic Design, Moscow••1993 Society of Russian Designers

Thonik Nikki Gonnissen, born Amsterdam, Netherlands, 1967; Thomas Widdershoven, born Maastricht, Netherlands, 1960. Live and work in Amsterdam **education** 1993 B.A., Art School, Utrecht (NG)••1993 B.A., Rietveld Academy for Fine Arts, Amsterdam (TW)••1988 M. Phil., University of Amsterdam (TW) **practice** 2001–present Professors, Rietveld Academy for Fine Arts, Amsterdam••1993–present Founding Partners, Gonnissen and Widdershoven; since 2000 Thonik••2000 Professor, Eindhoven Design Academy (TW)••1995–2000 Professor, Arnhem Art School (TW) **selected projects** 2003 Visual communication, *2003 van Gogh Year*, Van Gogh Museum, Amsterdam••2002 Identity program, City of Amsterdam, in collaboration with Eden, Amsterdam••2002 Book design, *Less and More*, 010 publishers, Rotterdam••2000 Visual communication, *Over the Edges*, S.M.A.K., Ghent, Belgium••1996 Identity program and communication, Centraal Museum, Utrecht••1996 Literary-magazine covers, *Tirade*, van Oorschot, Amsterdam **selected bibliography** 2003 *Type at Work: The Use* *of Type in Editorial Design*, Index Books ••2001 *Thonik®, New Dutch Graphic Design*, BIS Publishers, Amsterdam ••2001 *Apples & Oranges 01: Best Dutch Graphic Design*, BIS Publishers, Amsterdam ••2001 *HD: Holland Design New Graphics*, exhibition catalogue, ACTAR, Barcelona **selected exhibitions** 2003 *Super Woman*, Hong Kong Heritage Museum ••2003 *Reality Machines*, Netherlands Architecture Institute, Rotterdam ••2001 *010101—Art in Technological Times*, San Francisco Museum of Modern Art ••1999 *Mooi maar Goed: Graphic Design in the Netherlands 1987–1998*, Stedelijk Museum, Amsterdam **awards** 2003 Nederlandse Huisstijlprijs (Dutch Corporate Identity Award 2003), Grafische Cultuurstichting, Netherlands ••2001, 1999, 1997, 1996, 1995, 1994, 1993, De Best Verzorgde Boeken (The Best Book Designs), Stedelijk Museum, Amsterdam ••1997 Gold Award for Graphic Design, Art Directors Club Europe, London ••1998 Graphics Best of Category, *I.D Magazine*, New York Annual Design Review **memberships** 1993 Dutch Designers Association (BNO) ••1993 Art Directors Club Netherlands

TRUE

Born Los Angeles, USA, 1968. Lives and works in Brooklyn, New York **education** 1992–96 Design, Cooper Union School of Art, New York ••1991–92 Art and Psychology, Sarah Lawrence College, Bronxville, New York **practice** 1997–present Principal, HGX DESIGN, Brooklyn, New York ••2002 Artist in Residence, El-Hajj Malik el-Shabazz School, Brooklyn, New York ••2000–2001 Design Teacher, Parsons School of Design, New York **selected projects** 2002 "Japanese Internment Camps 1942, INS Detention Centers 2002—What's the Difference?," Guerrilla Art, New York ••1998–2002 Editorial illustrations, *Source* magazine, New York ••2001 "Oodles of Doodles for Your Noodle," American Institute of Graphic Arts (AIGA) / Art with Heart, Seattle ••1996 *GOD & us (an illustrated book of theosophy)*, self-published, New York ••1994 "Life Instructions," Guerrilla Art, New York ••1993 "Crosswalks," Guerrilla Art, Los Angeles, New York **selected bibliography** 2001 *How* magazine ••2001 *Eye* magazine 41, London ••2000 "*I.D. 40*," *I.D. Magazine*, New York ••1999 *Metropolis Magazine* **selected exhibitions** 2002 *Visions*, Museum of Contemporary African Diasporian Art (MoCADA), New York **awards** 1992 Full-tuition scholarship, Cooper Union School of Art, New York **memberships** 2000 Graphic Artists Guild

2x4

Michael Rock, born Rhode Island, USA, 1959; Susan Sellers, born Pennsylvania, USA, 1967; Georgie Stout, born New York, USA, 1967. Live and work in New York **education** 1998 B.F.A., Graphic Design, Rhode Island School of Design, Providence (GS) ••1994 M.A., American Studies, Yale University, Connecticut (SS) ••1989 B.F.A., Graphic Design, Rhode Island School of Design, Providence (SS) ••1984 M.F.A., Graphic Design, Rhode Island School of Design, Providence (MR) ••1981 B.A., Literature, Union College, New York (MR) **practice** 1997–2003 Lecturer in Design, Yale University, Connecticut (SS) ••1991–2003 Professor of Art, Yale University, Connecticut (MR) ••1995–99 Visiting Fellow, Jan Van Eyck Academy, Maastricht, Netherlands (MR) ••1995 Establishment of 2x4 (MR+SS+GS) ••1989–94 Bethany Johns Design (GS) ••1986–91 Adjunct Professor for Graphic Design, Rhode Island School of Design, Providence (MR) **selected projects** 2003 Environmental design, Dia Center/Beacon, Beacon, New York ••2002–03 Graphic and environmental design, Nasher Sculpture Center (with Renzo Piano Building Workshop), Dallas, Texas ••2001-03 Wallpaper and short films (with OMA/Rem Koolhaas), Prada Epicenter store, New York ••2001-03 Graphic and environmental design, Mori Art Museum, Tokyo ••2001-03 Graphic and environmental design, IIT Campus Center (with OMA/Rem Koolhaas), Chicago ••2001 Graphic and environmental design, Guggenheim Las Vegas, Nevada **selected bibliography** 2002 "Designer as Author," *Looking Closer Four: Critical Writings on Graphic Design*, Allworth Press and AIGA, New York ••2000 "Saving Jelly," *Emigre* magazine 54, Sacramento, California ••1999 "Forest of Signs," *I.D. Magazine*, September/October, New York ••1998 "Museum of the Ordinary," *Eye* magazine 28, London ••1996 "Mixed Messages," *I.D. Magazine*, September/October, New York **selected exhibitions** 2003 Design Triennial, Cooper Hewitt National Design Museum, Smithsonian Institution, New York ••2002 Artist Space, New York City **awards** 2000 Rome Prize, American Academy in Rome (MR)

Tycoon Graphics

Yuichi Miyashi, born Tokyo, Japan, 1964; Naoyuki Suzuki, born Niigata prefecture, Japan, 1964. Live and work in Tokyo **education** 1983–87 Graphic Design, Tokyo Institute of Art and Design (NS) **practice** 1991–present Art Directors/Graphic Designers, Tycoon Graphics, Tokyo ••1987–90 Graphic Designer for Contemporary Production (NS) ••1985–90 Graphic Designer, Diamond Heads Inc. (YM) **selected projects** 2002–present Lucky Strike, British American Tobacco Japan, Tokyo ••2002–present TyGun project, TyGun/Tycoon Graphics, Tokyo ••2002 Atehaca project, Toshiba Corporation, Tokyo ••2002 Versus Exhibition 02, Parco Museum, Tokyo ••2002 CD packaging, *Gokujo Hybrid*, by Bird, Sony Music Associated Records, Tokyo ••2001-02 Motion Element, Motion Element, Tokyo **selected bibliography** 1999 *A&D scan Tycoon Graphics*, Rikuyosha, Tokyo ••1995 *G-Men*, Little more, Tokyo **selected exhibitions** 2002 *Versus Exhibition 02*, Parco Museum, Tokyo 2002 *The Doraemon*, Suntory Museum, Osaka **awards** 1999 Gold Award for Graphic Design and Silver Award for Advertising, Art Directors Club, New York ••2000 79th Merit Award for Graphic Design, 78th Art Directors Club Awards, New York **memberships** Graphickers (MY+NS)

Rick Valicenti

Born Pittsburgh, Pennsylvania, USA, 1951. Lives and works in Barrington, Illinois **education** 1976 M.F.A., Photography, University of Iowa ••1973 B.F.A., Painting and Drawing, Bowling Green State University **practice** 1981–present Self-employed, Thirst (3st.com and thirstype.com) **selected projects** 2003 Apex sans Font Family, Thirstype.com, USA, in collaboration with Chester ••2002 Oxford, The Holly Hunt Collection, Gilbert Paper, USA ••2001 Infinity Font Family, Thirstype.com, USA, in collaboration with Chester ••1999–2000 Herman Miller Neocon Experience, Chicago, in collaboration with Joyce Mast ••1992 Manhattan Gentle Luv, Osaka ••1990 ESSE introduction, Gilbert Paper, USA **selected bibliography** *2002 Emigre* magazine, Sacramento, California ••2000 *Graphic Radicals/Radical Graphics*, by Laurel Harper, Katherine McCoy, Chronicle Books, San Francisco ••1999 *Typography Now: The Next Wave*, by Rick Poyner, Booth-Clibborn Editions, London ••1992 *Eye* magazine, London **selected exhibitions** 2001 First Seoul Typography Biennale, Seoul ••1997 Solo exhibition, Canon Digital Gallery, Tokyo ••1992 solo exhibitions, GGG and DDD Galleries, Osaka and

Tokyo••Selected Thirst works have also been included in the permanent collection of the Cooper-Hewitt National Design Museum, Smithsonian Institution **awards** 2001 Silver Medal, Art Directors Club New York••1995 *ID Magazine*, 40 top designers (first listing)••ACD 100, American Center for Design••Two-time nomination for Chrysler Design Awards **memberships** 1998 Alliance Graphique Internationale (AGI)••1981–83 President, Society of Typographic Arts (later known as the American Center for Design)••1985 Board Member, Chicago chapter, American Institute of Graphic Arts (AIGA)

Alberto Vieceli Born Zurich, Switzerland, 1965. Lives and works in Zurich **education** 1988–92 Graphic Design, School of Design, Zurich **practice** 2001–present, Cooperation with graphic designer Tania Prill, Zurich••1996 Founded own graphic design studio, Zurich••1995–96 Graphic Designer, Lars Müller Publishers, Baden, Switzerland••1992–94 Graphic Designer, Polly Bertram & Jul Keyser, Zurich **selected projects** 2003 Book design, *Inchoate, An experiment in architectural education*, ETH, Zurich and ACTAR, Barcelona (with Tania Prill)••2002 Posters for *Stand der Dinge: Neustes Wohnen in Zürich*, Federal Building Department of Zurich, Zurich (with Tania Prill) **selected bibliography** 2003 *Graphic Design for the 21st Century*, Taschen, Cologne••2001 *Swissmade*, Verlag Hochparterre, Zurich••2000 *Benzin: Young Swiss Graphic Design*, Lars Müller Publishers, Baden, Switzerland **selected exhibitions** 2001 *Swissmade, An Exhibition of Contemporary Swiss Design*, Museum of Applied Arts, Cologne••1997 Swiss Design Competition Show (Eidgenössischer Wettbewerb für Gestaltung), organised by the Swiss Arts Office, Basel **awards** 2003 Most Beautiful Swiss Books, Federal Office for Culture, Switzerland (with Tania Prill)••2003 Swiss Poster Award, APG, Switzerland (with Tania Prill)••2000 Most Beautiful Swiss Books, Federal Office for Culture, Switzerland••1997–98 Most Beautiful Swiss Books, Federal Office for Culture, Switzerland

Garth Walker Born Pretoria, South Africa, 1957. Lives and works in Durban, South Africa **education** 1976–78 Diploma, Graphic Design, Technikon Natal, Durban **practice** 1995–present Founder and Director, Orange Juice Design, Durban••1995–present Graphic Design mentor for Durban Institute for Technology, Vaal TriangleTechnikon, Imagination Lab Durban, Vega School of Design **selected projects** 1995–present Publisher of *i-jusi*, Orange Juice Design's experimental studio magazine, Durban••2003 Typeface and signage design, New Constitutional Court of South Africa, Johannesburg Development Agency, Johannesburg••2002-03 Ideas That Matter project, SAPPI Paper, Johannesburg••1998–2003 Unilever SA Pension Fund Annual Reports, Unilever South Africa, Durban••2002 Aids Management Standard identity, Liberty Life Limited, Cape Town **selected bibliography** *Design Week*, January, London•• 2001 *Issues—New Magazine Design*, Gingko Press, London••2000 *Étapes Graphique*s magazine, November, Paris••1999 *Creative Review*, September, London ••1997 *Emigre Magazine* 43, Sacramento, California **selected exhibitions** 2003 *No Boundaries: Visions of Design Today*, Palacio de Sastago, Zaragoza, Spain••2002 *Vive le Graphisme*!, Galerie Anatome, Paris••2000 *Graphistes Autour du Monde*, Echirolles, France••2001 *TypoJanchi 2001*, Seoul Arts Centre, Seoul••1998 *Forum Typografie*, Potsdam, Germany **awards** 2001 Grand Prix, Loeries, South Africa••1998, 2002 D&AD Annual, D&AD, London••1998 Silver Award, Art Directors Club, New York **memberships** 2002 Alliance Graphique Internationale (AGI)••2000 THINK (South African Design Council)••1998 British Design & Art Directors Club (D&AD)••1992 Type Directors Club, New York

Chris Ware Born Omaha, Nebraska, 1967. Lives and works in Chicago **education** 1991–93 Printmaking, School of the Art Institute of Chicago••1991 B.F.A., Painting, University of Texas at Austin••1989 Skowhegan School of Painting and Sculpture, Skowhegan, Maine **selected projects** 1993–present *The ACME Novelty Library*, Fantagraphics Books, Seattle••1986-present Weekly or daily newspaper cartoon strip••2003 *Quimby the Mouse*, by Chris Ware, Fantagraphics Books, Seattle••2003 *The Acme Novelty Datebook*, Oog and Blik, Amsterdam••2000 *Jimmy Corrigan, The Smartest Kid on Earth*, by Chris Ware, Pantheon Books, New York **selected bibliography** 2001 "The Book You Have to Read," *Entertainment Weekly*, 23 February, New York••2000 "After Wham! Pow! Shazam!," *New York Times Book Review*, 26 November, New York••2000 "Right Way, Corrigan," *Time* magazine, 11 September, New York••1999 "*Wie Musik auf Papier*," *Der Spiegel*, October, Hamburg **selected exhibitions** 2002 *American Comics*, Centre Angoulême de la Bande Dessinée, Angoulême, France••2002 Whitney Biennial, Whitney Museum of American Art, New York••2001 *Summer Reading: The Recreation of Language in 20th Century Art*, Frances Lehman Loeb Art Center, Vassar College, Poughkeepsie, New York••2000 National Design Triennial, Cooper-Hewitt, National Design Museum, Smithsonian Institution, New York **selected awards** Best Book of the Year (L'Alph d'Art), Angoulême, France••2001 Guardian First Book Award, London••2000 American Book Award, USA **memberships** 1998 American Banjo Fraternity

Martin Woodtli Born Bern, Switzerland, 1971. Lives and works in Zurich **education** 1996–98 Visual Communication, Academy of Art and Design, Zurich••1990–95 Graphic Design, School of Design, Bern **practice** 2002–present Teacher, Academy of Art and Design, Lucerne, Switzerland••1999–present Head of individual studio in Zurich••2002–03 Guest Professor, Staatlichen Akademie der Bildenden Künste, Stuttgart, Germany••2002 Workshop, School of Design, Biel, Switzerland••1998–99 Worked for Stefan Sagmeister, New York **selected projects** 2003 Poster for Jazzfestival Schaffhausen, Schaffhausen••2003 Poster for the Internationales Video and Film Festival VideoEx, VideoEx, Zurich••2001 Book design *Woodtli*, Die Gestalten Verlag, Berlin••2000 Poster for art event "onthespot," Bern••1999 Corporate design for contemporary-art space Stadtgalerie, Stadtgalerie Bern••1995 Corporate design for contemporary-art space Kiosk, Kunstkanal Bern **selected bibliography** 2001 *Woodtli*, Die Gestalten Verlag, Berlin••2001 *IDEA 285*, Tokyo••2000 *Benzin: Young Swiss Graphic Design*, Lars Müller Publishers, Baden, Switzerland••2000 "The I.D. Forty," *I.D. Magazine*, New York **selected exhibitions** 2002 *Postscript*, Künstlerhaus Wien, Vienna **awards** 2002 Most Beautiful Swiss Books and Book of the Jury, Federal Office for Culture, Switzerland••1999 Swiss Federal Design Prize, Swiss Federal Department, Section Art and Design, Switzerland **memberships** 2000 Alliance Graphique Internationale (AGI)

Michael Worthington Born St. Ives, United Kingdom, 1966. Lives and works in Los Angeles **education** 1993–95 M.F.A., Graphic Design, California Institute of the Arts, Los Angeles •• 1988–91 B.A. (Hons.), Graphic Design, Central Saint Martins College of Art and Design, London **practice** 1998–present Codirector, Graphic Design Program, California Institute of the Arts, Los Angeles •• 1995–present Design Faculty, California Institute of the Arts, Los Angeles •• 1991–present Practicing graphic designer **selected projects** 2003 "From B.J. With Love," essay on medalist Robert Brownjohn, AIGA 365 Annual, USA •• 2001 "Personal Modernism," *Restart: New Systems in Graphic Design*, Thames and Hudson, London •• 2001 "Right On!," essay, *Eye* magazine 41, London •• 2000 Book design (with Lorraine Wild), *In Between Places*, Henry Art Gallery, Seattle, Washington •• 1999 Book design, *Bas Jan Ader*, University of California, Irvine •• 1999 "Seduced by Stillness," essay, *Eye* magazine 33, London •• 1999 Catalogue design (with Geoff McFetridge), CalArts Bulletin, CalArts, Los Angeles **selected bibliography** 2002 *East coast/West coast*, Textuel, France •• 1999 "Designers in LA," *Eye* magazine 31, London •• 1998 *New Design: Los Angeles*, Rockport Press, USA **selected exhibitions** 2003 *Remix*, CENAR, San Salvador, El Salvador •• 2002 *Californian Dream, Graphic Designers in California*, Echirolles, France •• 2002 City of Los Angeles (COLA) fellowship show, Japanese American National Museum **awards** 2001–2002 Individual Artist Fellowship, City of Los Angeles (COLA) **memberships** 1996 American Institute of Graphic Design

Wang Xu Born Chaozhou, Guangdong, China, 1955. Lives and works in Guangzhou and Beijing **education** 1997 Graduated from Design Department of Guangzhou Fine Arts College, Guangzhou **practice** 1995–present Founder and Creative Director, Wang Xu & Associates, Beijing •• 1986–95 Graphic designer, Hong Kong •• 1980–86 Graphic designer, Guangzhou **selected projects** 2002–present Designer and Editor, *Lighter Magazine*, Exchange Publishing, China •• 2000 Book design and promotional posters, *Artistic Conception Writing*, China Youth Press, China •• 1986–2000 Designer, editor, and publisher, *Design Exchange* magazine, China •• 2000 Poster for Second International Ink Painting Biennial of Shenzhen, China **selected bibliography** 2002 *New AGI Members*, China •• 1998 *Graphis* 316, New York **awards** 1996–2003 Two Silver Medals, one Distinctive Award, and eight Merit Awards, Art Directors Club, New York •• 1998 and 2000 Golden Bee Awards, 4th and 5th International Biennale of Graphic Design, Moscow •• 1996 Icograda Excellence Award, 17th International Biennale of Graphic Design Brno, Czech Republic **memberships** 2000 Alliance Graphique Internationale (AGI) •• 1996 Art Directors Club, New York

Catherine Zask Born Paris, France, 1961. Lives and works in Paris, France **education** 1979–84 École Supérieure d'Arts Graphiques (ESAG), Paris **practice** 1986–present Freelance graphic designer **selected projects** 1997–present Visual identity and visual communications, L'Hippodrome de Douai •• 1993–present Visual identity and visual communications, Société Civile des Auteurs Multimedia (SCAM), Paris •• 2001 Visual identity, École d'Architecture Paris Malaquais, Paris •• 1994 Creation of "Alfabetempo Roma" •• 1998 Book design, *Les Cahiers de la Recherche Architecturale*, Paris •• 1998 Visual identity, École d'Architecture de Marne-la-Vallée **selected bibliography** 2002 "2 + 3D," *Polish Design Quarterly*, Krakow •• 2001 *TypoJanchi*, Seoul Typography Biennale, Seoul Art Center Desin Gallery, Seoul •• 1999 *New Design: Paris*, Rockport Publishers, Gloucester, Massachusetts •• 1996 *HOW, International Design Annual*, Cincinnati, USA **selected exhibitions** 2002 First Korea International Poster Biennale, Seoul •• 2002 20th International Biennale of Graphic Design, Brno •• 2002 Festival d'Affiches de Chaumont, Chaumont, France •• 2001 *TypoJanchi*, Seoul Typography Biennale, Seoul **awards** 2002 Grand Prix, 20th International Biennale of Graphic Design Brno, Czech Republic •• 1993–94 Grant from the Villa Medici, Académie de France, Rome •• 1988 Typography Excellence Award, Type Directors Club, New York **memberships** 1997 Alliance Graphique Internationale (AGI)

032c Joerg Koch, born Wuppertal, Germany, 1974; Petra Langhammer, born Seoul, Korea, 1967; Sandra von Mayer-Myrtenhain, born Vienna, Austria, 1966. Live and work in Berlin and New York **education** 1997 History and North American Studies, Freie Universiät Berlin and Technische Universität Berlin (JK) **practice** 2000–present Cofounder and Creative Director, 032c, Berlin (JK) •• 2000–present Co-founder and Project Manager, 032c, Berlin (SvM) •• 2000–present Art Director, 032c Magazine (PL) **selected projects** 2003 *032c*, issue 5, "Shanghai Desire," 032c workshop, Berlin •• 2002 *032c*, issue 4, "Embrace Instability," 032c workshop, Berlin •• 2000–2001 *032c*, issues 1–3, "Professionalism," "Destruction," "What's Next?" (with Vladimir Llovet Casademont), 032c workshop, Berlin **selected exhibitions** 2003 Group exhibition *Magasins*, Contemporary Art Center Marres, Maastricht •• 2003 *032c/Berlin Flair*, GAS, Tokyo •• 2001 *Destroy the Good Taste*, Colette, Paris •• 2001 *The Searching Stays With You*, The Pineal Eye, London **selected bibliography** 2002 "Red is the Colour," *I.D Magazine* 225, London •• 2001 *Vogue*, April issue, Paris •• 2001 "Better Read than Dead," *V Magazine* 11, New York •• 2001 "*Wir finde ich das? 032c*," *Die Zeit* 22, Hamburg •• 2001 "*Berlin la constructiviste*," *Le Monde*, 20 September, Paris **awards** 2003 Bronze Award, Art Director Clubs, Germany •• 2003 Visual Lead Award for Innovative Design of the Year, Germany

Viola Zimmermann Born Biel, Switzerland, 1962. Lives and works in Zurich **education** 1997–1998 MA, Communication Design, Central Saint Martins School of Art and Design, London •• 1978–1983 Graphic Design, School of Art and Design, Biel, Switzerland **practice** 2001–present Assistant professor for Graphic Design, Bern, Switzerland •• 1993–present, Self-employed graphic designer with own studio •• 1983–93 Art director of numerous companies, Bern and Zurich **selected projects** 2002–2003 Skateboard design, Airflow Skateboards, Switzerland •• 2002–03 Book design, *Outlet*, School for Design, Art and Conservation (HGKK), Bern •• 2002 Corporate design, Restaurant Zurlinden, Zurich •• 2002 Campaign for short story and poetry competition "*abgefahren*", VBZ, Zurich •• 2000 Design for card game Chuko, Inka Druck, Zurich •• 1997 Identity for a Drum'n'Bass club SNOT, Zurich **selected bibliography** 2002 *HELVETICA – Homage to a Typeface*, Lars Müller Publishers, Baden, Switzerland •• 2001 "Swiss Survey," *Wallpaper* magazine, May issue, London •• 1999 *Benzin, Young Swiss*

Graphic Design, Lars Müller Publishers, Baden, Switzerland **selected exhibitions** 2003 *Swiss Design—Traditionally Progressive*, New York • • 1999 *FRED*, Migros Museum, Zurich • • Viper Palace, Lucerne • • 1998 *Follow The Signs*, Museum für Gestaltung, Zurich **awards** 1998 ADC Award, Art Directors Club, Switzerland • • 1992–94 ADC Award, Art Directors Club, Switzerland

index

Page Numbers in *italics* refer to illustrations